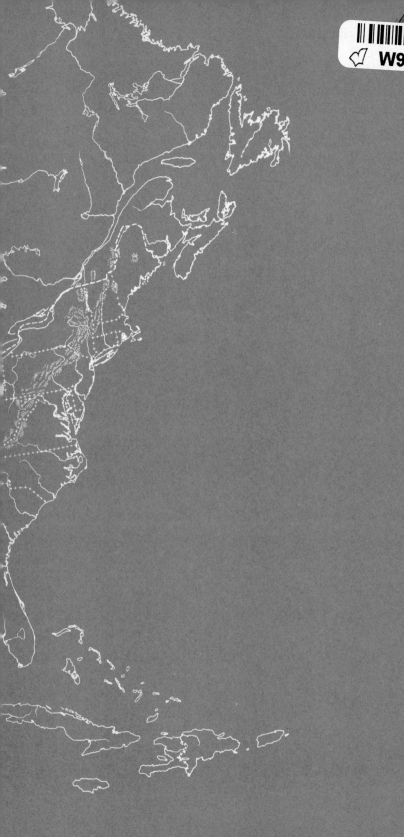

The United States

A HISTORY OF A DEMOCRACY

McGRAW-HILL SERIES IN AMERICAN HISTORY

Blake and Barck
The United States in Its World Relations

Gewehr, Gordon, Sparks, and Stromberg
The United States

Edited by **Wesley M. Gewehr, Donald C. Gordon,**

David S. Sparks, Roland N. Stromberg

with the special assistance of **Herbert A. Crosman**

all of the Department of History, University of Maryland

CONTRIBUTORS: *J. Leonard Bates   Whitney K. Bates   Verne E. Chatelain Herbert A. Crosman   E. James Ferguson   Wesley M. Gewehr   Donald C. Gordon R. Justus Hanks   Charles A. Johnson   Horace Samuel Merrill David S. Sparks   Phyllis Bate Sparks   Roland N. Stromberg*

The United States

A HISTORY OF A DEMOCRACY

Second Edition

McGRAW-HILL BOOK COMPANY, INC.

New York   Toronto   London   1960

*The text of this book has been set in Linotype
Garamond, a fine modern recutting of a classic French type
design. The displayed heads and titles are
Garamond Bold. Maps and charts were drawn by Felix Cooper.*

Preface

The United States: A History of a Democracy is the second edition of the book titled in its first edition *American Civilization: A History of the United States.* The textbook has grown out of several years' experience in teaching a required course in American history as part of an American civilization program at the University of Maryland. The course is normally taken in the sophomore year, but students in some of the colleges in the university register for it in their junior or senior years. During the first ten years in which the program was in effect, we experimented with several combinations of conventional texts (both the one-volume and two-volume types), supplemental readings, and the "problem" approach. This experimentation gave rise to the unanimous opinion that the time had come to tackle the problem of content in the college-level course. While we felt that some sort of text giving the basic outline of American history was essential, we also became convinced that most existing textbooks were not suited to present needs. Our experience has made us feel that a text should avoid too many minor details of names and dates. Rather than telling too little about too many things and repeating a good many facts with which most students are familiar by the time they reach college, we as teachers thought a text should point up significant trends, meanings, and interpretations.

From the outset, the instructors involved in the program began to consider a way in which this need for a different approach might be met. It was felt that a textbook which represented the collective effort emanating from the actual experience of teaching in the program might be an answer. So this book came to be written by a very busy group of teachers who were daily wrestling with the practical work of the classroom and its many related duties.

The decision to write this textbook required the definition of certain objectives qualifying the character of the book's content. The first of these was the elimination of needless or already familiar details which are frequently retained solely for the sake of convention. A second objective was to write enough about the topics presented to make them significant and meaningful to the student, and to offer them in clear and simple prose. A third objective was to give considerable emphasis to current historical scholarship and to make our writing reflect recent contributions wherever they were of significance to the narrative. In this respect, the various authors introduced interpretations growing out of their own research fields. Finally, a consistent effort was made to prevent the chapters from becoming a series of historical essays without unity or reference to a theme. While each chapter is a unit in itself, it is also part of a general pattern which makes a connected narrative, carrying one through the entire span of American history from European and colonial backgrounds to the present.

This is purposely a brief book as college texts go. The authors have designed it for use either in a one-semester or quarter course or in a full-year course. Its thirty chapters break evenly at the year 1865. For those using it for a two-semester course, it is suggested and expected that the text be supplemented by collateral reading or study, either by using one of the several volumes of collected readings and sources or by the special-problems method. Especially suited to this sort of supplementary use is the *Readings and Study Guide in American History,* compiled by Roland N. Stromberg, a selection of readings combined with student review material using the workbook technique and designed specifically to accompany the text. For the one-semester or quarter course, where time is a considerable factor, the instructor might be well advised to assign supplementary readings that fit into the framework of our topics. We feel that it is not unimportant that this book offers much more opportunity for the teacher to enrich class discussions by the introduction of significant relevant materials which in his judgment will contribute to the students' essential fund of knowledge. And he can assign research problems to the students themselves, depending upon available library facilities.

This textbook is a collaborative effort, but it has gained rather than suffered as a result. We have tried to avoid the common pitfalls of collaboration by assigning to an editorial committee complete authority and full responsibility for the final preparation of the manuscript. The editors have striven to achieve a uniform and simple style which they believe will appeal to their readers and have exercised their judgment in rewriting many portions of the manuscript to accomplish this result. In all instances their decisions have been final; therefore they must assume full responsibility for those aspects of the text which commonly come within the scope of editorial supervision.

The authors and editors are gratified that the success of their efforts has warranted this early opportunity to revise and enlarge their work. It makes possible the inclusion of many helpful suggestions by teachers, students, and reviewers who have had occasion to read or use our book. The response to our original determination to provide a text which minimized unnecessary detail and emphasized basic themes of American civilization has encouraged us to retain that approach in this edition.

Virtually every chapter has undergone some revision. Where there were rather major changes or additions, as in Chapter 18, our goal was to provide somewhat more cultural, social, and intellectual history. Chapter 29 has been rewritten and extended to include very recent events and issues, while the final chapter of summary and survey includes comment on some current social problems. The appendices have been revised and brought up to date. New aids in the form of charts, graphs, and tables have been added, as well as new pictures and maps which make the book more useful to students and readers. We trust also that our changes and revisions will meet the approval of the many teachers who found merit in our first edition. Finally, in keeping with our original purpose, the authors and editors have striven to incorporate in this revision the findings of the most recent historical scholarship and interpretation.

The work of the editors in no way minimizes the unique contributions of the several authors whose labors have made this book possible. The authors and the chapters for which they are responsible are: J. Leonard Bates, Chapter 16; Whitney K. Bates, Chapter 6; Verne E. Chatelain, Chapter 23; Herbert A. Crosman, Chapters 7, 17, 21, 28, and 29; E. James Ferguson, Chapters 2 and 5; Wesley M. Gewehr, Chapters 8, 9, and 20; Donald C. Gordon, Chapters 1, 4, 19 and 27; R. Justus Hanks, Chapter 22; Charles A. Johnson, Chapter 12; Horace Samuel Merrill, Chapter 26; David S. Sparks, Chapters 10, 13, 14, and 15; Phyllis Bate Sparks, Chapter 11; and Roland N. Stromberg, Chapters 3, 18, 24, 25, and 30.

The editors would like to express their special thanks to Virginia Daiker and Milton Kaplan of the Prints and Photographs Division of the Library of Congress, who generously gave both time and enthusiasm in the search for illustrations for this text. Thanks should also go to Phyllis Bate Sparks, who prepared the sketches from which the maps have been drawn, and Minna Weinstein, Graduate Fellow in the Department of History at the University of Maryland, who prepared the index.

Wesley M. Gewehr
Donald C. Gordon
David S. Sparks
Roland N. Stromberg

Contents

Preface   *v*

ONE   THE EUROPEAN HERITAGE   1
*Introduction   The Age of Discovery and the Expansion of
Europe   The Background of English Colonization in the
New World   Religion and Empire   The English Heritage
English Revolutions and American Liberties*

TWO   NEW WORLD ENVIRONMENT AND INFLUENCES   19
*Representative Government in the American Colonies
Attempts at Political Oligarchy   Theocracy and Dissent
in the American Colonies   Commerce, Credit, and
Currency   The Acts of Trade and Navigation   Population
and Labor Supply   Class and Sectional Conflict   Frontier
Protests   Political Life in the Late Colonial Period*

THREE   COLONIAL THOUGHT AND CULTURE: PATTERNS
OF AMERICAN CIVILIZATION   42
*The Diversity of Colonial Society   Virginia Gentry:
Southern Pattern   Puritanism: New England Pattern
The Great Awakening   The Enlightenment   Emerging
Americanism*

FOUR   THE EXPANSION AND DISSOLUTION OF EMPIRE   56
*War for Empire   British Colonial Administration
Problems of Empire   Crisis of Empire   The Fight for
Freedom   Toward Independence   Making the Peace*

FIVE   REVOLUTIONARY GOVERNMENT   81
*American Philosophies of Government   The State
Governments   The Articles of Confederation
Administration in the Revolution   The Counterrevolution
Financiers and Their Plans   Social Changes*

SIX   FROM CONFEDERATION TO UNION: MAKING A
NEW NATION   101
*The West in the Confederation   Economic Depression and
Recovery   The Movement for a Stronger National
Government   Making the Constitution   Problems of
Constitution Making   The Ratification Controversy
Launching the New Government*

viii

SEVEN **FEDERALISTS AND REPUBLICANS: TESTING THE NEW NATION** 126

Jefferson and the Opposition   Foreign Policy and the Origins of Political Parties   War with England? War with France?   Heroic Adams   Jefferson's Presidency   Jefferson and Randolph   Diplomatic Troubles

EIGHT **THE RISE OF AMERICAN NATIONALISM, 1809 to 1829** 151

The Breakdown of Peaceable Coercion   Causes of the War of 1812   The War of 1812   Peace Negotiations The New Nationalism after 1815   The Supreme Court and Nationalism   Sectionalism Again: The Missouri Compromise   The Monroe Doctrine An Era of Bad Feelings   The Campaign of 1828

NINE **WESTWARD EXPANSION: THE FRONTIER EXPERIENCE** 176

The First Frontier and the Birth of Sectionalism   The Old Southwest   The Old Northwest   To the Mississippi and Beyond   Far-western Frontiers   The Frontier Experience

TEN **THE DEMOCRATIC CHALLENGE** 202

Political Democracy   The Challenge of Majority Rule Preview of Sectional Conflict   Jackson and the Sectional Challenge   Economic Democracy

ELEVEN **ECONOMIC DEVELOPMENT—NORTH AND SOUTH** 223

The Progress of Agriculture   Southern Agriculture Slavery   The Transportation Revolution   The Emergence of Industry   The Role of Labor Economic Progress

TWELVE **INTELLECTUAL AND SOCIAL FERMENT, 1830 to 1850** 244

The Roots of Reform   The Democratization of Knowledge   Some Reforms and Reformers   The Antislavery Crusade   Slavery and the Southern Mind Utopian Vistas   The Literary Renaissance

THIRTEEN **THE POLITICS OF EXPANSION** 265

Slavery and Expansion   "Manifest Destiny" Tippecanoe, Tyler, and Texas   Polk and Slavery   Polk and Manifest Destiny   A "Glorious Little War" Manifest Destiny and Sectional Conflict

FOURTEEN   **SECTIONAL CONFLICT**   284
            The Slavery Issue   The First Symbol: The "Final"
            Settlement   The Second Symbol: The Fugitive Slave
            The Third Symbol: Kansas-Nebraska   The Fourth
            Symbol: "Bleeding Kansas"   The Fifth Symbol:
            "Bleeding Sumner"   The Sixth Symbol: "Black"
            Republicans   The Final Symbols: Dred Scott and John
            Brown   The Campaigns of 1860

FIFTEEN   **THE CIVIL WAR**   310
            Secession and the Failure of Compromise   Two
            Presidents   Cocky Confederates and Confident
            Yankees   Anaconda   The War in the West   The
            Civil War Soldier   War Politics   The Collapse of the
            Confederacy

SIXTEEN   **RECONSTRUCTION AND THE NEW SOUTH**   338
            The Defeated South   The Victors and Their Plans
            Johnson and the Radicals   Congressional
            Reconstruction   The Collapse of Black Reconstruction
            The New South

SEVENTEEN   **INDUSTRY,   FINANCE,   CAPITALISM,   AND**
            LABOR   358
            The Underlying Factors in Industrial Growth   The
            Railroads   Industrial and Finance Capitalism   Labor
            Ideologies of Capital and Labor

EIGHTEEN   **POLITICS AND SOCIETY IN THE GILDED AGE**   379
            Politics and Social Change   Degeneration of Politics
            Reform Efforts   Cleveland and the Tariff   Seeds
            of Political Revival   The Pattern of Corruption
            Thought and Letters

NINETEEN   **THE AGRARIAN REVOLT**   398
            Agriculture and Industrialization   Grievances of the
            Farmer: Marketing and Credit   Grievances of the
            Farmer: Currency and the Tariff   The Agrarian
            Protest: Grangers   The Agrarian Protest: Money and
            Politics   The Populist Movement   The
            Campaign of 1896

TWENTY   **THE LAST FRONTIERS**   417
            Mining Frontiers   Pioneering in Transportation
            The Passing of the Red Man   The Frontier of the
            Ranchers   The Peopling of the Plains   The
            End of an Epoch

TWENTY-ONE   AMERICAN IMPERIALISM AND ANTI-
                IMPERIALISM   432
                *Isolationist Interlude   Latin America   The
                Pacific   Imperialism and the Spanish War   A
                "Splendid Little War" and an Empire   Running
                the Empire   The Aftermath of Imperialism:
                Far Eastern Politics   Roosevelt and the
                Caribbean*

TWENTY-TWO   THE ERA OF PROGRESSIVISM   453
                *The Progressive Climate   The Muckrakers
                Intellectuals and Reform   City and State Reform
                President Roosevelt and the National Scene
                T.R.'s Policies   Taft and Leaderless Reform
                Roosevelt, Wilson, and the Progressive Dilemma
                Wilson's Reforms*

TWENTY-THREE   THE FIRST WORLD WAR AND ITS
                AFTERMATH   480
                *Wilson's Foreign Problems   American
                Neutrality Threatened   "Peace without Victory"
                or War?   Victory and Peace Terms
                Peacemaking at Paris   The Fight for the League
                and the Treaties   The Significance of the War*

TWENTY-FOUR   THE 1920s: NORMALCY AND ABNOR-
                MALCY   500
                *Harding and Coolidge   Issues of the Twenties
                Foreign Policy   The Social Scene   The
                Revolt of the Intellectuals*

TWENTY-FIVE   THE GREAT DEPRESSION   520
                *Fool's Paradise   False Prosperity   Economic
                Earthquake   The Hoover Policies   The Impact
                of the Depression on American Life*

TWENTY-SIX   THE NEW DEAL   537
                *Sources of Rooseveltian Reform   Roads to
                Recovery   Priming the Pump   Labor
                Agriculture   Other New Deal Programs
                Opposition and Criticism   The New Deal
                in Summary*

TWENTY-SEVEN   THE ROAD TO WAR   560
                *The Twenty-year Truce   The Mounting Crisis
                American Isolationism   The Crumbling of
                Isolation   The Spread of War   The Collapse of*

*Isolationism   All Aid Short of War   The
Road to Pearl Harbor   The Pearl Harbor Debate*

TWENTY-EIGHT   **WAR AGAIN**   580
*Organizing for Total War   High Tide of the
Axis   America Takes the Offensive   The War
in the Pacific   Unconditional Surrender
The United Nations*

TWENTY-NINE   **AMERICAN DEMOCRACY IN CRISIS, 1945
        to 1960**   601
*From War to Peace   Failures of Peacemaking
Containment and the Cold War   Truman's
Second Term: Korea   New Leadership   Recent
Economic Issues   Civil Rights and the
Segregation Issue   Foreign Affairs since 1952*

THIRTY   **THE COURSE OF AMERICAN HISTORY:
        CONCLUDING STATEMENT**   626
*American Traditions   American Achievements
American Dilemmas   Changes   American
History and World History   American Virtues*

General Readings   640

Appendixes   642

Index   687

The United States

A HISTORY OF A DEMOCRACY

ONE

The European Heritage

1215
Magna Carta granted by King John.

1485
Beginning of Tudor dynasty in England.

1486
Portuguese sail around the Africa Cape.

1492
Columbus reaches the New World.

1509
Accession of Henry VIII in England.

1519–1521
Magellan's voyage around the world.

1534
English Church separated from Roman.

1558
Queen Elizabeth becomes ruler of England.

1577–1580
Drake's voyage around globe.

1588
English defeat the Spanish Armada.

1603–1625
James I, first of Stuart kings.

1640–1647
Puritan revolution and English Civil War.

1653–1658
Cromwell Lord Protector of England.

1660–1685
Charles II King of England.

1685
James II becomes king.

1688
Glorious Revolution in England.

INTRODUCTION

NOT FAR FROM the present busy metropolis of London have been found in recent years the remains of the Swanscombe man, a human being who lived some 300,-000 years ago. Such is the ancientness of man in England, a part of that Old World of Eurasia which was the original home of man. In marked contrast, the New World of North and South America (so named by Europeans in the sixteenth century) developed no native human types; the first men to inhabit this hemisphere came over from the deserts of Asia probably no more than 15,000 to 20,000 years ago. These were the American Indians, found here by the Europeans when they arrived a few hundred years ago. These red men had developed, in Central and South America, some rather advanced civilizations, whose wealth attracted the first Spanish explorers to those areas; north of Mexico, they were largely a primitive nomadic people, sparsely distributed over the continent. Here was a virgin continent.

Even though man is very ancient in England, it is nevertheless true that England—and all of Western Europe—did not acquire *civilization* until relatively late. Civilization began, a mere 8,000 years ago or so, in the Near East, and thereafter made its way slowly westward to Europe. No one who wishes to understand our American heritage can afford to neglect the study of that supremely creative people, the ancient Greeks, or of the

1

Queen Elizabeth I (reigned 1558–1603)

John Locke (1632–1704)

Baron de Montesquieu (1689–1755)

The British House of Commons, 1793

The Great Charter (Magna Carta)
granted by King John in 1215

The American political tradition grew from European soil, with its deepest roots in the Middle Ages. Its English development combined a strong monarchy, represented by Queen Elizabeth, with a heritage of liberty and law stretching from Magna Carta to the Glorious Revolution of 1688, which established the supremacy of Parliament. John Locke summed up the meaning of the 1688 revolution. The French philosopher the Baron de Montesquieu, who was well known in America, was a staunch admirer of English liberty.

great Roman Empire, which spread Greco-Roman civilization to northern Europe. Here lie the seeds of European civilization; and America was the child of Europe.

Despite the varying fortunes through which this Mediterranean-European civilization has passed, despite the frequency of "times of trouble," its essential continuity has not been broken. It reached one of its higher levels of creativity in the years of the Roman Empire, but even with the spectacular breakdown of that great political structure, the civilized traditions of Greece and Rome, now combined with the unique religious contributions of Hebraic-Christian beliefs, carried on. The centuries following the collapse of the Roman Empire were characterized by feudal disintegration and were long regarded as the Dark Ages. After about A.D. 900 the life of Europe began to revive both economically and culturally. The culmination of the growth of this medieval civilization came perhaps in the thirteenth century. Its monuments of Gothic architecture, scholastic philosophy, the great Roman Church, emerging universities, and developing systems of law show us a vigorous and creative civilization. But great and significant as were many of the accomplishments of this period, the so-called medieval synthesis could not last; European civilization has always been dynamic, growing, changing, and a new order began to appear. By the time of Columbus, Europe was in the throes of a transition to the modern age—a transition which brought wars, revolutions, intellectual revolt, the decline of the authority of the Roman Church, and the emergence of the modern institution of the nation-state. All this belongs to European history, but in the larger and truer sense it is also part of

American history. In the long perspective of time, our cultures have a common ancestry. We share with Europeans, for all our differences, the great common heritage of Western civilization. The discovery and settlement of North America brought this civilization to our shores.

THE AGE OF DISCOVERY AND THE EXPANSION OF EUROPE

The discovery of America by Christopher Columbus in 1492 was not the result of chance; rather, it was an event for which Europe, unknowingly, had long been preparing. The epochal voyage of the great Genoese, who sailed under the banner of Spain, was the climax of the Age of Discovery. Like the birth of the Atomic Age in our time, the news of the discovery of two new continents stirred Europe, but in reality it was the logical result of slowly accumulating forces which had already affected many aspects of European life and thought.

Among the factors which made possible this unprecedented thrusting out of Europeans into the remotest corners of the globe were new ways of farming. At last there was enough to eat. For years, the specter of starvation and famine had aroused fear in the life of Europe. But by degrees Europeans improved their food-producing and -processing methods, utilizing, for example, such devices as the windmill and better methods of harnessing horses for plowing. Gradually they were able to produce enough food so that a division of labor was possible. Many who were no longer needed on the farms went into commerce, buying and selling surplus produce. Others entered manufacture, making goods that were needed for the betterment of living conditions. Europe was getting richer and therefore better able to organize and equip such ventures of exploration as that of Columbus.

Another element in the preparation of Europe for the Age of Discovery was the series of military-religious expeditions known as the Crusades. In their simplest form the Crusades were efforts on the part of European Christians to wrest from the hands of the Moslems the territory of the Holy Places in the land of Palestine, today in the state of Israel. To many of the devout Christians of the Middle Ages, it seemed sacrilegious that the land where Christ had lived and taught should be in the hands of the infidel Moslems. As European life became better organized and possessed of increasing wealth, a great series of expeditions was staged to bring the land of Christ back into Christian hands. The Crusades were only partially successful, but they did hasten the development of a number of important changes in European life. They reconquered strategically important parts of the Mediterranean, making it easier for Europeans to travel about that sea. Further, in the course of the Crusades, Europeans developed greater skill in seamanship and shipbuilding, arts which had been largely lost to European life during the earlier period of the Middle Ages. But perhaps the most important result of the Crusades was the fact that through them the people of Europe discovered the wealth of the Orient and determined to get their share. They found that the world of the Moslems and the great Asiatic continent that lay behind it had a greatly superior technical civilization and an array of luxury items such as fine textiles, wines, and spices, which Europeans eagerly sought. There was a particular need for spices, since the food of medieval Europe was frequently so bad

that only spices could make it palatable. And thus it was that the contacts which Europeans made with the Asiatic world through the Crusades led to a great expansion of European-Asiatic trade. This trade brought great profit to some of the merchant cities which had grown up on the shores of the Mediterranean. Venice, for instance, grew fabulously rich from its role of middleman in the trade which found its way to the markets of Europe. Merchants of other countries were eager to find some way of getting the goods from Asia without paying the prices charged by the Italian cities for the services they provided. However, before other Europeans could afford to dispense with the services of the Italians in their search for Asiatic trade, their strength had to be mobilized for the search for new routes to the east. The most significant agency for this mobilization was the nation.

The third factor in the transition of Europe and its preparation for the new age was the emergence of the nation-state. We are so accustomed to a world of nations today that it is difficult to imagine a time when there were none; yet that was the condition of medieval Europe. After the collapse of the power of the Roman Empire, Europe dissolved into feudalism. In some regards feudalism was little better than anarchy. There was no strong central government, and the men who held the greatest authority over the lives of other men were members of the local nobility who were powerful because they were the great landlords of their area. This pattern of feudalism was gradually supplanted by centralized governments, especially in such countries as Spain, Portugal, England, and France. In these lands, formerly weak feudal kings were able to build their domains into states which possessed a considerable degree of centralized power. With this new authority the kings were better able to direct the affairs of their realms and could more effectively pursue courses of national interest.

Another agency, the joint-stock company, was frequently used as a means of securing cooperation between the government and individuals with money who were willing to risk it in overseas exploration and settlement. The great advantage of the joint-stock company was that it provided a means by which, through the sale of shares in the company, wealth could be pooled for some major enterprise. Those who purchased shares could participate in the selection of the directors of the company and share in any profits according to the amount of their ownership. The Crown granted these companies charters, that is, legal statements which defined the privileges, rules, and conditions under which they were allowed to conduct their affairs. Ruler and wealthy subject each contributed his money toward the forma-

tion of companies in which each had a share of the wealth invested, and the companies, thus equipped, were among the devices by which Europeans sought to discover and explore the great world beyond their continent.

Other devices were needed too—technical devices such as navigating instruments, better maps, larger sailing ships, and new sailing methods. Some of these were developed in Europe; others, such as the compass, were perhaps adopted from non-European peoples. These new aids greatly eased the path of the explorer across the seas to unknown lands.

These, then, are a few of the circumstances from which the overseas expansion of Europe grew. It is not possible to take any one date or event as the beginning of this expansion, for history is a cumulative process. Each generation makes at least some use of the achievements of those that came before. But since a beginning must be made, there is some merit in starting the train of events of discovery with the

THE WORLD KNOWN TO EUROPEANS IN 1490 AND IN 1580

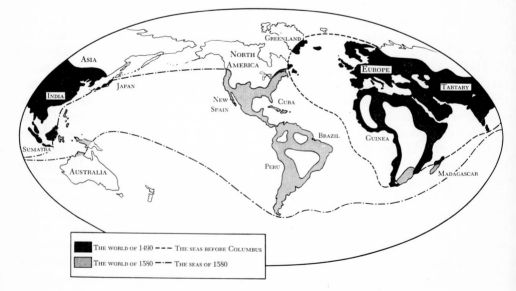

activities of Henry the Navigator, Prince of Portugal. In part because of his stimulus, Portugal took the lead in the exploration of the African coast line and in opening up the route south of the Cape of Good Hope into the Indian Ocean. Prince Henry established an institute for the study of geography, navigation, and seamanship. From this institute came a number of famous navigators, and on their achievements Portugal erected a great empire that included large areas of land in South America, Africa, and the Indonesian archipelago. The vestiges of that once powerful empire are still scattered about the globe, and the people of the large South American state of Brazil speak Portuguese, an inheritance from their colonial period.

If Portugal took the lead in the age of exploration and discovery, its neighboring state on the Iberian peninsula, Spain, was not far behind. The Spaniards were feeling rather pleased with the world and themselves at the close of the fifteenth century. They felt a sense of great triumph as their long struggle to end the existence of the Moorish Moslem states in Spain came to a successful close in 1492. Spain secured freedom from Moslem rule and a form of national unity at about the same time, so their sense of achievement was justified. In this flush of triumph, Spain was ready to embark upon great ventures. It was with Spanish aid that Columbus made his voyage of 1492, and it was under the flag of Spain that Magellan started on the first voyage around the globe, a voyage that he was not destined to finish, but which his second-in-command was able to complete. On the basis of these voyages and the conquests of men like Cortez in Mexico and Pizarro in Peru, Spain built a remarkable empire that straddled the Pacific, eventually includ-

ing most of the American continent and also the Philippines. The sixteenth century was Spain's "Golden Age" of imperial preeminence.

Both Spain and Portugal sought to exclude all other nations from the vast areas they claimed, and with the arbitration of Pope Alexander VI, and later by treaty, they tried to divide the newly discovered areas of the world between themselves. But England, France, and the Netherlands had no intention of allowing the Iberian states to monopolize the new colonial world. A period of lively competition for trade and settlement among the greater European nations ensued, and in this competition, the European states eventually became masters and rulers of the greater portion of the non-European world. For about four hundred years, many of the European states were the centers of great imperial structures, with colonies, dominions, protectorates, bases, and outposts of power scattered throughout the globe. From this fact of dominion they drew immense economic advantage.

While much of these vast colonial systems still exists, the twentieth century has seen the collapse and retreat of European power in many quarters of the globe. We live in what one historian has called "the passing of the European age." World leadership, for better or worse, has largely passed from the hands of the European states that so long dominated the globe into the hands of powers such as the United States and the Soviet Union.

Several nations shared in the colonization of the American continents. The Dutch influence is still discernible in the valley of the Hudson River, where the Dutch settlements were established. The great natural gateways to much of the North American continent, the St. Lawrence and Mississippi Rivers, were colonized by the French, who were to extend their power deep into the heart of the continent along the line of the rivers. The Spaniards planted their life and culture not only in the vastness of South America, but in much of the southern portion of North America as well. The influence and abiding effect of Spanish life is still apparent in such states as Florida, New Mexico, and California.

Of all the European nations, it was England that furnished the largest number of early settlers in the American colonies, and it was from English life, institutions, and historical experience that the basic institutions of American life were derived. The civilization established in the thirteen colonies either was English from the beginning or was to receive before the close of the seventeenth century a strong English flavor. Further, for over 150 years, the portion of colonial America from which the United States later developed was part of the British empire. These colonies were, because of this association, deeply influenced by developments that occurred in what was still the motherland.

As a distinguished student of American culture has commented: *

> For better or worse, we have inherited the fundamental qualities in our culture from the British. For that reason we need to take a long perspective of our history, a perspective which views America from at least the period of the first Tudor monarchs and lets us see the gradual development of our common civilization, its transmission across the Atlantic, and its expansion and modification as it was adapted to conditions in the Western Hemisphere. We should not overlook other influences which have affected American life, in-

* Louis B. Wright, *Culture on the Moving Frontier*, Indiana University Press, Bloomington, Ind., 1955, p. 241. Used by permission.

fluences from France, Holland, Spain, Germany, Scandinavia and the rest of Europe, and also influences from Asia and Africa. But we must always remember that such was the vigor of British culture that it assimilated all others. That is not to say that we have been transmogrified into Englishmen, or that we are even Anglophile in sentiment. But we cannot escape an inheritance which has given us some of our sturdiest and most lasting qualities.

THE BACKGROUND OF ENGLISH COLONIZATION IN THE NEW WORLD

The early great achievements of exploration and discovery had been the work largely of the Portuguese and Spaniards; the English had not contributed in any significant fashion. The beginnings of English concern and activity in colonial ventures coincide roughly with the years of the Tudor dynasty on the English throne. The Tudors, ruling from 1485 to 1603, provided England with some of her most vigorous and effective rulers, at least three of whom, Henry VII (1485–1509), Henry VIII (1509–1547), and Elizabeth (1558–1603), have substantial claims to greatness. During the years of the Tudors, the English people passed through a series of significant changes in their national life, many of which contributed directly to the entry of England into the sphere of colonial activity. This was a dynamic and expansive period of English growth, and the list of achievements is large and imposing; it includes several major developments which contributed to English maritime enterprise and colonization.

One of these is the emergence of a vigorous and fervent patriotism. There was a new sense of national pride and consciousness which permeated English thought. A considerable group of antiquarians, his-

STUART AND TUDOR MONARCHS OF ENGLAND

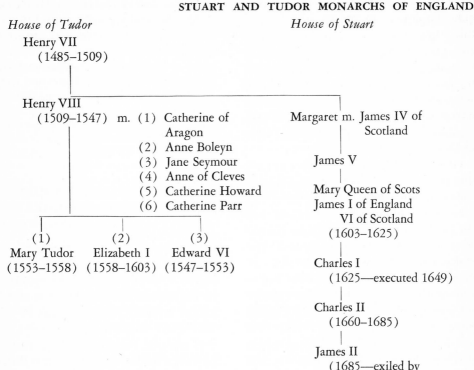

House of Tudor

Henry VII
(1485–1509)

Henry VIII
(1509–1547) m. (1) Catherine of
Aragon
(2) Anne Boleyn
(3) Jane Seymour
(4) Anne of Cleves
(5) Catherine Howard
(6) Catherine Parr

(1) (2) (3)
Mary Tudor   Elizabeth I   Edward VI
(1553–1558) (1558–1603) (1547–1553)

House of Stuart

Margaret m. James IV of
Scotland

James V

Mary Queen of Scots
James I of England
VI of Scotland
(1603–1625)

Charles I
(1625—executed 1649)

Charles II
(1660–1685)

James II
(1685—exiled by
revolution, 1688)

Dates in parentheses indicate reigns of the monarchs.
Numbers (1), (2), and (3) indicate mother-child relationship.

torians, and geographers enlarged on the greatness of the English past and sang the praises of the "opulent and ample realm" in which they lived. This strong feeling of national pride is revealed in the literature of the Tudor period, for English wits and writers were aflame with love of country, and the greatest of them all described his native land as

This fortress built by nature for herself
Against infection and the hand of war,
This happy breed of men, this little world,
This precious stone set in the silver sea.

Such national pride and satisfaction both encouraged and was encouraged by another major development of the Tudor

era. This was the great religious change brought about largely by Henry VIII in withdrawing the church in England from the authority of the Pope, the Bishop of Rome. This act of revolutionary nationalism appealed to many in England as being but another manifestation of the greatness and power of the English nation, and King Henry VIII was to some the "Majestic lord that broke the bonds of Rome." It was not the intention of the King to change the doctrines of the English Church. He sought, rather, to continue Catholicism without the Pope. But on the Continent, in the years after Martin Luther's break with the Roman Church, the air was vibrating with the noise of doctrinal clash and dispute. Although it was quite impossible to prevent the fury of this controversy from reaching England and profoundly affecting the minds of men, the Tudors exerted firm control over the affairs of their church. A church that was managed by the Crown naturally took on an increasingly nationalistic character.

Amidst all the changes of English religious life and their accompanying political controversies, England as a nation was getting richer. Not all Englishmen shared in the new wealth; indeed, many were driven into further impoverishment by shifts in the productive system. For the nation as a whole, however, there was greater wealth, and a large portion of it came into the hands of speculators and investors, who were willing to run the risks of financing trade and colonizing ventures overseas. It was a period in which the first English joint-stock companies were founded. Brave-sounding names such as the Muscovy Company, the Levant Company, the East India Company, and the Virginia Company reveal the new grandeur of their designs.

Central figures in this transition through which England was passing were the monarchs of the realm, the Tudor rulers. Just prior to the establishment of this family on the throne, England had been distraught and beset by a series of squalid civil wars that frequently took on the quality of feuds among the nobility. These wars were picturesquely, but inaccurately, known as the Wars of the Roses. Over the thirty-five-year period of these quarrels, there had been a general weakening of government in many areas of the nation—so much so that in many instances the ordinary processes of justice through the courts had been subverted by the power and influence of local nobility, no longer held in check by royal authority and pres-

tige. The first Tudor ruler, Henry VII, crafty and able, soon put an end to much of this "lack of governance," reasserted the power of the throne, and restored peace to the land, a peace that was essential for the effective work of the productive classes of the nation. Englishmen, tired of the brawling squabbles of the Wars of the Roses, accepted the new leadership of the monarchs with gratitude. Henry VII's successors to the throne built their policies on his example and generally showed a strong and jealous regard for their power of national leadership.

But the Tudor monarchs could not govern alone. Their power and policies were supported by a newly created nobility and by the newly emerging middle class of financiers and merchants who looked to the court for support, grants, and favors that might open their way to riches. The Tudor rulers for the most part were successful in cooperating with the dynamic and productive classes of the community, extending to them protection and care in return for their loyalty and support. It was this royal favor, as much as the new opportunities for trade in the expanding world of the period, that led a distinguished economist to comment in regard to this period, "Never in the annals of the modern world has there existed so prolonged and so rich an opportunity for the business man, the speculator and the profiteer."* It was this sustaining and supporting hand of the state that helped guide Englishmen into a period of industrial expansion which was unequaled until the eighteenth-century Industrial Revolution.

Yet the Tudor leadership—or despotism, as some have called it—was exercised without the usual apparatus of power.

* John Maynard Keynes, *A Treatise on Money,* Harcourt, Brace and Company, Inc., New York, 1930, vol. II, p. 159.

Nothing remotely resembling either a modern army or police force existed in Tudor England. In all the policies of state the rulers of the realm depended upon the cooperation of a host of unpaid local officials, without whose aid government would have virtually collapsed. Unpaid justices of the peace were the backbone of administration, but there were many other officers of various ranks who took on their shoulders duties of managing local affairs.

The results of the new vigor in English life were revealed in spectacular fashion in the exploits of the seamen. They treated with scorn the efforts of the Spaniards to hold a monopoly of trade and settlement in the Caribbean and Central American regions, and with reckless bravado they penetrated into the heart of this part of the Spanish empire, forcing the sometimes not unwilling Spanish colonial officers to trade with them. The greatest of these English seamen, Francis Drake, carried out the most daring of raids when he led a small command into the Pacific, up the western shores of South America, and into waters where Spanish ships had heretofore held sway. From this combination of buccaneering and exploration, Drake returned to England three years later with a hold full of loot. The Queen, Elizabeth I, daughter of Henry VIII, shared in the profits, which are estimated to have reached 4,700 per cent. Thirsting after such profits, Elizabethan sea dogs made the seven seas their empire and robbed at will.

Such depredations as these into the waters of the world that Spain claimed as her own were part of the reasons why the Spanish sovereign, Philip II, came eventually and reluctantly to the conclusion that England had to be conquered. There were additional reasons for this decision.

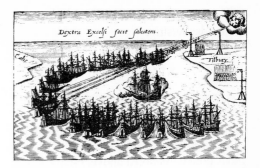

The Invincible Armada, from a book celebrating the glorious triumph of English arms over the mighty Spanish fleet. (Folger Shakespeare Library)

England, under Elizabeth, was active in support of the Dutch, who were in rebellion against their Spanish rulers. Further, England had in some measure become a champion of the cause of Protestantism in parts of Europe, and the Spain of Philip was the vindicator and champion of Catholicism. Philip's decision took the form of the preparation of a mighty fleet to carry a conquering army to English shores in 1588. This great enterprise and show of Spanish power is known in history as the Invincible Armada. But its purpose was never accomplished. The seamen of England bested it in a running fight in the Channel; they allowed the huge vessels of Spain no rest in the harbors of the Low Countries to which they fled. Rather than confront the English guns once again, the Spaniards sought to return home by sailing around the British Isles and to the west of Ireland, only to be buffeted by the gales of the North Sea and the Atlantic and damaged even more severely than they had been by the English guns. The shores of Scotland and Ireland were dotted with the wreckage of the Spanish ships, wreckage that also marked the collapse of the hopes of Philip II. The defeat of the "Invincible" Armada demonstrated to Europe the vitality of the English nation under Tudor leadership.

RELIGION AND EMPIRE

Queen Elizabeth governed a realm that perhaps had more national unity than any other state in Europe. The only major cause of dissension lay in the realm of religious policy. As noted above, Henry VIII's severance of the connection between the English Church and Rome had opened the doors to the furies of religious controversy. It was the policy of Elizabeth to still this fury by making the English Church as broad and comprehensive as possible. It was her goal to establish a religious body in which Englishmen could accept membership as readily as they accepted political membership in the nation. In this she and her theological advisers had mixed success. The vast majority of Englishmen accepted the state church, but there were islands of opposition which were not cowed by the combination of coercion and cajolery which the rulers used to impose the new religious order. On the one hand, there were the Catholics who refused to concede the Catholicism of the new state church and retained their loyalty to their traditional faith. The law sometimes bore on this group with great severity because some of their more fanatical members became identified with various plots and schemes, many engineered in Spain, to assassinate Elizabeth and replace her with a Catholic ruler. Patient endurance, however, of the state's religious policies was the choice of most Catholics. At the opposite end of the religious spectrum was the growing body of the Puritans, who were the English followers of the great French Protestant theologian John Calvin. To many of these Puritans the state church was a sorry compromise with the hated

Religious intolerance, a Roman Catholic illustration showing the persecutions with which the Reformation era was filled and of which both Catholic and Protestant were guilty. (Folger Shakespeare Library)

doctrines of Roman Catholicism. They pressed hard, especially in the Parliament, for a greater "purification" of the Anglican Church of what they regarded as "Romish" doctrines and liturgy. To Elizabeth and her advisers they seemed a cantankerous and contentious crew, quarrelsome disturbers of the religious peace that the Queen was trying to maintain. But their loyalty was not suspect. They might fulminate against the established church, but their actions fell far short of involvement in any plots against the Queen.

Other religious groups were to emerge as time passed, generally groups of more extreme Protestant character, including those who were called Separatists because they called into question the connection between the state and church. These groups found little comfort or solace in a religious policy that included the idea that the state must control much of the nation's religious life. For to the rulers of that time, European as well as English, the general policy of separation of church and state, or even of a wide religious toleration, seemed totally unacceptable. To the minds of rulers, national unity demanded religious conformity. In 1602, Elizabeth indignantly rejected a rumor that she was prepared to grant legal recognition to two religions rather than one within the state. Her successor, the Scottish James Stuart, who came down from Scotland to become James I of England, stated his policy, "I will have one Doctrine and one discipline, one Religion in substance and in ceremonie." As for dissenters, "I shall make them conform themselves, or I will harry them out of the land, or else do worse." And there existed a special court, the Court of the High Commission, for the policing and prevention of religious nonconformity.

Out of the nonconforming groups came many of the migrants to the early English colonies in America. They hoped to find in the colonies a freedom for faith and worship largely denied them in their native land. For however ardently the home government might defend the Anglican Church against both Catholics and Puritans, it placed no barrier to their migration to English colonies, and thus for many the colonial areas were havens of refuge. This idea that religious dissenters were acceptable in colonization produced a wide variety of religious beliefs in the English colonies of North America. It was in notable contrast with the general policies of France and Spain, which insisted on the doctrinal purity of migrants before they were permitted to settle overseas.

Woven from such strands as these came the pattern of English colonization: national pride, growing wealth, greater efficiency in government and the organization of business enterprise, a search for profit in mercantile ventures, a search for greater freedom of religious expression, and in some cases the simple urge for novelty and adventure. All these appear in the late sixteenth and early seventeenth centuries, and the pattern persists throughout much of the eighteenth century, but initially it was religion and the search for riches that brought the first English settlers to the shores of the New World.

THE ENGLISH HERITAGE

Whether Englishmen migrated from England for economic gain or for a larger measure of religious freedom, they brought with them well-defined concepts of law and government which they planted in colonial America.

Of course, the institutions which grew up in the American colonies were not wholly a product of Tudor or Stuart influences. English settlers in America brought with them traditions of much earlier origin, basic ideas and attitudes which had been a part of English political experience

Sir Walter Raleigh, the "learned knight," Renaissance cavalier and adventurer, servant of Queen Elizabeth and pioneer of New World settlement. (Library of Congress)

since medieval times. Of all the ideas which the colonists brought with them, none was more important than the concept of law. There were two chief concepts of law implanted in the life of colonial America. One was the idea of natural law and natural rights, and the other was the idea of the English common law. Both were part of the intellectual and institutional inheritance of the early American settlers, and both became living forces in American culture.

The ideas of natural rights and natural law had been part of the intellectual tradition of European life for centuries, ever since classical times. Under the concept of natural law, evolved chiefly by the lawyers and rulers of the Roman Empire in their task of governing many different peoples, it was assumed that there existed certain general rules of good conduct accepted by all men of reasonable understanding, whatever their race or culture. Of particular significance in this connection was the concept of natural rights— rights given to men by God or by Nature that could not rightfully be touched or infringed upon by any government.

In the comparatively simple society of early America, natural law, reinforced by scriptural law and injunction, seemed to be all that was needed. The English common law, with its concern for property rights, its rules of evidence, and its somewhat involved procedures, seemed unnecessary. This was especially true since its use required the employment of lawyers, a group regarded by most early settlers with beady-eyed suspicion. Early Americans were content with the simple ideas of natural and scriptural law, but as life became steadily more complex, as men acquired property and wished to place that property under protection of the law, the situation changed somewhat. Moreover,

toward the close of the seventeenth century, the British authorities began to manifest an interest in the colonies that they had not revealed before. With that new interest it became necessary for the American law to conform in some measure to the English law, the more so since English courts and law officers maintained a right of review over American legislation and legal decisions. They were likely to look askance at such enactments and decisions as did not conform to the principles of the common law. As the colonists lost their early simplicity, they were forced more and more by circumstances to the adoption and use of the English common law.

The code of common law was one of the great products of medieval English life. Its axioms and procedures had gradually grown through the long centuries of English corporate life, from the customs of the people, and the wisdom and discretion of the justices, into a complicated and sophisticated body of jurisprudence. It was a code that was not written down in statutes but was simply a recognized body of law based upon tradition and precedent.

Common law and natural law had these important meanings in common: both put limitations on the powers of the rulers, neither gave any support to the idea of absolutism, and each appealed to a principle of authority beyond the prince's reach. In English history there had been a long struggle between king and common law; kings had tried to escape from the limiting effect of the common-law courts by setting up their own special courts or by trying to intimidate the common-law courts. Once, for example, King James I, in an effort at such intimidation, was told by a doughty judge, Sir Edward Coke, that while the King was not under any man he was under God and the law. Coke was dismissed from his office for the boldness of his assertion, but the final result of the great constitutional struggle of the seventeenth century was the end of the special courts and the vindication of the independence of the common-law courts.

The protection thrown by the common law around private property, putting it in many particulars beyond the discretionary power of the legislature, may not always have been best for the public welfare, but in the integrity of the courts and the law there was security for the individual. The tradition of the common law, with its idea of the supremacy of the law, also carried with it a gradually accumulating protection for persons who run afoul of the law. This included the right of trial by jury, the use of the writ of habeas corpus (which prevented accused persons from being kept in jail at the whim of the arresting authority), the rigid rules concerning what was admissible as evidence in trials, the right to counsel, and the general principles that an accused person is innocent until proved guilty. These protections and guarantees of personal liberty became a vital part of the American tradition.

If English legal traditions were enormously influential in the development of our American institutions, the English parliamentary tradition was scarcely less important to the development of representative governments in America. The English Parliament evolved from very ancient roots; perhaps nowhere else is our debt to the Middle Ages more obvious. Parliament was an ancient institution when the vessels of Columbus hove within sight of the American shores. At the time of its beginnings, in medieval times, it was but one of a number of similar institutions scattered throughout Europe. But while the other legislative bodies of Europe languished and died, victims primarily of the demand for greater centralized power in the modern nation-state, the English Parliament alone grew in vigor and effectiveness, to become finally the most venerable of all the world's legislatures.

The great period of the early growth of Parliament was the fourteenth century. During that century the clumsy feudal council evolved into a recognizable parliament. The bicameral form of legislature made its appearance, and the office of the Speaker of the lower chamber, or House of Commons, emerged. More important, the legislative body began to assert its authority in matters of finance. When, in later generations and on far-off shores, Americans asserted their rights to no taxation without representation, they were appealing to a long-established tradition in English government. In addition, the fourteenth-century Parliaments tried to share with the monarch the general control of government policies; they attempted also to control the men designated for office by the king. One effort of Parliament to control such officeholders led to the first use of the device of impeachment.

Parliament declined in power in the next century, however, and it is one of the glories of the Tudors that during their reigns the Parliament recovered much of its former dignity and position in English life. Henry VIII, carrying out his revolution against the authority of the Roman Church, used Parliament most effectively to achieve his own ends. He overawed some members, cajoled others, but always acted as if Parliament were an important institution. He sensed the advantage in having the Parliament on his side for the job of helping to shape and form public opinion. Thus Parliament recovered in prestige because the Tudor rulers associated it with them in their policies, and by the close of Tudor period, even the imperious Elizabeth found it expedient on occasion to yield to the wishes of the legislative body.

All the American colonies had their legislative bodies, which were in fact if not in theory modeled closely upon the forms and traditions of the English Parliament. Many a British governor was to find out how seriously the colonial legislators regarded themselves, their duties, their powers, and the traditions of their colonial assemblies. Indeed, the growth and development of the colonial assemblies has been hailed as the outstanding feature of the old British system of colonial government. These bodies struggled valiantly, with all the weapons at their command, to rid themselves of any limitations that British law or other controls placed upon them. Throughout these struggles, the example of Parliament in its effort to secure dominance in English life was decisive. Nearly all the colonial assemblies could have echoed without reservation the assertion of the legislative body of Jamaica, "The House has all the privileges of the House of Commons in England and no instructions from King or ministers can either abridge or annihilate the privileges of the representative body of the people of this island."

As in the English Parliament, colonial assemblies established their power over the control of finance. With few exceptions, the moneys for the government of the colonies, even in some instances the funds necessary to pay the salaries of the royal governors, were dependent upon the taxes authorized by the colonial legislatures. In many of the colonies a form of running battle took place between the royal governors and legislative bodies over the issue of governors' salaries. The governors were anxious to have some permanent revenue set aside for the payment of

their salaries; the legislatures were desirous of creating or retaining a situation in which the governor was dependent on the legislature. In Virginia, for example, there was no reason for dispute over the governor's salary, for it was paid out of permanent revenue. But in 1753 Governor Robert Dinwiddie raised the issue of the power of the legislative body over revenue by claiming the right to collect a tax imposed by himself for the placing of the public seal of the colony on all documents which required the seal. The legislature protested against what was regarded as the invasion of its power over revenue, and despite the support he received from the British government, Dinwiddie was forced to retreat. The colonial legislatures took their power over taxes soberly and sought to protect and expand it whenever they could.

In addition to the traditions of common law and parliamentary government, personal freedom in the American colonies was increased by the great assertions of individual rights found in the Magna Carta, the Petition of Right, and the English Bill of Rights. We rightly cherish the bills of rights in our various state constitutions and in the federal Constitution, but these stem from a line of similar pronouncements made in English history. The Magna Carta, sealed in 1215, is the first of these great constitutional promulgations. Perhaps nothing better illustrates the continuing influence of the Magna Carta than to place side by side one of its more famous passages and a section of a constitution for a middle-western American state written in 1818. Among the clauses of the Magna Carta is one that reads as follows:

> No freeman shall be taken and imprisoned or disseised of any free tenement or of his liberties or free customs, or outlawed, or exiled, or in any other way de-

stroyed, nor will we go upon him, nor send upon him, except by the lawful judgment of his peers or by the law of the land.

Slightly more than six hundred years later, in a land unknown at the time of the writing of Magna Carta, some men sat down to prepare a constitution for the state of Illinois. Among the clauses they placed in the constitution was one that reads as follows:

> That no freeman shall be imprisoned or disseised of his freehold, liberties, or privileges, or outlawed or exiled, or in any manner deprived of his life, liberty or property, but by the judgment of his peers and the law of the land.

Certainly no one can argue that the barons of England who forced the Magna Carta on a reluctant king, and the men who drew up the first state constitution for Illinois, had as great a similarity in ideas as they had in language. Too much had happened in the intervening six hundred years for that to be possible. But at least there are certain principles of freedom for the individual from arbitrary

and misused power which connect the two documents like a golden thread running through the centuries. Subsequent generations of Englishmen added other great documents of freedom. One was the Petition of Right of 1628, and another was the Bill of Rights of 1689. Both embody principles which formed part of the legacy of freedom brought by British colonial settlers to American shores. This legacy, increased and enlarged by the democracy of the frontier, made the inhabitants of colonial British North America the freest people within the general body of European civilization.

ENGLISH REVOLUTIONS AND AMERICAN LIBERTIES

As will be shown in subsequent chapters, traditional English liberties found congenial soil and were nourished in the environment of the New World, but it cannot be properly overlooked that for 150 years the American colonies were part of the British Empire and the inhabitants were British subjects. Under these conditions political and institutional life

Royal Exchange, late seventeenth century, symbol of commercial enterprise and the speculative spirit, so significant in the establishment of New World colonies. (Folger Shakespeare Library)

was affected by developments in Britain. The growth of political freedom in the colonies would have been greatly impeded had the trend of government in Britain been toward absolutism, as it was, for instance, in France. That this trend did not triumph in England as it did in many European states was due largely to the great religious and constitutional conflicts fought out in England in the seventeenth century. These struggles increased the sum of English liberties and indirectly broadened the tradition of colonial freedom.

The course of these struggles need not long detain us. They began in the reign of Elizabeth's successor, James I (1603–1625), who was the first king of the Stuart dynasty to rule in England, and continued in the reign of his son, the unhappy Charles I (1625–1649). In the decade of the 1640s the conflict between King Charles and his supporters, on the one hand, and the Parliament, on the other, culminated in war. The forces of Parliament were victorious, and the world was amazed by the spectacle of the execution of Charles in 1649. But the victorious Parliament was unable to establish a stable civil government, and England was ruled chiefly through the power of a military dictatorship headed by Oliver Cromwell. On Cromwell's death in 1658 the dictatorship fell apart, and the way was opened for the restoration of the exiled Stuart dynasty in the person of Charles II, son of the executed king. England had its normal political arrangements of king, lords, and commons once more, but the claim to absolute rule on the part of the king was no longer asserted. There were, however, still more changes in the wind. After a reign of twenty-five years, Charles II was succeeded by his brother, James II, who made the mistake of trying to destroy the power of Parliament and establish a government after the despotic French model. He further offended the sensibilities of the masses of his subjects by extensive favors granted to Catholics. Within three years after mounting the throne, James was in flight from the "Glorious Revolution" in 1688. After this revolution, which further strengthened Parliament, England entered into a period of political equilibrium. The results were nevertheless momentous, and in the colonies their effect was scarcely less profound.

The two revolutions of the seventeenth century produced at least two important changes in England. One was an acceptance of the fact that it was folly to try to control, by state power, the religious life of the nation. After the 1688 revolution Parliament passed a Toleration Act which virtually acknowledged the futility of religious coercion. There remained the state-supported Church of England, but the right of other Protestant groups to have their own organization and worship was established. The position of the Catholics was less fortunate; many were still suspected of being agents of enemy powers. With this exception England was, in most aspects, a model of religious toleration during the eighteenth century, although this tolerance reflected in part the increasing indifference of the state to religious matters. Political wisdom had supplanted religious zeal as a guiding force in politics. The indifferent attitude of the government toward religion was, practically speaking, an embryonic form of separation of church and state. The other idea reinforced by the outcome of the revolutions was that of representative government. The victory of Parliament in these struggles naturally added to the power and prestige of that body. The monarchs still possessed great power and influence, but in the two overwhelmingly important areas of government—finance, and control of the armed forces—the power of Parliament as opposed to that of the king had been upheld.

It was, of course, largely on the basis of the English example that all the British colonies on the North American continent had strongly established legislative institutions. The "Glorious Revolution" of 1688 meant much to the colonies. In New England especially, the revolution brought a welcome change. James and his appointee as governor, Sir Edmund Andros, had carried out a consolidation of the New England colonies, combining them with New York and New Jersey into a so-called Dominion of New England. In the process of consolidation, the colonies were deprived of their charters and legislative assemblies. This experiment in arbitrary and centralized government collapsed, however, with the overthrow of James, and the traditional forms of government with elective legislative bodies were reestablished. Had the place of Parliament in English life not been vindicated by the revolutions in England, it is difficult to imagine that the colonial legislative assemblies would have developed the strength they attained.

Not the least important result of the 1688 revolution in England was that it found a great defender and theorist in John Locke. In the second of his *Two Treatises on Civil Government,* published in 1689, Locke argued that governments were established by men for the realization of certain ends, and that when they became destructive of these ends, the people governed had the right to alter or abolish their governments. Writing in magisterial and olympian style, Locke instructed all who read him that government derived its power from the people and expressed its will through the actions of representative legislative bodies. In no part of the world was there to be readier acceptance of these ideas than in the American colonies, for it was essentially the political faith in which colonial Americans had been reared.

FURTHER READINGS

Laurence Packard, *The Commercial Revolution, 1400–1776* (1927), and E. P. Cheyney, *European Background of American History, 1300–1600* (1904), are good introductions to the transplanting of European society to American soil.

There is much material on English colonial expansion in volume I of *The Cambridge History of the British Empire* (1929). Two books by A. L. Rowse, *The England of Elizabeth* (1950) and *The Expansion of Elizabethan England* (1955), are written with Elizabethan gusto. D. W. Waters, *The Art of Navigation in England in Elizabethan and Early Stuart Times* (1958),

discusses and gives cogent reasons for the maritime and colonial successes of the English nation.

Faith Thompson gives a good introduction to much of the tradition of Parliament in *A Short History of Parliament* (1953), and the works of Sir John Neale, *The Elizabethan House of Commons* (1950) and *Elizabeth I and Her Parliaments* (2 vols., 1953–1957), add much to the understanding of the political success of the Tudor queen.

Margaret Judson, *The Crisis of the Constitution* (1949), and George L. Mosse, *The Struggle for Sovereignty in England* (1950), are perceptive studies of seventeenth-century political development in England.

In the New American Nation series, Wallace Notestein, *England on the Eve of Colonization* (1954), is an invaluable picture of English society in the early 1600s. Louis B. Wright, *Middle Class Culture in Elizabethan England* (1935) and *Religion and Empire: The Alliance between Piety and Commerce in English Expansion 1558–1625* (1943), are important studies.

Standard accounts of the colonial period of American history by capable American historians are Max Savelle, *The Foundations of American Civilization* (1942), and Curtis P. Nettels, *The Roots of American Civilization* (1938).

A specialized study of considerable relevance here is Richard B. Morris, *Studies in the History of American Law* (1930).

In addition to these short lists of selected recommended readings at the end of each chapter, see the list of general works at the back of the book on page 640. For additional bibliography of an extensive nature, see the Oscar Handlin et al. (eds.), *Harvard Guide to American History* (1954). This work will be hereafter referred to as the *Harvard Guide*.

TWO

New World Environment and Influences

1587
Raleigh's colony at Roanoke Island.

1607
Settlement at Jamestown, Virginia.

1619
Virginia House of Burgesses meets.

1620
Plymouth settlement.

1628
Settlement of Massachusetts Bay.

1634
First settlements in Maryland and Connecticut.

1636
Roger Williams founds Rhode Island.

1643
New England Confederation.

1657
Persecution of Quakers in New England.

1663
Carolina granted to proprietors.

1676
Bacon's Rebellion in Virginia.

1682
Pennsylvania founded.

1691
Witchcraft mania at peak in Salem.

1732
Founding of Georgia.

1764
Paxton Boys in Pennsylvania.

1771
Regulator movement in North Carolina.

REPRESENTATIVE GOVERNMENT IN THE AMERICAN COLONIES

AMERICAN CIVILIZATION, as we have seen, was the offspring of Europe, inheriting a mixture of its characteristics and closely resembling it in fundamental traits. Institutions of government in America owed a particular debt to English accomplishments. But American civilization was not wholly a product of Europe. The primitive coast of North America was a different environment, and some of the beliefs and practices transplanted from Europe took root and flourished while others died. The American frontier chose some elements of European culture for survival and others for destruction. Between Old World culture and New World conditions there was an interaction out of which American society grew.

This interaction is apparent in the ease with which representative government took root in British North America. The fact that the British possessions were *settlement* colonies facilitated the process. Whereas the overseas dominions of other nations were occupied by a relatively small number of Europeans, who constituted a thin fringe of settlers sometimes vastly outnumbered by the native population, English colonization was marked by a flow of English people to America. Except in the very first years of settlement, it was impossible to regard these people as mere agents of the king or of anyone else in England, whom it would be proper to

19

George Frederic Lotter
1784.
W.A.E
L.R.W

A Virginia tobacco wharf
(from a map drawn in 1784)

A colonial kitchen

Drying fish in Maine

Making barrels

Colonial life was an adaptation of European ways to the New World environment. Though King James I called tobacco a "loathsome" weed, it proved to be the economic salvation of Virginia. In New England, fishing became an important industry. There were some employed artisans, but most colonial Americans "set up for themselves" as farmers.

direct from home. They formed an English society in the New World, and they expected to retain the customary rights of Englishmen. For the most part, English kings took it for granted that the colonists would exercise some rights of self-government.

Other circumstances under which early English colonization took place also encouraged self-government. The English colonies were not the work of the government itself, but rather of private groups or individuals. Unlike the colonies of other empire-building nations, which were ordinarily promoted or directly inspired by their home governments, the English efforts were initiated by private business concerns or by individual proprietors who were granted princely domains by the Crown. This fact was exceedingly important for the future of America: in the early formative period, the Crown did not closely direct the development of the colonies.

The foregoing factors can be seen at work in the process by which representative government was established in Virginia. Virginia, first of the English North American colonies, was founded by a joint-stock company. The importance of these companies in colonial enterprises was noted in the previous chapter. Because they operated in far and dangerous places, their charters gave them broad authority over the Englishmen under their control. Indeed, they exercised most of the customary powers of government in the overseas territories, such as waging war, coining money, and granting land titles. It should also be noted that these companies were organized in a way that was, for that time, extremely democratic. The stockholders, who invested money, wanted some measure of control over the business. All power to make laws for the company and elect its officers therefore resided in the stockholders. As a result, in theory at least, power flowed from the bottom up, rather than, as was characteristic of the times, from the top down. In practice, however, control of company affairs lay in the hands of the directors.

The Virginia Company was formed in 1606 by a group of Englishmen ready to invest in the chance of making profits from gold or other valuable products which might be found in that part of America claimed by their sovereign. They secured a charter from the Crown. In 1607 an expedition sent out by one group of the promoters headed into the James River and selected a place on its banks. After building an enclosure, the settlers began to explore the lush countryside for gold or exotic products which might yield a return to their backers in England. They found mostly death from disease and starvation. During the next few years, reinforcements from England barely kept pace with the death rate. By 1616, of 1,600 persons who had embarked for Virginia, there were only 350 survivors in the colony. Eventually, however, those who withstood malaria and dysentery acquired some immunity, and the settlers learned how to raise more food. The success of Virginia was definitely established when treasure was found, not in gold or spices, but in tobacco! The high profits of tobacco culture ensured that the settlement would not be abandoned.

During the first decade the Virginia settlement was ruled by agents appointed by the company. The colonists had no voice in government. In 1619, however, the company saw fit to give the residents of Virginia some of the privileges exercised by the stockholders in England. The governor sent out from England had orders to call together an assembly representing the "freemen" in Virginia, which was to have power to make laws, subject to the governor's veto. This first representative assembly in America, called the House of Burgesses, was modeled on the organization of the English joint-stock company. The continued existence of the House of Burgesses was for a time in doubt. Though the colony gained strength, the company itself fell into bankruptcy. In 1624 its charter was revoked by James I, who took Virginia into his own hands and sent out a royal governor. The King did not recognize the House of Burgesses. Royal governors, however, found it convenient to consult with the inhabitants and continued to summon the House of Burgesses in order to pass laws for the colony. In the end, the usefulness of the system impelled the king to give formal recognition to the Virginia representative assembly. In 1639 its privileges were confirmed, and Virginia had a representative assembly from that time on. Thus a precedent was established. During the next century, most of the charters originally granted to corporations and proprietors were revoked by the Crown. But the kings did not attempt to govern the colonies from England or reserve all power to their own agents. It became the rule that a "royal colony" should have a representative assembly, and the same principle was followed whenever the Crown granted new territory to companies or proprietors. Every colony founded after the establishment of the Virginia House of Burgesses had some kind of representative assembly.

ATTEMPTS AT POLITICAL OLIGARCHY

The joint-stock company was only one agency of colonization. A whole group of English settlements was established by proprietors. Beginning with Lord Baltimore in 1632, Charles I and his successors bestowed large areas upon favored individuals or groups of courtiers. Most of the North American colonies—New Hampshire, New York, New Jersey, Pennsylvania, Maryland, the Carolinas, and Georgia—originated as proprietorships. Whereas Virginia was a projection of English mercantile institutions, the proprietary colonies represented English landed interests. The powerful men who founded them were nearly all large landowners in England, who derived their wealth from ownership of land. In promoting colonies, their primary aim was to acquire enormous estates, which would grow in value as the population increased. Men of noble birth, they had ideas about society that were appropriate to their station. Democracy was not one of these ideas. Their ideal was a society composed of definite classes, based on ownership of land.

The charters which the proprietors got from the king gave them kingly powers. Lord Baltimore's grant is a good example. His powers were greater than those the king dared exercise in England. He owned all the land in Maryland. He was the head of the government and controlled all its branches. His lawmaking power was limited by the provision for a representative assembly, which must consent to all laws, but as he alone had power to propose legislation, the function of the assembly was, at first, only to approve or disapprove. Baltimore was also head of the church, captain general of the armed forces, and disposer of all offices, both civil and clerical.

Plans carried forward after the first settlement in 1634 reflect the idea that Maryland was to have a stratified society

CHRONOLOGY OF COLONIAL ESTABLISHMENT

Colony	Date of establishment	Motive	Government At time of founding	Eighteenth century
Virginia	1607	Commercial	London Company	Crown (after 1624)
Plymouth	1620	Religious	Church Assembly	Incorporated in Massachusetts (1691)
New York	1624 (seized by British 1664)	Commercial	Proprietary	Crown (after 1691)
Massachusetts	1628	Religious	Charter	Crown (after 1691)
Maryland	1634	Religious	Proprietary	
Connecticut	1636	Religious	Charter (1662)	
Rhode Island	1636	Religious	Charter (1663)	
New Jersey	1664	Commercial	Proprietary	Crown (after 1702)
North Carolina	1663	Commercial	Proprietary	Crown (after 1729)
South Carolina	1670	Commercial	Proprietary	Crown (after 1729)
New Hampshire	1679	Commercial	Crown	
Pennsylvania	1681	Religious	Proprietary	
Delaware	1702	Separation from Pennsylvania	Crown	
Georgia	1732	Humanitarian	Proprietary	Crown (after 1752)

based on land ownership, like that of the English countryside. To encourage gentlemen to settle in Maryland, the proprietor offered 1,000 acres to anyone who brought five able men to the colony at his own expense, and another 1,000 acres for each additional group of five men. It was expected that the large tracts disposed of in this way would be "manors," that is, that the owners would have certain monopolies and legal powers over the people who lived there. According to this scheme, Maryland was to be a land of large estates, owned by gentlemen and cultivated by a subordinate class of tenants whom the gentlemen had transported there. To balance the extremes of large landholders on the one side and landless tenants on the other, the proprietors hoped to attract a class of yeomen, that is, independent farmers who would own and work their own land. Thus, 100 acres were allowed to every man who migrated at his own expense, besides additional allotments for his dependents. The proprietor himself expected to live as the lord of this pastoral kingdom, supported by a perpetual income from quitrents.*

* In feudal times there was no such thing as private property in land, as we understand it today. The use of land was granted by a lord to a vassal on condition that the vassal would

The proprietors of the Carolinas had similar ideas. They were a group of eight courtiers, who in 1663 obtained a grant of the area now included in North and South Carolina. Their charter gave them powers similar to those conferred on Lord Baltimore, but in one respect it went further in authorizing them to create titles of nobility. The plans they drew up included a legally constituted nobility of ascending grades. There were to be barons who held 12,000 acres, cassiques who held 24,000 acres, and, highest of all, the landgraves with 48,000 acres. The number of such noblemen was always to be the same, and their estates were not to be divided into smaller units. The tenants who worked their lands, on the other hand, were to be like medieval serfs, bound to the land and subject to the nobleman's court. Their children were to inherit their status. The proposed government and legal system was a fantastic jumble of courts and assemblages, which relegated virtually all power to the proprietor and the noblemen, leaving only an insignificant place for representation of other classes.

The plans of the original proprietors of Maryland and the Carolinas were soon no more than historical curiosities. The Baltimore family made a large amount of money out of Maryland and managed to retain an exceptional degree of personal

authority over the colony, but they could not completely override the representative assembly, which contended for an increasing share in the government, nor could they execute for one moment their plans for disposing of land in such a way as to create a feudalistic society in Maryland. The same misfortune befell the proprietors of the Carolinas. They found that their conceptions were grounded in a mistaken notion of conditions in America. They could not impose rigid class distinctions. Indeed, they could hardly exert any authority at all. Unable to make a profit from their grant, they at length surrendered it to the Crown. The American colonies were not a fertile soil for the unreconstructed ideas of English noblemen. Repressive systems failed because the abundance of cheap land allowed people to move elsewhere if they did not like conditions where they were. The promoters of colonies were placed in the position of having to bid for settlers, and few people, it was discovered, would migrate to colonies where they could not easily own land, nor would they submit to feudal arrangements that were already vanishing in their homeland.

A more significant consequence of the abundance of land was the absence in America of a landless peasantry in the sense that it often existed in Europe. In England, the man who owned his own farm was a person of some importance. His position was superior to that of most of the people in the community, and he was likely to have a sense of pride and personal dignity. Unlike his landless neighbors, he was entitled to vote for members of Parliament, and if his fortunes prospered, it was not beyond the realm of possibility that his daughter would marry into the family of a country gentleman. In England, the yeomanry—small land-

perform services and make payments to the lord. After modern forms of ownership emerged, the notion persisted for a long time that one still owed something to the "lord" of the land, and it was customary to pay him a quitrent in lieu of all feudal services and obligations. Thus, though a person owned a piece of land in the full sense of the word, having bought it and being able to sell it or use it as he pleased, he still paid a quitrent to some individual—the king, or whoever was the nominal lord of the land.

owners—was a class that had a certain status, as well as a reputation for manliness and independence. The existence of a majority of yeomen of this sort set the tone of colonial American society. They owned, or at least cultivated, their own land. In New England land was granted to groups of settlers who applied to the legislature. The settlers would occupy the land as a group, dividing it among themselves, reserving some for late comers. In Virginia, land was conferred on the basis of headrights. Every free man automatically became entitled to 50 acres. Later, when this headright system was discontinued, land could still be bought on easy terms, particularly in the west. It was true of all the colonies, except possibly New York, that any man could easily get land. True, these farmers might be pressed with debts and carry on their lives under crude and isolated circumstances, but they displayed the habits of mind appropriate to men who lived off their own acres. There were poor people and incompetent people in the American colonies, but aside from the slaves there never was a large dependent and propertyless class. Even those who lived in towns and worked for others received, if they were not bound servants, perhaps three times the pay of a laborer in England. Underneath the formal political and social institutions brought from Europe, the presence of economic opportunity nourished democratic manners and habits.

THEOCRACY AND DISSENT IN THE AMERICAN COLONIES

Another experiment which failed to realize the aims of its sponsors was Massachusetts, founded in 1629. This was an attempt to organize a society in America on religious principles. The leaders were English Puritans, men filled with religious zeal, who intended to found a Christian commonwealth in the New World. Their motives, of course, were mixed; like nearly everyone who ever migrated to America, they were inspired with the hope of making their fortunes or at least bettering their condition. This consideration was, no doubt, paramount among the common people who formed the bulk of the population. Nevertheless, side by side with an economic motive was the idea of establishing a society in accord with religious principles.

In some ways these men were closer to the Middle Ages than to the present. Modern thought has a secular bias. Although we may wonder about the ultimate meaning of things, we go to science for most explanations of nature, society, and even human behavior. In the Middle Ages, however, the different branches of formal thought were saturated with theological concepts. The theology of the Puritans emphasized the doctrine of original sin. In common with other Protestant groups, the Puritans held that all mankind merited eternal damnation. Jesus' sacrifice had, they thought, atoned for the sins of only a portion of mankind—the elect destined for salvation. The remainder were unregenerate, bound for Hell. Moreover, the Puritans held to a belief in rigid predestination. No one by any act of his own could change his divinely appointed spiritual destiny or move into the ranks of the elect if not already chosen by God for such privilege. There were thus two kinds of men, the elect and the unregenerate, and their fates were irremediably fixed. This Calvinistic theology had been but slightly softened by the addition in England of the concept of a Covenant of Grace, offered to man by God, by which God promised to save all those who truly believed. In New England, the requirements accepted as evidence of saving grace were at first very strict indeed.

At a time when religion validated and upheld all governments, laws, and social relations, it was natural to translate these religious concepts into a system of government. In civil society, the elect of the Lord should hold the power of government; they should dictate the details of daily life for all in the society, for presumably they alone knew the purposes of God. The Puritan regime was therefore characterized by excessive regulation of personal behavior and by an inquisitorial prying into the state of people's morals. Toward other sects that appeared in their midst, the Puritan leaders displayed a fierce intolerance which amounted on occasion to brutal oppression, for their strength of purpose and their sense of election obliged them to scorn, despise, and stamp out such sects if they could.

The Massachusetts ministers attempted to maintain uniformity of doctrine and procedure by extending control over all the church congregations of the colony. The high point of this effort was the Cambridge Platform of 1648, a statement of creed enacted into law by the legislature and enforced by the civil authority. But it proved impossible in the long run to maintain discipline. Congregations chose their own ministers, and some of them always insisted on running their own affairs. Moreover, as time went on, the people spread farther into the hinterland, losing interest in the religious disputes that had provoked the first coming. There was a noticeable decline in piety. The first religious and civil leaders had thought of themselves as a chosen people, but there had always been—as one common man replied to a pastor who was haranguing

the congregation of a coastal village— many, who "had just come to fish." Amidst the opportunities presented by a growing economy, material goals gained primacy over spiritual goals. More and more people whose salvation was dubious were admitted into the church. By the eighteenth century, though the clergy remained influential and religion an important force, the idea of Massachusetts as a theocratic society, committed to a purely religious purpose, was dead.

Rhode Island, which along with Connecticut was an offshoot of Massachusetts, displayed Puritanism in a quite different aspect. Its founder was Roger Williams, who was a Separatist. One might describe the Separatists as the lower-class wing of the general group of Puritans, drawing their strength from farmers and workingmen. They were as zealous in religion as any other group, and not without their share of the bigotry characteristic of the times, but as lowly people they could not think of forcing their tenets on others or making their creed the official religion of the state. They conceived of a church only as a voluntary association of like-thinking people, divorced from the political organization of the community. Though not really very tolerant, they opposed the principle of authority in matters of faith and stood for the separation of church and state. One group of Separatists came to America in 1620 and founded the Plymouth colony whose quaint and picturesque beginnings have made it a favorite subject for writers. Never important, Plymouth was later absorbed by Massachusetts.

Roger Williams was fairly prominent among Puritans in England and received a cordial welcome from the leaders of the Massachusetts colony. Had he fully shared their ideas, he would have found a place among them. But Williams, a man of deep religious impulses, was disturbed by what he saw and not backward in voicing his objections. To him the religious organization in the colony was too much like the state church in England. He opposed the union of church and state in Massachusetts and the attempt to dictate religious belief and enforce uniformity. Finally, when the Massachusetts authorities were ready to deport him to England, he escaped with his followers and organized another settlement, which became the nucleus of Rhode Island. Here Williams's ideas were put into practice. Complete freedom of conscience was established. Rhode Island became the haven of minority sects like the Quakers and the Baptists, and in the eyes of respectable people of neighboring colonies, a sinkhole of religious and social radicalism. Rhode Island was an experiment in religious liberty dedicated to the idea that, though people may disagree in their principles, civil order can best be secured not by trying to force them all to believe alike, but by allowing them to disagree. Roger Williams himself became a "seeker," who did not believe any church was in sole possession of the truth. In an extended controversy with John Cotton, spokesman for the Massachusetts theocracy, he attacked the "bloody tenent of Persecution," and defended religious freedom.

The implications of a similar nonconformist creed were worked out fifty years later in Pennsylvania, founded in 1682 by Quakers under William Penn. Though Penn himself was a wealthy aristocrat, who secured a proprietary grant from the king, the majority of Quakers were poor workingmen or farmers in England. By contemporary standards, their doctrines were quite radical. Some of the religious ideas of the Reformation were carried

much further by them than by other groups. Believing literally in the "priesthood of true believers," the Quakers had no ministers and no well-defined dogma or creed. They sought as individuals that "inner light" by which each man would know God in his own way. On principle, they rejected authority in matters of belief. These ideas were shocking to the "better" sort of people. Moreover, on religious grounds, the Quakers refused to perform certain acts required by law and custom. They would not undertake military service. They refused oaths. No "respecters of persons," only of God, they would not doff their hats in the presence of superiors. Consequently, the Quakers drew persecution upon themselves and were herded into jails and prevented from making a living. Thousands of them from England and the Continent sought refuge in Pennsylvania.

The history of Pennsylvania displays the liberal influence of Quaker beliefs. No official or state-supported church existed in the colony, and there was complete toleration of other beliefs. Penn had great authority as proprietor, but he willingly granted a constitution which limited his own power. Of all the American colonies, Pennsylvania grew most rapidly in the eighteenth century, not only because of her fertile lands, but also because the colony welcomed and freely tolerated people of different nationality, religion, and opinion. The success of Pennsylvania highlights the American experience. Attempts to control religious beliefs by political authority met with no more success than efforts to transplant European feudalism into a primitive environment featured by an abundance of land.

The ancient controversies fought in the name of religion concealed issues of fundamental importance in the development of modern civilization. As has already been noted, the people of that time had the habit of thinking in theological terms. Differences in religion usually signified a conflict of ideas about government, law, property rights, and other social matters. The struggle for religious toleration was, therefore, a struggle to establish freedom of thought in all things relative to mankind and society. This conflict was not fought in the colonies alone, of course, but here the wide latitude in religious matters led to a similar tolerance of unorthodox views in government. This, then, was the impact of religious dissent and the contribution of religious reformers to American colonial development.

COMMERCE, CREDIT, AND CURRENCY

The major economic problem of a frontier area is to find a return, that is, some kind of goods or occupation that will yield a quick income, enable the settlers to buy the multitude of things they need from older countries, and so permit them to rise above the first primitive conditions. The southern provinces solved this problem by discovering a marketable agricultural staple. Virginia and Maryland became the tobacco colonies, raising vast quantities of this commodity, the exportation of which provided the funds used to buy manufactured articles from England. The Carolinas and Georgia were settled in a later period, and at first their economic growth was slow. South Carolina, however, eventually found profitable cash crops in rice and indigo, with production stimulated by a British bounty.

No such simple solution was available in New England, where good soil was scarce. The New Englanders employed other means of obtaining the money to

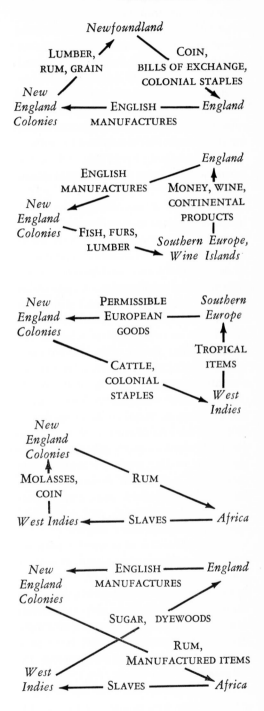

TRIANGULAR TRADE

pay for their imports from the mother country. They took to the sea as fishermen and traders. Near at hand were the Newfoundland Banks, one of the great fishing grounds of the world. New England's dependence on the fisheries was symbolized by Massachusetts' emblem, the codfish. But it was as traders and middlemen that New Englanders raised most of their money income. New England lay athwart the main shipping routes from the mother country to the more southerly provinces, and the merchants of Massachusetts played the role of middlemen, buying English goods and distributing them to other colonies. Much of the intercolonial trade fell into their hands. Illustrative of New England's early commercial growth was the so-called triangular trade. In one of these triangles, New Englanders distilled rum out of molasses and shipped the rum to the coast of Africa, where they traded it for slaves. The human cargo was then transported over the dreaded "middle passage" to the West Indies and sold. The New Englanders took part of the proceeds of the sale in cash and part in molasses—a by-product of the sugar manufactured in these islands. The last leg of the trading journey was the voyage home with a cargo of molasses destined to be manufactured into rum, which would start the process over again. This trade was vital to New England.

The middle colonies raised money by producing agricultural staples as well as by trade. Out of their rich hinterlands came harvests of cereal grains and other foodstuffs, which were shipped abroad. New York, Philadelphia, and, later, Baltimore became commercial centers, whose merchants engaged in general and diversified trade.

There were two main directions of colonial commerce. One was toward England, where the colonies bought nearly all their manufactured articles and the tobacco colonies marketed their crops. The other was toward the West Indies, whose trade was important to the middle colonies and New England. The West Indies, both British and foreign, had become huge sugar factories, crowded with slaves. So exclusively were these islands devoted to sugar production that they had to import foodstuffs. They took the fish, the barrel staves, and the slaves brought in by New England vessels and grain supplied by the middle colonies. It was largely the cash which the colonists derived from the West Indies that enabled them to keep buying English goods.

When trade fell off, everybody in the colonies suffered; nevertheless, much of the economic life of the country existed apart from the buying and selling of goods. America was not commercially developed and produced few manufactures. The largest cities, like Boston and Philadelphia, were but small towns by our standards, with populations of 25,000 or 35,000 at the end of the colonial period. They had a far greater importance than these figures would imply, however, as each was the metropolis and the capital of a province, and towns like these were still exceptional in a predominantly rural country. Perhaps 95 per cent of Americans practiced agriculture, and most of these people were small farmers who produced mainly for consumption and only a little for sale, getting most of the things they needed from the farm and the labor of their families.

The typical colonist was not a good farmer. He wasted the soil, let his livestock run in the woods, and refused to adopt better methods when they were hown to him. But living standards were imple, and the common things were heap. Nearly everybody enjoyed a rude abundance of things to eat.

As their economy grew, the colonies needed more capital and credit to exploit the opportunities which emerged. Thus began a process which continued up to recent times: the older countries of Europe, in this case England, made capital available to further the economic development of America. In colonial times, much of the business activity in the provinces rested ultimately on British credit. A chain of credit extended across the ocean to the remote inland settlements. English merchants sold goods to colonial merchants on credit, and these in turn passed the goods along on credit to country storekeepers. The storekeepers sold the goods to farmers on credit. A reverse chain of indebtedness paralleled the chain of credit. Farmers and planters typically owed money to colonial merchants, who, in turn, were likely to be in debt to English or Scottish merchants. Over the whole period, colonial indebtedness mounted steadily, particularly in the southern provinces. At the time of the Revolution, it was estimated that the planters of Virginia and Maryland owed some 3 million pounds to British merchants, a sum which it was unlikely they would ever be able to pay. Jefferson described the great planters who rose in Virginia as "a mere species of property annexed to certain British mercantile houses."

In order to increase the credit available to farmers and planters, as well as to supply the people with a medium of exchange, colonial governments resorted to various experiments with paper money. Colonial legislatures established "land banks," printing paper money and loan-

ing it to farmers, accepting mortgages on their land as security. This system was popular among farmers because it gave them capital to buy more land and improve their property. It was also popular with the general public as a way of curing economic depression. Whenever trade slackened, the people called upon the government to establish a land bank, which would put money in circulation, raise the price level and stimulate business. Later, the money could be retired as

COLONIAL ECONOMIC ACTIVITY

farmers paid back their loans to the government. Such land banks were adopted by all the colonies except Virginia.

Paper money was also emitted directly by colonial governments to pay their operating expenses, particularly in time of war. Unlike modern governments, they could not raise much money by borrowing from the people. Whenever an emergency arose, therefore, they simply printed enough money to pay their expenses. The money was redeemed, not by giving gold or silver in exchange for it, but by accepting it for taxes levied on the inhabitants. All the colonies used this system. In most of the colonies paper money worked satisfactorily and contributed to their economic growth. It was liable to abuse, however, and in some colonies, notably those of New England and the Carolinas, so much was issued at one time or another that the money depreciated to a fraction of its value. This gave rise to bitter conflicts between merchants and creditors, on the one hand, and farmers and debtors who benefited from depreciation, on the other.

In spite of the constant search for a circulating medium, the colonies remained chronically short of capital and credit, and as a result, they were in some ways distinctly backward. Up to the Revolution, there were no banks or business corporations. Merchants restricted their activities to local partnerships and small-scale operations. But wealth was increasing, and individuals were amassing substantial fortunes. At his death a few years before the Revolution, Thomas Hancock, Massachusetts merchant, left an estate valued at over $300,000, and fortunes of similar magnitude were not unknown among the Quaker grandees of Philadelphia or the great planters of the Old Dominion.

THE ACTS OF TRADE AND NAVIGATION

The colonial economy was regulated in a general way by the mother country. Crown and Parliament, like all other governments of this era, subscribed to the ideas of mercantilism, whose central principle was that economic life ought to be regulated in the interest of the state. One object of that regulation was to establish a favorable balance of trade with foreign countries in the belief that a continuous excess of exports over imports would build up a nation's industry at the expense of its rivals and draw from them their stores of gold and silver. Another cardinal principle was that of monopoly —the exclusion of foreigners from trade and economic opportunity within the empire. A third principle, no less vital, was the promotion of the oceanic carrying trade and the increase of the merchant marine, not only for the sake of the middleman's profits, but for the sake of defense. In the age of sail, fighting ships were not highly specialized and armed merchant vessels played a large role in wartime.

It was accepted doctrine that colonies existed for the benefit of the empire and that the interests of the mother country were paramount. The conditions under which the British settlement colonies had evolved ruled out any gross form of exploitation, however, and although Britain's welfare was always foremost, the home government's policy was guided by the desire to achieve an economically integrated and self-sufficient empire whose parts complemented one another to their mutual advantage. Britain was conceived of as the metropolis, the industrial and financial center, and the colonies as hinterland, markets, and producers of raw materials.

Apart from regulations intended to serve the interests of the empire and of Britain in particular in competition with foreign nations, there was a conscious effort to promote a reciprocal economic development within the empire. In some cases this involved prohibiting colonial activities which conflicted with those of the mother country, in other cases granting special inducements to stimulate enterprise which was complementary to British industry and useful to the empire.

Although foreshadowed in earlier acts, the grand design of British regulation was elaborated between 1650 and 1673 with the passage of successive Navigation Acts. Aimed directly at the Dutch, whose carrying fleets dominated the trade of northern Europe and England herself in the preceding century, they became landmarks of British maritime policy and were considered to be a vital factor in the emergence of Britain as a great commercial nation. The Navigation Acts comprehended two major principles affecting the colonies: the complete exclusion of foreign merchants and foreign ships and the channeling of colonial trade with Europe through Britain.

The Navigation Act of 1660, the "English Magna Carta of the Seas," barred all foreign merchants from the colonies and restricted colonial trade to English ships —English built and owned, under an English captain, three-fourths of whose crew was English. The colonists qualified as English under this act and shared in all privileges. The act also designated certain "enumerated articles" produced in the colonies, including sugar, tobacco, cotton, indigo, ginger, and dyewoods (the list was later extended), which could be shipped only to English or colonial ports. If destined for Europe, these articles had first to be landed in an English port and reloaded, with all duties paid, before they were carried to their destination. The system of regulation was completed in 1663 with the passage of the Staple Act of that year, which required all goods en route from Europe to America to undergo a similar process of deposit in England and payment of duties before proceeding. The system was designed to exclude foreigners from the trade of the empire, make Britain the intermediary of colonial trade with Europe, and increase royal revenues from port duties.

Besides the effort to control trade, Parliament tried to steer the economic development of the colonies by imposing duties and prohibitions upon some lines of enterprise to prevent their growth, while encouraging others with subsidies, bounties, and special privileges. The colonies were not allowed to export wool or wool cloth because these articles competed with British goods. In 1750 Parliament passed the Iron Act, which forbade the erection of iron-finishing mills; it was entirely acceptable to Britain that the colonies produce raw iron, but it was intended that they should buy their nails, tools, and other finished articles from British manufacturers. The efforts of the northern colonies to stimulate manufactures by laying duties on imported British goods were quickly suppressed. Along the same lines, the attempts of the southern colonies to restrict the importation of slaves were disallowed because the slave trade was profitable to Britain and it suited the purposes of the British government to foster the maximum production of such staple crops as tobacco in the southern colonies.

If the colonies were to consume British manufactures, however, they had to have something to sell. Hence, the tobacco colonies were given a monopoly of the British market; cultivation of tobacco was forbidden in England. A bounty upon indigo laid the foundation of South Carolina's prosperity. The Carolinas, along with Massachusetts and New Hampshire, benefited from subsidies for the production of naval stores. The requirement that all vessels in colonial trade be British built promoted shipbuilding in New England and the middle colonies. Northern merchants participated extensively after 1715 in the slave trade, in which Britain had won preeminence for its own merchants by military victory over Spain. The effect of the requirement that American cargoes destined for Europe be landed at a British port was mitigated by rebating all or part of the duties paid on them.

The most damaging restriction upon colonial enterprise was the Molasses Act of 1733, which Parliament adopted for the benefit of the West Indies planters. The British sugar islands, whose by-product of molasses was the basic ingredient in New England's rum industry, suffered early from soil exhaustion, declining productivity, and increased costs of production. New Englanders therefore bought molasses in the French and Spanish islands, where it could be obtained more cheaply. In an effort to sustain the British islands, Parliament laid a duty of sixpence a gallon on foreign molasses imported into the colonies. If enforced, this rate would have undermined New England's economy; however, it was evaded by smuggling on a grand scale—the colonists were skilled practitioners of the art.

The general effect of British regulation is difficult to evaluate. American interests were frankly subordinated, but in most cases it would appear that the regulations did not greatly interfere with the course which colonial trade would have followed in any case. Those regulations which did interfere were simply evaded. The discouragement of American manufactures counted for little; lack of capital and the high cost of labor were a greater obstacle. On the other hand, the colonists gained a great deal from association with Britain—not only the specific privileges afforded by the Acts of Trade and Navigation, but general and indirect advantages. British merchants supplied the basic capital for colonial economic development. The British navy protected the colonists and their oceanic trade without cost to themselves. The colonies were set within the empire of a powerful, dynamic nation destined for economic greatness. The growth and prosperity of the North American colonies in the eighteenth century hardly represented the spectacle of oppression, but rather the mildness of British rule and the benefits of the imperial connection.

POPULATION AND LABOR SUPPLY

In addition to the shortage of capital and currency, the economic development of the colonies was hampered by an inadequate labor supply—this in spite of the fact that people married young and bore many children. As one Englishman observed: "The Americans multiply with the fecundity of their own rattlesnakes." Family raising, in fact, was a sound investment. Within a few years the children could be put to work in kitchen or field. Thus the colonists arrived at a partial solution to the problem of labor supply. But this was not enough. Even though natural resources were abundant, economic development was limited by the scarcity of labor and capital. The need for labor early gave rise to the practice of importing indentured servants, that is, contract laborers, who bound themselves to work for a term of years in return for their passage across the ocean. Most indentured servants were drawn from the poorer classes of England. Many did not come willingly but were deluded or forced into emigrating. Thousands were kidnaped and placed on vessels sailing to America. Other thousands were convicts, sentenced to servitude. During the eighteenth century, there was a heavy migration of Germans and Scotch-Irish, and a good many of these came as contract laborers.

Those who ventured or were herded into the New World in this way faced an ordeal of hardship and danger. Crowded into the interior of ships, indifferently fed, they fell victim to diseases that swept through the immigrant vessels. Once in the colonies, the majority were put to heavy labor on farms and plantations. They suffered, and often died, in the harsh, strange climate. Frequently America did prove to be a land of opportunity for these lowly folk. The servant who had worked out his term found that no particular stigma attached to him because of his former condition. He could take his place with other freemen, get a headright or buy land, and rise in the world. Many ex-servants acquired wealth and position. On the other hand, however, many remained poor. So far as records are available, it appears that ex-servants were likely to stay among the lower ranks of the colonial population, and of the convicts who served their terms and became free, very few ever radically improved their fortunes. They did not always rise above the disabilities of habit and character stamped on them by their early condition, and since they started with less, it

was harder for them to gain a position of prosperity and respectability.

Negro slaves eventually took the place of white servants as the major labor supply of the southern colonies. Negroes were imported into Virginia as early as 1619, but slavery did not become predominant until after 1700, when England became the world's great slave trader. The Negroes were gathered on the coast of Africa and shipped to the West Indies. Those who survived the voyage, the new climate, and the rigors of despair, were trained to labor. In three or four years they could be sold as seasoned slaves to planters in the tobacco colonies. Unlike the white servants brought to America, the Negro was destined, whether slave or free, to occupy a place below and apart from the general body of white inhabitants. During the eighteenth century, the number of slaves increased rapidly in the southern colonies.

Growth in wealth and population owed much to a new wave of immigration in the eighteenth century, not primarily of English people, but of Germans and Scotch-Irish. The Germans came impelled by the desire to escape feudal conditions, religious intolerance, and destructive wars that existed in their own country and by the hope of owning their own land in America. Many of them were radical sectarians whose peculiar ways conflicted with the dominant religions in Germany. They wanted to practice their faith and live their own kind of life in peace. Since the Penns offered religious toleration and cheap land, the main body of immigrants flowed through the port of Philadelphia and took up land around the original Quaker settlements. The Pennsylvania "Dutch" soon became America's most skillful general farmers, delighting in orchards, two-story barns, and massive horses. They generally settled apart, keeping their language, customs, and religion. This migration was of such proportions that Benjamin Franklin once expressed the fear that Pennsylvania would become a German community.

As German migration reached its height in the 1720s, the Scotch-Irish were already arriving in large numbers. Like the Germans, and for the same reasons, most of them entered Pennsylvania. The Scotch-Irish came from Ulster, a district in northern Ireland. Early in the seventeenth century, the English government had wished to plant a colony there as a means of imposing some control over the Catholic Irish, who were periodically in rebellion. Almost all the colonists sent to Ulster were drawn from Scotland and were zealous Presbyterians who lived on terms of intense hostility with the Irish people ranged about them. Repeated massacres and reprisals on both sides provided a kind of environment which suitably prepared the Scots for their later role of Indian fighters on the American frontier.

The migration of the Scotch-Irish got under way early in the eighteenth century and continued until the Revolution. Unlike the pacific Germans, who got along well with the Quakers, the Scotch-Irish were a quarrelsome and unruly breed, violent, contemptuous of authority, and addicted to taking over land without paying for it. An agent of the Penn family once said that a single Scotch-Irishman caused him more trouble than twenty of any other nationality. The Quakers were only too willing to see these immigrants move off to the frontier, where they settled behind the Germans. As more immigrants arrived, the Scotch-Irish pressed farther inland, ultimately reaching the heads of the long Appalachian valleys that extend southwestward behind the first ridges. In decades that followed, they moved down these valleys into the back country of Virginia, the Carolinas, and even Georgia. The Scotch-Irish became America's typical frontiersmen, habituated to primitive life and Indian warfare, moving with the frontier as it edged westward.

On the eve of the Revolution the colonies had a population of perhaps 2,500,000 at a time when the mother country had no more than 7,000,000. Settlement had moved inland from the coast and was breaking across the Alleghenies into the valley of the Ohio. The growth and westward movement of the population was sustained and accelerated by an increasingly productive economy.

CLASS AND SECTIONAL CONFLICT

Few of the nobility and privileged classes of Europe migrated to the American colonies, but during the century before the Revolution, social and economic changes in the colonies gave birth to a native aristocracy. It was not a titled order, for no formal order of nobility was introduced into the colonies, but rather an aristocracy of wealth. It was not a leisure class, divorced from ordinary life and toil, such as existed in the Old World. A colonial aristocrat might be a merchant; in that case, he was a master of ships, who himself calculated the hazards of trade and supervised the work of clerks employed in his countinghouse. He might be a planter, who lived in a mansion seated on a great estate; nonetheless, he attended personally to the cultivation of fields and managed the numerous details of plantation life, dealing with common men and slaves. America lacked the accumulated wealth, tradition, and prestige, which allowed the Old World nobility to live on a plane removed from the lot of the common people. The American aristocracy was home-grown and provincial, and it imposed itself on a distinctly unservile population, whose ways reflected the assurance and self-respect of men who made their living off their own land. Nevertheless, in an age when the principle of social gradation was universally accepted, it was natural that as the colonies grew in wealth and population, men who acquired large possessions should arrogate to themselves a higher status. It was also natural that the common people, by and large, should acquiesce in these pretensions.

For example, in early Virginia the small farmer constituted the principal element of the population. Rich men came to the colony, and there were some who traced descent from gentle families in England; nevertheless, most of the people worked farms of moderate size with the help of their families and perhaps a few indentured servants or slaves. Tobacco prices stayed high during the first half-century, and small planters could prosper, pay their debts, and buy more land. Really large scale operations were handicapped by the scarcity and high cost of labor. Over a period of time, this situation changed, and the eastern part of Virginia became a land of large plantations, slavery, and aristocracy. Economic changes helped to bring this about. Tobacco was overproduced and prices fell. With a low margin of profit, small farmers no longer found it easy to pay their debts and advance themselves. The wealthier planters got credit from British merchants, which sustained them when others failed and enabled them to acquire land and slaves. The increasingly plentiful supply of slaves after 1675 was, of course, fundamental to the development of large-scale planting.

Another factor was the diminishing availability of land. There was no shortage of land in the early days. It was cheap and plentiful. Indeed, a large amount was required by the tobacco grower because his methods wasted the soil. No care was taken to avoid erosion, which soon ruined large areas. Moreover, tobacco planters neither fertilized their soil nor practiced crop rotation. They planted one tobacco crop after another, but after about five years the soil became useless for further planting. To stay in business, a tobacco farmer had to have reserves of land. Eventually, as population increased, good land within the settled area became scarce and expensive. Even the land farther west was likely to be the property of some large proprietor; it had become a common practice for the governor to make huge grants of land to favorites and wealthy men who could exert influence. The headright system was discarded. Ordinary men no longer had easy access to good tobacco land.

The declining fortunes of the small farmers and their resentment against the increasing sway of aristocracy were registered in Bacon's Rebellion, which occurred in 1676. The occasion was an Indian outbreak, during which the governor, Sir William Berkeley, refused to take proper measures for defense of the frontier plantations. There were other, more basic reasons for the rebellion. The autocratic Berkeley had systematically gathered around himself a party formed of the richer men of the province, whom he bribed with lucrative offices and special favors. For more than a decade, this clique ruled the colony. The common people saw their political rights taken away at the same time that their economic prospects were worsening. At last, however, the gathering resentment found a leader in Nathaniel Bacon, who raised a force against the governor and drove him out of the colony. Bacon was master of the province for a short while, but at a critical juncture he died, and the rebellion collapsed. When Berkeley regained power, he and his party took vengeance on Bacon's followers, executing many and taking their property for themselves. Berkeley was finally recalled to England in some disgrace, but the great planters who stood with him kept their power and continued to be the leaders of the province.

The rise of a planter aristocracy in Virginia gave birth to a sectional division which tended to coincide with class difference. During most of the colonial period, large-scale tobacco planting was confined to the tidewater, that is, the low-lying continental shelf which begins in the Chesapeake Bay region, broadens to a region more than 100 miles wide in South Carolina, and eventually merges with the Gulf uplands. On the west, the tidewater is bounded by the fall line, where the land becomes elevated and the rivers flow in rapids. In colonial times, this marked the end of easy transportation into the interior. Behind the fall line lies the piedmont, a region of rolling hills well suited to general farming. The hills become steeper up to the first of the great ridges that run across the interior of Virginia and the Carolinas. Behind the ridges, which enclose fertile valleys, lies the broad mass of the Appalachian highlands. The tidewater became a land of great plantations and slavery, dominated by aristocratic families. As population increased, the piedmont was inhabited by small farmers, who practiced agriculture largely for subsistence and whose interests were frequently opposed to those of the eastern planters. Sectional divisions of

Bradford House, Kingston, Massachusetts. Built in 1674 and still retaining its original appearance, this is a sturdy example of early Puritan domestic architecture. (Historic Buildings Survey, Library of Congress)

this kind were destined to play a large role in American development.

Despite the lack of large-scale agriculture, similar antagonisms appeared in New England. As we have seen, the most lucrative pursuits there were trade, fishing, and manufacturing, and these in time gave rise to individual fortunes. A distinctive aristocracy, such as one finds in the south, never developed in New England, which remained the most "democratical" of the colonial areas. Nevertheless, there was an upper class, accustomed to being foremost, standing apart from the ordinary run of people. In New England, as in the south, economic opportunity tended to contract as time went on. In the early days, free land had been available in the form of township grants to groups of settlers. As population increased and land prices rose in value, latecomers found that there was nothing for them. The original grantees kept for themselves what remained of the township land and would not divide it with others. New England towns were ridden with disputes between the original proprietors and the latecomers. Even in the frontier areas to the north and west, the township grant system did not function as it had in the early days. It had become a practice for the legislature to grant whole townships to one or a few individuals, who sought grants for speculative purposes, holding the land for sale to actual settlers. To this internal conflict was added sectional conflict. The back country was inhabited by subsistence farmers, typically in debt and exposed to Indian attack, whereas the people of the coastal cities lived by trade, fishing, and manufacture. The antagonisms between coast and frontier centered on such issues as frontier defense, taxation, and land ownership.

What has already been said about the rise of aristocracy and the existence of sectional cleavages in the south and New England is generally true also of the middle colonies. Fortunes were based on both commerce and landholding. After the Dutch yielded New York in 1664, the British governors who were sent out to the province granted such enormous tracts to individuals that much of the land up the Hudson River Valley was held by a few great proprietors. The landed magnates of the interior had their counterpart in the merchants of New York City, who amassed fortunes in trade.

In Pennsylvania, the poor Quakers who first sought refuge in the colony manifested singular business acumen and prospered in trade. Benefiting from the rapid growth of the colony, they became wealthy. Many of them, in accord with their religious tenets, still wore plain clothes and avoided display, yet their garments were of the choicest fabrics and the richest of them lived in finely appointed houses. Philadelphia became the capital of America, its most expensive and luxurious city. Its leaders in commerce and wealth comprised an aristocracy as well defined and as self-conscious as any that existed in the planter south.

FRONTIER PROTESTS

Everywhere the aristocratic clique sought to erect barriers against popular control of government through the denial of equal representation in the colonial legislatures to the frontier areas. When the first legislatures were set up, the assemblies consisted of delegates representing the counties of the coast, the region of early settlement. Later, as population increased and the back country filled up with farmers, the original eastern counties, now the seat of aristocracy, kept control of the government by refusing the interior counties the number of assembly delegates to which their population entitled them. An outstanding example is Pennsylvania. By the time of the Revolution, two-thirds of the population lived in the interior counties, yet these counties had less than one-third of the delegates in the assembly. With only one-third of the population, the original counties, including the city of Philadelphia, had more than two-thirds of the seats in the assembly. With the help of the German community in Pennsylvania, the Quaker minority retained political control.

The latent hostilities inherent in this political discrimination sometimes burst into violence. Such an incident was that of the Paxton Boys, which occurred in Pennsylvania in 1764. This grew out of the refusal of the Quaker-dominated legislature to extend adequate protection to exposed frontier areas against Indian forays. Infuriated by this neglect and the constant Indian menace, a band of Scotch-Irish frontiersmen massacred a group of friendly Christianized Indians whom they believed to have taken part in raids. They then proceeded to march on Philadelphia. It took all the persuasive power of Benjamin Franklin to persuade them not to attack the city. The incident closed without further violence, but it revealed the bitter feeling which the Presbyterian Scotch-Irish frontiersmen held against the existing merchant aristocracy of the Quakers.

A similar situation exploded into violence in North Carolina, just before the Revolution. In the background lay the familiar fact that the western counties were underrepresented in the assembly. Local government in the western counties was in the hands of a "courthouse ring" consisting of justices of the peace and sheriffs, leagued with the eastern planters who controlled the assembly. Government was notably corrupt. Officials charged improper fees, and a good share of the tax collections never got as far as the provincial treasury. Faced with such a situation, western farmers formed an association to "regulate" government. Among other things, the Regulators swore they would pay no more taxes until taxes already collected were accounted for. They called upon the tax officials to make public their accounts. They were met with blunt refusals and the seizure of goods belonging to Regulators who would not pay taxes. Thereafter, a series of provocative acts on both sides led toward an open break. The Regulators began to refer to their association as "our government," by implication denying their allegiance to a corrupt provincial administration. In 1771 the Regulators forcibly took over a court session in one of the western counties, held mock trials, and awarded judgments in favor of poor farmers against their creditors. The legislature responded by passing a number of acts which, in effect, outlawed the Regulators. The British governor, compelled by his duty to maintain law and order, collected a militia force, composed almost wholly of men from eastern counties, and marched into the interior. He met some 2,000 Regulators at a place called Alamance Creek. The Regulators wished to parley, but the governor refused unless they would surrender their arms. When the Regulators would not deliver up their weapons, the governor ordered his force to attack. Most of the Regulators fled at once, although a few held out for a time, fighting in a wood. The Regulator movement was crushed in this skirmish. Some of the Regulators refused to accept the liberal pardons offered by the governor and fled westward toward Tennessee. Those who remained were cowed, but they long harbored a bitter grudge against the easterners. This is one reason why there was an exceptional number of loyalists in the North Carolina back country during the Revolution. Since it was the eastern planters who led the resistance to Britain, many ex-Regulators took the side of George III.

In 1740 Massachusetts was divided by a controversy over a land bank. A group of men formed a private bank to issue notes on loans to farmers. This scheme was strongly opposed by Boston merchants, who pledged themselves not to accept the paper currency issued by the land bank. The struggle became intense when the merchants formed an opposition bank whose notes were backed by silver. The merchants appealed to Parliament, whereupon Parliament revived an old statute which had never been intended to apply to the colonies and declared that under its terms the land bank in Massachusetts was illegal. This arbitrary ruling, which gave victory to the merchants, brought financial ruin to the men who, in good faith, had organized the land bank. Feeling ran so high against Britain for a while that there was talk of resistance. Years later, John Adams wrote that the land-bank affair caused a greater stir in Massachusetts than the Stamp Act.

Such incidents suggest a growing degree of protest against aristocratic influences in American colonial society, a protest which usually emanated from the frontier regions. These episodes gain in significance when placed in conjunction with the democratic upheaval that occurred in some colonies during the Revolution.

POLITICAL LIFE IN THE LATE COLONIAL PERIOD

Over the course of decades, the leading families in each province were drawn together by intermarriage. Thus landed wealth merged with commercial wealth. In most of the colonies an identifiable group of families, with their allies and connections, both dominated economic life and monopolized political office. Politics was almost exclusively a gentleman's game. This was especially true in the provinces outside New England, where the county system of local government prevailed and where nearly all offices were appointive rather than elective. The highest office to which a colonist could ordinarily aspire was the governor's council. The dozen or so members of this body were almost invariably drawn from the richest and most influential families in each colony. Councilmen were appointed for life. They sat with the governor when he made executive decisions. They also acted as the upper house of colonial legislatures, thus taking part in the making of laws. Members of the council were powerful and influential men.

At the county level, government, as in England, was in the hands of justices of the peace, who were appointed for life. Except in the back country, those who held this office were men of wealth and family connections. Their power was great. They sat in judgment on civil and criminal cases in local areas, and several times a year the justices of each county assembled to try more important cases. Not only was the law in their hands, but they had important administrative functions. Justices of the peace took charge of nearly everything of a public nature that had to be done, such as assessing taxes, overseeing the construction of roads, building jails, and taking care of the poor. In practice, they controlled the appointment of the sheriff, the only other county officer of importance, and it was common for them to take turns at being sheriff. Frequently, the justices also served as officers of the militia, the military force of the colonies.

The lowest unit of local government was the parish, an administrative unit which existed in those colonies where the Anglican church was established. Parish affairs were managed by the vestry, a group of officers that handled, not only church matters, but also general public administration in the neighborhood. The vestrymen levied and collected taxes to support their activities. Vestrymen were not elected; when a vacancy occurred, the other members chose a replacement. As in the case of the justices of the peace, they came from wealthy and well-connected families of the area. Often, in fact, they were themselves justices of the peace.

The only elected part of the governments of the southern and middle colonies was the assembly, that is, the lower house of the legislature. In the early colonial period, the assemblies were overshadowed by the council and governor, but as time wore on, they became the most important branch of the government. It must not be thought, however, that because the assemblymen were elected, they were common men. This was an age when plain people deferred to their superiors. When the assembly of a province convened, the members who took their seats were the same class of gentlemen as those who filled the county and local offices. Politics was an aristocratic affair. The people had a vote, but in practice they had power only to choose between gentlemen.

The situation was considerably different in New England. Here the unit of local government was the town, rather than the county, and decisions were made in town meetings, which all the inhabitants could attend. The town meetings elected officials called selectmen, who handled local affairs. At the level of the province, too, government was more democratic than in the middle and southern colonies. In Connecticut and Rhode Island, which acted under their original charters all through the colonial period, the enfranchised male voters elected both the council and the governor. In Massachusetts, after 1691, the assembly elected the council, although the governor was appointed by the king. Not only was the structure of government more democratic in New England, but the gulf between social classes was not so wide. Nevertheless, political leadership lay with the "better" sort of people. The conduct of town affairs was in the hands of solid citizens whose wealth, sobriety, and social position compelled respect. It was the more prominent citizens of the town who were elected to the legislature. Social gradation was an accepted principle even in New Egnland.

In retrospect, the colonial experience taken all in all was generally fruitful and prosperous. Even the lowest classes shared the substantial economic well-being which prevailed throughout the colonial period. Inherited social customs in government and economic life were substantially modified in the direction of democracy and greater equality. The presence of abundant and cheap land created a social revolution. As a result, America from the very beginning was something apart; a new land where the characteristic institutions of the future, such as freedom and self-directed economic life, were developing more rapidly than elsewhere. Three thousand miles from the mother country, the colonists were forced to build self-government which assumed the characteristic representative forms preserved down to the present time. In a very real sense, America may be said to have been the first major self-governing nation in the world. Americans in 1776 were not fighting to win freedom; they were fighting to preserve freedom which they already enjoyed.

FURTHER READINGS

Able and attractive accounts of the various regions of colonial America are provided by James T. Adams, *The Founding of New England* (1921); Thomas J. Wertenbaker, *The Founding of American Civilization: The Middle Colonies* (1938); and Wesley F. Craven, *The Southern Colonies in the Seventeenth Century* (1949). A solid work by a great American historian, also, is

Charles M. Andrews, *The Colonial Period in American History,* especially volume I (1934). The same author's *Our Earliest Colonial Settlements* (1933) is a more popular presentation.

James T. Adams, *Provincial Society, 1690–1763* (1927), is volume III of the excellent History of American Life series. Another outstanding treatment of colonial civilization is Louis B. Wright, *The Atlantic Frontier* (1947).

Some special aspects of colonial life are dealt with in A. E. Smith, *Colonists in Bondage: White Servitude and Convict Labor in America* (1947); Marcus L. Hansen, *The Atlantic Migration, 1607–1860* (1940); Perry Miller, *Orthodoxy in Massachusetts, 1630–1650* (1933), one of the most discerning of many treatments of early New England Puritanism; Carl Bridenbaugh, *The Colonial Craftsman* (1950) and *Cities in the Wilderness* (1938), reissued in 1955; E. S. Morgan, *The Puritan Family* (1944); and W. F. Dunaway, *The Scotch-Irish of Colonial Pennsylvania* (1944). Some studies of economic life are Bernard Bailyn, *The New England Merchants in the Seventeenth Century* (1955); F. B. Tolles, *Meeting House and Counting House: Quaker Merchants of Colonial Philadelphia* (1948); and T. J. Wertenbaker, *The Planters of Colonial Virginia* (1922).

The political system and social conflicts receive first-rate handling in Charles S. Sydnor, *Gentlemen Freeholders: Political Practices in Washington's Virginia* (1952); W. E. Washburn, *The Governor and the Rebel: A History of Bacon's Rebellion in Virginia* (1957), a fresh appraisal of that event; Robert E. Brown, *Middle-class Democracy and Revolution in Massachusetts, 1691–1780* (1955); and Theodore Thayer, *Pennyslvania Politics and the Growth of Democracy, 1740–1776* (1953).

For additional bibliography, see the *Harvard Guide,* chapters 7–9.

THREE

Colonial Thought and Culture: Patterns for American Civilization

1517
Martin Luther begins Protestant revolt.

1535
First edition of Calvin's Institutes *published.*

1543–1625
Copernicus to Galileo: new theory of the universe.

1636
Founding of Harvard College.

1644
Roger Williams attacks intolerance.

1687
Isaac Newton demonstrates laws of motion.

1689
John Locke's works on government and philosophy published.

1693
College of William and Mary established.

1704
First American newspaper published in Boston.

1710
John Wise defends congregational liberty.

1733
First issue of Franklin's Poor Richard's Almanack.

1734
Great religious revival begins.

1747
Franklin begins experiments on electricity.

1754
Jonathan Edwards's major philosophical work published.

1768
American Philosophical Society founded at Philadelphia.

THE DIVERSITY OF COLONIAL SOCIETY

As INDICATED in Chapter 1, the Americans did not come to the New World culturally naked, but were the product of a very old and very rich civilization. They brought with them all sorts of beliefs, customs, and manners, and yet, as Chapter 2 has stressed, they were from the beginning affected by the New World environment. This complex interaction of heritage and environment shaped a nation. It was rendered more complex by new ideas being developed in Europe and constantly imported into the new land. When the New World was first being explored, the Renaissance and the Reformation were under way in Europe. During the seventeenth century other profound changes were going on there, not least in the area of government and state making and in the emergence of modern science. And when the colonies were maturing in the eighteenth century, European thought was producing that intellectual revolution known as the Enlightenment. The modern world, in brief, was being made. The years between 1500 and 1789 brought forth such typical master institutions of that world as the nation-state, science and technology, political liberalism, and democracy. It is small wonder that the colonial period is

42

one of the most significant in American history.

Colonial society was extremely sectional and separatist in character. Political separatism was illustrated in colonial times when, in the seventeenth century, the effort to establish a New England Confederation foundered, indicating that it was not even possible to unite New England in a close political alliance. Separatism showed up again at the Albany Congress of 1754 when Benjamin Franklin failed to get the various colonies to approve a plan of federation. Indeed, the seeds of later state loyalties—state rights, even state sovereignty—in the American experience is rooted in colonial times. Virginia, Pennsylvania, and Massachusetts were units which hardly knew one another, as was evident during the subsequent War for Independence. In addition, the back country, or frontier, was also often very remote and different from the older settled regions along the seacoast.

With geography as well as the diversity of origin making for disunity, there were striking cultural differences between the various sections. New England, the middle colonies, and the south were, broadly speaking, cultural units with the frontier everywhere an additional element. A comparison of these sections underscores the divergences. In a time when religion was almost all-important, the dominant churches were different: Virginia was the bulwark of the Anglican Church, Pennsylvania of the Quakers, and New England of the Puritan Congregationalists. The frontier was filled with Scotch-Irish Presbyterians and German sectarians, with other religious groups to appear before the end of the colonial period. Again, the pattern of local government contrasted the New England town system,

with its element of "town meeting" democracy, with the rural and aristocratic southern pattern, molded after the English "squirearchy." Philadelphia was more cosmopolitan and tolerant than Boston, and Virginia had no great city at all. The lingering influence of the Dutch in New York, the Swedes in Delaware, and the French in South Carolina gave those colonies a distinctive flavor. Pennsylvania, especially, had its world of the German pietistic sects, the Amish and Mennonites and Shakers, people who still in the twentieth century exhibit their unconquerable loyalty to a religious vision. Everywhere in colonial society, religious diversity was the hallmark; it was a land where nonconformists outnumbered conformists by a vast majority. If America later became, as some insisted, a land of conformists, it did not acquire this trait from its early heritage.

VIRGINIA GENTRY: SOUTHERN PATTERN

Each of the various American regions had its remarkable features. The agrarian south, its economy based on tobacco in Virginia and Maryland and other staple crops farther south, had produced an aristocracy of proud, self-reliant, plantation directors. This aristocracy was largely home grown. A somewhat sardonic historian has suggested that the first families of Virginia might more profitably search the registers of London's Newgate prison than those of the peerage for the names of their ancestors. They imitated the habits, however, of the English country gentlemen, as well as their mode of government. The legend of the gay cavalier has been overdone; this was a hardworking class, as it necessarily had to be. On the largely self-sufficient manors, such things as shoes

Religion was more important in colonial America than at any time since. Such thinkers as Williams and Edwards were products of a way of life in which Christianity and the church were all-pervading influences. Yet in the eighteenth century the Enlightenment brought a different emphasis, in some ways a direct challenge to the religious outlook. Whatever its direction, colonial intellectual life was sturdy and vigorous, keeping the colonial printing presses active.

Jonathan Edwards (1703–1758)

Roger Williams (1604?–1683)

A colonial hornbook

The *Almanack*
A colonial printing

Poor Rich_rd, 173_

A_

Almanck.

For the Year of Ch_

173_

eing the Firft af _LE_ _Y___:

And makes fince the Creation
_y the Account of the Eastern Gre___
y the Latin Church, when ⊙ ent.
y the Computation of ___
y the _Roman_ _Chronolog__
y the _Jewish_ _Rabbies_

_Wh__

he Lunations,
the Weather, Spri__
mutual Afpects, Sun_ _oon's_
ting, Length of Da_ _ime o_ _rh_ _
Fairs, Courts, and obf_ _e Days_

tted to the Lat_ _of_
and a Meridian of _ _s Welt from_
but may without fe_ _or,_ ferve all t_
jacent Places, even _ _foundland to_ _South_
Carolina.

and clothes had to be made. The planter was kept busy supervising the multifarious activities of this busy economic unit in a frontier society. Luxuries were difficult to come by even for the wealthy in America. Rich in land and slaves though the planter often was, he frequently had to do without commodities which relatively humble people took for granted in the more settled society of Europe. The Virginia gentry also served, as did their English counterparts and models, as justices of the peace, as colonels of the militia, as leaders of the parish church, and as members of the colonial legislatures and governor's councils.

They were, in brief, the leaders of society in all its aspects—economic, military, political, and administrative. There was little democracy here, except as between members of the gentry. Not unnaturally, this society developed a class of men, remarkable in its capacity for leadership and "habit of command." It was a relatively sober class; there was less neglect of religion than has been sometimes supposed. The Church of England was not an enthusiastic religion in the eighteenth century, but it was a serious one, earnestly seeking to inculcate a "sober, godly life," and Virginians read such popular Anglican tracts as *Holy Living* and *Holy Dying.* They had a strong sense of duty. Most people now know that such a representative Virginian as the great George Washington was no saint, but a man who had gambled, drunk, wenched a bit, and raced fine horses. The Anglican Virginians were not Puritans. They were seldom profligates, however, and Washington himself illustrates what qualities of strength, energy, and leadership they could produce. Edmund Burke, when he came to sum up the causes in his view of the revolution in America, attributed to

them a "fierce spirit of liberty" beyond that of any other group he knew. They were, the British were to learn, accustomed to giving orders, not to receiving them.

The planters' contacts with England were unusually close. They dealt directly with English merchants, having no merchant class of their own to speak of. Often their children went to school in England, and they bought English books. Though one wonders how they found time, some of the Virginia gentry, at any rate (and those in such a southern city as Charleston), did not neglect reading. They accumulated fine libraries and were men of some literary culture. Anglicanism had a mild and rational theology, so that the southern aristocracy showed a strong interest in the liberal ideas of the Enlightenment in the eighteenth century. Thomas Jefferson was not atypical in this respect, and the institution of higher learning founded in colonial Virginia, the College of William and Mary, stressed secular more than theological learning.

We may believe that most Virginia gentlemen treated the Negro slaves who toiled for them with reasonable humanity. They did not, at least, seek at this time to justify slavery as a positive good. Their leading lights, such as Jefferson and Madison, believed the institution could not be defended morally and looked forward to its gradual extinction. They had no objection to the education of slaves, and manumission upon the owner's death was common.

For the rough society of poorer whites who lived on the fringes and in the foothills—"lubberland," as a Virginian called it—they frequently entertained a considerable contempt, because this society was so slovenly, unlearned, and disorderly. The back country was another world from that of the tidewater aristocracy.

It was the gentry, however, which set the standards and prices in the marketplace of ideas and values. Aristocrats they certainly were to the core, yet the ideas of the Enlightenment had penetrated their ranks sufficiently to inculcate in them some of the humanitarian liberalism of the eighteenth century. They were prepared for this liberalizing influence by the moderation and rationalism of their traditional Anglican religion, by their aspirations to play the role of a cultured intellectual aristocracy, and no doubt, by the independence of mind and character which their social status bred in them.

The Virginia gentry differed from most other colonial Americans chiefly, perhaps, in their allegiance to a non-Puritan religious outlook. The Anglican Church had struggled with Puritanism in the civil wars of the seventeenth century and had emerged with a pronounced distaste for it. In America, the pre-revolutionary Anglican spirit could be found in places other than the south. In New York City, for example, one of the leading figures of colonial thought, Samuel Johnson, became a founder of King's College, which grew into Columbia University. Anglicanism was usually associated with the upper class, and there was a slight but significant tendency for the wealthier to "conform," that is, return to the Anglican fold, even in Quaker Philadelphia and in New England.

PURITANISM:
A NEW ENGLAND PATTERN

Puritanism was, of course, present from the beginning of colonial society and continued to be a mighty force, especially, but not exclusively, in New England.

Despite the strong element of discipline and authority which John Calvin had sought to inject into his creed and church in order to counteract the Protestant tendency to disunity, those who were loosely called Puritans could not always agree among themselves. The group which came to New England were Independents, or Congregationalists; others were Presbyterians, notably the Scotch who came to America in such numbers toward the close of the seventeenth century. We have noted how Roger Williams led his seceders from Massachusetts Bay, while other Puritan dissenters broke off and formed Connecticut. Other theological and ecclesiastical disputes arose from time to time among the earnest New Englanders. In general, the rigid orthodoxy of the first settlers, who wished to suppress nonconformity and keep the church under a tight discipline, gradually surrendered to liberalizing influences which the frontier environment encouraged, and which also stemmed from the expanding Enlightenment—a movement to be discussed shortly.

The earlier and purer Puritanism had been harsh and intolerant. Shaped at the very climax of the continental Reformation, the grim creed of Calvin held that men are helpless and sinful creatures, powerless to save themselves from the eternal punishment they deserve, unless by the free gift of grace from an omnipotent God. This doctrine of predestination did not, however, lead to paralysis of the will. Though subject to doubt and torment, the Puritan might find that assurance of salvation for which he sought inwardly and emerge from this experience confident that he was one of the elect. The Calvinist doctrine encouraged activism by suggesting strongly that the proof of a man's spiritual salvation lay in worldly success. It was not in the monastery nor in the sacraments that one found holiness, but in everyday life. The true Puritan was intolerant and somewhat undemocratic; he could not believe that men were equal, for the very marrow of his faith was the radical distinction between elect and reprobate, saved and damned. But he was a stubborn individualist, fortified by the belief that he acted according to God's will. And this belief hardened the souls of America's first pioneers, helping them to raise a civilization in the wilderness.

It gave them, also, a respect for education, for the word of God must be read and understood by all. And in one sense, the Puritan commonwealth was a republic based on consent. The Congregational church polity insisted that there must be no priests between man and God. Puritans held that the only true Church is a group of "true believers, joining together according to the order of the Gospel," owning only Jesus Christ as their superior. In New England, however, only the elect were originally supposed to belong to the Church. The Puritans in Massachusetts Bay, as we know, set about to organize a holy commonwealth, an ideal Christian society here on earth, in which the elect should rule with an iron hand, chastising the ungodly. But Roger Williams conceived the idea that this effort to force Christian perfection on human society was futile and false—God's kingdom is not of this earth. And though the rulers of Massachusetts drove Williams to Rhode Island, in the long run his views, and not theirs, prevailed. By 1700 the persecution of dissenters had largely ceased in Massachusetts, and the churches were tending to admit almost anyone to membership, not just a chosen few. A significant landmark was the adoption in 1662 of the "halfway covenant" after a furious debate: hereafter church membership would not be restricted solely to those who could provide evidence of having experienced an inner religious illumination.

Once the Puritan had abandoned the idea of the theocracy, he was apt to come over to the idea of a republican form of government. The most striking Puritan of the early eighteenth century is John Wise, a clergyman of Ipswich, Massachusetts, who transformed the church polity of Congregationalism into a theory of political democracy. Wise's contribution must be placed against a background of the weakening of the old Puritan theocracy coupled with a desperate last-ditch effort to save it led by Increase and Cotton Mather, foremost of the old Puritan clergy. After 1686, the Puritans of Massachusetts no longer operated under their charter and were forced to recognize the Church of England; the theocracy was formally at an end. Yet the real cause of the decay of Puritan influence was the weakening of the old spirit which was militantly religious and exalted spiritual goals above all others. Old Puritans made the pulpit ring with denunciations of the new flabbiness, but to little avail. From various directions came blows to the Mather "dynasty." Harvard College escaped from Mather control and began to teach things which shocked Increase and Cotton Mather. Thus clergymen were soon to be accused of abandoning Calvinism for "Arminianism," a milder doctrine which insisted that man was a creature of some intrinsic dignity, that he possessed free will and was not basically sinful.*

To combat this heresy the Mathers

---

* Arminianism was named after a seventeenth-century Dutch theologian who had challenged Calvinist control in the Netherlands.

Harvard College in the eighteenth century.
(Library of Congress)

wished to set up a system of central control over the Congregational churches, establishing in effect a Presbyterian system. It would then be easier to keep discipline in the ranks of the clergy. In 1710 John Wise wrote a stirring appeal in defense of the liberties of the individual congregations. What is interesting is the fact that he justified this independence by arguments that had little to do with religion, but placed all the stress on political liberty. Wise was concerned to show that the congregations are schools of liberty and of self-government, and that they promote human happiness because they promote liberty and self-government. It was a complete reversal of Puritan philosophy in that human happiness, rather than the will of God, was placed foremost. Wise's *Vindication of the Government of New England Churches* was republished by special subscription in 1772 as revolutionary propaganda.

With the death of the two great Mathers (1723, 1728), there died the last of the older Puritanism. The spread of a milder, Arminianized theology was not so pronounced as the tendency of ministers to follow Wise's example and talk primarily about political liberty. This was especially true in the era of the Revolution. Resistance to arbitrary government was preached from many a pulpit. John Locke was quoted more often than John Calvin. After it had all but forgotten its Calvinistic theology, Puritanism retained its spirit of resistance to any authority that sought to impair the individual's freedom. To obey God rather than man had always been deeply Puritan. In the later eighteenth century this came to mean preserving independence against King George III. Puritan preachers fed the fires of Revolution. Their motto was "Ye have been called unto liberty."

These Puritans were a strange combination of narrow intolerance and courageous love of liberty. They are alleged to have held a bleak and joyless philosophy which blighted the human spirit and was hostile to both art and philosophy. But the hardness and harshness at the heart of Puritanism produced a spirit that George III could not overcome. There can be no doubt about the debt which political liberty owes to the Puritans in both England and America. There can also be no doubt about the indelible imprint they left on the American mind. Their sobriety, their high regard for hard work, their aversion to idle pleasures and wasted time, and their tireless endeavor to "get ahead" formed an early endowment from Puritanism which suited the American environment very well. Much of this Puritan spirit emerges in the writings of Benjamin Franklin, who extolled the virtues of thrift and industry in his *Poor Richard's Almanack.*

Puritanism was chiefly responsible, perhaps, for a somewhat negative American attitude towards the arts and literature, though the simple facts of life in a frontier society no doubt aided. Music, though it was not unknown in colonial

America, can hardly be said to have flourished. The theater, however, invaded even Puritan and Quaker territory. Novels like Richardson's *Pamela* and others of the same slightly naughty genre competed with works of theology at Boston book sales. It would be wrong to suppose that our colonial ancestors, because they had religious interests, never amused themselves. But the muse of pure literature flourished only here and there, and mostly in private. Not only was Puritanism hostile to it, but the Enlightenment, too, tended to disparage poetry as vain and visionary, while it extolled the merits of practical science.

THE GREAT AWAKENING

Pennsylvania Quakerism underwent the same sort of spiritual crisis in the eighteenth century as did New England Puritanism; success and worldliness had weakened its religious fiber. In the south, the Church of England was as mild and listless an institution as it had become in its home country. As for the frontier region, it frequently was served by no church at all. William Byrd of Virginia, in 1728, found towns not too far from the coast without "any place of public worship of any sect or religion whatsoever." It was not until as late as 1751 that some remote areas of North Carolina were reached by a minister of any sort. In response to these challenges came the first great religious revival in American history, the so-called Great Awakening. Because religion then played so large a share in cultural and intellectual life, it was an event of major importance in colonial history.

Jonathan Edwards, the pastor of Northampton, Massachusetts, a somewhat lonely and withdrawn figure, was destined to become the most famous American writer of the colonial period after the renowned Franklin. He had extraordinary intellectual power, but also the soul of a mystic. He devoted these great gifts chiefly to combatting the spread of religious indifference and attempting to restore the Calvinist theology. He had learned from John Locke that ideas are implanted through the senses, and he wished to reach men's emotions as well as their minds, to present in vivid form those religious ideas he thought essential, especially the utter worthlessness of man without God and the supreme power of the deity. One famous sermon portrayed in frightful imagery the nearness of all miserable sinners, every moment, to Hell. He succeeded in arousing his congregation at Northampton to a frantic awareness of their sinfulness and need of salvation.

In response to his passionate preaching, a revival began at Northampton in 1734 which was made famous by Edwards's own book about it, *A Narrative of Surprising Conversions*. The revival was marked by emotional excitement, soul searching, the confession of sins, the reformation of conduct, and great interest in attending church. Edwards forced his congregation to anxious self-scrutiny and a deeply troubled feeling about their souls which later ages, more complacent and more sophisticated about religion, have thought ridiculous or even morbid. But to him, their tortured souls were signs of God's presence, offering the opportunity of salvation to people who were powerless without Him, yet able, with Him, to win their way to life everlasting.

The Northampton revival spread to a few other localities in the Connecticut Valley, but a few years later, in 1740, the seed germinated in a great revival which swept over all the colonies. Actually the Great Awakening in America owed more to the Englishman George Whitefield than to Jonathan Edwards. Whitefield was far more famous as a preacher, if less profound as a thinker, than Edwards. Edwards was the prophet of the Awakening, but this major cultural event in colonial history was part of a general religious movement, affecting England as well. In England it was largely the work of the great John Wesley, founder of Methodism, and his associate Whitefield, both of whom visited America. It was Whitefield's dynamic preaching which forced the skeptical Benjamin Franklin to empty his pockets into the collection box in spite of himself! The doctrines of Wesley were in some respects theologically different from those of Edwards, yet both men were great evangelists determined to rescue Christianity from the spiritual sterility into which it had fallen. They succeeded, in the opinion of some, all too well. In the 1740s, from Georgia to Massachusetts, the revival movement filled religious meetings with throngs of people and was a main topic of conversation everywhere. The methods used by some of the revivalists were wild parodies of the style of Edwards or Whitefield. Before long almost every community in America, and almost every religious denomination, was split into followers of the "New Lights" and the "Old Lights," the fervent evangelists who used emotional appeals and the more conservative who found such methods lacking in good taste.

Quite often this dispute between New and Old Lights had political and social overtones. In Connecticut, for example, one could draw a very clear line between the upper-class Old Lights and the Evangelical poor farmers, and the religious controversy blended right in with arguments about cheap money and political democracy. A study of the Great Awakening in Virginia brings out with special clarity the social significance of the revival. It reached, primarily, the poor farmers of the back country. This class really had no religion before this, one can say, for the Anglican Church, which was dominant in Virginia, made practically no effort to reach them, and there were few churches in the frontier country. The revival brought these simple folk a simple religion, which they fervently embraced, and it gave them a new sense of dignity and importance as individuals. Undoubtedly it served to strengthen democracy by strengthening the self-respect of the poor classes. It was inevitable that this sort of religion would appear to aristocrats and educated men as a crude, vulgar, and even dangerous thing. But it became in America the inspiration of the frontiersmen.

This religion played a part in that significant colonial conflict between seaboard aristocracy and upcountry small farmer. There was a large difference in the outlook of these classes. The former was in closer touch with European thought and with the Enlightenment. Its religion was a mild, rational one, stressing prudent conduct and abhorring "enthusiasm." But on the frontier, a simple, emotional evangelical faith came to fill the spiritual needs of the people. Years later, Abraham Lincoln said that he had no use for a preacher unless he preached as if he were fighting a swarm of bees. The frontier had no use for genteel and scholarly sermons or for elaborate ceremony. It demanded the shouting sermon and the excitement of the camp meeting. The frontier churches sometimes had to fight against Anglican persecution, and thus they contributed to the achievement of religious liberty. Methodists and Baptists, the most popular of the new sects which carried out the Great Awakening, seemed dangerously radical to some of the aristocracy. In fact, they were an excellent school of democracy for the frontiersmen.

Religion was a far more important part of life to colonial America than it is today. It was something without which a way of life simply could not be conceived. The weekly sermon and the theological tract were in many places the entire diet of the mind. The great majority of all printed books were religious. We cannot picture New England without the congregations, or Pennsylvania without Quaker meeting-houses, or even the Virginia gentleman without his Episcopal church. And after 1740 we can scarcely think of the frontier without the revival or the camp meeting.

All through this period we can see the growing separation of church and state, and the Great Awakening played a part in this too. The Puritan theocracy was the last major effort to regulate all society in accordance with Christian principles. The piety of the evangelical faith was entirely a personal piety. Thereafter, the whole trend of American development was toward separating religion from the state and denying its relevance to all except personal spiritual experience. This was indeed made absolutely necessary by the great number of different sects in America. Quaker Pennsylvania and Roger Williams's Rhode Island had always practiced substantial religious tolerance. Although Maryland was founded as a refuge for Catholics, it had a good record of tolerance —however, in the eighteenth century its range of tolerance did not extend to Roman Catholics (which was also true in England and most of the colonies). Massachusetts and Connecticut tried to maintain a monopoly for their Calvinist churches, but in fact they ceased to be able to do so after the first few decades. In England, the Act of Toleration (which accompanied the Revolution of 1688) granted freedom of worship, though not political equality, to all except Catholics and Unitarians. Despite this law, in Virginia, where the Anglican establishment was strongest, we find sporadic but unsuccessful efforts to persecute the unruly evangelical preachers. Before the end of the colonial period every colony had a diversity of faiths, slowly learning to live together in peace. Religious liberty, of which Americans have always been proud, was on its way to realization. The Great Awakening powerfully aided such liberty by making the stubborn frontiersman a determined defender of his own peculiar way of religion, whether he called himself Baptist, Methodist, or New Light Presbyterian. Religious individualism and frontier individualism went hand in hand.

THE ENLIGHTENMENT

Religious toleration and, indeed, defense of all kinds of unorthodox opinions flowed also from the eighteenth century's most remarkable intellectual movement, known everywhere as the Enlightenment. This veritable revolution in the European outlook stemmed ultimately from the scientific revolution of the seventeenth century. Men were forced to recast their thinking to suit a new universe, revealed by Copernicus, Galileo, and finally Isaac Newton—a universe in which the earth became only a planet in motion about the sun, and the sun perhaps only one of millions of suns. The earth and man were dethroned from their position as the center of the universe. But the genius of Newton had shown that this vast world machine did obey regular laws, that all bodies moved in fixed and measurable patterns. For the first time since the ancient world, the methods of science changed in the seventeenth century, and Western man was on the threshold of the stupendous discoveries giving him power over nature. The result was to produce an optimistic confidence in human reason clashing sharply with Calvinistic pessimism, and to suggest that this reason might find out all kinds of other "laws" about human nature, society, and politics.

The empirical philosophy of John Locke went hand in hand with the achievements of Newton to inspire the Enlightenment. Locke, the same illuminating writer who had summed up the English political faith so neatly, published (in the same year as his *Two Treatises on Government,* 1689) one of the most influential philosophical tracts in all history, the *Essay concerning Human Understanding.* It appeared to take philosophy down from the clouds and make it both understandable and useful. Real knowledge comes only from sense experience, Locke held, and all else may be dismissed as bootless. On this sound basis, applying the scientific principles which served Newton so well, we may build up a body of useful knowledge in every field. Men had the feeling, reading Locke, that all previous thinking had been on the wrong track, and now had come the dawn of a new day, unlimited in its possibilities. This was very much the spirit of the entire Enlightenment. Somewhat naïvely and arrogantly, it was prepared to dismiss the past, and all other wisdom except the scientific; confidently and optimistically, it felt that progress from now on would be literally limitless.

The Enlightenment philosophy fell on fruitful soil in America. A pioneer people was more than ready to accept the idea that man can master nature; a new society believed it might refashion social institutions towards a better life. That knowledge should be useful, not merely speculative, seemed eminently plausible to this youthful colonial society already so optimistic about its future on an almost boundless continent. The Enlightenment was an international movement, the force of which was felt in all the countries of Europe and in all branches of thought. But nowhere did it sink such deep roots— or last so long—as in North America. Colonial America responded eagerly to this optimistic faith and produced in Benjamin Franklin one of the great men of the Enlightenment.

Typical manifestations of the Enlightenment in America were an interest in science, in practical social reforms of various sorts, in a utilitarian education rather than a classical one, and in a softening of religious dogmas. Franklin, pioneer of electricity, was also an inventor, a creator of numerous "projects" for reform in government and administration, and a journalist, editor, printer, and essayist. Later he was diplomatist and statesman. This incredibly versatile man became an international idol, and many considered him the greatest man of the Western world. Later generations might find this hard to credit. There were few lofty ideals or passionate affirmations in Franklin. His deistic religion (a religion of reason, in which all the necessary moral truths were held to be available by the light of nature without need of any special revelation from God) was rather bleak and cold. Franklin's morality, like Locke's, is the morality of prudence. "Poor Richard," that delightful almanacker, is mainly concerned with being, "healthy, wealthy, and wise," with wisdom consisting of something akin to practical shrewdness.

It is not true that Franklin excluded all knowledge except the "useful," but it was on the useful that he placed the heaviest stress. In this emphasis, however, he perfectly represented the Enlightenment as well as the American spirit. To improve the lot of man through useful scientific knowledge and through political reform seemed no mean objective. His common sense led Franklin to become a democrat, on utilitarian grounds; you cannot make a government work well, he thought, unless most of the people feel they have some share in it. The political ideas of Locke and of the Baron de Montesquieu, author of the *Spirit of Laws* (1748), were well known in colonial America and stressed the importance of retaining liberty through checks on arbitrary power by separating the branches of government. On the whole, however, it would appear that the Enlightenment created a more eager interest in science than in politics. This interest may be seen in Thomas Jefferson, and indeed in all the leaders of American thought of the eighteenth century. (Even Cotton Mather and Jonathan Edwards were caught up in it; the last of the Puritan oligarchs was a pioneer in inoculation for smallpox.) The Philadelphia which produced Franklin sheltered many others with scientific interests, and by 1769 the American Philosophical Society had been founded and had made a notable contribution to science with its observations on the transit of Venus in that year.

By late colonial times the dissemination of knowledge through newspapers and magazines as well as books published in this country had grown to major proportions. No colony was without a newspaper. Subscription libraries, of the sort first organized by Franklin, ministered to the needs of an increasingly literate people. Men of wealth both south and north took pride in accumulating splendid private libraries. This thirst for knowledge was still relatively aristocratic; the day of mass education and great public school systems was a long way off. Private tutors and small pay schools were the common means of education in most places, though the New England Puritans insisted from the beginning on a sort of public education system, and ministers of religion everywhere, so vital a part of most communities, instructed both young and old in the reading of the Bible and of sermons. This religious training constituted the greater part of the people's education. A considerable majority of books published were still on religious subjects. But the Enlightenment was rapidly broadening this intellectual spectrum. Societies devoted to science and to the promotion of useful knowledge indicated the trend. The Enlightenment would expand until it almost pushed religious and metaphysical speculation out of the picture. For the human mind, as wrote Virginia's agrarian philosopher John Taylor of Caroline, now "disdains to worship a pageant or fear a phantom, and is only guided by views of interest and happiness."

EMERGING AMERICANISM

Colonial American society was, then, sectional in its tendencies, but with some forces making for unity. Of these forces, the strongest were doubtless cultural and intellectual. They were the ideas, embodied sometimes in institutions, which Americans held in common with other Englishmen and Europeans as part of a general cultural heritage. During the colonial period, vital foundations of American thought and culture were being laid down. This indeed was the "seedtime of the Republic," when basic traditions were es-

A view of Baltimore, 1752. (New York Public Library)

tablished, affecting all Americans and destined to persist long in the nation's history.

The Americans of the colonial period got their ideas mainly from England. But they put their own stamp upon them and contributed their share of great minds proportionate to their population—a Roger Williams, a Benjamin Franklin, a Jonathan Edwards. We must not think of them as isolated from all higher thought, utterly immersed in primitive practical tasks. Granted that "the labor of the hand had to take precedence over the labor of the mind," and libraries and universities had to be few; nevertheless, we find among early Americans a surprisingly vigorous intellectual life. Americans made significant contributions in this creative era of Western thought, giving as well as receiving in the exchange of ideas. In particular, they participated in what we might call the continuing Reformation and in the new movement of thought known as the Enlightenment. Both left deep marks on the American mind.

For some Americans at any rate, these systems of ideas were a bond of union. Franklin of Philadelphia and Jefferson of Virginia met on the ground of the Enlightenment, and their international scientific and cultural interests utterly transcended their regional characteristics. The religious revival, among humbler and less educated people, played a similar role, reaching as it did all over the colonies. A tradition of religious liberty was being created, while the essentials of American religious and moral life down to the present day were shaped from Puritanism and Evangelicalism. The previously neglected "lubberland" in the back country was drawn into the circle of civilization. Ideas, which knew no boundaries, helped to break down localism and provincialism.

The basic political organization of the United States, and the emergence of its self-consciousness as a nation, was to take place when these intellectual movements were at their peak. Such typical ideas as belief in human perfectibility, reason, education, and science all came through the Enlightenment. Puritanism contributed political individualism and a passion for liberty, as well as the gospel of hard work and steady habits as a means of self-improvement. The spirit of humanitarian reform owed much to Quakerism. It is no accident that Philadelphia was the capital of the American Enlightenment, leading in science as in trade and population, for the humane and tolerant policies of the

Quakers had encouraged such an atmosphere.

In the south, a liberal aristocracy contributed greatly to the American tradition, bringing to it in its own way a strong individualism and passion for liberty, with roots other than Puritan, but equally deep.

The New Yorker Crèvecoeur, author of the *Letters from an American Farmer*, pointed out near the end of the colonial period that the inhabitants of the American back country owed little to English civilization, since they had come largely from the dispossessed classes. He called these frontiersmen "new men," developing their own distinctive outlook as they rose to economic well-being in the New World. He did not think they were yet

Americans, but they were certainly not Europeans. They were on their way to becoming Americans. For these humble people on the frontier, the greatest cultural event in colonial history was the Great Awakening.

The common denominator in American ideas at the end of the colonial period was a buoyant optimism, receptive to ideas of liberty and progress. Americans knew that the great European intellectuals of the age, such as Voltaire, looked to their new society with high hopes. This vision of a new society, a heavenly city on earth, a secularized version of the Christian idea of progress toward perfection, was to be the most important idea around which American nationalism would develop.

FURTHER READINGS

Much has been written in recent times on colonial culture. L. B. Wright, *The Cultural Life of the American Colonies, 1607–1763* (1957), in the New American Nation series, is a recent survey, rich in factual material if rather deficient in interpretation. This deficiency is more than compensated, however, by the highly original theorizing of D. J. Boorstin in *The Americans: The Colonial Experiment* (1958), a book which many have found stimulating. More restricted studies are legion. Wright, *First Gentlemen of Virginia* (1940), has been supplemented by various works emanating from the Institute of Early American History and Culture at Williamsburg, among them Carl Bridenbaugh, *Seat of Empire* (1950), and Edmund S. Morgan, *Virginians at Home* (1952). Frederick P. Bowes, *The Culture of Early Charleston* (1942), takes us farther south.

The Puritans have always been interesting. Herbert Schneider, *The Puritan Mind* (1930), remains outstanding and has recently been reissued in an inexpensive edi-

tion. Samuel Eliot Morison, *The Puritan Pronaos* (1936), is another older classic recently reissued. A. M. Davis, *Foundations of American Freedom* (1956), is an examination of the influence of Calvinism. Perry Miller, an authority on colonial New England's intellectual life, has edited *The American Puritans: Their Prose and Poetry* (1956), an anthology in a paperback edition. For more detailed analysis, see also Miller's *The New England Mind: From Colony to Province* (1953), one of several works by him on this subject. Philadelphia has been treated handsomely by Carl and Jessica Bridenbaugh, *Rebels and Gentlemen: Philadelphia in the Age of Franklin* (1942).

Significant biographies include Kenneth Murdock, *Increase Mather* (1926); Perry Miller, *Jonathan Edwards* (1949); and Verner W. Crane, *Benjamin Franklin and a Rising People* (1955). The Great Awakening has inspired a considerable literature, including especially Wesley M. Gewehr, *The Great Awakening in Virginia* (1930) and E. S. Gaustad, *The Great Awakening in New*

England (1957). The theme of religious liberty was capably handled by such older works as Sanford H. Cobb, *The Rise of Religious Liberty in America* (1902), and H. R. McIlwaine, *The Struggle of Protestant Dissenters for Religious Toleration in Virginia* (1894). The Enlightenment background is luminously sketched in the distinguished books of the late Carl L. Becker, among them *The Declaration of Independence* (1942), recently reissued. Scientific development during that period has recently received much attention: see Brooke Hindle, *The Pursuit of Science in Revolutionary America, 1735–1789* (1956). In *The Lost World of Thomas Jefferson* (1948), Boorstin has tried to recapture the spirit of the Enlightenment.

For additional bibliography, see the *Harvard Guide,* sections 83, 88, 90, 91, 103, and 104.

The Expansion and Dissolution of Empire

1754
Beginning of the French and Indian War.

1759
Fall of Quebec to English.

1763
Treaty of Paris ends war.
Proclamation of 1763.

1764
Revenue Act (Sugar Act) passed by Parliament.

1765
Stamp Act passed and later repealed.

1767
Townshend acts passed.

1770
"Boston Massacre."
Townshend duties repealed except on tea.

1773
Boston Tea Party.

1774
Intolerable Acts passed by Parliament.

1775
Battles of Lexington and Concord, April 19.

1776
Declaration of Independence adopted, July 4.

1777
British defeated at Saratoga.

1778
Treaty of alliance with France signed.

1781
Cornwallis surrenders at Yorktown, Virginia, October 19.

1783
Treaty of peace grants independence to Americans.

WAR FOR EMPIRE

ONE OF THE CHIEF FACTS of eighteenth-century American life was the great rivalry between Britain and France for the domination of the colonial world. This rivalry lasted for approximately one hundred years and resulted in frequent hostilities that culminated in the great war for the continent, usually known as the French and Indian War. While this conflict was world-wide in scope, involving many powers and fought on four continents, in no area did it have more significant results than in North America. The victory ultimately won by the British over the French helped to assure the continuity of the institutions of freedom existing in American colonial life and enlarged that freedom by paving the way for the American Revolution and the consequent establishment of the United States. The defeat of the French thus ensured the survival and extension of religious toleration and diversity, self-government, free speech and press, and individual liberty.

Though there were other zones of friction, such as the southern frontier between Georgia-Carolina and the French influence emanating from New Orleans, the center of the rivalry between Britain and France in North America was the great inland empire of the Ohio and Mississippi Valleys. Its strategic heart was at the forks of the Ohio where the Monongahela and Allegheny Rivers join, at the present site of Pittsburgh. The natural corridors into

56

this heartland were the mighty St. Lawrence from the north and the Mississippi from the south. By establishing themselves at the mouths of these two great river systems at Quebec and New Orleans, the French acquired a stranglehold on the vital arteries of the interior of the continent. From these natural citadels the French moved inland to converge finally at the forks of the Ohio, where they clinched their control by the erection of Fort Duquesne. The British colonists, hemmed in by the mountain wall of the Appalachians, found no such inviting access to this coveted area. Their routes lay over the narrow mountain passes of Pennsylvania or the long portages of the Mohawk Valley of New York.

A second advantage possessed by the French in their effort to win control of the Ohio Valley was their concentration on fur trading as a livelihood. This concentration produced allies among the Indians for the French traders. The French depended upon the Indians' skill as hunters and trappers to supply them with furs, thus leaving the Indians in undisturbed possession of their traditional hunting lands. The Indians grew to depend upon the French for clothing, utensils, and weapons. The British did not have this advantage. They came as settlers and farmers, cut down the forests, and drove out the game upon which the Indians lived. Thus the English became the natural enemies of the Indian. The English, on the other hand, possessed two compensating advantages: the hostility of the Iroquois toward the French and the lower prices for English trading goods. French troubles with the Iroquois are partially explained by the fact that they attempted to bypass the Iroquois, who sought to become middlemen in the lucrative fur trade between the western tribes and the European traders. The Indians

soon discovered that their pelts bought more goods at English posts than at the French. Moreover, English rum was cheaper than French brandy.

French and British trade rivalry in the west was reinforced as American colonists speculated in lands west of the Appalachians claimed by the French. The most famous of the colonial land companies was the Ohio Company, which received from the British Crown a grant of 200,000 acres of land on the Upper Ohio in 1748. So rapid was the wave of speculation that by 1750 there were more than a score of colonial land companies seeking grants beyond the mountains. This speculation occurred at the very time the French were attempting to consolidate their authority in this disputed area. Regiments of French regulars were being sent to Canada. Old fortifications were being strengthened and new ones erected along the Upper Ohio and the shores of Lake Erie, and efforts were made to overawe the Indians with displays of military power. These efforts were so successful that by 1752 the hopes of colonial land speculators in the Ohio Valley dimmed as British influence beyond the mountains collapsed.

In the larger conflict between the British and French, two concepts of empire clashed. The French maintained a centralized control with authority flowing from the sovereign. This authority extended to the most trivial details of colonial government. Even the question of repairing the roof of a tiny parish church was referred to officials in Paris. In striking contrast, the affairs of the British empire were left largely in the hands of local governments and private enterprise. Even substantial questions involving the extension of the very frontiers of empire were controlled more by private initiative than by governmental decree.

In CONGRESS

DECLAR

By the REPRESENTA

NITED ST

In GENERAL

WHEN in the Courfe of human Ever with another, and to affume among Nature's God entitle them, a decent to the Separation.

We hold thefe Truths to be unalienable Rights, that among the among Men, deriving their juft Powers from the is the Right of the People to alter or to abolifh fuch Form, as to them fhall feem moft likely fhould not be changed for light and tranfient Ca fufferable, than to right themfelves by abolifhing th ably the fame Object, evinces a Defign to reduce t vide new Guards for their future Security. Such alter their former Syftems of Government. The direct Object the Eftablifhment of an abfolute Tyran

refufed his Affent to Laws, the moft wholefome a forbidden his Governors to pafs Laws of immediate and preffing Importance, unlefs fo fufpended, he has utterly neglected to attend to them. refufed to pafs other Laws for the Accommodation ature, a Right ineftimable to them, and formidable called together Legiflative Bodies at Places unufua them into Compliance with his Meafures.

diffolved Reprefentative Houfes repeatedly, for o refufed for a long Time, after fuch Diffolutions, t the People at large for their exercife; the State rema endeavoured to prevent the Population of thefe State ge their Migrations hither, and raifing the Condit obftructed the Adminiftration of Juftice, by refufi made Judges dependent on his Will alone, for the erected a Multitude of new Offices, and fent hither Swarms of Officers to harrafs our kept among us, in Times of Peace, Standing Armies, without the confent of our affected to render the Military independent of and fuperior to the Civil Power. combined with others to fubject us to a Jurifdiction foreign to our Conftitution, and Legiflation:

artering large Bodies of Armed Troops among us: tecting them, by a mock Trial, from Punifhment for any Murders which they fho ting off our Trade with all Parts of the World: pofing Taxes on us without our Confent:

Tom Paine of Philadelphia

Patrick Henry of Virginia

Samuel Adams of
Massachusetts

Fort Necessity in western Pennsylvania

The events that set in motion the American Revolution began at the apparently unimposing structure, Fort Necessity, where the French attacked Virginia troops, commanded by George Washington, in 1754. The ensuing war with France was victorious for the British and Americans. But to pay some of its costs, the British sought to impose a direct tax on the Americans by the Stamp Act, passed by Parliament in 1765. The colonists objected to the tax with unexpected fury. In the long controversy that followed, the colonies gradually moved towards independence, encouraged by the eloquence of "radicals" Paine, Henry, and Adams. Finally in 1776 came the great Declaration of Independence, explaining the circumstances under which rebellion is justified.

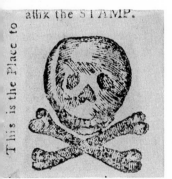

An American reaction to the Stamp Act

A stamp issued under the Stamp Act

The competition between France and England in North America had on several occasions broken out into open warfare. These colonial wars are known in American history, though not in European, as King William's War, Queen Anne's War, and King George's War. Men fought and died in these struggles without settling the basic issue of mastery of the continent. In the 1750s war broke out again between the English and the French in the strategic Ohio Valley.

In the early months and years of the war the French won a startling series of victories. The turning of the tide of battle in favor of the British and the ultimate defeat of the French in North America were due chiefly to the emergence of new and effective British political leadership in the person of William Pitt. This powerful and commanding personality forged his way to leadership in the British Parliament despite the hostility of the king and the opposition of mediocrities. By 1757 he had made his peace with the politicians. The British war effort against France, which

WAR FOR EMPIRE

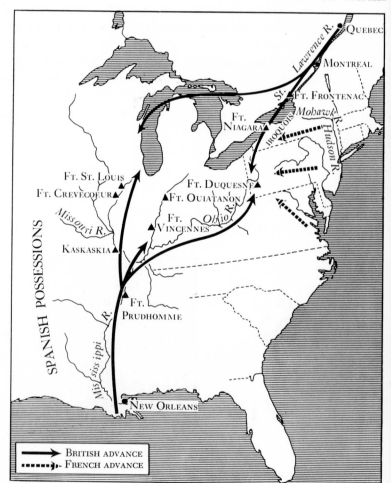

had been disorganized, began to take on direction and drive. Pitt decided that the chief theater of combat was North America rather than the European continent or India, where the war between France and Britain was also being waged. Under his invigorating leadership, new commanders were assigned to the British forces in North America, and greater contributions to the war began to come from some of the colonies.

The decisive period of the war came in 1759, when the British forces under young General James Wolfe, supported by a large fleet in the St. Lawrence River, took Quebec. With command of the St. Lawrence thus assured, and the great fortress dominating it in British hands, the taproot of the French power in North America had been cut. French Canada had little strength to carry on the war on its own resources. The next year Montreal fell, and the British were successful in forcing the French to evacuate Fort Duquesne.

By this time, the war which had started on the forks of the Ohio had extended throughout the globe. Almost everywhere, from the Ohio to the Philippines, Britain and her allies were successful. The Treaty of Paris of 1763, ending the war, registered these British successes, which were nowhere as great as in North America. In effect, the Treaty of Paris eliminated France as a power in North America. All

WARS OF THE EIGHTEENTH CENTURY IN EUROPE AND AMERICA

Dates	European name	American name	Adversaries	
1689–1697	War of the League of Augsburg	King William's War	England, Austria, Holland, Spain and many small powers	France
1701–1714	War of the Spanish Succession	Queen Anne's War (1702–1713)	England, Austria, Holland, Prussia and several small powers	France and one or two small powers
1740–1748	War of the Austrian Succession	King George's War (1743–1748)	England, Austria, and several small powers	France, Spain, Prussia, and several small powers
1756–1763	Seven Years' War	French and Indian War (1754–1763)	England, Prussia, and several small powers	France, Austria, Russia, Spain, and several small powers
1776–1783	War of the American Revolution		England	France, the United States, Spain, and Holland

French territory east of the Mississippi was ceded to Great Britain with the exception of New Orleans. Spain, which had entered the war belatedly and on the losing side, lost the Floridas to Britain. France ceded her claims west of the Mississippi to Spain, and of former French Canada she retained only two small islands in the Gulf of St. Lawrence, for the convenience of French fishing fleets. Thus the British government, dragged reluctantly into a great colonial conflict, came into the possession of a vast new colonial domain, which posed unprecedented problems of empire. British officialdom was psychologically unprepared to deal with the new state of affairs in North America. In addition, it was severely handicapped by having to work through colonial administrative machinery which was both cumbersome and antiquated.

BRITISH COLONIAL ADMINISTRATION

British colonial administration had developed in a clumsy and irrational way. Because the colonies were originally founded not by the government but by private individuals or companies, there was no settled plan of administration and no coherent policy. When the colonies became more numerous and important, it was felt necessary to exert more positive control over them. Several branches of the British government were given a voice in the supervision of colonial affairs. This led to inefficiency and division of responsibility. In the eighteenth century, for example, the main agency occupied with colonial matters was the Board of Trade, but the board could not act, it could only advise. All decisions and appointments were made by the Privy Council, composed of the king's ministers, a body somewhat like

our president's Cabinet. The Board of Trade, moreover, was by no means the only body that tendered advice and recommended policy to the Privy Council. It shared responsibility for colonial administration with many other agencies, including the Admiralty, the War Office, the Exchequer, the Secretary of State for the Southern Department, the Board of Customs, the Solicitor General, and the Bishop of London. Above all, from time to time Parliament passed laws which applied to the colonies.

The British government exerted control over the colonies in two principal ways: through governors appointed to the various provinces, and through disallowance of colonial laws. Governors were sent out armed with detailed instructions defining what they should and should not do; what they might concede to the Americans and what they must not yield. As governors, it was their right to veto acts of colonial legislatures, and their instructions charged them to refuse assent to certain kinds of legislation, while urging the passage of other laws. As a last resort, however, the Crown reserved the right of disallowance. Even though the governor signed an act of a colonial legislature, the law was still subject to review by the Privy Council. At any time within a specified number of years, the act could be annulled. During the colonial period, the Privy Council disallowed hundreds of colonial acts.

The king's councilors notwithstanding, British control was not very effective. Sometimes this was due to inefficiency or divided opinion at home. At other times, British administrators were content to follow a policy of "salutary neglect," or they were obliged to conciliate the Americans in order to win their support in wars against the French. The great reason why the British government failed to wield effective control, however, was that the American leaders were Englishmen, well versed in traditions of representative government, who thoroughly understood the technique of parliamentary resistance to royal authority.

In the long struggle for representative government, dating back to the Middle Ages, the major weapon of the House of Commons was control over taxation. It early became a tradition that whenever the king needed money beyond his customary revenues, he must procure the consent of Parliament, including the Commons. Control over taxation became the means of checking royal authority and bargaining for privileges. Historically, it has been the foundation of modern representative government. The colonists understood this perfectly, and they used the same weapons against the British government that Parliament had wielded against the king. From the beginning, colonial assemblies had the right to consent to taxation, and they used it to whittle down the authority of the governor, making him responsible to themselves rather than to his royal master. The governor's salary was under their control. When he refused to approve laws desired by the colonists, the assemblies would not vote money to pay his salary. If, on the other hand, the governor complied with all their demands, he was sometimes given a bonus. During the frequent wars against the French, the assemblies employed their bargaining power to wring further privileges and concessions from the governor, who represented royal authority in the colony. Charged with responsibility for defense of the province, the governors would plead with the assemblies to grant money for war. The assemblies, which frequently displayed singular indifference to enemy advances, would procrastinate and delay, making any grant of money

contingent upon some concession. Eventually, the assemblies took the expenditure of major revenues completely out of the governor's hands by establishing their own treasurers, who paid out money only by order of the assemblies. By a rigorous use of their power over revenue and a remorseless opposition to the governor's authority, the colonies advanced toward mastery over their own affairs. They were bound by general regulations of king and Parliament, formed for the whole empire, but within these limits the colonies achieved substantial self-rule. By the end of the colonial period the upper-class colonists, with some help from the lower orders, were practically self-governing in their local affairs. Having successfully mastered the royal governors, it was but a step to the rejection of Parliament's authority.

PROBLEMS OF EMPIRE

The stubborn fact which confronted the British government in the years immediately following the Treaty of Paris (1763), ending French power in North America, was that peace has its problems no less formidable than war. Ironically, the empire which had fought, among other things, for the security of its colonies in North America, fell asunder soon afterward, in large measure because of the very problems which victory brought. Had the war with France resulted in another stalemate, it is indeed doubtful whether there would have been any revolutionary movement in America against the British government. Nothing so enhanced the charms of the imperial connection as the nearness of a foe; the foe vanquished, things were seen in a different light. The elimination of France gave the English colonies the sense of a new birth of freedom. The French menace was gone, and the colonists were prepared to enter more fully into their inheritance.

To the British, the war had called attention to a pressing need for imperial reorganization. The war itself had been rendered difficult by the inadequacies of imperial administration; consolidation and rationalization were obviously in order. The British were anxious to eliminate the flaws in their system of colonial organization before another outbreak of war. The extent of the victory and the immensity of the new conquests made the task of reorganization even more difficult. The British government had gained a familiarity with the empire, as a result of the war, which it had not had before, and it did not like all that it saw. For one thing, the task of organizing for war the potential strength existing within the colonies had proved beyond the capacities of either the imperial or the colonial government. Some of the colonial governments had established a good record in the war; others had assumed an attitude as aloof as if the conflict were being fought on another planet. There had been a good deal of trade with the enemy, and French troops were in part fed with food purchased from American traders. Trading with the enemy was not considered as reprehensible in the eighteenth century as it is today, but it was an activity that aroused the British to some degree of annoyance. The simple fact was that despite the overwhelming numerical superiority of the population of the British colonies, it had not been colonial forces but regular British troops that had beaten the French. Here was a situation that seemed to cry aloud for some remedial action. The defense of the empire needed reinforcement.

Such reinforcement would mean a larger military budget for the British tax-payer. The normal expenditures of government had been swollen enormously by the demands of the recent war; taxation rates in Britain had reached dangerously high levels. If the new program of defense was to be established and maintained, then it seemed only fair that the colonists should bear some portion of the cost.

Of nearly equal importance with the establishment of a suitable defense against a return of French armies and fleets to North America was the British concern over the Indian menace. In 1763, at the close of the great war, came a terrifying outbreak, known to history as Pontiac's Conspiracy, which seared with flame much of the northwest frontier of the colonies. During the war, the British government had guaranteed possession of their lands to various Indian tribes, in efforts to wean them away from the French. These were treaties of full stature, ratified by the British Crown, and it was incumbent on the British authorities to see that they were carried out. If the Indians were to be assured the possession of their lands, migration across the mountains by the colonists would have to be brought under control. If trouble with the Indians was to be abated, the movement of settlers onto Indian lands would have to be halted until consent of the Indians had been secured.

The chief needs of the empire as seen from London, therefore, were (1) revenue from the colonies to meet the increased expenses of the defense program, and (2) a cessation of colonial movement into the west until relations with the Indian tribes of that area could be regularized. In order to secure the revenue, the idea of a stamp tax was proposed to the agents of the colonial governments in London, with a request for their reactions and any suggestions they might have concerning an alternative. In order to carry out the second feature of the program, the Proclamation of 1763 was issued. This prohibited further migration beyond the crest of the Appalachians except under rigid restrictions.

Public opinion in the colonies was not prepared for either of these measures. The need for the strengthened defenses, with the taxes that accompanied them, was certainly not apparent to the colonists. The French had been conquered; why then, the elaborate and belated precautions against them? As for the Proclamation Line, any attempt to control westward movement was completely out of harmony with the realities of colonial life. The empire had always before been underregulated rather than overregulated. It was certainly not a centrally disciplined and controlled state, in which the men of the frontier willingly accepted the edicts of London officials. The empire had left the advance of the frontier line to the discretion and enterprise of frontiersmen, speculators, and Indian traders. These adventurous spirits were not likely to be happy long under the restraints of an authority that seemed concerned chiefly with the security of the Indians. The whole policy of attempting to restrain the frontiersman and the speculator broke down before many months. But the attempt to control the frontier illustrates the lack of understanding of colonial realities by those in authority in London.

Though the policy of limiting frontier expansion was not carried out, the authorities were more persistent in the matter of taxes. Parliament passed a new revenue act in 1764, designed to increase the proceeds from taxation of sugar and molasses imported into the American colonies, by more rigorous collection of these often evaded duties. Since there had long been such a tax, the colonists were not on strong legal ground in opposing it, but were

nevertheless angry about the new measures. In the following year came the bitterly controverted Stamp Act, which imposed on the American colonists an obligation to buy from the British government stamps to place on legal documents, on printed newspapers, and on pamphlets. For the colonists this tax was an innovation. Heretofore, the efforts of the British government to raise any revenue from the colonial areas had been confined to the indirect taxes that were incidental to the control of trade. Even the revenues raised in this way had been negligible, for the trade and navigation laws had been laxly enforced. The only taxes that the colonists were accustomed to paying were the relatively light ones imposed by their own legislative bodies. Now the British government was attempting to tap a new vein of revenue, thus invading a field long held by the local legislatures. This was the first effort by the British government to impose a direct tax upon the colonists.

The tax was not only an innovation and an invasion of the prerogatives of the colonial assemblies, but fell upon the most articulate members of colonial society. These were the lawyers and editors of the colonies—a group never given to suffering silently. Further, as an additional sting in its tail, the tax would have to be paid with hard currency, which was exceedingly scarce in the colonies. This, in effect, substantially raised the rates of the taxes.

The entire project broke down in the face of colonial hostility. Mob action prevented the sale of the stamps in a number of cities, and a congress attended by delegates from nine of the colonial governments met in New York and drafted a protest against the tax as an invasion of the exclusive rights of the colonial legislatures to impose taxes on the people of the colonies. Confronted with this opposition,

BRITISH LEGISLATION AFFECTING THE COLONIES, 1763–1774

Name of act	Purpose	Reaction
Proclamation of 1763	To establish controls and prohibitions over western lands	Largely ignored by western pioneers
Sugar Act, 1764	To raise revenue	Local and sporadic hostility
Currency Act, 1764	To prohibit issuance of colonial legal tender	Resentment among debtor class
Stamp Act, 1765	To raise revenue	Widespread hostility and violence Stamp Act Congress
Declaratory Act, 1766	To assert Parliament's authority to make laws binding on Colonies in all cases whatsoever	Ignored in gratification over repeal of Stamp Act
Townshend acts, 1767	To raise revenue by taxing some colonial imports	Organized boycott of British goods
Tea Act, 1773	To give East India Company privileged position in American market for tea	Boston Tea Party and other demonstrations
Coercive or Intolerable Acts, 1774	To punish Massachusetts for Boston Tea Party	Growth of colonial unity and spirit of militant resistance
Boston Port Act	To close port of Boston	
Administration of Justice Act	To authorize transfer of trials of British officials in legal cases arising from the discharge of their duties in Massachusetts; trials to be held in Britain	Growth of colonial unity and spirit of militant resistance
Massachusetts Government Act	To make extensive antidemocratic changes in the government of Massachusetts	Growth of colonial unity and spirit of militant resistance
Quebec Act, 1774	To provide government for Canada and to extend Canada's boundaries to include Ohio Valley	Growth of colonial unity and spirit of militant resistance

and with a petition from a number of British merchants who feared the loss of their American markets, the British government repealed the Stamp Act. Thus the second of the major projects for imperial reorganization collapsed when confronted with the realities of American conditions and opinion. But the attempt at the taxation of the colonists had stung many of them into an awareness of their political traditions and had stimulated them to united protests through the convoking of a Stamp Act Congress. Even more important than that, however, this act had given new power to the slogan, "taxation without representation is tyranny."

The repeal of the Stamp Act did not mean the relinquishment of Parliament's right to tax the colonies. This was indicated by the passage of the Declaratory Act, which stated that Parliament "had, hath, and of right ought to have, full power and authority to make laws and statutes of sufficient force and validity to bind the colonies and people of America . . . in all cases whatsoever." The Declaratory Act revealed that the British Parliament regarded the empire as centralized under its supreme authority. They believed that the sovereign power of the empire was lodged solely in their hands, and that the various colonial legislative bodies were distinctly subordinate, possessing powers comparable only with those held by a town council in the British Isles. The Parliament can scarcely be blamed for holding such a conception, for nearly all the examples of empire, both ancient and modern, were highly centralized.

CRISIS OF EMPIRE

In actual practice, what had developed within the British Empire made it different from any empire of the past. The growth of elective legislative bodies throughout the Empire, their assumption of powers without any effective challenge coming from the imperial government, the development of a mature and sophisticated body of political opinion in nearly all the colonies, the practical schooling in the political arts which colonial leaders received through the management of their own affairs—all had tended to make the British Empire not the consolidated type of British imagination, but rather a form of political federation between largely coordinate and self-governing units. The task of

ruling such an empire was not so much one of legislation as of diplomacy; it was a matter less of giving orders than of joining in conference and consultation. The essence of good imperial government was not command but consent. The British possessed a system of laws and political customs that made them the freest of all European peoples. As we have seen, the inhabitants of the British colonies had an even greater measure of freedom, because so little of the aristocratic tradition that existed in Britain had been successfully transplanted into the New World. Among peoples of such traditions, the only effective basis of political unity was cooperation, not domination. The American Revolution must be largely explained as a result of this long tradition of freedom in the handling of their own affairs which had been the experience of the American people. A people trained in so many of the arts of freedom could not accept taxation by a legislative body in which they were not actually represented.

It is true, of course, that for years the American colonies had known certain formal limitations upon their freedom of action. The trade laws and Navigation Laws, enacted by the British Parliament, attempted to control the direction of American trade by confining that trade largely to buying and selling within the British Empire. Also, the British government retained the right to disallow, and thus in effect to declare null and void, laws passed by the colonial legislatures. In fact, however, these restrictions were more annoying than formidable. There can be no denying that they were, on occasion, a nuisance to the colonists, but a widespread agitation against them never developed. With regard to the trade laws, there were segments of the colonial economy which were deprived of economic opportunity because of the restrictions, but for the most part the laws did not disturb the normal development and direction of American trade. And, on the other hand, for many portions of the American economy, there were real advantages and security offered by the trade laws. As for the disallowance, most of the rejected laws were condemned for loose wording and faulty drafting. The disallowance, however irritating, did not bulk large enough to invalidate the assertion that the American colonists were a people schooled in freedom, the freest of the free people of the world at that time, and therefore poor material for experiments in consolidated empire making.

But the British government adhered to its own legalistic conception of the Empire. The needs for revenue were great. If the Americans attached so much importance to the difference between direct and indirect taxation that they would reject the first and accept the second because it was part of the accustomed system of trade laws, the British government was perfectly willing to go along, just as long as the revenue came in.

It was just the sort of situation that appealed to the sardonic Chancellor of the Exchequer of the British Cabinet, Charles Townshend, a gentleman known to men of affairs as "Champagne Charlie." In 1767, Townshend presented three acts to Parliament for passage. One would suspend the meetings of the New York colonial assembly until it complied with certain demands of British laws calling upon it to provide quarters and such supplies as candles, vinegar, salt, bedding, "and small beer or cyder, not exceeding five pints, or half a pint of rum mixed with water, to each man." The second called for the establishment of a board of customs commissioners in America to enforce the customs laws along the American shores. The

third proposed a series of customs duties or tariffs on goods imported into the American colonies. The last was designed to raise the revenue within the bounds of traditional trade regulations. This was done to placate American objections so vigorously expressed against the Stamp Act. Parliament accepted Townshend's program, and though he died shortly afterward, it was retained by his successors.

The Townshend revenue act had taken the American argument at its face value, and in effect scored a debating point by seeking to raise revenue within the framework of the trade laws. But running an empire differs from winning points in a debate. Townshend confronted the American people with the choice of accepting his new taxes, because they were within the scope of the trade-regulation system, or of rejecting the right of the British Parliament to bind the colonists through any type of law at all. What Townshend did was to make the idea of any parliamentary authority to make laws for America completely unpopular. John Dickinson of Pennsylvania condemned the Townshend acts on the ground that any act for raising revenue, even though disguised as a trade regulation, was a tax. Dickinson's distinction was too subtle for those extremists who preferred to reject the right of Parliament to make *any* laws at all binding the colonists rather than to seek to define that power by such fine discriminations.

Other aspects of the Townshend acts also aroused colonial feeling. The acts implied a direct attack upon the rights of the colonial legislatures. One of the assets possessed by most of the colonial legislative bodies had been their power of appropriation of funds for the salaries of the royal governors and judges. The Townshend acts proposed to set aside some of the revenue gained through the new taxes to pay the salaries of these officials. Thus royal officers would be freed from some of their dependence upon the legislative bodies, and the power of the legislatures would be diminished. But there was a more direct attack. One of the Townshend acts suspended the operation of the New York assembly, and the legislatures of Massachusetts and Virginia were dissolved by the royal governors of those colonies for activity in protest against the acts.

There were other protests against the Townshend acts. Attempts to collect the new duties led in some cases to public disturbance. Merchants of the Boston area resorted once again to the commercial boycott, the refusal to buy British goods, that had been used in the protest against the Stamp Act. Resistance to the collection of the new duties led to the stationing of two regiments of British troops in Boston to aid in the enforcement of the law. The presence of the troops evoked strong feeling and eventually led, in 1770, to a clash between troops and some of the populace in which three of the latter were killed.

"Boston Massacre" of 1770. (Paul Revere's engraving, Library of Congress)

Withdrawal of the "redcoats" from the city of Boston removed some of the bitterness arising from this "Boston Massacre," however, and in fact many leading Bostonians recognized that the troops in firing on the crowd might have acted in legitimate self-defense.

As for the commercial boycott, it cut substantially into the value of British imports. This time the British merchants did not feel it necessary to petition the imperial government to end the Townshend duties. Because of their expanding markets in other parts of the world, they did not suffer seriously from the decline in their American trade. The British government eventually repealed most of the duties because of the apparent folly of trying to raise revenue by taxing the sale of British goods to British colonies. Only the tax on tea was retained as a continuing claim of the right of Parliament to impose such indirect taxes.

THE FIGHT FOR FREEDOM

The years between 1770 and 1773 were a period of calm in the growth of revolutionary sentiment. In large measure this was owing to the general prosperity that prevailed throughout the colonies. Discontent does not usually grow during good times. On both sides of the Atlantic inertia and indifference prevailed where once there had been contention and bitterness. There was enough irritation, however, left in America to enable the radicals in American public life to keep alive some of the feeling against British policy. Samuel Adams, one of the most vehement of the voices raised against Britain, helped to organize the radicals by establishing a system of Committees of Correspondence throughout the colonies. This revolutionary mechanism managed to nourish some hostility toward the British government, in spite of the existing inertia.

Then, ironically, the British government came to Adams's aid. The long calm was broken, and the tension renewed between Britain and the people of the American colonies by the policy of the British government over tea. The duty on tea had been retained in 1770 when the government of Lord North removed the Townshend duties. Now the great and politically powerful British East India Company was floundering, and Prime Minister Lord North proposed to assist it. By an adjustment of various tax rates, the government in effect consented to give this great corporation a privileged and, indeed, a monopolistic position in the American market for tea. The tea of the East India Company would undersell all others. Further, the company proposed to sell its tea in the American market through its own agents and not through the established merchants. Not only was this policy a threat to the independent merchants, who would be damaged by the loss of their tea sales, but there was clearly a larger threat of monopoly. If, by the sort of manipulation proposed for tea, a monopoly on the sale of that commodity in the colonies could be granted to one company, similar monopolies in other commodities could also be established. The threat to the trade of colonial merchants and to the pockets of tea-drinking Americans seemed real. To the British government the new regulations about tea were apparently only a normal use of the power of Parliament to regulate the trade of the empire. To large numbers of Americans, the granting of a privileged position in the American market to a giant British monopolistic corporation was a menace to their freedom. This was an ideal issue for Samuel Adams. The first East India Com-

pany ships in Boston harbor had their cargo unceremoniously dumped into the sea in the famous "Tea Party" by a group of "Indians" led by Adams in 1773. There were demonstrations against the landing of the company's tea in New York and Philadelphia that forced the vessels carrying it to return to Britain with their cargo. In Annapolis, the owner of the tea ship *Peggy Stewart* was forced to set fire to it, and it was burned to the water line.

These were lawless acts, no matter what justifications they might have had in colonial eyes. Even friends of the colonists in Britain felt that the tea parties were of criminal character. Franklin, moreover, denounced the Boston affair as an outrage. And so a British government that seemed well fortified by public opinion moved to punish the colonists. Lord North proposed, and Parliament agreed, that the port of Boston be closed and that the customhouse be moved to Salem. The port of Boston was to remain closed until payment had been made for the destroyed tea. Another act diminished the degree of popular representation in the government of Massachusetts by requiring that members of the governor's council be chosen by the Crown, and forbade the usual town meetings in Massachusetts without the consent of the governor. In addition, British officers charged with capital crimes committed in connection with the discharge of their duties might have the place of their trial transferred to another colony or to Britain if the governor felt they would not receive justice in Massachusetts. The colonists speedily dubbed these the "Intolerable Acts." Enacted at about the same time was another measure, one that is often classified with the above legislation, the Quebec Act. This was passed by the British Parliament, however, not to punish the colonists for defiance of British

DIVISION OF BRITISH TERRITORIES IN NORTH AMERICA
AFTER THE QUEBEC ACT, 1774

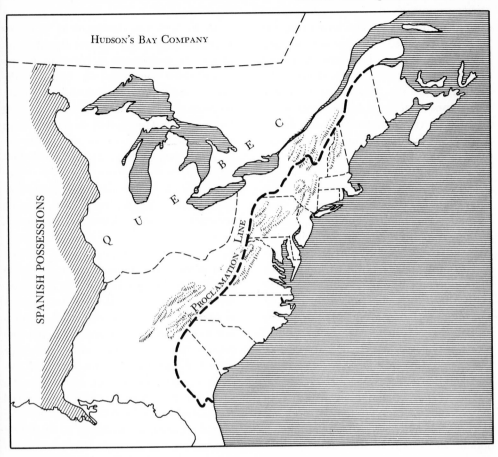

law but rather to provide a basic law for the province of Quebec. But the Quebec Act had features that aroused colonial fear and suspicion. For one thing, it granted a wider freedom to the Catholics of overwhelmingly Catholic Quebec than followers of this faith received anywhere else under the British flag. This concession to Catholics in Canada was regarded with great hostility in a New England which was militantly Protestant. Further, in view of the geographic unity between the St. Lawrence and the Ohio Valleys, the act placed control of the whole region north

and west of the Ohio River under the government in Quebec, thus striking a blow at the western land claims of such provinces as Virginia.

It is notable that Massachusetts alone was singled out for punishment. In order to enforce the closing of Boston's port, General Thomas Gage was sent there as military and civil governor with a fleet of naval vessels and four regiments of troops. Massachusetts had certainly been a center of resistance to British policy. The British government hoped, however, to prevent the formation of anything like a united front by punishing one of the colonies alone. They wished to do nothing to arouse the other colonies and drive them into a common front against the British. In this they failed. The Intolerable Acts brought the quarrel between the British government and the defiant colonists to a head. The closing of the port of Boston inflicted considerable hardship on the populace of that city, and contributions flowed in from all the other colonies to alleviate the suffering. In addition, there were numerous resolutions of support and sympathy passed by various political bodies throughout the colonies in support of Boston and Massachusetts. The most practical of these came from the Virginia House of Burgesses, which called for an intercolonial Continental Congress. The response to the plight of Boston revealed how abysmally the British government had failed. The other colonies were rallying to the support of Massachusetts. Every colony save Georgia was represented at the First Continental Congress when it convened in Philadelphia in September, 1774.

The virtually unanimous response of the colonies to the call for the congress did not, however, signify a unanimity of opinion in support of the radicals. There were many who hoped that the congress might devise some means of reconciliation with the British government. Joseph Galloway, a distinguished Pennsylvania representative in the congress, offered a plan for such reconciliation. It called, in effect, for the creation of a Grand Council that would be an all-colonial legislative body, and proposed that no act of Parliament was to apply to the colonies without the approval of the colonial Grand Council. This compromise effort was defeated by a vote of six colonial delegations to five, and the support given to the plan so embarrassed the more radical members of the

congress that they ordered all reference to it removed from the records of the gathering.

In the end, the Continental Congress took a strong stand against British policies. It drew up a Declaration of Grievances which demanded the repeal by the British Parliament of some thirteen laws, and which Britain could not have accepted without giving up the long-standing claim of the British Parliament to be the supreme legislative body of the British Empire. Further, the congress once more turned to the weapon of commercial boycott in order to bring pressure to bear on the British government to abandon its policies.

The Americans were resorting to other means of resistance. In New England, the militia was being refurbished, and weapons collected. The dissolved government of Massachusetts had reassembled as a provincial government, an extralegal and revolutionary body. It called on the people of the colony to drill and prepare their defense. General Gage decided to seize the arms that were being collected and stored at Concord, a few miles from Boston. The troops sent out on April 19, 1775, found the people of the countryside alerted against them. At Lexington, some eight miles short of Concord, the progress of the British forces was barred by a line of colonial militia. They resisted the order to disperse, and both sides fired. The militia withdrew, and the British moved on to Concord to seize the accumulated arms. But their return to Boston was like the passage through a long ambush, with the aroused colonial militia directing a stinging, harassing fire on them from every concealment along the line of march. The appeal to arms had begun. The colonial militia from much of New England swarmed in around Boston to lay siege to

Battle of Lexington, a contemporary American representation. (New York Public Library)

the town and the British regiments hemmed in there.

The fighting around Lexington and Concord nearly coincided with the date on which the Continental Congress reassembled. Before adjourning, the First Continental Congress had fixed a date in May, 1775, for the assembling of another such body. The Second Continental Congress met in Philadelphia, like its predecessor. Upon it, for lack of any other agency, fell the enormous task of directing the effort of the colonies in the Revolutionary War. Perhaps no decision this body made, aside from the adoption of the Declaration of Independence, was more important than their action in appointing George Washington Commander-in-Chief of the Continental Army, as it came to be called. This stouthearted, strong-willed man was to be the core of the American military effort. He was not a great strategist or tactician, but he was endowed in abundance with the qualities of personal character without which it seems likely the American cause would have collapsed.

The colonists were not united in the cause of the struggle against Britain. This war, which was destined to become a war for independence, also was a civil war. John Adams, the sagacious and cautious patriot leader from Massachusetts, made the widely accepted estimate that only one-third of the American people were strong in support of the war, while one-third were still loyal to the British Crown and one-third were indifferent. Out of a population that should have been capable of supporting a military force many times that number, Washington had great difficulty in holding together a force of more than four or five thousand. The British had some success in enlisting colonial volunteers into their forces. There were some fifty or sixty British military units of various sizes formed from recruits enlisted in the colonies, and it would appear that at times there were more Americans in the British armies than there were in that of George Washington.

If American opinion was divided, there was also division of thought in Britain over the war. In important circles of British opinion, the war was thoroughly un-

BATTLES OF LEXINGTON
AND CONCORD

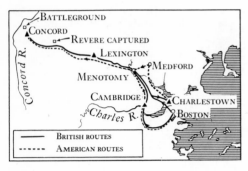

popular. Even the British government at times prosecuted the war as if it did not know whether it wanted to conciliate the Americans or coerce them. Fortunately for the American cause, there was no William Pitt to direct the British war effort. Indeed, Pitt, now the Earl of Chatham, was one of the severest critics of the policies of the British government, for in them he sensed the ruin of the empire which he had done so much to enlarge. The direction of Britain's war effort fell largely into the hands of the Colonial Secretary, Lord Germain, who was often at odds with the Secretary for War, and who in addition was a man possessed of a talent for bungling.

A basic feature of the strategy of the war was the British command of the sea. This permitted them to make landings almost at will along the length of the American coast, to support their troops with supplies and reinforcements when landed, and to withdraw them when desirable or needed. The one time that the British lost command of the sea, a temporary and local loss off the Virginia capes, disaster befell British arms at Yorktown. It was this command of the seas that permitted the British to shift the scene of fighting from New England to the middle colonies, and then later to the south.

When Washington assumed command

of the American forces, they were established in position around Boston and were holding the city under siege. The militia had already demonstrated much of its fighting quality in the stout resistance they had displayed to the British effort to drive them from Bunker Hill, one of the heights overlooking the town. It had proved so costly to the British that even though successful in capturing the heights, they had no appetite for further military effort. Thus the American forces continued to hold much of the town and the harbor under the range of their guns, and the position of the British was so precarious that eventually they withdrew their forces by sea. Accompanying them in their evacuation were numbers of colonists who, in the clash between the colonial cause and the traditional authority, chose to abide by the older loyalty. This closed the first phase of the war.

The ease with which victory was won in New England gave many colonists an illusory optimism and a false picture of the difficulties which lay ahead. The discomfiture of the British in the retreat from Concord and Lexington, the heavy losses inflicted by the colonial forces on the British in the latter's costly victory at Bunker Hill, and the eventual forced withdrawal of the British from Boston all worked to strengthen the idea of the Americans that all that was necessary for victory over the British was the summoning of the local militia. It was the militia of New England —the minutemen—who had won these victories. It seemed that there was no need for a regular military organization to defeat the British regiments. This belief was comforting to most Americans, who had no liking for military service anyway. They were particularly resentful of discipline, and they had been brought up with a hearty distrust of standing armies and professional soldiers. This attitude and its support from the events in New England greatly aggravated the difficulties which Washington and his officers confronted. Militiamen could no doubt fight, but they were here today and gone tomorrow—in the front line one moment, and back home with the plow the next. These factors made the maintenance of anything like morale and *esprit de corps* almost impossible. It was in this situation that the contribution of Washington was particularly important. His indomitable character and inflexibility of purpose provided sufficient morale for his whole army; his powerful personality furnished the rallying point that ordinary discipline might have provided in other circumstances. That anything at all of an American army remained in existence in periods of adversity was owing to Washington. Without him the war would probably have degenerated into a series of guerrilla actions, with the British eventually making a piecemeal reconquest.

After the retreat of the British from Boston, the initiative swung over to the Americans. With the object of bringing Canada into the conflict, and of creating a solid front against Britain among the British colonies on the mainland, two armies were sent northward. In addition, a propaganda campaign was directed at the Canadians to arouse them against their British rulers. Both the propaganda and the military campaign ended in failure. The Canadians showed a substantial reluctance to be drawn into the fight on either side, and despite tremendous sacrifices and displays of great courage, the American attempts were insufficient to capture the Canadian fortress of Quebec. An assault against this citadel was launched on the last day of the year 1775. The assault failed, the gallant General Richard Montgomery was killed, and his associate, Benedict Arnold, was wounded. Arnold held the small American force together in a continuing but futile siege that had to end in retreat when the thawing of the ice in the St. Lawrence made it possible for the British to send reinforcements to Quebec's relief.

TOWARD INDEPENDENCE

The actual resort to arms had led to a considerable hardening of American opinion against the British. At first, the Americans had been fighting chiefly for an acknowledgment of a place of equality within the British Empire. But the impact of war brought about a shift in sentiment toward outright independence. This change of opinion was greatly accelerated by the appearance of one of the great political pamphlets of the time, Thomas Paine's *Common Sense*. Couched in effective and easily understood language, it argued not from constitutional theories or legal abstractions but from what many colonists regarded as the simple facts of American experience. "Common sense" demanded American independence. It struck the proper note at just the right time, and Americans reading it put it down with a feeling that they had read the thoughts of their own inmost minds, heretofore unexpressed.

Perhaps equally important in the growth of idea of independence were the attitudes of General Washington and the army, from whom strong pressures came. Washington's motives were eminently practical: he was fighting a war, but he found that many things he needed to do—such as licensing privateers, hanging loyalists as traitors, creating a navy—could not lawfully be done unless he represented a sovereign state. Washington at length decided that the advantages of independence were greater than the disadvantages, and urged it upon the congress. The Continental Congress responded by adopting a resolution favoring independence. The resolution had been presented to the congress on June 7, 1776, by Richard Henry Lee on behalf of the delegation from Virginia. A committee was named to formulate a declaration that would be worthy of the occasion. On July 2, the congress formally adopted the resolution of independence offered by Lee, and two days later it adopted a declaration drawn up by the committee. This Declaration of Independence was largely the work of Thomas Jefferson.

The Declaration embodied the most effective statement ever made of the political philosophy underlying the American Revolution. It contained nothing new, only what has been described as the "intellectual commonplaces" of the period. The statements in it were all "self-evident" and needed no elaborate presentation of evidence or logical development in debate in order to make them acceptable to the multitudes. In a very real sense, Jefferson

wrote into the Declaration of Independence an American political creed. It was a creed that had grown from many sources. One source was the revolution in seventeenth-century English life which had received its intellectual justification in the writings of John Locke. The ideas of Locke permeated the phrases of the Declaration. Another influence was the American environment. This had encouraged an equalitarianism which was at substantial variance with prevailing British ideas and, further, had developed an atmosphere of freedom and self-reliance that led to a distrust of government and a feeling that it should be limited to certain essential fields. One of the greatest defenders and exponents of the common law, Sir Edward Coke of seventeenth-century England, had declared that reason was the life of the law, and it could be argued that if the law departed from reason, one could appeal from the law to the common sense of mankind. It was in order to appeal to this common sense of mankind that Jefferson submitted his Declaration "to a candid world." To this world Jefferson made

Signing the Declaration of Independence. (Library of Congress)

clear mankind's unalienable right to life, liberty, and the pursuit of happiness.

The Declaration of Independence, however, would have remained no more than an interesting historical relic had it not been sustained by military victory. Such victory must have appeared rather precarious in 1776 and 1777. The British had been forced to retreat from Boston, but in 1776 they seized control of another major colonial port, when General William Howe wrested New York and the entrance to the Hudson River from Washington and his forces in the battles of Long Island and Harlem Heights. Washington was forced to retreat to New Jersey. And it was by virtue of their possession of New York that the British were able to set in motion a grandiose plan for the reconquest of the northern colonial area. Howe was supposed to advance from New York City up the Hudson and make junction near Albany with an army under General John Burgoyne which was to advance from Canada down the line of Lake Champlain, Lake George, and the Hudson River to meet him. In addition, a small British force was to come from the western end of Lake Ontario along the line of the Mohawk River to meet Howe and Burgoyne. Three British forces would thus converge in the neighborhood of Albany. By these maneuvers, New England, which the British regarded as the center of the rebellion, would be cut off from the other states.

The conception of these plans was vastly superior to their execution. General Howe, who had some distaste for the whole task of crushing the Revolution and favored some form of compromise with the Americans, did not receive his orders to advance up the Hudson toward Burgoyne on time. Instead, he withdrew many of his forces from New York, sailed with

them into Chesapeake Bay, and then marched north and captured Philadelphia, the seat of the Continental Congress. He left Burgoyne and his forces stranded. Burgoyne had some initial success in capturing Fort Ticonderoga, which lay across his route from Canada, but from that time on his troubles multiplied. He met increasing difficulties from the terrain, for the obstacles to an advance through heavily wooded country with a European-style army were immense. Short of supplies, he sent large-scale foraging parties far afield, and one of these suffered a stinging defeat from the Vermont militia at the battle of Bennington. While Burgoyne continued to stumble forward, the comrade-in-arms whom he had hoped to meet coming up the Hudson was settling down in comfortable winter quarters in Philadelphia. The American forces finally closed in for the kill, and in a series of battles near Saratoga in October, 1777, Burgoyne was defeated and compelled to surrender the whole of his command. Nor had the other prong of the British offensive any better fortune. The small British force advancing from the west had been defeated at the battle of Oriskany and forced to retreat to Canada. The British grand design had utterly collapsed.

The American victory at Saratoga was decisive, for it brought France into the war as an ally of the United States. France had watched with sympathy during the early months of the struggle, partly because of the long-standing hostility toward Britain, and partly because of a sympathy among French intellectuals with the philosophy of the American revolutionary movement. A good deal of unofficial aid had already come to the American cause, and the presence of Lafayette and other Frenchmen serving with the American forces was living testimony to French feeling. But it was the hope of the American leaders that this concern and aid might turn into an effective alliance. A diplomatic mission had early been sent to France to push this project. Benjamin Franklin was a member of the delegation, but his popularity and ability, though immense, were not sufficient to get France to abandon official neutrality until after receipt of the news of Saratoga. France had been restrained by fear of joining the losing side of the struggle. Saratoga changed the picture. For the first time, there seemed to exist a real possibility of American victory. That was recognized even in London, for Lord North's government sent a secret emissary to feel out the American delegation in Paris about the possibility of peace on terms in which Britain would grant to the Americans everything desired except severance of the American ties with the Empire. The knowledge of the French that these feelers for reconciliation were being put out by the British hastened the French decision to enter the war officially, for certainly the French were hoping that one of the results of the war would be the dismemberment of the British Empire. Early in 1778, French representatives signed two treaties with the United States. One recognized the independence of the United States and granted important concessions in trade to the merchants and shippers of this country. The second treaty was a military alliance by which the two powers agreed to wage a concerted war until the independence of the United States was established. They also agreed that neither one would make peace without the consent of the other. In the early summer of 1778, a large French fleet came into American waters. This was the first tangible proof of the existence and value of the new French alliance.

Spain also eventually joined in the war against Britain. Spain was tied to the anti-British combination by a treaty with France but had no treaty with the United States.

These diplomatic triumphs of the United States came in the nick of time. While the victory at Saratoga was a decisive one, that victory must have seemed remote to the men suffering at Valley Forge in the winter of 1777–1778, at a time when the British were enjoying life amid the comforts of Philadelphia. Yet, though comfortable in Philadelphia, the large British military forces were doing little good there, and so a new British commander, Sir Henry Clinton, ordered a withdrawal across New Jersey to New York City. Despite the efforts of Washington to disrupt their movements, the British completed their change of base without serious damage. During the summer of 1779 the British made a number of desultory raids from New York into the surrounding regions, but no operations of any decisive character were fought.

By this time, however, the war had been extended into new areas of the west and south. In the Ohio Valley, George Rogers Clark won decisive gains for the United States which may have been of considerable importance in establishing American claims to that territory when the time came to negotiate peace. And the British, still confronting the task of reestablishing their authority over some extensive area of American soil, turned their efforts to the southern states. They took Savannah in 1778, and Charleston in 1780. Some savage and well-fought battles, such as King's Mountain, Cowpens, and Guilford Courthouse, were joined in the Carolinas, but nothing decisive was gained by either side until the British moved into Virginia. Lord Cornwallis, the British commander, led his forces to Yorktown so that he might secure further supplies from British transports and naval vessels. But he found himself trapped in Yorktown. French naval forces, not British, commanded the waters off the Virginia capes. And Washington quickly moved some 16,000 American

AREA OF MILITARY OPERATIONS IN THE SOUTH, 1763–1781

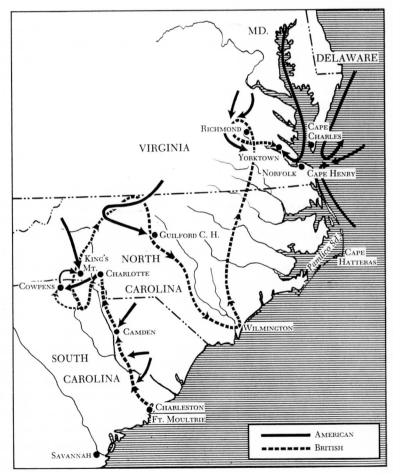

and French troops to hem Cornwallis in at Yorktown. Deprived of the support of sea power, the British position was hopeless, and in October of 1781 Cornwallis surrendered his command to General Washington. The major fighting of the war was ended.

In London, on receipt of the news of Yorktown, the British government which had been directing the war fell from power and was replaced by one willing to enter into peace negotiations with the Americans.

The revolutionary cause had triumphed. The richest and most highly developed portion of the British Empire had broken away from the ancient allegiance and its system of imperial controls and established itself as an independent state among the nations of the world. In so doing, it had blazed a path that many other colonial areas would follow in the coming centuries. The example of independence was to prove infectious. In seeking independence, the American people had adopted two ideas which were to have explosive potentialities: the idea of the right of revolution and the idea that government properly derived its power from the consent of the governed. Before many decades had passed, a number of other empires and governments would join eighteenth-century Britain in feeling the impact of these revolutionary doctrines.

MAKING THE PEACE

The peace negotiations conducted at Paris in 1782 were intricate. There was considerable suspicion in the minds of the American diplomats about the intentions of the French, whose position was ambiguous. They were bound by the treaty with the United States to make peace together, but they were also bound by their alliance with Spain not to make peace until Spain had recaptured the fortress of Gibraltar from the British, and that prospect seemed remote. John Jay, one of the American negotiators, also suspected that there existed some form of understanding between the French and the Spaniards to limit the territory of the United States to the area east of the Allegheny Mountains. To add to the American problems, there were for a time two sets of British emissaries to deal with.

Brilliantly represented by the team of Benjamin Franklin, John Jay, and John Adams, the Americans succeeded in winning "the greatest victory in the annals of American diplomacy." Under the terms of the Treaty of Paris, Britain acknowledged the independence of the thirteen colonies, and the new nation was recognized as possessor of a great western domain that stretched to the waters—then remote—of the Mississippi River. A stroke of the pen won what military power had not been able to conquer; for despite the heroic exploits of George Rogers Clark around Vincennes, the great expanse west of the Appalachians had not been won on the battlefield. The American agents gained these favorable boundaries by shrewdly exploiting the rivalry of France and Britain and by capitalizing on the British desire to diminish the link between the United States and France. Presented with the opportunity, our delegates decided, regardless of their instructions from the Continental Congress, to negotiate a treaty with the British without consulting the French. This was hard dealing, for the United States was committed by treaty and by moral obligation not to desert her ally in this way. In fact, the French did not much mind; it was not their interests, but those of their ally Spain, which had kept them from offering the Mississippi bound-

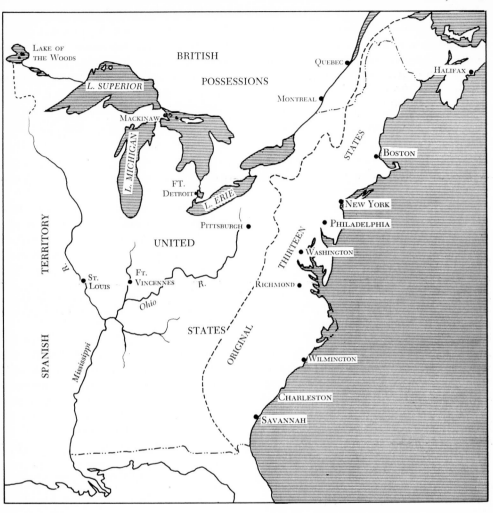

ary, and they accepted the situation with good grace.

The Treaty of Paris was a great diplomatic triumph, and the British delegates who had given away so much soon found themselves unpopular in England. Whether the young republic could actually make good her claim to so much territory, or even keep the independence she had won, was another question. The next decade was to indicate that, regardless of what the Treaty of Paris might provide, American authority did not replace British in the Ohio Valley. Claims to territory, like declarations of independence, require more than a paper authority to give them weight, and in the years after 1783, the political weakness and instability of the new republic made it somewhat doubtful whether the United States could hold the prizes won by its diplomats.

FURTHER READINGS

A massive work dealing with the history of the British Empire, especially with the struggle between France and Britain, is Lawrence Gipson, *The British Empire before the American Revolution,* volumes 1–9 (1936–1956). Gipson is currently engaged in revision of the first three volumes of this work. He has also written a volume in the New American Nation series, *The Coming of the Revolution, 1763–75* (1954). Also dealing with the rivalry between Britain and France is J. L. Rutledge, *Century of Conflict* (1956).

Other well-regarded accounts of the coming of the Revolution include C. H. Van Tyne, *The Causes of the War of Independence* (1922), and John C. Miller, *The Origins of the American Revolution* (1943). An especially valuable essay by a distinguished American scholar is Charles M. Andrews, *The Colonial Background of the American Revolution* (1924). Concerned with the legal and constitutional aspect of the dispute between Britain and her colonies is Robert L. Schuyler, *Parliament and the British Empire* (1929). See also Weldon A. Brown, *Empire or Independence: A Study in the Failure of Reconciliation, 1774–1783* (1941).

Other highly regarded works on various aspects of the causes of the Revolution are Oliver M. Dickerson, *The Navigation Acts and the American Revolution* (1951); Edmund S. Morgan and Helen Morgan, *The Stamp Act Crisis: Prologue to Revolution* (1953); and Edmund S. Morgan, *The Birth of the Republic, 1763–1789* (1956). A portion of Clinton Rossiter's interesting *Seedtime of the Republic: The Origin of the American Tradition of Political Liberty* (1953) has been reprinted in a paperback edition, *The First American Revolution* (1956).

Military aspects of the Revolutionary War are effectively presented in John R. Alden, *The American Revolution* (1954), one of the New American Nation series; Willard Wallace, *Appeal to Arms* (1951); and Christopher Ward, *The War of the Revolution* (2 vols., 1952). Most recent is Howard Peckham, *The War for Independence* (1958).

The important diplomatic history of the era is presented in Samuel F. Bemis, *The Diplomacy of the American Revolution* (1935). A rewarding biographical approach is C. P. Nettels, *George Washington and American Independence* (1951). The classic biography of Washington is Douglas S. Freeman, *George Washington* (6 vols., 1948–1954).

For additional bibliography, see the *Harvard Guide,* sections 97, 101, 107–109, 112–114, and 116–118.

FIVE

Revolutionary Government

AMERICAN PHILOSOPHIES OF GOVERNMENT

THE AMERICANS WON their independence in 1783, but the task of creating governments that would preserve and extend hard-won freedoms remained. During the quarrel with Britain, Americans had talked ardently of the rights of man, of government by consent of the governed, and of no taxation without representation. But the problem of giving reality to these ideas by incorporating them into institutions of government created serious disagreements. The formative period of the republic was torn by conflict.

War and independence intensified the class and sectional conflicts which were characteristic of colonial society. The governing classes of the American colonies initiated the resistance to Great Britain. Aristocratic legislative bodies drew up remonstrances. Planters and merchants, lawyers and newspaper editors, led protest meetings, acted on committees, and whipped up patriotic sentiment among the common people. The Stamp Act Congress of 1765 represented the ruling groups of the several provinces, acting in defense of colonial privileges from which they especially had benefited.

By degrees the resistance assumed what might be called a more *popular* character. In cities like Boston, New York, and Philadelphia, organizations arose, usually called Sons of Liberty, which were recruited largely from apprentices, laborers, shopkeepers, and other elements of the laboring population. Ordinarily, such working people took no active part in political

1774
First Continental Congress meets.

1775
Second Continental Congress meets.

1776
Congress votes independence.
States begin making constitutions.
Virginia bill of rights adopted.
Virginia law against entail passed.
Anglican Church disestablished in some states.

1777
Articles of Confederation adopted in Congress.
Loyalist estates confiscated.
Vermont abolishes slavery.

1780
States begin ceding western land to union.
Other northern states emancipate slaves.

1781
Ratification of Articles completed.
Continental money becomes worthless.

1783
Mutiny of unpaid soldiers in Philadelphia.
Movement to strengthen central government.

81

Robert Morris of Philadelphia

Financial instability plagued the young American government during and after the Revolution, and was a symbol of its inherent weakness. Its paper money became "not worth a Continental"; soldiers were often paid in western land, not money. After independence was won, men of substance supported a stronger central government partly in order to secure a stable currency. Morris was the leader of this movement. These men achieved their objective after several years, when a new central government was created and the Bank of the United States was established.

American paper money issued during the Revolution

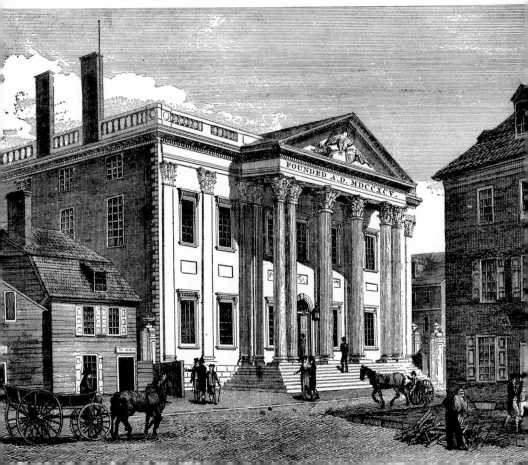

No. 16   MIAMI LAND-WARRANT.

THIS entitles *Jonathan Dayton* his Heirs or Affigns, to locate one Section, in which the Fee of 640 Acres fhall pafs, fubject to the Terms of fettlement.

Dated the *first* Day of *May* A.D. 178

Signed by *John Cleves Symmes*

Counterfigned by

A land warrant (Ohio), 1787

The First Bank of the United States in Philadelphia

affairs, which were regarded as above their station. Now they crowded town meetings, formed their own committees, and took issue with their betters on matters of policy. The Sons of Liberty were addicted to extreme measures. Holding aloft the banner of patriotism, they accused those who would go slower of being pro-British. Thus a division early materialized among patriots, which grew more definite as the quarrel with Britain progressed. Many a man of wealth and conservative temper felt his own ardor for opposing Britain cool as he witnessed lower-class stirrings and the spread of patriotic enthusiasm to the back country, now beginning to lift a crude hand in defense of American rights.

Independence crystallized some of the divisions among the American people. Thousands who had supported colonial protests now became loyalists, motivated by caution, love of the mother country, and distaste for the revolutionists. But even among the Whigs, that is, the patriots who stood firm against Britain, there were many who dreaded independence and hoped for reconciliation. Prominent individuals, such as Robert Morris, John Dickinson, James Duane, and others, especially in the middle colonies, embraced independence with regret and were carried forward unwillingly by the tide of events. Many of these reluctant patriots were destined to greatness in the affairs of the new nation. Having accepted the idea of independence, their loyalty to the United States was never in question. Nonetheless, they were a type of conservative revolutionary, who, though consenting to break with Great Britain, wished to preserve the social order that had existed in the colonies.

The Revolution fostered the growth of democracy. The people, having listened to the heady slogans of the day about liberty and natural rights, were never the same again. War and independence released democratic impulses long nourished by the traditions and ways of American life. It should be said that all patriots, of whatever rank and social degree, shared in some measure the glorious hope that independence would mean a chance to shake free of the Old World and found a more perfect society free of the evils of the past. For the ordinary folk especially, the Revolution assumed the character of a struggle against privilege and inequality at home as well as against oppression from abroad. This did not occur at once, for the forms and practices of colonial times often survived into the new era with slight apparent change. But in the long run it is apparent that the War for Independence breached the old colonial order beyond repair and dealt aristocracy a blow which proved mortal.

Not all patriots had the same motives, but they had a common fund of political principles and ideas about government, derived from English history and from their experience as colonists. In this "Whig" philosophy, the central idea was distrust of government. Such maxims as "power corrupts" and "eternal vigilance is the price of liberty" were the general beliefs of most Americans about government, expressing the wisdom taught by tradition, learned writings, and their own experience. They believed that government had an inveterate tendency to become tyrannical; that public officers, having tasted power, would grow intoxicated with it and would try to increase it. The rights of the people were always in danger and must constantly be defended.

Invasion of what Americans regarded as their private and political rights had come mainly from kings and governors; consequently, they expected abuses of power primarily from the executive. The elected representatives of the people had upheld local privileges and private rights; therefore, Americans looked to the assemblies for the defense of popular liberties. They had also learned to hate big government. War, standing armies, bureaucracy, big debts, and heavy taxes were the recognizable hallmarks of despotism—the instruments of oppression. Americans looked upon government as a necessary evil and thought that the less there was of it the better. Liberty was best preserved, they thought, when government was small and was conducted locally by the immediate representatives of the people, where its operation could be seen. Powerful and distant administrators were likely to become tyrants. On this point, their thinking was not altogether consistent. After the new nation was formed, different groups did not hesitate to seek government aid when it served their particular interest, even though this meant extending governmental functions and activity in social and economic affairs. Nevertheless, when most Americans set themselves to think in fundamental terms, they viewed individual liberty as existing in opposition to the power of government. Their conception was simple and negative: liberty consisted in allowing the greatest possible scope to the free action of the individual. They stood for private enterprise, civil rights, and weak government. These were the principles upon which their new governments were established.

THE STATE GOVERNMENT

The Americans began the process of forming their governments in the full flush of resistance to what they considered British tyranny, and the principles of liberty were fresh in their minds. They reg-istered their deep distrust of arbitrary power by drawing up written constitutions, which severely limited the authority of the government and specifically listed the rights of citizens. These state constitutions, with their prominent "bills of rights," were a higher law, supposedly above the reach of any set of men temporarily in office. And during the course of the Revolution, the Americans developed a procedure for creating this higher law by means of constitutional conventions, a new political device of great consequence for the future.

That government originates in a voluntary compact of agreement among the people and that it derives its authority from their consent were principles that Americans embraced with the deepest faith and emotion. In the world that they knew, however, there were no examples of a government actually being formed by the people. Authority had always flowed from the ruler. Where there were representative bodies and where individual rights were protected by law, as in Britain, these privileges and civil rights existed because the King had once granted them and they had become confirmed by the customs and traditions of the land. There were no examples, no precedents, available to Americans of a people constructing its own government and establishing the fundamental principles under which it would be governed.

When, in most cases, the colonial governments that had functioned under British rule lapsed or were thrust aside, Americans felt that the incumbrances of the past had been put behind, the slate swept clean, and that the opportunity was at hand to form government by a true compact or agreement. The processes by which early state constitutions were drafted and enacted up to 1780, however, did not allow the full expression of popular will. In no state was there an elected special convention for the specific and exclusive purpose of making a constitution, nor was any constitution submitted to the people for acceptance or rejection.

The complete procedure for translating the idea of social compact into reality was at length realized in Massachusetts, where, after the towns had voted on and rejected a constitution prepared by the legislature, a demand arose for a special convention to be chosen solely for the purpose of making a constitution. From first to last, the procedure by which the resulting constitution of 1780 was prepared and adopted rested squarely upon popular will. The people had a choice of whether or not they wished to have a constitutional convention. When, upon their approval, elections were held for delegates to a special convention, and when these delegates had drafted a constitution, the constitution was submitted to popular vote before it was put into effect. This procedure was probably the fullest expression of the idea of social compact which could be realized by any political community, then or later. It left no doubt that government derived its powers from the people and that it was a government of law, binding even upon the lawmakers.

Another device intended to safeguard liberty was the separation of powers. The new state constitutions usually provided for separate executive, legislative, and judicial departments, each clothed with its own authority and able to carry on its functions independently of the others. The purpose was to throw obstacles in the way of a seizure of power. An individual or a faction, though supreme in one branch, could not legally override the others and bring all parts of the government under single unified control.

It was typical, also, that the state constitutions made the executive weak and gave more power to the elected legislature. On general principles, the Americans were extremely reluctant to confer power upon a single man. They had had a long experience with British governors, whose presence had obstructed their efforts toward self-rule, and in drafting their state constitutions they severely limited the governor's power. All but one of the new constitutions denied the governor a veto over legislation. In several cases, he was not allowed to act even in an executive capacity, except as a member of a council, of which he was merely the president. His appointive powers were usually curtailed or taken away. It was said of the governor of North Carolina, for example, that he had power only to collect his salary. This situation prevailed in nearly all the states. Powers lost by the governor fell to the elected legislatures, which gained in importance. This result accorded perfectly with the prevailing notion that the representatives of the people were the best guardians of liberty.

The new constitutions did not always advance the cause of democracy. The extent to which state governments were more democratic than those of colonial times depended on local circumstances and upon the relative strength of competing groups. In Pennsylvania, the wealthy conservative Quakers and their allies lost political control in the opening years of the Revolution. City radicals and back-country leaders captured the patriotic movement, thrust themselves to the fore, and proceeded to write a new constitution embodying their views. The Pennsylvania constitution provided for a one-house legislature, which was made supreme. There were no effective checks on the power of the people's immediate representatives.

Early national architecture. The two houses, one in Salem, Massachusetts (left), and the other near Richmond, Virginia (right), indicate the substantiality of American life in the early national period. Sabine Hall, the Virginia mansion, was begun earlier but completed with the addition of the porticos in the 1790s. (Historic Buildings Survey, Library of Congress)

The governor was merely the president of an executive council; both he and the council were chosen by the legislature. The members of the all-powerful legislature were elected on the basis of broad suffrage. Property qualifications for voting were virtually eliminated; any free white male who was a taxpayer could vote, and, whereas before the Revolution the back country had been grossly underrepresented in the legislature, it was now just as grossly overrepresented. Control of the state passed to the back country and into the hands of the active leaders of the revolutionary party, who, if they did not always genuinely represent the people of the state, were at least steadfastly opposed to privilege and wealth.

The southern colonies, on the other hand, went into the Revolution under their aristocratic leaders, who were active in conducting the rebellion. There the break from the mother country did not greatly alter the existing balance of social forces, and the usual forms and practices remained. Under the new state constitutions, the frontier areas still did not have adequate representation in the legislature.

Property qualifications for voting and holding office significantly limited the participation of the common people in government. In Maryland, to give an example, one had to have a 50-acre freehold or a £30 estate to cast a vote for assemblyman. This was about the usual qualification for voters. However, the qualifications for holding office restricted political positions to the gentry. For a member of the assembly, the qualification was a £500 estate. Members of the senate were required to own £1,000. The governor had to be a wealthy man indeed, possessed of a £5,000 estate, of which £1,000 at least had to be property in land. In Maryland, as in most of the states, the constitution provided for an upper house or senate, chosen in this case not directly by the people but indirectly by electors. It was intended to represent wealth as opposed to human beings, and to act as a check on the lower house. Maryland was not completely typical, even of the southern states, among which North Carolina and Georgia present a quite different picture, but the example of Maryland illustrates the conservative features of several state constitutions, both north and south. It is apparent that their formal arrangements did not always advance political democracy.

In another and more fundamental way, however, the Revolution was a great democratic upheaval which eventually reshaped the country's political and social forms. The deepest change was psychological. Before the War for Independence, aristocracy and social inequality were accepted principles. Wealth and family commanded respect; the common people knew their place. Gentlemen exercised political leadership as a matter of course. After the Revolution, the change was unmistakable. High political offices were still occupied almost exclusively by gentlemen, but gentlemen as a class had to cope with an active popular movement that questioned what they stood for and would end by questioning their right to rule.

THE ARTICLES
OF CONFEDERATION

The first constitution of the federal union, the Articles of Confederation, was a fitting product of the revolutionary movement. Drawn up early in the war by committees of the Continental Congress, though not adopted until 1781, it reflected the principles of liberty which were uppermost in the minds of its framers. It provided for a weak central government, with several essential powers remaining in the hands of the states.

The Revolution had proceeded from the struggles of thirteen separate colonies for self-rule, carried forward to rebellion and independence. National feeling had but partially developed, and the goal sought by the foes of British authority in each province was self-rule of their particular colony. They were fighting for liberty, which they defined as the right of the

people of every colony or state to conduct their own affairs through elected representatives, without interference of any sort. They had learned to associate central governments with tyranny. Britain had formerly provided a central government over the colonies, which had checked and limited local aspirations toward self-rule. It was against this that patriots were contending. They thought that a central government, by its very nature, inevitably limited liberties and self-rule of the people in the states. Although by common consent a central government was established to help conduct war, the revolutionists had no intention of creating an authority reminiscent of Great Britain. They deliberately made their new central government as weak as possible. Their union was a league of states, in which the states retained essential sovereignty. This arrangement they looked upon as "a work of time and great wisdom," which incorporated the experience of centuries.

Notwithstanding their fear of central government, practicability and experience demanded that certain essential powers be granted to it. Among these were declaring war, making treaties, sending and receiving ambassadors, regulating the value of coins, fixing standards of weights and measures, and regulating post offices and postage weights. A most critical defect of the Articles lay in the lack of sanctions or enforcing authority. Congress had no coercive authority. It was dependent upon the will of the states to grant necessary revenue as well as levies of men in time of war. The new government was no sooner in operation than proposals were made to remedy its deficiencies. Significantly, most of these had to do with giving the Congress more adequate revenue, more control over commerce, and particularly some way to enforce obedience by giving to the

United States powers over the citizens similar to those exercised by the states. Another major shortcoming of the Articles was the impossibility of getting the necessary unanimous action by the states to amend them.

Still another basic flaw of the Confederation was the denial of taxing power to Congress. In previous chapters something has been said about the emergence of representative government in England and the way in which the House of Commons employed its control over taxation to wrest power from the kings. This history was better known to the revolutionary generation than it is to Americans of today. The American colonial assemblies had used this control of taxation as a weapon against the British governors. A fundamental maxim in their political philosophy was: "That power which holds the ﹖ purse strings absolutely must rule," and they had no doubt that the ability of the people to refuse or grant taxes to the government was the foundation and only defense of popular liberties. Accordingly, they denied Congress under the Confederation the right of taxation. Congress could levy upon the states for money, but could neither wring money from them against their will nor collect its own taxes. Without income Congress could scarcely carry out a policy or pursue an undertaking. Actually, these limitations were never quite so severe as they seem, because Congress did in fact acquire sources of income. Nevertheless, the denial of taxing power to Congress was a basic fact which shaped the character of the federal system under the Articles of Confederation.

It will be said at once that this union was too feeble, that Congress lacked sufficient powers, particularly in time of war. Many Americans came to believe that Congress ought to be strengthened. It should be kept in mind, however, that Americans of that time understood the consequences of weakness or strength, of localism or centralization in government. They knew that a weak government was less effective in war, but they chose a weak government because their minds were set on liberty. The Revolution, as one contemporary said, was "a struggle for liberty and not for power." They did not aim, most of them, at the creation of a powerful national state. They preferred that the union be a rope of sand, as it was called, rather than a rod of iron. The federal system under the Articles of Confederation was designed to secure liberty as Americans then understood it.

ADMINISTRATION IN THE REVOLUTION

The Revolution unloosed a business boom and price inflation that was to leave a deep mark on American society. The war was greater and far more expensive than any the country had known before. The armed forces needed unprecedented quantities of supplies—imported goods, such as powder and uniforms, as well as country produce, beef, pork, wheat, rum, and forage for the horses. The states and Congress bid against one another for the available supplies. Prices soared.

Coupled with advance of real prices was the effect of currency depreciation. Congress and the states issued paper money to pay their expenses. It was the only way they had of meeting the costs of war. This method had worked well in colonial times, but it was not equal to the strains of the Revolution. The new state governments were reluctant to impose taxes and frequently unable to collect those they levied. Many states had virtual civil wars on their hands and were subject to enemy invasion. Troops crossed the land; the coast was harassed and eventually blockaded. The enemy occupied commercial cities. Men left their farms to fight in the army. Under these circumstances, affairs were chaotic, and it would have been hard to collect taxes even had the states been so disposed. But the revolutionary governments were not firmly established at first, and they could not risk alienating support by imposing heavy taxes. Consequently, state revenues during the first two or three years of the war were inconsiderable. To meet this deficiency both Congress and the states issued huge quantities of paper money. The result was a spectacular inflation of prices. Once the paper money began to fall in value, people lost confidence in it, expecting it to decline further. Governments got less and less real value in return for the money they spent, and therefore had to issue larger amounts. At the beginning of 1778, a Continental dollar was worth about 25 cents. By January, 1779, it was worth perhaps 12 cents; a year later, 2 or 3 cents. In the spring of 1781, the Continental dollar passed out of circulation.

Before this, Congress had ceased to issue any more paper money and was virtually without income. The armies in the field were supported by impressments of material conducted by both state and federal officers. In camp or on the march, the military forces simply took whatever they needed from the inhabitants, relieving the farmers of their grain, their livestock, or their wagons. Farmers thus visited frequently grew bitter, and in some areas refused to grow anything more than they needed to feed their families. During the Yorktown campaign, the American forces advancing in Virginia seldom saw a wagon that was not made useless by being deprived of its wheels, and they could not

persuade the inhabitants to cooperate in rounding up horses.

The sacrifices of individuals whose property was taken or whose patriotism induced them to enlist in the army where they served virtually without pay, frequently in rags, and sometimes without thanks, stood in contrast to the conduct of many other individuals for whom the war provided an opportunity to get rich. Merchants often made enormous profits, banding together to raise prices or corner the supply of badly needed goods. Farmers charged extortionate prices when they could, arousing in some cases the resentment of the city population, whose wages lagged behind the rising cost of living. The anger against profiteers and monopolists was intense. General Washington, who as commander of the army felt the effects of these practices, declared that the United States had more to fear from profiteers and monopolists than from the enemy, and lamented that they had not been hunted down and hanged.

Attracted by high profits, a good many Americans did not scruple to revive the old colonial habit of trading with the enemy. Unlike the Continental forces, which could offer only paper money, the British paid in solid coin; consequently, they drew off supplies from the areas which they occupied. While Washington's army was starving at Valley Forge, wagonloads of country produce were being hauled into nearby Philadelphia, then in British hands. Illicit trade was carried on by prearranged captures of American vessels, which were taken into New York harbor and sold, with their cargoes, to the profit of both captive and captor. A vast trade with the enemy went on through neutral European ports, a traffic organized by American, British, and European merchants. John Adams reported from Europe in 1781 that

British customhouse receipts were climbing as a result of the recovery of the old trade with America. He said that American merchants who visited London could easily obtain loans from British merchants. The language of the British merchants was (he said): "We understand one another. Let the governments squabble."

The state governments made elaborate efforts to regulate economic activity in the public interest and to sustain the value of paper money. They adopted tender laws which fixed a legal value on paper money and required that the money be accepted at this value in private transactions and in payment of debts. They passed laws regulating the prices of labor and all sorts of commodities and made it an offense to charge more. They tried strenuously to check monopoly and profiteering, even authorizing the seizure of hoarded goods. They adopted embargo acts prohibiting the export of goods which were needed by the military forces. These efforts were mostly ineffective. By a sort of general agreement, the laws were evaded. Governments of those times lacked the power to control the economic life of the community. The main significance of the economic legislation of this time was that it served as a political rallying point, rousing the common people against the businessmen and propertied men whose interest compelled them to violate the laws. On the other hand, these laws caused unquenchable bitterness in the hearts of wealthier citizens who felt they were being deprived of their rights and property. Propertied men were further enraged by the fact that regulations were often enforced by local committees composed of poor men and farmers, who, as they thought, meddled and made trouble without cause, purely out of dislike of the wealthy.

A good share of the difficulties which beset the Continental government arose from inefficiency, waste, and corruption in the federal administration. Congress had been no more than a debating society in 1774, when suddenly it confronted the enormous task of waging war. The multitudinous details of supplying the army had to be taken in hand without any sort of organization to deal with them. Harassed and driven by the rapid pace of events, Congress met emergencies as they arose, creating by degrees the various agencies needed to handle foreign and domestic procurement of supplies, maintain the army, and conduct diplomatic affairs.

These agencies functioned in a loose and casual manner. Reluctant to delegate power, Congress first made committees of its own members responsible for executive functions. These members had many other duties. Some were not interested. Others were preoccupied with the notorious distractions of social life in Philadelphia. By the time they became informed and skilled in their duties, their terms had often expired and they had to go back to their states. The whole procedure was not one which appealed to a sense of managerial efficiency, and there was much ridicule of Congress for this reason, particularly on the part of merchants, who thought they knew how to run a business. This situation was not relieved before 1781, even though Congress replaced committees with boards, which included permanent administrative officials as well as members of Congress.

The same casual methods and undefined responsibility characterized the whole federal service. Frequently, the top officials did not appoint their deputies, who were selected by Congress. Thus the man in charge of the hierarchy of public servants in a department had no direct control over the lower officers who carried on the actual functions of the department. He very likely would not know how many minor officers were employed, who they were, or even what they were doing in a local area. Besides, Congress was in the habit of reorganizing such departments every year or two. This not only disrupted the services to a certain extent, but caused extreme rancor and jealousy among public officers who felt that their rank and status were being undermined by the plots of rivals. A great deal of inner rivalry for place and power existed among officers in the public service, both in the executive departments and in the army.

Congress's problems were eased, but in the end complicated, by the employment of merchants in the public service. Today we would be likely to question the propriety of giving an official appointment to a man who is actively engaged in the same kind of business with which he has to deal as a public officer. During the Revolution, however, it was the rule to appoint a wheat merchant to buy wheat for the government, a trader in tobacco to purchase tobacco, and so on. There were good reasons for the practice. Merchants had the necessary connections and knowledge to get business done, and Congress could hardly dispense with their service. But the result was that Congress's procurement agencies were staffed with merchants who traded furiously in all kinds of business at the same time that they acted as public servants. During the early years of the war, the entire procurement of supplies in Europe and the spending of the money received from France rested in the hands of a particular group of merchants, interlocked by partnerships and contracts. As agents of the Continental government, they disposed of official business, acting through their own commercial connections, mixing official transactions with their own, and using information at their command to further their own speculations. Within the United States, the purchase of supplies for the government was carried out by merchants, sometimes obscure traders traveling the countryside, virtually unsupervised by higher authority, who pursued a traffic in goods on their own account while acting as federal agents, thus earning a profit on each transaction in addition to collecting their normal compensation from the government.

This kind of administrative system was tolerated by the ethics of the business community of that time, and no doubt most federal officers, particularly in the higher echelons, observed a scrupulous regard for the public interest. But it does not need to be pointed out that such a system provided many openings for the pursuit of private gain. Moreover, such were the fluctuations in the value of currency, the disorder and improvisation that characterized the whole administration, that fraud and speculation were difficult, and often impossible, to detect. General opinion among the people was that the federal procurement services were shot through with corruption, and that an officer so engaged was to be assumed dishonest unless proved otherwise. Undoubtedly, this opinion arose in some degree from that natural suspicion with which the people of a democracy regard their rulers, as well as an ignorance of the real problems confronting public officers. However this may be, the belief in official corruption was so universal as to cause a decline in public morale and patriotic feeling. People would not willingly make sacrifices when others, as they thought, were lining their pockets. The loyal corps of officials who served with devotion and self-sacrifice did

TRAVELS OF THE CONTINENTAL CONGRESS, 1776–1785

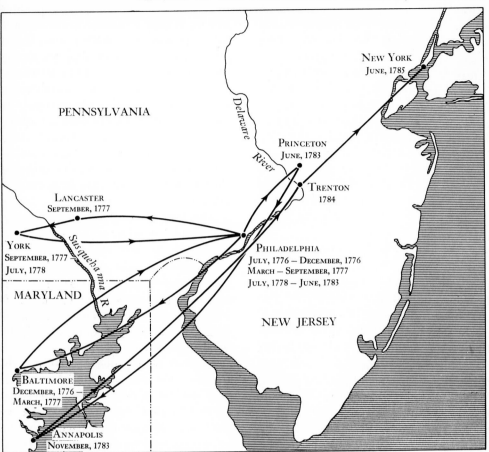

not escape the general odium attached to public service.

In the military forces there was a considerable amount of what we would call featherbedding, particularly among minor appointees and functionaries. Men were put on the public payroll to perform small duties that occupied only a fraction of their time. At military posts, it was a common sight to see three or four men lounging around, each assigned to a separate little part of some job that one man could have performed. Meanwhile, these men would consume supplies, perhaps retain a cook for their own separate mess,

use wood to keep two fires going all winter, draw forage for their horses, and, as the mood struck them, call on the services of carpenters and other workmen also on the federal payroll. This sort of thing amounted to such a public scandal that a member of Congress remarked that one half of the population was supporting the other half and its horses.

THE COUNTERREVOLUTION

A more serious handicap to the prosecution of the war was the factional rivalries and hatred among the patriots themselves. Conservatives in Pennsylvania, for example, never ceased to press their fight against the radical government, which was dominated by back-country delegates. They conspired to obstruct and defeat the measures of the radical administration and apparently felt little hesitation in making common cause with outright loyalists, who wanted America to lose the war. The radical government, on its part, took harsh and discriminatory steps in dealing with people who opposed it. Quakers and other pacifists who refused military service were heavily taxed, and the government was not always too careful about whose property it confiscated. Such ungenerous bickering in the midst of a struggle for liberty offended many patriots, who became disgusted with public affairs altogether.

Partisan conflict of this sort to some extent occurred in all the states. Writing from Virginia, Charles Lee voiced his contempt for back-country leaders now rising in public affairs. According to him, Virginia lived under misrule and tyranny. In so many words, he said that if he had to choose between the tyranny of the "mob" and the tyranny of Britain, he would prefer the latter. "We in Virginia live (if it can be call'd living) neither under Monarchy Aristocracy nor Democracy; if it deserves any name it is a Macocracy—that is that a Banditte of Scotch Irish Servants or their immediate Descendants (whose names generally begin with Mac) are our Lords and Rulers. . . ."

Such remarks illustrate the general attitudes of many men of wealth and station. Profoundly aware of the changes which had occurred since the Revolution, many of them looked back with regret to the peaceful order of colonial society, when America was safely anchored to Britain and a common man knew his place. How sharply those times contrasted with the epoch in which they were now living! "There is no order that has a will of its own," cried Alexander Hamilton; "the question is always what will please, not what will benefit the people." This was a common theme in the language of gentlemen. The "leather aprons" of the towns and the country bumpkins who now presumed to inflict their prejudices on the government, it was said, knew nothing of statesmanship or the general principles which ought to prevail in society. Seeing only the "narrow circle of their own concerns," the populace did not hesitate to sacrifice the general welfare of the community for the sake of any paltry gain. Men of mean abilities, ignorant and lacking in good manners, occupied public office. Under such circumstances, so gentlemen believed, nothing could be expected but confusion and injustice.

Some of the activities of state governments in this period lent weight to what these gentlemen were saying; nevertheless, behind their criticism was a rankling resentment at sometimes having to take second place to men whom they looked down upon as their inferiors. Besides, from what they saw of currency depreciation and tender laws during the Revolution, they were convinced that "the people" aimed to use political power to divest them of their property. Popular governments had never before been tried, and gentlemen's minds were full of the history of ancient Greek city-states which had been periodically rent by class war. They had no confidence in Thomas Paine's dictum that property was safe in the hands of the people. Believing as they did that unequal distribution of wealth and property was the main ground of conflict among human beings, they thought that only a strong government prevented different social groups from pillaging one another. Intensely conscious of law and order, they were acutely disturbed by the susceptibility of state governments to popular pressure, especially where property rights were concerned. At the beginning of the Revolution, they might possibly have been carried away by the generous enthusiasm for liberty, but before long paper money, radical committees, tender laws, and the violent and sometimes confiscatory practices of state governments convinced them that their fear of democracy was only too well justified.

The mounting dissatisfaction with the conduct of the war, the profiteering, and the waste, and the belief that many responsible for directing the war were using it to advance their own fortunes brought a shift in political leadership. The military crisis of 1780, culminating in the defeat of General Horatio Gates at Camden, South Carolina, hastened the crisis which brought a reaction. Conservatives acquired new strength in several important states, and these changes were reflected in the composition of Congress. One man who quickly grasped the significance of the new trend was Thomas Paine, an early radical in the Revolution. In 1780 he wrote that hitherto the war had relied upon the support of the poor. This had been possible, he said, as long as the war could be waged by emissions of paper money. But now that paper money was exhausted, the rich and propertied people must throw in their aid, or the cause would fail. As popular leadership was discredited by the apparent failure of the war effort, conservatives stepped forward and told the people that victory could be won only by adopting their program. They spoke not of liberty but of the need for authority and business principles in the conduct of public affairs. They hated paper money and blamed it as the source of the country's misfortunes. They held out instead the virtues of heavy taxation, sound money, and a rigorous enforcement of contracts. They called for an end to price controls, laws against monopoly, and all those other restraints on trade which, according to them, served no good purpose and created a host of evils. Only free enterprise, they said, could win the war. Finally, they urged the necessity of a permanent army, composed of men enlisted for long terms. In sum, they offered to the nation a program of authority, discipline, business efficiency, sound money, and economic *laissez faire*.

Men who held these views dominated Congress from 1781 to the end of the war. Much of their program was realized. After paper money went down to its final ruin, they abandoned it, along with tender laws and price controls, and tried to run the government by other expedients. They did all they could to form a permanent army, asking the states to enlist men for three years or the duration of the war. In the face of strong opposition from the New England states, they granted half-pay pensions to officers who would continue in service until the end of the war. In the name of greater efficiency, they undertook a reform of central administration, creating new departments of finance, war, foreign affairs, and marine, placing these departments under powerful single executives, who were not members of Congress. A change in leadership accompanied this shift of policy. Writing in 1783, a contemporary observer, who viewed these changes with disfavor, commented on the "strange turn" that affairs had taken. The "new and rising interests" were displacing the old revolutionary

leaders, whose disappointments and chagrin were "inexpressible." "Almost all
new appointments either state or congressional run in that line," he said, "so
that most of those who were much distinguished and known in times of our
great difficulty, are now in private station,
and the few left are daily falling in." The
disappointments and discouragements of
the war had discredited the radical patriot
leaders and given the "better sort" a
chance to grasp the helm of state.

The new regime drew support which
had not formerly been proffered to the
government. Merchants in Philadelphia,
Baltimore, and other cities voluntarily got
together to advance money on loan for the
public use. Commenting on these surprising developments, one member of Congress said that there seemed to be a new
spirit of patriotism rising. Men who for
years past had been concerned only with
making money were now rallying to the
cause. Although the sum actually raised
by these contributions was small, the fact
that merchants were taking the initiative
revealed a disposition to back a government whose policies they approved.

The trend of affairs came to light in
the resolutions adopted by a convention
of New England states and New York
held at Hartford in 1780. Formerly, such
conventions had occupied themselves with
fixing prices and framing common regulations for controlling trade and frustrat-
ing the schemes of profiteers. From this
convention emerged a set of resolutions
far different in character, all pointing toward stronger government as the cure for
the country's ills. One resolution proposed
that George Washington be given power
to collect supplies by force in states that
did not comply with the requests of Congress. Another resolution declared that
the weakness of Congress was a fatal flaw

in the system of government and went on
to demand that Congress be given power
to collect a duty on imports. Commenting
on the resolution to give Washington dictatorial powers, the old radical, James
Warren, wrote to Sam Adams: "If [that]
does not astonish you I have forgotten
my political Catechism." Surely, he went
on, history would not be believed when
it recorded that New England delegates
voted to give the military power coercive
authority over civilian government. "This
must have been done without recollecting
political Maxims, without attending to
Historical Admonitions and warning, or
the Principles on which our Opposition
to Britain rests."

A changed Congress had already begun
to revise its political catechism. The revisions were to become more drastic. At
this very time, the subject under discussion in Congress was a plan for a Continental impost (federal tariff). As finally
adopted in 1781, the plan called for a
5 per cent duty on imports, to be collected
by Continental officers and appropriated
to the uses of Congress, primarily to the
payment of interest on the federal debt.
Congress asked the states to "vest a
power" in the central government to collect such duty, and this power was to be
exercised as long as a debt existed. The significance of this proposal was vast, almost
revolutionary. It was, in fact, a modification of the federal system as contemplated
under the Articles of Confederation. As
we have seen, the exclusive right of
the states to levy taxes was basic to the
whole of that system. The Continental impost would have conferred the power on
Congress to levy taxes and would have
established the primary condition for the
growth of a stronger central government.
Since it was an amendment to the pending
Articles of Confederation, the impost res-

lution had to be ratified by all the states.

This proposal became the focus of a movement for a strong national government that had the backing of important segments of the population. From the beginning of the Revolution, the propertied and aristocratic classes, particularly in the middle states, had desired such a system. They were convinced that their personal and property rights were, and always would be, subject to the abuse of "an interested and overbearing majority."

FINANCIERS AND THEIR PLANS

The decision to finance the war effort out of borrowings from the public instead of through issuance of paper money resulted in the creation of a new group which had an economic stake in a stronger central government. These public creditors constituted an increasingly powerful voice in the affairs of the country. As the years wore on the debts of Congress increased and the public creditors bought larger quantities of federal securities. Unlike the bonds of World Wars I and II, these government obligations could be bought and sold between individuals. As time went on they became concentrated in fewer hands, as the original possessors sold them to others. Securities sold at a fraction of their face value because many lost faith in the government's ability to pay its debts. Speculators who were willing to gamble on the eventual ability of the government to pay its debts bought them in large quantities and stood to make handsome profits if Congress should ever meet its obligation.

The leader of these forces was a merchant in Philadelphia, Robert Morris, who during the next few years was to be one of the greatest political figures in America. Morris had acquired a fortune during the war by combining government office with private trade. Already one of the larger merchants of Philadelphia, he was put in charge of congressional agencies that handled procurement of supplies in Europe. It appears that he managed to place a large share of these government transactions in the hands of his own partners and business associates. His success in business brought him a reputation as the most prominent merchant in America, widely known, revered, envied, and hated in all parts of the country. "He has vast designs in the mercantile way," wrote John Adams, "and no doubt pursues mercantile ends, which are always gain; but he is an excellent Member of our Body."

Robert Morris typified a large and influential group of conservatives who feared democracy and who looked to the establishment of an effective central government as the only bulwark against domination by the back-country radicals. The fact that he and his associates owned federal securities provided an economic incentive for their demand for a stronger union. Thus the political and economic motives of this group caused them to become identified with the movement for a stronger union. They abhorred paper money, governmental restrictions on business, and waste and inefficiency in public administration. They were alert also to the economic possibilities created by the emergence of a new nation. They were aware of the advantage of commercial banks, insurance companies, and business corporations, though none of these had existed in colonial America. They understood the benefits which would derive from a well-financed public debt and a government that would promote business enterprise. Morris dreamed of an America that would take its place among the foremost nations of the world—a nation of "power, consequence, and grandeur" buttressed with armaments and public credit.

Appointed Superintendent of Finance in 1781, Morris acquired powers that made him almost a "pecuniary dictator," as some called him. His personal influence reached into all branches of the administration, and he so dominated Congress that to many he became the formulator of the federal policy which Congress merely sanctioned. Aided by a personal following within the government and in many states, Morris planned to introduce "correct principles" and sound management in the finances in contrast to the inefficiency and waste which prevailed when the radicals were in control. The times were favorable to these plans. The victory at Yorktown practically ended the war, thereby reducing expenditures. The Superintendent was further assisted by substantial French loans during his term of office. The hard money which these loans placed at his disposal freed him from some of the difficulties which had embarrassed Continental officials in the past. Even so, the problems were many, and Morris had ample opportunity to demonstrate managerial efficiency. He cut down on personnel, reduced expenses, and tried to introduce some degree of order into the confusion of government records. He even managed to reestablish a shred of public credit, which resulted in some restoration of confidence in the government's financial responsibility among those close to him.

Morris's larger aims centered on strengthening the central government, particularly in the interests of the business and financial community. The first step toward this was the creation, in 1782, of the Bank of North America. Failing to attract enough capital from private individuals, Morris invested government money in the stock of this bank in order to get it started. The bank, therefore, represented a joint enterprise, with most of the original stock owned by the government and by Morris's friends and associates. The bank was to serve as a depository for government funds and as a moneylender to Congress. It could help the government maintain credit, and its notes would provide a stable circulating medium under regulation of businessmen rather than of the inflation-minded state legislatures controlled by farmers. Morris hoped to be able to increase its capital and eventually draw within its orbit much of the private wealth of the country. If propertied men in all parts of the nation could be led to invest their money in partnership with the government, the result would be "to unite the several states more closely together in one general money connexion, and indissolubly to attach many powerful individuals to the cause of our country by the strong principles of self-love and the immediate sense of private interest. . . ." In this hope Morris was disappointed. Far from becoming a "principal pillar of American credit," the bank finally became a wholly private concern, operating principally in Philadelphia. But during most of Morris's term it was there, ready to play its role as one of those "useful institutions" on which the country's future would depend.

Morris's greatest goal—his grand design—was to free Congress from financial dependence on the states and on foreign loans by securing for it independent sources of revenue in the form of a federal impost or duty. This was needed in order to establish the public credit and pay the war debt; it would also require an amendment to the Articles of Confederation and would thus be the first step in constitutional reform directed toward strengthening the central government. Independent revenue was the mortar needed to hold his whole system together. Likewise, the revolutionary debt was a "national blessing" and a potential "cement to the union," for it justified the demand for federal revenues. In the plans of men like Morris, a government debt was of strategic importance. It was a potential source of capital which would aid in the economic development of the country. If the securities which represented the debt could be solidly funded and the interest regularly paid, they would rise in value. But propertied men would, therefore, gain wealth which would supply capital for banks and all kinds of business enterprise. In all Morris's planning the political uses of the debt went hand in hand with its economic uses. He argued that the debt could be paid only if the Articles of Confederation were altered to give Congress the power of taxation. Once the central government was provided with its own sources of revenue and the means of paying its debts, propertied men who owned securities would be drawn to its support.

Never for a moment did Morris disguise his purposes. They were given widespread publicity. But despite his vast influence, his exhaustive appeals to the state legislatures, the many letters and newspaper articles which went out under his direction, Morris fell short by one vote of securing the revenue amendment. Late in 1782 his grand design was ruined by the single negative of Rhode Island, whose legislature unanimously rejected the impost. When Virginia then revoked her previous grant, the nationalists were defeated. The ending of the war soon undermined their influence. The American people saw no need to risk the liberty they had won by establishing a strong central government.

In his views, his program, and his penchant for employing economic interests as "cement to the union," Morris anticipated the financial plans of Alexander Hamilton, who built upon the foundations the nationalists laid in the closing years of the war. Though it benefited from his genius, the nationalist movement under Morris paid the penalty of his leadership. It was too much the creation of Morris and his clique, savoring of personal aggrandizement and private advantage. It was a political machine, but a defective one because it operated from the middle states, slighting the interests and excluding the influence of New England and the south. For these reasons, many influential men who were generally sympathetic with Morris's aims did not believe that stronger government and economic reform could be safely accomplished under the auspices of Morris and his colleagues. Samuel Osgood, a bitter foe of centralized power, expressed an opinion by no means confined to agrarian radicals when he wrote to John Adams, then in Europe:

> In some of your letters you seem to be in opinion that there is an absolute necessity of bracing up the Confederation. That funds are necessary for supporting the Credit of the United States. I cannot collect your ideas precisely, but I am apprehensive that if you were here, you would find it very difficult to establish funds that would not have a tendency to destroy the liberties of this country. Our embarrassments are very great. Our danger lies in this—that if permanent funds are given to Congress, the aristocratical influence, which predominates in more than a major part of the United States, will finally establish an arbitrary government in the United States.

SOCIAL CHANGES

A sense of optimism permeates many of the writings of this period. It was a hopeful era, even for those persons who looked at America's growing democratic institutions and did not always like what they saw. Writing in the last year of the war, the French Minister to the United States conceded, despite his sympathies with the movement to strengthen the central government, that

> the people of this country are in general happy; that the tribunals have a sufficient authority; that there is room for all the world; that abundance reigns; that the most unlimited toleration does not engender the smallest religious dispute; that union and peace reign in families; and that the government is not faulty, except with regard to several great objects of internal administration and to those of foreign policy.

● The American Revolution was in many ways a conservative movement; it originated as a struggle to *preserve* rights and liberties supposedly existent. The war brought no violent upheavals or sweeping changes in government and law, religious and social ideas, class relations, or the organization of economic life—no abrupt departure from the colonial past. Nothing occurred in any way comparable with the upheaval of the French Revolution of 1789 or the Russian Revolution of 1917. Yet revolution is always destructive of the existing order, and in America it germinated seeds of change, seeds already planted in colonial society.

The departure of the loyalists removed a segment of the community inclined to conservatism and adherence to the *status quo*. When the war began and people had to make a choice of allegiance, some from every class became loyalists; however, loyalists were more numerous among the men of property and position than among the general population. If loyalists remained inactive and stayed at home, they were not usually molested, but if they fled to the British lines, they were outlawed and their property was confiscated. About 60,000 loyalists took refuge with the British forces during the war. Many of them migrated to New Brunswick, Nova Scotia, and Upper Canada, adding an English stock to the French population of Canada. Meanwhile, the revolutionary governments confiscated and sold their estates. Although purchased initially by wealthy investors who bought them in large blocs, the estates were ultimately broken up and sold to small farmers. The extensive lands of the Penns and the Baltimores were thrown upon the market. Thus land ownership was in some degree broadened, great estates became less conspicuous in the seaboard areas, and the gentry class suffered a loss in numbers and prestige.

Further alterations in the landholding system contributed to the same result. Quitrents were swept away, and within a decade after the Revolution, all the states had abolished primogeniture and entail, removing the legal props of landed aristocracy. More important was the elimination of British restraints upon western settlement. Lands formerly closed by British and proprietary injunction fell to the state governments, which rapidly opened them to purchase and settlement. America expanded farther into the hinterland, to and beyond the Alleghenies. The log cabin became more than ever the symbol of the American way of life.

War prosperity stimulated the development of business enterprise in the United States. Private fortunes were on a far greater scale than in colonial times.

WESTERN LAND CLAIMS AND CESSIONS BY THE STATES

Whereas the $300,000 owned by Thomas Hancock had once caused amazement, the estimates of Robert Morris's wealth ran into the millions. Business ventures in ships, cargoes, and land speculation were of a new level of magnitude. Formerly dependent upon Britain to provide marine insurance, American merchants now formed companies to supply it to themselves. Before the war, business enterprise had been limited to partnerships, formed almost always by merchants of a single port or locality. The war went far towards nationalizing business. Merchant capitalists, many of them new men raised up by war speculation, combined wide-ranging investments in land, state debts, and federal securities with trading ventures in all parts of the union. Having national interests, they were susceptible to national points of view.

The physical expansion of the country proceeded unabated. Throughout the war, population increased rapidly. The westward surge of people hardly awaited the end of active fighting before engulfing the western parts of existing states and breaking over the Alleghenies. A postwar economic depression dimmed the immediate joys of independence, and painful readjustments in maritime trade were necessary now that America was outside the British Empire. But blessed with a rich hinterland and a rugged, acquisitive population, America's prospects were immensely favorable.

The larger history of the Revolution epoch is not contained in the story of political movements and the need for constitutional reform. Too much has been said about the weakness of government, the divisions among the states, and their failure to cooperate during the war. When we consider the circumstances, the thirteen American communities exhibited a remarkable degree of cooperation. They recognized Congress as head of the country, took its paper money, accepted its rulings, and for the most part attempted to do what it asked. They sent their own citizens as soldiers to serve under federal commanders in distant parts of the land. Actually the common struggle helped vastly to break down local feeling and to stimulate a sense of national identity. The Confederation was slowly taking on the attributes of a national state.

FURTHER READINGS

J. Franklin Jameson, *The American Revolution Considered as a Social Movement* (1926), and Randolph G. Adams, *The Political Ideas of the American Revolution* (1922), are two well-established classics which have been reprinted in paperback editions. Information on the social and political side of the Revolution may be found in some of the books cited in Chapter Four: Edmund S. Morgan, *The Birth of the Republic, 1763–1789* (1956), and John R. Alden, *The American Revolution* (1954). Other standard works includes James T. Adams, *Revolutionary New England* (1923); H. J. Eckenrode, *The Revolution in Virginia* (1916); Charles H. Lincoln, *The Revolutionary Movement in Pennsylvania* (1901); and Carl Becker, *History of Political Parties in New York, 1760–1766* (1909).

The Loyalists have been dealt with by Isaac S. Harrell, *Loyalism in Virginia* (1926); Lewis Einstein, *Divided Loyalties* (1933); and C. H. Van Tyne, *The Loyalists of the American Revolution* (1902). A view of economic factors may be gleaned from Robert A. East, *Business Enterprise in the American Revolutionary Era* (1938). On the Articles of Confederation, one may profitably compare an older view such as A. C. McLaughlin, *Confederation and Constitution* (1905), with the ablest recent synthesis, Merrill Jensen, *The Articles of Confederation* (1940). An excellent study of a particular state is Richard P. McCormick, *Experiment in Independence: New Jersey in the Critical Period* (1950).

The best and most recent biography of Robert Morris is by Clarence L. Ver Steeg, *Robert Morris, Revolutionary Financier* (1954). Valuable here as well as elsewhere are the biographies of other major American statesmen of the period, such as Douglas S. Freeman, *George Washington* (6 vols., 1948–1954); Nathan Schachner, *Thomas Jefferson* (2 vols., 1951); Catherine D. Bowen, *John Adams and the American Revolution* (1950); R. D. Meade, *Patrick Henry,* volume I (1957); and Carl Van Doren, *Benjamin Franklin* (1938). For the whole period, interesting source material is to be found in E. C. Burnett (ed.), *Letters of Members of the Continental Congress* (8 vols., 1921–1936).

For additional bibliography, see the *Harvard Guide,* sections 119–121.

SIX

From Confederation to Union: Making a New Nation

1785
Land Ordinance of 1785 adopted.

1786
Virginia enacts statute of religious freedom.
Shays' Rebellion begins.
Annapolis meeting called to discuss union.

1787
Northwest Ordinance enacted.
Constitutional Convention meets at Philadelphia.
First Federalist *paper written.*
Delaware first state to ratify new constitution.

1788
New Hampshire ninth state to ratify, June 21.

1789
First presidential election.
First Congress meets.
Washington inaugurated, April 30.
Bill of Rights passed by Congress.

1790
Funding and Assumption Act passed.

1791
First Bank of the United States created.
Hamilton's Report on Manufactures *published.*
Ratification of Bill of Rights completed, December 15.

1792
Washington reelected unanimously.

THE WEST IN THE CONFEDERATION

THE ERA OF THE Confederation, from the end of the Revolution to the establishment of the new federal government under the Constitution, has been called "the critical period," the implication being that the country was foundering under an inadequate governmental system and that the whole future of the United States was in dire jeopardy. This view, once widely held, is an exaggeration.

To be sure, there were serious problems of economic depression, foreign relations, and clashes between social groups and sectional interests. But it is doubtful that these problems taken together constituted an emergency or endangered the existence of the United States. The nation was vigorous and hopeful. Where problems and difficulties existed, there was a will to cooperate and a group of leaders of unrivaled political talent to face them.

In the 1780s the United States had a foretaste of the sweeping expansion which within less than a century was to transform the country from a group of Atlantic provinces into a great nation spreading for 3,000 miles across the land mass of North America. Before the Revolution, a small trickle of migration had begun to spill across the Appalachians into the great basin of the Mississippi, and land speculators were scrambling for title to vast areas of this domain. But first British

101

We the People of the United States...

Article I.

Section 1. All legislative Powers herein granted shall be vested in a Congress of the United States, which shall consist of a Senate and House of Representatives.

Section 2. The House of Representatives shall be composed of Members chosen every second Year by the People of the several States...

Americans had known the meaning of representative government and constitutional practices from the very beginning of their history. But this had always been on the local and state levels. There were many who, identifying self-government with the states, refused to believe that it could be made national. Would not a super-government, set up over the states, take away their liberties and the liberties of the people? Those who boldly wrote the new federal constitution in 1787 were suspected of anti-democratic sentiments. Such was the opposition to the new government that only a national leader of General Washington's stature could assure its acceptance.

A New England town meeting

First meeting of the Virginia House of Burgesses, 1619

The Constitution

George Washington, the first President

policy and then the distractions of war had restrained this movement. Consequently, population had grown slowly, from 2,000 or 3,000 in 1776 to perhaps 25,000 in 1783. Now, however, the stream swelled rapidly, so that by 1790 the area had a population of about 250,000. Americans were on the move once again, attracted by greater farming opportunities on virgin soil or driven to escape from debts or unhappy lives.

The whole transmontane area was subject to numerous and conflicting claims among the various states, based upon differing interpretations of colonial charters, royal grants, and Indian treaties. The largest of these claims belonged to Virginia, but Massachusetts, Connecticut, New York, the Carolinas, and Georgia also had them. Those states without claims naturally wanted title to all western lands to be vested in Congress. Their view ultimately won out owing to the stubborness of Maryland speculators, who persuaded the state to refuse ratification of the Articles of Confederation until such an agreement was reached in 1781. This cession of western lands was of profound impor-

**TERRITORY NORTHWEST OF
THE OHIO RIVER, 1787**

tance. It gave the federal government an important source of future revenue. And not only did it avert dangers stemming from state rivalries, but it contributed substantially to the centralization of political power. The United States now controlled far more land than did any state, and it was possible to apply a single set of policies to the whole frontier.

Influenced by its need for money and the pressure of speculators, Congress decided upon the sale of federal lands in the territory beyond the mountains and north of the Ohio River as far west as the Mississippi. The decision to sell lands in this "Northwest Territory" required legislation for the survey of lands and the establishment of government. The resulting legislation was embodied in two of the greatest and most enduring enactments of the Confederation government. The first of these, the Land Ordinance of 1785, provided for the survey of the territory into townships of 36 square miles, subdivided into sections of 640 acres. One section of each township was to be "reserved . . . for the maintenance of public schools," and four others were to be held by the federal government for future sale. The remaining sections were to be sold at auction. The fact that the smallest unit of sale was an entire section of 640 acres, at $1 an acre cash, made it impossible for the average pioneer to purchase land under this ordinance. The result was that most of the land was sold to speculators. It remained for subsequent laws to modify the terms of sale sufficiently to make purchase from the government practicable for the small farmer; meanwhile he could buy from an intermediary or establish himself as a squatter, without legal title. If this portion of the act was unsatisfactory, that pertaining to the support of the public schools was wise. More mportant still was the provision for a egular method of survey, for the system dopted was subsequently applied to early all the area from the Appalachians o the Pacific Coast. Although the actual urvey proceeded slowly, it proved in the ong run far superior to the traditional nethod of delineating property lines by eference to familiar landmarks.

Government for the Northwest Territory was established by the Ordinance of 1787, which provided for an orderly progression from territorial status to full statehood. It included a bill of rights which barred slavery from the territory, abolished primogeniture, guaranteed freedom of religion, and defined carefully the individual's rights in court. Initially, the territory was to have a governor and judges appointed by Congress. When the adult male population of the territory reached 5,000, landowners would elect the

THE RECTANGULAR SYSTEM OF SURVEYS

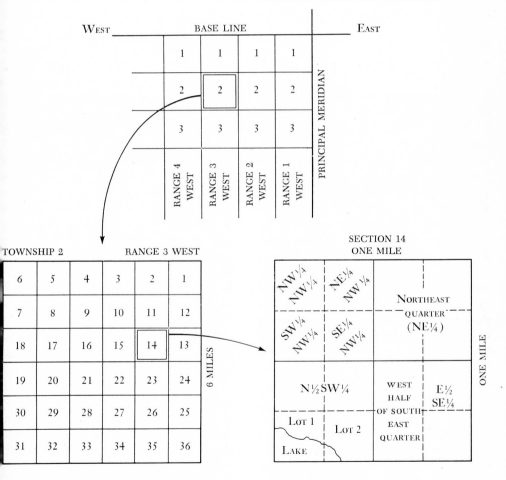

The system in use today has been only slightly modified since the Ordinance of 1785.

SECTION CONTAINS 640 ACRES
QUARTER SECTION CONTAINS 160 ACRES

lower house of a territorial legislature, and this assembly would in turn nominate ten men, from whom Congress would choose five for an upper house and governor's council. Enactments of the territorial legislature in this state of limited self-government could be vetoed by Congress or by the governor whom it appointed. Finally, when the population of a designated portion of the territory reached 60,000, and when its legislature ratified a constitution acceptable to Congress, it would be admitted to the union on a basis of complete equality with the original states.

This ordinance established a colonial policy new to the modern world. Instead of subjection, or at best limited political rights and economic exploitation, the territories could anticipate full equality within the union, to be achieved according to a regular and established pattern. So satisfactory was this arrangement that most of its important features were included in later territorial legislation under the Constitution. Except for a few special cases, this pattern was followed for all of the vast region west of the Appalachians. By establishing rules for land survey and government in advance of settlement, the ordinances of 1785 and 1787 assured more orderly and controlled settlement than had prevailed in the earlier settlements that were located south of the Ohio River.

ECONOMIC DEPRESSION AND RECOVERY

The end of the war found American and British merchants eager to profit from the resumption of normal trade, and merchants of Holland and France equally desirous of entering the newly free American market. It was this eagerness, combined with ignorance of the real circumstances which soon produced a first-rate commercial depression. Trade had been interrupted by the boycott on the eve of the Revolution, but by the spring of 1777 European goods from France and Holland, and from privateers, had begun to reappear on the American market. By 1780 considerable quantities of English goods were being received through the Dutch West Indies. Wartime prosperity was general except where actual fighting was going on. There were exceptions with many small businesses wrecked and the virtual ruin for a time of New England's fisheries and whaling industry. But ignoring the misfortunes of some individuals, American merchants as a group came out of the war far wealthier than they had gone in.

The situation in 1783 looked promising, especially since the British and French armies had bought supplies with hard money, and the end of the war found more specie in circulation than ever before. Many American merchants were in London as early as 1782 awaiting the restoration of peace, and when it came, they, along with British, Dutch, and French merchants, joined in a race to rush cargoes to what was rapidly becoming a buyer's market. Those fortunate enough to have their cargoes arrive early were able to cash in. But prices soon began to decline and the market was glutted. By the end of 1783, reports of poor markets and other ominous signs were numerous, with many predicting collapse. The oversupply of goods was first absorbed by the extension of credit to purchasers, but credit and specie soon dwindled so that Americans were no longer able to buy from Europe. By the middle of 1784, American wholesalers, unable to collect their own debts, could not pay their British suppliers. The atter lost heavily, many of them going into bankruptcy.

The fundamental problem of American importing merchants was quite simply that they lacked foreign markets for American products necessary to pay for future imports. This problem was highlighted by the difficulties of the southern tobacco grower. Freedom to sell his product in markets outside England, prohibited under the old trade and navigation laws, brought him no immediate gain. The lack of marketing facilities such as warehouses, credit, and auctions largely restricted the trade to the traditional markets of London and Glasgow. If he tried to sell his tobacco in France, the grower found himself limited by the monopolistic arrangements made between Robert Morris and a French syndicate, which held prices at a low level. Not until after the invention of the cotton gin in 1793 was the foundation laid for the recovery of the southern planters.

New England merchants, for their part, encountered the difficulty of being cut off from their former flourishing markets in the British West Indies because of their new status as "foreigners." Their lumber, fish, rum, and grains piled up on the wharves while the British tried to supply their West Indian possessions from Canadian sources. But Canada was neither sufficiently populous nor sufficiently developed economically to supply the British colonies. The United States was the obvious source. West Indian planters cooperated with American smugglers, and by 1785–1786 a trade revival was under way. Further, the British West Indian governors could admit American ships in case of "emergency." Pressure from island planters interested in low-cost supplies made such "emergencies" almost continuous. By the end of the decade New England trade with the British Caribbean possessions was at least equal to what it had been before the Revolution.

In other areas, too, commerce soon came to equal or exceed its prewar levels. Before the Revolution the colonies had operated within the commercial system of the Empire, and while the resulting arrangements were not always one-sided or suffocating, they were highly restrictive. Now Americans were free to trade throughout the world. France and Holland, among other nations, were eager to enter the American market, and in return France opened seven free ports to American goods, while Holland imposed no barriers whatever. By 1789 commerce with Holland had become more than half as important as that with England. And in the West Indies, trade with French, Dutch, and Spanish colonies revived. Nor was this all. Sweden and Prussia agreed to reciprocal trade treaties. The advantages of these agreements were not great, but American merchants soon opened up yet other new trade routes which quickly proved profitable. The most important of these came in 1784, when the *Empress of China* made the first passage from North America to China and the East Indies with a cargo of ginseng—reputed among the Orientals to have marvelous powers as a restorative of virility.

Before the end of the decade, then, foreign trade was booming, with the commerce of every American seaport considerably greater than ever before. It has been estimated that by 1790 American foreign commerce was triple that of the prerevolutionary era. Plagued though we are by the inexactness of commercial data before 1790, it seems fair to say that commercial growth had more than kept pace with the expanding population. This revival in turn brought new life to the lumber and the fishing industries, and a growing demand for agricultural commodities.

THE MOVEMENT FOR A STRONGER NATIONAL GOVERNMENT

Economic recovery came too late to save the Confederation. If the Articles, at least in the beginning, reflected in large degree the fears and aspirations of the majority, they nonetheless had weaknesses which in the end proved fatal. The most significant of these were their inflexibility, due to the difficulty of amendment, and the absence of that vital attribute of sovereignty, the revenue power.

We have already seen that Robert Morris tried in vain to remedy this major defect by securing for Congress the right to levy and collect taxes. By the end of 1783 the conservative counterrevolution, which he initiated, had temporarily stalled, but the dissatisfactions which had occasioned it remained and grew. As has been indicated in a previous chapter, this was particularly true of that influential group who held public securities and who continued to agitate for a national government that could pay its debts.

Other groups in addition to the public creditors objected to the impotence of the Confederation. Merchants wanted a government that could regulate and protect trade, while manufacturers desired a protective tariff for their "infant industries." Several states adopted tariffs against foreign goods, while admitting them freely from other parts of the United States. In a few cases trade barriers were erected against states, but these were mostly cases of petty retaliation. New Jersey, for example, imported most of her European goods through New York and Pennsyl-

vania. She understandably objected to the payment of duties on them to the treasuries of these states, and when New York refused to remit them, she imposed a tax on a New York lighthouse which stood on New Jersey soil. But such cases are exceptional. By 1785, the states were uniformly specifying in their tariff laws that duties were not to be applied to goods which were "the growth, produce, or manufacture" of the other states. Nevertheless merchants displayed a tendency to demand more coordinated trade policies and to blame state governments for difficulties which actually arose out of the transition to independence. Manufacturing was yet in its infancy in America, but it was beginning to grow in the 1780s, and manufacturing interests desired a national tariff program.

Strong dissatisfactions with the impotence of the Confederation arose on other than economic grounds. Ardent nationalists, impatient for the time when the United States would gain acceptance as an equal by the powerful nations of the world, blamed our failure to attain that end immediately upon the "weakness and ineptitude" of the Confederation. In so doing, they distorted reality. The monarchies of Europe looked with little sympathy upon this republican experiment in the New World; wartime aid from France and Spain had come not because they endorsed the principles of the Declaration of Independence, but because of their desire to weaken England. Of even more weight was the fact that, although with foreign aid we had been able to wrest independence from England, we still lacked the population and the economic strength to form the basis of genuine international power. Yet the nationalist argument was not completely groundless. Although the basic weakness lay outside the realm of governmental organization, the centrifugal tendencies of the Confederation brought a further loss of prestige and led several European powers to look hopefully for the day when the new nation would fall apart and its segments could be seized. Nationalists rightly believed that a more unified government would allow us to negotiate with other powers on more nearly equal terms.

Frontiersmen and those who speculated in western lands were disgruntled on other grounds. The Confederation was unequal to the task of ensuring the security of their lives, their property, and their commerce. Britain persisted, in violation of the treaty of peace, in maintaining her frontier posts in the northwest, insisting that her soldiers would not be removed until southern planters had paid their prewar debts to British merchants. Such payment had been agreed to in the treaty, but here again the Congress could recommend but not compel. Indians, who really needed no stimulus in their resentments against the frontiersmen, were aided and stirred into attacks by the British. To the southward, Spain controlled the mouth of the Mississippi River at New Orleans. Not only did the Spanish add to the Indian trouble on the American frontier, but they blocked the mouth of the Mississippi River by refusing the western settler the right to transship goods to ocean-going vessels at New Orleans. This right was vital to the west because of the great cost of transporting bulk goods by land eastward across the Appalachians. In 1786 John Jay negotiated a treaty by which the United States agreed with Spain to relinquish the right of navigation on the Mississippi River for a period of twenty-five or thirty years. It narrowly missed acceptance by the Congress, convincing westerners that their welfare was in jeopardy. Eastern merchants would have benefited from commercial concessions by Spain at the expense of the frontiersman. It is not surprising, then, that most westerners favored a national government strong enough to persuade or, if necessary, to compel the cooperation of England and Spain and end the Indian threat.

Events and circumstances within the states strengthened the determination of those who wanted a stronger national government. In most of the states the constitutions, though not fully democratic in the modern sense, left the way open to popular control. If this satisfied the agrarian majority, it chilled the spines of the commercial and financial groups, especially when such control was translated into legislative attacks on property rights. Conservatives, accustomed to governing, and deeply imbued with the long-established English view that the right to participate in government stemmed from property ownership, had once been able to call on England to help keep the "rabble" in check. Under the Confederation, the central government, even when controlled by conservatives, was powerless to intervene in the states. Legislative supremacy and annual elections in most states meant that, in spite of property qualifications for voting, yeoman farmers, when sufficiently aroused, could win elections.

All the states found themselves at the end of the war with tremendous debts. However handled, these led to trouble. In several states, such as Virginia, popularly controlled legislatures devalued their war debts, in effect repudiating part of them, and thus depriving the creditors of a portion of their expected return. This devaluation of some of the state debts was defended on the legitimate grounds that full payment at face value was beyond their resources. A basic difficulty in this matter of indebtedness was that the debts involved had often been incurred in inflated paper currency, when prices were high, and now were to be repaid in hard money when lower prices prevailed. To repay the face value of the indebtedness would mean the repayment by the states of much more in purchasing power than they had originally borrowed. Massachusetts, which was in this respect the epitome of conservative rectitude, contracted in the process a debt so large that the heavy taxes levied in an attempt to redeem it helped to produce Shays' Rebellion of 1786.

Equally serious to men of property was the matter of paper money. Paper currency, successful in the colonial period when used with discretion, had been discredited by the spiraling inflation of the Revolution. Hard money, or specie, became for a time the chief medium of exchange. The consequent fall of prices and scarcity of both money and credit caused severe hardships to farmers and other debtors, burdened with obligations contracted at high prices. Their circumstances were especially harsh in the depression years of 1784 and 1785. In seven states they captured control of the legislatures and managed in 1785 and 1786 to push through new currency issues which, of course, reduced the real value of their debts. Creditors, required to accept payment in inflated paper, complained that they were being cheated. Some legislatures also passed "stay" laws which postponed the payments of debts and suspended mortgage foreclosures. Such laws served further to convince creditors that all rights of property and of contract were becoming insecure.

A final impetus for enlarging the powers of the national government came from events in Massachusetts. There the state

constitution was weighted heavily in favor of conservative interests. Most of the state debt had been acquired by speculators, while the cost of its redemption fell mostly on farmers through land and head taxes. By mid-decade, the burden of taxes and private debt caused mounting distress. Many farmers lost their lands, and in 1786 others went to jail for unpaid debts; their bitterness increased because these debts often amounted to only a few dollars. Proclaiming itself firmly on the side of "honor" and "justice," the conservative legislature refused relief in the form of lower taxes, paper money, or stay laws. Faced with this harsh decision, farmers in the Connecticut River Valley, where distresses were most acute, took the law into their own hands; they began to force courts to close, thus preventing them from hearing debt cases. When, in the early autumn of 1786, the state government took action to protect the courts, a group of farmers in the central part of the state rebelled under the leadership of the revolutionary veteran, Daniel Shays. His forces never numbered more than a thousand or two, many of them armed only with pitchforks. The story of this rebellion was exaggerated by distance and fear, until some lurid contemporary accounts would have one think that this was equivalent to an invasion by all the armies of Europe. As a matter of fact, the rebellion was quickly crushed by a state militia amply financed by contributions from Boston merchants, and by early 1787 order was reestablished. Within Massachusetts, the spring elections of 1787 permitted the aroused and still discontented farmers to bring into office a new and more liberal legislature, which pardoned the rebels, lowered taxes, and gave some relief to debtors in the form of stay laws. In this process all efforts to pay the debt were abandoned. But Shays' Rebellion had political repercussions which extended far beyond the boundaries of Massachusetts. It produced a general alarm throughout the country and aroused concern for the orderly processes of government not only among the wealthy but also among ordinary citizens, opposed equally to aristocracy and mob violence. Thus it helped broaden support for the campaign for a stronger national government.

Some of the most forceful leaders in this campaign had meanwhile taken action at Annapolis. There a convention met in September of 1786 at the instigation of Alexander Hamilton, ostensibly to discuss problems of interstate commerce. When only five states sent delegates, those present decided that this representation was insufficient for decisive action. Concerned also with the final failure of efforts through the normal amending process to obtain a revenue for the national government, the delegates readily accepted Hamilton's suggestion that Congress should be asked to call a new convention of all the states to propose amendments to the Articles. By this time Congress was thoroughly impressed by its inability to govern so long as it lacked the power to tax. Further stimulated by the rebellion in Massachusetts, in February, 1787, it asked the states to select delegates to a convention to meet in Philadelphia "for the sole and express purpose of revising the Articles of Confederation."

MAKING THE CONSTITUTION

The Constitutional Convention opened its sessions on May 25, 1787. A total of fifty-five delegates attended the proceedings, which lasted through the sultry summer and on into September. All the states were represented except little Rhode Is-

land, obdurate to the last. George Washington lent his prestige as presiding officer. The contributions of his fellow Virginian, James Madison, based upon a great fund of knowledge and reflection about the history and theory of governments both ancient and modern, justify the traditional characterization of him as "Father of the Constitution." Among the many other prominent public figures in attendance were Alexander Hamilton from New York, Elbridge Gerry and Roger Sherman from New England, and a distinguished group of Pennsylvanians which included James Wilson, Robert and Gouverneur Morris, and the venerable Benjamin Franklin.

No single characterization would apply to all members of the convention, but in their background and in certain interests they displayed striking similarities. Most of this delegation, some of whom were in their twenties and thirties, were college-educated; nearly all were upper-class conservatives. Many among them were lawyers, wealthy planters, merchants, speculators in western lands, and holders of federal securities. A large number, of course, fell into more than one of these categories. Of the outstanding conservative statesmen of the time, only John Adams and John Jay, both in the diplomatic service of the Confederation, were absent. Thomas Jefferson, whose name has come to symbolize liberal democracy in the early republic, was in France as American minister. The other old "radical" leaders of the Revolution either were not elected or, like Patrick Henry—who stayed at home because he "smelt a rat" —refused to attend. Thus workingmen, ordinary farmers, debtors, the common people in general were not directly represented in the convention.

Much has been said and written about

the classic compromises of the convention, and it was these which occupied most of its time and provided the drama of conflict. Deliberations were held behind locked doors, and nothing approaching a full written account of the proceedings was publicly available until the release of Madison's notes half a century later. The debates were candid, unrestrained, and sometimes heated. But men must agree on some things if their disagreements are to be resolved in compromise, and the key to an accurate understanding of the convention lies in a knowledge of the common ground from which the framers proceeded. Though differing in detail and on a variety of lesser issues, there was stated or implicit agreement among most members on a number of fundamental issues: (1) a greatly strengthened central government must be created, a government with the power to tax, regulate trade, promote economic development, and protect American interests abroad—a government which could legislate in all matters of national concern; (2) the states must be restrained from interference in such matters, and particularly from attacks upon property; (3) control of the national government must be lodged primarily in the hands of the upper classes, of those whom Hamilton characterized as "the rich, the well-born, and the able." Although not opposed to liberty or to basic human rights, the founding fathers were more actively concerned with stability, order, and the protection of property rights from the "turbulent masses." It was common talk in the convention that the evils of the Confederation sprang from an "excess of democracy," as men such as Edmund Randolph of Virginia and Elbridge Gerry of Massachusetts insisted. Primarily suspicious of popular power, the framers were fearful also of

any sort of unrestrained power. This temper tempered their decisions, as did the realization that, if they went too far in limiting popular participation in government or ignoring the widespread sentiment for state rights, their proposals had little chance of acceptance.

Although called to suggest amendments to the Articles of Confederation, the convention from the beginning agreed that it would be easier to prepare a whole new constitution than to repair the frayed fabric of the Confederation. In so doing, the framers exceeded the powers intended in the call issued by the Congress, but they felt their task was otherwise nearly hopeless, and their action was in the end justified and sanctified by ratification.

To accomplish their ends, a few members of the convention, most notably Hamilton, would have taken the extreme step of abolishing the states or reducing them to the status of municipalities. This attitude was rejected by the marjority of the delegates in favor of a division of authority between the state and national governments. However illogical such a division of sovereignty has been regarded by some political scientists, it was in a real sense a compromise between conflicting ideas of local and national power. There was ample precedent for a distribution of power between a central and local government in the relationship between the colonial legislatures and the British imperial Parliament. Except for taxation, the powers granted by the framers to the new central government were strongly reminiscent of those exercised over the colonies by Parliament before the Revolution. In its own sphere of action, now much extended, the national government was given full sovereignty and a sweeping grant of additional authority. It had all the powers it had possessed under the

Articles of Confederation, including control of national defense and foreign policy. Among the most important new powers of Congress were those of federal taxation—the national government now had that all-important attribute of sovereignty, a revenue power—and exclusive jurisdiction over interstate and foreign commerce. Federal laws and treaties were to be binding on the states under a constitution which was to be the "supreme law of land." National authority was further extended by giving the central government direct coercive power over individuals, and state officials were required to take an oath to uphold the United States Constitution and could thus be held personally responsible if a state disobeyed national laws. And the door was left open, intentionally or otherwise, for a subsequent vast extension of national power through what have become known as the "elastic" clauses which stated that Congress may provide for the "general welfare of the United States" and can make any laws "necessary and proper" for carrying its specified powers into execution.

Several significant limitations on the states were imposed either by the grant of powers to the national authority or by specific restrictions on the states. Most important of these were assignment to the Congress of the control of interstate and foreign commerce and the sole right to coin money. Among the new restrictions were those forbidding states to impair the obligation of contract and to issue paper money, or make anything but gold and silver legal tender. By these provisions two of the favorite devices of the agrarian radicals, stay laws and paper money, were prohibited. It thus became unnecessary for conservatives to maintain control of state legislatures in order to forestall the radicals. Each state was guaranteed a "repub-

lican form of government," and state militia or United States troops could be used to suppress future uprisings such as Shays' Rebellion. Now made far less powerful than they had been under the Confederation, and subjected to numerous restrictions, the states were nonetheless allowed to retain revenues of their own and jurisdiction over a wide range of local affairs such as commerce within their own borders, religion, education, labor, and local police.

Such a distribution of governmental powers would naturally be welcomed by businessmen, glad to see a national currency and a uniform tariff replace the confusing and sometimes conflicting state systems. The new government would have the authority, and seemed likely to have the will, to protect and encourage the growth of a mercantile economy. Many of the well-to-do held securities, made newly valuable if the central government had an adequate income; care was taken to include in the Constitution a provision that the debts of the Confederation were to be valid obligations of the new government. Speculators in western lands could anticipate prosperity from a government strong enough to control the Indians and command the respect of European powers with possessions on our western borders. And a stronger national administration would enjoy greater prestige and influence abroad, giving firm ground for anticipating less danger from outside threats.

Such high hopes from a national government of ample powers might be doomed to frustration unless the structure of that government could be arranged in such a way as to guarantee it against tyranny and ensure upper-class control. Some safeguards against assaults on property rights had, as we have seen, been built into the Constitution directly. Believing in government by a paternalistic elite, the framers wanted to limit majority rule, which they thought would endanger property rights and destroy enlightened leadership. This distrust of democracy was expressed repeatedly in the Convention. The same philosophy appears in more veiled form in the *Federalist* papers, a group of essays by Hamilton, Madison, and Jay which appeared in the New York newspapers during the ratification controversy and which were widely reprinted elsewhere. Men of this period, including the framers, were profoundly convinced that political positions were firmly rooted in economic interest. This theory of the Constitution is best expressed in concise form in Madison's famous *Federalist, No. 10.* Madison argues that the varying talents of men result inevitably in the division of all societies into conflicting groups —the few and the many, the rich and the poor, creditors and debtors—according to their interests. Any one of these groups, which Madison calls "factions," must be prevented from gaining exclusive control of the government and using that control to oppress the others. This way, says Madison, lies tyranny. Democracy tends to lead the uninformed and credulous majority to become easy prey for demagogues, and thus to end in dictatorship, or to use the weight of numbers to oppress the minority. In the ideal society, the minority of the opulent must be protected against the majority; other minorities must also be protected. The rights of all can best be guaranteed by a balancing of conflicting interests. In particular, numbers and property must each be prevented from exploiting the other. Madison believed that balanced government could be more readily achieved in an extensive union than within individual states, since the union would include a greater diver-

sity of competing groups. The true statesman should himself be above parties and not identified with any particular group. The whole system of American political parties as it soon developed was thus not anticipated by Madison or the other philosophers of the Constitution. Perhaps ironically, this party system appears to have been the means through which policy making under our governmental structure has gained enough cohesive formulation and direction to make the system work. It should be added that our major political parties have, in fact, rather consistently been coalitions of "factions," and thus agents of compromise and a balancing of interests.

PROBLEMS OF CONSTITUTION MAKING

One of the problems of the delegates at Philadelphia was to create a balanced system of government in which neither a majority nor a persistent minority could ever secure unchecked control of the government and become tyrannical. Under the Confederation, power had been concentrated in a single branch of the government—a Congress whose members represented the states, with a nominal executive which was really the creature of Congress. The Constitutional Convention agreed readily on a different framework, making possible a system of "checks and balances" by separating the government into three independent and presumably coequal branches: executive, legislative, and judicial. Americans had become familiar with such a separation of powers during the colonial period and found further justification for it in the writings of the eighteenth-century French political philosopher Montesquieu.

In the system as finally crystallized, the

convention decided on a bicameral congress. The House of Representatives was to be the democratic part of the government, its members elected every two years by popular vote. There was some discussion of imposing limitations on the national electorate, but no agreement was reached. The delegates, who were conscious of the necessity of submitting a finished Constitution for ratification, left this matter to the states, with the provision that, in federal elections, qualified voters were to be those eligible to vote for the most numerous body of the legislature in each state. As for the Senate, some members of the convention proposed that it should directly represent wealth, through the imposition of high property qualifications. Advocates of this position insisted that it would make one house of Congress represent the people, and the other property, in fine Madisonian style. In the end this proposal was rejected. In a compromise with the federal principle of the Confederation, the Senate was to represent the states and each state was to choose two senators. Senators were to be made relatively independent of popular pressures through six-year terms. Their terms were staggered in such a way that only a third of the Senate would stand for election at any one time. They were further removed from popular control by a system of indirect election by which senators were to be chosen by the state legislatures.

In the choice of a chief executive, the principle of indirection, which Madison called "refining the popular appointments by successive filtrations," was used once again. The President and Vice President were to be chosen by electors in each state. These electors were expected to vote their judgments rather than merely reflect popular sentiments. Indeed, in the early years of the republic, the choice of a President was one step further removed from the people because the electors were chosen in several states by the legislatures rather than by popular vote. If no candidate had a majority in the electoral college, which was expected to happen frequently, the winner was to be chosen by the House of Representatives from among the five leading candidates (later changed to three by the Twelfth Amendment), with each state delegation having one vote. The framers believed that a President thus elected would be reliable, and gave him a relatively long term of four years, with no limitation on reelection. The President was given broad powers including the appointment, subject to Senate approval, of executive and judicial officers. His administrative authority was to be especially great in times of emergency. Executive participation in the framing of laws and the formulation of domestic policies was not clearly defined in the Constitution. The direction and formulation of foreign policy was placed almost exclusively in the President's hands, subject to Senate approval of treaties and full congressional consent to making war. These limitations illustrate the manner in which the major branches were to check each other. Another important restraint on excessive presidential authority was through congressional control of appropriations. Yet a final illustration of the system of checks and balances is the power given to the President to veto legislation, a veto which could be overridden only by a two-thirds vote in each house.

Even a limited popular participation in the choice of powerful officials was omitted in the creation of the third major branch of the federal government, the judiciary. Supreme Court justices, named by the President and confirmed by the

Senate, held office for life. Such an independent judiciary which has been, indeed, one of the marks of free government everywhere, would find it unnecessary to yield to popular pressures. It was expected that the courts would oppose those forces threatening stability and endangering order and property, and the Supreme Court under Chief Justice John Marshall after 1801 was to confirm this expectation beyond all hopes. Much discretion was left to Congress in establishing a system of national courts, with the whole inferior court structure left for later decision. Controversies have raged periodically on the question of judicial review: does the Constitution give the Supreme Court the power to examine state and national laws and rule invalid any which it finds in conflict with the Constitution? This power was not specifically given in that document, which was nonetheless sufficiently broad in its implications to enable Chief Justice Marshall to assert the doctrine in 1803 and establish a precedent for the future. The preponderant evidence appears to be that this was the intent of the framers, who favored a strong judiciary. Thus new laws would have to run the gamut of three different branches of a government in which only one house of the legislative branch was to be directly elected. Persistent popular opinion, though ultimately it might be supreme, would thus be delayed, checked, and "refined." And any group or individual bent on tyranny would have to capture all three branches of the government.

Definition of powers and the delineation of governmental structure were not the only problems of the convention. Although this work was more fundamental than the famous "compromises," the latter deserve consideration. The most important compromises involved the manner of apportioning representation in Congress, and certain sectional conflicts between North and South. So far as representation was concerned, delegates from the larger and more populous states supported the Randolph (Virginia) plan of basing representation in Congress directly on population. Delegates from the less populous states favored the Paterson (New Jersey) plan of giving each state equality in a unicameral congress. The system adopted and still in use was formulated in the so-called Connecticut compromise, which gave each state two senators and based membership in the lower house essentially on population.

The conflict between North and South was by no means as sharp as it became in the nineteenth century, though disagreements and, in some degree, a mutual distaste were often exhibited in the convention and in the early Congresses. These reflected a divergence of interests as well as of habit and background. One compromise concerned commerce. The South, as an agricultural section, was interested in European markets for its exports of such staple products as tobacco and in obtaining low-priced imported goods. Many northerners were interested in the promotion of shipping and some in the protection of manufacturing. As a concession to the South, the Constitution barred taxes on exports and prohibited restrictions on the slave trade for at least twenty years. As a concession to northern interests, the national government could make navigation laws and impose duties on imports. Another sectional compromise came on the counting of slaves for purposes of taxation and representation. Direct taxes, according to agreements already reached, were to be assessed on the basis of population. Northerners insisted that it was logical to treat slaves as property in apportioning representation in Congress, but wanted to count them as people for tax purposes. Southerners thought that the reverse should be the case, that is, slaves should count for purposes of representation; they should not count for taxation. Out of this disagreement came a mutually acceptable compromise, consistent if illogical: only three-fifths of the slaves should count for purposes both of taxation and of representation.

One final southern apprehension was that the Senate might damage southern interests through its use of the treaty power, since the southern states were outnumbered. This produced a successful insistence that treaties must be ratified by a two-thirds vote of the Senate rather than a simple majority. Southern and western support for this rule was related to the recent negotiations with Spain about Mississippi navigation, previously mentioned.

Anticipating the possible need for future change, the framers included in the completed Constitution a provision for amendment. But though they were desirous of some flexibility, they feared capricious or shortsighted change. They therefore made the amending process difficult and rather awkward. Amendments were to require the approval of a two-thirds majority in each house of Congress and ratification by three-fourths of the states, acting either through their legislatures or through conventions.

THE RATIFICATION CONTROVERSY

Having framed a Constitution to replace the Articles of Confederation, the founders faced the problem of getting it approved. Obviously, the Continental Congress had no power to change the organic law of the union. The delegates had no desire to reach their goal through force or a *coup d'état;* referral in some fashion to the people as the ultimate source of sovereignty was clearly necessary. Ratification by the state legislatures appeared unlikely, since they had a vested interest in the existing distribution of powers and several of them were controlled by radicals. The members of the convention were equally fearful of the results of a popular referendum in each state. Most of the people, while willing by now to grant limited additional authority to the central government, were farmers able to find their own remedies through the existing state legislatures and therefore unlikely to approve of a powerful central government weighted in favor of propertied interests and imposing severe restrictions on the states. The framers therefore decided that the most feasible approach would be through a convention in each state. Delegates elected to such conventions would likely be wealthier and more conservative than the average voter. In addition, many of the strongest supporters of the Constitution were not members of state legislatures but could be elected to the ratifying conventions and throw their weight behind the new plan. A tractable Confederation Congress made the appropriate recommendations to the state legislatures, and the battle was joined.

Conscious of popular fears of strong government, advocates of the Constitution were careful to call themselves, not Nationalists, but Federalists, implying that they favored a decentralized government in which state rights were dominant. Most of the educated and articulate members of American society in this era either belonged to or identified themselves with the upper classes, which gave the Federalists a powerful advantage. One manifestation of this was in the publication

RATIFICATION OF THE CONSTITUTION

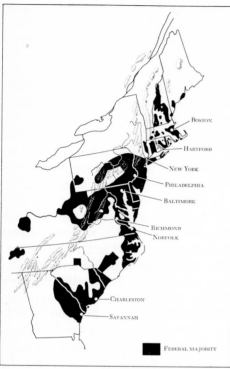

BOSTON

HARTFORD

NEW YORK

PHILADELPHIA

BALTIMORE

RICHMOND
NORFOLK

CHARLESTON

SAVANNAH

FEDERAL MAJORITY

of the highly influential *Federalist* papers. In making their public appeal, the authors of these essays, particularly Hamilton, judiciously tempered their expressions, pressed the advantages of the Constitution, and toned down their distrust of popular sovereignty.

Though on principle it could be argued that opponents of the Constitution were the true federalists, they were compelled in the circumstances to call themselves Antifederalists. They suffered other handicaps. State suffrage laws disfranchised landless laborers, indentured servants, and tenant farmers, most of whom might have been expected to vote for delegates opposed to ratification. At a time when many saw the need for some change, the

only positive counterproposal which the Antifederalists could offer was to suggest a second Constitutional Convention. Although they had able leaders in a few states, they were generally outmatched on this score. And, with rare exceptions, their advocates lacked the skill in expression and parliamentary maneuver possessed by the Federalists. The most notable literary expression of the Antifederalist position was in Richard Henry Lee's *Letters of a Federal Farmer*. Of the numerous objections raised to the proposed Constitution, two were most significant and consistently repeated: (1) the creation of what they ordinarily called a "consolidated" government, and (2) the omission of a bill of rights. On the first count, a powerful national government was central to the whole Federalist plan, and no real concession was possible. Federalists insisted that these fears were unjustified and stressed the urgency of circumstances. Regarding a bill of rights, Federalists insisted that freedom was guaranteed by the body of the Constitution, but they were not opposed to additional guarantees. Many felt that these were necessary because of the broad grant of powers to Congress to pass any legislation "necessary and proper" to carry out its delegated powers. Thus it became generally understood that a bill of rights would be an early order of business once the Constitution was adopted. This understanding eased the way to ratification in states.

The best evidence available indicates that, had the Constitution been submitted to a direct vote of all the people, or even of all qualified voters, it would probably have been defeated. But in the end the Federalists carried the day. Their victory required some skillful political infighting. In such states as Pennsylvania, where they had a majority when the convention assembled, they rushed through an early vote before the opposition could organize. In other states, such as Massachusetts, where they were at first outnumbered or the division was so close as to make the result uncertain, they adopted tactics of delay. By the end of 1787, three states had approved the Constitution. By early June of 1788, five more had ratified. Aware that efforts to amend the Confederation had failed repeatedly because of the rule of unanimity, the Constitutional Convention had taken the precaution of providing that the Constitution was to become effective among its adherents when nine states had ratified. Victory was therefore in sight. Still debating, however, were the powerful and populous states of Virginia and New York, in which the opposition was strong and effective. Without these states, there was the prospect of a divided and weakened union. By now, however, the Federalists could successfully argue that ratification was almost assured, and add to their arsenal in these states the insistence that if they stayed out they would be alone, while the one which ratified first would have the honor of casting the ninth and decisive vote. These arguments helped sway the balance, and the Virginians actually thought that they were the ninth state to ratify, on June 25, 1788. Word had not yet arrived that New Hampshire had ratified on June 21. New York agreed in July. North Carolina came to reluctant acceptance in 1789, while Rhode Island, recalcitrant to the end, held out until 1790, when lonely solitude and commercial pressure from the union brought a change of heart.

In a nation dedicated to the democratic credo, a critical appraisal of the framing and ratification of the Constitution, now

VOTE OF DELEGATES TO CONSTITUTIONAL RATIFYING CONVENTION

Order of ratification	Date of ratification	Convention vote
1. Delaware	Dec. 7, 1787	30–0
2. Pennsylvania	Dec. 12, 1787	46–23
3. New Jersey	Dec. 18, 1787	39–0
4. Georgia	Jan. 2, 1788	26–0
5. Connecticut	Jan. 9, 1788	128–40
6. Massachusetts	Feb. 6, 1788	187–168
7. Maryland	Apr. 28, 1788	63–11
8. South Carolina	May 23, 1788	149–73
9. New Hampshire	June 21, 1788	57–47
10. Virginia	June 25, 1788	89–79
11. New York	July 26, 1788	30–27
12. North Carolina*	Nov. 21, 1789	195–77
13. Rhode Island†	May 29, 1790	34–32

* Ratified in a second convention. The first voted 184–84 neither to ratify nor to reject, recommending a twenty-part bill of rights and proposing twenty-six amendments.

† Originally rejected the Constitution in a popular referendum on March 24, 1788, by a vote of 2,708 to 237 (of about 6,000 qualified voters). Rhode Island Federalists refused to participate in this referendum, which they claimed was illegal.

properly revered as the foundation stone of our freedom, is sometimes mistakenly interpreted as an attack on democracy. We must be prepared to accept and understand a paradox. From our twentieth-century perspective, it seems that founders built better than they knew. The Constitution, designed in part to protect the upper classes from the "tempestuous multitude," has since been transformed into a democratic instrument. It has been changed, and it is changing still. Indeed, one of its greatest virtues has been its peculiar combination of stability and flexibility. Were it completely flexible, it would bend too freely before the shifting and sometimes intemperate winds of popular opinion; were it as inflexible and unyielding as is sometimes implied, it would have long since shattered, for the survival strength of any human institution, however well conceived, must depend in part upon its adaptability. As it is, our Constitution has survived the profound change from an agrarian to an industrialized America.

The democratization of the American system of government has come about in a variety of ways: through formal amendment, through changes in state constitutions, through interpretation and custom, through shifts in party control, and through intangible changes in the American spirit. Many, though not all, of these changes took place in the half-century after 1787. For example, universal manhood suffrage was achieved gradually in the established states as they revised their constitutions, while most new states entered the union without property limitations on the suffrage. Direct popular election of senators is a consequence of the Seventeenth Amendment, adopted in 1913. Women achieved a vote through the Nineteenth Amendment, adopted in 1920. Meanwhile, the development of political parties and a rising popular interest and participation in the choice of the President changed the electoral system so that very soon by "custom of the Constitution," rather than through any formal change, electors began voting for party choices for the presidency rather than exercising an independent judgment.

The Bill of Rights, contained in the first ten amendments, all adopted in 1791, is another illustration of this process of democratic revision. The Tenth Amendment states that "the powers not delegated to the United States . . . nor prohibited . . . to the States, are reserved to the States respectively, or to the people." Events were soon to show that this was not the victory for decentralization which it appeared to be, although it established the basis for a powerful tradition. The other nine amendments in the Bill of Rights, deeply rooted in past experience with tyranny in England and America, guaranteed certain basic human liberties. To the assurance of the right of habeas corpus and the prohibitions on bills of attainder and ex post facto laws in the body of the Constitution, they made important additions. Congress is barred from interfering with freedom of speech or press, petition or assembly, or of religion. The right to bear arms and security of domicile are guaranteed. No person is to be deprived of life, liberty, or property without due process of law, and all are promised a fair trial. Finally, the Bill of Rights makes plain that the enumeration of certain rights in the Constitution is not to be interpreted as a denial of rights not enumerated, which are retained by the states or the people. Such a brief summary fails, of course, to more than hint at the long and bitter human experience which has necessitated such protections against the actions of arbitrary government.

LAUNCHING THE NEW GOVERNMENT

Though the Constitution defined the broad structure and some of the powers of the new federal government, many of its provisions were of a general nature. Much of its meaning would therefore depend upon future interpretations and the use made of powers granted. A note of self-conscious awareness of this runs through the debates and conduct of the early Congresses; they were especially cognizant of the fact that decisions must be made with care, because precedents once established were likely to be perpetuated. Much also depended on the attitude and conduct of those who controlled the government. Both the Federalists and their opponents were aware that the convention had been unable to build into the structure any absolute guarantee of upper-class control. Washington's great prestige won him the presidency virtually by acclamation, but congressional posts were hotly contested. As there were no definite political parties in the beginning, candidates ran as individuals, though the majority were publicly associated with either the Federalists or the Antifederalists. The latter were still disorganized and in some degree discredited by their defeat on ratification, and a strong majority of those elected were Federalists.

On September 13, 1788, the old Confederation Congress had provided for choosing the presidential electors on the first Wednesday in January, 1789, for the selection of the President on the first Wednesday in February, and for his inauguration on the first Wednesday in March (March 4). After this action, at-

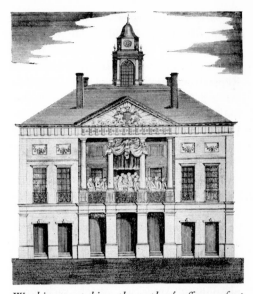

Washington taking the oath of office as first President, April 30, 1789, Wall Street, New York City. (New York Public Library)

tendance in Congress shrank and there was seldom a quorum. It was impossible to transact any business at all after October 10, but the executive departments of Congress continued to function and many of their personnel were carried over into the new government. Because of delays of travel in reaching the seat of government in New York City, there was no quorum in the new Congress until April 6, and the inauguration did not occur until April 30. It was certainly of major importance that the new government was to have the advantage of Washington's balanced judgment and granite-like integrity to give it stability, and of his great personal popularity to win acceptance for it.

Meantime in the Senate a serious debate had occurred over the form of a proper title for the chief executive. It was finally decided to designate him as "His Highness the President of the United States and Protector of the Rights of the Same." Even this was not sufficiently dignified for the aristocratic tastes of Vice President John Adams, but it did not sit well with the democratic instincts of some senators. The title was settled by the House of Representatives when James Madison pointed out that the constitutional designation was simply "President of the United States." And so it has remained.

The great task of the first Congress of the United States was to endow the Constitution with vitality by creating a functioning government. A bill was quickly passed providing for moderate tariff duties, averaging about 8 per cent, which were primarily for revenue. Also a tonnage act, providing for discriminatory taxes on foreign-built or -owned shipping, gave American vessels such great advantages as to severely curtail competition of foreign carriers. Having provided for revenue, Congress turned to the creation of executive departments to replace the organization that had been carried over from the executive offices of the Confederation Congress. Departments of State, War, and Treasury were established, and in the judiciary bill an attorney general's office was created, but not until 1870 did this official become head of a separate Department of Justice. Wash-

This was the original executive mansion, occupied by President Washington in 1789–1790 while the capitol was in New York. The White House at Washington was not occupied until 1800. (Library of Congress)

ington soon made his executive chiefs into a board of advisers, thus inaugurating the President's Cabinet, which was not anticipated in the Constitution. He established another precedent by almost immediately going beyond the strictly administrative function to urge legislative programs on Congress and use his influence to help obtain their adoption.

In the creation of the State Department the question of the removal power was settled. The Constitution was silent as to where the authority lay to remove administrative officials. In Congress some thought that the removal power should be identical with the appointing power and therefore shared with the Senate, whose province it was to approve presidential appointments. But it was feared that sharing the removal power would weaken the Chief Executive's responsibility as administrative head. The division on the issue was sharp, and it was settled only when the deciding vote of the Vice President was cast in favor of the President. This decision established a practice which has become a permanent feature of the American administrative procedure.

Similarly, in creating the Treasury Department, the status of the Secretary became the subject of serious debate. A question arose whether he should be permitted to report in person to the House of Representatives or whether he should transmit his recommendations in writing. The bill simply authorized him to "digest and prepare" financial plans. When, in 1790, the first Secretary of the Treasury sought to present his reports in person, he was required to do it in writing. The Secretary was never accorded an opportunity to appear on the floor of the House of Representatives to advocate his proposals. Thus, the decision was made to adhere in practice to the deep-seated concept of separation of powers.

Whether or not there was to be a system of lower federal courts was left by the Constitution to the discretion of Congress, out of deference to those who feared too much centralization as a result of the subordination of state courts. Congress was given the power to regulate the appellate jurisdiction of the Supreme Court, but that did not necessarily mean that there must be inferior federal courts. Appeals could come from state courts. But the wisdom of a dual or concurrent system of courts in a federal state where powers are shared by a national and many state governments is obvious. And so in the Judiciary Act of 1789 Congress set up not only a Supreme Court as required by the Constitution, but also two grades of inferior courts covering the nation. Thirteen district courts, each with its resident judge, were created. The districts were grouped into three circuits where a district judge would be joined by two judges of the Supreme Court "on circuit." It was expected that this would be the principal work of the six Supreme Court judges. The provision of the right to appeal to the Supreme Court was highly significant. Any case could be appealed whenever a decision of a lower court denied any right claimed under the Constitution or any law or treaty of the United States. The Judiciary Act of 1789 really represented a compromise in establishing concurrent state and national jurisdictions in its courts and incorporating the state courts into the federal system.

After completing its work of creating a governmental structure, Congress turned to the problem of straightening out the nation's tangled financial affairs. In doing this it relied heavily upon the first Secretary of the Treasury, Alexander Hamilton.

His proposals constituted the key legislation of Washington's first administration and had far-reaching and permanent effects upon the history of the nation. Although his special province was finance, it might fairly be said of Hamilton that his every move was self-consciously political. He visualized himself as Washington's prime minister and often functioned as such. Washington had great confidence in him but reserved to himself most of the important final decisions. The Constitution fell considerably short of Hamilton's ideal, and Hamilton wanted to use its latitude and uncertainties to create precedents which would extend and strengthen the authority and ensure the success of the new government. His specific proposals are strongly reminiscent of those of Robert Morris, and he drew from a fund of general ideas then current in both England and America. Thus the Hamiltonian financial program is less striking for its originality than for the boldness, force, and lucidity with which it was advanced, and for the fact that it formed a coherent and interrelated whole with strong political overtones. His prime objective was to provide a favorable milieu for the commercial, financial, and industrial groups in American society. He envisaged a strong and politically stable nation, with prosperity and economic expansion stemming from assistance to such groups. If these dynamic and powerful groups identified their economic interests with those of the new government, the success of the republic seemed assured. Although designed most significantly and deliberately to serve particular interests, these measures were not in the strictest sense "class" legislation. Hamilton himself cared little for the agrarian way of life and looked with disdain upon popular democracy and political decentralization, but he appears to have believed that the prosperity he anticipated from the adoption of his proposals would extend throughout the economy.

The new nation faced total public debts, both national and state, of some 73 million dollars. The public securities were past due and badly depreciated. In his *Report on the Public Credit* (January, 1790), Hamilton proposed exchanging the outstanding securities for new bonds. These were to be a "funded debt," with fixed revenues to be appropriated to the annual payment of interest and a small part of the principal, payable over a definite number of years. His intent was to shore up the government's credit, revive the price of securities, and bring public creditors under obligation to the national government. There was no dispute over paying at par the foreign debt of nearly 12 million dollars; all agreed that it was a debt of honor and should be paid in full. But heated debate over other parts of Hamilton's plan occupied about half the time of Congress from February to July of 1790. The internal debt of the national government, with back interest, amounted to about 40 million dollars. Much of it had been contracted at inflated price levels or in inflated currency, and in large part it was now concentrated in the hands of speculators who had purchased it at a few cents on the dollar. There was some sentiment in Congress for scaling it down, and serious debate over Madison's proposal of a "discrimination" whereby speculators and other current holders would be paid the price of their investment, with interest, and the balance would be given to original holders. In the end, this plan was rejected in favor of payment at face value to holders at the time of redemption. Even more controversial was Hamilton's proposal that the federal government assume outstanding state debts of about 21 million

dollars. These had in large part been contracted by the states as a part of their Revolutionary War expenditures, and they thus had some equitable claim to compensation. Once again Hamilton's object was partly political: he wanted the state creditors to look to the national government for payment. Some states, such as Massachusetts and South Carolina, were in serious financial trouble, especially since under the Constitution they had lost their tariff revenues. They eagerly supported this plan. Other states, such as Virginia, had already paid off the larger share of their revolutionary debts. Their view was that they would now be taxed through the federal government to pay the debts of others less vigorous. They also insisted that assumption would be a further step in the centralization of political power. In the end, a famous bargain was arranged. Hamilton agreed to have Robert Morris use his influence with the Pennsylvania delegation to swing enough votes to place the national capital in a southerly location on the Potomac; in return, Jefferson arranged for the switch of enough crucial votes within the Virginia delegation to pass the assumption of state debts.

Funds would obviously be needed to support the debt and pay the ordinary costs of government. As already noted, even before Hamilton took office, a tariff act had been passed. The national government also anticipated income from the sale of public lands, although actual receipts before 1800 were trivial. To raise additional funds, in December, 1790, Hamilton recommended an excise tax on distilled spirits. Over $200,000 was secured from this source in 1792. Hamilton also intended through the excise to emphasize the power of the federal government over individuals, even on the remote frontier. In this again he was successful, although in the process he created resentment and opposition which culminated in 1794 in the Whisky Rebellion.

A uniform system of coinage was clearly essential to both private commerce and public finance. Congress, in 1792, established a mint and provided for a coinage system which Hamilton modeled rather closely on an earlier plan advanced by Jefferson. The dollar was adopted as the basic unit, its silver content almost precisely the same as in the Spanish milled dollar of colonial days, while the decimal system now in current use was decided on in preference to the awkward English method of reckoning.

The mint was to coin money only of small denominations, and governmental paper currency issues had in the minds of men such as Hamilton been thoroughly discredited. In order to fill this gap and accomplish a number of other objects, Hamilton proposed the chartering of a national bank, which in its conception and specific features was based largely on English experience. This bank was to fulfill a variety of functions: (1) to issue notes which would circulate as money and thus help maintain an adequate and stable currency supply; (2) to assist the federal government by acting as its fiscal agent in such matters as the sale of new bonds, to act as a safe depository of public funds, and, on occasion, to lend money to the government; (3) to provide banking facilities for commercial transactions and to promote economic expansion by extending credit to businessmen.

Despite the strenuous opposition, the first Bank of the United States in 1791 received a twenty-year charter from Congress. One-fifth of its 10-million-dollar capital was to be contributed by the government and the remainder by private investors, who would thus predominate in the control of the bank despite strict governmental regulation and the authority given to the Secretary of the Treasury to inspect its affairs. Thus it was really a quasi-private corporation. It could issue bank notes to the amount of its capital stock. The government's subscription and 2 million dollars of the private subscriptions were to be in hard money, while the remaining 6 million dollars of private funds could be subscribed in federal securities received at par. This use of the federal debt as a source of credit was probably the neatest trick in Hamilton's bag. The use of federal bonds as a backing for currency issues may at first seem puzzling, although the operation is essentially the same as that involved in the modern issue of Federal Reserve notes. The procedure was sound so long as the bonds retained a relatively stable value. This was to be ensured by regular payment of interest on them and the use of public funds to buy up securities when their price threatened to fall substantially below par.

Desiring to stimulate and foster the growth of American industry, Hamilton, in December, 1791, submitted a *Report on Manufactures*. Arguing that "infant industries" in a young country needed protection from foreign competition, he proposed that they be aided by direct subsidies and a higher tariff. Southerners, whose economic interests required low-priced imports and a vigorous export trade, were joined in opposition to this measure by northern merchants, who feared that it would reduce foreign commerce and thus cut their profits. Congress agreed to a slight increase in tariff levels, but primarily to raise more revenue, and this proposal thus stands as the only part of the Hamiltonian financial program which was not adopted by Congress.

As the Hamiltonian program unfolded,

the importance of controlling the national government became ever more apparent. Opposition to the Federalists had at first been based on states'-rights grounds and on the belief of many that the Federalists' concept of rule by the "better people" might lead to monarchy. Madison began to split with Hamilton over the manner of funding the national debt and over assumption of the state debts. Jefferson, who was Secretary of State, developed a variety of objections to the Hamiltonian program. He and others, primarily agrarians, saw in funding, the bank, and similar plans, legislation designed to favor city over country. It gave aid to speculators, merchants, and men of wealth in general, but included no direct measures to benefit the common people. Jefferson thought, for example, that the bank would help create a monopoly in the hands of a small group of capitalists and become an agency which would give to this group too many opportunities for large profits and an impressive influence over the currency and credit of the country. Washington, as was his custom, asked his Cabinet members for written opinions on the bank proposals. Hamilton justified them as good policy and maintained that they were constitutional. Here he resorted to the doctrine of implied powers, namely, that the federal government could use any constitutional means to carry out specifically delegated powers. Jefferson, on the other hand, argued that the bank was unconstitutional, insisting that the national government must limit its functions to those explicitly authorized by the Constitution. Washington agreed with Hamilton, setting an important precedent for a wide latitude in constitutional interpretation. As such conflicts deepened, Jefferson's position in the Cabinet became increasingly uneasy. When new disagreements on foreign policy were added to differences over domestic policy, and as Washington inclined in his views more and more toward Hamilton, Jefferson resigned in December, 1793.

With the enactment of Hamilton's economic measures, the Federalist structure was complete. The decade had witnessed the rise of a nationalist movement, whose leaders had seized the prevailing sentiment in favor of strengthening the central government and driven it far beyond what most people expected. They had established a different form of government, one which was truly national, operating directly upon the citizens, and they had given it sinews of power which, though barely exercised as yet, were of the greatest strength.

FURTHER READINGS

A standard older account is Max Farrand, *The Framing of the Constitution of the United States* (1913). Readily available at the Government Printing Office in Washington is the volume of *Documents Illustrative of the Formation of the Union of the American States* (1927).

In 1913 Charles A. Beard challenged older views with his *An Economic Interpretation of the Constitution,* reissued 1935 and fol-

lowed two years later by his *Economic Origins of Jeffersonian Democracy.* A recent criticism of Beard's views contained in Robert E. Brown, *Charles Beard and the Constitution* (1955), is amplified and further documented by Forrest McDonald, *We the People: The Economic Origins of the Constitution* (1958). Some of the controversial issues may be followed in the collection of papers edited by Conyers Read, *The Con-*

stitution Reconsidered (1938). Merrill Jensen, *The New Nation, 1781–1789* (1950), should be consulted for the trend of recent scholarship.

Among other works, the following may be mentioned: C. M. Walsh, *The Political Science of John Adams* (1915); C. G. Haines, *The American Doctrine of Judicial Supremacy* (1932); and Walton Hamilton and Douglas Adair, *The Power to Govern* (1937).

An outstanding biography is Irving Brant, *James Madison* (1948, 1950), of which volumes II and III are relevant here. Other biographies of Founding Fathers include Nathan Schachner, *Alexander Hamilton* (1946); Frank Monaghan, *John Jay* (1935); and Charles Page Smith, *James Wilson, Founding Father* (1956).

Suggestive, finally, of the deeper historical roots is C. H. McIlwain, *Constitutionalism Ancient and Modern* (1947), reprinted in paperback form.

For additional bibliography, see the *Harvard Guide,* sections 121, 122, and 124–126.

SEVEN

Federalists and Republicans: Testing the New Nation

JEFFERSON AND THE OPPOSITION

1789
French Revolution begins.

1793
Proclamation of neutrality toward war in Europe.
Citizen Genêt visits America.

1794
Whisky Rebellion.
Jay's treaty with Britain.

1795
Pinckney's treaty with Spain.

1797
John Adams becomes second President.
XYZ correspondence published.

1798
Alien and Sedition Acts passed.
Kentucky and Virginia Resolutions.

1800
Treaty of 1800 brings peace with France.
Jefferson elected President.

1803
Marbury v. Madison decided.
Louisiana Purchase.

1804
Judge Chase and Pickering impeached.
Burr-Hamilton duel.
Jefferson reelected.

1807
Chesapeake-Leopard incident.
Embargo Act.

A S WE HAVE SEEN, Hamilton, with the acquiescence of the President, charted the course of Washington's administration. But the Hamiltonian program and the political philosophy underlying it encountered increasing resistance. This opposition began to crystallize behind Thomas Jefferson. The author of the Declaration of Independence was a worthy opponent for the brilliant and incisive Hamilton. Where the latter was neat, precise, and orderly, Jefferson was loose, rambling, and disjointed. But Hamilton's absolute command of the complex relations between public finance and politics was matched by Jefferson's profound knowledge of the law and governmental institutions. He had a breadth of political experience reaching back to the beginning of the Revolution. By 1790 Jefferson had served his countrymen as Governor of Virginia, member of the Continental Congress, drafter of the Declaration of Independence, and Minister to France. It was from the latter post that he returned to accept Washington's invitation to become the first Secretary of State under the new constitution. A man of remarkable versatility, Jefferson was accomplished in such fields as architecture, invention, agriculture, and natural science.

Jefferson was, in addition, deeply interested in political theory. His view of mankind was thoroughly optimistic. Man, for him, was essentially good and capable

126

of progress toward perfection. He believed in popular education and wrote a plan for education in Virginia which proposed educating all citizens up to the limits of their capacities by a system of scholarships for able students. Above all, he feared a ruling elite of property and wealth. Familiar with Europe, he had little desire to see his own country imitate her aristocratic ways. His own manners were simple and unaffected, and he had no respect for the formal ways which some of his countrymen were trying to import from beyond the sea. Thus Jefferson, familiar with European life and institutions as a result of his widespread travel and residence as a diplomat in Paris, came to embody the American faith and its democratic ideals. Hamilton, on the other hand, wished to import the aristocratic institutions and the social stratification of an England which he had never seen. Jefferson recommended to his countrymen who leaned toward Old World institutions that they go "to Europe to see something of the trappings of monarchy [and] . . . every man shall [come] back thoroughly cured" of any monarchical leanings.

His attitude toward the Hamiltonian program was simply that it was designed to cause wealth and power to gravitate toward a tiny commercial class whose antidemocratic prejudices made them a danger to the republic. When Jefferson entered the Cabinet in 1790 he found most of the Hamiltonian program in the process of enactment. He could see the advantage to the country as a whole of sound credit and therefore could approve the plan to pay the foreign and domestic debt at par, even though this represented a subsidy to the speculators whom he so bitterly condemned. Jefferson also supported the assumption of state debts by the central government. The new Bank of the United States, however, was quite another question. This bank became the focus of a violent clash of ideas. In it, Jefferson and his friends detected the intention of the moneyed clique to use the national government to subvert the Constitution. The foes of Hamilton feared the bank more than any other feature of his plans because of its apparent permanence. Jefferson frequently observed that the national debt might soon be paid, and the tariff might be reduced at any time, but the twenty-year charter of the new bank indicated that it was clearly designed to exert a continuing influence in American life. Jefferson's arguments against the constitutionality of the bank doubtless flowed from his fears of the uses to which the bank might be put in creating a permanent aristocracy of wealth. Jefferson argued, against Hamilton, that the bank was unconstitutional because it was nowhere explicitly authorized in the Constitution, and that stretching the "necessary and proper" clause to cover it, as Hamilton wished to do, would set a dangerous precedent. His feeling, evidently, was that "loose construction" would play into the hands of a moneyed elite.

The same fears prompted the Jeffersonian reaction to the protective tariff which Hamilton had advocated in his 1791 *Report on Manufactures*. The agrarians argued that a protective tariff discriminated against them because the farming population used most of the imported goods and therefore paid most of the taxes. As producers and exporters of raw materials, they feared retaliatory tariffs on their produce in foreign markets should the United States adopt such a protective policy.

The excise taxes, adopted at Hamilton's urging, seemed to justify the alarm of the Jeffersonians. Partly designed to raise

Alexander Hamilton

A view of New York City in 1794

The First Bank of New York

Thomas Jefferson

Clock designed by Jefferson

At the fountainhead of American political parties stand Hamilton and Jefferson. The rivalry between them was in part philosophical but in part rooted in economic differences. Hamilton's party was urban and commercial; Jefferson represented an agrarian society, though one with strong intellectual and scientific interests. There was a clash of interests over such questions as the tariff, the currency, and taxation.

Monticello, Jefferson's home in Virginia

revenue, these taxes were also intended to demonstrate the power of the national government. By levying taxes directly on the people and collecting them by force, if necessary, individual citizens were constantly reminded of the immediate presence of a new government capable of carrying out its will. The most objectionable of these taxes was one levied on the manufacture of distilled liquors. This bore with especial weight upon the poor frontiersmen who had to convert their grain crops to whisky in order to get them to market. Roads were bad or nonexistent, and whisky was compact. Moreover, it was so standard a commodity with so stable a value and market, that it passed as currency on the otherwise currency-barren frontier. The tax had, therefore, given rise to much protest all along the frontier, especially in western Pennsylvania, where the sturdy Scotch-Irish settlers had a long tradition of resistance to oppression. Old traditions were stirred, and a new "struggle for liberty" against this "new Stamp Act" was launched. The issue of special and distant courts was also raised. Since cases were heard only in the federal courts in Philadelphia, 200 miles away, the accused were tried far from the support and sympathy of their friends.

Most of these frontiersmen were Jeffersonians, and the political issues of the day were freely mixed in with the general resentment. The agitation continued for three years and came to a climax in July, 1794, when an attempt to arrest "moonshiners" resulted in bloodshed. Two thousand armed frontiersmen "demonstrated" in Pittsburgh, intimidating citizens and cadging free drinks. There was loose talk about attacking a national arsenal located nearby. Hamilton welcomed this chance to prove that the national government could enforce its laws and to teach a lesson to these independent frontiersmen.

Some 12,000 militia, collected from the eastern counties of the middle states, were dispatched to the scene of disorder. This "federal army" paraded its might about the frontier but found no one to fight. The responsible leaders of the protest movement, including Albert Gallatin, subsequently Jefferson's Secretary of the Treasury, took no part in the violence and warned against it. Hamilton went along with the army and directed the arrest of a score of ringleaders who were carried away to the east and tried for treason. Two were convicted and sentenced to death, but Washington magnanimously—and wisely—pardoned them.

To the Jeffersonians, the discriminatory nature of the tax and the inquisitorial methods of collection, in addition to the manner in which resistance to it was put down, smacked of tyranny. The whole Federalist program, which included taxes bearing heavily on the farmers and a tariff and banking system designed to aid the manufacturers and merchants, seemed to Jefferson and his followers the old story of a wealthy few exploiting the majority. It is not surprising, therefore, that one of the first acts of Jefferson when he later reached the White House was to bring about the repeal of the excise taxes.

The differences in political ideology between Hamilton and Jefferson have been somewhat exaggerated by political controversy. Both hoped that the people would have sense enough to choose their representatives from among the rich and well-born. Both were uncertain about universal suffrage and preferred the leadership of a "natural aristocracy." Jefferson displayed a greater confidence in the popular wisdom and virtue, but Hamilton was hardly the "enemy of the people" he was sometimes made out to be. So far as basic principles were concerned, Jefferson probably differed from his opponent chiefly in having received a strong influence from the French *philosophes* during his years in France from 1783 to 1789—an influence which was not so much democratic per se as it was anticlerical, deistic, and liberal in a more abstract and doctrinaire way than was the English tradition. Hamilton's attitude was in the tradition of English liberalism, with its practical, property-conscious spirit, while Jefferson had digested much of that larger if vaguer concern for the Rights of Man which France, on the eve of her great revolution, had discovered.

Nevertheless, to their contemporaries, excited by political controversies, the difference between Hamilton and Jefferson came to seem fundamental. It appeared to many as an issue between democracy and aristocracy, equality and special privilege; to others, as one between order and mob rule, intelligence and demagoguery. Aroused by the new democratic doctrines of the French Revolution, Federalist and Republican sharpened their feelings of an absolute mutual hostility during the tense 1790s. Modern Americans may well go back to the literature of these times to rediscover the arguments about the future and meaning of the American experiment, for these views are as fresh today as they were in the 1790s. The French Revolution raised similar questions on a world-wide stage, and it was only natural that this crucial event should have had a profound effect on America, raising to fever pitch the controversy in which Hamilton and Jefferson became the leading symbols.

FOREIGN POLICY AND THE ORIGINS OF POLITICAL PARTIES

A basis for the formation of political parties existed in the philosophical split just discussed, but party formation was accelerated by the impact of the French Revolution and the subsequent war, a war which broke out in 1792 and which ranged revolutionary France against the monarchical powers of Europe, including Great Britain. The Federalists sided with Britain and the conservative powers of Europe, while the followers of Jefferson, who were coming to be known as Republicans or Democratic-Republicans, favored France.

Jefferson, as Secretary of State in Washington's Cabinet, based his foreign policy upon the consideration that England hated and menaced the United States, and that we must use France and the French alliance to offset this enmity. The revolution in France, which was widely viewed in this country as based on principles similar to our own, strengthened this belief. Hamilton believed that England could be our friend, and that economic and other ties still united Britain and her former colonies. He felt that trade with Britain was essential to the success of his financial program. The fact that there was no early manifestation of this friendship after the Revolution did not discourage him. So great was his admiration for the British government, British business methods, and British social structure that he was able to ignore all indications of unfriendliness toward the United States which emanated from England. France's revolution strengthened his opinions. He saw there the threat of bloody upheaval and mob rule, about which he had so often warned his countrymen. The destruction of all the established forms of society, the rise of the common man, the danger to property and to the culture-bearing upper class filled him with strong feelings of disgust and fear.

The French Revolution swept all foreign affairs into one great basket. Before its coming, the two chief items of foreign policy which occupied the Washington administration were the Mississippi River mouth, involving Spain, and the northwest forts, which concerned England. By virtue of her ownership of the Floridas and the trans-Mississippi West, Spain controlled the mouth of the great river. The rapid settlement of the trans-Allegheny region, which had gone on during and after the Revolution, made this a vital issue. The natural outlet for the settlements along the Ohio and Tennessee Rivers was down these rivers, which flow into the Mississippi, and thence to the sea at New Orleans. The Spanish sometimes permitted this trade to pass through their territory and sometimes did not. The United States negotiated the question with Spain year in and year out. The Spanish dreaded the coming of Americans into the Mississippi Valley as a threat to their continued occupation of the continent and sought in every way to hamper the extension of American settlement. They even encouraged the frontiersmen to break their ties with the United States and to become dependent upon Spain.

The English controversy concerned a number of important frontier forts located within American territory, including Niagara and Detroit, which the British refused to abandon. London expected our loose confederation to break up and wanted to be in a position to grab territory if this occurred. The British in Canada also controlled a profitable fur trade with the Indians through these forts and were reluctant to give it up. Britain claimed that the forts were being held because Americans had failed to live up to the treaty which ended the Revolution. The treaty had provided that we would not impede the efforts of English creditors to collect debts owed them by Americans and that we would recommend to the states that the loyalists who had lost property through

confiscation during the Revolution be compensated.

When, early in 1793, the French declared war upon England and Spain, these problems became part of the general problem of America's attitude toward the war and the three belligerents with whom we were concerned. We had a treaty with France which obligated us to come to her aid in defense of her American possessions, if asked. In the meantime, no demand having been received, Washington proclaimed neutrality on April 22, 1793, and awaited developments.

While the revolution in France brought trouble and doubt to the administration, the country, at the outset, quite generally greeted it with enthusiasm. As John Marshall said, "In no part of the world was the Revolution hailed with more joy than in America." France was generally credited with a new birth of freedom, which presaged the downfall of authoritarian governments everywhere. In Baltimore, on December 29, 1792, when news was received that the French had beaten the Austrian and Prussian forces which were trying to put down the revolution, a "company of gentlemen, Friends of the Rights of Man," met to celebrate, and drank fifteen republican toasts. Bells were rung in New York, and a liberty pole was raised. In January, 1793, respectable Boston, stronghold of Federalist sentiment, held a feast to congratulate the French on their success "in their glorious struggles for Liberty and Equality." From 1789, when the revolution in France began, to the end of 1792, the sentiment for France was almost unchecked, although individuals like Hamilton and John Adams never shared the general enthusiasm. The years 1793 to 1794 saw the execution of the French king, and the excesses of the Reign of Terror which tempered the early enthusiasm in America. But the revolution continued to produce controversy between Federalists and Republicans.

Early in 1793 the French were at war with England, and the division in sentiment between the Federalists and the Republicans in this country was intensified. From that time forward, the French Revolution was the principal factor fomenting party strife in America. As one writer pointed out at the time, "It not merely divided parties, but moulded them, gave them their watchwords, and their bitterness." Party lines were established from the other side of the Atlantic. The more democratic Republican party in the United States frequently viewed the French revolutionists as fighting on their side in the struggle against the conservatives in America. To the Federalists, on the other hand, the entrance of England into the war was a mixed blessing. While they were glad to see the revolution resisted by English sea power, this threatened to disrupt trade. Since the great bulk of the government's income came from taxes on imports, of which nine-tenths came from England, the entire Hamiltonian financial structure was endangered.

The general tension was heightened in the spring of 1793 by the arrival of Citizen Edmond Genêt, representative of the revolutionary French Republic to the United States. This colorful character, a republican enthusiast to his fingertips, landed at Charleston after an adventurous crossing enlivened by the threat of the British navy. He assumed that all Americans, being republicans, were therefore warm friends of France. This illusion was no doubt fostered by the thunderous welcome given him wherever he went by the partisans of France. He was a vigorous speaker, a poet, and even sang patriotic songs. Such gifts were bound to make him

a popular performer at the public meetings which were organized everywhere in his honor. So popular did he become that Republicans began to call themselves "Citizen" in honor of the French revolutionary form of address. "Jacobin" clubs, named after similar radical clubs in France, appeared everywhere. A rash of liberty poles, liberty caps, and cockades followed Genêt wherever he went. Genêt had hopes of American cooperation in the stirring events which were shaking the world. The United States might conquer the Spanish possessions of Florida and Louisiana and the English colony of Canada while England and Spain were busy in Europe. If the American government did not wish to become involved, Genêt was prepared to direct and finance the operations of Americans who would volunteer for these schemes of conquest or for privateering. He carried commissions ready to be filled out with the names of such volunteers as should present themselves, nor were volunteers lacking.

His schemes failed partly because Hamilton refused to turn over to Genêt French funds which were deposited in the United States, money which came from American payments on our French debt incurred during the American Revolution. Also, they failed because Citizen Genêt incurred the wrath of the Washington administration. When this energetic Frenchman learned that the Federalist administration was not so warm toward France as he had supposed, he conceived the notion of forcing the government out and replacing it with Republicans, whose attitude was much more sympathetic. His meddling seriously threatened the neutrality that Washington and Jefferson were hoping to exploit. It made Genêt *persona non grata,* and Washington asked that he be recalled. The French government complied, but Genêt could not return to France, since his party had meantime fallen from power and the guillotine now awaited him. He became instead a citizen of the United States and married the daughter of a governor of New York.

WAR WITH ENGLAND?

In 1793, before the repudiation of Genêt, it had almost seemed as if sympathy for the French cause were going to drive us into war with England. Genêt's failure did not end this possibility. As the European war continued, problems of neutrality arose and brought new and even more serious complications. The rights which Americans claimed included (1) a narrow definition of contraband, (2) freedom from seizure of noncontraband goods carried on neutral ships, (3) freedom from impressment of American seamen by the British navy, (4) freedom from "paper" blockades,* and (5) freedom from the British Rule of 1756, which declared that trade not legally open in time of peace remained closed in time of war. British disregard of these neutral "rights" and her highhanded treatment of our ships on the high seas exasperated Americans, and for a time a break seemed near. Washington and the Federalist group, however, were determined to keep peace with England if at all possible. A crisis developed, in spite of American hopes, as a result of British seizure of American shipping. When England and France went to war, France had opened the trade of her sugar islands in the Carib-

* The American claim was that a blockade, to be legal, must involve the close guarding of the blockaded port by actual warships. A paper blockade, which was a mere statement that an area was under blockade, justified the blockading power in seizing ships on the high seas as well as close to ports.

bean to the United States, and American ships flocked to this new trade opportunity in great numbers. Without warning, a British fleet swooped down and swept up 200 of the American vessels to be carried off to prize courts. Despite American protests, 150 of them were condemned for violations of the Rule of 1756. Britain, while modifying her position a little as a result of the uproar which this action caused, nevertheless maintained in essence that she had the right to prevent neutrals from trading with her enemy, France. Outraged American shippers cited international law, the rights of neutrals, and the doctrine that "free ships make free goods," all to no avail. The British were determined to stop American trade with France and were willing to strain international law to do so.

British actions enraged Americans and set off a highly technical, hotly argued controversy about the rights of neutrals to trade with belligerents in time of war. The controversy lasted from 1793 until 1812, when we finally went to war with England, ostensibly because of her abuse of neutral rights. Leaving legal questions aside, what actually happened was that the British tried to prevent the Americans from trading with the French by any and all methods at their command, while maintaining as well as they could that their actions were perfectly legal. Urged on by high wartime prices which made trade very attractive, the Americans made every effort to trade by any available means, arguing that the British methods and actions were illegal.

British efforts to stop this trade included blockades, "paper" and real, seizure of our ships, occasional firing upon them, and impressment of our seamen into the British navy. American protests were strenuous and occasionally successful on minor matters, but we never succeeded in forcing the English to change their policy. Britain was hard pressed by the French Revolution and later by Napoleon in the war which lasted with brief interruptions from 1793 until 1815. Often fighting alone against a power which threatened to overrun all of Europe, the British could not afford to let us help her powerful foe with our trade. Britain's arguments may have been weak, but her navy was strong, and she was prepared to fight rather than let the French receive needed supplies from our growing commerce. As usual, Britain's chief weapon against European enemies was her navy, by means of which she hoped to choke France into submission. Despite their losses to the British navy, however, business for American shippers was good and profits were high.

President Washington, anxious to avoid war, in 1794 sent John Jay of New York, well known for his pro-English sympathies, to London to see if a settlement of all outstanding issues could be negotiated. In addition to the questions arising over neutral rights, Jay was instructed to secure British withdrawal from the northwestern posts, adjustment of the prerevolutionary war debts, and freedom to trade with Canada and the British West Indies. Jay faced enormous obstacles. He found the British adamant on neutral rights and little disposed to negotiate on the other matters. His task was complicated by the fact that Hamilton secretly supplied the British with information which made Jay's task immensely more difficult. As a result, the treaty which he brought back surrendered the "freedom of the seas" to British restrictions and directly contradicted our treaty of alliance with France on this score. The French, and their partisans in this country, were furious.

Also objectionable to American opin-

ion was the grudging concession to trade with the West Indies. American vessels of no more than 70 tons capacity were to be permitted to trade with the British islands on condition that the United States did not export to any part of the outside world in American vessels certain tropical products such as sugar and cotton. This restriction would have choked off America's budding cotton industry. In addition to these niggardly concessions the British promised to give up the frontier posts and to submit to "amicable negotiation" and arbitration questions of boundaries, debts, and claims. Since our right as neutrals to trade with belligerents was the most pressing problem of all, Washington and the Federalists were greatly disappointed with Jay's efforts. The Republicans were furious at this "insult to our shipping" and clamored for war. As the best, and perhaps the only, way to avoid war, Washington accepted the treaty and with the full weight of his personal prestige succeeded in gaining approval for it in the Senate without a single vote to spare. But even the President's influence was not sufficient to prevent the Senate from suspending the objectionable provisions concerning trade with the West Indies.

By his decisive action in accepting the Jay Treaty, Washington may well have saved his country from a war which in all probability would have been disastrous. But for the moment the President had to pay dearly for serving his country so well. His reputation was in shreds. The father of his country was vilified by exasperated superpatriots angry at his "cowardice" in the face of English insults. Most of these fire-eaters were Republicans, who no doubt were making political capital out of the situation. He was called a "supercilious tyrant" and an "American Caesar," said to be "in his political dotage" and "trampling

JAY TREATY, 1794

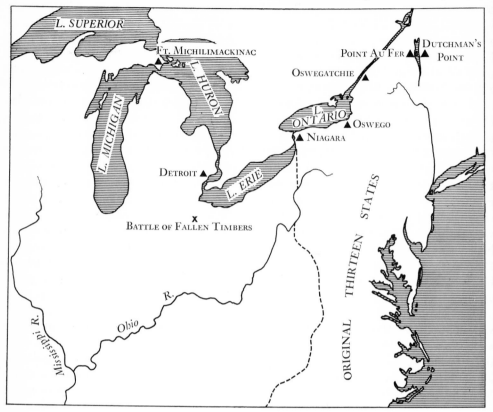

upon the Constitution." Benjamin Franklin Bache, grandson of Franklin, said "Washington has debauched America . . . deserted his great cause." Tom Paine declared that the question we must ask now was, "Has Washington deserted his principles or did he ever have any?" The great soldier who hated war and sacrificed himself to peace died four years later with these denunciations still ringing in his ears.

The much-maligned Jay Treaty went far to settle the problem of the northwest frontier. As settlement beyond the mountains progressed, the Indians in that region had become restless and troublesome. They had undoubtedly received at least moral support from the forts which the

British had refused to evacuate in spite of the Treaty of 1783. Two American expeditions were sent against the Indians, one in 1790 and another the following year. Both were badly beaten. A third force under General "Mad Anthony" Wayne defeated the red men at Fallen Timbers, near the western tip of Lake Erie, in the summer of 1794, but could not bring peace to the frontier. As long as the English forts remained, the Indians persisted in their hope of halting the advancing white settlements. Jay's agreement removed the British forts, and in 1795 a general peace was brought about in the Treaty of Greenville (Ohio). The treaty opened new land to settlement, and Indian troubles were ended for fifteen years; that is, until settlement along the Ohio made it necessary for the Indians to be pushed back again.

The Jay Treaty also contributed to the solution of the problem of free navigation of the Mississippi River. Spain in 1795 had quit the European alliance against France and was fearful that her former allies, especially England, might be in the mood for reprisals. She was aware that Britain and the United States had signed a treaty and was apprehensive that secret clauses might presage an attack upon her American possessions by the two treaty makers. As a result Spain was anxious to placate the United States in order to avert danger to her possessions. She therefore hastily acceded to all the terms which this country had been pressing upon her ever since 1783. The resulting Pinckney Treaty was signed, granting free navigation of the Mississippi River and permission to deposit goods at New Orleans for transshipment without paying tariff duties. The agreement recognized the boundary of Florida at the 31st parallel, and Spain promised to keep the southern Indians in check.

These three treaties entirely altered the western problem, opened new territory to settlement, pacified the Indians, and gave the westerners an outlet for their produce. They preserved the peace and secured the west from the danger of aggression and secession.

The Jay Treaty was successful in relaxing western tensions, but it plunged America into trouble with the French, who naturally disliked the treaty and felt, with some justice, that it violated the 1778 treaty between France and the United States. Our minister was recalled and France declared that she would henceforth treat our shipping to England exactly as England was treating our shipping to France. France had acted in this way previously, after Gênet's dismissal, but prior to the Jay Treaty her action had caused little harm and therefore aroused little resentment in the United States. After 1795, however, French seizures of our shipping became very troublesome. The two great powers, locked in deadly combat, were determined to coerce the cocky little neutral into accepting their concepts of right and wrong. Equally determined to participate in a profitable trade with the combatants, America was being badly buffeted on both sides. The angry French severed diplomatic relations, and danger of war now appeared from a new quarter.

Washington decided in 1796 that two terms in the presidency were enough for any man and that, after twenty years of almost continuous service to his country, he was entitled to spend his declining years in peace at home. His last solemn warning to his fellow countrymen urged them to keep out of the war which was raging in Europe. The retirement of Washington gave the Republicans their first real chance to test their strength. In the elections of 1796, John Adams and Thomas Pinckney received the Federalists' support against Thomas Jefferson and Aaron Burr, who had a strong Republican following. Adams received 71 electoral votes and Jefferson 68. It was apparent that the Federalists were badly weakened by Washington's retirement.

WAR WITH FRANCE?

Adams, who was eager to leave behind him a great name, was as anxious to keep the peace as Washington had been. Unfortunately for him, the Federalists, his own party, were not so opposed to war with France as they had been to war with

Britain. It was one thing to fight our best customer and quite another to war with revolutionary France. In fact, even as Adams was inaugurated, Federalists were demanding war. Adams determined to seek peace by sending a commission to France. The commission was composed of three members: C. C. Pinckney and John Marshall, good Federalists; and Elbridge Gerry, a political maverick, who had flirted with Antifederalism and was later to become Republican governor of Massachusetts. Gerry was Adams's personal choice, a fellow Bay Stater in whom he had faith.

The delegation reached France toward the end of 1797, at a very bad time for negotiating. French arms had been extremely successful of late. Italy had been conquered, Austria humbled, and parts of Germany were in French hands. It appeared to Talleyrand, the French foreign minister, that the infant American republic, which had been born with French aid and which had cynically deserted her patron, was now coming to seek favors. He was prepared to accept the United States back into friendship but was determined to make her pay. Through three emissaries, dubbed X, Y, and Z by the Americans, Talleyrand demanded a bribe of $240,000 for himself and associates and a large loan (actually a gift) for the French government. The clever Talleyrand had for once misjudged the situation. He had underestimated the recklessness of the Federalists who were ready, even anxious, to risk war with France. He was unaware that it was only President Adams who wanted peace and that his party did not support him. Although Talleyrand's demand was in keeping with common eighteenth-century practices in diplomacy, the Federalist war faction exploited it to whip up the war fever. Talleyrand's action was represented as an insult to a sovereign nation. The cry of "Millions for Defense, but Not One Cent for Tribute" became a national slogan. Joseph Hopkinson wrote "Hail Columbia, Happy Land," which almost became a national anthem. X, Y, and Z were denounced as so many brigands who had smirched the honor of the country. President Adams was popular, for once in his life, as he took a firm stand and called upon Congress to prepare for any emergency. Minister Gerry was summarily called home, and Adams announced to Congress, "I will never send another minister to France without assurances that he will be received, respected, and honored as the representative of a great, free, powerful, and independent nation."

War now seemed certain, and preparations were begun. The army was enlarged, and Washington was asked to head it. He accepted the task but, prompted by party leaders, demanded Hamilton as next in command. Adams reluctantly yielded to pressure and appointed him. Hamilton had large dreams concerning his future military role. A soldier of great promise, he had served during most of the Revolutionary War as Washington's secretary before he was given a combat command and retired as a colonel. Since Washington was well along in years, it appeared that Hamilton would have active command.

But where was the army to fight? Spain had been forced out of the coalition against France and was now her ally—or, better, her satellite. Florida, Louisiana, and perhaps the whole Spanish empire to the south of us therefore lay open to conquest. The trade of Spain's possessions in the New World had been the constant goal of British policy for 200 years, and Hamilton's commercial party cast eager eyes upon it. Any such venture to the south would require the help of the British fleet. While Europe was in the throes of revolution and war, these Spanish colonies in the New World were becoming restless and were ripe for rebellion. Perhaps the United States might aid them, earn their gratitude, and get in on the ground floor commercially. Hamilton and Henry Knox, the Secretary of War, had talked over the situation with Francisco Miranda, a leading Latin-American revolutionary leader, as early as 1784–1785 when Miranda was in the United States. The project was still alive. It was a big dream worthy of Hamilton's creative mind, but John Adams had other plans.

Prospective war with France made a navy imperative, and Congress established a Navy Department and provided for the construction of a fleet. As soon as the warships were ready they were rushed to sea to engage French naval vessels and to prey upon French shipping. A lively undeclared war on the sea ensued. Some very heartening victories were won, and news of these stirred American enthusiasm and flattered American pride—more perhaps than was strictly warranted. After all, the French navy was engaged in a struggle with the British navy.

One of the most attractive features of the "war" with France from the Federalist point of view was the opportunity which it afforded to strike a blow at the Jeffersonians. Federalists were motivated by hatred of the principles of the French Revolution and by fear of democracy at home as well as by French insults and injury to our shipping. Republican sympathy with the French at this time was interpreted as treason by Federalists. Since the presidential campaign of 1796, the war of words between the Federalists and the Republicans had been waged with ever-growing acrimony and virulence.

Each side had newspapers devoted to its cause, and the language of abuse used in these violently partisan sheets has seldom been equaled in the history of the press. Republican editors were led in vigor of vituperation by Philip Freneau, a poet and democrat who had set himself up in the newspaper business in Philadelphia. Freneau's pen had the power to sting and wound; his diatribes against monarchists, tyrants, aristocrats, pipsqueak gamesters, monopolists, and speculators, which were some of the names he called his political opponents, were widely copied by less gifted Republican editors.

The war scare and undeclared naval war gave the Federalists the opportunity to strike another blow at their "unpatriotic" political opponents. They had control of Congress and in 1798 passed a series of laws aimed particularly at the French and other foreigners allegedly influential in the Jeffersonian party and at the editors and writers of their press. A new naturalization act extended the residence requirements of an applicant for citizenship from five years to fourteen. This struck more heavily at the Republicans, who tended to attract the greater proportion of the recent migrants. More obviously partisan was an act which gave the President the power to deport any aliens whom he considered undesirable or order their imprisonment without trial. What made this law unusual was that it applied to peacetime, instead of the customary law which applied in wartime only, and it enabled the government to punish aliens of any country. Most objectionable of all to the Jeffersonians was a so-called Sedition Law which made it a crime, under penalty of fine and imprisonment, for anyone to "write, print, utter or publish" any "false, scandalous and malicious" statements designed to bring disrepute upon the government, either house of Congress, or the President. While it was not necessary to use the Alien Act, the Sedition Act was used for purely partisan purposes. Many were arrested, fined, or imprisoned; some even suffered brutal treatment. Newspaper editors, printers, and foreigners were special objects of attack. The partisanship of Federalist judges and the juries in the sedition trials further revealed the Federalist determination to use the foreign imbroglio to crush their domestic enemies.

The law against sedition backfired upon its users. The widespread animosity aroused by the injustice and questionable legality of the laws served to cement the opposition to the Federalists. Only convinced or rabid Federalists could support such tactics. All but the staunchest Federalists felt that the law violated the First Amendment to the Constitution as well as the spirit in which the whole of our fundamental document had been written.

The Republicans took quick advantage of the fact that their "tyrannically minded" opponents had now openly resorted to repressive measures. Jefferson vigorously organized this discontent and fear as he welded together agrarian sentiment in Virginia and directed and encouraged Republican party organizers in other states. Seizing the highest possible ground, Jefferson and Madison drafted resolutions declaring the acts unconstitutional. These resolutions were passed by the legislatures of Virginia and Kentucky. The Virginia and Kentucky Resolutions not only declared the Alien and Sedition Acts unconstitutional, but called attention to the fact that the Constitution had established a limited government and that Congress was not the sole judge of the extent of its powers. The resolutions strongly suggested that the states—perhaps even one state—had the power to declare an act of Congress

null and void. Here was an idea which, somewhat altered and greatly elaborated, and called "nullification," was to have a long and momentous history. It climaxed the constitutional argument of the two parties in this era, in which Federalists sought to enlarge the powers of the national government, while Republicans stood for the powers of the states.

HEROIC ADAMS

Things were not going well for the Federalists, but they relied upon the French war to repair their fortunes. They would then be in a position to crush opposition and rally the country behind themselves. Unfortunately this resource also failed them. John Adams's sturdy frame stood squarely in the path that led to war. Adams had recovered from his first seizure of war fever, and news from France encouraged him to move for peace. We had no representative in Paris, but our minister in Holland, William Vans Murray, was keeping an eye on developments in the French capital. At the end of the year 1798, he saw a change in the situation. Talleyrand had by then learned that he had sized up the American situation badly. Able diplomatist that he was, he began rapidly to shift his ground. He had thought that the Americans wanted peace and he planned to make them pay a stiff price for it. When he discovered that many in the United States apparently wanted war, Talleyrand abandoned his effort at blackmail and sought to negotiate a peace treaty. When this state of affairs was communicated to Adams, he appointed Vans Murray to negotiate a treaty, and an agreement was signed in 1800. This treaty abrogated the old French alliance of 1778 and ended the threat of war in return for assumption of French claims by the United

States government. In addition the French confirmed the American position that "free ships make free goods."

The stirring events of this near war with France came close to wiping out completely the enthusiasm for France which had existed in America. The role of the French Revolution as a stimulus to the formation of political parties was, nevertheless, not quite ended. The Alien and Sedition Acts, intended as a defense against subversive French ideas, put the finishing touches on the formation of the Republican party. Political parties now clearly existed.

By making peace with France, Adams had in fact destroyed the main hope for the Federalists in the election of 1800. The party of Washington, Adams, and Hamilton split apart upon the stubborn independence of the Chief Executive. By preventing war, Adams jeopardized the future of his party and sacrificed his own political career. The leading issue in his eyes, it appears, was that of "militarism," and he retained too much republican mistrust of a large army to go along with the plans of Hamilton's faction. Hamilton and his friends never forgave him. Adams himself believed that his action in seeking peace at the expense of his party and his personal ambition was "the most disinterested and meritorious action of my life." Historians have shown no disposition to disagree.

The French treaty laid open a split in the Federalist party which had always existed but which, up to this time, had been hidden. Hamilton had always been the real leader of the party, but he had achieved that position because of his influence over the party leaders, which in turn was the product of his vast ability and dominating personality. He really represented the beliefs of only a minority of the rank-and-file Federalists, the extremists who shared his doubts about popular government and his desire for a truly strong central government. In 1800 Federalist sentiment was strong, especially in New England, among people who were neither rich nor aristocratic. To these voters, "honest John Adams" was the party leader. Hamilton's bitter denunciation of Adams at the time of the French peace weakened the party but did not destroy Adams. In the election of 1800 the Federalists still had no stronger candidate, and ran President Adams for a second term. He had narrowly beaten Jefferson in 1796, and was only narrowly to lose to him in 1800, despite the fact that he led a divided party. The electoral college vote was 73 to 65. The only significant change between 1796 and 1800 was in the vote of New York State.

Jefferson and Burr again represented the Republicans, and the campaign was

PRESIDENTIAL ELECTION, 1800

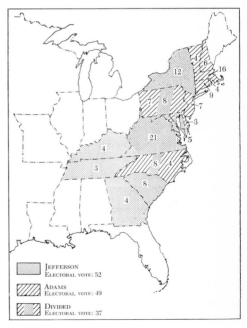

JEFFERSON
ELECTORAL VOTE: 52

ADAMS
ELECTORAL VOTE: 49

DIVIDED
ELECTORAL VOTE: 37

fought with extreme bitterness. Federalists called Jefferson an atheist, a leveler, and a revolutionary, while Republicans retaliated with their stock phrases, of which "monarchist" and "tyrant" were perhaps the least extreme. Each Republican elector cast two votes, one for Jefferson and one for Burr. Therefore, each Republican candidate had 73 votes, and there was no way of determining which should be President. The election went into the House of Representatives, where Federalist leaders, still determined to save the country from the monster Jefferson, tried to make a deal to elect Burr. Burr was considered an opportunist with no convictions which would prevent him from co-operating with Federalists. Hamilton prevented this scheme by persuading enough of his friends in Congress to cast blank ballots to ensure Jefferson's election. Burr, who four years later killed Hamilton in a duel, was already an old enemy. Hamilton distrusted Burr, and feared Jefferson less than did many of the Federalists. Hamilton had been willing to contemplate a desperate scheme to withhold the votes of New York from the Republicans, but he could not approve of the equally desperate Federalist plan to elect Burr rather than Jefferson as President. Thus ended one of the most famous presidential elections in American history.

The attempt of some Federalists to defeat the popular will by elevating Burr to the presidency led to the adoption of the Twelfth Amendment to the Constitution. Under the original provisions of the Constitution, there were no candidates for the vice presidency. The candidate who received the highest number of electoral votes, provided it constituted a majority, became President. The one who received the next highest number of choices became Vice President. The framers of the Constitution did not foresee the emergence of well-disciplined political parties which would cause the electors to vote a straight party ticket. But this had happened by 1800, with the result that Jefferson and Burr received exactly the same number of votes for President. This threw the election into the House of Representatives and might have brought about the defeat of Jefferson. The Twelfth Amendment made any such maneuvering impossible. It provided for separate ballots for the presidency and vice presidency, requiring a majority of the electoral college in each case. At the same time, this change diminished the importance of the vice presidency, for this office was now definitely relegated to a secondary position, and has often been a political sop to appease some faction disappointed in not winning the first place on the national ticket. It also made for the selection of second-rate men for this second-rate post.

JEFFERSON'S PRESIDENCY

The hysterical fulminations of the Federalists about "the beast," Jefferson, led people to believe that a radical change in government direction was to be expected. Indeed, the tumult of that day has not entirely died out. Some modern historians still speak of "the Jeffersonian revolution"; others accept the opinion of John Adams's great-grandson Henry Adams, whose historical volumes argue that Jefferson followed the Adams policy with very little change; that he won the election with high-sounding talk about the rights of the common man and then quietly did nothing about them. There is a measure of correctness in each of these interpretations. The succession of Jefferson to the presidency brought in an administration with views about the purposes and functions of government that were diametrically opposed to those of the Federalists.

Quite in contrast to the latter's reliance upon big government to effect its policies, it was Jefferson's conviction that "that government is best that governs least." While it should restrain evildoers, the government should leave the people free to regulate their own pursuits and activities "and shall not take from the mouth of labor the bread it has earned." It should dispense equal justice to all; should jealously safeguard the rights of election by the people; should acquiesce in the decisions of the majority; and should rely upon the supremacy of the civil over the military. There should be a careful preservation of the rights of the states, and a rigid regard for the constitutional limitations upon Congress and upon its delegated powers. Moreover, Jefferson envisioned a nation built upon foundations of prosperous small farmers rather than primarily upon businessmen, manufacturers, and financiers. He did not believe in equality of political rights, for not all men were qualified to vote or wise enough to hold office. But if he did not believe in the immediate political wisdom of all men, he had an abiding faith in the ultimate capacity of ordinary men to decide public questions wisely. Given equality of opportunity with wise direction under a simple government, the people would progress to a point where they could be entrusted with the full management of public affairs. That time had not yet arrived, and until it did, the management of the state must be entrusted to men of talent and merit.

More than anything else, Jefferson believed in the dignity of man and the obligation of the government to safeguard his liberties. Every individual should have complete freedom of religion, of speech, and of the press—freedom to express himself on all subjects, even to criticize the government. Indeed, criticism of the government was both healthful and desirable. There should be no censorship of thought or expression. Although the will of the majority must prevail, it could only be rightfully exercised if it recognized the equal rights of the minority or the advocates of unpopular causes. Underlying this belief in freedom as the foundation of society was Jefferson's faith that truth would always overcome error. "The public judgment," he stated, "will correct false reasonings and opinions, on a full hearing of all parties; and no other definite line can be drawn between the inestimable liberty of the press and its demoralizing licentiousness." The only effective weapons against error were reason and free inquiry. Such, in brief, was Jefferson's philosophy of government. It considerably extended the principles of English liberalism, adding generous measures of French revolutionary democracy. It challenged the pretensions of the so-called "ruling class."

In keeping with this new democratic spirit, Jefferson dispensed with ceremonies that were reminiscent of Old World pomp and custom, such as stiff levees like Washington's and ceremonial seating at state dinners. To avoid the latter, he used a round table to encourage a more informal atmosphere. When the British Minister once came on an official call dressed in high court regalia, he was greeted at the door by the President himself in ordinary clothes and slippers. The Minister was so disturbed that he reported to his government his belief that Britain had been given a calculated insult. In place of the customary formal address to the assembled Congress, the President sent a written message to be read by the clerk of the House. Thus did Jefferson make himself

Driving to the Capitol, 1800. The newly established seat of government at Washington was as yet little more than Capitol and White House connected by a dirt road. (Library of Congress)

a symbol of democracy, as he had made himself its philosopher.

But the new democracy was decorous and dignified, not crude, noisy, and vociferous, as when the people rode into power with the confident and boastful Andrew Jackson a generation later. If the new "republican court" functioned with simplicity and informality, it was none the less hospitable. Both at the White House and at Monticello, a lavish hospitality was extended—as is evidenced, for instance, by the wine bills of the first year, which amounted to nearly $2,800. The President's fine stable reflected the traditions of the Virginia aristocracy, and Jefferson himself was a man of discriminating tastes and unusual accomplishments. He was a skilled musician, a scientific farmer, and the foremost American architect of his time. His library of about 6,000 books, collected from all over the world and sold to Congress in 1815, testifies to his scholarly and literary interests. Before his death

in 1826 Jefferson had gathered another library of nearly 1,000 volumes. His collections were selected with utmost care and discrimination and covered a wide range of subjects. The pattern of Thomas Jefferson conforms neither to the ruling class of his generation nor to the later equalitarianism of Jacksonian democracy. Rather, he personifies the late-eighteenth-century liberalism and rationalism, with interests similar to those of a European liberal nobleman. "He seemed," wrote Henry Adams, "during his entire life to breathe with perfect satisfaction nowhere except in the liberal literary and scientific air of Paris of 1789."

The actual policies of the Jeffersonian administration represent no great political upheaval. At the time of his victory over Burr in the election of 1800, Jefferson seems to have given assurances that he would not disturb major Federalist legislation such as the bank, the tariff, and recently enacted provisions for enlarging the army and navy. This attitude reflected the closeness of his victory over the Federalists in the electoral college and his hope to introduce changes by degrees wherever he could. While Jefferson regarded the Federalist leaders as beyond redemption, moderate policies might gradually win over the rank and file of the opposition. And so the President sought to undermine the skeptics by his inaugural theme: "We are all Republicans; we are all Federalists." The inclusion of three New Englanders in the Cabinet, while disconcerting to some of Jefferson's own followers, constituted a gesture of conciliation.

It was not necessary for the Republicans to repeal the hated Alien and Sedition Laws, for they had expired by limitation in 1801. The Naturalization Act was repealed and the provision for five years of residence instead of fourteen was restored. The excise tax on whisky was repealed, because it bore hard on plain frontiersmen and its methods of collection were too inquisitorial. Along with it went the whole system of internal taxes. Strict economies were introduced into the government, particularly in the army and navy. Jefferson instructed his Secretary of the Treasury to keep the government's accounts in such a way that even a plain farmer could understand them. The Republicans might well have succeeded in paying off Hamilton's beloved debt had it not been for international complications which cut off all commerce and the income derived from it, and eventually brought us into another war with Great Britain. With the exception of the repeal of a judiciary act passed by the Federalists in the closing days of their control, these measures represented the sum total of the Republican changes. To the uncompromising members of the party, led by John Randolph of Roanoke, Jefferson's failure

to attack the Federalist financial structure was little less than treason. His mild policies and the inclusion of New Englanders in the cabinet were regarded as a surrender to Federalist principles—so much so that Randolph considered Jefferson to be nothing more than a Federalist spelled backward.

It was against the courts, which were the bulwark of entrenched Federalism, that the Jeffersonians launched their one vigorous attack. The Judiciary Act of 1801, which they repealed, had been in part designed to relieve Supreme Court judges from their duty of traveling around to various districts in order to hold circuit court. It had increased the number of district courts and provided for sixteen circuit judges with additional marshals and attorneys. This law was not the result of a Federalist plan to create jobs for defeated congressmen and senators, although a few were appointed. The reform had been under consideration for several years, but passage of a law had been delayed. The act made a much-needed improvement in the judiciary, but the circumstances of its passage and the fact that it would enable the Federalists to extend their party influence made the Republicans indignant. Indignation mounted when Adams appointed none but party members to the new offices ranging from judgeships to petty justices of peace. The Judiciary Act of 1801 was promptly repealed and replaced by a new one passed by the Republicans in 1802. The Jeffersonians had won the first skirmish in the battle for control of the courts.

The most important consequence of the repeal of the Judiciary Act of 1801 was the case of *Marbury v. Madison*. William Marbury was one of forty-two justices of the peace appointed by President Adams for the District of Columbia. John Mar-

ferred to the latter. Napoleon hoped to make it the basis for a new French empire in America, but in this he was thwarted by his failure to crush the revolt of the Negroes of Haiti. In 1803 he began to fear that it would fall into English hands by conquest, and he was therefore disposed to transfer it to the United States. Jefferson, who had naturally been disturbed by the prospect of a neighbor so aggressive as Napoleonic France, had sent James Monroe to Paris. He hoped to purchase New Orleans in order to prevent the Mississippi from being closed to us at some future date. Napoleon's sudden offer to sell the whole of Louisiana Territory for a price of $11,250,000, plus claims of American citizens against the French government, caught him unprepared.

Jefferson believed that the Constitution strictly limited the power of the federal government, and he could find in that document no authorization for the transaction he contemplated. He proposed to amend the Constitution, but that was a lengthy procedure, and Napoleon, like most dictators, was in a hurry. Unless the deal was quickly consummated, the golden opportunity might slip away. Jefferson had to choose which way he would strengthen democracy: by buying a great heritage for future agrarian democrats or by keeping the federal government weak. He must strengthen the hand of those who wished a powerful central government by finding authority to perform an act not specifically authorized in the Constitution, or he must forgo a chance to add millions of acres to the national estate. His Republican associates came to his rescue. They pointed out that the President and Senate may acquire territory by treaty. But Jefferson felt uncomfortable about the entire proceeding, for, in using an implied power

rather than one specifically granted by the Constitution, he was taking Federalist ground. To appease his conscience, he got the House as well as the Senate to vote on the treaty. And so the nation's interest prevailed. The national domain was doubled; the Mississippi flowed to the sea in American territory for its full length.

The acquisition of Louisiana was the fulfillment of a hope long nourished by Jefferson. Years before, while on a diplomatic mission in Paris, Jefferson had developed plans to have the western half of the continent explored. In 1786 he sought to have a noted adventurer cross Siberia and sail across the Pacific to the west coast of North America, whence he would journey overland through Spanish Louisiana to the United States. But the explorer, traveling mostly on foot, was turned back by the Russians. Then, after Jefferson became President, but before the purchase of Louisiana, he received permission from Congress to organize an exploring expedition to travel from St. Louis up the Missouri River to the northwest coast. Before this famous Lewis and Clark expedition started, the great purchase was made, and the explorers traveled chiefly in American territory.

JEFFERSON AND RANDOLPH

Jefferson's first administration won the widespread approval of the nation. His reelection in 1804 was a complete vindication of his policies. He received the votes of 162 electors to a mere 14 for his Federalist opponents, who carried only the two states of Connecticut and Delaware with some votes from Maryland. A rift had developed, however, within the ranks of his own party. The leader of the opposition was the bizarre but brilliant John Randolph of Roanoke. Moderation was no part of the temperament of this fiery Virginian, who boasted that the blood of Pocahontas ran in his veins. Perhaps no more apt characterization of anyone has ever been made than the three words of a biographer which describe Randolph as "a furious negative." Conciliation was no part of his creed, and it brought Jefferson little comfort to denounce the Randolph faction as "three or four in number and all tongue." Randolph's tongue cut to the quick with its barbs of caustic sarcasm. He used it to assail Jefferson as a traitor to true Republican principles. He seized every opportunity to expose what he considered to be the President's duplicity.

Randolph found such an opportunity when the President sought to claim West Florida as a part of Louisiana and to bluff the Spanish government into parting with it. The purchase of Louisiana had met with widespread approval despite the fact that Jefferson had stretched the Constitution and added heavily to the national debt. Jefferson was eager to have West Florida included within the boundaries of the Louisiana Purchase. Although the facts did not support his claim, after much study the President decided that we had in fact purchased this desirable territory. He even established a port of entry for customs above Mobile, despite Spanish protests. He acted rashly when, in a public message, he tried to force Spain's hand by calling upon Congress to resist Spanish "trespasses." In a secret message, however, he asked for 2 million dollars to *purchase* West Florida. Moreover, France was to be persuaded, for a financial consideration, to be the go-between.

This was too much for the acrid Randolph. It was nothing less than an attempt to bribe France into helping us blackmail Spain. As chairman of the powerful Ways and Means Committee, Randolph fought

John Randolph of Roanoke, spokesman of the state-sovereignty school. (Mellon Collection, National Gallery of Art)

to block the request for the 2 million dollars, but he was overruled by the House. He threw himself into the fight with fury and, supported by the Federalists, railed at the President and his Secretary of State, James Madison, even as he had once fulminated against the party which now supported him in his attacks upon Jefferson. The real cause of Randolph's running fight with the administration was that he saw in its policies an abandonment of the theories expressed in the Virginia and Kentucky Resolutions of 1798—principles which their very authors were now betraying. Randolph's criticisms of Jefferson failed to prevail in the Republican party, and he was regarded as representing virtually no one but John Randolph. Nevertheless, there was truth in his charges that Jefferson in power was a very different leader from Jefferson in opposition, and that the pure states'-rights position of 1798 had been considerably altered in the direction of nationalism.

DIPLOMATIC TROUBLES

The most serious of all the problems which Jefferson had to face were those which grew out of a renewal of the Napoleonic Wars in Europe. For, in 1803, after a brief lull, the European volcano burst forth again, and for the next nine years the same old scenes were enacted. Hundreds of American ships were lost. American sailors were impressed. American cargoes were seized. In 1805 the British were seizing our ships in the West Indies as they had in 1793. In 1806–1807 Napoleon countered the British blockade with his Continental System, which forbade anyone to trade with England. In return, Britain tightened her blockade of the Continent. Neutrals were forbidden by Britain to trade with the Continent without first submitting to British inspection, while France threatened their ships with confiscation if they did submit to the British rules.

The war was reaching a crisis, and America was caught in the middle, vainly insisting upon neutral rights and daringly dodging both sides in search of the golden rewards of trade. Britain, desperate for sailors, pursued her policy of impressment with increasing vigor; the search for alleged deserters from the British navy caused such incidents as the highhanded attack on the American warship *Chesapeake* in 1807, just off the Virginia coast, by the British frigate *Leopard*. After the *Chesapeake* affair, Jefferson determined to act, though not to go to war, for which the country was in no way prepared.

Jefferson therefore sought to compel respect for American rights by means of economic weapons. He remembered the effectiveness of the prerevolutionary boycott and determined to try this device again. Britain, he reasoned, was dependent upon American trade, and if it were cut off she would soon be brought to terms. This policy had much logic in it, for Britain was increasingly dependent upon American food as the war progressed. Congress passed an Embargo Act in December 1807 forbidding all American ships to leave port for foreign shores. If this did not bring terms, at least it would remove the principal provocations to war—if it could be enforced. There is a certain irony in the spectacle of Jefferson, the believer in weak government and full personal freedom, attempting such sweeping governmental control of trade. But he saw no other way of upholding national honor short of war.

Unfortunately for this policy, much of the nation did not agree that keeping out of war was the most important consideration. Farmers wanted to sell food, shippers wanted to make money, sailors wanted employment. This commercial paralysis brought outright opposition from New England. Daniel Webster, New England's leading spokesman in Congress, denounced the embargo in the language of the Virginia and Kentucky Resolutions as "a deliberate, palpable and dangerous exercise of powers." The Massachusetts legislature resolved that the act to enforce the embargo was "unjust, oppressive and unconstitutional and not legally binding on the citizens of this state." Connecticut and Rhode Island condemned the embargo in equally strong terms and upheld the right of the state to "interpose" against acts of Congress that were beyond the Constitution and designed to destroy the liberties of the people. Most people of these states, and other states as well, were far less interested in constitutional theories than in everyday business. Attracted by the lure of British gold, border farmers of Vermont and New York made a business of smuggling. They carried on a flourishing trade with Canada in beef, flour, pork, potatoes, and lumber. State militiamen and regular troops were used to enforce the law, and President Jefferson once declared the state of Vermont to be in rebellion as revenue officers and militiamen were murdered. Smugglers and murderers were even indicted for treason, but as the crimes were personal acts motivated by the desire for private gain they could not possibly fall in this category.

The economic paralysis was not without its compensations. With foreign competition eliminated, and with capital and labor available that had formerly gone into commerce and shipping, there began the transition to manufacturing that was to bring wealth and prosperity to the New Englanders. Mills and factories that had been closed in the face of British competition were reopened, and new ones were established. The 8,000 spindles in the cotton industry in 1807 increased to over 80,000 in 1809 and 130,000 in 1815. Much progress was made in other fields, particularly in the manufacture of woolen goods, as an enthusiasm for American-made goods spread among all classes. Ironically, northern manufacturing owed its revival to Jefferson, as an unintended result of the embargo. But these ultimate benefits were not so apparent while economic depression paralyzed business. The real feelings of New England were expressed when every New England state except Vermont voted Federalist in 1808.

Outside New England the Republican hold upon the people was not so badly shaken. Madison and George Clinton easily won this election. Nevertheless, the Federalists made sizable gains in Congress. Nor was all harmonious among the Republicans. Party unity was endangered by local splits and factions, and the widespread dissatisfaction with the embargo boded ill for party harmony. And so, just before Jefferson left office, it was repealed. Jefferson's "peaceable coercion" had proved politically impractical. Our first three Presidents had managed to keep us out of war by skillful and determined management of the powers at their disposal. But the world conflict was mounting in intensity all the time, and the pressures on American neutrality grew in proportion. Jefferson left for welcome retirement at Monticello early in 1809 with deep forebodings about the future, and the problems facing his successor and long-time friend James Madison were as grave as any that ever faced a new Chief Executive.

Many productive years remained ahead of Jefferson as he pursued his varied interests at Monticello. He was also to play the role of elder statesman, giving valuable advice to Presidents Madison and Monroe for the next fifteen years. Jefferson and democracy had won permanently over Hamilton and government by "the rich and well-born," but Hamilton's vision of an industrial nation with a strong central government had a better future than Jefferson's dream of a nation of small farmers jealously withholding powers from the government at Washington. The drama played out between the two in the formative years of the republic remains one of the most interesting and important in all of American history.

FURTHER READINGS

Jefferson and Hamilton was the theme of Claude Bowers's older work (1925) and has been the theme of many since. The recent works of unusual distinction include Dumas Malone, *Jefferson and His Time,* a projected four-volume study of which two volumes have appeared—*Jefferson the Virginian* (1948) and *Jefferson and the Rights of Man* (1951). Since 1950, *The Papers of Thomas Jefferson,* edited by Julian P. Boyd et al., one of the major historical undertakings of our time, have been appearing in many volumes (when completed to be about fifty). As for Hamilton, the centennial year 1957 produced several new studies, including the first volume of a large-scale biography by Broadus Mitchell, *Alexander Hamilton: Youth to Maturity, 1755–1788,* and Louis M. Hacker's sympathetic analysis, *Alexander Hamilton in the American Tradition.* Richard B. Morris has edited a useful inexpensive edition of *The Basic Ideas of Alexander Hamilton* (1956). Leonard D. White found a new perspective in his studies of administrative history, *The Federalists* (1948) and *The Jeffersonians* (1951).

Alexander DeConde, *Entangling Alliance: Politics and Diplomacy under George Washington* (1958), supplements older books by Samuel F. Bemis, *Jay's Treaty* (1923) and *Pinckney's Treaty* (1926). Gilbert Chinard, *Honest John Adams* (1933), is a topic continued recently by Stephen G. Kurtz in his *The Presidency of John Adams: The Collapse of Federalism, 1795–1801* (1957). The Alien and Sedition Acts have inspired much historical writing, including James M. Smith, *Freedom's Fetters: The Alien and Sedition Laws and American Civil Liberties* (1956), and John C. Miller, *Crisis in Freedom* (1951).

Jefferson in power after 1801 has also been a fascinating theme. Henry Adams's classic *History of the United States during the Administrations of Jefferson and Madison* (9 vols., 1889–1891) has been condensed by Herbert Agar under the title of *The Formative Years* (2 vols., 1948). Older surveys of this period, such as Edward Channing, *The Jeffersonian System* (1906), and Allen Johnson, *Jefferson and His Colleagues* (1921), are continued in such modern works as Adrienne Koch, *Jefferson and Madison: The Great Collaboration* (1950). Jefferson's leading critic is vigorously championed by Russell Kirk, *Randolph of Roanoke: A Study in Conservative Thought* (1951).

For additional bibliography, see the *Harvard Guide,* sections 131, 132, and 134–137.

EIGHT

The Rise of American Nationalism, 1809 to 1829

1808
James Madison elected President.

1810
Macon's Bill No. 2 becomes law.

1811
Battle of Tippecanoe.

1812
War declared on England.

1814
Hartford Convention meets.
Treaty of Ghent ends war.

1815
Battle of New Orleans.
End of Napoleonic Wars.

1816
*Second Bank of the United States
chartered.*
James Monroe elected President.

1819
Florida treaty with Spain.
Panic of 1819.
Dartmouth College v. Woodward;
McCulloch v. Maryland.

1820
Missouri Compromise.

1823
Monroe Doctrine announced.

1824
Election of John Quincy Adams.

THE BREAKDOWN OF
PEACEABLE COERCION

THE UNPREPOSSESSING James Madison took office as President of the United States on March 4, 1809. Three days before this, Jefferson's policy of embargo on all foreign commerce had been abandoned. In its place a rebellious Congress had substituted the Nonintercourse Act, which legalized trade with all ports of the world except those under British or French control. The boycott would be suspended against either of these that met the condition of ending its violations against our neutral commerce. For a brief moment it appeared that peaceable coercion would now be crowned with success. The British Minister David Erskine was instructed to offer the withdrawal of the British restrictions. Unfortunately, there were some conditions attached, one of which was that the United States must immediately restore nonintercourse with France, with the British navy helping to enforce it. Mr. Erskine did not communicate this condition to the President. Taking the Minister at his word, Madison announced that on June 10, 1809, commerce with Britain would be resumed.

Hundreds of American vessels left for British ports, many not even waiting for June 10. The jubilant expectations of renewed commerce were short-lived. Erskine was recalled by his government for violating his instructions, and his agreement with the United States was disavowed. In deep chagrin at the "Erskine fiasco," Madi-

151

A view of Fort McHenry, Baltimore

Though the War of 1812 was almost a national disaster, the United States emerged from it unscathed and promptly forgot the defeats, remembering only the victories. It led to a new spirit of nationalism. Political partisanship was for the moment forgotten, and James Monroe was elected President virtually unanimously in 1820. At this time the Supreme Court under John Marshall's leadership operated as a potent force for nationalism, increasing the Federal government's powers at the expense of the states. In the aftermath of the War of 1812 it proved possible to announce the Monroe Doctrine, symbol of American "continentalism."

Battle of Lake Erie

President James Monroe

Chief Justice John Marshall

Andrew Jackson at the Battle of New Orleans

son was forced to restore nonintercourse with Britain. Shippers heard the news with bitterness and were loath to obey the proclamation. With the repudiation of the Erskine agreement there passed the last chance of a prompt settlement with Great Britain. Erskine's successor proved to be so insolent that irate citizens cursed him and even threatened him with horsewhipping. He was soon recalled, and for the next two critical years the British refused to send another minister.

The final act of peaceable coercion was Macon's Bill No. 2, passed on May 1, 1810. Earlier measures to bring the European belligerents to respect neutral rights having failed, the exasperated Congress now went to the dubious extreme of placing American influence on the auction block. Macon's bill reopened commerce with both France and England but further provided that, if either of the belligerents repealed its offensive restrictions on American commerce, then the United States would reapply nonintercourse to the nation which continued to blockade our commerce. Napoleon saw an opportunity and directed his foreign minister to inform us that France was revoking the offensive decrees and would expect that either Britain would take similar action or the United States would renew nonintercourse with England. Madison fell into the trap and issued the desired proclamation containing the ultimatum to Great Britain. The President had acted precipitately without any official assurances that Napoleon had withdrawn his decrees. And the French Emperor never actually did withdraw them, as the British foretold. It has been suggested in explanation of Madison's action that it was done to win French support for the American seizure of West Florida. At any rate the occupation of West Florida did occur later in the same

year. On March 2, 1811, Congress ratified the President's stand by passing a new nonintercourse measure against Great Britain, and the last hope of avoiding an open break disappeared. Ironically enough, this was done despite a very rapid increase of our commerce under the Macon bill, and despite the fact that more than half our foreign trade was with Great Britain.

It is easy to write off peaceable coercion as harebrained and impractical. But there was a sound basis for the assumption that withdrawal of the trade of the greatest neutral nation might actually bring the European belligerents to respect our rights. Neither America nor Britain wanted war over the issue of trade. In fact Minister Erskine had been most anxious to avoid one, and both nations were eager to restore commercial relations. The hasty action of the British Foreign Secretary in disavowing Erskine's agreement was not a denial of England's desire to trade. Americans themselves never gave the embargo policy a real chance to succeed, although the policy was originally supported overwhelmingly in Congress and favored by most of the state legislatures. The embargo hurt American merchants, planters, and farmers, but it hurt Britain also. Her falling exports and rising debt led to increasing economic and political discontent. Petitions that poured in upon Parliament revealed real distress, with closed factories, unemployment, forced sales, and malnutrition as some of the common results of hard times. English manufacturers, faced with the loss of American markets, began to clamor for the withdrawal of trade restrictions, and on June 16, 1812, two days before Congress declared war, it was announced that all restrictions would be suspended. Formal action was taken on June 23. The expectation was that the United States would now repeal nonintercourse, but Congress had declared war on June 18. Why, then, was not the war halted before military operations actually commenced?

CAUSES OF THE WAR OF 1812

There is no simple explanation for the War of 1812. Many seemingly contradictory factors contributed to its causes. The close vote of 19 to 10 for war in the United States Senate indicates the measure of disagreement. Certainly the protection of our neutral maritime rights and the upholding of the principle of freedom of the seas were major issues. To have the right to export our products and to insist on the freedom of our ships from seizure and our sailors from impressment appealed to Americans everywhere as a question of our national honor. Even a congressman from Tennessee, far from the seacoast, called upon the country to recover impressed seamen "from British slavery," to procure indemnity for property "wrongly captured and condemned," and "to secure and irrevocably fix that grand maritime principle 'that free ships shall make free persons and free goods.'" Westerners as well as easterners resented the impressment of thousands of American seamen as an intolerable outrage against all Americans. Few appreciated or cared about the fact that thousands of British seamen deserted to serve under the more acceptable conditions of the American navy. At no time during the negotiations, which started as soon as the war began, did the British express any willingness to renounce the policy of impressments. The Czar of Russia, who, early in 1813, sought to effect a reconciliation between the opponents, found the British adamant on the issue. Certainly British unwillingness to make any concession in a matter which

stirred American patriotism must be regarded as a major reason for continuing the war. Resentment was further inflamed by the firing upon American ships and the resulting death of some of our seamen.

On the other hand, the greatest opposition to both the embargo and the war itself came from the maritime sections of the country which, it would seem, suffered the most from impressments and seizures. New England shipowners became much more excited about American restrictions on commerce than about British hindrances to it. The election of 1812 featured the war issue and found all New England except Vermont, together with New York, New Jersey, and Delaware, voting solidly for DeWitt Clinton, while the southern and western states cast their ballots for Madison and war. Once the war started, New England Federalists denounced it, and extremists among them even proposed secession from the union and withdrawal from the war. It is certainly a paradox that a war presumably waged for the commercial interests of the country was denounced by those very interests.

Maritime causes, however, are insufficient to explain western and southern enthusiasm for the war. People in these areas, particularly in South Carolina, suffered from falling prices and economic stagnation resulting from a decline in their export trade. British policies, and also those of Napoleon, were blamed for ruining their markets. Therefore, as time went on, a prolonged economic depression became a major factor in arousing the war fever. It is significant that South Carolina, Georgia, Tennessee, and Kentucky, all seriously affected by the economic decline, voted unanimously for war.

Westerners were also directly concerned with the Indian danger and with land hun-

INDIAN LAND CESSIONS

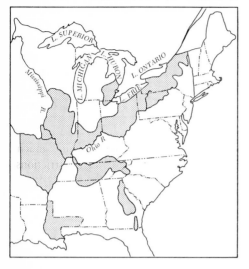

ger. The steady encroachment of the whites upon the preserves of the Indians made it evident that the latter were fighting a losing battle. A series of Indian treaties, culminating with a purchase of 3 million acres in 1809, pushed the white man's frontier far up the valley of the Wabash River in Indiana. Other and larger cessions in the half-dozen preceding years had given the United States title to eastern Michigan, southern Wisconsin, and most of Illinois. The over-all result was the loss by the Indians of nearly 110 million acres of their hunting grounds by bribery, intimidation, corruption, the playing of one tribe against another, and dealings with individual chiefs. Particularly distasteful was the 1809 cession, which aroused the Shawnee leader Tecumseh and his one-eyed medicine-man brother, known as "the Prophet." For several years these two had been traveling from tribe to tribe with the purpose of uniting the Indians from the Gulf to the Great Lakes in a vast confederation. There were to be no more tribal cessions, and a united front was to be presented to the white man. In

1808 Tecumseh established headquarters in "the Prophet's town," on the Wabash River. He established connections with the British at Malden, in Canada, across the river from Detroit. The Indians were convinced that British aid would be forthcoming in any new contest with the whites. The Wabash cession was the final straw. Tecumseh denied its validity in the light of the new Indian organization, which forbade cessions by individual tribes. To William Henry Harrison, governor of Indiana Territory and the man immediately responsible for Indian policy, Tecumseh's opinions meant nothing. But the Indians were in dead earnest, and soon a border war was in full swing. Canadian authorities, alarmed at the prospect of a general war, sought to restrain the warlike young braves. So did Tecumseh, as long as Harrison refrained from surveying the recently acquired Wabash lands. Meantime Tecumseh continued to organize his confederacy and urge resistance to further encroachments by the whites. His departure to organize the southern tribes gave Harrison his opportunity to inflict what he hoped would be a crushing defeat upon the Indians. Marching up the Wabash from Vincennes, Harrison's forces were surprised by an attack just before dawn on November 7, 1811. In the ensuing battle of Tippecanoe, defeat was averted when the more numerous and better-armed Americans rallied in time to beat off the attackers. They pressed their foe until the Prophet's town was abandoned, and then, before returning to Vincennes, they destroyed it.

The victory of Tippecanoe was not a decisive one. Harrison could not follow up his advantage, and even the Prophet's town was soon rebuilt. Tecumseh, to be sure, suffered a setback and never completed his grand design of a confederacy.

But instead of ending the Indian wars, the defeat at Tippecanoe aroused the red men to widespread attacks along the frontier. Whether or not there was any British complicity in inciting the Indians made no difference. To westerners it was enough that Harrison reported captures of English rifles and ammunition on the battlefield. There could be only one solution to this danger—the conquest of Canada.

Reports of Tippecanoe came just after the Twelfth Congress assembled in November of 1811. In this Congress seventy members sat for the first time, and prominent among them was a group of young westerners and southerners including Henry Clay of Kentucky and John C. Calhoun of South Carolina. These men represented the rising generation, and they immediately took control, Clay becoming Speaker of the House. John Randolph not improperly dubbed them the "war hawks." They were full of the spirit soon to be known as "manifest destiny." Clay openly called for the acquisition of Canada in order to acquire the fur trade and put an end to Indian warfare. He even announced that the Kentucky militia could do the job singlehanded. Such talk was popular in the West.

Associated with the demand of the westerners for Canada was the cry of the Southwest for both Floridas; the occupation of a portion of West Florida in 1810 had only whetted an appetite for the rest.

There is evidence that southern and western leaders were sometime interested in a deal that would bring about the successful culmination of their plans and that a tentative bargain was made, but it either broke down or had not included enough men to make it effective. Northern opposition defeated southern plans to annex Florida. Southerners shied on the issue of apportionment in Congress. If Canada were admitted it would increase northern strength in Congress out of all proportion to what the South would gain from the Floridas. The most vigorous pressure for annexation of Canada came from Congressman J. A. Harper of New Hampshire. Harper tried to get a pledge that Canada would be retained if it were conquered by the Americans. Significant too was the proposal of "war hawk" Congressman Peter B. Porter of New York for a provisional army of 20,000 men that could be used outside of the United States. Obviously this was to ensure the conquest of Canada, for state militias could not be relied upon to fight on foreign soil.

It is clear that both West and South were in an expansionist mood and were determined to extend our borders to the north and south. This may not appear logical in view of the fact that a large portion of the Ohio Valley was still unsettled in 1812, but popular demands are not always logical. So far as the Southwest was concerned, West Florida contained important river outlets for Alabama and Mississippi, an economic factor of some significance. East Florida was also an annoying sanctuary for runaway slaves. Thus western support of the war in 1812 may be explained by a variety of causes, ranging from national honor to Indian problems, land hunger, desire for the fur trade, and hope of forcing the British to remove restrictions on trade. The westerner was a man of action, and in that section there was solid agreement that the time had now come to end mere talk. Surely the stalwart frontiersmen could sweep aside the arrogant and decadent British!

THE WAR OF 1812

But the anticipated victories were not so easily won. If the United States did not

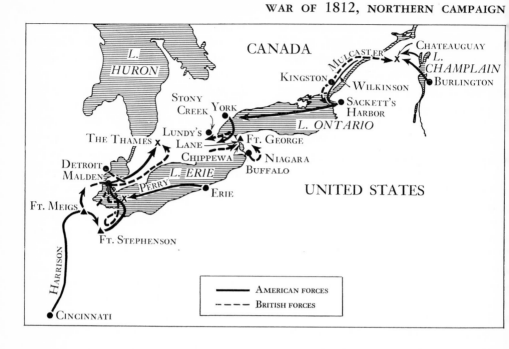

lose the war, most certainly it did not win it. By a stroke of good fortune Britain's principal enemy was Napoleon, who tied down the greatest portion of her military might. Indeed, in the same month of June, 1812, in which the American Congress declared war, Napoleon led a vast army into Russia. The fate of Europe hung upon the outcome of this campaign, and until Napoleon's defeat in Europe in 1814 ensured the safety of the Continent, the America war could not be taken very seriously. By that time, American control of the inland lakes made ultimate British victory doubtful, and Wellington ("the Iron Duke") counseled against full-fledged military operations to defeat America. There was little promise of power or glory to the war-weary British in the prosecution of the American war.

With such excellent prospects for victory, the American preparations for war were almost unbelievably halfhearted.

Even in a divided nation, there was no excuse for such a complete lack of military preparations. A regular army of some 36,-000 had been allowed to degenerate into a force of about 6,700 men, many of them raw recruits. These forces were stationed in garrisons from Mackinac in Michigan to Lake Champlain in New York. The principal generals were old and incompetent. One, James Wilkinson, whose past career verged on treason, had to be removed from command for incompetence. Another was so inept that at the very beginning of the war he surrendered Detroit to a force half as large as his own, losing his baggage and all the war plans therewith. It was not until the third year of the war that competent American commanders emerged.

The militia proved a most unreliable fighting force. In 1812 they refused to follow General Dearborn, another second-rate commander, in an invasion of Canada from the Lake Champlain area. When a call for volunteers to increase the regular army by 25,000 men was made, the response was so disappointing that the main reliance had to be placed on the militia. The President was authorized to call out 50,000 militiamen for federal service, but less than 10 per cent of the desired number responded to the call. As a result, the army had an aggregate strength of from 30,000 to 35,000 out of a population of about 1 million of military age. The maximum number of troops in any battle was about 4,000. Fortunately, the Canadian forces opposing the Americans were usually even smaller in number. Meanwhile, Congress, apparently not aware of the magnitude of the task, showed a great reluctance to vote money for the war. A request for additional funds for naval construction was defeated, and so we challenged the queen of the seas with some sixteen ships of war, plus a number of small one-gun boats suitable only for coastal defense, and whatever response might come from volunteers for privateer duty. Although the Treasury was empty and the war was on, Congress decided to postpone any increase of taxes, which left popular or bank loans as the only recourse. The charter of the United States Bank had been allowed to expire in 1811, which made bank borrowing more difficult. In 1813 Congress was forced to revive the Hamiltonian system of excise taxes; even a stamp tax was eventually levied. The war increased the national debt by about 80 million dollars.

To the handicaps of an incompetent military leadership, an inefficient military system, and an indifferent Congress was added serious national disunity. New England was disgusted with "Mr. Madison's war" and supported it as little as possible. The section subscribed far less than its

logical share of government loans and traded illicitly with the British in Canada. The governors of Massachusetts, Connecticut, Rhode Island, and Vermont refused to allow the President the power to call out their militia. Later in the war New England's discontent came to a climax with the Hartford Convention, which adopted a report stressing state sovereignty and proposing seven amendments to the Constitution, some of them aimed at the war powers of the President and the federal government. The Hartford Convention was ill-timed, coinciding as it did with news of Jackson's victory at New Orleans and the signing of the peace treaty. It must be conceded that some of the other states showed as little disposition to surrender their militia to the central government as did New England, but no other group matched the embittered Federalists of that section in their dislike of the whole business.

American strategy in the assault on Canada was badly coordinated. There were four obvious points of invasion: at Detroit, at Niagara, at the head of Lake Ontario, and from Lake Champlain toward Montreal. In each year of the war the principal military operations were launched in these areas. But in 1812, improper coordination and incompetent leadership, along with poor troop morale, caused failure at all four points. By 1813 incompetents were being weeded out, lessons had been learned, and better results were secured; yet bitter setbacks were to come. An important victory of 1813 was the recapture of Detroit, after a battle along the Thames River, by General William Henry Harrison, who had replaced the inept General Hull. This triumph removed the British and Indian threat from the entire area and paved the way for a rapid subjugation of the Indians along the Ohio River.

Meanwhile, the heroic Oliver H. Perry was defeating the British gunboats on Lake Erie with a fleet built at Erie, Pennsylvania, winning the vital mastery of the Great Lakes in a furious battle (September 10, 1813), after which Perry sent to Harrison his famous message, "We have met the enemy and they are ours." The battle of Lake Erie, coupled with Harrison's victory, compelled the British to abandon Detroit and Fort Malden. Command of the Lakes was to prove a decisive factor in the outcome of the war.

There were no other successes in 1813. A two-pronged advance from Lake Champlain toward Montreal met with reverses because of the incompetence of General Wilkinson, of whom a great American general was to write a two-word opinion:

WAR OF 1812,
CHESAPEAKE CAMPAIGN

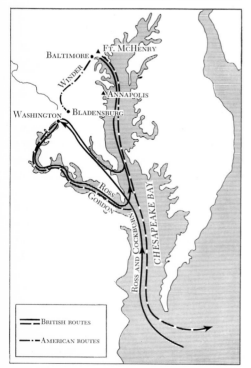

"unprincipled imbecile." Wilkinson was finally retired in the spring of 1814, ridding the command of the last of the incompetents. New and vigorous commanders in 1814 and the development of a body of seasoned troops gave promise of greater success in that last year of the war. There were limited successes at the battles of Chippewa and Lundy's Lane, where the Americans gave a good account of themselves, and American forces advanced into Canada from Niagara. Unfortunately, at the same time, the war in Europe drew to its close, and the British fleet began to bring over seasoned veterans of the European wars. An expedition sailed into Chesapeake Bay, marched toward Washington, routed the green militiamen sent to oppose them, and, one August evening, arrived at the capital, from which the government officials and many residents had fled. The Capitol, the President's house, and the executive offices were burned in retaliation for the burning of the Parliament House at York by Americans in 1813. From Washington the British sailed up the Bay to attack Baltimore, where they encountered sterner opposition and failed to reduce Fort McHenry by bombardment—an event which inspired the writing of "The Star-Spangled Banner." Meanwhile, an unusually formidable British army of 11,000 men invaded New York by the Lake Champlain route. National morale seemed to be sinking—the government's flight from Washington was a serious blow to the national spirit—and the New England states seemed ready to secede and make a separate peace. At this critical moment, young Captain Thomas MacDonough won a brilliant victory over the British lake fleet on Champlain. Control of Lake Champlain was decisive. The British retreated, and two days later they also abandoned the assault on

WAR OF 1812, JACKSON'S CAMPAIGNS, 1813–1815

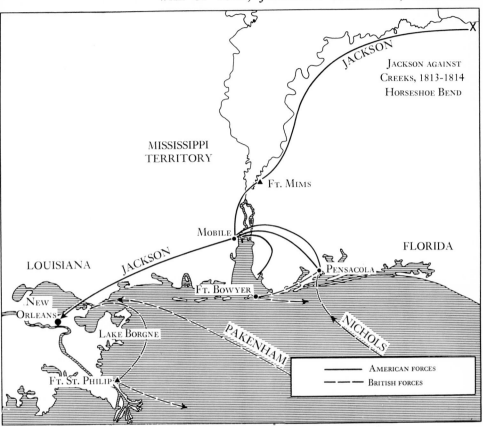

Baltimore, the two attacks having been part of a pincers movement.

There was another and final British offensive late in 1814. It was aimed at New Orleans and, possibly, control of the mouth of the Mississippi. The Gulf expedition, based on Jamaica, included fifty vessels and an army of 10,000 veterans. General Andrew Jackson, commander of the southwest military district, was off fighting Indians—his chief occupation—when the Jamaica expedition left for New Orleans, but he hurried back just in time to make preparations for defense. Jackson did a masterful job. During the ensuing engagement, the well-planned defense arrangements and superior American artillery fire

brought an overwhelming victory. The British were driven off with heavy losses, Jackson was a national hero, and from a very dubious war the United States had at least salvaged a great victory, and the last one. As a matter of fact, the battle did not affect the outcome of the war, for the treaty of peace had already been signed; had there been a cable, the battle would never have been fought. Yet the victory did much to salve the nation's wounded pride.

In complete contrast to the failures of the army in most of its campaigns, the deeds of the navy brought everlasting fame to that branch of the service. A dozen of the American ships were as good as any in the world. The commanding officers were superb. But as a fleet the sixteen seagoing vessels of the navy were unable to cope with the great sea power of the British, even though for the Royal Navy the American war was a diversion. Only five ships, including the *Constitution,* were left at the end of the war. All these were bottled up, and the British could bring reinforcements and supplies to our shores at will. The navy operated mostly far from our shores, the ships fighting sometimes singly, sometimes two or three together. Battles were fought in the far North Atlantic, off the shores of Africa, off the coast of South America, and occasionally in Britain's home waters. Significant indeed was the supremacy of the Americans in these engagements wherever the opponents were approximately evenly matched. British communications were so harassed that it was necessary to maintain a large convoy service to protect the slow-moving freighters of the West Indian trade. Heavier still was the blow to British pride as the tradition of the invincibility of her navy was shattered.

An important chapter was written by the hundreds of privateers that scoured the seas. The war reactivated unused ships and idle seamen. Profits were alluring, but risks were great and losses were heavy. Of more than 500 privateers sent out during the war, less than half took any prizes and only 60 were afloat under the American flag when the war ended. Although the privateers diminished greatly in numbers, their audacity never lessened. They carried the war to the very gates of the British ports, where one privateer burned fourteen vessels. Such activities were more irritating than damaging in view of Britain's vast trade, but they did contribute to Britain's war-weariness and subsequent desire for peace.

PEACE NEGOTIATIONS

When peace came, it was not the result of any clear-cut military decision. The only such victory was that of Jackson at New Orleans, which came after the treaty had been signed. With the ending of the Napoleonic Wars in 1814 the maritime policies and disputed questions of international law which had contributed most directly to the outbreak of war became dead issues. After that, both sides realized that it would be pointless to continue the indecisive contest. Direct negotiations began at Ghent in the Low Countries in August, 1814. The United States was fortunate in having such very able commissioners as John Quincy Adams, Henry Clay, and Albert Gallatin. They were more than a match for their British opposites. At one time the British demanded the erection of an Indian buffer state south of the Great Lakes, the cession of an area in northern New York and eastern Maine, and control of the Great Lakes through demolition of American fortifications and our relinquishment of the right to maintain armed vessels there. The Americans rejected these extreme demands, and the British at length abandoned them all. Their failures at Baltimore, and especially at Lake Champlain, deterred them; moreover, the European situation seemed threatening to Britain even after Napoleon's final defeat as the victorious allies quarreled among themselves at the Vienna peace conference. The treaty signed at Ghent on December 24, 1814, left all disputes for future settlement. It simply ended the war with mutual restitution of conquered territories and war prisoners. There was not a word about neutral rights or other disputed questions. These were left to settle themselves or were referred to commissions of adjudication. It was "peace in its simplest form," but it was welcome. The Senate approved t unanimously on February 15, 1815.

If the negotiations at Ghent left all major issues unsettled, not many years passed before most of them were liquidated. In April, 1817, Richard Rush concluded an agreement with the British Minister Charles Bagot regarding naval vessels and military establishments on the border lakes, which allowed each power one gunboat on Lakes Champlain and Ontario and two on each of the other Great Lakes. Too much has perhaps been made of the Rush-Bagot agreement; it did not provide for complete disarmament, and it was not until after the border troubles of 1871 and the Treaty of Washington of that year that the complete disarmament foreshadowed in the Rush-Bagot agreement actually came into effect. In the interlude the fear of war never wholly vanished. Both governments spent considerable sums strengthening their land and sea defenses. Not until after 1871 did demilitarization of the border gradually come to provide the world with a unique example of over 3,000 miles of unfortified frontiers between two nations once hostile to each other.

In 1818 a treaty settled almost all the active remaining disputes with Britain. In addition to extending a commercial agreement of 1815, the question of offshore American fishing rights, one of the bones of contention at Ghent, was adjusted satisfactorily. Although the Maine boundary remained undetermined until 1842, the border from the Lake of the Woods to the Rocky Mountains was established along the 49th parallel. Beyond the mountains, the Oregon country was to be under joint American-British occupation for ten years, subject to renewal, an arrangement which continued until 1846. In all these negotiations the Americans had acquitted themselves well. Above all, they set the precedent for peaceable settlement of disputes which was to govern British-American relations from that day to the present. If there were to be recurring misunderstandings, at least there was to be no more war.

If Americans had not gained a military victory in the War of 1812 they could take pride in the fact that, aided by Europe's dilemma, they had successfully held at bay the world's leading sea power. And they had successfully repelled Britain's effort to impose a disadvantageous and humiliating peace treaty upon the United States. They may not have achieved their boasted ambitions in the war, but they had held their own. The end of a long period of international involvements enabled the young nation, for the first time, to free itself from disturbing foreign issues. At the same time, American prestige was enhanced by the friendly attitude of Britain, which power sensibly did not permit the animosity of two American wars in one generation to warp the vision of her own national interests. This attitude added to the success of the United States in its foreign policy.

British diplomatic support for the United States was a silent factor in the background of our acquisition of Florida in 1819–1821. We had gone to war against Britain in part to acquire Florida; now Britain helped us to obtain it from Spain. During the war the acquisition of Spanish West Florida had been completed, with the reduction of the fort on Mobile Bay in the spring of 1813. Florida had long been an object of American desire, for obvious strategic and economic reasons. In 1810 President Madison connived at an uprising of American settlers, who set up a "Republic of West Florida," which promptly came under the jurisdiction of the United States. Our claim that the region belonged to us as part of the Louisi-

THE FLORIDA QUESTION, 1783–1819

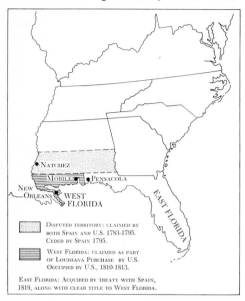

NATCHEZ

MOBILE • PENSACOLA

NEW
ORLEANS • WEST
FLORIDA

EAST FLORIDA

DISPUTED TERRITORY: CLAIMED BY
BOTH SPAIN AND U.S. 1783-1795.
CEDED BY SPAIN 1795.

WEST FLORIDA: CLAIMED AS PART
OF LOUISIANA PURCHASE BY U.S.
OCCUPIED BY U.S., 1810-1813.

EAST FLORIDA: ACQUIRED BY TREATY WITH SPAIN,
1819, ALONG WITH CLEAR TITLE TO WEST FLORIDA.

ana Purchase was flimsy indeed, and the American action was condemned by Britain and Spain. Spain was Britain's ally in the war against Napoleon, a fact which gave a certain justification for our seizure of Mobile in 1813. Completion of the West Florida occupation was the only territorial gain of the War of 1812. But Spain had not recognized our title to it, and, of course, East Florida remained in Spanish possession. The latter continued to be a thorn in the flesh because it harbored hostile Indians, outlaws, runaway slaves, and an assortment of renegades.

Spain was in no position to keep order there because her troops were involved in efforts to suppress rebellions in South America. In 1817 Andrew Jackson led a whirlwind campaign into Florida in which he routed the Seminole Indians, struck at Spanish posts, replaced the Spanish governor with an American, and executed two British traders guilty of inciting the Indians. Here was direct action indeed; but Secretary of State John Quincy Adams,

one of America's great diplomats, was able to turn this questionable action to our favor by pointing out that Spain obviously could not keep order in Florida and hence ought to relinquish the territory. Against this background the Adams-Onis Treaty was negotiated in 1819. Spain formally ceded all of Florida. In addition, this "transcontinental" treaty drew the western boundary of Louisiana in such a way that Spain relinquished her claims to Oregon while the United States gave up any claims it might have had to Texas. The United States compensated Spain by assuming claims of about 5 million dollars held by American citizens against the Spanish government.

The treaty of 1819 was of great significance to the expanding nation. It rounded out our boundaries to the south and east; it contributed to the rapid expansion of the southwest cotton kingdom; it strengthened the American claim to Oregon. Thus, within a few years after the almost disastrous War of 1812, the outlook was again favorable. The rivalries of Europe had once again been exploited to the advantage of the American republic, with the aid of some shrewd and fairly tough diplomacy.

THE NEW NATIONALISM
AFTER 1815

Many developments and policies on the home front bear witness to the emerging nationalism during the generation after 1815. So prominent were the changes and new tendencies that the War of 1812 has been labeled "the second war of independence." Purely American issues began to dominate the political scene, and distinctively American characteristics emerged. The rapid growth of the trans-Allegheny West contributed to the development of democracy and to the creation of new national issues. The birth of what might be called a genuine American spirit reflected a faith and confidence in the destiny of the nation. A new religious fervor, characterized by revivalism and the rise of many new sects, was soon to appear. A new romantic literature was soon born. In truth, after 1815 "new winds had begun to blow over the American people."

Politically, the period immediately after 1815 was marked by the absence of any well-defined opposition party. The Federalist party had died in 1816. The Republican James Monroe, last of the Virginia dynasty, who succeeded Madison in 1817, was reelected in 1820 by an electoral vote that was unanimous except for one elector who preferred John Quincy Adams. Monroe was a President of somewhat limited abilities, but his administration was favored by the fortunes of the time and records some significant achievements: the Rush-Bagot convention and the treaty of 1818 with Great Britain; the Spanish treaty of 1819; the Missouri Compromise of 1820, which averted serious consequences from a dangerous sectional controversy over slavery; and finally the Doctrine of 1823 which was to attach Monroe's name to what eventually became the basic tradition of American foreign policy. The President was unusually fortunate in the caliber of his Cabinet, which included John Quincy Adams, one of the ablest of all America's Secretaries of State, as well as the able William H. Crawford of Georgia and the brilliant John C. Calhoun. Dominating the House of Representatives as no one else ever has was the magnetic Henry Clay of Kentucky, whose long career was to be notable for the great compromises he fashioned in times of crisis. Calhoun and Clay as well as Adams and Crawford had presidential ambitions.

Clay's bitterest enemy and most successful rival was the popular border captain and Indian fighter Andrew Jackson of Tennessee. All these men were nominally members of the same political party, the now unchallenged party of Jefferson, which kept its unity for a few years before breaking up in factional quarrels in 1824. These few years of unity are known as the Era of Good Feeling.

Significantly, the Jeffersonian Republicans, once quite otherwise, now became strongly nationalistic, feeling that there was no other practical course to pursue. Even Jefferson gave his endorsement to the new orientation. Henry Clay became the most influential sponsor of the new national program to which the designation "American System" became attached. So strong was the confidence that the welfare of the nation was anchored to the new program that it received enthusiastic support from congressmen and senators from all sections. It called for a protective tariff, internal improvements, and a United States bank. Thus were introduced the issues which for years would be dominant in American politics. In 1816, even a large minority of southern congressmen, hopeful that their section would profit from industrialism, supported the protective-tariff bill introduced in Congress by William Lowndes of South Carolina.

The embargo and then the war had given a great boost to manufacturing. By 1816 it was estimated that the capital invested in manufacturing amounted to 100 million dollars, of which 40 million dollars was in cotton textiles. That industry had already entered the factory stage. But after the war a great influx of British goods threatened to destroy innumerable small American mills. The tariff of 1816, passed by Jeffersonians, was protectionist enough to have pleased Alexander Hamilton. Ample protection against foreign competition was given to all American industries. Once having tasted the fruits of protection, manufacturers persisted in their efforts to increase duties. They won another victory in 1824 and pressed their advantage to even greater lengths in the so-called "Tariff of Abominations" of 1828. By this time the issue had aroused bitter opposition, especially in the South. Far from uniting the parties, as was hoped in 1816, the tariff had by 1829 turned into the chief cause of sectional animosities.

The second big measure of the nationalists of 1816 was the recharter of the Bank of the United States. Originally granted in 1791 as a part of Hamilton's financial program, the charter of the first bank had expired in 1811. At that time the Jeffersonians, except for a faction headed by Secretary of Treasury Albert Gallatin, vigorously opposed the bank as unconstitutional—even un-American, because of the large number of shares held abroad—and on the grounds that the control of banking properly belonged to the states. Then came the costly and hazardous financial expedients of the War of 1812, which seemed to point to the need for a national bank. By 1816 opposition to the recharter of the bank was overcome. The bill was introduced by Calhoun and passed over the opposition of a combination of old Federalists and unreconstructed Jeffersonians headed by John Randolph of Virginia. The bank was rechartered for twenty years. Hamiltonians watched their erstwhile opponents now set up a bank capitalized at 35 million dollars, or three and a half times as much as the first bank. As in the case of its predecessor, the government subscribed one-fifth of the stock and appointed the same proportion of the directors. The bank was the depository of the United States government funds without paying any interest; in return it transferred public money free of charge. Its notes were receivable for all payments to the United States. It was exempt from taxation. For these privileges it paid the government a $1,500,000 bonus.

The bank very soon became most unpopular in the West. In 1819 a severe "panic," or depression, struck the country. An aftermath of the war, it hit the West especially hard. The easy money obtainable from state banks and the credit system of land purchases under the law of 1800 had both contributed to overspeculation in western lands. Then the bank had suddenly contracted state-bank currency, causing the bubble to collapse. Before long the bank was widely hated in the West as the "monster" which allowed the East to control money and credit and ignore the interests of the western farmer. Another chapter had been added to the long history of agrarian complaints about the money supply; and thus another measure passed in 1816 as a national measure became within a few years a source of sectional friction.

The third item in the new national program was internal improvements at national expense. The establishment of communications with the West was a vital problem. The building of roads and canals appeared to be projects too complicated and expensive for states or private corporations to handle. Yet the rapid growth of the West carried with it the possibility of disunity unless the country could be knit by a system of adequate transportation. The War of 1812 had revealed these inadequacies in a shocking way. By 1816 all that Congress had done was to construct some twenty miles of the Cumberland Road. Although the Constitution gave Congress the authority to provide for the common defense and general welfare and to "establish" post roads, Presidents Monroe and Madison both had strong constitutional scruples against the actual construction, maintenance, and upkeep of roads. Their reason was mainly that national control of the roads would constitute undue interference with the powers reserved by the states. Monroe, however, by 1822 came to the position that the "general welfare" authority of Congress justified appropriations for roads but that a constitutional amendment would be necessary in order to actually construct them.

Such an inconsistent position did not offer a practical solution to the problem. The building of the Cumberland Road, which was subsequently abandoned to the states, represented the extent of the national government's participation in the actual construction of internal communications. Calhoun's bill of 1816 to use the $1,500,000 "bonus" from the second Bank of the United States as a revolving fund for internal improvements passed Congress but was promptly vetoed by Madison. Thenceforth the government's role was principally confined to making surveys for internal improvements and purchasing stock in turnpike and canal companies. Another practice was to make grants of land to aid in various kinds of projects. But here again a national policy was to prove a source of dissension: the West thought the government did not go far enough; the South thought it went too far.

For a moment, however, an Era of Good Feeling seemed to prevail, where all was happy harmony. A look beneath the surface of one-party rule reveals many sources of potential conflict, but these did not burst forth for a few years after 1816. Meanwhile, as a force for nationalism, a strong influence was emanating from an-other direction—from the Supreme Court, dominated by the greatest of Chief Justices.

THE SUPREME COURT AND NATIONALISM

No period in American history is more significant for its Supreme Court decisions than the one under consideration. Many of the greatest decisions of Chief Justice John Marshall fall within its limits. The powers and authority of the national government were extended so as to leave no doubt that the purposes of the founding fathers to establish a "supreme" national government were to be realized. In a series of great decisions, four principles became established as a part of our constitutional system for all time: (1) the authority of federal courts to set aside any state laws in conflict with the United States Constitution or its laws or treaties, even though the highest state court had decided otherwise; (2) the right of the Court to receive appeals, even when a state itself was a party to the action; (3) the right to expand the national power and thereby to further restrict the states by an interpretation and extension of such words as "contract," "commerce," and "legal tender"; (4) the application of the "implied powers" doctrine in favor of the national government in such matters as, for example, the acquisition of territory and the creation of corporations.

An example of the first of these principles was the case of *Fletcher v. Peck* (1810), in which a land grant made by a corrupted Georgia legislature was upheld as valid and a repeal law of a subsequent legislature was set aside as unconstitutional. It was ruled that such a grant of land was a "contract" within the meaning of the Constitution, and no state may invalidate a contract, by the terms of the

Constitution. Many unsuspecting people had purchased the land in question in good faith; hence the validity of these purchases was sustained, despite the bribery of the legislature that had originally passed the law and the desire of the later legislature to erase the stigma of corruption. *Fletcher v. Peck* was the first case in which a state statute was held to violate the Constitution. Within the next fifteen years at least eleven acts of eleven states were pronounced invalid. The decision also exemplifies the third of the aforementioned principles.

The right of the Supreme Court to receive appeals was definitely established in the case of *Cohens v. Virginia* (1821). In this case the state rightfully prosecuted two brothers for selling lottery tickets in Virginia in violation of a state law. When the Cohens appealed to the Supreme Court, the state maintained that under the Eleventh Amendment a citizen could not sue a state. Marshall, however, ruled that in this case the state itself began the prosecution and, therefore, the appeal of the Cohens did not come within the meaning of the amendment. The citizen had not sued the state. On the actual prosecution of the sellers of the lottery tickets the state was upheld, as such sales were forbidden by Virginia's laws. But on the vital issue of the right of a citizen to appeal from the highest court of a state, the national authority was maintained.

The curtailment of the powers of the states is well illustrated in the famous cases of *Dartmouth College v. Woodward* (1819) and *McCulloch v. Maryland* (1819). In the first of these, the Supreme Court interpreted a college charter to be a contract. The state of New Hampshire was therefore forbidden to convert the college into a state-controlled institution, as such a step would have violated the origi-nal charter, which created a charitable school for whites and Indians. Marshall pointed out also that much property had been conveyed to the college on the assumption that this was a private institution supported by private donations. Therefore the property and funds of the college were inviolable as contractual obligations to the donors.

In the same year Maryland was prevented from taxing the notes of the Baltimore branch of the United States Bank when action was brought by the state against its cashier, McCulloch. In this case Marshall found full justification for the constitutionality of the bank. Like Alexander Hamilton, he justified the bank as constitutional under certain implied powers, in that it helped carry out such constitutional functions as paying the debts and establishing the credit of the nation. Furthermore, Marshall held that the power to tax involved the power to destroy and therefore no state could tax any instrumentality or agency of the United States. Notes of the bank were deemed to be in this category; hence the state law was unconstitutional. When, despite the McCulloch decision, Ohio forcibly attempted to tax the notes of branches of the bank in that state, the Maryland decision was sustained. The case of *Osborn v. the Bank of the United States* was really a suit against the state itself, except in the actual naming of the party in the record. Osborn was the auditor of the state of Ohio. Ohio, like Maryland, was forced to yield.

In another of his great cases, *Gibbons v. Ogden* (1824), the Chief Justice forbade the state of New York to grant a monopoly to operate steamboats in the waters of the state. Gibbons was allowed to run his steamboats between New Jersey points and New York on the grounds that he held his license under a law of Congress for regulating coastal trade between states. Ogden's counsel tried to limit "commerce" to the buying and selling of goods. Marshall extended its meaning to embrace commercial intercourse. "Commerce, undoubtedly, is traffic but it is something more—it is intercourse." As such, it included navigation. The emancipation of commerce from state control was completed by the case of *Brown v. Maryland* (1827). In this decision the state was forbidden to require importers to take out licenses. The reasoning was that such licenses were equivalent in effect to levying duties on imports, which was wholly within the domain of congressional powers. Imported goods could not be taxed by a state until they had passed from the importers' hands and entered into general circulation.

One final example of the extension of national authority came in the case of *American Insurance Company v. Canter* (1828), where it was necessary to determine the status of Florida territory which had been acquired from Spain in the treaty of 1819. The Constitution does not specifically empower the government to acquire territory. Marshall, like the Jeffersonians in 1803, found justification for the acquisition of territory under the treaty-making and war powers. The treaty with Spain was now "the law of the land and admits the inhabitants of Florida to the enjoyment of the privileges, rights and immunities of the citizens of the United States." Likewise, Congress had the power to govern the territory and to establish territorial courts by its legislative authority.

The decisions in some of these cases brought violent protests against the dicta handed down by the Supreme Court. This was especially true of the Cohens decision, at which time Virginia editors, publicists, and politicians vented their wrath upon their fellow Virginian who was Chief Justice. The period under review produced many proposals to curb the Court and its power over states. Jefferson, who had clashed with John Marshall as early as 1801 and who had then denounced the "usurpations" of the Court, attacked it again in 1819. He spoke of the "sappers and miners" of the Constitution, who by judicial interpretation were greatly altering that document, always in the direction of greater national power. Certain it is that the Supreme Court made law by the way in which it chose to interpret the often vague and general phrases of the Constitution. But John Marshall's long and amazing ascendancy over the Court and the logical trenchancy of his decisions were difficult to cope with. The question of judicial review, of just how far the power of the Court to override laws passed by states or Congress should extend, remained a most controversial one, destined to crop up on many future occasions, an inevitable result of the "separation of powers" principle in our government. It was Marshall who fully developed the inherent powers of the Supreme Court—powers which some feared as much too great and undemocratic, but which others, usually the conservatives, thought of as an invaluable bulwark against the menace of unrestrained "legislative tyranny."

SECTIONALISM AGAIN: THE MISSOURI COMPROMISE

While Marshall was steadily consolidating the powers of the central government by judicial interpretation, the latent strength of sectionalism was manifesting itself in a controversy which grew out of Missouri's application for statehood. This question agitated Congress from the beginning of 1819 through 1821. Outside Missouri and Illinois there seemed to be remarkably little public concern; the panic of 1819 was of much greater importance to the people. But heated tempers were aroused in Congress and veteran statesmen took a serious view of the threat to national unity.

It was not that Missouri's admission would upset the balance between free and slave states, for such was not the case when the question came up in December, 1818. It is true that the admission of Alabama in 1819 did inject this issue. But what was paramount in the Missouri dispute was geography. Mason and Dixon's line and the Ohio River marked the division between free and slave states. Missouri lay mostly north of that line if that line were to be projected across the Louisiana Purchase. Missouri thus lay in a sphere which the North regarded as rightly its own, and moreover it raised the question of the whole of the Louisiana Territory: if Missouri were allowed to come in as a slave state, would not the whole of that vast area be open to slavery? Missouri was a symbol. The climate and topography of Missouri made it unlikely that it would ever become a great slave state, but each side saw the importance of the precedent involved and looked forward to the possibility of extending its institutions across the Mississippi River.

Representative James Tallmadge of New York set the controversy in motion when in February, 1819, he proposed an amendment to the Missouri bill to permit no additional slaves to be brought into Missouri and to free, at the age of twenty-five years, those children of slaves born after admission of the state to the union. A constitutional debate immediately began: did Congress have the authority to impose restrictions on states as part of the

terms of admission? Was this a violation of the principle of the equality of states in the union? So southern spokesmen maintained, but northerners cited the precedent of the Northwest Territory, where slavery had been prohibited. The debate went on with much acrimony. A southern congressman said that Tallmadge had "kindled a fire which all the waters of the ocean cannot put out, which seas of blood can only extinguish." Something must be allowed for rhetorical exaggeration, but the issue was serious enough. The Tallmadge proposals were adopted in the House but defeated in the Senate, and thus the question was deadlocked.

When the Congress assembled in December, 1819, a bill to admit Maine was presented. In its origin the Maine bill had no connection whatever with the Missouri question. Strong sentiments for separation from Massachusetts had reached a climactic point in the district of Maine, which was grossly underrepresented in the legislature and which also felt that its development was being hampered by its attachment to Massachusetts. The frontier aspect of Maine, with its democratic aspirations, was another factor in the situation. At any rate, the Missouri issue, with the need of a free state to retain the balance now that Alabama had been admitted, made the demands of the people of Maine fortunately opportune in settling the crisis. Obviously the southerners would never vote for a Maine bill unless the restrictions on Missouri were withdrawn. This offered the basis for a compromise submitted by the Illinois slave-holding Senator Jesse Thomas. Missouri was to be admitted without restrictions as a slave state, but there should be no slavery allowed in the remainder of the Louisiana Purchase north of 36°30', Missouri's southern boundary. Thomas's amendment was accepted, as

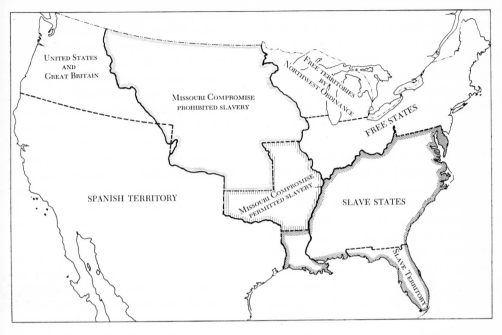

many northern congressmen joined southern members in its support. This compromise was perhaps the best solution that could have been worked out. The 36°30' line set legal limits to the expansion of slavery along a national boundary. The balance of states was kept even, and the South gained Missouri and, for the future, Arkansas. The land north of the line was wild and unsettled country, then considered a part of the great American Desert and regarded as unlikely to be organized for generations. It can be contended that on no other basis but the complete freedom of Missouri to determine her own institutions could the crisis of 1820 have been settled without danger of civil strife. The country was certainly not ready for a crusade against slavery. The Missouri Compromise became a great symbol of the settlement of the troublesome issue of slavery; thirty-four years later, its repeal inflamed passions and contributed directly to the division of the union in 1861.

The signing of the bill by President Monroe in March, 1820, did not quite end the matter, however. A new controversy flared up when in December, 1820, the Missouri constitution was presented for approval. It was found to contain a clause forbidding the admission of free Negroes to the state. This violated the clause of the United States Constitution which guaranteed to the citizens of each state "all the privileges and immunities of citizens in the several states." Another congressional deadlock ensued which was not broken until the adoption of Henry Clay's proposal to have Missouri's legislature agree to pass no law depriving citizens of other states of privileges and immunities to which they were entitled. The Missouri legislature accepted this condition but evidently did not regard it as binding. It subsequently made it impossible for free Negroes to migrate into the state. A minor dispute also arose concerning whether or not Missouri's electoral votes were to be counted in the election of 1820–1821, which took place while all this was going on.

The Missouri issues epitomized the sectional controversy over slavery which was eventually to widen into a complete rupture. For the time being, the stronger forces of nationalism prevailed, but not without arousing heretofore latent apprehensions in each section. For the South, the controversy marked the turn in the road from the natural-rights philosophy of Jefferson's age toward the unbending proslavery orthodoxy that took shape in the decades preceding the Civil War.

THE MONROE DOCTRINE

From 1820 on, the United States had reason to be seriously concerned about the possibility of European intervention in the New World. The ratification of the Florida treaty had been held up for two years by Spanish fear that the United States would recognize the independence of Spain's rebelling Latin-American colonies. Revolution had swept over that region, and there was indeed much popular sentiment in this country for giving help to fellow Americans who were struggling to throw off Old World rule. The larger question was whether the European powers of the Quadruple Alliance (a league of all the great European powers which was an outgrowth of the Napoleonic Wars) might intervene to restore Spanish authority in South and Central America. This alliance was committed to such a policy, and in 1820–1823, Austria and France had crushed revolts in Naples, Piedmont, and Spain. The Alliance was also considering intervening in the bloody Greek uprisings against Turkish misrule. It was rumored that powerful French and Spanish naval forces would be dispatched to South America in order to suppress the new republics there.

America's concern about European intervention in the New World was also related to another development: a Russian edict asserting Russian sovereignty over the entire Alaskan coast and the coastal waters as far south as the 51st parallel in the Oregon country. Americans were not much excited about this Russian edict except for the fact of Russia's association with the Quadruple Alliance. Both these things, however, raised very sharply the question of what the American attitude would be toward such threatening European encroachments.

The British had, in reality, nipped in the bud any possibility that European forces would be sent to South America. In approaching the problem of the Americas, the United States and British governments were in accord on the basic point of protecting the new Spanish American republics. George Canning, the British Foreign Secretary, proposed joint action, which received serious consideration. Even the elder statesmen Jefferson and Madison counseled cooperation with the British. But Canning had proposed delay in recognition of the new republics. Another one of his conditions was that none of these Spanish possessions should be transferred either to Britain or to any other power. This was a self-denying pronouncement which the Americans were unwilling to accept. Therefore, largely by the persuasions of Secretary of State John Quincy Adams, President Monroe decided to make a unilateral declaration. He put this famous declaration in widely separated portions of his message to Congress delivered in December, 1823.

Monroe's message proclaimed the diversity of the political systems of the two hemispheres. In view of this, he announced (1) "that the American continents, by the free and independent condition which they had assumed and maintain are henceforth not to be considered as subjects for future colonization by any European powers . . ."; (2) that, with reference to the newly established republics of Latin America, we would consider any attempts to suppress them "as the manifestation of an unfriendly disposition towards the United States." In order words, this hemisphere was closed to any further European colonization or the extension of Europe's political system. The doctrine did not assert that the newly established governments must be republics but simply extended to them the unimpeded right of self-determination. The Monroe Doctrine is often carelessly represented as a doctrine by which the United States renounced altogether European involvements in favor of a strictly stay-at-home policy. Not only must Europe keep hands off this hemisphere, but, we are told, the United States renounced all alliances and political associations with European nations. But the fact is that Monroe's message really stated that "With the existing colonies or dependencies of any European power, [that is, in the New World,] we have not interfered, and shall not interfere." Then came the warning to European powers that they must not interfere with any of the governments that had successfully revolted. With regard to Europe itself, the doctrine asserted: "Our policy . . . which was adopted at an early stage of the wars which have so long agitated that quarter of the globe, nevertheless *remains the same,* which is, not to interfere in the *internal concerns* of any of its powers; to consider the *de facto* as the legitimate government for us; to cultivate friendly relations with it. . . ." [Authors' italics.]

Monroe, be it noted, refers to this as our *historic* policy which "remains the same." It has continued to be our historic policy not to interfere in the internal affairs of any nation. The doctrine did not state that we should never become involved in European wars. "In the wars of the European powers, *in matters relating to themselves,* we have never taken any part, nor does it comport with our policy to do so. *It is only when our rights are invaded, or seriously menaced,* that we resent injuries or make preparations for our defence." Our interference in the European wars of the twentieth century in no sense violated the principles of the Monroe Doctrine which Monroe stated to be our established policy. In both world wars our rights were menaced or invaded before we became a belligerent. All this is not to say that the Monroe Doctrine was never extended beyond the literal assertions. Indeed, in the century that followed, the doctrine was extended in its application far beyond what Monroe ever intended. In fact, it is not too much to say that it became a shield for a peculiarly American brand of imperialism. Nevertheless its staunch affirmation of American freedom from outside aggression has afforded the most consistent strand in our foreign policy. And certainly it brought an unexpected fame to James Monroe. Yet this historic declaration passed relatively unnoticed at the time. Nor did it command any particular respect abroad. After all, its words meant no more than the enunciation of the views of any President on the foreign policy of his day. The world knew that the United States would have to depend upon the friendly cooperation of the British navy to make the announced policy effective. Only in later years did the doctrine take on great significance as the basic statement of American policy concerning the defense and security of the Western Hemisphere.

AN ERA OF BAD FEELINGS

In 1824 John Quincy Adams was elected President by the House of Representatives. In this election party lines were obliterated. The unprepossessing and politically inept Adams defeated three of the most able public men of the day. They were Andrew Jackson, William H. Crawford of Georgia, and the astute and popular Henry Clay. The latter ran fourth in the electoral vote and therefore was eliminated from consideration by the House. By throwing his support to Adams, Clay assured the latter's election. The alliance with Adams was both logical and natural, despite the charges of bargain and sale by the Jackson supporters. But Jack-

John Quincy Adams, sixth President of the United States. (Library of Congress)

son had received the highest electoral and popular vote, and his defeat in the House aroused his bitter resentment. He immediately began a campaign which, four years later, would sweep him into the White House on a tide of popular enthusiasm without precedent in American history.

John Quincy Adams was a brilliant statesman, though a poor politician. His public career had included early diplomatic appointments to The Hague and to Portugal. He had served in the House and in the Senate, from which his Federalist constituency in New England forced him to resign because of his support of Jefferson's embargo. From 1806 to 1807 he taught rhetoric and belles-lettres at his alma mater, Harvard. President Madison sent him as Minister to Russia, and at the close of the War of 1812 he served as one of the peace commissioners at Ghent. He then served as Minister to England and Secretary of State under Monroe. No man of greater experience or more solid integrity than John Quincy Adams ever occupied the White House. But his cold austerity and his refusal to play the political game, even in such a vital field as patronage, left him with few supporters in Congress. His appearance and personality carried no popular appeal, nor was there anything of the heroic or colorful in his long public life. His four years in the White House were both unproductive and unhappy. He was thwarted on every hand, and every issue was made the occasion to discredit him and further the cause of Andrew Jackson. His broad nationalistic program of internal improvements, which even included a national university and the promotion of science and art with federal funds, brought opposition from the South and only halfhearted support in Congress. His efforts to persuade Congress to participate in a meeting with Latin-American

The Capitol building. Begun in 1793, the unfinished Capitol was burned by the British in 1814 and was not completed until 1830. (Library of Congress)

powers at Panama was subjected to such long delays that nothing ever came of it. The purpose of this Panama Congress included consideration of means to make the Monroe Doctrine more effective and in general to establish closer relationships with the new nations to the south. When the President sought to protect the Creek and Cherokee Indians against ejection by the state of Georgia, he was met by defiance from Georgia and indifference from Congress. Presidential efforts gained a new treaty with fair provisions for the removal of the Creeks, but the more civilized Cherokees were left to the mercies of Georgia and Andrew Jackson, who combined to force their removal westward.

On all parts of his program President Adams was attacked bitterly by the Jackson forces who sought to make political capital for their standard bearer. The recommendation for internal improvements was bitterly depicted as a plan for the further concentration of governmental powers. The Panama Congress was portrayed as boding disaster to the southern states if the nation participated in a congress attended by the delegates from the Negro republic of Haiti and where plans would be discussed to free Cuba and Puerto Rico from Spain and emancipate their slaves. Finally, the tariff of 1828 was devised for the defeat of Adams in the scurrilous election campaign of that year. Its significance was purely political, and as John Randolph sarcastically remarked, the bill had to do with no other manufactures than that of a President.

THE CAMPAIGN OF 1828

Adams's sensitive spirit must have suffered its severest blow in the campaign of 1828. In this rough-and-tumble, knock-down, drag-out political brawl, Adams was accused of having sold a lovely American girl to a Russian prince while he was American minister in St. Petersburg. Accusations of drunken revelry and the keeping of concubines turned the air purple. He was also charged with having gambling tables in the White House and with misappropriating public funds.

The Adams faction also got in some low blows, however. Andrew and Rachel Jackson were accused of having lived together before they were legally wed. The General, it was charged, was no better than a cold-blooded murderer, having killed a man in a duel. As the campaign progressed the charges became more scurrilous.

Through the smoke and heat of the political battle, it became apparent that the Jackson forces were making political capital with three specific charges. The first was the corrupt-bargain charge. The process by which Clay swung his support to Adams for the presidency in 1825 and the subsequent appointment of Clay as Secretary of State in the Adams administration was attributed to a nefarious political deal by which Clay was to be put in line for the presidency. A second charge that served the Jackson forces well was the claim that the Adams administration had stood for excessive centralization of the government. The President's recommendations for internal improvements and a high tariff were evidence of a dangerous tendency towards consolidation, reminiscent of the long-repudiated Federalist doctrines. Such doctrines as these had led to the famous Virginia and Kentucky Resolutions of 1798 that were so important a part of the Republican heritage. And finally, Adams was charged with mishandling the patronage.

As a matter of fact, Adams was helping his opponents along by refusing to appoint to public offices men who were loyally working for his reelection. He insisted that merit, rather than party loyalty alone, was the proper basis for patronage appointments. To make matters worse, some of Adams's staunchest supporters were forced to stand idly by while the Postmaster General, a Calhoun supporter, carefully distributed the postal patronage to Adams's political enemies.

The result of the 1828 campaign surprised few observers. The Jacksonians were swept into office with both a popular and an electoral majority by a combination of the South, much of the West, and the Middle Atlantic states of Pennsylvania and New York. One of our most conscientious and honorable Presidents was defeated by the vast democratic upheaval which marked the arrival of Jacksonian democracy on the national political stage. One of the basic forces in this democratic upsurge was the westward movement and the settlement of the frontier.

FURTHER READINGS

The background of the War of 1812 is analyzed in Louis M. Sears, *Jefferson and the Embargo* (1927); Gaillard Hunt, *James Madison* (1902); Bernard Mayo, *Henry Clay* (1937); W. C. Eaton, *Henry Clay: Adventure in Politics* (1957); and Julius W. Pratt, *Expansionists of 1812* (1925). Volume I of Charles W. Wiltse's biography of Calhoun, entitled *John C. Calhoun: Nationalist, 1782–1828* (1944), and volumes IV and V of Irving Brant's biography of Madison, *James Madison: Secretary of State, 1800–1809* (1953) and *James Madison: The President, 1809–1812* (1956), cast important light on the same period.

Two important Canadian viewpoints on the War of 1812 are Alfred L. Burt, *The United States, Great Britain, and British North America* (1940), who takes sharp issue with Pratt's interpretation, and, on the military side, Charles P. Lucas, *The Canadian War of 1812* (1906).

From the American side, the war itself is surveyed by F. F. Beirne in *The War of 1812* (1949), dramatized by Theodore Roosevelt in *The Naval War of 1812* (1882), and analyzed by Alfred Thayer Mahan in *Sea Power in Its Relations to the War of 1812* (1905). See also H. A. DeWeerd (ed.), *The War of 1812 by Henry Adams* (1941).

A biography of special virtue is Glenn Tucker, *Tecumseh: Vision of Glory* (1955). The diplomacy of the period has been brilliantly reviewed by Samuel F. Bemis in his *John Quincy Adams and the Foundations of American Foreign Policy* (1949). The early career of the "General" has been vividly portrayed by Marquis James in *Andrew Jackson: The Border Captain* (1933). W. P. Cresson has given us a sympathetic biography in his *James Monroe* (1946).

George Dangerfield, *The Era of Good Feelings* (1952), is a well-written account chiefly of the period following the war. Edward S. Corwin's little book, *John Marshall and the Constitution* (1919), in the Chronicles of America Series, is by one of America's great students of the Constitution. It may be compared with W. Melville Jones (ed.), *Chief Justice John Marshall: A Reappraisal* (1956).

The best discussion of the Monroe Doctrine is undoubtedly by Dexter Perkins in *The Monroe Doctrine, 1823–1826* (1927),

New light has been cast on the complex story of the 1820 settlement by Glover G. Moore in *The Missouri Controversy, 1819–1821* (1953).

See also the *Harvard Guide,* sections 137–139 and 142–147.

Westward Expansion: The Frontier Experience

1769–1770
Daniel Boone explores Kentucky.

1788
First settlement in Ohio.

1803
Purchase of Louisiana territory.

1805–1806
Lewis and Clark expedition explores West.

1806–1807
Zebulon Pike explores Southwest.

1815
End of War of 1812 removes Indian danger.

1820
New public land law passed.

1822
Sante Fe Trail opened.

1826–1846
Indians removed to trans-Mississippi West.

1836
Texas gains independence.

1841
Preemption Act passed.

1845
Texas annexed.

1846
Oregon acquired from Britain, to 49th parallel.

1847
Mormon migration to Utah.

1848
*Utah, New Mexico, and California acquired from Mexico.
Gold discovered in California.*

THE FIRST FRONTIER AND THE BIRTH OF SECTIONALISM

SINCE SETTLERS FIRST LANDED upon the Atlantic shores, Americans had been pushing constantly westward. This process, which moved slowly during the colonial period, became a rush after independence was achieved. Whatever the pace of the westward movement, there was, for almost 300 years, always a frontier. The fact of the westward movement, of the existence of a frontier, has been perhaps the most characteristic and continuing feature of American history. One of America's great historians, Frederick Jackson Turner, pointed out more than a half-century ago that much of what was unique about the American experience derived from the expanding frontier. Turner presented the thesis that the greatest contribution to American democracy came from the existence of vast areas of good cheap or free lands, ever beckoning the hardy pioneer. On the frontier life began ever anew, generally under primitive conditions. In this constant reversion to the primitive and in the continuous re-forming and reshaping of institutions which resulted, Turner found the key to the development of the American, as contrasted with the European, way of life. Here man was shaped by his environment, and the product was the American. This thesis may have been overstressed by some historians, and it has received some searching criticism, but there can be no denying that here is one of the

176

great keys to the understanding of American history. In any case, the advance westward remains a story of epic proportions, vast in its magnitude and sweeping in its significance.

We may first set forth the facts of westward expansion before dealing with the fascinating subject of life on the frontier and its significance for American civilization. This movement to the West began, as we have seen, in colonial times. In the region later designated as the Old West, Americans encountered the first truly large-scale frontier problems growing out of the opening of a new area with interests opposed to that of older settled regions. The Old West consisted of the inland towns in New England, the Mohawk Valley of New York, the great Susquehanna and Wyoming Valleys of central Pennsylvania, the Shenandoah Valley of Virginia, and the upland portion of the South known as the piedmont, which lay between the Allegheny Mountains and the fall line of the rivers. In these areas there developed problems, special traits, social and economic patterns, and antagonisms suggestive of the experiences of later frontiers. In fact, such a community of interests existed in this far-flung belt that it is customary to regard the Old West as a single area with distinctive characteristics —to treat it as one region rather than as portions of the separate colonies scattered from New England to Georgia.

In New York, apart from German settlers in the Mohawk Valley, there was little immigration until the Yankee pioneers pushed into the western section, securing land titles from the Iroquois Indians. The vast estates in the Hudson Valley, which had their origins in the Dutch "patroonships," diverted settlement from this region. A few of these estates ranged in size up to a million acres, and the manorial

system existing there placed New York at a great disadvantage in competing for immigrants. In Pennsylvania, on the other hand, a flood of settlers poured into the Susquehanna and tributary valleys during the early eighteenth century; as land prices increased, pioneers pushed southward into western Maryland and the Shenandoah Valley of western Virginia, filtering southward into the back country of the Carolinas. These were mostly Germans and Scotch-Irish, the Germans belonging to many different nonconforming religious sects and contributing to that religious dissatisfaction with established churches which was so typical of the colonial frontier. Of those stubborn and unruly Scotch-Irish Presbyterians we have already heard. By 1760 a zone of Scotch-Irish lightly mixed with German settlements extended along the frontier line from Pennsylvania southward into the Carolinas. A secondary contribution to this zone came with the movement from the older coastal settlements into the piedmont and through the passes into the Shenandoah Valley of migrants who were mostly small farmers, many of them former indentured servants.

The most important consequence of the settling of the Old West was that it established a line of interior settlements which differed considerably from the coastal and tidewater regions. These differences led to antagonisms. Sectionalism had been born. The established coastal society was determined to retain control of the legislatures, and to that end they discriminated against the often more populous frontier. The earliest issue of sectional strife centered about property rule versus popular rule; minority privileges versus majority rights; "natives" versus foreigners. In New England the frontier towns protested against absentee ownership of land by the town

Log cabin near Sidney, Ohio

River scene at Cincinnati, 1853

Dubuque, Iowa, as painted in 1824

An Idaho homestead, photographed in the 1850s

Frontier life in its initial phase was primitive and lonely; its symbol was the log cabin in the forest. Within a generation, usually, towns and cities sprang up. But new frontiers constantly beckoned, and the frontier process was repeated many times as America expanded across the great continent. The cumulative experience left an enduring mark on the American character.

proprietors, against an unfair burden of frontier defense and taxes, and against being compelled to remain in the established towns instead of being permitted to migrate freely. Friction over unfair representation and lack of religious freedom also developed into movements of protest. Some of these conflicts were also prominent in the middle and southern colonies; in addition, the factor of nativism, not found in New England, was important in these colonies. The small farmers of the southern back country were opposed to slavery and unwilling to support an established church. Their society was more democratic than the seaboard's, and they resented political discrimination, which took the form of suffrage discrimination, high property qualifications for officeholders, and unequal representation. Thus the Virginia constitution of 1776 preserved tidewater domination by keeping as many seats in the upper house of the legislature for the east as for the more populous interior counties. In South Carolina, in 1790, the three counties in the low country,

ROUTES WESTWARD, 1800

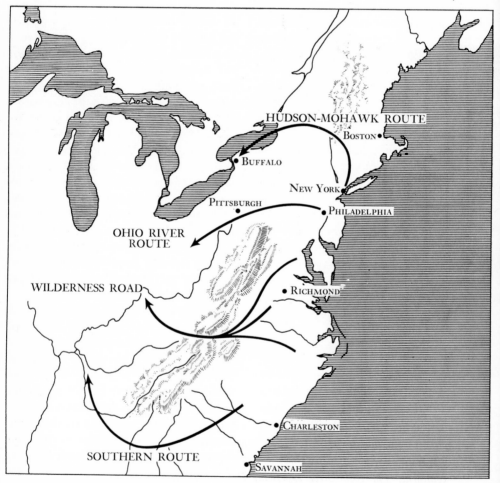

which had two-thirds of the slaves and seven-ninths of the wealth but only one-fifth of the white population, retained a majority of the seats in both houses of the legislature.

Such movements of frontier protest as the Paxton Boys of Pennsylvania in 1764, the Regulators of North Carolina, and the Massachusetts rebellion led by Daniel Shays in 1786 have already been referred to. Thus from very early times did democracy, liberalism, and revolt come out of the West. Later frontiers farther west repeated this pattern. The frontier region was always concerned with equality of treatment under the laws; it was sometimes ready to become independent if need be. It was always prepared to protest vehemently against discrimination.

THE OLD SOUTHWEST

The region between the Appalachian Mountains and the Mississippi River, and just beyond the river, has a certain unity by virtue of climate, soils, topography, waterways, and communications. The pattern of settlement in this vast area therefore showed a considerable uniformity. Within this general unity there were, however, variations of pattern. Thus the region north of the Ohio River developed the diversities associated with a varied economic pattern and with a society untrammeled by slavery. South of the Ohio and extending across the Mississippi into Louisiana, Arkansas, and Missouri, slave labor and staple crops, notably cotton, sugar, and tobacco, conditioned the development of society. They made for a more uniform economy, a more agrarian society, and the existence of a "slave oligarchy." Migration into the northern sections of the West was unimpeded by slavery, and there the familiar characteristics of a free society and

small-farm economy appeared. But at least until the building of canals in the 1830s and 1840s, which diverted commerce north and east via the Great Lakes and the Erie Canal to the eastern seaboard, the Ohio and Mississippi Rivers were the great arteries of commerce and travel, serving to hold the great valleys together north and south sufficiently to warrant treating them as a single region.

Nevertheless, the time of settlement makes it convenient to deal with this area as a series of successive frontiers, the first of which was the Old Southwest. The settlement of Kentucky and Tennessee was predominantly individualistic. In contrast to the Old Northwest, there was no plan for land survey or for organized government before the tide of settlement got under way. Consequently there was much land-grabbing and great insecurity of title. No provisions were made in advance for school lands, as was provided under the land ordinance of 1785. Nor was any previous provision made for organized government, as was done for the region north of the Ohio by the ordinance of 1787. As a result of this haphazard settlement, some of the most notable American experiments in spontaneous state making occurred in Kentucky and Tennessee. Strong tendencies to separate from the United States and join the Spanish empire developed here also.

The settlement at Sycamore Shoals in the Watauga Valley, one of the several streams that contribute to the headwaters of the Tennessee, provides an example of these tendencies. Beginning about 1768 settlers began to drift from Virginia and North Carolina into the Holston and Watauga Valleys. It appears that dissatisfaction resulting from the defeat of the Regulator movement impelled many to make this move. In 1772, in this remote settlement, the Watauga people, headed by James Robertson and John Sevier, drew up a set of articles of association. Under these articles the freemen of the several settlements chose representatives, who in turn selected a committee to carry on government, using the laws of Virginia to guide them. For five years the Watauga settlers managed their own affairs. In 1776, by which time there were 600 people in the community, they petitioned the North Carolina legislature for annexation, which was granted. The Watauga movement is an example of government by voluntary compact, a process which had begun with the Mayflower Compact. It was repeated in many forms in frontier communities, as a typical American adaptation to life remote from settled government.

In Kentucky, the Transylvania settlement, with which the names of Richard Henderson and Daniel Boone are most in-

THE OLD SOUTHWEST AND THE OLD NORTHWEST

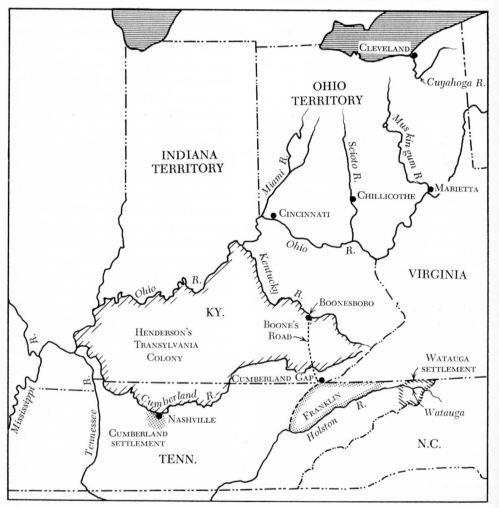

timately connected, made one of the earliest contributions to the settlement of that state. Judge Richard Henderson of North Carolina, one of the enemies of the Regulators, was a typical land speculator and promoter of his day. He engaged Daniel Boone to explore in Kentucky in 1769–1770. The Boones were Quakers who had migrated from Bucks County, Pennsylvania, going south up the Shenandoah Valley and eventually settling on the extreme western frontier of North Carolina. Daniel Boone, who has his place in history as a hunter, trapper, scout, Indian fighter, surveyor, road builder, and lawmaker, here began his role as an agent of colonization. One of that restless class of "foresters" who stayed in the vanguard of pioneer settlement, he found it difficult to settle down, always becoming restless and dissatisfied when population moved in and towns developed. It is characteristic of Boone that his last years were spent on the far western frontier of Missouri, to which he had fled when that region was still a part of Spanish Louisiana. In this, his last haven of refuge from stultifying civilization, he died at an advanced age in 1820, the year of the Missouri Compromise. There were many like him, the explorers, the scouts of civilization, who could not stand civilization themselves.

As Henderson's agent, Boone prepared the way for his principal to carry out colonization schemes in Kentucky. Indian troubles delayed the plans for several years, but in March, 1775, Henderson secured some 17 million acres by a questionable deed from the Cherokees. Meantime the Transylvania Company was formed by Henderson, and liberal terms were offered to attract settlers. Boone had been commissioned to blaze a trail across mountains and forest to erect a fort on the Kentucky River. Here, despite protests from the governors of North Carolina and Virginia, who were themselves heavy speculators in western lands, Henderson planted his colony. The proprietors granted settlers in the Transylvania colony a form of representative government and a degree of popular government, but retained a veto power. Transylvania provides another example of government by compact worked out by pioneers in the wilderness. This colony was short-lived; its bounds included several other settlements of pioneers who had preceded Henderson and who resented his authority, and these earlier settlers moved to get his grant annulled by the Virginia legislature. Their complaints, sent to this body, included such typical frontier grievances as the increase of land prices and the appropriation of all the best lands by the proprietors. It was in the interest of Virginia speculators to forestall Henderson, and so in December, 1776, the Transylvania purchase was voided. Such of its lands as lay in Virginia were erected into the county of Kentucky. As some compensation the proprietors received some 200,-000 acres farther west along the Ohio River.

Established as they were just when the War for Independence was starting, the settlers of Kentucky as well as those of Watauga rendered valiant service in warding off Indian attacks and saving the Old Southwest for the American cause, Boone's skill in Indian fighting being particularly valuable. Henderson soon turned his efforts south into the Cumberland Valley, where Nashville now stands. He sent one of his associates to lead a migration from the Watauga and Holston settlements into the beautiful Nashville bowl. Here, in the spring of 1780, articles of confederation drafted by Henderson were adopted as "a temporary method of restraining the licentious" until North Carolina could extend its authority. In 1783 North Carolina did so.

The most pretentious and significant of the separatist movements in the Old Southwest occurred in 1784. North Carolina had tentatively ceded its Tennessee lands to the United States by that time; the offer was to be withdrawn if not accepted within two years. Fearing neglect and danger from Indian attacks during this period when they belonged to neither the state nor the federal government, settlers in eastern Tennessee took steps to organize a new government. The people of Franklin— for this was the name they gave their new state—proceeded to set up a government with John Sevier as governor, but they were never able to get recognition as a state. Soon there was civil war between the Franklinites and the parent state, with two different sets of officials claiming the authority to govern. Sevier was once condemned for treason by North Carolina; yet a few years later he became Tennessee's first governor, serving six terms in all. The feud came to an end when Congress, in 1789, accepted responsibility for the Tennessee settlements, organized them into the Southwest Territory, and extended to the area the civil guarantees of the Northwest Ordinance, except for the prohibition of slavery. Three years later Virginia gave permission to the trans-Allegheny settlers in Kentucky to become the first state west of the mountains to be admitted to the union; Tennessee followed in 1796.

In addition to his activities as a colonizer and public servant, Sevier was a talented land speculator. Careful research reveals that the Franklin movement was little more than a bitter contest between two groups of land speculators. Separate statehood for Franklin was expected to remove the territory from the control and claims of the North Carolina speculators and give outsiders a chance. Sevier, the apparent leader of the protest movement, was actually playing a double game, with the purpose of blocking the separatist movement. The champion of the West was working for the eastern speculators against the interests of his own people. With such intrigue was the settlement of the frontier filled.

These separatist intrigues were dwarfed, however, by the greater threat that the Kentucky and Tennessee settlements would be lost to Spain. Nearly every one of the outstanding leaders in the Old Southwest at one time or another entered into negotiations with Spanish agents. Their actions, which have the flavor of treason, are better understood as a fight to promote the interests of their section. They invoked the principles of the Declaration of Independence in their defense, for their development was being hampered and their security threatened by distant leaders who denied their desire for statehood and for local control of their most vital concerns. Specifically, their grievances revolved around Spanish control of the mouth of the Mississippi, the great outlet for western commerce. The Spanish influence over the southwest Indians, and the inability of the central or state governments to provide for defense, was another cause for complaint. When, in 1788, North Carolina rejected the new federal Constitution, Tennessee was for a time out of the union anyway; her only allegiance was to the state of North Carolina. Agreement with Spain might solve the difficulties. In the Cumberland settlements, negotiations with Spain had reached such a stage that the settlements were organized into the Spanish District of Miro, named in honor of the Spanish governor at New Orleans. A Spanish conspiracy in Kentucky developed during these years also.

Virginia offered Kentucky statehood four times, and no fewer than ten conventions were held in Kentucky before statehood was achieved and a constitution adopted in 1792 to make Kentucky the fifteenth state in the union. The solution to the problem of the navigation of the Mississippi River in 1795 (Pinckney Treaty) brought an end to the economic crisis which had threatened western secession under Spanish influence. But some years later, after the purchase of Louisiana, the celebrated affair of Aaron Burr and his plot to detach the West from the United States indicated that western discontent was by no means entirely at an end.

THE OLD NORTHWEST

As has previously been noted, territorial organization of the region between the Ohio and the Mississippi Rivers was provided in the Northwest Ordinance of 1787. Although it was at first applicable only to that region, the Northwest Ordinance had a far greater significance in that it served as a pattern for all the territories that were organized after this date. It established principles in the governing of dependent territories that were something new in history. It contained the assurance that the western territories would all eventually be admitted to the American union as free republican states on a basis of equality with the original states. And during this period of preparation there would be orderly government from the outset. the ordinance authorized Congress to provide temporary government, vested in a governor, secretary, and three judges, when settlers began to arrive and to establish communities. In contrast to the region south of the Ohio River, this assured government *in advance* of settlement and made it unnecessary for the pioneers to cre-

ate temporary commonwealths such as those of Watauga and Franklin, already mentioned. The steps provided for on the road from territorial status to full statehood have already been described.* With the exception of Texas and California, neither of which ever passed through a territory status, all the western territories were organized on this pattern of orderly political evolution which the Northwest Ordinance set.

Besides providing for ultimate statehood, the Northwest Ordinance guaranteed in perpetuity full protection of civil rights for the people in the territories. These rights included freedom from arbitrary arrest, trial by jury, judicial proceedings according to law, right of bail, protection of everyone's property by regular judicial processes, full freedom of contract without government interference, and equal division of property among children of anyone who had failed to make his disposition by will. Moreover, full religious freedom was guaranteed to every person, and slavery was prohibited. One of the most magnificent pronouncements of principles of the American system of government is found in the statement: "Religion, morality, and knowledge being necessary to good government and the happiness of mankind, schools and the means of education shall forever be encouraged." These fundamental provisions guaranteeing individual rights could not be repealed and were to be continued even after statehood was granted. Therefore, the Northwest Ordinance was in a real sense a constitution for territories. It laid the foundations of the American territorial system for the entire West, except that southern territories did not accept the prohibition of slavery.

* See pp. 103–104.

A second basic feature of American territorial policy, first applied in the Northwest Territory, was the system of land survey. First embodied in the land ordinance of 1785,* it was incorporated in many subsequent land laws and established the principle of land survey into townships six miles square, each containing thirty-six sections of land. As the Northwest Ordinance of 1787 provided government in advance of settlement, so the land ordinances provided for survey before the settler could establish title. This tended to make for more regular settlement and more secure titles; it also permitted the government to set aside lands for certain specific uses and for future sale. Thus the land ordinance of 1785 reserved one section of everty township for the support of public schools. At the same time it determined that the vast national domain was to be sold primarily to settlers. A big problem, however, was to make the land really available to the poor man and keep it from falling too much into the hands of big speculators. The problem was never satisfactorily solved. As time went on, however, the minimum size of the tract that could be purchased was reduced by 1820 from 640 acres, obviously too large for the average settler, to 80 acres. The minimum price was generally $2 per acre, and to make it easier for settlers, a credit system was established in 1800 which allowed the purchaser three years to complete his payments. The credit system was designed to overcome the pioneer's shortage of cash, but it did not solve the problem and Congress had to pass many relief acts to protect the settler against loss of his land. Finally, in 1820, the credit system was abandoned. The price of land was reduced from $2 to $1.25 an acre and

the size of the tract from 160 acres to 80 acres. Thus, for $100, which might not be easy to raise at a time when the panic of 1819 had brought depression and closed many banks, the pioneer could establish himself on a farm. Additional protection to the small settler was subsequently provided by "preemption laws" which gave him a priority in the purchase of the land he occupied. Finally in 1862 the principle of free land to the actual settler was established in the Homestead Act. Thus the western idea of providing land to the actual settler gradually superseded the older eastern concept of using the land as a source of government revenue.

Ohio was the first fruit of statehood in the Old Northwest. The sale of a vast tract of over 1,500,000 acres to the Ohio Company of Boston, for the sum of 1 million dollars in depreciated Continental currency, provided the first impetus for colonization. The Reverend Dr. Manasseh Cutler, the persuasive lobbyist of the company, not only got Congress to grant a section in every township for schools but, in addition, two entire townships aggregating over 46,000 acres for a university. Grants for public schools, as we have seen, were foreshadowed in the land law of 1785, but the practice of donations for higher education was new and henceforth became an established practice as each new territory or state was organized.

Ohio was the first state north of the Ohio to be admitted into the union. The pattern of settlement there is illustrative of the general process which, with understandable variations, operated in each new territory. The pattern was a cosmopolitan one, drawing its elements from many and various sources. The New England origin of the Ohio Company drew an influx from that section to the first settlement at Marietta on the Ohio River in

* See pp. 102–103.

LAND POLICIES OF THE UNITED STATES, 1785–1862

Date of act	Minimum size of tract	Price per acre	Terms of settlement
1785	One section (640 acres)	$1.00	Cash in specie, loan-office certificates, or certificates of the public debt
1787	One section	2.00	Partial credit: 1/3 cash, balance in three months
1796	Half the townships sold in sections; alternate townships in blocks of eight sections	2.00	1/20 cash, 1/2 in thirty days; balance in one year
1800	Sold partly in sections, partly in half sections	2.00	1/4 cash, balance in four annual installments
1804	Quarter sections	2.00	No interest charges until payments became delinquent
1820	80 acres	1.25	Cash
1832	40 acres (smallest tract ever sold)	1.25	A typical special temporary preemption act
1841	160 acres	1.25	Permanent preemption act of general application lasted until 1891
1854	First graduation act to reduce price of unsold lands on graduated basis		
1862	160 acres	Free	Title after five years of residence and meeting minimum requirements of cultivation

1788. A second New England area was in Connecticut's Western Reserve along the shore of Lake Erie where, in 1796, the settlement of Cleveland began. In the western part of the reserve, lands were donated by Connecticut to inhabitants of towns that had suffered from British depredations in the Revolutionary War. Many Pennsylvanians drifted into the eastern part of the reserve, thus introducing a substantial German and Scotch-Irish element. Important communities developed just across the Pennsylvania boundary, which in time became highly important industrial centers.

By a strange turn of events a considerable French community came into existence at the western edge of the Ohio Company's purchase. This was associated with the activities of a group of speculators known as the Scioto Company. The Scioto group, promoted by Manasseh Cutler, counted among its members congressmen and government officials, including the Treasurer of the United States. The results were unfortunate. The plan was to sell lands to Frenchmen anxious to escape the French Revolution by flight to America. A land office was opened in Paris, but the whole transaction became honeycombed with fraud. The five or six hundred ill-equipped Frenchmen who, after many hardships, finally reached Ohio found that they were on lands belonging to the Ohio Company, for which they had to pay a second time. The Scioto venture was disastrous for all concerned.

Because of their geographical proximity to Ohio, and because they had no reserves of land west of the Appalachians, the middle states of Pennsylvania, New York, New Jersey, and Delaware contributed the largest portion of settlers to Ohio prior to 1840. Cincinnati, which was one of the earliest and most important settlements on the Ohio River, got its start in 1788 when

one of the territorial judges, who was from New Jersey, secured a huge option on lands in the Miami Valley. By 1850, Cincinnati was a thriving city of over 100,000 and was the principal packing center of the West. Its only rival in the entire Mississippi Valley was New Orleans.

The southern element in Ohio was second in size to that of the middle states. Virginia, in particular, contributed heavily to this influx because the state retained some 6,500 square miles as bounty lands for families of its veterans. The Virginia Military Tract extended from the Ohio River far up through the Scioto Valley. It was quickly settled, and its principal town, Chillicothe, was for some years capital of Ohio, both as a territory and a state. Chillicothe was a strong center of Virginian influence, and its leaders were very

THE OHIO COUNTRY

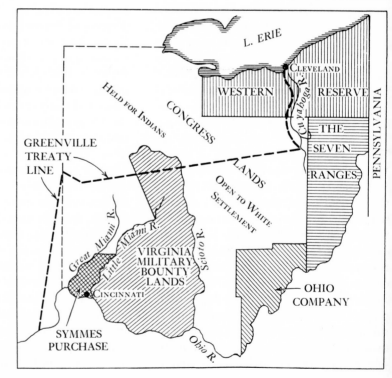

active in politics. It was also on one of the most important highways of the Middle West, connecting Pittsburgh and the Kentucky settlements. Settlers from the South spilled across into southern Illinois and Indiana, too. So many southerners migrated to Illinois that they were able to have slavery legalized in the first constitution (1818).

In 1800 the Northwest Territory was divided into two sections, Ohio and Indiana. Three years later, against the bitter opposition of the Federalists, who tried to delay the admission of another state that would strengthen the Jeffersonians, Ohio gained admission to the union. Thus it was the first state formed under the provisions of the Northwest Ordinance and set the pattern for the future growth of the union. Its first constitution, which lasted for nearly a half-century without amendment, was notable for its democratic provisions. Although the governor was elected by the voters, he was regarded with distrust. This suspicion of the executive was a logical outgrowth of experiences with the governor sent out by Congress and clothed with arbitrary powers in the territorial stage of government. His powers were rigidly limited. He had neither the veto nor appointing power. The legislature appointed all major civil officers, as well as the judges. Its extensive powers were checked by annual elections. Minor officials were elected. The Ohio bill of rights reflected the prevailing liberalism. The phraseology of its preamble echoed the words of the Declaration of Independence. Besides the usual guarantees of individual rights as embodied in the Northwest Ordinance, Ohio forbade involuntary servitude in the form of long-term labor contracts. Imprisonment for debt was forbidden in cases where a debtor had surrendered his estate to the creditor. Poll taxes were prohibited. There was to be no discrimination against poor people in schools supported by public lands. Neither compulsory church attendance nor official preference to any religion was allowed. One staunch Federalist who did not like the constitution sarcastically wrote: "It begins with we the people, and if we may judge from the judiciary Article few Constitutions were ever so bepeopled as it is throughout."

The many peoples and many cultural aspects of Ohio were typical of the entire Ohio Valley. From New England came the Yankee shrewdness in business, the Puritan morality, an interest in reform, an appreciation for education and learning, an interest in the church, and the township form of government. The southerners brought in an agrarian tradition, displayed much interest in political affairs, and held to the diversions of horse racing and lavish hospitality. The large element from New Jersey and Pennsylvania reflected the religious interests of Scotch-Irish Presbyterianism and the educational influences of Princeton College. All the major evangelical sects found hospitable environment in Ohio, and many of the small sects, notably the Shakers, Moravians, and Quakers, established their communities and missions there. The Catholics soon organized their parishes on solid foundations in cities and towns. There were also many European influences from groups like the French, Welsh, and Germans. This fusion of peoples and cultures, drawn from the older seaboard regions and Europe, freed men from their state localisms and provincialisms. They were no longer Virginians, Pennsylvanians, and New Englanders, but in the new atmosphere of the expanding West, they became Americans. In all these ways, and many others, Ohio was typical of middle-western development. What went on there was to be repeated again and again in middle America and beyond.

TO THE MISSISSIPPI AND BEYOND

A new Southwest developed apace with the Northwest. Drawn by the lure of cotton profits and by the speculative fever and aided by travel routes such as the Natchez Trace (from Nashville to Natchez) and the Federal Road, which led to the Southwest via the piedmont, settlers poured into Alabama and Mississippi after the War of 1812. Both territories were soon admitted to statehood. The Indian problem of the Southwest was more difficult than that of the Northwest. Defeat of the Indians by Andrew Jackson in 1814 and the cession of valuable lands in Alabama was followed by the removal of such civilized tribes as the Cherokees and Creeks. This removal to reservations in the Indian Territory was a feature of Jackson's policy after he became President in 1829; it was carried out with much cruelty and brutality. It was an agreed principle of the frontiersmen that the Indian had no rights which the white man was bound to respect. This cruel uprooting of the Indians completed, a new wave of migration swept in after 1830. During the first rush, nearly 5 million acres of land were sold in Alabama and Mississippi in the five years after 1815. The panic of 1819 checked migration for a time, but as soon as cotton prices began to recover, the advance was renewed. Settlers pushed across the Mississippi into Missouri and Arkansas. Soil exhaustion in the seaboard states contributed to the movement, and millions of new acres were taken up; the populations of Mississippi, Arkansas, and Missouri tripled in a decade. The rich tobacco lands of Missouri attracted immigrants chiefly from the older communities of Kentucky and Tennessee. The seaboard states of the Southeast, from which came most of the immigrants into the "cotton kingdom," barely held their own in population. This later migration included a considerable number of plantation owners with their slaves, and soon—an extremely significant process—the small farmers began to be crowded out. The cotton kingdom was being created.

At the same time, removal of the Indians after the Blackhawk and Winnebago wars cleared the way for further settlement of the Northwest after 1832. The opening of the Erie Canal in 1825, followed by a rapid increase of steamboats on the Great Lakes, made access to this area from New England and New York easier. Hundreds of towns were laid out in northern Illinois in the decade 1830–1840. At first the newcomers chose wooded areas, to which they were accustomed, as the most desirable sites. Only when latecomers were forced on to the flat prairies was the value of these fertile lands realized. Iowa soon had a line of towns along the Mississippi. Michigan Territory, hampered early by inaccessibility, Indians, bad administration, and a bad reputation concerning agricultural possibilities, flourished after the completion of the Erie Canal. It became a state in 1837, followed within a few years by Iowa and Wisconsin. Until 1837 virtually all the lands in the area that later became Minnesota belonged to the Sioux Indians, and the only commercial interest was a flourishing fur trade. As soon as the first cessions were made by the Sioux, lumbermen planted themselves in the St. Croix Valley. Pioneer farmers followed the lumbermen; the progress of Minnesota was marked by the supplanting of the fur trade by lumbering in the decade of the 1840s and the establishment of agriculture on an independent basis in the 1850s. The growth of Minnesota was phenomenal; by 1858 it had attained statehood.

Minnesota's admission completed the roster of states in the Mississippi Valley. Beyond this tier of states the pioneer encountered new and unfamiliar environments. There stretched a vast tilted plateau which gradually ascended to an elevation of 5,000 feet at the foot of the Rocky Mountains. Most of this region embraced the Great Plains, with their rich grasslands giving way to scantier and sparser vegetation as one proceeded westward into the semiarid regions of brush grasses, desert sagebrush, and mesquite. Lack of rainfall and of forests forced many new adjustments on the settler. His old tools were inadequate. So unattractive and difficult did farming and living on the Great Plains appear that migration for the most part passed over them and proceeded to the more attractive environments of Oregon and California. The Great Plains were to be the last American frontier. Pioneers were content to leave them to the Indians and the buffalo until there were no other frontiers to settle.

The great Rocky Mountain barrier fortunately could be crossed easily through the wide South Pass, reached by the most famous of all western routes which ran along the course of the North Platte and Sweetwater Rivers. Between the Rockies and the Pacific were the Columbia plateau and, farther south, the great plateaus of the Colorado River—mostly hot and dry, awaiting a program of water conservation and irrigation to make these millions of square miles of desert useful. But there were extremely attractive and fertile basins on the Pacific Coast. Above the Columbia River lay the fertile Puget Sound trough, and south of that river the broad, alluvial Willamette Valley of Oregon. To the south, in California, were the contrasting lush, productive coastal strip and the arid Great Central Valley of the interior.

Two famous exploring expeditions contributed much to the opening of the Great West. The first of these was the great Lewis and Clark expedition, conceived and sponsored by Thomas Jefferson even before the United States purchased the vast Louisiana Territory from Napoleon. The expedition, led by young Captain Meriwether Lewis, Jefferson's private secretary, and William Clark, followed the Missouri River 1,600 miles to near the present town of Bismarck, North Dakota, in 1804, and then in the spring of 1805 followed the Missouri to its source. They crossed the Continental Divide, obtained horses from the Shoshone Indians, and with the aid of a heroic Indian woman, made the difficult descent of the west slope of the Rockies into entirely unfamiliar country. The final stage of the famous expedition took the explorers by way of Clark's Fork of the Columbia to the trail through the Bitter Root Mountains to the north branch of the Clearwater, thence to the Snake River and the Columbia, reaching the Pacific Coast in November, 1805. They wintered at the mouth of the Columbia. Only one life had been lost on this remarkable voyage. On the return trip to St. Louis, Clark explored the Yellowstone while Lewis descended the Marias from the north. The expedition had carefully collected data and made maps and charts. Lewis and Clark gave much encouragement to the fur trade by their glowing reports on the upper Missouri and Columbia

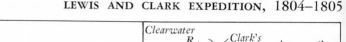

LEWIS AND CLARK EXPEDITION, 1804–1805

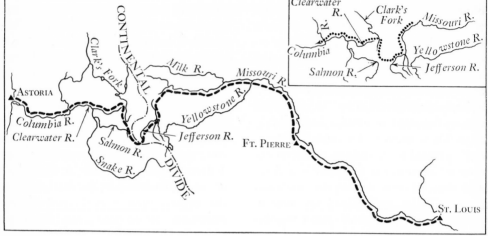

regions, which they considered the world's richest fur areas.

In 1806–1807 young Zebulon Pike, already a famous explorer, traversed the country drained by the Arkansas and the Red Rivers. Pike erected a post near Pueblo, Colorado, and discovered the great peak which bears his name, though he was unable to reach the summit. Traveling southward in search of the Red River, Pike reached the Rio Grande by mistake. Here he was made prisoner by the Spaniards, and his books, papers, and maps were taken from him, not to be recovered for a hundred years. It is possible, though not certain, that Pike's expedition was connected with the schemes of Aaron Burr, that political adventurer who fathered a plot at this time to further his fortunes and possibly to detach the western areas from the United States. Pike's explorations were of great importance. His report printed in 1810, based on notes concealed from his captors, aroused so much interest that it was reprinted in Dutch, French, and German editions.

No group was more important in the early history of the Far West than the fur trader. Between 1796 and 1822 the government maintained factories or trading posts, but finally it withdrew from the field. Operating from St. Louis, the Missouri Fur Company, organized in 1809, was the earliest of a number of private western companies. For a while it was a most important one, but it met with bad fortune which greatly restricted its activities. The next of the famous fur companies was the Rocky Mountain Fur Company, organized in 1822. Among its partners Jedediah Smith, a fervent Christian who carried his Bible as well as his gun always with him, was a renowned trail blazer. His explorations opened thousands of square miles of the central Rockies in the Wind River Valley, the Green River Valley, and the Salt Lake basin. In 1826, with a few men he made the arduous journey through desert and across mountains from Salt Lake to southern California. Later he traveled up the Central Valley and through the coastal mountains to Oregon. He, and not John C. Frémont, deserves the title of the "Great Pathfinder" of California. It was a partner of this company who drove the first loaded wagon from the Missouri via the Platte and Sweetwater to the rendezvous at South Pass—the entrance to the Oregon Trail.

But the most successful of all fur traders was John Jacob Astor. This German immigrant boy, who came to Baltimore in 1784 virtually penniless, had by the end of the century amassed a fortune estimated at $250,000—colossal for that time. It had increased to 20 million dollars at the time of his death in 1848. It was Astor who sent the first ship to the northwest coast in 1810, establishing the post of Astoria at the mouth of the Columbia River. He also sent an overland expedition, along a dangerous route, which helped to mark the Oregon Trail. Astoria was sold to the British during the War of 1812, but it was restored in 1818, at which time Britain and the United States agreed on common occupancy and exploitation of the Oregon country. Astor's American Fur Company went on to become the great corporation of its time, developing an almost complete monopoly of the fur business of the upper Missouri Valley. It had great posts at the mouths of the Yellowstone, of the Marias, and of the Bighorn, and it established the first steamboat connections with the upper

THE OREGON TRAIL AND THE OLD SANTE FE TRAIL

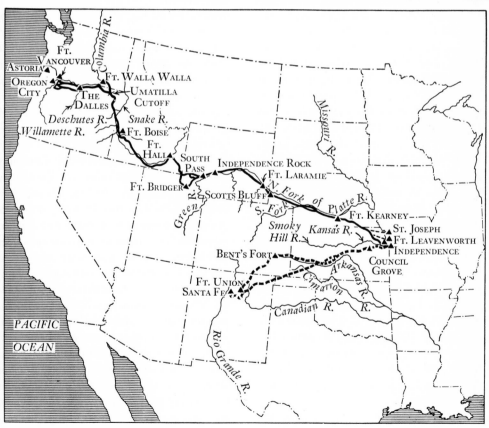

Missouri. The Astor company was bitterly hated by competitors, was regarded by independent traders as an oppressive monopoly, and was supported by a powerful and assiduous political lobby at Washington. It reaped enormous profits. Its trappers and agents explored widely throughout the Rockies and blazed trails that later emigrants were to follow in settling the Far West.

Meanwhile other traders were pushing into the southern plains and mountains to establish trade with the Indians, sometimes in defiance of Spanish and Mexican authorities. A regular caravan trade developed with pack mules along what was known as the Old Spanish Trail from Santa Fe and Taos to Los Angeles. Santa Fe, a drowsy little town hundreds of miles from the nearest settlement, had been founded in 1610 by the Spaniards. It had become the seat of the Spanish provincial government. Zebulon Pike had aroused the interest of Americans in the commercial opportunities there, and Santa Fe became the seat of a flourishing commerce with the American border towns. The prairie caravans carried cotton and woolen goods, shawls, velvets, cutlery, and hardware and brought back silver, furs, copper, and mules. Trading expeditions were organized as early as 1812, but the early traders generally met with misfortune. Some of them were seized as spies and imprisoned; others had their goods confiscated. After the establishment of Mexican independence in 1821 the trade began to flourish. A new and shorter route across the desert was discovered in 1822. Wagon trains drawn by oxen or mules were soon traveling this trail in long caravans, the wagons being drawn up at night in a hollow square for defense. This commerce, which at first was enormously profitable, came to be taxed heavily by the Mexican government, but

nevertheless continued to grow. The big annual caravan of 1846 comprised over 400 wagons with merchandise valued at $1,750,000. In that year American troops occupied New Mexico and it became American territory.

FAR-WESTERN FRONTIERS

What was known as the Oregon Country originally included all territory between 42° and 54°40′. As finally determined in 1846, the American portion extended to the 49th parallel on the north; subsequently the states of Oregon and Washington and Idaho were carved out of this imperial domain. There was a long history of conflicting claims to Oregon. At one time Spaniards, Russians, British, and Americans all laid claim to it by virtue of discovery and exploration. By 1825 America and Britain were left as the sole claimants, Spain having withdrawn south of the 42nd parallel as a consequence of the Florida treaty of 1819, and Russia having retreated to Alaska north of 54°40′. In 1818 America and Britain agreed on joint occupation of Oregon. It was in fact the great British Hudson's Bay Company that constituted the principal obstacle to American possession. For over a hundred years after its founding in 1670, the Hudson's Bay Company enjoyed unrestricted monopoly in exploiting the vast resources of Canada, except as it was challenged by the French, whose title was extinguished in 1763. In 1821, the Hudson's Bay Company absorbed its principal competitor and emerged as a most powerful and well-organized commercial monopoly. Its position was nearly unassailable, and for years it dominated the Columbia River Valley and the Puget Sound basin. Its headquarters were at Vancouver, where the benevolent but firm Dr. John Mc-

Loughlin ruled with a strong hand and successfully resisted all American efforts to break the company's monopoly. The company's activities were widespread, including in addition to the fur trade such things as agricultural development, stockbreeding, salmon fishing, lumbering, and milling. Its contributions in laying the economic foundations of this northwest region were of great benefit to the later American settlers.

No wonder, then, that the British were reluctant to yield their claims to this rich region. But, from the 1830s on, American interest in Oregon grew, and thousands of people began to migrate there. The famous Oregon Trail led from Independence, Missouri, via the North Platte and Sweetwater, through the broad South Pass in Wyoming to the winding Snake River, and thence through the Blue Mountains into the welcome valley of the Columbia. The distance was great, but propaganda stimulated interest in this far-off paradise. Early expeditions to Oregon met with indifferent success. They were not able to break the control of the powerful Hudson's Bay Company, whose agents and traders thwarted them in all their efforts. Not until the coming of the missionaries were the Americans able to establish permanent settlements. In the early 1830s the Methodists established a mission station in the Willamette Valley which proved to be more important as a factor in American colonization than in giving religious instruction to the Indians. They organized a joint-stock company, recruited capital and settlers, and agitated for American control of Oregon. Presbyterian and Catholic missionaries also took an interest in Oregon. In 1843 Marcus Whitman made a famous ride back east to prevent the closing of the Presbyterian mission stations, a ride which brought Oregon to the attention of many Americans. Jesuit missionary influence became important after 1840.

As a result of this widespread publicity, thousands migrated to Oregon in the 1840s. An Oregon fever swept the country, fed in part by the hard times which followed in the panic of 1837. This heavy American migration was the decisive factor in establishing our claim to Oregon as far as the 49th parallel, the boundary agreed upon by Great Britain and the United States in 1846. In 1848 Oregon Territory was organized, and five years later the northern part became Washington Territory. By that time there were 20,000 persons in the Oregon Territory, mostly in the Willamette Valley. In 1859 Oregon became a state.

There was no more significant movement northwest than that of the Latter-day Saints, perhaps better known as Mormons. While the Oregon pioneers were taking the trail to the Pacific Northwest, the Mormons were building a new Zion in Utah. Their remarkable story begins with the vision of Joseph Smith, who claimed that an angel of God had appeared before him in person, revealing to him the golden plates which became the Book of Mormon. This native-born religious sect was subject to constant persecution which was quite out of harmony with the religious liberty of the frontier. From their place of origin in upstate New York, the Mormons went on a hegira which led successively to Ohio, Missouri, and Illinois. Everywhere they were persecuted, and they suffered considerable losses in both lives and property. The explanation for this persecution may be found in the untrammeled authoritarianism characteristic of the Mormons, deriving from Smith's claim to have established his church under direct authority and instruction from the Almighty. This was not in accord with frontier in-

Under the powerful leadership of Brigham Young (above) the Mormons, driven out of Illinois in 1846 by mob violence, made their way to the shores of Great Salt Lake in Utah. Here their industry and zeal overcame extreme hardships. Below, the Mormon Tabernacle before its completion in 1867. (Church of Jesus Christ Latter-day Saints)

dividualism; moreover, the Mormon practiced polygamy, resented as immoral They invariably prospered but just as in variably incurred their neighbors' wrath

In 1844 the prophet was murdered b an enraged mob at Carthage, Illinois Smith's murder gave the Mormons a mar tyr, and Mormonism gained more follow ers as its devoted missionaries carried it gospel far and wide. In Brigham Young the Mormons found a new leader of out standing ability. Young laid plans to lead his people across the plains to a place where there would be peace and freedom from persecution. During the winter of 1845–1846 the Mormons began to prepare for the new migration. Near Florence, Ne braska, perhaps 15,000 refugees gathered during 1846 with wagons, cattle, tools, and other equipment. In July, 1847, Brigham Young and an advance guard reached the valley of the Great Salt Lake, which Young decided the Lord had destined for the seat of Zion. Fields were staked off The fresh-water creek was dammed to

THE MORMON FRONTIERS, 1830–1840

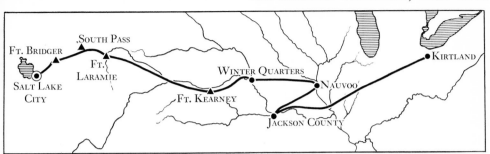

wash the salt and alkaline from the soil and begin the irrigation of the valley. The site of a temple was chosen, and preparations were made for the arrival of the first refugees.

The migration that followed was the best organized of any such movement in our history. The Mormons even had agents in Europe to assist emigrants, especially skilled mechanics and craftsmen. Despite all the great care they exercised, the Mormons met extreme difficulties and hardships during the first years. Indeed, the colony might have perished but for the discovery of gold in California in 1848. During the great gold rush which followed, Salt Lake City became a halfway station on the road to California; Mormon laborers and merchants reaped good profits repairing wagons and selling horses, and the church even organized a transportation company to carry freight and passengers from the Missouri River to the Pacific Coast. Although the Mormons organized the state of Deseret with Young as governor and applied for admission to the union soon after the Mexican War had transferred Utah to the United States, many years were to pass before Utah was admitted as a state (1896). In the 1850s President Buchanan waged a veritable "Utah war" against the Mormons, the outgrowth of friction between United States

officials sent to Utah and the stubborn Mormons under Young's vigorous leadership. The question of polygamy was long a troublesome one. Not until 1890 did the church submit, after a federal law passed against polygamy in 1882 caused hundreds of Mormons to be jailed.

The Mormons' secret of success lay in community cooperation, under direction of the church, leading to a social integration rare in frontier communities. The welfare of each member was the concern of all. At first, every individual was required to surrender his property to the church, retaining only what was necessary for his own support, while the surplus was used for the needy. Later this system was supplanted by tithing, or devoting one-tenth of one's income to the church. The church supervised the location of settlements and irrigation projects. Moreover, the Mormon Church took over the direction of cultural and literary life. Newspapers, societies, musical organizations, and other social groups remained under the surveillance of the church. Particularly strict was the careful supervision over the activities of the youth. In a day when the theater was generally tabooed by religious sects, the Mormons made it an ally of the pulpit and an instrument for building character and improving the tastes of the community. So different from the dominant theme of frontier individualism, these socially conscious Mormons, who made the desert bloom and managed to enjoy life too, occupy a wholly unique place in the history of westward movement, one that testifies to the limitless variety of frontier experience.

One of the last, and perhaps most colorful, westward pushes before the Civil War was the California gold rush. No movement in all American history surpasses it in drama. California had not yet been officially transferred from Spain when gold was discovered in the millrace forty miles from Sutter's Fort in January, 1848. As reports from California were verified, excitement mounted in the eastern states, and some of it spread to Europe, to South America, to Australia, even to China. In 1849 thousands of gold seekers flooded the village of San Francisco, which had a population of about 800 before the gold rush. The town was almost emptied at first as the inhabitants rushed to the mines, but before long it was booming and afforded fabulous business opportunities.

Most of the gold seekers took the perilous overland trail to California, at the risk of untold suffering in the torrid deserts

Mission of San Luis Rey de Francia, one of a score of Spanish missions built in California in the eighteenth century. (Library of Congress)

and sinks between Salt Lake and the Sierra Nevada. The carcasses and bones of dead animals and the graves of countless pilgrims lined the California trail. More than 5,000 perished from cholera alone. Those in no great hurry might take the long sea voyage around South America, which took six to nine months. There was also a Mexican gold trail; but the easiest, shortest, and most crowded route was via Panama. On this journey one was at the mercy of native guides and boatmen across the Isthmus, and one had to await one's turn for an overcrowded, insufferable boat from Panama to San Francisco. But none of these difficulties halted the flood of men drawn by the lure of gold.

The inrush of miners made the problem of government a pressing one. After the treaty with Mexico was ratified on May 20, 1848, it was expected that Congress would organize regular territorial government; but this question became so involved with slavery and sectional conflict in Washington that nothing could be done until the summer of 1850. In the meantime, the miners themselves organized their local governments and drew up mining regulations. In September, 1849, the Californians held a convention at Monterey, organized a state government, and set it up without waiting on Congress. The Compromise of 1850 admitted California and broke the balance of free and slave states.

The coolheaded businessmen, shrewd lawyers, and scheming politicians of San Francisco were likely to have an easier time making a fortune than the miners who panned gold as they stood knee-deep in streams under a blistering sun. In the early years of the gold rush conditions were chaotic. Prices were exorbitant; small frame houses rented for $2,000 a month, and all sorts of tents and shacks provided shelter. There were no public services at first. Streets were unpaved. Businessmen preferred to auction off their goods on arrival rather than hold them in the face of wild and unpredictable price fluctuations. Lawlessness and crime flourished, and to meet this situation, decent elements of the community formed a Vigilance Committee to administer quick justice. Five years later, in 1856, the committee was reorganized after the murder of a United States marshal and a public-spirited editor. The criminals were hanged. The underworld was thoroughly tamed so long as the Vigilantes maintained their organization, which included several thousand well-equipped members. This method of administering justice was to become a feature of mining camps throughout the Rocky Mountain region.

THE FRONTIER EXPERIENCE

From Puritan and indentured servant to Mormon and bearded miner, from Bacon's Rebellion to Vigilance Committee—it is time to consider the impact of this whole frontier experience upon the American character and American institutions. If Frederick Jackson Turner was right, it was the most significant experience in American history. From any viewpoint, it has left its enduring mark. One might first ask, in attempting to sum up the meaning of the frontier, "What were the characteristic conditions of frontier life?" They were, primarily, hardship, danger, isolation, and monotony. The struggle for existence was likely to be hard and the temptation to lawlessness strong. The frontier exalted the qualities of individualism and of personal worth. Daring, courage, initiative, and self-reliance bordering on recklessness characterized the westerner. The remark of Roy Bean, who in the 1880s dispensed liquor

with one hand and Texas justice with the other, "west of the Pecos," was doubtless exaggerated but carries a wealth of significance: "Everything is perfectly peaceful here," he told a visitor, "there hasn't been a man killed in four hours." Life was rough; but opportunities were unlimited, and the ideal of the self-made man took firm root. If the frontier often produced the type of Billy the Kid, only the American frontier could have produced an Abraham Lincoln.

"Do you think I could remain here and be a common man when I can go there and be a judge?" In this remark of a New Englander is revealed the pull which drew a legion of ambitious young Americans westward. Where land was easily available and where the opportunity to start life afresh beckoned constantly, ideals shaped by equalitarianism and individualism became deeply planted. Equality and opportunity were here not merely ideals, but living realities. Arriving penniless, one might soon be a man of substance. Or, if luck refused to smile, one might move on and try again.

All things were possible in such an expansive world, and so the spirit of the West was a thriving, hustling, boastful one. Its legends and its heroes were of gigantic proportions; the superman and the "tall tale" flourished. The frontier created the legend of Mike Fink, the keelboatman, who could drink a gallon of whisky a day and shoot a tin cup off a man's head at thirty paces, shooting from between his knees. "I can outrun, outhop, outjump, throw down, drag out, and lick any man in the country," Mike boasted. "I'm a salt-river roarer, I love the wimmen, and I'm chock full o' fight!" Out of the Minnesota woods came a similar giant, Paul Bunyan, and in the Southwest the legends of vast prowess clustered around Davy Crockett.

Nothing was more typical of the spirit of the frontier than the steamboat races, where, with reckless disregard of flimsy boilers and collisions, the boats vied for speed records amid immense popular excitement. Competition was the life of the frontier; it loved all kinds of contests, from cornhusking to the less innocent "no holds barred" fights, and including horse races, cockfights, and shooting matches.

But if competition was a main theme, so was gregariousness. The loneliness and monotony of much frontier life made it natural for the settlers to seize upon every possible occasion to satisfy their social instincts. They were prone to make a great occasion of the arrival of a new settler. They helped him build his cabin, cutting down trees and toting logs in what was likely to become a competitive event. The women took advantage of the "logrolling" to gossip and prepare a bountiful repast for the workers. The gregarious instinct also combined with the competitive at harvesting and husking time. Sugarings, housewarmings, weddings, quilting parties, and sewing bees provided opportunities for social contacts and display of skills. Weddings were apt to be celebrated by dancing parties which lasted far into the night to the tunes of the local fiddler, as whisky flowed freely. The twice-yearly local "militia musters" were big events for the whole family. When small towns appeared, county court days invariably attracted large crowds, partly because of interest in the trials but more for the sake of "visiting" or participating in some competitive match. Taverns became centers for the dissemination of culture as well as of social cheer. The social life of frontier people in the early years was largely a by-product of their need for assistance in performing the tasks necessary to their existence. Social life for its own sake came

later, when the country had become more thickly settled, and the most arduous labors of pioneering had been completed.

The reckless, whisky-drinking, even lawless spirit of the early frontier was soon opposed by forces of order, morality, and respectability. No frontier institution is more significant and more interesting than the church. Religious leaders on the frontier developed new techniques to cope with the problem of isolation and sparsely settled communities. These were the traveling preachers, known as "circuit riders," and the camp meeting. The Methodists particularly excelled in these new institutions and consequently reaped a good harvest of members; the phenomenal growth of the Methodist Church was largely a product of its success in bringing religion to the frontier. Using a system of circuit riders and local lay preachers, the Methodists found also, as did other frontier sects, that their teachings were well adapted to frontier life. Often uneducated, the ministry preached to the emotions rather than to the intellect; their direct fire-and-brimstone sermons could be understood far better than those of men better trained in theology. They emphasized salvation by work and faith, the equality of all men in the sight of God, and the freedom to make one's own choice. These teachings found a congenial response on the frontier, where self-help and substantial equality were every man's experience.

The great camp meetings were usually held in late summer and early autumn, and people came great distances to attend these "revivals." They brought provisions and camped out for a few days or even a week as preaching went on in tents or out in the open. Under the flickering torches and candlelight, amid the deep shadows of night, the direct, lusty, fear-arousing message of the preachers created the wildest

:motionalism. The "jerks" would spread ike a contagion until hundreds might be affected simultaneously by this muscular eflex. Those affected would sometimes lrop prostrate and lie for hours in a coma. Others shrieked and were convulsed, writhing and screaming. There was a tendency to appraise the genuineness of a conversion by the amount of violent physical activity which accompanied it. Religious ecstasy was so contagious in these revivals that it frequently spread to mere curious observers, and "those who came to scoff, remained to pray." In the course of time, however, the cruder and more violent aspects of the camp meeting in a given area wore off, and worship became more orderly and disciplined. The revivalism of the frontier is explained by the nature of the frontier environment: one of hardship, fear, monotony, and limited cultural and recreational outlets. Frontier people often exhibited profound religious imagination and deep emotional instincts, and these were encouraged by the passionate, uneducated preaching. The camp meeting came to be more than a focus for religious life; it was a center of social life, even a place of entertainment very welcome to people whose lives were so filled with toil and loneliness.

From the churches also came civilized restraints upon moral laxity and lawlessness. So rigid was the Methodist opposition to the use of intoxicants that this church became synonymous with the temperance crusade. The innumerable congregations afforded discipline and opportunities for training in leadership. Frontier ministers brought in books, sermons, tracts, and hymnals. There was a Methodist printing press as early as 1789, supplying religious literature to the frontiers. Beyond any doubt, this frontier religion, crude as it sometimes was, was the chief civilizing agent that "helped tame backwoods America." The Baptists, with their democratically organized churches and unpaid, uneducated but fervent ministers, also met with astonishing success on the frontier. Presbyterians and Congregationalists, significantly, suffered because of their insistence upon a well-educated clergy with thorough theological training. An insight into frontier life may be found in the greater percentage of small religious sects there than existed in older settled areas. For a variety of reasons, the small religious groups have always found the frontier environment more congenial. They attracted people on the economic fringe, and they often appeared as the spearhead of protest against both social injustice and theological exclusiveness. Some of them practiced varieties of community living, little experiments in "socialist" planning— "backwoods utopias." If a schism developed, a part of the group might leave to move farther westward and thus contribute another group to the increasing number of tiny sects who insisted upon going to Heaven in their own way— typical frontier individualists. The history of such sects as the Quakers, Dunkers, and Mennonites is filled with schisms that have fragmented the original body, and which reveal an ever-westward-shifting center of gravity.

Thus the frontier encouraged individuality and nonconformity. But as frontier conditions yielded to a more settled life, these sects tended to move on or to relax the vigor of their peculiarities. In longer-settled regions, the values of civilized life tended to be emphasized, and with that emphasis came a demand for more education. This demand produced the small denominational colleges which soon came to dot the middle-western countryside. Most of these colleges were established just as the frontier was ceasing to be a frontier; in the Middle West, from Kentucky to Michigan, the small-college era closed just before the Civil War, while in the trans-Mississippi region it continued until the 1880s. As frontier conditions wholly passed, scores of small schools went out of existence. The principal purpose of their founders was to provide adequate religious training along with the usual classical education. Many survived, and these denominational colleges expanded the opportunities for higher education in America, contrasting strongly with the limited number of universities in Europe.

And so civilization was re-created from primitive beginnings on the frontier, emerging as something distinctly American. What a wide variety of traits which are "typically American" can be gleaned from the frontier experience! The good as well as the bad: crudeness, acquisitiveness, a bumptious equalitarianism, a contempt for fine manners, and a respect for practical competence, but also simplicity, generosity, a plain and fervent faith in

God, individualism, a strong sense of family and group community, an aggressive patriotism, an optimistic nationalism—the list might be extended. Certainly the Old World was much farther away on the frontier, and the New World much newer —a place of infinite opportunity for the man bold and energetic enough to seize it. That "new man" whom Crèvecoeur had seen dimly emerging on the frontier of New York in 1780 was completed in the West. He was a unique creature indeed, somewhat disconcerting to European travelers who came to sniff at this strange new democratic society, but recognized by many of them as a new and striking type. Subtle and abstract thought was not his strong point, for he had his answers and did not need to search for them in metaphysics. Strength and energy were his virtues. He believed American civilization to be the best in the world and was prepared to take part in its endless expansion. He was also ready to challenge the political supremacy of the American East in the name of a more democratic political faith.

FURTHER READINGS

George R. Taylor (ed.), *The Turner Thesis* (rev. ed., 1956), contains the most satisfactory critical analysis of this subject. F. J. Turner, *The Frontier in American History* (1920), contains the principal essays of the proponent of the frontier thesis.

Very useful texts are R. E. Riegel, *America Moves West* (3d ed., 1956); Ray Billington, *Westward Expansion* (1949), unusually rich in detail, analysis, and bibliography; and most recent of all, Thomas D. Clark, *Frontier America* (1959), with a new and unique approach.

On Kentucky and the Old Southwest, see John Bakeless, *Daniel Boone: Wilderness Scout* (1939), and A. Henderson, *Conquest*

of the Old Southwest (1920). On the Old Northwest, typical of the many books are W. C. Buley, *The Old Northwest: Pioneer Period, 1815–1840* (1951), which has much social and cultural material; B. W. Bond, *Civilization of the Old Northwest* (1934); and Randolph Downes, *Frontier Ohio* (1935).

Louis Wright, *Culture on the Moving Frontier* (1956); Charles A. Johnson, *The Frontier Campmeeting* (1955); Everett Dick, *The Dixie Frontier* (1948); and W. B. Posey, *Methodism in the Old Southwest, 1783–1824* (1933), are significant.

Typical studies and literature on a few of the many facets of the trans-Mississippi

West which offer wide coverage on the fur trade are H. M. Chittenden, *The American Fur Trade of the Far West* (1902), reprinted in 1935; S. Vestal, *Mountain Men* (1937); and R. G. Cleland, *This Reckless Breed of Men* (1950).

On the Santa Fe trade, the great classic is Josiah Gregg, *The Commerce of the Prairies* (1845), now available in a modern edition (1954) edited by Max L. Moorehead. Less familiar but highly dramatic is N. M. Loomis, *The Texas–Santa Fé Expedition* (1958).

Of the vast literature on the Mormons, the student will profit much from W. J. McNiff, *Heaven on Earth* (1940), which is cultural and social in emphasis. W. Mulder and A. R. Mortensen, in *Among the Mormons* (1958), have assembled a fine collection of source materials and contemporary observations. Nels Anderson, *Desert Saints* (1942), covers the story of Mormon beginnings and migration to Utah.

On the Pacific Northwest, D. O. Johansen and C. M. Gates, *Empire of the Columbia* (1957), is the best and most recent history.

Bernard DeVoto, *The Year of Decision, 1846* (1943), has much merit.

On California the literature is endless, but for an introduction, see Stewart E. White, *The Forty Niners* (1918), or the composite diary compiled by A. B. Hulbert, *The Forty Niners* (1921). Also very readable and of good coverage are two books by Owen Coy, *The Great Trek* (1931) and *Gold Days* (1929). J. H. Jackson, *Anybody's Gold* (1941), deals with mining towns.

For additional bibliography, see *The Harvard Guide,* sections 128, 129, 140, 164, and 165.

TEN

The Democratic Challenge

1819
Panic of 1819.

1825–1829
John Quincy Adams's presidency.

1828
"Tariff of Abominations."
Jackson elected President.

1830
Maysville Road veto.
Webster-Hayne debate in Senate.

1831
Jackson breaks with Calhoun.

1832
Fight over Bank of the United States
begins.
Nominating conventions come into use.
Jackson reelected over Clay.
South Carolina nullifies tariff.

1833
Force Bill passed.
Government deposits removed
from Bank of the United States.

1834–1835
Antiabolition riots in North.

1836
Van Buren elected President.
Charter of bank expires.

1837
Independent Treasury Act passed.
Charles River Bridge case decided.

POLITICAL DEMOCRACY

THE GOOD ENGLISH GENTLEWOMAN Frances Trollope was a little shocked by the sights and sounds about her as she stood on the steamboat landing at Cincinnati in the late winter of 1829 and watched the Americans receive their President-elect. In spite of her several months of travel in the United States, Mrs. Trollope had not yet become accustomed to the "domestic manners" of the Americans. As Andrew Jackson stepped ashore she noted that he looked harsh and gaunt. She correctly attributed his haggard appearance, in part, to the recent death of his beloved wife, Rachel. She could hardly believe her ears when someone far back in the crowd shouted out the taunt, "There goes Jackson. Where is his wife?" Her pain and surprise at this impropriety were probably shared by the General, for neither really understood that a new day had dawned in American politics. Andrew Jackson was stopping the night at Cincinnati on his way up the river to arrive in Washington in time for his inauguration. This trip was unlike that of previous Presidents-elect. Gone were the impressive coaches and special steamboats which had carried the others to Washington. Gone were the pleasant stopovers in the mansions and country estates of friendly supporters. The people's choice must ride the public steamboats and rub elbows in the crowded hotel lobbies. He must learn to accept the crude kindliness and suffocating enthusiasm of his supporters as well as the jeers and insults of his opponents.

Understood or not, a new day had

202

dawned, and Andrew Jackson was its prophet. Jacksonian democracy, as historians have labeled the movement born in 1829, was a twofold challenge to the *status quo*. It first challenged the aristocratic domination of American politics in much the same way that the patriots had challenged the British imperial rule fifty-odd years before. Jefferson had said, to the evident satisfaction of most Americans, that all men are created equal, but the ideal of equality had not been realized. Gentlemen of wealth and leisure had been able to attain and preserve a fair approximation of minority rule. By the 1820s the plain people had decided that "life, liberty, and the pursuit of happiness" would be protected only when equal participation in government became a reality. Since equal participation meant that the average man, always outnumbering the privileged few, would be in the majority, the first tenet of Jacksonian democracy was an uncritical faith in majority rule.

The second challenge to the *status quo* was an economic one. Small farmers, city artisans, and middle-class businessmen wanted a freedom from mercantilist theories of business enterprise. To them, government-supported monopolies were undemocratic, while free enterprise and unrestrained competition were the only form of economic organization suitable for men who were "created equal" and "endowed by their Creator with certain unalienable Rights."

In reality, the entire rationale of Jacksonian democracy was borrowed from Jefferson. We look in vain for evidence of original theories concerning the relation of men to their government or to each other among the Jacksonians. Jackson himself was not a thinker; he was a man of action. He and his supporters adapted and fitted Jeffersonian democracy to a na-

tion that was fast becoming industrialized and one that now spread in fact, as well as on the map, to the Mississippi Valley.

Andrew Jackson was probably better equipped both by nature and by experience than any other man alive to lead an attack upon the established order. His life was the story of one fight after another. Some had been important, some had been silly, but all had been colorful. Before he was fifteen young Andy had graduated from village brawling to a real war. He fought both the British redcoats and the loyalist invaders of his home country in the western Carolinas. The ranks of revolutionary veterans had been considerably thinned by 1828, but those who remained considered Jackson one of their own. It is not recorded that the scar Jackson carried as a result of a saber blow by a British officer ever lost him a single vote. Jackson's duels were famous throughout the Southwest. He defended his own honor, his wife's honor, and that of his racing stable with equal vigor. A better measure of the man is deduced from the fact that after reaching manhood Jackson invariably resorted to the pistols of a gentleman rather than to the fists of a frontiersman and dueled only with those he considered his social equals.

Jackson came of Scotch-Irish stock. These were the folk who had come into the country through New York and Pennsylvania and gradually sifted out along the frontier in the search of free land and a free religious atmosphere. Caught by the mountain valleys, they moved southward until they had settled the whole frontier from Pennsylvania to the Georgia backwoods. In their exposed position, the Scotch-Irish bore the brunt of Indian attacks for generations. Sometimes called the "cutting edge" of the frontier, they were ambitious, able, and hard as cold-

Andrew Jackson

Henry Clay

Daniel Webster

John C. Calhoun

Jackson Forever!
The Hero of Two Wars and of Or'eans!
The Man of the People!
HE WHO COULD NOT BARTER NOR BARGAIN FOR THE
PRESIDENCY!

Who, although "*A Military Chieftain*," valued the purity of Elections and of the Electors, **MORE** than the Office of **PRESIDENT** itself! Although the greatest in the gift of his countrymen, and the highest in point of dignity of any in the world,

BECAUSE
It should be derived from the
PEOPLE!

No Gag Laws! No Black Cockades! No Reign of Terror! No Standing Army or Navy Officers, when under the pay of Government, to browbeat, or

KNOCK DOWN

Old Revolutionary Characters, or our Representatives while in the discharge of their duty. To the Polls then, and vote for those who will support

OLD HICKORY
AND THE ELECTORAL LAW.

A Jackson election poster, 1828

Jacksonian Democracy represented an upsurge of the "common man," but Jackson himself was a rather courtly Tennessee gentleman. With his election as President the political party system began to take on its modern characteristics, and the office of the Presidency was much transformed during the reign of "King Andrew." Jackson overshadowed even his great rivals of the Whig party, Clay and Webster.

rolled steel. Admired, respected, and feared, they were seldom loved. John C. Calhoun and Woodrow Wilson supply other examples of the vitality, idealism, and coldness of these people. Throughout his career, Andrew Jackson had the complete devotion of the Scotch-Irish, and the heart of his political strength in the West lay in the areas they had settled.

Orphaned by the Revolution, young Jackson came into a small inheritance. A fling down in Charleston, where visits to the race track and cockpits left him poorer and wiser, was followed by a year spent in picking up the rudiments of law. After practicing in a western village of North Carolina for a short time, Jackson moved on to Tennessee. There, in the midst of a collection of log cabins and taverns that was to become Nashville, he found that he was the second lawyer to arrive in the community. Since the first had assumed the role of spokesman and defender of the farmer-debtors in the neighborhood, the local merchants, speculators, and money-lenders were finding it difficult to collect their debts. Jackson was retained by one after another of these substantial citizens and creditors, and what was intended to be a visit stretched out into a permanent residence.

In the following years Jackson became, through legal fees, merchandising, land speculation, and a little private banking, something of a frontier aristocrat. His rise from penniless immigrant to Tennessee nabob was matched by his professional growth from journeyman lawyer to superior court judge. Jackson served as a member of the Tennessee constitutional convention and was subsequently elected to represent the new state in Congress, first as representative and then as senator. He gave up his Senate seat after only one year

as part of a deal by which he became a member of the Supreme Court of Tennessee. Never in a class with the eastern seaboard aristocrats (his free and easy ways with the conventions of orthography and grammar would have prevented that), Jackson was nevertheless a long way above the coonskin-cap democracy of the West.

Long before Jackson was seriously discussed as a presidential possibility by even his most ardent supporters, his home, The Hermitage, was known throughout the West for the luxury of its appointments and the hospitality of its owner. In all his political activities at the state level, Jackson was a close ally of the landed gentry and fought the debt-ridden farmers who sought relief in stay laws and paper money. Despite his aristocratic connections and inclinations, however, Andrew Jackson believed deeply in the plain people and even more in the principle of majority rule. Recent generations have been somewhat puzzled by the paradox of the obviously wealthy and aristocratic Jackson becoming the leader of a great popular movement against aristocracy and privilege. But Jackson's appeal was that of the poor orphan boy who had made good. The man who was elected to the presidency in 1828 was one who in his own career had proved that the American dream of back-country farm boy to plantation gentleman in one lifetime was possible.

But Andrew Jackson did not reach the White House because of what he did or did not believe. He was elected because he was a military hero. One of the prerogatives of prominent politicians in the West was appointment as an officer in the state militia. The rank of these appointments in the Tennessee militia was determined by the votes of subordinate officers; and, in this manner, Jackson was elected a major general, commander of the Volunteers. It was at the head of his Tennessee Volunteers that Jackson decisively defeated the Creeks at Horseshoe Bend in 1814, freeing the entire southern frontier from the stifling fear of Indian raids.

His victory over the Indians by itself would have made him the hero of the West. The victory over the British in the following year at New Orleans made Jackson the most popular figure since Washington. Immediately there was talk of the White House among Jackson's Tennessee friends and supporters. In days when it was a toss-up whether the Indians or the British were more hated, here was a man who had defeated both in spectacular and important victories. It looked like an unbeatable combination, and it was. The hero of New Orleans needed no political platform. He needed no finely spun theories of government and democracy. He did not even need political experience, although Jackson possessed the latter in abundance. Jackson's record was sufficient to win him the presidency; once President, his instincts and prejudices would serve him as well as theories and programs.

In the few years following Jackson's inauguration, it became apparent that here was a new kind of President. Only the perspective of history allows us to determine just what kind of Chief Executive he became. We can see now that he was a man of many "firsts." He was the nation's first modern President. Jackson was the first self-made man to occupy the White House, the first to become the leader of a tightly organized political party, and the first to use that party as a normal part of his administration machinery. He was the

first to use the veto power extensively, and the first to reach out over the heads of Congress and the Supreme Court to the people for support of his acts. He was the first to use a paid party press as a bulwark to his rule. In short, Andrew Jackson found the machinery with which to put Jefferson's ideal of majority rule into practice.

The General owed his election partly to the vast increase in the number of voters in the past few elections. Conventionally the broadened suffrage has been attributed solely to the changes in the state constitutions removing old restrictions on voting. Recent research has indicated, however, that, in addition to the constitutional changes which added many thousands of voters to the lists, the end of the one-party era and the return of genuine competition to the presidential canvass brought out many voters who had formerly stayed home on election day.

Jefferson had looked forward to the day when all freemen over twenty-one would possess the right to vote. That ideal had not been realized while Jefferson was in office, but great strides had been made toward its attainment during and since his administration. Vermont had made manhood suffrage a part of her first constitution. New Hampshire, Pennsylvania, and Georgia made payment of taxes the only restriction on use of the ballot. The western states uniformly provided for manhood suffrage upon or shortly after admission to the union. It must be remembered, however, that as late as 1840 eleven out of the fifteen eastern states still limited the vote to those who paid taxes or held property to a certain value. While such restrictions had been eased and would be modified further by the Jacksonians, we must look elsewhere for a complete explanation of the tremendous increase in voting between 1820 and 1836.

The administration of James Monroe marked the nadir of political interest in the United States. In the 1820 election, Baltimore, with a population of 62,738, cast 568 votes; while only 17 of Richmond's 12,067 inhabitants went to the poles. The whole state of Virginia, with a white population of over 600,000, had only 4,321 persons who bothered to vote; in Mississippi it was 751; and in Rhode Island the vote for presidential electors was 724. But a careful analysis of these statistics and comparison with other states indicates that political apathy rather than suffrage restrictions accounted for the small vote. The average voter going to the polls in 1820 found a single ticket of electors pledged to vote for Monroe. This

was all right if he liked Monroe, but since only a few votes were needed to elect him anyway, there was little incentive to go to the polls. If the voter disliked Monroe, there was no other name on the ballot (except in two of the states).

When the people were given a choice among several candidates in 1824, they turned out in large numbers. The total presidential vote in 1824 was more than double that of 1820. And in 1828, after four years of active campaigning, over 1 million people came out to vote on election day. The popular vote in 1828 represented a 300 per cent increase over that of 1824. The explanation for this unparalleled increase in the popular vote lies as much in the death of the one-party system, in the introduction of new and vital campaign issues, and in the rise of a popular

"The Country Election," by George Caleb Bingham. (City Art Museum, St. Louis)

leader such as Andrew Jackson, as it does in the reduction of restrictions on the suffrage.*

Perhaps some of the spread of popular participation in voting was due to the way in which politics suddenly became the national sport of most Americans. Outside of the few metropolitan centers or the great plantations, life in America was apt to be a pretty drab affair. All the energy and interest now absorbed by big-league baseball, college and professional football, movies, bowling, radio, television, and slick magazines was devoted then to politics and religion. Given the opportunity, Americans proved to be as interested in and capable of political hairsplitting as the French are reputed to be. The rise of the penny press before Jackson left the White House gave a nation that was just becoming literate something on which to practice its new skill at reading. The political stump became as popular a center of Saturday afternoon or early evening entertainment as the ball park has become for us. Even the traditional wedding, house-raising, and husking-bee festivities turned into political forums near election time. The golden age of the politician in American life falls between Jackson and Lincoln. Never before and seldom since have so many been so interested in the fate of parties, politics, and politicians.

THE CHALLENGE OF MAJORITY RULE

Andrew Jackson's victory in the election of 1828 constituted the first direct challenge to the *status quo* by the new democracy. The majority discovered that

* These data have been drawn largely from Charles S. Sydnor, "The One-party Period of American History," *American Historical Review*, vol. 51, pp. 439–451, April, 1946.

they might rule directly instead of trusting the talented few to govern wisely. But if the victory of 1828 was to be consolidated, the majority must be protected from the expected counterattack of the privileged minority. The need was to create an organization that could win elections even after the "Old Hero" was gone; a party which would retain the initial enthusiasm for the General in a more effective and permanent form. The obvious solution was a strong political party. National political parties were not entirely new to American experience; for they were in existence, in very rudimentary form at least, as early as the debates over the ratification of the Constitution. While Jackson did not originate the party system, he did, as in all other things, alter and fit the existing institution to the needs of his own day.

The most obvious change Jackson made in the organization of political parties lay in his use of patronage. Whereas earlier generations had been apologetic, Jacksonians took pride in defending the "spoils system." Jackson spoke of the fitness of every man for any public office and scoffed at the idea that statesmanship required some particular talent. To Jacksonians, new men "fresh from the people" seemed preferable to incumbents grown lax and supercilious in their long tenure; "rotation in office" brought new blood into the government. It also let out a good many experienced brains, retorted the opposition. Jefferson had talked of retaining ultimate authority in the hands of the people while reserving the actual operation of the government to men of talent. Even had he so desired, Jackson, under the pressure for jobs which beset him, would have found such reservations impossible. Furthermore, by offering government office to any and all citizens, Jackson was simply carrying the Jeffersonian faith in the common man to its logical conclusion. True democracy, the Jacksonians held, is best served when men in public office represent the majority. Some went further and defended the spoils system as good administrative procedure, since it established a clear connection between the responsibility and the authority for policy decisions.

Bitter opposition to Jackson's use of patronage arose from the then prevalent concept of tenure for officeholders. Prominent politicians expected to be continued in public office because of their character,

their standing in the community, their need for the office, or their general competence. This was particularly true throughout the South, where political office was a public responsibility joined to one's social position. Jackson's immediate predecessors tended to feel that long and faithful service *entitled* the supplicant to continued employment. While it is perfectly true that Jackson was the first President to frankly use the appointing power as a reward for party services and as a means of maintaining administrative dis-

PRESIDENTIAL ELECTION, 1828

MICHIGAN TERRITORY

ARKANSAS TERRITORY

FLORIDA TERRITORY

JACKSON AND CALHOUN
ELECTORAL VOTE: 171.
POPULAR VOTE: 650,050.

JOHN QUINCY ADAMS AND RUSH
ELECTORAL VOTE: 83.
POPULAR VOTE: 512,178.

cipline, it is not true, as was regularly charged by his enemies, that he invented the system. George Washington wrote to his Secretary of War that: "I shall not, while I have the honor of administering the government, bring a man into any office of consequence knowingly whose political tenets are adverse to the measures the general government are pursuing; for this, in my opinion, would be a sort of political suicide."

The extent to which Jackson used the spoils system has also been greatly exaggerated. The opposition made so much of every political removal that only in very recent years have scholars been able to restore a balance to the picture. One of Jackson's enemies, speaking in the Senate in 1830, charged Jackson with removing nearly 2,000 officeholders during the first year of his administration and implied that this high rate of dismissals was being continued. We now know that Jackson removed 252 out of 612 executive officers and about 600 out of 8,000 deputy postmasters. His total removals numbered just over 900 out of over 10,000 federal officeholders. Removal of one government worker in ten was scarcely "wholesale proscription" or a "clean sweep." It was the absolute certainty that every man removed would be replaced by a Jackson supporter, as well as an unashamed defense of the system by administration partisans, which so aroused "Old Hickory's" enemies.

It should be remembered that a distribution of the political loaves and fishes to the faithful was a *necessity* for the Jacksonians. The men who had organized the General's campaign in the various states were not men with independent incomes. If they were to remain in politics they must be given jobs to support them. The Virginia dynasty had been officered by wealthy gentlemen living on the income from extensive lands or mercantile enterprises while they spent their time at the national capital. Few such men joined the party of Jackson. Only a judicious use of the patronage could maintain a party based upon western farmers and eastern mechanics and shopkeepers. Every President since Jackson has been faced with the same problem, and every one has found the spoils system a political necessity.

Another way in which the Jacksonians sought to consolidate the victory for majority rule was by the use of party newspapers. Tradition held that freedom of the press could be preserved only if newspapers remained independent of all political ties. That tradition was so strong that when Jefferson found it expedient to encourage newspaper editors such as Philip Freneau and his *National Gazette* and Benjamin Franklin Bache and his *Aurora,* he took pains to keep the arrangements quiet. Jackson, on the other hand, was quite open in his support of certain newspapers and even brought several editors into high party councils. Amos Kendall of the *Argus of Western America* and Isaac Hill of the *Concord Patriot* became Jackson's personal advisers. Both Duff Green's *United States Telegraph* and its successor, Francis Preston Blair's *Washington Globe,* were supported by government printing contracts. The *Globe* became the capstone of a journalistic pyramid which rested upon party newspapers in cities and towns all across the country. These newspapermen in Jackson's "Kitchen Cabinet" wrote editorials favorable to his policies and sent them to the party press in the country, which then published the material as if it had been written by their editors. These articles were then reprinted in the *Globe* as if they had originated in the grass roots. Thus the Jacksonians were able to create the impression, if not the reality, of public opinion favorable to administration policies.

Andrew Jackson was also responsible for a marked increase in the personal power of the President. Much of this increase was simply the direct result of the open use of patronage and the development of an organized party press. Some of it was the impact of the old General's personality, for friends as well as enemies attest the highhanded manner in which he conducted affairs of state. Frequently overlooked, however, are the changes which Jackson introduced in the Cabinet. Unlike former Presidents, Jackson chose his official family in order to produce a nice balance among the contending factions within the party. Jackson also ended the nearly permanent Cabinet which had become a feature of the Virginia dynasty. From Washington to the second Adams, the same men crop up in one Cabinet after another. As the Secretary of State in one administration became the President in the next, he frequently asked his former colleagues in the Cabinet to remain and serve him in their accustomed places. This practice became so well established that officials began to look upon their positions as permanent appointments. William Wirt, Attorney General under both Monroe and John Quincy Adams, even questioned whether he ought to submit his resignation to President Jackson upon the latter's election. When he sought advice on the point from James Monroe, the ex-President agreed that there was much to be said for an independent Cabinet, in which tenure of office depended upon the competence of the Cabinet member. Only reluctantly did Monroe conclude that, as department heads, the members of the Cabinet were probably responsible to the President and that perhaps Wirt would have to submit

his resignation. There were no holdovers in Jackson's Cabinet; and the men who joined him in the Cabinet room were merely advisers and not makers of policy.

The increased power of the executive office during Jackson's administration is also apparent in his use of the veto. The first six Presidents vetoed a total of only eight different bills (the Adamses and Jefferson vetoed none). Jackson vetoed twelve different bills and used the pocket veto on seven occasions. His readiness to use the veto power undoubtedly stemmed from his view of the relative position of the judiciary, the legislature, and the executive under the Constitution. In his veto of the bill to extend the charter of the second Bank of the United States, he declared:

> The Congress, the Executive, and the Court must each for itself be guided by its own opinion of the Constitution. Each public officer who takes an oath to support the Constitution swears that he will support it as he understands it, and not as it is understood by others. It is as much the duty of the House of Representatives, of the Senate, and of the President to decide upon the constitutionality of any bill or resolution which may be presented to them for passage or approval as it is of the supreme judges when it may be brought before them for judicial decision. The opinion of the judges has no more authority over Congress than the opinion of Congress has over the judges, and on that point the President is independent of both.

In this Andrew Jackson stood precisely on the same ground as Jefferson: both agreed that each of the three coequal branches of the federal government must make its own decisions on the constitutionality of its acts. Here again, Andrew Jackson was making a practical application of the Jeffersonian ideal. Where Jefferson ignored the efforts of the Supreme Court to review his official acts, Jackson both ignored and defied the efforts of the Court and the Congress to curtail his generous view of the powers of the President.

PREVIEW OF SECTIONAL CONFLICT

Andrew Jackson was scarcely settled in the White House before it became apparent that he would have to use both his new party machinery and his extensive executive powers to check the sectionalism which once again threatened the national authority. The new President was quite familiar with the power of sectional appeals, for he had used them widely in his bitter four years' campaign to defeat John Quincy Adams's bid for a second term.

Sectional conflict had appeared first during the colonial period between the planters and merchants who dominated the tidewater and the yeoman farmers of the back country. Representation, taxation, frontier defense, and roads to market were then the chief bones of contention. The War of 1812 brought forth another form of sectional rivalry. New England, with money invested in commerce and shipping on the high seas, had little stomach for a war that was being fought to expand western territories. The abortive Hartford Convention (1814) climaxed a long effort to get out of "Mr. Madison's war."

When the battle of New Orleans and the Treaty of Ghent ended the threat to New England's commerce, Boston merchants joined with Carolina planters in electing James Monroe to two terms in the White House. Congress, basking in the warmth of a temporary nationalism, chartered the second Bank of the United States and passed a mildly protective tariff de-

signed to help New England manufacturers withstand the flood of British goods. The passage of the tariff and bank bills in 1816 are conventionally interpreted as symbols of the spirit of nationalism pervading the country as the various sections joined in the happy task of exploiting the resources of the western lands. This Era of Good Feeling can be more accurately described as a period of political confusion resulting from a rapid change in the economic foundations of the various sections. The Northeast was shifting from a land of small farms and commercial cities to an area of factory and mill towns. The South was shifting from tobacco, wheat, and rice to its great staple, cotton. The West was rapidly filling up with land-hungry settlers who were soon producing wheat and corn in quantities that swamped eastern markets and invaded European ones as well.

All three sections were badly hit by the panic of 1819. As the panic stretched into a major depression, the urge to find a scapegoat became irresistible, and each section quickly came to the conclusion that its interests were being sacrificed to the needs of the other two. The West was convinced that the South and Northeast were determined to withhold the capital necessary to develop the frontier and to deprive the western settler of access to the cheap lands vital to his existence. The South was certain that the Northeast and West had combined to raid the federal treasury for money with which to pay for grandiose internal improvements and to force a protective tariff upon the country. The Northeast, for its part, was fearful that a combination of West and South might effectively block a protective tariff and induce its factory labor to migrate into the West with promises of cheap land.

These issues played leading roles in determining the political attitudes assumed by each of the three sections during the 1820s and early 1830s. Politicians and statesmen who sought national prominence and power were constantly juggling these issues in an effort to produce a combination which would win friends in all three sections, or at least avoid alienating many voters. In the chart below, showing what each section favored, the issues are listed in order of their relative importance in each section.

Northeast (down to Mason and Dixon's line)
  High tariff
  High-priced land
  Internal improvements
Seaboard South
  Low tariff
  High-priced land
  No internal improvements
Northwest
  Low-priced land
  Internal improvements
  High tariff

The panic of 1819 brought the so-called Era of Good Feeling to an end. Revived sectional animosities bedeviled the plans for national progress projected by Presidents Monroe, Adams, and Jackson.

President James Monroe's 1822 veto of an internal-improvements bill which would have provided funds for the Cumberland Road illustrates the play of sectional rivalries. The veto was viewed in the West as an expression of the implacable hostility of the seaboard South toward western aspirations. John Quincy Adams found himself caught up in the same struggle and retired from the White House a defeated and embittered man. His broad nationalist program, which included internal improvements, a protective tariff, and a national university, won the support of only the Northeast and the Ohio Valley. Elsewhere it was regarded as a bribe tendered by New England to the

West as the basis for an unholy alliance. Many Jacksonians who did not share the General's personal animosity for John Quincy Adams joined in the campaign against the New Englander on sectional grounds. Adams and his program were swallowed up in the vortex of sectional strife.

As President, Jackson fully expected to face the problem of sectional politics, but he did not expect the challenge to be as personal or as prompt as it was. He had barely given orders for cleaning up the mess left in the White House by the "mob rampant" at the inaugural reception when he found he had another mess on his hands. This one involved his Secretary of War and old Tennessee friend John H. Eaton and an innkeeper's daughter, beautiful Peggy O'Neale. The "Eaton Malaria" or "Petticoat War," as the affair was soon dubbed, would have remained no more than a choice bit of gossip to help bored Washington wives through dull official receptions had it not become a focus for sectional politics.

The many descriptions of Miss O'Neale do not agree on whether she was vibrant, alluring, and witty or simply vivacious, charming, and clever, but they do agree on her many conquests. After at least two suitors were prevented from eloping with Peggy by her vigilant father, the young lady agreed to marry a man she had known less than twelve hours. At the worldly age of sixteen, and within a month after she had met him, Miss O'Neale married John B. Timberlake, a naval officer. While her husband was at sea, Peggy continued to make her home at her father's boardinghouse. There the star boarder was John H. Eaton, junior Senator from Tennessee. In the course of the next few years Eaton fell in love with Mrs. Timberlake. When news came that Mr. Timberlake had died while his ship was cruising in the Mediterranean, the question of Mr. Eaton's intentions was raised in the drawing rooms and kitchens of Washington. The news of Timberlake's death came just before the election of 1828. Immediately after the election, Eaton wrote General Jackson, "At a *proper time* I will tender her [Peggy] the offer to share my life and prospects." The return mail brought the General's reply, "Major, if you love Margaret Timberlake go and marry her at once and shut their mouths." A private messenger from The Hermitage followed shortly with the admonition that Eaton should marry Peg "forthwith" or leave the O'Neale boardinghouse. On January 1, 1829, Mrs. Timberlake became Mrs. John H. Eaton. There the affair would have ended had it not been for Eaton's close private and public connection with the President-elect.

The elevation of Peggy from innkeeper's daughter to wife of a Senator was hard to take, but the thought of seating her even closer to the head of table when she became the wife of the Secretary of War was more than many good ladies could accept. Soon after the inauguration it was apparent to all who were interested that Mrs. Eaton was being boycotted. And it appeared that this boycott was being led by Floride Calhoun, wife of the Vice President. General Jackson, still in deep mourning for his beloved wife, believed that Rachel's death had been caused, in part at least, by the malicious gossip that had charged her with adultery and bigamy. Jackson had killed men who cast aspersions on his wife's honor. While not ready to go so far for Peggy Eaton, he openly despised those who dragged a woman's reputation into a political fight. Washington was soon divided between those who had called on Mrs. Eaton and those who had not. The former were Jackson's political friends; the latter were his enemies.

Martin Van Buren, the wily new Secretary of State, was the representative of the upstate New York machine in the Cabinet, and he was unencumbered by wife or family in Washington. His small attentions and overtures of friendship to the Eatons were carefully noted by the President. Calhoun, South Carolina's spokesman, could not compel his wife to receive the Eatons. This, too, was carefully noted by Jackson. A rare situation had developed in which Washington politics and social life accurately reflected the shift in sectional alliances in the country at large. When Martin Van Buren brought his powerful New York faction to the support of the Jackson administration, fully intending to become Jackson's successor, he was using a combination of Northeast and West as his chief support. John C. Calhoun, who sought to speak for the seaboard South, had accepted second place on the Jackson ticket in the full expectation that Jackson would serve only one term and that Jackson's support would make him President in 1832. Calhoun planned to rely upon a combination of South and West. Jackson and Calhoun were probably further apart than either knew long before the Eaton affair muddied political waters in Washington and completed Calhoun's isolation. With the elimination of Calhoun, Jackson depended more and more upon Van Buren; and a coalition of Northeast and West ended by giving the presidency to the New Yorker in 1836. The tavern keeper's daughter had contributed much to making Martin Van Buren President of the United States.

JACKSON AND THE SECTIONAL CHALLENGE

Throughout Jackson's administration the protective tariff offered many opportunities for sectional horse trading. As

northeastern manufacturers won control
of that section's voice in Congress from the
merchants, they reversed its old opposition
to a tariff. Daniel Webster, who had
fought the tariff of 1816, now became an
advocate of the protective principle. New
England and Pennsylvania found the West
receptive to tariff arguments, for the West
possessed resources and an increasing labor
supply that together might well produce
factories and mills if foreign competition
could be reduced. In addition, the wool
producers of Ohio and the hemp planters
of Kentucky saw prosperity in higher
import duties. Only the seaboard South
found no virtue in the tariff. As a producer
of raw materials for foreign markets it
saw only that a tariff would raise the prices
on the goods the South bought which
consequently meant a reduction in the
value of its products. While the back-
country South seemed to ignore the tariff
question, the seaboard planters were
aroused, then defiant. Many southerners
appeared at Jackson's inaugural dressed in
homespun as a protest against the high
cost of textiles under the 1828 "Tariff of
Abominations." In order to hold the support of his planter friends, John C. Calhoun was forced to abandon his earlier
support of high tariffs and come out in opposition to protective duties. While offering to accept a fair and judicious tariff,
Calhoun condemned the recent bills, term-
ing them "grossly unequal and oppressive"
and an "encroachment upon the true spirit
of the Constitution."

Calhoun was fully aware of the sectional threat posed by the combination of
Northeast and West on the tariff question.
In an effort to protect a minority interest
while yet operating within the Union and
the Constitution, Calhoun worked out his
theory of nullification. As a youth Calhoun had learned his law at Yale and at
the great law school at Litchfield, Connecticut. There he studied under men who
were disseminating ideas of nullification
and secession because of opposition to Jeffersonian policies. Calhoun found precedents for nullification of congressional acts
by the states in the arguments of these
teachers and friends in New Haven and
Litchfield as well as in the Kentucky and
Virginia Resolutions of Jefferson and
Madison. Calhoun first wrote his theory
in the "South Carolina Exposition and
Protest" of 1828, but his authorship of the
document was not known until some time
after he became Jackson's Vice President
in March, 1829.

Starting with the premise that sovereignty is by nature indivisible and indestructible, Calhoun began his argument
for nullification with the then generally
held belief that sovereign states had combined to form a union in 1787. If these
states were sovereign in 1787, then they
must still be sovereign in 1828. This argument was questionable. Had the sovereign states, in ratifying the Constitution,
done nothing more than create an agent
to carry out their collective wills? If Calhoun's reasoning were accepted, however,
it was a small and logical step to uphold
the right of the people of a single state to
nullify an act of Congress when the
"agent" had exceeded the powers granted
it by the sovereign states.

When the tariff of 1832, passed by the
coalition of Northeast and West, became
law, South Carolinians concluded that
their section was hopelessly defeated on
this issue and that a protective tariff was to
be the settled policy of the government.
They then turned to Calhoun's doctrine.
Calling a special convention in late 1832,
South Carolina nullified the tariff, declaring, "That it shall not be lawful for any of
the constituted authorities, whether of this

State or the United States, to enforce the payment of duties imposed. . . ."

Calhoun had intended to establish his doctrine as a substitute for the more dangerous theory of secession advocated by New England extremists in 1813–1814. He hoped that the mere threat of nullification would be sufficient to protect the basic rights of a minority. Calhoun was dismayed when his more impetuous followers actually nullified the tariff of 1832 and brought the full force of Andrew Jackson's wrath down upon South Carolina and himself.

Calhoun and his nullifiers had committed a major error in strategy when they assumed that Jackson would accept their view of the limits of federal power. This error is understandable, for Jackson's own record was dotted with statements upholding the rights of individual states. His veto of a federal internal-improvements bill just two years earlier had been widely interpreted as a defense of states' rights. Furthermore, Jackson had just completed a vigorous presidential campaign in which he fought the Bank of the United States with every weapon at hand, including the right of states to regulate their own banking institutions. What the nullifiers overlooked, or forgot, was the General Jackson who had fought the national enemy at New Orleans. They also overlooked Jackson's devotion to the principle of majority rule, by which Old Hickory meant a majority of Americans, not simply the majority in one state. We, with the perspective of history to aid us, can also see what they could not: that no American President, however strong his sympathies for his own state or section, has failed to subordinate those sympathies to the national welfare upon his elevation to the White House.

Jackson's reaction to the nullifiers was quick and strong. He strengthened United States military forces in and around Charleston; he asked Congress for the authority to use the military to enforce the acts of Congress (the Force Bill); and he issued a proclamation to the people of South Carolina. The proclamation, one of the most forceful bits of prose in American political history, said in part:

> The constitution of the United States then, forms a *government*, not a league; and whether it be formed by compact between the States or in any other manner, its character is the same. It is a government in which all the people are represented, which operates directly on the people individually, not upon the States; . . . The laws of the United States must be executed. I have no discretionary power on the subject; my duty is emphatically pronounced in the Constitution. Those who told you that you might peaceably prevent their execution deceived you; they could not have been deceived themselves. They know that a forcible opposition could alone prevent the execution of the laws, and they know that such opposition must be repelled. Their object is disunion. But be not deceived by names. Disunion by armed force is *treason*.

Thus Jackson held the forces of sectionalism in check by a new assertion of the national authority. Throughout the nullification crisis, he had been sure of the support of the vast majority of Americans: his recent reelection by an even larger popular vote than he received in 1828 gave added authority to his words. Certain of his power, Jackson was content to allow the nullifiers to save face by withdrawing their ordinance in exchange for the promise of lower tariffs. Henry Clay's compromise tariff of 1833, which fulfilled the promise of lower duties, did not hide the fact that the seaboard South had been

PRESIDENTIAL ELECTION, 1832

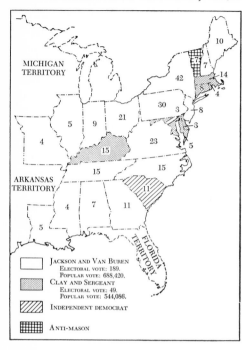

MICHIGAN TERRITORY

ARKANSAS TERRITORY

FLORIDA TERRITORY

JACKSON AND VAN BUREN
Electoral vote: 189.
Popular vote: 688,420.

CLAY AND SERGEANT
Electoral vote: 49.
Popular vote: 544,086.

INDEPENDENT DEMOCRAT

ANTI-MASON

isolated by a combination of West and Northeast just as effectively as Calhoun himself had been isolated by a growing entente between Jackson and Van Buren.

The famed Webster-Hayne debates are a last striking illustration of the way in which sectional questions plagued the Jackson administration. Here again, the end result was the emphasis upon the community of interest between Northeast and West and the consequent isolation of the South. The opening move in these debates came in 1829 when Senator Samuel A. Foot of Connecticut moved that the sale of western lands be limited to those already surveyed and that the office of surveyor general be abolished. Foot defended his resolution on the ground that the Northeast might soon be depopulated by westward migration if western land sales were not limited.

Senator Thomas Hart Benton, a staunch Jackson supporter from Missouri, answered for the West in a thundering attack upon the Foot resolution. Benton accused New England and the other northern manufacturing states of deliberately trying to limit the settlement of the West in order to keep a plentiful supply of cheap labor tied to their factories. Senator Robert Y. Hayne of South Carolina, a close friend of Calhoun, saw an opportunity to recoup the loss the South had sustained on the tariff issue. Hayne assumed leadership in the debate, siding with Benton against the northeasterners.

In January, 1830, the debate reached its climax. Daniel Webster, the acknowledged leader of the Northeast in the Senate, moved to drive a wedge between the West and the South. Webster's strategy was simple: he would change the whole basis of the discussion, for as long as the conflict remained a debate over public land policy, the community of interest between South and West was too apparent. By maneuvering Hayne into a discussion of the virtues of union, Webster and the Northeast could parade their newfound loyalty to the Union which the West, long loyal to the federal government, could admire and applaud. Webster pointed an accusing finger at the South and reminded it of southern readiness to "speak of the Union in terms of indifference, or even of disparagement." Many of Webster's listeners failed to note that the "godlike Daniel" had shifted the grounds for the debate from land policies to union. When Webster concluded his immortal second reply to Hayne with the "sentiment, dear to every true American Heart, —Liberty and Union, now and forever, one and inseparable," he meant a union dominated by a combination of Northeast and West.

Although the two men had little else in

common, Jackson shared Webster's views on the union. Two months after the debate, at a Jefferson Day dinner for the party leaders, the President offered a toast: "Our Federal Union—it must be preserved!" To which Calhoun replied, a little lamely, "The Federal Union—next to our liberty, the most dear!" Sectional conflicts continued and became more dangerous. When sectional rivalries over slavery and expansion became prominent in the 1840s they became increasingly more difficult to compromise, and in 1860 these same rivalries brought civil war. Unfortunately for the country, subsequent Presidents were unable or unwilling to reject sectional claims as forcefully as did Andrew Jackson.

ECONOMIC DEMOCRACY

The second major challenge of Jacksonian democracy to the *status quo* was economic. Until rather recently, Jacksonian democracy was interpreted by historians as a western movement. This understanding was based upon many detailed studies of the Jackson party in individual western states. In most instances, after carefully examining the new liberal state constitutions which broadened the suffrage in the West, these studies emphasized the increased participation of the "common man" in politics during the Jackson period. Jackson's reliance upon the spoils system and the general revolt against the caucus system as a means of choosing political candidates were interpreted as the result of a western revolt against the domination of eastern aristocrats. In the 1920s a new generation of historians began to investigate the Jackson parties in the eastern states. These historians found that Jackson was as popular with many groups in New York, Pennsylvania, and North Carolina, as he had been

anywhere in the West. Further research revealed new workingmen's parties endorsing Old Hickory—a rising group of "expectant capitalists" seeking freedom from domination by the agrarian aristocrats of the Virginia dynasty. A reexamination of the whole concept of Jacksonian democracy was needed to fill the gaps left by the previous interpretation.

Within the last twenty-five years that reexamination has been made. Little of the older view has been totally rejected. Students of the period continue to be impressed with the contribution of the western settlers who saw in Jackson the fulfillment of their own hopes and ambitions. The new view simply raises Jacksonian democracy to the level of a national movement rather than labeling it a sectional one. Jacksonian democracy becomes a movement for economic as well as political democracy. In such a light Jackson's veto of a bill to establish a road (the Maysville Road) in Kentucky was more than a personal slap at Henry Clay, it was a repudiation of government-sponsored privileges for certain businessmen. The long fight against the Bank of the United States is no longer regarded as a personal fight for political power between the President and Nicholas Biddle, the powerful president of the bank, but rather a war on government-backed monopoly in banking facilities. And, the importance of the general incorporation laws passed in many states by the Jackson supporters is seen as a part of the middle-class fight against government-backed monopolies and for laissez-faire relations between government and business, i.e., economic freedom and no special favors by government to anyone.

This reexamination of Jacksonian democracy was inspired by studies of the Jackson party in the eastern states. While these studies confirmed that the Jackson vote tended to come from areas of low land values, indicating support by the less prosperous farmers, they also revealed that many cities and towns dominated by middle-class businessmen regularly voted for Jackson. The Jackson party in Pennsylvania won its early strength in the Pittsburgh area, where the "expectant capitalists" and workingmen combined. In Massachusetts eager young men who migrated to Boston and made their fortunes found themselves ignored by the Federalist, and later the Whig, rulers, so they joined the Democratic opposition. Some historians, doing research on the subject of individual Jackson leaders in eastern states and cities, have found that the sons and daughters of wealthy New England merchants, well-to-do Philadelphia businessmen, and independent bankers worked together, rubbing shoulders with doctrinaire reformers and utopians in the Jackson ranks. Workingmen's parties were often discovered to be organizations of small shopkeepers, new factory owners, and small businessmen in general. As a result of much of this new examination of the role of Jacksonian democracy in American history, several events of that period take on added significance.

Jackson startled many of his western supporters early in 1830 by vetoing a bill which would have provided federal money for a road in Kentucky. The President defended his action upon the ground that the Constitution gave the national government no power to appropriate money for local internal improvements, and if there were surplus funds on hand, that money might better be applied to the reduction of the national debt. Those more familiar with the Washington scene saw the hand of Van Buren quietly slipping a knife between Henry Clay's ribs, but they also recognized that Old Hickory was assuming the traditional Republican position against internal improvements at national expense —the position held by Jefferson, Madison, and Monroe.

That none of these explanations adequately revealed Jackson's motive can be seen from his later actions. Shortly after his Maysville veto, Jackson vetoed two other internal-improvements bills. In his explanation of these vetoes Jackson clearly reiterated the laissez-faire doctrine that government and business ought to be totally divorced. Two of the three vetoed bills provided that the government, as its share of the cost of the projects, purchase stock in private road-building companies as it had in the Bank of the United States. This aspect of the problem particularly concerned Jackson:

> The practice of thus mingling the concerns of the Government with those of the States or of individuals is inconsistent with the object of its institution and highly impolitic. . . . If the interest of the Government in private companies is subordinate to that of individuals, the management and control of the public funds is delegated to an authority unknown to the Constitution and beyond the supervision of our constituents; if superior, its officers and agents will be constantly exposed to imputations of favoritism and oppression.

It was the "favoritism and oppression" in government-sponsored business enterprise which the rising generation of entrepreneurs feared. And Jackson's own earlier unfortunate mercantile operations and banking connections made him quite sympathetic with these fears of the business community.

The second Bank of the United States had been chartered in 1816 with a twenty-year charter, as we noted in a previous chapter. This was a private corporation with immense powers derived from the government. The directors appointed by the government were always in the minority, having no real voice in the operation of the bank. These directors, laughing at their title, said they should be called "directed" and openly declared they were ciphers on the board of directors. The monopoly granted the bank by the nature of its charter had long angered considerable portions of the business community. Many state legislatures had roundly denounced the two important decisions of the Supreme Court supporting the bank. While the steady improvement in transportation facilities throughout the 1830s extended the markets for manufacturers over large areas, these producers became more dependent upon credit and banking facilities. Men who had been indifferent to the first Bank of the United States were vitally affected by the operations of the second Bank of the United States, and a large proportion of them saw the big bank as a possible threat to their security. More important, the principle of government-granted monopolies was an actual threat.

Andrew Jackson relied upon the fear of monopoly to sustain him in his fight with the bank. When he vetoed its recharter bill in 1832, he put his most telling arguments against it into the form of an appeal to the laissez-faire convictions of small businessmen. He declared that he was "deeply impressed with the belief that some of the powers and privileges possessed by the existing bank are unauthorized by the Constitution, subversive of the rights of States, and dangerous to the liberties of the people." In concluding his veto message, the President made a classic statement of the free-enterprise doctrine.

It is to be regretted that the rich and powerful too often bend the acts of government to their selfish purposes. Distinctions in society will always exist under every just government. Equality of talents, of education, or of wealth cannot be produced by human institutions. In the full enjoyment of the gifts of Heaven and the fruits of superior industry, economy and virtue, every man is equally entitled to protection by the law; but when the laws undertake to add to these natural and just advantages artificial distinctions, to grant titles, gratuities, and exclusive privileges, to make the rich richer and the potent more powerful, the humble members of society . . . who have neither the time nor the means of securing like favors to themselves, have a right to complain of he injustice of their government. There are no necessary evils in government. Its evils exist only in its abuses. If it would confine itself to equal protection, and, as Heaven does its rains, shower its favors alike on the high and the low, the rich and the poor, it would be an unqualified blessing. In the act before me there seems to be a wide and unnecessary departure from these just principles.

The fact that the words of the veto message were probably a composite of contributions by members of Jackson's "Kitchen Cabinet" makes them no less authoritative. One of the members of that group, a man who contributed much to the veto message, was Roger B. Taney, then serving as President Jackson's Attorney General.

It was this same Taney who in 1837, as Chief Justice of the United States Supreme Court, handed down the memorable decision in the Charles River Bridge case. The decision drove another wedge between the government and those who sought legal aid in the winning of "exclusive privileges," and it was a vital part of the Jacksonian fight for free enterprise. The Charles River Bridge Company had received a charter to build a bridge between

Boston and Cambridge. The company was empowered to collect tolls. As the population in the area grew, the bridge became an extremely profitable bit of property. The company, originally capitalized at $50,000, had an estimated value in 1823 of $280,000, meaning that although the bridge had been paid for several times over, the public was still paying tolls for its use. In 1828, the Massachusetts legislature granted a charter to a second company to build a bridge just a few yards from the original bridge. Under the new charter this Warren Bridge Company was authorized to collect tolls up to a maximum of six years, or until the bridge was paid for. A free bridge next to the toll bridge would mean the end of profits for the Charles River Bridge Company. The latter took the case to court, contending that the Constitution of the United States protected its charter when it declared that no state might pass a law impairing the obligation of contract. The Charles River Bridge Company argued that the charter to the new bridge company violated its contract since it lowered the value of the property in the original bridge by allowing the development of ruinous competition.

The Supreme Court of Massachusetts decided against the Charles River Bridge Company, and the case was appealed to the United States Supreme Court. There the case was first argued in 1831, but it carried over and was not finally decided until 1837. By the time a decision had been reached, five of the seven members of the court were Jackson appointees. All five of these men concurred with the opinion of Chief Justice Taney in finding for the new or free bridge and against the toll bridge. In support of his decision Taney quoted from an English court which declared in a similar case:

This, like many other cases, is a bargain between a company of adventurers and the public, the terms of which are expressed in a statute; and the rule of construction in all such cases is fully established to be this—that any ambiguity in the terms of the contract must operate against the adventurers, and in favor of the public. . . .

Taney himself, in less formal language, said:

While the rights of private property are sacredly guarded, we must not forget that the community also have rights, and that the happiness and well-being of every citizen depend on their faithful preservation.

The decision was hailed by Jacksonians as a victory for the plain people over privilege. It was regarded as significant that the only justices dissenting from the majority opinion were the two members of the court held over from the pre-Jackson period. One of them, Justice Story, thought the decision a "manifesto of anarchy." A recent student of the Constitution observes that the decision encouraged "all business men who contemplated investments of capital in new corporate enterprise and who were relieved against claims of monopoly concealed in ambiguous clauses of old charters."

While the fight against economic privilege was being waged on the national level by Jackson and Taney, a host of Jacksonians in the state legislatures carried on their share of the struggle. On the state level the fight took the form of attacks against the requirement that every corporation charter be the product of a special legislative act. Since getting an incorporation charter through the state legislature frequently involved great expense, the corporation as a type of business organization was considerably handicapped.

In 1837, Connecticut passed a general incorporation law allowing any group of businessmen who could meet certain standard requirements to incorporate. Other states quickly followed suit, and the corporation, the most flexible method of business organization, was freed from its old alliance with government and made the instrument of the rising middle-class entrepreneur. The banking business gained its freedom at about the same time and by the same method. In 1838, New York passed a general banking law which allowed anyone to organize a bank upon the fulfillment of standard state requirements. In such fashion the way was gradually cleared for the great expansion of business which was to follow in succeeding decades.

The Democrats were not alone, however, in their interest in the business community. In fact, this was one of the primary concerns of the vigorous opposition created by Jackson's manner and measures. This opposition consisted of a combination of former nationalist Republicans and Antimasons who joined with a handful of old-line Federalists and a sprinkling of disgruntled Democrats to form the Whig party. Fundamentally a coalition of "outs" united chiefly in their antipathy to the "ins," the Whig party survived for almost twenty years and won the presidency twice before it was swallowed up by the Republican party in the 1850s.

One of the few things on which all Whigs agreed was their distrust of Andrew Jackson and all he stood for. The name Whig was chosen in a conscious effort to recall the age-old battle against the tyranny of kings. They attempted, without much success, to stigmatize the friends of "King Andrew I" with the label of Tory.

Behind a succession of talented leaders, beginning with Clay and Webster and in-cluding men like Abraham Lincoln and Horace Greeley, the Whig party sought to translate its optimistic and nationalistic views into a workable program. Dedicated to "sound" money and credit, willing to use the national government to promote the welfare of all classes of society, and abhorring radical or violent reforms, the Whigs thought Jackson's economic ideas primitive, his political principles moribund, and his general negativism quite out of keeping with the mission of America.

Undoubtedly, modern America is nearer the Whig than the Jacksonian dream, but it was Jackson who became the symbol for his age. The historic significance of Jacksonian democracy lies in its challenge to the economic as well as the political *status quo*. Jackson shared Jefferson's fear of the privileged few. But where Jefferson had sought to check the evil effects of minority rule by keeping government weak, Jackson reversed the strategy by creating a strong government to check the pretensions of the favored few. Jackson organized a rising tide of new voters into something very like a modern political party. By use of a party press, the "spoils of victory," party loyalty and discipline, and above all, by the weight of his imposing personality, Andrew Jackson led his party in the fight for greater political equality. The age of Jackson marks the end of the idea that America might be ruled by a political elite. Jacksonian democracy did not stop with its first victory. It used the great power of its new weapon to knock down the walls of economic privilege. Through these attacks upon government-created monopolies in banking and business, Jacksonians brought about a new freedom for American businessmen. Freedom to incorporate at will and freedom from monopoly competition were as fundamental to American economic democracy as was the right to vote to American political democracy. Jacksonians harnessed a political revolution to produce an economic revolution. Free enterprise and free speech became equal partners in the making of American democracy. Because of Jackson, government favors and responsibilities fell "alike on high and low, rich and poor."

FURTHER READINGS

The most recent and authoritative general account of the period is Glyndon G. Van Deusen, *The Jacksonian Era, 1828–1848* (1959). The older work of Claude G. Bowers, *Party Battles of the Jackson Period* (1922), is a very lively account, but it must be read with caution. A brilliant interpretation is A. M. Schlesinger, Jr., *Age of Jackson* (1945).

The best biographies of Jackson are those by Marquis James and John Spencer Bassett. James's is entitled *Andrew Jackson: Portrait of a President* (1937), and Bassett's is *The Life of Andrew Jackson* (2 vols., 1911).

For the controversy over banks and banking, see Ralph C. H. Catterall, *The Second Bank of the United States* (1903); Walter B. Smith, *Economic Aspects of the Second Bank of the United States* (1953); and Bray Hammond, *Banks and Politics in America* (1957).

The question of land policy is explored in Raynor G. Wellington, *The Political and Sectional Influence of the Public Lands, 1828–1842* (1914).

Outstanding biographies of leaders of the period include Edward M. Shepard, *Martin Van Buren* (1889); Frederic Bancroft, *The Life of William H. Seward* (2 vols., 1900); Charles M. Wiltse, *John C. Calhoun* (3 vols., 1944–1951); Claude M. Fuess, *Daniel Webster* (2 vols., 1930); Richard N. Current, *Daniel Webster and the Rise of National Conservatism* (1955); and Glyndon G. Van Deusen, *The Life of Henry Clay* (1937). William E. Smith, *The Francis Preston Blair Family in Politics* (2 vols., 1933), is a must.

Two provocative studies are Marvin Meyers, *The Jacksonian Persuasion* (1957), and John W. Ward, *Andrew Jackson: Symbol for an Age* (1955).

ELEVEN

Economic Development— North and South

1790–1791
First power-driven factory machinery in United States.

1792
Whitney's cotton gin invented.

1799
Interchangeable-parts system developed.

1807
First successful steamboat.

1814
Lowell cotton mills at Waltham, Massachusetts, established.

1825
Erie Canal completed; other canals under way.

1828
Railroad construction begins.

1837
Plank roads built.
Steam-powered threshers in use.
John Deere's steel plow in use.

1840
Hot-blast furnace used to produce pig iron.

1842
Commonwealth v. Hunt; growth of trade unions.

1846
Reapers come into use.
British repeal tariff on grain.
Sailing ships giving way to steam on ocean.

1855–1860
Rapid industrial expansion begins.

THE PROGRESS OF AGRICULTURE

AMERICANS OF THE YEAR 1800 were almost exclusively an agrarian folk, farming in a fashion some historians have likened to that of Biblical times. The manufactured products they needed were made within the household, produced locally by artisans, or imported from Europe. Obviously there was great reliance upon this last source, for domestic manufacture was rudimentary. Constant labor and effort were required to wrest a meager living from the soil. But there were economic developments in progress which were to broaden the vision and enlarge the scope of American economic life.

Within the half-century preceding the Civil War, the boundaries of the United States were pushed beyond the Mississippi River and extended from the Canadian border to the Gulf Coast. Within that same half-century Americans settled the new lands, bound the wide-flung reaches of the nation with a transportation and communication network, and laid the foundations for the economic primacy of the United States in future decades. In the years 1800–1860, the United States developed from a simple agrarian nation to one with a rapidly growing industry and a basic agrarian economy, progressing from primitive self-sufficiency to highly mechanized and specialized production. The progress of agriculture and the rise and growth of industry were certainly the ma-

223

The McCormick reaper, first used in 1831

A drawing of John Deere's
1837 steel plow

An earlier plow, made in
Massachusetts, 1783

A model of the McCormick reaper

Model of Eli Whitney's cotton gin

Improved agricultural tools, along with better farming methods, raised agricultural productivity and thus contributed to the growth in wealth of a nation still mainly agricultural. Without the new plow the farmer could not successfully cultivate the rich Midwestern prairie soil. The reaper with a two-man crew could cut as much grain in a day as four or five men with cradles, and further improvements in harvesting machinery were to follow. A simple piece of machinery, the cotton gin, opened up a vast future for American cotton in the textile factories of England. With labor scarce, machinery was the key to American economic progress.

Cutting grain with the cradle, in use about 1776–1830

jor economic developments of the first half of the nineteenth century. These developments were interdependent, and both were related to the spread of transportation and communication facilities during these same years.

There has been a tendency to emphasize the growth of manufacturing in the decades before the Civil War and, by contrast, to underestimate the importance of agriculture in early-nineteenth-century America. The spread of manufacturing throughout the nation, particularly in the older seaboard areas and certain sections of the West, was indeed a unique feature of these years. By 1860, the income from manufacturing and hand trades constituted about one-eighth of the national income, a figure testifying to the tremendous growth (and potential) of American industry. Yet, at the same time, the income from agriculture, over 1,200 million dollars, was twice that of manufacturing and made up over one-quarter of the national income. Many Americans turned to new economic activities in the years 1800–1860, but the great majority of them continued to seek their living in some manner from the soil. At mid-century almost 60 per cent of the nation's population were engaged in some sort of agricultural enterprise; East, West, and South, the nation was primarily one of free small farmers.

As late as 1820, most northern farmers still worked their land in a fashion little changed from that of their colonial grandparents. Conservative, continually hampered by lack of capital (or ready cash), ignorant of methods of scientific agriculture, they faced the added problems of inadequate transportation facilities and a scarcity of labor. But in the next thirty years their position was materially altered by the rapid improvement in transportation and the consequent opening of new markets, by the development of industry, and by technological improvements in farming methods.

The rapid growth of commercial and manufacturing towns throughout the Northeast gave the farmers their first stable markets. Soon the swift expansion and improvement of transportation methods presented them with a variety of domestic markets plus the possibility of selling surpluses to foreign customers. With this incentive, the farmers were moved to increase output by any possible means. To increase production, though, the farmers had first to overcome a serious handicap —a scarcity of labor.

This labor shortage plagued the American farmer as constantly as it did the American industrialist. The seemingly endless supply of cheap land in the early half of the nineteenth century had checked the rise of a landless class which would serve as a supply of agricultural laborers. The farmer soon found the source of help from within his own family disappearing as his sons moved out into the western lands and his daughters went off to the more lively and profitable factory towns. Few of the growing number of immigrants to the United States were attracted to farm labor, preferring the better pay in the mills or, if they had savings, the purchase of their own farms. In view of this labor shortage, the northern farmer sought ways in which both to improve his tools and to increase the productivity of his soil. By making hand tools lighter and by redesigning others, he found it possible to conserve his strength and energy. Thus horse-drawn wheelless hay rakes took over the work formerly done by six to ten men with hand rakes, cultivators simplified the growing of corn, and threshing machines replaced the flail and ended the use of livestock to trample out the grain.

In the last decades before the Civil War the farmer received his greatest boon from steel plows, grain drills and seeders, reapers and mowers. Colonial plows were heavy, with handles so vertically set as to give little leverage or control; they were particularly inadequate when applied to breaking prairie land. In order to cut through the heavy tough sod, with roots as large as a man's finger and reaching 12 to 15 inches underground, the farmer had to plow with five to ten yoke of oxen. Although patents for improved steel plows were issued early in the century, their production was negligible before 1850. Local blacksmiths and inventors constantly tried their hands at improving the iron plow; the Diamond, the Tobey and Anderson, and many other varieties were used at one time or another. But not until 1858, when John Deere's factory at Moline, Illinois, was finally averaging 13,000 steel plows a year, did the new tool begin to supersede the cast-iron plow on a wide scale.

With a reaper, a farmer no longer planted only that acreage of grain he could handle with a sickle and cradle. The average reaper, a great timesaver, allowed nine men to do a job that formerly had taken fifteen men. Threshing machines were equally valuable. One of the most time-consuming and wasteful operations on the farm was the threshing of grain by flail. By the old methods, threshing and cleaning the crop of a 10-acre farm was an all-winter job for a single farmer. But with the new machine and four men, the farmer could thresh 25 bushels of grain per hour, instead of the 8 bushels a day formerly processed by two men using the old hand methods.

New tools and machines, however, were not the only means by which the farmer's production was increased. Attention was given to soil improvement. After ignoring for many years the possibilities of fertilizers, even such crude ones as barnyard manure and rockweed, farmers began to realize that the use of gypsum, lime, or marl resulted in enlarged crop yields. By 1860, adding fertilizer to the soil had become such a standard practice in the East that commercial fertilizers were either imported or produced on a wide scale. In the West, though, despite constant advice from agricultural leaders, farmers never seemed to turn to new ideas like fertilizer and seed selection with the readiness with which they adopted mechanical improvements.

At about the same time, farmers began to pay more attention to the quality and care of their livestock. For the domestic demand for wool, hides, meat, and dairy products was also increasing, offering larger markets and stimulating production. Following the lead of a few wealthy gentlemen farmers who did much of the initial experimenting in livestock breeding, the average farmer tried to purify the breeding of his sheep and cattle and to improve their housing and feed. This required more cash and security than most could afford. They did, however, recognize the greater efficiency of horses and mules as draft animals and generally substituted them for oxen.

While each decade brought with it a substantial improvement in the farmer's life, there were recurring problems arising from the settlement of large areas of western land. Between 1820 and 1850, vast new regions were brought under cultivation, extending at length to the Mississippi and beyond. The western farmer had to sustain himself and his family during the years required to convert his 80 or 160 acres from forest to tillable soil. Only then might he expand his holdings, cultivating a portion of his acreage while raising livestock on the remainder for local and eastern consumption, or sending dairy products to river towns such as Cincinnati. With the arrival of the railroads in the 1840s, western farmers could undersell their eastern competitors in most agricultural products. They had learned to farm the fabulously fertile soil of the prairie lands—an environment which they had at first distrusted because of its lack of trees, scarcity of rivers and building stone, and the toughness of the prairie sod. Using this rich soil, the new agricultural machinery, and the rapidly developing transportation system, the western farmer by 1860 had become the nation's, and soon was to become the world's, major producer of wheat, corn, and livestock.

The prosperity of western farmers meant near disaster for many eastern farmers. In order to escape western competition, the latter turned to specialized farming, such as truck gardening, fruit growing, and dairying. In 1850 New York was the leading apple state, while the Middle Atlantic coastal states were famous for their peach crops. Dairy farming, together with the raising of hay as a winter ration for the dairy cows, absorbed the energies of more and more eastern farmers. Since milk could not as yet be transported long distances, its production tended to localize in areas near urban centers, such as southeastern Pennsylvania, Delaware, northeastern Maryland, and upper New York. The relative decline of eastern agriculture meant that many farmers migrated to the fertile West.

SOUTHERN AGRICULTURE

While the northern farmers were thus engaged in increasing their productivity, finding new markets, and mastering the prairie, their counterparts south of Mason and Dixon's line were striving for somewhat similar goals. There also, farmers turned to improved farming methods to compensate for labor scarcity and as a means of profiting from new and wider markets. Southern farmers, as well as northern, struggled with the problem of marketing, handicapped at times by markets which were inaccessible, expensive and difficult to reach, or fluctuating in price and demand. In both sections, too, farmers previously isolated by lack of transportation facilities found that the turnpikes, canals, and railroads opened up a new world to them.

Southern farmers had much in common with their northern neighbors. Despite the peculiar characteristics which set the ante bellum South apart from the rest of the nation, that section was, primarily, a region of independent small farmers. This preponderance of small farmers is often obscured by the social and political influence exerted by the plantation aristocracy in southern life. The planter group, chiefly cotton magnates, owning great tracts of land and large numbers of slaves, monopolized that section's wealth, yet fewer than 8,000 slaveholders, out of a total population of almost 10 million, owned 50 slaves or more. The great majority had fewer than ten apiece, and most had fewer than five. More numerous by far were the small farmers, tilling five to ten acres, rarely owning slaves, and living in small, crudely built houses. In all the prewar years, these made up nine-tenths of the South's landowners. Even in the "plantation" South small farms predominated—in the tobacco area around the Chesapeake Bay and in central Kentucky, in the sugar region of Louisiana, and in the rice and cotton sections of South Carolina and the Gulf Coast. Though it is true that in these plantation regions the small farmers frequently

Cotton plantation, by Giroux, an American painter of the mid-nineteenth century. (M. and M. Karolik Collection, Museum of Fine Arts, Boston)

lived on the "thinner" lands bordering the giant plantations, the old South was everywhere more a land of farms than one of huge feudal estates.

Where the South differed substantially from the North was in the domination of its economy by staples grown for consumption outside the South, in its climate and soil, in the influence exerted in its society by a small number of wealthy planters, and, of course, in the existence of Negro slavery. With the passing of years these distinctions tended to make the southern farmer's life different from that of the farmer of the East and West. But they did not eliminate the concern the southerners had in common with all farmers about the problems of transportation, marketing, increased productivity, and the competition of the West.

Nature in most respects had not favored the South as much as the North. Her clay or sandy soil was subject to constant erosion and unable to absorb and retain an abundant rainfall. The poorer soil and the heat made most of the South deficient in the grass and grain so necessary for the raising of livestock. Although not a tropical area, much of the section had lengthy summers of six to nine months, affording a growing season long enough in some places to allow the raising of three vegetable crops a year. It was these physical characteristics that made the South an ideal area for the raising of the great commercial staples: cotton, sugar, tobacco, and rice. Some general farming was done in small areas such as the Bluegrass country of Kentucky. But most of the South was devoted to the growing of staples: rice along the Carolina and Georgia coast and the Mississippi delta; sugar in Louisiana and Texas; cotton in the wide Deep South; and tobacco in the older states, Maryland, Virginia, Kentucky, and Tennessee. Tobacco, once the South's chief money crop, unable to compete in world markets, had become unprofitable in many areas early in the century. It was revived in certain limited areas after 1840, by which time new methods of curing gave American tobacco an edge in market competition. Virginia and Kentucky produced the greater portion of the country's crop, a crop worth 10 million dollars in 1850.

Rice, of necessity, was grown in a limited area; needing an ample supply of water, it was planted on the flood plains of rivers or streams. The rice fields were carefully weeded and tended during the growing season, and harvesting the year's crop was backbreaking labor. Four-fifths of the nation's rice crop was gathered annually in the coastal regions of South Carolina and Georgia. While rice growing was confined to flood regions, that of sugar cane was limited to a very warm climate, of the sort found in the southeastern part of Texas and southern Louisiana. Growing cane took more effort than raising tobacco or cotton. Cane fields had to be cultivated diligently all during the growing season, while harvesting required using a heavy knife and carting large loads of cane stalks to the mill. Harvest time was particularly arduous: at least one overseer of a large Louisiana sugar estate recorded that he kept his slaves in the field continuously at that time.

Until the advent of Eli Whitney's cotton gin in 1793, cotton culture in the South was confined to the sea islands and the coastal regions of the Carolinas and Georgia. There, a long-staple cotton, which could be economically cleaned by hand, had long flourished. Whitney's device, which separated the short-staple cotton from its sticky green seeds, now made possible the spread of cotton into the upland regions and beyond into the Mississippi Valley. The routine of "making a crop" of cotton was soon established over wide areas of the South.

Cotton proved a relatively simple crop to manage. Cultivation of the planted seed was not needed after the plants were too big to allow further hoeing. Picking started late in summer and continued through December. It was this operation which most frequently determined the amount of seed planted, for the Southerner knew "that a laborer could plant and cultivate about twice as much cotton as he could pick." In order to adjust the harvest capacities of his workers to their other work potential, the southern farmer usually supplemented this cotton crop with corn, peanuts, small grains, or sweet potatoes. But however completely he adjusted the work and ability schedule, the southern farmer was still at the mercy of insects, rainfall, frosts, and market prices, as indeed were farmers everywhere.

The marketing of cotton had improved little over that of colonial days and in many ways worked to the farmer's disadvantage. Most of the South's cotton crop was sold through factors or brokers who served both as commission merchants and bankers. For a commission, averaging 2½ per cent, the factors agreed to sell the crop, while holding accounts to which sale proceeds were accredited and against which the farmer could draw. Occasionally, farmers borrowed money from factors, mortgaging future crops and paying large interest rates for the favor. Under these circumstances planters found it easy to become embroiled in a never-ending cycle of debt. Most of the cotton crop was sold in the large southern export towns like Charleston. Small amounts of cotton were constantly marketed in interior cities or the mill towns of New England. While most farmers of this period were, to some extent, victimized by the existing marketing system, the southern cotton planter seemed to be an especially easy mark. The factor method took from him more and more of his profits as it became a traditionalized marketing scheme.

But too often the impression is created that the South's staple crops constituted its chief source of wealth. This is not true. Most southern farmers produced their own food supply and frequently a surplus. As late as 1850 the South still grew over one-half the country's corn crop and most of its hemp and bean product. In every decade of the first half of the century the upper South harvested large crops of fruit, while its garden crops were always equal to those of the North.

SLAVERY

The southern farmers, while constantly facing obstacles identical with those of the farmers of the East and West, found that certain problems were peculiar to their section, especially that of securing a steady, large labor force to ensure the consistent production of staple crops. While farmers of the North confronted the same problem, they found that their crops, primarily grain, lent themselves to the use of mechanical implements. They were able to make up for an inadequate labor supply by adopting new tools as soon as they became available. As an added factor, the northern farmers found that they still made a profit even though limiting their acreage, for their products were less subject to market fluctuations and slower in exhausting the soil. Not so the southerners. The staples grown in the South required cultivation and care which could not be provided by any machine then known. These crops so quickly ruined the soil that most planters found it unprofitable to try to counteract the process; the only alternative seemed to be the constant addition of new acreage.

The southern planter met most of his labor needs by a continued reliance upon the system of slavery. He did not create slavery; it was a heritage. Slaves had been in this country since 1619. Through the years the South had grown more and more dependent upon slavery as a labor system. By the time of the Civil War slavery was so firmly established in southern states that it had become "the great peculiar institution of the South." To a great extent, slavery was plantation labor. Having come into being primarily to meet a labor shortage, it was found mainly wherever the

THE INSTITUTION OF SLAVERY

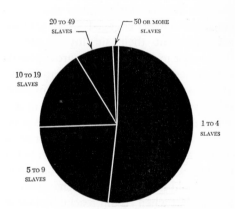

THE SLAVE-OWNING POPULATION OF 347,525 FAMILIES IN 1850.

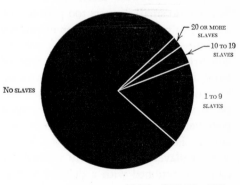

THE SOUTHERN WHITE POPULATION OF 7,981,000 IN 1860.

southerner could set up large "agricultural factories" for the raising of a staple crop. It is often mistakenly thought that the whole southern population had a stake in slavery; actually, a very small percentage were slaveholders. By 1850 less than one-third of the southern white population had any direct connection with slavery, and this number was steadily decreasing.

Since the African slave trade had closed in 1808, the slaveholders had had to draw their labor supply largely from the 1 million slaves then present in the United States and their descendants. The closing of the slave trade and the gradual migration of the cotton planters westward gave rise to an interstate slave traffic. Older eastern states, especially Virginia and Maryland, no longer engaged in large-scale planting, sent their surplus supply of slaves west to be sold to the great plantation owners in the cotton and cane belts. These slaves, carried to the new markets in coastwise vessels or sent overland in coffles (caravans), fetched slave traders sums closely tied to the current selling price of cotton: when cotton sold for 13 cents per pound in New York City in 1837, an able-bodied field hand cost his purchaser about $1,100, but when cotton reached a low of 5 cents per pound, the same slave brought only $500.

Many slaves were hired out by their owners—to small farmers too poor to buy a slave, to professional men or merchants needing helpers, or to others wanting domestic servants. Many slaves worked alongside, as well as under the control of, their owners. On smaller plantations and farms, where slaves were few, they worked and even ate in company with the master and his family.

Since slavery was basically a labor system, it functioned with a definite routine and discipline. Slaves were assigned tasks according to their strength and ability, serving as field hands or as blacksmiths, bricklayers, and the like. They had to observe fixed hours of labor or perform given amounts of work; a piece system was used most often on the rice coast, while time work or the gang system was best suited to sugar and cotton. The most irksome of rules involved in the system were those connected with discipline. The usual basis of discipline was a system of punishments and rewards, the rigors of which varied with the personality of the owner or overseer. Although most slaveholders agreed that whipping was essential to order and industry, and while all discipline was based ultimately on physical force, few slaveholders indulged in cruel and unusual punishment. But behind the slaveholder stood the law, and before it the slave was a thing of little consequence. His testimony was never accepted against whites; legal statutes generally ruled to his disadvantage; and, with the passage of years, his emancipation became more and more difficult to achieve.

Food and clothing were regularly issued to the slaves, and some attention was paid to their health, amusement, and housing. Housing was seldom good; slaves usually lived in small one- or two-room cabins, windowless and unfloored. If, on rare occasions, they were provided with well-built cabins, their carelessness and poverty soon reduced these to hovels. Food was adequate in quantity but unappetizing and monotonous, and probably not very nutritious. The diet almost always included bacon, bread, milk, cornmeal, and whatever vegetables the slaves could raise themselves. Clothing consisted of homespun cotton and shapeless brogans, the same things worn by the poorer whites. Provisions for amusement and care of health depended upon the nature of the individual slaveowner. While there were always those who neglected both, there were more who were both genuinely fond of and concerned for their slaves; in any event, the slave was at the least a financial investment to be kept in good working condition.

Whether slavery increased the planters' profits or limited them no one knows. While the advocates of slavery emphasized the fact that slaves, once purchased, worked for nothing but their subsistence, it is not fair to ignore the economic risks involved in slavery. Not all slave children were born healthy; owners could not count on a full life of work from each slave; and the slaveholder was responsible for all slaves too old to labor. Then there were the many threats to his labor force such as epidemics, fire, and escape. Finally, while the price of slaves rose rapidly in the years before the war, giving the planter a property wealth on the books, the price of his staple was fluctuating widely, sometimes so much so as to wipe out any observable profit for a given year. With the cost of slaves increasing, more and more southern planters were kept from adding to their labor supply, and thus to their yield.

Whatever the effect of slavery upon the planter and his income, the institution certainly worked hardship on the South as a whole. Naturally all the backwardness and poverty of the South could not be attributed solely to slavery, yet it was true that it was an "area of rude and wasteful agriculture" and that its methods of agricultural production were sadly lacking in foresight, intelligence, and thrift. The southern farmer, in a frenzy of waste, exploited his soil and slaves, gaining temporary wealth at the cost of sectional impoverishment. Both southern and northern critics of slavery felt that it immobilized

an excessive amount of capital, thus greatly limiting the development of industry and commerce, and that it discouraged the enterprise of nonslaveholding whites. Defenders of the system found that, on the contrary, slaves were both capital and labor, for the slaves served as collateral for the credit needed to move to market the crop they had produced.

Be that as it may, by making manual labor disreputable, by limiting wage opportunities, by denying the average southern farmer access to the richest lands, by withholding funds from education and general governmental activities, and by discouraging the diversification of industry, slavery put a blight upon the South.

Whether by adopting new tools and methods, by turning to specialized farming, or by the continued employment of slavery, American farmers tried to meet the problem of scarce labor. These means, however, only partially provided an answer. Nor were all farmers able to use these methods, for their adoption was contingent upon financial reserves, local conditions, and individual enterprise. In 1860 many were undoubtedly continuing to farm in the fashion of colonial days.

THE TRANSPORTATION REVOLUTION

There was one important area, at least, in which very substantial progress was made in the years before 1860—the providing of adequate transportation facilities. If the farmer could not get his product to market, both he and his customer lost. While much produce did reach market, it was at such cost in time and labor that prices were distorted or the condition of the product altered. Inaccessible markets plagued all economic producers in the early years of the century, but especially the farmer, the nation's chief entrepreneur. To make matters worse, the country steadily expanded, bringing even greater distances between producers and consumers. Yet by 1860 this separation was on its way to an end. The growth of transportation facilities enabled the farmers to get their product to market at lower cost.

Expansion of the transportation system began with the improvement of old roads and the construction of new ones; it ended with the establishment of a network of railroads. New methods of transportation substantially altered the conduct of trade and manufacture; yet it is worth noting that they did not eliminate, but rather supplemented, older transportation patterns. Thus in 1850, as in 1800, traders carried much of their produce by river, while peddlers, covering the roads of the North or moving from wharf to wharf along the rivers bordering southern plantations, brought the village store to the consumer's door.

By the 1820s nearly 1,200 miles of improved roads had been built in the United States. Since no state or community yet regularly appropriated funds for the purpose, road construction was undertaken by various private companies. Securing some aid from the states, turnpike corporations financed their projects through lotteries or by charging tolls. Following the pattern set by John L. McAdam, the famous road builder, many early roads were built by spreading crushed stone 10 inches deep, thus forming a roadbed that grew stronger with time and use.

With the opening of western lands, even this improvement seemed less than a drop in the bucket. Most new roads were built in the East; not one penetrated into the trans-Allegheny country. Manufacturers in search of cheaper raw materials and wider markets united with western farmers and pioneers in demands for internal improvements. In answer, Congress undertook early in the century to finance the construction of a transcontinental highway, the Cumberland Road. By 1852, the road extended as far west as Vandalia, Illinois, though its construction had been slow and haphazard. In the mid-1840s, travelers complained that the road beyond Terre Haute, Indiana, was "nothing more than a track . . . the timber cut down and removed, the stumps being left." Regardless of its condition, the old National Road was one of the great highways of the world. For decades it was crowded with emigrants moving westward and wagons bringing western produce to eastern markets.

By 1830, many roads and turnpikes had been built and many more were projected in anticipation of government assistance. But President Jackson's veto of the Maysville Road bill in 1830 put a crimp in some of the more grandiose road-building schemes. Most states were too poor to assume the burden and private road construction ceased to be profitable as steamboats, railroads, and canals appeared.

Canals as a means of inland communication had intrigued Americans since prerevolutionary days, but little actual work was completed until after the opening of the Erie Canal in 1825. This canal connected Buffalo with Albany, and thence (via the Hudson River) to New York. With the success of the venture, the nation succumbed to canal fever. Immediately most of the seaboard states tried to improve their western connections. Although Boston found that the topography of western Massachusetts made canal construction impractical if not impossible, Pennsylvania was able to solve the problem. In the 1830s Pennsylvania spent 10 million dollars tying Philadelphia to Pittsburgh with an elaborate system of canals complete with a 36-mile portage railway over the mountains. Canalboats were placed on cars and pulled over the crest by means of a series of inclined planes. The power was furnished by stationary engines. This "Pennsylvania system" was state owned. For twenty years it was the most important through route from the Ohio Valley to the East. But the railroad made it impractical except for limited purposes, and in 1857 the Pennsylvania Railroad Company bought it.

The other most notable project to link the east coast with the Middle West was the Chesapeake and Ohio Canal. Designed to connect the nation's capital with Pittsburgh via the Potomac, it was completed only as far as Cumberland, Maryland. The canal company met a bitter competitor in the Baltimore & Ohio Railroad, which eventually acquired control of the canal. It had only one period of prosperity—in the 1870s when, in conjunction with the

railroad, the transport of coal was highly important.

Canal fever raged just as severely in the West as along the seaboard. There one state after another, enchanted by visions of vast and profitable interior navigation, borrowed large sums of money to finance their schemes. Of the many western canals, most were feeders to main canals, designed to provide one continuous inland waterway to either New York City or New Orleans. Ohio led in the construction of two canals begun in 1825. Both were designed to link the Ohio River with the Great Lakes. The total cost of both—nearly 16 million dollars—was nearly three times the original estimates owing to unanticipated difficulties. But for thirty-five years the Ohio canals earned revenues, after which they succumbed to railroad competition.

The most important canal project in Illinois was the one to connect Lake Michigan with the navigable portion of the Illi-

CANALS IN THE UNITED STATES, 1785–1850

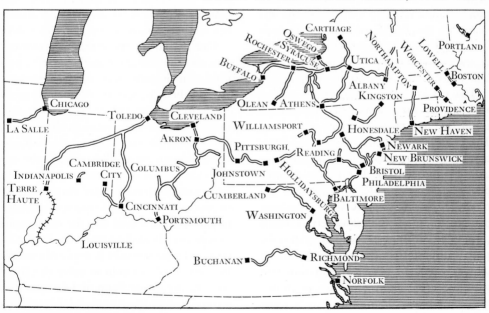

nois River and thus to the Mississippi. Construction began in 1836 but was not completed until 1848. Still another canal system resulted from the cooperative efforts of Ohio and Indiana. This canal system made connections between the Ohio River and the Great Lakes via the Wabash River. But railroad competition came too soon for the venture to be profitable. This was the usual fate of canals. But in addition to being unable to compete with railroads, which afforded faster transportation, canals suffered from other inadequacies. They were unable to keep pace with industrial developments; they served only certain localities; they were closed for part of the year; their management could not be divorced from politics, which resulted in loss of public confidence in them. Notwithstanding their failure to meet expectations, the canals of the Middle West resulted in a revolution in transportation. This was the diversion of much commerce, which formerly went downstream to New Orleans for export, to a northeasterly line of communications which might take the products ultimately to the eastern seaboard via the Erie Canal. This may well have been a factor in holding the loyalty of the trans-Allegheny Northwest to the Union when the Civil War came.

The passion for digging canals was at a peak when the steamboat added another factor to the transportation revolution. The country's navigable rivers had been one of the first means of transportation used by the settlers. With no (or very poor) roads available, the pioneer depended upon these rivers for reaching markets, using an endless variety of small craft. The steamboat completely altered river transportation. Before the nineteenth century opened, men had experimented with the application of steam to movement on water. Although this was success-

fully demonstrated by Fulton and his associates before 1810, steamboats did not become commonplace in the East until after 1812.

Although the first steamboat in the western rivers made a successful voyage in 1811, this new method of navigation continued in an experimental stage until 1817. In that year it was demonstrated that steamboats could successfully overcome the current in upstream navigation. The steamboat *Washington* made the 1,300-mile trip from New Orleans to Louisville in twenty-five days. By 1821, when steamboat tonnage at New Orleans port exceeded all other tonnage combined, the business was definitely established. The conquest of other western rivers was rapid. By 1839 there were 362 steamboats on the Mississippi and its tributaries, none more than seven years old. The effects of the steamboat in increasing western commerce is indicated by the fact that in the 1840s the tonnage of the Mississippi Valley was greater than that of all Atlantic ports. In 1843 New Orleans had twice the tonnage of New York and was the fourth city in population in the United States.

The heyday of the steamboat was before the Civil War, with the year 1859–1860 marking the peak of river prosperity. The first steamboats were slow, moving 4 to 6 miles per hour, or even less against the currents of a swift river. Flimsily constructed, steamboats were as liable to destruction from their own weak engines and poorly made boilers as from the many perils on the rivers. As time went on, the size of vessels increased, accommodations became more elegant, and speed records improved. The trip from New Orleans to Louisville, which required twenty-five days in 1817, could be made in a little over eight days in 1834, and in less than five days in 1853. At the same time, in-

The "De Witt Clinton," one of the first locomotive engines built in America, hauled its first passengers in August, 1831, from Albany to Schenectady. (New York Central)

creasing competition brought steadily decreasing fares. On the other hand, the accident rate continued high. More than a thousand steamboats were lost in the forty years from 1810 to 1850, involving the loss of well over two thousand lives.

Steamboats, canals, and turnpikes stimulated the settlement of new regions and gave real aid to both farmer and merchant, but they did not completely ease transportation troubles. Farmers far from great rivers, main roads, or canals still had urgent needs. Even better-situated farmers found these routes long, roundabout, and dangerous. It remained for the railroads to provide not a complete answer to the problem, but an exceedingly valuable addition to the transportation system. Early American railroads were often thought of as improved turnpikes, or railed roads, offering better facilities for vehicular transport by horsepower. "Railways" of wood with horse cars had been used around quarries and mines since the late 1790s.

After many trials and experiments, a 3-mile tramway was built from the Quincy, Massachusetts, granite quarries to the Neponset River. Soon several regular railroads were begun; among the first were the Baltimore & Ohio (1828) and the Charleston & Hamburg Railroad, in South Carolina. The latter was the first steam railroad opened for operation, and in its first year it carried an average of fifty passengers a day, as well as large quantities of raw cotton from the Georgia cotton belt.

Once the railroads were under way, their promoters spent many decades trying to overcome a host of obstacles, including mechanical and engineering problems, public prejudice and ignorance, and the need for financial support for construction. The first railroads followed existing roads and were full of sharp curves and steep grades. Roadbeds, inadequately laid, needed constant improvement to withstand the strain of increasingly heavy rolling stock. Rails, first made of wood and then of iron, never seemed strong enough. Only gradually, with the coming of more efficient locomotives and cars, did railroad travel cease to be a matter of acute discomfort and unreliability. A great boon to railroad travel came with the invention of the telegraph, making it possible to run trains with more speed and certainty. Using information obtained from others, Samuel F. B. Morse, artist and inventor, showed successfully in 1837 that there was no reason why "intelligence may not be transmitted instantaneously by electricity." Congress was eventually persuaded to build an experimental line from Baltimore to Washington, and soon after, telegraph wires became a permanent feature of the American landscape.

Money for building railroads was hard to find. Yet despite the scarcity of surplus capital in the nation, the enormous sum of 1 billion dollars had been invested in railroads by 1860. This private investment was supplemented by substantial aid from various governmental units. Cities, counties, states, and subsequently the federal government itself frequently gave land grants or stock guarantees. Before the Civil War most of the aid came from the states, which not only lent money to railroad builders but gave them land grants and permission to issue paper money to pay for labor and materials. The raising of capital was not the only problem, however. Railroad building was opposed not only by vested interests representing turnpike, steamboat, stagecoach, and canal companies, but also by great portions of the public. Many thought of this noisy new contraption as a "pestilential, topsy-turvy, harum-scarum whirligig . . . setting the whole world a-gadding." Farmers feared it would ruin the market for hay and horses. Those who warned of the per-

nicious moral effects of railroads were joined by others who asserted that the human heart could never function at speeds as great as 25 miles per hour! Nevertheless, by 1850 there were over 9,000 miles of railroads in the United States. More than three-fourths of this mileage was north of the Potomac and Ohio Rivers, perhaps because of the seasonal variation of southern cotton and tobacco freight and the greater use of navigable rivers in the South.

A burst of railroad building during the 1850s coincided with the expansion of other modes of transportation and worked startling changes in the nation's economy. With the opening of new avenues of travel, westerners no longer sent the bulk of their produce to nearby markets but instead dispatched surpluses to richer eastern and foreign markets. The new markets wanted western grain, so the farmer concentrated on raising that crop. New means of transportation had first swamped eastern farmers with western competition. This increased competition was offset, however, by greater accessibility to the expanding urban markets which created a growing demand for dairy and truck-garden products. The southern farmers did not benefit as greatly from the transportation revolution, for they already possessed one natural means of communication in their many navigable rivers. But the new modes of travel did not completely bypass the South. That section also built canals, roads, and railroads in order to facilitate the movement of its great staples to market.

The transportation revolution not only simplified the movement of raw materials to market, it also brought an expanding variety of manufactured goods to an ever larger number of consumers. While the American farmer was busy with his production problems, another segment of the American population was engaged in building a substantial manufacturing interest in the United States. Although the new industrialist competed successfully with the farmer for the nation's limited labor supply, he was creating many of the farmer's new markets and manufacturing new farm implements. As in most cases of economic development, each factor aided and stimulated the other. They were competitors in one sense and coworkers in another.

THE EMERGENCE OF INDUSTRY

Some manufacturing had been carried on in colonial times. Largely household production, such manufacturing expanded temporarily during times of crisis to compensate for the loss of imported articles. Except for these periods, American industry remained fairly primitive during the eighteenth century—the victim of jealously guarded technological innovations and a scarcity of labor and capital.

At the beginning of the nineteenth century, a number of small cotton mills opened in New England. After a short-lived prosperity during the Napoleonic Wars and the War of 1812, these had succumbed to world-wide depression and foreign competition by 1820. But revival soon followed. In the 1820s a host of new factories, equipped with more modern machines, began to dot the New England landscape. With the growing availability of technological improvements, both foreign and domestic, this impulse to manufacturing was soon general throughout the country. The first successful efforts to establish industry in the United States were in the field of textile manufacturing. Probably owing to the fact that textile produc-

tion had been more thoroughly mechanized than other industrial processes, this type of manufacture lent itself more readily to the factory system. With some knowledge of English inventions, the textile industry was employing by the 1820s a number of native technical improvements such as a power loom which combined the spinning and weaving process under one roof or another loom designed to weave patterned fabrics. Mechanical inventions, and other technical innovations such as the use of chemical bleaching instead of lawn bleaching and cylinder machines for printing, soon gave American textile manufacturers a strong competitive position in world markets.

Textile manufacture was not the only industry profiting from improved techniques. Much attention was paid to the production of primary metals and their finishing. In 1830, iron ore was successfully melted with anthracite coal, freeing iron production from its dependence upon the more expensive charcoal. In the next decade the "hot-blast furnace" replaced the old furnace. The biggest change in iron production came in the 1850s, when William Kelly, a Kentucky ironmaster, independently discovered the method used by Sir Henry Bessemer to make steel—decarbonizing molten metal by forcing air through it. Meanwhile, machinery was developed for turning out a variety of finished iron goods formerly produced by hand, such as screws and firearms. By expanding the principle of interchangeable parts evolved by Eli Whitney and Simeon North and applying it to other manufactures, Americans soon produced clocks and machine tools that surpassed in originality and efficiency those made in Europe.

In some instances where mechanical devices could not yet be applied to the production process, other modern industrial procedures were used. The division-of-labor system could be found in the Cincinnati packing houses as early as the 1830s. In these three-story buildings, covering several acres, the animal, most often a hog, moved down a "disassembly" line —from death blow through finished product. Lines of workers plied "the mallet, —the knife,—the axe,—the boiling caldron—the remorseless scraping iron, . . . [and] the fated porker, that was but one minute before grunting in full enjoyment of bristling hoghood, now cadaverous . . . hangs a stark and naked effigy among his immolated brethren."

During these years the motive power propelling the new machinery also increased in efficiency. Water was, of course, used at first, but by the 1830s the rivers of the older industrial areas were working at capacity and seemed unable to support additional demands upon them. In regions where water power was not abundant, mill and factory owners turned to the steam engine, a particularly fortunate substitute in industries such as glass manufacture or print works, where intense heat was needed. Industry in the Middle West was especially dependent upon steam power. As early as 1817, Steubenville, Ohio, had a steam-run woolen mill processing 38,000 pounds of wool annually, while Cincinnati newspapers advertised the opening of a woolen mill operated by a 20-horsepower steam engine. Wood was the main fuel for generating steam power until after the Civil War, although coal was being employed in increasing quantities. America scarcely awakened to the possibilities of coal as a fuel until after the War of 1812, when the decreasing supply of wood plus the known utility of coal began to overcome the public's reluctance to use the new fuel. Originally

most coal users preferred soft coal, obtaining it from the rich Virginia coal fields. As hard coal became more accessible, consumers in the East got their supplies from the Lehigh Coal Mine Co., one of the first companies to undertake the mining and selling of coal. Western coal users bought their coal from Pittsburgh at 12 cents per bushel or from the coal counties of Ohio and Illinois. By 1860 coal had become such a generally used commodity that the United States was producing over 14 million tons per year besides importing a considerable tonnage from abroad. The mechanization of production processes and the development of new, efficient sources of power were characteristic of the growth of American industry during this period.

Also characteristic of American economic growth before the Civil War was the evolution of an elementary system of corporate finance. Lack of capital handicapped all economic producers—the small farmer, the canal builder or railroad promoter, the southern planter, and most of all, the industrialist. The latter was required to put forth greater initial investment than the others in paying for his factory, his motive power, his machinery and his labor before any return could be expected from his enterprise.

Since most early factories were small establishments, they could be, and were, financed by individuals, families, or partners. Many early businessmen were former farmers, small merchants, or retired skippers who had amassed savings, ripe for investment. If the industrial undertaking required extensive capital, some would join together in a joint-stock company. As the nation grew, American industry became an attractive investment possibility even for foreign capitalists. Soon some industrial units, expanding with the stimulus of profits and available capital, changed from family enterprises to corporate organizations. In a corporate form an enterprise not only found capital funds easier to raise, but also found greater freedom from legal regulation. There was, indeed, little regulation or control of any kind before 1860.

Whether as corporations or family businesses, American industrial undertakings prospered and grew in the ante bellum years. During the twenty-year period from 1840 to 1860, the value of American manufactures doubled. At the same time the number of men engaged in industrial establishments increased from almost 800,000 to 1,300,000. Of a variety of products manufactured in the United States, ranging from iron rails to distilled liquors, textiles were at all times the most important. The greatest areas of industrial concentration were two: along the coast of the New England and Middle Atlantic states, and in the trans-Allegheny region.

While the South was as anxious for the benefits of manufacturing as was the rest of the nation, she was slow to develop it. Profits gained from cotton and tobacco may have been so large that it was cheaper to import manufactured goods than to produce them; in any case the capital of the region was tied up in land and slaves. Still there was some manufacturing in the South, as witness the factories in Columbia, South Carolina, and Atlanta, Georgia (where both white and hired slave labor worked side by side). At least a half-dozen cotton mills were in operation by 1825, while a good deal of iron manufacturing was done by companies like the Tredegar Iron Works of Richmond, Virginia, and the Nesbitt Manufacturing Company of South Carolina.

It was natural that manufacturing should do best in the populous eastern states. New England was the first region to turn to industry with enthusiasm; its abundant water power, poor soil, apt people, and accessible markets combined to make this impulse inevitable. Though New England always retained the primacy in this respect before 1860, a second belt of manufacturing soon began to appear in the trans-Allegheny section. A report to the Secretary of the Treasury on the condition of manufactures in the West in 1832 noted that "manufactures are only beginning to exist" and that factories were "few and far between." But many western manufactures developed. Establishments in towns near the Ohio River were prepared to offer the local consumer everything from woolen cloth to hats and glassware. On the eve of the Civil War, the West had become the nation's chief producer of agricultural machinery, flour, and distilled and brewed liquors, as well as the leader in meat packing.

Thus, although the American republic continued to be an agrarian nation until after the Civil War, the rise of manufacturing during the ante bellum decades was phenomenal. Lured on by seemingly extraordinary possibilities of profit and possessing unlimited faith in the future of the American economy, businessmen built factories, exploited the nation's natural resources, and contributed to a rising standard of living.

THE ROLE OF LABOR

A fundamental factor in this rising standard of living was the factory worker. Coming sometimes from American farms but in increasing numbers after 1830 from Europe, this group constituted a new force in American society. It made its significant contribution to the prosperity of America; it also tended to develop its own distinctive outlook and to have its own special needs. As was natural in a largely agricultural country, the first factory operatives came from the farms. To rural folk, especially in certain depressed areas in the East suffering from western competition, factory employment provided an opportunity to earn much-needed cash. By working in the factories, many a son and daughter helped a farmer father pay off the mortgage on his farm or earned extra money with which to educate a younger member of the family. It was a way, moreover, of escaping from a somewhat drab life on the farm. Employers preferred women and children as factory workers because they would accept lower wages, and these groups constituted the bulk of the labor force for many years, particularly in the textile industry. Children four to sixteen years old were regularly hired for factory labor. Such employment was generally considered beneficial, for it not only supplemented the family's income but was alleged to inculcate proper habits of work and thus make for sober, thrifty citizens. In addition, these conditions also freed the members of the community from concern for the orphan and the pauper.

The labor situation changed when, after 1830, a great wave of immigrants, despairing of Old World poverty and attracted by opportunities in the United States, increased the nation's population. While many Americans objected to these newcomers on grounds of race or religion, businessmen welcomed them, for they were a supply of cheap and unskilled labor. Soon these immigrants, including the Irish and French-Canadians, settled in groups in New England cities and villages and were displacing native workers in the mills and factories.

Whether native or immigrant, child or adult, the life of a factory worker was hard and monotonous. Working twelve to fifteen hours a day, the American wage worker earned only $1 to $6 a week, unless he happened to be on hand during a temporary boom in a mushrooming western city. For instance, in 1819 carpenters in Detroit were earning $2 a day; masons in Chicago in 1835 received $3 a day. Hours of work grew longer under the piecework system, so much so that in 1850, reformers complained that conditions of labor in the cotton mills were more severe than in the state prisons. Not only did the factory laborer not own his tools of production, he frequently lived in houses and traded at stores owned by his employer. Denied by law and public opinion the security of a labor organization, his life was close to the margin of subsistence. If adults fared badly, the lot of the children was worse. Spending long hours in poorly ventilated and poorly lighted mills, performing tasks too arduous for their strength, these working children rarely earned more than $1 a week and were soon broken in body and spirit, stunted, and denied the pleasures and advantages of childhood. Their plight was one of the first to catch the public's eye, and by the 1840's some states forbade hiring children under twelve. This was but slight improvement, and many years were to pass before substantial reform was accomplished.

Not all industrial working conditions were equally unpleasant. There were several factories, the most famous of which was the Lowell Mills in Waltham, Massachusetts, in which the life of the women operatives was considered idyllic. In Waltham, the operators lived in company-owned dormitories, earned about $2 a week plus board, and spent their leisure time after an average workweek of 70 hours in a variety of "cultural" activities. They appeared, to all visitors, in excellent health, dressed in the latest fashion, refined and cheerful. According to a distinguished Englishwoman, visiting some mills in Paterson, New Jersey, in 1835, "the girls were all well-dressed. Their hair was arranged according to the latest fashions which had arrived, *via* New York. . . ."

But even the pleasant life of the Lowell mill girls faded as businessmen, in an effort to reduce production costs and increase profits, demanded more labor for the same pay or turned to a cheaper labor supply, the newly arrived immigrants. In any case, there remained the daily labor from daylight to dark, the grind of work in noisy, stuffy rooms and the underlying insecurity of the workers' position. Employers were free in their use of the black list and other antiunion devices, while any combination of working people for the purpose of raising wages or bettering working conditions was held illegal. Naturally, labor unions were both slow to start and short-lived. There had been small local organizations of skilled workers for many years, but these groups were closely akin to guilds, paying sick and death benefits, setting standards for apprentices, and opposing the competition of untrained workers. Beyond this a workers' group rarely went, for any bolder action, such as a strike, was consistently regarded by the courts as an unlawful conspiracy. The public, encouraged by the businessmen, supported the court's view, believing that higher wages meant higher prices and that such labor organizations were un-American, radical, and dangerous.

Historians credit the Mechanics' Union of Trade Associations, organized in 1827 in Philadelphia, with beginning the American labor movement. The Union of Trade Associations, a city central union, grew out of an abortive strike by Philadelphia carpenters for a ten-hour day. Believing that all trades would have to cooperate to win strikes, labor leaders hailed the organization of the new union as the beginning of a new era of "respect" for the workingman's rights.

One of the greatest handicaps to the success of labor unions in the decades before the Civil War lay in the extension of the right to vote to increasing numbers of workingmen. It was natural for the laborer to seek his objectives through political action first rather than through militant trade unionism. During the 1830s, particularly, a number of labor parties sprang up in New York, Philadelphia, and other places, and, after achieving varied success, died out. Seeking such reforms as free education, equal taxation, and abolition of imprisonment for debt, these parties deserve part of the credit for a series of reforms made during the years 1830 to 1860: the extension of free public schools, abolition of imprisonment for debt, and enactment of mechanic's-lien laws in many states. These lien laws gave to the worker a prior claim to his wages ahead of other claims against the employer.

Labor parties were almost always short-lived. Rent by internal dissension, lacking political experience, and much distrusted by the general public, they saw their demands absorbed into the programs of older, traditional political parties— their thunder stolen. Perhaps the greatest weakness of the labor party lay in the fact that there was no distinct, cohesive "labor class." American laborers were primarily individualists, preferring to get ahead on their own rather than through collective action. This feeling was especially strong in the nineteenth century, when the still wide-open frontier and the boundless economic potential of a young nation seemed to justify the worker's faith in his own abilities and opportunities.

A burst of union activity followed the disruption of the workingmen's parties. The boom period preceding the panic of 1837 had caught the laborer in a vise between rising prices and trailing wages while, at the same time, his employer, eager for profits, boosted his production quotas. In the last years of the 1830s, a large number of labor organizations sprang up in the eastern industrial cities. Some of these, particularly combmakers and carpenters, even attempted to organize national unions. They also experimented extensively in the techniques of the labor strike.

These strikes, invariably either for a ten-hour day or for higher wages, were uniformly failures if for no other reason than that the courts still held strikes illegal. Not until 1842, when the Massachusetts Supreme Court, in *Commonwealth v. Hunt,* ruled that laborers had a legal right to organize and to use peaceful means to achieve their objectives, did they receive some protection. The panic of 1837 brought a severe setback to the majority of these unions, though enough of them survived to back the movement for the ten-hour day. Gaining some recognition of this objective in President Van Buren's 1840 order that all employed on public works work only a ten-hour day, and in subsequent state legislation setting a ten-hour day for certain industries, the union movement entered into a period of distinct decline lasting until the post-Civil War years. Yet the emergence of a self-conscious labor movement was indicative

of the growing complexity of economic life in America.

ECONOMIC PROGRESS

The transformation of the American economy was gradual and accompanied by the expansion of the nation's borders and the increase of its population. New economic activities, undertaken in response to the needs of this growing country, frequently stirred a series of other enterprises, all of which, in turn, contributed to the economic wealth and progress of the American people. Thus the farmer, the fundamental economic producer of the ante bellum years, found his markets expanding with the rise of industry and the establishment of a group of industrial laborers. Both were consumers of his product, the one to process it, the other to eat it. As his markets expanded, they became more accessible through the revolution taking place in transportation methods. The farmer, for his part, turned to improved methods of production—to machinery, specialization, and seed selection—in an effort to increase and improve his crop yield and thus take better advantage of his new opportunities.

The industrialist, in turn, using the abundant raw materials, many of which were produced by the farmer, manufactured an increasing variety of goods. His products were employed by the farmer or used in the expansion of transportation systems. Thus was set in motion an elaborate system of exchange: as each producer prospered, his demands grew and new products were manufactured or grown.

The growing economy was tied together by the establishment of an expanding transportation network. From turnpikes to railroads, the facilitation of movement allowed the complex system of economic exchange to function smoothly and to become more and more complicated. On the eve of the Civil War, the United States was a nation with a rich and fertile agriculture, a substantial industry, an efficient and growing transportation system, and an increasing supply of skilled and unskilled labor.

Thus the years 1800 to 1860 were dynamic ones in the evolution of the American economy—dynamic not only because of the actual progress made in all manner of production, but also because of the future economic potential of the United States implied therein. A once simple, agrarian economy, sufficient to the needs of a nation but lately released from its colonial status, was, by mid-century, well on its way to becoming a highly complex economic unit and a major world factor.

FURTHER READINGS

George R. Taylor, *The Transportation Revolution, 1815–1860* (1951), is a splendid review of the economic development of the country during this formative period.

General surveys of agriculture are available in L. C. Gray, *History of Agriculture in the Southern States to 1860* (2 vols., 1933), and in P. W. Bidwell and J. I. Falconer, *History of Agriculture in the Northern United States, 1820–1860* (1925). A lighter treatment of social and economic life on southern plantations is found in William E. Dodd, *The Cotton Kingdom* (1919), and a scholarly one in J. C. Sitterson, *Sugar Country* (1953).

Transportation problems are described in Louis C. Hunter, *Steamboats on the Western Rivers* (1949); P. D. Jordan, *National Road* (1948); and W. S. Sanderlin, *The Great National Project: The Chesapeake and Ohio Canal* (1946).

Manufacturing and the people who labored in the mills have received extensive study. Among the best of such works are V. S. Clark, *History of American Manufactures from 1608 to 1860* (rev. ed., 3 vols., 1929), Caroline F. Ware, *Early New England Cotton Manufacture* (1931), Norman J. Ware, *The Industrial Worker, 1840–1860* (1924), and Marcus L. Hansen, *The Atlantic Migration* (1941).

See also the *Harvard Guide,* sections 141, 142, and 148–150.

TWELVE

Intellectual and Social Ferment, 1830 to 1850

1805
Free School Society Organized in New York.

1819
Unitarian Church founded.

1824
Owen's New Harmony settlement.

1826
American Temperance Society founded.

1827
Repeal of Massachusetts law allowing religious instruction.

1828
American Peace Society founded.

1830
Mormon Church founded.

1833
American Antislavery Society formed.
Beginning of the penny press.

1835
Abolitionists gain free speech in Massachusetts.

1837
Emerson's Phi Beta Kappa address at Harvard.
Horace Mann begins school reforms.

1841
Brook Farm established.

1845
Know-Nothing party organized.

1846
First women's college, at Mount Holyoke.

1852
Uncle Tom's Cabin published.

1855
Walt Whitman's Leaves of Grass.
Henry Thoreau's Walden.

THE ROOTS OF REFORM

WE HAVE LISTENED too long to the courtly muses of Europe," Ralph Waldo Emerson announced in 1837, in the Phi Beta Kappa address at Harvard which has become known as America's "declaration of intellectual independence." Cultural nationalism, or the striving for a unique American thought, literature and art, had been somewhat evident ever since the achievement of political independence. It was demanded in the name of patriotic pride, but it was slow in coming. "Why," asked a spokesman of literary nationalism in the 1830s, "cannot our literati comprehend the matchless sublimity of our position among the nations of the world—our high destiny—and cease bending the knee to foreign idolatry . . . ?" The demand for a distinctive American culture was related to other manifestations of aggressive nationalism in this era. The spirit of "manifest destiny," the truculent ideology of democracy on the march, will be observed when we turn to the politics of the 1840s. The superiority of American democracy to all other forms of society and government was no longer debated; it was taken for granted. Why then should not American writers cease imitating the ideas and the styles of Old World writers? Democracy must have its own art, its own philosophy, its own culture.

Thus part of the notable intellectual ferment of the 1830s and 1840s stemmed

244

from confident nationalism. Another part of it, an even more important one, related to the all-pervasive spirit of reform. This was the theme of the day. Democracy must be made perfect. A host of evils remained, myriad tasks needed to be performed. It was an optimistic spirit. The Americans, God's chosen people, faced a bright future of greatness and prosperity. There was no limit to what such a nation could achieve. The young nation experienced a thrill as frontier after frontier was met and conquered. Such a people could march forward to eliminate all relics of a more shoddy past and to complete its ideals of perfect equality, freedom, and a great new civilization based on the common man.

The best in American thought has always sought improvement in human welfare. What set this reform movement apart was its universality and the religious zeal with which it was pursued. Reform reached out in all directions—to the group, and also to the spiritual life of the individual. The evils that beset man must be stamped out; temptations to sin must be eliminated; society must be reorganized so that it might produce good people. Humanitarianism captured the imagination of all thinking people. "What is man born for," Emerson asked, "but to be a Reformer, a Remaker of what man has made, a renouncer of lies, a restorer of truth and good . . . ?" Hardly a phase of American life remained untouched by the reform tide. A simple listing of the major movements reveals why a southern writer in the 1850s characterized the North as a "Land of Pernicious Isms." These included utopianism, anti-Catholicism, Mormonism, Millerism, perfectionism, Shakerism, spiritualism, nativism, prohibitionism, vegetarianism, pacifism, feminism, antipauperism, and abolitionism. Reform was everywhere. Every evil to which mankind is heir found its organized foes in the social and intellectual ferment of the 1830s and 1840s. "Not a man among us but has the blueprint of a new society in his vest pocket," Emerson observed in amusement.

The impulse toward reform had its origins in the eighteenth-century philosophy of the Enlightenment, which had produced the Declaration of Independence and was still very much alive in the age of Jackson. Every reform movement made its appeal to the natural and unalienable rights of man, and to the idea of the perfectibility of man. But the newer humanitarianism drew increased strength from the spirit of romanticism, an enthusiastic mood which fused easily with the exuberant optimism of the frontier. This was a major development in European thought of the period. Its stress was upon the free individual, part of an eternal order with fixed moral laws, constantly progressing as he learned to comprehend the eternal truths and to translate them into action. The European heritage of ideas joined with the American frontier experience to make the optimistic creed which has been named the "American democratic faith."

Religion also contributed to this spirit of reform. It is difficult to exaggerate the importance of the religious impulse to reform in this time of "infinite hope." Writing in the 1830s, the astute French commentator on America, Alexis de Tocqueville, observed that "there is no country in the world in which the Christian religion retains a greater influence over the souls of men than in America. . . ." The moral urge to improve man rested upon a burning faith in Christian ethics. At a time when belief in democracy was approaching the status of a national

*From about 1830 until the Civil War the northern United States exhibited
a rich and diverse intellectual pattern of social reform, cultural nationalism,
the democratizing of knowledge, and literary coming-of-age. The passion
for education created the public school systems; it also involved a fad for
adult education which could sometimes take bizarre forms. Cheaper newspapers catered to a widened reading public. Dedicated social reformers like
Miss Dix set out to right the world's many wrongs. The spirit of the age
was in general one of exuberant optimism, and its achievements were
remarkable despite a number of comic eccentricities and "projects for the
salvation of the world." This period produced the first truly notable
American literature.*

Education in the 1850s

religion, evangelical Protestantism, with its emphasis on the free will of the individual, was sweeping the nation. Religious leaders were prominent in every reform movement. The greatest revivalist of his age declared that clergymen "should set forth with determination to aim at being useful in the highest degree." Preachers acted as reform leaders, and church buildings were frequently used as lecture halls, sometimes serving even the despised abolitionists. The revival gospel cooperated with the reform crusade. Thus the force of Christianity was directed toward secular reform with a new zest.

Still another important stimulus to social reform came from the growing concentration of population—especially in the East. Industrial growth called into being grimy factory towns and smoky cities. Two new social classes, the factory workers and factory owners, emerged alongside the traditional small farmers, shopkeepers, and artisans. By 1860 there were 141 cities of over 8,000 population, and city dwellers made up 16.1 per cent of the nation's total population. Only 3.3 per cent had lived in cities in 1790, when the first federal census was taken. In the growing cities, problems cried out for reform: slums bred crime and disease, poverty and vice, and the degradation of the factory worker. Dangerous factory machinery, unhealthful working conditions, low wages, and brutally long hours (the fourteen-hour day was common) all made life hard for a great segment of the laboring population. The panic of 1837 and its aftermath made conditions dramatically worse, as wages declined almost 50 per cent in a five-year period while nine-tenths of the eastern factories closed their doors. Perhaps the plight of the city worker was no worse than that of many farmers, but it was far more obvious; it

spurred reform enthusiasts into action and led distressed workers to join the forces of reform. Laboring men began to organize unions, scan utopian schemes, and support such political demands as abolition of imprisonment for debt, free public schools, and the curbing of licensed monopolies.

Finally, in seeking the roots of American reform, it must be noted that the movement coincided with a similar trend in Europe—a matter of some importance, for the influence of Europe was always silently pervasive. In the aftermath of the French Revolution and the Napoleonic Wars, the forces of conservatism and reaction dominated Europe for nearly a generation. By 1830, however, authoritarianism was being challenged. The successful and moderate revolution of 1830 in France ushered in a period of constitutional government, and in the same year Belgium threw off the union with the Netherlands which had been forced on her in 1815. In 1832, after a long and tense crisis, Great Britain adopted a Reform Bill which broadened the franchise. An era of liberalism and radicalism came to a climax in 1848, a year of revolutions all over Europe. The deep interest Americans took in European struggles for freedom may be seen in the tumultuous reception given to Louis Kossuth, the Magyar patriot leader, in 1850, when he visited this country. The humanitarian reformers in England labored for antislavery, for prison reform, for universal peace, for temperance, and other causes and were in close touch with their counterparts in the United States. Democracy seemed on the march everywhere; countless distinguished visitors came to observe and report on the American experiment, and if some went away disillusioned, others, like the perceptive Tocqueville, considered American democracy a qualified success and pre-dicted its victory in Europe. The liberal ferment of this period was not confined to America but was, in varying degrees and in different guises, common to all the European world.

THE DEMOCRATIZATION OF KNOWLEDGE

The drive to make the masses literate and educated, in itself a great reform move-ment of the time, was basic to other re-forms, for it created a public intelligent enough to understand ideas and respond to them. In the field of education, a rev-olution took place in the second quarter of the nineteenth century. It was primarily a revolution in elementary education. By 1850 the principle of the free, tax-sup-ported primary school had been accepted in the North; the community had assumed responsibility for the education of its chil-dren. Moreover, the principle of compul-sory attendance to a certain age, very low at first, was established, thus recognizing the state's right to infringe on the parent's freedom of choice. In the northern states by 1850 even the tax-supported secondary school, the public high school, was be-ginning to emerge. By that date 6,000 public high schools were in operation, with New England leading the way. The basic principles of American education had been formulated. The southern states lagged behind. Here proponents of free public schools—and they were many— labored under serious handicaps: the low population density, which meant fewer heads to tax; the aristocratic tradition of upper-class education; the political domi-nance of the planter class, whose laissez-faire outlook led them to think of educa-tion as a private matter; and the apathy of southern farmers toward all "book learn-

ing." Of the southern states, only North Carolina and Kentucky developed public school systems before the Civil War. The 1850 census statistics revealed that 20.3 per cent of the native white population of the South were illiterate. But by that date the illiteracy rate had fallen to very low levels throughout the rest of the country —to less than 1 per cent in New England, and to about 3 per cent in the middle states.

The free "common school," as the pub-lic elementary school was then termed, was not established without a long and bitter struggle. This reform measure strug-gled against the well-organized opposition of church-supported schools and the wealthy. The latter quite naturally op-posed being taxed for the education of other people's children. The educational *status quo,* consisting of the private schools and paupers' schools, was hotly defended. This struggle for democracy in education, for the public school, was one of the most fiercely fought reform battles waged in the age of Jackson and culminated in an outstanding victory for democracy. Persons of property suggested that if free schools were established other "social" concessions would inevitably fol-low, bringing about socialism itself. Oth-ers argued that such schools should be blocked because they would furnish edu-cation to those "who were better suited to their station without it." An eminent spokesman of New England's industrial might insisted, however, that the duty of educating people rested on the firm foun-dations of morality, civic responsibility, and the necessity for an informed voting public. An intelligent electorate, he main-tained, is the only safeguard for the re-public. Educators won support from busi-ness and manufacturing interests with the utilitarian argument that a laborer imbued as a child in the common schools with the virtues of thrift, honesty, and obedience could always be relied upon to work "more steadily and cheerfully, and therefore more productively."

In state after state the educational debate continued; legislative halls rang with charge and countercharge. Advocates of the new educational philosophy included reformers like Horace Mann of Massachusetts, politicians like Thaddeus Stevens of Pennsylvania, and many lesser-known leaders of organized labor in the Atlantic coastal cities. The first crack in the wall of resistance to public education appeared when a Free School Society, later known as the Public School Society, was organized in New York in 1805. Its purpose was to provide schooling for poor children who had no other means of getting an education. The society established the first system of free public education in the metropolis. It raised funds, built schoolhouses, and even provided for the training of teachers. The master craftsman in the formation of the Free School Society was De Witt Clinton, who was mayor of New York City several times between 1803 and 1815, and later governor of the state for nine years. More than 600,000 pupils received instruction, and some 1,200 teachers were trained before the society surrendered its charter and turned over its work to the public school department of the city which had been organized in 1842. But another quarter of a century was to pass before the public schools were free to all children. In Baltimore, Philadelphia, Washington, and other cities in the East, public education systems were pioneered by privately supported societies, as in New York. In the newer states of the West, beginning with Ohio, the foundations of a public school system rested in part upon money received from the federal government consisting of proceeds from the sale of certain public land, as originally provided for in the ordinance of 1785. The battle for the free public school was not entirely won in the northern states, however, until the 1850s.

The Lancastrian system of instruction by pupils, named after its British innovator, Joseph Lancaster, was commonly used in early schools. It provided a quick and inexpensive method to meet the demands for mass instruction in the cities. The teaching was done by the older pupils serving as monitors under supervision of the teachers. Each monitor usually taught ten pupils. Thus the system had the double advantage of providing instruction and preparing a certain number of monitors to become regular teachers after they had served their apprenticeship.

The rapid spread of the public school system throughout the states created a special problem for the Catholics. A Massachusetts law of 1827 prohibited the long-established practice of religious teaching in public schools. It forbade the use of "any school books which were calculated to favor the tenets of any particular sect of Christians." The Bible might still be read, but the teaching of the fundamental tenets of Christianity as viewed by any particular denomination became illegal. The example of Massachusetts was followed in many states. Appropriations for church-controlled institutions which had hitherto shared in state support were soon withdrawn. In New York the Public School Society had already started this practice when it took over the distribution of the school funds in 1822. There was much bitter controversy over the issue, particularly with the Catholics. Feelings became so strong on the matter that extremists among them denied the right of the state to participate at all in the education of children. After a few ineffective attempts at compromise, by which the state was to assume a part of the support of church schools, the two systems of public and parochial education went their separate ways. Massachusetts hastened the process, especially after the Unitarian Horace Mann became secretary of the newly created Board of Education in 1837. After 1840 no demands by churches for a share in public school funds were successful anywhere. State after state now adopted constitutional amendments prohibiting state support for church schools.

The public elementary school, suited to an evolving democratic society, educated its pupils in republicanism and the acquisition of practical skills. Since they were "common schools," they served as a leveling and integrating force in American society. Noah Webster's *Blue Backed Spellers* and *Readers,* along with William McGuffey's *Eclectic Readers* (graded readers), molded little minds for generations, inculcating ideas of morality, patriotism, and Christian idealism. At the same time these books, through their many reading selections, introduced school children to the best in English and American literature.

Horace Mann, an environmentalist and a serious student of the advanced educational theories then practiced in Prussia, became the first secretary of the Massachusetts State Board of Education in 1837, and guided that state to leadership in American educational theory and teaching practice. During his first year as secretary, Mann spoke out in favor of the "entire exclusion of religious teaching" from the public schools in accordance with the 1827 Massachusetts statute; in his annual reports he also championed raising the salaries of the poorly paid teachers. Improving the quality of teaching soon attracted his attention. Mann played a decisive role in the establishment of the first state normal school in 1839 at Lexington, Massachusetts. It was here that professional teacher training in the United States began.

A lesser chapter in the story of the democratization of knowledge in this era is the expansion of higher education. Progress in this area was relatively slow until after the Civil War. Many small denominational colleges accompanied the advance of the frontier, reflecting the hunger for education. A small beginning in higher education for women was the establishment of the first college for women, Mount Holyoke Female Seminary, in 1837. Oberlin College in Ohio had the distinction of being not only the first coeducational college, but also the first to admit Negroes as students. But the day of the great state universities and the heavily endowed private institutions was, with a few exceptions, yet to come.

The establishment of the public grammar school in the United States was certainly the most significant step in the democratization of knowledge. But many other instruments of popular education were making their appearance at the same time. Among these were the cheap newspapers which came into being in the eastern cities during the 1830s. Urban growth, mechanical advances in printing, and improved methods of transportation and communication made the "penny press" possible. The *New York Sun,* founded in 1833, was not only the first successful penny daily, but also the first newspaper to derive its main financial support from advertising revenue, the first to try promotion stunts to raise circulation, and the first to play up sensational news —lurid stories of murder, robbery, and sex. Its success quickly inspired imitators, the most flamboyant being the sensation-mongering *New York Herald,* begun in 1835. The *New York Times,* established in 1851, was to set a high standard of accurate and objective reporting. In this day of great editors, men like Horace Greeley, who published the *New York Tribune,* commanded a nationwide audience. Greeley's editorials espousing many different reforms and ideas far overshadowed other features of the paper and reached a distant public through semiweekly mail editions. Other weekly and biweekly newspapers flourished, and the religious press grew. An amazing number of monthly popular magazines appeared. Some were truly literary, as the *Atlantic Monthly,* the *Dial* and *The Southern Literary Messenger;* many were feature or picture magazines, such as *Harper's,* or magazines for women such as *Godey's Lady's Book.* Subscription libraries and public libraries made their appearance. A new reading public was being created; what it read might not always be wholly edifying, but believers in democracy could not but hail the advance toward universal literacy.

Perhaps even more encouraging than the often uninstructive daily press was the remarkable growth of the lyceum movement, which instructed the adult public by means of public lectures. Starting in the small town of Millbury, Massachusetts, in 1826, the lyceum network expanded rapidly until, by 1834, some 3,000 village lyceums were functioning in fifteen states. Regional professional lecture bureaus were organized to schedule renowned speakers for lyceum audiences. Some of the leading figures in American intellectual life traveled the lyceum circuit during the twenty years preceding 1860. Related to the lyceum were other lecture societies that evolved into public forums: Lowell Institute (Boston), Peabody Institute

(Baltimore), and Cooper Union (New York). "Mechanics' institutes," beginning with the Boston Mechanics' Institution of 1826, served urban workers, enabling them to increase their earning power along with their technical knowledge. The lyceum was both a cause and a result of America's intellectual awakening. The lectures, debates, and scientific demonstrations that were a part of the lyceum promoted the common school movement. They stimulated the people to think, to purchase books, and to engage in library reading on political, economic, scientific, and literary subjects. On the other hand, the lyceum can be viewed as an institution whose existence was made possible by a people brought intellectually alive through the spread of public education. The lyceum was excellent training for democracy.

Finally, dissemination of popular literature, this time with a religious emphasis, came about through the activities of the American Bible Society, the American Tract Society, and the American Sunday School Union. Through the work of these agencies, millions of Bibles, tracts, and copies of Sunday school manuals and literature were circulated among the masses. Thus religious organizations had their part in the democratization of knowledge.

SOME REFORMS AND REFORMERS

Provided with a forum and an audience, the eager spirit of reform burst into glorious and eccentric action. The tendency of every man to become his brother's keeper amused some and disgusted others in this age. But among the myriad schemes for reform, some stand out as of unquestioned value and as monuments to individual courage. Dorothea Dix, semi-invalid mistress of a school for girls, achieved an international reputation for making America conscious of the plight of its mentally ill. After a three-year investigation of the jails and almshouses of Massachusetts towns, she submitted a report on the status of the "insane persons confined within this Commonwealth in *cages, closets, cellars, stalls, pens! Chained, naked, beaten with rods, and lashed* into obedience." This "memorial" to the Massachusetts legislature in 1843 led to legislation that began to separate the insane from criminals and provide for scientific care in asylums. Miss Dix traveled across America, into Canada, England, and even Japan, advocating improved training facilities for the insane, blind, deaf, and dumb. Her work was one example of the widespread interest in humanitarian reform.

No group of reformers were more earnest and assiduous than those who be-

lieved that Demon Rum was mankind's greatest enemy. This crusade won support from a variety of organizations: from religious societies and evangelists, of course, but also from the feminist or women's-rights group which saw in it a means of strengthening the home, and from industrialists who blamed the liquor habit, rather than low wages, for their workers' indebtedness and poverty. Opposition to alcohol can be traced back to the later eighteenth century, but the campaign against intoxicants did not move into high gear until the founding of the American Temperance Society in 1826. Urging at first only partial abstinence, by 1840 the reformers had shifted to total abstinence. They spread the gospel of temperance by means of tearful testimonials from reformed drunkards, by tracts, magazines, and novels. Temperance literature threatened to deluge the nation. Whisky-drinking Irish immigrants and beer-loving

The temperance movement. Anti-drink crusaders ranked among the leading reformers of the age of reform. Total abstinence or total degradation were the sole alternatives, they preached. (Library of Congress)

Germans proved hard to reform, but the "Cold Water Army" inviting people to "sign the pledge" continued its strenuous campaign. *Ten Nights in a Bar Room* became a popular play. Prominent national leaders from all fields supported the movement. Maine passed the first state prohibition law in 1846; within a decade six other states had passed "local option" laws, and "dry" areas spread through the nation.

Women were at all times prominent in such crusades. Indeed, it may be said that women entered public life for the first time as reform participants—not without bitter opposition from some male reformers. Miss Dix and the renowned lecturer and temperance leader Susan B. Anthony were among the vanguard of the host of women outstanding in the battle for reform. Soon these ladies were contending for the "rights" of their sex. In 1841 the refusal of the World Antislavery Convention in London to seat women delegates representing the United States sent Lucretia Mott and Elizabeth Cady Stanton home fighting mad. Seven years later, their battle for equality culminated in the first women's-rights convention in the United States, held at Seneca Falls, New York. This meeting produced a ringing female "declaration of independence" which insisted that "the history of mankind is a history of repeated injuries and usurpations on the part of men toward women." Included in the list of grievances were unjust divorce laws, limited educational and economic opportunities, denial of suffrage, and women's status of wardship in the eyes of the law, which precluded female control over property. The feminist movement received the jeers of many, who associated it with the costume of Amelia Jenks Bloomer, reformist editor and lecturer. Little progress was achieved

before 1860, though a few states passed laws allowing married women to own property, and some schools or "seminaries" for women were founded.

Like the fight for equality of the sexes, most reforms contended for greater freedom, more equality, fair play and free opportunity for all. But not all the propaganda drives of the period were so liberal. One which achieved wide popularity was a militant anti-Catholic campaign, a veritable "Protestant Crusade." Predominantly Protestant America feared the consequences of the large-scale Roman Catholic immigration between 1830 and 1850. Here seemed a threat to the traditional thought patterns of yankee Protestants. Religious freedom was an American ideal, but the countertradition of prejudice against Romanism was deeply rooted in our Puritan past. The wave of revivalism so prominent from the 1820s on represented in some respects a swing away from religious liberalism toward a rigid fundamentalism. This quickening of religious interest could encourage bigotry. A vigorous Protestant press was prepared to resent Catholicism as a hostile system. To this religious crusade was added the prejudice of workers who resented competition from cheap immigrant labor. This "nativist" movement began in New York in 1831 with the formation of a Protestant Association, whose newspaper shouted its message of hate. Soon national societies appeared, alerting the nation to the alleged dangers of "Popery." Anti-Catholic books were published by the score under the seal of the Protestant Reformation Society or the American Protestant Society. The misrepresentation, sensationalism, and fraudulent character of many anti-Catholic books did not prevent their wide circulation. The fruits of this campaign of hate were mob action, destruction of Catholic property, and bloodshed such as that which occurred in the burning of an Ursuline convent at Charlestown, Massachusetts, in 1834. Another reflection of this antiforeign and anti-Catholic hysteria was the bigoted Know-Nothing society, which produced a nativist political movement, the "American party" of the 1850s. On the other hand, many national leaders in the course of time spoke out against such un-American intolerance.

More typical of the generous humanitarian spirit of the age was the career of Elihu Burritt of Connecticut, the self-taught "Learned Blacksmith." Through his study of thirty foreign languages, this lecturer and reformer became convinced that the common origin of tongues sprang from the common origin of man. To further the interchange of ideas from man to man, he campaigned for "ocean penny postage," founded the League of Universal Brotherhood, in 1846, and organized the first world peace congress at Brussels. Through the printing of leaflets known variously as "Olive Leaves" and "Friendly Addresses," which were circulated to the American and English press, Burritt gained supporters for the cause of world peace. His propaganda techniques were also utilized in behalf of temperance, and he even found time to promote the raising of cotton by free Negro labor in the South as an answer to slavery.

The innumerable reform societies of this period had many common features; in fact, a sort of standard reform pattern evolved. That pattern included a national headquarters located in the East, usually New York City, exercising limited co-ordinating supervision over a network of local societies or "auxiliaries." The latter were organized independently at the grass-roots level and later at the state level. The national headquarters served often as the planning agency and central lecture bureau; it raised funds, recruited "important names" as sponsors, published the society newspaper, and hired agents to exert pressure on national church organizations and governmental bodies. Such was the structure of the interdenominational American Tract Society (1825), the American Temperance Society (1826), the American Antislavery Society (1833), the Protestant Reformation Society (1836), and many others. This unified effort enabled the reformers, a minority group at all times, to exert an influence out of all proportions to their number.

THE ANTISLAVERY CRUSADE

The most famous of all the reform movements of the century, the one destined to dwarf all others, was the crusade for the freedom of man, identified in the public mind by the one heated word "abolitionism." Actually, the antislavery cause, a highly unpopular movement among northerners, encompassed many different plans for freeing the Negro. Proposals advanced included voluntary and compensated emancipation with subsequent colonization of the Negro in Africa; compensated manumission by state law; and immediate, uncompensated abolition of slavery by law. The last was the proposal of the abolitionists of the 1830s. The antislavery crusade was conducted, almost simultaneously, on three different levels —by the moral philosophers, politicians, and professional reformers.

The "antislavery impulse" of the Jackson era stemmed from the intellectual convictions that human slavery was a "moral wrong," as well as a social evil. That was the new message of the abolitionist crusaders. This new identification of the slaveholder as a "sinner" aroused southerners far more than the mild criticism advanced by men like George Washington, Thomas Jefferson, and George Mason. There had long existed in America an antislavery tradition, one which showed its greatest strength in the period immediately after the Revolution, when, under the influence of the philosophy of natural rights, slavery was abolished by a majority of the northern states. Some talk was heard against that "necessary evil" in the upper South. Not until the 1820s, however, did the antislavery movement gather momentum.

During this decade many local antislavery societies were founded. Most of them had no rigid program, advocating only some form of gradual emancipation; some openly acknowledged that the South had a race problem that might delay the end of slavery. During this early period, freedom of expression was not yet fettered in the South, and many Quakers of the border slave states pioneered in this cause. As early as 1819 there was an antislavery paper in Tennessee; the Quaker Benjamin Lundy published in Baltimore; and James G. Birney, a converted Alabama slaveholder, was similarly active in Kentucky. Altogether, some 100 to 150 local antislavery societies were operating in America, largely in the border states. The antislavery papers tied these local societies together. Meanwhile, the American Colonization Society was demonstrating its futility by sending fewer than 4,000 ex-slaves to Liberia between 1820 and 1840, while the slave population increased by almost a million during these same two decades.

In 1833 a fresh impetus was given the antislavery cause by the abolition of slavery in the British Empire. English reformers now turned toward the goal of ending human bondage in the United States, Rus-sia, Brazil, and the rest of the world. There was considerable collaboration between English and American humanitarians. The victory of the antislavery forces in England convinced American crusaders that the time was now ripe to weld the many local and state antislavery societies into one powerful national organization. Accordingly, in December, 1833, the American Antislavery Society was organized in a convention at Philadelphia. One of the convention's outstanding leaders was the New England firebrand William Lloyd Garrison, who waged a lifelong battle against slavery, war, and intemperance.

The uncompromising Garrison has long been portrayed with considerable exaggeration as the most important antislavery name, a name synonymous with abolitionism. In January, 1831, Garrison became prominent with the publication of his militant Boston *Liberator,* whose first issue demanded the immediate freedom without compensation "of our slave population." He had no practical plan or interest in many social, economic, and political difficulties incident to emancipating millions of slaves (almost 4 million by 1860). The New England Antislavery Society which he organized the following year echoed his scheme of "immediatism," a doctrine imported from the contemporary British movement. The non-Garrison group of antislavery men, led by such New Yorkers as Arthur and Lewis Tappan, and middle-western campaigners like Theodore Weld of Ohio, saw the difficulties inherent in trying to attract support for such a radical doctrine. They sought a middle way.

The founding convention of the American Antislavery Society adopted the somewhat ambiguous doctrine of "immediate emancipation, gradually accomplished." As interpreted by Weld, this doctrine was recast as "gradual emancipation, immediately begun." Legal control of the master over the slave should be immediately abolished, slave labor made free labor, and the former slave placed under "a benevolent and disinterested supervision" of probably either the state or the federal government until he was trained to assume equal status with the whites, intellectually and morally. This compromise statement on "immediatism" helped lessen public hostility to the American Antislavery Society, although Garrison continued to advance his own brand of "immediatism."

Formulation of a reasonable statement of principle, not far removed from earlier Quaker proposals, brought no great rush to the antislavery banner. Abolitionists remained unpopular. Not only were they self-righteous and dogmatic, they had attacked the institution of private property. Their intemperate denunciation of slaveholding as a moral wrong, moreover, was seriously damaging relations between North and South. Ahead of the antislavery men lay a prolonged indoctrination program aimed at changing men's minds. Our aim, said Weld, is "to inform, indoctrinate, and arm at all points." Through lecture campaigns, magazines, pamphlets, songs, tracts, and poems, aimed at children as well as adults, the word about human freedom was spread. But just how the southern institution of slavery was to be ended by converting the population of the North was never quite explained by the abolitionists. Garrison, who was a pacifist, suggested a disruption of the union, the North drawing away from those parts contaminated by slavery—a scheme too radical for widespread appeal.

Among the most effective workers in the antislavery cause were some of America's greatest writers and preachers. The poets John Greenleaf Whittier and James Russell Lowell were clearly abolitionists, while Henry Wadsworth Longfellow, Henry Thoreau, and Ralph Waldo Emerson were on the fringe of the movement. Almost no one in the North was prepared to defend slavery as such, but a very great many questioned the practicality of Garrison's demand for immediate abolition, or questioned even the wisdom of agitating so dangerous a question. But in general, northern leaders of opinion defended the right of free speech for abolitionism. In 1835, for example, William Ellery Channing, the great Unitarian minister, staunchly defended Garrison's right to be heard, while deploring the fanaticism of the abolitionists. In the same spirit, John Quincy Adams, who had despised Garrison, took up the battle against curbs on the right to petition Congress, seeing here a dangerous attack on basic freedoms. Despite persecution, the abolitionists won their right to be heard in the North. Lowell aided the cause with his very successful antislavery *Biglow Papers* (1846–1848), while a few years later the wife of a Lane Seminary theology professor, Harriet Beecher Stowe, was to write that most popular of all antislavery tracts, *Uncle Tom's Cabin*. Southern defenders resented the criticism and bitterly replied.

The Ohio group led by Weld, leaders from the Lane Seminary at Cincinnati, and a host of others waged their campaign not by pamphlet, but by personal-appearance tours in the small towns of the East and Middle West. Moving sermons were preached against the "sin" of slavery by a loyal band of lecturers who had been trained in the catechism by the "New York group." Negro abolitionists, both escaped slaves and freedmen, were important contributors to the cause; the self-educated runaway slave Frederick Doug-

INTELLECTUAL FERMENT, 1830–1850

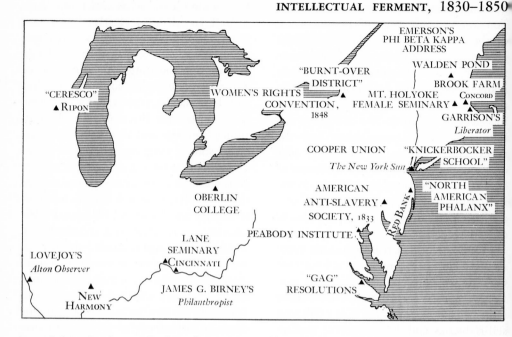

lass of Maryland was the best known of these workers. The aim was to blanket a town with lecturers until a sufficient number of converts were won who would organize a local antislavery society. Three years after the national society's founding it claimed 500 local auxiliaries. By 1840 the number of societies was reported at 2,000, with a total membership of 200,-000.

Abolitionist activity in the 1830s provoked a violent reaction in the North as well as in the South. Militant abolitionists were touching the pocketbook nerve of all those with an economic stake in slavery, and these included many northerners who traded with the South. Others in the border areas feared the social, economic, and political consequences of the abolition of slavery. Active abolitionists often had their presses destroyed, sometimes even their lives endangered. Civil liberties were being trampled upon by outraged citizens and law enforcement officers alike in states

bordering on both sides of the Ohio. Many of the antislavery militants—eagerly courting martyrdom in their Christian idealism—suffered violence, and some were killed. Feeling ran high against James G. Birney's establishment of an antislavery paper in Danville, Kentucky, in 1835; the next year, publication of Birney's *Philanthropist* near Cincinnati led to mob riots and destruction of his press. The first abolitionist killed in defense of his right of free expression was the intemperate Elijah P. Lovejoy, Presbyterian preacher and editor of the *Alton Observer*. A willing martyr, Lovejoy died on November 7, 1837, in Alton, Illinois, fighting off a mob bent on destroying his press.

Mob assaults on their freedom of speech, denial of the right to petition Congress (begun in 1836 with the "gag resolution"), and disclosure of the unofficial policy of federal censorship of the mails carrying literature to the South gained some sympathy for the abolitionists. They tood as champions of free speech and a ree press. Abolitionists remained a somewhat despised minority in the North until he Civil War. But here was the grandest ause of an age that gloried in the crusade against evil. There is no denying that abolitionism appealed to men and women of courage and ability. The charge against t remains that it aroused bitter passions, stimulated extremism in the South as a reaction, and thus fed the fires that were to flare up in civil war. Nevertheless, to the frequent demands from the South that he abolitionists be silenced, the North could give only one answer: its society was built on free expression, and every effort to suppress this noisy and, to conservatives, troublesome minority was doomed to fail. Those who are inclined to blame the coming of the Civil War on abolitionist agitation have yet to explain how, in this age, one could have forced people to remain silent on what was evidently an enormous evil crying for reform. And when it was a question of such fundamental liberties as freedom of speech and petition, the abolitionists won significant sympathy from people who would never have supported them had the issue been simply that of opposition to slavery.

SLAVERY AND
THE SOUTHERN MIND

The southern defense of slavery against northern criticism led not only to a ban on all criticism of their "peculiar institution" but, by extension, to "a ban on all analysis and inquiry, a terrified truculence toward every new idea, a disposition to reject every innovation out of hand."*

* From W. J. Cash, The Mind of the South, Alfred A. Knopf, Inc., New York, 1941.

The South drew in on itself and bade defiance to the hostile world of liberalism and reform, erecting a social philosophy which came close to rejecting democracy in favor of an ordered and aristocratic society. It found its ideals in the ancient aristocracies of Greece and Rome, it took its ideas from the British Tory writings of Sir Walter Scott and Thomas Carlyle, and it ended by denying the worth of a society based on freedom and equality. From suppression of the abolitionists as a menace to society, the road led straight to those proslavery ideologies which attacked the very idea of freedom as a delusion.

Abolitionist propaganda seemed in southern eyes to be inciting the Negro slave population to revolt, threatening southern society with a bloody race war. Therefore it must be suppressed. In the name of the security of society, southerners were prepared to justify drastic restrictions on freedom of expression. Salesmen and other travelers from the North found themselves suspect and were sometimes driven out of southern communities by force. United States mails were frequently opened and confiscated with the connivance of southern postal officials. The threat of mob action hung over anyone who dared to suggest criticisms of slavery. Professors and university presidents regarded as unsound on the slavery question were forced out of their positions. In brief, freedom of thought in the South, once vigorous enough, had virtually ceased to exist by about 1840 as a consequence of the need to defend the South's "peculiar institution."

Suppression of antislavery thought and speech was not wholly approved by all leading southerners; there were moderates who thought it wrong in itself and a grave strategic error, since it would, as they saw, only win sympathy for the abolitionists.

But as early as the 1830s the powerful influence of John C. Calhoun was thrown behind the silencing of all criticism of slavery. Calhoun also led in the bold assertion that slavery was not a necessary evil but a "positive good." The South must close ranks against the North and antislavery; it must not cringe on the defensive but, rather, proudly proclaim the superiority of its way of life over that of the North. Such a program gradually won mass support from among southern whites. It was far more satisfying to counterattack than to meekly accept the reproaches of the North. Those who looked for ammunition with which to defend an aristocratic order and to attack the industrial-democratic society of the North did not have to look far, for in the era after 1815 Europe produced many conservative philosophies hostile to democracy and liberalism.

These were taken up and revised for southern American consumption by a number of proslavery writers, elaborating on Calhoun's interesting thesis that slavery was no evil but a highly desirable basis of society. The proslavery arguments were more often negative than positive; they assailed the society of the North as a means of defending that of the South. Northern "wage slavery" was worse than southern slavery; the North's society was chaotic, selfish, materialistic, while that of the South was orderly, cooperative, gracious. The immigrant was mongrelizing the North, while the South remained racially pure. The North was breaking up in a perfect insanity of wild isms, many most shocking and immoral, while the South remained sound and serene, untroubled by fanatics. A typical argument in favor of slavery was the so-called "mud-sill" theory. It asserted that every civilization must rest on a class of servile labor; otherwise

there could be no civilization. The so-called free society of the North actually did so, in so far as it was worth anything; the factory workers were really a slave class, worse off than their Negro counterparts in the South. The South rested its social foundation squarely and frankly on social inequality between master and slaves; therefore, it was argued, southern civilization was sound and stable, while that of the North was unsound and confused. Such arguments were common among the writings of southern intellectuals. There was much talk, following Calhoun, of a "Greek democracy"; there was much striving after the virtues of a chivalrous aristocracy. None of these apologies for slavery was worth much intellectually; they are deeply significant as symptoms of that morbid sensitivity to criticism which slavery produced in the South and which led to a shrill and constant effort at self-justification.

Whether or not most southerners really believed that slavery was an asset to civilization, it is certainly true that southern society was by contrast with the seething North much more conservative and far less inclined to produce or to tolerate unorthodox ideas. Very few new religious sects appeared south of Mason and Dixon's line. The insistence on conformity in religion was related to the defense of slavery, for in the Bible, literally interpreted, slaveowners thought they had a powerful justification for the institution. Of 257 Unitarian churches in the United States in 1860, only 3 were south of the Potomac—a good measuring stick for religious liberalism, since Unitarianism was the most notably liberal of all the sects. Similarly, the utopian communities did not thrive in the cotton belt, nor did any other of the reforms and fads so numerous in the North, with one exception, that of temperance. There are other reasons for this conservatism than slavery. The South was predominantly rural, and the reforms and innovations everywhere did best in the cities. The South received fewer infusions of foreign immigration than did the North. The geography of the South made for more isolation than was true of most of the North. Slavery does not explain it all, but it was important. It became increasingly difficult to speak freely on anything that touched that sensitive issue.

And so, in a remarkable reversal of roles, that land of Jeffersonian liberalism turned into a land of stiff and narrow conservatism, while Puritan and Federalist New England was transformed into a place of liberal ferment. After some resistance, the Jeffersonian tradition in the South withered and all but died, blighted by the grim spirit of Calhoun, and the South proudly vaunted not its freedom of thought but its static, conservative, hierarchical society. At the same time, the grim old Puritanism of New England was melting before the free romantic optimism of Emerson. In both sections thought was active and new ways of life were taking shape, but they went in different directions. Ultimately the most significant thing about this age of intellectual development was that it widened the gulf between the sections. "Freedom's ferment" in the North had its counterpart in a movement toward southern nationalism and the pro-slavery ideology.

UTOPIAN VISTAS

A significant manifestation of the northern ferment of optimistic liberal doctrines was the persistent interest in establishing utopian communities. Several hundred such projects, affecting hundreds of thousands of people, sprang up in northern and western America during these years. These idealists proposed to build experimental societies according to their blueprints. Believing as they did in the perfectibility of man, they were sure that when the rest of society saw how successful their experiments were, the whole nation would embrace the idea. The forming of small communal societies was an old custom in Western civilization, with deep roots in the Judaic-Christian tradition as well as in Greek thought. It had appeared in Europe and also in early America. But in the breadth of its scope and the variety of its execution, utopianism was most remarkable during the age of Jackson. There were many kinds of such communal experiments, both religious and secular. What they had in common was the desire to prove that a more perfect society than the existing one was possible.

Those which persisted the longest and were the most successful were of religious inspiration. In the words of the founder of one such community, "it was the declared object of Christ's labors to inaugurate the kingdom of heaven ON THE EARTH; and it was the imperative duty of his disciples to pray and work earnestly for that sublime end." The creation of a perfect society was a part of the preparation believers must make to be ready when the millennium occurred. German pietistic sects, Moravians, Rappites, and Amish, had established little utopian commonwealths in Pennsylvania as early as 1694. In the Jackson period, hardy souls from the "Burnt-over District," an area from western Vermont across the Mohawk River Valley between Albany and Buffalo, which had long been the proving grounds for a variety of strange doctrines, proved susceptible to the experiments of

Mormons, Millerites, Inspirationalists, Shakers, and others. These religious communities usually shared their goods in common and sought to lead lives of primitive simplicity. But it remained for newer and more secular faiths of the age of progress to provide the most challenging experiments in group living.

The Scottish manufacturer Robert Owen, one of the founders of modern socialism, and his son Robert Dale Owen, had grown disillusioned with the possibilities of reform in England. In 1825 they purchased the properties of a Rappite group which had foundered in Indiana, and there in New Harmony on the Wabash an Owenite community attempted to grant all men equal treatment in society. Believing that all men are fundamentally equal and fundamentally good, the Owens organized their cooperative community on the socialist principle of "from each according to his ability, to each according to his needs." The project did not succeed, partly because the idea was incompatible with the individualistic American background and partly because neither the founders nor the members were trained in the ways of frontier life. Yet nine other Owenite communities were attempted.

Another group of utopian experiments derived from the eccentric theories of the French mathematician Charles Fourier. These were somewhat more complicated than the Owens' simple faith in human equality; Fourier proposed to find his "social harmony" in a scheme of living which combined the right number and kind of individuals, based on the twelve passions or desires which Fourier believed men to have. In these "phalanxes" a kind of socialism was also practiced: the highest returns were paid to those laboring in the least pleasant work, while more agreeable labors did not receive as much compensation. Each person could choose his own occupation and was supposed to retire after working diligently to his twenty-eighth year. Albert Brisbane, who wrote articles for Greeley's *New York Tribune,* popularized Fourierism as an answer to the "desertlike" society of the machine age. More than forty such organizations were started from 1840 on, including the North American Phalanx, near Red Bank, New Jersey; Ceresco, near Ripon, Wisconsin; and the famed Brook Farm, near Boston, to which numbers of the New England intellectuals resorted and which the skeptical Nathaniel Hawthorne later made fun of in his *Blithedale Romance.* Unhappily, these ideal communities, which were supposed to provide a richer community life, had a tendency to break up in discord.

Étienne Cabet's book *A Voyage to Icaria* (1840) inspired yet another wave of secular utopias. Icarian settlements, which were communistic in that all received the same economic rewards, seemed to fare better, and numbers of them were scattered through Illinois, Iowa, Missouri, Texas, and California. It is easy to laugh at this utopian vogue; it climaxed all the extravagant hopes and eccentric fads with which this age abounded. But it symbolized, too, the earnest faith in human progress, the burning zeal for a better life, and the unbouded belief in man's infinite possibilities which so marked the American spirit.

THE LITERARY RENAISSANCE

All this ferment of the spirit expressed itself in the first great creative period of American literature. Those who had long complained of American sterility in the creative arts and sciences now had their dreams fulfilled. American writers for the first time won international renown and produced a distinctive American tone in literature.

In 1828 James Fenimore Cooper had speculated upon the reasons why American literary production was so scanty— why, in the words of Emerson, "not a book or . . . not a thought" had appeared in America during the last quarter-century. It was not that Americans did not read. But they imported their books, and with them their tastes and ideas, from abroad. "The principal reason for this poverty of original writers," thought Cooper, "is that men are not yet driven to their wits for bread. Talent is sure of too many avenues to wealth and honors, in America, to seek . . . an unknown and hazardous path." All America's human resources were absorbed in the great task of building a new society in the wilderness. And America also lacked a literary tradition of her own. The literary age of the Enlightenment, of Franklin and Jefferson, had long passed, leaving no successors, and the founding fathers were no longer read. A new literary fashion, romanticism, had rendered eighteenth-century writers obsolete in style and so robbed them of a continuing audience.

There was no American aristocracy to patronize the literary men, as was the European custom, and, there being no international copyright law, American authors found that publishers preferred to print English authors free. Said Cooper, "A capital American publisher has assured me that there are not a dozen writers in this country whose works he would feel confidence in publishing at all, while he reprints hundreds of English books without the least hesitation." The American writer had to compete on unequal terms with Sir Walter Scott, Charles Dickens, and many another British master, whose pirated works were sold at ridiculously low prices. Moreover it was not generally considered honorable for normal healthy men to go in for literary careers. Although the Knickerbocker school had produced a few important writers (such as James Fenimore Cooper and Washington Irving), William Ellery Channing, writing in 1830, declared that "the few standard works which we have produced, and which promise to live, can hardly, by any courtesy, be denominated a national literature." In an oft-quoted passage, Sydney Smith, who was an English liberal sympathetic to the United States, asked, "Who reads an American book or goes to an American play?" He went on to question whether the world yet owed anything to American physicians and surgeons, to American scientists and scholars.

The 1830s and 1840s, however, saw

Nathaniel Hawthorne, the first significant American novelist, product of the Concord literary renaissance. (Mellon Collection, National Gallery of Art, Washington)

the emergence of a significant group of distinguished American poets, essayists, and historians.* To a large extent this literary renaissance was the "flowering of New England." The sleepy rural town of Concord, untouched by industrialism, where the sage Ralph Waldo Emerson dwelt, was the literary center of the American awakening. Emerson's electrifying plea for a native American literature in 1837 sounded the call, and his "transcendental" philosophy set the mood of the entire epoch. In one way or another practically all the writers of this "golden day" of American literature were his disciples. Among those whose works were to become treasured classics of world literature were Henry Wadsworth Longfellow, Nathaniel Hawthorne, Walt Whitman, Herman Melville, Henry Thoreau, and in the South, Edgar Allan Poe. With them America had come of age intellectually, boasting a literature of her own which interpreted the American scene, expressed national ideals, and found an audience in the outside world. To this could be added some encouraging changes in the world of science which had come since 1800 when Noah Webster had remarked that almost no research was being done or could be done in the United States. Before long, American inventors and scientists were to make their share of contributions.

If one of the great American minds of this splendid age is to be singled out for comment, that one must surely be Emerson, in consideration of the influence he exerted, the fame he won, and the representative philosophy he expressed. He presided like a benign Buddha over all this chaos of the spirit, approving every

* The historians William H. Prescott, John Lothrop Motley, George Bancroft, and Francis Parkman were among the products of this literary renaissance.

Ralph Waldo Emerson. (*Library of Congress*)

kind of doctrine for its own sake even if he could not agree with it. For Emerson held that the individual must dare to express himself, to be himself, obeying the inner laws of the soul. In that sense Emerson is the philosopher of democracy. Each man, he thought, has within him a spark of the divine. The doctrine of human inequality was very old and very deeply entrenched; in Western civilization it may be traced back to Aristotle. The view that all men are created equal had been stated in the Declaration of Independence and verified in the experience of the frontier, but it remained for Emerson to give it deep philosophic meaning. In this task, the Concord sage drew on a large variety of intellectual traditions—not least, on Christianity. Emerson was once a minister of the Gospel, though he left even the liberal Unitarian church because his absolute individualism would brook no institutional restraints or dogmas whatsoever. While the origins of Emerson's philosophy are diverse, certainly a central theme is drawn from the Christian tradition.

Emerson denied that men were unequal. They were different, to be sure; but each man had within himself a divine spark, a little piece of God's divinity, a gift which, if he were able and willing to develop it, would result in greatness. It is possible to have a society composed entirely of fully developed persons, each man and woman capable, creative, and responsible. This is the goal of democracy. Indeed, it is the only possible result of democracy. It is the American dream—the meaning of American history. It was in these terms that Emerson summed up the meaning of his age—an age of "restless, prying, conscientious criticism," of humanitarian experimentation and reform.

Emerson's most insistent message was the duty of the individual to be true to his own genius, to obey the inner voice, to be self-reliant. He preached the unlimited potentialities of the individual. The philosophy of transcendentalism asserted that all men were part of the divine. It was therefore optimistic in its view both of the individual and of the universe. The Emersonian message was the challenge to men to live up to this potentially godlike quality. In this respect his vividly written essays summed up this era of democratic strivings. A good part of America was undergoing an Emersonian striving for perfection, a striving which took the form of many schemes and panaceas looking toward the reform of society. The sage himself, strong individualist that he was, could not always approve these social schemes. But he did stimulate the whole movement by his insistent injunction to "reform thyself."

This optimistic spirit, this ferment of reform and thought we have discussed in this chapter, is related to Jacksonian democracy and to economic progress. At the same time that the nation expanded and developed, it was discovering its national soul. The idea of democracy took shape, both among the common people and among writers and philosophers. At all levels, a mood of confidence and pride appeared. The United States had shaken off its dependence on Europe and was on the way to national greatness. At no time in American history have all groups in society shared so enthusiastically the same creed of democratic progress. An outgrowth of this is the theme to be treated next: the ideology of national expansion, the spirit of "manifest destiny."

FURTHER READINGS

Surveys include Harvey Wish, *Society and Thought in Early America* (1950); Vernon L. Parrington, *Main Currents in American Thought,* volume II (1930); and Van Wyck Brooks, *The Flowering of New England* (1936), a paperback reprint of which is available. Perry Miller has edited a useful anthology of *The American Transcendentalists: Their Prose and Poetry* (1957) in a paperback edition. Lewis Mumford, *The Golden Day* (1934), also has been reprinted recently. Alice F. Tyler, *Freedom's Ferment* (1949), deals mostly with reform crusades.

F. O. Matthiessen, *American Renaissance* (1941), is a sensitive appreciation by a literary critic and historian. Useful studies of various special areas include Merle Curti, *The American Peace Crusade, 1815–1861* (1929) and *The Social Ideas of American Educators* (1935); Gilbert H. Barnes, *The*

Anti-slavery Impulse, 1830–1844 (1933); and A. A. Ekirch, *The Idea of Progress in America, 1815–1860* (1944). The abolitionist crusade in relation to civil liberties is the theme of Russel B. Nye, *Fettered Freedom* (1949). Henry S. Commager, *Theodore Parker* (1936), is an outstanding biography of a prominent reform leader. The flavor of the age is effectively conveyed by Carl Bode in his account of *The American Lyceum: Town Meeting of the Mind* (1956).

A. E. Bestor, Jr., *Backwoods Utopias* (1950), deals capably with the absorbing theme of the utopian communities. William W. Sweet's general history of *Religion in the Development of American Culture, 1765–1840* (1952) may be supplemented by

Timothy L. Smith, *Revivalism and Social Reform in Mid-nineteenth Century America* (1957), and Ray A. Billington, *The Protestant Crusade, 1800–1860* (1938), a study of "nativism." Of some interest also is William K. Dunn's study of *The Decline of Religious Teaching in the Public Elementary School, 1776–1861* (1958). Clement Eaton, *Freedom of Thought in the Old South* (1940), is standard in its area.

Everyone probably ought to read the classic examination of American democracy, Alexis de Tocqueville, *Democracy in America* (1835), republished in many editions since and now available in an inexpensive edition.

THIRTEEN

The Politics of Expansion

1836
Texas wins independence.

1840
Whigs win in "log-cabin" campaign;
Harrison elected.
Liberty party appears.

1841
John Tyler President upon death of
Harrison.

1844
Texas a leading campaign issue.
Polk wins over Clay.

1845
Texas annexed by Congress.
The phrase "manifest destiny" appears.

1846
Oregon treaty made with Britain.
Polk vetoes rivers-and-harbors bill.
Mexican War begins.

1847
Wilmot Proviso offered in Congress.
Scott captures Mexico City.

1848
Treaty of Guadalupe Hidalgo ends
Mexican War.
Free-Soil party appears.
General Zachary Taylor elected
President.

SLAVERY AND EXPANSION

SEVERAL GENERATIONS of American historians, impressed with the prodigious display of energy and activity in the United States during the decade of the 1840s, wrote and talked of the "Roaring Forties." Stories and statistics of new lands opened to settlement, new territories acquired by conquest, railroad and turnpike building, the development of factories, all attested the vitality of Americans. From the mills of Waltham to the mining camps of California, the country was alive with sights and sounds of industry and labor. Before the decade was done the United States had presented the census taker with 6 million new noses to count, over and above the 17 million counted in 1840. By conquest and treaty, the size of the country almost doubled in ten years. Railroad mileage increased 300 per cent to a total of over 9,000 miles in 1850. A dip into statistics, anywhere and of any type, showed the same results—increases of several hundred to several thousand per cent.

While more recent historians of the Roaring Forties continue to be impressed with the statistics of national growth, they have found new significance in many of the events of the decade. These students have been less concerned with describing the great changes than with determining what these changes meant to the American people. This new orientation seems justified, for it is now quite clear that while the 1840s truly roared they were also a decade of decision. One of the most significant developments of the decade was that slavery

265

General Winfield Scott

General Zachary Taylor

A sketch of General Scott's
U.S. Army landing near
Vera Cruz, 1847

A sketch of the Battle of Buena Vista, drawn by General Taylor's aide-de-camp

The theme of the 1840s was territorial expansion in the name of "manifest destiny." Oregon and Texas were acquired without bloodshed, but Mexico refused to sell California or recognize the Texas annexation. Even those who disapproved of President Polk's belligerent actions which resulted in war were excited by the prospect of military adventure and then delighted with the outcome of the Mexican War. In marked contrast to the War of 1812 there was brilliant military leadership. Mexico was completely defeated and a vast area taken from her. This western territory was to prove a bone of contention between the slave and free states.

became entwined with every public question of the day. Whether the discussion was of tariffs, land policy, civil rights, or foreign war, it was soon being examined for its relation to slavery, and some connection was regularly found. Until the 1840s, slavery had not had this association with other issues. It was possible to discuss it on its own merits, as a labor system, a social system, an educational system. Men could debate the morality and the economics of slavery. But after the 1840s this was no longer possible; slavery, increasingly an issue in itself, could not be separated from other issues. This sudden shifting of slavery to the center of the stage was not the result of any change in the institution of slavery itself but was the result rather of a change in men's attitudes toward slavery.

The whole subject of property in human beings had bothered some Americans for many years. Thomas Jefferson was only one among many Virginians troubled by the inconsistency between the Declaration of Independence and the ownership of human beings. In 1787 southerners joined with northerners in voting to exclude slavery from the Northwest Territory. Virginians led the efforts of the American Colonization Society to end slavery through voluntary emancipation of Negro slaves and their resettlement in Africa or the Caribbean. The private diaries and letters of many slaveholders reveal that property in human beings was a burden on the owners' consciences. But the fact remained that slavery survived in the South, while in the North it was disappearing. Because of the invention of the cotton gin, slavery grew stronger rather than weaker in the South, and the South increasingly accepted the institution as inevitable and permanent. The crisis resolved by the Missouri Compromise of 1820 revealed a widening gulf between the two sections on this issue, and though a settlement was reached at that time, the conflict was to be renewed at every new acquisition of territory.

Had slavery been confined to the original slave states of the Atlantic seaboard, it might have withered away and died quietly. It also might not have aroused any very violent antislavery opposition. But all this changed as slavery began to expand into the western lands, taking a new lease on life in the rich cotton lands of the Southwest. Thus slavery became bound up with westward expansion and manifest destiny. The failure of the antislavery agitation of the 1830s to win wide public support in the North indicates that public opinion in the North was by no means prepared to come to grips with the issue, preferring to hope that time would bring some peaceful solution. But each demand for new slave territory diminished this hope.

By 1850 the expansion of the country had brought to the fore a host of new problems while aggravating all the old ones. Homesteads for western settlers, the railroad to the Pacific, and the improvement of rivers and harbors in the burgeoning Middle West were problems demanding attention. But new needs as well as old issues could not be discussed apart from their effects on slavery. This wedding between the issues of slavery and expansion took place in the 1840s, and the result of that marriage was secession and war. The danger to the very life of the nation posed by the combination of slavery and manifest destiny was painfully evident in 1850, when a major effort by Congress was required to prevent the issue from boiling over and involving the nation in war. The great Compromise of 1850 resulted, however, in a mere postponement of the conflict.

"MANIFEST DESTINY"

Although expansion reached a climax in the 1840s, it had been a theme in American life since the beginning. One of the constant reasons for American expansion was land hunger. The desire for land was a magnet of immense power pulling generations of prospective landowners out of Europe as well as from the eastern areas of the United States into the American West. In addition to those who yearned for land to till, there were always the speculators dreaming of great profits to be made in holding land for the inevitable increase in value. An attempt to cut off access to western lands had been one of the more important causes of the American Revolution. George Washington and Benjamin Franklin are only two of our founding fathers who dreamed of fortunes to be won in western speculation. The War of 1812 was fought in some measure to remove the British check on our western dreams.

In the eyes of many expansionists, another important reason was the hope of eliminating European influence from the North American continent. Jefferson sought the Floridas and Louisiana in part because their acquisition would ensure the removal of European powers from our borders. Expansionists were quick to point out that so long as European nations retained powerful establishments in the American West they would be tempted to arouse the Indians, interfere with our fur trade, furnish asylum for renegades and runaway slaves, and generally make trouble. Only after we had expanded our authority over the western lands would we be free of this constant source of irritation. The later acquisition of Texas and California was also pushed in the expectation that European intrigues on the North

American continent would thus be ended.

National security and considerations of strategic defense were uppermost in the minds of many of the promoters of expansion. The Louisiana Territory was long coveted not only because its acquisition would give us control of the vital Mississippi Valley, but because it would give us the protection of the mighty mountains to the west. Our hankering for Florida is best understood as an effort to rid ourselves of the Indian nuisance, but our eagerness also stemmed from a desire to have a naval base from which to protect our whole southern flank. After we had filled out our natural boundaries to the Gulf Coast, we developed Mobile Bay as a first-rate naval base.

Of less importance, although still significant as a force promoting manifest destiny, was simply the habit of migration. No one can judge the power of a motive so personal as wanderlust, yet many of our westward-bound ancestors tell of itching feet, curiosity about things beyond the mountains or rivers, and a simple yen to move on. Of course, there were some whose sudden curiosity about distant places coincided with the sheriff's curiosity about their recent activities.

These were the real motives for expansion. Mixed with them were a wide variety of rationalizations and excuses which came to be summed up in the phrase "manifest destiny." It is perfectly clear that a great many Americans were deeply troubled by the manner in which the Indian was stripped of his ancient hunting grounds or the Spanish deprived of a goodly part of the empire that they had stolen from similar Indians. In an effort to appease the national conscience, attempts were made to win the approval of higher authorities; God and natural law were invoked in support of expansion. The phrase "manifest destiny" itself is a product of this effort to base the right of expansion on the highest authority. The literature of expansion is full of references to God's will and to Nature's laws which invariably directed Americans to go west. General William Henry Harrison, fresh from his victory over the Britith in Canada, used the language of manifest destiny when he asked: "Is one of the fairest portions of the globe to remain in a state of nature, the haunt of a few wretched savages, when it seems destined by the Creator to give support to a large population and to be the seat of civilization, of science, and of true religion?" The question was purely rhetorical to a good expansionist. In 1830, another northwesterner, Lewis Cass, of Michigan, assured Americans, "There can be no doubt that the Creator intended the earth should be reclaimed from a state of nature and cultivated." At the same time a Georgia congressman was declaring that Indian claims in the Southwest were invalid in view of the "Almighty's command to till the earth." This argument for fulfilling God's will through superior utilization of the soil appeared wherever expansion was advocated.

Those who remained unimpressed with the superiority of an agricultural over a nomadic civilization were assured that God's will and Nature's laws were easily discernible in other ways. For instance, invoking the law of gravity, some maintained that, since large bodies attract small ones in nature, surely large nations must attract small ones. Others consulted maps to prove that the Creator had laid down natural boundaries for nations; certainly appendages like Florida had been intended as part of the United States. There were many references to the appearance of symmetry in nature as a guide to symmetry in national boundaries. The country needed "rounding out" by the acquisition of Texas, California, and Oregon. Another law of nature was discovered to decree that all living things must either grow or die. This law prohibited a static boundary and justified continued expansion. In other instances, neighboring countries were likened to overripe fruit, ready to fall; it was the plain duty of Americans to harvest this fruit before it spoiled. Clearly some expansionists were not above shaking the tree a bit.

Perhaps the most convincing justification for manifest destiny, and undoubtedly a real motive for many, was the unshakable belief in the mission of America. It was felt that the United States had a unique origin and mission in the world. Since God and Nature had combined to place in a richly endowed wilderness a race of men equipped with the best government the world had ever seen, it was obviously God's will that this noble experiment be given every opportunity to succeed. Separated from the rivalries and jealousies of the Old World, America had a mission to preserve and expand the dominion of liberty and democracy. It was the doctrine of a chosen people, selected by God to regenerate, reform, and lead the world to freedom and equality. This was the "American democratic faith" in operation.

In 1827, a minor New York politician put this faith into the following words: "We may look forward to the period, when the spark kindled in America, shall spread and spread, till the whole earth be illuminated by its light." America was thus the testing ground for all mankind. Institutions and ideas, having proved their worth in America, were to be extended as far as possible. Expansion was indeed "manifest destiny." The tragedy of America was that the problems of expansion and slavery could not be kept apart.

TIPPECANOE, TYLER, AND TEXAS

The small boys of Columbus, Ohio, were popeyed one afternoon in 1840 when the big balls rolled into town. One ball, 12 feet high and covered with tin, had been rolled all the way down from Cleveland by relays of raucous supporters of old General Harrison, the Whig nominee for President. A second ball, 15 feet high and covered with cowhide, had rolled into town behind a team of twenty-four white oxen. It was as much fun as a circus. Throughout the country the campaign was turning out to be even more fun for the parents of small boys. Town meetings, debates on the courthouse steps, and speeches down at the fairgrounds suddenly became the occasion for barbecues, clambakes, and fish fries where hard cider flowed freely and politics took on a new glow.

The 1840 campaign had barely begun before it was apparent that it would go down in the books as the most boisterous and tempestuous campaign in America's short national history. The anti-Jackson party of National Republicans, now calling themselves Whigs, had shrewdly discerned two currents running through politics at the beginning of the 1840s. One was the tremendous increase in the suffrage which the Jacksonians had encouraged; the other was a new interest in westward expansion. Clever Whig party managers put together a campaign designed to win the approval of the great mass of new voters by suggesting that the Whigs were vitally interested in the West. Since the Whig party itself was hopelessly divided on all major issues, including the virtues of westward expansion, the western appeal was left to the candidate. William Henry Harrison was a natural choice for this task. A "hero" of battles against the Indians at Tippecanoe and against the British at the battle of the Thames during the War of 1812, he had been governor of Indiana Territory during Jefferson's administration. An anti-British Indian fighter from the West gave the aristocratic Whig party a

A TIPPECANOE PROCESSION.

(Library of Congress)

chance to campaign as the special friend of the little man who dreamed of a future home in the new western empire. The log cabin and the coonskin cap replaced the broadcloth coat as the symbol of the Whigs; hard cider in copious draughts made them look more like Jacksonian Democrats every day.

By contrast, the Democrats forgot their debt to the western dream and renominated Martin Van Buren of Kinderhook, New York. Whig campaign literature pictured Van Buren, in reality a self-made man, eating from his gold table service while he entertained his friends among the effete eastern aristocracy. Burdened down by charges of responsibility for the panic of 1837, the effects of which were still being felt all across the country, Van Buren tried to talk of the Democrats' friendship for farmers and workingmen. But his campaign was drowned out by the cry of "Van, Van is a used up man" and "Tippecanoe and Tyler too." Confused by the theft of their issues as well as of their campaign tactics, the Democrats tried vainly to humanize Van Buren by references to "O. K. [Old Kinderhook] Van Buren," but all they succeeded in doing was perhaps to give the language a new expression. Some Democrats, in a desperate effort to win a few temperance votes, were reduced to opening party banquets with ostentatious toasts of water, while old-time western Jacksonians shuddered.

The results of the campaign proved the political sagacity of the Whig managers. The number of voters had increased 50 per cent over the total vote of 1836, and a goodly portion of these new voters cast their first ballot for Harrison and Tyler. Overlooked by both the rejoicing Whigs and the dejected Democrats were the 7,000 votes for James G. Birney, aboli-

tionist candidate of the newly formed Liberty party.

The candidacy of Birney, a former Alabama slaveholder, was the first venture into national politics for the abolitionists. The tiny vote he received showed the essential dualism in the American attitude toward slavery. Many Americans, utterly devoted to the principles of equality and liberty enunciated in the Declaration of Independence, were equally dedicated to the preservation of the union formed under the Constitution. While the Declaration presumably bade them abolish slavery, the Constitution recognized and protected the institution from political interference, inasmuch as it was a local institution under control of the states. Thus the vast majority of Americans hoped and prayed for an end to slavery but were equally determined to uphold the Constitution. The minute vote for Birney in 1840 clearly revealed that northerners were no more interested than southerners in bringing the slavery question into the political arena. Yet that is precisely where it landed. Before the term for which Harrison had been elected ran out, the debate over the annexation of Texas had become a debate over the expanding political power of the slave states.

President Harrison died after only one month in office. He was succeeded by John Tyler, a Jeffersonian Republican from Virginia. With few friends or supporters among the regular Whig leadership, Tyler cast about for some new combination to strengthen his administration and perhaps allow him to win the presidency in his own right in 1844. In the process, he used up four Secretaries of State, four Secretaries of the Treasury, five Secretaries of War, and five Secretaries of the Navy. Tyler's fourth Secretary of State was John C. Calhoun of South Carolina. Ever since his rebuff by Jackson in 1830, Calhoun had been sitting on the sidelines of party contests. He had devoted his time and energies since 1832 to creating and directing a movement for the protection of southern rights. Convinced that the South must control the Union if its peculiar institution were to survive, Calhoun used his Senate seat both as a forum from which to spread the gospel and as a window through which to watch for weaknesses in the northern position. When Tyler offered him the State portfolio, Calhoun accepted with alacrity. The position would give him an opportunity to advance his cause and his career by reviving the question of the annexation of Texas.

Texas had sought annexation ever since she had first achieved independence from Mexico in 1836. But the prospect of several new slave states being carved from that vast territory aroused such fears in the North that Jackson had reluctantly postponed any effort at annexation. Van

Buren followed the same policy. Texas, forced to go her own way, approached England and France with offers of friendship and commerce. The chance to curb American westward expansion, plus a chance to buy cotton and sell manufactured goods without the annoying American tariff, was too good an opportunity to pass up. The two leading industrial nations of Europe signed treaties of amity and commerce with Texas.

When Calhoun came to the State Department, he saw that England's interest in Texas gave the South a golden opportunity. England's action could be interpreted as a restraint on manifest destiny. By organizing all the power of American expansionist feeling, coupling it with anti-British sentiment, and focusing it on Texas, Calhoun was able to override northern and antislavery objections to annexation. Calhoun's first attempt at a treaty of annexation failed of ratification in the Senate, but his second effort, reinforced by the

The Alamo, scene of the famous incident during the Texas revolution against Mexican rule, when a massacre of Texans stirred the Lone Star Republic to fight on for independence. (Library of Congress)

election of Polk in 1844 on an expansionist platform, was successful. Texas's annexation was assured by a joint resolution of Congress just two days before Polk was inaugurated. Calhoun had his immediate victory. Texas was on its way into the union and empowered to divide itself into five states should it so desire. Mexico refused to recognize the annexation and broke off diplomatic relations with the United States.

Northern antislavery elements received the Texas "deal" with rising anger. The joint-resolution method of bringing Texas into the union after the treaty had been clearly defeated in the Senate smacked of chicanery. In addition, in the course of the negotiations, Calhoun had written a letter to the British Minister in Washington. It was a harsh letter, reprimanding the British for their interest in seeing slavery abolished in the Republic of Texas and clearly implying that one of our major purposes in acquiring Texas was to prevent the abolition of slavery there. Many northerners, among them the most bitter opponents of abolitionism, began to wonder if the powers of the federal government were not being rather badly used by slaveholders. Finally, it was perfectly clear that the leadership of the Democratic party had slipped a few more degrees southward. The election and the administration of James K. Polk reinforced the belief that the Democrats had become a southern party, interested in expansion, but only in expansion that would add territory suitable for slavery.

POLK AND SLAVERY

When the Democratic convention met in Baltimore in May, 1844, Van Buren was known to have a majority of the delegates pledged to him. But Van Buren and Clay, his Whig counterpart, each had a major weakness. In April they had each announced that the questions of Texas and expansion would only divide the union and therefore should not be made party issues. Their announcements were issued simultaneously on April 20, one from New York and the other from Raleigh, North Carolina. But Democratic party leaders felt that Texas was simply too important an issue to be set aside by Van Buren. In spite of all advice from his friends, Van Buren refused to soften his attitude toward Texas. On the first day of the convention his "majority" was unable to prevent the old rule requiring a two-thirds vote for the nomination from being revived. Thus Van Buren needed to win over additional delegates to secure a two-thirds vote and the nomination; the delay gave the expansionists time to work. Under the leadership of ardent advocates of the annexation of Texas, a revolt was organized in the convention and Van Buren's candidacy was defeated.

The nomination was given to James K. Polk of Tennessee, who came out strongly for expansion and endorsed his party's demand for the acquisition of both Texas and Oregon. Here was a very neat political stratagem: to take the sting out of Texas, and out of the charge that manifest destiny was a slaveholder's plot, the Democrats threw in Oregon, with a ringing demand for the British to surrender their legitimate claims in that territory and cede us all of Oregon up to the tip of Alaska. But all the enthusiasm for Polk and expansion did not hide the fact that the Democrats had failed to include in their platform their traditional reaffirmation of the principles of the Declaration of Independence.

James K. Polk has been described as the first "dark-horse" candidate in American history. The title is misleading. He

President James K. Polk. (*Library of Congress*)

had long been prominent in Tennessee politics; a close friend of Andrew Jackson, he had been in and out of the "Kitchen Cabinet" and was frequently the Jackson spokesman on the floor of the House of Representatives. Political jobs that he had filled, like that of governor of Tennessee and Speaker of the national House of Representatives, had made him a well-known political figure. A tough, dedicated Puritan spirit drove Polk to live up to his high sense of duty.

Affable Henry Clay had a better grip on the Whig party in 1844 than Van Buren had on the Democrats. The Whigs dutifully nominated Clay and remained silent on Texas and Oregon. The 1844 campaign was 1840 in reverse. Now the Democrats set out to win a popularity contest. The failure of the Whigs to provide decisive leadership, the persistence of the long depression, and the proven popularity of expansion gave Polk a narrow victory. Few people this time missed the significance of the fact that the Liberty

party, again running James G. Birney, increased its 1840 vote ninefold. It had discovered 62,000 voters who were ready for some political action on the subject of slavery. Indeed, it managed to determine the outcome by tilting pivotal New York State to Polk.

Polk, one of the ablest men to occupy the White House, did a rare thing after his inauguration. He set out to translate his party's platform into legislation. The Democratic platform had called for Oregon, Texas, a tariff reduction, and the re-establishment of the independent treasury. When the hard-working Polk left office in 1849, all four objectives had been accomplished. In addition, the war against Mexico had been fought and won, and the country was reaching new heights of prosperity. In spite of these notable achievements, Polk returned to Nashville broken in spirit and health and died within four months after the end of his term. The explanation for this seeming paradox is to be found in the way that slavery was beginning to poison the political atmosphere.

Of all the programs which Polk advocated, only the independent-treasury plan was unaffected by the slavery dispute. With the unlamented demise of the second Bank of the United States, the Jacksonians were faced with the problem of a place to put government money between the time of receipt and expenditure. Jackson's deposits of government money in his "pet banks" had led to trouble when many of them failed. Van Buren had devised a system of depositing federal funds in the Treasury at Washington or in the vaults of the mints around the country. The Whigs abolished this independent-treasury system in 1841; Polk restored it in 1846. (Although considerably modified by the National Banking Act of 1863 and the Federal Reserve Act of 1913, the essential features of the independent-treasury plan are still in effect today.)

Tariff reduction, the second of Polk's campaign promises, became involved immediately with the question of slavery. The South had been demanding free trade since 1828. Protective tariffs put the South in the unenviable position of selling her great agricultural surpluses in a free market while she bought in a protected market. Whether it was calculated as higher prices for the things she bought or lower prices for the products she sold made little difference. Southern planters and farmers firmly believed that protective tariffs reduced their real income. The compromise tariff of 1833 with which Clay had tried to resolve the nullification crises satisfied no one. The gradual reduction of duties provided for by that tariff had taken place on schedule, but the Whig victory in 1840 led to a restoration of higher rates in 1842. Soon after Polk's election it became obvious that a powerful bloc of southern Democrats were planning a concerted drive for tariff reduction. The southern Democrats were just a little shy of sufficient votes to pass a low-tariff bill, so they offered to support a massive internal-improvements program for the Northwest in exchange for northwestern votes for a low tariff. The bargain was made, Polk cracked the party whip, and Walker's tariff of 1846 became law.

A brief glance at the votes on the Walker tariff shows how clearly Polk's action identified him with the southern slaveholding wing of his party. In the House of Representatives, the only congressmen from the Northeast who voted with Polk were those from the farming districts of New York, New Hampshire, and Maine. Massachusetts, Connecticut, Rhode Island, and New Jersey opposed the reduction

unanimously. In Pennsylvania, only one out of twenty-four congressmen voted for the reduction. On the other hand, southern representatives were as one in their approval of the measure. Northern editorials talked of a slaveholding conspiracy which exposed national interests to cutthroat competition with European manufacturers. Some northern newspapers carried the news of the Walker tariff on pages outlined in black. Dire warnings of eventual ruin for American industry under southern domination were freely made. Slavery and tariff were now seen as two sides of the same question.

The next public issue to run afoul of the slavery controversy was that of internal improvements. True to the bargain made on the Walker tariff, southern Democrats voted for a huge internal-improvements program in 1846. It was a perfect example of congressional logrolling, since there was something in the bill for practically everyone. There was money for the development of eastern and southern rivers. There was money for harbors on the Great Lakes and for the improvement of rivers in the Old Northwest. The smiles which greeted the news of the passage of the cherished rivers-and-harbors bill changed to scowls with the announcement that President Polk had vetoed the measure.

Actually Polk had never expressed a willingness to support the Whig program of internal improvements. His veto message was a carefully reasoned defense of the limitations on federal authority imposed by the Constitution. He was in distinguished company, for both Hamilton and Jefferson had doubted that the general government had the power to engage in internal improvements. Madison, Monroe, and Jackson had all vetoed internal-improvements bills similar to that which

Polk had turned down. But constitutional arguments meant little to men pressed by low prices, and the high cost of transporting wheat, corn, and meat to eastern markets had long ago convinced western farmers that improved transportation was their only chance for permanent prosperity. Polk's honest constitutional doubts were dismissed with a shrug, while much was made of his Tennessee slaveholding background. Typical of the northern reaction to Polk's rivers-and-harbors veto was the statement of the Chicago *Daily Journal:*

> The North can and will no longer be hoodwinked. If no measures for the protection and improvement of anything north and west are to be suffered by our Southern masters, if we are to be downtrodden, and all our cherished interests crushed by them, a signal revolution will inevitably ensue. . . . The North and West will look to and take care of their own interests henceforth. They will deal justly with the South, but at the same time they will see that they have equal justice, and that the power to oppress shall not again be entrusted to men who have shown themselves to be slave holders, but not Americans.

Within two months of Polk's veto, an immense Rivers and Harbors Convention met in Chicago. Over 10,000 delegates and friends listened to one prominent politician after another condemn the Polk veto and demand federal aid for northwestern rivers and harbors. "Polk the Mendacious" was soon the favorite title for the President in many areas of the West. By 1848, Democratic as well as Whig county conventions were calling for freedom from the slaveholder's yoke. Even the most loyal Democratic conventions adopted resolutions like that in the first congressional district of Iowa: "That the South has had the President for forty-eight out of sixty years. We think it is time to elect another from the North." Not until after the Civil War had decided the issue of slavery would Americans again be able to discuss internal improvements without also discussing slavery.

POLK AND MANIFEST DESTINY

The few northerners who remained unconvinced of the southern orientation of the Democratic party under Polk were easily converted by a third measure of the administration. Although it had not been a major factor in the 1844 presidential campaign, the Democratic interest in the acquisition of Oregon had been clear. The party platform had coupled demands for Oregon with those for Texas. Polk himself had expressed particular interest in getting clear title to Oregon. Both England and the United States had good claims to Oregon. Both claims were buttressed by settlement and by treaties with other powers. Unable to agree on a boundary dividing their claims, the two countries had decided in 1818 to occupy jointly the whole of Oregon. The terms of the decision, as amended in 1827, called for an indefinite joint occupation which could be terminated by either country after one year's notice.

During the late 1830s and the early 1840s, American settlers began to arrive in Oregon in appreciable numbers. The welcome which had been extended by the local representatives of the Hudson's Bay Company was withdrawn when it became apparent that American settlers were jeopardizing British claims to Oregon. Polk, in perfect sympathy with the aims of manifest destiny, set out to win Oregon for the United States. In his first annual message Polk asked Congress for the authority to give the British the required notice for the termination of the joint occupation. By April, 1846, Polk had the permission of Congress in his pocket and was dropping hints of American willingness to go to war for Oregon. Then, with little advance notice, Polk reversed himself and made a peaceful settlement with the British. To those familiar with the details of the conflicting claims over Oregon, Polk's compromise settlement seemed a sound and fair one. We acquired Oregon up to the 49th parallel, and the British retained the whole of Vancouver Island and the right to navigate the Columbia River. This settlement gave Polk's Whig enemies a beautiful opening. They were quick to charge that Polk had vigorously campaigned for the acquisition of Oregon all the way up to 54°40′, that "Fifty-four Forty or Fight" was a campaign slogan that pledged the Democratic administration to seek title to Oregon all the way to the Alaskan border.

Recent research reveals that "Fifty-four Forty or Fight" was emphatically not a campaign slogan in the 1844 contest and that, as a matter of fact, Oregon played a distinctly minor role throughout the campaign. This, however, gave Whig politicians little pause. They went right ahead and charged Polk with promising to fight for "all of Oregon," but "basely bowing the knee to England" when the chips were down. Polk had, it was charged, sold out the future generations of northern farmers who would make Oregon their home. Again the charge of "Polk the Mendacious" was heard. "All of Oregon and All of Texas" became a sneer rather than a cheer for manifest destiny. Through all the bitter recriminations ran the comparison of Polk's aggressiveness where the acquisition of slave territory in Texas was involved to his "sweet reasonableness" when free territory in Oregon was involved.

While the controversy between the North and the South grew more tense, Polk went ahead with his plans for expansion. No tool of the "slavocracy" was he, but a true disciple of the concept of manifest destiny. Polk cared not one whit whether the territories acquired were suited to slave or free labor. Expansion was an end in itself in his mind and not one to be defeated by petty haggling over future labor systems. Equally contemptuous of the spokesmen for the radical "slavocracy" and the abolitionists, Polk believed that their extreme charges and countercharges were dangerous to the union. In April, 1847, he confided to his diary that he thought "Mr. Calhoun had become perfectly desperate in his aspirations to the Presidency, and had seized upon this sectional question as the only means of sustaining himself in his present fallen condition, and that such an agitation of the slavery question . . . [is] not only unpatriotic and mischievous, but wicked." At the same time he noted that northern men have "unpatriotically . . . shown by their course that they desire to mount the same hobby in the North and hope to be successful by their opposition to slavery." His judgment of both was forthright: "I am utterly disgusted at such intriguing of men in high places, and hope they will be rebuked by the people." It is undoubtedly one of the minor ironies of history that a man so bitterly opposed to the sectional extremists of his day should have provided the area in which their animosities found full play. For his war with Mexico soon revealed that the sectional controversy over tariffs, internal improvements, and Oregon were mere preliminaries to the great conflict over the extension of slavery into new territories.

When the United States annexed Texas, the Mexican government broke off diplomatic relations. Pride as well as self-interest prevented Mexico from recognizing the Texas annexation as anything but theft. While Mexico considered herself wronged, the forces of manifest destiny, which had brought Texas into the union, were focusing on California and New Mexico. Spurred by the belief that England was interested in California, Polk moved rapidly. Barely six months after taking office he sent word to the American Minister in California that should the Californians "desire to unite their destiny with ours, they will be received as brethren." At the same time he was outlining plans to the Cabinet for a direct approach to Mexico. He had decided to send John Slidell to Mexico with an offer to purchase New Mexico and California. Polk felt that the price was of small consequence and expected to pay 15 to 20 million dollars, though he was ready to go as high as 40 million dollars for a favorable settlement. The boundary Polk hoped to purchase ran along the Rio Grande River to El Paso, then westward along the 32d parallel to the Pacific. A glance at the map shows that except for the minor addition of the Gadsden Purchase territory in the 1850s, Polk soon acquired, by conquest, the boundary he had hoped to purchase.

News came in January, 1846, that the Mexican government had refused to receive John Slidell. This could not have come as much of a surprise to the President. He had been too long in politics not to have realized that a government in so unstable a country as Mexico could not have remained in power a week after sell-ing nearly half its national domain to a foreign power. Polk must also have been aware that there was a technical diplomatic distinction between the commissioner whom Mexico agreed to receive and the minister plenipotentiary whom he sent in the person of Slidell. Receiving a minister would have been tantamount to recognizing the Texas annexation. The Mexican temper quickly showed itself when the mere presence of Slidell in Mexico City was seized upon as an excuse for another revolution forcing the tottering Herrera government from power and replacing it with a military junta.

The day after Polk received the news of Slidell's rejection, he ordered General Zachary Taylor to cross the Nueces River and move to the Rio Grande. By this move the President was attempting to reinforce the claim of Texas to the 200-mile-wide strip of territory between the two rivers. On the disputed theory that the Rio Grande had been the southern boundary of the Louisiana Purchase, Texans had claimed it as their southern border. The

TEXAS-MEXICAN BOUNDARY DISPUTE, 1836–1848

claim was feeble, for the Mexican province of Texas had always stopped at the Nueces, and Texas troops had never occupied the land between the two rivers. Polk's own doubts about the validity of the claim were apparent in his willingness to purchase the territory. The President now hoped that General Taylor's presence in the disputed territory would provoke the chest-thumping Mexican generals into an attack upon American forces.

Late in April, the President, despairing of getting any action out of the Mexicans, determined to force war upon them. He sat down to write a message to Congress asking for a declaration of war, based chiefly on the rejection of the Slidell mission. On Saturday, May 9, he told his Cabinet that the message was ready and would be sent to Congress on the following Tuesday. The Cabinet had barely left the White House when good news arrived from Taylor. The Mexicans had crossed the Rio Grande and attacked American troops before returning to the south side of the river. It was only a little skirmish, but Polk made the most of it. The President, overcoming his Puritan conscience, devoted the Sabbath to revising his war message. Now he could include, almost exultantly, the statement that Mexico had "invaded our Territory and shed American blood upon American soil."

So war came. It had come for a variety of reasons. The chaotic conditions prevailing in Mexico, which produced frequent revolutions with consequent loss of property to Americans residing there, contributed. Jingoistic Mexican generals, convinced that their tremendous armies could easily whip the feeble yankee forces, added their bit to the war fever. Hurt pride over the dismemberment of the young Republic of Mexico by the loss of Texas was high on the list of reasons. And in the United States, manifest destiny, in all its ramifications, must be charged with the credit or blame for our willingness to fight. In the last analysis, it was America's desire for California, and Mexico's refusal to sell it, which caused the war.

A "GLORIOUS LITTLE WAR"

For Americans, the Mexican War was short, glorious, and profitable. When it was over the United States had acquired more land than the combined area of France, Spain, and Italy. At a cost of 1,700 battle dead—as usual in all wars, the sick and wounded far outnumbered the battle deaths—the United States conquered more than half of Mexico and won recognition of the annexation of Texas. The war probably cost about 100 million dollars, including 15 million paid to Mexico for lands "deeded" to the United States in the peace treaty, as well as the $3,250,000 we agreed to pay our own citizens who had claims against the Mexican government.

But the ultimate success of the war was not at all apparent at its beginning. The regular army of Mexico was roughly ten times the size of the standing army of the United States. Polk may have been confident that the American regulars plus 20,000 volunteers could defeat Mexico, but he was soon forced to call for 50,000 volunteers. Before the war was over some 70,000 volunteers had fought alongside the regulars in Mexican campaigns. In most battles the American forces were outnumbered about three to one. Except for some of the Texas troops and the regulars, most Americans found that the plains and deserts of northern Mexico were hotter, dustier, and drier than anything they had imagined. It was not until the Mexican armies were discovered to be made up largely of badly equipped and poorly trained masses of Indian and mestizo conscripts with little interest in war that Americans began to view the action as a "glorious little war."

The first American campaign was an advance under General Taylor from the Rio Grande south along the Gulf Coast to Matamoros and then inland to the key city of Monterrey. After several skirmishes, a long march, and a serious battle for the city, Taylor's force was considerably weakened and it seemed advisable for him to assume the defensive until he could be reinforced with the volunteers just being recruited. During a winter of enforced idleness General Taylor was joined by small expeditions under General John E. Wool and Colonel A. W. Doniphan. Wool had moved out of San Antonio and cut inland across the disputed territory to make connection with Taylor some two hundred miles west of Monterrey at Parras. Doniphan's march was a remarkable overland journey from Santa Fe to Parras and Saltillo.

Taylor was probably a second-rate general. Even if he had been a third-rater, it would have made little difference to his men. He was loved and respected for his informality and the way he could put a Missouri mule skinner to shame when it came to swearing. He is reported to have worn a uniform on only two occasions during the campaign. He wore civilian clothes during his very infrequent reviews and campaigned without any insignia or mark of rank about him. The General fought at least one battle mounted on a mule. In an army of boisterous young men from the aggressively democratic areas of the West, Taylor's plain ways made him a great favorite. His early military successes, and letters written home by impressionable young recruits detailing the virtues of

"Old Rough-and-Ready," suddenly elevated Taylor to political prominence.

Whig politicians, learning that Taylor had no particular political beliefs but considered himself a Whig, were immediately interested in his possibilities as a presidential candidate. When it was learned that he was born in Virginia, was raised in Kentucky, and had recently bought a Louisiana plantation, they were overjoyed. The fact that he was a conservative southerner now identified with western expansion, as well as a war hero of major proportions, made Taylor seem an unbeatable nominee. Polk and the Democrats saw the same potentialities in Taylor and were worried. They could not make him lose a battle, but they might well stop him from winning any more victories. In an effort to counter the growing popularity of Taylor, the administration turned to General Winfield Scott. Scott was a first-class general and a lifelong Whig, but the President was assured that Scott's imperious ways would prevent his ever becoming popular with the troops. Scott, therefore, was sent to take command in Mexico. From the beginning of the war Scott had contended that limited campaigns in the northern provinces of Mexico would never win California and New Mexico and that only capture of the enemy's capital would assure conquest of the coveted territory.

Accordingly, he prepared a plan for a drive directly inland from the port city of Vera Cruz to Mexico City. The plan had two virtues: it was militarily sound, and it would leave Taylor high and dry hundreds of miles away from the main campaign. After innumerable delays, Scott got ashore at Vera Cruz. In a brilliant campaign, in which the enemy had all the advantages of the ground and numbers, Scott climbed the mountains and captured

MEXICAN WAR, 1846–1847

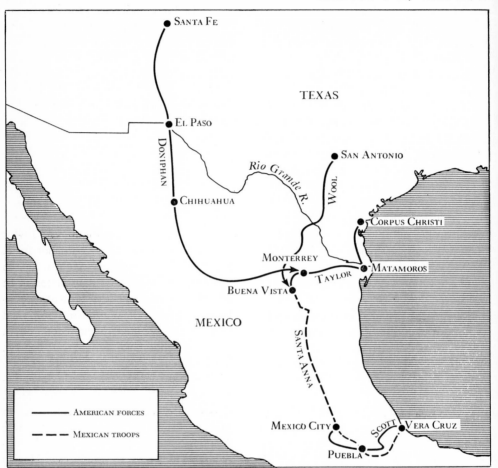

Mexico City. But Scott's great victory did not obscure the fact that Taylor, left with 5,000 raw recruits, had driven off 15,000 Mexicans at Buena Vista in February, 1847.

While Taylor and Scott were contending for honors in Mexico, California was falling into American hands. Colonel Stephen Kearny in a dramatic overland campaign took Santa Fe and then marched his troops across mountains and deserts to California. In the meantime, Commodore J. D. Sloat of the United States Navy heard of the declaration of war. He immediately landed forces at Monterrey and

declared California a possession of the United States. Just to the north, at Sutter's Fort, Captain John C. Frémont had finally consented to lead a handful of American residents of California who had declared themselves the "Bear Flag Republic" and independent of Mexico. Frémont was in California at the head of an expedition to make a geographical survey of the American West. Thus three American commanders, all with some evidence of authority, contended for the honor of taking California. The Mexicans in that territory entered into the spirit of the thing and gracefully retired after fighting a few skirmishes.

In this comic-opera atmosphere, California was won from Mexico.

The Treaty of Guadalupe Hidalgo, signed in early 1848, gave the United States legal title to all of Texas to the Rio Grande as well as Utah, New Mexico, and California. Although some Americans wanted to seize all of Mexico, most Americans agreed that we had got an impressive parcel of real estate at a bargain price. A few remembered the long acrimonious debates in Congress over every measure connected with the war and wondered if the bargain might not prove to be one of the most expensive in our history. The skeptics proved tragically correct, for the legacy of the Mexican War was the bitter contest over slavery in the territories which ended in the Civil War.

MANIFEST DESTINY AND SECTIONAL CONFLICT

In spite of the overwhelming vote for war in both houses of Congress (the Senate voted 42 to 2, and the House 174 to 14, for war), important opposition had developed almost immediately. This resistance naturally centered in the Northeast, where the possibility of new southern senators and representatives from states carved out of Mexico was a most unwelcome prospect. There was also opposition to the war in the South Atlantic states. Prominent politicians in Virginia, the Carolinas, and Georgia advised caution. Calhoun doubted that New Mexico and California would prove suitable for slave labor and feared that the new senators and representatives might well turn up in Congress speaking in western accents rather than southern. He feared that slavery might be destroyed rather than extended by the workings of manifest destiny.

Proof of the unpopularity of the war in the Northeast and seaboard South is to be found in the statistics on volunteers. Of the nearly 70,000 men who volunteered for service, fewer than 15,000 came from the eastern seaboard states. In contrast, there were 30,000 men volunteering for Tennessee's quota of 3,000, while in Kentucky the governor was forced to halt recruiting entirely when volunteers far exceeded both the quota and the state's ability to handle recruits. Yet even in the West there was some resistance to war. It was an obscure Whig from Illinois who rose in Congress and offered a series of resolutions against the war. Designed to embarrass Polk, the resolutions asked the President to indicate the spot on American soil where American blood had been shed. The obscure Whig was Abraham Lincoln, serving his only term in the House of Representatives.

The war was barely under way when those who opposed it found a rallying point for their resistance. It was a hot August night in 1846, and the House was debating the President's request for 2 million dollars to finance the war, when David Wilmot, a Pennsylvania Democrat, offered an amendment to the measure. The Wilmot Proviso, as it came to be known, would have provided that "neither slavery nor involuntary servitude shall ever exist in any part" of the territory acquired from Mexico "except for crime whereof the party shall first be duly convicted." The use of the words of the Northwest Ordinance which kept slavery out of the territory north of the Ohio River was intentional. The proviso was subsequently tacked on to a host of bills dealing with the war, but it was never adopted. Actually no one expected its adoption; it was a symbol, a statement of principle, a platform. As such, the proviso was tremendously effective. The discussion of the measure soon revealed a realignment of political forces in the nation. Democrats

MEXICAN WAR, DRIVE FOR CALIFORNIA, 1846–1847

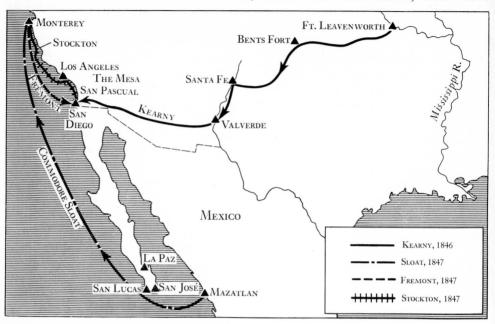

and Whigs became Northerners and Southerners. Party organizations split wide open as one northern legislature after another passed resolutions approving the proviso, while southern Whig and Democratic editors alike condemned it.

The discussion of the proviso gave extremists on both sides an unparalleled opportunity. Opposition to the war as such became hopelessly mixed up with opposition to the spread of slavery. In one of the most widely quoted speeches of the year, Tom Corwin, senator from Ohio, blamed an "aggressive slavocracy" for the Mexican War and declared: "If I were a Mexican, I would tell you, 'Have you not room in your own country to bury your dead men? If you come into mine, we will greet you with bloody hands and welcome you to hospitable graves.'" Walt Whitman declared that the proviso made it plain that the real conflict was between the millions of mechanics, farmers, and operatives of

the North and a few thousand southern slaveowners. At the same time, southern extremists emphatically denied the right of the North to exclude slavery from territories won by the common blood and treasure. They maintained that, on the contrary, Congress had a solemn duty to protect slavery in the territories. Between the two extremes the great majority of Americans sought a middle or compromise ground. They joined with Polk in denouncing extremists using the slavery issue as a "hobby" to carry them to power.

But the proviso would not be put down. The resentments and frustrations of years were bound up in it, and the extremists gained ground as they chipped away at the moderates. Next to war news, the proviso was the most discussed topic of 1847. Wilmot Proviso leagues were formed in the North which flooded their state legislatures and the Congress with petitions demanding passage of the proviso. Moderates like Stephen A. Douglas of Illinois and Daniel Webster vainly sought to point out that the nature of the soil would probably prevent the extension of the plantation system and slavery into the new territories. Even Calhoun, who had expressed such moderate sentiments less than a year before, found himself forced to take more extreme ground, now demanding the right of slaveholders to take their property anywhere in the territories.

The Wilmot Proviso debates marked the tragic marriage between slavery and expansion. Although discussion of the two issues would continue right down to the outbreak of war, the fundamental positions of North and South were never altered. The election of 1848, the Compromise of 1850, the Kansas-Nebraska Act, the birth of the Republican party, the Dred Scott decision, and the election of Lincoln were simply milestones in the great debate. Manifest destiny brought the United States great wealth, power, and opportunity; it also brought sectional rivalry and civil war.

As in Europe, where it was a year of revolutions everywhere, the year 1848 came to a close in America amid a sense of restlessness, crisis, and tension. Mutterings about secession came from the South, and talk of no more appeasement of slave drivers came from the North. The Wilmot Proviso was a dark cloud low on the horizon. This was the ominous situation which lay behind the great Compromise of 1850, in which the old leaders bestirred themselves mightily to save the union and stave off civil strife.

FURTHER READINGS

Three of the four Presidents of the 1840s have found excellent biographers in Freeman Cleaves, *Old Tippecanoe: William Henry Harrison* (1939); O. P. Chitwood, *John Tyler* (1939); Holman Hamilton, *Zachary Taylor* (2 vols., 1941–1951); and Brainerd Dyer, *Zachary Taylor* (1946). Charles G. Sellers, Jr., has covered the pre-presidential career of Polk under the title, *James K. Polk, Jacksonian, 1795–1843* (1957).

Other outstanding biographies include the following: Samuel F. Bemis, *John Quincy Adams and the Union* (1956), is the second volume of the best Adams biography. Arthur D. H. Smith, *Old Fuss and Feathers* (1937), is a readable account of Winfield Scott. Elbert B. Smith, *Magnificient Missourian: The Life of Thomas Hart Benton* (1957), and William N. Chambers, *Old Bullion Benton: Senator from the New West* (1956), treat one of the most remarkable men of the period in authoritative fashion. Russell B. Nye, *George Bancroft* (1944), is a splendid biography of one of the minor figures of the period.

The Mexican War is treated in a Pulitzer prize winner by J. H. Smith, *The War with Mexico* (2 vols., 1919), while a briefer and highly readable account is Robert S. Henry, *The Story of the Mexican War* (1950). Equally readable is Alfred H. Bill, *Rehearsal for Conflict* (1947).

The reaction of the country to the issues of slavery and expansion is thoroughly covered in Allan Nevins, *The Ordeal of the Union* (2 vols., 1947), and Charles Sydnor, *The Development of Southern Sectionalism, 1819–1848* (1948). Albert K. Weinberg, *Manifest Destiny: A Study of Nationalist Expansionism in American History* (1935), is a must for its subject. In the same category is Norman Graebner, *Empire on the Pacific* (1955).

FOURTEEN

Sectional Conflict

1850

Crisis of the union; Compromise of 1850 enacted.

Taylor dies; Fillmore becomes President.

1852

Franklin Pierce defeats General Scott for presidency.

Death of Clay and Webster; Whig party in eclipse.

1853

Gadsden Purchase treaty.

1854

Kansas-Nebraska Act passed.

Birth of Republican party.

1855

Struggle over Kansas—"Bleeding Kansas."

1856

Brooks attacks Sumner in Senate.

Buchanan elected President over Frémont (Republican).

1857

Dred Scott decision by Supreme Court.

1858

Lincoln-Douglas debates.

1859

John Brown's raid.

1860

Democratic party divides at Charleston.

Lincoln elected.

South Carolina secedes, December 20.

THE SLAVERY ISSUE

A NATION EXISTS only in the hearts and minds of its citizens. It is born when a people believe they are part of a nation, and it dies when they withhold their loyalty or transfer it elsewhere. The American nation was born for some men in the wet and cold of Valley Forge; for others, when George Washington became President of something called the United States of America. For most Americans a sense of loyalty and unity came only with the War of 1812. Just as the birth of a nation is a slow process, so is its death. A nation dies not when it ceases to occupy a portion of the map, but when men no longer think and feel themselves part of it. In the 1850s the American nation was threatened with death as several million citizens withdrew their allegiance from it.

Thus the search for the causes of the Civil War becomes an attempt to determine what ideas and events caused Americans to withdraw their loyalty from the United States and to give it instead to individual states or to something they called the North and South.

There can be no doubt that the existence of human slavery in one portion of the nation after it had been abandoned in the remainder was a constant threat to the life of the nation. The authors of the Constitution were aware of the threat which slavery presented, but they were unwilling to jeopardize the experiment in political federation by taking any determined action. They retreated from the advanced position taken by Jefferson in the Northwest Ordinance, when slavery had been prohibited

284

north of the Ohio River. Instead they left slavery in the hands of the states and provided no clear statement concerning its status in the territories. Sensing that anything so fundamental as property in human beings would inevitably divide the nation, they put a mild check on its future growth by limiting the importation of slaves after twenty years. They then sat back and hoped that something might happen which would lead the South to follow the North in its abandonment of the institution. But slavery did not die. The cotton gin made cotton production immensely profitable. Since cotton cultivation requires tremendous quantities of unskilled labor, the demand for slaves skyrocketed. The hopes of the founding fathers went glimmering as the ownership of human beings became more deeply entrenched in the South.

In 1820 Americans again found themselves confronted with the issue of slavery. The institution had become a social system as well as a labor system. It allowed a minority of white masters to live among and direct the great masses of black slaves and to retain a reasonable sense of security in the process. Few southerners defended the system on grounds other than economic necessity. Most apologized for the institution and pointed out, quite reasonably, that slavery was as much their heritage as was the language they spoke, the religion they professed, the nation they loved, or the lands they farmed. But the hard fact remained: slavery existed in only half the nation. When settlement spread beyond the Mississippi River, the question had to be faced again. Was slavery to expand with the nation, or was it to be confined to the area it already dominated? If it were to be confined to existing slave states, a severe strain would be placed upon the nation. Southerners who knew that both their

prosperity and way of life rested on chattel slavery were sure to weigh carefully the value of a nation that threatened both. But if slavery were allowed to expand, the question of a nation "divided against itself" was merely postponed, and a subsequent generation would have to face the problem again. When the Missouri Compromise was passed in 1820, many Americans feared that failure to limit the expansion of slavery threatened the very life of the nation. Jefferson described the decision as "a reprieve only, not a final sentence." He said the news came and "like a fire bell in the night, awakened and filled me with terror. . . . In the gloomiest hour of the Revolutionary War, I never had any apprehensions equal to those which I feel from this source." Other statesmen of the period shared Jefferson's fear for the fate of the nation.

Slavery, fundamental as it was, did not alone destroy the sense of unity which was the American nation. There was a conflict between two economic systems. The North was rapidly becoming industrialized. More and more of its capital and labor were being absorbed in the building of factories and railroads. Even though a majority of northerners still made their living tilling the soil, the spokesmen of the section increasingly represented the interests of industry and transport. The South, on the other hand, remained an agricultural economy. In spite of the zealous efforts of crusaders, the South was wedded to agriculture. While J. D. B. De Bow's *Review* extolled the virtues of a more diversified economy and a few others sought to convert the South to manufacturing by establishing successful factories as examples of what could be done, industry made little headway. The South possessed labor, raw materials, and water power, but it could not develop industrially

Stephen A. Douglas, the "little giant" from Illinois

A poster for *Uncle Tom's Cabin*

Smuggling slaves to freedom via the Underground Railroad

TO BE SOLD,
A Likely negro Man, his Wife and Child; the negro Man capable of doing all forts of

During the tense 1850s Douglas's Democratic party sought to preserve the Union by appeasing an angry South. But through the North the conviction slowly spread that the nation could not exist half slave and half free. Once a despised minority, the abolitionists gained respectability, as fugitive slave cases kept alive an indignation about slavery. At the end of the decade John Brown's resort to violence shocked the South but was admired by some in the North, and persuaded many in both sections that the two social systems could not live together in peace. Brown's militant spirit had prevailed over Douglas's moderation.

John Brown

Slave sale advertisement

for want of capital. Its capital was absorbed in a system whereby one portion of the population owned the remainder. Northern capital was not available to the South, since it was already drawing heavy profits from northern factories and railroads and from financing the southern money crops. "And anyway, why turn to industry when such handsome profits are to be made in cotton, cane, hemp, and tobacco?" asked the average planter.

The conflict between farm and factory showed up in a thousand ways. It was revealed in the sectional division over national legislation on tariffs, land, and internal improvements. During the 1850s it was at the heart of the bitter fight over an eastern terminus of the proposed transcontinental railroad. It filled the pages of southern newspapers as they sought to prove that northern capital, labor, and industry lived off the sweat of southern farmers. Books were published to prove that northern wage earners were more truly enslaved than Negroes. The conflict was presented as a phase of the traditional one between Jefferson's "chosen people of God" (the Virginia farmers) and Hamilton's "monocrats" (who lived on "paper and patronage"). The North replied that only southern backwardness prevented the United States from becoming the greatest industrial power in the world. Southern obstinacy deprived the western farmer of free land, a railroad to the Pacific, and a fair wage. Labor could never possess dignity in a land where only the slave worked with his hands.

There is no denying that this clash between two economic sections was one of the deeper causes of the destruction of national loyalties. But it must be remembered that southern crops sold in northern markets, just as northern crops and manufactured products sold in southern markets. The two economies complemented each other, and at the same time, they competed. Thus economic sectionalism, while doubtless an important cause of the Civil War, does not explain why Americans transferred their loyalty from the concept of a United States of America to the Union on one hand and the Confederate States of America on the other. Historians have also stressed the importance of the conflict over the rights of states in a federal union as an issue that pushed the sections apart. They noted that John C. Calhoun, leading southern spokesman until his death in 1850, consistently maintained that the issue of states' rights was more important than that of slavery. Even the fact that states' rights were most frequently used as a bulwark in the defense of slavery does not warrant dismissing them as no more than a southern rationalization. The conflict between the states and the central government was older than the union. Jefferson had devoted considerable thought to the problem of protecting the rights of local government from encroachment by a centralized government. New England had seriously considered secession when it thought its rights were being jeopardized during "Mr. Madison's war." Long after the Civil War was over, both Jefferson Davis and Alexander Stephens, in defending their roles as president and vice president of the Confederacy, maintained the moral and legal right of states to secede from the union when the federal government exceeded the authority granted to it by the Constitution. Stephens argued, quite cogently, that slavery was merely the vehicle that brought states' rights and national authority into open conflict. Abraham Lincoln lent considerable support to this concept when he wrote, in 1862,

My paramount object in this struggle *is* to save the Union, and is not either to save or destroy Slavery. If I could save the Union without freeing any slave, I would do it; and if I could save it by freeing all the slaves, I would do it; and if I could do it by freeing some and leaving others alone, I would also do that. . . .

Without taking issue with the statements of these great statesmen it is still possible to wonder why the rights of states, emphasized in 1798, 1814, 1828, and 1850, brought on civil war only in 1861. Some have answered that states' rights were strong enough to destroy national loyalties only when they coincided with major conflicts over slavery and economic sectionalism. Nevertheless, it is plausible to argue that the only way to explain why the war came *when* it did, as well as *why* it started, lies in a study of men's emotional reactions to events which became symbols of right and wrong.

It is a truism of history that men act on the basis of what they *think* has happened rather than what has *actually* happened. Applying this thought to the ante bellum period of American history reveals some very interesting attitudes. Starting with slavery, it is apparent to us today that the institution of American Negro slavery changed very little between 1850 and 1860. To be sure, the number of slaves in the South increased another 700,000 during the decade, to bring the total to about 4 million in 1860. But compared with the 2,600,000 immigrants who entered the country during the same period or the total population increase of 8,300,-000 during the decade, the increased number of slaves was not remarkable. In fact, the slave population was not increasing as fast as the free population. Slavery moved westward during the 1850s as new lands

were opened in Alabama, Mississippi, Louisiana, and Texas. The Black Codes which governed the conduct of slaves were tightened up in areas where the Negro population increased radically, and they were relaxed in those areas where the number of slaves dropped. There was no great upsurge in the number or intensity of slave revolts during the decade. Nor was there any apparent increase in the punishment meted out to slaves who resisted their bondage. The number of fugitive slaves escaping into the North increased very little after 1850. June of 1860 ended a year in which some 800 slaves were reported as runaways, while some 3,000 had been voluntarily manumitted by their masters. These annual figures on runaway slaves and manumissions were about the same for the two decades 1840–1860.

But Americans of the 1850s did not have the statistics and records available to us today. They thought slavery was changing radically. Southerners read the reports of runaway slaves in their newspapers or heard friends report losses. Rumor exaggerated the numbers until virtually every southerner was convinced that losses from this source alone were costing the South millions of dollars a year. Northerners read of the pathetic plight of poor old Uncle Tom and Eliza and visualized the inhumanity of Simon Legree. They watched the growth of southern pressure for a reopening of the slave trade and the acquisition of Caribbean territory and became convinced of the existence of a great "aggressive slavocracy." They fought off the demands of the South for access to the territories of Kansas and the Far West, little knowing that slavery would never seriously attempt to move beyond Texas. Both North and South worked themselves into a frenzy of opposition to the doctrine of popular sovereignty, unaware that popular sovereignty actually determined the limits of slavery throughout the entire United States and its territories. Slavery changed very little during the decade of the 1850s, but men's attitudes toward it changed radically. Reality was lost in a conflict over symbols.

Many historians are now convinced that civil war came to America when changing attitudes destroyed traditional loyalties to national churches, national political parties, and to the idea of a national government. In order more accurately to describe what happened, these historians have called the Civil War a "War for Southern Independence."

THE FIRST SYMBOL:
THE "FINAL" SETTLEMENT

President Polk had feared that northern and southern extremists, engaged in a bitter contest over the future of slavery in the lands won from Mexico, would ride their hobby so hard that war between North and South might result. His fears were realized, but the war he anticipated was delayed ten years by the spirit of union and compromise which prevailed in 1850. But it was a touch-and-go battle before the compromisers and nationalists won out over the radicals and sectionalists who put a very high price on their loyalty to the union.

In 1848 evidence from all sides made it clear that some sort of showdown between proslavery and antislavery forces was near. The presidential election which elevated the Whig General Taylor to the presidency over his Democratic opponent Lewis Cass had increased the power of both southern and northern radicals at the expense of moderates everywhere. Particularly disturbing was the surprising suc-

cess of the new and radical Free-Soil party which had received over a quarter of a million votes, almost all in the North. Its total vote south of Mason and Dixon's line was 219! Virginia gave the Free-Soilers just 9 votes. For the first time, northerners openly admitted voting for a presidential candidate because of their loyalty to a section. Southerners were doing the same. A Georgia politician in a campaign speech for Taylor said, "The General is identified with us in feeling and interest—was born in a slaveholding state—educated in a slaveholding state, is himself a slaveholder." In Charleston, the great southern radical John C. Calhoun urged his listeners to "rally a great southern republican party" and promised that "with such a party we can command our terms and control the North." Unless this trend was reversed the Union was in grave danger.

During 1849 radical sentiment increased rather than abated. The lame-duck session of Congress which convened in December of 1848 was plagued by sectional animosities. Moderates protested in vain that "from morning to night, day after day and week after week nothing can get a hearing that will not afford an opportunity to lug in something about Negro slavery." The reply of the extremists was to offer resolutions like that suggested by the old abolitionist representative from Ohio, Joshua Giddings, who proposed that the citizens of the District of Columbia, both black and white, be allowed to vote on ending slavery in the District.

In an "Address of the Southern Delegates in Congress to Their Constituents," written by Calhoun, southern radicals traced the history of what they regarded as aggression from the days of the Northwest Ordinance and the Missouri Compromise down to the Wilmot Proviso and the most recent attempts to abolish slavery in the District of Columbia. They declared that if this aggression were not halted the North would organize the territories and, with senators and representatives drawn from the new states, would have the power to amend the Constitution, control Congress, and free the slaves. Calhoun himself concluded that antagonism between the two sections had already gone too far to save the union.

Radicals in Congress were staunchly supported in their home districts. Northern governors, legislatures, and conventions adopted resolutions in an endless stream, all condemning the extension of slavery into territory already free and demanding an end to the slave trade, if not to slavery itself, in the District of Columbia. Southern governors echoed the sentiments of Governor Floyd of Virginia, who declared that if the Wilmot Proviso (which would have banned slavery from territories acquired from Mexico) were ever adopted, "then indeed the day of Compromise will have passed, and the dissolution of our own great and glorious Union will become necessary and inevitable." Committees of Safety and Correspondence were formed in many districts of South Carolina. The *Sumter* (South Carolina) *Banner* declared that the only reply to the proviso should be "the secession of slaveholding states in a body from the Union and their formation into a separate republic." The Cleveland *Plain Dealer* replied that, "rather than see slavery extended one inch beyond its present limits we would see this Union rent asunder." Moderates, fearful for the future of America, began to wonder if they would be able to halt the swing to this radicalism which threatened the nation. The extremists gave every appearance of possessing both the ability and the determination to press their sectional attacks to the point of disunion.

In the two years since Taylor's election, the conflict over slavery had settled on three issues. These were slavery in the territories, slavery and the slave trade in the District of Columbia, and fugitive slaves who escaped into northern states.

The debate on slavery in the territories centered on New Mexico and California. With the acquisition of the Mexican cession, the dormant question of the western boundary of Texas was revived; Texas had entered the union claiming a large portion of present-day New Mexico. Suddenly Congress was faced with the problem of drawing a boundary line between the two. Northerners hoped to limit the size of Texas, where slavery was established, and add the disputed territory to New Mexico, where the Mexican prohibition on slavery might be continued as the Wilmot Proviso wished to ensure. But it was California which occupied the center of the stage. The lure of gold had attracted so many settlers to California that in 1849 its 80,000 inhabitants entitled it to immediate admission as a state without undergoing the intermediate territorial status. The nature of the gold rush had prevented southerners from bringing their slaves to the gold fields, with the result that the population was staunchly against slavery. In the summer of 1849, Californians wrote a constitution excluding slavery, organized a state administration, elected representatives to Congress, and awaited admission to the union. But since the Missouri Compromise, every new free state had been admitted only when it could be paired with a new slave state, and there was no slave territory awaiting statehood in 1849. Two new senators from a free state were more than southern radicals were willing to face.

Only a little less knotty than the problems of New Mexico and California was the issue of slavery in the District of Columbia. While moderate northerners might repudiate the abolitionist demand for an end to slavery in the district, there was a widespread desire to end the slave *trade* there. Even moderate southerners deplored the sight of dejected gangs of slaves shuffling through the streets of Washington on their way to auction blocks and slave pens in the shadow of the rising Capitol building.

The other major bone of contention was the antiquated fugitive law of 1793. Under this law, which carried out a constitutional provision, fugitives from labor were to be restored to their masters. During the 1840s several northern states, under the whip of public opinion, passed "personal liberty laws" which virtually nullified the federal law within those states. This followed a Supreme Court decision which weakened the law by relieving the states of any obligation to help enforce it. On many occasions northerners openly defied southern owners coming north to retrieve their runaway property. Southern extremists demanded a new and more stringent fugitive-slave law as a matter of simple justice to the South.

Congress convened in an atmosphere of suspicion and distrust. A group of southern radicals had met in Mississippi and laid plans for a southern convention to meet in the following June in Nashville. The call for the convention made it plain that if northern radicals succeeded in passing the Wilmot Proviso in any form, the Nashville convention would attempt to lead the South out of the union in 1850. Added tension arose from the fact that Whig and Democratic strength in the new House was so evenly divided that Free-Soilers held the balance of power. By playing their cards properly, the latter hoped to win sufficient support from northern "Conscience" Whigs and "Proviso" Democrats to organize the House, control the all-powerful Committee on Rules, and push the proviso through. A stalemate quickly developed. The Free-Soilers were unable to win their game, and neither the Whigs nor the Democrats would give way to the other. Ballot after ballot was taken in a vain effort to elect a Speaker and organize the House. Tempers were short; congressmen came armed with knives and pistols, prepared for any eventuality. The Senate, unable to begin consideration of legislation until the House got to work, met day after day only to adjourn after dealing with minor executive matters. The country was appalled at the spectacle of the federal legislature paralyzed by sectional friction.

Yet, beneath the manifestations of sectional animosity, there was a deep desire for moderation. Loyalty to the nation was far from secondary to loyalty to a section for the majority of Americans. President Taylor was showing the same rugged strength he had displayed on the battlefield, and he was devoting all his energy to preserving the spirit as well as the form of the union. Henry Clay and Daniel Webster, nearing the end of their great service to the union, rejected Taylor's plan but approved wholeheartedly of his determination to let nothing destroy the nation. These were the great statesmen of "America's Silver Age." The work of their lives would be lost by secession and war. Only Calhoun, of the great triumvirate which included Clay and Webster, was ready to accept the end of the union.

The President hoped that the questions concerning slavery would be shelved for the time being, so that there would be no need for a prolonged debate which would only inflame the people. California should be admitted at once, the President thought. Although New Mexico lacked sufficient population, Taylor hoped it might be organized as a state at once. Mormon hostility to slavery precluded congressional discussion of the subject so far as that territory was concerned. Since few slaves actually escaped north, he felt that there was no reason to disturb the nation over a new fugitive-slave law. Taylor did feel that the slave trade in the District of Columbia might be abolished without vital injury to the South. Henry Clay differed with the President on the proper strategy for maintaining peace and unity. He felt that some grand gesture, some audacious and dramatic measure, was more likely to succeed. Daniel Webster inclined to Clay's view and promised his support. Sensing something big in the air, Washingtonians packed the little Senate gallery the day Clay arose to speak. Now an "elder statesman," Clay at seventy-three had let his burning desire for the presidency die out. He sought only preservation of the union and a chance to close his career with one more "great compromise." He called for forbearance on the part of North and faith in the union by the South. Since the North possessed the greater power, he offered a plan that slightly favored the South. He called for the immediate admission of California as a free state, as was her right. He paired New Mexico with Utah and suggested they both be organized as territories without reference to slavery. This was the principle of "popular sovereignty" which allowed the settlers themselves to determine the status of slavery in their territories. Clay asked that New Mexico be favored in the adjustment of her boundary with Texas and in return the Texas debt, left over from the days of the Republic, should be assumed by the United States. He proposed that the slave

trade be abolished in the District of Columbia, but that slavery itself never be abolished there without the prior consent of Maryland. Finally, Clay called on Congress to enact a more stringent fugitive-slave law and promise never to interfere with the interstate slave trade.

It was a scene of incredible drama when, on March 4, Calhoun tottered into the Senate chamber and took his seat. Again the public had been alerted, and there was scarcely room to breathe in the galleries. Calhoun's health had been declining for over a year, and everyone felt that this might well be his last appearance. Like Clay, he had devoted his life to America, but he had made it clear on many occasions that if forced to choose between his country and his section he would stand by the South. Friend and enemy alike were touched when Calhoun begged permission of the Chair to allow his friend Senator Mason, of Virginia, to read his speech, since he himself was too weak to do so. Sitting immobile throughout the reading of his speech, Calhoun seemed to be speaking from beyond the grave through the voice of his colleague on the floor. He rejected completely the Clay proposals. He again rehearsed the long list of "aggressive" actions perpetrated by the North, beginning with the exclusion of slavery north of the Ohio in the ordinance of 1787. He rejected Taylor's plan of dealing with slavery piecemeal and agreed with Clay that "a full and final settlement . . . of all questions at issue between the two sections" was necessary, but he offered no compromise proposals of any kind. He readily admitted that the bonds of union were snapping. He noted specifically that three of the four national Protestant church organizations had split into northern and southern factions, and he feared the great national political parties were very near a final division. With both spiritual and political bonds breaking, Calhoun saw little hope for the union.

It was quickly apparent that Calhoun's speech was too extreme to attract wide support. It contrasted sharply with the generous tone of the Clay speech. Clay had called for sacrifice, compromise, and understanding. Calhoun spoke of rights, justice, and the Constitution. Within three weeks Calhoun was dead and his cause was dying. One after another the great Senate leaders of the "Silver Age," both Whig and Democrat, arose and spoke for compromise. Webster's 7th of March reply to Calhoun was undoubtedly the greatest speech of his career. The "god-like Daniel" supported Clay's plan in every respect. In the flowing oratory so dear to nineteenth-century America, Webster denied the possibility of peaceable secession. "The dismemberment of this vast country without convulsion! The breaking up of the fountains of the great deep without ruffling the surface! Who is so foolish . . . as to expect to see any such thing?" he asked. Demanding that we "not be pygmies in a case that calls for men," Webster expressed what was deep in the hearts of many men—the belief that the strength, the liberty, and the prosperity of America were somehow bound up with the union. Webster, a Whig, was followed by Cass and Benton, both Democrats, bringing the support of the North and West to the compromise. Without detracting from the magnificent work of Clay and Webster in the cause of union, it should not be overlooked that the compromise measures were Democratic in origin, and that nearly all the measures advanced by Clay had been considered by the Senate's territorial committee, of which

Stephen A. Douglas was chairman. Moreover, throughout the battle Democratic votes were decisive in putting them through, and it was the Democrats who endorsed the Compromise of 1850 as a "final settlement" in their platform of 1852, while the Whigs wrote a plank that evaded the question of whether or not the settlement was to be final. The death of the obstinate President Taylor was more significant in paving the way for passage of the measures than was the leadership of Henry Clay.

Extremists, both North and South, were angered by what they both agreed (but for very different reasons) was a pact with the devil. John Greenleaf Whittier, the abolitionist poet, wrote of Webster in bitterness and sorrow:

> Oh, dumb be passion's stormy rage,
>   When he who might
> Have lighted up and led his age,
>   Falls back in night.
>
> Let not the land once proud of him
>   Insult him now,
> Nor brand with deeper shame his dim
>   Dishonored brow.

But the spirit of compromise had succeeded. Loyalty to the idea of a nation had won over competing loyalties. Americans served in one army, saluted one flag, looked to one capital, elected one President, and looked to one future. The nation sighed with relief and turned back to the more congenial tasks of opening new lands, building new factories and railroads, and enjoying the fruits of its toil. There were, however, signs that the "final settlement" might prove quite temporary —that the issue of slavery was a moral question which could not be compromised in nineteenth-century America. One of the provisions of the settlement began to cause trouble almost immediately. This was the new Fugitive Slave Law.

THE SECOND SYMBOL: THE FUGITIVE SLAVE

It is impossible to determine with any accuracy the number of fugitive slaves who escaped to the North. The census figures would indicate that the number was small. The 1850 report declares that about 1,000 ran away that year. Sixteen out of 400,000 slaves in South Carolina were listed as runaways. On the other hand, careful students of the subject have estimated that anywhere between 20,000 and 50,000 fugitive slaves were living in the North in 1850. Two things should be noted about the controversy over fugitive slaves. Foremost is the fact that the whole controversy centered on matters of principle and morality and was almost divorced from any factual knowledge of the problem. For example, the states of the Deep South, whose runaways had a very slim chance of ever reaching the North, were the loudest in their demand for a more stringent law. On the other hand, the extreme northern states, which never or rarely saw a slave catcher, were loudest in their objections to that more stringent law when it was passed. The border states, most directly concerned, were comparatively quiet on the whole subject. Secondly, the assumption that slaveowners were eager to regain their runaway property was false. Most owners were happy to be rid of runaways. The slave who ran away was, after all, apt to be the most clever and most courageous among the owner's slaves and therefore the most dangerous to the remainder of his slave force as well as to the owner himself and his family. It was a general practice to sell the slave "a-run-nin," which meant to sell title to the slave to a professional catcher for a fraction of his worth. This system gave the owner some return for his loss and produced a group of professional slave catchers.

Though the South lost few fugitive slaves and retrieved even fewer, the runaway slave became an important symbol of the deeper conflict between the sections. The new law aroused the hostility of men who feared what might be done under it far more than they feared disunion. It had three provisions which were particularly odious to most northerners. In spite of the constitutional provision that in all "suits at common law, where the value in controversy shall exceed twenty dollars, the right of trial by jury shall be preserved," the Fugitive Slave Law allowed no jury trial even though any slave was worth far more than $20 if considered as property. If by chance it was admitted that the slave was a person rather than chattel property, the new law was equally unjust, for it deprived a person of the protection of the Sixth Amendment guaranteeing a jury trial in all criminal prosecutions. Second, the penalties of the law were excessively harsh. Officers charged with the duty of arresting a fugitive were subject to a fine of $1,000 for refusal to execute their assignment, and citizens who refused to assist or who obstructed the officers recapturing runaways were subject to penalties totaling $2,000 and a six-month jail sentence. Finally, the fugitive was to be taken before a special commissioner, rather than a regular court, where the affidavit of the purported owner was sufficient to establish ownership. When the commissioner found the alleged fugitive to be the slave claimed, he received a fee of $10. If he found the charge false, he received only $5. In the light of these provisions, even moderate northerners were ready to agree with the abolitionists who had maintained all along that the South was ready to violate the Constitution in order to protect its "peculiar institution." And to cap it all, the South had now put the price of human liberty at $5. Ralph Waldo Emerson lost all semblance of philosophic calm and wrote of the new Fugitive Slave Law in his journal: "This filthy enactment was made in the nineteenth century, by people who could read and write. I will not obey it, by God!"

Northern resistance to the act began almost immediately and became widespread before the decade was done. The "personal-liberty law" adopted by Massachusetts is typical of the laws adopted in many northern states to nullify the Fugitive Slave Law. It provided that a writ of habeas corpus might be issued in cases involving a fugitive. It also provided for a jury trial and banned the testimony of both the claimant and the alleged fugitive while it put the burden of proof upon the claimant. The law thus made it necessary for the purported owner to prove his title to a particular Negro by affidavits from his friends and neighbors back home, and this before a Massachusetts judge and jury! The importance of the personal-liberty laws lies quite outside any question of their effectiveness, for they apparently did not free a single slave. Their significance rests on the fact that a majority of northerners were now ready to nullify a federal law on slavery, whereas prior to 1850 such action would have been countenanced by only the hard core of militant abolitionists. The new Fugitive Slave Law was making abolitionism respectable. The "Underground Railroad" which spirited slaves across the North to Canada and freedom now became more active, even fashionable.

Two things brought about this remarkable change in the moral climate of the North. The first was a series of well-publicized cases involving alleged runaway slaves. Eight days after the passage of the Fugitive Slave Act, a man appeared in New York City. He was armed with a power of attorney signed with an X by an illiterate Baltimore woman. He filed an affidavit that a certain James Hamlet was the runaway slave of his client. Hamlet was placed under arrest and sent off to Baltimore before his two children were even informed of his whereabouts. In 1851 Euphemia Williams, who claimed she had lived her entire life as a free Negro in Pennsylvania, was seized and carried off to Maryland by a man who swore she had run away from him twenty-two years before. He also demanded possession of her six children, including a healthy young lad of seventeen. The most famous case of the period was that of Anthony Burns, a Virginia slave. Burns managed to stow away in a ship at Richmond and reach Boston safely. There he foolishly sent a letter to his brother back in Richmond. His owner traced him to Boston, and since Burns readily recognized his master, there was no question of identification. He was taken before a federal commissioner, who ordered him remanded to his master. The people of Boston organized a protest demonstration, and the authorities, prompted by a fear that some attempt might be made to free Burns, called for extra police forces to escort Burns from the courthouse to the ship which was to carry him back to Virginia. In the end, the hapless fugitive was escorted by over 1,100 soldiers as well as a host of policemen and extra deputies. The total cost to the United States government of returning Anthony Burns to slavery was about $50,000.

Of even greater significance in solidify-

Harriet Beecher Stowe, author of Uncle Tom's Cabin. (*Library of Congress*)

ing and popularizing abolitionist sentiment in the North was the publication of Harriet Beecher Stowe's *Uncle Tom's Cabin*. Appearing in 1851 in serial form, it was published as a book the following year. Mrs. Stowe had little intimate knowledge of slavery, for she had never lived in a slave state. She had, however, lived in Cincinnati for seventeen years, just across the river from slavery. While there she had been active in helping runaways make contact with those who operated the Underground Railroad to the North. She had also visited with relatives in Kentucky who were slaveholders. Largely ignorant of the personal side of slavery, she made up in fervor what she lacked in knowledge. Daughter of one of the greatest American preachers of his day and sister of another, she was married to a classics professor who displayed the quiet courage of his convictions by many years of teaching in the abolitionists' Lane The-

ological Seminary. Neither Mrs. Stowe nor her publisher was prepared for the reception her story received. Within a year 300,000 copies had been sold and eight power presses were running night and day to meet the demand. Soon translated into half the languages of the world, its influence was nearly as great abroad as it was at home. Russian landowners, moved by her story, even freed some of their serfs. The book was soon transformed into a play which moved audiences in Oslo, Antwerp, and Rome quite as much as it did those of Philadelphia, Cleveland, and Detroit. Hostile reception by the press and leaders of the South did not prevent a great many southerners from reading of the fate of poor old Uncle Tom.

THE THIRD SYMBOL: KANSAS-NEBRASKA

The personal-liberty laws and *Uncle Tom's Cabin* served to make abolitionism respectable in the North. They also allowed northerners to maintain that they favored the "final settlement" while they resisted it in practice. Southerners were at a distinct disadvantage under the Compromise of 1850, for there was no single act of the bargain which they could isolate and resist. They were forced to either accept or reject the entire compromise. Since popular sentiment was obviously strongly supporting the settlement, southern radicals were forced to bide their time while the abolitionists were having a field day. When their opportunity finally arrived, these southern radicals embraced it with a fervor that stemmed from hopes long deferred. Their opportunity was the introduction of a bill to organize the territories of Kansas and Nebraska.

It was early in 1854 when Stephen A. Douglas, chairman of the Senate Commit-

SLAVERY IN THE TERRITORIES IN THE 1850s

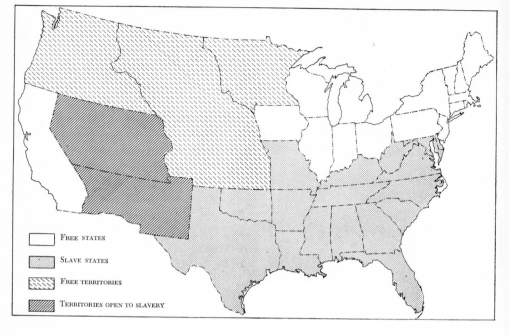

FREE STATES

SLAVE STATES

FREE TERRITORIES

TERRITORIES OPEN TO SLAVERY

tee on Territories, reported out a bill to organize Kansas and Nebraska. The action was long overdue. The country to the west of Iowa and Missouri had been owned by the United States since the Louisiana Purchase. It had remained unorganized after Texas and California had achieved statehood and the remainder of the Mexican cession had been organized into territories. Much of the delay was caused by failure to clear the land of the Indian titles to it, but this was rectified by a series of treaties in 1853. Some opposition to the organization had come from radical southerners who insisted that the barrier to slave expansion north of 36°30′ in the Louisiana Territory, established in the Missouri Compromise, discriminated against the South, which had shared in the cost of the Louisiana Purchase. Important opposition appears to have come from promoters of a transcontinental railroad who hoped to win federal

support for a southern route. So long as the territory west of the Missouri River remained unorganized, the federal government could not possibly support a northern route, and the southern plans were safe.

Pushed both by northern promoters of a Pacific railroad and by the settlers in Iowa and Missouri who were demanding access to the new lands, Douglas hoped to organize the territories without bringing the slavery question back into national politics. He attempted to do this by providing that the territories be organized under the principle of popular sovereignty. He reasoned that popular sovereignty had been applied to Utah and New Mexico in 1850 without serious protest, so there could be no reasonable objection in 1854. In point of fact, southerners had Douglas over a barrel, and they knew it. Their votes had killed previous attempts to organize the area, and they could kill the new attempt. They also knew that any future Douglas might have in the Democratic party (and he was being pushed for the presidency) depended upon them. Making the most of their advantage, they proposed that Douglas make a slight change in his bill. Since the system of popular sovereignty, which allowed the actual settlers to determine the status of slavery, revoked the Missouri Compromise prohibition by implication, they demanded that Douglas revoke the prohibition outright. Caught in the trap of his own logic as well as his political ambitions, Douglas agreed. The Kansas-Nebraska bill was amended to repeal the Missouri Compromise prohibition of slavery north of 36° 30′. Douglas firmly believed that popular sovereignty was right and just, and he was convinced that any opposition to it would come only from irresponsible abolitionist agitators, whom he despised.

Douglas had miscalculated the depth and intensity of northern opposition to the extension of slavery. For thirty-three years the North had believed that the 36° 30′ line constituted a permanent barrier to the northward expansion of slavery. Few agreed with Douglas that the establishment of popular sovereignty in Utah and New Mexico constituted a precedent for the Louisiana Purchase territory. They saw only that a solemn compromise, made and upheld in perfect good faith, had been broken by the South. Douglas himself was soon being burned in effigy by the same Chicago crowds which had lionized him a short time before. He was accused of selling out to the "slavocracy" in order to further his presidential ambitions.

The Douglas bill was a godsend to radical abolitionists and Free-Soilers. It made them even more popular than had the Fugitive Slave Law agitation. Typical of northern newspapers' reaction was the Ohio editor who called the Kansas-Nebraska bill "the scheme of a weak and imbecile administration; of a corrupt and ambitious demagogue; of grasping dishonorable slaveholders—[it] has filled the cup of bitterness which has been pressed to Northern lips so long. . . ."

In communities all over the North, anti-Nebraska meetings were called. Men calling themselves Anti-Nebraska or Independent Whigs and Democrats joined Conscience Whigs and Proviso Democrats in adopting resolutions condemning Douglas, the Democratic party, and southern slaveholders. Many announced their readiness to form a new political party. Soon these dissident elements succeeded in electing governors, representatives to Congress, and many local officials. The Kansas-Nebraska bill thus had a double significance: it hastened the disintegration of the two national political parties, just as Calhoun had feared, and it paved the way for the birth of the Republican party. As men shifted their loyalty from the national parties to a sectional one, they were abandoning one more of the bonds which held them to their nation.

In the crisis of the Kansas-Nebraska controversy the nation could no longer rely on the elder statesmen who had created the Compromise of 1850. Clay and Webster died within six months of each other in 1852. Thomas Hart Benton, defeated for the Senate in 1850, was now in the House, but his influence was gone. Cass was still in the Senate, but he had lost his fire. In their place was a new set of leaders, younger men with reputations to make. For example, Webster's seat was occupied by Charles Sumner, who would prove one of the most effective and determined enemies of slavery and the South. Of the great compromisers, only Douglas retained a position of leadership, and he had failed to judge the temper of the people.

While the attention of Americans was riveted to the symbols of sectional division, they were continually reminded of the deeper sources of the conflict. For example, President Franklin Pierce, elected in 1852, vetoed another rivers-and-harbors bill, which alienated the Northwest only a little less than Polk had done in 1846. The bill had passed Congress by a strictly sectional vote. The North had approved money for northwestern internal improvements and the South had opposed it. Northern Democrats found it impossible to defend their administration's failure to support them. Many northern Democrats, unimpressed with the agitation over slavery, were thus forced into the arms of the new Republican party.

The 1850s was a decade of railroad building. Until the depression of 1857 cut off the flow of capital, a boom in railroad construction had left the whole country gasping in wonderment. The crowning glory of the railroad promoters was to have been a transcontinental railroad to the Pacific. Since it was plainly impossible for private capital to finance so stupendous an undertaking, it was assumed from the beginning that the federal government would take the lead in providing the necessary money. The usual plan included grants of land by the government to the railroad owners, who would then sell the land and put the profits into constructing the road. Some plans also proposed cash loans by the government, secured by bonds of the railroad. It soon became apparent that even the federal government could afford to support only one railroad to the Pacific. The rivalry between the sections, and between cities within the sections, immediately became intense. St. Paul, Chicago, St. Louis, Memphis, and New

Orleans all vied to become the eastern terminus of the railroad. The northern cities showed some signs of joining forces, at least until they could prevent the South from winning the coveted railroad. Southern cities were doing the same. Northern promoters were alarmed at the power of their southern competitors, as evidenced in the Gadsden Purchase of 1854. The Gadsden Purchase was made for the sole purpose of getting the Gila River Valley as a route for a southern railroad through the Rockies. Northerners were also alarmed when Jefferson Davis of Mississippi became the Secretary of War under Franklin Pierce. In that capacity Davis controlled the Topographical Corps of the United States Army, which surveyed railroad routes through the mountains. Davis made no secret of his preference for a southern route to the Pacific. The Kansas-Nebraska bill was introduced, as we have seen, to help northern railroad promoters catch up with the southerners. Such men were grateful to Douglas for his assistance, but they wanted more: they wanted assurances that the northern route would be chosen. The Democrats could obviously make no such promise, but the new Republican party, untroubled by southern supporters, could and did promise that the transcontinental railroad would be a northern one. Northern railroad promoters joined the Republican party in wholesale lots.

A third source of conflict between North and South was the ancient problem of land. A homestead bill granting free land to those who would settle it was introduced in the House as early as 1846. Every session of Congress thereafter received a flood of petitions favoring the idea. At least one bill was pigeonholed in committee or defeated on the floor in every session. It was opposed generally by the East, but clever political footwork by the new Republican party gradually convinced most northwestern farmers that the southern-dominated Democratic party was alone responsible for the defeat of their cherished dream. And of course the Republican party promised a homestead bill if elected.

Thus the loyalty of Americans to the concept of a nation and national political parties was destroyed by economic competition as well as by the moral question of property in human beings. But nationalism in America was a hardy breed and it took a good deal to kill it. The storm over the Kansas-Nebraska bill had barely begun to moderate when new symbols appeared to stir up more trouble.

THE FOURTH SYMBOL: "BLEEDING KANSAS"

The Kansas-Nebraska bill provided that the settlers themselves would determine whether slavery would be prohibited or permitted in the new lands. Since the settlers would determine the status of slavery in the course of writing a state constitution, a race developed between North and South to push enough settlers into Kansas to win a majority in the coming constitutional convention. Before long, the air was thick with charges and counter-charges. Free states accused Missouri "border ruffians" of crossing into Kansas on election days and, after recording their vote, returning to their homes in Missouri. No one mentioned that Iowans were doing the same thing in Nebraska, for there was no conflict there. Southerners pointed to the Emigrant Aid Societies which were formed in the North to win Kansas for freedom by encouraging northern settlement there. Such societies were formed, but their contribution to the population of Kansas was negligible. The North was also accused of sending Sharps rifles, "not the ordinary weapon used in the chase, or for the protection of the domestic hearth, but a weapon of war," in boxes marked "Bibles." Before long reports of conflict began to filter back to the East: reports of the "Wakarusa War" and the "Sack of Lawrence."

Even today it is difficult to determine exactly what did go on in Kansas in 1855 and 1856. That there was bloodshed there can be no doubt. That some of it can be traced to competition between the friends and enemies of slavery is also true. But it is quite clear that much of the "bleeding" in Kansas had little or nothing to do with slavery. One careful student has discovered that most of the shooting in Kansas took place just when the land surveys were finished and men began to realize the extent of the conflict over titles to the land on which they had been squatting. Another has made a careful comparison of the reports of violence in Kansas with those of Nebraska. Since there was no proslavery element in Nebraska, the violence there can be attributed solely to claim jumping, horse stealing, and the dangerous combination of free-flowing whisky and excessive boredom so typical of the American frontier everywhere. This comparison indicates that there was a good deal of "bleeding" in Nebraska as well as in Kansas. Kansas was headline news in the eastern Republican press, however, while Nebraska was rarely mentioned. Even those cases of violence which did occur in Kansas were grossly exaggerated in the East. The "Sack of Lawrence" is a case in point. The word "sack" raises images of rape, murder, and burning. One visualizes something like the barbarian invasion of Rome. Actually, two newspaper presses were thrown in the river, a hotel and the home of "Governor" Robinson were burned down, and a few houses and shops were broken into in search of whisky. There was one accidental death. The headline of the *New York Tribune* was "Startling News from Kansas—The War Actually Begun—Triumph of the Border Ruffians—Lawrence in Ruins—Several Persons Slaughtered—Freedom Bloodily Subdued."

Fanatical John Brown, soon to achieve abolitionist martyrdom, arrived in Kansas in 1855 and settled on Osawatomie Creek. A few days after the "sack" of Lawrence, Brown and four of his sons descended upon a proslavery settlement on Pottawatomie Creek and killed five inhabitants in cold blood. Retaliation was swift, and Osawatomie was burned, with twelve lives lost. John Brown fled the territory, to reenter the headlines at Harpers Ferry three years later. Whether the "bleeding" in Kansas was the result of normal frontier lawlessness, open conflict between free-state and proslavery forces, or the work of a self-appointed "avenging angel," it was grist for the extremists' mill. The American people were further divided along sectional lines, and a new symbol helped them emotionalize that division.

THE FIFTH SYMBOL: "BLEEDING SUMNER"

On the day that Lawrence was raided, Charles Sumner was completing one of the most vituperative speeches ever heard in the Senate. Labeled "The Crime against Kansas," the speech was filled with venom and personal abuse. Sumner's two chief targets were Senator Douglas and Senator Butler of South Carolina. Butler, in particular, was widely respected in the Senate for his gentlemanly manners and moderation in debate. When Sumner accused Butler of taking to his bosom as mistress "the harlot, Slavery" and denounced

Senator Sumner attacked by Preston Brooks. (New York Public Library)

him with discharging "the loose expectoration of his speech" on the Senate floor, he had gone too far. Sumner was fast becoming the most unpopular man in the Senate, a fact which gave him no concern. Sumner hated slavery. The institution was a personal enemy as well as a moral wrong. A man dedicated to principle and absolutely sincere, Sumner was also completely devoid of humor; he was arrogant, and fanatical in his hostility to slavery. He differed with the abolitionists on the proper strategy to be used in destroying slavery but agreed wholeheartedly with their objectives.

The reply to Sumner was delivered by Senator Butler's nephew, Preston Brooks, a member of the House of Representatives. Two days after the Sumner speech, Brooks entered the almost empty Senate Chamber, where Sumner was still writing at his desk. Marching up to Sumner, he began to strike the Senator with a gutta-percha cane. The first blow, struck while Sumner was still seated, blinded him and prevented him from defending himself. As he rose, Sumner lurched forward, tore his desk from its moorings and stumbled forward ten or fifteen feet before collapsing. Brooks continued to rain blows on Sumner's head before he was finally restrained by other senators and the breaking of the cane. Sumner was carried to the cloak-room, where he was treated by doctors hastily summoned. He was badly injured, several stitches were required to close the wounds in his scalp, and he was out of action for over three years. Even though it was understood that he could not serve, the Massachusetts legislature reelected him by an overwhelming vote, and Sumner's empty seat in the Senate became a more effective attack on slavery than Sumner himself could ever have delivered. Brooks, on the other hand, was soon off on a triumphal tour of the South, feted and banqueted wherever he went. A prominent part of every celebration was the presentation of a new cane—preferably made of gutta-percha.

Newspaper reaction North and South can be imagined. Northern editors asked if this is what was meant by the term "southern chivalry." They declared that no place was safe from southern violence if the floor of the Senate was not. Many charged that Brooks's attack was the natural result of the lawlessness which the system of slavery encouraged. Southern editors were almost unanimous in approving Brooks's action. They felt Sumner had deserved the caning and that physical injury was the only way to stop his bitter invective. The incident gave Sumner recognition and support that he would never have won by his speeches or votes. "Bleeding Sumner" and "Bleeding Kansas" became the outstanding symbols of the sectional conflict. They were also the mainstay of the new Republican party's campaign in 1856.

THE SIXTH SYMBOL: "BLACK" REPUBLICANS

By 1856 the strange mélange of political bedfellows who had won local and state elections under the names of Fusionists, Independents, Anti-Nebraska Democrats and Whigs, and Free-Soilers was able to achieve a substantial organization under the name of Republican. Seeking a man new to politics, untainted by prior connections with any political faction, they chose John Charles Frémont, the western adventurer. With a campaign slogan of "Free Soil, Free Speech, Free Men, and Frémont" the Republicans embarked on a moral crusade. Democrats, badly scared by the obvious strength of the Republicans in the North, accepted Douglas's generous offer to step aside and chose James Buchanan. Favored by a long record of honorable service to the party, Buchanan was chosen because he had been out of the country as Ambassador to England during the Kansas-Nebraska debate and therefore was not identified with the bill in any way. He was also "available" through being a northerner from the critical state of Pennsylvania, whose nomination would help preserve the illusion that the Democrats were a truly national party in contrast to the sectional Republicans.

A third candidate was in the field. This was Millard Fillmore, who agreed to head the American party ticket. Its membership, better known as Know-Nothings, had grown in the vacuum created by the disintegration of the Whig party. As a way station for those in transit from the old national parties to some new party, it appealed to the antiforeign and anti-Catholic sentiment prominent in American life during the nineteenth century. The Know-Nothings had achieved startling successes in local elections in 1854 and 1855 but were unable to bridge the gap between their northern and southern wings and so never became a national party. The chief political significance of the Know-Nothings lies in their contribution to the further disruption of the Whigs and Democrats.

The campaign was quite unlike any presidential contest Americans had ever seen. It had all the buoyancy of the hard-cider campaign of 1840, but it also possessed the elements of a moral crusade and a religious revival. Republicans attacked slavery not only as a moral wrong, but also as an institution which blocked progress, blighted America, and prevented expansion, prosperity, and peace. Soon there were few ills that beset the country which could not be traced to the insidious evil of slavery. Southerners who had remained fairly complacent during the Kansas-Nebraska imbroglio sensed the danger inherent in the Republican appeal. A Mobile paper described the campaign as "internecine war—war to the knife and to the hilt." Soon the label "Black Republicans" was becoming as popular as

President James Buchanan. (Corcoran Gallery of Art, Washington)

"damnyankee" became a short while later. The southern press was sprinkled with comments like that of the *Southern Advocate* which called the Black Republicans "the mortal enemies of every man, woman and child in the Southern States." The excitement, both North and South, is revealed by the total vote, which was 28 per cent above that of 1852; nearly 1 million more Americans voted in 1856 than in 1852.

The results of the canvass were discouraging both to Democrats and to those who feared for the life of the union. Buchanan was elected as a result of narrow victories in Pennsylvania and Indiana. The Black Republicans, starting virtually from scratch, had won well over 1 million votes, or 33 per cent of the total vote cast. They had won eleven of the free states and naturally not a single slave state. There were few Democrats, North or South, who thought the Republicans, with four years in which to perfect their organization and broaden their appeal, could be prevented from electing a sectional candidate on a sectional platform in 1860. The South, for its part, ceased to see any difference among Free-Soilers, abolitionists, Conscience Whigs, and Proviso Democrats. They were all lumped together as Black Republicans, whose existence was a threat to the foundations of southern society.

THE FINAL SYMBOLS: DRED SCOTT AND JOHN BROWN

Most Presidents in our history have been allowed a few months in which to settle down in the White House, get their bearings, enjoy the cooperation of Congress, and generally get into shape for the four-year grind ahead. James Buchanan had no such luck. His presidential "honeymoon" was cut short after two brief days by a decision of the Supreme Court. It had been general knowledge in Washington that the Court was about to render a decision in the knotty case of Dred Scott.

Dred Scott was a Negro resident of Missouri who had been taken along by his master, an army surgeon, during tours of duty in the free state of Illinois and in Wisconsin Territory (later Minnesota). Some time after their return to Missouri, Dred's master died and Scott was persuaded by abolitionist friends to sue for his freedom on the grounds that his residence in a territory from which slavery was excluded by the terms of the Missouri Compromise (the area north of 36°30'within the Louisiana Purchase and excluding Missouri itself) made him free even after his return to a slave state. The local Missouri court freed Scott, but the Missouri Supreme Court reversed the decision on the ground that whatever his status while in free territory Scott was a slave when he returned to Missouri.

By arranging a fictitious sale of Scott to a New Yorker by the name of Sanford, Dred's friends hoped to get the case into the federal courts on the ground that it became a case of a citizen of Missouri suing a citizen of New York. The hope was to carry the case to the Supreme Court, where the entire question of slavery in the territories might be decided. Thus the heart of the case centered on the power of Congress to exclude slavery from the territories belonging to the nation. The Republican contention that Congress had always possessed this power, and had exercised it in the ordinance of 1787 as well as in the Missouri Compromise of 1820, was at issue. Scott's personal freedom was not at stake, for he was to be freed by his friends if he lost in the courts.

Southerners were confident that the court would uphold the Kansas-Nebraska Act repeal of the Missouri Compromise restriction on slavery and would deny the power of Congress to exclude the "peculiar institution" from the territories won with common blood and treasure. Seven of the nine justices were Democrats, five of whom were from the South. And there were indications that a majority of the Court were eager to use the power of the Court to get the whole subject of slavery out of the halls of Congress.

Chief Justice Roger B. Taney, the old Jacksonian, gave the majority decision, speaking for the seven Democratic justices. He declared that the lower federal court had lacked jurisdiction because, under the laws of Missouri, Scott was not a citizen. This much was in accord with precedent, and if he had stopped there Taney would have given the Republicans and abolitionists no opening. After all, if the lower federal courts lacked jurisdiction, so did the federal Supreme Court. But Taney went on to declare that Negroes had not been citizens at the time of the adoption of the Constitution and had not become citizens of the nation since. Thus Scott had been a slave even while at Fort Snelling, for Congress had exceeded its authority in adopting the Missouri Compromise probition on slavery. The corollary was that the Missouri Compromise restriction was contrary to the federal Constitution, and Taney so declared it.

Both Buchanan and the justices had hoped that a decision of the highest tribunal in the land would carry sufficient prestige and authority to bury permanently the entire question of slavery in the territories. Instead of pronouncing a requiem, the Court had exploded a bombshell.

Republicans were nearly speechless with anger (but they quickly recovered their voices), for the Court had struck down a solemn compromise. Strong words in the North soon evoked equally harsh replies from the South. The significance of the Dred Scott decision was soon apparent. Existing divisions within the Democratic party were greatly deepened. Many Democratic leaders, understanding that the only hope for union lay in the continued health and vigor of a truly national party, were helpless. The position of Stephen A. Douglas was typical. As the only national leader left to the party, Douglas's primary job was to reconcile northern and southern wings of the party. After the Dred Scott decision, this meant that he must try to get northern Democrats to acquiesce in the Dred Scott decision while he convinced southern Democrats that they must not insist on the abstract right to take their slaves into all the territories. Personally convinced that the issue of slavery in the territories was dead because the soil and climate would never make slavery profitable in the Far West, Douglas set out to find a formula which would unite the two wings of his party.

A plain-speaking popular attorney, nominated by the Republicans to go after Douglas's Senate seat in 1858, was quick to see the broad canyon Douglas was trying to straddle. Over and over again in a series of debates with Douglas, Abraham Lincoln asked how the people of a territory might prevent slavery from being established among them, since the Supreme Court in the Dred Scott case had decreed that slavery must be protected everywhere in the territories. Douglas's answer, which became known as the Freeport Doctrine, makes more sense to us than it did to his listeners. He pointed out that slavery required positive and friendly local legislation (such as it had received everywhere in the South); failure to pass such laws in

territorial legislatures would as effectively prohibit slavery as any act of the federal government. But the damage had been done. Lincoln and the Supreme Court made it impossible for southern Democrats to follow the lead of even so moderate a northern Democrat as Douglas. Dred Scott and the Lincoln-Douglas debates became two more milestones on the long road down to war. But it would take more heat, more emotion, and more misunderstandings before Americans would be ready to abandon their deeply ingrained loyalty to the union.

It was in October, 1859, that old John Brown with a small band of followers, black and white, tried to capture the United States Arsenal at Harpers Ferry, Virginia. Brown had some vague ideas of freeing and arming the slaves in the neighborhood, who would then provide the nucleus for a kind of chain-reaction slave revolt. Harpers Ferry, situated in the mountains at the northern end of the Shenandoah Valley and protected on two sides by the Potomac and Shenandoah Rivers, gives the false impression of being easily defensible. Because of its location at the head of the valley, Brown apparently thought it would be accessible to fugitive slaves coming from the South along mountain pathways. Whatever his plans were, none of them was realized. The arsenal was easily captured, but Brown foolishly allowed a train to go on to Baltimore after the conductor had seen the state of affairs in Harpers Ferry. The conductor spread the alarm, and militia and United States marines soon reinforced the townspeople who had trapped Brown in a firehouse. Seven citizens and soldiers were killed, several of Brown's followers were captured, ten were killed, and a few escaped. Brown himself, seriously wounded, was captured, tried for treason to the state of

Virginia, and speedily hanged. No slaves willingly joined Brown's revolt, but as with previous slave insurrections, the South took no chances. Governor Wise of Virginia called out the militia, took command of cadets at the Virginia Military Institute, issued proclamations, and marched his men back and forth across the state.

What John Brown did is unimportant; how Americans reacted to his action is of the first importance. The first reaction, of both North and South, was shock. Once that was past, everyone began to think of the implications of Brown's deed. Conservative northerners joined the South in deploring the whole affair. Men who had been fairly complacent about the abolitionists suddenly saw where extreme antislavery doctrines led. Even radical northern leaders like Seward and Greeley drew back before the awful reality of the Brown raid. They were particularly concerned with the fact that Brown would be inevitably blamed on the Republicans, for there were still too many moderates to make that politically profitable. But a tiny minority applauded, and their applause echoed all through the South. Emerson called Brown, a "new saint awaiting his martyrdom . . . who . . . will make the gallows glorious like the Cross." Louisa May Alcott called him "Saint John the Just," and Thoreau thought him "an angel of light." This minority grew rapidly as the calm courage with which Brown met his fate inspired widespread admiration.

Southern fire-eaters were in the delicious position of being able to say "we told you so." They had devoted years to warning their section that violence would follow abolitionist agitation. As far back as Calhoun, they had demanded that all discussion of the subject of slavery must be stopped in the North. Men who had long viewed the fire-eaters as alarmists began to support them. Most southerners, like most northerners, were primarily interested in what advantage might be gleaned from Harpers Ferry. This is perfectly illustrated by a letter written by James A. Seddon, a Virginia aristocrat who later became secretary of war in the Confederacy, to R. M. T. Hunter, who for a short while was secretary of state in the Confederate cabinet. Writing two months after Brown's attempt, Seddon said: *

I must venture however to say that in my humble opinion . . . the course of public conduct and opinion . . . , especially in V [irgini]a [has] been injudiciously and alarmingly mismanaged and misdirected, and I hold the unsound judgement, insatiate vanity and selfish policy of our fussy Governor [Wise] mainly responsible for them. The Harper's Ferry affair ought to have been treated and represented either in its best light as the mad folly of a few deluded cranks branded fanatics, or, more truly, as the vulgar crime and outrage of a squad of reckless desperate Ruffians. . . . Our honorable Governor, . . . by insisting on holding them as the chiefs of an organized conspiracy at the North, . . . has invoked the sympathy . . . of large masses and of established organs of public opinion at the North. . . . Wise has *exploited* this whole affair to his own selfish aggrandizement, to aid his vain hopes for the Presidency and to strengthen the fragment of a Southern party he heads. And as the result, has conjured a Devil neither he nor perhaps any other can lay, and, annoying the roused pride and animosities of both sections against each other, has brought on a *real crisis* of imminent peril to both.

* Charles H. Ambler (ed.), *Correspondence of R. M. T. Hunter, 1826–1876,* Annual Report of American Historical Association, Washington, 1918, pp. 281–282.

CHAPTER FOURTEEN

THE CAMPAIGNS OF 1860

As the Democrats prepared for the presidential campaign of 1860, it was perfectly apparent that *someone* had conjured a devil, and that it would certainly play hob with the Democratic party. Buchanan had proved too weak to hold the rending factions of his party together. In spite of all his efforts at conciliation, the southern "ultras" in the party refused to cooperate. In the North the President had been overshadowed by Douglas, who had regained much of his old popularity by his refusal to support a proslavery constitution for Kansas. Instead of one national convention, the Democrats ended by having several conventions in 1860. The first, meeting in Charleston in April, ran into hot weather, inadequate hotel space, and an atmosphere both hostile and alien to northern and western delegates. Local hotel keepers had agreed to charge the unheard-of price of $5 a day for room and meals. Four or five delegates were stuffed into each single room, with the temperature hitting 100 degrees. Some delegations faced catastrophe when their private supplies of whisky ran out as the convention dragged on. The numbers and success of the pickpockets surprised everyone, even those hardened by residence in New York and Chicago. Many delegates left before the voting began, simply because they had run out of funds. When the convention opened, the Douglas supporters had a plurality, but they lacked the necessary two-thirds majority to nominate. Southern radicals under the leadership of William L. Yancey of Alabama organized a drive to stop Douglas. They agreed to demand that the party pledge itself to the positive protection of slavery in the territories by Congress. The Douglas people refused to abandon the doctrine of popular sovereignty, which Douglas had long championed and upon which the party had campaigned in 1856. Yancey then led his Alabama delegation out, and six other southern states joined the secession movement. Douglas men kissed the bolters good-by, feeling that their exit would give Douglas the necessary two-thirds. The bolters, for their part, fully expected to be called back by some compromise proposal. The seceders took up their stand at a theater just down the street, called themselves a "Constitutional Democratic Convention," and waited for the peace overtures. Both sides had overplayed their hands. Douglas, it developed, could not be nominated, and the bolters waited in vain for some overture. Both conventions adjourned, one to meet in Baltimore in June and the other in Richmond. The upshot was that Douglas received the nomination of northern and western Democrats, while John C. Breckinridge of Kentucky was nominated by the radical group.

In the meantime the Constitutional Union party, a group of antique Whigs and die-hard Know-Nothings, had met in convention and nominated John Bell of Tennessee. In what was one of the shortest platforms in American political history, this group declared that it had "no political principle other than the Constitution of the country, the union of the states, and the enforcement of the laws." It would take important strength away from Douglas in the campaign that followed.

The split in the Democratic party augured Republican success. They had only to make sure of their own unity. To that end, strategy dictated the writing of a cautious platform and the choice of a moderate candidate. The Republican platform therefore played down the slavery issue and gave as much attention as possible to the homestead idea, protective tariffs, internal improvements, and a Pacific railroad. As for the candidate, there was intense rivalry at the convention, for he would almost certainly be the next President. The convention was held at Chicago, in a great rambling wooden structure built especially for the purpose and dubbed the "Wigwam." This location somewhat favored the chances of the western candidates, as also did the need to woo the doubtful middle-western states. There were five leading candidates when the convention opened; behind them stood several ranks of hopefuls, waiting for the lightning to strike.

The best known of the Republican possibilities was William H. Seward of New York, a senator and former governor of

William H. Seward of New York. (National Archives)

that state. Supported by one of the most experienced political bosses of his day, the canny Thurlow Weed, Seward was a former Whig who had joined the new Republican party at the time of Kansas-Nebraska in 1854. Because in 1850 he had made a famous speech asserting that there was a "higher law" than the Constitution which prohibited slavery in California and the territories, Seward was rather erroneously identified as one of the more radical Republicans, a fact which now told against him. Only a little behind Seward was Salmon Portland Chase, a former Democrat from Ohio, formerly senator and then governor of that state, long a leader in the antislavery movement and perhaps best known for his authorship of the "Appeal of the Independent Democrats" which had sounded the tocsin of the Kansas-Nebraska bill. An early Republican, Chase had many friends throughout the upper Middle West, the heartland of Republicanism. The third candidate was Abraham Lincoln.

Lincoln was less well known than either Seward or Chase, though he had recently been acquiring a national reputation. His debates with Douglas in Illinois and some speeches in New York and New England early in 1860 had received favorable notices in the national press. A former Henry Clay Whig, Lincoln was an old internal-improvements and protective-tariff man, whose years as a country lawyer and state politician had been interlarded with important jobs as a railroad attorney. All that was known of him as a personality indicated that he might be an eccentric: everyone noted the anecdotes, the squeaky voice, the awkward figure. But his political views as well as his geographical location were favorable. He was known as a fairly conservative Republican, opposed only to the extension of slavery; he had, unlike Seward, favored the Fugitive Slave Law. Rounding out the list or prominent candidates for the nomination were Edward Bates of Missouri and Simon Cameron of Pennsylvania. Bates was a Virginia-born jurist backed by the most conservative elements in the party, who wanted no more agitation of slavery; Cameron, a wealthy industrialist turned politician, had built a strong and somewhat rotten political machine in Pennsylvania and was devoted only to the protective tariff.

During the convention, Lincoln's supporters, ably seconded by some powerful railroad attorneys, quietly went about gathering promises that their candidate would be the second choice if the delegation's favorite was beaten. When a "stop Seward" movement was successful, Lincoln's supporters calmly counterfeited passes to the Wigwam and packed the galleries to shout for Lincoln. Seward and Chase were both passed over because they were considered too radical on the subject of slavery, Seward having the additional disadvantage of coming from a safe state. Lincoln received the nomination.

In the campaign that followed Douglas broke an old American tradition by personally taking the stump to speak in his own behalf. Lincoln, Breckinridge, and Bell quietly sat on their front porches, received callers, wrote letters, and conferred with their managers in the traditional way. The result was as expected:

	Popular vote	Percentage	Electoral
Douglas	1,375,157	29.40	12
Breckinridge	845,763	18.08	72
Lincoln	1,866,352	39.91	180
Bell	589,581	12.61	39

The results of this election have been repeatedly analyzed in an effort to discover their significance. Few facts are agreed upon, even by the best-informed students. Among those few are the following. Obviously, Lincoln was a minority President —probably no candidate could have received a majority vote in 1860. Then, Lincoln's vote came exclusively from the North; he received not a single vote from the states that joined the Confederacy, with the exception of a few votes in the area that later became West Virginia. Finally, the vote of 1860 was not a vote for disunion, but for preservation of the union; the conservative vote for each candidate outnumbered the radical vote. In the area of historical curiosities, it might be added that only Bell carried his own home county.

When all the analysis is done, the fact remains that the American people had elected a president who led a sectional party, and to the other section he was a symbol—a "Black" Republican. Because of that symbol, national loyalties were abandoned and sectional loyalties were built. A nation had come to war—against itself.

FURTHER READINGS

Much the best survey of the social, economic, and political history of this critical decade is to be found in Allan Nevins, *Ordeal of the Union,* volume II (1947) and *The Emergence of Lincoln,* volumes I and II (1950).

The theory that the Civil War resulted from a failure of statesmanship on both sides is impressively supported in Avery O. Craven, *The Coming of the Civil War* (2d ed., 1957), and in George Fort Milton, *The Eve of Conflict: Stephen A. Douglas and the*

Needless War (1934). That the war was the result of a fundamental conflict is the theme of Arthur C. Cole, *The Irrepressible Conflict, 1850–1865* (1934). A middle ground in this debate is taken in Roy F. Nichols, *The Disruption of American Democracy* (1948). See also Avery O. Craven, *The Growth of Southern Nationalism, 1848–1861* (1953).

Three studies of the 1860 election are of particular value: Reinhard H. Luthin, *The First Lincoln Campaign* (1944); Ollinger Crenshaw, *The Slave States in the Presidential Election of 1860* (1945); and E. D. Fite, *The Presidential Campaign of 1860* (1911).

Aspects of the secession crisis are to be found in Dwight L. Dumond, *The Secession Movement, 1860–1861* (1931); David M. Potter, *Lincoln and His Party in the Secession Crisis* (1942); and Kenneth M. Stampp, *And the War Came* (1950).

Biographies of particular value to an understanding of this period include Roy F. Nichols, *Franklin Pierce* (2d ed., 1958); G. T. Curtis, *James Buchanan* (2 vols., 1883); Albert J. Beveridge, *Abraham Lincoln* (2 vols., 1928); Carl Sandburg, *Abraham Lincoln: The Prairie Years* (2 vols., 1926); and W. E. Baringer, *A House Dividing* (1945).

A northern radical is carefully analyzed in Oswald G. Villard, *John Brown* (1943). A middle-states moderate is portrayed by J. H. Parks in his *John Bell of Tennessee* (1950), while two southern radicals have been the subject of intensive study in Avery O. Craven, *Edmund Ruffin* (1932), and Laura A. White, *Robert Barnwell Rhett* (1931).

For additional bibliography see the *Harvard Guide,* chapter 17.

FIFTEEN

The Civil War

SECESSION AND THE FAILURE OF COMPROMISE

1861
Confederate constitution framed,
February 8.
Fort Sumter fired upon, April 12.
Battle of Bull Run, July 21.

1862
Union forces win control of Mississippi
River.
Union forces defeated in Peninsular
campaign.
First Confederate invasion attempt ends
at Antietam.
Preliminary emancipation proclamation
issued.

1863
Final emancipation proclamation issued.
Second Confederate invasion attempt
ends at Gettysburg.
Failure of Confederate hopes abroad.

1864
Battle of the Wilderness.
Sherman's march through Georgia.
Lincoln reelected over McClellan.

1865
Lee surrenders at Appomattox, April 9.
Lincoln assassinated, April 14.
End of war, May 26.

IN 1861 THE AMERICAN people went to war. Virtually everyone, North and South, agreed that it would be a short war. They disagreed only on the outcome. Four years later they looked back on the greatest civil war in history and the bloodiest war Americans have ever fought. The number of men who were killed in combat or who died of wounds or disease is equal to the total of similar casualties suffered by Americans in the Revolution, the War of 1812, the Mexican War, the Spanish-American War, World War I, and World War II. No day in American history has yet matched the awful holocaust of Antietam, where 25,000 casualties were sustained in a single day. No war in our history has more significance for Americans past and present. It marked the end of our federal union in its old form and the beginning of the modern American nation. It ended slavery and began the search for more satisfactory relations between white and black Americans. It ended the dominance óf the farmer and planter in national councils and permitted industry, finance, and labor to share in directing the course of our political and economic development.

The election of Lincoln was the signal for which southern zealots had been waiting. In December, South Carolina went out of the union with a rush and a shout. With only a few more backward glances, the lower South followed during January and February. In South Carolina resistance to secession had been confined to a hand-

310

ful of sentimental unionists. In Georgia the division was between those who wanted to secede immediately and those who wanted to secede only if the remaining slave states agreed to leave the union. Secession won out in Georgia only after a bitter debate. The first test vote on secession in the Georgia convention stood 165 to 130 in favor of immediate secession. The 130 eventually concurred in the decision to secede, but many made it clear that they did so only in the hope that they might negotiate better terms with the union after they had left it than while they remained within it. In Alabama the issue of secession ran into the old sectional division within the state, the small farmers of the northern hill country and Tennessee River Valley being arrayed against the cotton princes of the "black belt" to the south. Of the 95 delegates in the Alabama convention, 34 voted against secession, and 33 of these refused to sign the Ordinance of Secession after it had been adopted by the majority. The familiar division between those ready for immediate secession and those ready to secede only in cooperation with the other slave states appeared in Mississippi. There being no sectional division comparable to that of Alabama, the "cooperationists" were far less determined and were quickly converted to immediate secession. Louisiana, Florida, and Texas followed the pattern established in Georgia and Mississippi, and by February the states of the lower South were ready to get on with the business of forming a new central government.

Significant as was the success of secession in the lower South, it did not obscure the fact that not a single state of the upper South had joined the movement. In North Carolina, Virginia, Tennessee, Missouri, and Arkansas, conventions called by the governors or legislatures either refused to consider secession or talked the idea to death. Maryland and Kentucky did not even call conventions to consider the subject. The decision of the upper South to reject secession for the time being was the result of the distinctive character of the people and institutions in the area. Several of these states were closely bound to the North by ties of trade and commerce. The Ohio River and its tributaries, the Tennessee and Cumberland Rivers, formed a great basin which was as distinct from the lower South as it was from the North. Pittsburgh, Cincinnati, Louisville, Nashville, and St. Louis were its trading and financial centers. Even distant Baltimore was closely linked to this basin by its heavy trade along the Baltimore & Ohio Railroad. Tied by economic interest to the factories and mills of the North, this central basin was equally bound to the plantations and farms of the lower South and particularly the lower Mississippi River Valley. Secession impaled these border states on the horns of a dilemma. If they joined the lower South, their markets, credit, and sources of manufactured goods in the North would be largely cut off. If they remained loyal to the union, their loans, markets, and sources of agricultural staples in the South would be lost. But it was more than economic factors which made the border states hesitate to commit themselves on secession.

The institution of slavery was much softer in the upper South than it was on the great rice, cotton, and sugar plantations of the lower South. The proportion of Negroes to whites in the total population was much lower, with a consequent easing of the tension between the races. Enforcement of the "Black Codes" was generally more lax in the upper South. To a surprising degree, slavery in the border states had become by 1860 a system for supplying

The unfinished Capitol, 1861

Seamen of the Union Navy

Railroads in military use at Atlanta

Abraham Lincoln

The American Civil War, bloodiest in the nation's history, was a test of courage, of industrial power, and of leadership. In courage the South was the equal of the North, but it lacked the industrial power and did not find the political leadership that the North discovered in Lincoln.

Death behind the stone wall,
at the Battle of Fredericksburg

house servants rather than plantation labor. Comparatively unexcited by the fugitive-slave problem in the 1850s, the border states remained equally complacent about the threat of Black Republicans in 1860.

A third factor in holding the upper South on the fence was the nature of its leadership. In Virginia particularly, but all through the border states, the concept of political rule by the "best" families retained considerable vitality. Such leadership was apt to be conservative and confident. Unlike the more strident leadership of the new cotton "aristocracy," the politicians of the upper South were slow to boil and careful to count the cost of any proposed action.

A final consideration holding the border states neutral was their desire to see the outcome of the many peace and compromise efforts which were then under way. Although they waited, several of the

border states made it quite clear they would secede at any moment rather than be *coerced* into remaining within the union.

The hope for peace and compromise was reinforced by the realization that the great majority of Americans, North and South, wanted neither war nor secession. Stephen A. Douglas sensed this spirit of moderation as he spoke to southern audiences. Douglas had learned of his defeat by Lincoln while in Mobile, Alabama, where he had ended his presidential campaign. On his way back to Washington, he made frequent speeches counseling union and compromise. One such speech, in Vicksburg, Mississippi, was nearly drowned out by applause. In succeeding months Douglas threw his full weight into the battle for compromise. President Buchanan, too, desperately wanted to hold the union together, but he labored under a

THE COURSE OF SECESSION

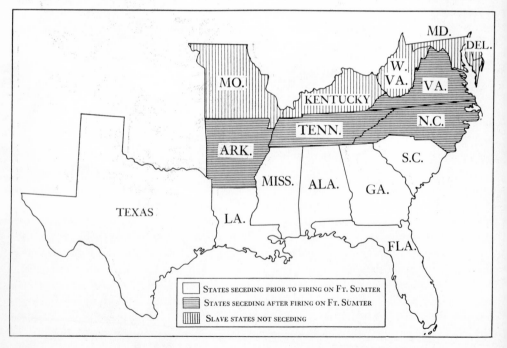

MD.
DEL.
MO.
W. VA.
VA.
KENTUCKY
N.C.
TENN.
ARK.
S.C.
MISS.   ALA.   GA.
TEXAS
LA.
FLA.

STATES SECEDING PRIOR TO FIRING ON FT. SUMTER
STATES SECEDING AFTER FIRING ON FT. SUMTER
SLAVE STATES NOT SECEDING

tremendous handicap. In addition to being rather prosouthern by inclination, Buchanan held the novel notion that the President possessed the authority to put down a small insurrection but none to suppress a large one. Kentucky's Senator Crittenden, seeking to inherit the mantle of the great compromiser Henry Clay, offered a compromise plan which became the basis for most of the subsequent efforts at settlement. The heart of the Crittenden plan was a series of constitutional amendments which were designed to take the issue of slavery out of national politics. Crittenden proposed to reestablish the old 36°30' line to divide free soil from slavery during the territorial stage, and to allow each state to determine whether or not it would have slavery at the time of its admission into the union. The final provision would have been a constitutional amendment which would have bound the nation to consider no future amendments to the Constitution on the subject of slavery. In spite of considerable popular support, the Crittenden Compromise received little support in the Senate. As a matter of fact, both the House and the Senate were visibly melting away, as southern members quietly bade their Washington friends good-by and hurried home to tend their political fences. A final effort at compromise achieved no more success. The Washington Peace Conference, called at the behest of Virginia, met in February, 1861. Several of the southern states refused to send delegates, and many of the delegates from northern states came only to defeat all compromise proposals.

By the end of February it was perfectly clear that compromise was impossible. During the months since Lincoln's election, the secessionists had made no offer that the President-elect felt he could accept. The secessionists were insisting on positive protection for slavery in all the territories owned by the United States. Lincoln, on the other hand, voiced the deep conviction of the Republican party and most people of the North when he said "that on the territorial question—that is, the question of extending slavery under the national auspices—I am inflexible. I am for no compromise which assists or permits the extension of the institution on soil owned by the nation." With Lincoln "inflexible" and the secessionists determined, all hope of compromise was dead. The American people had found an issue that could not be settled by the conventional methods of democracy. The issue of slavery could not be talked away, voted away, or compromised away. Few Americans wanted war, but most Americans were willing to go to war when the issue of slavery proved too complex and too divisive for solution by any other means.

TWO PRESIDENTS

On February 4, 1861, delegates from the seceded states of the lower South gathered at Montgomery, Alabama. Within a few days they had written a constitution, chosen Jefferson Davis provisional president, and declared themselves the provisional congress of the Confederate States of America. Within a month Abraham Lincoln was inaugurated in Washington, and what had been the United States had two new presidents. Both Lincoln and Davis were sons of Kentucky. In fact, they had been born within a year of each other in strikingly similar log cabins less than 150 miles apart. But there the similarity ends. Davis grew up as the protégé of a brother twenty-four years his senior who had become one of the wealthiest planters in Mississippi. Young Jeff was given the best education money could buy in the

Jefferson Davis, President of the Confederate States. (National Archives)

West. At the proper time he was handed an appointment to West Point. His graduation was followed by several years' service as a junior officer at a series of military posts in the Mississippi Valley. He found that military life suited him. He liked the order and security of a life in which one gave respect and obedience to one's superiors and expected the same from one's subordinates. Personally Davis was stiff and formal, wholly lacking a sense of humor, but dedicated to duty and considered by all an excellent young officer. The story of Lincoln's scratching for a little learning is too well known to bear repetition. Young Lincoln developed in the rough-and-tumble of frontier politics and preferred situations which called for original thought and gave freedom of action. Although no philosopher, Lincoln developed a rare skill in analyzing complex problems and putting them into simple language. He interspersed his conversation and speeches with homely illustrations which rang true to his listeners. In a day of great orators Lincoln habitually used his high squeaky voice in a conversational manner while making speeches.

In 1860 Davis had been a national figure for over a decade. A hero of the Mexican War, he had been a senator from Mississippi, Secretary of War in the Pierce Cabinet, and probably the outstanding champion of southern nationalism after the death of Calhoun in 1850. Lincoln's career included an undistinguished term as congressman from Illinois during the Mexican War, a substantial and increasingly prosperous law practice, and a succession of local and state offices to which he was elected as a Henry Clay Whig. Lincoln had achieved national recognition only in 1858, when he was defeated for the Senate by Douglas after a series of brilliant debates. A speech or two in New York and New England which attracted national press coverage followed, but beyond that, Lincoln was hardly known outside Illinois and the Old Northwest. Even the immense prestige of his election to the presidency did not entirely obliterate the slightly comic figure of the angular and ugly country lawyer. In March, 1861, there were few men who hesitated to predict success for Davis and failure for Lincoln in the difficult years ahead.

The problems which faced the two new presidents were quite similar. Each had to overcome very considerable opposition to his leadership from within this own ranks. The choice of Lincoln over able and ambitious men like Seward, Chase, and Bates still rankled with many Republicans, and in the crisis of 1861 Lincoln needed such men more than they needed him. Until he could count on their support, he could not even give serious thought to a plan to meet the secession movement. By careful attention to political appointments at the lower levels of government, as well as by carefully rewarding each of the major factions and their leaders, Lincoln soon created some semblance of Republican unity behind his administration. Even then, he was not master in his own house. Secretary of State William H. Seward, who had been the leading contender for the nomination which Lincoln had won in Chicago, expected to be the guiding light in the new administration. He capped several weeks of irregular negotiations with representatives of the Confederacy by proposing that Lincoln designate him to solve the secession crisis by allowing him to provoke a little war with France and Spain. And if France and Spain would not help us reunite, then perhaps we might pick a fight with England and Russia which would rally Americans under the Stars and Stripes once more! Lincoln's firm and kindly rebuff to Seward's wild schemes settled everyone down a bit, and Lincoln was soon master in his own house; Seward went on to become one of our most successful secretaries of state.

Jefferson Davis ran into similar trouble with his supporters. Davis had been the choice of southern moderates who managed to suppress the claims of the fire-eating radicals for the moment. It was soon apparent that their defeat had embittered the men who had done so much to create the Confederate States, and whatever support they gave Davis later they gave grudgingly. Davis attempted to conciliate this and all the other factions within the Confederacy, but lacking the fine political touch of Lincoln, as well as the patronage of a well-established and handsomely endowed government, he was in constant hot water with his cabinet, his congress, and his generals.

Lincoln entered the White House determined to save the union at any cost. Secession would solve nothing, for, as Lincoln pointed out, "Physically speaking, we cannot separate. We cannot remove our respective sections from each other nor build an impassable wall between them. A husband and wife may be divorced and go out of the presence and beyond the reach of each other, but the different parts of our own country cannot do this. They cannot but remain face to face, and intercourse, either amicable or hostile, must continue between them." In addition to providing no solutions to the problems that faced Americans, Lincoln felt that secession was wrong and that breaking up the union would destroy freedom; the noble experiment in self-government begun "four score and seven years ago" would "perish from the earth." In this devotion to the union, Lincoln was in perfect harmony with the deepest desires of the North. By contrast, Jefferson Davis worked under a severe handicap in trying to find a common ground upon which the South would stand. Southerners were equally devoted to the cause of freedom and self-government, but for most of them these concepts were bound up with old loyalties to the union and the Constitution. Even in secession, most southerners were striving to preserve the liberties they had known under the old Constitution and in the old union. The task of the new president was to convince southerners that the new Confederacy would be even more devoted to liberty and democracy than the union had been. Davis had to bind his people to a new loyalty, which is infinitely more difficult than holding a people to an older loyalty.

The initial contest between Lincoln and

Davis was over the allegiance of the border states. As we have seen, the upper South was sitting firmly on the fence. These states held the balance of power in peace or war. Neither Lincoln nor Davis could hope to win either a peaceful settlement or a victory in war if they lost all the border states. But the determination of the border states to resist both secession and coercion gave the rival administrations little leverage with which to work. It was apparent to both Lincoln and Davis that a waiting game was called for—Lincoln waiting while Union sentiment crystallized, Davis waiting for slavery and resistance to coercion to push the border into the Confederacy.

Unfortunately for everyone, the waiting game had a time limit. The first paper Lincoln had been handed after his inauguration was a message telling him that the federal garrison at Fort Sumter at the mouth of Charleston harbor was short of rations, and if it were not reinforced and provisioned it would have to withdraw by the middle of April. Fort Sumter had become the symbol of the Union. As long as it remained in federal hands, the Confederacy was not sovereign within its own boundaries. As long as the Stars and Stripes flew in Charleston harbor, secession remained a theory instead of a fact. The Confederate leaders made it quite clear that any attempt to reinforce the fort would result in hostile action. Lincoln could not abandon the fort without admitting the fact of secession as well as losing much of his most valuable support in the North. When Lincoln moved to provision Sumter, Davis, unable to withstand the pressure of South Carolina hotheads, was forced to give his consent to fire on the fort. Lincoln was clearly the victor in the first test of patience.

Now confident of united northern support, Lincoln issued a call for 75,000 state militia to suppress "combinations too powerful to be suppressed by the ordinary course of judicial proceedings." He also ordered the regular army expanded. The Treasury was authorized to pay out $2 million for military equipment, and a blockade of the southern coast was ordered. Except for the call for volunteers, none of Lincoln's actions are sanctioned by the Constitution, but he believed that violating the Constitution was justified by the necessity of preserving it. The call for volunteers was the signal for Virginia, North Carolina, Tennessee, and Arkansas to secede. Federal troops and pressure assisted pronorthern majorities in Maryland and Missouri to defeat secession movements. But Davis won the second round when Lincoln's call for troops was interpreted as coercion in much of the upper South.

Aside from Virginia, the greatest prize in the game of patience was Kentucky. If Kentucky seceded, the Confederacy would have the Ohio River as her northern boundary between the mountains and the Mississippi River. Combined with the Potomac in the east and the Missouri in the west, this would give the Confederacy defensible strategic boundaries along her entire northern border. But Lincoln won the third round; for his delicate handling of the Kentucky situation tried Confederate patience beyond the breaking point, and Confederate troops invaded Kentucky. Coercion from the South was no more welcome than from the North; federal troops were welcomed in Kentucky as defenders against foreign invasion. The Confederacy never achieved its river boundary in the west, and its military fortunes in that area never overcame this disadvantage.

With the exception of small areas in Maryland, Missouri, and Tennessee, the

American people in the winter of 1860–1861 had decided by majority vote within their states between secession and union. It remained for military force to decide whether a majority of Americans would accept these decisions.

COCKY CONFEDERATES AND CONFIDENT YANKEES

The fateful decisions of the spring of 1861 were made under the influence of a false glow of optimism. In spite of the dire warnings of many elder statesmen, both North and South went gaily to war. Each was certain of victory, and each was equally certain the war would be short. This easy optimism is only partly explained by the eternal confidence of youth. Both North and South had substantial reasons for expecting victory. The South looked at a map. The Confederacy controlled over 100,000 square miles more territory than did the North. A common border with Mexico offered the opportunity of drawing sustenance from that quarter. Even the expected blockade held no terrors, for it would take years to establish an effective blockade over the 2,000 miles of coastline with literally thousands of little coves, harbors, inlets, and river mouths through which goods could be shipped. In any case, the blockade was expected to collapse as a result of the need of Europe and the North for cotton. So confident was the Confederacy that "Cotton Is King," that the export of cotton was prohibited long before the Union blockade was established.

Closer examination of the map gave Confederates added hope. The mountain chain of the Appalachians covered the Confederacy from Virginia to Alabama. They reasoned that invasion would be confined to the narrow Atlantic shelf in Virginia or the Mississippi River Valley. They calculated that the latter route would be virtually impossible because an invading army would bog down completely in the swamps, bends, and bottom lands of the river valley. Behind their mountain barrier the Confederates were well equipped with natural waterways which, coupled with the defensive strategy they expected to pursue, gave them the advantage of interior lines with good communication between strong points on their defensive perimeter. The expectation of a defensive strategy led the Confederates to discount the obvious numerical superiority of the North. The popular idea that "any Reb could lick ten Yanks" was seconded by serious military leaders who knew the North would have need of every one of its additional men to carry an offensive war into enemy territory. Finally, the South was confident of victory because it had always before it the example of the American Revolution in which the Americans had lost nearly every battle and yet won their independence. The Confederacy had only to remain in existence to win its objective of independence, while the federal forces had to destroy the Confederate government in order to preserve the Union.

The optimism of the North was equally well founded. Unionists knew that their young men of military age outnumbered the Confederates by about four to one. They were confident of their ability to blockade and isolate the South from outside assistance. They knew that wheat had become as important to England and Europe as southern cotton. The enlisted personnel of both the federal army and navy had remained thoroughly loyal, and the bulk of West Point graduates appeared to be loyal. The Union counted on widespread disaffection in the South as soon as the concrete problems of setting up a new government were faced, and fully expected wholesale desertion from Confederate ranks as soon as Union forces had inflicted one decisive defeat on the rebel army.

Both the North and the South overlooked several factors which were much more decisive than any of the sources of strength on which they based their calculations. The first was the railroad. The North possessed twice the mileage found in the South. Moreover, the North was tied together by four through lines connecting the east and west, while the South possessed only one through line between east and west and the outline of a second. Of equal importance was the fact that the northern roads were better built, with heavier ballast and rails; besides, the North possessed the machine shops and skilled manpower to operate its system. The North was quick to learn to gear its railroads to the needs of war. Lincoln had had considerable experience as a railroad attorney. At one time, the President, his Secretary of War, the first commanding general of the Union armies, and a whole host of lesser Union generals were ex-railroad men. Men with railroad experience were brought into national service solely for the purpose of utilizing their skill in railroad building or management. Before the war was a year old, the northern railroads had become an integral part of the northern war effort. In sorry contrast was the Confederate position. Unable to use effectively even the railroads it possessed, the Confederacy stood helplessly by and watched its railroad plant deteriorate under the pounding of wartime use.

The second factor overlooked by both North and South in calculating their chances of victory was the industrial superiority of the North. Just as the Civil War was the first in which railroads played a major role, so was it the first in which industrial power became a major factor in determining the outcome of a war. Whether it was shoes, guns, ships, or plows, the North produced what it needed. Northern industry was far stronger in 1865 than it had been at the outbreak of the war. The significance of the famous battle in 1862 between the *Monitor* and the *Merrimac* was not the use of armor plate on naval vessels but the fact that in a little over six months the North had been able to design, build, and deliver a wholly new weapon. A quick look at the design reveals what the North was able to do. A weapon which could penetrate the heavy defenses of rivers and harbors was called for. Since such waters would give a vessel a minimum of area for maneuver, the ship had to be built to move in both directions with equal ease and fire in all directions. This led to the revolving turret. Shallow rivers called for a light-draught vessel, but Confederate gunners in harbor fortifications or along river banks would know their firing ranges perfectly, so a heavily armored ship was necessary. This difficult requirement was met by the design of a heavily armored turret set on a lightly armored flush deck with the resulting "cheese box on a raft" silhouette of the *Monitor*. By contrast, even the brilliant improvisation of the Confederates in remodeling the old *Merrimac* was crude. The North had both the skill and the industrial capacity, while the South had only ideas and hopes in the field of war production.

The great intangible which neither the North nor the South could properly evaluate at the onset of the war was the element of leadership. On the face of it, the Confederacy had a distinct advantage in Jefferson Davis's West Point training, his Mexican War experience, and the secretaryship of war he had held. But the Civil

War called for leadership far beyond conventional matters of choosing generals and directing strategy. This first modern war demanded complex financing and long-range industrial planning. As a civil war it emphasized the need for winning and holding the support of a deeply disturbed and confused people. Also as a civil war it produced more than the usual quota of knotty diplomatic problems, which required a delicate and sure hand in control of foreign relations. Such requirements were almost made to order for the peculiar skills and talents of the consummate politician Abraham Lincoln. As the war dragged on, it became apparent that Lincoln was the master and Davis the apprentice in the conduct of modern war.

Thus, in all three of the factors overlooked or too intangible for ready calculation at the beginning of the war—the adaption of railroads to war, the conversion of industry to war production, and the role of leadership—the North turned out to possess complete superiority. With that superiority went victory, but not until the country had experienced the greatest blood bath in its history.

ANACONDA

The strategy of both the Union and the Confederacy was dictated by politics and geography. The problem of the Confederacy was largely defensive, for if it remained in existence after the last battle had been fought, the victory belonged to the South regardless of who won the battles. Most southerners agreed that outside help would be necessary if they were to defend themselves successfully. They did not agree on how that help was to be obtained. Some Confederate leaders were under the impression that the world would beat a path to southern shores in quest of

cotton and because of sympathy for a people who were resisting aggression. They advocated that the South do nothing except perhaps cut off cotton exports in order to hasten the steps of those who were bound to come in search of the precious fiber. Others proposed doing everything possible to break the blockade and devoting all energies to winning recognition by France and England as a prelude to gaining their economic assistance. There was general agreement that on land the Confederacy ought to confine itself to defensive operations. This strategy was so thoroughly endorsed by every southern state that the Confederacy was forced to spread its little armies over the full length of its northern boundary as well as along the Atlantic coast and the Gulf Coast. The result was that it rarely had sufficient strength to meet the northern attacks, which were naturally concentrated in small areas. Thus the fears of individual southern states and their insistence on a perimeter defense of the entire Confederacy handed Union commanders one of the most prized of all military weapons—the initiative. Only General Lee in Virginia and General Bragg in Kentucky were ever able to wrest the initiative from the Union; Bragg did so only once, and Lee managed it but twice.

The problem of the Washington government was in finding the best way to reunite the Union. General Winfield Scott, now so fat and feeble that he could no longer mount his horse, retained the military brilliance that had brought him fame in the War of 1812 and the Mexican War. As General in Chief, Scott went to work to prepare a plan for putting down secession. He prepared one, only to find that Lincoln and his advisers were not very interested. Scott's plan, soon derisively dubbed the "Anaconda" by an impatient public, called

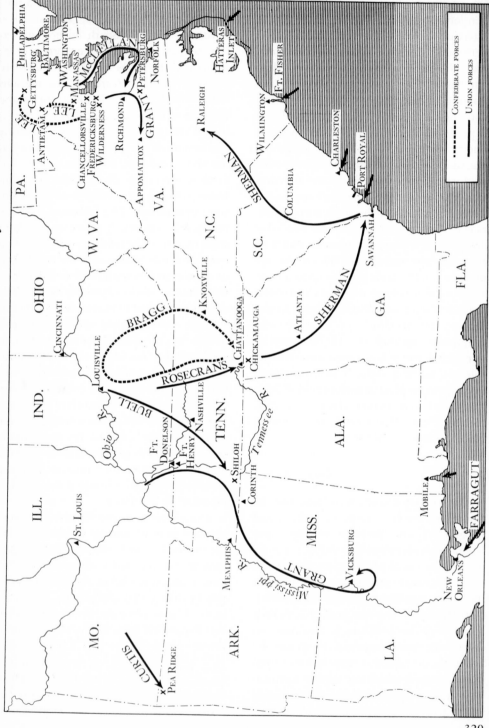

MAJOR CAMPAIGNS OF THE CIVIL WAR

for wrapping coil after coil around the Confederacy and then waiting until a tremendous force could be organized to mount an invasion, hoping, in the meantime, that Union sentiment in the South might crystallize and make an invasion unnecessary. The confident North preferred the stirring phrase "On to Richmond" to the slow but sure Anaconda. The first part of Scott's plan proposed a blockade of the southern coast with amphibious operations to keep the Confederates off balance, close up their ports, and provide close-support bases for an extended blockade if that became necessary in the future. This was the only part of Anaconda immediately adopted. While the blockade was being battened down, Scott urged that huge armies be organized and trained in preparation for a spring campaign in 1862. "Old Fuss-and-Feathers" fully expected the Confederacy to concentrate its strongest forces in northern Virginia, so he planned a holding operation around Washington while Union armies in the West pushed down the Mississippi to cut off the western portion of the Confederacy. With the Confederacy squeezed between the Mississippi and the sea, Scott was sure it could not hold off a second attack through Tennessee and Georgia, which would confine the resistance to Virginia, North Carolina, and South Carolina. If the Richmond government was able to continue the fight, Scott assumed that a third attack mounted in South Carolina and moving northward could hammer Richmond against the anvil of the holding force he planned to keep above Richmond. While Scott alone was responsible for Anaconda, it should be noted that a good many federal commanders were thinking along identical lines. But an impatient public forced leaders to adopt plans promising quicker suc-

cess. Only later, after many failures, did grand strategy fall into the Anaconda pattern, and Union armies in the West threw one coil after another around portions of the Confederacy while the eastern armies pounded each other to death along the Atlantic shelf between Gettysburg and Petersburg.

The summer and fall of 1861 witnessed the formation of the greatest armies the continent had ever seen. In the East the Confederate Army of Northern Virginia and the Union Army of the Potomac began to take shape. The terrain of the eastern theater was largely gently rolling farm country, from the wheat, corn, and hog lands of southern Pennsylvania to the old tobacco country along the James below Richmond. On the west the theater was walled in by the Appalachian highlands and the great Shenandoah Valley tucked in between the Blue Ridge and the highlands proper. On the east it was hemmed in by Chesapeake Bay. Its entire length of 250 miles was cut up by a series of rivers and streams which made every campaign seem like am amphibious operation to the men in the ranks. The only sizable battle of 1861 was the brief "blooding" at First Manassas.* The Confederates were spread out along Bull Run, covering the vital rail junction at Manassas. Undertaken by a reluctant Union commander who was convinced his army was not ready for battle, the federal foray out of Washington against them ended disastrously for the Union. But the picture of Union troops

* Many of the Civil War battles come to us with two names, because the Confederates fell into the habit of naming battles after the nearest settlement, while the Union frequently named the same battle after a nearby creek or other landmark. Hence the Confederate First Manassas is the same as the Union First Bull Run and the Union Antietam went on Confederate records as the Battle of Sharpsburg.

PRINCIPAL OFFENSIVE DRIVES IN THE EASTERN THEATER

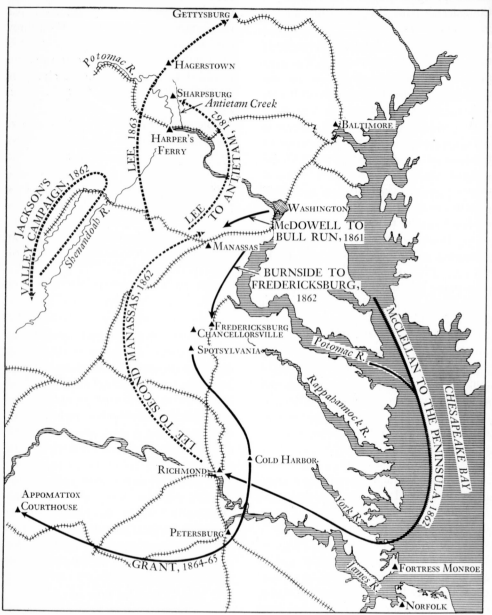

streaming back to Washington, defeated and broken, shocked and aroused the people of the North. They quickly abandoned all idea of a short and cheap war and buckled down to the business of raising an army in earnest. So much in earnest were they, that by April, 1862, they were able to land an army of 100,000 men on the peninsula just a few miles below Richmond, while another 30,000 to

40,000 remained in northern Virginia to counter any Confederate moves toward Washington. It appeared that the Union troops under the command of General George B. ("Little Mac") McClellan were about to clamp a giant pincers on the Confederates defending Richmond. In an early battle of this campaign, the Confederate commander Joseph E. Johnston was seriously wounded, and the command devolved upon Robert E. Lee. Lee, with the brilliant assistance of Thomas J. ("Stonewall") Jackson, made hash of the Union plans for northern Virginia and then concentrated against McClellan, bluffing and beating him into a retreat from the gates of Richmond. Before 1862 was over, Lee had defeated a second Union commander, John Pope, and had crossed Virginia and invaded Maryland, where he suffered his first major defeat at the hands of a restored McClellan. "Little Mac" failed to follow Lee back into Virginia with vigor and was soon replaced. The year closed with Lee springing a vicious trap on the Army of the Potomac, now under the command of General Burnside, whose muttonchop whiskers won him a permanent place in American dictionaries.

The campaigning of 1863 opened with a brilliant maneuver by the new commander of the Army of the Potomac, Joseph Hooker, which came to grief when Hooker lost his nerve and Lee proved as audacious as ever. This battle of Chancellorsville was followed by Lee's second attempt at invasion of the North, which ended disastrously at Gettysburg. With George Gordon Meade in command of the Army of the Potomac, and Ulysses S. Grant brought from the West to command all the Union armies but giving his special attention to "Marse Robert," the war in the East entered its final phase. Wielding the huge army of raw recruits and hard-

General Robert E. Lee. (Library of Congress)

ened veterans that now made up the Army of the Potomac, Grant spent 1864 grinding down the Army of Northern Virginia, depriving Lee of his mobility, never giving up the initiative, and generally acting like a blacksmith who had picked up the anvil and found it more effective than his hammer in bending and breaking iron. By continual bludgeoning, Grant forced Lee back into Richmond, then cut off Lee's supplies and pried him out of Richmond, and finally brought the proud Army of Northern Virginia to bay at the little crossroads of Appomattox Courthouse, a few miles to the southwest of the Confederate capital, in April, 1865.

THE WAR IN THE WEST

One of the ciritical shortages in every war is a lack of first-rate commanders. Davis was more fortunate than Lincoln in finding good men quickly for his eastern army. Many West Pointers resigned from the "old army" and offered their services to the Confederacy. This fact takes on added significance when it is remembered that every single first-rate military reputation made during the Civil War was made by a West Point graduate. Within the first year of combat Davis had chosen for top command the great triumvirate of the Army of Northern Virginia: Lee, Longstreet, and Jackson. In contrast, Lincoln dismissed four commanders, one of them twice, before he found a man who could handle the Army of the Potomac and use its numerical superiority against the agile Lee.

Davis's success in finding good commanders in the East was matched by Lincoln's success in the West. By all odds, the greatest commander the Union produced turned up in command of a half-tamed regiment of Illinois volunteers. Ulysses S. Grant was a West Point graduate who had been only a mediocre student. His service

General Ulysses S. Grant. (Library of Congress)

in the Mexican War was excellent but not of the kind that attracts many headlines, since a good share of it was devoted to tending a string of army mules. His regular army career after the war consisted of assignments at a series of dull army posts in the Middle West and on the Pacific Coast. This service was a disappointment to Grant and to the army. His subsequent efforts at farming, selling real estate, and working in his father's leather store were equally disappointing. When war broke out, Grant offered his services to the War Department (from which he received no reply—the letter was found only many years later) and to the state of Ohio. The Governor of Illinois finally found a spot for him and gave him command of a regiment which had just cowed its previous commander. Grant soon had the rowdies in line, all signed up for three years' service, and marching off to war.

The war Grant expected to fight was going to be governed by certain facts of geography as familiar to westerners as the lines on the palms of their hands. In spite of the advent of the railroads, westerners still thought in terms of great rivers. The broad Ohio, the Tennessee and the Cumberland leading from the Ohio into the heart of the Confederacy, and finally the "Ole Man" of them all, the great Mississippi, determined the course of military operations in the West. From Grant's headquarters on the Mississippi at Cairo near the confluence of all these rivers, the strategy to be followed seemed perfectly plain: tie up both the Tennessee and the Cumberland Rivers by occupying Paducah, and then get permission from his commander to use his growing little army to cut into the Confederacy by moving south along the rivers. This strategy seemed almost inevitable, since the Confederates as yet had no armed vessels on the rivers, and Grant could count on the close cooperation of the navy's growing fleet of armed river boats. If successful in breaking the Confederate hold on the Tennessee and Cumberland Rivers, Grant could outflank their entire position in Kentucky and force a retreat deep into Tennessee. Early in 1862 Grant carried out the plan to attack the Confederate defenses on the Tennessee at Fort Henry. When Henry fell with only a token resistance, Grant moved against the much stronger Fort Donelson, which the Confederates had built on the Cumberland to protect the approaches to Nashville. When asked for terms upon which the Donelson garrison could surrender, Grant replied that his "terms" were "unconditional surrender." Thus the slouching, unkempt, stogie-smoking little man from the West became a national hero known as "Unconditional Surrender" Grant.

The remainder of 1862 in the West saw the Confederates stop the southward advance of Grant at Shiloh in a crazy-quilt sort of battle in which a confused mass of civilians in Confederate uniforms won what appeared to be a decisive victory on Sunday only to find an equally confused mass of civilians in Union uniforms come back on Monday to drive off Sunday's victors. Shiloh stopped Grant's drive, but at such a cost that the Confederates were never able to shake his grip on western Tennessee. To the east a bit, the Confederate commander Braxton Bragg conducted a remarkable late-summer campaign which took him ranging far to the north in Kentucky, but by the end of the year he was back in Tennessee with little to show for his effort. By the end of 1862 the Union commanders in the West were getting ready to resume their drive southward along the Mississippi and southeast-ward toward Chattanooga. Union armies in the West were even more eager to get on with the business when they were reminded by their slightly superior naval friends of the brilliant campaign under David G. Farragut and David D. Porter, which had opened the Mississippi as far north as Port Hudson and had handed the army an undamaged New Orleans to occupy. In spite of friendly bantering, the Union operations in the West were marked by the closest kind of cooperation between the army and the navy.

Active campaigning in 1863 opened with Grant trying to find a way to get at the great fortress city of Vicksburg which was the key to the southern hold on the Mississippi. Foiled by the destruction of his supply base in his attempt to approach from the interior of Mississippi in late 1862, Grant turned to the navy for help in getting at Vicksburg via the river. In a campaign that violated all the textbook rules, Grant crossed the Mississippi twice, cut loose from his base of operations, fought five battles against two armies, and captured Vicksburg. Over and over again during the campaign Grant had shown brilliance, audacity, and mobility, handling his army as though it were a rapier. Grant must be rated one of history's great commanders; he showed at Vicksburg he was as much a master of a war of movement as his later campaigns in Virginia showed him a master of a slow grinding war of attrition. The victory at Vicksburg in July, 1863, was the decisive battle of the Civil War, though public attention was riveted on the almost simultaneous Confederate defeat at Gettysburg. With Vicksburg gone, Port Hudson quickly surrendered, and the Mississippi flowed "unvexed to the sea."

The remainder of 1863 in the West

PRINCIPAL OFFENSIVE DRIVES IN THE MISSISSIPPI VALLEY

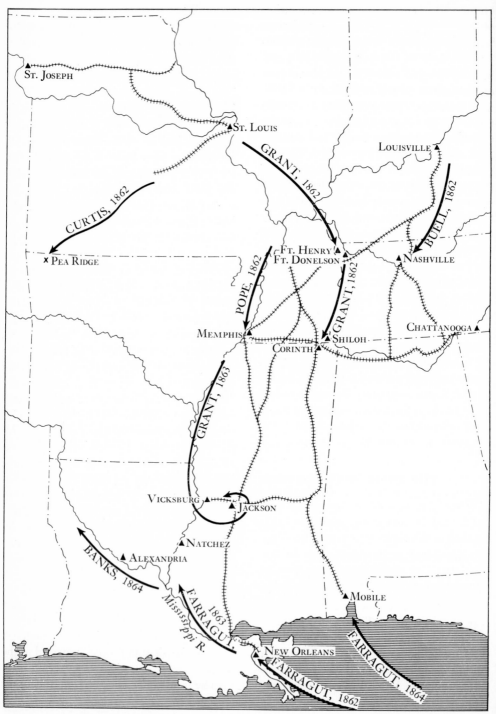

found Grant, leaning heavily on Generals George H. Thomas and William T. Sherman, punching his way southward out of Chattanooga. With two of the top men on anybody's list of Civil War generals, and with troops that accomplished the impossible in their attack straight up a sheer mountainside, Grant succeeded in preparing the way for a Union drive eastward through the mountain barrier and into the "soft underbelly" of the Confederacy in Georgia and South Carolina. With affairs in the south left in the more than capable hands of Thomas and Sherman, Grant was brought to Virginia and placed in command of all Union forces. While 1864 and 1865 provided battles, casualties, and death in sickening numbers, it was largely an anticlimax, for the pattern of the war strategy had been firmly established in 1863. Union forces held Lee by the throat in the Virginia theater, while great slashing attacks cut ever larger chunks out of the Confederacy and left it by the spring of 1865 a head without a body. With all its false starts, temporary defeats, and frequent stalling, the Union campaign in the West remains one of the longest sustained offensives in the history of warfare.

THE CIVIL WAR SOLDIER

While the Lincolns, Davises, Grants, and Lees were designing grand strategy, the men in the ranks were acting very like the soldiers of every other war. In the initial burst of enthusiasm "they went to war with an air, as if they went to a ball." They were

Dress-uniform boys who rubbed their buttons brighter than gold,
And gave them to girls for flowers and raspberry-lemonade,
Unused to the sick fatigue, the route-march made in the cold,

The stink of the fever camps, the tarnish rotting the blade.*

The dress uniforms soon faded and the flowers wilted. The three-month volunteers went home, and those who remained could never explain why they stayed. But even those who volunteered to stay were not enough; the South began conscripting men for service in 1862, and the North followed suit in 1863. Those responsible for getting men into service during the Civil War ran into all the usual problems and then some. Draft dodging was widespread, encouraged by the substitute clause which allowed a man to hire another to go into service in his place or buy outright exemption for $300. Open resistance to the draft occurred in New York City and in scattered communities elsewhere in the North. The pernicious effects of the northern "bounty system," which allowed states, counties, and towns to add cash rewards to those offered by the federal government as an inducement to enlistment or reenlistment, were felt everywhere. "Bounty brokers" who could direct a man to the places offering the highest bounties were soon in business. For a percentage of the bounty, they directed men to places offering the most generous rewards. Such brokers frequently provided the means by which one of their enlistees could desert and sign up again in another town or state, which provided the broker with his cut of a second bounty. Bounty jumpers were usually more trouble than they were worth to the army, but by 1864 a good proportion of the Union army was made up of conscripts, purchased substitutes, and bounty jumpers.

* From *John Brown's Body,* copyright 1927, 1928, by Stephen Vincent Benét. Copyright renewed, 1955, 1956. Published by Rinehart & Company, Inc., New York. By permission from Rosemary Carr Benét.

Southern conscription problems were aggravated by the provision that any man who owned twenty slaves was exempt from service. Large planters were known to divide up their 200 or 300 slaves into twenty-slave parcels and thus provide exemption for a long list of sons, cousins, nephews, or friends. Then there was the provision of the conscription law which exempted, among others, schoolteachers and druggists, which caused a rush for pupils and drugstores such as the South had never seen. Both North and South placed conscientious objectors in noncombatant positions.

In the ranks, the Civil War recruit or "strawfoot" was bewildered by his new life. He was issued a uniform that was frequently sewn together by the patriotic women of his home town or provided by some dealer in "shoddy" who had just sold the town fathers a carload of trousers with two left legs. Only in the fall of 1861 did good-quality government issue begin to reach the armies. His firearm was a single-shot smoothbore musket, little changed from the gun his grandfather had carried in the American Revolution. Like his uniforms, his weapons improved and he was soon equipped, both North and South, with muzzle-loading Springfields or Enfields which had been rifled to increase range and accuracy. A few Union outfits were equipped with copper-cartridge repeating rifles, but the men who received them were not entirely happy about it, for they soon discovered that they were regularly thrown into the hottest spots in a battle. These were the weapons that led the Rebs to complain that the Yanks had a gun they could load on Sunday and shoot all week. The shining bayonet issued to every recruit was used first and last for cleaning game, digging trenches, trimming fingernails, and whittling

whistles, but almost never in combat. By 1865 infantry firepower had been boosted by the general adoption of trench mortars and land mines, but the machine gun had been given only a trial run.

The knapsack, sewing kit, mess kit, and sundry other articles issued to a recruit were quietly dropped on the first field march. A veteran could be easily distinguished by the paucity of goods he carried: a huge slouch hat to keep out the sun and rain and use for bathing; his gun, ammunition, bayonet, tin cup, water bottle (the tin canteens were blown apart with a little powder and made into two nice light cook pans); the clothes on his back; and his blanket wrapped in a rubber poncho. The veteran thus had reduced his load from the 40 to 50 pounds he had been issued to a more reasonable 15 to 20 pounds.

Combat tactics during the Civil War underwent a greater change in four years than they had in the previous 400 years since European armies had adopted gunpowder. At the beginning of the war approved tactics called for long lines of troops to march into battle in formation and to march from place to place on the field in formation. The battle consisted of lining up 200 or 300 yards from the enemy line and firing away until his line or your line broke and ran. Artillery was used simply as an oversized shotgun. Cannon were loaded with grape, canister, solid balls, chains, rusty scrap iron, or anything else handy when the ammunition ran out, and were fired point-blank at the enemy infantry lines. Because of the flat trajectory and limited range of the artillery, the big guns were regularly posted in front of the defending infantry line. Since the infantry weapons outranged the artillery, life expectancy for a cannoneer was short.

As the war progressed, artillery weapons increased in size, and with the introduction of rifling, their range lengthened substantially. By the end of the war, artillery had a rather modern look about it, as explosive shells came into general use, and artillery was increasingly used in counter-battery fire, interdiction missions, and infantry support. By 1865 the only thing that had not changed on the battlefield was the use of black powder. It required both the infantryman and the cannoneer to follow every shot by a quick step to the side or ducking down to peer around the cloud of smoke his firing had created to see how his aim had been. Otherwise an 1865 battleground looked very like a modern field. The long lines of infantry and artillery had disappeared into the ground or behind natural cover. Small units had taken over much of the offensive work, and defense in depth had begun to appear. The cavalry had disappeared from the fire fight. Except for scouts or raiding missions in enemy rear areas, it was now used exclusively to give added mobility to men who fought as infantrymen when contact with the enemy had been established.

The Civil War saw the introduction of many minor improvements in the lot of the private soldier. His natural worry over wife and family was somewhat alleviated by special leaves and furloughs, unknown in earlier armies. A few northern states sought further to ease the burden for families whose sole support was in uniform by providing cash payments to supplement the money the soldier could send home out of his pay. Debt moratoriums for men in service were also provided for. The obvious inadequacies of the medical services at the outbreak of the war led to energetic private efforts to establish hospitals and recuperation centers for the wounded. The United States Sanitary Commission, which was deeply involved in this work, also performed many of the recreational functions of the modern special-services branches of our armed forces. Women appeared in considerable numbers in the field as

Union troops in the trenches before Petersburg, Virginia, near the end of the war. (National Archives)

nurses; by 1865 they were so completely accepted that women had found a new and challenging profession. Religious needs of the troops received some attention. At first, individual clergymen volunteered and frequently served alongside men from their own congregations at home. Before long, chaplains were being regularly assigned to the troops, and both the Union Army of Tennessee and Lee's Army of Northern Virginia were swept by great religious revivals.

The war was equally remarkable in the conduct of the troops. Around the fringes of the main theaters of war, in the areas where guerilla fighting was general, the fighting became brutal, with prisoners tortured and killed, civilians murdered and raped, and rather general pillaging. But in the areas of the major campaigns, including Sherman's operations in Georgia and South Carolina, civilian lives were safe, women were honored and protected, and even property was comparatively safe in cases where owners remained at home and asserted their rights. Ransoms were levied on cities during Lee's invasions of Maryland and Pennsylvania, but no widespread destruction of property took place. Even when civilians were caught in places like Gettysburg, Vicksburg, or Fredericksburg, there was almost no loss of life, for the civilians were given opportunities to move out before any bombardment began. By comparison with any other war of its size in modern history the Civil War was quite "civilized."

WAR POLITICS

Few governments in history have countenanced as much open criticism of their war efforts as did the Confederacy and the Union. One of Richmond's most prominent newspapers was a constant thorn in the side of the Davis government. Commanders on both sides found reading the enemy press a valuable source of intelligence information. Several northern newspapers were closed down because of their opposition to the war, but on the whole there was not much press censorship. In the North, the constant sniping of antiwar Democrats, popularly called Copperheads, plagued Lincoln. Opposition to the war in the Confederacy took the form of a states'-rights movement which found some state governors openly charging the Confederate government with establishing a tyranny exceeding anything the government at Washington had ever sought to impose in former days. Both the Davis and the Lincoln governments were the targets of constant criticism from various quarters. Both leaders had to exercise the utmost political skill.

The way Lincoln handled political problems was noteworthy. His early difficulties with Seward, and the firm yet tactful way in which the presidential authority was asserted, have already been described. But Lincoln's troubles had only begun. One wing of the Republican party constantly demanded a bolder policy toward prosecution of the war and especially toward emancipation of the slaves. But even after Lincoln issued his famous proclamation of September, 1862, opinion in the North remained deeply divided on the subject of freeing the slaves. Especially strong in the border areas was the conservative opinion that the object of the war was to preserve the Union "as it was," and that emancipation would be most unwise. Abolitionists argued that the sacrifices of war would be meaningless if nothing more substantial was achieved than turning the clock back to 1860. Furthermore, abolitionist sentiment increased with every passing month. Lincoln had to step warily, resisting the

premature demands of the radical abolitionists, lest public support for the war be
lost, yet moving in the direction of emancipation when the time was ripe. On one
notable occasion he faced a crisis in his
Cabinet between the conservatives led by
Seward and the radicals whose spokesman
was Secretary of the Treasury Chase. This
he surmounted by a typical piece of political legerdemain, securing the resignations
of each and holding them as a weapon
over the quarreling factions.

A decision on the great question of
emancipation was hastened by the problem
of the slaves who appeared at Union bases
in the South. The problem became acute
as Union lines advanced in 1862. Many
of these Negroes had simply been abandoned by their masters who fled with the
retreating Confederate troops. In a few
places the Union troops were met by
hordes of black folk who greeted the soldiers as liberators and who then followed
the army. Others wandered about the countryside searching for friends and relatives
sold "down river" under the operation of
the slave system. These Negroes, with
their hopes and dreams as well as their
need of food and shelter, were a concrete
problem rather than a theoretical political
question. They were soon a target for the
activities of several different sorts of people from the North: humanitarians who
wished to give the Negroes education and
guidance, speculators interested in making
a financial killing out of the abandoned
slaves and cotton lands, and devisers of
fraudulent schemes who were interested
only in relieving the hapless Negro of
whatever small bits of cash he might
possess. These elements were a constant
headache to many Union commanders in
the South. Some policy was obviously
needed, for further procrastination threatened to produce complete chaos.

The Second Confiscation Act of July,
1862, was an effort to establish some sort
of national policy toward the slaves and
meet the immediate problem. It provided
for the liberation of slaves abandoned by
rebels, or captured from them, as well as
those whose masters were convicted of
treason or rebellion. In his preliminary
emancipation proclamation of September,
Lincoln went beyond this only in announcing freedom for slaves beyond Union lines,
where Union authority actually could not
reach. The issuing of the proclamation was
in fact dictated by other factors, especially
public opinion at home and abroad.

Lincoln, who had never been an abolitionist, continued to be reluctant about
embracing that cause. But in addition to
public opinion in the North, there was the
important matter of European attitudes to
consider. In spite of the protests of our
Minister to Great Britain, Charles Francis
Adams (son of a President of the United
States), the formidable commerce raider
Alabama had been built in British shipyards and put out to sea to be handed over
to the Confederacy. It was soon to do great
damage to northern commerce at sea. This
action underscored the whole question of
European aid to the Confederacy. If the
Confederacy could secure enough ships,
arms, and money from abroad, as it
counted on doing with the aid of "King
Cotton," the course of the war might be
changed. Confederate representatives in
England and France played with some
success on the need for cotton and upon
upper-class fears of too much democracy.
They pictured the war as one between a
democratic mob and a conservative republic. Lee's victories and the gradual depletion of British cotton reserves made the
prospects of Confederate diplomacy look
good in 1862. Emancipation fitted into this
picture of diplomacy for high stakes. Pub-

lic opinion in England was strongly anti-slavery, and if the war were proclaimed clearly as one for the removal of slavery, then the North would receive a great deal more sympathy there and the British government would hesitate to grant recognition and further aid to the Confederacy. Here was a powerful reason reinforcing the pressure to issue a statement on emancipation of the slaves.

The preliminary proclamation was issued on September 22, 1862, announcing that, except within specified areas behind Union lines where slaveholders were presumed loyal, slaves would be forever free in all states still in rebellion on the first of January, 1863. The final proclamation was issued on the latter date. President Lincoln himself had doubts about the constitutionality of this act, and continued to hope for a plan of compensated emancipation. In making a plea for such a scheme to Congress he declared that "We, even *we here,* hold the power and bear the responsibility. In *giving* freedom to the *slave* we *assure* freedom to the *free*—honorable alike in what we give and what we preserve. We shall nobly save or meanly lose the last, best hope of earth." Slavery did not legally end in the states of the Confederacy until December, 1865, when the Thirteenth Amendment to the Constitution was ratified. Despite the misgivings of many about emancipation, and the original statement of war aims as not involving slavery, the war had irresistibly encompassed the doom of slavery in the United States.

While such crucial decisions of war policy had to be decided by Congress and the President, there was another aspect of politics almost equally significant during the war. This concerned the enacting into law of the Republican party platform. During the 1860 campaign, the Republi-cans, it will be recalled, had played down the slavery issue and talked about an economic program which included a protective tariff, internal improvements, a transcontinental railroad, and a homestead law. This program offered something to every important economic group, the manufacturers as well as the farmers. The departure of southern representatives from Congress following secession gave the party a unique opportunity for enacting its program into law. First to be passed was the Morrill Tariff Act. Though not a high protective tariff, it marked an appreciable increase over the 1860 level of about 20 per cent to about 47 per cent at the close of the war. These increases were defended on the ground of need for war revenue and were accompanied by assurances that the high duties would be abandoned when the national emergency was over. This was not to happen, however. The protective tariff on manufactures, so long and bitterly resisted by the agrarian South, became an accepted feature of American policy, reflecting the victory of manufacturing interests.

The long-coveted Homestead Bill became law in May of 1862. It provided that 160 acres of unoccupied land would be granted to anyone who would actually settle the land and work it for five years, paying only a nominal fee. By the end of the war, 2,563,000 acres had been settled, providing some 20,000 new farms to strengthen the Union. Ever-increasing quantities of land were to be settled in the postwar years in spite of corruption in the administration of the act. By another significant land act, the Morrill Land Grant Act, federal land was given to the states in order to provide an income for establishing the now famous "land-grant colleges," thus giving a much-needed stimulus to higher education in the years after the war.

The secession of the South also paved the way for a decision on the route of the transcontinental railway, long the object of competition between North and South. The Republican majority quickly decided on a route from Omaha to San Francisco, to run through the thin strip of settlement in Nebraska, Utah, and Nevada. Lavish land grants and a government loan of 50 million dollars in federal bonds were to back the enterprise. The Union Pacific was chartered to build westward from Omaha, while the Central Pacific was to build eastward from Sacramento. These and other companies formed at this time were not able to lay much track until after the war was over, but they were to take full advantage of the generous subsidies immediately thereafter.

Major banking legislation was also passed during the period of Republican hegemony in the federal government. In 1863 Congress approved a national banking system proposed by Lincoln's Secretary of the Treasury, Salmon P. Chase. The new banking system was advocated as a means of assisting the government in its attempts to borrow money for the war effort, as a means of stabilizing the currency, and as a means of providing the additional credit needed for the wartime expansion of the economy. Since the death of the second Bank of the United States, the country had possessed no adequate circulating medium. The bullion supply was being constantly drained off to pay our debts to Europe. The only paper money was the note issue of hundreds of local banks which fluctuated radically and circulated at discounts that increased proportionately with the distance from the bank of issue. The war stimulated the need for a circulating medium as well as the government's need for revenue. Congress sought to provide both with the creation of the United States Notes, or "greenbacks." The first of the legal-tender acts provided for the issue of 150 million dollars in greenbacks, and subsequent acts in 1862, 1863, and 1864 increased the greenback limit to 450 million dollars. The constant increase in the number of greenbacks brought about radical fluctuations in their value. In 1864, after Grant's repulse at Cold Harbor and Early's raid on Washington, the greenback was worth only about 35 cents on the dollar. The average value was about 66 cents, as greenbacks usually wandered between 46 and 74 cents on the dollar. The national banks which were chartered under the 1863 law were allowed to issue up to a total of 300 million dollars in bank notes against the security of government bonds owned by these banks and deposited with the United States Treasury. The operations of the entire system were under the supervision of the Comptroller of the Currency. Rigid requirements for note redemption and reserve funds gave the national bank notes a remarkable stability, and the system provided an enlarged market for government securities as well as additional credit for the expanding economy. Several major defects showed up in the system almost immediately, but it served the needs of the dominant groups in the business and banking community well enough so that it was not replaced until the Federal Reserve Act was passed in 1913.

THE COLLAPSE OF THE CONFEDERACY

The Civil War legislation of the Republican party, thus, was truly remarkable in its scope and permanence. It helped sustain a flourishing wartime economy and lay the foundations for a great industrial boom afterward. In Lincoln the North had found, if almost by accident and unexpectedly, a leader of increasingly great stature, combining the qualities of political shrewdness and genuine depth of soul. Problems existed, nevertheless, and could not be entirely exorcised even by Lincoln. In 1864 Lincoln's Republican party did not feel strong enough to reelect the war president, but formed a coalition Union party, nominating a Union Democrat, Andrew Johnson of Tennessee, as vice presidential candidate with Lincoln. The sickening losses and failure to bring the war to an end made for a serious decline of public confidence. Nominating the deposed General McClellan, the Democrats boldly called for an immediate peace. Atlanta fell in time to save Lincoln, but only a few weeks before the election his defeat seemed quite possible. Then within a few months, the Confederacy collapsed and the long war was over.

The end of the Confederacy came from a variety of causes. The failure of Lee to stop Grant after the Wilderness and above Richmond made it clear that Virginia would soon be knocked out of the war by superior military force. The ease with which Sherman moved through Georgia and South Carolina made it equally clear that the will to resist had been broken in those key states. The blockade had become increasingly efficient as the Union navy grew, and additional southern ports were captured and converted to bases for the blockading fleet. In 1861 about 90 per cent of the vessels attempting to run the blockade were successful. That percentage had been reduced each year until, in the last year of the war, only about 50 per cent were successful. It is estimated that over 8,000 successful trips through the blockade were made, but that figure must be balanced against the fact that these trips were made by small fast vessels

whose cargo capacity was extremely limited and that many of them brought in wines, laces, and other luxuries instead of the medicines and munitions so vitally needed by the South. No improvement appeared possible after 1863, for all real hope of European intervention or aid died in that year. Thus, by 1865, the Confederacy was being systematically strangled, and her armies were falling back everywhere. At this critical juncture the Confederacy began to come apart at the seams.

Disaffection and desertion in the Confederacy increased substantially during the latter portion of 1864. In January, 1865, the Confederacy counted 445,000 men in service, but the number who remained to surrender in April was something like 200,000. Over half the Confederate armies apparently evaporated in three months, which explains why those who remained "to stack arms at Appomattox" were so long remembered and honored in the South. The men who deserted the Confederate service during the final months of the war did so for a number of reasons. Most were worried about conditions at home. Reports of food shortages and other hardships pulled many a loyal Confederate out of his place in the ranks. Dissatisfaction with Confederate leadership made many more lose hope. Tax laws which discriminated against the farmer, and other laws which favored the larger planters, gave substance to the bitter observation that it was a "rich man's war and poor man's fight." The failure of the Confederate government to establish and maintain a stable currency had been both a cause and a result of a lack of popular faith in the government. In January, 1865, Confederate officials reported large quantities of food available in southern Virginia and in North Carolina, but the farmers would sell only for gold or for

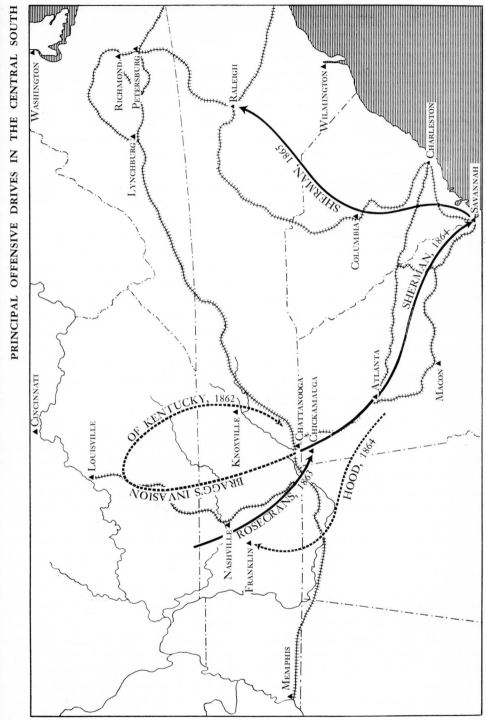

Union money. It appears that there was no over-all shortage of food or forage in the Confederacy at any time, but the breakdown in transportation can be traced to excessive wartime use, lack of repair facilities, and a marked lack of cooperation between the Confederate states and the Richmond government.

All through the story of the collapse of the Confederacy runs the thread of states' rights and resistance to a central government, which raises a fundamental problem of democratic society. On the eighty-fifth anniversary of the Declaration of Independence, Lincoln sent his war message to Congress. Lincoln's message contained a brilliant analysis of this problem.

And this issue embraces more than the fate of these United States. It presents to the whole family of man, the question whether a democracy—a government of the people, by the same people—can, or cannot maintain its territorial integrity, against all its domestic foes—it presents the question, whether discontented individuals, too few in numbers, to control administration, according to organic law, . . . [can] break up their Government, and thus practically put an end to free government upon the earth. It forces us to ask: "Is there, in all republics, this inherent, and fatal weakness? Must a government, of necessity, be too *strong* for the liberties of its own people, or too *weak* to maintain its own existence?"

The collapse of the Confederacy and the victory of the federal government partially answered Lincoln's questions.

FURTHER READINGS

General surveys of the Civil War include the very thoughtful interpretation of Carl R. Fish, *The American Civil War* (1937); the sprightly yet perceptive *Conflict: The American Civil War* (1941), by George F. Milton; and the textbook treatment by James G. Randall under the title of *The Civil War and Reconstruction* (1937). Perhaps the best single book ever published on the war is Stephen Vincent Benét, *John Brown's Body* (1927).

Northern politics and politicians have attracted a host of able students. Among the best are Burton J. Hendrick, *Lincoln's War Cabinet* (1946); William B. Hesseltine, *Lincoln and the War Governors* (1948); T. Harry Williams, *Lincoln and the Radicals* (1941); Allan Nevins, *The Statesmanship of the Civil War* (1953); David Donald, *Lincoln Reconsidered* (1956); and Richard N. Current, *The Lincoln Nobody Knows* (1958).

The two great biographies of Lincoln are Carl Sandburg, *Abraham Lincoln: The War Years* (4 vols., 1936–1939), and James G. Randall, *Lincoln: The President* (4 vols., 1945–1955). The best one-volume life of Lincoln is Benjamin Thomas, *Abraham Lincoln: A Biography* (1953).

Southern politics and politicians have been getting increasing attention. There is still no satisfactory biography of Jefferson Davis, but he can be seen at work in Rembert W. Patrick, *Jefferson Davis and His Cabinet* (1944), and Burton J. Hendrick, *Statesmen of the Lost Cause* (1939). General works on the Confederacy include Clement Eaton, *A History of the Southern Confederacy* (1954); Clifford Dowdey, *The Land They Fought For* (1955); and R. S. Henry, *The Story of the Confederacy* (1931).

The military story has been widely explored. There is nothing to surpass Douglas Southall Freeman's classic biography *Robert E. Lee* (4 vols., 1934–1935), and his study *Lee's Lieutenants* (3 vols., 1943–1944) has become a model. On the Union side, Kenneth P. Williams attempted a similar extended study of the problem of command with Ulysses S. Grant as his focus in *Lincoln Finds a General* (5 vols., 1949–1959), but death prevented the completion of his study.

More readable is Bruce Catton's trilogy on the Army of the Potomac, which appeared under the titles *Mr. Lincoln's Army* (1951), *Glory Road* (1952), and *A Stillness at Appomattox* (1953).

The life of the man in the ranks is treated in two books by Bell I. Wiley, *The Life of Johnny Reb* (1943) and *The Life of Billy Yank* (1952).

SIXTEEN

Reconstruction and the New South

1865

Death of President Lincoln, April 15.
Andrew Johnson becomes President.
Congress refuses seats to southern
representatives.
Thirteenth Amendment abolishes slavery.
"Black Codes" passed in southern states.

1866

Congress and President Johnson quarrel.
Ku Klux Klan organized.
Radicals win congressional elections.

1867

Tenure of Office Act passed over veto.
Reconstruction Acts passed over veto.

1868

Johnson impeached and tried.
Fourteenth Amendment becomes
effective.
Grant elected President.

1869

Fifteenth Amendment sent to states.

1872

Freedmen's Bureau discontinued.
Grant reelected over Greeley.

1876

Disputed Hayes-Tilden election.

1877

Last Union troops leave South.

THE DEFEATED SOUTH

THE DEFEAT OF THE SOUTH brought inevitable tragedy and readjustment in its wake. Most defeated powers suffer as a consequence of war. It was natural that the conquered region would cling to its old system as much as possible, thus antagonizing its conquerors; it would, for instance, try to hold the Negro in continued subservience despite the verdict of the war which had "freed" him. The industrial-urban North, meanwhile, under the guidance of the Republican party would certainly oppose a resurgence of the Democratic party, whose main roots had been in the agrarian South. The average Republican politician would struggle to maintain his advantage, the Democratic or southern politician would attempt to regain political power, and both parties would employ fine phrases to justify their actions. And the people of both regions would harbor feelings of bitterness and hate as the aftermath of so bloody a war.

In the long run, there was one important factor which would tend to bring about a *rapprochement* between northerners and southerners: the South of its own volition began to accept the economic system of its erstwhile enemy, the superiority of which had been proved in four years of fighting. A "New South" of sprawling railroads, country merchants, absentee corporations, textile villages, tobacco towns, smoky cities, and the tenant-farm system slowly developed. While the

338

overwhelming majority of people in the traditionally rural South continued to farm or live in small towns, the idea of industry and "progress" became a shining grail to many. In the long run, the industrial revolution in the South was to prove more important than the military and political phases of Reconstruction. Even before the last Union troops had departed (in 1877), political control of the old Confederacy had shifted from the planter agrarian group to new, dynamic business overlords.

The Civil War has been characterized as a second American Revolution, in which the capitalists and the plain people of the North and West broke the power of the plantation aristocracy of the South. This was in part the result of physical destruction visited on the South by the war, which was considerable despite the relative humanity with which the war had been fought. Where General Sherman's army had marched from Atlanta eastward through Georgia to the sea, the countryside was dotted with torn-up rails and burned-out houses and barns. The Shenandoah Valley had been systematically devastated, and large areas in the Tennessee Valley were badly shattered. Guerrilla bands—the backwash of war—raided and plundered indiscriminately. Important towns like Charleston, Richmond, Columbia, and Atlanta were all or partly in ruins. Since railroads had been military objectives of high priority, they were badly damaged, but many had been partially rebuilt in order to supply the advancing Union armies, and the federal government was eager to turn these captured and rebuilt properties back to their southern owners. Such manufacturing establishments as had existed in the erstwhile Confederacy were largely destroyed. Not a single bank or insurance company was

solvent. For those who had money there was little to buy.

But the backbone of the South had been agriculture, and it sprang back with surprising rapidity. In spite of the dislocation of the agricultural labor force caused by the emancipation of the slaves, and in spite of the lack of capital, the land remained fruitful, and production figures indicated that in one crop after another southern agriculture soon regained prewar positions.

The political and social system was more seriously damaged. As the war ended, Jefferson Davis was apprehended and put in jail, and other military and political leaders fled the country or made themselves as inconspicuous as possible. Schools and churches closed in many places. The old ruling class faced ruin; slave property, in which a little over half of southern capital had been invested, was wiped out, and of course investments in Confederate bonds and money were lost. With land values a fraction of what they had been, there was little hope of economic salvation from that quarter. George Fitzhugh, the proslavery philosopher of the Old South, lived in a shanty among his former slaves. Such instances as these were hardly typical, but they do reveal the breakdown of the old southern aristocracy. The new leaders of business or agriculture rose more frequently from the middle class than from the old planter group. The chief social revolution wrought by the Civil War was, however, the freeing of 4 million slaves, who, whether of the ignorant mass or the literate few, were aware of the "day of jubilee" and hoped to begin a climb toward genuine citizenship and equal rights.

The freedman was the central figure in the social cauldron of the postwar South. How would he fare at the hands of northern conquerors, the broken southern aris-

A photograph of Richmond
at the close of the war

Cartoon (by Thomas Nast)
of Negro voting, 1867

Admission of first
colored lawyer before the
Supreme Court

enator Charles Sumner of Mass.

Rep. Thaddeus Stevens of Pa.

War damage in the defeated South was small by standards of later wars, as the picture of the shelled Confederate capital indicates. Reconstruction was primarily a social, political, and moral process. How could the freed Negroes be fitted into the social system of the South? And how could national unity be restored between North and South? Stevens and Sumner, leaders of the northern Republican Radicals, asked for continued Federal control over the South to protect the freed men and bring about basic social changes. Largely adopted in 1867, this program aroused deep resentment in the white South and was completely abandoned by 1877. The Negro was then pushed back down. The Civil War had brought him nominal freedom, but he would have to wait many more years for full civil and political equality. For him the years of Reconstruction were years of illusory hope.

The Ku Klux Klan
pays a visit

tocracy, and the white middle class? Calhoun had warned that if the Negro were freed from individual masters he would become the slave of society, and this was not far from the truth. While some northerners were genuinely interested in securing rights for the Negroes, the truth is that most of them were indifferent. Evidence of this may be seen in the fact that at the close of the war, many northern states themselves denied Negroes the vote. If relatively few northerners were basically concerned about civil and political rights for the freedmen, those southerners who were willing to see the Negro advance along these roads were even fewer in number. To the present day it remains one of the South's frightful dilemmas that most kindness and sympathy toward the Negroes is to be found among the upper class, rather than among the masses of people. Tolerance is most common among those who can afford it. In the defeated, impoverished South of the immediate postwar years, it was a rare virtue.

There was a continuing class struggle in the South. More than two-thirds of the whites had been nonslaveholders, sturdy farmers for the most part, envious of the power concentrated in the hands of great slaveowners. Many of them, as for example in upcountry North Carolina, had hated the planter and his slaves of the "black belt." The postwar struggle often resolved itself into white counties against black-belt counties where the planters and their black labor force raised cotton or other staples. Poor whites and Negroes hated or distrusted each other more than they did the aristocrats. The prejudices of race crossed and complicated those of class. The Negro was frequently a pawn in a conflict in which aristocrats were willing to help him while using him, and in which poorer whites wished to overpower both

the master and his black laborer, with whom they competed. Into this picture the motivations of northern policymakers intruded to make it yet more complex. It may also be said of northern policy that on occasion it *too* used the Negro as a pawn for preventing the political resurgence of the South and the Democratic party.

To enable the Negro to become a full-fledged citizen in the immediate postwar years would have required patient and careful planning for his education and economic rehabilitation. This the leading politicians, North and South, were unwilling or unable to do. Some southern leaders, Governor J. L. Alcorn of Mississippi among them, could understand the necessity to "vote with the Negro, discuss politics with him, sit, if need be, in council with him." But such cooperation was indicative of a practical approach to the political problems of the white South rather than a recognition of the freedmen's critical condition. Before the end of his career Alcorn lost the support of the Negroes in his state.

In searching for the causes of the failure to plan for the Negro it is necessary to look beyond the personalities and ideas of individual leaders. At least two prevailing attitudes of the times have bearing. First, the Reconstruction era was one of opportunism and *laissez faire* in business. Planning, social or economic, was not regarded as a proper or useful function of government. Second, the accepted theories concerning race did not accord the Negro a place in society equal to that of the white man. The old theoretical basis upon which slavery had rested before the war accounted in large measure for the Negro's subordinate position after he had secured his legal freedom. Even the former abolitionists acceded to these racial views. Senator Charles Sumner stood almost alone among the pre war abolitionists to combat these views during the Reconstruction period.

THE VICTORS AND THEIR PLANS

That a new power dominated the central government at Washington was clear from the legislation of the war years. No sooner were the low-tariff southerners out of the union than business interests of the North obtained tariff increases previously impossible, and the trend of rates was steadily upward after the war. The National Banking Acts of 1863 and 1864 were also attractive and lucrative to northern capitalists. Financing the northern war debt provided immense profits to investors. The Contract Labor Law of 1864 permitted the recruiting abroad of cheap immigrant labor. Subsidies to business were granted, notably the huge land grants and loans to railroads. But the Republican party of the North could not be so foolish as to reward its business friends and wholly neglect the tillers of the soil; these were rewarded not only by the railroad policy, which was approved in the earlier years by pioneering farmers of the trans-Mississippi area, but also by the Homestead Act of 1862 and the Morrill Land Grant Act. The latter granted 30,000 acres of the public lands to each state for each representative and senator, to be used for the support of agricultural and mechanical colleges.

The power of the Republican party rested, then, on its sympathetic concern for the interests of northern farmers and especially northern capitalists; it also lived on its reputation as the architect of victory and on the identification of the opposition party with the rebels. "Waving the bloody shirt" came to be a familiar Republican campaign device. Hard-pressed Republican candidates could always revive memories of the Civil War, expose the wounds made by Democratic rebels, and urge their audiences to "vote as you fought"—vote for the party of Union—vote Republican. For decades northern Democrats were at a disadvantage because of this political demagoguery employed against them. The developing reconstruction program of the Republican party was a strange mixture of idealism and materialism. This program was to be motivated by the fact that, despite their successes, the Republicans faced the possibility of defeat if the South was not Republicanized and if many disgruntled and doubting people in the North were not won over. Western farmers, for example, often disliked the laws passed for the benefit of banks and capitalists. A Democratic South restored to the union might easily combine with northern Democrats to regain control of national affairs. To most Republicans, for reasons both good and bad, such a result was a thing to be avoided at any cost and by the use of almost any means. And so ultimately they came to think that only through the Negro vote could the feared restoration of Democratic rule be averted.

Abraham Lincoln represented the early idealism and the wisest leadership of the Republican party. In beginning the program of reconstruction he showed himself to be practical as well as charitable and humane. He had entered the war to save the union, and he continued to think chiefly of binding up the nation's wounds, of saving and preserving the union. He was not primarily interested in preserving merely the Republican party or the interests of its creditor and big-business friends. As he saw it, southerners must be welcomed back into the union whenever they were ready to support it, even though possibly they might be able again to control it. On the Negro question he counseled moderation. Three days before his death he expressed a wish that the very intelligent Negroes and those who had served in the Union army be given the suffrage. Lincoln had, as a practical matter, to deal with the question of reconstruction almost from the day the war began. In Louisiana, Arkansas, Virginia, and Tennessee, which Union forces controlled early, temporary provisions for rehabilitation and for government were necessary. The President's permanent plan, calling for reconstruction under presidential supervision, was offered in a proclamation of December 8, 1863. All Confederates except high-ranking leaders were to be pardoned on taking an oath of allegiance to the United States; and as soon as one-tenth of the number of voters of 1860 took such an oath, each Confederate state might start the process of reconstructing its government. As Lincoln saw it, this loyal nucleus would organize a state government, show its good faith by abolishing slavery and taking right actions toward the Negroes, and soon command the support of both its own people and those of the North. In announcing this program he tried not to offend Congress. Each house of the Congress, he pointed out, must determine the qualifications of its members, including those to be elected by the newly re-created states; and moreover, he said, while this plan was the best that occurred to him, it was not necessarily the only satisfactory one.

Even Lincoln's caution and tact did not suffice to prevent severe attacks on his plan. The Radical* wing of the Republican party was deeply suspicious of the charitable treatment of rebels. The Wade-

* The Radicals derived their name from their attitude on the Negro and southern policy solely; on other questions they were usually conservative.

Davis bill, offered in Congress as a substitute plan, proposed a harsher mode of reconstruction, according to which Congress would supervise the organization of the new state governments. This plan insisted upon a majority, rather than just 10 per cent, declaring their allegiance to the union. Moreover, actual participation in the new governments would be denied to those who had borne arms against the union, and Negro rights would be carefully safeguarded. When Lincoln blocked this bill with a pocket veto, enraged Radical leaders bitterly attacked him in a manifesto which declared that it was the President's function to obey and execute the laws, not to make them. Thus began an epic struggle between President and Congress which lasted all through Reconstruction and reached its bitter peak under Lincoln's successor in office, Andrew Johnson. The American system of divided powers always makes for a certain rivalry between President and Congress, but never before or since has it reached such a stage of hostility as it was to reach in 1867. For the time being, in 1864, a stalemate existed: the Radicals could not have their way, but on the other hand when congressmen elected under Lincoln's plan in Louisiana and Arkansas arrived in the capital, they were denied their seats.

The reasons for congressional resistance to Lincoln's plan were numerous. There was, of course, the pride and honor of the Congress at stake; at all times senators and representatives are jealous of their prerogatives and determined to guard against executive usurpation, and inasmuch as during the war Lincoln had been compelled to exercise many extraordinary powers, they were particularly jealous at this time. Many people also could not rise to Lincoln's exalted magnanimity, above the hatred engendered by a bloody war; they wanted a tougher policy for vindictive reasons. Another important factor was the motive mentioned earlier, that of protecting the Republican party and its legislative program against a return to power of the Democratic party. Yet some of the Radical opponents of Lincoln were sincere idealists, interested in the cause of Negro rights and in breaking down caste barriers; they feared, with much justification, that a South left to reconstruct itself under the old leadership would not make a democratic society or give the ex-slave his rights as a citizen. Whatever their exact motives, these Republicans who took issue with their President made up a formidable group.

Inevitably the question arises whether Lincoln, had he not been hit by an assassin's bullet, could have prevailed against the extremists. Could he, by using his rare qualities of shrewdness, diplomacy, and good humor, have carried the country with him for a policy of moderation and thus have prevented the excesses of Radical Reconstruction which were to follow? About the best answer that can be provided is that his chances were, for a number of reasons, far more promising than those of his successor, Andrew Johnson of Tennessee.

JOHNSON AND THE RADICALS

By a strange and unfortunate turn of events it was a southern Democrat who engaged the Radicals in the critical struggle over the nature of reconstruction. Andrew Johnson had been a senator from Tennessee in 1861 but had refused to go with his state when it decided to secede. He had remained in the Senate until 1862, when he had been appointed military governor of Tennessee. In 1864 the Republicans, looking for a likely man to run with

President Andrew Johnson of Tennessee.
(Library of Congress)

Lincoln on a "Union" ticket, selected Johnson as vice-presidential candidate, and thus in April, 1865, he acceded to the presidency and was confronted with the major problem of reconstructing his own native South. In many respects Johnson was an admirable figure, a splendid example of the vigorous commoner of the South who often rose to positions of power. An ex-tailor, he had educated himself and had risen swiftly in politics, becoming Governor of Tennessee and then Senator before obtaining the highest position in the land. Johnson was a product of the agrarian way and the class struggle in the South; a Jacksonian democrat, believing in real democracy for white people, he was suspicious of bankers and corporations, and hostile toward the plantation aristocrats, whom he blamed for guiding the South down a ruinous path. As a hill-country Tennessean, he had fought the slaveowners for control of his own state. Following the war, he wished to punish this class by refusing to pardon, except through special action, all Confederates worth $20,000 or more. But toward the Negroes Johnson's attitude was that of the plain whites, whose interests he stood for; at best he was willing to give the vote to only a few of the ablest ex-slaves. A key to Johnson's actions in the White House was a consistent and burning belief in states' rights and strict adherence to the Constitution, a product of his Jeffersonian heritage. The war having ended, he believed in bringing to a halt the extraordinary powers of the central government; but the Radicals felt that the times were still extraordinary and that extensive federal powers would be needed to reconstruct the South. Johnson's southern and Democratic background, his states'-rights philosophy, and his blunt, often tactless manner were to be obstacles in the way of workable relations with the Radical leaders in Congress. Honest and forthright, Johnson notably lacked Lincoln's skill in diplomatic dealing with difficult people.

The new President wasted little time in inaugurating a reconstruction program which in broad outline was Lincoln's plan, generous toward the South and under presidential direction. It was to his advantage, or so he thought, that Congress had recessed and would not meet again until December, 1865. Knowing its mood, Johnson chose not to call it into special session. He had eight months in which he hoped to accomplish the reconstruction of the southern states, and in December he would be able to present Congress with an accomplished fact. His plan was in one respect more lenient than Lincoln's; it was unnecessary for even 10 per cent or any specified number of the citizens of a state

to be loyal. This was to be left to the discretion of provisional governors appointed by the President. Loyal citizens were to elect delegates to a state constitutional convention. This convention must meet certain conditions: it must declare invalid the secession ordinances, repudiate the debt acquired in rebellion, and accept the Thirteenth Amendment freeing the slaves. Thereafter elections would be held and reconstruction would be finished—except for one possibility. Congress might refuse admittance to the representatives and senators arriving from southern states. So it came about. By December all southern states except Texas were reconstructed, in Johnson's opinion. But Congress refused to approve.

The trend of public opinion in the North favored the Radicals during the summer and fall of 1865. A hostile reaction toward Johnson's plan gathered strength. Some charged that the southerners had not accepted defeat, that they were still rebellious, and that therefore the Johnson program was too fast and too easy. Others at least wondered if this might not be so. Unfortunately, some actions of the Johnson state governments played into the hands of their enemies. Suffrage was denied to all Negroes, in spite of Lincoln's and Johnson's recommendation that some of the intelligent and educated receive it. Worse than this, "Black Codes" were passed, severely restricting the rights of freedmen. In some respects these laws were defensible; they were intended to clarify the status of the Negroes and regulate the employment and movements of these 4 million largely illiterate and backward people. Most of the codes conferred on the Negro such privileges as the right to own property (with some restrictions), to make contracts, and to sue and be sued in the courts. In some states the codes were quite mild. But in others a number of provisions smacked of peonage, or semi-slavery. In Mississippi, for example, Negroes could not carry firearms, nor own property except in incorporated towns, nor assemble together "unlawfully," nor break a contract for labor. There was a system by which Negro children allegedly unprovided for, and Negro adults unable to pay fines for minor offenses, could be bound out to the service of white masters; in fact, the Mississippi legislature went so far as to reenact a large part of the old slave code, merely providing for appropriate changes in the manner of trial and punishment. It was not the aristocrats of Mississippi who were responsible for these severe measures. We now know that the legislature represented and expressed "the feelings of the small farmers and the poor whites of the hills, a group now thoroughly aroused and beginning the advance that was to give them control of the state after 1890."*

But in the North no distinction of this sort was made. "We tell the white men of Mississippi," snarled the *Chicago Tribune,* 'that the men of the North will convert the state of Mississippi into a frog pond before they will allow any such laws to disgrace one foot of soil in which the bones of our soldiers sleep and over which the flag of freedom waves." When Congress convened, the Radicals lost no time in capitalizing upon the trend of events. First, rebuffing Johnson, they refused to admit southern representation to either house of Congress. Next, arguing that more information was necessary, they called for an investigation to map the course of reconstruction. The result was the Joint Committee on Reconstruction, made up of nine

representatives and six senators. The body was under the control of Radicals, whose real purpose was to destroy Johnson's program and substitute in its place military control of the South for the purpose of a long period of drastic reconstruction under control of a Radical Congress. As the months passed, this body became an effective sounding board for Radical doctrine. Dominating it was the ablest of the Radicals, grim Thaddeus Stevens of Pennsylvania, bearing in his soul a relentless hatred for the southern slave system.

The developing struggle between Johnson and the Radicals has led one historian to designate 1866, appropriately, as "the critical year." This was the year in which the Johnson program might have prevailed, but instead was lost forever in the congressional elections. The odds were with the Radicals from the start. Already they controlled Congress and much of the patronage. Organizing, spreading propaganda, bringing pressure to bear on wavering members of Congress, they succeeded in one skirmish after another and finally won the battle. When Johnson vetoed a bill to continue the Freedmen's Bureau,† they mustered the necessary two-thirds vote to pass it over his veto. Then they pressed through the Civil Rights Bill, aimed at protecting the freedmen against discriminatory actions by individuals or states. Again Johnson vetoed the bill but saw it passed over his veto, as he entered into an immoderate battle of invective with congressional leaders. The crowning achieve-

---

* Vernon L. Wharton, *The Negro in Mississippi, 1865–1890,* The University of North Carolina Press, Chapel Hill, N. C., 1947, p. 90.

† The Freedmen's Bureau was established to administer relief and resettle some ex-slaves on abandoned or confiscated lands. It did notable work with a most difficult problem, but it was increasingly suspected by white southerners of being a tool of political propaganda. Johnson opposed it on states'-rights grounds, seeing in it a dangerous extension of federal power over the states.

ment of this phase of the battle was the Fourteenth Amendment, which elevated the civil-rights principle and made it part of the Constitution. It was passed by Congress and sent to the states for ratification in June, 1866, Johnson again vainly protesting. This was a most significant amendment; its influence was later to reach far beyond what its framers dreamed, and it became in the 1880s a bulwark of property rights, not human rights. At the time, however, it was a burning issue in the battle over reconstruction and in the elections of 1866. It contained several sections. Section 1 defined citizens so as to remove all doubt that Negroes were now citizens. Most important were the provisions aimed at denying the power of states to deprive any person of "life, liberty, or property, without due process of law" or "the equal protection of the laws," or to "abridge the privileges or immunities of citizens of the United States." In section 2, Negro suffrage, while not required, was encouraged by a provision, never to be enforced, which declared that states depriving citizens of the vote shall have their representation in Congress reduced proportionately. Section 3 contained the most bitter pill of all for the South to swallow. It deprived the great body of southern leaders of the right to hold federal or state offices, which disability could be removed only by a vote of two-thirds of each house of Congress. This would bar the most able men of the defeated Confederacy from taking part in the difficult task of reconstruction. Finally, the Fourteenth Amendment made payment of the federal war debt and repudiation of the Confederate debt a part of the Constitution, a provision intended to quiet the fears of northern creditors about what the Democrats might do if they got back into power. Here, then, was a good deal of security against the future and a measure

of protection for the Republicans' friends in the South. It appears to have been agreed that if the southern states accepted this amendment there would be no further requirements. Led by President Johnson, however, all the states of the former Confederacy except Tennessee defiantly rejected it and so further hardened the hearts of Radicals against them and determined them to pursue an even more drastic policy.

The campaign of 1866 was highly emotional. The Radicals frantically waved the bloody shirt and employed every possible device to defeat Johnson. They had on their side the financial and industrial interests and the powerful conservative press, for while these interests might care little for Negro rights as such, they mistrusted the agrarian ideas of Johnson and his friends. Johnson was subjected to severe abuse; he was falsely accused of being a drunkard, for example. Yet the President, who undertook a famous "swing around the circle" speaking tour, was often his own worst enemy, for when subjected to heckling and abuse on this tour he lost his temper and spoke in a manner which even his friends admitted was inconsistent with the dignity of the presidency. Unfortunate also for Johnson and for the cause of moderation was an outbreak of race riots in the South, which shocked northern opinion and gave plausibility to Radical claims that no governments worth the name existed in the rebel states and that there was no security for friends of the Union there. All this contributed to a decisive victory for the Radicals. The way was cleared for a thoroughgoing program of Radical Reconstruction.

Johnson's leadership during the "critical year" was not what it might have been. His tactlessness and indiscretion have been noted. He failed to mobilize moderate opinion behind him. In the elections of

866 the northern voter was far too often onfronted with a choice between a Radical Republican and a doubtfully loyal, prosouthern Democrat. On some occasions ohnson compromised, as in keeping the Radical Edwin Stanton as Secretary of War. But where he might well have compromised and might thereby have shaken he Radical cause, as by accepting the Freedmen's Bureau Bill or urging a limited Negro vote in the South, he was uncompromisingly stubborn. On the whole, his demand for the restoration of normal constitutional government at a time when conditions were still abnormal does not appear to have been realistic. While the Radicals were too vengeful and too extreme, Johnson in his own way was prejudiced and unyielding. The sad state into which affairs fell here provides an example of how our system of divided powers demands the utmost in wisdom and tact on both sides.

CONGRESSIONAL RECONSTRUCTION

If Congress and the President are often at war under our system, 1866–1868 certainly marked the greatest victory Congress has ever won over its rival. Under Radical leadership, Congress moved boldly ahead in 1867 and 1868 to jettison the Johnson state governments and to create its own. The theory was that no republican institutions existed in the South, except for Tennessee where local Radicals had gained the ascendancy and secured ratification of the Fourteenth Amendment. Therefore military force was necessary. Five military districts were created, each under a major general, and military authority was to be supreme until new republican governments, in which Negroes could vote and hold office, were functioning. The states could escape military control only after black and eligible white citizens elected delegates to a constitutional convention which drew up a satisfactory constitution, and after the legislature chosen under the new constitution accepted the Fourteenth Amendment. Reconstruction governments of this sort were created in seven states by 1868 and in the remaining four by 1870. The Reconstruction Acts of 1867 which authorized this program were denounced by President Johnson as unconstitutional, which they plainly were; yet they went into effect. For a time the Radicals were invincible. Congress was under their control, and Thaddeus Stevens was not far from being the real ruler of the country; a sort of "congressional dictatorship" prevailed.

Even the Supreme Court was partly cowed into acquiescence by the congressional offensive. In 1866 the Court ruled that use of martial law in Indiana during the Civil War had been illegal (*ex parte Milligan*); but in the McCardle case of 1868, involving the suspension of habeas corpus rights in Mississippi, the Court sidestepped the issue and refused to invalidate the Reconstruction Acts, bowing instead to a new law passed by Congress denying Supreme Court jurisdiction. In *Texas v. White* (1868), the Court risked criticism of the Radical regime by declaring that the union was indestructible and that the action of secession was "absolutely null," but its decision did not deter Congress from continuing to treat the former Confederate states as "conquered provinces."

President Johnson was, of course, the special target of Congress under Radical domination. His power was fundamentally circumscribed by the presence in Congress of a two-thirds majority against him. With this voting strength the party passed such

This is the committee of Republican congressmen who managed the impeachment of President Andrew Johnson. Chairman Thaddeus Stevens sits second from left. (National Archives)

unprecedented acts as the Command of the Army Act, which denied the President his constitutional powers as Commander-in-Chief and lodged control over the army in the hands of General Ulysses S. Grant, who was working with the Radicals. Congress also passed, in 1867, the Tenure of Office Act, according to which Cabinet members, among others, could be removed only with the consent of the Senate. There was a question, however, whether this law applied to the appointees of Lincoln. When Johnson at last decided to remove the Radical Edwin Stanton, a holdover from the Lincoln government, as Secretary of War, the Radicals were prepared to use this "violation" of the Tenure of Office Act as grounds for impeachment. On the basis of this and a number of other trumped-up charges, Johnson was brought to trial before the Senate in the spring of 1868, Chief Justice Salmon P. Chase presiding. For the first and thus far only time in American history, Congress had impeached a President. Despite the dubious nature of the charges brought against Johnson, there was a very good chance that he might be convicted by the necessary two-thirds vote of the Senate and removed from his office. (In this case the Radical Benjamin Wade, Speaker pro tempore of the Senate, would have taken his place.) But despite intense pressure from the more fanatical party leaders, the case against Johnson was so flimsy that some Republicans refused to vote for conviction and he escaped by a single vote the 35-to-19 vote for conviction just missing the required two-thirds. The Radicals argued that the proceedings were political not judicial, but Chief Justice Chase enforced judicial proceedings. Johnson's lawyers demolished the accusations against him, and seven Republicans refused to vote him guilty.

In general, the dramatically close failure to convict the President marked the beginning of the ebb of Radical domination. Nevertheless, the election of 1868 gave the Radicals virtual control of the presidency, for General Grant, who was elected, was compliant to the wishes of the party bosses. Popular though he was with the people as the military hero of the recent war, Grant won only a small majority over his rival Democratic nominee, the able governor of New York, Horatio Seymour. It appeared that without the Negro vote the Republicans would not be able to stay in power. This ominous fact led its leaders on to the Fifteenth Amendment, attempting to guarantee Negro suffrage, and to other measures designed to perpetuate Republican control of the South. But the end result of "Black Reconstruction" was to be failure. The effort to build stable governments in the South on the basis of the Negro vote was destined to failure.

In the last analysis, these governments always rested on the force provided by the presence of federal troops; but such a policy could prevail only if the force were continued indefinitely. The experiment of Black Reconstruction was a "desperate venture." The vote was given to about a million freedmen, of whom 75 per cent or more could not read or write. Meanwhile, almost 200,000 whites were barred from political privileges, while others boycotted the elections. The chance, Radicals argued, had to be taken; a slave-minded regime in the South had forced such action by refusing to give former slaves access to land, education, or physical freedom. The effort to elevate the Negro and establish in the South a democratic society with rights for all regardless of color was one which enlisted the efforts of sincere idealists. But the experiment eventually foundered on the hostility of the white population. The masses of Negro voters had to be directed mainly by northern "Carpetbaggers," an additional affront to the embittered white southerners. The extent of Carpetbag control is indicated by the fact that in the seven states reconstructed by 1868, four governors, twenty representatives in Congress, and ten senators were Carpetbaggers, that is, northerners who came to the South after the war. Negroes, while supplying most of the votes, usually received only the minor offices, although some went higher.

Much misgovernment and corruption existed, the result in part of the fact that inexperienced Negro voters had legislative majorities in five states of the lower South. In South Carolina, a particularly flagrant example, the state debt rose in ten years from about 7 million dollars to 29 million. Legislators engaged in an orgy of using state money for personal use; business privileges and favorable court decisions were openly bought and sold. More or less systematic looting of the treasury occurred in some other states, such as Louisiana. There is no doubting the considerable corruption of these years, yet some extenuating circumstances should be pointed out. First, southerners of high position shared in the responsibility for the corruption by being quite willing to accept the profits of corruption, as in fraudulent issues of railroad bonds. Second, political corruption was becoming rampant all over the United States in this era, not just in the Carpetbag South. The new capitalism was tending to corrupt politicians as a general pattern, and the South was hardly worse than the North in this respect. Coupled with this as an extenuating circumstance was the devastation of the South and the consequent need for extraordinary expenditures to rebuild a war-torn country. Certainly many of the Carpetbaggers were able and honest. Governors D. H. Chamberlain of South Carolina and Adelbert Ames of Mississippi, for example, each had an honorable though controversial career. Many of the Carpetbaggers were men with a mission, particularly teachers and preachers who came hoping to uplift the South. And a number of able, educated Negro leaders emerged also.

A fundamental weakness in the Radical program was the concentration on political reforms and the failure to include economic ones, such as providing the freedmen with land and economic security. Only a few Republicans, including Thaddeus Stevens, seriously advocated such a program; most Reconstruction "Radicals"

Senator Hiram R. Revels, Negro Senator from Mississippi, 1870–1871. (Library of Congress)

were economic conservatives, disinclined to experiment with land reform. The problem was not lack of land, for millions of acres of public land existed in the South, and other land could have been bought cheaply and turned over to the Negroes under some federal guidance. In the perspective of time it is obvious that many Negroes would have succeeded with this land, though many would have failed, and that the whole country would have benefited. Impoverished, ignorant, diseased Negroes were no blessing to the South or to the nation. In the last analysis, the failure to solve this economic problem was perhaps the greatest blight on the whole experiment of Reconstruction. If the Radicals seriously hoped to make the Negro a self-reliant citizen, they would have had somehow to raise him in the economic scale from the level of dependent laborer, and also to raise the white South with him. But in the atmosphere of the times, at least, this was impossible. And so, as one Carpetbagger later put it, the experiment was a hopeless effort to build "bricks without straw."

THE COLLAPSE OF BLACK RECONSTRUCTION

Thus, almost from the start, Radical Reconstruction began to break down. The resistance of whites in the South, factional struggle within the Radical regimes, and growing doubts in the North itself about the program meant inevitably the collapse of the policy of force. As early as 1871 the native whites had regained control in North Carolina, Georgia, Virginia, and Tennessee; the same had occurred in Alabama, Texas, and Arkansas by 1874, and in Florida, South Carolina, and Louisiana in 1877. These dates show that Radical Reconstruction was a brief, if turbulent, interlude in the majority of states. The return to power of southern whites was easily accomplished in such states as North Carolina, where conservative whites were clearly in the majority. They simply voted the Radicals out of office. Since few whites in any state were disfranchised, this was the easiest method. Another southern weapon of great notoriety was the secret terroristic societies, such as the Ku Klux Klan or the Knights of the White Camelia. Their aim was to frighten the Negroes away from the polls. To combat this the Grant administration obtained special legislation in 1870 and 1871 which virtually crushed these organizations; nevertheless, in one form or another the practice of terror continued. An outstanding study of the Negro in Mississippi notes the fascinating way in which Negro organizers arose from the anonymity of slavery but also the frequency with which these men met death at the hands of white opponents. The motives for intimidating or assaulting Negroes were not always the same; a strong tendency in the cotton belt was to keep Negroes on the land, if necessary by coercion, while in the area of small farms a common motive was economic competition between whites and blacks. There was a "three-cornered battle" among planters, Negroes, and poor whites. In any event, it meant repression of the Negro and the failure of Radical plans.

In 1870 the Republicans lost their two-thirds majority in the House. Two years later a strong Liberal Republican movement developed, embodying a protest against Radical Reconstruction policies, among other things. Among the leaders of the Liberal Republican movement were men who had been ardent antislavery advocates before the war. Some had been founders of the Republican party back in the 1850s. Now for the first time they voted against the regular Republican ticket and sought to defeat it with Democratic aid. This was really not strange. Some of these men had been Democrats before the war and opposed Republican economic policies. Others found the corruption of the Grant regime intolerable and had made a futile effort before breaking with the party to reform it from within. No longer in good standing in the Republican ranks, they now sought votes in the white South for the Liberal Republican movement in return for amnesty. This Liberal Republican movement was an important indication of a disunity within the Radical faction, which was probably never as unified as it appeared to be. This helps to account for the ultimate failure of the Radical program in the South.

The Liberal Republicans combined with the Democrats to support Horace Greeley, famed editor of the powerful *New York Tribune,* for the presidency. Grant easily defeated Greeley, but the trend of events and opinion called for concessions. The Amnesty Act of 1872 restored political privileges to all but a handful of Confederates. In the same year the Freedmen's Bureau, which had lent support to Negroes, ceased its functions. These actions tended to weaken the Negroes and Carpetbaggers and to strengthen southern whites. By 1876 the only states remaining under Negro-carpetbag rule were South Carolina, Florida, and Louisiana. It remained for the national election of 1876 to bring to a close the "desperate venture" of Black Reconstruction. It also meant the abandoning of the Negro to his fate, while the masters of capital, North and South, ascended to greater power.

The Republican nomination in 1876 went to Rutherford B. Hayes, Governor of Ohio. Governor Samuel J. Tilden of New York received the Democratic nomination. The Democrats were committed to a termination of Reconstruction; both candidates were conservative on economic questions. As the first returns came in, it appeared that Tilden had won the election. But the Republicans surveyed the vote of four states, in which there were disputes, and took heart. Three of these states were those where Carpetbag governments and Union troops might give them victory—Florida, South Carolina, and Louisiana. Although the Democrats claimed victory in these states, Republican-controlled election boards disputed the claim. On both sides intimidation and corruption were rampant, and as the uncertainty continued for many months, some saw the threat looming of another civil war. Democrats seemed in no mood to be cheated out of their long-awaited victory. The Constitution provides no remedy for conflicting sets of election returns; Congress therefore provided for a special electoral commission which originally was intended to consist of seven Republicans, seven Democrats, and one independent. As it turned out, the independent withdrew and there were eight Republicans. Eminent though these men were—there were five senators, five representatives, and five Supreme Court justices—they voted the straight party line. Every contested state was given to Hayes, and therefore, by a margin of one electoral vote, he gained the majority. Democrats cried "fraud," yet they accepted the fraudulent count and submitted quietly.

The reasons for this singular behavior lay in negotiations which went on behind the scenes—negotiations which brought about a compromise between the capitalists of the Republican party and capitalists in the South from the old Whig and Democratic parties. Because of the failure of the military occupation to establish a Republican party in the South, Hayes hoped to create more solid foundations

for his party there. The troops were withdrawn, and Hayes appointed a southerner to the Post Office Department, with virtually a free hand to dispense patronage among old Confederates. Hayes also cooperated with the southerners in their need for capital, for aid to railroads and appropriations for improving rivers and harbors. The dollar bill was to ease the way to reunion. An era of some concern for human rights was terminated in what was essentially an economic deal, the chief beneficiaries of which were cotton planters, railroad barons, lawyers, employers of convict labor, and the like. But it is obvious that by 1877 Radical Reconstruction was a failure and the Republicans were ready to take any easy road out of it.

The compromise of 1876–1877 between southern and northern conservatives that brought about the election of Rutherford B. Hayes and the end of the process of political reconstruction was not the result of a sudden deal to relieve the South of the burden of northern occupation. Rather it was the culmination of developments that had been taking shape throughout the Reconstruction period. Soon after the war southern advocates of a New South, modeled on the industrial North, had shown their willingness to cooperate with Radicals and Carpetbaggers. To be sure, resistance movements in the South had their effect in the failure of Radical rule. But the fact of resistance should not obscure the amount of cooperation that existed throughout the era. Long before the Civil War, John C. Calhoun had recommended the cooperation of southern planter capitalists with northern industrial capitalists in order to preserve the social and economic stability of the nation. Considering the plight of the wage earner in the North and of the sharecropper in the South after the war, it appears that Calhoun's views were not so fantastic as they might have seemed to his contemporaries.

The Reconstruction era had come to its end, leaving behind a long-lived legacy of hate and violence. Any evaluation of this turbulent decade after 1865, ought, as scholars increasingly realize, to be placed in a broader perspective; to understand Reconstruction it is helpful to survey a longer period of time than just the Radical decade and also to look at the South in comparison with the rest of the nation. These years may, indeed, be considered as embracing a twofold revolution—the first toward political democracy, the second toward industrialization and urbanization. Before the war, the South was moving toward a fuller democracy—a democracy in which, however, the Negroes did not participate. Nonslaveholders had begun to make efforts to diminish planter power by taxing the slaves and by prohibiting the counting of slaves as a basis of representation in the state legislature. This democratic movement was carried on in some ways by the Radical program: taxation on a more equitable basis, governmental reorganization, establishment of decent public school systems, poor relief, and other humanitarian measures. Perhaps suffrage changes should also be included, even though these were carried out through military force. Contrary to a common belief, large numbers of whites continued to vote during these years. Thus, in the balloting of 1867, while 200,000 whites were disfranchised, those who did vote numbered almost 700,000, only slightly less than the total of 1860. Obviously many whites had voted who had not done so before. Out of the turmoil of Reconstruction the white masses emerged with some gains.

Yet an important result of Reconstruction was the one-party system in the South. For a time it seemed possible that a permanent two-party system might develop. After all, in the Old South there had been two parties, Whigs and Democrats, who fought bitterly on almost even terms; and following a difficult period of cooperation in the Confederacy, they resumed their partisanship. That the Whigs, whose views on economic questions were almost identical with those of the Republicans, should join the latter party was not an impossibility. The rivalry of classes among the planter-aristocratic group, the small-farmer democracy, and the new industrialists pointed to a natural dual- or multiple-party system. But the shadow of race fell across the picture to blur it; the Negro was the block. As a slave he had been ignored by the white men, who could freely air their differences; but as a free man he was a threat to white supremacy, compelling the whites to form a solid front. As reconstruction went on, with northern men and northern organizations backed by Union troops being employed to guarantee Republican victories through the Negro vote, former Democrats and former Whigs —white men of all sorts—joined together in a party of resistance. President Hayes's efforts to implant the Republican party in the South by a policy of conciliation and national aid for internal improvements came to naught despite two trips to the South in 1877 to further this end. Fear of the Negro acted as a cement compelling solidarity among whites of otherwise conflicting views. The "Solid South" emerged after 1876, its one-party system hardly a healthy situation for the growth of democracy and the solution of social problems in a democratic way.

THE NEW SOUTH

Joseph E. Brown of Georgia provides an example of one who "lived through it" and held high offices successively under the Confederacy, under the rule of the

Radicals, and in the era after the Carpet-baggers left. Such occurrences were not uncommon. Yet, in the main, a new class of leaders arose out of Reconstruction. They are variously called Bourbons, New-departure Democrats, Redeemers, or merely Conservatives. In any event, they represented a new business viewpoint. They regarded themselves as the saviors, or redeemers, of the South from Carpet-baggery. Originating mostly in the old middle class, they were pushing types who sought to rise in society. Though professedly believers in *laissez faire,* they controlled the state governments to their own advantage; tax exemptions, special franchises, "giveaways" of state property, and similar favors to business interests were common. At the same time, they demanded retrenchment to save money and reduce taxes, and under their control public schools and other services suffered severely. Corruption was not uncommon. There were shocking cases of embezzle-ment and scandal in many southern states after 1876; the worst was in Louisiana, where the state treasurer systematically de-frauded the state of about a million dollars before absconding to Honduras. Despite their sins, the Redeemers stayed in power, virtually unchallenged, for many years. The reasons are not hard to find. Allied with northern capital, they were dynamic leaders in a movement for industrialization and diversification of the economy. Few could resist the arguments for industriali-zation, as picturesquely put forth in such stories as that of the "Pickens County Funeral," often told by Henry Grady of the Atlanta *Constitution.* It was the story of a southerner whose tombstone came from Vermont and his pine coffin from Cincinnati, with nails from Pittsburgh:

> The South didn't furnish a thing on earth for that funeral but the corpse and the

hole in the ground! . . . They buried him in a New York coat and a Boston pair of shoes and a pair of breeches from Chicago and a shirt from Cincinnati, leav-ing him nothing to carry into the next world with him to remind him of the country in which he had lived, and for which he had fought for four years, but the chill of blood in his veins and the marrow in his bones.

The story illustrates another talent of the Redeemers. While engaging in a cam-paign to copy the industry of the North and to make southerners into yankeelike shopkeepers and corporation directors, they also appealed to the hallowed mem-ories of the Old South and the brave boys of the Confederacy. Impoverished gen-erals lent their names to business enter-prises; though Lee refused to do this, oth-ers such as P. G. T. Beauregard, Jubal Early, and John B. Gordon endorsed a variety of schemes—some of them rather dubious. Politically the Redeemers or-ganized tight machines prepared to main-tain their power by a variety of means. They used the Negro much as the Carpet-baggers had formerly used him, mobilizing his vote on occasion against the small farmers and poor whites of the hills and mountains, though they posed as leaders of white supremacy. Many of the Re-deemer group were sufficiently wealthy and secure to show some friendship for the ex-slaves. But it was practical politics rather than friendship for the freedmen which led them to support Negro suffrage. Consequently, opposition to the rule of the Redeemers among the poorer farmers included opposition to the Negro vote. Such opposition appeared in a small way during the 1870s and 1880s, the era of Granger-Greenback agitation in the North as well. The second and major phase of the anti-Redeemer movement occurred in the late 1880s and early 1890s, merging with the great Populist movement of the northern West. Southern farmers were desperate enough to join the Populists of the West in organizing a third party in 1892.

Behind this discontent lay the sad plight of farmers in the postwar era. Tenant farming arose as a natural result of labor problems following the war. Capital was short. Also, Negroes naturally detested working in gangs, because it reminded them of the days of slavery. Therefore, in order to utilize their land capital, landowners organized their property into tenant holdings. By this means land and labor were made productive in spite of the shortage of money capital. At the top of the "tenancy ladder" were some who simply paid rent, owning their own equipment; at the bottom were sharecroppers who offered nothing but their labor, turned over perhaps half their crop to the owners, and were at worst in a status of peonage. The crop-lien system was closely associated with tenancy in that farmers too poor to pay cash for food and supplies were forced to obtain these necessities by mortgaging their as yet ungrown crop. From top to bottom, pressure was exerted to grow the money crops, such as cotton or tobacco, so that the cropper could pay the merchant landowner, the merchant could pay the local bank, and (very likely) the latter could pay a northern lending institution. The pressure of debt and tradition and the lack of sufficient money capital kept the South at this gloomy routine, a form of debt slavery to many farmers, both white and black. Hookworm, pellagra, malaria, the lack of medical attention, and the lack of a friendly government contributed to their sorrows. Slowly the small farmers organized themselves to fight Redeemer governments which had little sympathy

for their troubles but represented the interests of landowners and merchants.

It was a tragic fact that white democracy seemed irreconcilable with Negro democracy. Some of the early Populist leaders advocated biracial cooperation of all the underprivileged against the upper classes. But those who tried this were beaten by the control which the latter exercised over the Negroes. The party of "white supremacy" marched the Negroes to the polls and defeated the spokesmen of the poorer whites. In North Carolina during the Populist years, it is true, a coalition of Republicans, rebels from the Democratic ranks, and Negroes joined to oust the Redeemers. But by 1900, these same Redeemers, waving the flag of white supremacy, had swept back to power. And so the independents and Populists reached the conclusion that they must expel the Negro from politics; they must render it impossible for the Redeemers to control his vote; they must eliminate the fraud an violence that had resulted from the rivalry for Negro votes. In many cases the white factions got together to do the job, both Redeemers and lower classes expecting to benefit from the operation in one way or another. From 1890 on, the southern states, Mississippi being the first, began to deprive Negroes of the vote. This was done in a variety of ways, including the poll tax, literacy tests, and the "understanding" clause, based on ability to read and interpret the state constitution. It was understood that registrars would approve any white man's interpretation of the constitution but would reject that of even a highly educated Negro. Still another part of the disfranchising machinery was the white primary. Only whites could participate in the Democratic primary, which was ordinarily tantamount to election. By such stratagems the Negro vote was reduced almost to nil. At the same time many whites, who could not pay the poll tax or meet other requirements, were also barred from voting. But in some states illiterate and propertyless whites were rescued from this disfranchisement by the famous "grandfather" clause, which allowed anyone to vote who had an ancestor who had voted before the day of Negro suffrage.

The era of farmer revolt against the Bourbons or Redeemers thus brought reaction as well as progress to the South. The average white man had gained some power, but at the expense of the Negro. "Jim Crow" laws became common. Race baiting flourished. Demagogues rose to political power, commonly champions both of white supremacy and economic reforms to benefit the poor whites—the red-necks, crackers, and hillbillies. In the Progressive era of Bryan, Theodore Roosevelt, and Wilson, which came to America around the turn of the century, the South experienced a progressive trend along with the rest of the country, and yet this liberal spirit did little to benefit the Negro, who in some ways was worse off than ever before.

The hope of the future obviously lay in economic progress which would break up the old patterns and raise the living standards of black and white alike. By 1900 industrial patterns were established which did not become significantly altered until the New Deal and World War II. There was an unhealthy concentration in a few industries: textiles, tobacco, iron and steel, furniture, cottonseed oil, lumbering, and mining. Even within the leading industry, textiles, there was too much concentration on cheap cloth rather than on the finer products that yielded large profits. A characteristic of southern industrialism was paternalism, perhaps more accurately called a form of feudalism. The mill-village authority resembled the plantation,

with owners dispensing justice or punishment to their workers in accordance with a southern tendency to believe that the kindness of a superior to an inferior is preferable to democratic relationships. Labor unions gained few converts in such an atmosphere; profits were satisfactory, but wages were low. Another characteristic was northern investment and control; southern railroads and steel mills fell under the control of the great New York banking concerns whose influence was expanding so enormously over the whole nation in this period. The interests of the South suffered in consequence; though the South needed capital, the increasing migration southward of northern capital was not an undiluted blessing.

Yet the rise of industry and the city brought much that was beneficial. Slow as was the South's industrial progress, it produced some significant alterations in the old agrarian way of life. In the twentieth century, and especially following World War II, enormous strides in business brought diversified economic life and promised for the first time to ease the tensions that poverty had produced in southern society. It was noteworthy that in 1948 about 700,000 southern Negroes were able to vote, roughly the same number as had voted in 1867. It is true that federal pressure had hastened the day, operating through the Supreme Court and through the fair-employment policies of the New Deal. But, hopefully, much of the change was internal. Although there still remained those traditionalists who declared that all this threatened the South with the loss of its uniqueness, its very soul, for the first time since the grim days of Reconstruction, the possibility of Negroes and whites working harmoniously together in the building of a truly New South seemed to exist.

FURTHER READINGS

For a general coverage of the Reconstruction period see Allan Nevins, *The Emergence of Modern America, 1865–1878* (1927); James G. Randall, *The Civil War and Reconstruction* (1937); Walter L. Fleming, *The Sequel of Appomattox* (1919); and Francis B. Simkins, *The South Old and New* (1947). Claude Bowers, *The Tragic Era* (1919), and G. F. Milton, *The Age of Hate* (1930), are marked by strong partisanship; so, in another direction, is W. E. B. Dubois, *Black Reconstruction* (1935), which brilliantly represents the Negro viewpoint. E. M. Coulter, *The South during Reconstruction, 1865–1877* (1947), is a recent scholarly treatment by an outstanding southern historian, while William A. Dunning, *Reconstruction, Political and Economic, 1865–1877* (1907), is an older study by one of the great pioneers of historical research in this area. H. K. Beale, *The Critical Year, 1866* (1930) is standard.

More specialized studies include C. Vann Woodward, *Reunion and Reaction* (1951), an authoritative examination of the disputed election of 1876; Vernon L. Wharton, *The Negro in Mississippi, 1865–1890* (1947); Joseph B. James, *The Framing of the Fourteenth Amendment* (1956); and George R. Bentley, *A History of the Freedmen's Bureau* (1955). Among biographies, Richard N. Current, *Old Thad Stevens* (1942), is worth special mention.

Two interesting analyses of southern attitudes as shaped in part by Reconstruction experiences are W. J. Cash, *The Mind of the South* (1941), and Henry Savage, Jr., *Seeds of Time: A Background of Southern Thinking* (1959). Woodward has surveyed the post-Reconstruction epoch in *Origins of the New South, 1877–1913* (1951). A distinguished Negro historian has written the sometimes tragic history of his own people in John Hope Franklin, *From Slavery to Freedom* (1947), and another, Rayford W. Logan, has written *The Negro in American Life and Thought: The Nadir, 1877–1901* (1954).

Industry, Finance, Capitalism, and Labor

THE UNDERLYING FACTORS IN INDUSTRIAL GROWTH

1859
First oil well, at Titusville, Pennsylvania.

1861
Morrill Tariff passed.

1862–1864
Land grants made to railways.

1863–1864
National Banking Act passed.
First Bessemer steel plant in United States.

1869
Transcontinental railroad completed.

1873
Depression begins.

1877
Great railroad strikes.

1878
Knights of Labor organized.

1879
Standard Oil trust formed.
Henry George's Progress and Poverty *published.*

1886
American Federation of Labor organized.
Fourteenth Amendment used to protect corporations.
Strikes and riots in Chicago.

1890
Sherman Antitrust Act passed.

1892
Mesabi iron-ore range begins operation.

1895
Electricity used for factory power.

THE CENTRAL THEME of postwar America was the industrial development of the nation. Industrialization, which had made steady progress during the 1850s, had been given a tremendous impetus by the war, and this impetus continued into the postwar period. By 1900, America was the foremost industrial nation of the world. The predominantly agricultural nation of the prewar epoch was transformed beyond belief; an urban, industrial land took its place. Between 1850 and 1910 the value of manufactured products increased thirty-nine times, and the number of wageworkers became seven times as great. Such startling increases made this period indeed one of an American "industrial revolution."

The great industrial region which carried the United States to the first place among the nations of the world in industrial production lay in the northeast corner of the country. A line drawn on the map from Chicago to St. Louis and thence east to Baltimore would roughly define its limits. This small region, 1,000 miles long and from 300 to 500 miles wide, contained well over one-half of the country's population and more than three-fourths of its wealth. It was the industrialized hub around which the rest of the country was ranged as satellite feeder regions—the "heartland" of a great industrial country. The wealth of this heartland ruled and

358

levied tribute upon the rest. Containing within itself coal, iron, and other minerals, timber, and some of the nation's best agricultural land, this region is mainly a great plain whose low mountains at the eastern end presented no insuperable obstacle to transportation. This magnificent area was further endowed at its eastern border with the splendid ports of New York, Philadelphia, and Baltimore, which were natural outlets to the markets of Europe. For the period under consideration, this heartland was America; the rest was important only in its relation to the heartland and in its promise for the future when the relative importance of this region should have waned.

The policies of the federal government —high tariff, the Homestead Act, unrestrained immigration, the National Banking Act of 1863—laid the legislative foundations for this rapid industrial growth. Governmental influence upon economic life was pervasive. Favorable immigration laws supplied hands and markets; the Homestead Act assisted the development of the West, which provided a wealth of cheap resources. Federal and state governments subsidized railroad builders with a lavish hand. A friendly government prevented the enactment of laws harmful to business, and federal courts interpreted existing laws in the same spirit.

There were other factors favorable to industrial growth. These factors may be classified as resources, markets, and social conditions. Little need be said about resources other than that they were available in abundance and at relatively little cost. The further fact that the bulk of the raw materials used during this period were compactly grouped in or near the industrial heartland has already been noted. Pennsylvania contains iron, coking coal, and limestone for iron and steel produc-

tion. When the unrivaled iron deposits of the Mesabi Range in Minnesota were opened up, a center for iron products was established on the southern shores of the Great Lakes, connected with the Mesabi by cheap water transport. Coal was plentiful almost everywhere in the Middle West. Immense stands of virgin timber were located in Maine, Michigan, Minnesota, and Wisconsin on the edge of the heartland. Most products of agriculture, save cotton and cattle, were produced within the region in great abundance. Most of the copper used prior to 1885, and half of that used up to 1900, came from Michigan's Lake Superior shores. Of the lesser metals, supplies were found in or near the region at the beginning of the period; later, supplies had to be brought in from farther west.

The cost of these materials was low because they were located within easy water or rail haul to the place of manufacture and because the land in which they were located cost practically nothing. The bulk of the raw materials was in undeveloped lands, much of which belonged to the federal or state governments. These governments, anxious to promote business, disposed of their holdings for a song. Often, under the Homestead Act, valuable mineral-bearing or timber lands were fraudulently obtained. As a result, capital during this period was not burdened with heavy initial outlay for its raw materials.

This industrial region also had a vast and growing market for its goods. The South remained an essentially agrarian region, very slowly turning to industrialization, and had to import almost all its needs except food. To the west and southwest, the rapidly expanding frontier provided an ever greater market. The Far West and Pacific Coast were added to the market of the heartland by construction of

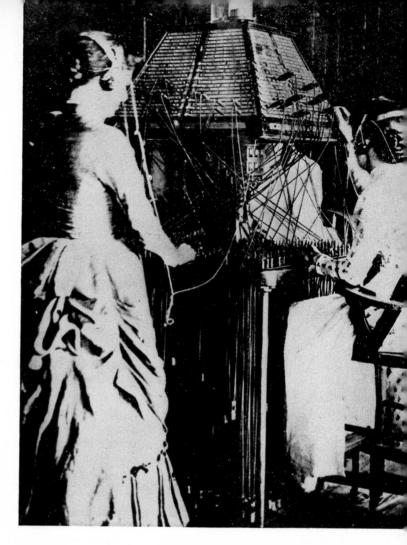

An early
telephone switchboard

Dormitory cars for railroad construction workers in the 1880s

John D. Rockefeller

The first oil well, Titusville, Pa.

Economic changes came with bewildering speed to America after the Civil War. New industries, industrial booms and busts, industrial empire-builders, and the emergence of an industrial working class— these were features of an age dominated by industrialism. Industrialism meant a growth in national wealth, but it also brought a host of social, economic, and political problems, most of them connected with the vast power of men like Rockefeller and the contrasting distress of the workers.

First Labor Day parade, 1882

a transcontinental railroad at the beginning of the period of expansion (1869). Other railroads quickly followed. The population of the country during these years, by natural increase and immigration, expanded rapidly and steadily. The factor of demand, sometimes overlooked, is really crucial to an understanding of the unique economic development of the United States. The capitalist system is the most flexible organization of economic life ever devised by man; it responds with sensitive and selective accuracy to the presence of a demand for goods. When the demand is steady and strong, miracles of production at once appear to meet it. Enterprise, capital, and technology rush in to harvest the golden crop. Steadily increasing demand has been the real key to the success of the capitalist system.

A further stimulus was the relatively high standard of living which had always been maintained in the United States. The farms, the mines, the railroads, the factories were clamoring for workers; and wages, by European standards, were good. There never was any tendency in the United States to develop the subsistence kind of life so common in Europe. Despite the efforts of employers to keep wages low, many workers had money to buy the products of industry; and farmers, too, often sunk in hard times though they were, bought much more than their contemporaries in other lands. The mechanization of farming, begun in a large way during the Civil War, continued all through the later nineteenth century. The need for farm machinery created a continuing market for manufacturing; agriculture in general was in a depressed condition during all this period, but the more efficient farmers enjoyed a reasonable living standard, and all farmers needed machinery to compete in the fight to reduce costs.

The great age of railroad building securely bound the customers of the hinterland to the industrialized heartland. Goods were transported everywhere, rapidly and cheaply. Manufactured goods moved south and west, while raw materials flowed east into the maw of the machine and from the port of New York to the outside world. The availability and cohesiveness of this market brought about by railways, and the consequent smooth flow of goods in all directions, greatly increased the value of the market itself. The enormous expanse of our country was overcome by rapid communications. A factory located anywhere had the whole economy at its disposal. This vast market gave American producers important advantages over Europeans, who were almost forced by the limits of their own small lands to seek markets in the outside world. This is not to say that the existence of foreign markets was unimportant to the industrial development of the United States. Europe provided America with markets for wheat, cotton, and other agricultural surpluses. These products were paid for, not in a return of goods, but in money. This capital, plus the stored-up profits of European industrialization, poured into the American economy. It was used to build railroads, dig mines, fell timber, and provide a fillip to industrial development in general.

Another important cause for the rapid industrialization of the United States was the social organization of the country itself. Our ancestors had bestowed upon us a form of government without many of the barriers to change which existed in older lands. Furthermore, the dead weight of the past in the form of guilds, of traditional patterns of work, of an aristocratic disdain for manual labor, of antiquated marketing procedures, of attachment to the land —all these features of an older manner of life, while perhaps not completely absent, pressed very lightly upon Americans. Traditionalism presented no real obstacle to rapid change. Americans took it for granted that a man should rise, should change his type of work and his social status. Nor were there any legal bars to the development of capitalism. After the eclipse of the supporters of agrarianism in the Civil War, there was not even a widely accepted body of ideas to hamper industrial growth. A free, rich land full of hardy, self-reliant men and women, who had never been trained in servility, who did not "know their place" but sought to find it somewhere higher up—this was the American heritage that made industrialization rapid and easy. It was the free, fluid, and open society, inherited from our democratic past, that provided the foundation for economic greatness.

Fortunately, this wholesome and vigorous but rather crude and unformed society received guidance and intellectual stimulus from the Old World. From the older, more intellectually advanced countries of Europe flowed the fruits of scholarship and learning. The basic scientific knowledge upon which the industrial system rests was not elaborated in America, nor could it have been. The discoveries in mathematics, chemistry, and physics which made American inventions possible came from Europe, where scholarship and learning held an honored position and where wealth and leisure for research existed. This fund of knowledge lay ready to our hands, offered by the freemasonry of the scholarly mind. Americans drew upon it heavily. It was to be a long time before, in the process of cross-fertilization of ideas, the United States would begin to repay Europe and to pull its weight in research and scholarship. The world was interdependent in the nineteenth century, and

Americans were then largely the recipients of the benefits of this interdependence.

From Europe also flowed the workers who made the factory system possible in the United States. Thirty-five million immigrants came to our shores during the eighty years after 1850. These people—English, Scotch, Irish, Germans, Poles, Italians, Scandinavians, Austrians, Hungarians, Russians—provided the hands and backs with which our industrial society was built. As older American stocks moved westward, or upward in the economic scale, their places were taken by new Americans from Europe. An early example of this was found in New England, where the factory system first evolved, at a time when the exhaustion of its soil and the competition of the West made farming a losing game. Thousands of older Americans, during the twenty years after the opening of the Erie Canal, deserted their homes. In families, in groups, whole villages sometimes, they migrated to the agricultural Middle West. Their places were taken by the Irish who, because of their lack of capital, were forced into the dreary and ill-paid routine of the early factory system. The Irish were followed by other peoples who in turn took up the burden, providing the cheap, plentiful labor which industrialism needed and which it could not easily have found in sufficient abundance among the older American stocks. Without these once-despised foreigners, industrialism in America would have been greatly hampered.

Almost all the forces operating in American society were favorable to the development of industrialism. The results were staggering. Mechanization (successfully applied to farming, also) produced goods in such abundance that the primary problem of the future would become that of getting rid of them. The factory altered

GROWTH OF MANUFACTURING IN THE UNITED STATES COMPARED TO THAT IN GERMANY AND GREAT BRITAIN

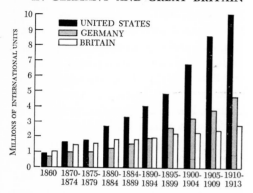

Though Britain, the original leader, continued to increase her manufacturing and Germany made extraordinary progress, by the turn of the century the United States had outstripped both of the other two industrial leaders put together. (After Colin Clark, The Conditions of Economic Progress, *Macmillan & Co., Ltd, London, 1957)*

the way of life of millions. It brought them from the farm and huddled them together in tenements and slums. It introduced millions to new ways of earning a living which demanded greater intelligence and more education. Changes were so rapid and so profound that other institutions, political and social, could scarcely keep up.

The impact of industrialism upon pre-existing institutions was greater because industrialization came in the form of big business. From 1850 to around 1880, industrial growth worked through small and medium-sized competing businesses, usually operated by a single individual or a partnership. The period of rapid consolidation began in the 1880s, and soon the whole structure changed. In all the main lines of production small businesses tended to disappear or be eclipsed, and the characteristic industrial form became the

large corporation, which was able to command larger quantities of capital than previous forms. Competition among a large number of small producers disappeared over large areas of the economy. These huge businesses, which became the basic economic organization of our times, dominated their fields. They were not merely small businesses growing big—not merely the substitution of millions for thousands—but an entirely new system, a system wholly unforeseen by the early philosophers and economists of capitalism.

A study of the way in which industrialism developed, the problems it had to solve, and the manner in which it solved them is fundamental to any understanding of the American economic system. The railroad industry provides an outstanding example of the new capitalism.

THE RAILROADS

Developed in England in the 1820s and 1830s, the railroad was transplanted to this side of the ocean almost at once. The Railway Age in the United States really began in the 1850s, when the primary roads in the heartland were built. By 1861 over 30,000 miles of road had been constructed, but the great age of the iron horse in America was only beginning. There were at that time scarcely any integrated lines. There were hundreds of small roads which had yet to learn not to compete. These roads did not even fit together. There were many different gauges; standard gauge (4 feet, 8½ inches) had not been generally accepted. Rolling stock was not interchangeable, and short hauls and frequent reloading were the rule. The distance between those days and the present has been bridged by thousands of inventions, by standardized equipment, by standard operating rules, and by consolidation of lines into vast, integrated systems.

Under the conditions which existed in the early days of railroading, consolidation became necessary to combat a set of evils which severely limited the usefulness of the railroad. Consolidation might well have come as an effort to increase efficiency. Actually it occurred in an effort to increase profits and to eliminate competition, but the results were the same. Railroads had to cope with technical problems growing out of the haphazard way in which they had been built. Flimsy bridges, soft iron rails, inadequate ballasting, tortuous grading, sketchy signaling, and inadequate safety inspection made early railroading a nightmare. A new group of railroad financiers were able to use these chaotic conditions as a defense for consolidation which produced both immense profits and increased efficiency.

But consolidation required considerable quantities of initial capital. Even the early railroads had required large outlays compared with other business ventures of the

time. Thus, from the beginning, most railway enterprises had assumed the corporate form. They sold stocks and bonds, and in that way invited the general public to supply the necessary capital. These securities were bought and sold through the stock market, particularly the big stock exchange in New York City. Later refinements were introduced by large-scale banking, but this remained the fundamental system of capital collection. In its early days financing by stock sale was a relatively crude process filled with hazard and trickery. Some of the railroad consolidators like Daniel Drew, James Fisk, Jay Gould, and Cornelius Vanderbilt not only obtained the funds for their railroad ventures from this source, they also manipulated the price of their stocks in such a manner as to victimize the legitimate investors in their businesses. Railroads, during the period directly following the Civil War, were in good part financed by the gambling instincts of the American public. Most of the speculators lost their money, which, as in

FEDERAL LAND GRANTS FOR RAILROADS

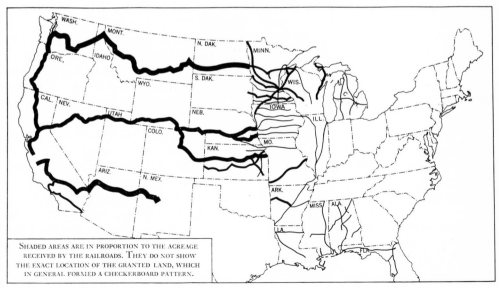

SHADED AREAS ARE IN PROPORTION TO THE ACREAGE RECEIVED BY THE RAILROADS. THEY DO NOT SHOW THE EXACT LOCATION OF THE GRANTED LAND, WHICH IN GENERAL FORMED A CHECKERBOARD PATTERN.

all gambling games, found its way into the hands of the insiders—those who ran the game. The picturesque stories of the skinning of the public by these early magnates of railroading are so well known as to have become a part of American folklore; they illustrate the rowdy days of unregulated capital collection. It was in reference to these times, when P. T. Barnum himself lived, that the great showman gleefully exclaimed: "There's a sucker born every minute."

One of the best of these stories concerns old "Commodore" Vanderbilt, one of the earliest of the consolidators of the railroads. Vanderbilt put together the great New York Central Railroad. Combining a number of existing shorter lines, he created a single road which ran from New York to Buffalo, and ultimately, after his death, to Chicago. At one stage of the process of consolidation, in order to get a terminal for his railroad in New York City, he bought the franchise of a streetcar line. News of this fine stroke of business reached the public and sent the price of the shares in Vanderbilt's railroad from $8 to $70. Some New York City councilmen also heard and thought they saw a fine chance to make a financial killing. Their plan was to sell the stock short* and then rescind Vanderbilt's recently acquired franchise. When the public learned of the loss of the franchise, the stock would drop and the councilmen could buy it back cheap, at a nice profit. Vanderbilt, however, fooled them by buying up all the stock of his railroad and holding it. When the time came for the councilmen to deliver the stock which they had sold short,

* Selling short is selling for future delivery stock you do not have, in the hope that it will go down in the meantime so you can buy it later at a lower price and make delivery at a profit.

they could not buy any and faced jail. Vanderbilt saved them from jail by selling them some of his stock at $179 per share. Members of the state legislature were also in on the short-selling deal. They had to pay $285 per share for their stocks! Vanderbilt chuckled: "I busted the whole legislature."

With the money he made on that deal Vanderbilt went on with his consolidation. There were other short roads between New York and Albany, and Vanderbilt bought them up to prevent competition. Then quietly he began to buy the stock of the competing Erie Railway which ran from New York to Buffalo. This road was "owned" by Drew, Gould, and Fisk, three professional riggers of the market who could match even the Commodore in skulduggery. They let him buy the stock, but slowly, so that his continuous purchases made the price go up and up. They sold out their own holdings at a good stiff price. When Vanderbilt finally controlled the railroad and the price of the stock was high, the rascally trio dumped 10 million dollars' worth of forged certificates on the market and broke the price down to the bottom. They almost ruined the old man. He sued, and they bought up the judge; he sued in another court and bought his own judge. The resulting mess finally reached the state legislature, and both sides had to bid furiously for the votes of the lawmakers. Those legislators who had been caught previously in the short dealing probably got their money back. The Commodore fought so hard that the four rascals finally had to get together to patch up the quarrel. But the old man was so badly burned that he went back to fleecing amateurs. Measured by the size of his private fortune at his death, 100 million dollars, he must have been a past master at this game.

This wild and disorderly process of capital collection and railroad consolidation began to settle down in the 1880s to more orderly methods under the influence of the investment bankers. The bankers and their clients suffered along with the investing public at the hands of these rapacious "industrialists." Investment bankers, who ultimately controlled and regulated the process of capital collection, reached national prominence during the Civil War with the rise of the house of Jay Cooke. They developed a market for stocks and bonds by familiarizing the general public with the notion of investing in United States bonds. J. P. Morgan built upon the foundation laid by Cooke; it was he who finally regularized the chaotic business of collecting capital and incidentally reserved the job for the bankers. In the 1880s he began to teach the Vanderbilts how to consolidate railroads without so much excitement and danger. By 1885, when the New York Central Railroad reached Chicago in its consolidating march, Morgan had perfected his system; during the next two decades he dominated the process of consolidation, which spread rapidly to other types of business.

When one considers the early condition of the railroads, consolidation made good sense. It is no wonder that efforts to bring order out of the jigsaw puzzle of rail lines were undertaken by the vigorous railroad magnates of the day. A shipper could obviously get better, quicker, and cheaper service from one road covering the entire distance from Chicago to New York than from a half dozen. Economies of many kinds were achieved. As a result, profits were increased. Standardized rates were set. The advantage of size to all concerned in this business was obvious; and consolidation of railroads may be viewed as a step in the direction of providing better service to the public, effecting economies in operation, and reducing rates. Big business as applied to railroads was a result of technological and financial needs as well as of the drive for greater profits.

These reforms were not sufficient to silence public criticism of the railroads. In fact, consolidation increased such criticism because it strengthened the monopoly position of the railroad operators. Like the "robber barons" of old, the railroad owners were in a position to levy upon the rest of society a tribute which could not be avoided. Goods had to be shipped, and a monopoly price could be exacted. "Pools," a sharing of available business or profits in order to avoid competition, became common. The farmers in particular, as perhaps the railroads' largest customer, developed a sense of acute grievance against the railroads and attempted political action to control railroad rates. To the farmer, obviously, every railroad was a monopoly since he could ship his produce only on the one that ran nearest his farm. Early attempts to regulate the railroads by state action having failed, those increasingly concerned about railroad rapacity turned in the 1880s to national control. They thought they had won a great victory when Congress at length passed, and President Cleveland reluctantly signed, the Interstate Commerce Act in 1887. But the law was written in such a manner as to make effective enforcement virtually impossible for the next fifteen years, nor was there much of a will to enforce it.

The great railroad magnates were able

INCREASE IN RAILROAD MILEAGE, 1860–1890

1860 30,000 MILES
1870 52,000 MILES
1880 93,000 MILES
1890 167,000 MILES

to fight off the governments, but they could not so readily dispose of the bankers. After forcing consolidation and respect for the rights of investors on the railroads, Morgan and the bankers began to insist upon many of the reforms which the public had been demanding. They felt that the rugged individualists who controlled the railroads were undermining public confidence and would ultimately, if not controlled, destroy the railroads themselves. The bankers, who had interests in all businesses, took a much broader view than the railroaders. Beginning in 1889, Morgan successfully exerted pressure to regularize the railroad business. The bankers controlled the process of capital collection, and the mightiest of the railroad tycoons were brought to heel. The wild old days of railroading ended; responsibility became the watchword. Rates were still too high; defenseless farmers, at least, continued to be gouged. But the immediate job of regulation, reducing chaos to order, had been achieved by business forces themselves. What Morgan had done for railroads he would later do for steel and other industries. These services of the Morgan combine had to be paid for by very high fees. Morgan settled a single dispute between the mighty combines of the New York Central and the Pennsylvania Railroad at a fee of around 2 million dollars. The mighty robber barons of the roads had at last met their master.

Thus the railroads succumbed to the "rationalizing" processes which were transforming all business in the age of industrialism. In response to the requirements of efficiency and to the urge for profits, they became great corporations. The picturesque ruffians who had ruled them disappeared and were replaced by boards of directors, largely influenced by bankers. The economist, the engineer, the technician, the banker—these assumed control. In much the same manner other businesses grew, were consolidated, and became corporations and congeries of corporations. The typical development which we have traced for the railroads is to be found in all the other basic industries. In some of them we even see the same guiding hand—that of J. P. Morgan, the organizing genius. Morgan's firm had special connections with the European money markets, from which it obtained vast sums which were invested in American industry. This firm also developed in the United States organizations for the distribution of stocks to investors, who trusted their judgment. These circumstances placed the bankers at the center of the whole system and gave them, in the end, substantial control over it. Successful industrialists themselves went into banking. The bankers' reward for their services was twofold: a quick profit for themselves and steady profits for the investors whose money they handled.

INDUSTRIAL AND FINANCE CAPITALISM

The railroads illustrate one of the techniques upon which the growth of American industry rested. The development of the oil industry provides examples of two more of these techniques: business management and market control. While the railroads became immense concerns, no one of them was able to control the whole industry. The Standard Oil Company was able to do this and was thereby able to survey and largely control its market.

The great promoter and organizer of the oil business was John D. Rockefeller. Rockefeller had none of the "sparkle" of the most colorful of the railroaders. He was a quiet, modest, retiring little man, a good churchman with an excellent Sunday school training which remained with him throughout his life. He avoided the limelight and the gaudy public battles of finance, but he could shoulder a competitor out of his way with the best of them. Rockefeller must be considered as an organizing force rather than as a man. He had some of the dream of Morgan in his head. When he started in business the oil industry comprised a large number of small, fiercely competing concerns for the refining and selling of oil, which was largely used as kerosene in lamps. When he finished his "rationalization" there was one big concern which dominated the refining, shipping, and selling of petroleum products. Many of his former competitors were absorbed into this new organization, while others were squeezed out of the industry entirely. The motivating force behind Rockefeller was a passion for the economies of bigness. He discovered the great truth that control of the market and of the sources of supply gave him a central position from which he was able to extract the maximum profit. He squeezed both buyers and sellers and forced them to operate as cheaply and efficiently as possible in order to stay in business. A big enough concern could utilize the best methods and iron out the multitude of duplications inherent in uncoordinated competition. A typical Rockefeller stratagem was to force the railroads to give him lower shipping rates in the form of rebates. This single "economy" enabled him to rid the market of most of the competition, since preferential shipping rates to one company in a highly competitive market gave that company an immense advantage over its rivals. The railroads discovered that the large and steady supply of shipments which Rockefeller sent more than repaid them for the lowered

rate, since oil by the trainload is cheaper to handle than oil by the barrel. Both Rockefeller and the cooperating railroads prospered, while only the competitors suffered.

Rockefeller had begun his business career as a grocery clerk at an age when most youngsters of today would be in grammar school. Within a very few years, the talented young businessman was ready to go into the wholesaling of groceries. He was twenty-one when the Civil War brought its boom to business in general, and Rockefeller was able to take full advantage of it. In 1865 he was a man of substance with some ready capital, looking for larger fields of operation. The oil industry seemed inviting, and with two experienced associates he went into the business of refining oil in Cleveland, Ohio. Five years later the concern had 1 million dollars in surplus through the accumulation of profits and had become the Standard Oil Company of Ohio. It was from this base that Rockefeller launched his grand attack. He bought, by exchange of stock and for cash, all the refineries in the Cleveland area. Those who resisted absorption were forced to the wall by ruthless price competition; those who accepted stock in Rockefeller's company in exchange for their businesses never had cause to complain. By the use of his railroad-rebate idea he caused such havoc among refiners elsewhere that he was able to take over nearly all of them. In 1878 he owned 80 per cent of the refining facilities of the industry. He was thirty-nine years old, with most of his creative life (he died at the age of ninety-eight) before him. His conquest of the direct selling field and the subsequent forays of the Rockefeller associates into steel and banking, while tremendously important for the economic history of America, are something of an anticlimax compared with the brilliant performance of his youth.

Rockefeller knew little about the technical problems of oil production. His contribution was in the field of business management. In bigness he found the key which opened the door to the economies inherent in centralized management and in the control of supply and of the market. The oil industry did not require the intervention of the bankers to achieve rationalization. It developed its own organizing genius.

The story of steel produced its folk hero in the person of Andrew Carnegie. But many-sided as this Scotch immigrant was, he did not carry the task of unifying steel production through to the end. The services of the old professional consolidator, J. P. Morgan, were required for the last step. It may be that Carnegie's failure to complete the job was related to his lack of singleness of purpose. He was not in later life much interested in money, and he took a passionate philosophical interest in the development of the institutions of democracy in his adopted land. Unlike Morgan and Rockefeller, he was seriously concerned with the destiny of man and the development of America's institutions, so different from those he had known in his youth in Scotland. Though no great writer, he attempted to put his ideas into print in numerous articles and books, one of which he titled *Triumphant Democracy* (1886). Beginning in the 1880s, Carnegie operated several newspapers in Great Britain dedicated to the spread of social democracy in that land. Carnegie was a rare specimen indeed among the folk heroes of the industrial age.

The immigrant boy began his American career as a bobbin boy in a textile mill. Four years younger than Rockefeller, he had arrived in America with his family in 1848 at the age of thirteen. By 1863 he was superintendent of a division of the Pennsylvania Railroad and had a bit of money tucked away, as was usual among aspiring young men of those days before the advent of the income tax. The rapid extension of railways was straining the infant iron business to the utmost, and Carnegie, in 1873, decided to go into business for himself in the manufacture of iron axles for railway cars. It was but a step to iron bridges, rails, and locomotives—always more business than he could handle. He came to see the potential future of steel, the cost of which was rapidly being reduced by the Bessemer process. In the Pittsburgh area, where ample supplies of iron, coal, and limestone were located and which was well served by railroads, he set up a modern steel plant. He tactfully named the plant after his friend J. Edgar Thomson, president of the Pennsylvania Railroad. The road became his best customer. Entering business at the very moment when railroads were converting their rails from iron to steel, a vigorous man with connections like Carnegie's could hardly fail. A half-dozen years later, in 1880, his steel plant was producing over 100,000 tons a year and was far ahead of all its rivals. And the mechanical civilization just emerging was built on steel. Railroads and oil were important, but steel was the heart of the matter.

By the end of the century, Carnegie's plant was making a profit of 40 million dollars a year, and its owner was one of the fabulously rich men of his day. But his real achievement lay in applying the bigbusiness idea to a new industry. Steel manufacture is in itself a large-scale operation. Even a single furnace is large. Vast economies were achieved by size and by continuous operation. The market was there; and in his attempts to serve it (and gobble it all up) Carnegie discovered that the more steel he made, the less it cost per unit. In the normal process of endeavoring to lower costs he discovered the relationship which, in the steel industry as in so many others, exists between large operations and economy. Carnegie produced steel cheaper than ever before, and cheaper than any of his contemporaries. In the process he became by far the largest producer.

Consolidation in America, as we have seen, proceeded through the elimination of small businesses by competition, and through the subsequent amalgamation of the survivors by purchase. Carnegie pushed out his competitors, just as Rockefeller did. He, too, used the favorite Rockefeller trick of railroad rebates, and later purchased the plants of other steel operators. He also branched out, acquiring fleets of ore boats and railroads, controlling iron and coal mines. His partner, Henry Clay Frick, was a coke magnate. Carnegie's experience reveals another factor in the amazing success of the American "captains of industry." Far more than either the railroaders or Rockefeller, Carnegie capitalized upon the advantages which arise from bigness in the manufacturing process itself. He was one great pioneer of what is commonly called mass production.

While Carnegie's firm was by far the largest, other steel companies also had grown to great size. In 1901, under the guidance of the Morgan banking firm, the majority of these, including Carnegie's, were organized into the United States Steel Company, a "combination of combinations" which has remained the largest producer of steel down to the present time. Finance capital rationalized the steel industry as it had the railroads. The profits of the consolidation were enormous. The trust which resulted was the largest single

business the world had ever known. The great industrialists had discovered the secret of big business in these four principles: mass production, business management, capital collection, and marketing control. These were innovations which rank with the significant technological inventions of the Industrial Revolution. Morgan contributed the secret of large-scale capital collection. Rockefeller pioneered in the field of business management and control of the market, while Carnegie opened the way to mass production. This trio, Morgan, Rockefeller, and Carnegie, whose experiences sum up the meaning of big business as it developed in the post–Civil War era, were much more typical of business in their time than were the railroad magnates who dominated the earlier part of the period. They were businessmen on the grand scale, business innovators who created businesses too large for their personal control and invented other methods of control.

What Morgan did for railroads, what he and Carnegie did for steel, and what Rockefeller did for oil, others were doing elsewhere in the world of industry. Around the packing of meat in Chicago rose the beef trust; around the refining of sugar, the sugar trust. Morgan and his railroads monopolized the anthracite coal fields. And so in many of the principal branches of business, corporations, trusts, pools, and banking syndicates took over basic American economic enterprise. Prior to 1890 relatively small individual businesses, controlled by individual entrepreneurs, made up the bulk of American business. In the next two decades the transformation was completed. A new type of business organization based upon efficiency, monopoly, and size appeared. This new type was not so much a big business as a cluster of closely related businesses welded together by great finance capital organizations. The startling report of a congressional committee in 1913 showed that Morgan controlled "forty-eight corporations, including forty railroad corporations, with at least one thousand subsidiary companies, and 16,000 miles of track; three banks and trust or insurance companies, five industrial and public service companies." This Pujo committee also revealed that the Rockefeller interests were twice as great as those of Morgan. Approximately half of this huge empire was controlled indirectly through the National City Bank. The controllers of these groups of industries developed a view nation in its scope. Finance capitalism had created a "money trust" which concentrated control of the vast industrial capacity of the country in the hands of a relatively few persons. While big business had solved the problems of production and distribution with such economies as to benefit all Americans, finance capitalism had created a national economy.

Almost as significant as the accomplishments of these giants was the attitude they took toward their achievements. All of them were remarkable men. The results that they achieved were staggering. The Standard Oil Company and United States Steel were wondrous constructions, and the services that they and the other trusts supplied at ever-decreasing costs were marvelous to behold. But the American business magnates tended to consider that the credit for the success of the American industrial system belonged to themselves alone. They credited the whole industrial system to their own initiative, self-reliance, and ability, rather than to the social forces of invention and scientific discovery, to the ample resources to which they had free access, or to the great free institutions which former Americans had provided for them. Much less did they give credit to the millions of immigrants upon whose broad backs their industries were built. The idea frequently expressed by Carnegie that the greatness of industrial America was a social product, the work of all Americans living and dead—and some Europeans too—occurred to few of them. They spoke in terms of "building America" with their own hands, of "giving work" to labor. They believed that they had created industrial America and that it was only right that it should belong to them; that they were public benefactors who richly deserved the emoluments and adulation which they received. Jay Gould, one of the worst of the early railroad pirates, said: "*We* have made this country *rich; we* have developed it." Even Andrew Carnegie, who recognized that social forces had contributed to his business success, said that even though these men had "monopolized everything, it was well that it was so. The man had arisen who could manage, and the tools belong to him." James Wharton, the nickel monopolist, was indignant when it was suggested that the tariff—that is, government support—had helped him create his immense business: "I have supported and aided the government more than it has supported and aided me. . . . I am one of the men who create and maintain the prosperity of the nation and who enable it to survive even the affliction of wrong-headed and cranky legislators." John D. Rockefeller gave credit for aid received, but he gave it to no man: "God gave me my money," he said. Here may be detected the old spirit of Puritanism, doughty and individualist, ready to equate worldly success with spiritual good health.

LABOR

Those who labored long hours in the mills got in return little credit, thanks, or money. They were in large part newly arrived immigrants. The only way in which America had been ill-suited to industrialization was in the lack of a ready supply of cheap factory labor. This lack was remedied by the great flood of immigrants who now came to her shores. After 1740, there had been about a century during which immigration was relatively very light, following the initial period of settlement. It was during this period that American civilization took on its mature characteristics. It will be remembered that the coming of fairly large numbers of Irish and Germans in the 1830s and 1840s created a rather serious problem of assimilation, expressed in the "nativist" movement of those times aimed at the foreigners, chiefly Catholics. Between 1820 and 1860, 6 million immigrants came in, and by 1860, 13 per cent of the population was foreign-born. (In 1952 the foreign-born comprised only 6 per cent.) The tide continued to roll in after the Civil War. From 1861 to 1900, 14 million entered the country. They came from Ireland and, to a decreasing extent, from Germany; from England and Scotland came a steady if unspectacular flow. After 1890, when the old sources began to dry up, Italy and eastern Europe took up the slack. In all, there came 5 million British; 2 million Scandinavians; 5 million each of Germans, Irish, and Italians; and 7 million eastern Europeans—Hungarians, Russians, Poles, and South Slavs. To these were added smaller numbers from every other country of Europe and the Near East, and scattered representatives from the other parts of the world. The population of the United States in 1860 was 31 million; an almost equal number of immigrants entered the country between the Civil War and World War I.

Many of the Irish, Italian, and east Europeans were brought over on labor contracts. Agents for industries needing workers recruited them all over Europe. The fares of these contract laborers were paid for them in return for a contract to work for the firm until the money advanced had been paid off. This practice was legalized in 1864 and became illegal in 1885, but it was continued for years after the latter date despite the law. The English, Scotch, Germans, and Scandinavians usually paid their own way and thus were able to make their own working arrangements on arrival. The remainder, however, arrived penniless in most cases and were at the mercy of the employers. They occupied, for a generation or more, the lowest rank of the working class; as they moved up the social scale, their places were taken by new immigrants. In all the industrial centers a great mass of penniless foreign workers lived in teeming slums and worked for low wages—which were, however, frequently higher than they had been used to in the old country. The fact that the industrial workers of America were recently arrived foreigners goes far to explain the unfavorable attitude of native Americans toward "labor." To an antagonism of class were added those of variant cultures. It also helps to explain the difficulties which industrial workers had in forming labor unions and raising their standard of living. They were a heterogeneous mass of despised foreigners, ignorant of the language and customs of their adopted country and often not understanding each other.

In all countries which experienced the Industrial Revolution, the first phase of that system bore heavily on the "operatives" who tended the machines, and drove them at times to violent protest. Not owning their own tools as the earlier working class did, having only their hands to sell (for the skill was now largely built into the machine itself), they were at the mercy of the owners of the machines, whose economic power enabled them to offer only the lowest wages. As compared with earlier employer-employee relations, the new giant corporations were far more impersonal in their attitude toward their workers. The intimate relationship likely to prevail where one owner hired a few employees was replaced by one in which the thousands of workers hired by a huge enterprise were merely costs of production, figures on an accounting sheet. The fierce competition characteristic of early industrialism helped cut wages to the minimum. Working conditions were likely to be miserable and dangerous; living conditions were likely to be deplorable, as the workers clustered in overcrowded areas around the congested factory district. Under unrestrained capitalism, labor was a commodity—to be bought as cheaply as possible, subject to the laws of supply and demand. And the supply of hands was made so plentiful by unrestricted immigration that wages were inevitably low. Statistics, to be sure, show that the real wages of labor increased in the industrial age; but those statistics do not show the slums, nor do they reckon with the cruel impersonality of the system.

It was to be expected that poorly paid workers thrown together in the factory would attempt to combine in unions to secure higher wages and better working conditions. But early unions, as will be recalled, had to contend with the legal tradition which held such combinations to be unlawful conspiracies. Before the Civil War, workers had also turned to political action, seeking state regulation of factory conditions and such other aids to opportunity as free education. Such efforts continued through and after the Civil War. But after the war, such hard-won gains as labor had made were wiped out. The great

depression of 1873 to 1878 dealt severe blows to the precariously situated labor unions; foreign immigration completed the job. In 1880 small numbers of skilled workers were organized into craft unions, but within the factories of the new industrial era there was virtually no organization. Moreover, the obstacles to unionization were more formidable than ever.

A basic American tradition, never stronger than in this period, was the idea of individual opportunity and self-help, which saw the democratic ideal as a process in which each man raised himself a notch or two in the social scale by hard work and initiative. There were always many who thought of unionism as somehow un-American—an effort to substitute the Old World principle of class conflict for the American principle of individual self-reliance. And indeed, in some measure the myth of unlimited opportunity corresponded to reality in this period. Millions of workers did graduate from the ranks of labor; some even became great capitalists. The stories of Carnegie, Rockefeller, and others might be the exception and not the rule, but they showed what could be done. Waves of new foreigners came in to take up the lowest places in society which their predecessors abandoned as they found better jobs. A worker who thought of himself as a potential capitalist was not so easily organized; and a public which was convinced of the reality of infinite opportunity was not so likely to sympathize with union activity. But there were, in addition to this general philosophic attitude, a great many more concrete obstacles to unionization. The courts were unsympathetic. The local police were likely to be in the pay of the factory owners. Employers, tough in this age, organized themselves to fight unionism by any means, legal or otherwise. They hired strikebreakers and thugs, they made up "blacklists" of troublesome workers whom they would not hire, they required their workers to sign an agreement, soon known by workers as a "yellow-dog contract"—a promise, as condition of employment, not to join a union. This was an age in which the machinery of government—courts and lawmakers—belonged largely to the great capitalists. To all this must be added the difficulties inherent in organizing for collective action a working class which included so many different nationalities, religions, and races. Employers were accused of practicing "divide and rule" by placing incompatible groups of workers side by side—Poles and Russians, say, or Irish and Italians.

The conditions were ripe for an era of lawless and bloody strife between capital and labor. Difficult as it was to organize and go on strike, working conditions were so bad that strikes occurred year after year. A mass of immigrant labor, ineffectively organized but prone to violent protest, encountered the hostility of the early capitalists, a hard-boiled class not likely to show mercy to any antagonist. The period from 1873 to 1896 (and even beyond) was so troubled on the industrial front that it can be described as a period of labor warfare. There was violence on both sides. In 1877, during the depression, a spontaneous strike of the railroad workers in the East, protesting the fourth wage cut within a few years, caused riots in Pittsburgh, Reading, Buffalo, and other places. The governor of Maryland called out the militia, and President Hayes sent federal troops to several states. Some of the public sympathized with the desperate workers, but others saw a revolutionary plot, and a shudder of horror swept the nation. The strike was broken, but workers remained embittered. A great labor organization, known as the Knights of Labor, grew almost overnight

to national proportions dedicated to the solidarity of the laboring class against the capitalists. The Knights had a large number of rather cloudy objectives, but their great goal was the uplift of the entire mass of labor. They soon became involved in a series of bloody strikes, culminating in the railroad strikes of 1886. The Haymarket affair, in the same year, grew out of the eight-hour-day campaign which the Knights had been organizing. On May 4, in Haymarket Square in Chicago, a mass meeting of workers ended in a fight in which a bomb was exploded, resulting in seven deaths and many wounded. The nation was shocked, and because some Chicago anarchists, preachers of violent revolution, had been associated with the meeting, the Knights were discredited and soon declined as rapidly as they had arisen. Eight anarchists were rounded up and given the death penalty, although there was no proof that any of them actually threw the bomb that touched off the Haymarket riot.

The warfare of capital and labor was not thereby ended; it reached almost epic proportions in 1892 to 1894, when two great strikes rocked the nation. One was at the home of Carnegie Steel, at Homestead, Pennsylvania, a long fight at the conclusion of which H. C. Frick observed that the steel interests had taught their employees a lesson they would never forget —a rather inept prophecy, unless taken in a different sense from that intended by the ironmaster. The other, the Pullman strike, was even more sensational. It spread to affect the railways of almost the entire country. President Cleveland, at the behest of the railroads, sent federal troops, although the governor of Illinois declared they were not needed to keep order. The violence which broke out, workers alleged, was deliberately incited by company

The Homestead Strike, which erupted into violent clashes between strikers and strike-breakers, is depicted in details from a contemporary print. (U.S. Department of Labor)

agents. The leader of the railwaymen, Eugene Debs, was sent to jail for defying a court order. This use of the injunction was a new and most effective employer tactic, which involved getting a sympathetic judge to issue a writ against the strike under the Sherman Antitrust Act. Here, too, in Pullman, Illinois, the strike was broken, but bitterness remained. Labor sank back into temporary apathy after these two staggering defeats.

Only among the skilled craftsmen was unionism at all successful in this period. In 1886 a union of unions, the American Federation of Labor, was created to co-ordinate a number of craft unions. The remarkable Samuel Gompers, a man determined to avoid violence and pursue moderation, was the organizer—and until 1924, president—of this federation. Shrewd management and conservative tactics of the AFL under Gompers paid dividends. These unions gained recognition by management and won better conditions and higher wages. But the AFL too seldom regarded the mass of unskilled factory hands as part of its responsibility; it was, on the whole, content to gain a greater reward for the skilled craftsmen. Even here progress was slow, though steady; by 1902 there were a million workers enrolled in the AFL, while the American "proletariat"—the total of the skilled and unskilled industrial workers—comprised eight or nine times that number. In the warfare of labor and capital, capital kept the upper hand in this first age of industrial growth.

IDEOLOGIES OF CAPITAL AND LABOR

Was there such a thing as a proletariat, a separate class which, according to the socialist prophet Karl Marx, ought to recognize that its interests stood unalterably opposed to those of the capitalist class? Was there a natural and chronic state of war between these classes? We have already observed that the "American" habit of thought was otherwise, whatever new ideas "foreigners" might bring in.

The ideology of individualism held that every man might rise in a fluid society with no fixed social classes. It stressed individual initiative, not collective action. This ideology was a product of the frontier, but it also received the weighty support of economic theory, which, as elaborated mainly in England and Scotland (from Adam Smith, through David Ricardo and J. R. McCulloch, to Alfred Marshall), held that the greatest wealth will be produced and will be most equitably distributed where individual enterprise is left free from all restraints or controls. Moreover, it received yet another buttress in this period from the great popularity of that system of thought known as "social Darwinism." The British philosopher Herbert Spencer had an immense vogue, and Americans like William Graham Sumner and John Fiske spread this gospel of rugged individualism. The most exciting and challenging scientific discovery since Newton's time was Charles Darwin's mass of evidence for the fact of biological evolution and his suggestion that the method which nature used in order to bring about progression from lower to higher forms of life was a ruthless elimination of the unfit —"natural selection." Applied by others to human society, Darwinian concepts produced an ideology which asserted that progress came through competition, or as Sumner put it, "root, hog, or die." It was not a very logical philosophy, but it suited the mood of the age, and it apparently had the impressive backing of that new god, Science. The struggle for survival without

any hindrance from soft-headed sentimental reformers was erected into a law of life, the only way of progress.

Thus fortified by eminent authority, American employers stood firmly against any interference with the competitive order, whether by labor unions or by government regulation. As one of them put it, "It is perfectly right for the wage earner to get all he can . . . but after all one inexorable law finally settles this as it does so many other economic questions, and that is the law of supply and demand." "Strikes," said the *New York Times*, "are un-American . . . and those who employ them have no real conception of what American citizenship is or implies." The *New York Herald* denounced workers for the "presumption that they had a moral, if not a legal, right to a living wage. . . . This is an entirely un-American presumption. . . . No man is entitled to a living. . . ." Another newspaper went so far as to declare that strikers ought to be met with "bullets and bayonets, canister and grape." The great Homestead and Pullman strikes had been brought on by the refusal of the owners to recognize the existence of labor unions, or to deal with them at all—"there is nothing to negotiate," George Pullman had said. Time and again it was asserted that recognition of labor unions would constitute a deadly blow at private property itself, since it would prevent an owner from doing as he wished with his own. It would also wreck the economic order by destroying the freedom of the market in labor. A formidable combination of moral, legal, economic, and even scientific reasons persuaded the employing class of what it already felt in its bones—that labor agitators were un-American, unions were subversive, and strikes were a conspiracy against civilization.

The most striking and effective manifestation of this big-business ideology was provided in this era by the Supreme Court. Dominated by conservative judges who felt it to be their duty to defend capital from any sort of interference, the Court produced an extraordinary series of decisions in which it consistently found that regulation of big business was unconstitutional. The Court's power to invalidate legislative acts, heretofore used very rarely, was erected into a powerful defense of property rights. In the 1890s the Court threw out the income tax, explained away antitrust laws, and, most remarkable of all, developed a strained interpretation of the Fourteenth Amendment which enabled it to reject state regulatory acts. It was consistently unfriendly not only to labor unions, but to laws attempting to remedy unhealthy conditions of labor. In connection with one such case a few years later, Justice Oliver Wendell Holmes, in a minority criticism of the decision, remarked that "this case is decided upon an economic theory which a large part of the country does not entertain." The judges, he said, were reading into the Constitution their own economic and social views. They did so in this period to an unusual degree, and it reflected how deeply those conservative views had penetrated into the mind of the owning class in industrial America.

As against this official ideology, the birth of a new radicalism was the most significant trend in social thought. Socialism, in a variety of forms, had already arisen in Europe. In its early days, it had taken the form of Christian or utopian socialism as we have already seen. Some of these doctrines had been brought to America in the 1830s and 1840s and had led to many experiments in socialist communities. Since those days European socialism had hardened under the influence of

Karl Marx, who predicted as a scientific certainty the overthrow of the capitalists by the oppressed workers, their seizure of the state through revolution, and the establishment of publicly owned industries producing for consumption alone and not for private profit. Marxian socialism never got very far in America. Eugene Debs, after his harsh experience in the Pullman strike, became a moderate socialist. A very popular view of the moderate position appeared in Edward Bellamy's novel *Looking Backward,* which painted the glories of a socialist civilization as Bellamy imagined it to be in the year 2000—some time after the revolution. But perhaps more significant was the unique radicalism of Henry George. Many read his *Progress and Poverty* in the 1880s; and those who could not take very seriously George's panacea of a single tax on surplus land values (to deprive the landlord of his unearned increment and allow every worker to have the fruits of his own toil) might nevertheless reflect on the challenging thesis that while more and more wealth was being produced, more and more people were living in misery—the giant paradox of progress along with poverty.

With such as these, reform, not revolution, was to be the American way. The revolutionary Socialist Labor party, despite Daniel De Leon's vigorous leadership, never had more than a tiny membership. A few years later there appeared the radical, colorful, and revolutionary IWW (Industrial Workers of the World) movement, which won scattered successes for a few years, mainly because the mass of industrial workers had no responsible labor unions to represent their interests; but the career of the IWW was ephemeral. Debs's Socialist party was pledged to win state ownership of industry by ballots, not bullets. It managed to win a fairly substantial vote from 1900 to 1912, but never seriously threatened to supplant the major political parties. It is worth noting that George's radicalism had an agrarian slant, with affinities to Jeffersonian ideals; and in fact it was to be the American farmer, not the American factory worker, who led the greatest movement of social protest in this era.

While socialism never made much progress in the United States, from 1880 on the assumptions of *laissez faire* were increasingly challenged on more conservative grounds. Christian ministers of the "Social Gospel" challenged it in the name of morality; and a new school of economists in the universities challenged its claim to scientific validity. Carefully distinguishing themselves from socialists, these people thought that a case could be made out for government regulation in various specific areas, on the basis not of dogma but of common sense. They accused

theoretical *laissez faire* of being too rigid and doctrinaire. They disagreed equally with those who said the state should do nothing and those who said it should do everything, but in suggesting that it could here and there do *something* useful, economists and sociologists were preparing the way for moderate social reform, in the long run more effective than militant radicalism. This was to emerge later in the progressive era.

This ferment of liberal and radical thought stemming from social reformers, social gospelers, and social scientists represented an undeniable discontent about the consequences of unmitigated private control of the vast new industrial system. The system seemed to grind out vast profits for a few, but the great wealth being created was not being properly distributed. The power of the industrial tycoons seemed too great, and their sense of public responsibility too small.

FURTHER READINGS

Among broad and general works, B. J. Hendricks, *The Age of Big Business* (1919), and John Moody's two volumes in the Chronicles of America, *Masters of Capital* (1919) and *The Railroad Builders* (1919), are useful. W. M. Daniels, *American Railroads* (1932), is a good introduction to a large field. Matthew Josephson, *The Robber Barons* (1935), is colorfully written and even on the sensational side in stressing the sins of the great capitalists. More specialized studies are also available: Allan Nevins, *John D. Rockefeller* (2 vols., 1940); Ralph W. Hidy and Muriel E. Hidy, *Pioneering in Big Business: The History of Standard Oil Co., 1882–1911* (1956); and . Grodinsky, *Jay Gould: His Business Career, 1867–1892* (1957), a work which finds that the Mephistopheles of Wall Street was

not *quite* as villainous as usually depicted.

Edward Kirkland, *Business in the Gilded Age* (1952), and Robert G. McCloskey, *American Conservatism in the Age of Enterprise* (1951), are stimulating studies in the personalities and ideas of the "capitalist class." In the other camp, David A. Shannon presents *The Socialist Party of America: A History* (1955), and Chester M. Destler, *American Radicalism 1865–1901: Essays and Documents* (1946), is a useful collection. Foster R. Dulles, *Labor in America* (1949), is an attractive popular history of the labor movement. A recent examination by Philip Taft, *The American Federation of Labor in the Time of Gompers* (1957), is based on solid research. Henry George, undoubtedly the most significant figure in the movement of anticapitalist protest in this era, has been handled in a distinguished manner in Charles A. Barker, *Henry George* (1956).

On the margin between economics and history are some of the great public "problems" connected with industrial growth: W. E. Clark and J. W. Jenks, *The Trust Problem* (1917), and A. R. Burns, *The Decline of Competition* (1932), suggest one of them. See also H. B. Thorelli, *The Federal Anti-trust Policy* (1955).

For additional bibliography, see the *Harvard Guide,* sections 202, 205, 206, 217.

EIGHTEEN

Politics and Society in the Gilded Age

1868
Ulysses S. Grant elected President.
Tweed Ring in New York City.

1872
Grant reelected over Greeley.

1873
Crédit Mobilier and Whisky Ring exposed.

1875
Johns Hopkins University founded; educational reform under way.

1876
Hayes defeats Tilden in disputed election.

1880
Garfield elected President.

1881
Assassination of Garfield.
Chester Arthur to presidency.

1882–1883
Pendleton Civil Service Act passed.

1884
Mugwump revolt in GOP; Cleveland defeats Blaine.

1887
Interstate Commerce Act passed.

1888
Benjamin Harrison defeats Cleveland.

1890
McKinley Tariff enacted.

1892
Cleveland defeats Harrison.
People's party created.

POLITICS AND SOCIAL CHANGE

WITH THE END OF the Civil War and the coming of the industrial age, politicians no longer occupied the center of the stage. "Our age may be called the Age of Utility," a shrewd journalist commented shortly after the war. "We are not prolific of statesmen or orators, and politics has degenerated into a poor strife between speculators and mediocrities. But for all this the country is safe." Orators were no longer needed. The great political drama had closed, and the scene had shifted. What went on in Washington seemed relatively unimportant. What mere senator could compete with the building of a transcontinental railroad or with the activities of a John D. Rockefeller or Jay Gould? The new hero was no longer the statesman but the millionaire.

The years from 1868 to 1892 were years of comparative political lethargy, marked by a succession of colorless Presidents and dull campaigns. The lack of great issues reflected the industrial pattern discussed in the previous chapter. Neither party was prepared to oppose the new industrialism. Both parties had an agrarian wing, but in neither was it usually dominant. The Democrats were for a long time deeply mistrusted in the North as a party of rebellion and repudiation, but in fact the national leadership of that party was rather firmly in the grasp of northern conservatives. All the Democratic presiden-

379

Grover Cleveland

A caricature of James G. Blaine

President Cleveland's ample girth symbolizes the fatness of an era of fabulous money-making, high living, and the emergence of a new ruling class of business barons. Cleveland was notably honest, but most of politics was permeated with corruption. The "plutocracy" was cynical about politics, and thought nothing of bribing lawmakers and judges.

"Diamond Jim" Brady

Hoffman House bar,
New York, 1870

Society leaders
of the 1890s

tial nominees of the period, at least, from Horatio Seymour to Grover Cleveland, were of this stripe. The Republicans, for their part, stood proudly on their record as saviors of the union and sponsors of northern interests such as the protective tariff on manufactures, sound money, and railroad subsidies. As a national party, the Democrats did not often challenge any of these. Their basic traditions, after all, lay in the direction of limited government and *laissez faire.*

Industrialism did indeed bring its hardships and problems, as we have seen, along with its boons, but the political parties were reluctant to make issues out of them. Organized labor was too new, too alien, and too apparently radical to exert strong political influence as yet. The farmers took a generation to analyze their grievances and gird for political battle against urban capitalism. Over everything there was spread the influence of nineteenth-century liberalism, which mistrusted the state and put its faith in sturdy individualism as the mainspring of all progress. It was a faith Americans shared with their English cousins and with much of Europe in this epoch.

Meanwhile, there was a noteworthy trend towards the professionalization of politics, continuing a process begun in the Jacksonian era—control by highly developed organizations run by political "bosses." These calculating careerists found it convenient and profitable to stay on good terms with the incredibly wealthy overlords of the business world.

The rapidly growing cities produced the worst evils of political bossism. The most prominent social change of the era was this process of urbanization, creating for millions of Americans a new environment and breeding innumerable social problems. Between 1870 and 1910 the percentage of Americans living in large cities more than doubled; in concrete numbers, 16 million human beings were added to that small group of cities having more than 100,000 population. It is true that urbanization had been going on ever since the nation's birth, climbing at a fairly steady rate. But there now came a point at which the magnitude of cities in the "megalopo-

Mulberry Street, New York City, around the turn of the century: immigrant America in the crowded tenement areas. (Library of Congress)

is" class brought wholly new problems
into existence. The fact that a large majority of the urban increase came from
immigration added to the difficulties. And
the new industrialism produced congestion, smoke, dirt, and ugliness. Overcrowding was a function of factory economics in
this industrial era; power and transportation needs pulled great industrial com-
plexes into the same small area, and urban
congestion then tended to feed on itself.
Such vital human requirements as recrea-
tion and presence of beauty in one's environment were not met; sanitation and
health often suffered.

The steady influx of immigrants who
arrived penniless and only gradually
worked their way to a decent level of
existence—to be replaced by fresh arrivals
—made a permanent market for habita-
tions of the most abominable sort. The
slum gained its place of dishonor on the
American scene. Ultimately, movements
of social reform would be powerfully
stimulated by the fact that drab poverty,
and the stark contrast of riches and poverty, was so dramatically obvious in the
great cities. But immigrant Americans
could for a time be ignored by respectable
people, and their degradation explained
away as the result of their racial backwardness. Public attention tended rather
to focus on the gaudy symbols of wealth
flaunted by the new millionaires. It was a
time when the public generally admired
the glamorous rich, those fabulous makers
and spenders of money whose glittering
society found its chief symbol in the mansions of Park Avenue and of Newport,
Rhode Island. The most fashionable intellectual philosophy of the day, that of social
Darwinism, regarded life as a struggle in
which the successful were to be admired.
The less philosophical satisfied their instinct of hero worship by gaping at the

exploits of the Vanderbilts and Goulds.
Newport was what Hollywood later became, and Mrs. Astor and her friends, the
diamond-covered circle of the "four hundred," were the equivalent of film stars.
"Diamond Jim" Brady and the gorgeous
Lillian Russell were the more scandalous
counterparts of the Astors. This was the
epoch Mark Twain named the "Gilded
Age." Its popular idols were the millionaires, its goddesses the millionaires' wives
and mistresses.

That politics should mirror this mood
was only natural. The politicians were of
no mind to challenge the supremacy of
the new economic order, but preferred to
share its splendors. Not for a generation
was there a great grass-roots impulse of
reform to stir them from their lethargy.
Working closely with the business community, politicians tended in the easy atmosphere of the Gilded Age to fall into
relationships which were to be branded
corrupt. Corruption was, unhappily, the
chief political theme of the age.

DEGENERATION OF POLITICS

Corruption in politics had been known
earlier in American history, and it would
be easy to assemble much evidence that
political life was far from pure before the
Civil War. Writing in 1860, Horace
Greeley declared it to be his considered
opinion after much experience of politics
that the only officeholders who did not
steal were those who were so rich that
money was no temptation. In the early
years of the republic, politics had tended
to be "the avocation of a privileged minority," with leading statesmen being
drawn from the leisured classes. But since
Jackson's day the officeholding class had
become professional politicians set apart
from the rich and respectable, a group

avid for the spoils of political office and often none too scrupulous about the way they took their rewards. A tendency toward corruption exists in all governments. In a large democracy the danger is that inferior men may seize the machinery of politics and that the masses of people, busy with their own tasks, may find it difficult to keep check on them.

But obviously the situation became much worse right after the Civil War. Some of the leading political figures of the Lincoln era quit politics in disgust, declaring that no honest man could any longer stay in the game. Corruption at the national level burst into the open during Grant's second term (1873–1877), when a series of unprecedented scandals, including the Whisky Ring and *Crédit Mobilier,** shocked the nation and sickened idealists. The 1876 election perhaps marked the lowest depths of degradation. But local politics were even more corrupt, and in the cities "boss" government of a scandalous sort became the rule, not the exception. The spectacular plunderings of a man like New York City's Boss Tweed, whose ring set a record for theft, were perhaps not so important as the setting of all politics into a mold of systematic corruption. That system was later described as "invisible government," or a "new feudalism," by means of which a few ruled as dictators in the name of democracy.

The reasons that political corruption grew worse at this time are obvious. Opportunities for corruption increased, and human resistance to it weakened. Opportunities were provided by the rapid growth of wealth and the emergence of the new industrial capitalism. The vigorous, tough

robber barons of capitalism's heroic age, engaged in fierce competition for economic power, were prepared to offer irresistible temptations to lawmakers and law enforcers. To a Rockefeller, a lawmaking body was just another rival to be bought up or bought out; a wit remarked that Standard Oil refined everything except the Pennsylvania legislature. The Goulds and Vanderbilts regarded judges as a cost of production, to be paid off like any other employee. Wherever the government, local, state, or national, had anything to offer, the new capitalists were prepared to bid for it; wherever there was a threat of government intervention in any way to lessen profits, they were ready to offer bribes to prevent such action. One of the insiders boasted that he had reduced the buying of legislators to an exact science, paying each exactly what he was worth and no more. These tycoons of capital had enough money to hold legislatures in the palms of their hands and to own their private judges. "We have 38 one-horse legislatures in this country," Wendell Phillips wrote, "and we have a man like Tom Scott [of the Pennsylvania Railroad] with 350 millions in his hands." The result of such an unequal contest was a foregone conclusion. The *Crédit Mobilier* scandal found the railroads reaching into Congress and even to the Vice President of the United States in order to obtain subsidies and conceal their flagrant profiteering by what amounted to bribery.

The other side of the coin was the low caliber of the politicians. To a large extent this must be attributed to the unhealthy political conditions left over from the war, and especially to the demoralization of the opposition party along with the too great prosperity of the Republicans. The long shadow cast by the Civil War lay over this period. Old battle cries

---

* The *Crédit Mobilier,* a name borrowed from the French, was a company which built the Union Pacific Railroad and paid fabulous dividends on its stocks, many of which were found to be in the hands of congressmen.

rather than fresh issues prevailed. The Democrats were tarred with the brush of secession and Copperheadism, while the "Grand Old Party," for its part, assuming that any tactics were justified to keep the Democrats out, fell back on the stock bloody-shirt argument, the appeal to war hatreds. The Democrats were scarcely respectable in the North. Their effort in 1868 to make an issue out of paying off the Civil War bonds in greenbacks rather than in gold further alienated them from respectable northerners, and the Republicans stood forth as the defenders of property as well as of the union, against a band of rebels, radicals, and repudiators. This was the period when, as the popular humorist "Mr. Dooley" recalled, "gin'rally speakin' a Demmycrat was an ondesirable immygrant that had got past Ellis Island." Needless to say, the Republicans made the most of this sentiment. "He who cries against the Republican party," one of them calmly asserted, "cries only from the rebel standpoint." In the Senate, in July, 1876, the Indiana Republican boss, Oliver Morton, replied to a Democratic attack by simply asking contemptuously, "What good thing has been done or suggested by the Democratic party in the last twenty-five years?"

The Democrats were always able to make a close race of it for the presidency in this period, because of grave Republican sins, and because large numbers even in the North were "ondesirable immygrants" and not bondholders. Indeed, in four of the six presidential elections between 1876 and 1896, the Democrats had more popular votes than the Republicans, although they won the presidency only twice. But on the whole, their party principles were in sad condition and they were vulnerable to every oratorical waving of the bloody shirt. The situation was one calculated to corrupt the Republican party. President Grant's sorry record in the White House illustrates the point. Elected in 1868, the military hero of the Civil War lacked the political ability to control the forces of corruption surrounding his administration. When honest men rebelled against the thievery, the cry went up that they were weakening the GOP and hence were no better than traitors to the union. To this logic Grant always submitted. "The party became a sort of Church," as one writer has put it; to question its leaders was shocking heresy. The high priests of the Republican "church" were now men like Oliver Morton, ruthless and arrogant. When Grant's honest Attorney General tried to clean out the nefarious "Whisky Ring" which stole money from the revenue tax on alcoholic beverages, the President failed miserably to follow through his first promise to "let no guilty man escape." The guilty men turned out to be prominent Republican politicians, and they had to be protected because nothing was so dangerous as to impair the reputation and threaten the unity of the party that was the bulwark of the union.

Everyone knew that Grant was not personally dishonest, and many were touched by his pathetic last message to Congress, where he in effect confessed the sins of his administration and pleaded his own political inexperience. If he was a victim of his own inexperience and naïveté, Grant was also a prisoner of the powerful Republican bosses and of the circumstances of the times.

REFORM EFFORTS

In 1872, a group of Republicans shocked by "Grantism" broke away from the party. The respectable element in the Republican party, alarmed to see the party falling into evil hands, hoped to restore decency to politics. They nominated the amiable editor Horace Greeley, and the Democrats, too dispirited to name their own candidate, followed suit in nominating Greeley. But this Liberal Republican movement was easily beaten by the regular GOP behind Grant. The people were still influenced by emotions derived from the late war, and the big money was with Grant. Greeley died not long after the campaign. One of the earliest of the Black Republicans, he found himself assailed as a rebel in disguise for daring to suggest that the Republican bosses could do wrong.

Between 1873 and 1876 a whole series of scandals came to light, and this on top of an economic depression threatened the GOP's hold on the national government. The Democrats returned to the attack

with high hopes. They chose a ticket headed by the New York Governor Samuel J. Tilden, who had attained considerable fame by his successful prosecution of the Tweed Ring. For Vice President, the Democrats chose a former Copperhead and inflationist from the middle-western prairies. The Republicans, needing an untainted name, settled on the fairly obscure Rutherford B. Hayes of Ohio. The fantastic election that followed illustrated the corruption of postwar politics. It will be recalled that a unique dispute occurred concerning the result of the election, with the outcome hinging on several Carpetbag governments in the South. The Democrats accused the Republicans of stealing the election, but during the controversy it was disclosed that Democrats as well as Republicans were offering to buy electoral votes. Before the disputed election

PRESIDENTIAL ELECTION, 1876

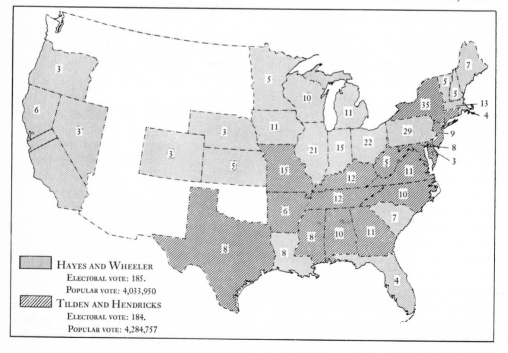

HAYES AND WHEELER
ELECTORAL VOTE: 185.
POPULAR VOTE: 4,033,950
TILDEN AND HENDRICKS
ELECTORAL VOTE: 184.
POPULAR VOTE: 4,284,757

of 1876 was finally decided, all the sordid features of political corruption and manipulation were revealed. Hayes and Tilden, the two candidates, were both men of honor, as Grant had been. But they were simply surrounded by political corruption.

Decent citizens were aware of the rottenness of politics. After such exposures as the Whisky Ring frauds and after experiencing the 1876 election, it was difficult not to be. Yet the public in general remained apathetic. This apathy was opposed by the zeal of a few reformers. Crusading editors such as George W. Curtis of *Harper's* and E. L. Godkin of *The Nation* attempted to mobilize public opinion. These reformers were inclined to blame chiefly the spoils system. Certainly this system reached its peak under Grant and was openly defended by prominent Republican leaders. The idea of taking federal jobs out of the reach of the spoilsmen by placing them on the "merit system," proposed earlier by Senator Sumner, was given lip service by both major parties in their platforms. But in practice, jobs continued to be handed out to deserving party workers as a reward for their services.

Hayes, taking office in 1877, made some effort to get away from the spoils system, though he rewarded the men who had corruptly aided his election in the South. For his efforts he was bitterly criticized by such powerful Republican senators as James G. Blaine and Roscoe Conkling. These two personal enemies, leaders of rival factions within the GOP, agreed in regarding the spoils system as necessary because without it no political party could be held together. How could you win elections without the "sinews of war" in the form of offices to be held out as rewards for loyal party workers? And

Rutherford B. Hayes of Ohio, eighteenth President of the United States. (Library of Congress)

were not any means justified by the great end of keeping the Republican party in power? Roscoe Conkling, the arrogant, colorful, red-bearded giant from New York, poured scorn on the "man milliners" of politics who thought you could run a political party on "mush and gush." In the face of such professional opposition, Hayes's halfhearted campaign for civil-service reform made little headway.

But a series of events between 1877 and 1881 had the effect of weakening the worst of the spoilsmen and inaugurating the merit system. Hayes, who had pledged himself to a single term in any event, was not wanted back in 1880. A conservative gentleman of the old school, the Ohioan had proved "sound" on the currency question and the labor question, but had been troublesome on matters of patronage. He had, after a bitter struggle, overthrown Conkling's right to control appointments to the rich New York City customs house. In 1880 the feudal satellites of the rival chieftains Blaine and Conkling ("Half-Breeds" and "Stalwarts" in the language of the day) quarreled over the presidential nomination. After numerous ballots there was recourse to a dark horse, James A. Garfield of Ohio. His selection did not please the overbearing Conkling, though Conkling's loyal lieutenant, Chester A. Arthur, was allotted the vice-presidential nomination.

Garfield was elected in a dull campaign, notable for the complete lack of issues separating the two parties. He immediately fell into a quarrel with Conkling over matters of patronage. Conkling was defeated and forced from public life, but a few months after the inauguration Garfield was killed by a bullet fired by a crazy Stalwart follower of the New York spoilsman, who apparently reasoned that to make Chester Arthur President would solve all his problems of job seeking. A shocked public then forced passage of the Pendleton Act, which introduced the merit system. With the defeat of Conkling and the enacting of the Pendleton Act in 1883, the worst days of the spoils system seemed over. In fact, the number of jobs placed under the merit system was at first not large, nor was the Civil Service Commission really effective for some time. But a start had been made, and gradually, in the course of time, the list of jobs to be filled by examination and not by the test of political affiliation grew. It was long, however, before the merit system was widely adopted on the state level. Thus it took the murder of a President of the United States to bring about the mere beginnings of political reform—surely a

tribute to the depth of the era's political degradation.

The election of 1884 also had a certain significance in the nation's gradual recovery from this degradation. With Conkling in disgrace, the way was cleared for the nomination of James G. Blaine. To his admiring followers the man from Maine was a "plumed knight," but by this time large numbers of Americans thought his plumes somewhat bedraggled. His chief weapon was the bloody shirt; he had defended the spoils system, and he had been accused of implication in the railroad scandals of 1873. During the 1884 campaign, painful evidence was uncovered showing the accusations to have been all too true. In protest against Blaine's character, a section of the Republican party broke away and supported the Democratic nominee, Grover Cleveland. The influential magazine *Harper's* flayed Blaine as a crooked politician. This revolt of the "Mugwumps," as they were called, stood out in a campaign outstanding for its bitter personal attacks. The party platforms, as usual, read about the same. A large section of big business quietly supported Cleveland, who as a conservative Democrat was regarded as even "sounder" than Blaine. But, as a business journal remarked, it did not really matter too much which man won, for "a good president cannot make the country; a bad president cannot ordinarily mar it."

Yet the revolt of the Mugwumps, the defeat of Blaine, and the election of the first Democratic President in the twenty years since the war had a considerable significance. It meant that the long and politically demoralizing shadow of the Civil War was passing. It was no longer possible to rely on the bloody shirt, and it was a handicap to be known as a spoils-man.

CLEVELAND AND THE TARIFF

Grover Cleveland, who won the torrid election by a very narrow margin, had compiled a notable reform record as governor of New York State before coming to the presidency, and his rugged honesty sets him somewhat apart from most statesmen of the Gilded Age. Like Hayes, he was partly frustrated in his efforts to keep appointments away from the spoilsmen. For his own party was starving, ravenous for jobs after twenty-four years of famine, and the pressure was enormous. "You cannot serve God and the Democratic party at the same time," a Republican senator taunted Cleveland. Cleveland at least tried. He showed his courage also in appointing two ex-Confederate southerners to his Cabinet, and he incurred the wrath of Union veterans by offering to return captured Confederate flags and even more by his attempting to curtail veterans' bonuses. The bluff New Yorker had, above all else, integrity and political courage.

He showed these qualities most when he deliberately raised the issue of the tariff. According to the veteran politician Carl Schurz, Cleveland had come to him and asked, "What is the use of being elected and reelected if you don't stand for something?" Schurz recommended the tariff, and Cleveland took it up. His desire to find some distinctive principles for his party was certainly most commendable, and his effort to make a political campaign meaningful was refreshing in this age. In seeking to lower the tariff he again showed rare political courage. For here was one of those issues the ordinary politicians always avoided like a plague. It was political suicide, they thought, to antagonize all the many industrial interests which profited by the protective duties. Since the war, under Republican auspices, the duties had crept up. More and more products were included, and tariff bills were framed in accordance with no plan except that of "logrolling," or mutual back scratching, by which everybody voted for everybody else's favorite tariff duty. It was time, Cleveland felt, for reform. He did not suggest abolishing all duties, of course, but he did think they should be scaled down and made more rational. Somewhat to the dismay of the politicians in his own party—and to the delight of the Republicans—he forced this issue into the open.

Cleveland lost the 1888 election on the issue of the tariff. The educated classes appreciated the soundness of arguments against excessive protection, but the manufacturers poured money into the coffers of the GOP. Since the tariff is one of those issues which is perennial in American history, and since it is still with us, we may conveniently review here the arguments for and against it. The indiscriminate granting of high duties was a source of corruption and evidence of eagerness to give handouts to every business interest, which demoralized politics in the Gilded Age. A tariff is a form of monopoly, not truly consistent with the "free competition" often proclaimed as an American ideal. It involved the exploitation of many farmers, whose prices for manufactured goods were raised and who derived no benefit from tariffs. The economic arguments offered in behalf of the protective system are theoretically unsound; it is not difficult for economists to show that everyone would be better off if all barriers to trade were removed. It is not true that freer trade would mean, as tariff advocates never tire of predicting, the ruin of all our industries. Only those would be ruined which deserved to be because of their inefficiency, while the others would do better than ever, profiting from the increased foreign markets. The case against high tariff duties on all our manufactures is thus very strong. An argument that sounds odd to modern ears was also offered by Cleveland when he declared that tariffs brought too much money into the Treasury. This money became a demoralizing influence on Congress, since it would be ladled out to be spent in the districts of as many congressmen as possible.

On the other hand, in this early period of our industrial development the "infant-industry" argument seemed persuasive. American industry needed to attract capital, and the existence of tariffs, virtually guaranteeing profits by keeping off competition, helped attract it. A tariff is a subsidy, but such a special favor might be justified in the national interest if it fostered an industry valuable to the nation. However, the problem of foreign trade was not yet acute, for American manufactured goods had a huge domestic market; thus some of the present arguments against tariff protection did not exist in Cleveland's time. Basically, however, the tariff system grew up and proved difficult to root out not because of enlightened arguments in its favor, but because individual congressmen and senators were seldom able to take the larger view of the question. They had to look after their local interests, and they could not well vote against a duty which protected local industry. The familiar process of logrolling then guaranteed that a tariff bill would come out of Congress bearing

something for everybody. It was politically difficult to attack this system, as Cleveland found out. And some arguments in favor of the tariffs were superficially plausible.

Nevertheless, Cleveland had forced an issue into the open, and the campaign of 1888 stands out as one of the few in this era which was marked by a fairly intelligent discussion of a real problem. To many it did not, however, seem the most vital question that could have been raised. A few years later the Populist farmers, who hated Cleveland for his general conservatism, called it a "sham issue." It was hardly that, but it was not quite strong enough to arouse the voters from their lethargy. Cleveland failed to arouse popular emotions against the tariff and was beaten in 1888, though this election is noteworthy as one in which the defeated candidate got more popular votes than his victorious rival. The Republicans celebrated their victory by passing the McKinley Tariff Act, raising duties to a new high. The election was a notably corrupt one, with the use of money to buy votes never more in evidence. Clearly, the purification of politics had a long way to go. But to many the victory of Benjamin Harrison in 1888 was evidence of the permanent dominance of Republican principles. The Indianapolis *Journal* ventured to predict that "this is a Republican country, and there is not a middle-aged voter now alive who will ever see the Democracy again in control of the national Government."

SEEDS OF POLITICAL REVIVAL

Despite the prophecy of this newspaper, Cleveland was to return to office at the next presidential election. Harrison was a feeble and uninspiring leader, and moreover the tariff message of the Democrats seemed to bear some belated fruit: increases in prices following the high McKinley Tariff impressed farmers and consumers unfavorably. Yet in a sense the *Journal* was right; unless the Democrats could find a better issue than the tariff, they were not likely to win any lasting triumph over the GOP. The Republicans had identified themselves with the new capitalism, and in general it was bringing prosperity and a higher living standard to wide areas of the nation. There were indeed forces of profound discontent beginning to arise, chiefly among disgruntled farmers and exploited workers. But the Democrats had shown little tendency to identify themselves with these elements.

Evidently, if they hoped to unseat the Republicans, the Democrats would have to dethrone this conservative leadership and develop a program of reform that would be attractive to farmers and workers. A tradition of militant defense of the "common man's" interests against a privileged minority also existed in the party— the Jacksonian tradition. Such a program, as some were beginning to realize, would have to involve the use of the federal government in a new way. Populism, the rising political force, boldly demanded that government help the farmers and workers to control the corporations and that it enact measures for the assistance of farmers and workers. It was not easy for a Bourbon-ridden Democratic party to adopt such a program. As a matter of fact, it could do so only after a revolution in the party which, in 1896, deposed Cleveland and raised to power insurgents from the West. With this revolt was to come a great revival of interest in politics.

The great political question that emerged, after a generation of relative quiet, was that of the control of big business. Rather suddenly, about 1890, there was a popular awareness of this problem —the "trust" problem, as it was called. Monopoly seemed to be spreading everywhere. Typical was the comment of old Rutherford Hayes, who had advocated strict *laissez faire* toward business when President a decade earlier; he now wrote that the country could not "leave uncontrolled a power that buys your councils, your legislatures, and your courts. Shall the will of monopolies take the place of the Government of the people?" Thus was the question posed in the minds of many. Interest in it had been aroused by investigations which disclosed the extent of monopoly and some of the dubious practices of the great trusts. A New York State investigating committee produced sensational evidence in 1887–1888, and in 1888 a House of Representatives committee investigated the Standard Oil Company, the sugar trust, the whisky trust, and the beef trust. More widely read were the writings of the pioneer "muckraker" Henry Demarest Lloyd, who told the story of Standard Oil, "the greatest, wisest, and meanest monopoly known to history," in no admiring terms. But concern about the power and influence of monopolies was not confined to left-wing journalists like the brilliant Lloyd, who soon became a Socialist. As the cited example of Hayes indicates, many conservative Americans became alarmed. The state supreme court of Michigan asserted that "it is doubtful if free government can long exist in a country where such enormous amounts of money are allowed to be accumulated in the vaults of corporations. . . ."

The new concern about the power of big business led directly to interest in freeing politics from its control. The new political hero was to be the man who could not be bought, who fought the "interests" and smashed the "machine." Such men had existed in the postwar years, but they had not been common. The political reformer as a type was just appearing at the end of the 1880s, typified by such men as John P. Altgeld in Illinois and Robert M. La Follette in Wisconsin. Altgeld wrote a bitter epitaph on the older politicians of the Gilded Age, or what he called the "officeholding class":

> It is difficult to point out wherein it does anything that can be regarded as raising the standard of public morals, creating a healthy public sentiment, or solving in a proper way any of the great questions, both economic and social, that are calling for solution. . . .

To be noted is the assumption that there *were* "great questions . . . calling for solution," for this was the critical factor. Most of these questions were connected with a rising uneasiness about the power of the great corporations, power both economic and political. The day of negative statesmanship—the day when it did not matter much what politicians did or did not do—was, in the opinion of many, drawing to an end. It was ending with the passing of free land, the growth of population, and the rise of giant industrialism. Lloyd wrote that the American people must now seek the "good society" not through frontier individualism but through conscious political effort.

The railroads were the first target of an uprising against predatory and monopolistic capitalism; the uprising was led by farmers who suffered directly from their practices. In 1884 each party paid tribute to the theory of government regulation of the railroads. In 1887 the Interstate Commerce Act was passed as a bipartisan measure, despite the doubts of President

Cleveland. It required railroad rates to be "reasonable and just" and forbade a number of discriminatory or monopolistic practices, such as "pools" and rebates. Then, in 1890, the Sherman Antitrust Act was put through in response to a tide of public indignation against all trusts. This significant act declared, in language drawn from the English common law, that every combination in restraint of interstate or foreign trade was illegal. It is to be doubted that these acts were intended to be very effective. For example, the Interstate Commerce Commission was given no authority to set rates. Young Robert La Follette, then a fledgling congressman, struggled in vain for a bill more thorough and enforceable than the Interstate Commerce Act; the act as passed proved ineffective until amended twenty years later. Conservative leaders said privately that the measure was intended to have no real force but was only to appease "the clamor of the ignorant and unreasoning." Much the same could be said of the Sherman act. Conservatives in both parties did not believe in regulation of big business and hoped to satisfy popular opinion with ineffective measures. Those who did sincerely believe that some control was desirable lacked the experience necessary to go about obtaining it. The vaguely worded Sherman act was virtually a dead letter for more than a decade.

Popular protest against big business did not die away, as some hoped; it was to reach an almost frenzied peak in the political uprising of the farmers a few years later. During the Gilded Age rumblings of protest had occasionally disturbed the complacency of the two major parties. An "Antimonopoly" ticket had appeared during the depressed 1870s, and then a more significant Greenback party, winning a million votes in 1878 with its demand for cheap money, only to decline greatly with the return of prosperity and the successful "resumption" of 1879. The Granger movement of the 1870s had attempted to bring about regulation of railroad rates. Now again in the 1890s the soft-money fever arose among the farmers, accompanying their hatred of the monopolies and their distrust of the two big political parties. The Populist farmers declared that both parties were tools of big business and must be swept aside to make way for a People's party. As it turned out, the old parties were to survive, but not without major alterations. This farmer-labor movement opened a new chapter in American politics. Politically speaking, the Gilded Age came to an end in 1896 when the two major parties ceased to be Tweedledum and Tweedledee, when the people reasserted their control over politics by becoming interested in a great issue, and when the supremacy of big business and the bosses was challenged by a grass-roots movement of protest against both.

THE PATTERN OF CORRUPTION

Something more must be said about that systematic corruption of political life which, particularly at the local level, sank such deep roots in these times. The treasured heritage of democratic government gradually slipped into a dismal swamp of corruption. Democracy seemed to disappear without people even being aware of it, for where the "boss" ruled there was no such thing as popular government. By common admission, bossism and corruption were worst in the cities, but at all levels they exhibited a common pattern. There were state machines as well as city machines; and in the Senate

of the United States sat the great state bosses, looking after the interests of the "interests" which they were paid to defend.

That a democratic constitution means nothing in itself is dramatically exhibited by the fact that the two greatest totalitarian states of this century, Soviet Russia and Nazi Germany, operated under "democratic" constitutions. In both, great party machines controlled the electoral process, leaving no freedom of choice to the voter. In the United States after the Civil War, something similar began to take place in a more haphazard manner. In city after city and state after state, the pattern was remarkably similar. The forces involved were the same: professional politicians of doubtful virtue and business interests willing to dispense money for a variety of favors. Keen students of the system distinguished between the "ruling" and the "governing" classes—the capitalistic interests which provided the goals and the money, and the politicians who actually manipulated the machinery of government. The barons of business preferred to deal with the bosses, who for the most part understood the bargain and kept to it. A famous remark attributed to Horatio Seymour expressed the ideal of the business class; put cynically: "Our people want men in office who will not steal but who will not interfere with those who do." The boss naturally insisted on his share of the "boodle" but was not ordinarily unreasonable about it. The code of the politician decreed that a man might take money if he earned it, that is, if he gave the capitalist something worthwhile in return. We have the testimony of Thomas Platt, writing of Matthew Quay of Pennsylvania (one boss commenting on another): "He believed that business men had a right to profit, and therefore

The Tweed Ring, which plundered New York City shortly after the Civil War, was eventually routed with the help of the famous cartoonist, Thomas Nast. The original caption read: "A Group of Vultures Waiting for the Storm to Blow Over— 'Let Us Prey.'" (*Library of Congress*)

railway and other concessions from local governments. The political boss took the money ladled out for these purposes and passed it down the line to the lesser bosses, who controlled the machinery of government from the local caucus on up. The system was nonpartisan. As the president of the American Sugar Refining Company once testified before the United States Senate, corporations gave their money to whichever party was locally dominant, and in case of any doubt they donated to both. The barons of business privately defended this system on the grounds that if the "masses," stirred up by "demagogues," were permitted to interfere with the delicate mechanism of business, they would ruin it. Since the capitalists were not themselves interested in going into politics, they dealt with the half-world of political bosses.

The latter were a class apart. They provided some of the most picturesque personalities of the Gilded Age, such as Matthew Quay, the fabulous half-Indian Pennsylvania boss, or Thomas Platt of New York, the "easy boss" who boasted that he ran New York State from a corner of the lobby of the Algonquin Hotel in New York City. These two sat in the Senate of the United States, controlling patronage, and through that and their local connections, dominating their states. Such men were the robber barons of politics and often got almost as rich as their counterparts in the world of big business. But there was a difference: Quay (whom Platt called the ablest of all politicians, technically speaking) died poor, though we know that he filched hundreds of thousands. Unlike a John D. Rockefeller or a Jay Gould, Quay and his kind did not hoard their gains. They were generous, open-handed, and good entertainers. Therein lay the boss's secret: a genial

could always command money in any amount when he desired it." This meant that Quay always delivered to business what it wanted and hence could always count on obtaining money from business. Among the corrupt politicians it was a breach of "honor" to take the capitalists' money and not deliver the goods. There was a fair amount of honor among these thieves, and a "boss" who was not as good as his word did not last very long.

Industrialists wanted "to control, as they saw fit, hours of labor, working conditions, competition, also to be free from drastic regulation." Sometimes they wanted more specific favors, such as street-

good fellow, he stole money from the public and extracted it from tycoons of business, but he had to distribute it among his innumerable friends and henchmen with a lavish hand. It has been suggested that, at a time when the rich were not heavily taxed by the government, the political bosses played the role of Robin Hood, taking from the rich and distributing to the poor—redistributing income, in a way. Certainly in the places where they were most firmly entrenched, in the large cities, the bosses made much of their role as friends and guardians of the poor.

Thomas Jefferson had predicted that the mobs of great cities would be as sores on the body politic. Even Jefferson could scarcely have foreseen Boss Tweed. The Tweed Ring of New York City became the most notorious of all the city "rings," yet it is not necessarily the most illuminating example. For Tweed and his gang were too crude to last. They stole recklessly, fantastically, with both hands in the loot—200 million dollars, in a few years, 1868–1872. Tweed himself, with his race horses housed in stables with stalls built of solid mahogany, lived in Oriental magnificence during his brief riotous career. His overthrow was inevitable because his thievery was too obvious. But the point is that within a few years after a surge of public indignation swept away Tweed and his gang, the system was back, with another boss reigning, cleverer and almost equally dishonest. Students of the system noted that a wave of indignation would be followed by public relaxation and the return of the bosses; reform was temporary only. It was obvious that only constant and active participation by the citizens in government could ensure its honesty. But busy urban Americans were not prepared to participate. They did not, Lincoln Steffens was forced to conclude in his famous study of *The Shame of the Cities,* really want self-rule; they wanted somebody to *give* them good government.

Many drew from this the possible conclusion that the "machine" was a natural growth, with deep roots in the realities of the new urban life. Looking at a number of cities, one found the same pattern. Boss government was the normal state of affairs. The boss was a regular feature of urban life, and in fact many intelligent people accepted the inevitability of at least some police graft, "boodle," and ballot-box dishonesty. Some people even took a perverse pride in the efficiency of their local machines. It was argued in defense of the system that the boss provided certain necessary services. He was quite often a kindly man with a wide acquaintance, and he served as a sort of informal social-security agent, lending a hand to any of his "people" who needed it. A political club like Tammany of New York was a social institution providing a sense of community for the urban masses of the slums. If a catastrophe such as a fire or accident struck a family, the boss's boys could be relied upon to lend a helping hand. They found jobs for the unemployed, got people out of trouble with the law, and donated money to all the churches. In these and innumerable other ways the boss played the role of a big brother to the city poor who had nowhere else to look for such services and comforts.

It would be well, of course, not to exaggerate the benevolence of the boss. The "kindly" leader was usually corrupted by power into a greedy tyrant who dealt in crime, throve on vice, and sacrificed such things as schools and hospitals to the demands of the machine for graft. He was, however, able to govern and willing to provide certain social services which no other institutions were providing. If the people abdicated their social and political responsibilities, something as loathsome as the boss system would fill the gap. "Someone had to lead, and the knave and the demagogue took over."*

Boss rule and crooked government persisted into the twentieth century as a stubborn feature of American city life—an unwelcome legacy from the Gilded Age and a challenge to the idea of democracy. As James Bryce, British author of the influential book *The American Commonwealth* (1888 and many subsequent editions), commented, "No government demands so much from the citizen as democracy." In the last analysis, the boss ruled where the people had abdicated. During the Gilded Age politics unfortunately almost ceased to be a respectable profession. It was abandoned to men of doubtful character. A vicious circle was established in which rogues took over

* Dennis T. Lynch, *The Wild Seventies,* Appleton-Century-Crofts, Inc., New York, 1941, p. 53.

politics because respectable people neglected it, and then respectable people scorned politics because it was a profession of rogues. This attitude has persisted down to the present as a legacy of this era. It was revealed in a recent public-opinion poll which showed that people tend to place politics well down toward the bottom among the careers they regard as desirable for their children to pursue.

THOUGHT AND LETTERS

Fortunately for the United States, her reputation in the later nineteenth century did not rest wholly on the morals of her businessmen or politicians. While the hum of new industry was the most audible sound, and politics was dominated by the new ruling class of businessmen and bosses, other phases of society showed real development. Learning, literature, and the arts by no means perished. Higher education made large gains, and American scholars and scientists made notable contributions to the world. A significant literature, art, and architecture appeared.

Vanderbilt residence, Newport, Rhode Island. Built in the 1890s at a cost of some 3 million dollars, The Breakers was but one of numerous palaces housing the Vanderbilt clan, and was the scene of some of the most lavish entertainments of the Gilded Age. (Library of Congress)

For the country which Tocqueville, a few decades earlier, had doubted could ever produce anything of real intellectual distinction, this was an achievement. There is something startling in the fact that Josiah Royce, one of the world's foremost philosophers, was born of a California-gold-rush family and grew up amid the rough-and-tumble of mining camps. He nevertheless got his education in Germany, as did many leaders of American thought in this era, and became a professor at Harvard, where he taught future Presidents of the United States. The example is not an isolated one. William and Henry James, William Dean Howells, and other notable writers continued the New England–New York intellectual traditions. Eastern universities perhaps still dominated the scene; the best of the new graduate schools was at Johns Hopkins in Baltimore. But the West, no longer so raw, was also heard from. A Missouri farm boy who grew up on "the river," became a steamboat pilot, and then knocked about the mining West for some years "roughing it"—Samuel Clemens, alias Mark Twain—was the most famous American writer of the age, and his name became a household word in parts of the globe where nothing else much was known about the United States of America.

Europeans were still shocked at the rawness of American culture, and the greatest American novelist of the age, Henry James, fled to live in England because the American scene offered, he thought, no place for the true artist. Less fastidious writers experimented in all directions and in all regions. The general impression of American letters is one of considerable vitality. European influences merged with native themes to produce some interesting literature. Naturalism, which sought to describe life in a grimly realistic manner, was the leading literary fashion. Hamlin Garland applied it notably to the lives of frontier farmers. *Maggie: A Girl of the Streets* and *The Pit: A Story of Chicago* were other significant titles—themes of human passion, greed, and degradation, set forth with frankness. Business tycoons and fallen maidens seemed, indeed, among the favorite subjects of this new realism. It fitted in with the dominant influences in this age, science and Darwinian evolutionary theories. Literature became empirical, exact, unsentimental, and a little grim.

The quantity and exuberance of such literature, if not always its quality, testified to a creative spirit working in America. In art and architecture and in science there was similar evidence. Henry Hobson Richardson was the foremost of the American architects who, in tune with European fashion, went in for the revival of older styles in a way often not pleasing to later taste. The mansions of the Gilded Age millionaires were reproductions of classical, Gothic, or Renaissance forms. For those with other tastes, Frank Lloyd Wright was already in the 1890s experimenting in the modern style he was to make famous.

As for science, the Michelson-Morley experiment of 1887 might be singled out for mention as an example of American contribution to the most advanced levels of science. One of the critical steps along the road to modern theories of light, motion, and matter, the experiment indicated that no such thing existed as an "ether" which could serve as a standard of absolute space; it thus prepared the way for Einstein's theory of relativity. In all fields, the growth of graduate schools and specialized institutes signaled that the United States was progressing toward the top in advanced areas of thinking and scientific research.

In the 1870s and 1880s educational reform was in full flight at a number of American universities; Harvard, Michigan, Cornell, and the newly established Johns Hopkins may be mentioned. The stress was on creative learning and original research rather than passive memorization. Modern literature, history, and political science were given preference over the older favorites, mathematics and the classics. Johns Hopkins boasted, in addition to its great medical school, a graduate school in history and political science from which emerged eminent historians, jurists, editors, and a future President of the United States, Woodrow Wilson. At Harvard, Royce and William James were part of a brilliant team which produced, among other things, the new philosophical doctrine known as pragmatism. The social sciences were especially active; the best known names were perhaps Lester Ward in sociology and Thorstein Veblen in economics, both genuine pioneers. They were many others. A theme of practical concern about solving real social problems, bringing pure theory down into the arena of actual human affairs, ran through much of this, and contributed greatly to the epoch of political and social reform that followed the Gilded Age.

There is sometimes a misguided tendency to search for the ideas and achievements that are specifically "American." Generally speaking, American scientists, social scientists, philosophers, and historians took their place, as they should, in the ranks of an international scholarly community. That William James's pragmatism and Thorstein Veblen's institutionalism were somewhat original is less important than that they were significant contributions to this larger world of thought. James was well acquainted with the European intellectual leaders, often visited Europe, and brought Europeans to Harvard. In these years cultural contacts between Old World and New were becoming closer. Mark Twain's *Innocents Abroad* might not seem to suggest it, but Twain himself was one of the many Americans who made a significant rediscovery of their European heritage in these years. While Frederick Jackson Turner of Wisconsin defiantly affirmed that America was unique because it had had a frontier, most American historians of this period were engaged in exploring the European roots of American institutions.

A catalogue of names and titles is not especially edifying, and there is unfortunately no space to provide here the history of all these ideas and achievements in the arts and sciences. But the student of American history ought not to be left with the impression that greed, corruption, and materialism were the only motifs in the so-called Gilded Age. The cultural and intellectual record was by no means a sad one. America was still undoubtedly behind Europe in this respect. She did, however, produce a respectable number of men who could bear the comparison, while one of the world's greatest systems of higher education was laying the foundation for additional progress.

This educational system provides us with one link between the often arrogant plutocracy of the times and the promising cultural developments. The untaxed millions which Rockefellers and Carnegies were extracting from industrialism found their way eventually into intellectual and educational projects. The University of Chicago was a Rockefeller creation, and numerous other private institutions of learning and research received endowments. Possessing money they could not possibly spend all on themselves, the great fortune makers often chose to leave behind some enduring and honorific monument to their names. A surprising number of them, who certainly knew little and cared less about art, became important collectors of paintings and other art objects. Across the United States, from the Mellon Gallery in Washington to Leland Stanford University in California, magnificent cultural institutions today remind us of the good use which hard-fisted barons of business sometimes made of their gains. At the same time, the public lands which subsidized the railroads also helped build the state universities of the nation. Thus did material and intellectual culture advance together.

FURTHER READINGS

Older and classic accounts of the American political system include James Bryce, *American Commonwealth* (1888), since reissued many times, and M. Ostrogorski, *Democracy and the Party System in the United States* (1902). To these might well be added William Allen White, *Masks in a Pageant* (1928), and Matthew Josephson, *The Politicos* (1938). Henry J. Ford, another keen student of American politics, wrote *The Cleveland Era* (1919), one of the Chronicles of America. More detailed studies of politicians include Allan Nevins, *Grover Cleveland: A Study in Courage* (1932); H. F. Gosnell, *Boss Platt and His New York Machine* (1924); Harry Barnard, *Eagle Forgotten: The Life of John Peter Altgeld* (1938); and Harold Zink, *City Bosses in the United States* (1930). Most valuable are the memoirs of such men as Carl Schurz, Robert M. La Follette, George W. Curtis, and William Allen White. Leonard D. White, *The Republican Era, 1869–1901: A Study in Administrative History* (1958), stresses the gradual growth of a professional bureaucracy at the expense of the spoils system. F. W. Taussig, *Tariff History of the United States* (1923), traces that persistent issue.

Literature, thought, and society are reflected in such works as V. L. Parrington's *Main Currents in American Thought,* volume III (1930); Charles E. Merriam, *American Political Ideas, 1865–1917* (1920); Richard Hofstadter, *Social Darwinism in American Thought, 1860–1915* (1944), now available in an inexpensive edition; Morton White, *Social Thought in America* (1949), also available in a paperback edition. Among numerous useful anthologies of American literature are Oscar Cargill (ed.), *The Social Revolt: American Literature from 1888 to 1914* (1933), and Perry Miller (ed.), *American Thought: Civil War to World War* (1954). See also Merle Curti, *The Growth of American Thought* (1943), chapters 20–24, a work which has an excellent bibliography; and Harvey Wish, *Society and Thought in Modern America* (1952).

Constance M. Green, *American Cities in the Growth of the Nation* (1957), and Bessie L. Pierce, *A History of Chicago, 1871–1893,* volume III (1957), represent interesting explorations of American civilization as a story of the rise of cities. The significant changes in higher education that took place during this epoch can be approached through the histories of major universities, such as Samuel E. Morison (ed.), *The Development of Harvard University, 1869–1909* (1930). See also Richard J. Storr, *The Beginnings of Graduate Education in America* (1953).

NINETEEN

The Agrarian Revolt

AGRICULTURE AND INDUSTRIALIZATION

1873
Silver demonetized—the "Crime of '73."

1877
Granger cases decided.

1878
Bland-Allison Act passed.
Greenback party reaches high point.

1879
Greenbacks redeemed in gold.

1885
Farm prices decline.

1887
Interstate Commerce Act passed.
Farmers Alliance movements grow.

1890
Sherman Silver Purchase Act passed.

1893
Depression begins.
Sherman Silver Act repealed.

1894
Pullman strike; march of Coxey's Army.
Populist movement grows.

1896
Bryan wins Democratic and Populist nominations.
"Battle of Standards" election won by GOP.

1900
Gold Standard Act passed.

THE GREATEST ACHIEVEMENT of the United States in the post-Civil War period was its rapid advance to the position of the leading industrial nation of the world. Perhaps nothing is more indicative of this surpassing industrial growth than the fact that by the 1890s American iron and steel products could be sold on better than even terms with British products not only in the general world market, but in Britain itself, the home of the Industrial Revolution. After a frenzy of construction in the two years 1882 and 1887, the trackage laid amounted to two-thirds of the total rail mileage existing in the nation in 1860. In 1860, slightly over 6 million tons of bituminous coal were mined in the United States; by 1900, well over 200 million tons were being mined each year.

As we have seen, a variety of factors made this miracle of industrial growth possible. The United States possessed one of the most highly concentrated and richest areas of diversified raw materials anywhere on the globe. It had a stable political and social system that allowed the businessman the widest possible freedom, and one that awarded to the successful the greatest measure of approbation and prestige. Immigration provided an abundance of labor. Vast sums of investment capital flowed into the American economy from foreign sources. The American economy carried no heavy burden of defense and armaments. The favorable climate for business expansion and the atmosphere of social mobility helped produce a group

398

of business leaders who startled the world with their managerial ability, financial acumen, and ruthless lust for power.

The skyrocketing growth of industry, however, carried with it the increasing subordination of agriculture in the nation's economic life. While the absolute value of farm production in the postwar decades continued to mount, its proportionate contribution to the nation's income diminished in relation to that of industry. The share of the national income going to the farmers of the nation dropped from 30 per cent in 1859 to slightly over 15 per cent in 1889. And yet this declining importance of agriculture occurred despite the growing efficiency of farming. Greater use of the reaper, the binder, and other farm machinery, the increasing availability of scientific information for the farmer through the expanding number of agricultural colleges, extension services, and experiment stations—all these worked to make American farming more productive. The possibility of acquiring cheap land under the provisions of the Homestead Act also increased the output of the American farmers by tempting them to add to their acreage.

The fortunes of the nation's industrialists and farmers were closely interlocked. The farmer's machinery was produced by American manufacturers. Without these tools that industry was placing at his disposal, he would not have been able to expand production. The extension of rail lines into the farm areas of the nation, and the resulting connections with the great urban centers, made it possible for the farmer to ship his livestock over hundreds of miles to the great markets and to send his wheat to regions hitherto inaccessible. Along with this, the lowering of the costs of steamship transportation on the world's oceans made the American farmer truly a part of the world's economy. It was the prospect of becoming part of the world market that led most farming communities in the nation to await the coming of rail lines into their area with the keenest anticipation.

The dependence of the farmer on the products of industry was counterbalanced by the industrialist's dependence on the labor of the farmers. There were some areas of industry where this dependence was apparent. The textile industry could not have flourished without the abundance of cotton and wool coming from the farms. The meat-packing industry was based on the flow of cattle and hogs to the slaughterhouses. The brewing and distilling industries required grains from the farms. But the American farmer made contributions to the growth of industry, both European and American, that were perhaps not so apparent. For one thing, the growing efficiency of farming, its expanding productivity, released a supply of labor from the farms that became available to industry. The hands not needed on the farm were free to produce other goods and services. Without the abundant produce of American farms it would not have been possible in either America or Europe to bring together vast numbers of people in industrial centers with the happy assurance that there would be food for all. Some European economists have compared the flow of foodstuffs from the United States to Europe in the decades after the Civil War with the flow of gold from the New World to the Old in the aftermath of the Age of Discovery. Both made possible a vast enrichment of European life.

The production of these vast surpluses of foods and raw materials on American farms aided industrial development in the United States in yet another way: it in-

Reaper with mechanical
rake, 1864 model

First practical
self-binder, 1876

William Jennings Bryan in 1896

Coxey's Army on the march toward Washington

The farmer was unable to market his increased agricultural production at satisfactory prices during most of the years from 1873 to 1896. The result was agrarian near-revolution in the 1890s, climaxed when the young Populist orator Bryan stampeded the Democratic convention in 1896 with his indictment of the gold standard and demand for cheaper money via "free silver."

McKinley as a tool
of the "trusts": a popular
cartoon by F. Opper

creased the possibility of attracting invest-ment capital from Europe. Billions of dol-lars were lent for a variety of enterprises. This willingness of European capitalists to invest in American industries was one of the greatest factors in our industrial ex-pansion. But it was not only the possi-bility of profits from industry that made American investments attractive; it was the added assurance that American farm surpluses afforded adequate guarantees of repayment of their interest and profits. Europe lent its billions with every antici-pation they would be repaid with profit or interest because the American economy could repay these loans chiefly out of farm surpluses.

In addition to all these contributions to industrial growth, the American farmer made another significant contribution to the industrialization of the nation. This contribution was extorted from him by the excessive prices he was charged for the services rendered by the financial and industrial sectors of the American econ-omy. Each excessive charge for farm ma-chinery, rail haulage, grain storage, and interest on loans was a subsidy paid by agriculture to finance and industry. Much of this was perhaps inevitable. The crea-tion of an industrial system in the midst of an agrarian economy has never been a painless process, and in some nations it has been accompanied by social tensions that have led to violence. In the United States the process may have been less painful than elsewhere because of the abundance of available resources. But un-der any circumstances, it was a process that required the accumulation of capital in vast amounts. In the United States some of this capital came from the profits of industry itself, plowed back into invest-ment. Some came from European borrow-ings, to be paid for by American farm

surpluses. And some came from excessive fees, charges, or taxes imposed on the nonindustrial sectors of the economy such as labor and agriculture. But the indus-trialists were in control of American eco-nomic life. They were a strong-willed, cohesive, and disciplined group, with great financial resources at their disposal. Many of them were deeply imbued with a sense of mission and an exaggerated conscious-ness of their role in American life. They constituted the dominant influence in na-tional political life, and the politicians of their day were frequently their willing servants. With these powerful weapons in the industrialists' hands, the farmers had little choice but to serve the needs of in-dustrial expansion.

THE GRIEVANCES OF THE FARMER: MARKETING AND CREDIT

Harnessed as he was to the service of industry, the American farmer in the post-war decades harbored an increasing sense of indignity that eventually exploded into one of the great political movements of American history. But not all of the farm-er's woes flowed from the subordinate status he was being forced into in Ameri-can life. Much of his difficulty came from the very abundance of his production, for he was growing surpluses that were mar-keted at decreasing prices. The years from 1865 to the middle of the 1890s saw a long-term downward trend in commodity prices, so that the farmer was caught in an ever-tightening vise of lowered returns and increased costs of production. He operated under conditions of the freest of free competition. Without any of the con-trols over production available to the industrialist, without any monopolies "pools," or under-the-table deals for the setting of prices, the American farmer sold his product in competition with the hosts of his fellows, and in competition with the farmers of other countries of the world. He sold under terms of maximum disadvantage to himself and maximum gain for the buyer.

In the United States, many of the forces in the economy stimulated higher farm production. The widening measure of scientific skill available to the farmer, the production of farm machinery and its increasing use, the cheapness of new land and the possibilities of profit from the appreciation of land values all led the farmer to try to solve his problem by producing more. He continued to force excess products into an already glutted market. The answer of the industrialists to this problem would have been to curtail production, but this was a remedy not then available to the farmer. His isolation and lack of detailed market information, along with the very nature of agriculture, made it impossible for him to control production. And so the surplus products continued to flow to the market.

Not all the difficulties of the farmer, however, came from the production of surpluses or from such normal uncertainties of farm life as the weather. Many of his problems were created for him by the practices of the emergent industrial society and the burdens these placed on the farmer. To change these practices through political action seemed easier than to control overproduction, and so the farmer increasingly turned his energies in that direction. Eventually he became irate and turned with such vigor to a political attack on the industrialists that he threatened to unseat them from the place of power they had held since the days of the Civil War.

Perhaps the leading object of agrarian discontent and wrath was the railroads.

The happy anticipation with which the extension of rail lines to farm areas had been awaited in many regions turned to anger as the farmer felt victimized by railroad practices. There was no railroad regulation of any sort at either the state or federal level; no effective controls were to be imposed until after 1900. The farmer was overwhelmingly dependent on the railroads for the marketing of his crops, and this usually meant the one railroad that served his area. In most farm communities, there was little competition from other means of transport. Thus the railroads were able to charge all that the traffic would bear, and the farmer's needs were the railroads' gains. In general, it would be assumed that the farmer would have to pay the price of one bushel of wheat to get another carried to market. In 1869 it was calculated that the wheat shipped out of the state of Minnesota would bring the farmers of the state 8 million dollars and the roads that carried it 12 million. Farmers in the Middle West could but wonder about their plight when corn for which they were offered 15 cents a bushel sold in New York for $1. Frequently, the railroads owned the grain elevators at the rail sidings, and the farmers were also charged excessive fees for storage.

With the growing efficiency of rail operations, and the economies available because of technical innovations such as the adoption of the standard gauge, the charge for hauling farm produce to the market gradually diminished. Indeed, freight rates as a whole declined during the postwar decades. But the farmer's anger was not abated, because other grievances existed to fan the flames of his resentment. Foremost among these was rate discrimination. The roads had a policy of giving lower rates to big shippers than were available to small, and the farmer

AGRICULTURAL PRICES, 1880–1896

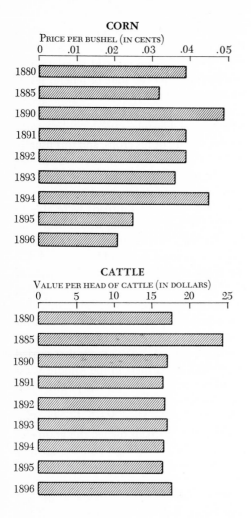

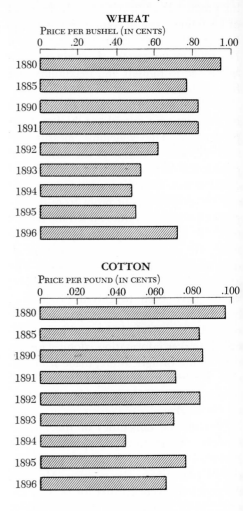

was the small shipper par excellence. They also frequently gave lower rates for carriage of freight between points where competition for traffic prevailed than were available in areas which were served by one line only. Thus the farm communities of the nation were again discriminated against. The railroads therefore became the first object of their attack.

The trend in taxation of the nineteenth century also added to the farmers' grievances. As the number of banks, railroads,

and industrial corporations increased, so did the amount of a stock they issued. This form of personal property was easily concealed from tax assessors. But the real property held by the farmer could not be hidden. A distinguished economist commented that "the farmer bears not only his share [of taxes] but also that of other classes of society." The customs and the excise taxes used so extensively in the period were, of course, taxes that were passed on by the importer or manufacturer to the consumer in the form of higher prices. This added yet more to the tax burden of the farmer.

The farmer was further the victim of his optimism and the lack of effective credit facilities in the nation. Far too frequently, he borrowed money at excessive rates of interest in order to buy new lands. Many a farmer calculated that even if he could not make a profit on the production and sale of farm produce, he might manage to stay afloat financially by what was essentially real estate speculation. So he borrowed money for land purchase in the hope of selling it later at a profit. A great deal of this farm indebtedness was encouraged by eastern land-mortgage companies which urged the money on the farmer in reckless disregard of his shaky financial position. Exorbitant rates of interest were frequently charged on the loans. But the fact that the farmer sometimes got into difficulty because of practices of this sort should not obscure the fact that the farmer's legitimate need of credit was almost completely overlooked in the basic banking legislation of the period.

The operations of the National Banking Act of 1863 were not designed to aid the farmer. No bank chartered under the act could be established with less than $50,000 capital or in a town of less than 6,000 population. These terms ruled out the establishment of national banks in most of rural America. Further, the state banks that had once furnished the farmer with much of the credit he needed were crippled by an 1865 law which imposed a 10 per cent tax on their note issues and thus taxed many of them out of business. Even had the farmer been able to find a national bank from which to seek a loan, these banks were forbidden to extend credit on the type of security most farmers could

offer, a mortgage on land. Some of the western states had banking acts which allowed state banks to operate with less capital than was required by the federal law and which also allowed the banks to lend on farm mortgages. But the amount of capital was so small, and the loans were, of necessity, for such long periods of time, that these banks afforded little relief. To be successful, such banks would need to have a ready market for the sale of the farmer's notes, but larger banks looked upon such securities with suspicion and preferred not to deal in them. Thus the state banks were, in practice, dominated by the larger banks and forced to do business according to their pattern. The farmer remained without adequate credit at reasonable rates of interest.

GRIEVANCES OF THE FARMER: CURRENCY AND THE TARIFF

Another aspect of the national economy that worked hardship on the farmer was the currency system, or the amount and kinds of dollar in circulation. Normally the ideal amount of currency in circulation is that which will achieve and maintain a stable dollar. Such a dollar did not exist in the years following the Civil War. Rather, there was a dollar that increased in purchasing power and diminished in debt-paying power—that is, an appreciating dollar. At a period when the population of the nation was expanding with great rapidity, when the nation was producing an ever-increasing volume of goods, when the farmers were growing more crops, the actual money in circulation diminished. Each dollar in circulation had to do a greater amount of work, had to carry a greater load, or in other words, purchase a greater amount of the nation's production. As the purchasing power of each dollar rose, the general level of prices went downward. The reasons for this hard-money condition lay substantially in the nation's adherence to the gold standard. This tied the value of the United States dollar and of the world's leading currencies to legally stated amounts of gold bullion. Thus gold was the common denominator defining the value of the world's various currencies, and to a large degree it was this common value of gold that aided so much in broadening the path of world trade in the nineteenth century. But gold itself is a commodity that may be scarce or plentiful, depending on the success of gold-mining ventures. In the period between the middle of the century and its last two decades there were no important gold discoveries throughout the world, and the world's gold supply was inadequate. As long as this situation prevailed in the face of an increasing population, the supply of gold-supported currency would remain inadequate unless other means of increasing it could be found.

In addition to these gold notes, there were other kinds of dollars in the United States. Under the National Banking Act, bank notes might be issued by qualified banks up to 90 per cent of the bonds of the United States which the bank owned. These notes circulated as legal tender and constituted a valuable addition to the nation's supply of dollars. But they did not furnish the farmer with the type of currency necessary to provide a stable dollar. The reason for this was that the amount of national bank notes did not vary with the volume of business or the amount of national production. The volume of bank notes depended on the size of the national debt, which was represented by the bonds. After the Civil War, provision was made for payment of the national debt, and con-

sequently the bonds were retired and the national bank notes diminished correspondingly. Further, not all the government bonds were in the hands of national banks. They were, of course, regarded as good investments, and many private individuals sought them. When owned by private investors, they could not serve as backing for currency.

National bank notes also had a tendency to be in plentiful supply just when they should have been getting scarcer and not to be available at all when they were most needed. In boom times, when the speculative fever was running strong, private holders of bonds were likely to sell them to banks in order to get cash to put into more promising investments. The banks, consequently, with bigger holdings, could now issue more notes just when the boom was under way and the reverse should have been taking place. When, on the other hand, investments were turning sour, investors turned to government bonds as sound security. Their price went up, and banks sold them for the sake of the profit on the sale, thus diminishing their capacity to issue bank notes at the moment when the declining markets should have been stimulated by an addition to the currency. The system of national-bank-note issuance therefore worked directly against the creation of stability in the nation's currency. Since this was a period of steadily declining farm prices, the operation of the money market served further to depress prices for wheat, corn, cotton, and in fact everything the farmer sold.

There was a third kind of dollar in use in the United States. These were United States notes, commonly known as greenbacks and first issued in the Civil War. Unfortunately for the farmers, the number of greenbacks in circulation was set by law. The Resumption Act of 1875 in effect limited them to about 350 million dollars. Thus, as with the gold notes and the bank notes, the number of dollars in actual circulation did not increase in step with the growth of the nation's business, and each dollar had to buy and sell more goods.

A fourth kind of dollar, one based on silver, might have increased the money supply of the United States and helped raise farm prices, but there was resistance to its use. At one time the United States and many other nations had used silver as the basis of currency. But silver had become even more scarce than gold. In a routine reexamination of the currency laws of the nation in 1873 it was established that for some years in the past silver had been even scarcer than gold, and relatively more costly to the United States mint. The silver miner could get more for his silver in the open market than he could at the mint. Therefore little or no silver was offered to the mint, and since most other nations of the world now used gold alone as the bullion basis of their currencies, the revision of the currency laws by the Congress in 1873 simply discontinued the authority of the Treasury to buy silver. This decision, under the circumstances quite reasonable, was later called the "Crime of '73." The demand that the government reestablish silver as the basis of currency issuance became one of the great controversial issues of politics.

The protective-tariff policies of the post-Civil War period also added to the farmer's burdens. Perhaps the tariff did not provoke as active a resentment among farmers as did their other economic difficulties, but its effects were still serious. By the creation of an artificially protected market, the producers of industrial goods were able to charge higher prices. For the farmer, the increase in prices he paid for farm machinery because of the tariffs generally ran from 30 to 60 per cent. Further, the tariff policies of the United States that tended to shut out European goods met with retaliatory action by many European nations. They raised tariffs against American goods, and since most of these goods were farm products, the American farmer's foreign market shrank. He felt increasingly the competitive pressure exerted by other agricultural exporting nations such as Canada, Russia, Australia, and Argentina.

While the farmers suffered from the fact that the prices of their products were set in the open world market, the tariffs assured the industrialists the opportunity of selling in a noncompetitive domestic market. To the security that the tariff gave them, the industrialists frequently added further security through one form or another of monopoly. Thus the farmer was pinched between the artificially controlled prices of the things he bought and the free and competitively set prices of the products he sold.

Perhaps all of this might have been borne had it not been for the general decline in farm prices. Discriminatory treatment from the railroads, lack of adequate credit and currency, burdensome taxes and tariff policies all might have been endurable if prices had been high. But with the constant downward movement of prices the farmer's indignation mounted. When, in the decade of the 1890s, he was confronted with the spectacle of 5-cent cotton, 15-cent corn, and 50-cent wheat, his anger knew no bounds. Partially a victim of his own excessive production, he was also a sufferer from legislation that gave much to the industrialist and financier and little to the farmer. This he was determined to change.

THE AGRARIAN PROTEST: GRANGERS

Confronted with the accumulating difficulties that arose from governmental policies, many of the nation's farmers moved toward united action through farm organizations in order to better their lot and force concessions from the government. The first such farm organization was the Patrons of Husbandry, commonly called the Grange. The Grange was founded in 1867 by Oliver H. Kelley, an employee of the Department of Agriculture. Kelley had traveled extensively in some of the major farming areas of the country, and he was persuaded that one of the blighting factors in the lives of farmers was the isolation which prevailed in the rural areas. He established the Grange and devoted years to its development in order to give the farmers a new focus of social life, hoping that in contact with their neighbors they would find wider social horizons and a fuller life. The growth of the Grange lagged until the depression of 1873; then it expanded rapidly. Farmers turned to it not for social contact, but rather in the hope that they might use it both as a political weapon in the legislative halls and as an agency for self-help. To many a farmer, the middleman was the most hated person in the economy, and the formation of producers' and consumers' cooperatives seemed to afford an effective way to bypass him. In this form of cooperation the members pooled their buying power in order to purchase from the producer, thus eliminating the customary middleman by assuming the role of distributor themselves. By buying and selling together they hoped to find mutual protection and security. A list was compiled of manufacturers who were willing to deal directly with state and local Grange organizations. In this way, the members hoped to escape the squeeze between fast-falling farm prices and the prices of machinery and other essentials which generally remained more stable.

The success of these cooperative efforts was at best spotty. In some instances groups of farmers did well, but far more frequently their cooperative activities ended in disaster. In many cases the ventures were initiated with too little capital, and in some cases the established manufacturers or distributors chose to compete with the cooperatives in a price war and farmers were squeezed out of business. In other instances, simple lack of business experience or effective management created difficulties for the cooperators and led to the collapse of one venture after another. Cooperation, even when well handled and developed, was not an answer to many of the farmer's most pressing problems. It furnished relief only in the purchase of a limited range of his needs, and it gave him no escape from the pressure of railroad rates, the lack of sufficient credit, and the general and frequently disastrous fluctuations of the market.

A more important result of Granger activities was the effort to use the power of the state governments to bring the railroads under public regulation. In a number of western states, where the farm vote was powerful, state legislatures enacted statutes to compel the railroads to correct the most flagrant practices. Various methods were used for this purpose. The most effective was to establish a state commission with regulatory authority. A less effective approach was to prohibit various railroad abuses by law, as the laws generally left ample loopholes discernible to the trained eyes of the railroad lawyers. Naturally, the railroads used every weapon in their armory to prevent enforcement of these laws. Such regulation of business enterprise was far more novel and therefore less acceptable then than it is today. Even so, the railroads deemed it essential to begin campaigns of "education" designed to produce in the public mind an antipathy to the idea that it was a proper function of government to supervise the activities of the railroads. One prominent editor, thinking of the Irish membership of the legislative bodies of some states, declared it abhorrent that rail rates should be set by "our Murphys and Caseys."

Despite this determined use by the railroads of both open and underhanded tactics to destroy the Granger laws, these laws emerged from their first great legal test unscathed. The state of Illinois had passed legislation which regulated not only rail rates, but also the charges made for the services of grain elevators. An owner of such an elevator brought suit to test the constitutionality of the law, and in 1877, in the case of *Munn v. Illinois,* the Supreme Court of the United States upheld the right of the state to pass such laws. The Court stated that when private property is devoted to a public use, it is subject to public regulation, and that the operation of grain elevators fell appropriately within this definition. The elevators in question were partly used for interstate trade, but the Court stated that until Congress acted to control such commerce, the state possessed full powers of regulation over them. This victory of the Granger laws at the bar of the Court was not to endure. In the case of *Wabash Railroad v. Illinois* in 1886, the Supreme Court ruled that regulation of interstate commerce was a congressional function under the terms of the commerce clause of the Constitution. Under this ruling, the Munn doctrine was made ineffective.

By the time the Court had given its decision in the Wabash case, however, Congress was on the verge of enacting railroad legislation. In the period after the Civil War many bills dealing with various aspects of railroad legislation by the federal government were introduced in Congress, but none was passed. The failure of state enactments to give adequate protection to the farmer and other small shippers against the discriminatory practices of the roads built up pressure for national action. Congress, permeated with orthodox laissez-faire doctrines, approached such legislation with reluctance. One committee, taking refuge in the established doctrine that regulation of business should be not by governmental agency but by the "unseen hand" of competition, suggested a vigorous program of deepening and improving internal waterways, so that barge transport might furnish competition to the railroads. This suggestion did not still the clamor, and eventually pressure was strong enough to bring the Senate, in 1885, to the establishment of a special committee on the problem of railroad regulation. After extensive hearings in all parts of the country, the committee reported that public opinion was determined upon the need for federal regulation of the railroad industry.

As the result of this report and of the pressure of public opinion, Congress passed the Interstate Commerce Act of 1887. This act was more important for its implications than for its immediate effects, as we have already seen (see page 390). But public opinion had forced a reluctant Congress to go through the motions of regulating one area of big business. Moreover, a significant addition was made to the number of businesses subject to public authority. Under the traditions of the English common law, certain types of business activity were appropriate subjects of control by public authority because their operation was of public consequence. The decision of the Supreme Court in *Munn v. Illinois* had extended the category of such businesses to include grain elevators and, by inference, railroads. Now the Congress, with constitutional authority, had accepted by statute law the doctrine set forth in the case of *Munn v. Illinois.* The favorite doctrine of the supporters of *laissez faire,* that the government could not regulate business, was given a body blow.

THE AGRARIAN PROTEST: MONEY AND POLITICS

While the Grangers had been leading the fight against the farmer's main enemy the railroads, other groups had been concentrating upon the farmer's money problems. In the 1870s and 1880s a Greenback party sought to promote currency reform. They argued that the prevailing low agricultural prices and high interest rates were in part due to the scarcity of money. The essential proposition of the Greenback party was simply that the wartime expedient of greenback currency be retained in large amounts as a form of legal tender. The Resumption Act of 1875 provided for the redemption of the greenbacks in gold and thus prevented further inflation. The plea of the Greenback party was for more greenbacks to be printed, unsupported by gold. It was, in effect, a program of currency inflation, suitable to the needs of a debt-ridden farm population, and the party drew most of its support from the upper Mississippi Valley states. It never had enough support, however, to make it anything more than another third party.

But the agitation for the printing of more greenbacks was soon drowned out by the larger demand for the free coinage of silver at a 16-to-1 ratio. Advocates of this idea demanded that the United States government buy all the silver offered to it, at a price set at one-sixteenth the amount that it would pay for a similar quantity of gold, and then use this silver as the basis for new currency. This would result in significant increases in the volume of currency and thus bring about inflation and consequent price increases. As the farmers were primarily sellers, this would better their economic status.

By a timely coincidence, just about the time that Congress gave up the purchase of silver for the Treasury because of its scarcity, great new quantities were discovered in the mines of the western states, and the silver-mining interests were now only too anxious to get the government to buy once again. Their anxiety to get the government to buy their product coincided nicely with the agitation of the farm groups for currency inflation. This combination of forces formed a powerful congressional bloc which was able to secure some partial victories.

The Bland-Allison Act of 1878 was a compromise which obligated the United States Treasury to buy not less than 2 million dollars' worth of silver each month. The silver purchased was to be coined into dollars. As the price of silver declined, the 2 million would bring in more of the metal and thus have an inflationary ef-

SILVER PRODUCTION, 1870–1895

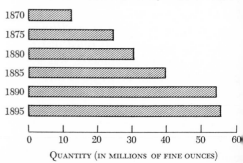

QUANTITY (IN MILLIONS OF FINE OUNCES)

fect. But the limitation on purchases did not satisfy the free-silver advocates, who wanted the government to purchase all that was offered—"free and unlimited coinage of silver." In 1890 a further concession was made to the silver bloc. The Sherman Silver Purchase Act of 1890 authorized the purchase of 4,500,000 ounces a month—practically all the silver mined at that particular time. The amount paid for the silver (not the quantity of silver itself) was to be added to the nation's currency in the form of Treasury notes. The Sherman act did not provide the expected inflation. The reason for this was the continuing decline in the price of silver. As a consequence, less and less had to be paid for the fixed monthly quantity of silver under the Sherman act. By 1894 silver was so cheap that, whereas the monthly inflation under the Bland-Allison Act would have been $4,073,319, under the Sherman principle only $2,880,000 was added to the currency in Treasury notes. These disappointing results, along with the continuing decline in farm prices, brought renewed agitation. The depression of 1893 was the last blow.

The panic of 1893 began with two business failures, one on each side of the Atlantic. Over in Great Britain, the prominent banking firm of Baring Brothers caused a scare in the ranks of British investors by coming perilously close to complete collapse, and in the United States, the failure of the Reading Railroad gave a similar shock to Americans. By the next year, farm prices were matters of anguish to the farmer. His sense of accumulating outrage broke out in political campaigns that had all the fervor of a religious revival and a battle against sin. The Middle West was aflame with protest and demands for reform. The appalling fact of wheat at less than 50 cents a bushel meant ruin for many farmers in the United States, and comparable declines carried doom to the growers of cotton and other crops. The disaster that such prices brought is revealed in fearful clarity by the growing lists of sheriff's sales in such states as Kansas and Nebraska, and the actual decrease in population of many western states in the early 1890s. Thirty-five of the ninety-eight counties of Nebraska declined in population between 1890 and 1900. Defeated hopes, frustrated ambitions, despair, and desolation stalked the land. The situation was aggravated by a ten-year drought from 1887 to 1897. The *Kansas Farmer* declared in 1896 that, if relief did not come soon, "every trace of settlement will be swept away."

There was no aid forthcoming from Washington. President Cleveland's conservative administration was more concerned about the decline of the gold reserve than about the threatened disappearance of the American farm in large sections of the West. From the Secretary of Agriculture, spokesman for the farmer in the Cabinet, came advice, but it was scarcely of a type to win the farmers' admiration. He urged the farmers to become better acquainted with the laws of economic behavior by reading Adam Smith's *The Wealth of Nations*. This might not heal their wounds, but it would, he felt, explain to the farmers what had hit them and drive home the lesson that there was nothing that could be done about their plight. This cold comfort provided no balm for the farmers' injuries, and the ranks of the armies of western protest swelled apace. The deaf ear turned by the Democratic administration in Washington added to the irritation, and explains why the western farmers formed a third party. To leave the Republican party of Harrison in favor of the Democrats led by

Cleveland was, they felt, to choose Tweedledum over Tweedledee.

While Grover Cleveland's administration rubbed salt in the wounds of the nation's agrarians by answering their complaints with lectures on academic economics, at the same time he seemed to show the tenderest solicitude in the handling of the bankers of Wall Street. Because the Treasury gold reserves had dropped below what was regarded as a safe minimum, Cleveland forced through a reluctant Congress the repeal of the Sherman Silver Purchase Act and thus deprived the farmers of a statute which they regarded as one of their chief triumphs. In order to replenish the Treasury supply of gold, which he felt essential to economic stability, Cleveland further sold United States bonds to a group of bankers on terms that left large profits in the pockets of the banking interests without at first appreciably filling the Treasury needs for more gold.

THE POPULIST MOVEMENT

The repeal of the Sherman Silver Purchase Act, coinciding with the depression of 1893, filled the farmers' cup of woe to overflowing and set off the great political revolt known as Populism. This was the greatest third-party movement in American history up to that time. Predominantly agrarian, it also enlisted some support from the industrial working class.

While he was incurring the wrath of the farmers, President Cleveland also managed to alienate labor. Workingmen, like farmers, felt that they were being denied opportunity to secure a fair share of this world's goods. Unable to help themselves, multitudes were ready to follow any leader who seemed to have anything to offer. One of these was Jacob S. Coxey, of Massillon, Ohio, a wealthy self-made businessman who was a congenital reformer. In 1894 he became leader of a movement to persuade the United States to lend money without interest to any state or local government unit for the purpose of constructing public improvements. These loans would be made in greenbacks secured by non-interest-bearing bonds to be deposited with the Treasury and retired in twenty-five years. By this means, a double objective of giving employment to millions of workers and inflating the currency would be accomplished. Coxey led an army of the unemployed to Washington, but he accomplished nothing (nor did any of the other "industrial armies" that took to the road in these years). Only a few thousand men reached Washington, where some of them established camps and finally had to be dispersed. But they were a sign of the unrest created by the great depression.

The most serious break with the labor groups came with the great strike at the Pullman car works near Chicago. The Pullman Company was a well-entrenched system of industrial feudalism, with some benevolent aspects. But when the panic of 1893 came, it decided to cut wages rather than to reduce dividends or dip into surplus funds. The company also refused to discuss grievances with the workers' leaders, and even discharged them. When the American Railway Union decided to boycott trains carrying Pullman cars, Cleveland's Attorney General (himself an influential railroad attorney) obtained an injunction. This sweeping injunction forbade interference by strikers with the transport of United States mails. Thereupon Pullman cars were attached to mail-carrying trains in order to bring them under the protection of the United States government. When the strikers sought to prevent the Pullman cars from moving, President Cleveland, without consulting the state governor, called out federal troops to protect the trains and prevent violence. Eventually the strike was broken after severe suffering, which left labor angry and embittered.

Meantime, it was becoming clearer that Cleveland's marked conservatism augured ill for the Democrats in the election of 1896. Certainly the Democrats could hardly hope to win another election without the support of the discontented of the land, both laborer and farmer. This meant that they must come to an agreement with the great new farmers' movement, the Populist party.

The Populist movement had its start in a number of sources. The decline of the Grange, following its failure to find a remedy for the farmers' complaints, helped pave the way for the creation of new farm associations. The more important of these were the Southern Alliance and the Northwestern Alliance. By 1890, both these organizations were counting their members by the millions. Both were militant bodies dedicated to the idea of bringing about a change in government to make it more responsive to the farmers' needs. The alliances were soon deeply engaged in political activity. They were shortly organizing local political parties. In the western farm states, new party names began to appear on the ballot. In Kansas it was the People's party; in Nebraska, the Peoples' Independent party. The formal establishment of the Peoples' party out of the various state parties came about in St. Louis in February, 1892.

The formal platform of the Peoples' or Populist party called for a variety of reforms, which, had they been adopted, would have wrested the political control and direction of the national life from the entrenched power of the men of wealth who had been dominant since the Civil War. It demanded, in finance, a flexible currency and the elimination of the role of the national banks in the creation and distribution of currency, a graduated income tax, free and unlimited coinage of silver at the ratio of 16 to 1, and an increase in the amount of money in circulation to $50 per capita. (At the time, there was about $20 per capita in circulation.) In transportation, the platform called for the public ownership of the railroads, telegraph, and telephone systems of the nation. The last major demand was that speculation in land should be eliminated, along with corporate and alien land ownership. This was the formal platform. It was, on the whole, a serious and well-considered effort to find legislation to rescue the farmers of the nation from their economic slough of despond. Populists also had a more informal program for the farmers, expressed in the simple words of one of the leaders of the movement in Kansas, Mary Elizabeth Lease. Her advice, repeated in speech after speech to the embattled farmers of her state, was to "raise less corn and more hell." There was also a form of Populist folklore reflected in the writings of some of their spokesmen that attributed many of the farmer's griefs to the nefarious influence of foreigners. The British investors in American land companies were the butt of much of this attack. Jewish bankers and merchants were also condemned in tones of virulent anti-Semitism.

Perhaps the most interesting feature of the Populist program was the minor place accorded to the free-silver idea, in view of the enormous hullabaloo that was to be raised over the issue before many months had passed. Free silver was inserted into the platform chiefly because it seemed a means by which some inflation and consequent price increases might be secured. But with its inclusion there developed a closer unity of purpose between the farm movements and the discontented silver-mining interests.

Not all the leaders of the Populist movement subscribed to the free-silver cause. C. W. Macune, prominent in the Southern Alliance and editor of the journal of that organization, had a plan for currency reform which was superior in many points to the silver program. Macune's plan called for the establishment of both a government warehouse and a sub-treasury branch in every county of the United States which grew annually $500,-000 worth of nonperishable farm produce. The farmer might, if he so desired, take his products to the warehouse for deposit and receive certificates of deposit which would be exchangeable at the subtreasury for currency that would be legal tender. This process would bring into existence a new form of currency, endowed with some flexibility because the amount of notes issued under the scheme would vary with the amount of farm production. (The present system of currency in the United States has more points of similarity to the Macune idea than to the theories of the silverites.) The Macune plan failed to win the support of many farmers. In addition, the plan did not have the support of the silver-mine owners, to whom it offered nothing at all. Since party campaigns cost a lot and the farmers had little, the wealth of the silver miners helped hold the Populists to the "Silver Crusade" and left the Macune plan high and dry.

THE CAMPAIGN OF 1896

The election of 1896 revived political life in the United States. After thirty years of "sham" campaigns, wooden candidates, and general political lassitude, the American people had found an issue. The issue would be called "free silver," but this was merely a symbol of the pent-up protests of farmers and others who had spent thirty years in fruitless fights against railroad tycoons, grain-elevator combines, monopoly implement makers, and chronic low prices. Greenbackers, Grangers, and a wide variety of splinter parties had vainly sought to arouse the American public. Each had failed, but each, in passing, had contributed its favorite reform to the cause. Now, in the 1890s, the Populists gathered in these dissident elements and sought to challenge the business and industrial leaders who had so long ruled America.

The growth of the Populist movement presented both an opportunity and a threat to the existing Democratic party of the western states. A real opportunity existed if some way could be found to channel the discontent into the service of the party. The threat was that the Populists might supplant the Democrats as the major party of opposition to the Republicans. The reality of this danger was clearly evident in the dimensions of the Populist vote in the elections of 1892 and 1894. Six Populists were elected to the United States Senate in 1894, and between 1892 and 1894 the new party's popular vote showed a gain of 42 per cent. In some southern states, where conservative Democratic organizations had been strongly established since the end of Reconstruction, there was a life-and-death struggle between the old leadership and the new men who were associated with the Populists in spirit and sometimes in name. In the West and in the South, Populism was something which the Democrats had to either join or fight. A decision to fight would throw the local Democratic politician into the arms of Grover Cleveland, which was political suicide. To come to terms with Populism, repudiate Cleveland, and harness the anger of the West to their party seemed to many local Democrats the only conceivable course. That would mean that some of the Populist party platform would have to be taken over by the Democrats, a course which many western Democrats had been advocating in Congress for many months.

Many regular Democrats found it easy to accept portions of the Populist platform. William Jennings Bryan, a Nebraska Democrat, had long advocated raising farm prices through the free coinage of silver. John P. Altgeld, reforming Democratic governor of Illinois, while not enthralled by the possibilities of free silver, was a Populist at heart and accepted the basic tenets of the Populist position. Altgeld had a substantial following among liberal Democrats by reason of his opposition to Cleveland's use of federal troops in the Pullman strike. This influence served to bring added strength to the Populist element within the Democratic party. The conflict between these reform Democrats and the conservative "goldbugs" of the party was rapidly making free silver the "hottest" issue of the hour.

Within Republican ranks there was little of the tension that plagued the Democratic party. The Republicans felt no need to cater to the free-silverites, for Populism had made relatively few converts among western Republicans. In its 1896 convention, the party nominated William McKinley, an able congressman from Ohio, whose name was linked with the highly protective McKinley Tariff of 1890. There were a few disgruntled western Republicans from silver-mining states who soured on the party for its hard-money platform and candidate, but the bulk of the party stood firm against free silver or any other inflationary device. For the first time the Republicans came out flatly in their platform for the gold standard.

It was otherwise at the Democratic convention. By convention time so many Democratic delegates had decided that free silver was the magic key to the farmers' vote that the Gold Democrats, the eastern "Bourbon-Cleveland" wing of the party, were snowed under. Not only did the Democrats write free silver into their platform, but they chose as their candidate the dynamic leader of the silver crusade, William Jennings Bryan, who had electrified the convention with his ringing peroration, "You shall not press down upon the brow of labor this crown of thorns, you shall not crucify mankind upon a cross of gold." Bryan brought more than his eloquent tongue to the cause. He had displayed a capacity for winning votes in usually Republican territory. He was young, one of the most youthful candidates in American history. He personified an optimistic faith in the simple and established virtues; he was an outstanding representative of an America that was still largely agrarian, Protestant, and unsophisticated.

To the Populists, the nomination of a Democratic candidate who could truly be regarded as a spokesman for the forces of agrarian discontent, and who could present the cause of the farmer to the nation in compelling language, presented a horrid dilemma. For all the protestations of the Democrats that they had accepted the farmers' cause as their own, they had actually adopted only one plank of the Populist platform, free silver—a plank which many of the Populist leaders regarded as the least important of their demands. On the other hand, there was the tantalizing prospect of victory if the Populists united their strength with that of the older party organization. The temptation was too great, and the Populist convention en-

PRESIDENTIAL ELECTION, 1896

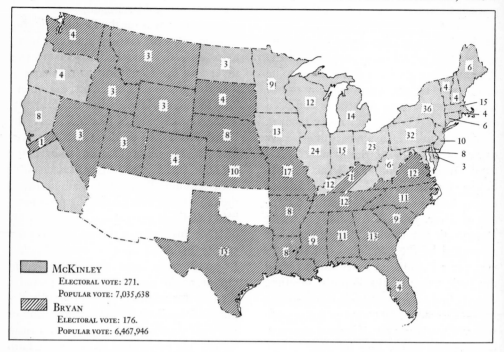

McKINLEY
ELECTORAL VOTE: 271.
POPULAR VOTE: 7,035,638
BRYAN
ELECTORAL VOTE: 176.
POPULAR VOTE: 6,467,946

dorsed Bryan, although they tried to maintain their own separate identity in the campaign by the relatively feeble device of nominating their own vice-presidential candidate. To many of the Populist leaders the choice was a tragic one, for it involved the sacrifice of principle to expediency, and the jettisoning of their program of reform for the weak cause of silver. But politics had frequently made stranger bedfellows than the Democratic-Populist alliance of 1896.

The campaign that ensued was the most memorable and exciting since that of 1860. For the first since the Civil War, there was a real issue at stake. In effect, it was the agrarians' last stand, an effort to wrest control of the government from the hands of the industrialists and financiers who had seized it during the period of the Civil War. In view of the di-

minishing proportion of the nation's population found on the farm, there was a quality of "Custer's last stand" about the whole affair. The agrarians were not only at war with their political foes but also at odds with the Industrial Revolution and the forces unleashed by that development.

Bryan fought a magnificent campaign. He traveled some 18,000 miles, made over 600 speeches, and reached audiences in twenty-nine states. His effectiveness caused conservatives to show signs of panic. Eastern newspapers pictured the "wild men" of the West undermining the foundations of property and progress with their radical soft-money ideas. Solid citizens were warned that a debased currency would rob them of their savings. Fearful Republicans, haunted by nightmares of a disintegrating society, rallied to Mark Hanna's carefully nurtured symbol—the quiet, stable McKinley. Hanna, the successful Ohio industrialist who had become the Republican master strategist, realized full well that his candidate could not match the oratorical thunders of Bryan and built his whole campaign around a contrast between the two men. He confined McKinley's campaign efforts to the front porch of his Canton, Ohio, home. Carefully selected audiences were conducted to McKinley's front door, to hear the candidate deliver carefully contrived speeches. These sedate utterances of McKinley were in sharp contrast with the stump speeches of the Democratic candidate, and large numbers of independent voters came to believe that McKinley sounded more statesmanlike than Bryan. At the same time, Hanna was collecting a large war chest from aroused conservatives. With unlimited funds, he managed the best organized political campaign in the nation's history. In the end, Bryan carried the agrarian states of the South and West, and McKinley the eastern industrial belt. In the decisive groups of states lying between the Ohio and Mississippi Rivers, the verdict went to McKinley by narrow margins. Here the new industry had outweighed the older established farming, and it was apparently in this area that the armies of industrial labor gave Bryan his smallest measure of support. In states where McKinley had a majority, the bulk of the city vote went to Bryan, but in the Bryan states, the city vote went to McKinley, indicating a high measure of rural-urban tension. Had the Populists been more of a farmer-labor party, had their program held a place for the worker, the result might have been different.

With the close of the election, the farmers' tempers subsided. The campaign had in itself been something of a great purgative, releasing tensions that had long been building. The long travail of the farmer was soon to be eased by substantial price increases. Prices began to rise for American farm produce. Coupled with crop failures abroad was the discovery of gold in the Yukon and South African areas, and the development of a new process for the refining of gold ore. This made a vast difference in world price levels. A considerable increase in the world's supply of gold meant that strict adherence to the gold standard was no longer a severe limitation on the amount of currency in circulation, and prices rose accordingly. They were to continue to rise through World War I with its demand for foodstuffs at almost any price. The Populist party had shot its bolt. With agrarian distress diminishing, an agrarian party had no basis for popular appeal. The party and the movement gradually sank into insignificance, but not without having made an important contribution to the American political scene.

The vigorous demand for economic and social reform voiced in the 1896 campaign did not pass away. It is apparent that the progressive movement soon to develop was in part Populism rewritten to meet the conditions of an increasingly industrialized and urbanized society. The Populist movement had played its part in the reawakening of the American social conscience, sharing that role with the "muckrakers," the new academic economists, the teachers of the "social gospel" in church pulpits, and the philanthropists concerned about city slums. Populism had helped to jar a complacent nation into a consciousness of social evils in American life yet to be grappled with and mastered. It stands in retrospect as the great divide separating a thoroughly individualistic economic order from one leavened by an increasing amount of social regulation, designed to protect the economically disadvantaged from the unimpeded exploitation of those who happened to be on top. It stands also as a stimulator of the democratic process, for it injected a live issue into American politics for perhaps the first time since the Civil War and thus helped rescue politics from that state of apathy and corruption into which it had fallen.

FURTHER READINGS

Fred A. Shannon, *The Farmer's Last Frontier, 1860–1897* (1945), is comprehensive and thorough. See also E. L. Bogart, *The Economic History of American Agriculture* (1923). Standard accounts of the farmers' movements of protest are S. J. Buck, *The Granger Movement* (1913), and J. D. Hicks, *The Populist Revolt* (1931). Also useful is Buck, *The Agrarian Crusade* (1920), in the Chronicles of America. C. Vann Woodward, *Origins of the New South, 1877–1913* (1951), has much material on Populist activity in the South. Helpful also are Richard Hofstadter, *The Age of Reform: From Bryan to F. D. R.* (1955), and Eric Goldman, *Rendezvous with Destiny: A History of Modern American Reform* (1952), both available in paperback editions.

The background for the emergence of an agrarian wing of the Democratic party is developed by H. S. Merrill, *The Bourbon Democracy of the Middle West, 1865–1896* (1953).

A good account of one of the chief episodes in the troubled 1890s is Almont Lindsey, *The Pullman Strike* (1942).

Biographies of the colorful Populist leaders include C. Vann Woodward, *Tom Watson: Agrarian Rebel* (1938), and F. B. Simkins, *Pitchfork Ben Tillman* (1944). The best biography of Bryan is probably M. R. Werner, *Bryan* (1929).

For additional bibliography, see the *Harvard Guide,* sections 200, 201, 209, and 210.

TWENTY

The Last Frontiers

1858
Pikes Peak gold rush begins.

1860
Pony express in operation.

1862
Homestead Act passed.
Pacific Railway Act passed.

1863
Montana gold rush begins.

1867
Beginnings of the range-cattle industry.

1869
First transcontinental railroad
completed.

1873
Timber Culture Act passed.

1874
Mining boom in West at peak.

1876
War with Sioux Indians.

1877
Desert Land Act passed.

1886
Final defeat of southwestern Indians.

1887
Dawes Act changes Indian policy.
Range-cattle industry declines.

1889
Oklahoma opened to settlers.

1890
Census report indicates end of frontier.

1894
Carey Act provides for irrigation
projects.

1902
Newlands Act for federal irrigation
projects.

1934
Indian Reorganization Act passed.

MINING FRONTIERS

WHILE INDUSTRIALISM WAS making over the eastern half of America, while the politicians of the Gilded Age were playing their sordid if picturesque games, and while the farmers of the nearer West and South were girding for a battle against exploitation, another drama was going on. It was somewhat less noted in the more populous areas, but in the opinion of very distinguished historians, it was possibly the most significant of all. The American frontier was coming to an end in a final burst of adventure, romance, lawlessness, and sometimes heartbreak. But between 1850 and 1890 there was a variety of frontiers, all displaying the flavor of frontier life in a most emphatic manner. Here in the plains, mountains, and deserts of the trans-Mississippi area was the "Wild West" of the cowboy and the cattleman, the Indian, and the prospector.

The purchase of the Gila River Valley from Mexico in 1853 had completed a remarkable half-century of continental expansion which began with the Louisiana Purchase and included the acquisition of the Floridas (1819), the annexation of Texas (1845), the winning of undisputed possession of Oregon to the 49th parallel (1846), and the great Mexican cession of 1848. But much of the land between Missouri and California remained unoccupied. The Great Plains with their dry, subhumid climate and lack of forest led into the wild Rocky Mountains; and between the Rockies and the Pacific coastal ranges lay such regions as the dry Great Basin and the

417

Geronimo, famous Apache leader

The slaughter of the buffalo:
a pile of skins

Desert land in the American West

The sod house frontier: settlers in Nebraska, 1888

The treeless Great Plains with their scarcity of rainfall, their swarming buffalo and fierce Indians, were a barrier to the advancing frontier for a number of years. But after the Civil War the railroad builders, then the cattlemen, and finally the hardy homesteaders penetrated this region. By 1890 the last of the frontiers had been settled and an epoch of American history had come to an end.

Completing the transcontinental railroad: ceremonies in Utah, 1869

even drier deserts of the Colorado plateaus. It will be recalled that the settlers avoided these to seek the fertile valleys of the Pacific Coast first. California and Oregon were states long before the Dakotas, Wyoming, or Oklahoma.

The great area of plains, mountains, and deserts first attracted people because of its mineral wealth. Gold prospecting became an established vocation in the 1850s. Throughout the Rocky Mountain region and into Canada, prospectors probed for gold after a number of "strikes" were reported. More often than not, the results were disappointing, as abandoned camps and half-worked diggings mutely testify. During the autumn of 1858 gold was discovered in Cherry Creek, near present-day Denver. The region was commonly referred to as Pikes Peak, although that mountain is actually about 90 miles to the south. To the natural excitement and urge of a gold discovery was added the fact of hard times after the panic of 1857. Colorado was not so far away as California; there were no mountains and deserts to cross, and if a person was lucky and had the necessary cash he might have gotten a seat on the new stagecoach service and made the entire journey with little effort. By the spring of 1859, thousands of people were leaving the Missouri border for the trek of 700 miles by wagon, carriage, pack horse, or even handcart. Perhaps 100,000 gold seekers took part in this greatest of all migrations across the plains. Most of the "fifty-niners" were to experience bitter disappointment. The great gold deposits were in quartz veins, so expensive machinery and chemical processes were required to extract them. The capital that was needed to exploit these mines could be furnished only by large corporations. And so most of the gold seekers could only return to the East

and leave the fortunes to others. The hopeful signs "Pikes Peak or Bust" which were displayed on vehicles en route to Colorado now expressed bitter disappointment— "Busted by Gosh!"

Far from the territorial capital at Topeka, the population of the many mining camps in eastern Colorado illustrated the capacity of American frontiersmen for orderly government. A convention of representatives of the camps first decided to request statehood for a great area under the name of the state of Jefferson. But by the time a referendum on the question was taken, so many people were leaving that the petition was changed to one for a territorial organization. Pending such a decision, elections were held in the fall of 1859 for a legislature and governor. The deadlock over slavery postponed action until after the secession of the southern states, whereupon Kansas was admitted to statehood in 1861 and Colorado Territory was organized—none too soon, as the authority of the temporary territorial government over outlying camps was uncertain. Yet the frontiersmen had improvised a reasonably successful government. It remained for Colorado to find its economic salvation, after some difficulties, in agriculture and dairying and as a grazing ground for Texas cattle en route to the northern ranges. By the end of the decade, 1 million cattle and 2 million sheep were reported in eastern Colorado. Never again did mineral development attract so many people as it did in 1859.

During the year of the Pikes Peak rush, discoveries of gold and silver in Nevada caused a dash to the eastern slopes of the Sierra Nevada. Carson City and Virginia City sprang up after the discovery of the great Comstock lode in 1859. Virginia City was a typical mining town. Pits, shafts, tents, shacks, and hovels of all sorts scarred the landscape; then, as in all mining communities, came the saloons, the dance halls, the gambling houses. Mark Twain came to Virginia City in 1861, leaving us an immortal account of his journey in *Roughing It* and a prize description of the town. Nevada Territory was organized in 1861 and brought in as a state only three years later, although political considerations much hastened its entrance. The mining rushes were all much the same and produced similar results. Thousands of miners invaded the Rockies. New territorial governments were created. Idaho received territorial status in 1863, and Montana was cut off from Idaho in 1864. Agitation for separation from New Mexico brought territorial status to Arizona in 1863. Some enduring towns sprang up at mining centers such as Lewiston in Idaho and Helena in Montana; others became ghost towns as the miners drifted away. Some fabulous strikes were made as old diggings were reopened and new ones discovered. At Alder Gulch, for instance, in the Gallatin River Valley, placer mining yielded about 30 million dollars in three years.

Thus in the 1860s, through the spread of mining, the nation became familiar with its least-known regions. The dramatic discoveries of precious metals brought settlers to regions of the West that would, no doubt, have been otherwise neglected for years. The political map was completed by the organization of several new territories, and even statehood was hurried along by the sudden influx of population. There remained only one more big gold rush, and that was to the Black Hills of Dakota in the late 1870s. Here the great metropolis was Deadwood, last and possibly the most turbulent of the mining towns. The Black Hills rush contributed a western center of population to balance an agricultural population in eastern Dakota, although the area had to wait for the railroads before it could come into its own. The miner with his pan looking for sudden wealth—sometimes finding it, more often not, but always hopeful—wrote his own chapter in the American story besides opening up new areas of settlement previously spurned.

PIONEERING IN TRANSPORTATION

No easy inland-waterways system invited settlers into the trans-Mississippi West as it had into the Ohio and Mississippi Valleys. Vast overland distances, high mountains, rugged plateaus, and dangerous deserts deterred settlement until some method could be found of overcoming these barriers. The first such means were the stagecoaches and overland freighters. The Southern Overland Mail started from St. Louis and, taking the southern route, reached San Francisco in a scheduled time of 23 days, beginning in 1858. This and the Central Line carried mail and passengers. After the outbreak of the Civil War, Ben Holladay of the Central Line was for a few years the transportation mogul of the West. At his peak, he operated nearly 5,000 miles of daily mail stages with about 500 coaches and express wagons, 500 freight wagons, 5,000 horses and mules, and thousands of oxen. In addition, he operated a fleet of steamers on the Pacific. Holladay made a fortune and spent it lavishly, but his career was short. The picturesque horse-drawn transcontinental stages fell afoul of Indian depredations and suffered heavy losses. Holladay sold out to Wells, Fargo & Company in 1866. During these same years freight was also handled in wagons, the overland freighting concerns sending out trains of huge wagons, each carrying 5,000 to 16,-

000 pounds and drawn by six to twelve yoke of oxen. The bullwhackers and mule skinners who drove these wagons were a distinctive frontier type; so were the freighters themselves, a group noted for their integrity and courage. With wagons costing $800 to $1,500, mules from $500 to $1,000 a pair, and harness equally expensive, this was a business with a large capital investment. The greatest of the freighters, Russell, Majors, and Waddel, at one time operated 6,000 big wagons with 75,000 oxen.

This company also instituted the famous "pony express," which was the most picturesque attempt to link East and West. Carrying no more than 20 pounds in their rainproof pouches, the riders traveled at full speed on their ponies for usually 10 miles before changing quickly to a fresh mount. These riders had to be men of endurance, prepared to travel day and night under all circumstances of weather and danger. The pony express was amazingly successful; it usually covered the distance from St. Joseph, Missouri, to Sacramento, California, in nine or ten days, cutting the stagecoach time by more than half, and proved most reliable. But operating costs were heavy, and within two years the pony express was replaced by the first telegraph line to the Pacific Coast, which was completed in October, 1861. There was no longer need for the express, but its swift and romantic journeys had demonstrated man's courage and initiative and added another saga to the frontier experience.

For all the enterprise shown by the horse-drawn vehicles and the riders of the pony express, much of the Far West would have remained unsettled indefinitely had it not been for the arrival of the railroads. The project of a transcontinental railroad had been a lively topic ever since 1845. Although surveys were made in the 1850s, final decision on the best route was delayed for many years because of the bitter rivalry between northern and southern delegations in Congress. The fateful Kansas-Nebraska Act owed much to Senator Douglas's ambition to organize this territory so that a railroad might be built from Chicago to the Pacific. But all railroad bills met defeat in the 1850s because of sectional rivalry. The secession of the South and the withdrawal of its congressional representatives not only paved the way for passage of the railroad bill, but gave the North victory on the location of the route. The Pacific Railway Act became law on July 1, 1862. It provided for generous subsidies, since the possibilities of profit in building a line through uninhabited territories were slim. For each mile of construction the railroad companies were to be given 20 sections of land arranged alternately on both sides of of the track, each section consisting of 640 acres, as well as a grant of the right of way. In addition, the government made loans ranging from $16,000 a mile to $48,000, depending on the terrain, and took a second mortgage as security for railroad bond issues. The whole question of subsidies to the railroads led to sordid financial scandals which, as congressional investigations later revealed, besmirched the reputations of a number of men high in public life and ended by making the railroads cost the government far more than was necessary. Nevertheless, the transcontinental road went forward. The Central Pacific Railroad, a California corporation, broke ground at Sacramento in 1863 but encountered such difficulties in construction that it completed only 60 miles in the first three years. Among many problems, that of a labor shortage stood out; by 1865 the importing of Chinese coolies solved this difficulty.

The eastern end of the railroad started from Council Bluffs, Iowa. Here also there were formidable construction problems, but demobilized veterans provided an ample and valuable labor supply; they could also stand guard against Indian attacks, a constant danger. As the railroad progressed across the plains, construction towns were hurriedly built to feed and house the thousands of workers. Every few weeks the town was dismantled, packed on freight cars, and moved ahead, leaving behind a scar to mark its last resting place. The rail town showed all the worst features of the mining camp or cow town; it was aptly described as "hell on wheels." Ahead of the construction gang, ambitious speculators laid out town sites, hoping to profit thereby. Most of these real estate booms never materialized. The Union Pacific built 500 miles in two years. The Central Pacific speeded up when it got across the mountains and on the flat deserts. The two lines raced to meet each other, but in order to avoid overlapping lines, Congress had to intervene and order the race to be ended near Ogden, Utah. Here the rival tracks joined, and the last spike was driven on May 10, 1869. Great was the national excitement. Large crowds waited in the eastern cities to learn the news of the completion. A continent had been bridged.

Nothing, perhaps, presents more forceful evidence of the passing of the trans-Mississippi frontier than the fact that by the middle 1880s there were four adequate trunk lines affording through connections with the west coast. Far to the south was the Southern Pacific, which joined the Texas and Pacific at El Paso. Between these lines and the Union Pacific was the Santa Fe, which entered California at Needles. The Union Pacific–Central Pacific followed the historic route via the Platte River and Salt Lake. Far to the north, connecting Duluth, Minnesota, with Portland, Oregon, was the Northern Pacific. Meantime, the federal land grants proved a continuing source of scandal until the hostility of the Granger movement of the 1870s made their continuance politically unwise. Before it ended, the government had given away in all 158 million acres of land for the building of 21,500 miles of track, most of which was for lines west of the Mississippi. The value of the land and its resources equaled the total cost of construction. In 1940 many thousands of acres which the railroads had never patented or sold were restored to the government under a law of that year, but according to reports of the U.S. Government Land Office, total federal grants to railroads were more than 131,000,000 acres. This policy of land grants seemed logical at the time, and was in fact a continuance of previous grants made for wagon roads and canals. It was an answer to the problem of developing transportation facilities across a sparsely settled expanse of territory. There was then little reason for thinking about the conservation of seemingly endless resources. Meanwhile the coming of the railroads stimulated new industries and new settlement in a vast region previously almost empty. There remained, however, one other obstacle to be removed: the Indians of the Great Plains.

THE PASSING
OF THE RED MAN

Until after the Civil War the Great Plains and the prairies remained for the most part the domain of the red man. Oregon immigrants, Mormons, forty-niners, and fifty-niners all passed them over, although farmers were edging into the eastern parts of Kansas and the fertile valleys of southeastern Dakota. The great central heartland of the trans-Mississippi West was the Indian's paradise. Subsisting on a simple buffalo economy, he had ample supplies of food and raw materials to meet all his needs. The flesh of the buffalo supplied him with abundant quantities of meat; the skins gave the hide necessary for tepees, leggings, thongs, and bowstrings. The horns could be fashioned into useful implements, the hair woven into belts and cords; the buffalo pelt made a warm blanket, and dried buffalo manure even supplied fuel. There were millions of buffalo on the plains. They sometimes blackened the landscape as far as the eye could see; an observer reported in 1868 that he rode for three consecutive days through one continuous herd. A herd might delay a train for hours as it crossed a track; it might even charge the cars and become entangled in doors and windows. It was the extermination of these vast herds that doomed the Plains Indians. That extermination was virtually accomplished in about fifteen years. By the middle 1880s nothing but scattered remnants remained. As the Union Pacific was built, the herd was divided; and before long the great slaughter began, with shooting excursions organized by the railroads. The sale of robes and hides became a big business; the largest St. Louis firm collected 200,000 skins in a single year. Buffalo steaks, hams, and tongues found a steady market in the East. The business of bone gathering on the plains was a large-scale activity for years; hundreds of tons might be seen stacked beside the tracks at shipping points. Freight trains sometimes carried nothing but loads of bones for the fertilizer factories.

The slaughter of the buffalo, along with destruction of the deer, antelope, and other wild game, was a basic cause of the innumerable Indian outbreaks and wars that were so unfortunately prominent during this period. The Indian watched with alarm and resentment this encroachment on his hunting grounds and this destruction of his means of survival. Relations with the Indians were marked by many other sources of trouble. The federal government seemed powerless in the face of persistent pressure from the frontiersmen. Thus a record of broken promises marred the American record. Indians were shunted from one reservation to another. Discovery of gold on an Indian reservation more than once brought an inrush of miners who regarded treaty rights with contempt. Illicit traders often supplied Indians with liquor, guns, and ammunition in defiance of government regulations. The government itself was shot through with corruption in this era, of course, and dishonest and unscrupulous government agents used their position to enhance their own fortunes. Outlaws, particularly along the international border, made deals with Indians to plunder settlements or steal cattle. All in all, it was a shameful situation, which was caused by the incapacity of a weak and corrupt government to cope with an aggressive white frontier population unwilling to regard the Indian as having any rights a white settler was bound to respect. To this was added a confused government policy, for the War Department and the Interior Department often clashed. But these Plains Indians were more formidable than any known in the older areas, and bitter battles took place before the last of the red men submitted to the white man's overwhelming power. After a number of pathetic "last stands," Indian control of the plains was definitely ended in the 1870s.

Until 1887 the principal purpose of government policy seems to have been to place the Indians on reservations and maintain peace as best it could by stationing garrisons of soldiers at strategic forts. It was not a happy policy. In 1887 there came a new approach with the passing of the Dawes Act, which provided for individual allotments of lands to Indians, safeguarded by government trusteeship for twenty-five years in order to protect the Indian landholder. Allotments could be made whenever the President decided that reservation lands might be advantageously utilized for agricultural or grazing purposes. The maximum size of grants for agriculture was 80 acres and for grazing 160 acres. This act also conferred citizenship upon all Indians who qualified for allotments. The act looked forward to the absorption of the Indian into white society rather than his treatment as a member of a foreign nation. The operation of the act eventually produced a considerable surplus of land for the government, the most desirable of which was in Oklahoma; this was opened for whites in 1889 and produced the last great land rush of the prairies. Between 1887 and 1923, through forced allotments of lands, 90 million acres of the best Indian-owned lands passed to the whites. Only 51 million acres, nearly half of which was semiarid desert, remained in possession of the Indians. In 1924 all remaining Indians were granted citizenship, though reservation Indians remained wards of the government, and control of the suffrage lay, as always, with the states.

The later history of Indian policy has as a landmark the Indian Reorganization Act of 1934, which was another reversal of objectives. It looked toward the restoration and preservation of Indian culture. Indians were to be encouraged to form tribal corporations and adopt tribal constitutions; further allotments were forbidden, and surplus lands were restored to the tribes. In contrast to the authoritarian philosophy of the Dawes Act, the new legislation was based upon the principles of complete local autonomy and cultural diversity. The 1934 statute became operative only after approval by the Indian tribes through a referendum based upon universal manhood and woman suffrage. Twenty years later it was the law for more than three-fourths of the Indians of the United States and Alaska. Self-governing constitutions had been adopted by 100 tribes. At the same time, some 200 tribal economic organizations had been chartered, for the Reorganization Act provided a revolving fund for loans to enable Indians to improve their economic status. Except for individual loans mainly for educational purposes, the loans have been made to tribal organizations. Through this assistance Indian tribes have been able to promote basic agriculture and livestock industries; salmon canneries in Alaska; at least one oyster-culture project; as well as such enterprises as producers' and consumers' cooperatives, arts and crafts organizations, stores, and trading posts. Thousands of Indians (many from relief rolls) have been rehabilitated by this Indian New Deal. Tribes that have lived on barren and bleak desert reservations under conditions of such extreme isolation that but few of their members ever learned the English language have benefited much from the assistance given under the Reorganization Act. Conditions of illiteracy, malnutrition, extreme poverty, disease, and high mortality rates have been alleviated.

However, by mid-century many of the gains made by the Indians under the 1934 act were seemingly threatened by the increasing tendency to end federal protection over the Indian tribes. Control of many aspects of Indian affairs was returned to the states in which the tribes were located. With the plea that it was insulting to the Indian to regard him as needing the special tutelage of the federal government, he was "freed" from many of the controls that had formerly been designed to protect him. Whether or not he was really prepared for this new freedom and could stand on his own feet in the white man's culture has yet to be seen. The Indian problem remains a troublesome matter for the white man's conscience.

THE FRONTIER
OF THE RANCHERS

The destruction of the buffalo, the removal of the Indians, and the coming of the railroads made possible the great cattleman's frontier. For the same grasses that nourished millions of buffalo could sustain cattle both on the ranges and on the long drive to northern ranches and cow towns. Texas was the great breeding ground for the longhorn cattle. The story of the range-cattle industry begins during the Civil War when northern control of the Mississippi and the blockade of the Gulf ports cut off the markets of the Texas drovers. The coming of the railroads opened new possibilities. Eastern markets were waiting, and by 1866 the Kansas Pacific Railroad had reached Junction City, Kansas; the Union Pacific reached Cheyenne, Wyoming, the next year. When it was now demonstrated that the herds could be driven north, feeding on the nourishing grasses, and could then be shipped by railroad in good condition to eastern stockyards, a new chapter in the history of the Great Plains opened. Besides creating large profits for cattlemen, the range-cattle industry gave to America,

and to the world, that most romantic of figures, the cowboy.

The cow business was a time-honored Latin-American vocation long before Americans took it up in Texas; the Spanish influence is evident in the cowboy's vocabulary, in such words as ranch, lariat, chaps, bronco, rodeo, and mustang. But nowhere did it develop the proportions and significance that it did on the Great Plains. The cowboy has become a legendary figure. In fact, much of his picturesqueness has a very utilitarian explanation. The physical environment of the range was one of space, lonesomeness, and lawlessness. Life on horseback, including the long drives, the roundups, and the use of lariat and branding iron, was merely a part of the business. His costume, distinctive as it might appear, was also dictated by utility: the broad-brimmed felt hat served both as sunshield and umbrella and could be tied down over the ears for winter protection, the silk handkerchief around the neck gave protection against hot winds, the wide chaps that loosely covered the front of his legs protected the rider against thorns and branches. The high-heeled boots with light soles were intended for riding, not walking, and helped to keep the feet in the stirrups. The lariat and six-shooter were indispensable.

Lack of normal social contacts and associations was apt to cause the cowboy to carry to extremes his gregarious instincts when he reached town after long months spent on the range. The northern cow towns became famous for both business and lawlessness. They sprang up almost overnight. Their location was determined by the railroad and by the proximity of the range. Abilene, Kansas, was the first great shipping center, changing from a sleepy village into a center doing a business of millions of dollars a year. After 1871, Abilene surrendered the lead to Dodge City, farther west. These cow capitals became meccas not only for cowmen, but for gamblers and desperadoes of all sorts; the problem of law and order defied the sheriff's office. Other cow towns of renown were Ellsworth and Hays in Kansas and Ogallala in Nebraska. Between 1866 and 1885, nearly 5,750,000 cattle are estimated to have been driven north from Texas, with the big boom coming in the 1880s, when the trail was pushed farther and farther westward, until finally the Texas Panhandle and the eastern third of Colorado became the route of the long drive. Cattle companies multiplied; with free grass and a minimum of operating expenses, a small outlay promised great returns. But the boom carried the dangers of overspeculation, overtaxing of the range, and careless handling of stock due to absentee ownership. The increased costs of operation, as the ranges became overstocked, necessitated such expensive measures as fence building. Moreover, by 1885 the price of cattle had begun to fall seriously in eastern markets. By this time it was clear that the business had outgrown its frontier stage and, indeed, had extended far beyond the margin of safety.

The decline of the range was as sudden as its sensational rise. In addition to grave overcrowding of the range, there were other weakening factors. One was the appearance of the hated sheepherder, as sheep ranching became more profitable. More and more sheep pressed upon the range; they could be grazed on hillsides and where inferior grasses grew. In 1886–1887 a disastrous winter caused terrific losses to the cattle industry and all but paralyzed it. The cattlemen did not surrender the range to sheep without a battle,

CATTLE TRAILS OF THE 1870s

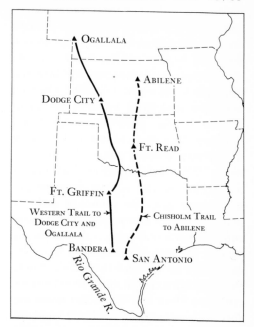

and for the years the rival groups engaged in bitter range wars. The feud was particularly bitter in Wyoming, where the cattlemen had great political influence. Other factors contributing to the decline of the cattle business included the enclosing of grazing areas after the invention of barbed wire, blocking the trails and resulting in heavy winter losses, and quarantine restrictions against Texas fever. The winter of 1886–1887 was the last blow of many, and the business never revived. Soon the hated "nester" or homesteader was in possession, and the law was on his side. The frontier of the range was replaced by the farmers' last frontier.

During their heyday the cattlemen created an interesting organization, the Stock Growers' Association. The vast extent of the cattle domain and the unusual problems which arose, and which no regular territorial or state courts could have handled, led to the development of extralegal machinery. Rules protecting cattle ownership, rules concerning disposition of mavericks and unbranded calves, protective measures against rustlers, wild animals, and disease—such problems as these the cattlemen's association handled through voluntary agreement. In 1886 the membership in the great Wyoming Stock Growers' Association represented property worth 100 million dollars in nineteen states. With headquarters at Cheyenne, it maintained its own regular detective bureau, made rules for roundups and appointed foremen to supervise them, helped enforce quarantine laws, and secured the passage of other laws beneficial to cattlemen. Here at the Cheyenne Club, where the association maintained headquarters, cattlemen dined and drank and made big deals. It is a commentary on the rapid decline of the industry that the association passed out of existence soon after the bad winter of 1886–1887. Its work was turned over to a Board of Livestock Commissioners, but the board never commanded the respect once accorded the powerful Stock Growers' Association, whose authority was feared more than that of the government itself.

THE PEOPLING
OF THE PLAINS

As the cattleman retreated, the heir to the range was the homesteader, finally ready to tackle the plains region. It will be recalled that, under the Homestead Act of 1862, the actual homesteader was entitled to 160 acres of free land. On the plains such a tract was not large enough. More land was needed in the semiarid regions to allow room for grazing. From time to time, Congress passed legislation to make this possible. But the whole administration

of the Homestead Act was shot through with that fraud so typical of the age. Although it was intended that the lands should be used only by the grantees, individuals were sometimes able to acquire vast holdings running to many thousands of acres. But the Homestead Act did stimulate migration to the plains after the Civil War. The eastern fringes of Kansas, Nebraska, and South Dakota had begun to be settled before the Civil War. Temporarily slowed by the panic of 1873, the movement to these areas between 1878 and 1886 was one of the greatest in our history. Into Kansas, Nebraska, the Dakotas, and the southern plains of Texas the people poured in an endless stream. Thus, between 1870 and 1890, the population of Kansas, Nebraska, and the Dakotas increased from about 500,000 to 1,600,000.

Many factors in addition to the promise of free land contributed to this tide. The fear of the Great American Desert had vanished; it was now firmly believed that the rain belt had moved permanently westward and that farming could be ventured safely in formerly semiarid regions. Both states and railroad companies engaged in campaigns to attract settlers, joined by local chambers of commerce, real estate men, churches, and newspapers. States were interested in settling their areas; railroad companies now wished to dispose of their vast land holdings acquired from the government. The railroads scattered their agents through eastern cities to offer such inducements as free transportation, free seed, and temporary housing. Their lithographed pictures were accompanied by exaggerated descriptions of the country and its opportunities. This advertising even induced groups of hopeful immigrants from Russia, Germany, and Scandinavia to settle in America.

The new settlers found, to their sorrow,

hat life on the plains was filled with unac-
ustomed hardships. This "sod house fron-
ier" was practically treeless and, save for
he Black Hills section of Dakota, flat.
Fencing was made possible by the inven-
ion of a practical barbed wire in 1874,
and dried buffalo and cattle chips, as well
as hay and corn, could be used for fuel.
Here eventually developed the world's
greatest corn and wheat belt. One of the
early obstacles, however, was the grasshopper. The year 1874 lives in plains his-
ory as "grasshopper year." From the Dakotas to northern Texas, the insects came
in great clouds, sometimes darkening the
skies for miles. Nearly everything green
was devoured; trees were stripped of their
bark; water became unfit to drink. Even
rains were brought to a halt, because of
the slippery rails. The area received relief
from the United States government in
small amounts and contributions poured
in from other states. There is an 1877 law
on the books of the state of Nebraska
which declared grasshoppers to be public
enemies and required all able-bodied
males of 16 to 20 years to contribute labor
in eradicating them. Such were the difficulties of life on the prairie.

Yet the boom continued. It was easy
enough for people to get capital from the
scores of mortgage companies that flooded
the country with credit at 6 to 8 per cent.
In five states the number of mortgages
averaged more than one per family. Real
estate booms developed in the cities, with
lively speculation and sometimes fabulous
profits. Many projected communities never
advanced beyond the blueprint stage.
Huge amounts of municipal bonds were
sometimes floated. The whole movement
was dangerously inflationary and came to
a dramatically sudden end; the bursting of
the bubble coincided with the final collapse of the cattle business in 1886–1887.

The cattlemen had been wiped out by a
terrible winter, but in the case of the farmers, calamity came in the form of a long
period of drought. Crops could not be
grown, and a trek back to the east, beginning in 1887, depopulated large areas.
Fully half the people of western Kansas
deserted the region within the next five
years. Entire towns were reported left
without a single inhabitant, and disappointed pioneers expressed their feelings
in such inscriptions as "In God we trusted,
in Kansas we busted," emblazoned on
their covered wagons. Much the same
thing happened in Nebraska and South
Dakota. In the eastern section of the prairies the population remained more stable.
But as a result of all this, farmers of the
"middle border" were burdened with debt
and discontented, ready to give eager response to those doctrines of Populism
which promised them relief. It is no accident that Kansas was the birthplace of the
People's party.

Four new states were admitted to the
union in 1889 and two more in 1891:
Washington, the two Dakotas, and Montana first; then Wyoming and Idaho. With
the admission of Utah in 1896, following adjustment of long-standing difficulties
with the Mormons, no areas remained as
territories except the Indian Territory in
Oklahoma and the territories of New
Mexico and Arizona. The settlement of
Kansas and Nebraska and the penetration
into central Texas close to the line of arid-
ity left the Indian Territory as the most attractive lure to land-hungry pioneers. For
years the pressure to open these lands to
white settlers had been growing. The
Santa Fe Railroad carried on a vigorous
propaganda campaign, and their lobby in
Washington kept the issue before Congress. The cattlemen, however, opposed
this, for they had no desire to see their

Date of act	Maximum size of tract	Price per acre	Terms or conditions of settlement
1873 Timber Culture Act (repealed in 1891)	160 acres	Free	Must plant and successfully grow 40 acres of timber (reduced to 10 acres in 1872) for 10 years
1877 Desert Land Act (applied to eleven states and territories where Homestead Act was not suitable because of scarcity of water)	640 acres (reduced to 320 acres in 1891 to better control fraudulent practices)	$1.25	25 cents per acre at filing; balance in three years, by which time the land must be irrigated
1878 Timber and Stone Act	160 acres	$2.50 min	Must be for personal use only and not for speculation
1891 Repeal of the old Preemption Act of 1841 (see p. 184			
1904 Enlarged Homestead Act for Nebraska	640 acres	Free	
1909 Enlarged Homestead Act, by this date extended to twelve states west of 100th meridian	320 acres	Free	Must cultivate 160 acres (one-half of the tract)
1912 Three-year Homestead Act			Reduced time of residence from five years to three and permitted absence for five months of year
1916 Cattlemen's Law	640 acres	Free	Land purely for grazing and not to contain timber or water for irrigation purposes

leases from the Indians canceled by an in-rush of homesteaders. But in both Kansas and Texas borderlands, prospective immigrants or "boomers" were well organized, eyeing the choice lands in the middle of the territory. They found able leaders. At one time the government ordered the dispersion of the boomers and arrested their leaders. But the boomers and the railroads won their battle in Congress after the Dawes Act of 1887 and the ruin of the cattle business. In 1889 President Benjamin Harrison proclaimed the opening of nearly 2 million acres in the Indian Territory. As the appointed day and hour approached (April 22, 1889, at noon) wildly excited throngs of hopeful immigrants lined the northern and southern borders of the promised lands; the eagerly awaited bugle signal brought a pellmell rush. From both north and south, in all possible conveyances, people raced across the prairies to stake their claims. The Canadian River, which bordered the coveted area on the south, proved to be no effective obstacle. Before nightfall cities of tents and shacks had sprung up along the railroad. Confusion, quarrels, and fights occurred as homesteaders rushed to establish claims. Many disappointed boomers were forced out, for there were only 12,-000 homesteads available for perhaps 100,000 applicants in this initial rush.

Oklahoma Territory was organized in 1890. It grew rapidly as additional millions of acres were purchased and opened. Except for the northwestern cow country, Oklahoma became a land of farmers whose sod houses and dugouts in the hillsides dotted the frontier. In 1907 the two territories, Oklahoma and Indian Territory, were merged into the state of Oklahoma. To Oklahoma the twentieth century was to bring another mad rush, this time for oil, and with it new frontiers

undreamed of in the days of the boomers. But with the settling of Oklahoma by white farmers there passed the farmer's last frontier in the United States. The restless hunger for new lands continued despite the closing of the frontier, and in the next decade thousands of Americans moved across the northern border into the prairie provinces of Canada to find the land that was no longer so abundantly available in the United States.

THE END OF AN EPOCH

The closing of the frontier marked the end of an epoch in American history. One of its many consequences was in the field of conservation policy. The apparently limitless land of the United States, that land that Jefferson thought was great enough to leave the American people with a frontier for a thousand years, was now recognized by many as needing careful husbanding. Reckless squandering of natural resources would have to be replaced by careful management and development of the remaining resources for later generations. It was difficult for some to make this readjustment in their thinking. For generations the policy of the government of the United States had been to transfer the public domain into private hands as quickly and as cheaply as possible. The Homestead Act of 1862 is the best illustration of that principle. It was now necessary to modify that tradition.

The first real effort to encourage land management came with the passage of the Carey Act in 1894, which granted to the states proceeds from the sale of arid lands. This was designed to get states to engage in irrigation projects for the reclamation of arid lands. Irrigation had been successfully used by some of the early Spanish missions in the Southwest, and also by the Mormons in their desert home on the Great Salt Lake basin. The Carey Act produced meager results, and in 1902 the Newlands Act authorized the federal government to undertake irrigation projects of its own. In addition to these measures, Congress in 1891 authorized the President to reclaim lands that had been fraudulently conveyed into private hands. Cleveland was the only President who used this authority with any vigor, and the only one before 1900 who showed any interest in the problem of conservation. The creation of a broad conservation program and the development of a national consciousness about the problem awaited the coming of President Theodore Roosevelt to the White House.

The census of 1890 called attention to the fact that a continuous area of unsettled land no longer existed in the United States. Within a few years, the historian Frederick Jackson Turner, in speaking of the frontier, declared that the most striking and typical factor conditioning the rise and development of American democracy had ceased to operate, after more than three hundred years. This filling up of the land had exerted intangible but certainly significant influences on a number of aspects of American life. The frontier, so Turner thought, had long provided a "safety valve" for the alleviation of all kinds of social discontents. His "safety valve" theory has been challenged at many points in the light of more detailed research, which indicates, for example, that at no time was it very common for wageworkers to trek to the fron-

tier. Still, it is difficult to doubt that the existence of plentiful cheap land contributed to a more individualistic and democratic social order in America. Turner, for one, feared that the ending of the frontier meant that the United States would soon have to experience European forms of radicalism and statism, losing, as it were, her unique democratic soul. However that might be, the ending of the frontier was certain to bring changes. A great environmental force in America had ceased to operate.

The end of continental expansion is also related to the emergence of a more aggressive foreign policy looking toward overseas empire. For a century the United States had had the habit of constant expansion. That expansion had taken place within the continental areas contiguous to the original thirteen states, but it had been constant and aggressive, involving us in wars with the Indians and with Mexico and in serious disputes with European powers. Between 1853 and 1898 the United States acquired no new territory, except Alaska, to which it attached no importance. It had been engaged in filling up the vast unoccupied regions acquired mostly in 1846 to 1848. Once that task was accomplished, the nation looked from long habit for new areas of expansion. It was no accident that the drawing to a close of the open frontier about 1890 was followed within a few years by a renewal of expansionism and its accompanying ideology of manifest destiny. The last continental frontiers were gone, but new frontiers beckoned from over the seas.

FURTHER READINGS

See again such readable modern texts as Robert E. Riegel, *America Moves West* (3d ed., 1956), and Thomas D. Clark, *Frontier America* (1959). In the Chronicles of

America series, see also Emerson Hough, *The Passing of the Frontier* (1918).

The most thoughtful work on the area of the Great Plains and the problems it presented is Walter P. Webb, *The Great Plains* (1931). A most interesting survey of trans-Mississippi foundations is Everett Dick, *Vanguards of the Frontier* (1941), a reissue of which appears under the title *The Story of the Frontier*. Everett Dick has given us the best social history of the northern plains in *The Sod House Frontier* (1937).

The following titles are significant in connection with the Indian problem: E. D. Branch, *The Hunting of the Buffalo* (1929); L. B. Priest, *Uncle Sam's Stepchildren* (1942); and Harold Fey and D'Arcy McNickle, *Indians and Other Americans: Two Ways of Life Meet* (1959).

On the cowboy, see Mari Sandoz, *The Cattlemen* (1958), an excellent survey; J. B. Frantz and J. B. Choate, *The American Cowboy: Myth and Reality* (1955); E. E. Dale, *Cow Country* (1942); and E. S. Osgood, *The Day of the Cattlemen* (1919).

On other topics, the following titles are significant: Roy Gittinger, *The Formation of Oklahoma* (1939); Glen C. Quiett, *Pay Dirt* (1936); J. V. Frederick, *Ben Holladay: The Stagecoach King* (1940); Arthur Chapman, *The Pony Express* (1932); and Robert G. Athearn, *William Tecumseh Sherman and the Settlement of the West* (1956), which discusses the role of the army.

James P. Shannon, *Catholic Colonization on the Western Frontier* (1957), deals with a phase in the settlement of the last prairie frontier.

For additional bibliography, see the *Harvard Guide,* sections 196–199, 207, 208, and 212.

TWENTY-ONE

American Imperialism and Anti-imperialism

1867
French withdraw from Mexico.

1872
Alabama claims arbitrated.

1889
First Pan-American conference held.

1893
Hawaiian annexation defeated.

1895
Venezuela boundary dispute with Britain.

1898
War with Spain.
Puerto Rico, Guam, Philippines, and Hawaii acquired.

1899
Philippine insurrection begins.
Open Door notes sent.

1900
Boxer uprising in China.

1901
Platt amendment to Cuban constitution.
Hay-Pauncefote Treaty with Great Britain.

1903
Colombian senate rejects canal treaty.
Panama revolution occurs with United States aid.

1904
Roosevelt corollary to Monroe Doctrine announced.

1905
Russo-Japanese peace treaty made at Portsmouth.

ISOLATIONIST INTERLUDE

AFTER THE CIVIL WAR the persistent interest in expansion that had characterized the American republic since its very beginning came to a sudden halt, and the United States turned inward upon itself, ignoring the rest of the world to a remarkable degree. Events conspired to concentrate attention upon internal affairs. The two classes whose interests had been most bound up with the outside world, the slaveowners and the merchant shippers, were casualties of the war; slaveholders were no more, and our merchant marine had all but disappeared from the seas. The internal development of a vast continent occupied all our energies. A host of pressing social and economic problems accompanied the rise of industrial capitalism and tended to divert attention to internal matters. A succession of weak Presidents showed little interest in any sort of vigorous policy. The products of our burgeoning industrial plant were absorbed by our rapidly growing population. Since we were not yet an exporter of capital, economic factors did not yet draw us toward foreign areas.

These facts help to explain our singular lack of interest in foreign affairs between 1865 and 1898. In addition, this period of American isolation coincided with an era of peace and stability unusual in the history of mankind. No major European war occurred between 1871 and 1914, and in the absence of any great world

432

disturbance, America's preoccupation with herself was not interrupted from the outside. Between 1871 and 1914 Europe was not only at peace, but basking in comparative prosperity; at the same time, she had her own international rivalries, which kept her attention away from interference in American affairs. Further, during these years Europe's expansionist energies were directed toward Africa, and later toward Asia. Thus it is not surprising that our foreign policy from 1865 until the 1890s was largely an unexciting narrative of trivial episodes. It had no general direction or aim, for none seemed to be needed.

Not all Americans were disposed to allow the tradition of an expansionist policy to lapse. Secretary of State Seward, who served in Johnson's Cabinet as well as Lincoln's, had taken part in the manifest-destiny movement of the 1840s and was unwilling to believe that American growth had ended with the Gadsden Purchase of 1854. He and others still dreamed of annexing Canada and also of rounding out the American zone with numerous outlying islands. Seward's ambitions for his country resulted, in 1867, in the addition to American territory of the immense northern land of Alaska, purchased from Russia. But this purchase was widely ridiculed and the territory long virtually ignored. Seward, and after him President Grant, continued to advocate the acquisition of foreign territories in the face of public indifference and even hostility. During the period before 1876, the executive department attempted to acquire the Midway Islands, the Danish West Indies, Santo Domingo, and a site for an interoceanic canal. During these years the groundwork was laid also for possession of Samoa and Hawaii. But in the face of public apathy, which was reflected in senatorial opposition, virtually all these efforts came to naught. Some of them, as in the case of Santo Domingo, became unfortunately involved with the notable corruption of the times, and this helped to discredit the whole idea of expansion. Grant eagerly sought to acquire Santo Domingo, only to meet with failure.

The only exciting diplomatic episodes of this period were provided by some disputes left over from the Civil War. Most notable was the American case against Great Britain growing out of the cruisers built for the Confederacy in British yards. The famous *Alabama* and two other commerce destroyers had done enormous damage to Union shipping. The United States held the British government guilty of behaving illegally in allowing their construction, and an angry public backed politicians who demanded huge indemnities from Britain, sometimes hinting that nothing less than Canada would balance the account. For several years this issue caused bitter feelings on both sides of the Atlantic. But finally, in the Treaty of Washington, 1871, it was agreed to submit the matter to an international tribunal of arbitration. After some further bickering, the result was an acceptance by both governments of an opinion which held the British guilty of violating international law but which scaled down the American claims to a moderate sum. This was a compromise in which Great Britain had gone far to appease American wrath. The settlement also was a rare example of the successful use of arbitration as a means of settling a fairly important international dispute. But, as many pointed out, Great Britain had perhaps not really yielded anything contrary to her interests; for in the event of war with some other power, she would not want the United States building *Alabamas* for her enemy.

After 1872, the year in which the Ge-

OFFICES IN AMERICA:

All Offices (21,000) of the Western Union Telegraph Company and its Co

OFFICES IN GREAT BRITAIN:

LONDON:
No. 21 Royal Exchange, E. C.
No. 109 Fenchurch Street, E. C.

LIVERPOOL: No. 8 Rumford Str
GLASGOW: No. 29 Gordon St. a
BRISTOL: Backhall Chambers.

200 0 PR GVT   93

RECEIVED at

305 A.M. Feb 16-98 Washington D.C. Fe

Havana,

Feb 15 Midnight,
Assistant Secretary of State,
Washington

Maine blown up and destroyed tonight at 940 PM. explosion

forward under quarters of crew consequently many were lo

ll officers saved but Jenkins and Merritt Not yet accoun

f explosion yet to be investigated Captain General and A

fficers have rendered every assistance Sigsbee and most

n Ward Steamer City of   Man

ity Am with Sigsbee no   artm

(above) Cable reporting *Maine* disaster
(below) Theodore Roosevelt

Landing light artillery at Daiquiri, Cuba, during Spanish-American War

Pressure from public opinion forced the United States into war with Spain in 1898. The sinking of the Maine *(from causes unknown) turned excitement into hysteria. Theodore Roosevelt, then Assistant Secretary of Navy, was one of the few government leaders who welcomed the war, as a chance to acquire colonies. Spain, fighting reluctantly, put up only token resistance, and the war was soon over. Out of it America got an empire.*

U.S. troops parade through surrendered Havana, January 1, 1899

neva Tribunal settled the *Alabama* claims and in which President Grant's Santo Domingo project died an ignominious death, foreign affairs entered on a period of torpor which lasted for twenty years, until the 1890s. It was once seriously suggested that the diplomatic service be abolished as an unnecessary waste of money. But this isolationist interlude was, in the perspective of time, only a moment's pause in the history of a nation which always had many ties—economic, cultural, and political—with the outer world. Interest in foreign areas never quite died.

LATIN AMERICA

Mexico, our nearest neighbor to the south, bordering us for more than 1,500 miles, was a land of largely undeveloped economic possibilities and of unstable government—factors likely to invite foreign intervention. Following the war of 1846 to 1848 with the United States, Mexico experienced a dozen years of bloody civil war. Then in 1861, taking advantage of this situation and of the outbreak of civil war in the United States, Napoleon III of France launched a grandiose scheme for the establishment of a French-controlled monarchy in Mexico. French troops installed as rulers of Mexico the ill-starred Emperor Maximilian and his beautiful wife Carlotta. Despite the weakness of its military opponents, the new regime was unable to consolidate itself and was maintained in power only by French bayonets. This French-supported empire, so close to our borders, excited the liveliest disapproval and fear in the United States. Busy as we were with our fratricidal struggle, there was little that we could do. But as soon as the war was over there was preparation for action. Putting an army on the Rio Grande, the United

States government asked Napoleon to withdraw French troops from Mexico. Our belligerence, coupled with the hopelessness of the French design and gathering war clouds in Europe, produced the desired effect, and Mexico in 1867 again attained her freedom.

Thereafter the economic development of Mexico was rapid, and the United States played a major role in it. American dollars and American skills developed railroads, mines, and agricultural and grazing lands. American engineers built bridges, power plants, and lighting systems; they sank wells and laid pipes. American promoters and bankers floated stocks and bonds for Mexican enterprises. By the end of the century, oil was discovered south of the border, and Americans shared with the British the development of this new source of wealth. During the thirty-four years of the presidency of Porfirio Díaz (1876–1911), Mexico was a happy hunting ground for United States capitalists and technicians.

A similar economic interest in Cuba, principally in sugar production, led during these years to the investment of 50 million dollars of American capital in that island. By 1895 annual trade with Cuba amounted to 100 million dollars. Similar investments and trade relationships, though on a smaller scale, were beginning to develop in the countries all around the Caribbean and in other Latin-American republics as well. Latin America as an area of trade and investment took on new importance. With this came a revival of the Monroe Doctrine. Even before 1890, the United States began to formulate a program which was later to develop into a Pan-American policy. Secretary of State James G. Blaine, especially, took an interest in the idea. Why could not the republics of the South be wooed away from their traditional attachment to Europe and England? Why could not the United States become the leader of a group of nations of this hemisphere, bound together by ties of commercial and cultural sympathy? Blaine launched his campaign for hemisphere solidarity with a call for a Pan-American conference to be held in Washington in 1881. The plan was nipped when President Garfield's death ended Blaine's tenure as Secretary of State; but he was back in that post in 1889 and proceeded at once to revive his scheme.

In that year the first of a long series of Pan-American conferences met in Washington. Its agenda included plans for reciprocal-trade agreements to facilitate trade and suggestions for a system of arbitration between the nations of the Western Hemisphere. The meeting, however, got no further than exploratory discussions. The idea of introducing tariff reciprocity into our tariff legislation met protectionist opposition in Congress and suffered a serious setback in 1898, when the reciprocity provisions of the Dingley Tariff were killed in the Senate. As for arbitration, the discussion on this topic revealed the significant fact that the Latin-American republics were mistrustful of their great neighbor to the north. They remembered too well such events as the dismemberment of Mexico in 1848, the designs on Cuba in 1854, and the filibustering expeditions against other Latin-American countries which had sailed from our shores in the 1850s. Proposals for arbitration and reciprocity looked suspiciously like an American plot to impose economic and political domination over the smaller countries, the more so since the United States was prompt to reject agreements which would limit its own sovereignty.

The fact that the United States was unwilling to transform her Monroe Doctrine into something more acceptable to Latin America was a stumbling block. The Monroe Doctrine, which had warned European powers that the United States would oppose any new colonial establishments on this continent, had not been opposed by Latin America at the time when it was proclaimed in 1823. Fifty years later, many of the southern republics were beginning to feel that the wording of the doctrine was perhaps a little insulting to their national dignity. They had no objection to receiving the support of the most powerful of the republics of the Western Hemisphere if it should become necessary, but they did not want to be wards of the United States. The Monroe Doctrine was far less welcome as a unilateral statement of United States policy than it would have been as a multilateral statement of the desire of the hemisphere to stand together against outside aggression. The United States, which had always viewed the Monroe Doctrine from a purely domestic angle, was as yet quite unconscious of any need for change. The policy of Pan-Americanism proposed by Secretary Blaine did not, therefore, receive unqualified acceptance at that time. American relations with her neighbors to the south were to receive many setbacks before a policy was pounded into acceptable shape in the second quarter of the twentieth century.

Yet the United States played an increasingly strong role in Latin America in the 1890s. Sometimes American intervention was welcomed and promoted good will; more often not. A revolution in Chile in 1891, in which the United States extended aid to an unpopular dictatorship, led to bad feeling between the two countries. On the other hand, intervention in the affairs of Brazil two years later turned out better, when a republican government was able with American aid to suppress a monarchist revolt backed by British and German warships.

Much more important was the assertion of American interest in Latin-American affairs that occurred in 1895 in connection with Venezuela. The British colony of Guiana borders Venezuela on the east. The boundary between the two states had never been determined because the territory through which it ran was thought worthless. The British discovered gold in the area, and Venezuela claimed that the gold-bearing lands were on her side of the boundary. The two countries broke off relations, and in 1895 Venezuela seemed on the verge of declaring war against England. President Cleveland determined to act vigorously to forestall war, which might have resulted in a settlement dictated from London. Despite the Monroe Doctrine, all through the nineteenth century the British had played the dominant role as arbiter, supplier of capital and technical knowledge, and principal trader in Latin America, and their influence seemed to be growing rather than declining. The Cleveland administration, agreeing with its Republican predecessor that it was time for the United States to replace England in that role, took advantage of the opportunity to state in ringing terms our aims in Latin America. A bombshell note was sent to England in which Secretary of State Richard Olney demanded arbitration. In extremely undiplomatic language he warned that "the United States is practically sovereign on this continent." Cleveland and Congress set up an independent fact-finding commission and were determined to settle the matter by forcing arbitration upon the two contestants, with or without their consent.

Such cavalier treatment of one of the world's great powers was rash, to say the least, but fortunately the British were at this moment unwilling to force the issue. Britain was fully occupied in other areas. She therefore agreed to arbitration and from that time on accepted America's dominant position in the Caribbean.

The Olney statement climaxed a quarter-century of increasing American interest in Latin America and stated a policy toward that area which remained basically unchanged for another thirty years. Until the formulation of the Good Neighbor policy in the late 1920s, America's attitude, frequently acted upon, bore the unmistakable brand of Olney's words. During all these years she assumed that her natural role was that of leader in this hemisphere, and that the hemisphere, especially the Caribbean, was the natural area for expansion of her capitalistic enterprise. Olney's victory served notice on the nations of the world that the United States was the dominant power in the New World. But it did not endear her to most of her Latin-American neighbors, who gave her little credit for defending Venezuela. In their eyes the United States seemed an alarmingly aggressive neighbor rather than a good friend and benevolent protector.

THE PACIFIC

When the west coast came into its possession, the United States became a Pacific power. The full implications of this fact developed much more slowly than the statesmen of the 1840s and 1850s had expected. In those days the United States had an important merchant marine and a promising whale and fur trade in the Pacific. Trade with China was increasing; America took the lead in opening Japan to world commerce. An interoceanic canal, which would give the east coast ready access to the Orient, seemed to be only a few years away. It appeared that the Pacific was to play an important part in the national life. But the Civil War and industrial development altered this. For almost a half-century after 1860, the development of the immense continental wealth took first place. International trade was largely confined to the production of raw materials for Europe, carried in foreign vessels. The west coast was bound to the rest of the country by a network of railroads, and Pacific commerce was nearly forgotten.

Nevertheless, interest in the Pacific never really died. The navy, during Grant's administration, became interested in the strategic importance of the Samoa Islands and attempted to obtain a naval base at Pago Pago. For many years after 1872, representatives of the United States, Germany, and Great Britain engaged in a lively and somewhat shabby intrigue for possession of these islands, which kept the natives in a turmoil and almost led to war among the three powers. Having failed to outmaneuver one another, they decided upon joint administration of the islands in 1889. This arrangement did not prove altogether satisfactory, and in 1899 Samoa was divided between the United States and Germany, England receiving compensation in the form of other Pacific islands and territory in West Africa. America's sphere included the island of Tutuila with its fine harbor, Pago Pago. Thus in a small way the United States was involved in world politics and Pacific empire during these years of "isolation."

The story of the Hawaiian Islands was somewhat similar, except that American influence was preponderant there at all times. These volcanic islands had been a port of call for American traders and whalers ever since the birth of the United States. American missionaries came in the early nineteenth century, and their descendants remained to trade and acquire land. The primitive social organization of the native Hawaiians was no match for the advanced techniques of the energetic newcomers. Their numbers declined, and their lands came into the possession of the white man. Before the end of the century, the foreigners, led by the pushing yankees, dominated the economic life of the islands. A prosperous sugar industry had grown up, with its market in the United States, owned mostly by a few thousand Americans and worked by a docile population of 100,000 native Polynesians, Japanese, and Chinese. This paradise of enterprise received a crushing blow from the bounty-supported beet-sugar industry of the United States, which with government aid was providing stiff competition for the islanders. After 1890, the American owners of plantations and mills were in serious trouble. Many, if not all of them, saw in annexation a solution to their economic difficulties. Already the United States had what amounted to a protectorate over the Islands, having in 1875 exacted a promise from the native king that he would never cede his territory to any other power and having in 1887 acquired the use of Pearl Harbor for the American navy. It was clearly time to speed the natural drift toward annexation.

The Hawaiian situation was brought to a head when, in 1891, the ruling potentate, Queen Liliuokalani, decided to return to the good old days by withdrawing some of the privileges which the Crown had granted in the past to foreigners. The white leaders promptly responded with a revolution. Aided by a few American marines who were landed from a warship,

THE UNITED STATES IN THE PACIFIC

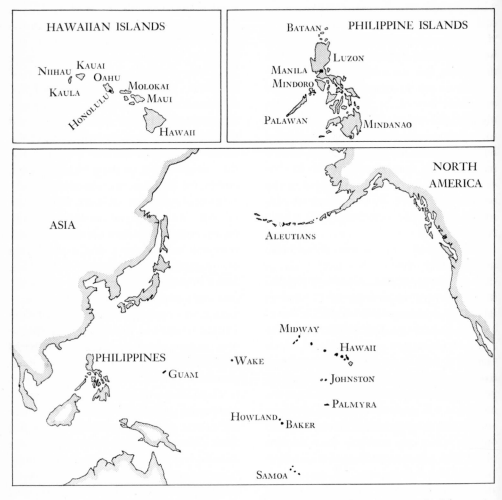

the revolution was a complete success. A government was formed and a delegation sent to the United States to request annexation.

These events occurred while Benjamin Harrison was President. However, before the annexation could be completed, the Democrats and Cleveland had succeeded to office. After an investigation, the new President became convinced that the American minister to Hawaii had been the principal organizer of the revolution,

and that he and his marines had been the chief force behind its success. Under these circumstances, the high-minded Cleveland could not bring himself to let annexation proceed. At the same time, the President did not wish to withdraw protection from American citizens endangered by a vindictive native ruler. So the matter dragged awkwardly along until 1894, when the revolutionists set up an independent republic. A month later the United States recognized the new nation. But Hawaii had to wait another four years until, on July 7, 1898, while Admiral Dewey's exploits at Manila Bay were still warming American hearts, the Islands were annexed by joint resolution of Congress for "the defense of our western shores."

Thus in the last decade of the century American interest in the Pacific was reviving. As in the case of Latin America, this new interest was motivated in part by commercial needs and desires and in part by strategic ones. At about the same time, a similar combination of causes was leading the powers of Europe toward imperialism. They were engaged in a keen competition for markets, fields of investments, sources of raw materials, and strategically situated naval bases. Each of them, like the United States, was striving to obtain spheres of influence, areas in which its exclusive or predominant influence might be exercised. The desire for colonies, which had gone somewhat out of fashion during the earlier nineteenth century, had revived and by 1880 was becoming a dominant force in world history. Within a few years the continent of Africa was divided, principally among France, Britain, Germany, and the king of Belgium. The powers next turned their attention to Asia. At the end of the century the European powers, along with Russia and Japan, were evidently preparing to carve up China.

The example was not lost upon the United States. If being a world power required the acquisition of colonies, the United States must follow suit. The nation was becoming aware of its strength and international stature. Surely the time had come, after a generation of apathy, to make that fact manifest. In the interest of national prestige and honor as well as profit, the feeling began to spread that, as Captain Alfred T. Mahan said, "America must look outward."

IMPERIALISM AND THE SPANISH WAR

In the 1890s the spirit of manifest destiny was again on the move. The old arguments about the destiny of a gifted people to spread their beneficent civilization over lesser peoples revived. The idea became very popular in intellectual circles; it fitted in very well with the fashionable doctrine of social Darwinism. Echoes of the Aryan myth were also heard—the theory that the Teutonic peoples constituted a superior race bearing the higher culture of the world. The United States, in any case, was a big nation, and ought to have an equally large policy, one with world scope. Abandoning the counsel of Washington and Jefferson, American thinkers and politicians began for the first time to advocate intervention in the affairs of Europe and Asia.

Naval Captain Mahan, in his books on sea power and on foreign policy, pictured the world closing in around the sleeping United States and warned that in the race for survival the devil takes the hindmost. The United States needed a great navy to protect her shores; the country was being drawn into world affairs whether she willed it or not. Certain missionary clergymen and professors of political science joined Mahan in ringing the changes upon the theme of the Anglo-Saxon world mission. Young Theodore Roosevelt and his friends were intimates of Mahan and warm admirers of his work. This group of young politicians tied their rising political careers to the new imperialism. They were weary of their stodgy and provincial elders and took the "large view."

Imperialism appealed to them also because it might be expected to turn men's minds away from troublesome issues at home, distracting attention from the great depression of 1893 and the rising political radicalism that accompanied this depression. The new imperialism, they felt, would heal class divisions and divert workers and farmers from radical ideas. As a matter of fact, some of the agrarian radicals of the 1890s actually were drawn toward a blustering foreign policy. Imperialism was in the air.

There began to develop in the United States a fervent sense of patriotism, previously lacking. It was not until the late 1880s that it became customary to rise at the playing of the national anthem or the passing of the flag. Only at this time did schools begin systematically to teach patriotism. American history was then only beginning to be generally taught in the schools. Military drill in colleges had not yet come into vogue, and patriotic societies were largely unknown before the 1880s. In 1891 the United States had practically no army, and the navy was so small that in that year the west coast had a fright at the prospect of an attack by the Chilean navy. During the dozen years after 1880, a more militant spirit was working to transform this slack and peaceful nation.

While America was hearkening to the call of destiny and trembling on the verge of great adventure, the Cuban revolution broke out in 1895. Cuba had been one of the objects of our earlier manifest-destiny movement. Some Americans had long cast fond eyes on this "pearl of the Antilles," so near our shores. Some attempts had been made to acquire this desirable piece of property during the years before 1860, but they were associated with the expansionist plots of slaveowners and thus discredited in the eyes of the North. American policy had long been content to let Cuba remain in the hands of Spain, too weak to constitute any threat to us. But the revolution of 1895, coming as it did at a time when the American people were developing an intense interest in the entire Caribbean area, was bound to induce in so susceptible a body a violent annexation fever.

Revolution had been endemic in Cuba ever since the early part of the century, when the other Spanish possessions in this hemisphere had attained their independence. The basic cause of discontent was that intangible thing called nationalism which has been working within many peoples for the last two centuries. But there were other causes at work: Spanish misrule, heavy taxes, denial of local self-government, the blighting poverty of the islanders. This situation had already produced the Ten Years' War, a terrible uprising between 1868 and 1878 which had been beaten down only with the use of savage force. The immediate cause of the 1895 revolution was our tariff act of that same year—the Wilson-Gorman Tariff—which, by heavily taxing imported sugar, caused the price of raw sugar in Cuba to fall drastically. Sugar had become the basis of the economic life of the island. It was raised on large plantations, owned by a few great landlords, some of them American corporations, and worked by poor peons whose condition was little better than that of slaves. Widespread depression and suffering among these peons provided an opportunity for nationalist agitators. The island burst into flames.

The center of the revolution may be said to have been in New York City, where a colony of Cuban revolutionaries, refugees from their homeland, had maintained a "junta" or revolutionary government for many years. After the fighting began in Cuba, this junta became a headquarters for propaganda and fund raising, and the source of filibustering expeditions from American ports. The activity of these Cubans in the United States, many of them American citizens, caused a series of incidents endangering American neutrality. American sympathy was enlisted on behalf of the suffering Cubans, and demands for intervention were soon heard on all sides. The new popular or "yellow" press found a gold mine in the Cuban affair. Atrocities of the most lurid nature were ready at hand. In case of any temporary shortage, they could easily be fabricated. The Spanish commanding general was dubbed "Butcher"—a title not entirely undeserved. President Cleveland, who was opposed to imperialism on principle, was aware that atrocities were being committed by both sides and tried to be scrupulously neutral. It was his opinion that an epidemic of insanity had the United States in its grip, an epidemic which he sternly withstood even when evidences of it came from the Congress itself.

William McKinley, who took office in March, 1897, was also determined to maintain peace, although he had been elected on a platform demanding freedom for Cuba. But he was not formed in the same rigid mold as his predecessor; the tide of events proved too strong for him. In Cuba a war of extermination was at its height. At home the press was in full cry. Although advocates of intervention were ever more insistent, McKinley was able to hold off the warmongers for a year. Two incidents, however, occurring almost simultaneously, toppled the well-meaning but too pliant President into the war camp. On February 9, 1898, a letter

written by the Spanish Minister in Washington and stolen by an enterprising reporter was published in a New York newspaper. The letter described McKinley in the most uncomplimentary terms. The country was outraged; the Spanish Minister resigned. While this incident was straining relations between the two countries, news arrived of the sinking of the battleship *Maine* in Havana harbor on the night of February 15. The *Maine* was at Havana to "provide protection for American interests." Two hundred and sixty lives were lost, and although the cause of the explosion has never been determined, few Americans then doubted that the haughty Spaniards were to blame. The war party now had a slogan: "Remember the *Maine!*" Congress appropriated 50 million dollars for "defense."

With the United States practically at war, Spain gave up and agreed to end the war in Cuba on whatever terms the United States should determine. On April 10 our minister to Spain cabled that Spain would agree to autonomy, independence, or cession to us, whichever we wished. But on April 11 McKinley sent his war message to Congress. Fearful that his failure to achieve a war might lose for him the control of his party, the President had yielded to the popular clamor.

The Spanish-American War must be judged a product of mass mania. It could not be blamed on the capitalists, for American business as a whole was by no means convinced of its need for foreign markets and was quite unconcerned about Cuban business possibilities. The old guard of the Republican party, led by Mark Hanna and McKinley, thought little of the arguments of the young radicals that America should thrust herself into the stream of power politics. Most newspapers, while neglecting no opportunity to increase circulation by playing up the sensational aspects of the Cuban revolution, felt that they were following rather than leading public opinion. America was caught up in the spirit of the times and was swept into war on a tide of hysteria which perhaps registered the emotions of a people who had experienced no such excitement for a generation.

A "SPLENDID LITTLE WAR" AND AN EMPIRE

Since the appearance in 1890 of Mahan's book on the influence of sea power on history, the United States had been building up its navy. One of the men responsible for this growth was an energetic and alert Assistant Secretary of the Navy named Theodore Roosevelt. In 1898 we had a much enlarged, mostly new and up-to-date navy to meet the challenge of the occasion. This navy won all the honors that the Spanish War afforded. The Spanish navy managed to cross the Atlantic to Cuba, where it was blockaded in the harbor of Santiago by half the Atlantic fleet. The other half of the fleet was held in reserve to protect the Atlantic seaboard against possible attack by this Spanish fleet. The American cities of the eastern seaboard had a delicious thrill of apprehension, which was all the better for the absence of any real danger.

When hostilities began, the Pacific fleet was conveniently located at Hong Kong, only a short sail from the Spanish islands of the Philippines. Most of the American public, it is safe to say, had never heard of the Philippines; fewer still knew where they were. But Assistant Secretary of the Navy Roosevelt knew. Roosevelt had made Commodore George Dewey commander of the fleet. Two months before war broke out, Dewey's fleet was ordered to Hong Kong. In that Chinese-English port Dewey met Emilio Aguinaldo, exiled leader of an independence movement which was in progress at the time in the Philippine Islands. Under the impression that the Americans were coming to give his country its freedom, Aguinaldo promised cooperation. When news of the declaration of war arrived, Dewey steamed to Manila and there destroyed the Spanish fleet on May 1. Then, assisted by the army and by the forces of Aguinaldo, Dewey took Manila on August 13, one day after the signing of the armistice with Spain.

The war in Cuba was brief and decisive. The Spanish fleet under Admiral Cervera broke out of the harbor of Santiago and was destroyed in four hours (on July 3, just in time for the celebration of the Fourth). American troops were landed, and a few skirmishes fought —enough to produce a hero, Colonel Theodore Roosevelt, who had raised a company of Rough Riders which charged, horseless, up San Juan Hill, one of the three hills commanding the port of Santiago. Puerto Rico was captured without a fight—"Gin'ral Miles' Gran' Picnic and Moonlight Excursion," as Mr. Dooley called it. Their hearts never having been in the war, the Spanish soon sued for peace, and the preliminary agreement was signed on August 12. John Hay, the new Secretary of State, wrote to his friend Roosevelt: "It has been a splendid little war." Fifty-five hundred Americans lost their lives, mostly from disease, not counting those who perished in the Philippines fighting against the patriot Aguinaldo, who continued to fight for independence against the Americans as he had against the Spaniards.

The final peace treaty was signed in Paris on December 10, 1898, after about two months of negotiating. The most important decision concerned the disposal of the Philippines, where our forces were occupying the capital city, Manila. Imperialistic sentiment had been growing in the United States, not least in high circles within the Republican party. In response to this sentiment, President McKinley had convinced himself, not without soul searching, that the Far Eastern prize must be kept. In fact, the alternatives were not very attractive. Having embarked upon the great venture of conquest, there was no ready way out of it. The islands could not be left with Spain; it seemed impossible that the Filipinos could govern themselves; France and Germany were waiting to seize them if the United States should abandon them. Japanese influence was also feared. American business interests were enthusiastic over the economic possibilities of the islands. Lying so close to the potential market of China's millions, Manila with its spacious harbor might become the American Hong Kong! Therefore, it was decided to pay Spain 20 million dollars and to annex the Philippines.

Almost as if by magic, the United States had acquired an empire. She had a protectorate over Cuba and outright possession of Puerto Rico, the Philippines, and Guam. On the way to the Philippines in the summer of 1898, an expeditionary force had taken the vacant island of Wake. Midway, which had been claimed earlier but forgotten about, was quickly reclaimed. Hawaii was annexed while the war was in progress, and at its close the islands of the Samoan group. The United States had gained her long-cherished dreams in the Caribbean and, in addition, possessed a chain of islands all the way across the Pacific. The European powers, except perhaps England, were somewhat disturbed at the sudden appearance of so hardy a newcomer in international affairs; and the Japanese protested that the balance of power in the Pacific had been upset.

The new empire was not decided upon without serious heart searching by the American people. The agreement which ended the war in August, 1898, had provided for Cuban freedom and the annexation of Puerto Rico. The Philippines, which had apparently fallen into our hands by chance, presented a new problem. If America was embarking upon a new imperial policy, if she was determined to bid for her share of Asian trade, it was obvious that a chain of islands across the Pacific culminating in the strategically located Philippines was essential. But did the United States want an empire? Was it consistent with her basic traditions? Did she desire an aggressive Far Eastern policy? Despite the action of the government during the half year from April to October, 1898, these questions were still unanswered. The issue of imperialism was aired for American public opinion by the debate in the Senate over ratification of the peace treaty. Ostensibly, the United States had fought the war for the sole purpose of freeing Cuba. The treaty thrust her into the complexities of the Orient at a time when most of her citizens were uneducated in the subtleties of power politics and were, by long usage, accustomed to isolationist thinking.

A group of senators who vigorously repudiated the new turn of events rose to defend America from her imperialistic leaders by attacking the treaty. The Senate debate set off a nationwide political battle—imperialism versus anti-imperialism—which raged for two years and reached a climax in the election of 1900. The treaty itself was ratified in the Senate by the intervention of Bryan, the Demo-

CHAPTER TWENTY-ONE

cratic leader. While a convinced anti-imperialist, Bryan felt that national honor required the Senate to accept the treaty and was apparently looking ahead to the election of 1900. The leaders of the two parties whipped into line enough of their followers to get the treaty approved.

The anti-imperialists now essayed the much more difficult task of trying to stem a tide already in motion. They were not without hope. There seemed an excellent chance that, if properly informed of the dangers, America might reject the new departure in foreign affairs. The new imperialism presented problems theoretical and practical, political and constitutional, for which no ideal solution appeared possible and which promised sweeping and uncomfortable changes in the American way of life. Could the Filipinos be citizens? If not, how could they be governed? Did the Constitution provide for the rule of dependent peoples? Would the inclusion under the American flag of millions of subject people endanger the freedom of American citizens? The foreign policy of a world power would involve large navies, large armies, a large bureaucracy, and heavy expenses. And, as critics of the new policy pointed out, America's oldest political principle condemned "government without consent of the governed."

All these questions were hurled at the prospective voters in the election campaign of 1900. The Democrats fought the campaign on the issue of anti-imperialism. Bryan, again the Democratic candidate, demanded that the Filipinos be prepared for independence as soon as possible. In their attempts to discredit the Republicans by attacking their imperialistic program, the Democrats found allies outside their own party. Anti-imperialists appeared in both parties and in all groups of society. The country's intellectual leaders were especially well represented. College presidents, idealistic politicians, literary figures, some of the leading editors, labor leaders, historians, philosophers, clergymen—a brilliant company took up the cause of defending old American ideals from the threatening new national policy. Aguinaldo was compared to Washington; the Filipinos, to the embattled Americans of 1776. The atrocities, the "water cures," and the concentration camps so reminiscent of the "Butcher" had appeared in the Philippines and received the same thorough press coverage as before—only this time the United States was cast in the role of oppressor. The Republicans, undismayed by the avalanche of criticism, nominated McKinley and stood pat on his record in both domestic and foreign policy. America must accept the responsibilities thrust upon her as a result of the war with Spain. The flag must not be hauled down! It had been raised in the Philippines and fired upon. The natives must be subdued and then civilized.

McKinley was elected; but whether his foreign policy or the renewal of prosperity in the agrarian West was the decisive cause, no one could say. He was assassinated in September, 1901, and succeeded by his Vice President, Theodore Roosevelt. Whatever the desires of the American people, and there was much evidence that by election time in 1900 they were already tired of the whole question of imperialism, the work of the year 1898 was not to be undone.

RUNNING THE EMPIRE

A few paragraphs concerning the way in which the United States handled her imperial possessions are appropriate here. On the whole, the American record as colonial administrator was a good one. Much was done for the peoples under American control. Public health and sanitation, particularly, became the hallmark of American administration. In Cuba, which was ruled by the army until 1902, American doctors under Walter Reed's leadership discovered the cause of yellow fever and wiped out that disease in Havana. The building of schools, hospitals, roads, and sanitation facilities also improved conditions in backward Puerto Rico and in the Philippines. Determined to live up to the doctrine of trusteeship, put forward as a justification for imperialism by many of its advocates (the "white man's burden"), the American government spent more money on its colonial possessions than it collected from them. It often introduced other salutary reforms; for example, that of breaking up many of the huge landed estates in the Philippines and giving the land to heretofore landless cultivators. On the other hand, in Puerto Rico the system of great plantations, owned by a few and employing low-paid peon labor, became even more pronounced under American rule, and during the Great Depression of the 1930s this led to extreme distress.

A sterner test of the trusteeship doctrine was whether the territories would be allowed to develop institutions of self-government. Promises in this respect were eventually fulfilled, for the most part. In 1902 Cuba was provided with a constitution based on that of the United States, but the Cubans were forced to accept the Platt amendment to this constitution, which granted the United States rights of intervention in times of trouble and also a veto power on matters of foreign policy

and finance. This right of intervention was exercised in 1906, 1912, 1917, and 1918. But the amendment was formally abrogated in 1934, and Cuba became fully independent. Puerto Rico also received limited self-government, which has grown steadily, until today she enjoys complete home rule. In 1917 Puerto Rico got an elected legislature as well as a seat in the House of Representatives; in 1948 she began to elect her own governor; in 1952 Puerto Ricans adopted a new constitution written and approved by themselves. Only a small minority has continued to clamor for complete independence. Among the smaller island possessions, Guam has had an elective legislature since 1950, Samoa since 1948, and the Virgin Islands (purchased from Denmark in 1916) since 1936. The natives of Guam and the Virgin Islands as well as Puerto Rico are citizens of the United States.

Alaska and Hawaii were self-governing territories until, in 1958 and 1959, they were both admitted as states, the first admissions since 1912 and the first states ever to be made from territory not contiguous to the continental union. The Philippines, largest of our colonial possessions, provided the biggest test in the matter of self-government. A bitter war between Filipino patriots and American troops lasted until 1902 and left a legacy of hatred. Subsequent American rule in the Philippines proved economically favorable to the islands, but the demand for freedom continued to come from their leaders. America responded with a series of measures looking toward independence. A native assembly was in existence by 1907, and in 1916 it obtained considerable authority, though the American-appointed governor still had a power of veto. The promise of eventual freedom was repeated at this time, and President Woodrow Wilson was on the point of granting it in 1920 when he went out of office. The Republicans were more reluctant, but by 1932 they too were ready to grant independence. Certain American agricultural interests, especially beet- and cane-sugar producers, were always supporters of Philippine independence from motives of self-interest, while isolationists never liked the involvement in the Far East these distant possessions brought. The Filipinos, frightened at the prospect of remaining outside the American tariff wall, were reluctant to accept the offer of independence. But they did so in 1934, under an act which provided that full independence would come after ten years. After World War II this went into effect. But until 1974 the new Philippine republic will have preferential treatment under our tariff laws, while the United States retains military bases in the islands.

The grandiose dreams of 1898 in regard to an American empire never materialized. The "illimitable markets of China" of which so much was then heard never became a reality; nor was any great amount of American capital invested in the Philippines themselves. Strategically, possession of the Philippine Islands proved an embarrassing liability. The American taxpayer was never willing to foot the large bill required to fortify and defend them. Exposed and vulnerable, they considerably weakened American diplomacy in the Far East and involved us in the threat of war. Plainly the American people had not carefully thought through the consequences of extending their empire so far. Hawaii and the Caribbean islands, on the other hand, clearly lay within the American sphere of defense, and were without question of great strategic value. Except for the Virgin Islands and the Panama Canal Zone, America was to acquire no more overseas possessions until after World War II. But critics were to claim that she soon developed a system of indirect control in the Caribbean area which was imperialism without annexation. For American interest in this region was to wax, not wane, in the next few years.

THE AFTERMATH OF IMPERIALISM: FAR EASTERN POLITICS

America's sudden entry into the race for colonial empire in 1898 was not to be followed up by other conquests, as many assumed would be the case. On the contrary, America wanted no more conquests and tended to draw back from some of the implications of what she had done. But it was difficult to retreat. At the time when she appeared on the imperial scene, the great powers had finished carving up the continent of Africa and were sharpening their knives for China. In the 1890s Japan, Russia, Germany, Britain, and France had already obtained special concessions there, and after China's defeat by Japan in the war of 1894–1895 they were engaged in establishing spheres of influence preparatory to an outright partition of the ancient empire. The alternative prospects of entering this contest or else being left out of the treasury of China's wealth while the other powers engrossed it all were both unappealing to the United States and sent her searching for another solution. Not willing to go further down the road of great-power imperialism, yet anxious to enter the China markets, the United States found an answer to her dilemma in the Open Door policy, enunciated by Secretary of State John Hay in

1899.* Hay sent a note to the various governments involved, suggesting that there be no discriminatory tariffs and railroad rates in the leased ports and spheres of influence which had been established in China. Alarmed by the aggressive attitude of the other powers and at the possibility of a world war which the situation invited, Great Britain sympathized with our policy. All the powers except Russia accepted the policy on condition of unanimous approval. Russia demurred, thus releasing the others from their commitment. Hay chose, nevertheless, to claim that all had accepted, and he proclaimed establishment of the Open Door policy.

Less than a year later, the situation in China reached a crisis in the Boxer rebellion. The Boxers, an antiforeign and anti-Christian society bent upon ridding China of these foreign influences, started a revolution within the country. The lives of thousands of whites were threatened; about 300 were killed. Since the Chinese government would not do anything to control the Boxers, the powers organized an international expeditionary force in order to rescue the foreigners besieged in Peking. American troops formed part of this expedition, which after achieving its mission engaged in brutal reprisals against the Chinese. It looked as though the Europeans might seize this opportunity to increase their influence, or even to make an attempt at partition. To avoid such a solution, if possible, Hay sent out another note stating that the purpose of the United States was to maintain the *status quo* in China. This action in all likelihood pre-

* The Open Door policy was in fact not a new one; it only received a new emphasis at this time. Equality of trading rights and maintenance of China's independence as the foundation of American policy may be traced as far back as the 1840s.

vented some of the eventualities America had feared. China's integrity was saved, but she was saddled with a huge indemnity. The United States later returned to China most of our share of this indemnity in the form of scholarships for properly trained Chinese students to complete their education in American schools.

These events and actions set the pattern of United States policy toward China which was maintained until very recent years. Equal treatment for trade and maintenance of China's territorial integrity have been her aims. The influence of the United States and Britain and the rivalries of the other powers kept China independent. Moreover, cooperation by these two powers in the Open Door policy built up Anglo-American friendship, a friendship which had begun at the time of the Spanish-American War and which was to continue thereafter almost uninterrupted. In her China policy the United States repudiated imperialism via annexation and returned to an older policy of equal trading rights for all. It is doubtful whether the Chinese fully appreciated our policy, for the Open Door did not necessarily mean an end of economic imperialism as embodied in the "unequal treaties" forced on China by the Western powers.

The assassination of President McKinley in 1901 brought to the presidency a leader fully devoted to imperialism and a "large policy." Theodore Roosevelt's handling of foreign affairs, like everything else he did, was vigorous. In the Far East Roosevelt supported the Open Door as well as he could and attempted to increase American influence. In 1904 a major war broke out between Russia and Japan, brought on by a clash of imperial ambitions in the region of Manchuria and Korea. American diplomacy as well as American public opinion supported Japan. At a moment calculated to achieve maximum gains for Japan, Roosevelt stepped in with an offer of mediation, which the Russians, faced with revolution at home, accepted reluctantly. The peace conference was held at Portsmouth, New Hampshire, and Roosevelt was awarded the Nobel peace prize. It could be argued that support of Japan helped the Open Door, inasmuch as Russia had been the more aggressive of the two in her Far Eastern imperialism.

But it was not long before we were quarreling seriously with our recent friend, Japan, for the Japanese did not intend to open to other nations the door to Korea and southern Manchuria. Roosevelt was willing to recognize their special position in Korea in return for a Japanese promise to respect our possession of the Philippines. But in Manchuria friction developed. At the same time there was trouble in connection with Japanese immigration to the American west coast and the action of San Francisco in excluding Japanese from public schools. All this led to talk of war. In 1907 Roosevelt conceived the dramatic gesture of sending the entire American fleet around the world in an action construed by many as an effort to impress the Japanese with our strength. Nevertheless, the President worked for peace; an agreement with Japan followed (1908), by which Japan was to respect the Open Door in China but had her privileged position in Manchuria silently recognized by the United States. It was obviously not going to be easy to persuade the rising nation of Japan, which had westernized its technology in an amazingly short period of time, to abandon her "manifest destiny" in Asia. Roosevelt's Far Eastern diplomacy had been astute, but his position was weak compared to Japan's.

President Taft, Roosevelt's successor, made a blundering effort to gain access to Manchuria for American railroad capital; Russia and Japan now joined in slamming the door shut. And during World War I, while the European powers were preoccupied, Japan greatly strengthened her position in China. In spite of these discouragements, American policy remained officially pledged to the Open Door policy and the territorial integrity of China.

ROOSEVELT AND THE CARIBBEAN

It was not only in the Far East that the events of 1898 had significant consequences. America's new status in the Caribbean and in the Pacific made mandatory the realization of the old dream of an isthmian canal, and toward this goal President Roosevelt proceeded with his customary vigor. One obstacle to the construction of a canal by the United States was the half-century-old Clayton-Bulwer Treaty with England, which specified that no

Roosevelt and the Panama Canal, 1906. The ebullient President runs a steam shovel helping to dig the big ditch. (Library of Congress)

such canal could be under exclusive American control. The British, who were bidding for our friendship in the Far East and elsewhere, were willing to revise this treaty. A new one, the Hay-Pauncefote Treaty of 1901, was approved, giving the United States exclusive control of any canal she should build. The location of the proposed canal was then enthusiastically debated. Most experts had favored a Nicaraguan route, but the Panama route was finally agreed upon. A French company which had been operating in Panama for a dozen years was now bankrupt and was anxious to sell its concession along with the work already done. A group of Americans had purchased some of the stock of the defunct company and formed a lobby which brought pressure for the selection of the Panama route. An erupting volcano in Nicaragua obligingly helped them, and Congress made its decision for Panama. The rights of the French company were to be purchased for 40 million dollars if arrangements could be made with the republic of Colombia, in whose territory the canal was to run. A treaty was signed in Washington between representatives of the two governments giving the United States a 100-year lease on a 6-mile-wide strip of land across the Isthmus in return for 10 million dollars and subsequent annual payments of $250,-000.

Dissatisfied with the terms of the bargain, the Colombian senate delayed approval of the treaty. Roosevelt became impatient, as did American opinion in general. When the agent of the French company, M. Philippe Bunau-Varilla, visited him, the President evidently gave him to understand that in the event of a revolt in Panama the United States would do all it could to see that the revolution did not fail. Agents of the company in as-

sociation with local Panamanians then promoted a revolution in Panama with the object of gaining independence from Colombia, a goal most Panamanians probably favored. American warships were sent to the area, and Colombian troops which arrived to put down the revolt were dissuaded by the Americans. Quickly the United States recognized the new government and negotiated with it substantially the same treaty Colombia had refused.

Speaking some time after the incident, Theodore Roosevelt said, "I took Panama." The rather highhanded means employed have generally been considered a blot on the record of American diplomacy. Certainly it did nothing to calm Latin-American fears of their powerful neighbor to the north. Nor were these fears stilled by Roosevelt's subsequent Caribbean policies. Many of the governments in this area were notoriously unstable. They had all borrowed money in Europe and, for reasons usually connected with their political instability, were often unable to remit scheduled payments. When this occurred, standard procedure (used throughout the nineteenth century) was for the creditor nation to force payments or reforms to make future payments possible. Now that the Caribbean was an American sphere of influence, such intervention was embarrassing to the United States. Great Britain and Germany used armed force in Venezuela in 1902–1903 in order to collect defaulted debts. Venezuela asked Roosevelt to force arbitration. Much as he disliked seeing foreign gunboats throwing shells ashore from "our lake," Roosevelt refused. The incident, however, set him to thinking. In his annual message of 1904 he outlined a plan for preventing the intervention of foreign powers. In cases where intervention was required because of the wrongdoing or

THE UNITED STATES IN THE CARIBBEAN

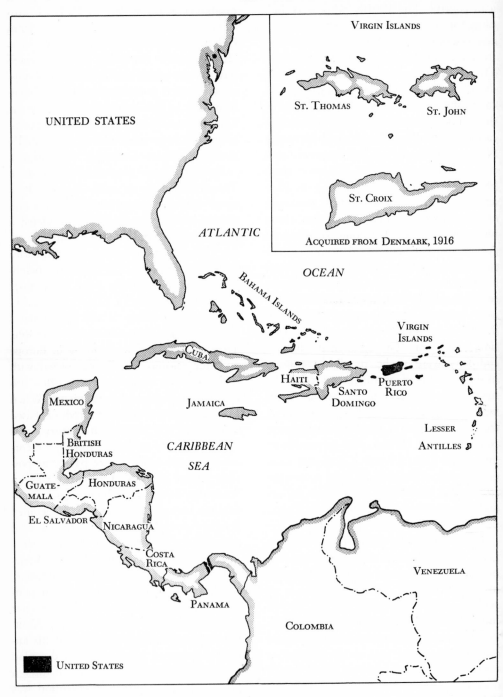

the impotence of a government within her sphere of influence, the United States might "exercise . . . an international police power."

In the following year an opportunity for the exercise of such "police power" occurred. Santo Domingo could not pay her debts, and European intervention loomed. Roosevelt sprang to action and announced his "corollary" to the Monroe Doctrine. Since the United States did not wish to permit foreign powers to meddle in her sphere, she must herself intervene whenever necessary. Roosevelt placed a receiver-general in charge of the Santo Domingo revenues and soon had its finances in good order. The Roosevelt Corollary was soon being invoked regularly and extensively. Roosevelt intervened in Cuba in 1906, under the Platt amendment. In 1908 it was Nicaragua's turn. After Roosevelt's "big stick" had been laid down, the precedent which he had established continued. In 1911 Honduras and Nicaragua received financial advice, in the latter case accompanied by marines. In 1915 the marines landed in Haiti after a tussel which cost some lives. In 1916 intervention occurred in Santo Domingo again, in 1920 in Guatemala, in 1924 in Honduras. In 1927 the marines, who had been briefly absent, returned to Nicaragua. Between 1900 and 1927 the United States intervened in one way or another in each of the eleven Latin-American republics bordering on the Caribbean, with the single exception of Costa Rica.

The policy of the United States during this period was called "dollar diplomacy" by those who assumed that the cause of armed intervention was the protection of American capital and the imposing of its greedy grip on the Caribbean. There was some truth in the charge. But the chief reason for intervention was military. This area, so close to the canal and to our Gulf Coast, was considered to be of great importance to the defense of the United States. It was therefore important to have it politically stable and to prevent any excuse for foreign intervention. This logic, based on national defense, was accepted by so liberal a President as Woodrow Wilson, who did not believe in promoting the interests of American capitalists overseas by such means. However, whatever its motives, American intervention under the Roosevelt Corollary poisoned our relations with Latin America. The policy was finally abandoned about 1930, none too soon from the point of view of good relations with the rest of the hemisphere.

Some of the excessively noisy and belligerent methods associated with American policy in this critical era may be attributed to the fact that the young giant had just arrived on the world scene. Not yet accustomed to her new role and inclined to make awkward mistakes, the United States was unmistakably announcing to the other great powers that she had "arrived." Roosevelt, whatever mistakes he may have made, had the insight to see that the nation had no choice but to play the part of the great power which it now was. After the excitement of 1898 passed away, a good many Americans were not so sure that they wanted to abandon their comfortable old policy to swim in the icy waters of world politics. Yet in fact 1898 was the turning point in America's evolution from the old foreign policy to the new.

FURTHER READINGS

On American relations with Latin America, Dexter Perkins, *The Monroe Doctrine, 1867–1907* (1937), is a more specialized treatment than his *The United States and the Caribbean* (1947). Wilfrid H. Callcott, *The Caribbean Policy of the United States, 1890–1920* (1942), is a reliable and balanced survey. Samuel F. Bemis, *The Latin American Policy of the United States* (1943), expresses some vigorous opinions by one of the most distinguished American historians. A. L. P. Dennis, *Adventures in American Diplomacy* (1928), covers the Venezuelan affair as well as other incidents, while a most lively account of an engaging subject is provided by D. C. Miner in *The Fight for the Panama Route* (1940).

Tyler Dennett, *Americans in East Asia* (1941), is a good introduction to its subject, now supplemented by Paul A. Varg, *Missionaries, Chinese, and Diplomats* (1958). The background of American imperialism is examined by Julius W. Pratt in *Expansionists of 1898* (1936). Walter Millis, *The Martial Spirit* (1931), remains the classic account of the war itself, such as it was. Charles S. Campbell, Jr., *Anglo-American Understanding, 1898–1903* (1957), is a recent authoritative account of the Open Door diplomacy and may be compared with Lionel M. Gelber, *The Rise of Anglo-American Friendship, 1898–1906* (1938).

Pratt, *America's Colonial Experiment* (1950), is a competent summary of America as an imperial power. The foreign policy of Hay and Roosevelt is acutely analyzed in portions of George Kennan, *American Diplomacy, 1900–1950* (1951), and of Samuel F. Bemis, *The United States as a World Power* (1950). A very important work for many aspects of Roosevelt's policies is Howard K. Beale, *Theodore Roosevelt and the Rise of America to World Power* (1956). More restricted in theme, but nevertheless interesting, is Edward H. Zabriskie, *American-Russian Rivalry in the Far East, 1895–1914* (1946).

A special topic of much significance and interest has been ably handled by Harold Sprout and Margaret Sprout in *Rise of American Naval Power, 1776–1918* (1944). Attention should also be called to the peace movement, notable in this era: see relevant portions of Merle Curti, *Peace or War: The American Struggle, 1636–1936* (1936). P. C. Jessup, *Elihu Root* (2 vols., 1938), sheds much light on affairs diplomatic, military, and otherwise.

For additional bibliography, see the *Harvard Guide,* sections 194, 220–225, and 236–238.

TWENTY-TWO

The Era of Progressivism

1901
United States Steel Corporation organized.
President McKinley assassinated.
Theodore Roosevelt becomes President.

1902
Roosevelt intervenes in coal strike.
First state workmen's compensation law.

1904
Theodore Roosevelt returned to White House.

1905
Lochner v. New York decided.

1906
Hepburn Act and Pure Food and Drug Act passed.

1908
William Howard Taft elected President.

1909
Payne-Aldrich Tariff enacted.

1911
Standard Oil Company ordered dissolved.

1912
Revolt of Progressive Republicans.
Wilson elected over Roosevelt and Taft.

1913
Sixteenth and Seventeenth Amendments ratified.
Federal Reserve Act passed.
Underwood Tariff enacted.

1914
Clayton Antitrust Act passed.

THE PROGRESSIVE CLIMATE

At THE TURN of the century, Americans viewed their national achievements with a complacency which was at least partly justifiable. They could take pride not only in an unprecedented material and economic expansion, but also in the success of their religious and educational institutions, in intellectual and scientific achievements, in the survival of representative government, and in a generous amount of individual freedom. But there was also a growing and uncomfortable sense of things left undone and of things which should not have been done. "The evil," as Woodrow Wilson expressed it, "has come with the good, and much fine gold has been corroded. . . . The Nation has been deeply stirred . . . by the knowledge of wrong, of ideals lost, of government too often debauched and made an instrument of evil." Of these evils accompanying the rapid pace of industrial growth in the United States since the Civil War we have already had glimpses—especially the corruption of government and the unequal distribution of the rewards of the new industrial wealth. It should be noted that throughout the Western world industrialism had created similar problems, which led to mounting pressure for a better distribution of the benefits of industrialism and for a greater popular voice in its distribution. In fact, Americans were slower to protest and slower to act than most other Western nations undergoing similar industrial transformation—a fact which suggests that the evils were less in America.

Working in a sweatshop factory
scene on Mulberry St.,
New York City, around 1900
strikers, 1900

In the Progressive Era, America's social conscience awakened to a variety of evils. Political reform was a prominent interest; another was a new concern with "how the other half lives." This "other half" was immigrant America, coming from depressed parts of the world with hope which was sometimes blasted by deplorable working and living conditions in the crowded tenements of eastern cities.

An immigrant family arriving in America

In Great Britain the new liberalism had begun as early as the 1880s to secure such welfare legislation as workmen's compensation laws, and by the early 1900s it had obtained unemployment insurance and old-age pensions. Unregulated *laissez faire* was everywhere on the defensive against those who demanded deliberate planning for a more equitable distribution of income.

Reformers of the American progressive period focused their indignant attacks upon two major sets of conditions: political corruption and the concentration of wealth and economic power. The two things were intimately related. The political system had, it appeared, simply caved in at certain points under the ponderous weight of pressure and privilege. Cities, counties, states, and even the national government had succumbed to an invisible, undemocratic control by bosses, behind whom stood special-interest groups. Politics had become the tool of a few, violating the spirit of democratic representative government. This undemocratic domination had been aided by the existence of antiquated and inefficient governmental machinery. It was the intention of progressives to simplify this machinery and restore government to the people. This problem, the analysis and solution of which were to occupy much of the interest and energy of the progressive movement, was more complex than it seemed; for this elaborate system of "invisible government" interlocking the interests of professional politicians and great economic lords had taken deep root during the Gilded Age, and its perpetuation served the purposes of powerful groups.

The second and related target of reform was the concentration of economic power itself. Industrial growth after the Civil War, as we have seen, was marked by a fierce competitive struggle in which the only standard seemed to be that might makes right. One of the main objects of the struggle was to reduce, if not to eliminate, the power of one's competitors. There gradually emerged certain companies which commanded broad areas of economic activity. This concentration of control threatened to destroy competition. The first wave of consolidation and the resultant protest brought passage of the Interstate Commerce Act in 1887 and the Sherman Antitrust Act of 1890. The early combinations, however, were rather insignificant when compared with those of the prosperous years around the turn of the century. By 1904 there were 318 industrial trusts, the result of mergers by almost 5,300 separate concerns, which were capitalized at over 7 billion dollars. To put this figure in perspective it is necessary to realize that the total capitalization of all American industry in 1900 was about 10 billion dollars. Most of this consolidation occurred between 1897 and 1904 in such industries as steel, copper, sugar, tobacco, and oil. The formation in 1901 of the United States Steel Corporation, the largest in the nation, drew the widest attention, but popular indignation was aroused by combinations controlling such basic products as sugar, tobacco, meat, whisky, and woolens. It was not only the concentrated industrial and financial power that aroused concern. That power, it was felt, must aggravate the already unequal distribution of wealth, which was revealed to be not radically different from that prevailing in Europe. Many Americans felt uneasy that only 20 per cent of the population owned most of the nation's abounding wealth, that one family in every hundred owned more than the remaining ninety-nine, that between one-half and two-thirds of the wage-earning working class received annual incomes less than was necessary to maintain minimum family-living standards. These extremes of wealth and poverty were especially disturbing since there seemed so little promise of improvement if existing trends continued.

Any attempt to describe progressivism should probably begin with the warning that it is not susceptible to any simple definition. There were numerous progressive movements working in different areas, on different levels of government, and toward a great variety of goals. Emphasizing the free individual as it did, progressivism was many things to many men. Diverse and divided, it contained a variety of intellectual, reformist, agrarian, and faddist elements, resembling in some respects the reformers of the 1840s. It possessed much of the buoyancy, faith, and optimism of the eighteenth-century Enlightenment in its belief that man was basically good and reasonable and through the use of reason could gradually perfect society. In the Jeffersonian tradition, the progressives placed great emphasis on the dignity and freedom of the individual, which they felt was being threatened by the growing imbalance of economic and political power. In the Jacksonian tradition, the progressives reasserted a faith in a free economy, public opinion, and majority rule, with a new and increasing emphasis on the national majority. They believed in political democracy and equality of economic opportunity in a genuinely competitive system. In spite of the potential contributions to human welfare that lay in the tremendous material and technical progress, progressives lamented that political democracy was not working and that economic democracy in the American sense was not being realized. The progressive movement drew its ideas and attitudes from protest movements which had grown up since the Civil War, from the discontent of farmers, workers, and reformers of the later nineteenth century.

If there was anything new in progressivism, it was a tone of respectability which the impatient and embattled farmers and the socialistic radicals of the preceding decades had lacked. Progressivism brought the middle class into the reform movement, making the cause of reform more articulate, more respectable, and even fashionable. Such respected university men as the economist Richard T. Ely were found attacking *laissez faire*. Such an impeccable middle-class group as the General Federation of Women's Clubs picked up the scent of reform; its president in 1904 announced to the assembled ladies that "Dante is dead . . . and I think it is time that we dropped the study of his *Inferno* and turned our attention to our own!" At the same time, ministers began to preach reform from the pulpit, giving to modern reform a traditional flavor of religious piety; this "social gospel" movement threatened for a while to turn the American churches into reform clubs.

Confident, complex, and often ambiguous, progressivism was distinctly a middle-class revolt, attempting to negotiate a compromise between old traditions and new realities. It wanted to have its cake and eat it too—to protect the values of competitive individualism and political democracy while also embracing the material benefits of a more intricately organized and interdependent industrial system. In this new industrial society lurked many new opportunities to thwart individual opportunity and freedom and to corrupt democratic politics. But the average middle-class progressive sought few radical changes. For the most part, he professed to be perfectly willing to abide by the decisions of free competition if that competition could be guaranteed free and equal. He was indignant at the arrogance and vulgar materialism of the new industrial rich, who undermined the traditional prestige and status of the prosperous middle class—the class from which was drawn many a progressive leader. The progressive displayed, furthermore, a typical middle-class attitude of superiority and suspicion toward the working class. He was no strict equalitarian. What he sought was quality more than equality, and the necessary quality of thought and leadership, he believed, could not be expected from the working masses, who should acknowledge and acquiesce in enlightened, progressive, middle-class leadership. By quality, the average progressive probably meant, above all, moral quality, which often gave to progressivism the strong flavor of a moral crusade. This emphasis on morality would, however, prove something of a handicap to the later survival of progressivism. It placed too much naïve faith in reform by the method of applied personal morality. Too much American popular moral idealism was built on the quicksands of enthusiasm, ignorance, and mediocrity, and on the romantic conviction that the right and the good could be clearly perceived and would triumph regardless of knowledge and intelligence.

Probably the main differences within progressive ranks arose over the questions of how to control the big corporations and of the role which the national government should play in protecting or assisting farmers and workers—a difference which would find its major national expression in the 1912 political battle between Theodore Roosevelt and Woodrow Wilson. Throughout the period, as throughout the progressive movement, there was a constant and fundamental tension between tradition and change, between city and country, between freedom and regulation, between a simple, agrarian, Protestant moralism and a newer urban sophistication, more intellectual, more experimental, more relativist.

THE MUCKRAKERS

In the late nineteenth and early twentieth centuries, more people were reading more things—and more people were reading the same things. The rapid advance of devices of communication and transportation was reflected in the stupendous growth in circulation of newspapers and magazines. This press was both progress and an instrument of progress, to use the magic word of that period. In the 1890s parlor tables still displayed the genteel fare purveyed by the old leaders in the periodical field—*Harper's, Scribner's*, the *Atlantic, Century*, and the *North American Review*. These journals were exclusive and expensive—appealing only to the educated or to the pretentious. The former group, if not the latter, was limited in numbers. But newer periodicals were appearing, designed for mass circulation at a low price. By experimenting with lighter, more timely, and more varied— to say nothing of lurid—literary fare, *Munsey's, Cosmopolitan, Collier's, McClure's* and others were shouldering their way toward new circulation records. Such advances could be maintained only by a constant sensitivity to, and stimulation of, reader interest.

To measure accurately the importance of these periodicals is, of course, virtually impossible. One can never be fully sure whether the periodical is leading in the formation of opinion and interest or whether it is primarily reflecting and catering to an already existing interest. But, s in the case of the chicken and the egg, we can at least know that the relationship s intimate. These new periodicals gave focus to matters of increasing public concern, and it was through them that the "muckraker" cast his beam of prose into sordid and fascinating corners of American life, revealing blemishes which some crusader was ever ready to exploit. The "horrors" of American life suddenly revealed by the muckrakers had existed for some time; so, for that matter, had muckraking, which was defined as the dramatic disclosure of social evils. The muckraking of the first decade of the twentieth century is differnt only in that it had such a rapid and broad impact. It stirred the middle class to a realization that political corruption and economic concentration were a threat to the aims and values of that class itself. From all corners of the land, amazingly diligent young writers showered the reading public with evidence of corruption in political and economic circles. They explored city politics, local politics, and national politics. They examined the business methods and the labor conditions that lay behind the increasing productivity of the American economy. And, more important, they showed the intimate relationship that existed between business and political corruption. They discovered that the American city was the weakest girder in the structure of American representative government. State governments came in for their share of exposure, thus further rounding out the picture of the workings of "invisible government" and machine politics.

Ida Tarbell's *History of the Standard Oil Company* and Ray Stannard Baker's *Railroads on Trial,* the investigation of the meat-packing trust by Charles E. Russell, Samuel Hopkins Adams's unappetizing truths about patent medicines—all appeared in the periodical literature of the times. Even the dignity of the United States Senate was punctured with thrusts from the pen of David Graham Phillips, who reviewed for *Cosmopolitan* the business connections of many members of the Senate. Riding off in all directions and displaying varying degrees of ability, these journalists revealed, if they did not always clarify, the very complex and tangled relationship between corrupt politics and the economic jungle. Lincoln Steffens indicted not only the corrupt politician, but also the people who corrupted him. The corruptor was frequently the businessman who, in order to maintain or enhance his competitive business position, bought favors from political chieftains. The system of political corruption was geared into the competitive economic system, usually for the purpose of eliminating its competitive features.

The journalistic muckraker was joined by the muckraking novelist who could fill in with imagination what the libel laws and a sense of objectivity often prevented the journalist from saying. The "exposure" novels, however, were not entirely the product of a simple desire to muckrake. The first decade of the twentieth century nursed to vigor the idea of "naturalism" in literature, portraying man and nature without Victorian reticence. And novelists were also infected with the all-pervasive concern with political and social problems. The fictional treatment of problems of the day varied all the way from the popular and romantic individualism of New England's Winston Churchill to the stark and bitter realism of Upton Sinclair. Sinclair's most powerful book, *The Jungle,* which was almost more a tract than a novel, was an indignant and passionate indictment of the conditions of labor in the meat-packing industry. There was irony in the fact that, while Sinclair was attempting to portray a great social injustice, his readers read *The Jungle* with their stomachs and were nauseated by the incidental picture of how meat products were prepared in the packing houses. Other talented novelists also worked the vein of naturalism and social problems—Frank Norris, Robert Herrick, Jack London, Theodore Dreiser.

What muckraking actually accomplished is difficult to define. It provided the publicity that, coupled with new leadership, made the cause of reform a national phenomenon. For a time, muckraking became a sort of fad. Its popularity attracted the unscrupulous as well as the careful journalist and investigator, and thus opened the field for exposés that were little more than unsubstantiated innuendoes and smears. It was this tendency that provoked Roosevelt's deliberately uncomplimentary reference to these publicists as "muckrakers." Finally, it must be considered that muckraking was, after all, a response to certain temporary needs and demands. The initial shock and horror was soon blunted, but not before a middle-class "social conscience" had been created which provided foundations for progressive political power. The work of the journalistic and literary muckrakers was largely descriptive rather than analytic, and thus had its limitations when it came to developing a concrete program. Into the breach stepped progressive political scientists to set up new political forms and progressive historians to correct past historical interpretations which supported the *status quo*.

INTELLECTUALS AND REFORM

Progressives after the turn of the century felt that Americans were being forced to cope with the domestic environment on terms established by and favorable to a wealthy minority. This minority justified itself by the use of traditional American doctrines of liberty, individualism, and free competition, bolstered in the late nineteenth century by social Darwinism and the all-embracing gospel of wealth. The disturbing picture of America being reshaped on the anvil of a rapid industrial revolution inspired a massive discussion and reevaluation of American history and society—a great intellectual revival. Progressive intellectuals mounted a frontal attack on the citadels of conservative thought, complacent behind its imposing monetary, legal, and philosophical fortifications. They rejected the determinism of a social Darwinism which claimed that progress would be automatic as long as government or any other form of collective action did not tamper with individual economic and competitive freedom. While these progressives accepted the evolutionary concept of natural life and of history, they scorned a conservative determinism that was so obviously contrived to justify and to serve not the freedom of the many, but the privileges of a few.

The intellectuals were concerned with preserving and expanding individual freedom and opportunity, which they felt were threatened. What was needed was a responsible individualism and a recognition of the fact that in a complex society individual actions could have far-reaching effects on the lives of many. Americans were quite prepared to deal with individual crimes like assault, theft, and murder. But what about the company which exploited child labor, or produced adulterated food products, or misrepresented medicines, or "watered" its stock to cheat stockholders for the benefit of a few insiders? American thinking and American law were not accustomed to considering s a sinner and criminal the gentleman who loved his wife, gave candy to children, and was kind to dumb animals, but whose business was producing shoddy, dangerous, and misrepresented goods by the use of underpaid and overworked employees, many of whom were children. When the businessman departed for his office in the morning, he left behind him the world of individual relations, governed by a traditional and well-formulated code, and entered the world of economic competition, where the rules of conduct were often as elastic as a new rubber band, and where the dazzle of success could justify many evils. As sociologist E. A. Ross demonstrated, a moral code adequate to the new needs had not yet developed.

In their approach to such questions, the progressive intellectuals owed much to the philosophy of pragmatism developed by William James and John Dewey. Pragmatism rejected either religious or scientific determinism. Its position was relativist in contending that there was no eternal and unchanging truth. There were simply truths, in restless conflict and change. Pragmatism was a method more than an explanation, constantly searching among competing thoughts and theories for the truths that were relevant to man's experience and practical in meeting his moral and physical needs. Thus philosophy was to become an instrument of man's critical and creative intelligence in weighing and seeking his goals. According to pragmatism, an idea is a truth if it works, but only as long as it works. "Progress is not automatic," said Dewey. Social change and progress could be achieved only through the rational, constructive cooperation of free, creative individuals. Man is the maker of change. Through pragmatism, then, many progressives found a bridge between scientific law and human

values, between individual freedom and collective political action, between democracy and industrial society. Here was emerging the philosophy of "positive" government. Lester Ward, a pioneer in the new field of sociology, condemned *laissez faire* and "survival of the fittest" as wasteful, irrational, and inconsistent ideas. Man, he contended, had always transformed his environment; why, then, should he not do it in a more rational and organized fashion instead of by the haphazard method of *laissez faire?* Using his rational abilities, man could employ government and social regulation to free, not fetter, individual liberty. Competition and struggle might not be the instruments of civilization. On the contrary, Ward argued, the advance toward higher levels of civilization was bringing about the elimination of the struggle for existence, and cooperation should become the basis upon which society is built.

Since the traditional individualist philosophy thus seemed under modern conditions to be a barrier to genuine individual freedom and development, most progressive critics looked to some measure of government regulation as the principal method of collective action in equalizing individual opportunity and in thus realizing what have been somewhat loosely called the Jeffersonian ideals of American national tradition. The progressive journalist and social philosopher Herbert Croly contended that the means to reach these goals must be taken from the other great tradition in our history—the Hamiltonian tradition, which had been identified with strong government. In brief, Hamiltonian means (that is, strong government) were to be used to accomplish Jeffersonian ends (that is, liberty and opportunity for the individual). Progressives usually agreed that the basic threat to freedom came from the area of economic rather than political affairs—that the concentration of economic power was corrupting politics and destroying individual freedom.

In reexamining American history, the historian Charles A. Beard and the political scientist J. Allen Smith startled and shocked many Americans by their assertions that the Constitution was not a sacred revelation of early American demigods assembled in convention in 1787. It was an undemocratic document written in the ink of the experience and personal interests of the upper class, seeking to protect their status and enlarge their property. Such an interpretation might have been more comprehensible to the men of the Constitutional Convention than it was to Americans of the early twentieth century, who revered their Constitution and its guardians on the Supreme Court. To constitutional and legal thought, Justice Oliver Wendell Holmes, Jr., and a future Justice, Louis D. Brandeis, applied the concept of juridical relativism. Law, they contended, was not based upon fixed and unchanging principles, but was an expression of human experience and of those dominant needs, interests, and prejudices of the times which were shared alike by the judges and the judged.

The new emphasis on the economic and class bases of social values and political ideas brought intellectual reenforcement to the progressive writers who were bombarding the current methods of acquiring and using money. Former heroes of American business enterprise were scathingly exposed as robber barons, unethical specialists in the pursuit of profit, selling their souls and their society to the devil in the headlong rush to accumulate money and power. In revealing the plundering and exploitation by which the great fortunes of Vanderbilt, Rockefeller, Mor-

gan, and others were built, muckraker and historian Gustavus Myers weakened the idea that property was a reward of virtue and a kind of divine and inviolable right. In this period the iconoclastic economist Thorstein Veblen began his attempts to shatter completely the conventional beliefs in the existence of certain fundamental unchanging economic laws, which businessmen quoted to justify their freedom from all restraint. Veblen pointed up the irrational, disorderly aspects of economic behavior, which was governed by shifting social values rather than by economic laws.

The work and the ideas of these progressive intellectuals did not, of course, reach a mass audience. But they did reach students, scholars, writers, journalists, lawyers, and other leaders of public opinion. They provided a strong ideological foundation for progressivism, convincing many that some traditional values and methods stood in the way of progress. The work of these intellectuals gave a depth to progressivism and challenged the naïve ideal of popular progressivism that simple political reform alone would enhance democracy. This great revival of intellectual activity and of social introspection also helped to ignite a literary and artistic renaissance that would rise and burst brilliantly upon the American scene in the twenties. Novelists, poets, and painters were stimulated to a fresh portrayal of the newly revealed realities of American life. And much of this new writing was emerging not from the "decadent" cultural centers of the East, but from the raw, productive West, with Chicago as its center. It was new, experimental, antimaterialist, and often anticapitalist. The artistic phase of this renaissance saw American artists, like novelists and poets, taking a new look at life and expressing themselves in more naturalistic terms. Their new preoccupation with more common subjects brought them the derisive name of the "ash can school" of art. It reflected, however, that passionate concern for social truth and social justice which marked the whole era.

CITY AND STATE REFORM

The call to action sounded by muckrakers and intellectuals expressed and reinforced the groping attempts at reform in boss-ridden cities and states. In the Gilded Age reform had put down half-starved roots, finding some sustenance primarily in middle-western soils, fertilized by the growing discontent of farmers. Reform impulses tended at first to manifest and organize themselves on the local level in the cities, whence, in concentric ripples of revolt, they gradually engulfed states, sections, and finally the nation. Unfortunately these ripples of reform often seemed as truly unsubstantial and short-lived as the ripples on a placid pond. Mr. Dooley once commented: "As a people . . . we're the greatest crusaders that iver was—f'r a short distance. . . . But th' throuble is th' crusade don't last afther th' first sprint."* Bossism and machine politics returned after every reform ripple and seemed to have proved themselves the only practicable alternative to chaos, leading Cleveland's reform mayor Tom Johnson to comment, "It all depends whether a boss is a good one or a bad one." The wave of municipal reform during the progressive years, however, almost reached the proportions of a tidal wave. Social evil in the cities was the favorite target of muckrakers, who pictured the city as a

* Finley Peter Dunne, *Mr. Dooley at His Best,* edited by Elmer Ellis, Charles Scribner's Sons, New York, 1938, pp. 117–118.

social worker's frontier and a modern city planner's nightmare, ruled in the interest of a powerful and wealthy minority. To tackle the mammoth task of scrubbing up the cities came ardent, moral, cursading mayors—Hazen Pingree in Detroit, "Golden Rule" Jones in Toledo, and Tom Johnson in Cleveland—determined to replace bossism, corruption, crime, and poverty with a government that was responsible and responsive. To this end they sought home rule for their cities, municipal ownership of utilities, civil service, improved schools, parks and playgrounds, and more democratic control of municipal political life. Picturesque and vigorous crusaders they often were, with greater stamina than any that had gone before. They brought about various experiments in more rational, nonpartisan government and city planning by experts.

City reformers soon discovered the truth in Lincoln Steffens's remark that "no matter what kind of reform it undertakes, an honest city administration, if it proceeds logically, has to appeal sooner or later to the corrupt state government back of the corrupt city government," for state jurisdiction severely circumscribed municipal action. Thus the progressive tide swept onward to the states, engulfing New York, Ohio, California, Iowa, Oregon, and Wisconsin, among others. Willaim S. U'Ren of Oregon and Robert M. La Follette of Wisconsin achieved national and historic prominence for their zealous and extraordinarily successful attempts to limit the power of state and national political bosses allied with big business interests. Seeking morality and democracy in government, the progressives battled for the Australian secret ballot, the Swiss devices of initiative and referendum, the recall, open primaries, civil-service systems, and corrupt-practices laws. Progressive legislation attempted to guard the public welfare through state commissions supervising the business of transportation, public utilities, and even of industry. Income taxes, inheritance taxes, labor laws, social-welfare legislation, and conservation laws were also part of this burgeoning activity.

It was on the city and state level of government, too, that the first tentative steps were taken on the path of social and economic legislation, calculated to improve the conditions of life for millions of underprivileged Americans. To a greater degree than political reform, however, social and economic reform required momentous shifts in American thought, shifts in the direction of accepting government action to improve and protect the lot of those who labored and of those who lived in poverty. In these years American cities, following a British precedent, developed the social settlement house and the professional social worker, devoted to the task of providing some constructive activities for people caught in the deadening frustration of the slums. In state legislatures there began to appear bills seeking action on child and female labor, health and safety standards in industry, wages and hours regulation, social insurance, and most notably workmen's compensation (which made employers liable for most accidents on the job happening to low-paid employees). Maryland enacted the first state workmen's compensation law in 1902; by 1920 nearly all the states had them. Yet, beyond this, such social legislation encountered slow going because of its novelty and because of the many political and legal obstacles. A conservative judiciary applying old-fashioned legal ideas consistently frustrated progressive legislation. For example, in the significant *Lochner v. New York* case in 1905,

Supreme Court Justice Oliver Wendell Holmes, great jurist and trenchant critic of traditional laissez-faire social philosophy in the Court. Holmes's long and distinguished career was at a peak in the progressive years. (Fabian Bachrach)

the Supreme Court ruled against a New York statute limiting employment in bakeries to sixty hours a week and ten hours a day on the grounds that it interfered with the liberty of contract guaranteed by the Fourteenth Amendment. That the Court would "protect" against his will the "liberty" of a man to work more than sixty hours a week seemed to many an ironical commentary on the obsolescence of the legal code.

Nevertheless, such legislation was a hint of the future, just as it was the result of great pressure for more political and economic equality. Such progressive legislation began at the local level and made its way upward. But many things, including Supreme Court decisions, pointed to the fact that it was not sufficient to have reform in the cities and states; a national movement influencing the national government was essential. Fortunately, perhaps, for the progressive cause, a political accident in 1901 suddenly placed in the White House a man who accepted much of the philosophy of the progressive movement.

PRESIDENT ROOSEVELT AND THE NATIONAL SCENE

Until 1901 the McKinley administrations had been conspicuous, if not for peace, at least for prosperity and patriotism. There was considerable dispute in the 1900 campaign over the issue of imperialism, but not enough to threaten the easy Republican victory. McKinley returned to his quiet life in the White House, reserved and dignified. William Allen White, the Emporia, Kansas, editor who became a sort of spokesman for the middle way in American politics and American life, suggested that very early in his youth McKinley had "buttoned himself up" for good. In September, 1901, the President was assassinated while attending a Pan-American exposition at Buffalo. While, in harmony with the occasion, he was speaking of trade reciprocity as a tool for strengthening Pan-American relations, a pistol shot shattered the placid surface of American life. The horror at McKinley's death was for many conservative Republicans a mild tremor compared to their feelings about the elevation of Theodore Roosevelt to the presidency. Mark Hanna was reputed to have been beside himself at the thought of "that damned cowboy" in the White House.

Roosevelt's accession to the presidency must indeed have given pause to many who saw in his career and personality streaks of authoritarianism, militarism, and a seeming dedication to discipline, action, and adventure for their own sake. Those who were better acquainted with his background, however, were able to balance against these characteristics his sense of duty and obligation, his concern with political morality, his feeling for history, and his ideal of enlightened political leadership. These would combine to give to his presidency and to his political theories a strong paternalistic flavor. One of Roosevelt's friends, Elihu Root, hit the nail on the head when he remarked that Theodore's bark was worse than his bite. The famous Roosevelt vigor rattled things up a bit, but it brought few really radical changes, a fact of which many of the more sophisticated conservatives were well aware. Roosevelt was no radical. But the nation had been treated since the Civil War to a unique series of sedentary and docile Presidents. Thus, quite apart from his ideas, Roosevelt was bound to arouse greater interest and greater antagonism. As much as anything, it was his metabolism that was progressive, while his brain fostered a sort of enlightened conservatism, deeply concerned with resolving current problems that might be potential threats to the American political and economic system. Nothing was more disturbing to him than the picture of "malefactors of great wealth" endangering the very system under which they had gained so much. Though Roosevelt frequently lectured big business with severity, he was no champion of the lower class. He came from an upper-middle-class background of such long standing as to be practically aristocratic. Not especially wealthy by the newer standards, the Roosevelt family nonetheless enjoyed a substantial and secure financial and social position in New York, a genteel background that looked askance at the raw new frenzy of business and politics in the Gilded Age.

It was hard indeed in those times for intelligent and well-bred young gentlemen to plunge into the rough-and-ready strife of political affairs. But Roosevelt was vigorous, idealistic, and ambitious—"I intended to be one of the governing class." With the aim of high statesmanship and with some sense of *noblesse oblige,* he plunged into the heaving current of New York politics. No man to hide his light under any bushel, Roosevelt quickly developed a reputation for energy and versatility. Following a brief period in New York assembly, Roosevelt went ranching in the Dakotas. Back home in 1886, he lost a three-cornered fight for the mayoralty of New York City. From 1889 to 1895 he exposed the prim precincts of the Civil Service Commission in Washington to his aggressive leadership, then he returned to New York City as police commissioner, a position which gave him some national prominence and an intimate acquaintance with urban problems and progressive thought. This was followed by a short period as an impatient Assistant Secretary of the Navy in the McKinley administration, and finally by a brief, frenetic, and glorious spell of organizing the Rough Riders. He returned from Cuba with a somewhat inflated military reputation which was sufficient to elect him Governor of New York in 1898. His one term as a highly independent and unpredictable governor brought considerable unhappiness to some of the leaders of his party in New York, especially to the New York Republican boss, Senator Thomas Platt. To get rid of Roosevelt, Platt used his influence in having the Governor consigned to the political tomb of the vice presidency in 1900. With some misgivings, Roosevelt accepted the assignment and settled into the quiet vacuity of that office which usually has been tantamount to political oblivion.

Through these years of political activity Roosevelt wrote numerous volumes of history and essays, and his mind clung firmly to the personal philosophy and practice of the "strenuous life," to the cultivation of the heroic virtues, and to the pursuit of action for its own sake. An adolescent determination to improve his poor physical condition never left him. He moved through life leaving behind him a turbulent wake strewn with physical-culture apparatus and preaching this "gospel of salvation by sweat" to urchins and ambassadors alike. When applied to government, such activism had fairly definite implications. On the domestic level active government meant government that would violate the hallowed business doctrine of *laissez faire.* On the level of foreign relations it involved, as we have seen, the intensification of American participation in international affairs.

Roosevelt served the progressive movement by the dramatic and active spirit which he brought to the executive branch of the government. For the first time in decades, the executive office was vibrant with interest in the welfare of all citizens and in the achievement of such traditional ideals as equality of opportunity. It was more for this sound and fury, for the drama and publicity, than for concrete legislative achievement that Roosevelt became known as a progressive leader. His was a "rhetorical radicalism," explosive but far from lethal. No doctrinaire, he was rather an astute and vigorous politician who, with amazing facility, could balance the thrust of progressivism and the drag of conservatism. He snatched the banner of reform from the hands of Bryan's Populism and led the middle class on a fresh attack against the commanding position of the trusts.

The year that Roosevelt took office marked a high point in the economic consolidation of business and industry. It was the year that the United States Steel Corporation, a holding company and the first billion-dollar corporation, was formed to dominate the steel business. This was only one of many industrial consolidations which had aroused anxiety and frustration first among the farmers of the West and South and then, after 1890, among large segments of urban, middle-class America. Roosevelt, who knew an issue when he saw one, proceeded to build popular support with a series of truculent attacks on the problems ushered in by this consolidation movement. From the very beginning, however, there was a certain equivocation in Roosevelt's position. On one hand, he held that large corporate enterprise was an inevitable and characteristic feature of the times. On the other hand, he launched an antitrust attack not, to be sure, against "good" trusts, but against "bad" ones. It was Roosevelt's belief that these large concentrations of economic power were not inherently bad. It was their behavior rather than their form that should be the focus of governmental concern. In the end, Roosevelt's great contribution lay in his belief in a stronger government that could meet this new economic power on its own grounds and assure protection to the public welfare.

At the same time the youthful President (he was less than forty-three when fate thrust him into the office) seemed determined to indicate to uneasy and skeptical conservatives in his party that he possessed the capacity for cautious conservatism. He reassured his fellow Republicans that he intended to carry out McKinley's policies, and the quip of a wit who said that "he carried them out and

Teddy and the Trusts. "The President's dream of a successful hunt" is Cartoonist Berryman's caption. (Library of Congress)

buried them" is not entirely fair. He retained McKinley's Cabinet and tactfully sought the advice of such men as Mark Hanna, who ran the party organization, and the "old-guard" senators, who held the confidence of the more substantial financial and industrial interests. Roosevelt ignored the tariff and eschewed monetary reform. He placed curbs upon his flamboyant rhetoric but did not succeed in dissipating the suspicion and distrust of some conservative Republicans, suspicion and distrust that grew as the years went by. But if the conservatives did not trust him, no more did the progressives. Roosevelt's ambition was to ride and control both groups by standing in the middle and seeming indispensable to both sides. In 1903 and 1904, concerned with his reelection, the President moderated the vigor of his statements and speeches to hold conservative support. But he underestimated his own power and appeal to the voters. The election not only showed him how popular he was, it also pointed unmistakably to the strength of progressive sentiment in the nation.

T. R.'S POLICIES

The second term saw an increase in the tempo of Roosevelt's actions and in the progressive tenor of his statements. Nevertheless, not all progressives were satisfied. The Democratic leader, William Jennings Bryan, conducted a running fire of criticism, challenging the President to act on such issues as the eight-hour day, the use of the injunction in labor disputes, the direct election of senators, and the regulation of railroads. Similar pressures came from progressives within the President's own party. Through the jungle of pressure and resistance, Roosevelt sought the middle way, "moderate action," as he put it. He feared that the arrogant and foolish resistance of conservative economic interests would push moderate reformers into collaboration with radicals. There was widespread fear of a world socialist plot, and Roosevelt was a strong believer in moderate reform to prevent the development of a more revolutionary situation. He spiritedly blamed conservatives for increasing the danger of radicalism. In this spirit, Roosevelt in his second term called for child-labor legislation, direct income and inheritance taxes, workmen's compensation for government employees, a curb on the use of labor injunctions, and further regulation of the railroads. Under the impact of the panic of 1907, the President became almost radical in his demands for reform measures. Congress was aware of his temporizing tactics, however, was able to relax after his political error of indicating that he had no intention of being a candidate in 1908. Congress had no fear of him in the twilight of his power.

The record of Roosevelt's administration was not a total blank when it came to concrete action. The administration could point to definite achievement in the new and fuller use of the executive power. Having accepted the proposition that large-scale business enterprise must not ignore the public welfare, Roosevelt proceeded to inject some spirit in the Sherman Antitrust Act and announced his intention of enforcing the law. He shocked business circles by moving against the Northern Securities Company, a railroad holding company organized by railroad magnate James J. Hill and financier J. P. Morgan. Minnesota had tried to prevent this combination in 1901, but effective action had to wait for the federal government in 1902. Two years later, the Supreme Court ordered the dissolution of the Northern Securities Company as an undesirable monopoly, one which in no way served the interests of the public.

After this highly publicized event Roosevelt began to be known as the "trust buster." In all, during his two administrations, Roosevelt carried out forty-three proceedings for violations of the Sherman act. Action was taken against the oil, tobacco, and beef trusts and against some railroad monopolies, though this record would appear less impressive when set against the ninety antitrust actions in the one term of Roosevelt's successor, President Taft. Furthermore, there is little evidence that much was accomplished by these actions. The restrictions on competition continued; consolidation slowed down somewhat between 1903 and 1917, but this was more for business reasons than for political ones. When business combinations were dissolved by government action, combination itself usually took a new form, for Roosevelt tended to view antitrust action more as a threat to hold over business in order to persuade it to behave or to accept regulation.

An early manifestation of the President's growing interest in federal regulation was the establishment of the Department of Commerce and Labor, including a Bureau of Corporations to investigate corporation activities. Railroad regulation was given a slight boost by the passage in 1903 of the Elkins Act, prohibiting rebates to railroad customers. Probably the most important development, however, was the Hepburn Act of 1906. Passed only after an intricate political minuet by both Congress and the President, the Hepburn Act was a major triumph for Roosevelt. It was, to be sure, a compromise between progressive and conservative objectives, but the Hepburn Act enabled the Interstate Commerce Commission effectively to set railroad rates and to investigate railroad books. While the act placed on the railroads the burden of proof to show why rates should not be lowered, the ultimate decision in all such cases still lay with the courts. The Hepburn Act was thus an early milestone in the evolution of federal regulation. Modest though they were, the Bureau of Corporations and the newly strengthened Interstate Commerce Commission gave evidence of Roosevelt's

emerging leadership in the progressive groping for a new federal executive power over the conduct and processes of private business.

Roosevelt flexed his executive muscles in the area of capital-labor relations, where he referred to his middle-of-the-road program as the "Square Deal." His handling of the strike in the anthracite mines in 1902 was an illustration of his belief that government should be an instrument for assuring a "square deal" to all groups in society, and that the President should employ his full powers to that end. In that year he applied the thumbscrew of presidential power and prestige to the mine operators of the Pennsylvania anthracite fields to persuade them to negotiate with the striking miners, whose plight had aroused much public sympathy while the arrogance of the operators induced the opposite. He threatened to send federal troops to take over the operation of the mines. In his second administration, Roosevelt was a force in using federal action to protect public health against the increasing adulteration and contamination of foods and medicines, a situation with which state legislation was unable to cope. Agitation and publicity, coupled with administration support, brought the passage

EXTENT OF MONOPOLY

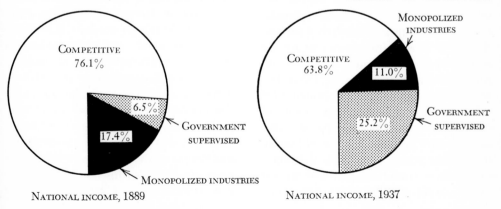

NATIONAL INCOME, 1889 — COMPETITIVE 76.1% — GOVERNMENT SUPERVISED 6.5% — MONOPOLIZED INDUSTRIES 17.4%

NATIONAL INCOME, 1937 — COMPETITIVE 63.8% — MONOPOLIZED INDUSTRIES 11.0% — GOVERNMENT SUPERVISED 25.2%

in 1906 of the Federal Meat Inspection Act and the Pure Food and Drug Act, first steps in curbing the philosophy of "Let the buyer beware."

A major achievement of the second Roosevelt administration was the creation of an effective policy looking toward the conservation of the nation's natural resources. For almost 300 years Americans had exploited—and had been free to exploit—the continent's resources as rapidly as possible. One result was the rapid and prodigious development of the American economy, with higher standards of living and greater economic opportunity than human history had ever known. By 1900, however, there was growing awareness that reckless and wasteful use of land, minerals, oil and gas, timber, and water held potential dangers for a nation that was fast becoming economically mature. Roosevelt's attention was brought to these matters by his own interest in the West as historian and ranchman and by his Secretary of the Interior, James Garfield, and his Director of the Forestry Service, Gifford Pinchot. In 1902 recognition of the problem appeared in the passage of the Newlands Act, which set up the Reclamation Service and provided that proceeds from the sale of public lands in the West be used for irrigation purposes. In 1907 Roosevelt established the Inland Waterways Commission to investigate the problem of conserving and improving the use of land, mineral, timber, and water resources. Since it was patent that state cooperation would be necessary, the President called a White House Conference on Conservation in May, 1908, at which the governors of twenty-four states joined with members of Congress, representatives of government bureaus, and other interested individuals to consider the question of the use of natural resources. This conference

led to the formation in 1908 of the National Conservation Commission and the National Country Life Commission. The President also withdrew from private entry many millions of acres of the public domain. This action rested on rather slippery legal ground and did not receive congressional benediction, but it did express a popular concern for the public interest.

Probably the stirring of public interest was Roosevelt's major contribution to the progressive movement while he was President. It is difficult to classify him as a progressive in any broad sense. He was often equivocal and compromising when it came to concrete action. He did not always exercise his full power to drive through legislation about which he talked so boldly. Certainly there were issues which he chose to ignore—most notably the tariff and banking—as too politically divisive. If Roosevelt's progressivism was not all that it seemed to be, however, it must be recognized that it was probably easier for a Republican to be a progressive out of office than in. After all, Roosevelt headed a party which was still predominantly conservative, and he had to temper the wind to the shorn lamb if he wished to continue as its leader. Furthermore, progressivism on the national level was as yet largely unorganized. In any case, Roosevelt's administrations provided definite contrasts with the past in at least proposing the idea that the federal government must increasingly intervene in the private affairs of a complex society to assure a "square deal" and a measure of welfare to all the citizens of the commonwealth.

Roosevelt's presidential career was, however, only the first phase of his national political career. His grasp of party leadership and the increasing scope of his reform proposals in his last year in office were but the opening salvos in a battle over progressive legislation that would culminate in 1912 with his New Nationalism and political revolt.

TAFT AND LEADERLESS REFORM

This "lighted torch" was placed by Roosevelt in the hands of his chosen successor, William Howard Taft, former judge, former Governor of the Philippines, and Secretary of War in Roosevelt's Cabinet. Undoubtedly somewhat chagrined at denying himself another nomination in 1908, Roosevelt settled on Taft as the most acceptable heir and executor of the Roosevelt policies. The Republican party platform pledged a continuation of Roosevelt's policies, promising tariff revision and the strengthening of antitrust laws and vaguely mentioning currency reform and limitations on labor injunctions. Though progressive efforts to obtain a more advanced party platform had failed, progressives saw in Taft a candidate who would consolidate the gains made under Roosevelt. Conservatives, on the other hand, were delighted at being rid of the unpredictable Rough Rider. To the West, furthermore, Taft appeared progressive, while in the East his candidacy seemed a favorable omen for greater stability of the conservative Republican variety. In the race against Taft, the Democratic party returned to its old leader and champion, William Jennings Bryan, on a platform less equivocal and more progressive than that of the Republicans. The issue of progressivism was, however, somewhat confused. The campaign was summed up in the Oriental dialect of humorist Wallace Irwin's *Japanese Schoolboy:* "Hon. Taft say, 'A President should be like Hon. Roosevelt, only less so.' Hon. Bryan say, 'A President should be like Hon. Roose-

velt, only more so.'" Taft won with a popular vote of 7,677,788 to Bryan's 6,407,982 and Socialist Eugene Debs's 420,890. The majority seemed to prefer a more diluted Roosevelt.

In more placid circumstances Taft would probably have made an excellent reputation as President. Amiable and charming, he was honest and exceedingly judicious. He did not seem physically constructed for the tasks of an active President. He was far overweight, and his mind and his metabolism were in marked contrast to Roosevelt's. Taft was slow, willing to let others carry much of the burden of his job. Though he believed himself to be a progressive, he was more of the judge than the political leader, and thus more innately conservative. His limited conception of the presidential office seemed, therefore, to emerge quite naturally from his personality. A comparison of the legislative policies and achievements of the two administrations, however, suggests that Taft was hardly less progressive, or more conservative, than Roosevelt. Where Taft seemed to fail was as politician and party leader. Under him the Republican party rapidly disintegrated. This was partly the result of simple misfortune, for Taft was heir to a party in which progressive strength was growing, especially in the Middle West. The new wing sought to control the party which had so long been led by those who represented business interests and the American version of *laissez faire*. Under Roosevelt the middle-western progressives in the Republican party were a minority, to whom Roosevelt needed to pay scant attention. But Roosevelt was an adept politician, able to appeal effectively for popular support, skilled in avoiding the issues that would generate antagonism in the party. Taft, in contrast, was a miserable politician, distrustful of appeals to the public, too inactive to offer real leadership. Taft himself recognized his limitations as political leader and entered his administration with a somewhat pessimistic attitude. Since Taft himself did not assume control, it fell into the hands of the conservative "standpat" Republicans in Congress.

All this gives, however, a somewhat false impression of the achievements of the Taft administration. Progressive ideas had gained such momentum that the standpat Republicans were more willing to compromise. The result was more concrete progressive action and legislation in the four years of the Taft administration than during the seven and a half years of charging all over the landscape with Roosevelt. The passage of the Mann-Elkins Act for further railroad regulation, the division of the Department of Commerce and Labor into two separate departments, establishment of parcel post and postal savings, creation of the Children's Bureau, creation of a tariff commission, and legislation to give publicity to political campaign expenditures were the major accomplishments. Moreover, two great progressive dreams were realized in the passage of the Sixteenth Amendment, authorizing an income tax, and the Seventeenth, providing for the popular election of senators. In the field of conservation Taft's activity compared favorably with that of his predecessor. He was the first President to withdraw oil lands from public sale. He was responsible for creating the Bureau of Mines. He purchased forest lands in the Appalachians and backed legislation which would permit the federal government to conserve mineral as well as surface resources. In contrast to Roosevelt, however, Taft was unwilling to push the limits of executive power in accomplishing these objectives but preferred to await leg-

islative initiative and sanction, and thus much credit for the new legislation must be given to the progressive leadership of both parties in Congress.

Probably only in the area of antitrust prosecutions did the Taft administration take vigorous and forceful executive action. In four years it prosecuted some ninety cases of violations of the Sherman Antitrust Act. Even in this area, however, the administration was partially overshadowed. The most momentous decisions on antitrust policy came not from the President but from the Supreme Court, which, in 1911 in the Standard Oil and American Tobacco cases, both clarified and obscured the future of antitrust action. The Court's decision brought industrial combinations definitely within the scope of the Sherman act. Even more important was the Court's application to these antitrust cases of the "rule of reason." The Court, in effect, gave new meaning to the Sherman act by holding that the law prohibited only "unreasonable" and "undue" restraints of trade. By this decision the Court not only limited the application of the law, but assumed for itself the power and responsibility of defining "unreasonable" and "undue." On balance this may have been a necessary and rational clarification of antimonopoly policy, but it aroused the ire of many progressives and lent substance to Roosevelt's distrust of antitrust policy and of judicial interference with the development of general public policy.

Taft's role in supporting or advancing progressive policies was not, therefore, large enough to placate progressives or to lend progressive coloration to his unhappy incarceration in the White House. There was some irony in the fact that what Taft supported and accomplished while President would ten years previously have been considered the actions of a radical. But history had sped beyond Taft; he thought himself abreast of the times, only to discover that ideas had forged ahead of him. He faced a widening cleavage within the party, where the progressive bloc had increased its power beyond that of Roosevelt's time. Progressive power and progressive proposals simply outran the President. To his contemporaries, there were several notable events which seemed to demonstrate his political limitations and innate conservatism. Partisan dust raised by these squabbles obscured the picture somewhat, but it was not difficult in each of them to discern the corpulent form of President Taft standing behind the conservative barricades.

The most important of these skirmishes was another of those great tariff battles which stud American history and which provide examples of the massive economic conflicts within a rapidly expanding nation. Republican policy since the Civil War had embraced the idea of a tariff protecting and fostering American industry. Progressives tended to oppose a high degree of protection, partly because of the advantages it gave to big business and partly because the progressives (at least

those in the Republican party) came principally from middle-western and far-western agricultural areas, where protectionism meant higher prices for industrial products. On assuming office in 1909, Taft called a special session of Congress, which proceeded to ignore the campaign pledge to reduce the tariff. The Payne bill, which had been hurried through the House, did provide for a moderate reduction of tariff rates. Senate leadership, however, was less inclined to heed public opinion. Here the tariff bill was subjected to the lethal ministrations of the Senate Committee on Finance, dominated by the multi-millionaire Nelson Aldrich. Mutilating the House bill in secret sessions, Aldrich's committee paid extensive heed to the lobbyists of special interests and added over 600 amendments to it, restoring and increasing former duties. After a monumental assault on the floor of the Senate, a few concessions were won by the progressives, led by Senator La Follette, but the Aldrich bill was carried essentially unchanged into the Senate-House Conference Committee, whence it emerged still adorned with the Aldrich amendments. Its final passage prompted Mr. Dooley to comment that Congress had now brought within the reach of everyone such essential free-duty items as "curling stones . . . sea moss . . . newspapers, nuts an' nux vomica . . . pulu . . . canary bird seed . . . spunk, apatite, hog bristle, wurruks iv art more thin twinty years old, kelp, marshmallows, life boats, silk-worm eggs, stilts, skeletons, turtles, an' leeches."[*]

The Payne-Aldrich Tariff was not quite that bad, but it was a huge disappointment to those who had expected real reform. Throughout this tariff debate, Taft

[*] Finley Peter Dunne, *Mr. Dooley at His Best*, edited by Elmer Ellis, Charles Scribner's Sons, New York, 1938, pp. 88–89.

GROWTH OF BIG BUSINESS

PERCENTAGE OF TOTAL MANUFACTURED
PRODUCT ACCOUNTED FOR BY FIRMS
WITH MORE THAN $1,000,000 ANNUAL
VALUE OF MANUFACTURED PRODUCT

70
60
50
40
30
20
10

PER CENT

1904   1909   1914   1919   1924   1929

had played a negative role, refusing to exert pressure or to veto the bill when passed. Disturbed by critical public reaction, he decided to embark on a speaking tour. In a hastily prepared speech delivered at Winona, Minnesota, in the heart of middle-western progressive country, he praised the Payne-Aldrich Tariff extravagantly and added some slighting remarks about the progressive senators who had opposed it. Such political ineptitude was potent ammunition for the western "insurgents."

Their quarrel with Taft had other grounds as well. In 1909–1910 insurgency within the Republican ranks threatened to crack the party when the progressives fought to democratize the rules of the House of Representatives, which gave virtually autocratic powers to the Speaker. These efforts finally met with success, as Democrats joined with the progressive Republicans in stripping the rustic and reactionary Speaker, "Uncle Joe" Cannon, of his membership on the powerful Rules Committee and of his power of appointing committee members. It had revealed an open breach between progressives and conservatives of the GOP, and again Taft seemed inertly to side with the latter. A third episode in this development of insurgency was the so-called Ballinger-Pinchot affair, a confused and emotional fracas over conservation policies. Gifford Pinchot, a close associate and appointee of Roosevelt's, brought charges that Taft and Secretary of the Interior Ballinger were disregarding and betraying Roosevelt's conservation policies. There was less truth than there seemed in these charges, but a congressional investigation, while clearing Ballinger, turned up some embarrassing facts about Taft's handling of the situation. Not his policies, but his political ineptitude again got Taft in hot water.

Insurgency was at white heat, and the political situation was passing beyond Taft's control. It is possible that no amount of political skill would have sufficed. A deep popular revolt against the domination of politics by great industrial and financial interests was under way, and the "old guard" which had kept control of politics ever since the Civil War was slipping from power. The revolution tore the Republican party asunder. In the congressional elections of 1910 the Democrats won control of the House, while in the Senate old-guard Republican losses, assisted by the popular direct-primary election of senators, gave the balance of power to insurgents. A pathetic political figure clinging to traditional ideas of strict legality and limited executive power, Taft was caught in the middle of this swirling pattern and was to be politically destroyed.

ROOSEVELT, WILSON, AND THE PROGRESSIVE DILEMMA

Insurgency made Taft's last two years in office a nightmare. Under the leadership of La Follette and other western senators, the National Progressive Republican League appeared, with the obvious intention of defeating Taft and capturing control of the party. La Follette, who had many claims to the title of the original Mr. Progressive, had definite ambitions to be the next Republican presidential nominee. In this picture Roosevelt was an unmistakable but uncertain factor. After Taft's election he had considerably removed himself from the scene and embarked upon a prolonged tour, including an African safari, on which he delightedly cut short the lives of nine lions, five elephants, thirteen rhinoceroses, and seven hippopotamuses. Concluding with a triumphal visit to Europe, Roosevelt returned in 1910 to be received with a great ovation. Though still relatively young, vigorous, and ambitious, Roosevelt remained aloof from the Republican conflict until the end of 1911, when it was too late for mediation. Disgusted with Taft, bored by private life, and confident of his own popularity, Roosevelt became receptive to progressive pleas that he run again for the Republican nomination. Able as he was, La Follette did not appear to have sufficient popular appeal, and a temporary physical breakdown early in 1912 was a signal for his followers to abandon him with unseemly haste and jump on the T.R. bandwagon. Roosevelt's hat was in the ring by late February.

There ensued four months of a bitter preconvention battle for delegates, a battle in which the former bonds of friendship between Roosevelt and Taft were completely severed. The Republican national convention opened with many seats still contested. Though Roosevelt was probably the choice of the majority of Republican voters, the Taft forces controlled the National Committee and awarded most of the contested seats to Taft delegates. Taft received the nomination on the first ballot. The outraged Rooseveltians, with cries of "theft," bolted the convention, held their own convention in August, and dubbed themselves the Progressive party—popularly known as the "Bull Moose party" from a phrase used by Teddy to describe his strength. Having told his followers that "we stand at Armageddon and we battle for the Lord," Roosevelt found himself leading an emotional crusade reminiscent of Populism in the 1890s. The convention delegates fervently sang "Onward Christian Soldiers," adopted an eminently progressive platform, and nominated T.R. It was one of the most

exciting moments in American political history. But behind this fog of political revivalism was concealed tragedy for the Republican progressives as well as for the Republican conservatives. At Baltimore the Democrats took the progressive path too, nominating Thomas Woodrow Wilson of New Jersey and Virginia. With the Republicans divided, they could hardly lose.

The story of Woodrow Wilson's rise to the White House was the rather unusual one of a metamorphosis from intellectual, scholar, and university president to politician and President of the United States. For a man with such a background to rise to the political pinnacle was unprecedented since the early days of the republic. Of Scotch-Irish Presbyterian background, the Virginia-born Wilson was an intense, orderly, almost ascetic man. To many he appeared aloof and even vain, though to his intimates he displayed warmth and sociability. In his speaking Wilson displayed a clarity and precision to match his personality. A graduate of Princeton, with a law degree from the University of Virginia and a Ph.D. from Johns Hopkins, he had had a distinguished career in both teaching and writing in the field of political science. Wilson had been largely the political theoretician, believing strongly in fixed moral principles and their application to the political process.

Having attracted attention as a reforming president of Princeton University, Wilson had been seized upon by the decrepit and moribund Democratic party of New Jersey as a likely vote getter. The illusion of some New Jersey Democrats that the professor would be an easily controlled political amateur was dispelled by the firmness and ability with which he took over the party and the state. He turned out to be both politically shrewd and philosophically progressive. He put across a notable legislative-reform program in New Jersey, including the direct primary, a corrupt-practices act, workmen's compensation, a public-utilities act, and several bills placing some limitations on the notorious freedom of corporations chartered in New Jersey. Overnight this spectacular performance gained him a national reputation, and from there the path to the presidential nomination, while not without its obstacles, was fairly obvious, for the logic of 1912 called for a fresh and a progressive Democratic personality. The Democratic platform assailed the protective tariff, called for legislation to destroy monopolies, supported the amendments for an income tax and direct election of senators, and proposed that labor unions be exempted from the provisions of the antitrust laws.

In the ensuing campaign, Taft and the conservatives were rudely pushed aside to make room for the main bout between Roosevelt and Wilson, between what the former called the New Nationalism and the latter the New Freedom.

While the progressive movement had thus split into two major blocs, the election of 1912 was the high tide of the progressive era. Certainly a campaign which included Roosevelt, Wilson, and Taft provided more political color and intelligence than had been seen on the national rostrums for many a decade. Both Roosevelt and Wilson felt that the major problem facing Americans was the concentration of private economic power, commonly referred to as the "trust problem." Both were concerned with the effect of this power on individual opportunity and on the orderly and just expansion of the American economy. There were, however, significant differences in the ideas of the two men. To grapple with the new society Roosevelt

offered his New Nationalism—a synthesis of ideas which he had been publicly expounding since his days in the White House. This New Nationalism was distinctively the product of the urban, industrial world and was sensitive to new intellectual trends in America and Europe. It reflected Roosevelt's paternalistic approach —his faith in the application of intelligence, power, and organization to public affairs. His Osawatomie speech of 1910 was his first call for a New Nationalism which would place human rights above property rights and which would augment the power of the national government to promote social justice. He would limit the power of the courts and make the President a "steward of the public welfare." Roosevelt's ideal was an efficient, stable, integrated society under the paternalistic supervision of a national government which would regulate the strong and protect the weak. Like Croly, Roosevelt believed that Americans should abandon their simple devotion to the ideal of personal material advancement in favor of a larger ideal of national improvement and unified national purpose. He accepted what he considered the inescapable fact of the growth of big business and its consolidation—"the result of an imperative economic law which cannot be repealed by political legislation." The answer, he thought, lay not in fruitless efforts to prevent such combinations, but in controlling them. As with Herbert Croly, whose book *The Promise of American Life* much impressed him, Roosevelt would use Hamiltonian (nationalist) methods to gain Jeffersonian ends. To protect individual opportunity and security against great private power, Roosevelt was, in effect, proposing to abandon traditional individualism for a kind of democratic collectivism and the welfare state. Accordingly, the Progressive party platform advocated the establishment of new federal agencies to regulate business; it endorsed such objectives of the social-justice movement as child-labor legislation, workmen's compensation, and social insurance; and it supported such political reforms as the initiative, referendum, recall, direct primaries, and the recall of judicial decisions.

Wilson's New Freedom took a different approach. Where Roosevelt had accepted industrial consolidation as in the very nature of modern industrial development, Wilson saw consolidation as the product of unregulated and unfair competition. His compelling prose constantly stressed protection of the competitive opportunities of the small farmer and businessman, with the aid of government, but without turning the government into a highly centralized regulatory mechanism. Wilson did believe in vigorous and dynamic political leadership, but only to serve the purpose of removing artificial barriers to competition. A firm believer in the individualist, competitive ideal, Wilson denounced Roosevelt's paternalism as incompatible with freedom. The New Freedom sought democracy and social justice along the well-worn paths of the liberal, Jeffersonian, states'-rights tradition. Wilson, of course, recognized that modern industrial society required some increase in federal power, but he believed that the national government should use its power more as an umpire than as a regulator and supervisor. He rejected the Rooseveltian idea of direct national intervention in economic and social arrangements and placed his faith in national protection of a fair and free competitive process. While Wilson brought to his campaign a magical eloquence, his New Freedom was somewhat vague and lacked the specific proposals of the New Nationalism. The difference between the

two programs represented a real dilemma that would haunt American progressive and liberal thought for some decades.

In 1912 the dilemma was more apparent in the New Freedom than in the New Nationalism. Industrial society and the growth of private power undoubtedly required some compensatory and protective expansion of government power in the public interest. But where was that obscure path of public policy that avoided both the tyranny of the trusts and the tyranny of government? When government controlled the trusts and promoted the welfare of farmers and workers, who was to control the government? Roosevelt grasped the nettle and declared his willingness to take his chances with enlarged government power guided by enlightened leadership. While Wilson made some concessions to this position, his eyes were fixed with anguished nostalgia on the American past. His position in 1912, however, was not fixed; it was a stage in the evolution of his experience and thought toward an ultimate synthesis of the New Freedom and the New Nationalism. In his very uncertainty and dilemma Wilson probably represented better than Roosevelt the bulk of progressive thought—suspended between the past and the present, regarding with nostalgia the simpler competitive ways of the past, but excited and stirred by the challenges of the present, desperately wanting to preserve the free, individualistic, competitive ideals of the past, and reluctantly acknowledging the need for new measures of public policy which would compromise between tradition and reality.

It is a remarkable tribute to Roosevelt's popularity that he received more votes than Taft, though he had almost no political organization. Crippled by this lack of organization and smothered by the Democratic victory, the Progressive party gradually expired between 1912 and 1916. It had been too much the product of one man's political glamour, and it could not survive Roosevelt's desertion of it four years later. By that time new issues had arisen; the mercurial Teddy was again interested in war, not reform—as indeed were most Americans. This left the Democratic party in undisputed leadership of the progressive cause. Although the schism in the Republican party was healed by 1920, the conservative standpatters were in firm control. Roosevelt's attempt to revive some of the old reformist tradition in the Republican party had met with abject failure. Powerful forces of conservatism in the Republican party ensured this failure. But the results of the 1912 election reflected a momentous majority for progressive ideas. Wilson received 6,300,000 votes to Roosevelt's 4,100,000, Taft's 3,500,000, and a surprising 900,000 for the Socialist candidate, Eugene Debs. Such a victory for the progressive cause, if not the Progressive party, meant that, given adequate leadership from the new President, Congress, whatever its feeling, could hardly obstruct the enactment of a progressive program.

WILSON'S REFORMS

Swiftly and adroitly Wilson mounted the crest of the progressive wave, using its swelling, if temporary, strength to establish his leadership of party and Congress in implementing the New Freedom. In his inaugural address Wilson asserted the duty "to cleanse, to reconsider, to restore, to correct the evil without impairing the good, to purify and humanize every process of our common life. . . ." Greater justice and opportunity for all was to be achieved by a legislative program the chief points of which were reduction of the

tariff, reform of the banking system, new and stronger antimonopoly legislation, assistance to agriculture (though not subsidization), and conservation of natural resources. No moss was permitted to grow on these proposals; Wilson did not temporize or try to "get along" with Congress. He promptly called a special session of Congress, broke long-established precedent by going to Capitol Hill personally with a message on legislation, and generally followed his theories of the role of the President in uniting party strength behind his program. Wilson had long admired the parliamentary form of government, in which executives and party leaders exercised more leadership.

The first item which he proposed was tariff reduction, a logical move in the attempt to restore more competitive conditions. The Democratic Congress responded with the Underwood Tariff, the first important general reduction of duties since the Civil War, reducing the Payne-Aldrich average of 37 per cent to about 27 per cent. The Underwood Tariff further revised tariff practice by establishing rates on

Inauguration Day, 1913: Woodrow Wilson takes over from William Howard Taft. (Library of Congress)

the basis of the value of a product (ad valorem) rather than on the basis of some quantitative measurement like yardage or tonnage. Included in this bill was a new principle in federal taxation, a tax on individual incomes, authorized by the recently adopted Sixteenth Amendment to the Constitution.

The second major interest of Wilson and his Congress was in a reform of the nation's banking, credit, and currency system. Since the turn of the century, it had been increasingly recognized by businessmen, bankers, and legislators that there had been substance to the Populist concern over currency in the 1890s. The existing system of national banks which could issue currency only against federal bonds did not provide the nation with an adequately elastic currency or with adequate reserves in case of economic crisis. While progressives were concerned with these factors, they were also concerned with the high degree of concentrated control over banking and credit that had been revealed in 1912 by the so-called Pujo Committee of the House. The Federal Reserve Act that resulted was probably the greatest single achievement of Congress and the administration in the Wilson years. It was a compromise between those who wanted a centralized banker-controlled system and those who wanted a more regional system from which the bankers would be excluded but over which the federal government would have ultimate control. The nation was divided into twelve regions, in each of which was a Federal Reserve bank whose funds were contributed by member banks. All national banks had to be members; for others membership was optional. The Federal Reserve banks were strictly bankers' banks, issuing money in the form of Federal Reserve notes backed by a 40 per cent gold reserve and by commercial notes presented as security by the borrowing member banks. Local banks could thus meet currency needs by borrowing at a reasonable interest rate from the Federal Reserve banks. In this way, the supply of money was to rest on the need for credit rather than on a fixed supply of federal bonds. Since member banks could not borrow money for trading in securities, it was hoped that the credit system would thereby rest more directly upon the needs of business than on the stock market. It was hoped and expected (too optimistically, as it turned out in 1929) that this system would do much to flatten out the business cycle and reduce the intensity of panics and depressions. To supervise and coordinate this system was a Federal Reserve Board, which exercised control chiefly by setting interest rates at which member banks could borrow money. By the late 1920s about 80 per cent of the nation's banking resources were controlled by member banks.

Although this system furnished the nation with a more elastic and responsive credit and currency system, it did not recognize the importance of and greater necessity for long-term loans, especially for agriculture. Nor did the act take to heart the findings of the Pujo Committee and attempt to regulate the securities market or to separate commercial from investment banking. Such reforms would not come until the New Deal, when the Great Depression had reinforced the need for such changes. But the Federal Farm Loan Bank Act of 1916 did improve the agricultural-credit situation by making long-term mortgage loans available to farmers at relatively low interest rates. Moreover, agriculture received assistance through such legislation as the Federal Highway Act of 1916 granting federal aid in the construction of rural roads, and through the Warehouse Act of 1916 providing warehouses in which farmers might deposit crops as collateral for obtaining bank loans.

Having promised in his inaugural message a strengthening of the antitrust laws, Wilson obtained the passage of the Clayton Antitrust Act and the Federal Trade Commission Act. Attempting to plug up holes in the antitrust legislation, Congress tried to make the Clayton act more specific than the Sherman act. It forbade price discrimination and exclusive selling or leasing contracts. It placed restrictions on interlocking directorates and the holding of stock in another company. As it worked out, however, the whole program would still have to run the gauntlet of judicial interpretation. Nor was Wilson or Congress willing to write laws so comprehensive that they might have an adverse effect on business conditions. Samuel Gompers, president of the American Federation of Labor, prematurely hailed the act as the "Magna Carta" of labor, since labor and farm organizations were specifically exempted from the operation of the act; the joker lay in later pronouncement of the courts that Congress intended only to exempt the organizations (which were already legal) and not the activities of such organizations. The Federal Trade Commission was set up to meet the demand for some criteria by which business activity could be measured and the existence of monopoly determined. The FTC was to investigate, collect information, and issue "cease and desist" orders to persons or corporations indulging in unfair methods of competition, though such orders were subject to review by the courts.

Congress began to edge into the field of labor legislation with the La Follette Seamen's Act of 1915, which initiated government supervision of labor conditions in the merchant marine; the Adamson Act, establishing an eight-hour day for operating employees on the railroads; and the Keating-Owen bill, barring the products of child labor from interstate commerce, although this was later voided by the Supreme Court. From the whole of the progressive movement, the laborer may be said to have gotten least. In accepting such measures as these, Wilson gradually moved in the direction of greater government intervention, which he had hesitated so long to espouse. Though he had ridden to victory on the tide of reform and had used its surging strength to establish his leadership, he quickly found the limitations of his power when he tried to call a halt. He was not enthusiastic about excluding labor and farm organizations from the operation of the antitrust laws, or about the FTC. Wilson gave even chillier reception to such proposals as workmen's compensation, rural credits, woman suffrage, the La Follette seamen's bill, and child-labor legislation. He endorsed racial segregation in the government departments, sacrificing to his southern supporters the advances in this area made under Roosevelt and Taft. In Wilson's mind social legislation which gave direct aid or protection to special groups exceeded the limits of social desirability, if not of federal power. Wilson would have preferred that the states handle these matters, though it must be emphasized that he was prepared to have the federal government move into this area should the states fail. The combined pressures of political necessity and of national problems, however, drove him to embrace more of Roosevelt's New Nationalism, causing the embittered T.R. to denounce him as that "damned Presbyterian hypocrite." By 1916, therefore, Wilson had moved from his limited program of 1912 and was leading his party in the formation of a new progressive coalition which supported the most advanced program of economic and social reform before the New Deal.

In its very moment of triumph, however, this progressive coalition and its program was confronted with defeat. Any further development, if such there might have been, in Wilson's concept or program of reform was precluded by the intrusion of foreign affairs and World War I. Though Wilson himself had been guilty of dragging his feet on some proposals for domestic reform, the war was to have a devastating effect on both the progressive spirit and progressive accomplishments. Out of the war erupted problems and ideas that challenged the confident, tidy, middle-class morality of American progressivism. Issues of foreign policy, of the

American role in international affairs, cut across party lines and set progressive against progressive. The blighting spirit of intolerance and the necessities of mobilization made it necessary—or at least possible—to ignore such things as antimonopoly legislation. And Wilson recognized what all this would mean to liberal and progressive ideals. To Frank Cobb of the *New York World*, Wilson lamented the illiberalism that would almost be required by war: "To fight you must be brutal and ruthless, and the spirit of ruthless brutality will enter into the very fibre of our national life, infecting Congress, the courts, the policeman on the beat, the man in the street." This was the very antithesis of tolerance and of the spirit of liberal reform and change.

FURTHER READINGS

General accounts of progressivism include Harold U. Faulkner, *The Quest for Social Justice* (1931) and *Decline of Laissez-Faire, 1897–1917* (1951); Richard Hofstadter, *The Age of Reform* (1955); and Eric F. Goldman, *Rendezvous with Destiny* (1952), the latter two works putting progressivism in somewhat longer perspective. Two volumes in the New American Nation series, George E. Mowry, *The Era of Theodore Roosevelt* (1958), and Arthur S. Link, *Woodrow Wilson and the Progressive Era* (1954), are in every respect distinguished books. Mowry has also written *Theodore Roosevelt and the Reform Movement* (1946), and Link, the outstanding biographer of Wilson, covered his early career in *Wilson: The Road to the White House* (1947), followed by *Wilson: The New Freedom* (1956).

Important aspects of progressivism are dealt with in the following valuable studies: C. C. Regier, *The Era of the Muckrakers* (1932); Charles H. Hopkins, *The Rise of the Social Gospel in American Protestant-*

ism (1940); Russel B. Nye, *Midwestern Progressive Politics* (1951); and David W. Noble, *The Paradox of Progressive Thought* (1958), which is concerned with the philosophical ideas found in progressivism.

Heroes of reform are presented in Louis Filler, *Crusaders for American Liberalism* (1950). The personal narratives of some of the reform leaders are vital documents: William Allen White, *Autobiography* (1946); Ray Stannard Baker, *American Chronicle* (1945); and Lincoln Steffens, *Autobiography* (1931). Alpheus T. Mason has written a notable life of Louis Brandeis, *Brandeis: A Free Man's Life* (1946). John M. Blum, *The Republican Roosevelt* (1954), is a penetrating and sympathetic appraisal of T.R. Less sympathetic is the older study by Henry F. Pringle, *Theodore Roosevelt: A Biography* (1931), reprinted in paperback edition. A meticulous job of collecting and editing was performed by John W. Davidson in *A Crossroads of Freedom: The 1912 Campaign Speeches of Woodrow Wilson* (1956).

TWENTY-THREE

The First World War and Its Aftermath

WILSON'S FOREIGN PROBLEMS

1914

Americans occupy Vera Cruz, Mexico.
World War begins in Europe, August 1.

1915

Lusitania sunk by German submarine.
Austrian ambassador expelled from
United States.

1916

Virgin Islands purchased from Denmark.
Wilson reelected President.
United States offers mediation in
European war.

1917

Germans declare unrestricted submarine
warfare.
Zimmermann note published, March 1.
Russian Revolution begins.
War declared on Central Powers,
April 6.

1918

Wilson offers Fourteen Points peace
program.
United States troops help check
German offensive.
Armistice signed, November 11.

1919

Treaty of Versailles signed, June 28.
Treaty defeated in Senate, November 19.

1920

Treaty again defeated in Senate,
March 19.
Harding (Rep.) defeats Cox for
President.

ON JUNE 28, 1914, A SHOT fired in Sarajevo, in the Balkans, set off a sequence of events which brought almost all Europe, and subsequently almost all the world, into a long and terrible war destined to cost millions of lives and do incalculable damage. The United States was to enter it a little less than three years later, after a long struggle to keep out. When the European war began at the end of July, 1914, the great majority of Americans regarded it as a rather remote event and had little doubt that the United States could and would remain aloof. By long custom and hallowed tradition, Americans looked upon any "entanglement" in European politics as a disaster from which, fortunately, the broad Atlantic and the excellent advice of George Washington protected them. The new interest in world affairs which flared up around the turn of the century was directed toward Latin America and the Pacific, not toward Europe. The active policy of Theodore Roosevelt led him to take an interest in Europe's affairs; on one occasion, it brought the United States into an important conference in Spain in 1906 which managed to settle one of the prewar diplomatic crises, known as "the first Moroccan crisis." But even Roosevelt could not make this action very popular with the American people, and Congress made it clear that this was to form no precedent for depart-

480

ing from "traditional American foreign policy." On no other occasion did the United States play any significant role in European international relations during the years preceding 1914.

We have already noted Woodrow Wilson's great role as a progressive reformer in domestic affairs. He was also called upon to face the most serious problems in foreign affairs any President since Madison had confronted. The war in Europe, of course, provided the foremost of these. But at about the same time, a great revolution in Mexico brought diplomatic headaches which seemed hardly less severe than those caused by the European war. This problem was on our very doorstep. The revolution had begun in 1911, with the overthrow of the long-time dictator Porfirio Díaz, ruler of Mexico since 1877. There followed a decade in which Mexico knew little relief from civil strife as the various revolutionary and counterrevolutionary factions struggled for power. Popular passions were notably directed against foreign capitalists in general and Americans in particular. Considerable damage was done to American property, and a number of Americans were killed, while others fled the country. Under such circumstances, demands arose in this country for a vigorous policy designed to protect American interests in Mexico. Would Wilson apply the big stick to turbulent Mexico?

In the course of a controversial Mexican policy, Wilson attempted to avoid intervention and war with Mexico. Applying the principles of democracy to foreign policy, he declared that the Mexican people must have the government they wanted. In 1913, a counterrevolutionary dictatorship under General Victoriano Huerta succeeded in gaining control of the Mexican government. Wilson insisted that, inasmuch as this government was not based on popular consent, he would refuse to recognize it. He was so firm in this determination to secure the overthrow of the Huerta regime that he went so far as to bombard and occupy the Mexican port of Vera Cruz in 1914. Huerta was forced to resign, but this did not bring peace to Mexico. In 1916 American troops engaged in an invasion of northern Mexico in order to catch and punish the troublesome guerrilla leader Pancho Villa, who had raided American border towns. Thus, on two occasions Wilson actually intervened in Mexico; his object was not, however, to take over the country but to help establish a democratic government there.

Wilson's well-intentioned efforts met with limited success, and there was a great deal of criticism of his handling of this situation. Ex-President Roosevelt declared that Wilson was a "mollycoddle" pacifist, and those with economic interests in Mexico were outraged. Nor did the Mexicans themselves at first appear to appreciate Wilson's efforts; they remembered the interventions and not the relative forbearance. Yet, with all its apparent errors, Wilson's Mexican policy holds a notable place in the history of the development of better relations with Latin America. He had refused to follow the pattern of dollar diplomacy and had shown a respect for the aspirations of the Mexican people. On one occasion he also consulted with other Latin-American states in an effort to find a joint solution. There was much clamor in this country for war, which Wilson courageously and wisely resisted. A few years later his policy was to be substantially vindicated when a democratic and reasonably stable Mexican government finally succeeded in consolidating its position.

An idealist with no high regard for big

The German Kaiser as murderer:
an American reaction
to the *Lusitania* sinking

American machine gun platoon in action in Meuse sector, October, 1918

General Pershing reviewing
returning troops, New York
City, March, 1919

German submarine warfare cost the lives of many Americans in the
Lusitania tragedy and was probably the most important single influence
in our gradual drift towards involvement in the great European war of
1914–1918. The United States entered the war in time to take part in the
last six months of fighting and swing victory to the Allies. Then President
Wilson went to Europe to try to make a lasting peace.

The "Big Four" at the
ris Peace Conference:
lando, Lloyd George,
Clemenceau, Wilson

business, Wilson made a point of repudiating dollar diplomacy; he declared that his administration would not look after the interests of American capitalists in foreign countries. Nevertheless, the President was capable of considerable realism in foreign policy. He did not hesitate to use the power of intervention in the Caribbean as vigorously as Roosevelt had done. Drastic action leading to occupation in Haiti and Santo Domingo was taken, in the name of our "paramount interest" in that strategically sensitive zone. In order to strengthen our position there, Wilson also concluded a treaty for the purchase of the Danish Virgin Islands in 1916.

These actions were strongly influenced by the fact that a great war had begun in Europe. Whatever comfortable illusions Americans had when the war started, it was soon apparent that so huge a conflict would pose grave problems for American neutrality. The war was too big to be ignored, and it began to impinge upon American interests in very direct ways. At the beginning of the war the President solemnly asked the American people to be "impartial in thought as well as in action." This proved to be exceedingly difficult, and Wilson himself did not always succeed in following his own request. For the next two and a half years, however, he strove bravely to accomplish the twin objectives of upholding American interests and honor while at the same time keeping out of war.

AMERICAN NEUTRALITY THREATENED

Neutrality in thought was not likely to be realized. Most Americans had strong feelings about the great European war; as a nation of immigrants, millions of them fairly recent ones, Americans were emo-

tionally close to the Old World. The majority of Americans tended to side with the Allies. This was the group that included Great Britain, with whom our relations had been unusually friendly for some time, and France, a nation to which the United States had strong sentimental attachments reaching back to our Revolution. To be sure, another of the Allies was Russia, whose despotic czarist government had become unpopular in America chiefly because of its brutal persecution of minorities. The other side, the Central Powers, included Germany, Austria-Hungary, and Turkey. Japan and Italy eventually joined the Allies. There were many German-Americans whose sympathies lay naturally with Germany, and the numerous and politically vociferous Irish-Americans were always anti-British. But a powerful factor swaying sentiment against the Central Powers was the belief that they had been responsible for starting the war.

Scholarly research after the war indicated that it was far more difficult to determine who was responsible for the war than most people thought at the time. It is a fact that the Germans believed they were fighting a defensive war. Nevertheless, German troops had struck first, and in doing so had violated the neutrality of Belgium. Before the western front settled down to a long and bloody stalemate toward the end of 1914, German armies overran Belgium and swept deep into France, coming very close to Paris itself before being halted. The gallant defense by the French and British aroused sympathy, and stories were heard of German brutality in treatment of the occupied areas. While later investigation proved many of the stories about German "atrocities" to be Allied propaganda, they were readily believed at the time, and Germany's position as invader and occupier of

France and Belgium rendered her vulnerable to such charges. Because of Belgium particularly, there was a good deal of resentment against Germany from the beginning.

Allied propaganda, which was extensive in America, was perhaps more astute than that of the Central Powers. It had an advantage in that Germany had not had a good press in this country for some time before the war. Glowing with pride from her recent unification, completed only in 1871, Germany had been in a boastful mood before the war. The speeches of Kaiser William II were notoriously tactless, and there had been occasions when he rubbed American fur the wrong way. During the war, Allied propaganda succeeded in persuading much of America that the Kaiser and the Prussian war lords headed a giant conspiracy against the liberties of mankind. This was a considerable travesty of the truth. But the Germans were often their own worst enemies; the behavior of certain German and Austrian representatives in the United States during the war was most unfortunate, involving some instances of sabotage in American industrial plants. They bungled the job, were caught at espionage, and expelled from the country, the episodes doing considerable damage to the German cause.

This propaganda battle was less significant than the issues raised by German submarine operations. As early as March, 1915, there was an outcry in the American press when an American life was lost aboard a torpedoed British ship. Then on May 7, 1915, the British liner *Lusitania* was sunk off Ireland by a German submarine with the loss of 1,198 lives, among them 128 Americans. These passengers had indeed been warned to stay off the vessel because it was carrying munitions. But such a tragedy inevitably aroused the most intense reactions. No such disaster occurred again, but the memory of the *Lusitania* could not be erased. President Wilson could not do less than issue a grave warning to the German government, demand reparations, and insist that American citizens had an unqualified right to travel on the high seas, whether in American or British ships.

Before this exchange of notes was completed, a fresh sinking, that of the British liner *Arabic,* added fuel to the flames and brought the United States close to war as two more Americans were drowned. Germany, acting on the advice of its ambassador in Washington, Count von Bernstorff, now promised that large passenger ships even of belligerent powers, would not be sunk without warning or without making provision for the safety of noncombatant passengers, provided such ships offered no resistance and did not try to escape. Then in May, 1916, after the sinking of a French steamer (the *Sussex*), Germany promised also to spare cargo vessels in the same way. This German pledge quieted the rising storm and postponed America's entrance into the war, as Germany considerably restricted the use of her strongest weapon on the seas. The submarine was a new and terrible weapon of war which most Americans were inclined to regard as too barbarous to be used at all by a civilized state. But a nation at war is not likely to forgo its strongest weapon for humanitarian reasons, especially if it is hard pressed. Germany was to reconsider her decision at a later date, with momentous consequences.

Behind Germany's eventual decision to ignore American feelings on the submarines was an economic factor of considerable importance in making the United States seem, to the Central Powers, not truly neutral. America's booming war industries were beginning by 1915 to pour into the Allied countries an indispensable portion of their war supplies. America did not start out with the idea of selling to the Allies only. It was simply a case of selling to any belligerent who could buy. This practice was felt to be within the bounds of strict neutrality. Even William Jennings Bryan, who was Wilson's Secretary of State until he resigned in 1915 because he felt we were abandoning our neutrality, conceded that "a citizen . . . can sell to a belligerent government . . . any article of commerce which he pleases." American industrialists and bankers wasted no time in exploiting the opportunity. As was traditional, the United States was strongly in favor of the widest possible rights of trade. But it quickly became apparent that not much trade with Germany was going to develop because Britain controlled the seas. In the case of the Allies, there was no limit to the amount which could be sold and delivered—except their ability to pay. That obstacle was overcome when, in 1915, private loans were permitted.

A study of the war-trade statistics reveals that vast quantities of goods were sold to the Allies and that vast profits were made. For example, the du Pont Company furnished during the war 40 per cent of all the explosives used by the Allies, increasing its shipments 160-fold

between 1914 and 1918. Americans sold 7 billion dollars' worth of goods to European belligerents prior to our entrance into the war. Those who shared in this large and profitable war trade were not merely industrial concerns, for the American farmer also did well; wheat exports more than quadrupled in value from 1913 to 1915. So large was the buying that by the fall of 1915 the Allies had all but exhausted their cash and credits. In 1914 the government had opposed, as contrary to "the true spirit of neutrality," loans by American bankers to belligerent nations. But in 1915 the pressure to permit loans so that the lucrative trade might continue was too great to resist. It was not just a case of Wall Street, but of the entire national economy, now being geared to the war trade and in no mood to abandon it. For the sake of American business, as well as to help the Allies, the President and the State Department granted permission for private loans. The war trade went on; without it, the Allies probably could not have continued the war. It should be stressed, however, that neither trade with belligerents nor private loans to them was inconsistent with international law. Since these privileges were formally open to both sides, the United States was being legally neutral. In fact, of course, Americans were helping one side only, and though this was no fault of theirs, it an-

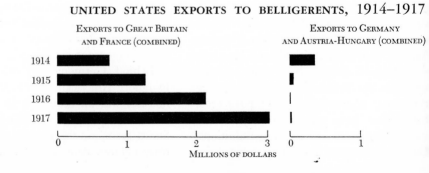

UNITED STATES EXPORTS TO BELLIGERENTS, 1914–1917

EXPORTS TO GREAT BRITAIN
AND FRANCE (COMBINED)

EXPORTS TO GERMANY
AND AUSTRIA-HUNGARY (COMBINED)

MILLIONS OF DOLLARS

PRESIDENTIAL ELECTION OF 1916

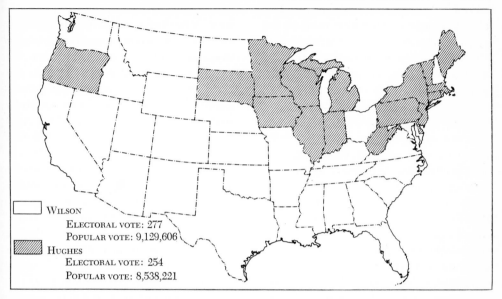

WILSON
ELECTORAL VOTE: 277
POPULAR VOTE: 9,129,606
HUGHES
ELECTORAL VOTE: 254
POPULAR VOTE: 8,538,221

gered the Germans, who saw American supplies helping to kill their soldiers.

In the development of his policies, there is no doubt that Wilson made an honest effort to be neutral, consistent with the defense of American rights and interests. The United States government protested to the Allies as well as to the Central Powers over violations of American rights. As she had done a century earlier, Britain used her naval power in a way that strained international law; indeed, international law went by the boards early in the war, each side claiming the other had abandoned it. British blockades and her search-and-seizure practices angered Americans and elicited strenuous protests from Washington, so heated that they sometimes alarmed the Allies seriously. So also did British practices of economic warfare, especially the black-listing of American firms who were trading with Germans. A few voices even demanded war with Britain. Yet, in the last analysis,

it was pretty clear that America would never go to war with Britain because of technical illegalities which accompanied so profitable a trade; and she was fast becoming virtually the arsenal for the Allied nations. Meanwhile, Germany's naval weapon, the submarine, had outraged public opinion and drawn forth threats of war from the United States. It is hardly possible to say that the United States, for all her efforts, was strictly neutral during the first two and a half years of the war. But the question might well be asked whether in such a conflict there could be, for a nation so great as America, any such thing as actual neutrality.

"PEACE WITHOUT VICTORY" OR WAR?

Wilson campaigned and won in the election of 1916 on a "He Kept Us Out of War" slogan. Bryan had resigned from the Cabinet because he said Wilson was too pro-Allied; the Republicans led by ex-President Roosevelt said he was not pro-Allied enough. They also attacked the administration for neglecting American necessary military preparations. It is quite true that our existing armed strength could command no great respect from the powers of Europe. It was nevertheless Wilson's most earnest hope, and certainly a noble one, to compel or persuade the warring powers to call off their senseless struggle and accept a compromise peace. To assume the role of an impartial mediator and bring about a settlement became for Wilson his "great mission." He made a number of attempts to sound out the two sides, and early in 1916 he sent his trusted friend Colonel Edward M. House to England with proposals for peace. He made another effort in December, 1916. But it is never easy to stop a war that has once started. In a speech on January 22, 1917, Wilson sternly demanded of both sides "peace without victory." Peace without victory is not something that nations at war will readily accept. Each side demanded terms which the other would never accept. To have forced peace on Europe would probably have required both far more diplomatic skill and far more military strength than Wilson commanded.

Neither side would give up hope of victory, and the war took a terrible toll from both. The loss of life was shocking; in 1916, 500,000 men fell in a few weeks in the great battle at Verdun, yet neither side was able to win more than a few square miles of ground. In the east, where backward Russia was unable to meet the demands of modern war, Germany won great victories, but she could not win the war without reaching a decision in the west. The unprecedented sacrifices in both blood and wealth put a strain on the mo-

rale of the peoples of all the warring nations. This was "total war," unlike anything seen before. Austria-Hungary, a polyglot state whose numerous minority groups were of doubtful loyalty, showed signs of cracking under the strain. On the Allied side, so did Russia. The Allies bribed Italy into the war with generous offers of enemy territory, but on the Austro-Italian front the battles were bloody but indecisive. The Allied blockade was a formidable weapon which caused severe shortages in Germany, yet the Germans proved ingenious in devising all sorts of substitutes. In sum, both sides were often in despair but often had their hopes raised by difficulties in the enemy camp. Victory seemed likely to come only when one or the other collapsed from utter exhaustion; and Europe was likely to be a shambles after the war.

Under such circumstances, Wilson's desire to bring about a compromise peace which would leave Western civilization still alive was obviously enlightened. As late as January, 1917, Wilson was still talking of "peace without victory." At just the moment when this last bid failed, the Germans made the decision which was to prove decisive in bringing America into the war on the Allied side. The German military leaders persuaded the Kaiser to let them use unrestricted submarine warfare. Germany now had a large submarine fleet, and its use seemed to offer a way of attaining victory. The United States was so unprepared for war, the Germans reasoned, that even if she did declare war it would be many months before she would be able to fight in Europe. Meanwhile the submarines might succeed in cutting Great Britain's lifeline and force her to sue for peace. The fateful plan was adopted, and Germany announced on January 31 her decision to begin U-boat action against all ships—including neutral ones—in the war zones around Britain specified by the Germans.

Three days later, evidently after some heart searching, Wilson broke off diplomatic relations with Germany. In this the great bulk of public opinion enthusiastically backed him. But Wilson was no McKinley, and he had not simply bowed to popular sentiment. In recent months he had not been pronouncedly pro-Allied. No doubt, he felt that, since his peace bids had failed, it would be next best to end the war by American intervention. The United States could then take part in the peace and help hate-ridden Europe to make a decent peace settlement. Wilson's "great mission" changed from that of bringing about a compromise peace through American mediation to that of using his moderating influence in the post-war settlement.

War did not come immediately. For six weeks there were no sinkings of American ships such as might provide the occasion for a declaration of war. Meanwhile, however, the sensational episode of the Zimmermann note occurred, keeping anti-German feeling at fever pitch. The British intercepted and published, at a very timely moment, a note from the German foreign office to the Mexican government trying to interest Mexico in going to war against the United States as the ally of Germany in the event of a German-American war. Then, on March 12 an American ship was sunk, and on March 19 three others.

After weeks of tension and anxiety, war finally came to America on April 6. Four days earlier, the President had appeared before the Congress and requested a formal declaration. His war message pointed to "the wanton and wholesale destruction

WORLD WAR I WESTERN FRONT OPERATIONS, 1914–1916

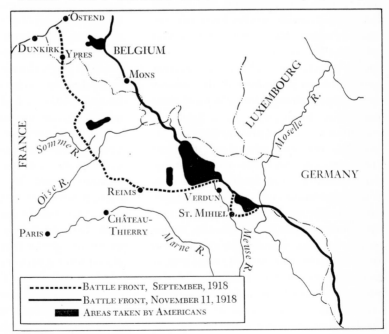

- - - - - - BATTLE FRONT, SEPTEMBER, 1918
————— BATTLE FRONT, NOVEMBER 11, 1918
▓▓▓ AREAS TAKEN BY AMERICANS

of the lives of non-combatants"* and spoke of the German submarine as "a warfare against mankind." But he went on to put the case upon a broader basis— that of vindicating "the principles of peace and justice in the life of the world as against selfish and autocratic power," in order to "make the world safe for democracy." As proof of its unselfishness, the United States would seek "no indemnity" and "no material compensation." This formulation of the war aims was influenced by an event of the previous month, which the President mentioned in his message—the first phase (as it turned out) of the Russian Revolution. No effort to cast the war as an ideological struggle between the democracies and the autocracies was possible so long as the worst of all despotisms, czarist Russia, fought as one of the Allies. But the March revolution, which was headed by liberals and offered hope of a constitutional regime, seemed to indicate that Russia had cast off the yoke of despotism in order to embrace a democratic system. Later events proved that this was an illusory hope, but in view of Wilson's idealism and the American people's strong desire to see a clear moral purpose in any war they undertook, the chance offered to proclaim a crusade for democracy cannot be dismissed from the list of reasons why the United States now decided to participate directly in the war.

The vote for war was not unanimous and was indeed resisted bitterly by a handful of rather distinguished senators, mostly of the "progressive" camp. The vote in the Senate was 82 to 6; that in the House, 373 to 50. The United States was at war with Germany and her allies and would, in the event of victory, be able to participate in the peace settlement. Perhaps there

* German submarine activity had caused the loss of 266 American lives.

Woodrow Wilson could carry out his "great mission" of bringing a fair peace to a troubled world.

VICTORY AND PEACE TERMS

As it turned out, American entrance into the war came just in time for the Allies. For a few months it appeared that the reckoning of the German High Command might have been well calculated in that submarine operations threatened to destroy the British supply line. Allied shipping losses mounted ominously until the autumn, when they were brought under control by new British and American countermeasures (one of which was the American-developed magnetic mine) and an increased rate of Allied ship construction. But then the November revolution in Russia brought in a regime determined to make peace at any cost, a dictatorship headed by the extreme left-wing Bolsheviks, pledged to violent revolution and liquidation of the old ruling class. Soon Russia was out of the war altogether, as the Bolshevik leaders, Nikolai Lenin and Leon Trotsky, to the great consternation of the West, signed away to Germany huge territorial concessions in the treaty of Brest Litovsk (March 3, 1918). Immediately thereafter, the Central Powers mounted a giant offensive on the western front, designed to crush the weary Allied armies.

Throughout all this, the moral support of America and, by 1918, the arrival of fresh American troops sustained the Allies' spirit. The United States, starting almost from scratch, swung into her war effort. A general-conscription act was passed after much opposition on May 18, 1917, more than a month after the declaration of war. Eventually about 4 million men were actively enrolled in the army and another 500,000 in the navy.

Approximately 2 million men went overseas without the loss of a single troop ship. But American forces in substantial numbers did not participate in military action in Europe until the late spring of 1918—just in time to help stem the great German offensive. General John J. Pershing, who had directed the Mexican campaign of 1916, was named commander-in-chief of this great army.

Congress created a Shipping Board in 1916 to secure, by lease, purchase, or loan, such vessels as could be employed for transport. Later an Emergency Fleet Corporation for building ships was organized. Yet by March, 1918, only two ships had been completed and commissioned. By July, however, nearly 100 vessels were in service, and by the war's end in November, nearly 500. There was bitter criticism over the failure to get American aircraft into production and over slowness in producing artillery and machine guns. A Council of National Defense set up in 1916, including leading men of industry and labor, had the chief responsibility for mobilizing the nation's industrial and transportation facilities for war. The entire American railroad system was taken over and operated by the government as a war-emergency measure. Agricultural and fuel-control commissions were established. The nation was organized for war under direction of the federal government. Despite many problems, war production at length got into high gear.

Propaganda was also organized: a public information bureau under the ex-Socialist journalist George Creel saw to it that Americans were well instructed in the purposes of the war, the wickedness of the enemy, and the need to buy war bonds. There was little tolerance for anyone suspected of not supporting the war, and freedom suffered. The Sedition Act of 1918 did away with peacetime freedom of speech and press, and another act authorized a general censorship of the mails. Leaders of the Socialist party, who declared the war to be a contest of rival capitalists for profit, were imprisoned. Never before had Americans submitted to such curtailment of their much-prized basic liberties of free expression.

These are but some of the highlights of a wholly unique experience for the American people, organization for a modern war. It was a rather exciting experience, and the war was popular with the majority, but it had its hysterical side. Did the people really know what they were fighting for? There was a great deal of singing, marching, and speechmaking. Patriotism was at a peak. Before long there were victories to cheer about. The last supreme German offensive in the west had not been stopped when American forces in substantial numbers began to participate in the action. At first brigaded in small units within larger British and French groups, these troops were soon formed into separate American divisions. They took over that part of the front from the Swiss border to the Moselle and Meuse Valleys below Verdun and parts of the line in the Argonne Forest, Aisne, and Champagne-Marne districts. In the later summer and fall these troops were chiefly responsible for wiping out the important St. Mihiel salient south and east of Verdun. They fought a large-scale battle through the Argonne Forest that broke the enemy's key communication system. Belleau Wood, Château-Thierry, Cantigny, and Montdidier became monuments to American military prowess. Americans actually fought in this war only a few months, and suffered relatively few battle casualties—about 50,000 killed, when Europe was counting its total dead by the

World War I: (above) hauling ammunition to the front through the mud; (below) wounded being treated in what is left of a church, Meuse sector, September, 1918; (opposite page) American gunners, St. Mihiel salient. (National Archives)

millions. But they exerted a decisive influence on the outcome. Of even more importance than the actual fighting was the psychological effect—raising the morale of the weary Allied forces and shattering that of the Germans.

By late September, 1918, the failure of their offensive and the impossibility of

winning the war faced the Central Powers. It must be remembered, however, that the front was still on French soil, and the German armies were still formidable, or apparently so. The Germans were ready for peace if it could be had on favorable terms. They appealed to the principles of Wilson's "Fourteen Points" as a basis for peace. Wilson had expounded these principles in January, 1918, as his idea of a just and lasting peace. They might be called war propaganda, for they had been designed to weaken the German will and also counter the Russian Bolsheviks, who after their seizure of power in Russia seriously embarrassed the Allies by publishing various secret treaties disposing of territory after the war. But the points reflected Wilson's characteristic ideals of a peace without vengeance, without vindictiveness, without annexations or reparations. They also included his dreams of a world without trade barriers, armaments, imperialisms, and nationalist diplomacy,

one in which every national people had the government it wanted and the peoples of the world were leagued in an international union. Some of this was sheer utopianism, wishful thinking without much relationship to reality. But the underlying idea of a peace between equals, not a conqueror's peace, had caught the imagination of many people in the world and had unquestionably helped weaken the German will to fight on. Under the Fourteen Points, Germany would have to return Alsace and Lorraine to France and presumably some territory in the east to the restored Polish nation, but would incur no further penalties. It remained to be seen whether the Allies, having shed so much blood and having felt so much hatred, would accept such a clement peace.

The vengeful mood of the French was certain, and that of the British was revealed in the elections of 1918. At home, ex-President Roosevelt attacked Wilson for being too "soft" toward the "Huns." The very popular AEF commander, General John Pershing, was against anything short of an unconditional surrender in order to impose a peace that would make future German aggression impossible. Numerous others also urged the necessity of complete defeat lest the Germans immediately begin to prepare for the restoration of their military power. "There is only one way to chasten Germany and that is to defeat her so completely that the memory will not pass out of her mind for many generations," wrote Henry Morgenthau, Sr. Gifford Pinchot feared the German armies might escape "and the German military caste would claim its victory and survive." Many fears were expressed that Germany would recover quickly at the expense of her neighbors unless she could be made to bear the financial burden of restoring France and Belgium, whose industrial potential her armies had destroyed. Although Americans did not generally favor the extreme demands of the French for the permanent dismemberment of Germany, there was much sentiment in responsible quarters in 1918–1919 for a strong peace.

The handling of the request for an armistice was left in the hands of the Allied commander-in-chief Marshal Foch. Meanwhile, in Germany, popular morale and the Kaiser's government were collapsing rapidly. The German people had lost faith in their government and were sick of the war. The Kaiser was forced to abdicate and flee to Holland. The Germans who faced Foch in the forest of Compiègne on the morning of November 11 were not representatives of the old imperial government, but of a revolutionary government led by Social Democrats, soon to become the Weimar Republic. This change of government made no impression upon Foch, to whom a German was a German. The armistice terms were severe. Germany must agree to withdraw behind the Rhine; to surrender all her submarines, most of her navy, and all her heavy artillery, and to allow the establishment of Allied bridgeheads east of the Rhine at Mainz, Coblenz, and Cologne. With their country in chaos and revolution, the German delegates, though protesting, could do nothing but sign. The war was over, and Germany lay helpless.

Meanwhile, the old empire of the Hapsburgs was also dissolving in revolution, never to be reconstructed. The war thus had caused the collapse, by revolution, of three great empires: Russia, Austria-Hungary, and Germany. The democracies had proved stronger. It remained to be seen whether they would use their victory wisely.

PEACEMAKING AT PARIS

The drafting of permanent peace terms went ahead without delay. President Wilson sailed for Europe in December—an event wholly without precedent, no previous American President ever having gone overseas while in office. He was given an enthusiastic reception by the people of Europe. Great throngs turned out everywhere to give him a hero's welcome. Undoubtedly he had become the moral leader of a distressed world. But these heartening ovations may have caused Wilson to overlook the dangers ahead in his supreme effort to impose the kind of a peace settlement he wanted. He continued in his speeches to stress the idealistic approach outlined in the Fourteen Points, though this conflicted with certain treaty commitments of the Allies. The other Allied leaders cannot be said to have regarded the Wilsonian ideas with enthusiasm. "We must stand together. . . . We cannot be separated in interest," Wilson declared of the Allies; but plainly there were serious differences. The experienced statesmen of France, Britain, Italy, and Japan felt that Wilson knew very little about the world or about practical statesmanship, in which view there was some truth. They had their own solutions to offer, and some of these contradicted the Wilsonian Fourteen Points.

The President, great man though he was in many respects, lacked some of the qualities that make for a skillful diplomat. He certainly was at a disadvantage in this respect when dealing with the brilliant Welshman David Lloyd George and the experienced Georges Clemenceau of France. In the light of later events, Wilson's decision to participate personally in the conference was perhaps a mistake. Wilson's whole position was weakened by his party's loss of the 1918 elections on the eve of his departure to Europe. Theodore Roosevelt was stating publicly that Wilson did not represent the American people. In selecting his members of the American peace delegation, Wilson had unwisely ignored Republican leaders in the United States Senate who were in a position to defeat any treaty he brought home. Of the four peace commissioners, only one, Henry White, was a Republican, and he, a career diplomat, was not an outstanding party leader. The obvious candidate was Senator Henry Cabot Lodge, but Wilson was not on friendly terms with him. Not the most tactful of men, Wilson had made powerful enemies in Congress. This fact weakened his position at Paris. Nevertheless, throughout the conference which convened on January 18, 1919, and eventuated in the signing of the Treaty of Versailles on June 28, Wilson fought stubbornly for his principles. He could not, after all, expect to win every point. Though American aid had been decisive and was likely to be needed still further in the reconstruction of Europe, the European Allies had certainly made far heavier sacrifices. France had lost over a million men and suffered extensive devastation. Britain, too, had made great sacrifices. Day after day, Wilson was closeted with Lloyd George and Clemenceau, the other members of the "Big Three" on whom the burden of peacemaking fell. Certainly Clemenceau, the French representative, did not get all that French opinion demanded—the dismemberment and economic crippling of Germany. What came out was, not unnaturally, a compromise between Wilsonian idealism and French realism.

The final terms of the Treaty of Versailles proved to be far from the peace of vengeance which France wished; but in the opinion of many they also diverged considerably from the "just" peace for which Wilson had contended. Germany was deprived of Alsace and Lorraine and a small amount of territory on the Belgian frontier, while the Saar valley, rich in coal, was turned over to an international administration for fifteen years, with France to have primary economic rights. In the east, the newly reconstituted state of Poland was given some former Prussian territory, with provision also for a free state of Danzig and a corridor through Germany to give Poland access to that seaport—apparently an economic necessity for Poland. In numerous other areas, plebiscites were to be held to determine the wishes of the population; these, unfortunately, were not always fairly conducted. But all these territorial arrangements, galling as they might be to Germany, could be defended on rational grounds, and they did not add up to that partition for which some French had hoped.

Unfortunately, in other, and sometimes petty, respects, the treaty went out of its way to inflict humiliations on a proud people who never were convinced that they had caused the war or lost it. Germany was to be substantially disarmed; she lost her colonies (a clear violation of the Fourteen Points); and by the notorious article 231, she had to accept the proposition that was commonly interpreted to mean that Germany alone was responsible for the war. She was never consulted in framing the treaty, though this seems to have been intended originally; in effect, she was called in and told to sign. Finally, perhaps the most criticized and most unhappy aspect of the treaty was the levying on Germany of a vast reparations bill—a sum which was to include all civil damages done in the war, which was construed at the peace conference as including soldiers' pensions so that Great Britain as well as France could be compensated. The Treaty of Versailles was not a settlement that a future Germany was likely to accept as permanent; yet neither, as we know, was it a treaty that left Germany permanently shorn of her might. Germany was also to be occupied, along the west bank of the Rhine, for fifteen years, while the east bank was to be demilitarized for a distance of 50 kilometers.

Regardless of the "justice" of the treaty —and that term is almost impossible to define in international affairs, since what is just to one country is often unjust to another—what really mattered was the enforcing of it. France reluctantly gave up her demands for the partition of Germany in return for a Wilsonian pledge to join with Britain in guaranteeing the new frontiers. Would the United States stand by this agreement to join in upholding the new boundaries—including perhaps those embodied in the treaties with Austria (St.-Germain), Hungary (Trianon), Bulgaria (Neuilly), and Turkey (Sèvres) —or would she repudiate Wilson and retire to nonentanglement? Upon this question really hinged the stability of Europe. For the United States was now the foremost power in the world, and Europe after Paris certainly had less strategic stability than before. The old Austrian empire now was divided into a half-dozen small states, some of them economically hopeless. The Russian empire had also collapsed. Italy had quarreled seriously with the other Allies at the peace conference over rewards she was to receive from the war and was now in spirit hostile to the Paris settlement. All this meant a rather gloomy outlook for future peace and stability in Europe when the embit-

tered losers should regain strength enough to challenge the terms of the peace. Wilson predicted that unless the United States joined in guarding the peace, there would be another European war within twenty years—a remarkably accurate prophecy. But to join in such guardianship would be a huge step for the American people, who by long tradition eschewed all alliances and "foreign entanglements."

There was a way, so Wilson and others felt, of bringing America into the world order without violating her traditions. A League of Nations, conceived as the chief and indispensable guarantor of the peace, was perhaps Wilson's chief interest at Paris. He thought it should be written into the treaties themselves. During the war there had been much discussion of this idea both in America and in Europe; it had received bipartisan support in the United States, with leading Republicans such as ex-Presidents Taft and Roosevelt endorsing it. Indeed, the League to Enforce Peace, headed by Taft and Harvard's President A. Lawrence Lowell, did most of the American spadework, cooperating closely with a British group headed by Lord James Bryce. Many other circles were discussing various versions of the idea of all nations, united in a new world organization of some sort, outlawing war and somehow enforcing the ban on it.

The idea was a vague one, but it appealed mightily to world idealism as a means of escape from the old order of alliances, secret treaties, balance of power, and "selfish nationalism." America might join such a world organization without impairing her purity. Wilson took up the idea and battled for it at Paris. Perhaps the European statesmen were more skeptical, but they had no serious objections to a plan that would bring America into the picture as an ensurer of the peace. The idea was approved and a committee authorized to draw up its Covenant. Wilson himself was chairman of the committee. With the aid of American experts, the draft was rushed to completion, approved in the plenary session, and embodied in the Treaty of Versailles.

But when Wilson had returned home for a short visit in February, 1919, he had found a group of Republicans in Congress prepared to ask searching questions about this League Covenant; and when later that year he came back from Paris bringing with him the treaties for approval by the Senate, he discovered that this was the major stumbling block in the way of such approval. Here, Wilson thought, was the most important achievement of the peace conference; the treaties themselves might be imperfect—though he thought they were as good as could have been obtained —but all would be set right by the new world organization. His critics in Congress thought otherwise, and they sharpened their knives for an attack on the League.

THE FIGHT FOR THE LEAGUE AND THE TREATIES

Wilson was aware of the opposition developing at home against the League, but he had determined to force the issue by completing the Covenant and putting it into the treaties. He was also aware when he came home in July that he faced "the fight of his life," but he was ready to wage it in behalf of his "great mission," so long as his strength held out. Nevertheless, some observers thought him disillusioned and discouraged, and as it turned out he was near the end of his strength. His enemies and critics of the League of Nations were numerous and confident.

We cannot go very far into the details of the League of Nations Covenant. There was a Council, which had the power to make decisions and on which the five great powers, France, Britain, the United States, Italy, and Japan were to have permanent seats. The Covenant provided for an Assembly, useful mainly as a world forum, where all the member states of the League would be on an equal footing. There was also to be created a permanent Secretariat, located at Geneva, Switzerland, which would serve to direct the work of the League. There were many committees which were to study and report on a variety of world problems, such as health, crime, labor standards, and narcotics control, and promote world cooperation in solving them. The League's great task of "enforcing peace" was to be carried out by requiring all member states to submit to arbitration all disputes which threatened war. Any member state then going to war in violation of the Covenant might, by a unanimous vote of the Council, be subjected to either economic or military penalties. The most controversial part of the Covenant was Article X, which required each member to "undertake to respect and preserve as against external aggression the territorial integrity and existing political independence of all Members of the League." To Wilson this was the heart of the Covenant. The question raised by opponents was whether a member state was bound by the Council's decision. If so, the sovereignty of the state was impaired. The United States might be required to go to war anywhere in the world at the request of a foreign body. The somewhat obscure language of Article X spoke of an "obligation" in this connection. Wilson did not think that this did require us to go to war, but he was not able to explain very clearly just what the "obligation" was. The issue quickly became bogged down in a great deal of fairly technical argument. Out of it emerged the conception that while most Americans favored "international cooperation" in principle, they were quite dubious about signing up to wage future wars.

The enemies of the League made the most of its uncertainties and possible perils. They had the support of a general public reaction against the whole wartime mood of idealism. In 1919 Americans were already drawing back in disgust from the situation in Europe, only too glad that the crusade was over, already questioning whether it had not been a mistake. When the soldiers came home from Europe, as they did very quickly after the fighting was over, their mood was that expressed by service organizations like the American Legion—"Never again." Communism seemed to be spreading over Europe, and the American fear of it managed to help discredit all ideas smacking of internationalism. The people were in no mood to enter upon the job of permanent policeman of strife-torn Europe.

America had not been properly prepared for the assumption of world leadership, and so Wilson's great plan was tragically premature. The League and the treaties were doomed. The moderate and international-minded Elihu Root, former Secretary of State, observed when the Treaty of Versailles was submitted that if the League Covenant were not "materially amended" then "a great opportunity has been wasted in the doing of a futile thing." To the demand that he go back to Paris and secure certain amendments designed to clarify obligations under the Covenant, Wilson always answered in the negative. He did not propose to reopen the whole peace conference. His only re-

course was to undertake a great speaking tour of the country to stir up public opinion in support of the League. In the course of this tour Wilson collapsed, after a speech at Pueblo, on September 26, 1919, and many months of lingering illness followed. Even had he kept his health Wilson could not have pushed ratification through without reservations it seems clear.

Chief of Wilson's foes and untiring opponent of the League—unless altered by certain reservations—was Senator Henry Cabot Lodge, Republican chairman of the powerful Committee on Foreign Relations. Lodge masterminded the fight against ratification, his strategy including first delay and then framing of "reservations"; he came up with fourteen of the latter. Article X must be clarified, the Monroe Doctrine must be placed beyond the reach of the League, and a number of other minor questions must be cleared up. The reservations did not appear unreasonable. Indeed, at one time Wilson appears to have approved of most of them. Article X proved the stumbling block. Wilson refused to repudiate the "obligation," and Lodge demanded that we should. Time and events were working against Wilson, and it has been the consensus of many experts that he should have given in. If he had done so, the United States would have entered the League with the Lodge reservations. Wilson held that our European allies would not agree to this, at least not without a new conference, but it appeared that they were willing to if necessary. Wilson was ill and was isolated from close touch with public and congressional opinion, a factor which may have contributed to his uncompromising stand. He ordered Democratic senators to stand firm against the reservations.

Twice, in November, 1919, and March, 1920, the treaty with the Lodge reservations came before the Senate and failed to secure the necessary two-thirds majority. On the second vote, it did receive a majority, as some Democrats broke ranks seeing that it was a question of the reservations or no ratification at all. Only a small number of senators were the "irreconcilable" foes of American entrance into the League on any terms; and since even Wilson agreed to some "interpretive" reservations, the issue was essentially on what seem rather fine points of wording the reservations. Most recent historians have assigned blame to the stubbornness of both Wilson and Lodge, but it is only fair to point out that each man felt a vital principle to be at stake.

The United States finally made a separate peace with Germany in August, 1921, on the basis of the Versailles Treaty without the League and with a few other provisions. The treaty of guaranty with France and Great Britain, which Wilson had signed at Paris, never even got to the Senate floor. The United States would take no part in enforcing the terms of the Paris settlement.

THE SIGNIFICANCE OF THE WAR

Thus did the great crusade for democracy and a new world order end in a somewhat shabby squabble between Congress and President, and in a seeming indifference on the part of the people of the United States toward their world responsibilities. Men have discussed ever since whether it was Wilson's fault, or Lodge's, or a combination of both; others have suggested the immaturity of the American people as the best explanation. The following conclusions seem well founded: First, the Americans never had a clear and rational idea of why they went to war, but

had marched off in a cloud of slogans and hysterical emotions which quickly evaporated after the war, leaving them confused and a bit disgusted. The great German statesman Bismarck had once warned against waging a war for reasons which would not hold water afterward. There may have been excellent reasons for America's going to war, reasons connected with her security and national interest. In the last analysis, the European power balance was threatened and American security was involved. But this was not clearly explained to the American people. Second, it probably did not matter so much in itself whether the United States joined the League of Nations or not; what mattered was that she should play an active role in world affairs, which she could do in the League or out of it. Unless the nation was ready to depart from her traditional reluctance to join in alliances and in the game of world politics, taking a seat at Geneva would mean little. And in fact, America was not ready for such a role, tragic though this was for the world. The roots of noninvolvement were too deep in the national tradition to be torn up overnight. It was not, after all, so surprising that the United States reverted to her old attitudes and policies, for these were time-honored, time-tested, and indeed almost sacred traditions. To change them would require an experience more sharply defined than the confused one of 1917–1919.

Though the United States was to show signs of drawing back into her shell after the war, the fact is that this war signaled a change in the world equilibrium of power which could not be undone. Europe was economically and physically drained and divided by poisonous hatreds. Russia had gone Communist, and the colonial world was beginning to stir against its European masters, thus further weakening them. The United States had made substantial economic gains during this war at the expense of Europe, and emerged from it the world's foremost economic power. Great Britain in particular, though nominally a victor, never regained the proud position she had formerly occupied as the world's chief creditor. She had lost markets and liquidated overseas assets in payment for the terribly expensive war. While Europe was to make a substantial recovery in the 1920s, there was now little question about the American economic supremacy, which was reflected in her mounting surplus of exports of goods and capital. In the long run, these fundamental facts were bound to force the United States into a different world role, however reluctant she might be to depart from traditional habits.

In many other ways the war was a turning point. Wars have always stimulated social change, and modern total war especially does so. The federal government had undertaken duties and exercised coercions hitherto unknown. Women had been drawn into employment on a scale previously unheard of. The "cake of custom" was broken through in these and other ways; the new habits induced by the shock of total war tended to persist after the war was over. New products and new industrial techniques emerged from the war. A new generation of American writers came out of these years too, obviously much affected by their experiences in Europe and by the thoughts this great crisis in Western civilization had induced.

In brief, much of the flavor of the 1920s, which is to be described in the next chapter, derived from the war. All in all, it was a major watershed in American history, and after it the directions of many streams of life would be altered. Less definitely perhaps than in Europe, yet nonetheless unmistakably, the war marked the end of one era and the beginning of another.

FURTHER READINGS

Among an almost inexhaustible supply of road-to-war studies, the following may be mentioned: Charles Seymour, *American Neutrality, 1914–1917* (1935) and *American Diplomacy during the World War* (1934); Arthur S. Link, *Wilson the Diplomatist* (1957) and portions of his New American Nation volume, *Woodrow Wilson and the Progressive Era, 1910–1917* (1954); and E. H. Buehrig, *Woodrow Wilson and the Balance of Power* (1955). More critical accounts are C. C. Tansill, *America Goes to War* (1936), and A. M. Arnett, *Claude Kitchin and the Wilson War Policies* (1937). On Mexico, Howard F. Cline, *The United States and Mexico* (1953), is a good survey which is rather critical of Wilson's Mexican diplomacy.

On the war itself, standard guides include F. L. Paxson, *American Democracy and the World War,* volume II (1939), and J. G. Harbord, *America in the World War* (1933). H. C. Peterson and G. C. Fite have recently written *Opponents of War, 1917–1918* (1957). Problems of the war may be approached through Frederick Palmer's biography of Wilson's Secretary of War, *Newton D. Baker* (2 vols., 1931); through Herbert Hoover's interesting *Memoirs,* volume I (1951); or through Palmer's study *John J. Pershing, General of the Armies* (1948). Lawrence W. Martin, *Peace without Vic-*

tory: Woodrow Wilson and the British Liberals (1958), is an interesting recent contribution to the topic of war aims.

The making of the peace and the fight over the treaty are described in two books by Thomas A. Bailey, *Woodrow Wilson and the Lost Peace* (1944) and *Woodrow Wilson and the Great Betrayal* (1945). Ruhl J. Bartlett's account of the League of Nations movement, *The League to Enforce Peace* (1944), is most sympathetic to Wilson. More critical of Wilson is John M. Blum, *Joe Tumulty and the Wilson Era* (1951)

(Tumulty was Wilson's long-time private secretary), while J. A. Garraty, *Henry Cabot Lodge: A Biography* (1953), seems scrupulously fair. Illuminating also are portions of Richard W. Leopold's study *Elihu Root and the Conservative Tradition* (1954), for Root was the real Republican strategist on matters of foreign policy.

For additional bibliography, see the *Harvard Guide,* sections 238–243. The volumes in the New American Nation series also contain up-to-date annotated bibliographies.

TWENTY-FOUR

The 1920s: Normalcy and Abnormalcy

1920
Prohibition amendment goes into effect.
Harding elected.
Red scare.

1922
Washington Conference concludes.
Prosperity begins.

1923
Scandals in government.
President Harding dies; Coolidge President.
Rise of Ku Klux Klan.

1924
Immigration Act passed.
Dawes Plan reduces reparations.
Coolidge elected President.

1925
Scopes trial in Tennessee.

1927
Sacco and Vanzetti executed.
Lindbergh flies Atlantic.
McNary-Haugen bill vetoed.

1928
Kellogg-Briand Pact signed.
Hoover defeats Smith in presidential election.

HARDING AND COOLIDGE

WARREN G. HARDING, the man whom the Republican party succeeded in nominating and electing in 1920, made himself the prophet of a return to what he called "normalcy." There should be no more reforms and no more crusades; the time had come to relax. This suited the national mood very well during the years just after the war. The Republican national convention of 1920 was a remarkable reflection of this spirit. The old guard was firmly back in the saddle, and observers noted a "back to McKinley" atmosphere. The erstwhile "Bull Moose" rebels made their peace with the conservatives, the more easily because these "progressives" were the most fanatical of the isolationist League of Nations haters. Such leaders of the Republican left wing as William E. Borah of Idaho, Robert M. La Follette of Wisconsin, and Hiram Johnson of California were ready, for the moment, to forget their progressivism on domestic issues in return for party support of their conservatism on international ones. Conservatism in domestic politics and isolationism in foreign affairs was the formula for reuniting the Republican party, which had come apart in 1912 and still showed signs of the wound in 1916. For both of these things, by a happy coincidence for the GOP, the country was more than ready in 1920.

How a few men met in a "smoke-filled room" to decide upon a rather ob-

500

scure Ohio politician for the presidential nomination has become one of the legends of American political history. The truth is that a tired convention finally chose Harding because, as one of them related, "there was nothing against him, and the delegates wanted to go home." A deadlock had ensued, and no obvious leader had emerged. Republican politicians, scenting victory if only they did not make a serious mistake, were ready to approve a harmless candidate. The old guard met with no strong challenge from the once militant left wing of the party. And Harding's Ohio friends, led by one Harry Daugherty, promoted his candidacy with shrewd skill. But there was no conspiracy of sinister forces to get the weak Harding nominated; the whole episode only provides a good example of the strange results that can sometimes come out of a nominating convention.

Ill and disillusioned, Woodrow Wilson lay inactive in the White House, while rumors circulated that he had gone mad. Lacking leadership, the country careened uncertainly through the difficulties of postwar economic adjustment. A great strike took place in the steel mills. Excited by the Russian Revolution and embittered by the short sharp depression of 1921 and wartime bans on free speech and action, radicals and labor's left wing were in a dangerous mood. The most active personality in Washington was Wilson's Attorney General, A. Mitchell Palmer, who set about to purge the country of the Red "menace"; but this policy, carried out with much enthusiasm, disheartened many of Wilson's liberal supporters, already disillusioned by the Versailles Treaty. At their nominating convention, the rather discouraged Democrats chose former governor James Cox of Ohio, and as his running mate young Franklin D. Roosevelt

of New York, wartime Assistant Secretary of the Navy, who tried to make an issue of the League of Nations.

As an issue, the League was rather confusing because many voters held Wilson's stubborn refusal to compromise to have been responsible for the deadlock, and because some Republicans claimed there was a better chance to enter the League if Harding won. During the campaign the Harding forces gave the impression that they would, if victorious, bring the United States into the League, or at least a similar league, with adequate safeguards. Cox followed Wilson in refusing to consider any reservation that would materially weaken the League as an enforcer of the peace. But the League idea was rapidly weakening. Chiefly to blame for this, probably, was the profoundly disillusioning state of the world, which seemed to have gone from bad to worse in the aftermath of the war. There were wars and revolutions. The savage strife between English and Irish in Ireland was only the foremost of a number of similar developments which seemed to show that the United States ought not to become a policeman for a world torn by conflict and full of injustice. After the election, the GOP quietly dropped the whole thing, to the evident satisfaction of a large majority. The most obvious political emotion of the hour was a revulsion against Wilsonian idealism and a return to what Harding called "triumphant nationalism."

Warren Gamaliel Harding, thus allowed to become the Chief Executive by an indifferent public, proved to be one of the feeblest of all Presidents. A friendly small-town newspaper editor, he had few qualifications for the presidency other than a handsome appearance, a certain talent for what he himself called "bloviating" (orating in meaningless platitudes)

H. L. Mencken

Spirited if somewhat irresponsible, the 1920s brought thrills and novelties:
automobiles, speakeasies, and heroes who could fly the Atlantic or hit sixty
home runs in one season. Most Americans enjoyed prosperity and forgot about
the world's problems. Some, like Henry Mencken and Sinclair Lewis, partici-
pated in a vigorous literary revival which reacted strongly, pulling no
punches in its criticism of American life. Mencken's Mercury *was the bible*
of the "civilized minority." The entire mood changed when the Great
Depression struck in 1929.

Charles Lindbergh and his plane

Model T Ford

A speakeasy of the 1920s

(above) Sinclair Lewis
and his wife, Grace

Babe Ruth in action

a long record of loyalty to his party, and a weakness of character evidently much prized by some of those who helped push him into the White House. These same sinister elements ruined Harding's reputation and drove him to his grave. This President, who had an illegitimate daughter and loved to hold poker-playing and drinking parties at the White House (despite prohibition), was nevertheless well-meaning and honest. He was also, as Wilson had once acidly noted, not very intelligent, and he was easily victimized by his many doubtful friends. Harry Daugherty, whom Harding appointed Attorney General, sold favors at the Department of Justice; the Veterans Administration was shot through with corruption; and, in the most famous of the Harding scandals, Secretary of the Interior Albert B. Fall accepted gifts from the oil interests in return for handing over public lands to private exploitation. This last affair was soon exposed to view with pitiless severity by the able Democratic Senator Thomas J. Walsh of Montana, head of a Senate investigating committee. Soon everyone had heard of Teapot Dome, the Wyoming naval oil reserve. As a result of these exposures, Cabinet member Fall eventually went to jail. Other Washington figures committed suicide or fled the country. Amid these dismaying events, President Harding died. Rumors whispered of suicide or even murder, but Harding's death was probably natural; it was hastened by worry over the sickening scandals hanging above his administration. Anxious to protect the reputations of her husband and his friends, Mrs. Harding burned his presidential papers. Harding will always be compared to that other postwar President, Grant—both victims of their cronies.

The whole sordid story provided many headlines, but it did not give the Democratic party victory in 1924. Harding's death was opportune for his party. It brought in, before the 1924 election, a President whose integrity was something of a public legend. Tight-lipped and wary, the prim little yankee Calvin Coolidge had first gained national prominence by standing firm against a strike of policemen when he was Governor of Massachusetts. Stepping up from the vice presidency upon the death of Harding, he proceeded to show energy in cleaning up the mess in Washington. The notorious "Ohio Gang" was in full flight by 1923. The Republicans nominated Coolidge in 1924.

The Democrats, demoralized by the pronounced public reaction against Wilson's idealism, turned out to be a deeply divided party also. They were split by the new issue of prohibition, for while their big-city following hated the ban on alcoholic beverages which was now a part of the Consitution, a strong rural bloc from the South and West was pronouncedly "dry." There was also the issue of the Ku Klux Klan, an amazing revival of "nativist" hatred for all things foreign, now strong in the West as well as the South. Here again the big-city Democrats parted company with the rural wing; the former despised the Klan and pressed for a plank in the party platform against it, which the rural delegates would not accept. It was the Democrats' turn to show the deep divisions that can exist in a great national political party. In 1924 they avoided a split by nominating a compromise candidate, after a deadlock between Governor Alfred E. Smith of New York and Senator William Gibbs McAdoo of California. This candidate, John W. Davis of West Virginia, was so conservative in his views that the remnants of progressivism created a third party, finding no possible home in either Coolidge Republicanism or Davis Democracy. Old "Fighting Bob" La Follette headed this Farmer-Labor ticket, and he got the support of even the conservative American Federation of Labor. The nearly 5 million votes La Follette polled probably hurt the Democrats more than the Republicans. The Republicans preferred to say little in this campaign; Davis complained of a vast conspiracy of silence. They did not need to talk. Again they won handily. The nation had decided to "Keep Cool with Coolidge."

Prosperity was in full stride. Business was good, and the country wished to forget all else. The business of America is business, Coolidge announced. The people rather liked the little man whose brevity became proverbial, whose political shrewdness was not in doubt, and who had the good sense to do nothing when doing nothing seemed just right. *A Puritan in Babylon,* William Allen White called his biography of Coolidge; he noted the curious fact that the riotous, golden twenties, a time of big money and high living, were presided over by an old-fashioned, frugal yankee reared in the "social museum" that was rural Vermont. Coolidge believed firmly that nothing could go amiss so long as men worked hard, saved their money, invested it, collected their profits, and reinvested them. His function was to see that no wild and ignorant men interfered with this happy law of nature. Coolidge felt that the whole duty of government was "to prevent crime and preserve contracts." With business booming, although a few protests were heard, not many cared to question this philosophy.

ISSUES OF THE TWENTIES

Those who protested most strongly against the Coolidge philosophy were farmers. The agricultural community did not share in the good times. Agricultural prices were falling, not rising. Under conservative Republican rule, there was an end to the antitrust policies pursued during the progressive era, and big-business cartels and combinations set prices unchecked, so that while farm prices fell, prices of manufactured goods rose somewhat. Also, the GOP gave its blessing to a return to high protective tariffs, reversing the Wilsonian policy. The Fordney-McCumber Act of 1922 was a foretaste of the Smoot-Hawley Act of 1930, each in succession raising tariffs to new heights. The return to high protective tariffs hurt the farmer by making it more difficult for foreign nations to buy American products; thus the great staple crops, produced in overabundance in the United States, could not be disposed of in foreign markets. Income taxes were reduced by the

Issues of the 1920s: the Democrats usher in Teapot Dome to join the others. (Clifford Berryman cartoon, Library of Congress)

Republicans; this helped the wealthy more than the poor. And the farmers were staggering under a burden of debt as usual; in the booming times during the war and immediately after, they had taken on new obligations for land, machinery, and public services. Then they watched the descending prices of wheat and cotton and once more thought of themselves as among the underprivileged. They asked why other producers got advantages, such as monopoly and the tariff, while the farmers did not. They developed schemes for remedying this unfair situation, schemes which involved the active help of government. The only noise which spoiled the placid serenity of Coolidge prosperity was made by the farm bloc.

Coolidge vetoed the farm bloc's favorite measure, the McNary-Haugen bill, which proposed to raise prices by having the government buy up surplus farm products. The farmer declared that some way must be found to solve the problem of too much wheat on the world market, which depressed prices. There was no way in which millions of farmers scattered over the whole country could organize to control production; the government must find a way to provide the farmer with a "fair" income. Farmers thought the year 1920 provided a fair standard. The farm bloc was bipartisan, supported by agricultural congressmen and senators from both parties. The farmers' reasoning impressed Coolidge no more than that of the Populists had impressed McKinley. Congress passed the McNary-Haugen bill twice but could not find the two-thirds majority necessary to override the President's veto. The farmers remained a discontented minority.

Organized labor had supported La Follette in 1924 and was to support Al Smith in 1928; it certainly could not approve the antiunion attitudes and policies of the Republicans. But organized labor was not very strong, and perhaps not very unhappy, at this time. Real wages did not rise as much as profits, but they did not fall, as farm income did. The well-organized AFL still represented the "aristocracy of labor," which was not doing badly during the 1920s with its great building boom. The unskilled and semiskilled remained largely unorganized. The grim struggle in the steel mills during the great strike of 1919–1920 had ended disastrously again for the steelworkers. They, as well as the coal miners, worked long hours for comparatively low wages and often lived in semifeudal conditions of complete dependence on the "company." The "company town"—owned, governed, and completely controlled by the business corporation involved—was typical of coal and steel enterprises. That organization which before the war had been doing most to organize the less skilled and mass-production workers, the IWW was now discredited and crushed because of its associations with wartime disloyalty and revolutionary radicalism.

For these reasons labor was not a very formidable adversary of the reigning conservatism of the 1920s. But beneath the surface a good deal of bitterness was accumulating. To prevent the spread of unionism, employers still commonly depended upon such devices as the use of spies and strikebreaking thugs, the injunction, and the yellow-dog contract. During this period some new chapters were written in the long and bloody history of labor violence in the United States. The "open-shop" principle was still enshrined as sacred in the law, and the Supreme Court also continued to uphold the legality of the yellow-dog contract and of the labor injunction. The latter was finally to be prohibited in 1932 in the Norris–La Guardia Act. The Republican party at this time was frankly opposed to the growth of trade-unionism, and in this it undoubtedly had the support of the dominant middle classes. They believed in the liberty of the employer to hire and fire as he saw fit and to pay what wages the market would bear. Agreeing with this philosophy, a conservative Supreme Court on several notable occasions in this decade threw out laws regulating the conditions of labor, wages, and working hours. Such were, for example, the much discussed cases of *Bailey v. Drexel Furniture Co.* (1922), involving child labor, and *Adkins v. Children's Hospital* (1923), involving minimum wages. Against this there echoed the cry of organized labor: "The labor of a human being is not a commodity." In the strife between owner and employee, which the Industrial Revolution had unhappily accentuated, the owner was on top during the 1920s, though the industrial worker gave indications that he resented the fact and thought it had been brought about by unfair means. But with relatively little unemployment and no general fall in wages, the 1920s produced no major labor question.

Judged by the amount of public comment, the leading issue of the times was prohibition. The war against alcohol was not a new one in the United States. The temperance movement before the Civil War will be recalled, and in 1884 there was a national Prohibition party which, so one explanation of that famous election runs, took enough votes away from Blaine in New York to lose him the presidency. In the days of progressivism, the idea of prohibition was to be found in many areas along with other sorts of reform. The organization of the Anti-Saloon League in 1895 was a landmark in the crusade for a national prohibition amendment. The Eighteenth Amendment to the Constitution finally was approved in the atmosphere of the Great Crusade, with its stress on sacrifice and abstinence to further the war effort, with its high-minded idealism and slight overtone of hysteria. After all, the Germans were addicted to beer. A most assiduous and effective "dry" lobby helped put it across, and some thought the absence of 2 million young men had something to do with it. In fact, this does not seem to have been true; the job of lining up enough states had already been done, in the main, before 1918.

In the last analysis, such a regulation was a tribute to the enduring Puritanism of America. A similar movement in Great Britain met overwhelming defeat and became a national joke. Within a few years, prohibition almost became a joke in this country too, and one wondered how it had ever been passed. H. L. Mencken thought it probably the most foolish law ever passed by a civilized state, and many less addicted to a sociable glass of beer than the famous Baltimorean were inclined to agree. Was it not, at least, properly a local matter? If the dry belt wished to be dry, why should it impose its standards on other parts of the country? In many circles, the glass of beer or the highball was a gregarious habit not easily broken, and the law which sought to prevent it was likely to be regarded with irritation and contempt. Prohibition nevertheless found impassioned defenders. In the age of the automobile, no one could have a right to drunkenness. It became all too clear, however, that the law was not only impossible to enforce, but productive of much evil in the form of gangsterism and graft. The rise of organized crime as big business was perhaps the most sensational feature of the decade, and certainly the least savory. The traffic in illicit liquor, a billion dollar business, was the chief cause of this unhappy development.

In 1928 the Democrats, as they nominated the colorful Al Smith, product of the city of New York, took up the cause of repeal of the Eighteenth Amendment. Their platform was ambiguous, but the vigorous Smith did not conceal his "wet" opinions. As a notable reform governor of the State of New York, he was somewhat progressive in his political views and tried to make an issue of the GOP's big-business conservatism; but far more people, evidently, were interested in his views on alcohol and in his religion. Smith had triumphed over the rival faction within his party partly because the lesson of 1924 seemed to teach clearly that the Democrats must be a progressive party, and partly because his rival McAdoo had fallen under a cloud of scandal. Yet the party had not healed its breach, and to southern Democrats a candidate from New York who was both a Roman Catholic and a wet was most unsatisfactory. The rural South and West was the citadel of "nativism" as well as of Prohibition: no "Popery" and no strong drink. As it turned out, the courageous Smith was to pay the price of his religion. No Roman Catholic, it appeared, could win the presidency. Vicious attacks on him as "Alcohol Al," who would destroy the public schools and turn the country over to the rule of Rome, helped send Smith down to defeat.

"Silent Cal" had, ironically enough, opened his mouth just once too often and had said the wrong thing: "I do not choose to run." He probably expected to be coaxed to accept another term, but to his private annoyance the party took him at his word and looked about for a more impressive but equally "safe" candidate. At Kansas City, in 1928, the GOP chose Herbert Hoover, who had served in both the Harding and Coolidge Cabinets, after gaining fame as an able war administrator under Wilson. Hoover was a mining engineer and businessman himself and was the favorite of businessmen. He was never a politician's politician, but support for him was too great to be denied by the professionals. As Secretary of Commerce he had worked vigorously in cooperation with business, helping it to find export markets and to organize trade associations. His administrative ability was not in doubt. Once considered something of a liberal, he was now conservative to the core. The country would surely be safe in his cool, efficient, conservative hands. Hoover never had popular glamour; some called him a cold fish. But, running on a platform pledged to continuation of "safe and sane" Republican policies, he easily defeated Smith. The Democrats even lost, for the first time since 1876, some states of the Solid South.

This election of 1928, in which religion, prohibition, and economic issues were so curiously mingled, was surely a tribute to the apparently solid success of Republican rule. That rule had been accompanied by extraordinary economic prosperity. It was difficult to get a hearing for any kind of reform issues in such a situation. The Harding and Coolidge administrations had raised tariffs, reduced income taxes, left the trusts alone, and thrown their weight against both labor unions and farmers' movements, in the name of an economic philosophy of unadulterated "free enterprise." And it seemed to work—for a few years.

FOREIGN POLICY

The United States had refused to enter the League of Nations primarily because this had seemed too great a commitment to assume in a violently unstable world. American opinion swung sharply away from the almost ecstatic mood of a holy war which had prevailed in 1918. The mood of the times was one of complete disillusion with the recent Great Crusade. America was disgusted with Europe, and with herself for having been so foolish as to have become involved in a European war. The reason for this was, no doubt, that the war had been oversold. It had not been put forward as a sober matter of national interest, distasteful but necessary; inevitably, perhaps, it had been presented as a highly moral and idealistic crusade. To "save the world for democracy," to produce a "just and lasting peace," to create a wholly new spirit of "world community"—these were laudable objectives, without which America would never have entered the war. But the real world which was to be seen at Paris in 1919, and in later world developments, hardly agreed with this ideal world seen through a haze of Wilsonian rhetoric. In the postwar world there seemed less democracy in the world, not more; there was just as much selfish nationalism. The old tradition of noninvolvement, which was at the bottom an assertion of moral superiority to Europe, now came back.

During the 1920s, moreover, serious doubt was thrown by historical research on that simple faith held by Americans during the war that the Central Powers had been the unmitigated villains of the piece. A vast amount of information became available about the origins of the war; and as scholars (and some pseudo scholars) sorted it all out, they reached conclusions which might differ in detail but certainly agreed in a broad rejection of wartime propaganda. Some British officials even confessed that American opinion had been played upon by deliberate lies and deception. All this led to a fresh wave of disgust and disillusion, a reaction which was quite as irrational as the earlier anti-German hysteria and almost equally strong.

An interminable and corroding quarrel with the erstwhile Allies about "war debts" helped poison relations between the United States and Europe. But this was itself a reflection of the new American attitude. Popular opinion now demanded, in effect, that Europe be punished for her sins by being made to pay back every cent (or almost) of the money we had loaned her. To the British and French, "U.S." now seemed to stand for "Uncle Shylock," demanding his pound of flesh from peoples who had shed their blood in the common cause while America mostly reaped profits. Coolidge responded with a dry "They hired the money, didn't they?" Behind this apparently mercenary attitude was a feeling that Europeans might not indulge in bouts of pointless bloodshed if they knew they could not finance them with dollars. When they protested an inability to pay, we pointed sternly to their continuing expenditures on armaments. Coolidge would have been astounded if he could have seen ahead twenty-five years to a time when, after another great war, America would press money on Europe for armaments. Very different was the situation in the 1920s.

Throughout the 1920s and into the next decade, the United States remained deeply suspicious of anything that looked like an attempt to get it involved in an

"You Can't Have Both." Americans found it hard to understand why Britain and France, especially the latter, refused to pay their war debts yet insisted upon expensive military preparations. (By Rollin Kirby, Library of Congress)

"entangling alliance." Most Americans were convinced that there should be no political cooperation with the League. The United States did cooperate freely with its nonpolitical agencies, engaged in a variety of economic, humanitarian, and technical activities. But so intense was the suspicion of the League that the Senate refused to permit American association with the World Court, though Presidents Coolidge, Hoover, and Roosevelt recommended it. Accepting the jurisdiction of the court was purely voluntary, yet the bare possibility that it might involve us in the League's political activities, via the court's right of issuing advisory opinions requested by the League, was enough to kill American membership. An almost pathological fear of being trapped into some commitment in Europe by the wiles of the French foreign office was a feature of American policy and opinion until

about 1938. One seldom found so much unanimity as there was on this point— that the United States would not again desert her traditional neutrality and form an alliance of any sort.

On the other hand, this did not mean a complete rejection of interest in peace. Americans assured themselves that they stood ready to do what they could in other ways. If this attitude often seemed hypocritical to Europeans, it was nonetheless sincerely held. And in fact, the United States displayed some activity in world affairs. In 1924 and again in 1929 American cooperation was evident in the Dawes Plan and the Young Plan, which scaled down German reparations and provided for loans to Germany. The irony often noted in this solution is that American loans to Germany paid for reparations, which in turn paid for war debts—so that we were in effect paying ourselves and might have profitably canceled the whole cycle of debts which plagued international trade and caused bitter resentments. Yet American opinion remained strongly set against any cancellation, and as late as 1932 the war-debts question continued to be a source of recriminations across the Atlantic. In that year of world depression the European debtor nations simply stopped paying, in spite of energetic American protests. They argued that towering American tariff walls, exemplified in the Smoot-Hawley Act of 1930, made it virtually impossible for them to pay in the only way international payment is ultimately possible, namely, by shipment of goods. If the United States was to be the great creditor nation of the world, she should adjust her economic policies to that role and should buy the goods and services of others.

In the 1920s America's chief contribution to world peace was to the cause of disarmament. She participated actively in several disarmament conferences, among which the great Washington Conference of 1921–1922 was the most important. Charles Evans Hughes, Harding's Secretary of State, was an able man, not content with a wholly passive policy. Impelled by the adoption of a Senate resolution, he called a conference at Washington to discuss general disarmament in 1921. This conference ended by concluding significant treaties dealing with the Far East as well as with the reduction of certain types of naval armaments. Japan took advantage of the European war to play a most aggressive role in the Far East, and we at all times looked upon this area in rather a different light from that in which we viewed Europe. The Open Door policy was threatened with extinction. By several treaties and agreements the powers concerned with Far Eastern problems sought to stabilize the situation. For one thing, they agreed to respect the territorial integrity and Open Door in China and to give China the fullest opportunity to develop and maintain a stable government. In keeping with this attitude, the same powers agreed to adjustments in the Chinese tariffs which prepared the way for tariff autonomy—a goal attained in 1929. While Japan kept some of her wartime gains, especially possession of the former German islands in the north Pacific, she agreed to withdraw from the Shantung peninsula and from Siberia. The principal naval powers—Great Britain, the United States, France, and Japan —agreed to consult with each other about any threat to the existing balance of power in the western Pacific.

The disarmament goals of the Washington Conference were partly achieved by an agreement on a naval ratio for capital ships between the major powers, in which Japan accepted a ratio of three ships to five for the United States and five for Great Britain. This 5:5:3 ratio was not wholly unfavorable to Japan, in view of the fact that in any Pacific war she would be operating in her home waters. And the United States also agreed not to fortify her possessions in the western Pacific, that is, the Philippines, Guam, and Samoa. The Washington treaties seem on the whole to have been a fair compromise in which each side gave up something. Contingent, like all treaties, on the good faith of the parties concerned, they worked well enough in the 1920s, when Japan under moderate leadership was not aggressive. They broke down in the 1930s when Japan, no longer willing to accept the *status quo* they represented, embarked upon an aggressive course.

Other American proposals for disarmament failed. The conference showed that it was much easier to get an agreement in principle on the desirability of disarmament than it was to work out the details. France and some other European states would much rather have had America arm herself and help police Europe, but this was not the American position at that time. During the 1920s the United States was generally to be found preaching sermons on disarmament to unappreciative French listeners. France persistently argued that she could not risk disarmament unless the United States were willing to help guarantee European stability. But this America had no intention of doing; never had public opinion been more strongly in favor of the old policy of "staying out of Europe's quarrels." The cause of disarmament was popular, and France was usually condemned for her attitude. The United States set an example for the cause by herself heavily slashing military expenditures, against the

Coolidge signing the Kellogg Pact. (World Wide Photos)

vain protests of army and navy people.

This attitude toward the problem was seen at its peak in the American-sponsored Kellogg-Briand Peace Pact of 1928. The original suggestion for a Franco-American nonaggression pact came from France, but in the form it finally took, the pact followed American thinking, and in fact the French were disappointed at the outcome. Under this pact, sixty-two nations pledged themselves to "renounce war as an instrument of national policy" and settle their disputes only "by pacific means." The Kellogg Pact agitation affords evidence against the view often expressed that Americans had lost all interest in world affairs at this time. It attested to considerable popular concern, whatever view one might take of its wisdom. Millions of earnest people, organized in dozens of peace societies, backed the great crusade to outlaw war, and literally forced the pact on a somewhat

reluctant government. They greeted its promulgation with hosannas of joy.

The significance of the pact was uncertain. Some advocates of enforced peace ridiculed it as a meaningless gesture. It was indeed a treaty without visible means of support, no procedures of any sort for carrying it out being mentioned. On the other hand, it could have sweeping consequences. Three years later, at the time of the Sino-Japanese dispute over Manchuria, Secretary of State Stimson pointed out that the pact had abolished neutrality in the old sense; hereafter, in any war, one or both of the belligerents would be treaty violators, and all other states must treat them as such. Eleven years later, the Kellogg Pact became a strong argument used by those who sought repeal of our neutrality laws in order to give all possible aid to one side in the European war. By "outlawing war," obviously, the pact greatly altered the legal conception of war and opened up alternate paths of policy. In 1928 many Americans believed it was the first cautious step toward a closer American approach to European political affairs. American participation in the Geneva Disarmament Conference, and in the League deliberations of 1931–1932 relating to Manchuria, somewhat encouraged this hope.

Within the Western Hemisphere, there seemed a significant evolution of good will. The decade brought its misunderstandings, but it also brought progress toward neighborly relations with Latin America. When Calvin Coolidge used American marines in 1926 to put down a revolution in Nicaragua, he was only doing what custom had decreed ever since the time of Theodore Roosevelt. But this time there was an outcry in this country of surprising proportions. Since the United States was playing the role of righteous critic of European political morality, it could not afford to be cast in the role of imperialist. We must stop bullying our smaller neighbors to the south, no matter what provocation they gave us. Herbert Hoover may reasonably claim to have inaugurated the "Good Neighbor" policy for which his Democratic successor got most of the credit. It was obvious by 1930 that the United States had renounced, probably for all time, the "big stick" policy of direct intervention in the internal affairs of Latin-American states.* The ill will it aroused was simply too great, nor would American opinion now tolerate it. In fact as well as in theory, the United States now began to assume the "moral leadership" of this hemisphere. Even when Mexico expropriated American property without compensation in 1938, few seriously proposed our using force. But by that time events in Europe and Asia were again ominous, and the friendship of Latin America became most important.

That story we must leave for another chapter. The first real sign of a renewal of international conflict on a serious scale was to come in 1931, when Japan would clash with China in Manchuria and when in Germany the violently nationalist party led by Adolf Hitler would suddenly increase its strength. The years between 1924 and 1929 were hopeful ones, marked by encouraging signs of Franco-German reconciliation in Europe. Perhaps had the great economic depression not poisoned the diplomatic soil, this peace plant might have taken root and flourished. But it was all too fragile. There were to be many who later reproached powerful America, now

the world's greatest nation, for a sad failure to assume her share of the responsibility for maintaining world stability in this decade after World War I. Her record in the 1920s was not, as we have seen, a wholly negative one, yet on the whole it seems reasonable to agree that a desperately unstable world badly needed more American help in all its pressing problems if another costly war was to be avoided. For this, however, American opinion was simply not ready.

THE SOCIAL SCENE

What politics lacked in energy and creativity was offset by other phases of life in the 1920s. No decade in American history has offered more to the social historian or to the student of ideas and literature. The "Jazz Age" has been much emphasized. This was the era of "speakeasies," of "flaming youth," of the "lost generation," in which, as an aftermath of Armageddon, a kind of desperate desire for amusement prevailed. This decade coined the word "ballyhoo" and reserved its greatest enthusiasm for events like the Dempsey-Tunney prize fight and Charles A. Lindbergh's transatlantic flight. It was the time of the big money, when speculators pushed stock and land prices up to the sky; when, also, gangsters shot it out with machine guns on city streets for the control of vast empires of alcohol and sin. All this, and more, lent to the era a slightly insane air. H. L. Mencken, the Baltimore writer whose sardonic cynicism was a part of the era, called it the greatest show on earth. Perhaps this aspect has been exaggerated by some writers. Certainly it is not true that all or most Americans lost their sobriety, made gin in their bathtubs, or sat on flagpoles. But in the absence of more serious issues, pop-

* In the Far East, also, the United States showed marked patience during the stormy Chinese Revolution culminating in 1927, and refused to intervene with military forces.

Ku Klux Klan. The weirdly hooded clansmen assemble in West Virginia for their favorite pastime, the burning of fiery crosses. Other Klan activities were less innocent. The national revival of the Reconstruction order for several years in the mid-1920s was a sign of the times. (Library of Congress)

ular interest as reflected in the chief newspaper headlines of these years did seem to be directed toward a variety of frivolous topics, while a number of significant changes in manners and morals disturbed the even tenor of life.

Much of this period was not very edifying. The decade began, as we noted, in fear and bewilderment. It will always be associated not only with a cheerful gaiety but also with a narrow nationalism and a fierce spirit of intolerance toward any nonconformity. It started off with a "Red scare," the intensity of which was certainly out of all proportion to the real threat of revolution. Communism was indeed abroad in the world, but election figures indicated that fewer than one American in every 2,000 sympathized with its doctrines. But IWW "Wobblies" were lynched, and there was a wholesale de-

parting of alleged "subversives," some of whom were certainly anti-Communist. This tendency to see Communists lurking under every bed, which was likely to victimize perfectly innocent liberals and pinch off freedom of expression, had a dramatic climax in the Sacco-Vanzetti case, a celebrated trial which was heatedly discussed all over the world. A robbery near Boston in 1920, which resulted in the murder of two guards, was pinned on two Italian anarchists, who were convicted of the crime and eventually executed for it. The suspicion existed at the time and has since grown that the evidence was insufficient and that the jury, the public, and the judge himself were deeply prejudiced against the accused. If, as most students of the case have concluded, there was a serious miscarriage of justice here, it was due to the hysteria about radicalism.

Behind this hysteria lay fear, detached observers agreed—although what it was that powerful America was afraid of is harder to say. Irrational fear was directed against more things than merely communism, though the latter—along with all forms of social radicalism—was a prominent target. There were many fears. Popular books dwelt on fear of the "yellow peril," fear of racial "mongrelization," fear of a Jewish conspiracy, a Catholic one, an atheist one. In Chicago, Mayor "Big Bill" Thompson aroused a crusade based on fear that the British were corrupting American patriotism, and in Detroit, Henry Ford's newspaper solemnly gave credence to a notorious forgery concerning the Jews which Adolf Hitler was to use with good effect in Germany. In flight from a confusing world, America reached back to an older nativism and embraced what a foreign observer called the cult of the native-born—"America fo

Regular Americans." The most extraordinary manifestation of this was the remarkable revival of the Ku Klux Klan.
This organization became a power not
only in the southern states but in the Middle West; it was strong enough to capture
political control of several middle-western
states in the mid-twenties before declining
after exposure of extensive fraud in its
higher circles. The renewal of racial violence in the South, while alarming enough,
was not so surprising as the spread of
racial and also religious bigotry across the
whole country. It was an astonishing sight
to see citizens of the state of Indiana arming themselves against a rumored invasion
by the Pope. Into this picture of prejudice,
of course, fits the election of 1928 with its
vote of religious intolerance against that
firm Democrat, Al Smith.

This same spirit aided materially the
passing of acts (1921, 1924) which finally ended the days of extensive immigration. While many who were not bigots
supported restriction of immigration, this
debate was marked by a great deal of
racial prejudice. The "new" immigration
from eastern and southern Europe which
was the target of restrictionists was frequently called "biologically inferior,"
"degraded," "foul and loathsome." Since
about 1890 there had been a persistent
but heretofore largely unsuccessful campaign to reverse the traditional policy of
allowing almost unrestricted entrance into
the United States. Some had alleged, and
others denied, that the influx of immigrants resulted in a lowered standard of
living for "native" Americans. It had been
asserted, and denied, that the immigrants
were responsible for such evils as political
corruption. The Chinese had been excluded in 1882, and the Japanese by
agreement with Japan in 1907. Cleveland, Taft, and Wilson had all vetoed a

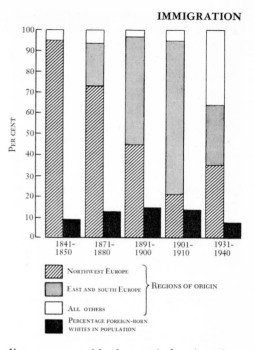

IMMIGRATION

NORTHWEST EUROPE

EAST AND SOUTH EUROPE } REGIONS OF ORIGIN

ALL OTHERS

PERCENTAGE FOREIGN-BORN
WHITES IN POPULATION

literacy test, with the reminder that thus
to discriminate against the poor was not
the American tradition and that our best
citizens today came from groups once
themselves called "undesirable." The coming of a million immigrants a year gave
some the impression of a tidal-wave
"invasion," but in fact the percentage of
foreign-born in the country increased but
very slightly between 1860 and 1920.
The place of origin of most immigrants
did shift very markedly from northern
and western Europe to southern and eastern. Majority opinion before the war was
probably reaching the conclusion that
certain types of unskilled labor should be
excluded. But the legislation of the 1920s
was strongly affected by the illiberal anti-
alien sentiment of the period, the same
sort that produced the Ku Klux Klan.
In 1924, a quota system was adopted,
aimed at choking off immigration from
the "less desirable" countries by basing
the number who could enter on popula-

tion percentages in the year 1890, prior to the major influx from the new areas.* In 1929 new restrictions were inaugurated which limited the total number of immigrants and favored northern Europeans, thus making the quota system permanent.

Intolerance was thus one aspect of this period, but a spirit of gay abandon was another. What William Allen White had in mind when he called it "the gaudy, bawdy, hell-roaring decade" were the speakeasies, the gangsters, and the abandonment of moral restraints. On its worst side, this gave rise to an alarming wave of criminal violence. The gunmen of Mr. Al Capone gave Chicago a reputation for lawlessness it has had difficulty living down, but racketeering and gangsterism were far from unknown in other cities. The gangsters waxed fat on the profits from the vast illegal trade in bootleg liquor. Until its repeal in 1933 the Eighteenth Amendment was certainly a prominent cause of gangsterism, but not the only one. A serious decline in civilized standards was indicated by the fact that gangsters and gunmen evidently moved in the most respectable circles of society. The free-and-easy atmosphere of this period seemed to approve success, no matter how attained, and to sneer at any sort of moral scruples as hopelessly old-fashioned.

The younger generation especially, filled with a vague sense of revolt and with exciting new ideas provided by Sigmund Freud and Karl Marx, shocked conservatives by their apparent willingness to flout conventional morality. Flaming youth emerged among the respectable

* The Japanese were singled out for complete exclusion in 1924, despite the protests of Secretary of State Hughes, who pointed out that this was a needless insult to that nation and violated an agreement with Japan. This action gave great offense to the Japanese and caused a violent anti-American reaction there.

middle class. Perhaps the war had done as much as the psychological theories of Freud (which were interpreted as suggesting a casting aside of inhibitions) to introduce new standards of sexual behavior; and some students of the question were inclined to assign some credit or blame to the automobile. At any rate, old standards of social behavior appeared to be breaking down. Girls smoked, wore lipstick and short skirts, and indulged in "petting parties." Though no Kinsey then appeared to provide thorough documentation of the trend, it was widely realized that a sexual freedom had begun to prevail which some found shocking, though others regarded it as a constructive freeing of sex from an injurious hypocrisy. Salacious sex scandals provided many of the headlines of these years.

There were other, more innocent diversions. Babe Ruth's hitting of sixty home runs, Lindbergh's spectacular flight across the ocean, and Floyd Collins trapped in a cave often seemed far more interesting than political or international issues. Perhaps the most notable story of a decade which was rich in sensational happenings occurred in Dayton, Tennessee. There, in the summer of 1925, William Jennings Bryan, veteran Democratic political leader and a deeply religious man, took part as prosecutor in a trial on which all America turned its eyes. The defendant was a Tennessee schoolteacher named John T. Scopes, who had violated a state law prohibiting the teaching of the theory of evolution. His attorney was the famous lawyer and religious skeptic Clarence Darrow, and the case turned into an argument between Bryan and Darrow on the issue of religious "fundamentalism," or the Bible versus modern science and scholarship. This was not exactly a frivolous matter, and the fact that the whole nation found it absorbing does not seem to testify to the flightiness of this era, as some would have it, but rather the opposite. But it was not altogether flattering to the nation to find such laws as this being passed, and such arguments as Bryan's being used, in the twentieth century.

More important perhaps than all these sensational stories, deeper changes were going on in American society. The American economy, always dynamic, now ushered in what some called "the second industrial revolution." Based on new techniques of mass production, productivity soared to new heights. Between 1885 and 1930 the average output of the American worker just about doubled. "In America," a French visitor commented, "the daily life of the majority is conceived on a scale that is reserved for the privileged classes anywhere else. . . . One could feed a whole country in the Old World on what America wastes."* For example, the American people owned 81 per cent of all the automobiles in the world, and President Hoover was predicting two cars in every garage as an early probability. The application of vast quantities of machinery to the production of goods was accompanied by scientific efforts to maximize the efficiency of the factory workers who tended the machines. Symbol of this new America to all the world was Henry Ford, mass-production wizard of the automobile industry. During this prosperous decade the journals were full of optimistic economic theories which reasoned that with the aid of mass production a way had finally been found to avoid slumps and create perpetual prosperity. After 1929 such thinking appeared bitterly ironic, and in

* André Siegfried, *America Comes of Age*, Harcourt, Brace and Co., Inc., New York, 1927, p. 160.

the light of cold analysis the fabled prosperity of the 1920s turned out to have had some decidedly weak spots. Yet the remarkable growth of new industries, including radio and motion pictures as well as automobiles, sustained an exciting boom which brought many people handsome profits in speculation on rising land and stock values. It also brought America an international reputation as the land of industrial miracles and an unbelievably high standard of living.

The great Florida real estate boom, during which a lot might change hands dozens of times a day, and the great "bull" market on Wall Street, which sent security prices soaring to delirious peaks, were typical of this decade. Then came the great crash and a quick sobering up, in the light of which all that had happened seemed like a weird dream. Judgments often pronounced on the irresponsibility of this "incredible era" were made in the atmosphere of the years of the Great Depression. Irresponsible, childish, and sometimes alarming it often was. It was also exciting and creative. The second industrial revolution did hold out the possibility of "the final abolition of poverty," however badly it got off the track in 1929. And in another field, that of literature and ideas, this decade proved to be an unusually rich one.

THE REVOLT OF THE INTELLECTUALS

No decade in American history has been more fruitful in ideas and creative literature than this one. American writers for the first time since Emerson's day became widely known all over the world in considerable numbers. The novels of Sinclair Lewis, Ernest Hemingway, William Faulkner, John Dos Passos, and others had tremendous vitality. The magazine *Poetry* served as midwife to the birth of a vigorous American verse. Older writers such as Theodore Dreiser, Edwin Arlington Robinson, and Edith Wharton were stimulated to do some of their best writing at this time. The literary critic who has surveyed this period with perhaps the greatest care holds that "rarely in history has there been such a release of the creative spirit as there has been in our time in America." This judgment may be too enthusiastic, yet it is hardly too much to say that the 1920s brought American literature and thought to a new stature. Achievements in the writing of philosophy, history, and related branches of thought were also notable.

The stimulus to these achievements had been provided in large part by the crumbling of old values and the need to find new ones. Something like an intellectual revolution took place during and after the great war. Manners and morals underwent a change, as we have seen; old truths no longer stood, and the younger generation felt impelled to search for new values. A general uneasiness had come over Western civilization, for the war had dealt a blow to that easy faith in unlimited progress which that civilization had held for a century. Prophets of despair appeared; the idea of violent revolution emerged. Brilliant as it was, this generation of writers was restless, rootless, and critical.

Most especially it was ready to engage in a remorseless criticism of American life. The literary renaissance long awaited by thoughtful Americans arrived in these years only to be associated with a spirit of cynicism and despair which resulted in searing attacks on American civilization. An important manifesto published in 1922 by a large group of the younger in-

tellectuals, called *Civilization in the United States,* was savagely critical. Many of these younger literary radicals then made their way across the Atlantic, to spend the next few years roaming Europe. Americans of the "lost generation" in Europe form the theme of one of the great novels of the decade, Ernest Hemingway's *The Sun Also Rises.* They were voluntary exiles from a civilization in America which, they charged, was narrow, materialistic, and without appreciation of art or beauty. The symposium referred to above spoke of "emotional and esthetic starvation" in the United States. Those who stayed at home wrote scorching satires on American life, such as Sinclair Lewis's notable series of novels about small-town life, or engaged in vituperative criticism, as did the acknowledged leader of the "civilized minority" of dissident intellectuals, the talented Henry L. Mencken.

Mencken, a spirit so uninhibited and a writer so gifted that the Baltimore *Sun* soon gave him a free rein, reached his peak in the 1920s, when he was editing *Smart Set* and *Mercury* in addition to serving as editorialist, reporter, and columnist for the newspaper. He was deeply influenced by Nietzsche, George Bernard Shaw, and the beer halls of Baltimore; his love was the English language and his mission to "debunk" nearly everything. Mencken was among those who announced that the United States had as yet produced no literature beyond that of a "respectable mediocrity." He held this to be the result of a "national distrust of ideas" that was a product of Puritanism, democracy, and materialism. For their mediocrity and hypocrisy he hated businessmen and clergymen, but he was no lauder of pedagogues and political reformers. Mencken's role as the American Voltaire had a climax in his covering of the Scopes trial, when he corched Bryan and the "gaping primates" who idolized the Great Commoner. His spirited nonconformism opened the eyes of many young people in the 1920s, encouraging them to think for themselves and join in the "revolt of the intellectuals."

Though new in its magnitude, this revolt had some precedents in the past. The aesthetic weakness of American civilization had been noted often; some traced it back to the Puritans. The low regard in which creative literature and art were held had long disturbed American writers. In his book *Portrait of the Artist as American* (1930), Matthew Josephson stressed the plight of unhappy, isolated American writers of the preceding generations, all studies in frustration. The writers he dealt with (Stephen Crane, Emily Dickinson, Lafcadio Hearn, Ambrose Bierce, E. A. Robinson) are now all recognized as among America's greatest literary figures, but they were for the most part neglected and bitter while they lived. Against this neglect of the artist the younger generation of literary rebels, growing to maturity in the restless atmosphere of the war, now protested.

They protested particularly against a business civilization, dominated by purely material values and by the machine. "I hate your city," someone says in Sinclair Lewis's novel *Babbitt*. "It has standardized all the beauty out of life. It is one big railroad station." The machine seemed to be conquering men. The urban masses, constituting now three-fourths of America, had more leisure and more money than ever before, but the culture which nourished them was cheap and mass-produced, consisting of stereotyped movies, radio programs, magazines, and newspapers, all as standardized as the breakfast food on the morning table. America had been transformed by the march of industry into a place with more wealth but less joy. The sharp pen of Sinclair Lewis created, in George W. Babbitt, small-town businessman, the classic type against which the intellectuals were in rebellion. Babbitt led an essentially joyless life, devoted wholly to the tedious game of money making and keeping up with the neighbors. The writers of this rebel generation repeated in their own way the cry of Emerson and Thoreau: if American civilization is to realize its potentialities it must escape from the grip of moral timidity, smallmindedness, and an ignoble materialism. It is noteworthy that a large number of these writers came from small towns; a whole school of novels in the 1920s could be categorized as "the revolt against the village." It was in the smaller cities that community pressure could be exerted against any sort of nonconformity. The novels of the 1920s often depict unusual individuals frustrated by or crushed under the tyranny of a small-minded public opinion.

Intellectual groups in their criticism of American life adopted a variety of different positions. On the left, the psychological theories of Sigmund Freud or the views of Karl Marx, as now thrust upon the world through the medium of the Russian Revolution, provided rallying points for those who emphasized their rejection of a stale pattern of culture by becoming "bohemians." Best-known home of this literary left wing was Greenwich Village in New York City, where unconventional behavior was the norm. But there were others who deplored the new freedom and yearned for an older, more stable, and aristocratic order. Such, for example, was the southern agrarian group, with headquarters in Nashville, who damned the modern industrial and democratic world in the name of the plantation-aristocracy tradition. In 1931 they issued their manifesto, entitled *I'll Take My Stand.* These conservative movements regretted the decay of religion, the breakdown of standards, and the tendency toward naturalistic frankness in literature. From the literary Marxists to the literary reactionaries, American *avant-garde* thought displayed a wide range of attitudes, and stimulating controversy was common among the intellectuals themselves.

One thing in common among these groups was a sharply critical attitude toward the existing pattern of civilization in America. A decided cleavage existed between the "civilized minority" and the masses. The former underscored their separation from the latter by generally refusing to take much interest in political questions; Walter Lippmann complained that "no intelligent man can afford to be caught holding the illusion that any public event matters very much." As for the general public reaction to the writers, it was put to a test when at the end of the decade Sinclair Lewis won the Nobel prize for world literature. There was a decided uncertainty about whether America ought to cheer the honor to an American or resent the recognition of a critic of American life.

In the end, a majority cheered. Emerson, Walt Whitman, and Mark Twain had also refused to treat some American characteristics as sacred.

The America of the 1920s stood in considerable need of criticism. The bigotry of the Ku Klux Klan, the ignorance displayed in the Scopes case, the moral irresponsibility indicated by the rise of gangsterism, the silliness reflected in the popular worship of movie stars and sports heroes— all this was nothing to be proud of. The intellectuals who were repelled by it were perhaps also guilty of certain sins: an overly supercilious attitude, a false sophistication, a tendency to sneer rather than provide responsible criticism. They were, however, not the least interesting and significant part of a decade that seemed always to produce extremes. Lying sharply delineated between the end of World War I and the collapse of the Wall Street market in the autumn of 1929, it had its own special flavor, and it was colorful in the highest degree. A certain nostalgia for these carefree days may be found in most people who lived through them. But one day in 1929 the spectacular crash of the stock market and the onset of the Great Depression brought the Jazz Age to an abrupt end.

FURTHER READINGS

The 1920s have become legendary. Such political accounts as Samuel Hopkins Adams, *The Incredible Era* (1939); William Allen White's biography of Coolidge, *A Puritan in Babylon* (1938); and Karl Schriftgiesser, *This Was Normalcy* (1948), leave the impression of a descent into the abyss. Descriptions of the social scene in the manner of Frederick Lewis Allen, *Only Yesterday* (1931), or Lloyd Morris, *Postscript to Yesterday* (1947), delightfully ex-

plore the lighter side of this era, which other books characterize by such phrases as "aspirin age," "fantastic interim," and "era of wonderful nonsense." In foreign policy, such books as Denna F. Fleming, *The United States and World Organization, 1920–1933* (1938), perpetuated the view that a sort of criminal irresponsibility existed.

More serious scholarship has scarcely caught up with much of recent history, but a number of works may be mentioned. A recent monograph of value is Robert K. Murray, *Red Scare: A Study in National Hysteria, 1919–1920* (1955). Two other recent studies of interest are Herbert Asbury, *The Great Illusion: An Informal History of Prohibition* (1950), and Edmund A. Moore, *A Catholic Runs for President* (1956). A number of excellent works on foreign policy have appeared, among them Robert H. Ferrell, *Peace in Their Time: The Origins of the Kellogg-Briand Pact* (1952) and *American Diplomacy, 1929–1933* (1957); John Chalmers Vinson, *The Parchment Peace* (1956) (the Washington Conference) and *Senator Borah and the Outlawry of War* (1958); Dorothy Borg, *American Policy and the Chinese Revolution* (1947); and Alexander DeConde, *Herbert Hoover's Latin American Policy* (1951).

Oscar Cargill, *Intellectual America* (1941), is a stimulating survey of American thought and letters, with emphasis on this fruitful decade. Such documents of the times as Malcolm Cowley, *Exile's Return* (1934), convey the flavor of the period as felt by the writers. One example of a writer's work presented in selected and accessible form is Alistair Cooke (ed.), *The Vintage Mencken* (1955), in a paperback edition. Industrial America, which the writers did not like but which made such great progress in this era, can be approached through Allan Nevins and Frank E. Hill, *Ford* (2 vols., 1954, 1957), and George H. Soule, *Prosperity Decade* (1947), volume 8 of a series on the economic history of the United States. Finally, John Higham has exhibited the "patterns of American nativism" in *Strangers in the Land* (1956).

For additional bibliography, see *Harvard Guide,* chapter 28.

TWENTY-FIVE

The Great Depression

1928
Stock market at peak.
Hoover defeats Smith in presidential
election.

1929
Agricultural Marketing Act passed.
Collapse of stock market, October 29.

1930
Smoot-Hawley Tariff passed.
Bank failures soar.

1931
Hoover moratorium on war debts.
Great Britain leaves gold standard.

1932
Unemployment reaches 15 million.
Reconstruction Finance Corporation
set up.
Bonus army driven out of Washington.
Moratorium on mortgage foreclosures.
Roosevelt defeats Hoover in landslide.

1933
Twentieth and Twenty-first Amendments
to Constitution.
Bank holiday.
New Deal begins.

FOOL'S PARADISE

BEGINNING IN 1929, the American people were plunged violently from the complacent dream of "the final victory over poverty" into the severest test of their courage and endurance, and of the stability of American institutions, since the Civil War. Their experiences during the bitter years of the Great Depression left a mark on the nation which was to last for decades. America's politics and her social and economic institutions were to be profoundly altered by this experience.

This Great Depression was unique not only because of its severity, but because, coming on top of a prosperity widely hailed as permanent, it brought bitter disillusionment and demands for action. During the 1920s men had become aware for the first time in history, perhaps, of a vision of real economic progress. The "second industrial revolution" with its technological miracles—in engineering, metallurgy, chemistry, electricity, fuels—suggested infinite possibilities for actually multiplying wealth. The Great Depression of 1929–1933 interrupted a dream of economic triumph and therefore seemed intolerable. It would be a mistake, of course, to think that economic depressions were new. It has been calculated that there were thirteen previous ones in American history, some mild but others, as, for example, those of 1873–1878 and 1893–1897, quite severe and quite long. They were invariably international in scope, with western Europe especially showing a close correlation with the United States. Economists took the "business cycle" for granted as an inevitable concomitant of

520

the free economic order, and people seem to have accepted depressions with a certain resignation, like bad weather.

If the economic freeze of 1929–1933 was not to be greeted so passively, the reason may well be found, first, in the point just made, that economic progress was now expected and a permanent abolition of poverty was regarded as possible for the first time in history. Second, there was the greater suffering which economic dislocations brought to a more specialized and urbanized economic order. Men had become dependent on the system and far less adaptable as individuals to economic distress. They could not so readily take up some other occupation, or go back to the farm, or migrate to another part of the country where opportunity might be greater. Caught up in an incredibly complex and interdependent economic pattern, they were almost helpless when it broke down.

We have mentioned how generally prosperous the 1920s seemed. In retrospect, after the great crash of 1929 and the severe depression that followed, it appeared that much had been wrong with the picture in this supposedly cloudless period. The "lords of creation," the leaders of business and government who presided over the American economy, were bitterly reproached for failures to observe warning signals. Very few people of any sort, however—though there were some—had seen the Depression coming. Most wisdom appeared, unfortunately, after the event. Beyond any question it would have required superhuman wisdom to have foreseen and provided a remedy for all the factors that seemed so obvious later. Yet it appears that the sluggishness of the government contributed to the coming of the Depression. Official policy during the 1920s encouraged a kind of complacent optimism. The same spirit prevailed after

the Depression had struck. Optimistic statements to the effect that "the worst is over," "business is fundamentally sound," and "prosperity is just around the corner" (a phrase that pursued the Republicans to defeat in 1932) issued from the White House and from prominent business circles with soothing regularity, while the economic machine was grinding to a halt, until finally an angry public turned bitterly on the men who uttered them.

It must be admitted, however, that virtually all previous economic theory supported these utterances. The Great Depression was to bring something of a revolution in economic thought, so that there is today a far greater readiness to consider business depressions as preventable or curable by government action of various sorts. But before 1929 there had scarcely been a challenge to the well-entrenched view of traditional economic theory that the economic mechanism is self-adjusting toward full or nearly full employment. Professional economists, with some few and hardly respectable exceptions, taught that to leave competition free, and not to meddle with the free and natural operation of economic laws, was a rule which, if followed, would ensure speedy recovery from any temporary kinks that might develop in the economic system. This was the great illusion under which almost all men lived: the illusion that a complicated economic system required no engineering but would automatically run itself if left untended. The course of the Great Depression which began dramatically in October, 1929, was to discredit this venerable theory.

FALSE PROSPERITY

A glance back at the prosperity of the "golden twenties," taken later from amid the shambles of the world's greatest de-

Unemployed occupy the Pennsylvania legislature at Harrisburg, 1936

Selling apples, a familiar Depression sight

A sharecropper's shack in southeast Missouri

A bread line

These pictures tell their own story. Want was nothing new, but the Great Depression of the 1930s, coming right after the supposed "final victory over poverty," was not to be suffered in silence, and an aroused people demanded that something be done about it. Poverty amid plenty was an intolerable paradox. What to do, however, was another question.

Slums in the nation's capital

pression, revealed that unhappily there had been flaws not much noted at the time. There were significant portions of the economy which were not prosperous at all even during the "prosperity decade." Most especially, as we have noted, agriculture had labored under difficulties ever since shortly after the war, the victim of falling world prices following the wartime boom, especially in wheat. These falling prices resulted from increased production by such grain-producing nations as Canada and Argentina, which began to outstrip the United States in the harvesting of wheat. At the same time, European nations became impressed with the wisdom of trying to become self-sufficient in foodstuffs in order to avoid the fate which had nearly overtaken blockaded Britain during the war. They sought self-sufficiency through the adoption of protective tariffs. At the same time, there were increases in yield per acre, the result of new machinery and improved breeds. All these factors made for excess supply. The American farmer was unable to curtail production because of the tremendous debt he had assumed in buying land and implements to meet the wartime demand. He was forced

to maintain or even expand production in the hope that the cash return might be sufficient to pay interest and principal on his mortgage. The circle of the farmer's trouble was completed with the fact that the taxes on his land and the prices he paid for the things he bought refused to follow farm prices downward. The decade of the twenties saw some American farmers squeezed dry between fixed costs and falling prices.

There had been a number of other sick industries, such as coal, railroads, and textiles. Significant pockets of unemployment appeared in areas where such industries were located. An accurate appraisal of unemployment throughout the nation is not possible, for the government did not then compile such figures. But some authorities state that an average of 10 per cent of the available labor force was unemployed in the 1920s, compared to a 4 or 5 per cent who would be out of work in normal full-employment conditions. It was to be pointed out that in actuality the prosperity of the 1920s had been sustained in very large part by two great industries which provided millions of jobs and absorbed huge quantities of investment capital:

THE TROUBLES OF THE FARMER

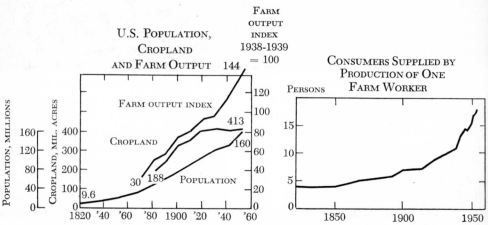

U.S. POPULATION, CROPLAND AND FARM OUTPUT

FARM OUTPUT INDEX 1938-1939 = 100

CONSUMERS SUPPLIED BY PRODUCTION OF ONE FARM WORKER

(1) automobiles and all the related fields, a great new industry at this time; and (2) the construction industry, undergoing a boom to catch up with a backlog accumulated during the war. But these industries could not continue long at their initial level; they naturally tended to taper off. Thus, by 1928, there was a slackening of the demand for automobiles, and the heavy initial investment in plant had been made. No new industries of any such magnitude were ready to take over the job of sustaining prosperity.

Upon examination, the prosperity of the boom years turned out to have yielded its returns rather unequally. A disproportionate share had gone into the hands of a small number. Profits got the lion's share of the rewards, while wages did little more than hold their own, and farm income did not even do that. Neither workers nor farmers had been strong enough to get their share of the cake. The meaning of this unequal income distribution is a matter for expert economists to dispute. As *the* explanation for the Depression, no crude "underconsumption" theory would pass inspection. But an unequal income distribution has its dangers. The rich save more and spend proportionately less of their income. Modern economic theory holds, however, that money saved must be invested by someone if there is to be full employment, and this demand for a high level of investment may not always be met.

Contributing to such a failure in the United States in the late 1920s was a decline in the rate of growth of consumption. Such a fall discourages businessmen from investing and expanding production; both expanding investment and expanding consumption are essential elements of a dynamic economy. A factor in this falling off of consumer demand was the fact that nearly 70 per cent of American families had an annual income of less than $2,500. While to most other peoples of the world this would have been almost a princely income, by American standards it was low. Furthermore, it represented a maldistribution of income; the upper 10 per cent had as much income as the lower 70 per cent, and this upper 10 per cent provided almost 90 per cent of family savings. Clearly, too, this accumulating wealth at the top went to feed the Wall Street bubble. Vast sums of untaxed corporate wealth, and not the money of little investors, contributed much more to the heavy demand for securities which bid stocks up to the sky in the 1920s. It is generally agreed that the stock-market crash was not itself the cause of the Great Depression but was a symptom of underlying ailments. The most important of these, to which the stock-market situation called attention, was the unequal distribution of income.

The process of speculation on the stock exchange had been assisted by lax rules on the exchange and possibly by too easy credit. As a result of the debacle which occurred in October, 1929, Congress in the New Deal era passed laws restricting such practices as the purchase of stocks "on margin" (actually paying only a small down payment). No such restrictions applied at the time of the crash, and the practice was very common. As for credit, the Federal Reserve Board, which today has considerable power to affect the credit situation by its decisions, then had less; it had been slow to impose restraints, and indeed in 1927 it had done the opposite. There was to be controversy about its policies on the eve of the crash, with the verdict in some doubt. But the situation on the stock exchange, one would think, cried out for some attention. Afterward, the activities of such promoters as Samuel Insull, who had piled holding company upon

BALANCE OF UNITED STATES—
FOREIGN TRADE, 1919–1952

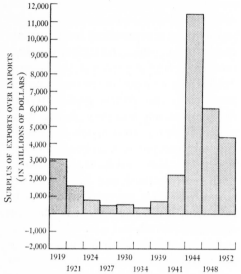

ternational trade exposed the unsoundness of the trade balance between Europe and America. The United States had now become the world's great creditor, without whose capital resources war-battered Europe, once the center of world capitalism, could hardly survive. But the United States did not readily adjust to her new role. A creditor nation must import, but America seemed not to need many imported goods and certainly discouraged them by erecting towering tariff walls.

The last and most extraordinary of these tariffs was the Smoot-Hawley Tariff, pushed through in 1930 over the objections of almost every American economist. More than 1,000 economists signed a solemn protest against it, for which they were denounced by the Republican National Committee as "communists, socialists, and radicals." No more revealing example exists of the economic blindness of the big-business-dominated Republican party at this time. For at the very moment when Europe was being suddenly deprived of American loans, she also found her goods more strictly excluded from American markets. The Smoot-Hawley Tariff has been authoritatively called one of the three great economic disasters of the postwar era. The shock to world trade which resulted from a combination of the stopping of loans and the tariff policy (plus the collection of war debts, which America insisted upon and began to get in 1928) was sufficient to demoralize it completely. During the Great Depression the passing of the international gold standard registered the downfall of the era of stability in world trade. In view of the fact that all through the 1920s the United States was showing a heavy surplus of exports over imports, this problem might well have been tackled, but it was not.

holding company in a fantastic structure of paper, were exposed to view and excited general indignation. Such activity, which was often criminal, reflected lax regulation of the securities market.

Another area where an abnormally bad situation existed was that of foreign trade. Abroad, Great Britain, once the leading financial and industrial nation, had known serious unemployment all during the 1920s. Such problems plagued most European countries in the wake of the great war of 1914 to 1918, which had diminished their assets, robbed them of markets, and subjected them to severe problems of readjustment. Large exports of American capital helped sustain Europe, besides providing an outlet for American surpluses of capital, during the 1920s. This took the form of private investment in European bonds. There was a certain contraction in this investment even before 1929, and a very sharp and swift one after the stock-market crash. The ensuing collapse of in-

ECONOMIC EARTHQUAKE

October 29, 1929, was the day of doom for the great "bull" market. The catastrophe that befell the stock exchange on this day, amid scenes of great confusion, had been preceded by several weeks of storm warnings, and it was to be followed by some eight months during which the stock market staggered still further downward. By June, 1930, the price of securities stood at an average of about 20 per cent of what it had been—a deflation of security values without precedent.* Yet, as was soon pointed out, the price of stocks had been much too high, far above what they were worth by any normal standard of value. They had been pushed up nearly 500 per cent between 1923 and 1929, riding on a wave of optimism. One might say, then, that what had happened was only the restoration of sanity. Indeed, the dramatic crash of the stock market was for many months thought to herald no general economic disaster, and it is today agreed that the crash was not itself the only cause of that disaster. Undoubtedly, though, it was a symptom of the deeper instability of the whole economic structure.

Such a drastic and sudden deflation of values necessarily had disturbing consequences, in addition to the personal ruin of heavy investors. Banks, for example, were "caught short" with too many of their assets invested in securities. The number of banks going broke soon climbed far above normal and reached serious proportions. The unsoundness of the banking system was a prominent characteristic of this depression—and an ominous one, for

* Between 1929 and 1932 the Dow-Jones industrial average fell from a high of 381 to a low of 41.

nothing did more to destroy popular confidence and create a mood of panic. Losses in the stock market affected the solvency of many great corporations, too, which had invested their surpluses in presumably good-as-gold stocks. Nevertheless, something more fundamental than this had evidently been wrong with the economic system; for as the months passed, factories closed, unemployment grew, farmers went into bankruptcy, and the country experienced the pains of a depression at all levels of society. The confident predictions of those who declared that "the country is basically sound" and all would soon be well failed to materialize. Things got worse, not better. In 1931 the American slump had repercussions in Europe, which in turn bounced back on America. By 1932 industrial production was down by half, foreign trade declined 70 per cent, and at least 12 million workers were unemployed. The whole economic world had gone awry. For millions of Americans stark economic tragedy had struck, bringing with it the loss of jobs, the extinction of life savings, and even the threat of starvation.

By this time the nation was talking of virtually nothing else but the Depression, why it had happened, and how it could be cured. Bearing in mind what has just been said about certain unsound conditions in the preceding years, we should consider the significant fact that in some areas this was a depression on top of a depression. The farmers, especially, had already been in bad shape; it is not too much to say that many were now totally ruined. In regard to foreign trade, again, the impact of the Depression came on top of an already unsound situation, and the result was to be not just a disruption but a catastrophe, with the international gold standard crash-

AMERICAN ECONOMIC SCENE DURING THE DEPRESSION YEAR!

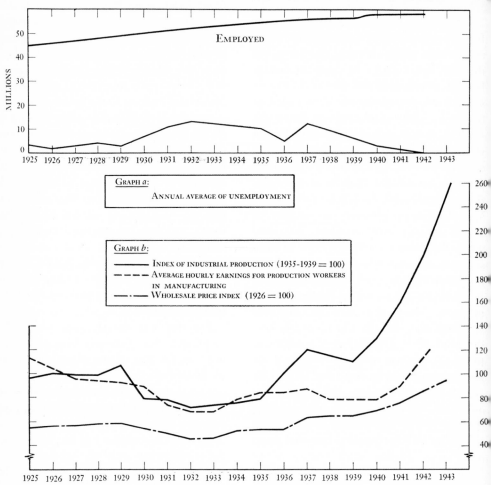

GRAPH *a*:

ANNUAL AVERAGE OF UNEMPLOYMENT

GRAPH *b*:

———— INDEX OF INDUSTRIAL PRODUCTION (1935-1939 = 100)
– – – – AVERAGE HOURLY EARNINGS FOR PRODUCTION WORKERS
        IN MANUFACTURING
—·— WHOLESALE PRICE INDEX (1926 = 100)

ing to the ground after a century in which it had been a symbol of world economic stability. Also, the United States had a very high debt burden before the slump; not only farmers had gone into debt, but manufacturers too, and consumers, buying on the new "installment-plan" system. This existing burden of indebtedness made the Depression all the more severe.

Economists had long been familiar with the ups and downs of the business cycle, but the scope, severity, and magnitude of this depression is what must be explained.

The full explanation would have to include a bewildering number of different factors. But above all it would have to reckon with the fact that a series of unprecedented disasters finally destroyed all confidence. Recovery had always come before when businessmen lost their timidity and decided to invest or to stock up, reasoning that the bottom had been reached. This time, one economic tremor after another shattered the structure of confidence until there was none left. First the unnerving stock-market crash; then the failure of banks; revelations of trickery in Wall Street, which tended to destroy confidence in the nation's economic leaders; the severe and continuing fall of agricultural prices, leading to widespread agrarian bankruptcy; the complete disruption of world trade and the world money system, an unprecedented thing; and finally the deep rumblings of discontent from a people not willing to wait patiently for "nature" to restore prosperity —all these things, successively and cumulatively, caused the growth of fear. The most intense and damaging fall was in capital-goods production, a decline of nearly 60 per cent between 1929 and 1933. Businessmen simply refused to build factories or expand production. Today, government in a similar situation would be quick to rush in with a large spending program, but at that time this was not contemplated, for the old economic theories forbade it. The decline of investment, probably the most significant aspect of the Depression, could be explained in part by the exceptional amounts that had been invested in the 1920s, but in large measure it also rested on fear. Money must be spent if there is to be prosperity. Between 1929 and 1933 anyone with extra money hoarded it, waiting for an end of fear. Such a cycle of stagnation can become self-perpetuating: the more fear, the more depression, and the more depression, the more fear. President Franklin D. Roosevelt recognized this when he announced in March, 1933, that there was nothing to fear but fear itself. It was, however, a very formidable enemy.

No doubt, had men had sufficient patience to endure, recovery would have eventually come. But in so dreadful a situation this was too much to expect. As the Depression deepened and suffering grew, there arose a chorus of protest. These voices came from all classes, including many business leaders. For all classes suffered from this depression; if the farmers were perhaps the hardest hit and unemployed factory workers the most miserable, the middle classes also sustained severe blows, with investments and savings lost, retail trade in sharp decline, factories no longer profitable. Few were willing to sit by and do nothing as long as there existed the grim paradox of millions unemployed while factories lay idle, of farmers letting their wheat rot in the fields for want of a market while men went hungry in the cities. A torrent of articles, books, and speeches attempted to supply a course of action. The most remarkable thing about this depression, next to its extreme severity, was the widespread demand it produced that the government do something about it.

No one was exactly sure what. The Depression was variously blamed on the war, on Europe, on the capitalist system, on Wall Street, on the Republicans, and on the alarmists who destroyed confidence by demanding drastic action. Even those who attributed it to such absurd causes as sunspots or a conspiracy of the Jews could get a following amid the confusion. Responsible public figures spoke of "the grave imperfections in an economic system which makes possible the awful contrast of vast fortunes and breadlines," of the need to "coordinate production and consumption," to "provide security for the workers of the nation," and to alleviate the "unequal distribution of the nation's income." There was also a lively demand to punish the wrongdoers on the stock exchange. Monopoly, too, came in for renewed attack, as some economists blamed the failure of the economy to right itself on "stickiness of prices," pointing out that the automatic-adjustment theory demands free competition if it is to work properly. All these demands and analyses were later to bear fruit in legislation, but they were rather too vague to point a clear way out of the Depression. Many panaceas were brought forth, but it was difficult to choose scientifically among them. This depression that broke all the rules stimulated an important reappraisal of economic theory at the most advanced level of thought; but the "new economics" cannot be said to have found its feet until the publication in 1936 of the Englishman John Maynard Keynes's significant book *The General Theory of Employment, Interest, and Money.*

Confused though the answer might be, it was urgent that a way out be found. All over the world, war and revolution were consequences of depression-bred misery. Japan seized Manchuria, and the previously obscure demagogue Hitler marched toward dictatorial power in Germany. The United States suffered as severely from the Depression as any country in the world, more severely than most. There were stirrings of violence in many places. So moderate a man as William Green of the American Federation of Labor announced that he would not be responsible for the peacefulness of the workers unless something were done speedily.

THE HOOVER POLICIES

Naturally the Depression rebounded against the party in power. The man in the White House became a target for much of the bitterness such a depression was certain to unloose. The tent and shack villages of the unemployed which sprang up on the fringes of great cities were "Hoovervilles"; old newspapers were "Hoover blankets." The Republicans had taken credit for the sunshine of prosperity and they now had to absorb the blame for the snowstorm of depression. Mr. Hoover had once predicted "a chicken in every pot and two cars in every garage." In 1931, the cartoonist of the *New York World-Telegram* drew a picture of two chickens scratching around in an empty garage. Such was the burden which Herbert Clark Hoover had to bear during his unfortunate term in the White House.

In some ways he was well equipped to bear it; in others, poorly so. Hoover was one of the more intelligent of our Presidents, he was deservedly famous as a brilliant administrator, and his record as relief administrator in Europe after the war had given this Quaker President a reputation as a great humanitarian. He was not a skilled politician and often did not get along well with Congress or the public. There are many apparent paradoxes and unsolved problems concerning Hoover, not all of which have been disposed of by his able volumes of *Memoirs,* written many years later. With an international business and engineering background and a good deal of economic intelligence, he signed and defended the Smoot-Hawley Tariff, which severely curtailed international trade—though at the same time he always declared that the Depression was international in its origins. He criticized the selfishness of certain powerful economic interests, yet his social philosophy favored giving them substantial freedom from any social control. In the area of foreign policy, he initiated a "Good Neighbor" policy by repudiating imperialistic tactics toward Latin-American countries; on the other hand, he sternly opposed independence for the Philippines. Hoover had a strong and independent mind and a keen sense of his own abilities. He was not likely to be swayed by popular emotions, in which respect he was like the

Democrat under whom he first came to public life, and whom he always admired, Woodrow Wilson.

Hoover's economic and political philosophy was not that of the more conservative and laissez-faire Republicans. He had criticized the inertia of Coolidge and Secretary of Treasury Mellon in not taking various actions earlier, especially against the runaway stock market. But Hoover shared with most academic economists a strong scepticism about the efficacy or desirability of government intervention in the economic order. He did act, but with some reluctance as well as hesitation, and he always felt that the main impluse to recovery must come from "natural forces," not from government. There are those who insist that Hoover really began the New Deal, but this is an honor he emphatically declines. The phrase "last of the old Presidents and first of the new," used to describe his role between 1929 and 1933, points to the fact that under the pressure of events he did take action, some of it precedent breaking. Yet in 1932 the Democrats were effectively to charge him with having been painfully negative in his approach to the Great Depression, and he even got the undeserved reputation of being "Hardhearted Herb," indifferent to the sufferings of the people. The fact is that Hoover, while no dogmatic believer in *laissez faire,* wished to confine government intervention in economic affairs within strict limits. He believed that his victorious rival in the 1932 election introduced the elements of a "collectivist economy," thus starting on the "road to serfdom" by expanding the authority of government. Whether Hoover was in this respect a misguided reactionary or a prophetic liberal may still remain for the future to decide.

It was, at any rate, an unpopular position to try to maintain in the atmosphere

President Herbert C. Hoover. (Fabian Bach-rach)

of the Depression, and Hoover reaped the rewards. He did, to repeat, sanction some emergency measures. The Reconstruction Finance Corporation, which lent government money to banks, corporations, and municipalities, was almost unprecedented. A farm program, under the Agricultural Marketing Act of 1929, bought up wheat and cotton in an effort to raise prices. Hoover gave his approval to a public-works program, though a relatively small one, hardly adequate to restore prosperity.* All these measures would be enlarged upon by the New Deal administration. If Hoover, adhering to economic orthodoxy, tried to keep the federal budget balanced, the Democrats, little anticipating their later policy, attacked him not for

* Expenditures on public works by the federal government rose by about $275 million from 1929 to 1932. In the same period, by contrast, the total decline in all construction, including private was about $8,500 million.

The bonus army encamps near the Capitol, July, 1932. (National Archives)

too much economy in government, but for too little. Most post-Keynes economists regard the balancing of the government's budget as a shibboleth to be disregarded in time of depression, when what is needed is some stimulation of investment and purchasing power. But this line of thought still lay in the future, and Hoover was not alone in rejecting the idea that government spending could defeat a depression. His own policies, however, had little effect, and he refused to adopt others which were very much in demand.

Hoover's Farm Board was unable to stem the decline of agricultural prices, which brought wheat as low as 25 cents a bushel cash in 1931. Without crop control the program was doomed to failure. The board asked farmers to reduce their acreage, but without success. It found itself stuck with large quantities of produce while prices continued to plunge. Some of this surplus was released to the unemployed. But Hoover would not agree to bring the government directly into crop control; in the 1932 campaign his Democratic rival promised this and undoubtedly won votes thereby. Legislation was passed under Hoover to ease the burden of mort-

gage foreclosures, which averted the threat of agrarian revolution but hardly answered the basic problem of farm surpluses, falling prices, and impossibly low agricultural income.

Above all, Hoover set a stubborn face against the disbursing of federal funds for relief of the unemployed—the "dole," as he called it. He was also opposed to unemployment insurance. There was a place for private charity, but there could be none, he felt, for a huge subsidizing of idleness by the state. The old view that the stick of starvation must be held over men to make them work persisted in Hoover's thinking. But this was a misreading of the depression situation, when millions of willing, skilled workers sought jobs in vain. These idle workers swamped local relief rolls and made even hardheaded businessmen look to Washington for help out of an impossible predicament, for bankrupt cities and towns could provide no relief, and violence sometimes threatened. Hoover's opposition to the idea of grants to the unemployed stemmed in good part from the automatic-adjustment theory, for on the premises of this theory workers must be compelled to accept lowered wages in order to bring about the necessary adjustments. Yet in this depression, disconcertingly for the orthodox economists, wages fell without reducing unemployment; there seemed no bottom to the slump. With the RFC giving "relief" to big corporations, it seemed grossly unjust to deny the workers relief, and the GOP was hit hard by Democratic propaganda for favoring capital over labor. Finally Hoover wavered and approved federal grants of relief money to the states, but this came too late to be of much help in the 1932 campaign.

Apart from his opposition to relief funds, Hoover's reputation for a stony indifference to depression suffering stemmed chiefly from his unwise handling of the "army" of about 15,000 ex-soldiers who assembled in Washington in May, 1932, in order to dramatize their demand for a soldiers' bonus. In 1924 they had received a twenty-year endowment policy, and in 1931 they were allowed to borrow up to half on this policy. They now wanted the other half. Franklin D. Roosevelt later felt as Hoover did in opposing such demands; but regardless of the merits of their case, the veterans might have been handled with courtesy and tact, whereas instead they were routed by armed force without a hearing. Blood was shed on the banks of the Anacostia River in Washington.

One should nevertheless read Hoover's defence of his policies before condemning him. "We have provided a series of measures unprecedented in the history of the Republic," he claimed on the eve of the 1932 election. To go even further, he feared, would be to undermine the foundations of a free society and fasten on it the hand of a corrupt and inefficient government bureaucracy. Much more conservative than Roosevelt, Hoover was in

Burning the shacks of the bonus army. The ex-soldiers who came to Washington demanding cash bonus payments during the worst months of the Depression were finally removed by force and their makeshift shelters destroyed. (National Archives)

his own eyes, and those of some Americans, an intelligent liberal, standing somewhere between the blind conservatism of an Andrew Mellon and the irresponsible radicalism of a Franklin Roosevelt. Hoover at any rate felt that the issues were deeply drawn: "This election is not a mere shift from the ins to the outs. It means deciding the direction our nation will take for a century to come."

During this 1932 election campaign the Democratic candidate Franklin D. Roosevelt promised to break precedents and scorn timidity. He made himself a symbol of energetic action, while charging the Hoover government with having "held out no hope and pointed out no path" back to prosperity. Economic laws, Roosevelt declared, are not made by nature but by human beings. Dubious though this proposition might be, it had a ring of courage about it which Hoover's statements lacked. Roosevelt promised "bold leadership" in distributing relief; a farm program based on curtailing production; putting a million of the unemployed back to work on reforestation; and—oddly enough, in the light of later events—

INDUSTRIAL PRODUCTION IN THE DEPRESSION

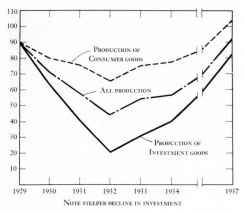

Production of Consumer goods

All production

Production of Investment goods

1929 1930 1931 1932 1933 1934 1937

NOTE STEEPER DECLINE IN INVESTMENT

economy in government. It is likely that the great majority who voted him into office paid less attention to his specific proposals than to his general confidence in his ability to take action toward "a new order of competence and courage." They registered a protest vote against the Hoover policies because these policies had not halted the disastrous downward plunge of the nation's economy. That was perhaps unjust, but it was inevitable. With this blow the Republican party, normally in the majority since the Civil War, was to be thrown into the minority position for about twenty years. The Republicans had once waved the bloody shirt of the Civil War successfully at the Democrats; now the situation was reversed, and for a generation the Democrats would wave at them the tattered shirt of the Depression.

Meanwhile, the period between the election in November, 1932, and the inauguration of the new President in March, 1933, saw the very bottom of the terrible economic collapse reached. All indices of economic activity touched bottom, and the nation was doubtless saved from some sort of revolutionary explosion only by the knowledge that a new administration was

on its way in, pledged to take bolder action against the Depression. This lameduck period of four months, an obsolete provision of the Constitution carried over from the days when it took that long for the new President to travel to the capital, was to be done away with soon by the Twentieth Amendment. On this occasion it proved to be most damaging. Hoover and Roosevelt tried to agree on an interim policy but were unable to do so. The climax of the Depression was reached when, on the eve of Roosevelt's assumption of office, a banking crisis threatened the solvency of every bank in the country. People had lost confidence in all banks, and a panic-stricken rush to withdraw money caused the banking system of the entire country to collapse. It was this situation that confronted the new President on the very day he took up his duties. All over the world men turned anxious and desperate eyes on him.

THE IMPACT OF THE DEPRESSION ON AMERICAN LIFE

Coming to office in the midst of the Depression's worst crisis, Hoover's successor was to meet that crisis and go on to have more success or luck than Hoover had had. Nevertheless, the Depression lingered on until 1940 in the form of unemployment (or underemployment) and other afflictions. The New Deal program, vastly significant as it was, remains to be examined. Any consideration of the social consequences of the Depression must include the whole period, though the worst of it was in the years 1931 and 1932.

There was a silver lining, however thin, in the Depression; not all its effects were purely bad. We have mentioned the stimulus to economic thinking, in all countries, which was to produce a new and presumably more intelligent school of economic thought. Today the onset of a depression would be met in an entirely different way, and though the theories have not yet been put to the test exactly, there is much confidence that their application would avert the worst features of a depression. A variety of techniques would be used, but all would involve the action of the federal government. Basic reliance would be placed on the government's ability to pump fresh spending power into the economic body before it succumbed to the attack of the depression virus. From the Great Depression, it is fair to say, economic science learned more than it had learned in the previous century. Not merely the *cure* of a depression, but, more important, its *prevention* by wise fiscal policies is now believed feasible.

There was also a pronounced tendency for the nation to exhibit a new seriousness of thought at all levels. The gay party of the 1920s was over, and the people sobered up. There were even some who claimed on such grounds that the collapse of prosperity was a good thing; it had brought the people "back to fundamentals." Churchgoing underwent a modest revival, there was more neighborliness, libraries reported an increase in reading. College students were said to be more serious, though more worried. The intellectuals ceased to be aloof, came home from exile, and began to take a serious interest in public affairs. The 1930s were to produce a rich and exciting literature, which contrasted sharply with that of the previous decade in its stress on the social theme. The representative novelists of the Depression years wrote sympathetically of the common people, of strikes and the battle for social justice; a good example is John Steinbeck's remarkable portrait of ruined farmers and migratory workers, *The Grapes of Wrath,* which found a wider reading public than almost any great American work of literature had ever found. The Depression stimulated a good deal of interesting work in other branches of the arts, as well as in sociology and in social philosophy. Politics, finally, became exciting once again. The battle between the New and the Old Deal brought public interest in politics to a degree of intensity comparable to the days of Andrew Jackson or the years before the Civil War.

Nevertheless, taken all in all, the Depression was a destructive force. For millions of Americans it was an agonizing experience, bringing in some ways tragedy even more bitter than that of war. In war the enemy is tangible and identifiable; for the victims of the Depression the forces that struck them down were intangible and could not be fought. The toll of human anguish and frustration mounted steadily as months passed with no lifting of the clouds of economic collapse. The suffering caused by the Depression cannot be more than suggested. For millions, prolonged unemployment, often stretching into years, meant the loss not only of material possessions but also of pride, of self-respect, and, through disuse, of skills. For many there was also loss of health; diseases stemming from nutritional deficiencies rose alarmingly. Hundreds of thousands of children went to their schools hungry each morning. The free wards of hospitals were overcrowded. The depths of the ignominy were revealed in the suggestion that the hungry might be fed by the collection of scraps left from restaurant meals.

In the major industrial cities of the nation, social problems springing from the Depression took on alarming dimensions.

In Detroit, automotive capital of the nation and the city that symbolized the prosperity of the 1920s, there were in the early 1930s more than 200,000 dependents on the relief rolls of the city. Fifteen banks had closed, impounding 34,000 deposits. It was estimated by the mayor that 4,000 children stood in the daily bread lines and that 18 per cent of the school children suffered from severe undernourishment. The suicide rate in the city rose 30 per cent above the previous five-year average, and there were 7,500 eviction proceedings a month. In some of the great automobile plants, wage rates for those fortunate enough to have jobs dropped as low as 12 to 15 cents an hour.

Almost every major city in the nation could match Detroit's tale of tragedy. It was a common experience for public employees to go without their pay for months, dependent on credit extended to them by their landlords and grocers. For such as these, the only consolation was that the shame of poverty tended to disappear as millions of Americans shared its bitter bread.

Amid these conditions, violence was bound to develop. In many cities, demonstrations of the unemployed seeking jobs or relief were an almost daily occurrence. Mobs could easily be recruited from the long bread lines or the melancholy areas of tarpaper and tin-can shacks that sprang up on the outskirts of nearly all cities. The danger of a major explosion of violence haunted the minds of public officials. Nor were things better in the rural areas. There violence lurked as menacingly as in the cities. In 1932 roads leading to many cities were patrolled by angry farmers, intent on seeing that food and milk did not get to the city markets until they brought higher prices. Milk and produce trucks were overturned by these striking farmers in futile endeavor to secure higher prices. Farmers also took action to prevent the dispossession of their neighbors through mortgage sales. Many a farm family was at least spared the final humiliation of seeing their small possessions dumped by the roadside because their neighbors gathered at the sheriff's sale to see that no one bid for the property to be sold.

One of the chief casualties of the Depression was family life. Both marriage and birth rates fell heavily in these difficult years as people of marriageable age feared to take on the responsibilities. Many existing families broke up as the mother was forced to take what work she could get, and the children left home rather than remain a burden on the family. Every major railroad yard or terminal in the nation had its hundreds of boys and girls waiting for a chance to "ride the rods" to somewhere, drifting aimlessly about in search of work, food, and adventure. They were youthful derelicts of a society that apparently had no place for them.

Among many such demoralizing social consequences of the Depression, its impact on minority groups deserves mention. "Last to be hired and first to be fired," as it was said with only slight exaggeration, the Negroes had a higher unemployment rate than the whites. A substantial migration of Negroes from the South to the northern cities had also occurred in these years. During the 1920s, in the North, the hopes of Negroes for advancement beyond the traditional level of the lowest unskilled labor had been growing. Now these hopes suffered a cruel setback. Economic insecurity was nothing new for the Negro in industry; it was greatly intensified by the Depression. The result was sometimes to produce embittered radicalism. Still, one could find instances where common misery drew Negro and white workers together, thus helping to dispel racial prejudice.

Thus were the good and evil consequences of the Depression mixed together, but few could doubt that the latter outweighed the former. The fabric of American society could hardly have survived many years of such conditions as existed in 1932. The result would be personal and social demoralization, so severe as to destroy democracy. Some form of totalitarianism would be the final product; for if democracy could not give men jobs and a living, they would assuredly look to some other system. In Germany, the only other Western nation to suffer as much as the United States from the Depression of 1929 to 1933, this happened. There the apparent incompetence of the existing government to deal with the Depression caused a torrent of votes to flow in the direction of the dangerous rabble rouser Adolf Hitler, who profited by not being identified with the government and who was willing to promise anything. The consequences for the world were to be great and tragic. In the United States, fortunately, the two-party system made for a less precarious situation. While extremist parties did spring up, producing all sorts of wild slogans and led by such redoubtable demagogues as Huey ("Kingfish") Long, they remained relatively insignificant. One did not have to vote for such parties to express protest; one could vote for the great rival party to the Republicans, the Democratic party. The impact of the Depression drove the Democrats toward reform and social experiment as they took up the cause of opposition to Hoover's cautious policies and promised bold action. But as an old and traditional party with deep roots in the American past, the Democratic party was not likely to become irresponsible—certainly not to abandon the democratic system. Though party passions ran high, the American political system was hardy enough to survive the impact of the Depression.

The Depression was responsible for a notable progressive thrust in American thought and politics. On the extreme left, even the Communists were able to make some gains by pointing to the absence of a depression in the state-controlled economy of Soviet Russia. Big business had long been a target of American reformers, while Socialists had long predicted the collapse of the "capitalist system." The faith of American conservatism, contrariwise, had been closely linked up with *laissez faire,* and a belief in the virtues of 100 per cent private enterprise. That was now pretty severely shaken by the 1929 crash, which was evidently the result of leaving things alone and trusting in the "lords of creation." Though conservatives declared that there were other causes of the Depression, such as the European war, they were very much on the defensive. A variety of liberal, progressive, and radical groups sprang forward in the 1930s—farmer-labor movements on the prairies which harked back to Populism, socialist and trade-union splinter groups, intellectuals intrigued by various social theories. One example of the changed outlook may be given, among many that might be cited: in his book *The Old Individualism and the New,* America's most famous philosopher, John Dewey, turned his attention to social problems and described how modern technology had destroyed the world of Adam Smith. Rugged individualism, he observed, had become ragged individualism. The welfare of the individual remained the chief concern of a democratic society, but that welfare must be sought through planned cooperative action, not through the anarchy of private selfishness. The trend was toward the social principle, unrestricted individualism.

The most extraordinary consequence of the Depression was to be the New Deal administration of Franklin D. Roosevelt, which reflected the new spirit of social welfare. The New Deal was to show the influence of John Dewey's pragmatism, or instrumentalism. This philosophy was nondogmatic, having no pat answers; it believed in constant experimentation. It tended to deny that there is any such thing as truth in the abstract, but thought of truth as a matter of constantly shaping

ideas to meet particular problems. Holding that social institutions must be constantly adapted to a changing reality, the New Deal too was dynamic, always ready to try something new. It felt, with Dewey, that the key to enrichment of the individual personality was in the improvement of society. For the next eight years, as the following chapter describes, the United States was to be a laboratory for the experiments of this progressive American philosophy. In all phases of life and thought the Depression encouraged a spirit of change and revolt, the natural result of so great a social catastrophe.

FURTHER READINGS

J. K. Galbraith, *The Great Crash* (1955), and W. Arthur Lewis, *Economic Survey, 1919–1939* (1950), are among works of economists bearing on the Depression. Harold G. Moulton, *Controlling Factors in Economic Development* (1949), a Brookings Institution study, is another. Alvin H. Hansen, *Fiscal Policy and Business Cycles* (1941), is a Keynesian analysis, while Lionel C. Robbins, *The Great Depression* (1934), represents a more traditional, conservative approach. James W. Prothro, *The Dollar Decade: Business Ideas in the 1920s* (1954), attempts to set down the views of business leaders during the intoxicating atmosphere of the great boom. A brilliant description of the Depression's impact on life and thought is contained in Charles and Mary Beard, *America in Midpassage*, volume I (1939). A less weighty work is Gilbert Seldes's charming and ironic *The Years of the Locust* (1933).

The best defense of the ill-starred Hoover policies is by Hoover himself, in the third and last volume of his *Memoirs* (1952), a vigorous and interesting work. The effective attacks on Hoover by Franklin D. Roosevelt in the 1932 campaign were printed as *Looking Forward* (1933). Typical passages

at arms for or against Hoover are the unfriendly treatment in Thomas L. Stokes, *Chip Off My Shoulder* (1940), and the admiring Eugene Lyons, *Our Unknown Ex-President* (1948).

Sociologists using techniques of "cultural anthropology" offer us much insight into a process such as the impact of the Depression on American life. See Robert and Helen Lynd, *Middletown in Transition* (1937), for the best example. Also shedding light on the social effects of the Depression are E. Franklin Frazier, *The Negro Family in the United States* (1939); Maxine Davis, *The Lost Generation* (1936); and Marie D. Lane and F. Steegmuller, *America on Relief* (1938).

Donald R. McCoy, *Angry Voices: Left-of-center Politics in the New Deal Era* (1959), is a lively and scholarly account of some of the radical movements thrown up by the Depression. Alfred Bingham, *Insurgent America* (1935), is by one of the "insurgents." Harnett T. Kane, in *Louisiana Hayride* (1941), has chronicled the career of Huey P. Long.

For additional bibliography, see the *Harvard Guide*, sections 254, 264, 267, and 268.

TWENTY-SIX

The New Deal

SOURCES OF ROOSEVELTIAN REFORM

DURING THE HALF DECADE from 1933 to 1938, startling changes took place in America, precipitated by the Great Depression and carried out by President Franklin D. Roosevelt and his New Deal aides. While much of the New Deal was the culmination of forces long apparent in American history, it inevitably bore the impress of Roosevelt's character and personality. Even yet, historians can do little more than suggest definite circumstances and experiences which molded his character and trained him for political leadership, but it is now perhaps possible to examine some of the influences which shaped Roosevelt as he threaded his way through a political career which has already become legendary. Fate, which seemed to be fashioning him for nothing more than a well-to-do, aristocratic Hudson River country squire, changed her mind and made him into an astute politician, a bold reformer, a champion of the forgotten man, a defender of world democracy—a man to be violently hated or worshipfully admired. Important, no doubt, in forming his character, but still impossible to evaluate, were a doting and protective mother; his student days at Groton and Harvard; his admiration for distant cousin Teddy Roosevelt; a brief experience as a lawyer; his membership in the New York legislature; his marriage to Theodore Roosevelt's niece, Eleanor Roosevelt, who was at least his equal in capacity and willingness to assume ever-greater responsibilities; contacts with Wilsonian progressivism and

1933

National Industrial Recovery Act passed.
Agricultural Adjustment Act passed.
TVA, CCC, and other New Deal agencies created.

1934

Additional New Deal legislation passed.
Some economic recovery occurs.

1935

NRA and AAA invalidated by Supreme Court.
Social-security legislation enacted.
National Labor Relations Act passed.
Works Progress Administration created.
CIO group breaks away from AFL.

1936

Roosevelt reelected in landslide.

1937

Supreme Court fight.
Economic recession.
Automobile and steel strikes.

1938

Second AAA establishes "parity" principle.
Wages and Hours bill passed.

Artist working on WPA art
project in San Francisco

Picketers in automobile workers' strike, 1937

*Aroused by the Depression and encour-
aged by favorable legislation, American
industrial workers organized and fought
anti-union employers in the 1930s. The
New Deal carried on many other activities; conservatives lamented the Government's intrusion into such diverse
fields as art and electrical power. Soil
conservation, in this decade of drought
and dust storms, received more general
support. To others the New Deal meant
old-age pensions or a WPA job.*

A "stay-in" demonstration
by aircraft workers

A part of the Tennessee Valley
Authority power system

Gully erosion in Wisconsin

A dust storm in eastern Colorado

President Franklin D. Roosevelt. (Fabian Bachrach)

administrative responsibilities while Assistant Secretary of the Navy in the Wilson administration; the mental, emotional, and physical experiences that followed a crippling attack of poliomyelitis in 1921 which kept him out of active public life until 1928; and election to the New York governorship that year, which office he held until he became a candidate for the presidency in 1932.

While serving as governor, Roosevelt and his associates made preparations for his presidential bid. In the 1932 campaign Governor Roosevelt had the help of intellectuals, especially college professors, in formulating policies and preparing speeches. Many of these people moved to Washington in 1933 with their principal and became popularly identified as the "brain trust." His chief political managers were newspaperman Louis Howe, who had devoted his remarkable talents to

Roosevelt's political career for many years, and James A. Farley, an experienced Tammany-trained politician whose personal honesty, shrewdness, and capacity to command friendship and loyalty were to win for him a deserved reputation as the ablest political manager since Mark Hanna. Farley maneuvered the conservatives out of control of the party machinery in the months before the convention, and at the national convention itself he engineered a deal with the backers of John Nance Garner of Texas which resulted in the victory of the Roosevelt-Garner ticket. The ticket rode into office in November on the tidal wave of public discontent. The Democrats carried all but six states, with an overwhelming popular vote which buried the hapless, depression-battered Republicans. They also captured both houses of Congress by large majorities.

The American people voted emphatically against Hoover and the Republican party, but they had no very clear idea for whom or for what they were voting. Even the relatively few who had tried to look deeper into the shape of things to come had found Roosevelt's campaign speeches highly puzzling. Having come into power as a result of the Depression, the Democrats had no intention of prejudicing the future by being too specific. In one of his September campaign speeches, Roosevelt had given what turned out to be a sketchy preview of the major aspects of the New Deal. But, as one distinguished commentator later remarked, "He said so many other things during the campaign that I didn't know till Inauguration Day whether he meant it or not." A study of Roosevelt's campaign utterances would not on the whole have given a very clear idea of the policies he was to follow. He promised to cut taxes, balance the budget, reduce the size of the bureaucracy, and stop giving doles to the unemployed. It took the public and, indeed Roosevelt himself, a long time to discover just what the New Deal was to be like. Roosevelt, above all else, was not a dogmatic person, and he sought to do what seemed best to meet each particular emergency.

As the pattern of the New Deal began to appear, it proved to be quite similar to what farmers and laborers had been demanding ever since the Civil War. The New Deal may be fitted into the picture of struggle against entrenched privilege which has frequently been a feature of American politics. It had something of the aspect of the back country's fight against the tidewater in colonial times, of the agrarian protest against business control in the age of Jefferson and Jackson, and of the Greenback and Populist revolt against monopoly after the Civil War. Most of all, perhaps, it resembled the progressive crusade of the years before 1914. The New Deal drew largely on American precedents.

In the foreground were the professional reformers who had for years been advocating their particular remedies for various evils. Farm leaders wanted better prices and cheaper interest rates; workers wanted better wages and the right to bargain collectively; social workers wanted slum clearance; everybody wanted the end of the Depression. Reformers and quacks offered panaceas without limit. The New Deal embraced many of these ideas. Roosevelt's primary role was political. Out of the discontents of the time he fashioned a political program for achieving the people's demands—one which stood for twenty years, until the forces which had called it into being had spent themselves and had been replaced by others. Roosevelt was unquestionably a political genius. He perhaps never fully understood the

economic problems with which the New Deal sought to cope; certainly he did not understand them in the way that the theoretical economist might. He understood people and their problems, and he made people work together in the vast jerry-built system which was the New Deal. The real New Dealers were a number of men whom Roosevelt gathered around him —such people as Harry Hopkins, social worker; Harold Ickes, lawyer and reformer; Henry Wallace, farm specialist; Rexford Tugwell, city planner; David Lilienthal, public power expert; Robert Nathan and Mordecai Ezekiel, economists; and a host of others who at one time or another were pulled into the circle of influence. Presiding genially and skillfully over this group was Roosevelt, the political manager, whose gaiety, persuasive voice, personality, and gift for phrasemaking headed the show. At his side was his wife, Eleanor, a most remarkable figure in her own right, lending valuable aid.

The new strong-minded, self-confident President did not select a Cabinet of men with outstanding reputations. The most notable figure in his Cabinet was low-tariff advocate and party wheelhorse Cordell Hull, Senator from Tennessee, who was made Secretary of State. The most important northern party leader to enter the Cabinet was national party chairman James A. Farley of New York, who became Postmaster General. Three leading members of the Cabinet were from outside the circles of the Democratic party: Secretary of Agriculture Henry A. Wallace of Iowa and Secretary of the Interior Harold Ickes of Illinois were Republicans, and Secretary of Labor Frances Perkins of New York was a professional social worker. Like Jackson, Roosevelt depended more heavily upon his "brain trust" for policy decisions than upon his official Cabinet. The man who had denounced Hoover for relying upon "crackpot professors" was himself to draw freely, although not exclusively, on the advice of such experts. Before long, enemies of the New Deal were making it a principal item of criticism that the President did not employ the counsel of "practical" men, that is, businessmen. Actually, he took his counsel where he could find it. Like his cousin Theodore, he held businessmen in no particular awe.

Roosevelt's first effort was his most important and most dramatic—giving new life to a prostrate nation on Inauguration Day, March 4, 1933. In the nation's capital that day, the sky was overcast and an unfriendly wind drove a chilling mist across the faces of the thousands of distraught people gathered for the ceremony. Those somber listeners, and the countless others throughout the land huddled close to radios, terribly wanted and desperately needed leadership. And Roosevelt seemed to be their last, their only, hope. Millions appeared willing to accept even a dictatorship. The seeming endlessness of the searing Depression had gradually, remorselessly, dangerously eroded people's confidence in themselves and in their governmental and economic institutions. Each failure had brought more physical suffering and mental torture than previous ones. At hand now, to haunt everyone, was the stark, inescapable fact that our banking machinery had actually come to a complete standstill. During the preceding weeks the banks in state after state had had to be closed. On the morning of inauguration, the sole remaining states with open banks, New York and Illinois, joined the others.

But with magnificent eloquence Roosevelt addressed the nation with such buoyant confidence and with such convincing promises of positive action that countless hearers began to feel somewhat ashamed of their surrender to panic fear. In ringing words he reminded the people that "the only thing we have to fear is fear itself." "Plenty is at our doorstep," and if its use was languishing, that was because "rulers of the exchange of mankind's goods have failed through their stubbornness and their own incompetence. . . . They have no vision, and when there is no vision, the people perish." Roosevelt promised "action, and action now. . . . Our greatest primary task is to put people to work." He hinted that if necessary he would ask Congress for extraordinary powers to deal with the emergency. America had found a leader. Immediately following this address came action—action so vigorous and so rapid that it stirred the whole nation. A great part of the populace was roused to hope after more than three years of deepening fear. A smaller segment, watching in growing apprehension while familiar landmarks of the past were blasted one by one, received a shock from which they never really recovered. Some of these became, and remained, bitter critics who looked upon Roosevelt and his coterie of New Dealers as irresponsible, dangerous, and wasteful destroyers of the American free-enterprise system and of democracy. Among the hopeful, many took the opposite view and began to regard Roosevelt as something of a savior. Only a few were able to maintain any perspective and to adopt a wait-and-see attitude. The crisis was severe, nerves were strained, and emotions for the most part were violent.

Roosevelt's first action following his inauguration as President, a bold attack on the financial crisis, was acclaimed by nearly everyone. Through executive order and then by the Emergency Banking

Act, passed in a special session of Congress, most of the banks were systematically examined, after which the apparently sound ones were reopened within a few weeks. Other banks were first placed in the hands of "conservators" and later opened on a restricted basis. To relieve the strain, Federal Reserve banks were permitted to obtain liquid funds by issuing more stock, which they then sold to the Reconstruction Finance Corporation. Collateral requirements for the issue of Federal Reserve bank notes were liberalized. An important factor in the success of the new bank program was the spirit of cooperation which prevailed. Treasury department personnel of the Hoover administration stayed on after March 4 to help the new officials. Bankers gave their support, because the program was aimed not at socializing the banking business but rather at saving it for private enterprise. The public accepted in good faith the decisions made regarding the soundness of the banks, and that confidence made it possible for reopened banks to function. Roosevelt contributed greatly to public confidence by his first "fireside chat," delivered over the radio on March 12. In this he said, "I can assure you that it is safer to keep your money in a reopened bank than under the mattress." One "brain truster" later reported:

> It cannot be emphasized too strongly that the policies which vanquished the bank crisis were thoroughly conservative policies. The sole departure from convention lay in the swiftness and boldness with which they were carried out. . . . If ever there was a moment when things hung in the balance, it was on March 5th, 1933— when unorthodoxy would have drained the last remaining strength of the capitalistic system. Capitalism was saved in eight days. . . .

Other banking measures followed. The Glass-Steagall Banking Act, which was enacted in June, 1933, gave the Federal Reserve increased power to control member banks, to prevent the granting of excessively risky loans, prohibited commercial banks from engaging in investment banking, and established the Federal Deposit Insurance Corporation (FDIC), which guaranteed depositors against loss in case of bank failure. At first the FDIC insurance completely guaranteed deposits up to only $2,500; in 1934 the figure became $5,000; and in 1950 it was extended to $10,000. All this brought about tighter federal regulation of individual banks. Banking was further affected by the activities of various government agencies which directly participated in granting or refinancing of loans. RFC loans to banks and businesses were greatly extended. The Home Owners' Loan Corporation (1933) and other subsequently established agencies took the government further into the field of home financing. An expansion of the Federal Farm Loan Bank system and the newly created Farm Credit Administration supplemented private bank credit. Direct federal participation in banking saved many homeowners, farmers, and businessmen from financial ruin and brought about a much needed lowering of interest rates on mortgages and other types of loans.

These banking changes, while they seem conservative enough, effectively broke what critics since the Civil War had called the "banking monopoly." By going into the banking business, especially by using its credit to guarantee loans, the government had effectively lowered the interest rate to small borrowers—principally homeowners and farmers. For the first time small borrowers were able to obtain money at rates between 4 and 5 per cent instead of from 6 to 12 per cent. Through its control over the Federal Reserve System, the Treasury kept the general interest rate for all borrowers, large and small, very low for years to come.

While the banks were being reorganized, other measures were pushed through the legislative mills at breakneck speed. During the first "Hundred Days" of the Roosevelt administration, more sweeping changes in policy occurred and more items of important legislation became law than in any comparable period in the nation's history. During this period Roosevelt demonstrated such ability for getting what he asked for from Congress that that body acquired a reputation for being a mere "rubber stamp," rushing important bills into law almost without debate and in many cases without study. For the most part, the bills were drawn up by Roosevelt's "brain trusters," with a minimum of consultation with congressional leaders. This was a "honeymoon" period for Roosevelt, during which time most congressmen, naturally conscious of their constituents, were in no mood to defy the popular President. The speed with which he responded to demands for action, and his disarming personality reflected in his speeches and in his relations with newspapermen, kept Roosevelt's popularity high with the public. Any Democratic congressman, moreover, who entertained the thought of revolt against the "dictatorship" was aware that Roosevelt's political henchman, Jim Farley, was watching carefully, prepared to withhold patronage from anyone who wandered off the reservation.

ROADS TO RECOVERY

Any such program as the New Deal was in danger of going off in all directions at once, so that its various parts might cancel each other out. In the all-important matter of attacking the Depression, one fundamental question was whether to deal with it as a world problem or as a domestic one. President Hoover had concluded that basic remedies required an international approach. Roosevelt at first accepted the idea that, while the main attack should be domestic, there was also good reason to explore the possibility of cooperation with other nations. But before long he was forced to conclude that the New Deal could not function within the framework of international agreements involving world currency and exchange stabilization. This dilemma was brought to a head at the London Economic Conference, held in the summer of 1933. Arrangements for the meeting had begun during Hoover's administration, and Roosevelt sent a delegation headed by Secretary of State Hull, an enthusiastic internationalist. While the conference was in session Hull received from his chief a reversal of instructions, which startled both him and the world and in effect wrecked the conference. Roosevelt instructed the United States delegation not to commit our government to international currency stabilization. It was, he felt, essential to home recovery that his government be free to act independently. Early New Deal measures for recovery were based on a purely nationalistic approach. The consequences of this decision have been much discussed; some believed that Roosevelt thereby contributed much to the political and economic deterioration of Europe, while others have doubted that the action was so serious in its effects. However that may be, the United States had in effect decided to "go it alone."

Political and economic orthodoxy had always insisted that in time of depression t was no part of the government's responsibility to take active measures to bring about economic recovery. Thus during the preceding severe depression, during the 1890s, President Cleveland held stubbornly to the precept that the government should confine its activities to conserving gold and balancing its budget, and on no account use the federal power to soften the blow of depression or assist anyone who had fallen victim to economic catastrophe. Hoover, as we have seen, moved a few reluctant steps beyond this philosophy. Roosevelt himself during the election campaign had promised economy and, while indicating that he favored more extensive government activity, had not expressed any willingness to unbalance the budget or leave the gold standard. In one of his very early official acts as President he attempted to set up a conservative budget program. At his request Congress passed an Economy Act reducing ordinary governmental expenditures. Though forced to ask for increased appropriations for unemployment relief, he seemed at first to be thinking of an orthodox financial approach so far as it was possible. Before long all this was to be changed; under the pressure of events and with the approval of a new school of economic thought, the New Deal would boldly decide on a revolution in fiscal policy and would be prepared to spend freely in order to put men to work and resources to use. Nevertheless, in 1933 and 1934 the New Deal approach to recovery, while scarcely orthodox, was hardly yet converted to that philosophy which unfriendly critics were to call "the handout state."

Devaluation of the dollar, which involved abandoning the gold standard, was a moderately unorthodox device designed to bring about controlled and moderate inflation; it did not seem to have much effect, but it was certainly one reason for F.D.R.'s attitude toward the London Economic Conference. Of greater importance was the much publicized National Recovery Administration set up in 1933. The idea of the NRA originated among businessmen who were troubled by the "cutthroat" competition which a depression struggle for scarce markets created. The danger was, they thought, that everyone would be forced into a fierce and destructive competitive race for what little business remained. Statistics indicate that big business had been able to safeguard its profits during the first three years of the depression, though small business had not; but by 1933 things had become so bad that even big business felt itself endangered. The administration accepted the proposition that employers should be protected from cutthroat competition. The NRA set up what amounted to a system of government-regulated monopolies. This was, of course, a reversal of the official government policy in operation ever since passage of the Sherman Antitrust Act in 1890. But it carried forward the tradition of interpreting antitrust legislation very generously; in particular, it related to Herbert Hoover's policy of encouraging the activities of "trade associations," which often established what amounted to price-fixing agreements by and for specific industries. Business leaders urged Roosevelt to utilize the association idea as a means of raising the price level of industrial products and thereby rehabilitating the whole of business. The result was the NRA, which exempted participating businesses from prosecution under the antitrust laws and provided for the establishment of cartel-like price-fixing arrangements among businesses. Director Hugh S. Johnson was empowered to call upon the various industries to submit what were called "codes of fair competition." These codes were agreements concerning what price manufacturers and dealers were to charge for their products; they also set up minimum-wage and maximum-hour scales for workers. Upon approval by the NRA and the President, they would have the force of law; no business could then legally cut prices below the agreed level or depart from the standards of wages and hours for employees.

The NRA was inaugurated with great fanfare, and patriotic appeals were made to the public to support it as a great crusade against the Depression. Blue Eagle emblems, the symbol of cooperation with NRA, appeared everywhere. It was not long, however, before the initial enthusiasm waned, to be replaced by widespread hostility. Workers were dissatisfied with their share of the plan, and it is a fact that employers had played a dominant role in drawing up the codes; consumers were not happy with rising prices; many small-scale businessmen complained that the codes favored big business. Above all, NRA did not seem to solve the problem of recovery. Nor was its director, General Hugh Johnson, any administrative genius; he was better at publicity. For all these reasons there was widespread relief when, in 1935, the entire law was declared unconstitutional in the Schechter case. The Supreme Court held that Congress had gone beyond its constitutional power in delegating legislative authority to the executive branch of the government, and also that the federal government had assumed too much power over intrastate commerce. The NRA was thereby effectively buried, and very few people wished to revive the corpse. The New Deal henceforth reverted somewhat to the antimonopoly tradition, bringing some antitrust

suits and subsequently holding a vast in vestigation into the problem of monopol As a means of inducing recovery, th NRA, while not a complete failure, ce tainly was not so successful as its sponso had expected. Much more needed to b done in the industrial segment of ou economy, especially in ending the shock ingly large industrial unemployment.

PRIMING THE PUM

The basic decision that the federal gov ernment should, in so far as it was able assume economic responsibility for th welfare of its citizens in times of crisis wa undoubtedly hurried along by the ecc nomic plight of the army of unemployec When the Democrats came into office, be tween 12 and 15 million persons wer out of work—roughly one-third of th labor force. These people had spent thei savings long ago, and the resources of state local, and private charities were also nea exhaustion. Hoover had already utilize federal funds in this emergency, but much larger federal effort could not b avoided. A large number of federal wor projects were initiated for the purpose o putting all classes of persons immediatel on the federal payroll. By 1935 the Work Progress Administration (WPA), unde the direction of Harry Hopkins, had re placed earlier emergency programs. It se out to find immediate employment fo such diverse skills as those of nurses, li brarians, engineers, statisticians, lawyer salesmen, and in fact, members of almos every occupation. The WPA was really a auxiliary economic system, operating be side the regular one. If a person could no find a job in the private economy, h might apply to the WPA. If possible

WPA workers were engaged in the kind of work for which they were trained, thus utilizing their skills. Here was a reservoir for excess workers until the economy could absorb them. Despite all the controversy that raged about the kind of projects WPA sponsored, this program accomplished much valuable work once its organization had been established and the peak load of unemployed had been reduced by the partial recovery of the nation's economy.

While the WPA took care of surplus labor, a Public Works Administration (PWA) was set up to assist the regular economy to expand. It had what became known as "pump-priming" duties. This was the job of spending our way out of depression by stimulating business and industry through spending money for capital equipment and construction. At its head was that incarnation of the New Deal, the irascible, colorful, able, and honest Secretary of the Interior Harold Ickes. At his disposal was over 3 billion dollars, to be spent in creating business. He conscientiously forbade "boondoggling" and concentrated on projects requiring large expenditures for materials rather than labor. These materials were purchased through regular business channels, thus stimulating production. Thousands of public buildings were erected, highways constructed, waterways improved, and dams, bridges, and harbors built or repaired through the PWA. These projects often involved collaboration with local or state government, which assumed a part of the costs by, in effect, selling bonds to the PWA. Into the stalled economy were thus injected billions of dollars, providing business for staggering private concerns to perform at a profit; at the same time, numerous

WPA employment. One of the most interesting and controversial activities of the Works Progress Administration was its employment of out-of-work artists and actors. (National Archives)

needed public improvements were created.

The price of such large-scale government spending was a budget deficit, most alarming to conservatives of the old school; there was also the threat of higher taxes on the rich. A corollary of pump priming was the redistribution of national income—the attempt to increase demand by placing a larger percentage of the national income in the hands of the poor, who, of necessity, usually spend it rather than save it. The New Deal theorists argued that a wider distribution of money would benefit all, because if more people received more, more would be spent, with a consequent stimulation of the economy. If too large a proportion of the money continued to flow into the coffers of the relatively few, those few would have more than they needed for sound spending on goods and services. It was pointed out that

PERCENTAGE OF GROSS NATIONAL
PRODUCT DIVERTED INTO
GOVERNMENTAL EXPENDITURES

Year	Total percentage diverted	Percentage in Federal expenditures	Percentage in state and local expenditures
1913	6.4	1.8	4.6
1919	29.8	26.0	3.8
1929	9.8	2.4	7.4
1932	18.1	5.2	12.9
1937	16.3	7.2	9.1
1942	39.6	34.2	5.4
1945	43.2	39.0	4.2
1950	21.4	14.3	7.1
1952	27.1	20.4	6.7

one cause of the great 1929 crash had been an excess of money at the top, which went to feed the inflation of stock values. Critics of the New Deal denied this line of argument entirely and expressed fear that such policies would distribute the national income so widely that not enough money would remain in private hands for necessary capital investments; anyhow, high income taxes, it was claimed, would remove all incentive to invest. In 1936 New Deal deficit-spending practices received the support of a new school of economics, headed by the British economist Lord Keynes, whose views supported both an unbalanced budget and income redistribution as methods of combating economic stagnation. But while Keynesian economics spread and had many notable followers in this country, it remained shocking heresy to the older orthodoxy and to most businessmen. Put forward as a means of saving capitalism by using a minimum of government regulation, it was to deep-dyed conservatives the road to socialism.

Thus were the seeds of bitter controversy sown.

LABOR

In accordance with its belief that income in the United States should be more evenly distributed, the New Deal desired to raise the pay of industrial workers. The first approach to this idea was in the NRA; the codes which were written specified minimum wages for each industry. Since labor did not receive an adequate hearing in the formation of the codes, laborers felt that their interests were not properly looked after. Especially during 1934, labor discontent was manifested in numerous and violent strikes. Even before NRA was outlawed it was decided that further aid to labor was necessary. The result was the Wagner Act of 1935. This aid to workers came in the form of legislation to help workers organize so that they would thereafter be strong enough to take care of their own interests. The Wagner Act not only recognized the right of laborers to have unions of their own choosing for purposes of collective bargaining, but it also provided elaborate governmental machinery to aid them in achieving this purpose. A National Labor Relations Board of three members was to administer and enforce regulations which allowed laborers to organize and, in so far as possible, aided them to do so. The board, for instance, had power to decide which organization of workers within a given plant was the official representative of the workers. This provision was to guard against unions that did not actually represent the workers but were dominated by employers or by labor-union racketeers. The board conducted elections in the plants to determine which union was desired and then compelled the employers to bargain collectively with the designated organization. Needless to say, the result was a tremendous growth of unionization.

Difficulties nevertheless arose. Some employers refused to cooperate and held out against the unionization of their plants until the Supreme Court, in a 5-to-4 decision, validated the act in April, 1937, two years after its passage. Trouble also grew out of conflicts, often in the form of serious jurisdictional strikes, involving the issue of which particular union was to have jurisdiction in particular industries. The most important conflicts arose as a result of rivalry between the two major organizations—the American Federation of Labor (AFL) and the Committee for Industrial Organization (CIO). This battle was an outgrowth of a long-smoldering discontent within the ranks of labor over the nature of the AFL organization and leadership. William Green, who had been president of the AFL since the death of Samuel Gompers in 1924, had failed to provide dynamic leadership or to adjust to changing times. Mass production and assembly-line techniques had long since resulted in a great increase in the number of semiskilled and unskilled workers and in a relative decrease in the number of skilled craft workers. But the AFL had continued to confine its membership very largely to the craft unions and had few unions that embraced all the workers in a given plant or industry. When the New Deal finally came to the rescue of labor, by providing a real opportunity for widespread organization, the AFL was the logical agency to supply the leadership. The AFL hierarchy was not flatly opposed to industry-wide unions as long as the existing craft unions were not disturbed, and it was willing to accept industrial unions

GROWTH OF LABOR UNIONS UNDER THE NEW DEAL

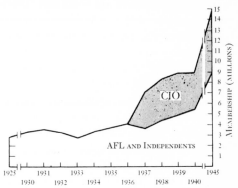

into the AFL if the old craft unions could continue to run the federation. Champions of industrial unions were not content with such subservience. In 1935, a group of leaders, including John L. Lewis of the United Mine Workers, David Dubinsky of the International Ladies' Garment Workers, and Sidney Hillman of the Amalgamated Clothing Workers, all industrial unions, led their organizations out of the AFL and set up a separate body. They formed a new union of unions which was named the Committee for Industrial Organization (CIO) and which began organizing all workers in a plant into a single union. This new organization, headed at first by the brilliant, egotistical, and pugnacious John L. Lewis, soon embraced an enormous membership, including such newly formed or greatly expanded unions as the United Steel Workers and the United Automobile Workers. The AFL, thus jolted out of its complacency and threatened with a loss of leadership to the CIO, began to make concessions to noncraft workers, and a race for members between the two groups ensued. While in 1932 the AFL membership was but 3,500,000, by 1941 it boasted a total of 4,500,000. At that time the CIO had 5 million members. These great organizations of workers have proved amply able to aid their members against even the largest of the great corporations.

Later in the New Deal era, legislation was enacted recognizing the need for economic protection for millions of workers not affiliated with any union. Minimum-wage laws were passed which were designed to force all employers to pay at least a living wage. This action helped many workers, especially in regions where unions had failed to become established; but unionization remained the most important force in raising wages. In 1953 there were only about 16 million unionized workers among a working force numbering more than 60 million. Yet unorganized workers in general received as much pay, or almost as much, as their unionized brothers. As organized workers made gains, these were automatically passed on to other wage earners. Employers realized, of course, that any marked difference between the pay of unionized men and others would speedily result in driving the unorganized into unions. In this fashion unionization has aided all workers whether they are members or not. Help for nonunionized labor came in the form of a wages-and-hours law, called the Fair Labor Standards Act. It provided for an eventual 40-cent-an-hour minimum wage and a forty-hour week for workers employed by enterprises engaged in interstate commerce. Since then, the minimum wage has been raised to keep pace with the mounting cost of living. It reached $1 an hour in 1956.

Working people also received benefit from the Social Security Act (1935), one of the most important measures enacted in the New Deal period. Its benefits were never confined only to laborers and have been extended to include most segments of the population. With its passage, the federal government at last assumed the responsibility for insuring citizens against the economic hazards of unemployment, old age, and disability. Although long overdue by the standard of other industrial nations, this step might have been postponed even longer if political leaders had not been frightened into action by the mounting popularity of ill-conceived schemes such as that put forward by Dr. Francis G. Townsend of California. Dr. Townsend, who wanted to give every old person $200 a month, competed with such other demagogues as Senator Huey P. Long of Louisiana, whose "Share the Wealth" organization proposed to redistribute wealth so that every family would receive an annual income of at least $5,-000. The passing of the Social Security Act illustrates how legislation comes about in a democratic society, and also how the New Deal measures were often very modest compared with what might have been foisted upon the nation if moderate men had left the field to the real "crackpots." Although the Social Security Act naturally fell far short of the extravagant demands being made by demagogues such as Long and Townsend, it did give the American workers a much needed cushion against unemployment and old age.

AGRICULTURE

Along with the New Deal projects to aid industry, labor, and the unemployed, went a program for the rehabilitation of agriculture. In an earlier chapter we have traced the struggles of the farmer between the Civil War and the end of the century. We have also noticed that, while from that time to the end of World War I he farmer did better, he was again in rouble after 1920, sinking into a chronic state of depression during that supposedly prosperous decade. After years of struggling with the problem, farm leaders were ready to propose a program by which the government should direct the fight against overproduction. The New Deal leaders recognized that the surpluses could not be disposed of by selling them abroad, although they hoped that in the long run agricultural exports might be greatly increased. It was equally clear that within the foreseeable future, the purchasing power or desire of urban America would not be great enough to absorb the total agricultural output. It was obvious also that such artificial devices as the protective tariff, which had given manufacturers a privileged position, could be of no significant help to farmers; indeed, tariffs were a hindrance to farmers because they meant high prices for the goods they purchased. It was not foreign-grown but home-grown produce that glutted the markets. The only alternative, it appeared, was somehow to reduce production. This could be accomplished either by allowing "nature to take its course," starving enough farmers out of production through mass economic failure, or by a controlled program allocating limited production goals to all farmers.

The farmers were hardly in a mood to be starved out. Already normally conservative farmers, through strikes and threats of violence, had been demonstrating a spirit of frustrated anger reminiscent of Shays' Rebellion. Production control appeared to be the only feasible alternative. There was nothing really revolutionary about production control. The industrial branch of our economy regularly operated that way. Protective tariffs guarded against a flood of foreign goods, and many industrial concerns were large enough to survey the whole economy and thereby make it possible for each manufacturer to measure with reasonable accuracy the amount of goods he could make and sell. Industrialists had even advocated such a controlled "national economy" in the NRA. It was, however, boldly experimental to attempt application of this principle to agriculture. The nature of agriculture, with its numerous widely scattered farms under separate management, made it impossible for farmers themselves to organize and conduct such a comprehensive program. Only the power of the federal government could administer the program, and the farmers demanded that it act.

In May, 1933, the Agricultural Adjustment Act, which established an Agricultural Adjustment Administration (AAA), was passed. This organization in the Department of Agriculture, of which Henry A. Wallace was head, embraced subordinate groups in the various states, counties, and townships. Through this pyramided arrangement, each individual farm was allotted a certain number of acres for the production of basic crops that came under the program. A prescribed percentage of acres on each farm was to be kept out of production under this plan, which was similar in principle to a layoff in a factory when production was outrunning consumption of a particular manufactured article. To avoid employing police-state methods, to assure farmer compliance, and at the same time to raise farmer income, the AAA gave cash benefit payments to farmers as an inducement to participate in the plan. This money was to come from what was called a "processing tax," which was a tax levied on the processors of farm-grown products. Hence, meat packers, flour millers, and textile manufacturers paid the tax and passed it on. In arriving at this decision it was reasoned, as farmers had reasoned since Jackson's day, that the very large gap in prices between what the farmer received and what the consumer paid for a given agricultural product was due largely to the excessive profits of the middleman.

Farmers were paid to hold down production. Lower poduction, resulting in scarcity, was expected to raise prices. The farmer, gaining both ways, would have his income substantially raised. And so it worked out for two years, assisted by the general rise in prosperity. But in January, 1936, the AAA was declared unconstitutional. Thus the AAA shared the fate of the NRA in the field of industry. Since the farmers, unlike the industrialists, could not operate without it, a stopgap measure was immediately substituted. Under this law, production control was approached through utilization of the clearly constitutional power of the federal government to promote conservation of our natural resources—one of which was land. The government simply paid farmers to conserve the growing power of their land by resting it or growing soil-rebuilding crops. This resulted in the limitation of production. All farmers who agreed to participate, and almost all did, were granted benefit payments for engaging in this conservation. They were paid, in effect, to raise more of such soil-building crops as grass and hay, and less of certain crops which were being overproduced. Five overproduced crops were controlled in this manner—cotton, wheat, corn, rice, and tobacco. In 1938 a new Agricultural Adjustment Act was passed. This act provided for emergency marketing quotas, which limited the amount that farmers could sell without penalty. In addition, the government agreed to support the

price of certain farm products. Farmers could obtain loans on crops that they withheld from the market when prices were too low. These loans could be repaid with the product itself, which was valued at a price level set by the government as constituting a fair return to the farmer.

This so-called parity was a basic feature of the entire AAA, for the whole program was aimed at achieving parity for the farmers. Parity was the estimated return that would place farm income on a par with other segments of our economy. This involved an administrative decision on just what proportion of our total national income should go to agricultural producers. It was decided that 1909 to 1914 constituted a well-balanced, equitable, normal period in our economy, and hence "parity prices" should be the average of those years. Secretary Wallace also succeeded in placing in the act an "ever-normal granary" provision, which expanded warehouse facilities where crops could be stored in order to reduce price fluctuations by evening out the flow of produce into the market; at the same time, it ensured the nation against shortages which might occur in years of crop failure. The act also provided partial (50 to 75 per cent) crop insurance for wheat growers. The program, then, provided for curbs on production, payments to farmers for producing less, a guaranteed minimum price, and storage facilities to prevent famine if production were cut too low. The farmers had received substantial relief. Production control, helped by serious droughts in 1934 and 1936, resulted in substantially less production and therefore in increases in farm prices. By 1937 the average had risen 86 per cent above the 1932 level. Farmers' real income was then about equal to the 1929 level.

Despite this success, there were many

criticisms of the program, of more or less validity. Some farmers themselves, especially among the older generation, grumbled over the "regimentation" imposed upon them. The first AAA aided the owners of large farms while few benefits accrued to smaller and tenant farmers. Subsequent legislation rectified this condition to some extent. Some nonfarmers scornfully attacked the program as basically unsound because it was based on economics of "scarcity" instead of "plenty." It seemed to many to be ridiculous that production was being cut while millions at home and abroad were not getting enough food to eat. Defenders of the AAA argued that the same criticism could be applied to manufacturers, who by no means produced at plant capacity all the time. Industrialists, and many consumers, complained that it was unjust that they were taxed to pay for subsidies to farmers. This objection could be answered by the reminder that in effect manufacturers had long had the advantage of subsidies through protective tariffs and through monopoly practices which the government did nothing to prevent. There was also much partisan controversy over the degree to which political favoritism, inefficiency, and graft accompanied the elaborate farm program.

Those wedded to the theory that expanding foreign trade was of basic importance to the nation's farmers were distressed over the purely nationalistic nature of the AAA. It was contended that limiting production to the home market and artificially fixing prices higher than world prices would result in the permanent loss of foreign agricultural markets. The only response to this contention was the negative, resigned statement that substantial world markets were in any case lost forever. The tremendous exports of farm produce during the years following 1939 were paid for almost entirely by the American taxpayer and could hardly be considered as normal exports. Some people opposed the AAA on grounds that it sustained inefficient farmers and kept in production marginal land which should have been retired. That criticism was impossible to answer on purely economic grounds, but perhaps it could be answered by suggesting broader considerations of the general welfare.

The New Deal program for agriculture also included legislation to ease the burden of farm debt, to reverse the alarming trend toward tenancy, to move farmers from submarginal land and resettle them on more productive acres, to provide better housing in blighted areas, and to bring electricity to farm areas where private companies had shown no interest. The most important of all these was farm debt relief. In 1932, two-fifths of the farms carried mortgages, many of which were extremely burdensome. Government agencies and funds helped thousands of farmers by refinancing mortgages and making short-term loans. The result of the program was that it raised the farmer from the lowest level in the economic scale to a position which was envied by some other groups.

OTHER NEW DEAL PROGRAMS

The New Dealers considered that they had a mandate not only to bring about economic recovery, but to overhaul thoroughly the old order that had collapsed so disastrously in 1929. Growing directly out of the stock-market crash was a regulatory agency, long overdue, to safeguard investors and the whole economy. This was the Securities and Exchange Commis-

sion (SEC), created in 1934. All new security issues sold in interstate commerce
had to be registered with the SEC, providing accurate information for the benefit of investors; the commission also was
given power to control the stock ex-
changes in order to prevent the manipulation of security prices and to prevent an
excessive flow of money into the security
market. Loans to brokers might be restricted, and the act which created the
SEC also gave to the Federal Reserve
Board power to control margin requirements in the purchase of securities. In the
same category may be placed the 1935
Utilities Holding Company Act, directed
at abuses stemming from monopolistic
control of the electric-power business.

One of the most challenging of New

Deal ideas was the reclamation, through
regional planning, of a great rural slum
area in the valley of the Tennessee River.
Here soil erosion and soil depletion, the
results of generations of unscientific farming, had wasted what had once been one
of the fairest agricultural regions in the
land. The valley became the scene of a
bold experiment in federal-government-
sponsored regional planning—the Tennessee Valley Authority (TVA). This
project, authorized in May, 1933, grew
in part out of a long-standing debate during the 1920s over what to do with the
Muscle Shoals power site, which the government had begun to develop during
World War I as a source of power to produce nitrates for explosives. Senator
George W. Norris of Nebraska for years

THE TENNESSEE VALLEY

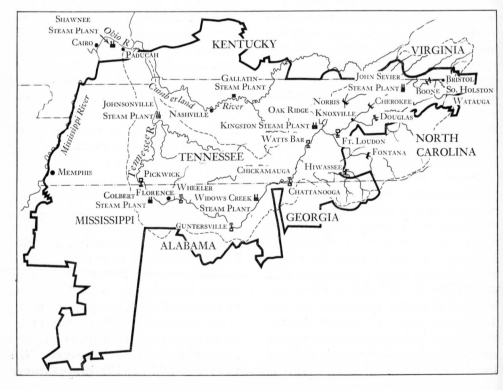

led the crusade to develop and reclaim the area as a public project. When the New Deal took up the idea, the TVA was authorized as a public corporation, with such broad powers that it eventually directly affected the lives of 4,500,000 people in an area of some 40,000 square miles which included parts of the seven states of Tennessee, Kentucky, Alabama, Mississippi, Virginia, North Carolina, and Georgia. TVA brought about a substantial reduction in the rates charged by electric companies throughout the nation. Moreover, as a bold experiment in social planning on a regional basis, it attracted world-wide interest. At the core of the TVA's many activities was a series of dams on the Tennessee River and its tributaries. Eventually there were over a score of these, most of which were constructed by the TVA itself. The dams provided electricity and flood control and contributed to the development of river navigation.

As the law was written, Congress provided that TVA sell electricity wholesale to other agencies, giving "preference to states, counties, and municipalities, and cooperative organizations of citizens or farmers, not organized or doing business for profit, but primarily for the purpose of supplying electricity to its own citizens or members. . . ." This placed the TVA in competition with private companies of the region, and so caused a bitter controversy. The chief battle was with the Commonwealth and Southern, a holding company with subsidiaries in the region, which had the moral support of outraged businessmen everywhere. The president of that corporation, Wendell Willkie, conducted a spirited fight which earned him great renown, especially among conservatives. The struggle took place in the courts, with TVA winning a series of court decisions. In the end, TVA bought out the Commonwealth and Southern holdings and other private utility companies operating in the region. Lowered power rates, promotional activity, and increased capital investments resulted in a remarkable development of the region through the use of electricity.

One of the purposes of TVA was to provide a yardstick to determine what electricity rates should be charged by private companies. The utility companies contended that this was not realistic, because, unlike the TVA, in their rate making they had to consider taxes and a fair profit. TVA countered with the argument that it allowed for these factors, and also that it had its own special costs in the form of interest and amortization payments made on the bonds issued, which offset taxes paid by private corporations. Various complexities, however, kept the yardstick a subject for disagreement. TVA argued that if the power industry would lower its rates it could do more business and make more money. Meanwhile, electrical rates throughout the country did drop markedly. TVA Director David Lilienthal said that during the seven years following 1933 there was about a 35 per cent decrease in the nation, compared with a 2 per cent decrease during the preceding seven years. This improvement was due in part to an aroused public and to improved regulatory legislation and enforcement, but also to the example set by the New Deal's Rural Electrification Administration (REA), which gave the industry lessons in how to find new customers, as well as to the example set by the TVA. Its rate policy, which has been one of TVA's greatest contributions to the welfare of the industry and its customers, was to set electricity prices so low as to induce increased consumption. Between 1934 and 1942 electrical consumption in the nation just about doubled.

The TVA also carried out a vast flood-control program. The river dams, designed with this in mind, were to hold back water in the spring and thereby make possible a more even flow of water. Land in the valley was also improved so that it would hold moisture and would not erode. Reforestation, crop rotation, and strip farming held water on the land, preventing floods and saving the land from erosion. When, in 1937, the Ohio River flooded and caused great damage, the same torrential rains did not bring a devastating flood along the Tennessee River. Transportation facilities were also developed, and an educational program, improved library facilities, and new and improved houses and factories helped lift the Tennessee Valley from a slum into a national asset. Population increased, and there was a marked improvement in the standard of living. Nevertheless, the TVA remained an object of criticism because it seemed so close to socialism. An effort to extend the idea to other great river valleys such as the Missouri and Columbia was defeated in Congress in 1938. Startling and suggestive, the TVA was also wholly new and controversial—and in these respects it was very much a symbol of the whole New Deal.

Reflecting the same interest in conservation of natural resources shown by the TVA were a number of other programs. Franklin Roosevelt, inspired by the example of Theodore, had long been interested in conservation, and so was the hardworking "old curmudgeon" Ickes. The early Civilian Conservation Corps (CCC) project, established to give work and training in a healthful environment to jobless young men, did work in the field of flood prevention, forest-fire prevention, and reforestation. The Soil Conservation

Service, created in 1934, promoted, among other things, strip farming and terracing in order to prevent land erosion and floods. Many huge dams were built to provide flood control, electric power, and water for irrigation. Though none of these projects was as ambitious as the TVA, on the Columbia River some huge industrial developments sprang up near great government-built dams which supplied cheap power. Extensive new agricultural regions were developed too—to which that captious group whom the New Deal could never please would rejoin, "Why increase the area of agricultural land while at the same time limiting agricultural production?" Such inconsistencies were no doubt as characteristic of the New Deal as were its energy, imagination, and innovating genius.

OPPOSITION AND CRITICISM

The New Deal continued in 1936 to receive the same public endorsement indicated in 1934, when it had startlingly increased its majority in Congress. It had brought hope out of despair, and skillful Democratic propaganda was able to contrast Democratic vigor with Republican confusion. The Republicans were indeed in much confusion, and did not know whether to denounce all the New Deal (which was unwise) or approve some of it (which was weak). Nevertheless, the "honeymoon" period was over, and an opposition was rising which made up in vehemence what it might lack in numbers. This opposition was most marked in business circles. For a while during the sad days of 1933 business had given the new administration its warm support; by 1935 that had changed. Too much regimentation; too much confusion; too many professors making policy; above all, financial unorthodoxy and higher taxes—these were the commonest complaints from businessmen.

Irked by such criticism, and wishing to press ahead with his ambitious reform program, the President shifted the New Deal's emphasis more and more toward the interests of the lower- and middle-income groups. Thus the emphasis of the farm program had shifted to aid small farm owners and tenants; labor had received a great boost in the Wagner Act; the plight of workers and the aged was recognized in the Social Security Act; and following the death of NRA, some fire was directed against monopoly in big business. "Pump priming" and social reforms cost money, and as the national debt spurted up to 34 billion dollars, many began to fear that this threatened the long-term position of persons in the upper-income brackets. John D. Rockefeller himself announced sadly that there would be no more millionaires. Wealthy foes of the New Deal could find some support among average Americans who feared the death of the old tradition of individualism and self-help.

An especially aggressive anti–New Deal group was the Liberty League, organized in 1934 by wealthy industrialists and supported by some disgruntled Democrats, including the embittered Al Smith. Most newspapers were hostile to the New Deal. But, as in 1800, the wealthy and the well-born were apparently out of step with the masses and without effective political organization. In the election of 1936, the GOP showed considerable confusion in its platform and speeches, while the candidate it selected, Governor Alfred M. Landon of Kansas, did not prove a very effective vote catcher. Renominating Roosevelt and Garner, the Democrats won a landslide victory, exceeding even that of 1932

—they carried every state but two, Maine and Vermont. The electoral vote was 523 to 8; the popular vote, 27,750,000 to 16,680,000. The New Deal was overwhelmingly victorious at the polls. But this did not mean that the minority lessened the bitterness of its opposition.

One important stronghold of minority opposition was the Supreme Court, which played a role reminiscent of Jefferson's times. Four of the nine justices (Justices Mc Reynolds, Sutherland, Van Devanter, and Butler) were extreme economic conservatives of the old school; only three (Brandeis, Cardozo, and Stone) were liberals. The other two, Owen Roberts and Chief Justice Charles Evans Hughes, were middle-of-the-road, but Roberts generally veered to the right on important decisions. Since 1934 there had been a series of 5-to-4 or 6-to-3 decisions in which New Deal measures were killed or rendered ineffectual. The Court majority relied upon various theories, perhaps chiefly on the old one of states' rights. It continued, as in the 1920s, to invalidate regulations of wages and hours on the grounds that they infringed on property rights, using again that venerable refuge of property, the Fourteenth Amendment. Roosevelt declared bitterly that the Court had created a "no-man's land" wherein neither the states nor the federal government could legislate on important economic questions, and he added that "we have been relegated to the horse-and-buggy definition of interstate commerce." It became evident that the chief challenge to the New Deal was to come from the Supreme Court.

The President, after receiving his overwhelming mandate at the polls in the election of 1936, determined to strike boldly at the Court. Some sort of constitutional amendment had been suggested to clip the Court's wings, but this seemed both impractical and time-consuming. How could the New Deal, evidently the will of the people, be saved from a reactionary Court? Roosevelt proposed a scheme which, under the guise of a general reorganization of the judiciary branch, would increase the membership of the Supreme Court beyond nine justices. This "court-packing" bill aroused heated debate, in and out of Congress, and it incurred unfavorable comment from many who had heretofore been friendly toward the administration. Like Jefferson, Roosevelt was to find the Court a tough nut to crack. Opponents of his plan were irritated by his lack of frankness and concerned over the threat to the judiciary's independence. After long debate in the Senate, the bill could not be passed, and an ominous split appeared in the Democratic party itself. No doubt many, even in the Democratic party, had long been waiting for so infallible and all-conquering a leader to make a bad mistake. The judiciary bill is generally held to have been Roosevelt's first serious blunder, and his first major defeat. Nevertheless, he could claim to have lost the battle but won the war, for the Court, astutely prodded by Chief Justice Hughes, began to hand down decisions favorable to the New Deal, as Hughes and Roberts voted with the liberals; and soon conservative Van Devanter resigned, affording an opportunity to replace him with a liberal. Other vacancies and new appointments followed, and there was no more trouble from the Court. Yet from this time forward, Congress, including a dissident anti–New Deal group of Democrats, began to examine new proposals in a more critical spirit.

At about the same time, in the summer of 1937, an economic "recession" occurred. After four years of rather steady economic gains, the New Dealers thought they had the Depression well on the way to being licked. Feeling that the pump had been sufficiently primed, the President cut spending and attempted to balance the budget. But business indices plunged sharply, and the number of unemployed rose in 1938 more than 3 million. Plans for a balanced budget had to be abandoned, as federal spending again increased to pour money into the stalling economy. In 1938 federal expenditures rose to 7 billion dollars—an all-time high, and about twice the normal rate during the 1920s. Not until the advent of World War II, with its stimulus of defense spending, was it safe to abandon huge expenditures for public works and relief. The economy responded to the new stimulus, and by the end of 1938 had reached a new high for the 1930s, which was lower, however, than that of 1929. The question that remained was whether economic prosperity did not demand, on New Deal terms, a perpetually unbalanced budget, spending without end. If so, it was a disturbing thought, even to many New Dealers, who had assumed that only a temporary injection of government money would be necessary.

As we shall see, foreign affairs, rather than domestic, had begun to absorb most of the President's attention as early as the fall of 1937; before long, they would hold the center of the public stage. The mid-term elections of 1938 were still, however, mostly concerned with domestic issues. They revealed a certain dissatisfaction with the reform program. In this election Roosevelt made an effort to "purge" such Democrats critical of the New Deal as Senators Millard Tydings of Maryland and Walter George of Georgia by asking the voters to replace them with New Deal Democrats. He was rebuffed. The Democrats saw their majority in Congress considerably reduced in this election, and a number of Democrats could be relied upon to vote against most New Deal policies. Henceforth Roosevelt followed a more conservative course; but a reason for this, in addition to the signs of public dissatisfaction, was his need to concentrate ever more attention on the world political situation.

THE NEW DEAL IN SUMMARY

By mid-century, the greater part of the New Deal reforms and innovations seemed certain to become permanent in American life. The new distribution of the nation's annual income was here to stay, sustained by the credit and tax structure. New Deal laws, agencies, and heavy government spending affected every significant economic segment of our population. Lower- and middle-income groups received more, while higher-income groups received relatively less. For example, in 1929 the upper 1 per cent of our population received 13.6 per cent of the total personal income, after taxes, but by 1948 the same group was receiving only 6.2 per cent. Any political party which advocated a reversal of the new income structure would be inviting defeat. The beneficiaries of the New Deal held an overwhelming voting majority. There were few politicians in either the Democratic or Republican parties who would risk advocating, openly, the elimination of such things as TVA, social security, the Fair Labor Standards Act, farm-price supports, the Securities and Exchange Commission, or the Federal Deposit Insurance Corporation. Modifications might be expected, but no outright scrapping of the great bulk of New Deal reforms. Moreover, the New Deal attack on the Depression

PER CAPITA NATIONAL INCOME

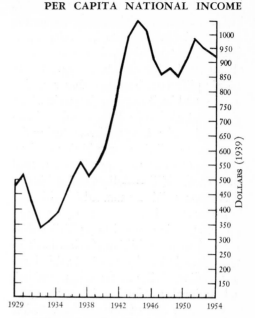

would be remembered as a movement that restored hope to a terribly frightened people and provided invaluable experience upon which to draw in case another devastating depression threatened.

The New Deal experience was not entirely conclusive as a blueprint for the future handling of depressions. It brought about what seemed at the time a rather large public debt (about 40 billion dollars), large enough to frighten businessmen, without achieving complete recovery. In 1939, after the New Deal had been curing the Depression for six years, there were still more than 8 million unemployed and national production was less than it had been in 1929. The New Deal might claim credit for a long and fruitful list of badly needed reforms; it could point with pride to the economic progress made since the horrible days of despair in 1933; but it could not claim that it had conquered the Depression or restored the nation to complete economic health. Subsequent experience, however, seemed to indicate that Keynes and the New Deal had been on the right track. What the New Deal could not do by itself, Hitler forced America to do, and the results were phenomenal. Keynes had argued (to oversimplify considerably) that a nation could spend itself out of a depression. The New Deal tried to do this very thing. Average yearly federal expenditures during the 1920s were a little over 3 billion dollars. From 1934 to 1940, expenditures ranged between 6.5 billion dollars and 9 billion. This amount did not succeed in achieving full recovery, but from 1942 to 1945 federal spending soared to 34 billion dollars and then 98 billion, falling back to 39 billion dollars by 1948. At this level of spending, full recovery was attained, and national production in 1953 more than trebled that of 1939. The question of just how much spending would have been required to cure the Depression was still unanswered.

The New Deal did not entirely cure the Depression, but it may be said to have saved capitalism. In the depth of the Depression, frantic Americans with votes to cast were demanding remedies. In less conservative hands, those remedies might have been very radical indeed. During the years between the two wars, economic crisis in Europe was profound enough to make it impossible for capitalism to work. In those countries, from one-half to three-fourths of the voters embraced socialism or communism. Germany took up Hitler's National Socialism, England drifted toward socialism, France moved to the verge of national disunion. The New Deal, by altering the income structure and by encouraging labor unionization, which would protect that change in the future, preserved the conservative spirit of America's workers. Farm policy did the same for the farming population. Other New Deal reforms, as in banking and social security, benefited lower-income groups and helped preserve the opportunity to rise in the economic scale, which has always been so prominent a feature of the American system. Since 1938 the American economy has experienced its longest period of uninterrupted progress and has attained a productivity undreamed of in the prosperous 1920s. Much of this prosperity can be traced to the stimulation supplied by two wars and a continued cold war, but some of it must be credited to the readjustments within the system made by the New Deal. An unconverted opposition will continue to insist, we may be sure, that all this progress will prove to have been made at the cost of liberty, bringing eventually full socialism and the death of private enterprise. The New Deal era was full of excitement and full of controversy, and the marks of that controversy are sure to remain on the American people for a long time.

FURTHER READINGS

Dixon Wecter has covered this period, for the History of American Life series, in *The Age of the Great Depression, 1929–41* (1948). In the more popular Chronicles of America, D. W. Brogan does a good job in *The Era of Franklin D. Roosevelt* (1950).

On Roosevelt himself, Frank Freidel's biography *Franklin D. Roosevelt* (3 vols., 1952, 1954, 1956) is the most thorough and objective, but the story has thus far been carried only to 1932. Also valuable are J. M. Burns, *Roosevelt: The Lion and the*

Fox (1956); Rexford G. Tugwell, *The Democratic Roosevelt* (1957); and John Gunther, *Roosevelt in Retrospect* (1950). Especially dramatic is A. M. Schlesinger, Jr., *The Age of Roosevelt:* volume II, *The Coming of the New Deal* (1958).

From a large amount of personal narrative and memoir material, Robert Sherwood, *Roosevelt and Hopkins* (1948), and Raymond Moley, *After Seven Years* (1939), should be singled out for mention. A unique and fascinating record is *The Secret Diary of Harold L. Ickes* (3 vols., 1954).

The literature on the New Deal in all its manifold aspects is understandably immense. Joseph Alsop and Turner Catledge, *The 168 Days* (1938), and C. H. Pritchett, *The Roosevelt Court* (1948), are useful on the judiciary. M. S. Eccles, *Beckoning Frontiers* (1951), deals with banks and banking. Selig Perlman, *Labor in the New Deal Decade* (1945), and Milton Derber et al., *Labor and the New Deal* (1957), cover this field well. Russell Lord, *The Wallaces of Iowa* (1947), is a biography of F.D.R.'s Secretary of Agriculture. Leo Gurko, *The Angry Decade* (1947), stresses literary and intellectual currents. Such tracts of the times as Alfred M. Bingham, *Insurgent America* (1935), and Charles A. Beard and G. H. E. Smith, *The Old Deal and the New* (1940), as well as the already cited Beard work, *America in Midpassage,* convey the outlook and mood of the era.

For additional bibliography, see the *Harvard Guide,* sections 256–264

TWENTY-SEVEN

The Road to War

THE TWENTY-YEAR TRUCE

1931
Japanese seize Manchuria.

1935
Italians attack Ethiopia.
First American neutrality act passed.

1936
Spanish civil war begins.
Germans remilitarize Rhineland.

1937
Japanese attack north China.

1938
Nazis overrun Austria.
Sudeten crisis; Munich agreement.

1939
Nazi-Soviet pact announced, August 23.
Germans invade Poland; World War II
begins, September 1 to 3.
American arms embargo repealed.

1940
Germans invade Denmark and Norway.
France defeated in six weeks.
Destroyers-for-bases deal with Britain.
Selective Service Act passed.
Roosevelt reelected for third term.

1941
Lend-Lease Act passed in March.
Germany invades Russia, June 22.
Japanese-American negotiations in
Washington.
Japan attacks Pearl Harbor, December 7.

FOR THE SECOND TIME within a generation, an administration engaged in a vast program of economic recovery and domestic reform was forced by events to turn from these conerns to face the problems of a world drifting rapidly into war. Preoccupied as the American people were with the New Deal, they and their leaders were distracted by the growing menace of world war. By 1937, the Roosevelt administration had to take a serious view of the foreign situation, and from that time on, foreign policy increasingly became the main concern of the President and his advisers.

Since the end of World War I, there had been little security in the world. A brief period of hopeful peacemaking in the 1920s, which saw the settlement of the tangled reparations dispute and the writing of treaties guaranteeing the security of the Franco-German frontiers, ended with the coming of the Depression in 1929. The Depression greatly weakened the new democratic or semidemocratic governments that had been established in Europe after World War I. In their stead, governments of a dictatorial and militaristic character appeared.

The disappearance of these democratic states occurred in a Europe in which the traditional values of Western civilization had been already substantially weakened. Great states had been captured by novel political movements that rejected in great measure the ethics of the West and the ideals of Christianity. The Marxist Communists had seized control of Russia in

560

1917, and the Italian Fascists under Benito Mussolini had taken power in 1922. Both these movements rejected much that heretofore had been regarded as essential to a civilized society. The Communists were stridently antireligious and condemned the existing code of morals as capitalistic or "bourgeois." In pursuit of their goal of world-wide revolution, they acted upon the doctrine that the end justified the means. The Fascists of Italy were professedly anti-Communist and sought to present themselves to the world as defenders of European life against Communism. But they rapidly developed a form of totalitarian government, organized a police state, and preached the idea that force was the final, and indeed, desirable factor in human relations. Both the Communists in Russia and the Fascists in Italy tried by propaganda to instill a warlike and military spirit in their people. The Communists did so in the interests of revolution; the Fascists, in the interests of Italian expansion in the area of the Mediterranean.

Despite the belligerent harangues that frequently came from Moscow or Rome, Europe gradually learned to live with these nations. But the coming of the Depression helped create a new and more menacingly warlike government in Europe. The democratic Germany that had come into existence at the close of World War I had its limited popular support eroded away by the economic distress of the Depression. Growing numbers of Germans looked for new leadership and radical solutions of their problems. They found such leadership in Adolf Hitler and the National Socialist party. Hitler became the leader of the German government in 1933. With his coming to power, the march of Europe to war moved at an accelerating pace. The Nazi state which he

led was perhaps the most fearsome dictatorship known to history. While both Communists and Fascists were ruthless in their elimination of all opponents and critics, they tried as a rule to keep their cruelties hidden from the rest of the world. The Nazis seemed rather to glory in their shame and to take a sadistic pride in their cruelties. But of even greater import to other European nations, the Nazis were fanatical racialists, full of hatred and contempt for the non-Germanic peoples of Europe. Under Hitler's leadership, Germany embarked on a tremendous program of rearmament, to the accompaniment of oratory in which the dictator of Germany spoke in menacing terms of the German need for greater living room in Europe. Alarm in Europe mounted with the increasingly powerful might of German arms and with the often hysterical tone of Hitler's speeches.

Europe was not the only area, however, threatened by war. In the Far East, Japan embarked on a course of aggression. There the government seemed to fall increasingly under the control of cliques of militarists who were determined to secure for Japan domination of much of the area of China and southeast Asia. Growingly contemptuous of the limitations on Japanese naval power established in the Washington naval conference, the Japanese terminated this agreement and started upon the enlargement of their navy and the fortification of strategic islands in the Pacific. In 1931, Japanese troops clashed with Chinese forces in Manchuria and speedily overran the country. Disregarding Chinese sovereignty in the area, the Japanese set up a satellite state, feeling a need to protect their economic interests there. The League of Nations, in a well-documented report, while conceding that Japan had grievances in Manchuria, con-

Adolf Hitler speaking in Vienna

After the assault on Austria in early *1938*, few could doubt the brutal nature of Hitler's Nazi government. But neither the will nor the weapons were ready to oppose the German dictator in the western democracies. "America Firsters" were convinced that American interference in any European quarrel could lead to no good. By *1940* most Americans thought otherwise to the point of favoring all-aid-short-of-war to the enemies of the Axis powers. It took the Pearl Harbor raid to get them into a shooting war.

Charles A. Lindbergh addressing an America First rally in Fort Wayne

The Pearl Harbor attack: an American ship exploding

Another burning ship during the Pearl Harbor attack, Dec. 7, 1941

President Franklin D. Roosevelt
signing the declaration of war
against Japan

demned the resort to force as a means of righting them. Stung by the rebuke, Japan left the League as speedily as possible. But aside from the rebukes of the League and the condemnation of public opinion in most countries of the world, Japan suffered little and, indeed, seemed to gain much. Aggression had been profitable, and Japanese armies remained in Manchuria, threatening northern China by their presence. The only American action was to promote a movement to withhold recognition of the conquest.

An uneasy truce prevailed in this area until 1937, when the tension in north China again flared into war, with Japan once more the aggressor. Japanese armies invaded north China, thus beginning a war that lasted until 1945. The Japanese were to learn to their cost that China was a large country, easy to overrun but hard to conquer as long as any Chinese national feeling existed to keep alive resistance to the invader. And Japanese aggression had done much to arouse the long-dormant patriotism of the vast Chinese masses.

By the time Japan's forces were launched against China in 1937, the outlook for peace in Europe looked precarious. In 1935, the Italian dictator had finally lived up to the menace in his speeches and alarmed the world by starting an unprovoked invasion of the independent African kingdom of Ethiopia. Again aggression seemed to bring swift and profitable returns. The Italian army quickly defeated the poorly armed forces of Ethiopians, and the pathetic appeal of the ruler of the invaded land to the League of Nations for assistance met with little more than an embarrassed silence that was testimony to the helplessness of that body. Various suggestions to halt Italian aggression by cutting off oil supplies met with defiant replies from that government

and seemed to unite the Italian people more solidly behind their rulers. In the end, nothing was done to halt Italy, and aggression seemingly paid off.

The chances for peace became even bleaker with the outbreak of civil war in Spain in 1936. The two sides in this bitter conflict soon received support from outside sources. Germany and Italy sent supplies and military units to assist the antirepublican groups under the leadership of General Francisco Franco. The republican moderate and left-wing groups received some support, though in much smaller amounts, from Communist Russia. The open efforts to support one side or the other of the Spanish conflict divided Europe into armed camps, with the prospect that an incident might plunge the continent into war at any moment. The collaboration of Germany and Italy in supporting General Franco in the Spanish war was indicative of a developing alliance between these two nations. Annoyed by the hostile attitude shown by France and Britain toward his Ethiopian venture, Mussolini turned to Germany for support and formed with Hitler the so-called Rome-Berlin Axis. This Fascist-Nazi combination constituted a power bloc menacing to the peace of the world.

We know today, because of the disclosure of secret German documents, that by 1937 the German dictator had decided to launch Germany upon a course of expansion which made war inevitable. Hitler had consolidated his hold on the German people by a huge program of rearmament that gave employment to many and that gave Germany a measure of economic recovery. His critics and political enemies had been silenced by a fearsome program of terrorism. The nations threatened by the new Germany seemed paralyzed by weak and hesitant leadership. In March, 1936, Hitler sent German forces into the Rhineland, which had been demilitarized by the Versailles treaty and by the Locarno pacts of 1925. There was no effective protest against this action from either Britain or France. In Europe, as in Asia, the forces of aggression were on the march; the antidemocratic states were apparently sweeping on in an unimpeded march to increasing power which the democratic states of Europe seemed helpless to halt.

THE MOUNTING CRISIS

If the democracies seemed helpless against the advance of the dictators to greater power up through 1937, the next two years saw an even more dismaying deterioration of the position of the democratic world. Early in 1938, Hitler launched the German army on yet another venture of aggression. He used brutal tactics of intimidation to annex Austria, whose government was able to offer no effective resistance. Soon there came out of Vienna, the capital of the formerly independent nation, the ugly tales of brutality and murder that accompanied the forces of Nazism wherever they moved.

Then the shrill demands of the German dictator were turned against another of Germany's neighbors, Czechoslovakia, one of the states newly created as a result of World War I. Hitler appeared determined to smash the Czech democratic state through the threat of waging a war designed to "liberate" the German people who lived in that nation and were supposedly suffering from brutal Czech oppression. But the Czech government was not intimidated by the German demands, and prepared to defend its independence. The Czech government also called on its ally France to aid it in the swiftly gather-

Munich Conference. (World Wide Photos)

ing crisis. But neither France, the ally of Czechoslovakia, nor Britain, the ally of France, was prepared to defend the position of the small nation threatened by Hitler. Instead their leaders, especially the British Prime Minister, Neville Chamberlain, decided to appease Germany by sacrificing the German portions of Czechoslovakia and transferring them and their peoples to Hitler. Amidst an atmosphere of ever-mounting crisis, an agreement to this effect was signed at Munich in September, 1938. This Munich pact was later to be condemned as arrant folly on the part of the leaders of the democratic states, but it should be realized that neither Britain nor France was prepared for war and that public opinion in both countries strongly supported this last desperate attempt to avert a terrible war. Peace, with or without honor, seemed preferable to the mass destruction of human life another war would inevitably bring.

But the war momentarily averted at Munich was bound to come. Though at Munich Hitler had declared that he would respect the remnants of Czechoslovakia, he was soon dissatisfied with his bargain. In a few months the German army swallowed up what had been left of that unhappy little country. This action destroyed whatever hopes had been left in the minds of British and French leaders that peace could be secured by appeasement of the German dictator. There could be no peace with a government led by a man who knew no law but his own insatiable appetite for conquest. The British government promised to come to the aid of other states which were threatened by the Germans. Guarantees of aid were extended to Poland and Rumania. But these states were too remote for any British aid to be effective. In order to buttress the anti-German front, Britain sought an alliance with the Soviet Union. Here alone was the power in eastern Europe that seemed great enough to check the sweep of German might. This decision was a decided reversal of the policy of Britain. The British had up to now felt that Russia, under the grim dictatorship of Joseph Stalin, should not be invited to play a large role in European affairs. For this reason Russia had been excluded from any share in the settlement of the Czechoslovakian crisis.

The belated British effort to form a common anti-Hitler front with the Soviet state ended in debacle. Russia, rebuffed at the time of Munich, was deeply suspicious of the diplomacy of the Western democratic nations and listened instead to the furtive blandishments of Hitler, who up to that moment had been stridently anti-Communist. In August, 1939, the world was astonished and dismayed at the news of a grand Soviet-German pact, in effect dividing up eastern Europe between the two dictatorships. Seemingly free now from the danger of any Russian intervention, Hitler began a campaign of hate against Poland. That nation refused to bow before the storm of abuse, and on September 1, German forces moved across the Polish border and the German dive bombers began their attacks on Warsaw and other Polish cities. Two days later, Great Britain and France declared war on Germany.

Thus World War II began, destined to be bloodier and more destructive than any war in history. Its coming was the logical conclusion to a period of years in which antiliberal dictators, maddened by a thirst for conquest and power, held the upper hand in world affairs, while the strength to resist them seemed not to exist. The failure of the appeasement policy had demonstrated that no peace with these dictators was possible save on the basis of unresisting compliance with their demands. This price was more than even the most peaceably minded democracy was willing to pay.

The forces of aggression in Europe and those in Asia soon came into alliance. The forging of this alliance received a momentary setback with the making of the Soviet-German agreement, but in 1940 the Rome-Berlin Axis was extended to Tokyo in a so-called "pact of steel" which seemed at that time to confront the rest of the world with the threat of domination by the dictatorships.

AMERICAN ISOLATIONISM

The American people watched the growth of international terrorism and the march of the aggressors with mounting horror, made more real because the development of short-wave radio, spanning the Atlantic, brought the very voices of European leaders into millions of American homes. But coupled with horror was a widespread gratification that the American people were not involved in the crises that seemed likely to engulf Europe. The descent of much of Europe and Asia into war was a grim drama of which the American people were witnesses and in which they were not participants. President Roosevelt did not share the sense of assurance apparently held by many Americans. Alarmed by the increasing measure of international violence, in October, 1937, he tried to warn the American people of the dangers converging on them. He warned that "the political situation in the world . . . is such as to cause grave concern and anxiety to all peoples and nations who wish to live at peace and amity with their neighbors." He further cautioned:

Innocent peoples and nations are being cruelly sacrificed to a greed for power and supremacy which is devoid of all sense of justice and human consideration. . . .

If those things come to pass in other parts of the world let no one imagine that America will escape, that it may expect mercy, that this Western Hemisphere will not be attacked, and that it will continue tranquilly and peacefully to carry on the ethics and the arts of civilization. . . .

But the warnings of the President met with a chilly response. The general public reaction only served to indicate the deeply entrenched isolationist feeling in the nation. This isolationist feeling was widespread in the decade of the 1930s. Most Americans, the public-opinion polls indicated, thought that our participation in World War I had been a mistake and that the American people in the future should take no sides in any war of foreign origin. Isolationism had its roots deep in the American past.* There was a strong American opinion that democracies did

* "Isolationism" is used chiefly to mean noninvolvement in European political affairs. It should be understood that the United States had always had important economic and cultural ties with Europe and the rest of the world.

Fear of war. Many liberals were isolationists because they saw American liberties as unique in an increasingly totalitarian world and were sure that involvement in war would bring severe restraints on those liberties. (By permission of the St. Louis Post-Dispatch)

not wage war or practice deceitful diplomacy, as the "despotisms" of Europe were reputed to do. There was a feeling that the Atlantic Ocean imposed such substantial barriers between Europe and America that events in the older continent had no import for the new. What interest could the United States have in European wars, when her own interests lay so obviously in continental expansion in this hemisphere? Reinforcing the hold of this traditional isolationism on the American mind was the mood of disillusionment which sprang up in the years after World War I. The feeling that we had been tricked into that war against our own and the world's best interests was widespread in the 1920s and even more popular in the following decade. The tawdry wrangle over the matter of war debts contributed greatly to this feeling. Perhaps on no other policy were the American people so generally agreed as on that of hostility to any participation in any more wars of European origin.

In looking back on the reasons for American entrance into the war in 1917, increasing numbers of Americans were persuaded that our policy had been dictated by the economic ties that had developed with the Allied powers of Britain and France. Loans made by American investors to those belligerent governments, the sale of American products in large quantities to these warring nations without any parallel sale to Germany and her allies had created a vested interest in an Allied victory that the United States government had eventually underwritten by entering the war as a combatant. The widespread acceptance of this economic explanation for our entry into the first world war clearly suggested the manner in which we might avoid involvement in a second. The way to stay out, it appeared, was to prevent the growth of economic ties with any belligerent nation in a future conflict. In order to stay out of war, Americans had to abandon their traditional rights of travel and commerce on the world's oceans in time of war and be prepared to forgo the profits arising from wartime trade. These attitudes were eventually translated into law. In 1935, when Italy attacked Ethiopia, Congress prohibited American citizens from selling or carrying arms to belligerent nations after the President had proclaimed the existence of a state of war. Some time later, a prohibition of loans to belligerents was also written into law. With the outbreak of the civil war in Spain, Congress passed a joint resolution forbidding the sale of arms to either side in that conflict. All shades of political opinion, from right-wing Republicans to left-wing Democrats, supported this legislation. In May, 1937, these temporary acts were replaced by a permanent law. This law retained the prohibitions of the sale of arms and the giving of arms to belligerent nations, but included in this new law was the so-called cash-and-carry principle. Rather than enact a complete embargo of the sale of all products to belligerents, the law allowed certain raw materials to be sold to warring nations, provided they were paid for in cash and carried from the United States ports in vessels of foreign states.

This law was attacked from two quarters. There were those who maintained that it assumed there were no real issues that concerned the American people in any foreign conflict. It legislated with fine impartiality against aggressor and victim alike. Those who voiced this criticism would have preferred a law that allowed the President to discriminate in controlling arms shipments against an aggressor nation. On the other hand, there were those who maintained that the law did not establish a true neutrality, for in the cash-and-carry provision the law clearly favored those nations which held control of the seas through dominant sea power.

While these laws testify to the avid desire of the American people to escape embroilment in any future conflict, American sympathy with the victims of aggression abroad was also to be reckoned with. The desire to stay out of war frequently conflicted with the contrary impulse to sympathize with people who were attacked by aggressive nations. This conflict is clearly revealed in American policy in Asia. Despite the clear intent of Congress in passing the neutrality law, President Roosevelt declined to apply it in the conflict between Japan and China on the legalistic ground that neither side in the struggle had issued a formal declaration of war. The real reason for this decision was the belief that the prohibition of arms to the belligerents would harm China a great deal more than it would hurt Japan. American sympathy for China as the victim of attack checked any serious criticism of the President for his choice in this matter.

On the other hand, the administration was completely unwilling to take any positive action to check the course of Japanese aggression, despite some violently provocative acts on the part of the Japanese. Japanese bombings of American ships in Chinese waters, even in one instance a sinking of an American naval vessel, elicited nothing more vigorous than verbal protests from the American government, which were met by profuse apologies from the Japanese. The people of the United States were not going to be provoked into war by any Japanese activities in a portion of the globe in which most Americans felt little immediate interest. Even the Japanese rejection of the long-established American policy of the Open Door in China, and the promulgation of a so-called New Order in Asia, in which Japan would clearly be dominant, brought little more reaction from the American government than the statement that the United States did not recognize any new order in Asia created by the Japanese alone.

Thus it was that both Congress and the Chief Executive generally followed what was called the "storm cellar" approach in the face of actual war in Asia and impending war in Europe. The isolationist inclinations of the American people had brought about the writing into law of acts that abandoned traditional American policies about freedom of travel and trade. The hands of the President in dealing with foreign affairs had been somewhat tied by the neutrality legislation. When he tried to warn his fellow citizens that they would not be safe in a world of growing lawlessness, the reaction to his speech revealed that public opinion allowed him very little room to maneuver. Americans seemed prepared to confront the growing world crisis by clinging firmly to the program of the storm cellar.

THE CRUMBLING OF ISOLATION

Apparently firmly committed to staying out of the impending second world war by the applications of techniques that might have prevented our entry into World War I, the American people were to find neutrality an increasingly difficult position to maintain. A basic factor was that Americans could not be neutral in thought as they were trying to be in action. The character of the Fascist and Nazi states of Italy and Germany, the acts of brazen aggression carried out by them, the barbarous policies they enforced against their enemies, and the open contempt revealed for ordinary decency shocked and horrified Americans. In the Asiatic areas, the aggressions of Japan aroused the hostility of the American people.

So, somewhat paradoxically, Americans were both passionately opposed to the militaristic course of the aggressor states and strongly isolationist. While they hated totalitarian dictatorship, they hated war even more. It was pointed out that in the event of another war, America too might lose her democracy. It was argued that ideas like fascism and nazism could not be defeated by military power, only by ideas. Some argued that, for all its brutality, Nazi Germany stood as a barrier against Russian Communism, which was a greater threat to Europe. This argument died out after the signing of the Nazi-Soviet pact in 1939. Others alleged that, behind their military façades, the aggressor states were too weak economically to stand the strain of a protracted war and therefore were no real threat to the United States. The argument was also frequently heard that the victorious powers of 1918 deserved little sympathy, for had not their treatment of Germany after World War I sown the seeds for World War II? Were not Britain and France imperialist powers, who were only trying to hang on to past plunder against a new set of robbers? America could have no legitimate interest in what was once referred to as "another chapter in the bloody volume of European power politics." Thus was the powerful emotion of isolation nourished by a variety of illusions about the possibility of living peacefully in a world of lawlessness. But considering the traditions of the American people and the obvious horrors of any impending war, isolationism seemed as reasonable as appeasement once seemed to the British and French.

It was in this apprehensive state of mind that Americans watched the coming of war in Europe. They observed the great Czechoslovakian crisis of 1938 with breathless interest and greeted the Munich pact with genuine relief. There were voices raised, however, to point out that Hitler could apparently gain anything he wanted through blackmail. And it was obviously difficult to be neutral when Hitler's Munich victory was followed by a shocking outburst of terrorism against the Jews in Germany. Open condemnation of this discriminatory brutality was voiced by many in America, from President Roosevelt on down. Both countries called their ambassadors home "for consultation," and relations between the United States and Germany were charged with greater bitterness than had prevailed at any time since 1919.

Certainly it was not until after the Munich pact that the administration began seriously to fight against the prevailing isolationist doctrines. A limited amount of naval rearmament was begun late in 1938. President Roosevelt was now thoroughly convinced that the foes of Axis aggression had to be given as much American support as possible, lest they too fall before Axis power and America confront the dictatorships alone. In the spring of 1939, the administration put on a major drive to get a modification of the Neutrality Act of 1937. The cash-and-carry principle written into that law had expired after two years. The administration proposed to revive that provision of the law and apply it also to the sale of munitions. Thus France and Britain would be permitted through their command of the sea to secure armaments from American sources, to the limit of their capacity to pay, and to carry them from our ports in non-American ships.

A bitter debate ensued, with the supporters of the administration arguing that American neutrality and its consequent denial of American-made weapons to the democracies of Europe encouraged the aggressors. The modification of the neutrality law would contribute to the prevention of war in Europe. But isolationist ideas triumphed. By the narrowest of margins, 12 to 11, the measure was finally killed in the Senate Foreign Relations Committee, and an influential Republican member of that body stated that, contrary to the opinions of the State Department, his sources of information in Europe told him there would be no war in Europe. The Senator was misled by his informants. War came in September, 1939. President Roosevelt invoked the Neutrality Act and issued the usual statement of neutrality. But he revealed his own state of mind and spoke for an overwhelming number of the American people when he said in a nationwide address: "This nation will remain a neutral nation, but I cannot ask that every American remain neutral in thought as well. Even a neutral has a right to take account of facts. Even a neutral cannot be asked to close his mind or conscience."

THE SPREAD OF WAR

By the time American citizens had had a chance to ponder the meaning of the President's words, German troops had won their first major victory. Striking with devastating swiftness, the Germans speedily overran Poland. They were joined in this enterprise by the Russians, and the two great powers divided the territory of their hapless neighbor. But with the close of the Polish campaign, the war moved into a new period. Aside from patrolling activities and some small clashes at sea, the blitzkrieg with which the Germans had laid Poland low seemed to degenerate into a "sitzkrieg." French and British forces confronted the Germans across a very peaceful battlefront, and in the United States there were references to the "phony war."

There was a war, however, which aroused the deepest emotions of Americans and provoked them to a great outpouring of sympathy for an attacked people. Continuing the policy of expansion revealed by their sharing in the despoiling of Poland, the Russians attacked the little neighboring nation of Finland. Despite the overwhelming disparity of power with which they were confronted, the Finns put up a tremendous resistance, and during the winter of 1939–1940 they amazed the world by their capacity to hold the power of Russia in check. The

sympathies of the American people were greatly aroused by the fighting Finns' defiance. The League of Nations expelled Russia from membership, but aside from this gesture of condemnation, little was done to aid the beleaguered Finns, and in the spring of 1940 they succumbed to the massive strength of the Soviet Union.

By the time the remnants of the Finnish army were returning to their battered homes, the German forces were again on the move. Without warning, on April 9, 1940, neutral Denmark and Norway were attacked and speedily conquered. And before the rest of the world had time to recover from the shock of these moves, the Germans launched their great offensive on the western front against France. Again striking without warning or declaration of war, the Germans seized control of Belgium and Holland, and then struck at the central section of the French line. Pierced by the speeding columns of German tank forces, the French went into what was first a retreat and then a rout. Within the short space of six weeks, the Germans defeated France, something they had not been able to achieve in four years of fighting in World War I. In the closing agonies of defeat, the French were attacked by the Italians too.

With ruin all around them, French leaders sent desperate appeals to President Roosevelt for arms shipments. All he could do, however, was to send expressions of sympathy, remind them that shipments of arms could be authorized only by Congress, and make a strongly worded speech condemning Italy for striking its neighbor in the back. But in their great need, this was of little encouragement. The French were forced to sign an armistice, and Hitler dramatically staged the ceremony in the same railroad car, located in the same spot, in which the Germans had signed the armistice terms in 1918. The French were effectively out of the war.

The Germans ruled most of France through military occupation, but they tolerated the existence in southern France of a French government with its capital at Vichy. This Vichy regime was formed of varying elements of French politics. Some of these were genuine Fascists, anxious to the point of servility to cooperate with the victorious Germans. Others were French patriots who felt that France had to accept the fact of defeat and learn to live in the new European order being created by the Germans. They hoped, however, to cooperate with this "new order" with some measure of dignity, and they wished to use what was left of French power, such as naval forces and possession of a large North African empire, to protect what they could of French independence. But the freedom of action of the Vichy regime was exceedingly small; France was largely reduced to the status of a German satellite state.

The British had been able to pull back most of their small army from the defeat in France by heroic improvisation and because of their command of the waters of the Channel. But it was an army without weapons, and the British position seemed hopeless. In the crisis of defeat, however, new leadership had emerged in Britain. Winston Churchill, who had spent weary years warning the British of the impending dangers of German power, was at last summoned to lead the British people in the most dangerous hour of their history. He spoke in language of unsurpassed eloquence to rally the courage of his countrymen, and his dauntless resolution aroused a new fighting spirit in Britain, but even Churchillian oratory seemed powerless to stay a German at-

tack if it were launched at British shores.

With France prostrate and with Britain apparently momentarily threatened by an invasion she seemed helpless to halt, American complacency was shaken to its foundations. Nothing in our history had prepared the American people for the situation that suddenly developed on the shores of the North Atlantic. The United States had grown to greatness and power in a world in which the North Atlantic area had been controlled by Britain and France. With these nations the United States had had its differences, but nothing they had done for years had impeded in any fashion the growth of the United States. As long as Britain and France had been powerful, the United States had devoted a smaller proportion of its manpower and wealth to military preparation than any other major state. And now this entire structure of power was threatened. One of its bastions was knocked out, and the other seriously menaced. Not for generations had Americans had to think so seriously and realistically of their relations with the rest of the world. The fearful possibility loomed large that, in President Roosevelt's words, the United States might become "a lone island in a world dominated by a philosophy of force."

THE COLLAPSE OF ISOLATIONISM

The first reaction of the American people, Congress, and leaders was to look to their own defenses. Within a few months of the defeat of France, the Congress had appropriated for defense nearly as much as had been spent by this country in the whole of World War I. President Roosevelt called for the construction of 50,000 airplanes, a number generally derided as being impossibly large. But in the subsequent war years this figure was greatly exceeded by American productive efforts. Even more significant than the mounting sum of defense appropriation was the decision of Congress to draft manpower for defense. The adoption of our first peacetime conscription law in September, 1940, even though it was passed over strenuous opposition, was clearly indicative of the mounting alarm at possible German victory. Certainly no such action would have been taken had it been French and British armies rather than German that had won the recent battles in Europe.

With Denmark, Holland, and France under German control, the question of the fate of their colonies in the Caribbean and on the adjacent South American mainland became of crucial importance. To see them occupied by German military or naval units would create a "knife at the throat" threat to the Panama Canal and other American defenses. Expressing this alarm was the congressional resolution of June, 1940, opposing any transfer of territory in this hemisphere from one non-American power to another. Conscious also of continental defense to the north, the United States set up a Joint Defense Board with Canada, despite the fact that Canada was a belligerent in the struggle and the United States officially a neutral. Thus did the movement of events and the necessities of defense override considerations of both neutrality and isolation.

Meanwhile the resistance of the British overseas bought time for the United States to attend to these duties of defense. The assumption of many, friends as well as foes, that the fall of Britain was imminent proved false. At first hoping for some sign of British surrender, Hitler came reluctantly to the conclusion that an attack would have to be staged across the narrow waters surrounding the British Isles. Air supremacy was essential for such an attack, and here the Germans were foiled. The British Royal Air Force, though outnumbered, was not outmatched by the Germans and held the air of Britain against German efforts to seize control. The resort by the Germans to massive bomber raids at night was the confession that their battle to seize the mastery of the daylight skies had failed. London and the other great cities of Britain might stagger under the weight of nighttime bombings, but no German soldiers put foot on British soil save as prisoners of war.

With Britain and her associated nations of the Commonwealth still fighting Hitler, and with the majority of American citizens fearful of an inevitable conflict with his power, the case for sending arms to the British became well-nigh irresistible. She was the last bastion lying between us and the power of the Axis. If she collapsed, Hitler might easily acquire command of her fleet and be in a position to strike across the Atlantic. Impelled by this fear, the administration sought for every loophole through which to get arms into the hands of Britain and her allies. Some hundreds of thousands of rifles and hundreds of pieces of World War I artillery were rushed to the beseiged British Isles as rapidly as possible.

But all these efforts to aid the British paled into insignificance with the negotiation of the destroyers-for-bases deal. By executive agreement with the British authorities, the President agreed to turn over to the British fifty overage American destroyers to help them in their fight to control the waters of the Atlantic against the prowling German submarines. In return, the British agreed to the lease of a series of outposts of the North American continent, stretching from Newfoundland down to Trinidad, on which the United States might build air and naval bases for the defense of the continent. Certainly no one questioned that both sides were the gainers from this agreement. The need of the British for the destroyers was great, and the gain in American security from the bases was immense. What could be, and was, questioned was the means by which the deal was achieved and the reality of any American neutrality after it was entered upon. If the President's action was essentially without the sanction of law—and many argued that it was—it could be defended as essential for American defense against the lawlessness reigning in the outside world. But it was irreconcilable with neutrality. Events had pushed the American people and government from neutrality to quasi belligerency in a few short months.

BASES ACQUIRED BY THE UNITED STATES THROUGH DESTROYER DEAL WITH GREAT BRITAIN, 1940

ALL AID SHORT OF WAR

The echoes of the controversy were still ringing in American ears when the nation was plunged into a presidential election contest. It was testimony to the crisis atmosphere that the election had many unusual features. The Democrats discarded the two-term tradition that had existed since the days of Washington and nominated Roosevelt for a third term. They hailed the President as the man best qualified by experience to deal with the international crisis the nation confronted. The Republican nomination was almost equally novel. The GOP nominated Wendell Willkie, who was practically a political unknown. He had long been head of an electric-power company which had fought the advance of the Tennessee Valley Authority. The fight he put up endeared him to many businessmen opposed to the public power projects of the New Deal. Willkie also had a pleasing personality, a forthright manner in the discussion of public events, and the further advantage of not being associated with the more obviously old-guard faction of the Republican party. The appealing qualities of the man and his politically refreshing naïveté created immense popular support for him among rank-and-file Republicans, and their pressure forced his nomination on a reluctant convention.

While the Republican candidate attacked President Roosevelt on many domestic issues, he indicated he agreed with the administration about the need of strengthening the forces of democracy opposing Hitler, although he condemned many of the methods used by the President. But all Willkie's vigorous campaigning was largely futile. Despite the anti-third-term feeling that influenced many, the majority of the voters preferred the

ISOLATED ISOLATIONIST

This cartoon by Vaughn Shoemaker, titled "Isolated Isolationist," indicated the trend during the election campaign of 1940. (Library of Congress)

experienced Roosevelt to the untried Willkie in an hour of crisis, and the President was elected for a third term.

Encouraged by the vote of confidence given him, President Roosevelt moved more boldly on a program of aid to the British and their allies. Aware of the desperate need of the British for American arms, and aware also of the diminishing capacity of the British to pay for these arms, the President proposed that the United States provide them on a "lend-lease" basis; that the arms be furnished the foes of Hitler in the common cause of embattled democracy; and that the manner and time of repayment be shoved aside until the crisis was past. The President used the homely analogy that one did not worry about the ownership of the hose when it was needed to put out the fire in a neighbor's house. The bill to put such a lend-lease program into effect was significantly labeled "An Act Further to Promote the Defense of the United States." Despite bitter opposition from the isolationist elements in the Congress, the bill became law by large majorities, and the day after its passage the President asked for an appropriation of 7 billion dollars to buy the arms to send to the foes of the Axis powers.

But if the manufacture of arms was essential, their delivery was equally so. The prowling wolf packs of German submarines made shipping across the Atlantic ever more dangerous, and it was a logical extension of American policy that American naval power should be used to protect the movement of convoys crossing the dangerous waters of the North Atlantic. American troops took over from the British the task of the defense of Iceland as a necessary bastion in the defense of the North Atlantic crossing, and soon American naval vessels were joining the British, Canadian, and other combatant navies in the Atlantic convoy operations. Shooting incidents and some sinkings inevitably occurred, and by the close of the summer of 1941, American naval forces were engaged in a shooting war in their patrolling operations. Secretary of State Hull frankly said the United States had abandoned the law of neutrality for the law of self-defense.

In the summer of 1941, as Americans were entering the struggle for the control of the North Atlantic, a tremendous change occurred in the war. In June, Hitler started a terrific military assault upon the Soviet Union. The apparently solid front among the dictatorships of the world was shattered. The Nazi-Soviet pact of 1939 had always been a marriage of convenience. The expansionist ambitions of the two powers in southeast Europe, the

Balkan Peninsula, and in the Middle East all too obviously clashed. Hitler, facing the probability of a long war brought about by stubborn British resistance and the mounting American aid to his enemies, resolved to eliminate any possible Russian threat by war and conquest. The defeat of Russia would also assure Germany of a supply of raw materials from the great natural resources of that nation. And so, in June, the mighty German army, the *Wehrmacht,* attacked Russia.

In the United States a majority of the people thought that Hitler was on the way to another smashing triumph. The dismal record of the Russians in the early weeks of the war against Finland had established in the American mind a low opinion of the fighting prowess of the Russians. This evaluation was reinforced by the early achievements of the Germans in Russia. Great Russian armies were apparently slashed to pieces and millions of prisoners taken as the long German tank columns swept on into Russia. Months of the struggle were to elapse before any true conception of the massive endurance of the Russians and of the magnitude of their military power was to form in the American mind and supplant the former picture of ineptitude. In the fall of 1941, Hitler seemed on the verge of a triumph that would place the vast resources of Russia at his command.

THE ROAD TO PEARL HARBOR

Despite the fact that great masses of their forces were bogged down in laborious military operations in China, the events of the European war provided the Japanese with an opportunity for further expansion that they were quick to seize. In the throes of her defeat, France was confronted with Japanese demands for the right to construct air bases in French Indochina and to move troops across French colonial soil to facilitate attacks upon southern China. Japan pressed her demands on the defeated nation with great persistence, and in September, 1940, France was forced to yield. These air-base concessions greatly strengthened the position of Japan in southeast Asia. The Japanese were already established on Hainan Island, which lay athwart the sea routes between Singapore and Hong Kong, from which she could also threaten the Philippines.

With this strengthening of her strategic position, Japan increased the pace of her diplomatic offensive. Thailand, the independent Asiatic nation bordering on French Indochina, was encouraged to renew an ancient quarrel with the French over boundaries. The Japanese hoped the dispute would further weaken the position of the hapless French and at the same time lead the Thai people and government to look to the Japanese for support. Thus they might be led to accept Japan's leadership in what the Japanese called the Co-prosperity Sphere of Southeast Asia.

At the same time, the Japanese were reaching further south to gain the yet more fabulous prize of the oil-rich Dutch East Indies. But here they had less success. Even in the hour of defeat and the occupation of their homeland by the Germans, the Dutch government in exile in London stubbornly refused to yield to Japanese pressure. The Japanese entered into an elaborate "war of nerves" against the Dutch, but the sturdy Netherlanders resisted all Japanese pressure. Not that the Dutch felt they had any real chance of resisting a Japanese attack, but they were determined they were not going to lose their colonial empire piecemeal by infiltra-

tion and subversion. If the Japanese wanted the Dutch East Indies, they were going to have to fight for them.

But the Japanese were not anxious to get by war what might be obtained by less costly methods. Further, the evident facts in the spring of 1941 that Hitler was not able to invade Britain and that the war was likely to be a long one added to Japanese caution. To German urgings that the Japanese attack the British base at Singapore, the Japanese replied that they would do so when German troops invaded Britain. But in the meantime, and without any great added risk of war, there were further concessions that might be wrested from unfortunate France. Naval-base sites and the privilege of stationing large Japanese forces in southern Indochina were secured from France in July, 1941. When the time came, these were excellent jumping-off points for a Japanese attack on Singapore and the Dutch East Indies.

The American authorities in Washington watched these Japanese advances to the south with mounting alarm and apprehension. The American government was not prepared to ignore the lawless course of the Japanese. Aside from the obvious peril that it presented to the Philippines, it also threatened the long-standing American interest in the maintenance of an independent Chinese nation. In order to place some restraint upon Japan, the American government had started in July, 1940, to exert a mounting economic pressure on Japan. Restrictions were placed on the exports of certain strategic goods. The severity of these restraints increased until a large number of important strategic goods were embargoed altogether. There were many in high official circles who would have made the embargoes even more strict by imposing a ban on the sale of oil. Others disagreed and maintained that embargoes would force the Japanese into more aggressive actions.

Whatever the effect of the American embargo, the Japanese government remained firm in its expansionist course. On July 2, 1941, an Imperial Conference (a meeting of high Japanese officials presided over by the Emperor) resolved to continue on the program of southward expansion, even if it might involve the risk of war with the United States and Great Britain. Shortly after this decision came the further pressure on France that led to the granting of bases from which an attack on Singapore and the Netherlands Indies would be possible.

What the Japanese did not know at this juncture was that their secret code had been broken by the American intelligence service and that their purposes of further expansion and ultimate attack on the Dutch and British colonial areas were known to the American government. This American knowledge of Japanese intentions rendered nearly all diplomacy useless. American officials could place little or no credence in the value of Japanese proposals and promises; certainly the secret information did not encourage them

to ease the effect of the embargo on Japan. Yet in its increasing severity, the American embargo encouraged further Japanese aggression. The fact that an embargo was placed on oil in August by the United States greatly alarmed the Japanese leaders, for they knew that such an embargo would have a crippling impact on the Japanese economy. The Japanese became more determined to secure access to an oil supply that the United States could not deny them. Such a supply source was to be found in the Dutch Indonesian archipelago.

Warned as they were of Japanese plans for southward expansion, American officials could see little purpose in most Japanese diplomatic proposals. The Japanese even proposed on one occasion that President Roosevelt and the Japanese Premier should have a face-to-face meeting somewhere in the mid-Pacific. The only terms which would be agreeable to the United States for the settlement of Pacific tension called for the abandonment not only of plans for further conquests, but of nearly all that Japan had seized since starting on its course of aggression in 1931. Even had the American government displayed any

As the Japanese saw it. Photograph taken from Japanese plane during Pearl Harbor attack, December 7, 1941. (Navy photograph)

tendency to compromise with the Japanese, it is doubtful that public opinion would have permitted any "Far Eastern Munich," to quote the phrase that was current at the time. There was less of a division of opinion concerning Far Eastern matters than prevailed about European ones. Isolationism was much less pronounced about Pacific affairs than over participation in European matters.

By the last week of November, the Japanese fleet was in motion, not so much to strike toward the south as with the idea of so crippling the United States Pacific fleet in the Hawaiian Islands that it would be unable to impede or intercept planned Japanese moves for overrunning the Philippines, Malaya, and Singapore, and— most prized of all Japanese objectives— the Dutch East Indies. The Japanese forces began to move out of the Sea of Japan toward the bases in the Kurile Islands. By November 21, Japanese submarines were in the mid-Pacific, moving toward the American naval bases. They later formed part of a massive force of aircraft carriers, cruisers, destroyers, and various support ships that moved toward Hawaii. On the morning of December 7, the strike was launched, and by the close of the morning's activity, the Japanese had achieved their objective. The bulk of the main American naval force in the Pacific was either sunk or lying crippled in the ruins of the American naval base at Pearl Harbor.

THE PEARL HARBOR DEBATE

Why had Japan attacked us? And why had she been able to succeed in the surprise attack on our fleet at Pearl Harbor? These questions were to supply food for much subsequent controversy. Even after fifteen years, some questions remained not entirely answered, but the principal facts seemed clear. During 1940 and 1941 the United States had stood more and more firmly athwart the ambitions of Japan in Asia. By a policy of firmness we had hoped to restrain Japan, thus preserving the Open Door and the Pacific balance of power while also aiding Great Britain against Hitler and Mussolini. For the raw materials of southeast Asia were vital to Britain's war effort and to our own war industries. With Britain wholly engaged in Europe, and France and the Netherlands prisoners of Hitler, it appeared that only the United States could prevent the whole of Asia from falling into Japanese hands.

Unfortunately, a policy of firmness had its dangers. America was rearming and was fortifying her Pacific possessions of Guam and the Philippines. The military extremists who were powerful in Tokyo argued that, since America was an implacable foe in any case, it would be better to begin the war before America grew too strong. The American embargo, applied in the summer of 1941, gave them a chance to argue that Japan must obtain supplies of oil and other raw materials by conquest, since she would not be allowed to buy them. It is clear that in deciding on a policy of firmness the American planners underestimated the capacity and willingness of Japan to wage war. Despite scattered warnings, few thought the Japanese capable of such a blow as the one they struck at Pearl Harbor on December 7, 1941. They were thought to be in trouble in China. If they attacked anywhere, it was felt, it would be against British Malaya or the Dutch Indies, or perhaps they might fall on Soviet Siberia when Russia was defeated by Germany.

The United States might conceivably have purchased peace from Japan in 1941; but, as has been noted, public opinion was decidedly hostile to "appeasement." The administration has been criticized for making no concessions in the teeth of evidence that Japan might well resort to war. But it would have been even more severely criticized for any "Far Eastern Munich," and concessions might have failed to keep Japanese expansion within bounds. It is important to note that we did have a vital stake in this region, strategically as well as economically.

While the American leaders may have lacked foresight, the more reckless charges occasionally hurled by irresponsible partisans are certainly not true. It has been alleged that, wanting to join the war but finding Hitler uncooperative, Roosevelt and his Cabinet deliberately and knowingly provoked Japan into an attack and thus took the "back door to war." The evidence fails to support this theory. On the contrary, it strongly supports the view that the administration was confident Japan would not attack us. One reason for the unpreparedness at Pearl Harbor was the widespread conviction that Japan would attack British or Dutch possessions, which is precisely what Japan did simultaneously with her attack on Pearl Harbor.

In retrospect, the Japanese strategy in attacking Pearl Harbor seems most plausible. Only the United States fleet stood in the way of their Asiatic plans; if they destroyed it, they could proceed for a long time without serious opposition. War warnings were sent out on November 27, as the American-Japanese talks broke down and the intercepted Japanese messages indicated military moves of some sort on foot from the home islands. The warnings were not couched in sufficiently urgent language and appeared merely routine to the commanders in Hawaii. It was subsequently disclosed that the army and the navy (not yet unified even in theory) were not in close cooperation and had a fatal misunderstanding about which was responsible for reconnaissance and radar warning over the Hawaiian Islands.

There was indeed negligence, at all levels, involved in the failure to be ready for the Japanese attack. It seems most plausible, however, to blame that failure on our long neglect of military preparations, a guilt shared by virtually the entire nation. Only since 1940 had the country been engaged in building a military machine. In a year and a half it was necessary to try to do everything that had not been done in the previous twenty years. The result was confusion and inadequate organization, as well as inadequate supplies. General George C. Marshall, Chief of Staff, testified later that his office thought Pearl Harbor to be well equipped and alerted. This was wrong, but it would be perverse to blame Marshall. He was trying to do the work of ten men, trying to supply shortages everywhere and create a vast war organization virtually from scratch. In the debate about Pearl Harbor, which too often has been on the level of personal attack, the clearest lesson that emerges is that a great power ought not to ignore military preparations. To have military strength is necessary to successful diplomacy. The best way of preventing war is to be prepared for it; to be unprepared may invite attack.

FURTHER READINGS

Standard works on general international relations between the two world wars include Edward H. Carr, *International Relations between the Two World Wars*

(1948), and Geoffrey Gathorne-Hardy, *A Short History of International Affairs* (1950).

On the relationship of the American people and their government to the growing crisis in Europe, there are a host of works. Of major import are the first three volumes of Winston Churchill, *The Second World War* (6 vols., 1948–1953). They are *The Gathering Storm* (1948), *Their Finest Hour* (1949), and *The Grand Alliance* (1950). Part of the American reaction to the European crisis is found in Robert E. Sherwood, *Roosevelt and Hopkins* (1948), available in a paperback edition; in *The Memoirs of Cordell Hull* (2 vols., 1948); and in Henry L. Stimson and George Mc-Bundy, *On Active Service in Peace and War* (1954). Of the battle in shaping public opinion, Walter Johnson, *The Battle Against Isolation* (1944), and Wayne Cole, *America First* (1953), tell of the two major organizations which sought to influence government action.

Also of major importance are Gordon Craig and Felix Gilbert (eds.), *The Diplomats, 1919–39* (1953), and the two works of Walter Langer and S. E. Gleason, *The Challenge to Isolation, 1937–1940* (1952) and *The Undeclared War* (1953). Donald F. Drummond, *The Passing of American Neutrality, 1937–41* (1956), is also important.

For Japanese-American relations prior to the Pearl Harbor attack, Joseph C. Grew, *Ten Years in Japan* (1944), gives the views of one in a unique position to know events and weigh their significance. Herbert Feis, *The Road to Pearl Harbor* (1950), is a judicious account. F. C. Jones, *Japan's New Order in East Asia, 1937–45* (1954), is a well-done survey. Walter Millis, in *This Is Pearl!* (1947), gives an admirable summary of an exciting hour in American history. A more recent work is Paul W. Schroeder, *The Axis Alliance and Japanese-American Relations, 1941* (1958).

Of the many volumes critical of the foreign policy of the Roosevelt regime, Harry Elmer Barnes (ed.), *Perpetual War for Perpetual Peace* (1953), is notable in that it gives most of the arguments of these critics. A work of an outstanding American historian is Charles A. Beard, *President Roosevelt and the Coming of the War, 1941: A Study in Appearances and Realities* (1948).

TWENTY-EIGHT

War Again

1941
German drive on Moscow checked,
December 6.
United States enters war following
Japanese attack.

1942
Japanese conquer southeast Asia.
Battle of Coral Sea.
Allies invade North Africa.

1943
German army surrenders at Stalingrad.
Allies invade Italy.
Guadalcanal campaign ends.

1944
Invasion of Europe across Channel,
June 6.
United States forces invade Philippines.
German counteroffensive, Battle
of the Bulge.

1945
Yalta Conference held in the Crimea.
Death of President Roosevelt, April 12.
United Nations Conference at
San Francisco.
German surrender, May 7.
Atomic bombs dropped on Japanese
cities, August 6 and 9.
Japan surrenders.

ORGANIZING FOR TOTAL WAR

THE ATTACK ON PEARL HARBOR plummeted the United States into war. In stunned surprise and anger, the American people forgot their differences and united to meet the challenge. Capital and labor pledged themselves to work in unison. Party politics were, for the moment, forgotten.

Unity of effort was highly essential, for the nation had been seriously preparing for war only since the fall of France in June, 1940, and was far from ready. Uncertainty about America's role in the world had translated itself into a half-hearted defense effort. War production had not been going well. Conscious of the danger, the administration had long been trying to enlist the cooperation of the business fraternity. The New Deal, which had belabored business leadership so long, had brought to Washington prominent leaders of industry to organize production for national defense. Yet the defense effort had been carried on without any real sense of urgency. The American people lacked consciousness of the magnitude of the effort required of them, as did their leaders. But the basic difficulty lay in trying to build a great military organization virtually overnight; for, after World War I, the nation had, as usual, sadly neglected its armed forces. The building of the highly complex military mechanisms necessary to modern war requires years rather than months.

After the events of December 7, the nation plunged feverishly into its task,

580

spurred on by continued bad news from the Pacific. The Japanese swept through the South Pacific and southeast Asia almost unopposed, taking Wake, Guam, Hong Kong, Burma, Malaya, Thailand, and finally the Philippines, despite heroic resistance on the peninsula of Bataan and the island fortress of Corregidor. As early as February, the great British base at Singapore fell and the Indonesian Archipelago (the Dutch East Indies) was occupied by the enemy. Allied forces fell back upon India and Australia.

The battle for production on the home front was really joined only after Pearl Habor. A Defense Commission to coordinate national defense had been set up in 1940 and later replaced by the Office of Production Management, headed by William Knudsen, chief of the General Motors Corporation. In May, 1942, this board was replaced by the War Production Board, under the chairmanship of Donald M. Nelson, an executive of Sears, Roebuck and Company, which gave the country for the first time the economic leadership it needed. The WPB, staffed by dollar-a-year men from industry and bright young New Dealers, was not always a harmonious body, but it managed to harness production with such success that, by mid-1943, war material was being produced faster than it could be used. Automobile production stopped on January 31, 1942, and the plants were converted to military production. After a fumbling start and many crises, a whole new industry was created to produce rubber synthetically. Existing factories changed their output and new ones were rapidly built. Shipyards were expanded. Airplanes, tanks, guns, and ships poured forth. Americans began to understand the miracle of mass production in a new sense as production figures rose to more than

double what had previously been considered full capacity. Steel production doubled, oil output rose 50 per cent, aluminum production increased sixfold, magnesium fortyfold, synthetic rubber increased from nothing to 750,000 tons a year. Agricultural production, aided by good growing weather, kept pace with rising needs at home and abroad. Labor pledged full support, worked longer hours, and forbore for the most part to strike. The experience of the war justified President Roosevelt's words that Americans were primarily builders, not destroyers.

Taxes were increased, and vast sums of personal savings went into the purchase of war bonds. Unemployment disappeared as almost 7 million new workers were added to payrolls in the first years of the war. The war was fought under conditions of almost staggering prosperity. There was production enough for guns and butter too. Meat, sugar, fats, coffee, and some other foods were rationed, as were gasoline and tires; but rationing served more as a blessing than a hardship. Its principal effect was rather to prevent prices from rising than to distribute hardship. The general level of prices rose during the war only some 20 per cent, despite full employment at high wages. The average standard of living actually improved: workers' real income rose and farm income doubled. Shortages in housing, especially in the neighborhood of new plants, perhaps caused the greatest hardship on the home front. A whole new industry arose to produce trailer homes which helped to fill this need. The shift to war production introduced violent dislocations; but the economy was flexible enough to cope with the changes without undue strain.

The war proved that the bitterness between the business community and the

Weary Marine drinking coffee
after fighting on Eniwetok

Marines and supplies at a Marianas port

The ruins of Hiroshima after the atomic bomb

Roosevelt and Churchill confer at Yalta

*World War II tried human
courage to the utmost, destroyed life and wealth on an
awesome scale. At its end
the atomic bomb—since made
many times more potent—
announced that either war or
the human race would become
obsolete. Men again sought a
lasting peace.*

The U.S. First Army's drive to the Rhine

Flame throwers on Kwajalein Island

New Deal was much less deep than the prewar strife had seemed to indicate. The rapidity and essential good humor with which Americans closed ranks was noteworthy. Industrial management met the challenge magnificently and was repaid by excellent profits as well as by the personal satisfaction of patriotic duty well done. Large corporations received the largest orders because of their greater resources and the convenience of centralized dealing with large firms. The facilities of smaller firms were used to supply the major producers, so that orders "trickled down" to small business. To the consternation of progressives who were alarmed by the close cooperation between government and big business, the war resulted in a speeding up of the concentration of economic control. Management took a long step in the direction of industrial democracy, however, by accepting the principle of labor-management committees, thereby widening the basis of authority to include labor. These committees proved that cooperation in management between capital and labor was possible and prevented long and costly strikes.

Thanks to the two years of defense production prior to our entrance into the war, the armed forces were not entirely unready, as had been the case in 1917. The army numbered 1,600,000, and officer-training programs were well advanced. The air forces were growing rapidly. Education centers for 30,000 fliers a year had already been set up. Bases had been built, and plans for many more were ready. The navy, which had begun preparations earliest and which had been fighting a limited war in the Atlantic for a year, was nearer to fighting readiness before Pearl Harbor than any other arm of the services. Horizons had to be almost indefinitely expanded, however, when the

full size of the task of beating the Axis was realized. Before the end of the war, over 15 million men and women had served in the armed forces, and at the war's end some 12 million persons were in uniform. The selection and training of this enormous force was begun at once, although no offensive could be launched till near the end of 1942. All men between eighteen and forty-five years of age were registered for the draft, and 17 million were examined for physical fitness. Five million, almost one-third, were unable to pass the examination, a fact which shocked Americans who were so proud of their supposed high standard of health and well-being. The navy and the marine corps were able to fill requirements for the first year of the war with voluntary enlistments. WACS, WAVES, SPARS, and WASPS (women auxiliaries of the armed forces) were not drafted. The training of men for the army and navy air forces, which ultimately numbered 3 million, was much more complex and costly than any similar project America had ever undertaken.

That all these tasks of creating a superb striking force in so short a time should have been accomplished was no less grat-

THE EFFECT OF WORLD WAR II AND THE POSTWAR PERIOD ON CONSUMER PRICES

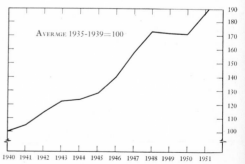

ifying than surprising. Challenged, America was able to throw back into his teeth Hitler's gibes about the decadence and inefficiency of democracy.

HIGH TIDE OF THE AXIS

While the battle for production was being won, the real war was being fought, at first under the most unfavorable conditions. Strategy demanded that the European theater, the seat of the greatest danger, be dealt with first, while expending such effort as could be spared in what was essentially a holding action in the Pacific. Nevertheless, the limited action that could be sustained in that area proved remarkably successful. In May, 1942, our crippled navy was able to engage an enemy fleet in the Coral Sea while our planes turned back Japanese ships off Midway. By September the marines were on Guadalcanal, and before the end of the year Australian and American forces were attacking on New Guinea. The objective of containing the Japanese and protecting Australia and New Zealand while preparing for a later offensive proved eminently practicable.

Elsewhere, the year 1942 saw for the most part only the war of production and preparation. Supply lines to our allies were established: 3,000 miles long to England, 5,000 miles long to Archangel, and 12,000 miles long to Calcutta and Abadan (in the Persian Gulf). Over these extended routes, supplies were delivered to England, Russia, and China. Meanwhile, troops were moved into the British Isles, and American planes based in England began their three-year bombardment of the Continent.

The war was already two years old in Europe when the Pearl Harbor disaster brought the United States into it, and the Axis powers had enjoyed almost uninterrupted success. As we have pointed out, first Poland had been crushed; then, in the spring of 1940, Denmark, Norway, the Low Countries, and France fell before the German onslaught. Britain, standing alone, was subjected to the first all-out attempt at conquest by air power. Hitler, believing firmly in the decadence of the democracies and encouraged by his easy success in France, was confident that England could be persuaded to capitulate or become his ally. The great German air force, which Hitler believed could destroy British morale, bombed England night after night for months. But England in "her finest hour" endured, and in the end the "invincible" German air arm was blunted by superb British fighter planes. While Britain was being tested in the air, enemy submarines, mines, and surface craft sought control of the Atlantic. Despite American aid, the German Atlantic effort came within an ace of cutting the indispensable supply lines from America and the Commonwealth.

Britain remained master of the Atlantic by a narrow margin, but in the Mediterranean, through which ran her traditional life line to the east, her position was even more precarious. Italy had claimed the shores of this inland sea for her own. As a first step toward the restoration of the ancient Roman Empire, she had annexed Albania in 1939 and subsequently attacked Greece. At the same time, from her colonial possessions in Libya and Ethiopia she proposed to possess herself of Britain's ally Egypt as a first step toward the conquest of all North Africa. The troops which she brought to this task numbered half a million, five times as many as England could bring into the field in that theater of war. The task demanded of the British navy and the 100,000 poorly equipped soldiers stationed in the Mediterranean seemed almost hopeless. Fortunately, Italian power proved inadequate to the opportunity. The fighting men of tiny Greece stalled the Italian legions completely, while the British met the advancing Italians at the Egyptian border and destroyed them in a magnificent series of desert battles. In February, 1941, the victorious British were at Benghazi, halfway across Italian Libya.

The threat of the Italian surface fleet was also successfully met. Engagements at Taranto and Matapan demonstrated that Italian seamen were no better able to match the British than their soldiers. The Germans thus received a further setback from the failure of their ally. German strategy had depended upon the Italians to close up the Mediterranean and so force upon the already overstrained British shipping the exclusive use of the long route around Africa. An alternate strategy would have been to get Spain into the war, which might have resulted in the capture of Gibraltar, long coveted by many Spaniards. With the great rock fortress of Gibraltar in hand, the narrow entrance to the Mediterranean could easily have been closed. Failing to persuade Spain to enter the war, the Germans had to rely upon Italian submarines and land-based planes to halt British shipping in the western Mediterranean. The tip of Sicily lies a scant hundred miles from Tunis, where the Vichy French, under German dominance since the fall of France, held sway. Through this narrow channel British shipping had to move. In these waters England held an island naval base at historic Malta. The Malta base and British surface ships took a terrible beating, but the life line was not broken, though it never was adequate to the needs of Allied defense in

OPERATIONAL AREAS, WORLD WAR II, ESTABLISHED BY THE COMBINED CHIEFS OF STAFF

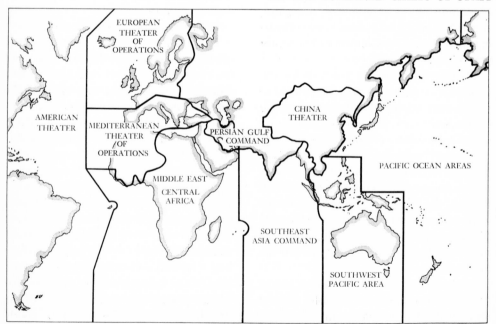

the eastern Mediterranean. German planes based upon Sicily made the route even more precarious.

Mussolini's resounding failure forced Germany herself to take up the Mediterranean problem. In the fall of 1940 began the occupation of the Balkans, which ended with the defeat of Yugoslavia and Greece by Germany in April, 1941. Although the regular armies of these countries were conquered in a matter of weeks, guerrilla resistance in the mountains kept thirty Axis divisions occupied all during the war. None of the other countries in that area ventured to fight. When the occupation of Greece threatened the British life line at its eastern end, British troops had to be diverted from North Africa to the defense of Greece and Crete. But the Greeks and the British were not able to stop the onrushing German forces. King George of Greece and the remnants of the Greek army went back to North Africa with their allies. Even here they were no longer safe. The German general Erwin Rommel, nicknamed "the Desert Fox," had come to Africa with German reinforcements, and after reorganizing the Italians, he pushed the British back to Egypt, where they made a successful stand (April–May, 1941).

The balance had swung back to level. British control of the Mediterranean was precarious, subject to constant pressure and danger until the crucial battle of El Alamein (October, 1942, to January, 1943). Since the failure of the Crete gamble, the British had slowly built up their African army, now led by General Bernard Montgomery, until it was finally able to fling the German-Italian forces back again across the Libyan desert. This operation was facilitated by the invasion of North Africa on its western end by the British and Americans.

England was really saved in the Mediterranean, and perhaps even at home, by Hitler's crucial decision to go to war against Russia. After June 22, 1941, the great bulk of German resources were committed to the vast Russian campaign, and Rommel could not get the reinforcements he needed to win victory in Africa. The ultimate ambitions of the Nazis had always been to conquer the rich agricultural lands held by the "inferior" Slavic peoples. The Nazi-Soviet pact of 1939, as we have seen, had never been more than a marriage of convenience, marked by much mutual mistrust. The ambitions of Stalin and Hitler clashed in the Balkans. Hitler felt that he could scarcely trust Russia to wait until he had conquered England and made the Mediterranean a German lake. France was out of the way, England was fully occupied in maintaining the defensive, America was neutral and seemed likely to remain so; it was time for Russia. Intoxicated by previous successes, the German leader assumed that barbaric Russia could be smashed in a blitzkrieg campaign.

The Russian campaign tested the tactics of the Germans to the fullest. During the first month, in a series of gigantic battles, the Nazi tanks and planes cut the Russians to pieces according to plan. Huge enveloping movements were completely successful. But the Russians did not surrender—they drew back. Even surrounded armies fought on and had to be destroyed. The equipment of the Russians and the number of their soldiers proved surprisingly greater than had been expected. In the bloodiest war in history, the Nazi armies rolled steadily forward, but the Russian armies still remained in existence, and the plains of Russia seemed endless. The Germans captured 1,500,000 prisoners in the first three months of the war. During

those three months the Germans conquered all of western Russia and arrived at
the gates of Moscow and Leningrad,
fighting on a front 2,000 miles long. By
the middle of October they had received
their first check before Moscow. On the
outskirts of their capital the Russians
poured everything into the defense. Untrained, ill-equipped soldiers built a wall
of bodies, while trains from the east
brought fresh troops to replace the killed.
In December the Russians were able to
counterattack, thus proving for the first
time that the *Wehrmacht* was not invincible.

Thus, when America declared war on
Japan and Germany in December, 1941,
the bulk of the German army was a thousand miles from home, frozen in the midst
of a Russian winter, suffering its first reverses. During the next year, while America was preparing her striking force for
entrance into the fighting, it was the same
story. The line from Leningrad to Moscow
swayed but remained relatively fixed while
the Germans plunged another 1,000 miles
forward in south Russia to Odessa and
Sevastopol. In the fall and winter of 1942,
the story of Moscow and Leningrad was
repeated at Stalingrad. Before Stalingrad
the German Sixth Army of 330,000 was
surrounded and cut to pieces. Acting upon
Hitler's orders, the German army refused
to retreat. The value of knowing when to
retreat was something Hitler never understood. The high tide of German power
broke at Stalingrad in the winter of 1942–
1943. From that time on it was all ebb in
Russia, while in the west a new military
machine from America was creating a
second front.

The Germans and Japanese were at all
times suspicious allies, and there was little
cooperation between them. Had they
planned their military drives as a joint

effort, they might have effected a juncture
in the Middle East in 1942 that would
have been fatal to the Allies. As it was,
their defeats in late 1942 constituted the
turning point of the war. But this was not
obvious at the time, and a glance at the
map indicated how much fighting would
have to be done if the Axis was to be defeated. To judge from the bitter resistance
the Japanese were putting up in Guadalcanal and New Guinea, it would not be
easy work.

AMERICA TAKES THE OFFENSIVE

The first major American military action in the European theater occurred in
the Mediterranean area. It had long been
agreed by most American military and political leaders that the European theater of
operations would have prior claim over
the Pacific. This was based on the idea that
the defeat of Germany would ensure the
defeat of Japan, but not vice versa. But
further decision was necessary. Was the
first large-scale American offensive to be
directed against the continent of Europe
itself, or against German forces in the
Mediterranean area, with the idea that
this would open southern Europe to further attacks? Perhaps, also, Italy might be
easily knocked out of the war. Outside the
United States, the chief concentration of
American power was in England. The island, at its nearest point only 26 miles
from the mainland, had become a central
base for our planes and for our sea and our
land forces. Across the English Channel
lay 100 miles of invitingly level beaches.
Nevertheless, the first attack upon Fortress
Europa was made in North Africa. The
reason for the decision to make the first attempt in the Mediterranean is related to
the events of the war in that theater which

we have been discussing. Of primary importance, however, was the question of strength. The Allies were still unable, at the end of 1942, to provide the power necessary to assure success in northern France, as the costly Dieppe raid had demonstrated. The Germans had heavily fortified the French coast, and while the American leaders hoped for a 1942 second front in France, they were forced to concede that the time for it had not yet come.

On the other hand, there were powerful arguments in favor of the southern location. The British had a force in Egypt which had been painfully built up to match Axis power in that area. A simultaneous attack from east and west would stand an excellent chance of clearing North Africa entirely. Success would have political as well as military importance, since liberated Morocco, Algiers, and Tunis would provide a base from which a free French government could operate. From North Africa, via Sicily, Italy could be invaded. Here political considerations also were strong. Mussolini's government was tottering to its fall. The war had seen nothing but defeats for Italy's armies, and her people were heartily sick of it. The possibility appeared of converting an enemy into an ally by eliminating Italy's pompous dictator. Once Italy was in the hands of the Allies, the war could be extended into the Balkans and southern France, hitting Europe in her "soft underbelly" and causing Hitler to relinquish his hold upon Russia in order to protect his vital flank. Air bases in southern Europe and North Africa would increase the effectiveness of our bombers. Such were the reasons for, and the objectives of, the North African campaign. American overall war planning was officially in the hands of General George C. Marshall, Admiral Ernest J. King, and General Henry H. Arnold, respectively chiefs of staff for the army, navy, and air forces. But the President and his two principal advisers, Harry Hopkins and Admiral William D. Leahy, took an active part. Secretary of War Henry L. Stimson has expressed the opinion that Roosevelt's capabilities as a strategist rank with the highest, and, of course, the final decision rested with him. The closest cooperation existed with the British, and Churchill, who was no mean strategist, participated in all major decisions. In the decision to invade Africa, Churchill's opinion was important, for the Americans had long favored a cross-Channel attack.

The North African campaign began in November, 1942. At that time northern Africa was held in the west by the Vichy French, allied with Germany but perhaps not too loyal to their hated masters. The central portion was occupied by German and Italian troops commanded by General Rommel, who was exerting constant pressure upon the British covering the Suez Canal in the east. A joint attack from east and west was planned by the Allies. General Montgomery was to attack from his position at El Alamein, while British and Americans should effect landings in Morocco and attack from the west. The invasion, executed by General Dwight D. Eisenhower, was carried out by American, English, and Free French forces. It was hoped that the Vichy generals in command of the French troops in Morocco might be won over to our side, an object which was in fact achieved after some delay, but not before heavy military opposition had been encountered. After the capitulation of the French had been arranged, Eisenhower raced toward Tunisia. Although few German reinforcements were available because of the Russian campaign, Rommel fought hard for Tunisia. But with half a million Allies in front and Montgomery's British at his back, the Desert Fox had at last met his match. Rommel fled, leaving 300,000 troops to become prisoners of war.

This was in May. Two months later the Allied army moved into Sicily. On July 25, Mussolini was deposed, and Italy capitulated, only to become an occupied country held in subjection by German troops. On September 2 the Allies invaded the mainland of Italy. The long, hard battle for Italy took more than a year of the heaviest kind of fighting, and its value has been disputed. In sometimes rather heated disputes within the Allied camp, the Americans generally wanted an early in-

vasion across the Channel, while the British pointed to its difficulties and urged that the initial effort be made in southern Europe. There is no doubt that Churchill's view was influenced by his concern about Stalin's postwar ambitions in eastern and central Europe. To the Americans such considerations did not seem proper; we were concerned only with winning the war as speedily as possible.

But the Allies had agreed in 1943 that the cross-Channel invasion would finally come in the spring of 1944. It was prepared for by almost continuous bombing of Fortress Europa. Since August, 1942, the Royal Air Force had been supplemented by American air power. The

MAIN ALLIED THRUSTS OF THE EUROPEAN WAR

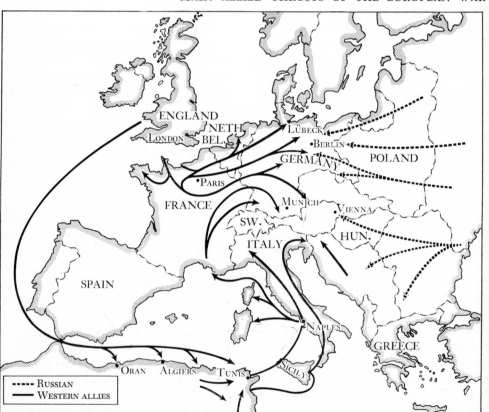

RAF went out at night and hit large industrial targets in "saturation" attacks, while the Americans in heavier-armed planes went out by day to bomb strategic targets ("pinpoint" bombing). Between them, the task of reducing northern Europe to rubble, of impeding the German war effort, and of softening her up for invasion went systematically forward. Some military experts had hoped that bombing alone would bring the enemy to his knees. While this hope proved futile, the damage inflicted was spectacular if not crippling. Five years after the war was over, the central portion of almost every German town of over 25,000 population was still a mass of rubble. In one week-long raid,

Hamburg was destroyed as a port, the center of the city of 1,500,000 population gutted, and 60,000 civilians killed. Yet, in the opinion of competent persons, German morale was hardly affected. One of the more startling and less noticed phenomena connected with modern warfare is mankind's frightening ability to tolerate it. As in Germany, so in England, the terrible bombings which the British endured from July, 1940, to June, 1941, seemed to have increased the civilian population's will to fight rather than to have diminished it.

But by spring 1944, the cumulative effect of the bombings on Germany was considerable. Transportation, so vital in

D-Day, June 6, 1944, day of the long-awaited and long-planned-for invasion of Europe. Men and supplies are pouring onto the Normandy beaches. (U.S. Army photograph)

modern war, was in bad shape, and shortages of strategic supplies, especially petroleum, had become hampering factors. The
Allied cross-Channel offensive, called
Operation Overlord, which was under the
supreme command of General Eisenhower, began on June 6th. The French
coast opposite England was heavily fortified, and formidable German forces—
some 60 divisions—were stationed in the
vicinity, under command of the redoubtable Rommel. The successful landing of
the army on the forty-mile stretch of the
Normandy shore in the face of opposing
armies and fortifications was one of the
most stupendous single undertakings ever
accomplished by man, especially when
one considers that most of the soldiers
participating had never before been under
fire. Stalin called it "grandiose in scale
and . . . masterly in execution." On the
morning of the 6th, troops began to storm
ashore from thousands of craft. The Germans had been deceived into expecting the
attack farther east, so that initial landings
were everywhere successful. At Utah
Beach, the western end of the invasion,
the landing was relatively easy, but the
Americans at Omaha Beach and the British farther east ran into heavy fighting.
Nevertheless, over 100,000 troops landed
the first day and held beachheads, while
hundreds of thousands more, with equipment and material of all kinds, poured in
behind them. Two months later, a million
men were in France, and Germany was
again fighting a two-front war.

The Germans, by the middle of 1944,
were everywhere being pressed back. On
the eastern front they had lost the initiative before Stalingrad in the terrible winter of 1942–1943 and had since been unable to recapture it. By June, 1944, when
the second front was launched, German
troops were being swept out of Russian
territory, steadily retreating. The landing
in Normandy was taking place just as the
Russian armies moved into East Prussia.
In Italy, the Allies were halfway up the
peninsula and gaining ground. The end
appeared to be in sight.

THE WAR IN THE PACIFIC

Despite the priority given to the European theater, the situation in the Pacific
slowly but steadily improved from the
time in mid-1942 when the high tide of
Japanese expansion had been checked by
our navy in the Coral Sea and at Midway.
In those battles the Americans had shown
that they knew how to use carrier-based
aircraft—air power in combination with
sea power. In the months that followed
they learned how to add land power in a
type of amphibious warfare, or "island
hopping," which maintained constant
pressure on the Japanese empire and gradually pushed it back. Amphibious warfare
was the combination of land, sea, and air
power in campaigns from island to island.
American forces were perfecting this new
kind of warfare, with which the marine
corps had long been experimenting. The
advent of aircraft allowed troops landing
on the beaches to be supported by bombers as well as naval gunfire. Before the
war was over, military men were attempting to "envelop" the enemy by bringing
troops into the enemy rear areas by para-
chute simultaneously with frontal attacks
by land and sea. Island-jumping was slow,
dirty, backbreaking work, in which victories were frequently bought at heavy
prices. It took six months to win the island
of Guadalcanal, key to the Solomon Islands, control of which would split the
southern Pacific holdings of the Japanese

in two. In the South Pacific war the Americans were joined by forces from Australia and New Zealand.

The Japanese were dislodged from New Guinea only after a full year of fighting in tropical jungles. American commanders in the Pacific naturally complained about not getting enough supplies; they nicknamed the Guadalcanal campaign "Operation Shoestring." For strategic reasons already indicated, Europe had priority. In any case, the supply problem in the Pacific was enormously difficult. The distances were tremendous, and amphibious warfare presented special problems. But fortunately for the United States, Japan had to face much the same difficulties, and Japanese war production was not equal to the strain. America could give only one-

fifth to one-third of her strength to the Pacific war, but when it rolled into high gear, American military production was ten times as great as Japan's. Although they did not have as much as they would have liked—no army ever does—the Americans in the Pacific had enough to force back Japan, despite the very great courage of individual Japanese soldiers. In their defense against the American counteroffensive the Japanese were handicapped by not knowing which of the many islands would be attacked; they seemingly had to prepare to defend all of them, while American strategy was to leapfrog over many of them.

This strategy resulted in a steady shrinking of the area held by Japan. The long and bitter struggle for the Solomons was

WAR IN THE PACIFIC, 1944–1945: STRATEGY OF THE UNITED STATES

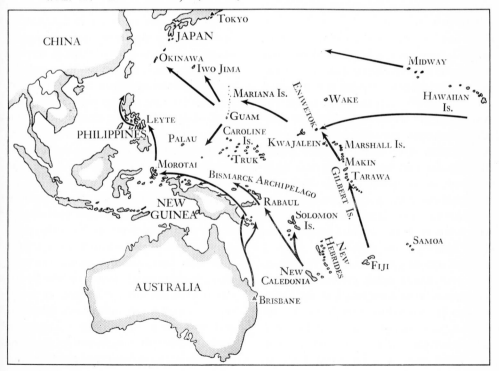

Japanese suicide dive bombers set fire to this American battleship, the U.S.S. Franklin, *in the late stages of the Pacific war. (U.S. Navy photograph)*

finally won. Victories in New Guinea and capture of the Admiralty Islands left the great Japanese base at Rabaul surrounded and neutralized. Leapfrogging north, the Americans did the same to the powerful enemy stronghold of Truk in the Carolines. Island after island in the Gilbert, Marshall, and Mariana groups fell. During two years of fighting, more than 100,000 Japanese were left to "wither on the vine" on fortified islands behind our lines, where supply ships could no longer reach them. The final objective of this creeping advance was to get bases close enough to Japan to make large-scale air bombardment possible and, from such bases, perhaps to launch a final attack on the softened-up homeland of the enemy. In a desperate effort to keep the Americans at bay, Japan risked a major air-sea battle in the Philippine Sea in June, 1944, only to be beaten.

This first battle of the Philippine Sea was followed by a greater one in the fall. On October 20, General Douglas MacArthur, carrying out his "I shall return" pledge, led American forces ashore at Leyte in the Philippine Islands. The Japanese risked almost all they had on a naval battle in Leyte Gulf in the hope of cutting off MacArthur's army. A great battle resulted, in which the Japanese were so badly mauled that they never attempted another major naval engagement. On land, MacArthur's forces had the aid of Philippine guerrillas, who seemed to rise from the ground. The civilian population showed by action that it had never become reconciled to the Japanese occupation. By Christmas, all was ready for the move on Luzon, the main Philippine island where Manila is located. Manila itself fell in February, 1945.

The final jump in the great island-to-island campaign was to Iwo Jima and Okinawa, which, along with the already captured island of Saipan in the Marianas, were to be used as bomber bases against Japan itself. The enemy fleet did not come out to defend these islands, but the planes did and brought with them a new suicide technique (kamikaze), in which the pilot crashed his plane on the target ship in order to lessen the chance of missing. The new tactic was terribly effective. Almost 200 of our ships were badly damaged in the taking of these two tiny islands. Once they had been taken, the final softening-up process could begin. Heavy bombers were based on Guam and Saipan, medium bombers and fighters on Okinawa, and fighters on Iwo Jima. Japan was pounded day and night, as Europe had been. The target was so compact that maximum results could be expected. Here, if ever, the air arm might prove its power to win a war unaided.

This island route to Japan seemed the only one available. If Burma had not fallen to the Japanese, and if the ground forces used in Europe had been available, a base for the assault on Japan might have been found in China, with perhaps very different results for future history. But the efforts made in 1942 to open a path to China through Burma failed. The Americans made a contribution to the fighting in Burma in 1944 when the campaign was renewed. General Joseph Stilwell, with an army made up mostly of Chinese trained in India, helped in the land fighting, while American airmen flew supplies through the mountains—"over the hump"—into China. By early 1945 it was possible to send in a greater volume of war supplies to China through Burma. Nevertheless, the Chinese had little success against the Japanese. Playing a part in this failure was the internal division in China, with Generalissimo Chiang Kai-shek's government refusing to cooperate with the Chinese Communists. The latter controlled some areas of China, and they were growing in strength. The increasingly conservative Chiang Kai-shek government fought the Communists as well as the Japanese, incurring the wrath of General Stilwell, who saw the problem in terms of securing maximum military efficiency against the Japanese. Once again, "politics" arose to bedevil the war effort, and again the Americans showed themselves less concerned about the nature of the postwar world than about the quickest way to victory.

American naval leaders believed that an invasion of Japan would not be necessary, for a blockade could starve the Japanese into surrender. They lost the argument, and it was decided that after extensive bombing there would be an invasion of Japan, and that Russia should, if possible, be brought into the war to conquer Manchuria.

UNCONDITIONAL SURRENDER

The defeat of the Japanese navy in the Philippine Sea and the American landing on Saipan caused the fall of General Tojo's government and the cautious emergence of a peace party, which included the royal family itself. Japan had clearly lost the war with the breaching of her inner defense line. By the summer of 1944 Germany was in the same situation. Unable to prevent the Allied invaders from bursting out of the Normandy beachhead and pouring across France, the Germans held them for a while behind their Westwall defenses along the German border; but all sane men knew that the war was lost. On the eastern front, the Balkans were falling and German troops were in steady retreat before the Russian advance.

Germany made an effort to free herself from the grip of the Nazis, but failed. A determined attempt to assassinate Hitler took place, led by the professional soldiers. This dramatic plot of July 20, 1944, tragically miscarried, and hundreds of its leaders, men high in German life, were brutally executed. General Rommel, who had sought to negotiate with Eisenhower, was forced by Hitler to commit suicide. Hitler, of course, would listen to no talk of ending the war, but was determined to fight on to the complete destruction of Germany. Nor could the Allies possibly make any sort of terms with his regime, even now as it faced defeat intent on the

Man's inhumanity to man reached an all-time depth in the Nazi concentration camps, where systematic murder was practiced on a vast and ghastly scale. This is a mass grave found at the notorious Belsen camp. (U.S. Army photograph)

total destruction of all remaining Jews.* But in Japan the possibility of appealing to a more moderate group by offering terms short of unconditional surrender certainly existed. Although fanaticism of the Nazi sort was a strong force there, it was never able to establish a dictatorship like Hitler's.

In this war, however, Allied policy was not to hold out the offer of generous terms, as Wilson had done in 1918. On the contrary, from a series of wartime conferences among the Allied chiefs of state there emerged the formula of no terms at all—"unconditional surrender." The feel-

* According to the careful estimates of Gerald Reitlinger in his book *The Final Solution* (London, Vallentine, Mitchell, 1953), pp. 489–501, the number of Jews killed by the Nazis or because of Nazi pressure was somewhere between 4,194,200 and 4,581,200—about half of these, Polish Jews.

ing was that the Axis powers must be taught a terrible lesson. It was agreed that there should be a complete occupation of Germany and Japan, perhaps the partition of Germany; the trial of "war criminals" in both countries; and the reconstruction and reeducation of society under Allied control. Nothing less than this, it was widely believed, would suffice to stamp out the seeds of militaristic aggression from these offenders against the peace. So strong was this feeling that for a short time official American policy toward Germany was the Morgenthau Plan, devised by Secretary of the Treasury Henry J. Morgenthau, Jr., of stripping Germany of all heavy industry and turning her into a largely agricultural state, a plan which its enemies charged implied the starvation of millions of Germans.

Although its emotional basis in hatred of such a bestial regime as Hitler's can be understood, the policy of unconditional surrender appears in retrospect to have been a most dubious one. The total defeat of Germany would certainly leave the Soviet Union the predominant power in Europe. The total defeat of Japan would offer almost equally tempting prospects for Soviet influence in Asia. It is easier to see why Stalin wanted unconditional surrender than why President Roosevelt and Secretary Hull backed it so enthusiastically. At the time, however, there can be no doubt that American public opinion overwhelmingly supported the policy. Balance-of-power thinking was still alien to the American mind, which tended to see international issues in a strong moral light. Roosevelt and Hull reflected that bias when they spoke of putting faith for future peace not in the balance of power, but in a United Nations—a new version of the League of Nations, which America would join this time. The cooperation of Soviet Russia in such an organization would be essential, and Roosevelt gambled that Stalin was, as he put it, "get-at-able," that suspicious Russia might be drawn into fruitful collaboration with the West. If the wartime Big Three remained firmly united, they could together build a better world.

Therefore peace bids were ignored, and the drive to inflict total defeat on the hapless Axis peoples went remorselessly ahead. In Europe, the Allies were held up both by Germany's Westwall defenses and by their own supply problems. And another argument broke out between the British and the Americans; the former favored gambling on a single thrust to break through in the direction of the Ruhr, while the Americans preferred a slower, more methodical, less risky advance on all fronts. The American point of view prevailed. In this controversy the Americans again displayed a nonpolitical approach which some Europeans thought naïve. A part of the British case was the belief that the Allies ought to beat the Russians to Berlin, but the Americans, including Generals Eisenhower and Omar N. Bradley, thought that this was mixing politics with war too much. The sole object, as America saw it, was to win the war; the future might be left to take care of itself. And there was a strong desire not to break faith with our Russian ally, a desire which the more realistic Winston Churchill did not entirely share, knowing as he did that Stalin was not overly sentimental in such matters.

Late in 1944, the Germans launched a last desperate counterattack in the Ardennes sector and achieved temporary success in the famous Battle of the Bulge. But the drive failed of its chief objectives and exhausted the last German reserve strength. By February the Allies were advancing on all fronts. The Americans crossed the Rhine on March 7. In Italy the Allied offensive at last broke out of the mountains into the plains of the Po; on April 28, Benito Mussolini, who had been restored to power by the Germans, was captured and executed by Italian partisans while trying to escape to Switzerland. The Germans were now too weak to offer any coordinated defense, and the rapidly moving Allied columns raced eastward while the Russians plunged into Germany from the other side. There was a last desperate defense of Berlin against the Russians, directed by Hitler from his underground bunker in that city. Three days after Mussolini's death, the Nazi *Führer* committed suicide, and German resistance was at an end. Russian armies "liberated" Berlin, Vienna, and Prague. It remained to be seen whether they would cooperate with their allies or

Albert Einstein, the great scientist famous for his contributions to theoretical physics, became even more famous for his contributions to the American development of the atomic bomb. Shocked by the actual use of the dread weapon in 1945, Einstein later opposed development of the even more destructive H-bomb. (Fabian Bachrach)

whether they would prefer to keep their vast gains in eastern Europe for themselves.

"Unconditional surrender" was also remorselessly applied to Japan. In April, 1945, Franklin D. Roosevelt, exhausted by labors unprecedented for an American president, had collapsed and died of a brain hemorrhage, thus depriving America and the world of a great leader at a crucial moment in history. The previous November, Roosevelt had been reelected to a fourth term, with Senator Harry S. Truman as his running mate. With the death of Roosevelt the relatively inexperienced Truman was thrust into a difficult role. In July, President Truman met Stalin and Churchill at Potsdam, near Berlin. At the Potsdam Conference the Allies tried to work out arrangements for their joint occupation of Germany, among other problems; they also sent to Japan a demand for surrender—indicating, however, that Japan after surrender might expect to be treated with some clemency. At this time Japan's leaders were seeking to negotiate with the Allies through the mediation of Russia, still at peace with Japan. What the Japanese did not know was that Stalin had promised Roosevelt at the Yalta Conference, early in 1945, to enter the war against Japan as soon as possible after Germany was defeated. The Russians were therefore deaf to the Japanese approaches, and meanwhile Japanese official reaction to the Potsdam proposals was interpreted in this country as a rejection.

On July 16 the atomic bomb had been successfully tested in New Mexico. The brains that put together the bomb, and thus unleashed atomic energy with all its potentialities for good and evil, were largely exiles from the Europe of Hitler and Mussolini—including the Italian Enrico Fermi, the Austrian Jews Lise Meitner and her nephew Otto Frisch, the great Albert Einstein, and the brilliant Dane Niels Bohr. Thus did Nazi intolerance accomplish its own doom, for had these scientists not been driven out they might have provided the dictators with the atom bomb. But it was on Japan rather than on already defeated Germany that the terrible weapon was to be used. On August 6, an A-bomb was dropped on the city of Hiroshima; three days later we dropped another on Nagasaki. The casualties from the Hiroshima bomb numbered 130,000; of these 78,150 were deaths.

Russia declared war on Japan on August 8. Since Japan was already a beaten power, virtually pleading for capitulation, both the use of the atomic bomb (a terrible precedent to set) and the bringing of Russia into the war have been subjected to strong criticism. But it must be recalled that the Russians did not fully inform us of the Japanese peace overtures. At the Yalta Conference, Russia won promises of Allied support for her recovery of Port Arthur and other privileges in Manchuria in return for her promise to enter the war; at Potsdam, the Americans helped Russia find a pretext for violating her pact of friendship with Japan. In defense of this, it can be said that the military situation was not as clear as it later became, and most of the American military chiefs thought Russian help would be invaluable in driving the Japanese out of Manchuria. At any rate, these twin blows, the atom bomb and the Russian declaration of war, brought Japan to quick surrender on August 15, 1945. While America was to play a dominant role in the occupation of Japan, Russia, through her brief entrance into the war, became the occupying power in Manchuria and northern Korea.

The most terrible war mankind had ever produced was over. It had cost the lives of around 22 million people and had caused hundreds of billions of dollars of property damage. It left millions homeless, helpless, and on the verge of starvation. Yet it was over; the frightful regime of the Nazis was crushed, as were the arrogant Japanese warlords, and most people, celebrating wildly, assumed that a better world was on its way.

THE UNITED NATIONS

There was no question after this war about the willingness of the United States to join an international organization. The lesson had been driven home that without powerful America's full participation in world politics there could not be a peaceful and stable world. During the war, isolationism had virtually ceased to exist. Preparations for a new international organization, to replace the defunct League of Nations, went on even while the conflict was in progress. President Roosevelt, always extremely conscious of this need, forecast a new world body as early as 1941. He and Prime Minister Churchill gave encouragement to the idea in the Atlantic Charter of August of the same year. Promises that the Allies who were fighting the Axis states would cooperate in the postwar period were exchanged at Teheran, in 1943, when Roosevelt, Churchill, and Stalin met to plan the progress of the war. At the Dumbarton Oaks Conference, in Washington, the three great powers and China carried the planning forward in 1944. At Yalta, in February, 1945, further details were agreed upon. The meeting which took place at San Francisco in April, 1945, was the climax of five years of hopes and plans in which, once again, the United States played the leading part. The hope was that the mistakes of 1919 might be avoided by completing the organization before the end of the war, while the spirit of cooperation among the powers was still strong.

Fifty nations sent delegates to the San Francisco Conference. It lasted two months, and while many sharp disputes marked its progress, it ended with a charter for world cooperation ready to be presented to the nations for ratification. The United States Senate ratified the United Nations Charter in July, 1945. The presence of leading Republicans at San Francisco emphasized that the United Nations had bipartisan support in the United States, and the Senate vote was all but unanimous (89 to 2), after only six days of debate. No more marked contrast to 1919 could be imagined. The United

Nations now was the center of all hopes for a permanent peace.

Its charter was much like that of its predecessor, the League of Nations. On its Security Council, which had to make the major decisions, the United States was one of five permanent members, along with Great Britain, France, Russia, and China. This Council was given powers greater than those possessed by the League of Nations Council to take action against any "breach of the peace." But there had to be unanimity; the veto of any one of the permanent members was sufficient to block action. Thus, if the great powers were as one, they could act freely as policemen of the world. But if they fell into a serious disagreement, the United Nations was not likely to prove very effective. It was the somewhat optimistic expectation of millions throughout the world that the "Big Three" would remain as united in peace as they had been in war. Stalin, however, had already remarked that it was much easier for the powers to maintain unity in war, when they had a common enemy, than it would be when that enemy was removed.

Signs of this melancholy truth appeared even before the war was over. There had been some controversies between Great Britain and the United States during the war. But these were minor in comparison to the mistrust that arose between Soviet Russia and the West. Between the suspicious Communist rulers of Russia and the Anglo-American team there had never been a very intimate meeting of minds during the war, and in 1945 the cordial relations established personally between Churchill, Stalin, and Roosevelt were broken first by Roosevelt's death and then by Churchill's defeat in the British election in 1945, which took place in the very midst of the Potsdam Conference. The abrupt curtailing of lend-lease aid on May 12 gave offense to Russia, as did our insistence upon the admission of Argentina to the United Nations and the giving of a zone of occupation and a seat on the German reparations commission to France. The Potsdam Conference produced some arguments, particularly over the Western powers' effort to scale down Russia's claim for huge reparations from Germany. And we were becoming deeply concerned, above all, at Russian behavior in the countries of eastern Europe which they had "liberated." Especially resented was the installing by strong-arm means of a completely pro-Communist government in Poland. England and America considered this to be a violation of a portion of the Yalta agreement, which declared that the Polish government should be democratic. It appeared that the Russian rulers were bent on keeping control of the countries bordering Russia—Bulgaria, Rumania, Poland—by the use of armed force and Communist puppet governments. To the West this was a betrayal not only of the Yalta agreement, but also of the spirit of the United Nations. It was an ominous sign for future world peace.

In fact, the Russian leaders, from a coldly realistic point of view, had every reason to play a waiting game. The United States was engaged in dismantling its great war machine during the last half of 1945. Wasn't the war over? "Bring the boys home" was apparently a cry few congressmen could fail to heed. Europe, after the terrible war, lay bleeding and impoverished. Great Britain was almost as economically exhausted as France and Germany, having used up all her overseas assets and lost her world markets. If the Americans went home, what could prevent the whole continent from falling into Russian hands? Communism could be counted upon to rise amid poverty and misery. As the war came to an end, Winston Churchill watched with something like horror the eagerness with which America was apparently preparing to take her troops home. The experienced British statesman knew that American military and economic strength would be needed for a good while, but he was unable to make his voice heard in the United States, where it was gleefully assumed that the war was over and "normalcy" might now begin.

The nations were far from united, and the postwar years were to bring many disillusionments. The mere creation of an international body called the United Nations could not magically solve the world's problems; for that, a good deal more of Churchill's formula of "blood, toil, tears and sweat" would be needed. It actually took the American people almost two years after the end of the war to understand this, and this failure was almost a fatal one for Western civilization. Nevertheless, the organization whose headquarters were to be in New York City became the center of the world diplomatic stage and the cynosure of the world's attention. In the age of the atomic bomb, no one could doubt that the prevention of still another world war was a necessity for mankind, taking precedence over all else.

FURTHER READINGS

There is a very large literature on World War II, including a War Department history which will eventually run to ninety-one volumes and a fourteen-volume *History of United States Naval Operations in World War II,* now almost completed, written by the distinguished historian Samuel Eliot Morison. More widely read are such personal accounts as Winston Churchill, *The Second World War* (6 vols., 1948–1954), and Dwight D. Eisenhower, *Crusade in Europe* (1946). Generals Mark Clark, Omar Bradley, H. H. Arnold, and Joseph W. Stilwell and Admirals E. J. King and William D. Leahy are among other outstanding American military leaders who have contributed important books. From the British side, the outspoken Field-Marshal Bernard Montgomery (Viscount Montgomery of Alamein) may be singled out, while Germany's General Hans Speidel, later a NATO commander, is among the Axis leaders whose military memoirs have received attention in this country.

Chester Wilmot, *The Struggle for Europe* (1952), is a very able single-volume account which is often critical of American strategic concepts. S. E. Morison, *Strategy and Compromise* (1958), defends the American position. The military literature is vast, but hardly much larger than that connected with political and diplomatic decisions of the war. Here Herbert Feis has contributed a valiant attempt at synthesis, *Churchill—Roosevelt—Stalin* (1957). Much more critical of Allied decisions is Edward J. Rozek, *Allied Wartime Diplomacy: A Pattern in Poland* (1958). R. J. C. Butow, *Japan's Decision to Surrender* (1954), is a work of sound scholarship. Published in 1955 amid considerable controversy, the official records of the Yalta Conference (appearing in the series *Foreign Relations of the United States,* U.S. Department of State) are a valuable source of information. The inception of the United Nations has been carefully traced in a Brookings Institution study by Ruth B. Russell, *A History of the United Nations Charter* (1958). In *Brighter Than a Thousand Suns* (1958), the journalist Robert Jungk has put together the story of the atomic scientists and the creation of the great bombs.

A general account of America at war stressing the problem of mobilizing for all-out economic effort is Eliot Janeway, *The Struggle for Survival* (1951). Cordell Hull, *Memoirs* (2 vols., 1948); Henry L. Stimson and George McBundy, *On Active Service in Peace and War* (1954); and Robert Sherwood, *Roosevelt and Hopkins* (1948), are examples of the large memoir literature of political figures, works which are invaluable but should be used with caution.

For additional bibliography, see the *Harvard Guide,* sections 269–272. An additional bibliographical aid is Henry L. Roberts (ed.), *Foreign Affairs Bibliography* (1955), an annotated bibliography covering books published from 1942 to 1952.

TWENTY-NINE

American Democracy in Crisis, 1945 to 1960

1946

Quarrels between Soviet Union and Western powers.

1947

Truman Doctrine; United States rearmament.

Marshall Plan announced.

Taft-Hartley Act passed.

1948

Communists seize Czechoslovakia.

Berlin air lift.

Truman defeats Dewey for presidency.

1949

North Atlantic Treaty signed.

Communists win in Chinese civil war.

1950

Korean conflict begins.

Red China intervenes in Korea.

1951

General MacArthur recalled.

Korean armistice negotiations begin.

1952

Eisenhower wins over Stevenson.

1953

Korean armistice signed.

1954

Supreme Court rules against discrimination in public schools.

First H-bomb exploded.

Indochina crisis.

1956

Suez crisis.

Hungarian revolution.

Eisenhower reelected.

1958

Middle East crisis.

Democrats sweep congressional elections.

FROM WAR TO PEACE

THE SUDDEN DEATH of President Franklin D. Roosevelt on April 12, 1945, stunned the nation and thrust a crushing burden on a hitherto obscure little man from Missouri who happened to be the Vice President of the United States. The war was drawing to a close, and all sorts of crucial decisions had to be made. Harry S. Truman had been a United States Senator and had done excellent work as chairman of an important Senate committee which served as watchdog over war production. But his selection as Roosevelt's running mate in the 1944 campaign owed more to the jealousy of other rivals for that post than to his own fame. Truman had scarcely settled back in the comfortable obscurity of the vice presidency when a fateful telephone call from Warm Springs, Georgia, informed him that he had inherited the loneliest and toughest job in the world.

At the outset of his administration Truman was able to count on more than the usual "honeymoon" granted a new President because of his friendships in the Senate and because of the sympathy felt by nearly everyone for a man caught in an impossible job. It was widely known, for example, that Roosevelt had not kept him adequately informed of the many momentous decisions that were being made and discussed, as for example at the recent Yalta Conference with Stalin and Churchill. With little or no advance preparation,

601

Delegates of the Big Three in an argument at the United Nations

U.S.A.F.'s SM-62 SNARK long-range strategic missile

Boeing B-52 "Stratofortress"

President Truman

Senator McCarthy and aide Roy
Cohn at a Senate hearing

"To save succeeding generations from the scourge of war" the victors of World War II set up the United Nations. But they seemed able to quarrel as well within the UN as outside it. Within a few years bitter hostility between an Eastern and a Western bloc led to an arms race and to a "limited" war—in Korea. The harassed Chief Executive, Harry S. Truman, was the target of criticism from some who sought a scapegoat for the disappointments of the postwar years. Most savage of the critics was Wisconsin's ambitious Senator McCarthy.

The grief of a soldier in the Korean War for a lost buddy

Truman set out to "do his darndest" on the problems that lay ahead—the task of finishing the war and winning the peace. To these tasks he brought a deep humility, a capacity for hard work, and a readiness to take the responsibility for the hard decisions that were to come.

Some measure of the problems of war and peace which faced Truman upon his accession to the presidency can be gained from a quick glance at the chronologies of this and the previous chapter. The war in Europe was drawing to a close, amid arrangements concerning the military areas to be occupied by Soviet and by Anglo-American forces. In later years, decisions made at this moment were to be looked upon as crucial for the future fate of Europe. The United Nations Conference at San Francisco was about to convene; in fact, the first major decision the new President made was to announce that this conference would meet on schedule in spite of Roosevelt's death. Before he had been in office four months, Truman was in Potsdam on the outskirts of Berlin settling the fate of Europe with Churchill, Clement Attlee, and Stalin. At this same time Japanese surrender terms had to be decided, and in late July Truman made the decision to use the atomic bomb on Japan.

These were fateful matters, about which men would long debate in later years. At the time, President Truman shared the faith of the vast majority of his countrymen that the crushing of the Axis nations, together with the inauguration of the United Nations, in continuation of the wartime Big Three alliance, opened a rosy future for world peace. There were to be many disillusionments, until two years later President Truman was forced to signal a great shift in American policy. In the meanwhile, domestic problems ac-

tually seemed of greater importance. With the Japanese surrender ceremonies aboard the *U.S.S. Missouri* on September 2, Americans assumed the war was all over and they could turn their attention to completely different matters. The vast process of demobilizing the armed forces, reconverting industrial capacity to peacetime uses, and satisfying the pent-up demand for goods assumed priority.

There was a good deal of apprehension about the social and economic difficulties that might attend this transition. Many experts expected a severe postwar depression. The nation's leaders worried lest the enormous expansion of industrial capacity leave the country with more than could be maintained in peacetime. These fears proved groundless, fortunately. Twelve million men were mustered out of the armed forces and absorbed into civilian employment with scarcely a ripple of disturbance. Production, stimulated by accumulated savings and wants, continued at the high wartime level. It was turned smoothly to the job of providing consumer goods rather than weapons of war. Few of the expected economic difficulties appeared.

The most troublesome and persistent postwar economic problem was inflation. With heavy demand straining every productive muscle, prices in what was now a seller's market began to creep upward. As prices rose, wages tended to follow, impelled by the bargaining power of 15 million organized workers; prices climbed ever higher, and inflation became serious. At the beginning of 1946, wartime price controls were relaxed and then altogether suspended, releasing pent-up inflationary forces with explosive energy. The price index (1935–1939 = 100), which stood at 130 at the war's end, rose to 155 by the end of 1946; and in August, 1948, it was up to 175. Nor was this the end. The index leveled off in 1949, during a brief economic recession, but in mid-1950, under the impetus of the Korean conflict, it began to rise again. Heavy defense spending made it difficult to balance the vast government budget and contributed some inflationary pressure. Big government, organized labor, monopolistic features in the field of business enterprise—these were most often proposed as causes of an inflation that continued through the 1950s, though at a diminished rate.

A moderate rate of inflation had its advantages, according to some economists, but also its disadvantages. Postwar inflation led to unrest on the part of industrial workers, resulting in frequent strikes. The single year 1946 showed 116 million man-days lost from strikes, as compared with only 36 million man-days lost in the four years of the war. Strikes were notable in the great industries of automobiles, steel, and coal, where the workers won significant gains, but at the cost of arousing some public antagonism and inviting government intervention. The government took over the coal mines and fined John L. Lewis's union $1,500,000, and an attempted railroad strike was prevented by the President's threat to use the army. These moves were taken under wartime emergency powers still in effect in 1946. In 1952, however, President Truman's effort to seize the steel industry in order to forestall a strike was frustrated by a notable Supreme Court decision.

In 1947 the Republican-controlled Congress passed a new labor law, over Truman's veto and the strenuous protests of most of organized labor. This Taft-Hartley Law was much less favorable to labor than had been the New Deal's Wagner Act of 1935. Yet organized labor continued to thrive, while at the same time industrial strife, so rampant in the re-adjustment year of 1946, was less apparent after that. The wartime experience of cooperation between worker and manager had had its effect, and efforts on both sides to avoid industrial strife began to succeed. Strikes were too costly, and both big labor and big management were too strong to fight without the danger of wrecking society in general. The only alternative to damaging strikes was government intervention, which neither the unions nor the corporations much liked. The result was a tendency to seek agreements, sometimes long-term ones, with adjustable clauses which were often tied to productivity, but were more often tied to the cost-of-living index. These agreements stressed cooperation, social welfare, and responsible behavior on both sides. The auto workers and managers took the lead in these efforts. Responsible union officials —a far cry, now, from the ragged and radical labor leaders of yore—were able to work with like-minded management officials—most of the time, at least.

Success in handling the problems of economic reconversion and labor-management relations typified the general success of the United States economically in the postwar era. These were years of substantial prosperity, nearly full employment, and rising productivity. In spite of inflation, the national standard of living rose considerably. The American economy had amply proved its flexibility and dynamism. As of 1960, the great postwar depression had never appeared. While the public held its breath, the economy rode buoyantly over three recessions, each publicized as possibly *the* great depression. In 1949–1950, 1952–1953, and 1957–1958, symptoms of economic crisis appeared, but the recessions proved relatively mild and short-lived. High government spending, and the cushions built into a social welfare state, might provide one explanation. Whatever the causes, the results were gratifying. The economic situation will be discussed in more detail further on in this chapter.

FAILURES OF PEACEMAKING

While internal economic developments in the postwar period were such as to inspire pride and confidence in the minds of thoughtful Americans, events in the world at large were so menacing that most Americans were given to apprehension and discouragement rather than to satisfaction and hope. After the destruction of Germany and Japan, only two first-class powers remained, and these two seemed destined to a struggle for supremacy which threatened to destroy civilization.

The real danger to America, the real challenge to her leadership, lay outside her borders. The Axis danger had been laid to rest; but it remained to be seen whether an equally or even more dangerous enemy might arise. At the close of the war everything depended upon Russo-American relations. Most Americans were prepared to get along with Russia. Many were even inclined to hope that the years had softened Communist intransigence, and that the shared experience of a horrible war would bind the two nations together. If nothing else, the frightful destruction and the resultant war-weariness in Russia, attested by many American visitors, seemed to guarantee a long period of peace which could perhaps be utilized in a search for workable relations with the Soviets. America was herself war-weary and in no mood to coerce her former ally.

Thus the policy of friendly toleration established at Teheran and Yalta became

our official postwar policy, and was to last with diminishing cordiality for about two years. In November, 1945, General Eisenhower wrote: "American-Soviet friendship is one of the cornerstones upon which the edifice of peace should be built. To achieve this friendship nothing is more important than mutual understanding on the part of each, of the institutions, traditions and customs of the other." The majority of Americans sincerely wished to try to maintain friendly relations as the best hope of a permanent peace. They were, moreover, extremely reluctant to face the consequences of any other belief. If Russia should be considered a dangerous enemy, we must assume new responsibilities and expenses which we were reluctant to undertake. We would need, for instance, to maintain a permanent and costly military establishment. The rejection of President Truman's request for universal military training showed the temper of the times. People wanted peace, demobilization, peacetime goods, tax cuts —and wanted them at once, without regard for the consequences. The result of this attitude was the dismantling, with undue haste, of the greatest war machine the world had ever seen. This was far less the policy of the administration that governed during these years than the demand of the American people. It appears that neither people nor leaders had any clear idea of the nature of international affairs or the disturbing forces that were abroad in the world.

America's postwar intentions were certainly pacific; what Russia's intentions were in 1945 we have no way of knowing. But circumstances alter intentions, and soon hard political realities drove a wedge between the two great powers who had never quite trusted each other even as wartime allies. Joint occupation of Germany, an awkward arrangement at best, produced specific disagreements. The Yalta and Potsdam Conferences of 1945 tried to lay the basis for the occupation system and to provide for the reestablishment of the defeated nations. Those nations which the Axis had destroyed or converted into satellites were to be re-created on the basis of "democracy" and "free elections," terms which, as it developed, were all too likely to mean different things to East and West. The Russian armies were present in force in the areas of eastern and central Europe which lay between their border and Germany. It soon appeared that the Soviet government was prepared to convert this area, including Albania, Rumania, Bulgaria, Czechoslovakia, Hungary, and Poland, into satellite states, in apparent violation of the wartime agreements. It appeared that Russia understood this to be her "sphere," the spoils of hard-won victory, the necessary guarantee to her future security. To Americans, these actions seemed proof of ill will and aggressive intentions to extend Communism over all Europe.

As for Germany and Austria, joint occupation quickly led to serious quarrels in that area. Although there were four territorial spheres of occupation—one each for the United States, the Soviet Union, Great Britain, and France—there was supposed to be a cooperative four-power policy, so that the entire area would remain an economic and social unit. But such cooperation between the Russians and the other powers soon broke down. The most serious quarrel concerned reparations demanded by the Soviet Union in vast quantities, and American reluctance to foot the bill for these, as the United States was in effect doing by having to support the industrial areas of Germany. Soon the zones governed by the three

Western powers were combined into one, later to become the semiautonomous Western German Republic; the Russians, for their part, proceeded to draw the east zone more and more into the Soviet orbit. Germany was split in two, to become a standing menace to the peace of Europe; the ill-starred policies of unconditional surrender, reparations, and joint administration by the victors had bred fresh quarrels. Europe was split in two, the eastern half wholly dominated by Communist regimes ideologically hostile to the West and dogmatically convinced that they could never compromise with capitalism. The collapse of Germany had let Russia into Europe; who was to get her out? Americans, who had gaily demobilized most of their military strength, now had to answer the bitter question, "Who could prevent Russia taking over all Europe?" Western Europe lay exhausted by the war, her economy ruined, wracked by internal political strife, and apparently vulnerable to military or ideological attack.

Communism was also on the march in Asia, taking advantage of nationalist hostility to Western imperialism and the decay of old political orders brought on by the war. Signs of Soviet aggressiveness appeared in 1946 in Iran, Russia's neighbor in the Middle East, which Soviet troops evacuated only after protests, and where Communist agents sought to foment revolution. The Soviet Union also put pressure on Turkey for territory and a share in the control of the Dardanelles. In the Far East, Soviet troops stripped the factories of Manchuria and then turned this valuable area over to the Chinese Communists. In Korea north of the 38th parallel, there was an apparent effort to install a government of pro-Soviet puppets. In Japan, where the American authorities under General MacArthur were able to run the show, Russia nevertheless sought to obstruct our policies.

The three years following the war were, then, full of disillusionment for the non-Communist world. The disagreements in Germany revealed the width of the chasm separating East and West. Russia's conversion of her neighbors into satellites was deeply disturbing; even more threatening was the possibility of revolution in western Europe engineered by local Communist parties. Such parties were especially strong in France and Italy. The conduct of the Soviet Union in the United Nations also aroused fear and criticism. Her use of the veto, while legal, seemed to indicate a stubborn desire to deny cooperation with the West. America had placed extravagant hopes in the United Nations, hopes which revealed her optimistic belief that after victory would come Utopia. The United Nations, was, of course, only a beginning; it was perhaps a step in the direction of world peace, but not the achievement of it. In the present phase of history no organization can put an end to the struggle for power among nations.

The postwar world was actually divided into two great spheres of influence. The center of one of these spheres, soon to include China, was the Soviet Union. Embracing the might of the Soviet Union and her east European satellites, while 500 million Chinese were falling under the rule of Communism, this sphere seemed dominant on two continents and upon the point of sweeping the world. The other sphere depended upon the United States. She must organize it and draw it together if it was not to disintegrate. The Monroe Doctrine had once stated a doctrine of "two spheres"—the Americas against all of Europe. The new version of the two spheres was quite different; it was America and her cultural motherland in western Europe against the East and Communism.

CONTAINMENT AND THE COLD WAR

The apprehensions evoked by these conditions led the United States to abandon the "get along" policy, now increasingly labeled "appeasement." By the middle of 1947, the practical difficulties of cooperation were becoming so great that the administration began to shift to a new policy, to be called "containment." This meant building up our armed forces and also the economic and military power of the threatened nations, especially of western Europe. At the same time, we and our allies would determinedly block any attempt at further advance by the Soviet Union. To combat the threat of subversion from within and armed pressure from without, the European democracies had already begun to try to combine their strength and enlist American aid. Some of their principal problems were economic ones, and the Soviets were known to count heavily upon the economic collapse of the West to do their work for them. The economic rehabilitation of disorganized Europe was essential to the defense of the West.

A first step in this direction was taken in 1947, when sixteen European governments formed the Organization for European Economic Cooperation. A second step was initiated by the United States itself. Convinced that the Russian advance must be halted, and recognizing that the fall of Europe would be a thrust at America, the administration launched its European Recovery Program. The germ of this aid program was contained in the now-famous Harvard speech of General George C. Marshall, Secretary of State, in June, 1947. Aroused by the danger of economic collapse in Europe, the Congress appropriated 6 billion dollars for the year 1948, and during the next four years some 12 billion dollars in all was allocated to the Marshall Plan. In order not to widen the breach between East and West more than was necessary, the offer of aid was extended to all of the European nations. Russia indignantly refused, and her satellites followed her lead in refusing to participate. She characterized the plan as an attempt to enslave Europe by bringing it under American economic control. Sixteen nations accepted, however, and at a conference in Paris, September, 1947, goals were set up for a four-year drive to increase production, foster economic cooperation and integration, and increase trade. The ERP provided aid to seventeen nations in all. The aid program raised the tempo of East-West rivalry as the Soviets used every effort of propaganda to prevent the restoration of political and economic prosperity in Western Europe.

The "cold war," as the impasse between the Russian and American blocs was beginning to be called, became ever more intense. Russia increased the directness and vigor of her control over her satellites. In Czechoslovakia a semi-independent democratic regime had managed to survive up to this time, but in February, 1948, this government was ousted from power and replaced by Communist party members. Czechoslovakia, for a second time within a decade, fell under a conqueror's heel. Of the east European states, only Yugoslavia maintained real independence.

The American policy of economic aid to nations threatened by Communist expansion was intended to promote economic recovery, to prevent the spread of Communism, and to cement the "free world" so that it could present a common front to Communist aggression. It is obvious that the program was designed to protect the United States by enlarging the sphere of her influence and shrinking the sphere of her potential enemy. Where needed, economic aid was supplemented by military aid. Already, in March, 1947, President Truman had announced a security policy which was quickly dubbed the Truman Doctrine. To those countries whose national integrity was being threatened by aggression from abroad, he pledged American financial and military aid. Congress quickly appropriated 400 million dollars to bolster Greece and Turkey, which were being bled white by their efforts to maintain the military establishments demanded by their position on Russia's flank.

In 1949 the United States invited the European nations to join her in a military alliance. Ten of the principal nations of Europe, together with the United States and Canada, formed the North Atlantic Treaty Organization (NATO). If one should be attacked, all would go to her aid. In 1950 these nations began to form an army which would be a European army for the defense of all under a single commander. General Eisenhower was appointed commander and labored two years at his task. He encountered immense difficulties, but much progress toward military integration was made. The vigorous foreign policy of Truman's administration, the work of his two Secretaries of State, Marshall, and Dean Acheson, and of Dwight D. Eisenhower, checked the advance of Russia and restored confidence to the free world. When President Truman left office the United States had bound herself in defensive alliances to some thirty states; his successor, President Eisenhower, extended this system of alliances to an additional nine. This great alliance system represented a colossal American effort to check the spread of Communism and contribute to world stability by uniting around her like-minded nations in defense of the values in which they believed.

If the Truman policies bore some encouraging fruits in Europe, they seemed less successful in Asia. The democracies of western Europe were already on our side in the fight against Communism; they shared with the United States a mature system of political democracy and individual freedom. In the troubled colonial world the situation was otherwise. These peoples had, in the main, never known self-government; they were inflamed with hatred of "imperialist" states, wanted their freedom, and beyond that wanted some measure of economic advancement. Communism did not necessarily appear to them obviously reactionary and frightening; they had watched backward Russia raise herself to economic power with its aid. Soviet Russia had always posed as an enemy of imperialism, and the propaganda which identified imperialism with the "capitalist system" had been most effective. Although the interlude of Japanese ascendancy had loosened old colonial ties, the Dutch in Indonesia, the French in Indochina, and the British in Malaya tried after the war to regain control. The result was civil war, with the West appearing in the role of "imperialist enslaver." True, the United States freed the Philippines, and Britain in a notable act of statesmanship granted independence to India and Burma; on the other hand, colonial wars raged in Indonesia, Indochina, and Malaya.

In China, the West was confronted with the problem of sustaining a non-Communist regime identified with defeatism and corruption, in the face of a rising tide of revolt which native Communists

had succeeded in capturing. It was not easy to give adequate aid to such a crumbling regime as that of Chiang Kai-shek, short of assuming the enormous burden of an outright protectorate. Critics of the Truman policies cried bitterly that Chiang's government had not been given enough aid at the right time. The fact is—and it later became a source of embarrassment to the administration—that in China as well as in Korea, American policy from 1945 to 1947 was aimed at getting the Nationalists and Communists to cooperate in some sort of coalition government.

The administration replied to its critics by asserting that no amount of aid could have saved so unpopular a government as Chiang Kai-shek's, and that Europe had to have prior claims on limited Amer-

First Bikini Atoll test of atomic bomb July 1, 1946. Huge as this blast was (note navy ships at base of explosion), it was later dwarfed by H-bomb tests. (U.S. Navy photograph)

ican resources. Arguments about our China policy continued to rage; but the fact was that the Communist-led revolution had succeeded by 1949 in overthrowing the Nationalist government of Chiang, which sought a precarious refuge on the island of Formosa. Clearly, the problem of saving Asia for the free world was fraught with many difficulties, and its solution was hardly in sight.

Over the period of postwar strife hung the shadow of universal destruction. The atomic uranium bomb, which in 1945 brought destruction and at least 130,000 casualties to Hiroshima, threatened a new form of total warfare. But for technical reasons, the size of this bomb limited its use. Within a few years, scientists had discovered a means of making an atomic explosion of unlimited size—the hydrogen bomb. A large airplane could carry enough to produce damage at least 100 times as great as the largest possible uranium or plutonium bomb. Experimental blasts suggested that as an aftermath of the explosion itself, there might be clouds of radioactive material capable of killing over a huge area. Both the United States and the Soviet Union now possessed vast quantities of fissionable material capable of producing nuclear weapons with power enough to destroy all life. To this nuclear revolution was added the development of missiles with nuclear warheads, capable of delivering this destructive power across oceans and continents to the enemy. Since 1954, the revolution in striking power has held the center of the stage, producing spectacular developments in missiles and rockets.

Under such circumstances, war—at least total war—was clearly obsolete. Even in World War II, the nominal victors hardly "won" anything, and in a future war there would certainly be no victors—

perhaps not even many survivors. The knowledge that this was so was probably the greatest factor deterring nations from war. But bitter hostilities, rivalries, and conflicts continued to exist among nations; the world had little strategic stability, and the fear that it might quite literally blow itself up was—and is—a dreadful one in the Atomic Age.

TRUMAN'S SECOND TERM: KOREA

Despite economic prosperity and some Truman successes in dealing with a troubled international situation, observers thought they saw unmistakable signs of a change in administrations as the presidential election of 1948 drew near. Truman's "Fair Deal" was only the New Deal under another name; and after sixteen years of left-of-center government, a swing of the pendulum seemed due. President Truman had encountered steady opposition to his domestic program, even from many Democrats. Conservative opposition had defeated him on taxes and on price controls, the Eightieth Congress voting lower taxes over the presidential veto. The Taft-Hartley Act also passed over the veto, representing a conservative revolt against the pro-labor policies embodied in the Wagner Act. In the elections of 1946, the Republicans had won control of both houses of Congress. The popularity of Truman and the Democrats seemed to be steadily waning, and all signs pointed toward their defeat. To make matters worse, Truman had to face rebellions from both wings of his own party in 1948. In one wing, old New Dealer Henry Wallace led a revolt and created a Progressive party, which stressed "getting along with Russia" and charged Truman with being too conservative in domestic policy. Wallace seemed sure to attract large portions of the labor and Negro vote. In the other wing, a movement of southern "Bourbon" Democrats (dubbed "Dixiecrats"), who protested against policies to end racial discrimination, raised the banner of states' rights and nominated Strom Thurmond of South Carolina. Truman's hand at the helm seemed too weak to hold the Democratic party together. Pollsters, bettors, and newspaper pundits universally agreed that he had no chance of reelection. The Republican party shared this view and chose their defeated 1944 nominee, Thomas E. Dewey, to make a second campaign for the presidency. Deluded by their confidence, the Republicans made only slight effort to win additional support.

Harry Truman, in contrast, stumped the country undismayed by the gloomy prophecies, belabored conservatives in both parties, and ridiculed the record of the Republican-controlled Eightieth Congress. He pointed to his record: effective rent control, federal aid for slum clearance and low-cost housing, an increase in the minimum-wage scale, unification of the armed forces under a Department of Defense, establishment of a council of economic advisers, and the Marshall Plan and the Truman Doctrine designed to contain Russian expansion. This record, forcefully presented by Truman in his famous "whistle-stop" campaign, looked pretty good to a majority of American voters. The prophets were spectacularly wrong. Newspapers and magazines reached the newsstands announcing Dewey's victory before red-faced editors had learned that Truman had contrived a major political upset. Truman's margin of victory was narrower than Roosevelt's had ever been, but the coalition of labor, farmers, urban liberals, and racial and religious minority groups had won another presidential contest.

Among the troubles which a second term held in store for President Truman, those connected with Asia were by far the most difficult. In the center of Asiatic problems was the unhappy country of Korea. The Korean peninsula, with its 30 million people, had been annexed by Japan after 1905 and, with the defeat of Japan in 1945, was supposed to regain its independence. Unhappily, like Germany and Austria, Korea was partitioned; the northern half was occupied by Russia and the southern half by the United States. These two powers were unable to agree either on a common policy of occupation or on unification. The two sides did manage to concur in the withdrawal of their occupation troops in 1948, but before leaving, the Russians had organized a fairly large (175,000) and efficient North Korean army and had established a government of Moscow-trained Communists. The army of South Korea was not nearly so large. A nationalist movement had been smoldering in Korea for half a century, and both sides were extremely anxious for national unity, but they found themselves frustrated by their differing political systems.

On June 25, 1950, the North Koreans, claiming to act to forestall a South Korean attack, crossed the border with 60,000 to 80,000 troops. The remoter origins of the decision to attack must remain obscure until we learn the secrets of the Kremlin. It seems probable that the Russians approved the operation. The United States had shown so little interest in South Korea that is possible the Communists thought there would be no vigorous reaction in Washington. It is also possible that they expected resistance and calculated on drawing the United States into a war which would weaken her in Europe and alienate Asiatic opinion. It is even possible that the Soviet Union wished to cause a war between China and the West, to bind China more firmly to Russia. All these remain mere hypotheses; what is certain is that as the South Korean army was driven rapidly southward, the American government, backed by an aroused public, determined to act to prevent another bastion from falling to the forces of Communism. General MacArthur's Eighth Army, stationed in Japan since 1945, was dispatched to the port of Pusan on the southern tip of the Korean peninsula. The Security Council declared the invasion an act of aggression and authorized action by United Nations members; about a dozen members subsequently sent small forces to aid in the fighting. The resolution in the UN Security Council was passed because the Soviet delegate was temporarily absent, and thus the Soviet veto was not applied. This absence has been taken by some as evidence that possibly the Kremlin was willing to see the conflict develop. But until other UN forces could arrive, it was the Eighth Army with what was left of the Republic of Korea (South Korea) forces which managed to hold a small beachhead around Pusan.

From mid-July to mid-September, these forces, despite lack of training, armor, and sufficient numbers, managed to hold on. Reinforcements and tanks arrived, and on September 15 a counteroffensive was launched. A brilliantly conceived landing at Inchon further up the peninsula, together with a breakout from the Pusan perimeter, threatened to catch the North Koreans in a giant pincers. Before this pincers movement the North Korean forces soon gave way. This pincers forced a North Korean withdrawal, which

THE UNITED NATIONS ACTION IN KOREA

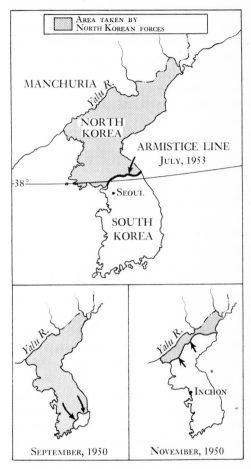

AREA TAKEN BY NORTH KOREAN FORCES

MANCHURIA

NORTH KOREA

ARMISTICE LINE JULY, 1953

38°

SEOUL

SOUTH KOREA

Yalu R.

SEPTEMBER, 1950

Yalu R.

INCHON

NOVEMBER, 1950

soon became a rout. There was nothing to oppose a United Nations advance beyond the 38th parallel, the boundary between North and South Korea, and toward the Manchurian frontier. But as the UN forces moved rapidly northward beyond the 38th parallel, a new element was injected into the situation: the intervention of Chinese Communist armies. The Chinese were first encountered in force about 70 miles south of the Manchurian border. The effect of their attack on the dispersed UN troops was disastrous, and only by a narrow margin was complete defeat in Korea averted.

The Chinese intervention in response to MacArthur's approach to their frontier might have been expected; it doubtless rested in general on a deep mistrust of American motives and more specifically on a concern for the safety of the electric generating plants on the Yalu River, which supplied power for a whole industrial region in Manchuria. The United States had refused to recognize the Chinese Communist government and had blocked its entrance into the United Nations, while recognizing and protecting the rival regime of Chiang Kai-shek on the island of Formosa. It was probably not hard for the men in the Kremlin to persuade their fellow Marxists in Peiping that the United States was a hostile power bent on destroying Chinese industry in Manchuria. Our government apparently took no steps to assure them that our aims were limited to repelling aggression by North Korea. Proud, and aspiring to leadership of an "Asia for the Asiatics" movement, Red China was in no mood to accept American forces on its doorstep, whether with UN sanction or not. Violent nationalism and deep-dyed suspicion of the "imperialist" states, among which the United States was included, certainly characterized the thinking of the new Chinese rulers.

By February, 1951, when the Chinese offensive had outrun its primitive supply system, it was brought to a halt at the Han River, about 100 miles south of the 38th parallel. General Matthew B. Ridgway, now commanding the UN forces, was able to regroup and launch counterattacks. By April he had recovered all of South Korea and had advanced some distance into North Korea; but during April and May the Communists maintained the of-

fensive, mounting massive attacks which dented, but could not break, the UN lines. By June the UN forces seemed to have regained the initiative in bloody fighting. At this point, upon the suggestion of Soviet Russia's delegate at the United Nations, a truce was accepted and hostilities largely came to an end pending the outcome of peace talks. These talks were to continue for two years, while each side built its lines into impregnable fortresses; the only fighting that continued consisted of local efforts to gain strategic hills along the stabilized battle front. At length, on July 27, 1953, final armistice terms were signed, after almost endless difficulties— terms which in effect accepted the continued division of Korea along a line not far removed from the original one.

Why, Americans were inclined to ask in some bewilderment, had they stopped fighting short of complete success? The answer was chiefly that there was fear of Russian intervention and a global war. MacArthur's original unwillingness to stop short of complete victory had resulted in Chinese intervention, thus enlarging and prolonging the war. Refusal to accept armistice proposals might have brought the Russians in. The effort for complete victory would have involved carrying the war into China, and Russia was China's ally, bound to her side by treaty. Victory at the cost of full-scale war with China, and perhaps World War III with Russia, seemed less desirable than acceptance of a stalemate. It could be said, at least, that aggression had been repelled and South Korea's independence had been maintained. Nevertheless, American opinion showed signs of impatience and frustration at the outcome, and there was ever-growing criticism of our Far Eastern policies.

All of Korea was thoroughly devas-

Korean refugee children, innocent victims of the frightful war which swept over a land left divided by the dissolving of the wartime partnership between Russia and the Western powers. (U.S. Department of Defense)

tated during this war, and its unhappy people suffered untold agonies. To many observers, this rehearsal for conflict in Korea drove home the lesson of the obsolescence of war under modern conditions. It was not a popular war, despite valiant efforts to depict it as a necessary defense of world security against aggression. An unpleasant aftermath of the stalemate in Korea was the discontent of the South Korean government, which wished to continue the war at any cost; the United States was placed in the rather embarrassing position of having to threaten its ally to prevent her from resuming the war.

NEW LEADERSHIP

In 1952 the expected swing of the political pendulum at last occurred, and after twenty years in power, the Democratic party was defeated and replaced by its rival. The decision of the American

people was undoubtedly connected with the fears, disappointments, and frustrations of the postwar years in foreign policy. Although billions of dollars had been spent on foreign aid and on defense, the "Russian menace" remained, undiminished in size. One could hardly say we had won the cold war, even if we had not lost it. The policy of "containment" had resulted in a war which cost 100,000 casualties without bringing a decisive result. Wiser and older nations might have thought the results satisfactory, but the American people were accustomed to victory—to "licking" problems, not living with them. Republican criticism of the conduct of our foreign affairs found fuel upon which to feed, though some of this criticism bordered upon the demagogic. Charges were hurled that our foreign policy failed because the Truman administration was filled with numbers of pro-Russians and even Russian spies. In the development of this myth, the "lunatic fringe" did not hesitate to involve such distinguished Americans as General George C. Marshall. Clearly, the situation had reached an alarming stage when such men could be accused of treason.

The "Red scare" hysteria was dismaying to those who felt that in the midst of a crisis in the cold war, internal unity was all-important. No one doubted that the Soviets had spies in the United States, as we doubtless had in Russia; no one doubted that American Communists, small in numbers, but dangerous, helped them. The spectacular revelations seemed to suggest that there might have been some Communist infiltration even into high government posts. It was another matter to charge the entire leadership of the State Department with softness toward Communism because it had not been able to prevent the growth of Communism in

Asia. The fact was widely publicized that for a time after 1945 the Truman administration had seen no need for elaborate security measures. It, and the entire nation, now was made to suffer for that attitude as the nation seemed to embark on a "witch hunt." Reckless charges were widely believed. Such professional demagogues as Senator Joseph R. McCarthy of Wisconsin hoped to ride the swelling tide of the Red scare into national prominence. The implication of McCarthy's arguments was that many government employees were Communists—in fact, all New Dealers and Fair Dealers were slightly disguised Communists. For a time, these exaggerated charges were given great prominence and considerable acceptance. The damage to American civil rights was great.

Many who voted for the Republicans in 1952 thought they were voting to throw out an administration shot through with Communist traitors; but interestingly enough, many others felt that only a distinguished Republican could ease the national hysteria and control the dangerous force of McCarthyism. The man they had in mind was America's outstanding military hero, five-star General Dwight D. Eisenhower, formerly Commander-in-Chief of the Allied Forces in Europe of World War II. Eisenhower's sincerity, integrity, and simplicity made him a national idol. He was persuaded to stand for the nomination, and the younger and more liberal wing of the Republican party adopted him as their own and guided his nomination campaign to victory after a sharp struggle with the party's old guard, who rallied behind the veteran conservative, Senator Robert A. Taft, "Mr. Republican." The Democratic candidate, Adlai Stevenson of Illinois, was also a man of outstanding abilities, a brilliant speech-

maker with a flair for witty but thoughtful discussion of real issues. Other issues of the campaign were provided by signs of Democratic corruption in Washington, which led many to suspect that the party had been in power too long, growing fat, complacent, and corrupt. Stevenson pointed to prosperity, and "Don't Let Them Take It Away" was a Democratic slogan to place against the Republicans' concentration on "the mess in Washington" and Korea. Both candidates on the whole discussed foreign affairs with gratifying sobriety and intelligence. The outcome was probably in the main a tribute to Eisenhower's personal popularity: he ran far ahead of his ticket, and even cracked the Solid South by carrying Virginia, Florida, Texas, and Tennessee, while in the races for Congress the Democrats came very close to holding their own. They lost control of the Senate by one seat and of the House by 20 but actually polled more aggregate popular votes than their rivals.

Whether Dwight D. Eisenhower would be another Grant or another Washington, unbiased observers honestly did not know; he had had no political experience. In his first administration he certainly marked up some substantial successes. The death of Joseph Stalin was followed by a shift toward a less intransigent Soviet policy, and the truce in Korea was finally achieved. This and a measure of economic recovery in Europe made it possible to reduce federal expenditures somewhat and pass a small tax reduction. Eisenhower, while making some gestures toward the conservative wing of his party, showed no desire to dismantle the great basic reforms of the New Deal. The President's most vocal opposition came from the conservative members of his own party, headed chiefly by Senator McCarthy. A bitter struggle developed between the White House and McCarthy over the right of the Senate to investigate administrative policies and decisions. It reached its climax in a series of Senate hearings, televised throughout the nation, which greatly discredited the Senator from Wisconsin. Shortly afterwards, McCarthy was censured by the Senate for conduct unbecoming to a member of that body.

The impact of the Eisenhower administration upon the domestic political scene was better revealed in statements of purpose than in major policy changes. The indecision of the average American voter, revealed in most elections since 1945, made it highly unlikely that any fundamental change would take place in domestic politics. Eisenhower, in milder tones than those of Truman, chided Congress and urged it to be reasonable and follow his lead, but he had little more success than his predecessor.

The most violent critics of President Eisenhower flayed him for his failure to offer effective leadership, and yet he remained one of America's most popular Presidents. The explanation apparently lay in the desire of the American people for a cessation of extreme partisanship and a general reluctance to engage in crusades of any kind. They found Eisenhower's obvious sincerity much to their taste. His emphasis upon the unity of Americans rather than upon divisive partisanship was met with a grateful warmth. His large and reasonable generalizations and his lofty, and occasionally pedestrian, idealism were called nothing more than fuzzy thinking by his critics, but the public found them to its liking.

While sharp political controversy developed over such issues as public power, defense spending, aid to education, and civil rights, the net result was to leave the line between Eisenhower's administration and its opponents quite indistinct. The immense majorities which Eisenhower piled up in both 1952 and 1956 were matched by increasing majorities for congressional Democrats. The reasons for this state of affairs appear to have been a kind of moral fatigue after the great crusades of World War II and the Korean conflict, heavily reinforced by the sense of well-being that accompanied the continuing prosperity of the decade of the fifties. A contributory factor was the refusal of the administration to make domestic policy the area of decision, preferring instead to base its reputation on the preservation of peace in a hostile world. The American people trusted the Democrats more in domestic policy, the moderate Republicans, in foreign policy.

RECENT ECONOMIC ISSUES

The decade of the 1950s saw the nation's economic system continuing to function well. The gross national product, the value of the total output of goods and services in the economy, was higher at the end of the ten-year period than at the beginning. The rate of capital investment was high. Whether it was high enough to meet the challenge to the capitalist system presented by the Communist economies was a question which troubled many thoughtful Americans. In this, as in so many other aspects of our national life, the atmosphere of the cold war colored the thinking of many citizens. The United States was in competition with the Soviet Union, many people felt, throughout broad areas of the non-European world, as a matter of prestige and influence.

In the course of the decade there were interruptions to the general theme of prosperity. There was a business recession in 1953–1954 and another, this time more severe, in 1957–1958. The latter brought serious unemployment into the national life again, a phenomenon all too reminiscent of the bitter days of depression in the thirties. Some 7 per cent of the working force was idle in 1958, and in some areas the percentage was much higher. The system of unemployment insurance, established during the New Deal era, did much to cushion the shock of this unemployment and to limit the disastrous effects on family life which would otherwise have been inevitable. But in some instances the unemployment-insurance funds were exhausted, and the ugly spectacle of the breadline once again appeared in some American cities.

Such conditions were not widespread. With the end of 1958, there were numerous indications of business revival. Many of the indices of economic activity showed an upward trend, and the total of unemployed began to decline. But there were still pockets of severe unemployment in several areas, especially where the business recession had hit industries already somewhat vulnerable to trouble because of technological changes or shifts in buying habits. Nor could it be overlooked that, regardless of whether recovery came swiftly or slowly, the loss of national wealth and income due to the recession would run into billions of dollars.

The business recession of 1957–1958 was undoubtedly a major factor in the growth of widespread criticism of the Eisenhower administration, a dissatisfaction which was demonstrated by the impressive Democratic gains in Congress in the mid-term elections of 1958. There was much demand that the federal government embark upon a broad program of compensatory spending to take up the slack in the economy created by the decline in private expenditure. Yet, despite the pressure of the election results, the administration held to the generally conservative view that the depression was not yet severe enough to warrant large-scale spending, and that before any such action could properly be taken, sufficient time should be allowed to see if the "natural forces" of recovery could assert themselves. The administration's leaders and supporters felt that the eventual up-turn vindicated the cautious policy followed, while its critics attacked it for a "do-nothing" attitude and pointed out that despite the business revival, full employment did not exist. Significant in all the debate was the fact that even a Republican administration expressed willingness to take action against the recession, undertaking deficit financing for large-scale government pump priming should the circumstances warrant this. Americans looked to the government to maintain a flourishing economic life. Politicians were well aware of this, however much many of the more conservative might resent it.

In general terms, the basic economic policies of the Eisenhower administration did not differ greatly from those of preceding Democratic ones. One difference was the greater concern about inflation, and the effort to balance the government budget as well as to use the powers of the Federal Reserve Board as a check on inflation. The pressures exerted by all sorts of demands, for needs of national defense, from powerfully entrenched groups in the nation, and for the generally multitudinous needs of an expanding population, did not leave much leeway for trimming federal expenditures. But the administration did show a reluctance to add to the federal expenditures, even in the face of strong demands from the opposition party to do so in the name of public welfare.

The Eisenhower economic policies placed greater reliance on the classical device of trying to regulate the national economy by manipulation of the rate of interest on bank borrowing. The Federal Reserve Board in particular sought to check inflation by raising the rediscount rate, which Democratic administrations had tended to keep low. To raise the interest rates in this manner would mean that banks could not lend so much money at cheap rates. The Republicans here again displayed a stronger desire to stabilize the dollar than to promote a number of popular interests. They argued that, in the long run, inflation was the greater evil. Democrats countered with charges that the administration was more sensitive to the profit margins of banks and other lending institutions than it was to the needs of the home builder, the small businessman, local school boards, and the many others who had to borrow for legitimate reasons. Thus the somewhat complex and mysterious operations of the Federal Reserve became something of a political issue, behind which lay an old American conflict between orthodox sound-money conservatism and the interests of various debtor groups.

An area of the national economic life in which the Eisenhower administration would have liked to make many more changes was that of agriculture. Secretary of Agriculture Ezra Taft Benson, holder of that office in both Eisenhower terms, was outspokenly hostile to much of the system of subsidies for the nation's farmers. But his efforts to bring about a return to some form of free-market pricing for agricultural products met with little suc-

cess, and may have cost the Republican party a good many votes. Despite its somewhat diminishing numbers, the so-called farm bloc in Congress, a group that included both Republicans and Democrats, was usually able to hold the Benson program in check and to protect the substantial vested interests that their farm constituents had in the existing legislation.

But an increasing number of Americans grew critical of the existing structure of farm legislation. The basic principles of the system, to keep farm income high by government subsidies designed to reduce production through limitation of acreage planted, was an obvious failure. Increased efficiency in farming made it possible both to limit acreage and at the same time to increase production. With the guaranteed income that many farmers had from their participation in the acreage-limitation program, they made greater purchases of new machinery or other devices which increased efficiency and thus

Mechanical corn picker. Such machinery increases the already fabulous efficiency of American agriculture. (U.S. Department of Agriculture)

added to the surplus. A great proportion of the national farm output of major crops could not be sold on the domestic market, and thus found its way into the warehouses and storage facilities of the nation. By mid-1958, it was costing the government just about 1 billion dollars annually in storage charges to cope with the outpourings of this farm cornucopia. Nor did overseas markets exist for any major portion of this enormous quantity of agricultural products. While some of it might be disposed of in programs of economic aid to other countries, this was something that had to be done with great caution, for any such program immediately caused resentment among other food-exporting nations, many of them valued friends and allies, who in part made their national living by the sale of similar crops from their own farms to overseas markets. And so the production of farm surpluses continued, the bill for farm subsidies mounted, the warehouses groaned with their great plenty, and the American people seemed to be the only people in history plagued and bedeviled with an overabundance of the good things of life.

CIVIL RIGHTS AND
THE SEGREGATION ISSUE

The most serious social issue in the mid-1950s grew out of the Negroes' battle for equal civil rights in the public school system. In many states the Negroes had long been denied the equal legal rights conferred by the Fourteenth Amendment. When, in 1883, in the civil-rights cases, the Court ruled that the restrictions of the amendment applied only to states and not to private individuals or groups of individuals, the Negroes were left without adequate protection. Many discriminatory restrictions imposed by individuals, cor-

porations, and organizations effectively deprived them of equal rights. Even the right of the *state* to pass discriminatory legislation was upheld in the all-important *Plessy v. Ferguson* decision (1896), which allowed "separate but equal" accommodations in railroad trains (Jim Crow laws).

The Plessy decision became the legal cornerstone of racial policy for a half-century. But the New Deal years, with their heightened social conscience, brought a breach in the wall. In a series of decisions, the United States Supreme Court held that state laws which discriminated against Negroes and other minority groups by denying them admission to tax-supported universities and professional institutions were unconstitutional. As a result of these decisions, a small number of Negroes were admitted to institutions which had previously been closed to them. Thus, in form at least, the separate-but-equal doctrine in the field of higher education was discarded. The ruling of the Court clearly implied that a separate Negro institution, even if physically the equivalent of the white state university, would not be of equal standing or quality because of its segregated status.

Then, in 1954, in one of the most historic and important of all the decisions on civil rights, *Brown v. Board of Education,* the Supreme Court unanimously overthrew the entire *Plessy v. Ferguson* doctrine. Following lines of thought developed in some of the decisions affecting higher education, it ruled that regardless of facilities, segregation is in itself discriminatory and in complete violation of the Fourteenth Amendment. "We conclude," said the Court, "that in the field of public education the doctrine of 'separate but equal' has no place. Separate educational facilities are inherently unequal."

The Brown decision was followed by many court actions at all levels, as Negro leaders, sponsored by the National Association for the Advancement of Colored People, sought to claim their rights under the new constitutional interpretation and to end the long-established practice of racial segregation in the public schools. The region most involved in this problem consisted of the border states, including the District of Columbia, and the states of the Deep South and the Southwest. The areas on the extremities of this region generally complied with the ruling of the Brown decision, as in the District of Columbia and Maryland in the East and Missouri and Oklahoma in the West and Southwest. In a group of states farther south, where southern traditions of racial segregation were more solidly entrenched, the tactics were to maintain segregation as long as possible, but to give a measure of compliance, as in North Carolina, Arkansas, Tennessee, and Texas. Virginia, along with six states of the Deep South, embarked upon a policy of "massive resistance" to the ruling of the Supreme Court, on the grounds that public school policies were exclusively the province of the states.

In those states which sought to delay integration, or which decided upon a program of total opposition, the pattern of resistance was similar. Resolutions of nullification or interposition declaring the Supreme Court order unconstitutional were adopted by state legislatures. New state constitutional amendments and legislation were adopted which required segregation in the schools. Commissions on constitutional government or state sovereignty undertook "to enlighten the public on the functions and duties of state and federal governments" and to resist "federal encroachment." In order to prepare for the establishment of private school systems, laws for compulsory attendance in public schools were repealed. Public funds were withdrawn from schools that had admitted Negro students in compliance with federal court orders. Provision was made in all these states for the use of public funds to support private school systems in communities where integration was ordered. Pupil placement laws authorized local school boards to assign pupils on the basis of such standards as availability of space and teaching personnel, effect on established programs, suitability of curricula, scholastic aptitude, relative intelligence or "mental energy" of pupils, and their home environment and social or psychological backgrounds and attitudes. In addition, loyalty oaths were imposed upon teachers, and they were required to disclose their organizational connections. In all, about two hundred laws and resolutions designed to preserve existing segregated school systems were passed in twelve states between May, 1954, and the fall of 1958.

In September, 1958, the Supreme Court unanimously set aside an order of a federal district court granting a two and a half years' delay in admitting Negroes to Central High School in Little Rock, Arkansas. This precipitated a clash between federal and state power. The segregationist Governor of Arkansas called out the National Guard, not to protect and escort the nine Negro pupils who had been admitted, but to bar their attendance. He asserted that "it isn't the duty of state authorities to enforce federal laws or federal orders." And furthermore, he contended, such a policy would have brought opposition from the people and would have stirred up violence. When an injunction was obtained compelling withdrawal of the National Guard, and it was apparent that local police protection could not be relied upon if the Negroes attempted to attend school, President Eisenhower decided to intervene and to use his constitutional power to uphold federal authority. United States troops were dispatched to Little Rock, and the National Guard was federalized. Federal troops thus kept open the doors of Central High School. But rather than comply with the order of the court to make a "prompt and reasonable start" on a program of gradual desegregation, state authorities closed Little Rock's four high schools at the end of the 1958–1959 session.

Public opinion in Arkansas appeared to support Governor Orval Faubus and the segregationists. But after a year without schools there were signs that a reaction was setting in. This was true also in Virginia, where a program of "massive resistance" in defiance of desegregation had been supported by the dominant political machine in the state. The Virginia Supreme Court declared the state school-closing laws unconstitutional, and a somewhat moderate plan was instituted which accepted nondiscrimination in the public schools but continued tuition grants from public funds to those who wished to send their children to segregated private schools.

Elsewhere in the border states, desegregation sometimes went more smoothly. Nashville, Tennessee, provided an example of successful desegregation as a result of effective leadership and enlightened Negro-white cooperation. But most southern cities and areas throughout the Deep South appeared determined not to concede a single point in the direction of desegregation. This was in spite of the pleas of some distinguished southerners, such as the great American novelist William Faulkner. Both moderate believers in gradual desegregation and embittered segregationists tended to agree that the South stood at the crossroads of its destiny on this pregnant issue.

In this connection it might be noted that the Supreme Court did not demand immediate desegregation. It sought to leave much to the determination of the local authorities and declared that "once a start has been made, the courts may find that additional time is needed to carry out the ruling in an effective manner." The road to compromise on this thorny question was not closed. Many thinking Americans argued that the issues went beyond the South itself and profoundly affected the position of the Western world in its struggle against Communism. The nations of Asia and Africa watched developments in the United States to see if the opportunities of American freedom and equality were available to the colored peoples of the land.

FOREIGN AFFAIRS SINCE 1952

Though in the eight years after the close of the Korean conflict in 1953 there was no major or protracted military action involving the great powers, a series of crises and conflicts kept apprehensions constantly alive. No year passed without its alarms, and few of the major problems left over from World War II were solved. The Far East, which had produced the Korean civil war and turned it into a major world crisis, produced a somewhat similar situation in Indochina, which caused weeks of anxiety in 1954 but was resolved without another Korean-type intervention. The ambition, power, and hostility of China under Communist leadership remained a source of worry. The United States continued to recognize and support heavily the Nationalist Chinese government on Formosa, despite a certain amount of domestic and world criticism of this policy. In 1956, and again in 1958, troubled flared up in the Formosa Straits islands. For the time being, the strength of the American position seems to preclude a major Communist assault aimed at Formosa, and the skirmishing over the off-shore islands was in itself relatively minor. For the future, the prospect is perhaps less bright. No such bastion of strength against the Communist colossus as the NATO alliance had been created in the Far East.

Throughout the Afro-Asian world of peoples emerging from colonialism into young nationalism and struggling for a place in the sun economically as well as politically, the challenge of Communism was more serious than in Europe. Many of these people lacked the cultural and social foundations for Western-style liberal democracy. Certain features of Communism undeniably attracted them, while the West had to live down a heritage of earlier imperialism. At best, they were apt to feel no great stake in the conflict of the superpowers, and they occasionally sought to exploit it to their own ends.

In 1956, and again in 1958, the Middle East suddenly assumed the center of the stage in the drama of world politics. This was a region of new, unstable governments and of violent young nationalistic movements accompanied by a "revolution of rising expectations" that brought acute discontent with the poverty so long endured. It also harbored the Arab-Israeli feud, embittered by a large population of Arab refugees expelled from the Jewish state. This feud had led to one war in 1948 and had continued afterward in the form of constant bloody frontier incidents. The Russians touched a match to this powderkeg by intervening in the area with the sale of arms to Egypt. Already deeply

The Cabinet officer whom President Eisenhower trusted and respected perhaps more than any other advisor was John Foster Dulles (right), Secretary of State from the beginning of Eisenhower's administration until Dulles's death in May, 1959. (Wide World)

distrustful of President Abdel Nasser of Egypt, the Israelites found in this move reason enough to consider preventive war. At the same time, Great Britain was aroused to hostility when Nasser nationalized the Suez Canal, while the French believed that Egypt was keeping alive the rebellion in neighboring Algeria. All the details of this complex situation cannot possibly be set down here; suffice it to say that the world was startled late in October, 1956, to learn that Israel, Britain, and France had suddenly attacked Egypt, the Israeli troops quickly overrunning much Egyptian territory while the British and French took Port Said. Confusing though the situation was, the American people undoubtedly agreed with their government's position that the aggression must be stopped, even though our friends and allies were committing it. They had some second thoughts when they found the United States joined by the Soviet Union in this demand. The British people were equally divided and confused; some blamed their own government for a bad blunder, while others bitterly reproached the American government for having deserted them.

The outcome of this affair was eminently unsatisfactory. Nasser and the Arabs were indignant at what seemed a conspiracy to commit aggression against them, the Israelis, who were forced to withdraw, were also unhappy, and the Western alliance was badly strained. The United Nations ultimatum, backed by the United States and the Soviet Union, had restored the *status quo* but had not solved the problems. With this fiasco the British and French were on the way out in the Middle East, where for many decades they had played the leading role, and the United States was forced to shape a more positive Middle Eastern policy.

Two years later, oddly enough, the United States found itself committing an act similar to the one it had condemned in 1956. Unwilling to come to terms with Egypt's ambitious Nasser, American policy was to give energetic support to governments in Jordan, Lebanon, and Iraq, which were anti-Nasser and more friendly to the West. But Nasser's star was rising on a crest of Arab nationalism, and in the summer of 1958 there were Nasser-incited revolts in Iraq and Lebanon. In support of these governments, President Eisenhower ordered the marines into Lebanon while British troops entered Jordan. The ensuing crisis set nerves once again on edge, for it seemed possible that Nasser, backed by the Russians, might counter with armed force and touch off a war. Fortunately, all was peacefully resolved, with everyone showing some restraint. Neither the West nor the Communists thought the Middle East worth a war, but the instability of this oil-rich region makes it always a potential

trouble spot. Certainly it was now more definitely an American concern than ever before. The venerable Monroe Doctrine, which forbade American intervention in the "internal affairs" of non-American states, had been a silent casualty of these new responsibilities.

The Russians, for their part, showed how little they accepted any self-denying ordinance when they openly intervened with massive power to crush brutally a revolution in Hungary against the puppet Communist regime there. This tragic event blighted hopes that Soviet Communism might prove more reasonable following the death of Stalin. Following the sensational denunciations of Stalin's regime by Nikita Khrushchev early in 1956, some loosening of the reins had, in fact, been noticed, but apparently the Hungarian revolt had frightened the Soviet leaders back into the policy of iron repression of the satellites. They were in the uncomfortable position of not being able to let go lest they reap the harvest of hatred and lose face. Informed opinion was unanimous in agreeing that Communist rule was unpopular in almost all the satellite countries and would be overthrown by angry peoples if Soviet force were withdrawn. With the city of Berlin shared by East and West in the middle of Soviet-dominated East Germany, the problem of "disengagement" was an extremely dangerous one, and was apparently no nearer a solution than it had been since World War II had been allowed to end with Russians and Anglo-Americans meeting in the middle of Europe. In 1959, the question of Berlin's—and Germany's—ultimate fate loomed ominously on the diplomatic horizon.

Some important objectives of American policy in Europe, on the other hand, made satisfactory progress. Since World War II, and especially since the creation of NATO in 1949, Americans had worked and hoped for a union of the states of western Europe. Such a union would make Europe both more defensible and more prosperous, in each case taking some burden off the United States. A strong, confident, prosperous Europe would stand as a bulwark against Soviet Communism and might provide a framework within which the troublesome German problem could be solved. In a major example of political evolution, the proud and ancient nations of Europe moved steadily in the direction of integration. Economic integration advanced further than most people had dreamed possible, at least for the six countries associated in the Coal and Steel Community, Euratom, and the Common Market, the countries of West Germany, France, Italy, and BENELUX. For Free Europe as a whole, a number of organizations promoted cooperation and prepared the way for future political integration. The whole movement is still young enough to leave doubts about its ability to withstand a real trial. But under the *Pax Americana* and with generous American economic assistance, Europe has responded nobly, and apparently needs only time to achieve the tremendous task of making a real European Community out of most of the former sovereign states. If this were to be achieved, it would introduce a powerful new factor in world affairs.

If at the close of the 1950s disastrous war seemed a little less likely, however, it was chiefly because of the weapons situation, in which a "balance of terror" had evidently been achieved. Uneasy though such a peace must be, it is at least clear that both the great world protagonists now have so much destructive power in their hands, and so little chance of keeping it from hitting them, that neither can

Cape Canaveral, Jupiter IRBM. These became familiar words to Americans rather suddenly in 1958. Dramatic Soviet achievements in missiles and rockets challenged the United States to keep up in the space race as well as the weapons-delivery race. (U.S. Army photograph)

willingly risk all-out war; the result would be certain suicide for both. To count on this as a permanent prevention of war is foolish, but it is a factor making for peace so long as it lasts and might provide a breathing-space during which understandings can be reached. Some optimists hold that Soviet Russia is in evolution toward a society less dogmatic and dictatorial than that of the Stalinist phase, and that its new leaders are bound to be more reasonable and more cautious in their foreign policy. There can be less confidence in the leadership of Red China, however, and no confidence at all that a world in the rapid ferment of change will be devoid of conflict and crisis. The challenge thrust upon the United States to preserve in such a world a benevolent leadership for Western civilization is surely the greatest challenge that tomorrow holds.

For in spite of optimistic views about changes in Soviet policy, it must be recorded that few authorities see any significant change in the unremitting hostility of the Communists to the West, in their determination to destroy the West in a final great competition of ideologies, and in their belief that, in the long run, they hold most of the cards for this game.

Compromise seems most unlikely, and between the two worlds there can be at best, in Walter Lippmann's words, a kind of mutual toleration. Whether such toleration can develop far, in view of the dynamism and fanaticism of Communism and the volatile state of so many parts of the world, must remain a matter of the greatest uncertainty. For the citizen of tomorrow there is little room for complacency.

FURTHER READINGS

A general survey is attempted by Eric F. Goldman, *The Crucial Decade 1945–55* (1956). A. A. Berle, Jr., has discussed the new American economy in *The Twentieth Century Capitalist Revolution* (1954), as has Thomas C. Cochran in *The American Business System: A Historical Perspective, 1900–1955* (1957). M. R. Benedict, *Farm Policies of the United States, 1790–1950* (1953), focusses on the contemporary farm problem. Other stimulating discussions of the economic situation are Sumner Slichter, *The American Economy: Its Problems and Prospects* (1948), and John K. Galbraith, *The Affluent Society* (1958).

On foreign policy, the survey by William Reitzel, M. A. Kaplan, and C. G. Coblenz, *U.S. Foreign Policy, 1945–1955* (1956), is serviceable. More specific areas are covered by Herbert Feis, *The China Tangle* (1953); W. P. Davison, *The Berlin Blockade: A Study in Cold War Politics* (1958); and Harry B. Price, *The Marshall Plan and Its Meaning* (1955). McGeorge Bundy has edited the Acheson record in *The Pattern of Responsibility* (1952). Henry Kissinger, *Nuclear Weapons and Foreign Policy* (1957), is now available in an inexpensive edition. John C. Campbell, *Defense of the*

Middle East: Problems of American Policy (1958), is a recent analysis of that particular trouble spot. George F. Kennan, *Russia, the Atom, and the West* (1957) (the Reith lectures), is a masterful examination of the continuing cold war and prospects for ending it. The annual volumes of *The United States in World Affairs* (since 1947) provide much detailed information on American foreign policy. L. W. Koenig, *The Truman Administration* (1956), is a documentary record.

Carl B. Swisher, *The Supreme Court in Modern Role* (1958), and Alpheus T. Mason, *The Supreme Court from Taft to Warren* (1958), deal brilliantly with an important topic. Rayford W. Logan, *The Negro in the United States* (1957), is a discerning work in paperback form. C. V. Woodward, *The Strange Case of Jim Crow* (1954), gives background for the desegregation controversy. Among other works called forth by the desegregation controversy are J. B. Martin, *The Deep South Says "Never"* (1958); Harry Ashmore, *Epitaph for Dixie* (1958); Virgil Blossom, *It Can Happen Here* (1959); and Henry Savage, Jr., *Seeds of Time: A Background of Southern Thinking* (1959).

Among the more interesting of the memoir literature in recent years are Arthur H. Vandenburg, Jr. (ed.), *The Private Papers of Senator Vandenberg* (2 vols., 1952); Harry S. Truman, *Memoirs* (2 vols., 1956); and Walter Millis (ed.), *The Forrestal Diaries* (1951). To these might be added Robert J. Donovan, *Eisenhower: The Inside Story* (1956).

For additional bibliography, see the *Harvard Guide,* sections 272–277.

The Course of American History: Concluding Statement

*I have been . . . in lands where one
felt the pervasive foreboding of
violence; . . . where government is
conducted not by compromise, but
by coup d'état. And I have looked
back with contentment to my own
country, distracted as she might be by
a Babel of many voices, uncertain of her
purposes and her path; where yet there
can be revolution without machine guns,
and men may quit a public office and
retain a private life.*

Judge Learned Hand,
The Spirit of Liberty
Knopf, 1954

AMERICAN TRADITIONS

PLAINLY, THE WHOLE of the American experience can not be summed up in any single statement. Few things true of the early America bear much relevance to the mid-twentieth-century one. Not only the physical aspects of the nation have changed —from rural to urban, log cabin to skyscraper, homespun to nylon, mule wagon to jet plane—so has the mental make-up of the people and the institutional characteristics of society. The Puritan with his psalm book could not have felt at home in twentieth-century society. The frontier has vanished except in novels, and with it has vanished a way of life. The maxims of the founding fathers in foreign policy have finally yielded to a diplomatic revolution, and those who had once assumed that the United States ordinarily kept aloof from Europe would rub their eyes in the 1950s to see American troops all over that once forbidden continent and American commitments all over the world. A country which once feared to have any standing army now takes for granted the necessity of keeping nearly 3 million men under arms. The small group of colonists who had rebelled and won their independence have changed into a people holding colonies of their own.

John Marshall's long-treasured pronouncements about the absolute sanctity of private property against government have also passed into the realm of the obsolete, despite the laments of some Ameri-

626

cans. Paine and Jefferson, who had thought that hardly any government at all would be necessary in a free society, would doubtless be much amazed at the apparatus of modern big government. It is a far cry, too, from the earlier literature, the gentle and genteel writings of Emerson and the good, gray Victorian poets, to the brutal realism of the modern American novel. These are only some of the ways in which mid-twentieth-century America differs drastically from that of 1776; there are obviously many others. Change has been the law of life in Western civilization generally, but most particularly in America. Constant experimentation, the evolving of new institutions and ideas, the pragmatic philosophy—here is the very genius of the United States.

Into its relatively short history the United States has crammed much action. The peopling of a continent, the winning of independence, the making of a suitable political system, a great civil war, the travail of industrialism, then the trials and responsibilities of becoming a great power—amid all these experiences there has been little time to rest or stand still. The American people have been drawn from the least tradition-conscious classes of Europe and confronted with frontier conditions. One school of American historians placed the greatest stress on the frontier as molding American character, but perhaps equally important has been the factor of selection in the great migration from the Old World. For it was mostly "common men" who came, often under circumstances which led them to reject their old country. Both factors worked together to produce a people without much regard for old ways and forms. To cultured Europeans the United States has always seemed rootless and chaotic—"all sail and no anchor," as one of them once put it. The American Revolution was in part a revolt against the upper classes of European derivation, and as time went on the cult of the common man grew until it became the typical American philosophy. The goal of America has been the economic improvement of the masses, and this remains a goal which requires social and economic change.

On the other hand, it is possible to find some important areas of persistence and continuity. The basic idea of democracy has persisted, though it may meet different obstacles and take varying forms. The energy and drive of the American people, leading them to ignore the past and push impatiently into the future, is itself a permanent feature, noted by outsiders as often in 1950 as in 1850 or 1750, sometimes admired and sometimes not. (European friends often object to the brusqueness, the lack of patience, the defiant "frontier" note in American diplomacy, which seem to them dangerous in an era when the world is as potentially lethal as an atomic bomb.) The basic legal aspects of a free society, while sometimes threatened under conditions of modern life, still count for much—the Magna Carta is still alive; the Bill of Rights is still appealed to. The Constitution of 1787, though altered by amendments and even more by usage, still functions as the permanent basis of government. In fact, the United Sates Constitution is the oldest written constitution of any major state in the world—a remarkable tribute to the strength of tradition in the sphere of government in the United States. The constant experimentation, the eagerness for novelty, so apparent in many aspects of American life is not displayed in government. Here, at least, Americans have exhibited an unusual reverence for the past and its ac-

Perhaps the greatest problem facing Americans midway in the twentieth century is that of preserving, in a world which has changed drastically both materially and spiritually, the basic principles on which the nation was founded. Although far more Americans than ever before own homes, drive automobiles and travel abroad, the increase in the incidence of juvenile crime for example, is a symptom of unsolved spiritual and educational problems. "Equal justice under law" is more nearly a reality despite the persistence of some racial bigotry.

Steve Poster prevented from entering Texarkana Jr. College

The Supreme Court

American tourists in Paris

View of Levittown, Pa.

Juvenile delinquents being booked by police

Evening rush hour in Chicago

complishments, a conservative trait which has lent a needed stability to American life, otherwise so volatile and mobile.

The basic idea that the common man is entitled to some share of the good things of life has also persisted. To many of our colonial ancestors it meant the hacking of a farm out of the wilderness; to the present generation it seems to mean the owning of a small suburban home, a new automobile every few years, and a share in social security. While the forms have changed, the goal is still that of providing a decent living for everyone. In this respect, the great corporations, the labor unions, and the subsidized agriculture of the present day, so different from the carefree individualism of the past, may be seen to seek the same end—a good life for the mass of the American people. Indeed, the whole present mass-production system is based on this essentially democratic concept. And in this economic drive for a high general level of prosperity many writers have found the most significant part of the American dream. This ideal of mass economic welfare has been an element of continuity, binding together early and modern America.

AMERICAN ACHIEVEMENTS

A society dedicated to the economic improvement of the common man may well leave out some of the higher achievements of art and literature, achievements which almost require a leisure class and a highly cultivated audience. The Puritan heritage of America combined with the needs of the frontier and the great ideal of material progress to give American minds a strong utilitarian cast, with a contempt for the frills of civilization. Even in the twentieth century, the most typical American philosophical school, on the highest level—the pragmatism of William James and the instrumentalism of John Dewey— seems to foreigners to reflect the national desire to honor only what "works" and to dismiss the quest for pure truth and beauty as meaningless. It is perhaps significant that in the recent great scientific conquest of matter, in the development of atomic power, the theoretical contributions came from Europe—from Einstein, Rutherford, Fermi, Bohr, and others—while American technological genius achieved the practical applications of these theories.

Whatever its weakness in the realm of abstract thought, the United States in its special field has given the world something to think about. The goal of achieving a decent standard of living for all men, of abolishing poverty and inequality, has come closer to realization in the United States than was dreamed possible. It has largely eliminated those class conflicts which have plagued almost all societies. That "classless society" which Marxian socialists held up as the goal of proletarian revolution has been largely achieved by American "capitalism," mixed with a good deal of government welfare activity. The American standard of living is many times the world average. With less than 10 per cent of the world's population, the United States possesses about 40 per cent of the world's wealth. This amazing material success is a justifiable cause of pride. Some of it, we must admit in all fairness, has been due to good luck, most especially to a fortunate geographic isolation from destructive wars. It seems reasonable to believe that had western Europe escaped her two frightful wars of this century, she would have reaped the rewards of industrialism and come close to achieving the same standard of living. And in mid-twentieth century it seems possible that Soviet Russia, operating under

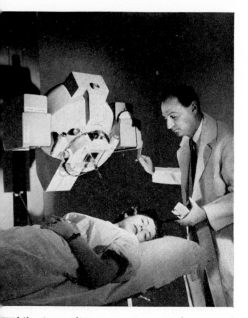

While its military use is a nightmare of modern man, atomic energy for peaceful uses promises all kinds of industrial and medical progress.

a political and economic system most Americans have been taught to abhor, might eventually match the American miracle of industrial progress. But when all is said and done, the fact remains that nothing has ever approached the American record in producing wealth and distributing it with reasonable equality. This goal has not been reached without many struggles, failures, and false starts, but in the middle of the twentieth century it appears to have been attained.

Their own great success has led the American people to be enthusiastic advocates of the export of their ways to the rest of the world. They have felt that sufficient doses of American individualism and ingenuity will suffice to transform the "backward" areas of the globe into miniature replicas of the United States. They have tended to become impatient with

these peoples for not showing a quick enough appreciation of the virtues of Americanism. But these other peoples, often to the astonishment of Americans, have sometimes been critical of Americanism. In large areas of the outer world, it is unhappily true that "Americanism" stands for much that is ugly and uninspiring along with much that is promising. The American is accused of being a mere materialist, of lacking a rich civilization of the mind, of having created a rich and powerful but drab society, in which everyone has plenty of gadgets but no ideas of culture. The objective historian might agree that the United States in the twentieth century has no literature or art or philosophy to compare with certain older countries of the world. She is still young, and has never yet had time and repose for the formation of a rich intellectual civilization. Some argue that a democratic society can never achieve this, but Americans have never conceded the point. They have placed a high valuation on learning; they have supported universities and endowed centers of research rather generously. And the United States has always produced its own critics of some of the apparently inescapable vulgarities of a commercial civilization. There is hope for future achievement in the sphere of culture.

Other skeptics ask if the American record of achievement, admittedly impressive in the past, can be maintained in the future. Exuberant and optimistic, even to the extent of possessing what an eminent British student of American affairs called a "myth of omnipotence," the American people face more difficult frontiers than those they have overcome in the past. The American past is the story of a successful people, subduing a continent by main strength, fortunate in having an abundance of human and physical resources and no problems which were not solvable. An unstable outer world full of explosive tensions, a world in which H-bombs have made war obsolete while conflict is still endemic in it—such a world may not be so easily subdued. It now looks to the United States for leadership in solving these problems. Getting used to a permanent crisis which has to be lived with is not easy for America. The subtlety and the patience necessary for the problems of diplomacy are qualities a frontier people had not much developed. Energy and will power alone cannot bring peace to a troubled world, and a good part of the world looks to America to maintain its peace and freedom.

Fortunately, the greatest of American achievements—greater, surely, than the merely material conquests—is the maintaining of political freedom and government by discussion. The roots of this achievement go back to Europe, and especially to England, but the United States has successfully adopted and added to this heritage of liberty. At its best, the American political system makes possible the use of public discussion and free expression as a means of education, of finding the answers to new and difficult questions, and of avoiding any antilibertarian movement that might seize power in moments of panic. At times seemingly wasteful and slow-moving, democracy has always held within itself the possibility of growth. The lines of communication between men have been held open in America, despite an occasional lapse. As long as it is possible to speak freely, the wisdom to meet new problems will be forthcoming and may be expected to prevail in the public arena. In an age of big government, big armies, and cold war, freedom of thought and discussion are more difficult to maintain than

they were in Jefferson's time, but they are being maintained. This is no guarantee that the right answers will be found at the right time. It is, however, the best hope for continued American progress in the long run. In view of the scarcity of successfully functioning free societies in the world, America's ability to preserve her basic civil and political liberties in the twentieth century is her greatest achievement.

To most Americans the close corollary of political freedom is elective government, under the unique American system of Congress and President. Most other democracies in the world have adopted the British cabinet system, which possesses certain advantages in harmonious relations between the legislature and the policy-making body. Some students of political systems have suggested improvements designed to bring our President and Congress into closer cooperation. Details may be changed, but the American Constitution in its basic form seems certain to remain. It is a going institution with roots now deep in the past. A powerful element of stability is the two-party system, almost an unwritten part of the Constitution. Despite their pride in self-government, Americans in the past have often exhibited an alarming indifference to political issues and a tendency to disparage politics and the politician. Public-opinion polls indicate that an astonishing ignorance about important public questions still too often exists. But the American political system has been tough enough to surmount many tests and is likely to continue to provide reasonably good government. Writings on the democratic system in mid-century are not so exuberant in their claims as they once were, but the more moderate statements of faith are firm and impressive. Judge Learned Hand, in a notable essay remarked that democracy may not be an ideal system, but it is a tolerable one, and in the last analysis all others are intolerable. While perhaps not an inspiring system, counting heads is still better than breaking them. In the stability of her political institutions America can take pride in a considerable achievement.

Over the years since 1789, the checks and balances of the original Constitution have undergone many changes. The states have declined in power, while the federal government has increased its authority in ways undreamed of by the founding fathers. The vote has been extended to almost all adults. The presidency has steadily enlarged its powers, and the Supreme Court exercises a right of judicial review which, according to some, had never been contemplated by the original framers. Nevertheless, no one fears that the constitutional system could lead to tyranny. The habits of a freedom-loving people are, after all, the best check against tyranny. And the American people continue to give signs that at bottom their instincts are always in the direction of freedom. The government of the United States is still one that derives its power from the consent of the governed, and that consent is still secured and expressed through the arts of persuasion rather than by force. The right of opposition to the party in power is secure. Defeated candidates for office do not find it necessary to take to the hills to flee from the wrath of their victorious opponents; rather, they take themselves to Miami for rest and recuperation. Though occasionally seriously threatened or even forgotten, the rights of minorities have been generally protected, and in certain key areas, such as the legal position of the Negro, there have been notable advances in recent years.

Despite the growth in the complexity of our legal system, and the development of new forms of legal practice in the many hearings before administrative agencies of the government, the basic legal protections established in American life by the transplanting of the English common law to these shores have been retained. The right of counsel to assist those involved in legal difficulties; the right to a fair trial or hearing, with all that phrase involves in the way of definite charges rather than vague accusations; adherence to time-tested rules of evidence—all this and much more is commonplace in American life.

AMERICAN DILEMMAS

Yet during the postwar years a great threat to free expression appeared in the United States, giving anxious alarm to many for a time. The roots of this panic, which led Americans to question each other's loyalty in a hysteria of suspicion and fear, lay in the perplexities faced by the nation. The United States had frightening world responsibilities. There were serious problems, internally as well as externally, but it was probably the outer world that gave most concern. It has become commonplace to say that an extraordinary burden has been laid upon the United States today, as she shoulders her world responsibilities. It would be well to indicate exactly what this means. Two vast historical processes have come to a climax: the collapse of Europe and the revolution in Asia. Western Europe, for hundreds of years the center of world power, has lost its ascendancy and has been hard put even to maintain its economic solvency. Those tasks of maintaining world order which it once performed have now fallen on the United States. Two terrible world wars have brought about the passing of the European age, leaving a huge vacuum of power in the world. It quickly became evident that this vacuum would be filled by Soviet Russia's totalitarian system unless America met the challenge. And so the defense of Europe and of Western civilization, and in large measure the performing of Europe's functions throughout the world, have very suddenly had to be taken up by the United States.

At the same time, there has occurred a movement among non-European peoples of vast significance. It is a movement against European domination, but also a revolution in which old societies are being transformed into new ones in partial imitation of the European pattern. Asia is "out of control"—in revolt, on the move, in a process of turmoil which makes for additional world instability. Once again, this restless turmoil in Asia and Africa provides an opportunity for Russian Communism and a terribly difficult but clear challenge to the United States. In brief, the world is in ferment and transition everywhere, and only the United States and Soviet Russia seem to have the strength and dynamism necessary to restore stability. The democratic world looks to the United States for the leadership necessary to prevent a universal breakdown in which civilizations are at stake. At the same time it is vital to avoid a third world war which would only end in universal ruin.

Since 1945 the most earnest and important debates within the United States have been about foreign policy. They went on at the level of specific decisions—about China, or Korea, or Indochina, or the Middle East—but also at a general and philosophical level, dealing with such questions as whether the ideal of democracy and the reality of international politics could be squared with each other. It seems likely that out of this discussion America

will learn much about how to play her role of world leader.

Many other questions have to be dealt with. Old issues and problems persist. Farm income; the tariff; monopolies; public power; racial discrimination; immigration policy—these are perennials. Agricultural overproduction, leading to impossibly low farm prices, the New Deal had met finally by guaranteed prices set at a level high enough to bring the farmer a decent income. The war created huge new markets at attractive prices, but after the war the old problem of the surplus returned. The government holds huge unsalable surpluses. Once again, it appears that farm production will have to be cut down in some way, or that the farmer will have to accept a fall in his income, or that much increased export markets will have to be found. The latter solution, unfortunately, runs up against the fact that the rest of the world cannot buy as many goods as it likes or as America would like to sell, because America cannot or will not accept enough goods in return. The tariff, today as in the days of Alexander Hamilton, is a live topic. Many thoughtful people believe that further reduction in our protective duties will be a necessary contribution both to American interests and international economic stability. But as so often before, it is politically difficult to overcome the opposition of entrenched economic interests well represented in Congress. However, considerable progress has been made in recent years. A notable development of the later '50s was the balancing of the foreign trade account by expanded imports.

This is but one example of continuing basic American dilemmas, most of which can hardly ever be "solved," in any final sense, but have to be adjusted by each generation, using the techniques of democratic discussion and compromise. Sometimes old political controversies do die away. Republicans in office after 1952 accepted and even expanded much of what they had once criticized as New Deal legislation. The role of the federal government in guaranteeing a minimum of economic security for most citizens is here to stay; so are strong labor unions, big government budgets, and use of the government's fiscal policies to guard against a possible depression. What has sometimes been called the "Keynesian Revolution," meaning government's active responsibility for maintaining economic prosperity, almost certainly cannot be reversed. The so-called welfare state, too, emerging from the experiences of depression and then further entrenched by total war, is undoubtedly a permanent fixture. This means that a certain minimum of human needs formerly met by individuals or private organizations will now be met by the government, perhaps even as a matter of right and obligation, and perhaps including a substantial number of services (housing and medical care as well as food and education). How far the welfare state might carry Americans in their search for security from the hazards of life in modern industrial society is still an open question, with such issues as health and housing under debate. It cannot be said that conservatives are any more reconciled than they had been to an increasingly state-directed system.

While controversy about economic policy continues, the continuing high level of prosperity reduces its urgency somewhat. Other national problems, perhaps the most urgent ones, seem to suggest spiritual rather than economic needs. Racketeering has invaded the labor movement and the business world. In 1955 a Senate report recognized juvenile deliquency as a national problem; the rate of crime shows

an alarming increase, most notably in the restless younger generation. As one cause of this disquieting phenomenon—which seems to make nonsense out of the old theory that poverty alone is the cause of crime—this report noted the need for more schools and teachers, a better educational program.

Perhaps there is a broader cultural explanation for crime and delinquency. With more leisure than any people have ever had before, Americans seem not to know exactly what to do with it. If such things as the average level of television and movie offerings reflect the cultural level, it is not a high one. Americans talk a great deal of the "American way of life," but there is a doubt whether it means more than a multiplying of mechanical gadgets. The ultimate goal of the democratic ideal is to free and enrich the individual. Economic well-being is no more than a means to that end. Matthew Arnold saw and said long ago that the "grave question" of modern times was, "What would these individuals *do* with their freedom and power?" Increased leisure, coming with the emancipation of man from grinding labor through the use of machines, would mean only increased boredom, and consequently moral breakdown, unless real intellectual and spiritual values were present. Conceivably, this is the deepest problem which confronts America in the years of the great prosperity at mid-century.

CHANGES

In view of the fact that for the United States change is a tradition, perhaps it is not amiss to include a brief description of what might be the most dynamic age of all. Whether all the changes that have taken place in mid-twentieth-century America can be called "progress" is open to question, but of the rapid and ceaseless pace of change there is no doubt.

The most obvious and striking manifestation of change was in growth as a sheer physical phenomenon. There were more people; men spoke of "the population explosion," which sent birth rates soaring and population suddenly bearing down on the 200 million mark, after a period in which it had seemed to level off at around 150 million. Predictions now are for a continuation of this rapid population growth over the next half-century, barring the unexpected or the catastrophic. For these additional people there were more homes—millions of them (the 1950s maintained an average of more than a million dwelling units built each year). The percentage of Americans who owned their own homes rose spectacularly. Most of these new homes were built on the outskirts of the great cities, where there rose vast "suburbias," one for each level of income. The growth of technological efficiency, which was the basis of the new wealth, continued to lessen the numbers of persons in agriculture, and so the city suburbs became the chief repository of the swollen population. Every large metropolitan area grew, some at a prodigious rate.

Other shifts in population occurred. The West Coast, the Rocky Mountain states, Texas, and Florida grew very rapidly; other regions, such as the older South and portions of the Northeast, formerly dominant in the nation, showed signs of population stagnation. The changing face of the economy led to the industrialization of new regions, especially along the Gulf of Mexico and on the West Coast. Industry was becoming much more widely diffused, and was no longer a monopoly of the Northeast. For this there is no one

explanation, but clearly both people and power had become much more mobile. Vast regional projects, such as the Columbia River Basin power and irrigation and the St. Lawrence Seaway, opened up whole regions to new economic potentialities.

Possibly the most startling effect of the increase in wealth and population was on education. While Americans found themselves hard pressed to provide elementary and high schools for the flood of children —one of a number of growth problems that afflicted suburbia—the most dramatic effect of the educational revolution was being felt in the colleges and universities. Not only were more children born—the universities began to get the first of the bumper crops of wartime babies about 1959—but the percentage of those going to college increased. Virtually all classes could now afford to send

Grand Coulee Dam and power project, Washington state. Projects such as this one in the Columbia River Basin, in addition to reclaiming land for agriculture, create new industrial centers and thus make for significant population changes. They represent a dynamic partnership between government and private enterprise. (U.S. Bureau of Reclamation)

their children to college. In 1958 almost half the total number of boys born in 1941 entered college. Americans would soon be living in a world where every second person had had a college education. When one considers that in 1920 only about 5 per cent graduated from colleges, and that today the British are talking of raising their percentage from about 4 to 7 per cent, the dimensions of this change can be appreciated. It is true that this tidal wave of students has created enormous problems of staffing and equipping universities to maintain the quality of education—problems which will not be easily solved.

State universities which had 5,000 students just a few years before, had 15,000 in 1960 and expected to have 40,000 by 1970. The Chancellor of the University of California has observed that this is more than mass education, it is massive. It represents something new in the history of the world, assuredly. American colleges have their chance to try to create, through the spread of learning, a better and more civilized nation.

The growth of population at so rapid a rate imposed other severe demands on American communities. Discerning critics pointed out a grave disparity between the private and public sectors of the economy. The child went from a comfortable home, full of all the latest gadgets, to a crowded school to be taught by inadequately paid teachers. The sprawling suburbs, with their high standards of comfort in living, proliferated along the edges of a metropolitan center slowly strangling to death because of hardening of the traffic arteries and afflicted with other serious social problems as a result of inadequate taxes. Taxes remain, as they were described by a great American jurist, the price we must pay for civilization. The mass movements

St. Lawrence Seaway. (*World Wide Photograph*)

of peoples to suburbia left behind massive problems of urban welfare and finance.

Modern America seems to represent mass—numbers, wealth, growth, sheer size—to many modern intellectuals. To these people, not least the American representatives, the "mass man" in a mass culture is a frightening thing. Most notable American writers of recent times have expressed a despairing protest against massism. William March, Henry Miller, and many others have indicated this quality. Such nonconformists actually stand in a long American tradition, reaching back at least to Henry Thoreau and finding converts in every generation, but perhaps never before was defense of personal integrity so needed as in the Machine Age, the age of the masses. A glance at American thought and letters at mid-century shows that there is no dearth of riches here, and that a distinguished list of writers are determined to leaven the mass with a little quality and preserve spiritual values in a world where all might seem transitory. It has been observed that the dominant note of serious American literature in recent years has been almost exactly the opposite of the alleged American characteristics of optimism, materialism, superficiality, and a cheerful conformism. The writers have exhibited in their works a pessimism, a complexity, a profundity and a concern for the unique individual that puts them somewhat at cross purposes to their culture, but which would seem to exert a healthy influence.

AMERICAN HISTORY AND WORLD HISTORY

An America in the flux of twentieth-century change can be sure of one thing at least: that it is far less an isolated unit and is far more bound up with the fate of the world than ever before. Though by cultural heritage part and parcel of European civilization, the United States through most of her formative years has had little to do with Europe, and has maintained toward her a tradition of cultural defiance. The powerful forces shaping the national character and traditions were isolationist, springing from a rooted conviction that only here in the New World was the great society to be created. Economic relationships with Europe and other parts of the globe were always significant, and there was also a very close cultural affinity. These facts were overlooked, however, and could be overlooked when during the long nineteenth century America's destiny seemed to lie wholly in the hands of her own vigorous westward-looking pioneers, and all that lay beyond the oceans seemed relatively insignificant. President Herbert Hoover once roundly declared

that America owed nothing to Europe. All Americans might not have believed this, but they did strongly feel that America was very different from Europe, and that the future hope of man rested here in the New World; the Old was not any longer of much consequence.

But in the twentieth century the United States has been led back into the world. Her great strength, growing as Europe's lessened, has brought this about. A vain effort to stay out of two great wars by clinging to an outmoded detachment has convinced Americans that they cannot separate their destiny from the rest of the world's. Much of the rest of the world, too, understands very well that American power and wealth are inevitably a great factor throughout the present world. With power goes influence; and influences emanating today from America to all parts of the globe are far greater than ever before. The best as well as the worst of America—from important state policies to grade B movies—is now regularly exported. Little that happens here is unobserved abroad, whereas formerly the United States was not considered very important by Europe or Asia.

By the same token, Americans are learning to appreciate the views of others as never before. The fact that America is now the center of world attention has had a profound effect on many American policies. For example, recent determined efforts to end racial discrimination owe much to world opinion and to the new American role in world affairs. A distinguished Negro has remarked that racial discrimination was formerly a backdoor problem but has now become a front-door one. With opinion in Asia of such great importance, the United States simply cannot afford to give offense to the colored peoples of the world, who considerably out-number the whites and who are increas-ingly aware of their group interests.

Despite isolationism, Americans have always believed in a world mission for their democracy. "We Americans are the peculiar chosen people, the Israel of our time," Herman Melville wrote. "We bear the ark of the liberties of the world." It has been noted that this "mission of American democracy to save the world" was a prod-uct of Puritanism, "a secular version of the destiny of Christianity to save the world from the governance of Satan." Once, most Americans believed that the rest of mankind would eventually adopt demo-cratic institutions of the American type. Her new world role, therefore, appealed to something in the American missionary spirit. But there were to be disillusion-ments. Much of the world, it appears, is perverse enough to refuse to accept Ameri-can ways. Some of it actually went com-munist, to the intense dismay of Americans. It has become evident that democracy is not always a panacea, that social and economic conditions are not always fa-vorable to it. The world is far more complex than most Americans had be-lieved in their isolationist era. The Ameri-can mission may still exist, but it is not simply a matter of converting everyone else to Americanism. America must re-ceive, as well as give influence, and can solve the world's problems not alone, but only in cooperation with others.

All can agree that the future of the United States is mixed up with that of the rest of the world. In these years Ameri-cans have rediscovered the ties that bind them to the parent civilization of Europe and to all other civilizations as well. It seems evident that the Old World and the New World will stand or fall together.

If democracy fails in one it is in danger of failing in the other. America's eco-nomic system and military security are interlocked with Europe's. For better or worse, the old days of American separate-ness and aloneness are certainly over. Here-after the stream of American history will flow on with that of world history.

AMERICAN VIRTUES

Though Americans have their share of defects, it seems fitting to conclude this book about their history with a reference to some of their merits. First on such a list might well be placed their generosity. All through American history runs a thread of openhandedness, expressed in dozens of ways: not only in the familiar hospitality of pioneer or plantation owner, but in such matters as overseas missions, where the American philanthropic im-pulse led the world. Private philanthropy in the United States has always been re-markably large, and continues to be so despite the emergence of the welfare state. For instance, millions of American citizens have given generously to relieve distress

AMOUNTS SPENT BY PRIVATE AND
PUBLIC SOURCES ON WELFARE

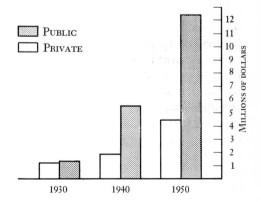

throughout the world through the facilities of the CARE program. History perhaps has no parallel of such mass generosity growing out of the good will and charity of a people toward erstwhile enemies and suffering humanity in uttermost parts of the earth. In the area of government-sponsored relief, the Marshall Plan provides an example of lavish aid generously given to foreign peoples in need of it; the program of economic assistance to undeveloped areas is another example. That these programs are, arguably, in the long-term interest of the United States, and hence not purely charitable enterprises, does not diminish the impulse of sympathetic benevolence that lay behind their enactment. As a nation and as individuals, Americans can claim to be as unselfish as any in history. And abroad the claim is freely granted these days.

The virtue of tolerance, notable in colonial times, has always characterized America. She has been tolerant of religion, of people, of new ideas. The tradition of religious freedom, from Roger Williams and William Penn on down, has been honored and cherished, with Catholic and Jew and all manner of Protestants living peacefully together along with many other religious minorities. The same has been true of races and cultures. Immigrants from every part of the world have come to the United States, and it is remarkable that the history of this vast intermingling has been marked by as little violence as has been the case. The United States is thus in itself an example of successful internationalism, and this success has been based on an unusual degree of tolerance. The reverse is often alleged, but when one looks at all the facts one is forced to conclude that the amount of racial and religious bigotry in the United States has

been small in relation to the problems involved. No other portion of the globe has a comparable record of success in the peaceful coexistence of so many different kinds of peoples. Nor is it true that Americans are inhospitable to new ideas. On the whole, they have welcomed and embraced a great diversity of faiths and opinions, and unorthodox views have been tolerated except in times of very unusual tension. If the record here is far from perfect, the ideal of toleration is a goal toward which America continues to aim.

As a third in the trinity of American virtues we may put faith. Faith in the future of mankind, most especially, has been the American habit of mind. It stems ultimately from the Enlightenment, and it is today somewhat less prevalent in Europe than formerly; too many tragedies there have undermined it. But America is still optimistic, still feels that through education and the spread of reason mankind will win through to a final triumph over all kinds of evil. The vision of universal peace continues to exist here. The "true grandeur of nations," Americans have always felt, lies in peace, not war; in social improvement, not military glory. This optimistic hope that a final utopia of enlightenment, of world peace, of universal brotherhood will prevail may be naïve, but it is a powerful force for good in the troubled world of today. This secular version of the Christian ideal of the millennium comes as close as any one thing to summing up the meaning of American history. A land where miracles have happened, and unhappy men have become happy, America is a country with a national faith that this can go on happening, until democracy, in the words of Walt Whitman, has fashioned "a new earth and a new man."

FURTHER READINGS

The innumerable appraisals of American civilization as a whole might be approached by way of Henry S. Commager (ed.), *America in Perspective* (1947), an anthology of foreign views on America. For interesting recent reactions, see Geoffrey Gorer, *The American People: A Study in National Character* (1948), and J. B. Priestley, *Journey Down a Rainbow* (1955). Commager is also author of a book on *The American Mind* (1950) that has been widely read. Another recent interpretation is that of David M. Potter, *People of Plenty: Economic Abundance and the American Character* (1954).

Two voluminous works, both with a somewhat left-wing slant, one by an Englishman and one by an American, are H. J. Laski, *The American Democracy: A Commentary and an Interpretation* (1949), and Max Lerner, *America as a Civilization: Life and Thought in the United States Today* (1957). The various contributors to Dixon Wecter (ed.), *Changing Patterns in American Civilization* (1949), represent a cross section of views and opinions.

An eloquent survey of the American political tradition may be found in the essays of Judge Learned Hand, *The Spirit of Liberty* (1952). Individual liberties in an age of big government and cold-war conflict is the theme of many recent books, among them Walter Gellhorn, *Individual Liberties and Governmental Restraints* (1957). Arthur A. Ekirch, *The Decline of American Liberalism* (1956), is a provocative work in this connection. A short book by the distinguished columnist and commentator Walter Lippmann, *The Communist World and Ours* (1959), based on a visit to Russia, appraised chances for peaceful coexistence between the two spheres.

William H. Whyte and the editors of *Fortune* magazine cover a significant aspect of recent America in *The Exploding Metropolis* (1958). Another book by Whyte, *The Organization Man* (1956), is a challenging contribution to the continuing discussion of American traits and values. *The New Partisan Reader, 1945–1953* (1953), edited by William Phillips and Philip Rahv, contains selections from a leading contemporary literary periodical, the *Partisan Review,* the issues of which are a good place in which to keep up with American literature and *avant-garde* thought. Harrison E. Salisbury, *The Shook-up Generation* (1959), is a discussion of modern youth and its problems by an eminent American journalist.

A List of Important Books on American History and Civilization

In addition to the end-of-chapter suggestions for further reading, which are usually books relating to that specific phase of history, the following general works are basic in study of American society in its historical development. For additional books on special subjects, see the *Harvard Guide,* section 61.

CONSTITUTIONAL HISTORY

E. S. Corwin, *The Constitution and What It Means Today* (12th ed., 1959)
A. C. McLaughlin, *A Constitutional History of the United States* (1936)
Bernard Schwartz, *American Constitutional Law* (1955)
C. B. Swisher, *American Constitutional Development* (1943)

POLITICAL HISTORY

Herbert Agar, *The Price of Union* (1950)
W. E. Binkley, *American Political Parties: Their Natural History* (1943)
Richard Hofstadter, *The American Political Tradition and the Men Who Made It* (1948)

FOREIGN RELATIONS

S. F. Bemis, *A Diplomatic History of the United States* (4th ed., 1955)
J. W. Pratt, *A History of United States Foreign Policy* (1955)
W. A. Williams (ed.), *The Shaping of American Diplomacy* (1956)
Robert E. Ferrell, *American Diplomacy* (1959)

ECONOMIC HISTORY

Joseph Dorfman, *The Economic Mind in American Civilization* (3 vols., 1946–1949)
J. F. Dewhurst and associates, *America's Needs and Resources* (1955)
Sidney Fine, *Laissez Faire and the General-Welfare State* (1956)
F. A. Shannon, *America's Economic Growth* (1951)
H. A. Smith, *Economic History of the United States* (1955)

LITERATURE AND THOUGHT

M. C. Curti, *The Growth of American Thought* (1943)
R. H. Gabriel, *The Course of American Democratic Thought* (2d ed., 1956)
Vernon L. Parrington, *Main Currents in American Thought* (1930)

H. W. Schneider, *A History of American Philosophy* (1946)
R. E. Spiller et al., *A Literary History of the United States* (3 vols., 1948)
Stow Persons, *American Minds: A History of Ideas* (1958)

MISCELLANEOUS

R. E. Dupuy and T. N. Dupuy, *The Military Heritage of America* (1956)
Z. Chafee, *Free Speech in the United States* (1948)
R. E. Cushman, *Civil Liberties in the United States* (1956)
R. A. Billington, *Westward Expansion* (1949)
J. H. Franklin, *From Slavery to Freedom: A History of the American Negroes* (1947)
M. L. Hansen, *The Immigrant in American History* (1940)
G. Myrdal, *An American Dilemma: The Negro Problem and Modern Democracy* (1944)
E. B. Greene, *Religion and the State: The Making and Testing of an American Tradition* (1941)
W. W. Sweet, *Religion in the Development of American Culture* (1952)
O. W. Larkin, *Art and Life in America* (1949)
A. E. Meyer, *An Educational History of the American People* (1957)

The Declaration of Independence

When in the Course of human events, it becomes necessary for one people to dissolve the political bands which have connected them with another, and to assume among the Powers of the earth, the separate and equal station to which the Laws of Nature and of Nature's God entitle them, a decent respect to the opinions of mankind requires that they should declare the causes which impel them to the separation.

We hold these truths to be self-evident, that all men are created equal, that they are endowed by their Creator with certain unalienable rights, that among these are Life, Liberty, and the pursuit of Happiness. That to secure these rights, Governments are instituted among Men, deriving their just powers from the consent of the governed. That whenever any Form of Government becomes destructive of these ends, it is the Right of the People to alter or to abolish it, and to institute new Government, laying its foundation on such principles and organizing its powers in such form, as to them shall seem most likely to effect their Safety and Happiness. Prudence, indeed, will dictate that Governments long established should not be changed for light and transient causes; and accordingly all experience hath shown, that mankind are more disposed to suffer, while evils are sufferable, than to right themselves by abolishing the forms to which they are accustomed. But when a long train of abuses and usurpations, pursuing invariably the same Object evinces a design to reduce them under absolute Despotism, it is their right, it is their duty, to throw off such Government, and to provide new Guards for their future security.—Such has been the patient sufferance of these Colonies; and such is now the necessity which constrains them to alter their former Systems of Government. The history of the present King of Great Britain is a history of repeated injuries and usurpations, all having in direct object the establishment of an absolute Tyranny over these States. To prove this, let Facts be submitted to a candid world.

He has refused his Assent to Laws, the most wholesome and necessary for the public good.

He has forbidden his Governors to pass Laws of immediate and pressing importance, unless suspended in their operation till his Assent should be obtained; and when so suspended, he has utterly neglected to attend to them.

He has refused to pass other Laws for the accommodation of large districts of people, unless those people would relinquish the right of Representation in the Legislature, a right inestimable to them and formidable to tyrants only.

He has called together legislative bodies at places unusual, uncomfortable, and distant from the depository of their public Records, for the sole purpose of fatiguing them into compliance with his measures.

He has dissolved Representative Houses repeatedly, for opposing with manly firmness his invasions on the rights of the people.

He has refused for a long time, after such dissolutions, to cause others to be elected; whereby the Legislative powers, incapable of Annihilation, have returned to the People at large for their exercise; the State remaining in the mean time exposed to all the dangers of invasion from without, and convulsions within.

He has endeavoured to prevent the population of these States; for that purpose obstructing the Laws of Naturalization of Foreigners; refusing to pass others to encourage their migrations hither, and raising the conditions of new Appropriations of Lands.

He has obstructed the Administration of Justice, by refusing his Assent to Laws for establishing Judiciary powers.

He has made Judges dependent on his Will alone, for the tenure of their offices, and the amount and payment of their salaries.

He has erected a multitude of New Offices, and sent hither swarms of Officers to harass our People, and eat out their substance.

He has kept among us, in times of peace, Standing Armies without the Consent of our legislature.

He has affected to render the Military independent of and superior to the Civil Power.

He has combined with others to subject us to a jurisdiction foreign to our constitution, and unacknowledged by our laws; giving his Assent to their Acts of pretended Legislation:

For quartering large bodies of armed troops among us:

For protecting them, by a mock Trial, from Punishment for any Murders which they should commit on the Inhabitants of these States:

For cutting off our Trade with all parts of the world:

For imposing taxes on us without our Consent:

For depriving us in many cases, of the benefits of Trial by jury:

For transporting us beyond Seas to be tried for pretended offences:

For abolishing the free System of English Laws in a neighbouring Province, establishing therein an Arbitrary government, and enlarging its Boundaries so as to render it at once an example and fit instrument for introducing the same absolute rule into these Colonies:

For taking away our Charters, abolishing our most valuable Laws, and altering fundamentally the Forms of our Governments:

For suspending our own Legislatures, and declaring themselves invested with Power to legislate for us in all cases whatsoever.

He has abdicated Government here, by declaring us out of his Protection and waging War against us.

He has plundered our seas, ravaged our Coasts, burnt our towns, and destroyed the lives of our people.

He is at this time transporting large armies of foreign mercenaries to compleat the works of death, desolation, and tyranny, already begun with circumstances of Cruelty & perfidy scarcely paralleled in the most barbarous ages, and totally unworthy the Head of a civilized nation.

He has constrained our fellow Citizens taken Captive on the high Seas to bear Arms against their Country, to become the executioners of their friends and Brethren, or to fall themselves by their Hands.

He has excited domestic insurrections amongst us, and has endeavoured to bring on the inhabitants of our frontiers, the merciless Indian Savages, whose known rule of warfare, is an undistinguished destruction of all ages, sexes, and conditions.

In every stage of these Oppressions We have Petitioned for Redress in the most humble terms: Our repeated Petitions have been answered only by repeated injury. A Prince, whose character is thus marked by every act which may define a Tyrant, is unfit to be the ruler of a free people.

Nor have We been wanting in attentions to our British brethren. We have warned them from time to time of attempts by their legislature to extend an unwarrantable jurisdiction over us. We have reminded them of the circumstances of our emigration and settlement here. We have appealed to their native justice and magnanimity, and we have conjured them by the ties of our common kindred to disavow these usurpations, which, would inevitably interrupt our connections and correspondence. They too must have been deaf to the voice of justice and of consanguinity. We must, therefore, acquiesce in the necessity, which denounces our Separation, and hold them, as we hold the rest of mankind, Enemies in War, in Peace Friends.

WE, THEREFORE, the Representatives of the UNITED STATES OF AMERICA, in General Congress, Assembled, appealing to the Supreme Judge of the world for the rectitude of our intentions, do, in the Name, and by Authority of the good People of these Colonies, solemnly publish and declare, That these United Colonies are, and of Right ought to be FREE AND INDEPENDENT STATES; that they are Absolved from all Allegiance to the British Crown, and that all political connection between them and the State of Great Britain, is and ought to be totally dissolved; and that as Free and Independent States, they have full Power to levy War, conclude Peace, contract Alliances, establish Commerce, and to do all other Acts and Things which Independent States may of right do. And for the support of this Declaration, with a firm reliance on the Protection of Divine Providence, we mutually pledge to each other our Lives, our Fortunes, and our sacred Honor.

The foregoing Declaration was, by order of Congress, engrossed, and signed by the following members:

John Hancock

NEW HAMPSHIRE
Josiah Bartlett
William Whipple
Matthew Thornton

MASSACHUSETTS BAY
Samuel Adams
John Adams
Robert Treat Paine
Elbridge Gerry

RHODE ISLAND
Stephen Hopkins
William Ellery

CONNECTICUT
Roger Sherman
Samuel Huntington

William Williams
Oliver Wolcott

NEW YORK
William Floyd
Philip Livingston
Francis Lewis
Lewis Morris

NEW JERSEY
Richard Stockton
John Witherspoon
Francis Hopkinson
John Hart
Abraham Clark

PENNSYLVANIA
Robert Morris
Benjamin Rush

Benjamin Franklin
John Morton
George Clymer
James Smith
George Taylor
James Wilson
George Ross

DELAWARE
Caesar Rodney
George Read
Thomas M'Kean

MARYLAND
Samuel Chase
William Paca
Thomas Stone
Charles Carroll, of Carrollton

VIRGINIA
George Wythe
Richard Henry Lee
Thomas Jefferson
Benjamin Harrison
Thomas Nelson, Jr.
Francis Lightfoot Lee
Carter Braxton

NORTH CAROLINA
William Hooper
Joseph Hewes
John Penn

SOUTH CAROLINA
Edward Rutledge
Thomas Heyward, Jr.

Thomas Lynch, Jr.
Arthur Middleton

GEORGIA
Button Gwinnett
Lyman Hall
George Walton

Resolved, That copies of the Declaration be sent to the several assemblies, conventions, and committees, or councils of safety, and to the several commanding officers of the continental troops; that it be proclaimed in each of the United States, at the head of the army.

APPENDIX II

*The Constitution**

PREAMBLE

We, the people of the United States, in order to form a more perfect Union, establish justice, insure domestic tranquillity, provide for the common defence, promote the general welfare, and secure the blessings of liberty to ourselves and our posterity, do ordain and establish this Constitution for the United States of America.

ARTICLE I

Legislative powers; in whom vested.

House of Representatives, how and by whom chosen. Qualifications of a Representative. Representatives and direct taxes, how apportioned. Enumeration. Vacancies to be filled. Power of choosing officers, and of impeachment.

Section 1. All legislative powers herein granted shall be vested in a Congress of the United States, which shall consist of a Senate and House of Representatives.

Section 2. (1) The House of Representatives shall be composed of members chosen every second year by the people of the several States, and the electors in each State shall have the qualifications requisite for electors of the most numerous branch of the State Legislature.

(2) No person shall be a Representative who shall not have attained to the age of twenty-five years and been seven years a citizen of the United States, and who shall not, when elected, be an inhabitant of that State in which he shall be chosen.

(3) Representatives and direct taxes shall be apportioned among the several States which may be included within this Union according to their respective numbers, which shall be determined by adding to the whole number of free persons, including those bound to service for a term of years, and excluding Indians not taxed, three-fifths of all other persons. [*"Other persons" meant the slaves.*] The actual enumeration shall be made within three years after the first meeting of the Congress of the United States, and within every subsequent term of ten years, in such manner as they shall by law direct. The number of Representatives shall not exceed one for every thirty thousand, but each State shall have at least one Representative; and until such enumeration shall be made, the State of New Hampshire shall be entitled to choose 3; Massachusetts, 8; Rhode Island and Providence Plantations, 1; Connecticut, 5; New York, 6; New Jersey, 4; Pennsylvania, 8; Delaware, 1; Maryland,

* The explanation and the information as to ratification are taken from the *World Almanac*.

6; Virginia, 10; North Carolina, 5; South Carolina, 5, and Georgia, 3.

(4) When vacancies happen in the representation from any State, the Executive Authority thereof shall issue writs of election to fill such vacancies.

(5) The House of Representatives shall choose their Speaker and other officers, and shall have the sole power of impeachment. [*Power to prefer charges against an administrative or judicial officer, which upon conviction by the Senate, would result in removal from office. Not applicable to military personnel or members of Congress.*]

Senators, how and by whom chosen. How classified. State Executive, when to make temporary appointments, in case, etc. Qualifications of a Senator. President of the Senate, his right to vote. President pro tem., and other officers of the Senate, how chosen. Power to try impeachments. When President is tried, Chief Justice to preside. Sentence.

Section 3. (1) The Senate of the United States shall be composed of two Senators from each State, chosen by the Legislature thereof, for six years [*Chosen directly by voters since 1913, as result of Amendment XVII.*], and each Senator shall have one vote.

(2) Immediately after they shall be assembled in consequence of the first election, they shall be divided as equally as may be into three classes. The seats of the Senators of the first class shall be vacated at the expiration of the second year, of the second class at the expiration of the fourth year, and of the third class at the expiration of the sixth year, so that one-third may be chosen every second year; and if vacancies happen by resignation or otherwise, during the recess of the Legislature of any State, the Executive thereof may make temporary appointment until the next meeting of the Legislature, which shall then fill such vacancies. [*Modified by Amendment XVII providing for direct election.*]

(3) No person shall be a Senator who shall not have attained to the age of thirty years, and been nine years a citizen of the United States, and who shall not, when elected, be an inhabitant of that State for which he shall be chosen.

(4) The Vice President of the United States shall be President of the Senate, but shall have no vote unless they be equally divided.

(5) The Senate shall choose their other officers, and also a President protempore, in the absence of the Vice President, or when he shall exercise the office of the President of the United States.

(6) The Senate shall have the sole power to try all impeachments. When sitting for that purpose, they shall be on oath or affirmation. When the President of the United States is tried, the Chief Justice shall preside; and no person shall be convicted without the concurrence of two-thirds of the members present.

(7) Judgment in cases of impeachment shall not extend further than to removal from office, and disqualifica-

tion to hold and enjoy any office of honor, trust, or profit under the United States; but the party convicted shall nevertheless be liable and subject to indictment, trial, judgment, and punishment, according to law.

Times, etc., of holding elections, how prescribed. One session in each year.

Section 4. (1) The times, places and manner of holding elections for Senators and Representatives shall be prescribed in each State by the Legislature thereof; but the Congress may at any time make or alter such regulations, except as to places of choosing Senators.

(2) The Congress shall assemble at least once in every year, and such meeting shall be on the first Monday in December, unless they shall by law appoint a different day. [*See Amend. XX.*]

Membership, Quorum, Adjournments, Rules. Power to punish or expel. Journal. Times of adjournments, how limited, etc.

Section 5. (1) Each House shall be the judge of the elections, returns, and qualifications of its own members, and a majority of each shall constitute a quorum to do business; but a smaller number may adjourn from day to day, and may be authorized to compel the attendance of absent members in such manner and under such penalties as each House may provide.

(2) Each House may determine the rules of its proceedings, punish its members for disorderly behavior, and with the concurrence of two-thirds expel a member.

(3) Each House shall keep a journal of its proceedings, and from time to time may publish the same, excepting such parts as may in their judgment require secrecy; and the yeas and nays of the members of either House on any question shall, at the desire of one-fifth of those present, be entered on the journal.

(4) Neither House, during the session of Congress shall, without the consent of the other, adjourn for more than three days, nor to any other place than that in which the two Houses shall be sitting.

Compensation. Privileges. Disqualifications in certain cases.

Section 6. (1) The Senators and Representatives shall receive a compensation for their services to be ascertained by law, and paid out of the Treasury of the United States. [*Salaries of senators and representatives are now $22,500 per year fully taxable; the Speaker of the House and the President pro tem of the Senate each receive $35,000 per annum plus $10,000 for expenses.*] They shall in all cases, except treason, felony, and breach of the peace, be privileged from arrest during their attendance at the session of their respective Houses, and in going to and returning from the same; and for any speech or debate in either House they shall not be questioned in any other place.

(2) No Senator or Representative shall, during the time for which he was elected, be appointed to any civil office under the authority of the United States which shall have been created, or the emoluments whereof shall have been

increased during such time; and no person holding any office under the United States shall be a member of either House during his continuance in office.

Section 7. (1) All bills for raising revenue shall originate in the House of Representatives, but the Senate may propose or concur with amendments, as on other bills.

(2) Every bill which shall have passed the House of Representatives and the Senate shall, before it becomes a law, be presented to the President of the United States; if he approve, he shall sign it, but if not, he shall return it, with his objections, to that House in which it shall have originated, who shall proceed to reconsider it. If after such reconsideration two-thirds of that House shall agree to pass the bill it shall be sent, together with the objections, to the other House, by which it shall likewise be reconsidered; and if approved by two-thirds of that House it shall become a law. But in all such cases the votes of both Houses shall be determined by yeas and nays, and the names of the persons voting for and against the bill shall be entered on the journal of each House respectively. If any bill shall not be returned by the President within ten days (Sundays excepted) after it shall have been presented to him, the same shall be a law in like manner as if he had signed it, unless the Congress by their adjournment prevent its return; in which case it shall not be a law.

(3) Every order, resolution, or vote to which the concurrence of the Senate and House of Representatives may be necessary (except on a question of adjournment) shall be presented to the President of the United States, and before the same shall take effect shall be approved by him, or being disapproved by him, shall be repassed by two-thirds of the Senate and the House of Representatives, according to the rules and limitations prescribed in the case of a bill.

Section 8. (1) The Congress shall have power:

To lay and collect taxes, duties, imposts, and excises to pay the debts and provide for the common defense and general welfare of the United States; but all duties, imposts, and excises shall be uniform throughout the United States.

(2) To borrow money on the credit of the United States.

(3) To regulate commerce with foreign nations, and among the several States and with the Indian tribes.

(4) To establish a uniform rule of naturalization and uniform laws on the subject of bankruptcies throughout the United States.

(5) To coin money, regulate the value thereof, and of foreign coin, and fix the standard of weights and measures.

(6) To provide for the punishment of counterfeiting the securities and current coin of the United States.

House to originate all revenue bills. Veto. Bill may be passed by two-thirds of each House, notwithstanding, etc. Bill not returned in ten days, to become a law. Provisions as to orders, concurrent resolutions, etc.

Powers of Congress.

(7) To establish post-offices and post-roads.

(8) To promote the progress of science and useful arts by securing for limited times to authors and inventors the exclusive rights to their respective writings and discoveries.

(9) To constitute tribunals inferior to the Supreme Court.

(10) To define and punish piracies and felonies committed on the high seas, and offences against the law of nations.

(11) To declare war, grant letters of marque and reprisal [*authorization to private vessels to act as public vessels in waging war, making captures, and disposing of prizes captured at sea. No longer practiced*] and make rules concerning captures on land and water.

(12) To raise and support armies, but no appropriation of money to that use shall be for a longer term than two years.

(13) To provide and maintain a navy.

(14) To make rules for the government and regulation of the land and naval forces.

(15) To provide for calling forth the militia to execute the laws of the Union, suppress insurrections, and repel invasions.

(16) To provide for organizing, arming, and disciplining the militia, and for governing such part of them as may be employed in the service of the United States, reserving to the States respectively the appointment of the officers, and and the authority of training the militia according to the discipline prescribed by Congress.

(17) To exercise exclusive legislation in all cases whatsoever over such district (not exceeding ten miles square) as may, by cession of particular States and the acceptance of Congress, become the seat of Government of the United States, and to exercise like authority over all places purchased by the consent of the Legislature of the State in which the same shall be, for the erection of forts, magazines, arsenals, drydocks, and other needful buildings.

(18) To make all laws which shall be necessary and proper for carrying into execution the foregoing powers and all other powers vested by this Constitution in the Government of the United States, or in any deperatment or officer thereof.

Provision as to migration or importation of certain persons. Habeas corpus. Bills of attainder, etc. Taxes, how apportioned. No export duty. No commercial preference.

Section 9. (1) The migration or importation of such persons as any of the States now existing shall think proper to admit shall not be prohibited by the Congress prior to the year one thousand eight hundred and eight, but a tax or duty may be imposed on such importation, not exceeding ten dollars for each person.

Money, how drawn from Treasury, etc. No titular nobility. Officers not to receive presents, etc.

(2) The privilege of the writ of habeas corpus [*freedom from arbitrary arrest and detention*] shall not be suspended, unless when in cases of rebellion or invasion the public safety may require it.

(3) No bill of attainder [*punishment by legislative rather than by judicial processes*] or ex post facto law [*law which alters rules of evidence or terms of punishment after a crime has been committed, i.e., "a retroactive criminal law which works to the detriment of any individual"*] shall be passed.

(4) No capitation or other direct tax shall be laid, unless in proportion to the census or enumeration hereinbefore directed to be taken.

(5) No tax or duty shall be laid on articles exported from any State.

(6) No preference shall be given by any regulation of commerce or revenue to the ports of one State over those of another, nor shall vessels bound to or from one State be obliged to enter, clear, or pay duties to another.

(7) No money shall be drawn from the Treasury but in consequence of appropriations made by law; and a regular statement and account of the receipts and expenditures of all public money shall be published from time to time.

(8) No title of nobility shall be granted by the United States. And no person holding any office of profit or trust under them shall, without the consent of the Congress, accept of any present, emolument, office, or title of any kind whatever from any king, prince, or foreign state.

States prohibited from the exercise of certain powers.

Section 10. (1) No State shall enter into any treaty, alliance, or confederation, grant letters of marque and reprisal, coin money, emit bills of credit [*paper money issued solely on the credit of the state*], make anything but gold and silver coin a tender in payment of debts, pass any bill of attainder, ex post facto law, or law impairing the obligation of contracts, or grant any title of nobility.

(2) No State shall, without the consent of the Congress, lay any impost or duties on imports or exports, except what may be absolutely necessary for executing its inspection laws, and the net produce of all duties and imposts, laid by any State on imports or exports, shall be for the use of the Treasury of the United States; and all such laws shall be subject to the revision and control of the Congress.

(3) No State shall, without the consent of Congress, lay any duty of tonnage [*charge based upon the tonnage of a vessel*], keep troops or ships of war in time of peace, enter into agreement or compact with another State, or with a foreign power, or engage in war unless actually invaded, or in such imminent danger as will not admit of delay.

ARTICLE II

President: his term of office.
Electors of President; number
and how appointed. Electors
to vote on same day. Qualifi-
cation of President. On whom
his duties devolve in case of
his removal, death, etc. Presi-
dent's compensation. His oath
of office.

Section 1. (1) The Executive power shall be vested in a a President of the United States of America. He shall hold his office during the term of four years [*two terms limitation imposed by Amendment XXII, adopted in 1951*] and together with the Vice-President, chosen for the same term, be elected as follows:

(2) Each State shall appoint, in such manner as the Legislature thereof may direct, a number of electors equal to the whole number of Senators and Representatives to which the State may be entitled in the Congress; but no Senator or Representative or person holding an office of trust or profit under the United States shall be appointed an elector [*no direct vote of citizens for either President or presidential electors; suffrage was wholly for state legislatures to determine*].

The electors shall meet in their respective States and vote by ballot for two persons, of whom one at least shall not be an inhabitant of the same State with themselves. And they shall make a list of all the persons voted for, and of the number of votes for each, which list they shall sign and certify and transmit, sealed, to the seat of the Government of the United States, directed to the President of the Senate. The President of the Senate shall, in the presence of the Senate and House of Representatives, open all the certificates, and the votes shall then be counted. The person having the greatest number of votes shall be the President, if such number be a majority of the whole number of electors appointed, and if there be more than one who have such a majority, and have an equal number of votes, then the House of Representatives shall immediately choose by ballot one of them for President; and if no person have a majority, then from the five highest on the list the said House shall in like manner choose the President. But in choosing the President, the vote shall be taken by States, the representation from each State having one vote. [*A compromise between large and small states at the Constitutional Convention to give the smaller states an advantage, on the assumption that in the absence of political parties no candidate would usually receive a majority on the first ballot. In such an event the election would be determined by the House of Representatives voting by states.*] A quorum, for this purpose, shall consist of a member or members from two-thirds of the States, and a majority of all the States shall be necessary to a choice. In every case, after the choice of the President, the person having the greatest number of votes of the electors shall be the Vice-President. [*No separate ballot for Vice Presi-*

dent until Amendment XII went into effect in 1804. See Amendment XII for changes in the method of choosing the President and Vice President and for qualifications of the latter.] But if there should remain two or more who have equal votes, the Senate shall choose from them by ballot the Vice-President.

(3) The Congress may determine the time of choosing the electors and the day on which they shall give their votes, which day shall be the same throughout the United States.

(4) No person except a natural born citizen, or a citizen of the United States at the time of the adoption of the Constitution, shall be eligible to the office of President; neither shall any person be eligible to that office who shall not have attained to the age of thirty-five years and been fourteen years a resident within the United States.

(5) In case of the removal of the President from office, or of his death, resignation, or inability to discharge the powers and duties of the said office, the same shall devolve on the Vice-President, and the Congress may by law provide for the case of removal, death, resignation, or inability, both of the President and Vice-President, declaring what officer shall then act as President, and such officer shall act accordingly until the disability be removed or a President shall be elected. *[Amendment XX authorizes Congress to provide for the presidential succession. In 1947 Congress delegated the succession first to the Speaker of the House, then to the President pro tem of the Senate, and then to Cabinet heads in the order in which the departments were established.]*

(6) The President shall, at stated times, receive for his services a compensation which shall neither be increased nor diminished during the period for which he shall have been elected, and he shall not receive within that period any other emolument from the United States or any of them. *[In 1953 the salary of the President was set at $150,000 per year fully taxable as income; an additional $40,000 is allowed for traveling expenses and official entertainment. The Vice President's salary was set at $45,000 in 1955, fully taxable as income; no official residence is provided for him.]*

(7) Before he enter on the execution of his office he shall take the following oath or affirmation:

"I do solemnly swear (or affirm) that I will faithfully execute the office of President of the United States, and will, to the best of my ability, preserve, protect, and defend the Constitution of the United States."

President to be Commander-in-Chief. He may require opinions of Cabinet Officers,

Section 2. (1) The President shall be Commander-in-Chief of the Army and Navy of the United States, and of the militia of the several States when called into the actual

etc., may pardon. Treaty-making power. Nomination of certain officers. When President may fill vacancies.

service of the United States; he may require the opinion, in writing, of the principal officer in each of the executive departments upon any subject relating to the duties of their respective offices, and he shall have power to grant reprieves and pardons for offences against the United States except in cases of impeachment.

(2) He shall have power by and with the advice and consent of the Senate to make treaties, provided two-thirds of the Senators present concur: and he shall nominate and by and with the advice and consent of the Senate shall appoint ambassadors, other public ministers and consuls, judges of the Supreme Court, and all other officers of the United States whose appointments are not herein otherwise provided for, and which shall be established by law; but the Congress may by law vest the appointment of such inferior officers as they think proper in the President alone, in the courts of law, or in the heads of departments.

(3) The President shall have power to fill up all vacancies that may happen during the recess of the Senate by granting commissions, which shall expire at the end of their next session.

President shall communicate to Congress. He may convene and adjourn Congress, in case of disagreement, etc. Shall receive Ambassadors, execute laws, and commission officers.

Section 3. He shall from time to time give to the Congress information of the state of the Union, and recommend to their consideration such measures as he shall judge necessary and expedient; he may, on extraordinary occasions, convene both Houses, or either of them, and in case of disagreement between them with respect to the time of adjournment, he may adjourn them to such time as he shall think proper; he shall receive ambassadors and other public ministers; he shall take care that the laws be faithfully executed, and shall commission all the officers of the United States.

All civil offices forfeited for certain crimes.

Section 4. The President, Vice-President, and all civil officers of the United States shall be removed from office on impeachment for and conviction of treason, bribery or other high crimes and misdemeanors.

ARTICLE III

Judicial powers. Tenure. Compensation.

Section 1. The judicial power of the United States shall be vested in one Supreme Court, and in such inferior courts as the Congress may from time to time ordain and establish. The judges, both of the Supreme and inferior courts, shall hold their offices during good behavior, and shall at stated times receive for their services a compensation which shall not be diminished during their continuance in office.

Judicial power; to what cases it extends. Original jurisdiction of Supreme Court. Ap-

Section 2. (1) The judicial power shall extend to all cases in law and equity arising under this Constitution, the laws of the United States, and treaties made, or which shall

*pellate. Trial by jury, etc.
Trial, where.*

be made, under their authority; to all cases affecting ambassadors, other public ministers and consuls; to all cases of admiralty and maritime jurisdiction [*jurisdiction over ships and shipping*]; to controversies to which the United States shall be a party; to controversies between two or more States, between a State and citizens of another State, between citizens of different States, between citizens of the same State claiming lands under grants of different States, and between a State, or the citizens thereof, and foreign states, citizens, or subjects. [*Restricted by Amendment XI.*]

(2) In all cases affecting ambassadors, other public ministers, and consuls, and those in which a State shall be a party, the Supreme Court shall have original jurisdiction. In all the other cases before mentioned the Supreme Court shall have appellate jurisdiction both as to law and fact, with such exceptions and under such regulations as the Congress shall make.

(3) The trial of all crimes, except in cases of impeachment, shall be by jury, and such trial shall be held in the State where the said crimes shall have been committed; but when not committed within any State the trial shall be at such place or places as the Congress may by law have directed.

*Treason defined. Proof of.
Punishment of.*

Section 3. (1) Treason against the United States shall consist only in levying war against them, or in adhering to their enemies, giving them aid and comfort. No person shall be convicted of treason unless on the testimony of two witnesses to the same overt act, or on confession in open court.

(2) The Congress shall have power to declare the punishment of treason, but no attainder of treason shall work corruption of blood or forfeiture except during the life of the person attainted. [*That is, no penalty could apply to a traitor's family or descendants, such as forbidding inheritance of property.*]

ARTICLE IV

*Each State to give credit to
the public acts, etc., of every
other State.*

Section 1. Full faith and credit shall be given in each State to the public acts, records, and judicial proceedings of every other State. And the Congress may by general laws prescribe the manner in which such acts, records, and proceedings shall be proved, and the effect thereof.

*Privileges of citizens of each
State. Fugitives from justice
to be delivered up. Persons
held to service having escaped,
to be delivered up.*

Section 2. (1) The citizens of each State shall be entitled to all privileges and immunities of citizens in the several States.

(2) A person charged in any State with treason, felony, or other crime, who shall flee from justice, and be found in another State, shall, on demand of the Executive authority of the State from which he fled, be delivered up, to be removed to the State having jurisdiction of the crime.

(3) No person held to service or labor in one State, under the laws thereof, escaping into another shall in consequence of any law or regulation therein, be discharged from such service or labor, but shall be delivered up on claim of the party to whom such service or labor may be due.

Admission of new States. Power of Congress over territory and other property.

Section 3. (1) New States may be admitted by the Congress into this Union; but no new State shall be formed or erected within the jurisdiction of any other State, nor any State be formed by the junction of two or more States, or parts of States, without the consent of the Legislatures of the States concerned, as well as of the Congress.

(2) The Congress shall have power to dispose of and make all needful rules and regulations respecting the territory or other property belonging to the United States; and nothing in this Constitution shall be so construed as to prejudice any claims of the United States, or of any particular State.

Republican form of government guaranteed. Each State to be protected.

Section 4. The United States shall guarantee to every State in this Union a Republican form of government, and shall protect each of them against invasion, and, on application of the Legislature, or of the Executive (when the Legislature cannot be convened) against domestic violence.

ARTICLE V

Constitution: how amended. Proviso.

The Congress, whenever two-thirds of both Houses shall deem it necessary, shall propose amendments to this Constitution, or, on the application of the Legislatures of two-thirds of the several States, shall call a convention for proposing amendments, which in either case, shall be valid to all intents and purposes, as part of this Constitution, when ratified by the Legislatures of three-fourths of the several States, or by conventions in three-fourths thereof [*Only Amendment XXI provided specifically for ratification by conventions*], as the one or the other mode of ratification may be proposed by the Congress, provided that no amendment which may be made prior to the year one thousand eight hundred and eight shall in any manner affect the first and fourth clauses in the Ninth Section of the First Article; and that no State, without its consent, shall be deprived of its equal suffrage in the Senate.

ARTICLE VI

Certain debts, etc., declared valid. Supremacy of Constitu-

(1) All debts contracted and engagements entered into before the adoption of this Constitution shall be as valid

tion, treaties, and laws of the United States. Oath to support Constitution, by whom taken. No religious test.

against the United States under this Constitution as under the Confederation.

(2) This Constitution and the laws of the United States which shall be made in pursuance thereof and all treaties made, or which shall be made, under the authority of the United States, shall be the supreme law of the land, and the judges in every State shall be bound thereby, anything in the Constitution or laws of any State to the contrary notwithstanding.

(3) The Senators and Representatives before mentioned and the members of the several State Legislatures, and all executives and judicial officers, both of the United States and of the several States, shall be bound by oath or affirmation to support this Constitution; but no religious test shall ever be required as a qualification to any office or public trust under the United States.

ARTICLE VII

What ratification shall establish Constitution.

The ratification of the Conventions of nine States shall be sufficient for the establishment of this Constitution between the States so ratifying the same.

George Washington, President, and Deputy from Virginia

NEW HAMPSHIRE
John Langdon
Nicholas Gilman

MASSACHUSETTS
Nathaniel Gorham
Rufus King

CONNECTICUT
William Samuel Johnson
Roger Sherman

NEW YORK
Alexander Hamilton

NEW JERSEY
William Livingston
David Brearley
William Paterson
Jonathan Dayton

PENNSYLVANIA
Benjamin Franklin
Thomas Mifflin
Robert Morris
George Clymer
Thomas Fitzsimons
Jared Ingersoll
James Wilson
Gouverneur Morris

DELAWARE
George Read
Gunning Bedford, Junior
John Dickinson
Richard Bassett
Jacob Broom

MARYLAND
James M'Henry
Daniel Jenifer, of St.
* Thomas*
Daniel Carroll

VIRGINIA
John Blair
James Madison, Junior

NORTH CAROLINA
William Blount
Richard Dobbs Spaight
Hugh Williamson

SOUTH CAROLINA
John Rutledge
Charles Cotesworth Pinckney
Charles Pinckney
Pierce Butler

GEORGIA
William Few
Abraham Baldwin

Attest. William Jackson, Secretary

The Amendments to the Constitution

The Bill of Rights was ratified by the States as follows—
New Jersey, (Nov. 20, 1789); Maryland, (Dec. 19, 1789);
North Carolina, (Dec. 22, 1789); South Carolina, (Jan. 19,
1790); New Hampshire, (Jan. 25, 1790); Delaware, (Jan.
28, 1790); Pennsylvania, (March 10, 1790); New York,
(March 27, 1790); Rhode Island, (June 15, 1790); Vermont, (Nov. 3, 1791); Virginia, (Dec. 15, 1791); Massachusetts, (March 2, 1939); Georgia, (March 18, 1939);
Connecticut, (April 19, 1939).

ARTICLE I

*Religious establishment pro-
hibited. Freedom of speech,
of the press, and right to
petition.*

Congress shall make no law respecting an establishment
of religion, or phohibiting the free exercise thereof; or
abridging the freedom of speech or of the press; or the
right of the people peaceably to assemble and to petition
the Government for a redress of grievances. [*The Bill of
Rights was intended to limit only the powers of Congress;
states were limited by their own constitutions and, after
1868, by Amendment XIV. Beginning in 1925, the Supreme Court has ruled that all the rights guaranteed by
Amendment I against the national government are now protected by Amendment XIV against encroachment by the
states.*]

ARTICLE II

Right to keep and bear arms.

A well-regulated militia being necessary to the security
of a free State, the right of the people to keep and bear
arms shall not be infringed.

ARTICLE III

*No soldier to be quartered in
any house, unless, etc.*

No soldier shall, in time of peace, be quartered in any
house without the consent of the owner, nor in time of war
but in a manner to be prescribed by law.

ARTICLE IV

*Right of search and seizure
regulated.*

The right of the people to be secure in their persons,
houses, papers, and effects, against unreasonable searches
and seizures, shall not be violated, and no warrants shall issue
but upon probable cause, supported by oath or affirmation,
and particularly describing the place to be searched, and the
persons or things to be seized.

ARTICLE V

Provisions concerning prosecution, trial and punishment —private property not to be taken for public use without compensation.

No person shall be held to answer for a capital or other infamous crime unless on a presentment or indictment of a Grand Jury, except in cases arising in the land or naval forces, or in the militia, when in actual service, in time of war or public danger; nor shall any person be subject for the same offence to be twice put in jeopardy of life or limb; nor shall be compelled in any criminal case to be a witness against himself, nor be deprived of life, liberty, or property, without due process of law; nor shall private property be taken for public use without just compensation.

ARTICLE VI

Right to speedy trial, witnesses, etc.

In all criminal prosecutions, the accused shall enjoy the right to a speedy and public trial, by an impartial jury of the State and district wherein the crime shall have been committed, which districts shall have been previously ascertained by law, and to be informed of the nature and cause of the accusation; to be confronted with the witnesses against him; to have compulsory process for obtaining witnesses in his favor, and to have the assistance of counsel for his defence.

ARTICLE VII

Right of trial by jury.

In suits at common law, where the value in controversy shall exceed twenty dollars, the right of trial by jury shall be preserved, and no fact tried by a jury shall be otherwise reexamined in any court of the United States than according to the rules of the common law.

ARTICLE VIII

Excessive bail or fines and cruel punishment prohibited.

Excessive bail shall not be required, nor excessive fines imposed, nor cruel and unusual punishments inflicted.

ARTICLE IX

Rule of construction of Constitution.

The enumeration in the Constitution of certain rights shall not be construed to deny or disparage others retained by the people.

ARTICLE X

Rights of States under Constitution.

The powers not delegated to the United States by the Constitution, nor prohibited by it to the States, are reserved to the States respectively, or to the people.

ARTICLE XI

Judicial powers construed.

The following amendment was proposed to the Legislatures of the several States by the Third Congress on the 4th of March, 1794, and was declared to have been ratified in a message from the President to Congress, dated Jan. 8, 1798.

The judicial power of the United States shall not be construed to extend to any suit in law or equity, commenced or prosecuted against one of the United States, by citizens of another State, or by citizens or subjects of any foreign state.

ARTICLE XII

Manner of choosing President and Vice-President.

The following amendment was proposed to the Legislatures of the several States by the Eighth Congress (Dec. 12, 1803), and was declared to have been ratified in a proclamation by the Secretary of State (September 25, 1804). It was ratified by 12 of the 17 States, and was rejected by Connecticut.

The Electors shall meet in their respective States and vote by ballot for President and Vice-President, one of whom at least shall not be an inhabitant of the same State with themselves; they shall name in their ballots the person voted for as President, and in distinct ballots the person voted for as Vice-President; and they shall make distinct list of all persons voted for as President, and of all persons voted for as Vice-President, and of the number of votes for each, which list they shall sign and certify, and transmit, sealed, to the seat of the Government of the United States, directed to the President of the Senate; the President of the Senate shall, in the presence of the Senate and House of Representatives, open all the certificates and the votes shall then be counted; the person having the greatest number of votes for President shall be the President, if such number be a majority of the whole number of Electors appointed; and if no person have such majority, then from the persons having the highest number, not exceeding three, on the list of those voted for as President, the House of Representatives shall choose immediately, by ballot the President. But in choosing the President, the votes shall be taken by States, the representation from each State having one vote; a quorum for this purpose shall consist of a member or members from two-thirds of the States, and a majority of all the States shall be necessary to a choice. And if the House of Representatives shall not choose a President, whenever the right of choice shall devolve upon them, before the fourth day of March next following, then the Vice-President shall act as President, as in the case of the death or other constitutional disability of the President. The person having the greatest number of votes as Vice-President shall be the Vice-President if such number be a majority of the whole number of Electors appointed, and if no person have a majority, then, from the two highest numbers on the list the Senate shall choose the Vice-President; a quorum for the purpose shall consist of two-thirds of the whole number of Senators, and a majority of the whole number shall be necessary to a choice. But no person constitutionally ineligible to the office of President shall be eligible to that of Vice-President of the United States. [*Date of inauguration changed to January 3 by Amendment XX.*]

ARTICLE XIII

Slavery abolished.

The following amendment was proposed to the Legislatures of the several States by the Thirty-eighth Congress (Feb. 1, 1865), and was declared to have been ratified in a proclamation by the Secretary of State (Dec. 18, 1865). It finally was ratified by 33 of the 36 States.

President Lincoln signed the joint resolution of Congress proposing the 13th amendment, although such resolutions (proposing amendments) are not submitted to the President. The U.S. Supreme Court decided, in 1798, that the President has nothing to do with the proposing of amendments to the Constitution, or their adoption.

(1) Neither slavery nor involuntary servitude, except as a punishment for crime whereof the party shall have been duly convicted, shall exist within the United States, or any place subject to their jurisdiction.

(2) Congress shall have power to enforce this article by appropriate legislation.

ARTICLE XIV

Citizenship rights not to be abridged.

The following amendment was proposed to the Legislatures of the several States by the Thirty-ninth Congress (June 13, 1866), and was declared to have been ratified in a proclamation by the Secretary of State (July 28, 1868). The amendment got the support of 23 Northern States: it was rejected by Delaware, Kentucky, Maryland, and 10 Southern States. California took no action. Subsequently it was ratified by the 10 Southern States and Delaware.

The 14th amendment was adopted only by virtue of ratification subsequent to earlier rejections. Newly constituted legislatures in both North Carolina and South Carolina, respectively (July 4 and 9, 1868), ratified the proposed amendment. although earlier legislatures had rejected the proposal. The Secretary of State issued a proclamation which, though doubtful as to the effect of attempted withdrawals by New York and New Jersey, entertained no doubt as to the validity of the ratification by North and South Carolina. The following day (July 21, 1868), Congress passed a resolution which declared the 14th amendment to be a part of the Constitution and directed the Secretary of State so to promulgate it. The Secretary waited, however, until the newly constituted legislature of Georgia had ratified the amendment, subsequent to an earlier rejection, before the promulgation of the ratification of the new amendment.

Rights of citizens protected. *

(1) All persons born or naturalized in the United States, and subject to the jurisdiction thereof [*Indians were not considered citizens by Amendment XIV; they were in a special category as wards of the government until Congress conferred citizenship upon them; all Indians were finally included in an act of 1924*] are citizens of the United States and of the State wherein they reside. No State shall make or enforce any law which shall abridge the privileges or immunities of citizens of the United States, nor shall any State deprive any person of life, liberty, or property, without due process of law; nor deny to any person within its jurisdiction the equal protection of the laws.

Apportionment of Representatives in Congress.

(2) Representatives shall be apportioned among the several States according to their respective numbers, counting the whole number of persons in each State, excluding Indians not taxed. But when the right to vote at any election for the choice of Electors for President and Vice-President of the United States, Representatives in Congress, the executive and judicial officers of a State, or the members of the Legislature thereof, is denied to any of the male inhabitants of such State, being twenty-one years of age and citizens of the United States, or in any way abridged, except for participation in rebellion or other crime, the basis of representation therein shall be reduced in the proportion which the number of such male citizens shall bear to the whole number of male citizens twenty-one years of age in such State.

Power of Congress to remove disabilities of United States officials for rebellion.

(3) No person shall be a Senator or Representative in Congress, or Elector of President and Vice-President, or hold any office, civil or military, under the United States, or under any State, who, having previously taken an oath, as a member of Congress, or as an officer of the United States, or as a member of any State Legislature, or as an executive or

* Without any question this portion of Article XIV was intended for the protection of the Negro freedmen against discrimination by southern states. Later, however, it was effectively used to defend business corporations against regulation by the states.

judicial officer of any State, to support the Constitution of the United States, shall have engaged in insurrection or rebellion against the same, or given aid or comfort to the enemies thereof. But Congress may, by a vote of two thirds of each House, remove such disability.

What public debts are valid.

(4) The validity of the public debt of the United States, authorized by law, including debts incurred for payment of pensions and bounties for services in suppressing insurrection or rebellion, shall not be questioned. But neither the United States, nor any State shall assume or pay any debt or obligation incurred in aid of insurrection or rebellion against the United States, or any claim for the loss or emancipation of any slave; but all such debts, obligations, and claims shall be held illegal and void.

(5) The Congress shall have power to enforce, by appropriate legislation, the provisions of this article.

ARTICLE XV

Equal voting rights for white and colored citizens.

The following amendment was proposed to the Legislatures of the several States by the Fortieth Congress (Feb. 26, 1869), and was declared to have been ratified in a proclamation by the Secretary of State (March 30, 1870). It was ratified by 31 of the 37 States, and was rejected by California, Delaware (March 18, 1869) and Kentucky. New York rescinded its ratification (Jan. 5, 1870). New Jersey rejected it in 1870, but ratified it in 1871. Delaware ratified in 1901.

(1) The right of the citizens of the United States to vote shall not be denied or abridged by the United States or by any State on account of race, color, or previous condition of servitude.

(2) The Congress shall have power to enforce the provisions of this article by appropriate legislation.

ARTICLE XVI

Income taxes authorized.

The following amendment was proposed to the Legislatures of the several States by the Sixty-first Congress (July 12, 1909) and was declared to have been ratified in a proclamation by the Secretary of State (Feb. 25, 1913). The amendment was ratified by 42 of the 48 States, and was rejected by Connecticut, Rhode Island, and Utah.

The Congress shall have power to lay and collect taxes on incomes, from whatever sources derived, without apportionment among the several States, and without regard to any census or enumeration.

ARTICLE XVII

United States Senators to be
elected by direct popular vote.

The following amendment was proposed to the Legislatures of the several States by the Sixty-second Congress (May 16, 1912) and was declared to have been ratified in a proclamation by the Secretary of State (May 31, 1913). The amendment was adopted by 37 of the 48 States, but was rejected by Utah.

The Senate of the United States shall be composed of two Senators from each State, elected by the people thereof, for six years; and each Senator shall have one vote. The Electors in each State shall have the qualifications requisite for Electors of the most numerous branch of the State legislatures.

When vacancies happen in the representation of any State in the Senate, the executive authority of such State shall issue writs of election to fill such vacancies: Provided, That the legislature of any State may empower the executive thereof to make temporary appointments until the people fill the vacancies by election as the legislature may direct.

This amendment shall not be construed as to affect the election or term of any Senator chosen before it becomes valid as part of the Constitution.

ARTICLE XVIII

Liquor prohibition amendment.

The following amendment was proposed to the Legislatures of the several States by the Sixty-fifth Congress (Dec. 18, 1917), and (Jan. 20, 1919) the United States Secretary of State proclaimed its adoption by 36 States, and declared it in effect (Jan. 16, 1920). The amendment ultimately was adopted by all the States except Connecticut and Rhode Island.

(1) After one year from the ratification of this article the manufacture, sale or transportation of intoxicating liquors within, the importation thereof into, or the exportation thereof from the United States and all territories subject to the jurisdiction thereof for beverage purposes is hereby prohibited.

(2) The Congress and the several States shall have concurrent power to enforce this article by appropriate legislation.

(3) This article shall be inoperative unless it shall have been ratified as an amendment to the Constitution by the legislatures of the several States, as provided in the Constitution, within seven years from the date of the submission hereof to the States by Congress. [*Rescinded by Amendment XXI.*]

ARTICLE XIX

Giving nationwide suffrage to women.

The following amendment was presented to the Legislatures of the several States by the Sixty-sixth Congress, having been adopted by the House of Representatives (May 21, 1919) and by the Senate (June 4, 1919). The Secretary of State (Aug. 26, 1920) proclaimed it in effect, it having been adopted (June 10, 1919–August 18, 1920) by three-quarters of the States.

(1) The right of citizens of the United States to vote shall not be denied or abridged by the United States or by any State on account of sex.

(2) Congress shall have power, by appropriate legislation, to enforce the provisions of this article.

ARTICLE XX

Terms of President and Vice-President to begin on January 20; those of Senators and Representatives, on January 3.

The following amendment was proposed to the Legislatures of the several States by the Seventy-second Congress (March, 1932), a joint resolution to that effect having been adopted, first by the House, and then (March 2) by the Senate. The Secretary of State (Feb. 6, 1933) proclaimed it in effect, 39 of the 48 States having ratified. By Oct. 15, 1933, it had been ratified by all of the 48 States.

(1) The terms of the President and Vice-President shall end at noon on the 20th day of January, and the terms of Senators and Representatives at noon on the 3rd day of January, of the years in which such terms would have ended if this article had not been ratified; and the terms of their successors shall then begin.

(2) The Congress shall assemble at least once in every year, and such meeting shall begin at noon on the 3rd day of January, unless they shall by law appoint a different day.

(3) If, at the time fixed for the beginning of the term of the President, the President elect shall have died, the Vice-President elect shall become President. If a President shall not have been chosen before the time fixed for the beginning of his term, or if the President elect shall have failed to qualify, then the Vice-President elect shall act as President until a President shall have qualified; and the Congress may by law provide for the case wherein neither a President elect nor a Vice-President elect shall have qualified, declaring who shall then act as President or the manner in which one who is to act shall be selected, and such person shall act accordingly until a President or Vice-President shall have qualified.

(4) The Congress may by law provide for the case of the death of any of the persons from whom the House of

Representatives may choose a President whenever the right of choice shall have devolved upon them, and for the case of the death of any of the persons from whom the Senate may choose a Vice-President whenever the right of choice shall have devolved upon them.

(5) Sections 1 and 2 shall take effect on the 15th day of October following the ratification of this article (Oct., 1933).

(6) This article shall be inoperative unless it shall have been ratified as an amendment to the Constitution by the legislatures of three-fourths of the several States within seven years from the date of its submission.

ARTICLE XXI

Repeal of the Eighteenth (prohibition) Amendment by conventions in the States.

The following amendment in the Constitution, embodied in a joint resolution of the 72nd Congress (Senate, Feb. 16, 1933, by 63 to 23; House, Feb. 20, 1933, by 289 to 121), was transmitted to the Secretary of State on Feb. 21 and he at once sent to the governors of the States copies of the resolution. The amendment went into effect on Dec. 5, 1933, having been adopted by 36 of the 48 States—three-quarters of the entire number.

(1) The eighteenth article of amendment to the Constitution of the United States is hereby repealed.

(2) The transportation or importation into any State, Territory, or Possession of the United States for delivery or use therein of intoxicating liquors, in violation of the laws thereof, is hereby prohibited.

(3) This article shall be inoperative unless it shall have been ratified as an amendment to the Constitution by convention in the several States, as provided in the Constitution, within seven years from the date of the submission hereof to the States by the Congress.

ARTICLE XXII

Limiting presidential terms of office.

The following amendment in the Constitution, embodied in a joint resolution of the 80th Congress (House, Feb. 6, 1947, by 285 to 121; Senate, March 12, 1947, by 59 to 23). Signed by the Speaker of the House, Mar. 24, 1947, and by the President protempore of the Senate, Mar. 24, 1947. Presented to the Secretary of State, Mar. 24, 1947. Went into effect Feb. 26, 1951, when Nevada became the 36th State to ratify. Utah had ratified earlier the same day, and Minnesota, Feb. 27th.

No person shall be elected to the office of the President

more than twice, and no person who has held the office of President, or acted as President, for more than two years of a term to which some other person was elected President shall be elected to the office of the President more than once. But this Article shall not apply to any person holding the office of President when this Article was proposed by the Congress, and shall not prevent any person who may be holding the office of President, or acting as President, during the term within which this Article becomes operative from holding the office of President or acting as President during the remainder of such term.

This article shall be inoperative unless it shall have been ratified as an amendment to the Constitution by the legislatures of three fourths of the several States within seven years from the date of its submission to the States by the Congress.

Amendment at Present Before the States

Child Labor.

Section 1. The Congress shall have power to limit, regulate and prohibit the labor of persons under eighteen years of age.

Section 2. The power of the several States is unimpaired by this article except that the operation of State laws shall be suspended to the extent necessary to give effect to legislation enacted by Congress.

Submitted to the legislatures of the several States June 2, 1924.

Entrance of States into the Union

State	Entered Union
Delaware	December 7, 1787
Pennsylvania	December 12, 1787
New Jersey	December 18, 1787
Georgia	January 2, 1788
Connecticut	January 9, 1788
Massachusetts	February 6, 1788
Maryland	April 2, 1788
South Carolina	May 23, 1788
New Hampshire	June 21, 1788
Virginia	June 25, 1788
New York	July 26, 1788
North Carolina	November 21, 1789
Rhode Island	May 29, 1790
Vermont	March 4, 1791
Kentucky	June 1, 1792
Tennessee	June 1, 1796
Ohio	March 1, 1803
Louisiana	April 30, 1812
Indiana	December 11, 1816
Mississippi	December 10, 1817
Illinois	December 3, 1818
Alabama	December 14, 1819
Maine	March 15, 1820
Missouri	August 10, 1821
Arkansas	June 15, 1836

State	Entered Union
Michigan	January 26, 1837
Florida	March 3, 1845
Texas	December 29, 1845
Iowa	December 28, 1846
Wisconsin	May 29, 1848
California	September 9, 1850
Minnesota	May 11, 1858
Oregon	February 14, 1859
Kansas	January 29, 1861
West Virginia	June 19, 1863
Nevada	October 31, 1864
Nebraska	March 1, 1867
Colorado	August 1, 1876
North Dakota	November 2, 1889
South Dakota	November 2, 1889
Montana	November 8, 1889
Washington	November 11, 1889
Idaho	July 3, 1890
Wyoming	July 10, 1890
Utah	January 4, 1896
Oklahoma	November 16, 1907
New Mexico	January 6, 1912
Arizona	February 14, 1912
Alaska	June 30, 1958
Hawaii	March 12, 1959

Presidential Elections

Year	Candidates	Parties	Popular vote	Electoral vote
1789	*George Washington* (Va.)			69
	John Adams*			34
	Others*			35
1792	*George Washington* (Va.)			132
	John Adams*			77
	George Clinton*			50
	Others*			5
1796	*John Adams* (Mass.)	Federalist		71†
	Thomas Jefferson	Democratic-Republican		68
	Thomas Pinckney	Fed.		59
	Aaron Burr	Dem.-Rep.		30
	Others			48
1800	*Thomas Jefferson* (Va.)	Dem.-Rep.		73†
	Aaron Burr	Dem.-Rep.		73
	John Adams	Fed.		65
	C. C. Pinckney	Fed.		64
	John Jay	Fed.		1
1804	*Thomas Jefferson* (Va.)	Dem.-Rep.		162
	C. C. Pinckney	Fed.		14
1808	*James Madison* (Va.)	Dem.-Rep.		122
	C. C. Pinckney	Fed.		47
	George Clinton	Dem.-Rep.		6
1812	*James Madison* (Va.)	Dem.-Rep.		128
	De Witt Clinton	Fed.		89
1816	*James Monroe* (Va.)	Dem.-Rep.		183
	Rufus King	Fed.		34
1820	*James Monroe* (Va.)	Dem.-Rep.		231
	John Quincy Adams	Dem.-Rep.		1
1824	*John Q. Adams* (Mass.)	Dem.-Rep.	108,740	84†
	Andrew Jackson	Dem.-Rep.	153,544	99
	William H. Crawford	Dem.-Rep.	46,618	41
	Henry Clay	Dem.-Rep.	47,136	37
1828	*Andrew Jackson* (Tenn.)	Democratic	647,231	178
	John Q. Adams	National Republican	509,097	83
1832	*Andrew Jackson* (Tenn.)	Dem.	687,502	219
	Henry Clay	Nat. Rep.	530,189	49
	William Wirt	Anti-Mason		7
	John Floyd	Dem. (S.C.)	‡	11

Year	Candidates	Parties	Popular vote	Electoral vote
1836	*Martin Van Buren* (N.Y.)	Dem.	761,549	170
	William H. Harrison	Whig	549,000 ⎫	73
	Hugh L. White	Whig	146,000 ⎬ 736,656	26
	Daniel Webster	Whig	41,000 ⎭	14
	W. P. Mangum	Dem. (S.C.)	‡	11
1840	*William Henry Harrison* (Ohio)	Whig	1,275,016	234
	Martin Van Buren	Dem.	1,129,102	60
	James G. Birney	Liberty	7,059	
1844	*James K. Polk* (Tenn.)	Dem.	1,337,243	170
	Henry Clay	Whig	1,299,062	105
	James G. Birney	Liberty	62,300	
1848	*Zachary Taylor* (La.)	Whig	1,360,099	163
	Lewis Cass	Dem.	1,220,544	127
	Martin Van Buren	Free Soil	291,263	
1852	*Franklin Pierce* (N.H.)	Dem.	1,601,274	254
	Winfield Scott	Whig	1,386,580	42
	John P. Hale	Free Soil	155,825	
1856	*James Buchanan* (Pa.)	Dem.	1,838,169	174
	John C. Frémont	Republican	1,341,264	114
	Millard Fillmore	American (Know-Nothing)	874,534	8
1860	*Abraham Lincoln* (Ill.)	Rep.	1,866,452	180
	Stephen A. Douglas	Dem.	1,375,157	12
	John C. Breckenridge	Dem.	847,953	72
	John Bell	Constitutional Union	590,631	39
1864	*Abraham Lincoln* (Ill.)	Rep.	2,213,665	212
	George B. McClellan	Dem.	1,802,237	21
1868	*Ulysses S. Grant* (Ohio)	Rep.	3,012,833	214
	Horatio Seymour	Dem.	2,703,249	80
1872	*Ulysses S. Grant* (Ohio)	Rep.	3,597,132	286
	Horace Greeley	Dem. and Liberal Republican	2,834,125	66
1876	*Rutherford B. Hayes* (Ohio)	Rep.	4,036,298	185
	Samuel J. Tilden	Dem.	4,300,590	184
	Others	Greenback, etc.	93,898	
1880	*James A. Garfield* (Ohio)	Rep.	4,454,416	214
	Winfield S. Hancock	Dem.	4,442,952	155
	James B. Weaver	Greenback	308,578	
1884	*Grover Cleveland* (N.Y.)	Dem.	4,874,986	219
	James G. Blaine	Rep.	4,851,981	182
	Benjamin F. Butler	Greenback & Anti-Monopoly	175,370	
	John P. St. John	Prohibition	150,369	

Year	Candidates	Parties	Popular vote	Electoral vote
1888	*Benjamin Harrison* (Ind.)	Rep.	5,439,853	233
	Grover Cleveland	Dem.	5,540,309	168
	C. B. Fisk	Prohib.	249,506	
	A. J. Streeter	Union Labor	146,935	
1892	*Grover Cleveland* (N.Y.)	Dem.	5,556,918	277
	Benjamin Harrison	Rep.	5,176,108	145
	James B. Weaver	People's	1,041,028	22
	John Bidwell	Prohib.	264,133	
1896	*William McKinley* (Ohio)	Rep.	7,104,779	271
	William Jennings Bryan	Dem.	6,502,925	176
	John M. Palmer	Nat. Dem.	133,148	
	Others	Prohib., etc.	182,250	
1900	*William McKinley* (Ohio)	Rep.	7,207,923	292
	William Jennings Bryan	Dem.	6,358,133	155
	John C. Woolley	Prohib.	208,914	
	Others	Socialist, etc.	101,270	
1904	*Theodore Roosevelt* (N.Y.)	Rep.	7,623,486	336
	Alton B. Parker	Dem.	5,077,911	140
	Eugene V. Debs	Soc.	402,283	
	S. C. Swallow	Prohib.	258,536	
	Others	People's, etc.	149,432	
1908	*William Howard Taft* (Ohio)	Rep.	7,678,908	321
	William Jennings Bryan	Dem.	6,409,104	162
	Eugene V. Debs	Soc.	420,793	
	E. W. Chafin	Prohib.	253,840	
	Others	(Misc.)	126,493	
1912	*Woodrow Wilson* (N.J.)	Dem.	6,293,454	435
	Theodore Roosevelt	Progressive	4,119,538	88
	William Howard Taft	Rep.	3,484,980	8
	Eugene V. Debs	Soc.	900,672	
	E. W. Chafin	Prohib.	206,275	
1916	*Woodrow Wilson* (N.J.)	Dem.	9,129,606	277
	Charles Evans Hughes	Rep.	8,538,221	254
	A. L. Benson	Soc.	585,113	
	J. F. Hanly	Prohib.	220,506	
	Others	Soc.-Labor, etc.	126,493	
1920	*Warren G. Harding* (Ohio)	Rep.	16,152,200	404
	James M. Cox	Dem.	9,147,353	127
	Eugene V. Debs	Soc.	919,799	
	P. P. Christensen	Farmer-Labor	265,411	
	Others	Prohib., etc.	274,960	
1924	*Calvin Coolidge* (Mass.)	Rep.	15,725,016	382
	John W. Davis	Dem.	8,386,503	136

Year	Candidates	Parties	Popular vote	Electoral vote
1924 (cont.)	Robert M. La Follette	Prog.	4,822,856	13
	W. Z. Foster	Workers' (Communist)	36,386	
	Others	(Misc.)	119,177	
1928	*Herbert C. Hoover* (Calif.)	Rep.	21,391,381	444
	Alfred E. Smith	Dem.	15,016,443	87
	Others	Workers', etc.	69,280	
1932	*Franklin D. Roosevelt* (N.Y.)	Dem.	22,821,857	472
	Herbert Hoover	Rep.	15,761,841	59
	Norman Thomas	Soc.	881,951	
	W. Z. Foster	Communist	102,785	
	Others	Prohib., etc.	175,699	
1936	*Franklin D. Roosevelt* (N.Y.)	Dem.	27,751,597	523
	Alfred M. Landon	Rep.	16,679,583	8
	William Lemke	Union	882,479	
	Norman Thomas	Soc.	187,720	
	Earl Browder	Communist	80,159	
	Others	Prohib., etc.	50,624	
1940	*Franklin D. Roosevelt* (N.Y.)	Dem.	27,244,160	449
	Wendell Willkie	Rep.	22,305,198	82
	Norman Thomas	Soc.	99,557	
	Earl Browder	Communist	46,251	
	Roger Q. Babson	Prohib.	57,812	
1944	*Franklin D. Roosevelt* (N.Y.)	Dem.	25,602,504	432
	Thomas E. Dewey	Rep.	22,006,285	99
	Others	Soc., etc.	336,051	
1948	*Harry S. Truman* (Mo.)	Dem.	24,105,695	303
	Thomas E. Dewey	Rep.	21,969,170	189
	Henry A. Wallace	Progr.	1,156,103	
	J. Strom Thurmond	States' Rights	1,169,021	39
	Norman Thomas	Soc.	139,009	
	Others	Prohib., etc.	149,391	
1952	*Dwight D. Eisenhower* (Kans.)	Rep.	33,824,351	442
	Adlai E. Stevenson	Dem.	27,314,987	89
	Others	Progr., etc.	412,640	
1956	*Dwight D. Eisenhower* (Pa.)	Rep.	35,581,003	457
	Adlai E. Stevenson	Dem.	25,738,765	73
	Others		707,272	1

* Washington was without opposition for the presidency in 1789 and 1792; the electoral votes cast for other candidates were intended for the election of the Vice President. See article II, section 1, in effect until 1804.

† Elected by House of Representatives, no candidate having had a majority in the electoral college; see Constitution, article II, section 1, replaced by Amendment XII in 1804.

‡ South Carolina electoral votes determined by state legislature.

Presidents and Their Cabinets

Dates indicate year official assumed office. Where no date is indicated the tenure of the official coincides with that of the President. Note that there were frequent carry-overs during the first six presidencies.

GEORGE WASHINGTON 1789–1797

V.P.	John Adams	
Sec. of State	Thomas Jefferson	1789
	Edmund Randolph	1794
	Timothy Pickering	1795
Sec. of Treas.	Alexander Hamilton	1789
	O. Wolcott	1795
Sec. of War	H. Knox	1789
	Timothy Pickering	1795
	J. McHenry	1796
P.M. Gen.	Samuel Osgood	1789
	Timothy Pickering	1791
	Joseph Habersham	1795
Att. Gen.	Edmund Randolph	1789
	William Bradford	1794
	Charles Lee	1795

JOHN ADAMS 1797–1801

V.P.	Thomas Jefferson	
Sec. of State	John Marshall	1800
Sec. of Treas.	Samuel Dexter	1801
Sec. of War	John Marshall	1800
	Samuel Dexter	1800
	R. Griswold	1801
Sec. of Navy (Est. 1798)	B. Stoddert	
P.M. Gen.	Joseph Habersham	
Att. Gen.	Theophilus Parsons	1801

THOMAS JEFFERSON 1801–1809

V.P.	Aaron Burr	1801
	George Clinton	1805
Sec. of State	James Madison	
Sec. of Treas.	Albert Gallatin	
Sec. of War	H. Dearborn	

Sec. of Navy	Robert Smith	1801
	J. Crowninshield	1805
P.M. Gen.	Gideon Granger	
Att. Gen.	Levi Lincoln	1801
	Robert Smith	1805
	J. Breckenridge	1805
	C. A. Rodney	1807

JAMES MADISON 1809–1817

V.P.	Elbridge Gerry	1813
Sec. of State	Robert Smith	1809
	James Monroe	1811
Sec. of Treas.	G. W. Campbell	1814
	Alexander J. Dalbs	1814
	William H. Crawford	1816
Sec. of War	William Eustis	1809
	J. Armstrong	1813
	James Monroe	1814
	William H. Crawford	1815
	I. Shelby	1817
Sec. of Navy	P. Hamilton	1809
	W. Jones	1813
	B. Williams	1814
P.M. Gen.	R. J. Meigs, Jr.	1814
Att. Gen.	William Pinkney	1811
	Richard Rush	1814

JAMES MONROE 1817–1825

V.P.	D. D. Tompkins	
Sec. of State	John Quincy Adams	
Sec. of Treas.	William H. Crawford	
Sec. of War	George Graham	1817
	John C. Calhoun	1817

Sec. of Navy	S. Thompson	1818
	S. L. Southard	1823
P.M. Gen.	John McLean	1823
Att. Gen.	William Wirt	

JOHN QUINCY ADAMS   1825–1829

V.P.	John C. Calhoun	
Sec. of State	Henry Clay	
Sec. of Treas.	Richard Rush	
Sec. of War	J. Barbour	1825
	P. B. Porter	1828
Sec. of Navy	S. L. Southard	
P.M. Gen.	John McLean	
Att. Gen.	William Wirt	

ANDREW JACKSON   1829–1837

V.P.	John C. Calhoun	1829–1833
	Martin Van Buren	1833
Sec. of State	Martin Van Buren	1829
	E. Livingston	1831
	L. McLane	1833
	J. Forsyth	1834
Sec. of Treas.	S. D. Ingham	1829
	Louis McLane	1831
	W. J. Duane	1833
	Roger B. Taney	1833
	Levi Woodbury	1834
Sec. of War	J. H. Eaton	1829
	Lewis Cass	1831
	Benjamin F. Butler	1837
Sec. of Navy	J. Branch	1829
	Levi Woodbury	1831
	M. Dickerson	1834
P.M. Gen.	William T. Barry	1829
	Amos Kendall	1835
Att. Gen.	John M. Berrien	1829
	Roger B. Taney	1831
	Benjamin F. Butler	1833

MARTIN VAN BUREN   1837–1841

V.P.	R. M. Johnson	
Sec. of State	J. Forsyth	
Sec. of Treas.	Levi Woodbury	
Sec. of War	J. R. Poinsett	
Sec. of Navy	J. K. Paulding	

P.M. Gen.	John M. Niles	1840
Att. Gen.	Felix Grundy	1838
	H. D. Gilpin	1840

WILLIAM HENRY HARRISON   1841

V.P.	John Tyler	
Sec. of State	Daniel Webster	
Sec. of Treas.	Thomas Ewing	
Sec. of War	John Bell	
Sec. of Navy	George E. Badger	
P.M. Gen.	Francis Granger	
Att. Gen.	J. J. Crittenden	

JOHN TYLER   1841–1845

V.P.	——	
Sec. of State	H. S. Legaré	1843
	A. P. Upshur	1843
	John C. Calhoun	1844
Sec. of Treas.	Walter Forward	1841
	John C. Spencer	1843
	George M. Bibb	1844
Sec. of War	J. McLean	1841
	John C. Spencer	1841
	J. M. Porter	1843
	William Wilkins	1844
Sec. of Navy	A. P. Upshur	1841
	D. Henshaw	1843
	T. W. Gilmer	1844
	John Y. Mason	1844
P.M. Gen.	Francis Granger	1841
	C. A. Wickliff	1841
Att. Gen.	H. S. Legaré	1841
	John Nelson	1843

JAMES K. POLK   1845–1849

V.P.	George M. Dallas	
Sec. of State	James Buchanan	
Sec. of Treas.	Robert J. Walker	
Sec. of War	William L. Marcy	
Sec. of Navy	G. Bancroft	1845
	John Y. Mason	1846
P. M. Gen.	Cave Johnson	
Att. Gen.	John Y. Mason	1845
	Nathan Clifford	1846
	Isaac Toucey	1848

ZACHARY TAYLOR 1849–1850

V.P.	Millard Fillmore	
Sec. of State	John M. Clayton	
Sec. of Treas.	W. M. Meredith	
Sec. of War	G. W. Crawford	1849
	Edward Bates	1850
Sec. of Navy	W. B. Preston	
Sec. of Inter.	Thomas Ewing	
(Est. 1849)		
P.M. Gen.	J. Collamer	
Att. Gen.	Reverdy Johnson	

MILLARD FILLMORE 1850–1853

V.P.	———	
Sec. of State	Daniel Webster	1850
	Edward Everett	1852
Sec. of Treas.	Thomas Corwin	
Sec. of War	Charles M. Conrad	
Sec. of Navy	William A. Graham	1850
	J. P. Kennedy	1852
Sec. of Inter.	James A. Pearce	1850
	T. M. T. McKennan	1850
	A. H. H. Stuart	1850
P.M. Gen.	Nathan K. Hall	1850
	S. D. Hubbard	1852
Att. Gen.	J. J. Crittenden	

FRANKLIN PIERCE 1853–1857

V.P.	William R. King	
Sec. of State	William L. Marcy	
Sec. of Treas.	James Guthrie	
Sec. of War	Jefferson Davis	
Sec. of Navy	J. C. Dobbin	
Sec. of Inter.	Robert McClelland	
P.M. Gen.	James Campbell	
Att. Gen.	Caleb Cushing	

JAMES BUCHANAN 1857–1861

V.P.	J. C. Brekenridge	
Sec. of State	Lewis Cass	1857
	J. S. Black	1860
Sec. of Treas.	Howell Cobb	1857
	Philip F. Thomas	1860
	John A. Dix	1861
Sec. of War	John B. Floyd	1857
	Joseph Holt	1861

Sec. of Navy	Isaac Toucey	
Sec. of Inter.	Jacob Thompson	
P.M. Gen.	A. V. Brown	1857
	Joseph Holt	1859
	Horatio King	1861
Att. Gen.	J. S. Black	1857
	Edwin M. Stanton	1860

ABRAHAM LINCOLN 1861–1865

V.P.	Hannibal Hamlin	1861
	Andrew Johnson	1865
Sec. of State	William H. Seward	
Sec. of Treas.	Salmon P. Chase	1861
	W. P. Fessenden	1864
	Hugh McCulloch	1865
Sec. of War	Simon Cameron	1861
	Edwin M. Stanton	1862
Sec. of Navy	Gideon Welles	
Sec. of Inter.	Caleb B. Smith	1861
	John P. Usher	1863
P.M. Gen.	Montgomery Blair	1861
	William Dennison	1864
Att. Gen.	Edward Bates	1861
	T. J. Coffey	1863
	James Speed	1864

ANDREW JOHNSON 1865–1869

V.P.	———	
Sec. of State	William H. Seward	
Sec. of Treas.	Hugh McCulloch	
Sec. of War	Edwin M. Stanton	1865
	U. S. Grant	1867
	L. Thomas	1868
	J. M. Schofield	1868
Sec. of Navy	Gideon Welles	1865
Sec. of Inter.	John P. Usher	1865
	James Harlan	1865
	O. H. Browning	1866
P.M. Gen.	William Dennison	1865
	A. W. Randall	1866
Att. Gen.	James Speed	1865
	Henry Stanbery	1866
	William M. Evarts	1868

ULYSSES S. GRANT 1869–1873

V.P.	Schuyler Colfax	1869
	Henry Wilson	1873

Sec. of State	E. B. Washburne	1869
	Hamilton Fish	1869
Sec. of Treas.	George S. Boutwell	1869
	W. A. Richardson	1873
	Benjamin H. Bristow	1874
	Lot M. Morrill	1876
Sec. of War	J. A. Rawlins	1869
	W. T. Sherman	1869
	W. W. Belknap	1869
	Alphonso Taft	1876
	J. D. Cameron	1876
Sec. of Navy	Adolph E. Borie	1869
	George M. Robeson	1869
Sec. of Inter.	Jacob D. Cox	1869
	C. Delano	1870
	Zachary Chandler	1875
P.M. Gen.	J. A. J. Creswell	1869
	James W. Marshall	1874
	Marshall Jewell	1874
	James N. Tyner	1876
Att. Gen.	E. R. Hoar	1869
	A. T. Ackerman	1870
	George H. Williams	1871
	Edward Pierrepont	1875
	Alphonso Taft	1876

RUTHERFORD B. HAYES   1877–1881

V.P.	William A. Wheeler	
Sec. of State	William M. Evarts	
Sec. of Treas.	John Sherman	
Sec. of War	G. W. McCrary	1877
	Alexander Ramsey	1879
Sec. of Navy	R. W. Thompson	1877
	Nathan Goff, Jr.	1881
Sec. of Inter.	Carl Schurz	
P.M. Gen.	David M. Key	1877
	Horace Maynard	1880
Att. Gen.	Charles Devens	

JAMES GARFIELD   1881

V.P.	Chester A. Arthur
Sec. of State	James G. Blaine
Sec. of Treas.	William Windom
Sec. of War	R. T. Lincoln
Sec. of Navy	W. H. Hunt
Sec. of Inter.	S. J. Kirkwood

| P.M. Gen. | T. L. James | |
| Att. Gen. | W. MacVeagh | |

CHESTER A. ARTHUR   1881–1885

V.P.	———	
Sec. of State	F. T. Frelinghuysen	
Sec. of Treas.	Charles J. Folger	1881
	W. Q. Gresham	1884
	Hugh McCulloch	1884
Sec. of War	R. T. Lincoln	
Sec. of Navy	W. E. Chandler	
Sec. of Inter.	Henry M. Teller	
P.M. Gen.	T. O. Howe	1881
	W. Q. Gresham	1883
	Frank Hatton	1884
Att. Gen.	B. H. Brewster	

GROVER CLEVELAND   1885–1889

V.P.	T. A. Hendricks	
Sec. of State	Thomas F. Bayard	
Sec. of Treas.	Daniel Manning	1885
	Charles S. Fairchild	1887
Sec. of War	W. C. Endicott	
Sec. of Navy	W. C. Whitney	
Sec. of Inter.	L. Q. C. Lamar	1885
	William F. Vilas	1888
P.M. Gen.	William F. Vilas	1885
	D. M. Dickinson	1888
Att. Gen.	A. H. Garland	
Sec. of Agric.	N. J. Colman	
(Est. 1889)		

BENJAMIN HARRISON   1889–1893

V.P.	Levi P. Mortin	
Sec. of State	James G. Blaine	1889
	John W. Foster	1892
Sec. of Treas.	William Windom	1889
	Charles Foster	1891
Sec. of War	R. Proctor	1889
	S. B. Elkins	1891
Sec. of Navy	Benjamin F. Tracy	
Sec. of Inter.	John W. Noble	
P.M. Gen.	J. Wanamaker	1889
Att. Gen.	W. H. H. Miller	
Sec. of Agric.	J. M. Rusk	

GROVER CLEVELAND   1893–1897

V.P.	Adlai E. Stevenson	
Sec. of State	W. Q. Gresham	1893
	Richard Olney	1895
Sec. of Treas.	John G. Carlisle	
Sec. of War	D. S. Lamont	
Sec. of Navy	Hilary A. Herbert	
Sec. of Inter.	Hoke Smith	1893
	D. R. Francis	1896
P.M. Gen.	W. S. Bissell	1893
	W. L. Wilson	1895
Att. Gen.	Richard Olney	1893
	J. Harmon	1895
Sec. of Agric.	J. S. Morton	

WILLIAM McKINLEY   1897–1901

V.P.	Garret A. Hobart	1897
	Theodore Roosevelt	1901
Sec. of State	John Sherman	1897
	William R. Day	1897
	John Hay	1898
Sec. of Treas.	Lyman J. Gage	
Sec. of War	R. A. Alger	1897
	Elihu Root	1899
Sec. of Navy	John D. Long	
Sec. of Inter.	C. N. Bliss	1897
	E. A. Hitchcock	1899
P.M. Gen.	James A. Gary	1897
	Charles E. Smith	1898
Att. Gen.	J. McKenna	1897
	J. W. Griggs	1897
	P. C. Knox	1901
Sec. of Agric.	James Wilson	

THEODORE ROOSEVELT   1901–1909

V.P.	C. W. Fairbanks	1905
Sec. of State	John Hay	1901
	Elihu Root	1905
	Robert Bacon	1909
Sec. of Treas.	Lyman J. Gage	1901
	Leslie M. Shaw	1902
	G. B. Cortelyou	1907
Sec. of War	Elihu Root	1901
	William H. Taft	1904
	Luke E. Wright	1908
Sec. of Navy	John D. Long	1901
	William H. Moody	1902

	Paul Morton	1904
	C. J. Bonaparte	1905
	Victor H. Metcalf	1907
	T. H. Newberry	1908
Sec. of Inter.	E. A. Hitchcock	1901
	J. R. Garfield	1907
P.M. Gen.	Charles E. Smith	1901
	Henry C. Payne	1902
	Robert J. Wynne	1904
	G. B. Cortelyou	1905
	G. von L. Meyer	1907
Att. Gen.	P. C. Knox	1901
	W. H. Moody	1904
	C. J. Bonaparte	1907
Sec. of Agric.	James Wilson	
Sec. of Com. and Labor (Est. 1903)	G. B. Cortelyou	1903
	V. H. Metcalf	1904
	O. S. Strauss	1907

WILLIAM H. TAFT   1909–1913

V.P.	James S. Sherman	
Sec. of State	P. C. Knox	
Sec. of Treas.	F. MacVeagh	
Sec. of War	J. M. Dickinson	1909
	H. L. Stimson	1911
Sec. of Navy	G. von L. Meyer	
Sec. of Inter.	R. A. Ballinger	1909
	W. L. Fisher	1911
P.M. Gen.	F. H. Hitchcock	
Att. Gen.	G. W. Wickersham	
Sec. of Agric.	James Wilson	
Sec. of Com. and Labor (Divided 1913)	Charles Nagel	1909

WOODROW WILSON   1913–1921

V.P.	Thomas R. Marshall	
Sec. of State	William J. Bryan	1913
	Robert Lansing	1915
	Bainbridge Colby	1920
Sec. of Treas.	W. G. McAdoo	1913
	Carter Glass	1918
	D. F. Houston	1920
Sec. of War	L. M. Garrison	1913
	N. D. Baker	1916

Sec. of Navy	Josephus Daniels	
Sec. of Inter.	F. K. Lane	1913
	J. B. Payne	1920
P.M. Gen.	A. S. Burleson	1913
Att. Gen.	J. C. McReynolds	1913
	Thomas W. Gregory	1914
	A. M. Palmer	1919
Sec. of Agric.	D. F. Houston	1913
	E. T. Meredith	1920
Sec. of Com.	W. C. Redfield	1913
	J. W. Alexander	1919
Sec. of Labor	W. B. Wilson	

WARREN G. HARDING 1921–1923

V.P.	Calvin Coolidge	
Sec. of State	Charles E. Hughes	
Sec. of Treas.	Andrew W. Mellon	
Sec. of War	John W. Weeks	
Sec. of Navy	Edwin Denby	
Sec. of Inter.	Albert B. Fall	1921
	Hubert Work	1923
P.M. Gen.	Will H. Hays	1921
	Hubert Work	1922
	Harry S. New	1923
Att. Gen.	H. M. Daugherty	
Sec. of Agric.	Henry C. Wallace	
Sec. of Com.	Herbert C. Hoover	
Sec. of Labor	J. J. Davis	

CALVIN COOLIDGE 1923–1929

V.P.	Charles G. Dawes	1925
Sec. of State	Charles E. Hughes	1923
	Frank B. Kellogg	1925
Sec. of Treas.	Andrew W. Mellon	
Sec. of War	John W. Weeks	1923
	Dwight F. Davis	1925
Sec. of Navy	Edwin Denby	1923
	Curtis D. Wilbur	1924
Sec. of Inter.	Hubert Work	1923
	Roy O. West	1928
P.M. Gen.	Harry S. New	1923
Att. Gen.	H. M. Daugherty	1923
	Harlan F. Stone	1924
	John G. Sargent	1925
Sec. of Agric.	H. M. Gore	1924
	W. M. Jardine	1925

Sec. of Com.	Herbert C. Hoover	
	W. F. Whiting	1928
Sec. of Labor	J. J. Davis	

HERBERT C. HOOVER 1929–1933

V.P.	Charles Curtis	
Sec. of State	Henry L. Stimson	
Sec. of Treas.	Andrew W. Mellon	1929
	Ogden L. Mills	1932
Sec. of War	James W. Good	1929
	Patrick J. Hurley	1929
Sec. of Navy	Charles F. Adams	
Sec. of Inter.	Ray L. Wilbur	
P.M. Gen.	Walter F. Brown	
Att. Gen.	William D. Mitchell	
Sec. of Agric.	A. M. Hyde	
Sec. of Com.	R. P. Lamont	1929
	R. D. Chapin	1932
Sec. of Labor	W. N. Doak	1930

FRANKLIN D. ROOSEVELT 1933–1945

V.P.	John N. Garner	1933
	Henry A. Wallace	1937
	Harry S. Truman	1945
Sec. of State	Cordell Hull	1933
	E. R. Stettinius	1944
Sec. of Treas.	William H. Woodin	1933
	Henry Morgenthau	1934
Sec. of War	George H. Dern	1933
	H. A. Woodring	1936
	H. L. Stimson	1940
Sec. of Navy	Claude A. Swanson	1933
	Charles Edison	1940
	Frank Knox	1940
	James V. Forrestal	1944
Sec. of Inter.	Harold L. Ickes	
P.M. Gen.	James A. Farley	1933
	Frank C. Walker	1940
Att. Gen.	H. S. Cummings	1933
	Frank Murphy	1939
	Robert H. Jackson	1940
	Francis Biddle	1941
Sec. of Agric.	Henry A. Wallace	1933
	C. R. Wickard	1940
Sec. of Com.	D. C. Roper	1933
	H. L. Hopkins	1939

	Jesse Jones	1940
	Henry A. Wallace	1945
Sec. of Labor	Frances Perkins	

HARRY S. TRUMAN   1945–1953

V.P.	Alben W. Barkley	1949
Sec. of State	James F. Byrnes	1945
	George C. Marshall	1947
	Dean G. Acheson	1949
Sec. of Treas.	Fred M. Vinson	1945
	John W. Snyder	1946
Sec. of War	Robert H. Patterson	1945
(See Sec. of Defense)	K. C. Royall	1947
Sec. of Navy (See Sec. of Defense)	James V. Forrestal	1945
Sec. of Inter.	Harold L. Ickes	1945
	Julius A. Krug	1946
	O. L. Chapman	1949
P.M. Gen.	Robert E. Hannegan	1945
	Jesse L. Donaldson	1947
Att. Gen.	Tom C. Clark	1945
	J. H. McGrath	1949
	J. P. McGranery	1952
Sec. of Agric.	C. P. Anderson	1945
	C. F. Brannan	1948
Sec. of Com.	W. A. Harriman	1946
	C. W. Sawyer	1948

Sec. of Labor	L. B. Schwellenbach	1945
	M. J. Tobin	1948
Sec. of Defense (Est. 1947)	James V. Forrestal	1947
	Louis Johnson	1949
	George C. Marshall	1950
	Robert A. Lovett	1951

DWIGHT D. EISENHOWER 1953–

V.P.	Richard M. Nixon	1953
Sec. of State	John F. Dulles	1953
	Christian A. Herter	1959
Sec. of Treas.	Geo. M. Humphrey	1953
	Robert B. Anderson	1957
Sec. of Interior	D. McKay	1953
	F. A. Seaton	1956
P.M. Gen.	A. E. Summerfield	1953
Att. Gen.	Herbert Brownell	1953
	Wm. P. Rogers	1957
Sec. of Agric.	Ezra T. Benson	1953
Sec. of Com.	Sinclair Weeks	1953
	Frederick H. Mueller	1958
Sec. of Labor	M. P. Durkin	1953
	J. P. Mitchell	1953
Sec. of Defense	Charles E. Wilson	1953
	Neil H. McElroy	1957
	Thomas S. Gates, Jr.	1959
Sec. of Health, Educ., & Welfare (Est. 1953)	Oveta C. Hobby	1953
	M. B. Folsom	1955
	A. S. Flemming	1958

APPENDIX VI

Chief Justices of the Supreme Court

John Jay, N.Y. 1789–1795
John Rutledge, S.C. 1795
Oliver Ellsworth, Conn. 1795–1799
John Marshall, Va. 1801–1835
Roger B. Taney, Md. 1836–1864
Salmon P. Chase, Ohio 1864–1873
Morrison R. Waite, Ohio 1874–1888

Melville W. Fuller, Ill. 1888–1910
Edward D. White, La. 1910–1921
William H. Taft, Conn. 1921–1930
Charles E. Hughes, N.Y. 1930–1941
Harlan F. Stone, N.Y. 1941–1946
Fred M. Vinson, Ky. 1946–1953
Earl Warren, Calif. 1953–

United States *Population, 1790-1950*

Division & State	1790	1800	1810	1820	1830	1840	1850	1860
UNITED STATES	3,929,214	5,308,483	7,239,881	9,638,453	12,866,020	17,069,453	23,191,976	31,443,321
NEW ENGLAND	1,009,408	1,233,011	1,471,973	1,660,071	1,954,717	2,234,822	2,728,116	3,135,283
Maine	96,540	151,719	228,705	298,335	399,455	501,793	583,169	628,279
New Hampshire	141,885	183,858	214,460	244,161	269,328	284,574	317,976	326,073
Vermont	85,425	154,465	217,895	235,981	280,652	291,948	314,120	315,098
Massachusetts	378,787	422,845	472,040	523,287	610,408	737,699	994,514	1,231,066
Rhode Island	68,824	69,122	76,931	83,059	97,199	108,830	147,545	174,620
Connecticut	237,946	251,002	261,942	275,248	297,675	309,978	370,792	460,147
MIDDLE ATLANTIC	958,632	1,402,565	2,014,702	2,699,845	3,587,664	4,526,260	5,898,735	7,458,985
New York	340,120	589,051	958,049	1,372,812	1,918,608	2,428,921	3,097,394	3,880,735
New Jersey	184,139	211,149	245,562	277,575	320,823	373,306	489,555	672,035
Pennsylvania	434,373	602,365	810,091	1,049,458	1,348,233	1,724,033	2,311,786	2,906,215
EAST NORTH CENTRAL		51,006	272,324	792,719	1,470,018	2,924,728	4,523,260	6,926,884
Ohio		45,365	230,760	581,434	937,903	1,519,467	1,980,329	2,339,511
Indiana		5,641	24,520	147,178	343,031	685,866	988,416	1,350,428
Illinois			12,282	55,211	157,445	476,183	851,470	1,711,951
Michigan			4,762	8,896	31,639	212,267	397,654	749,113
Wisconsin						30,945	305,391	775,881
WEST NORTH CENTRAL			19,783	66,586	140,455	426,814	880,335	2,169,832
Minnesota							6,077	172,023
Iowa						43,112	192,214	674,913
Missouri			19,783	66,586	140,455	383,702	682,044	1,182,012
South Dakota								4,837
Nebraska								28,841
Kansas								107,206

Division & State	1790	1800	1810	1820	1830	1840	1850	1860
SOUTH ATLANTIC	1,851,806	2,286,494	2,674,891	3,061,063	3,645,752	3,925,299	4,679,090	5,364,703
Delaware	59,096	64,273	72,674	72,749	76,748	78,085	91,532	112,216
Maryland	319,728	341,548	380,546	407,350	447,040	470,019	583,034	687,049
District of Columbia	……	14,093	24,023	33,039	39,834	43,712	51,687	75,080
Virginia	747,610	880,200	974,600	1,065,366	1,211,405	1,239,797	1,421,661	1,596,318
West Virginia	……	……	……	……	……	……	……	……
North Carolina	393,751	478,103	555,500	638,829	737,987	753,419	869,039	992,622
South Carolina	249,073	345,591	415,115	502,741	581,185	594,398	668,507	703,708
Georgia	82,548	162,680	252,433	340,989	516,823	691,392	906,185	1,057,286
Florida	……	……	……	……	34,730	54,477	87,445	140,424
EAST SOUTH CENTRAL	109,368	335,407	708,590	1,190,489	1,815,969	2,575,445	3,363,271	4,020,991
Kentucky	73,677	220,955	406,511	564,317	687,917	779,828	982,405	1,155,684
Tennessee	35,691	105,602	261,727	422,823	681,904	829,210	1,002,717	1,109,801
Alabama	……	……	……	127,901	309,527	590,758	771,623	964,201
Mississippi	……	8,850	40,352	75,448	136,621	375,651	606,526	791,305
WEST SOUTH CENTRAL	……	……	77,618	167,680	246,127	449,985	940,251	1,747,667
Arkansas	……	……	1,062	14,273	30,388	97,574	209,897	435,450
Louisiana	……	……	76,556	153,407	215,739	352,411	517,762	708,002
Texas	……	……	……	……	……	……	212,592	604,215
MOUNTAIN	……	……	……	……	……	……	72,927	174,923
Colorado	……	……	……	……	……	……	……	……
New Mexico	……	……	……	……	……	……	61,547	93,516
Utah	……	……	……	……	……	……	11,380	40,273
Nevada	……	……	……	……	……	……	……	6,857
PACIFIC	……	……	……	……	……	……	105,891	444,053
Washington	……	……	……	……	……	……	……	……
Oregon	……	……	……	……	……	……	13,294	52,465
California	……	……	……	……	……	……	92,597	379,994

Division & State	1870	1880	1890	1900	1910	1920	1930	1940	1950
UNITED STATES	39,818,449	50,155,783	62,947,714	75,994,575	91,972,266	105,710,620	122,775,046	131,669,275	150,697,361*
NEW ENGLAND	3,487,924	4,010,529	4,700,749	5,592,017	6,552,681	7,400,909	8,166,341	8,437,290	9,314,453
Maine	626,915	648,936	661,086	694,466	742,371	768,014	797,423	847,226	913,774
New Hampshire	318,300	346,991	376,530	411,588	430,572	443,083	465,293	491,524	533,242
Vermont	330,551	332,286	332,422	343,641	355,956	352,428	359,611	359,231	377,747
Massachusetts	1,457,351	1,783,085	2,238,947	2,805,346	3,366,416	3,852,356	4,249,614	4,316,721	4,690,514
Rhode Island	217,353	276,531	345,506	428,556	542,610	604,397	687,497	713,346	791,896
Connecticut	537,454	622,700	746,258	908,420	1,114,756	1,380,631	1,606,903	1,709,242	2,007,280
MIDDLE ATLANTIC	8,810,806	10,496,878	12,706,220	15,454,678	19,315,892	22,261,144	26,260,750	27,539,487	30,163,533
New York	4,382,759	5,082,871	6,003,174	7,268,894	9,113,614	10,385,227	12,588,066	13,479,142	14,830,192
New Jersey	906,096	1,131,116	1,444,933	1,883,669	2,537,167	3,155,900	4,041,334	4,160,165	4,835,329
Pennsylvania	3,521,951	4,282,891	5,258,113	6,302,115	7,665,111	8,720,017	9,631,350	9,900,180	10,498,012
EAST NORTH CENTRAL	9,124,517	11,206,668	13,478,305	15,985,581	18,250,621	21,475,543	25,297,185	26,626,342	30,399,368
Ohio	2,665,260	3,198,062	3,672,329	4,157,545	4,767,121	5,759,394	6,646,697	6,907,612	7,946,627
Indiana	1,680,637	1,978,301	2,192,404	2,516,462	2,700,876	2,930,390	3,238,503	3,427,796	3,934,224
Illinois	2,539,891	3,077,871	3,826,352	4,821,550	5,638,591	6,485,280	7,630,654	7,897,241	8,712,176
Michigan	1,184,059	1,636,937	2,093,890	2,420,982	2,810,173	3,668,412	4,842,325	5,256,106	6,371,766
Wisconsin	1,054,670	1,315,497	1,693,330	2,069,042	2,333,860	2,632,067	2,939,006	3,137,587	3,434,576
WEST NORTH CENTRAL	3,856,594	6,157,443	8,932,112	10,347,423	11,637,921	12,544,249	13,296,915	13,516,990	14,061,394
Minnesota	439,706	780,773	1,310,283	1,751,394	2,075,708	2,387,125	2,563,953	2,792,300	2,982,483
Iowa	1,194,020	1,624,615	1,912,297	2,231,853	2,224,771	2,404,021	2,470,939	2,538,268	2,621,073
Missouri	1,721,295	2,168,380	2,679,185	3,106,665	3,293,335	3,404,055	3,629,367	3,784,664	3,954,653
North Dakota	2,405	36,909	190,983	319,146	577,056	646,872	680,845	641,935	619,636
South Dakota	11,776	98,268	348,600	401,570	583,888	636,547	692,849	642,961	652,740
Nebraska	122,993	452,402	1,062,656	1,066,300	1,192,214	1,296,372	1,377,963	1,315,834	1,325,510
Kansas	364,399	996,096	1,428,108	1,470,495	1,690,949	1,769,257	1,880,999	1,801,028	1,905,299
SOUTH ATLANTIC	5,853,610	7,597,197	8,857,922	10,443,480	12,194,895	13,990,272	15,793,589	17,823,151	21,182,335
Delaware	125,015	146,608	168,493	184,735	202,322	222,003	238,380	266,505	318,085
Maryland	780,894	934,943	1,042,390	1,188,044	1,295,346	1,449,661	1,631,526	1,821,244	2,343,001

Division & State	1870	1880	1890	1900	1910	1920	1930	1940	1950
District of Columbia	131,700	177,624	230,392	278,718	331,069	437,571	486,869	663,091	802,178
Virginia	1,225,163	1,512,565	1,655,980	1,854,184	2,061,612	2,309,187	2,421,851	2,677,773	3,318,680
West Virginia	442,014	618,457	762,794	958,800	1,221,119	1,463,701	1,729,205	1,901,974	2,005,552
North Carolina	1,071,361	1,399,750	1,617,949	1,893,810	2,206,287	2,559,123	3,170,276	3,571,623	4,061,929
South Carolina	705,606	995,577	1,151,149	1,340,316	1,515,400	1,683,724	1,738,765	1,899,804	2,117,027
Georgia	1,184,109	1,542,180	1,837,353	2,216,331	2,609,121	2,895,832	2,908,506	3,123,723	3,444,578
Florida	187,748	269,493	391,422	528,542	752,619	968,470	1,468,211	1,897,414	2,771,305
EAST SOUTH CENTRAL	4,404,445	5,585,151	6,429,154	7,547,757	8,409,901	8,893,307	9,887,214	10,778,225	11,477,181
Kentucky	1,321,011	1,648,690	1,858,635	2,147,174	2,289,905	2,416,630	2,614,589	2,845,627	2,944,806
Tennessee	1,258,520	1,542,359	1,767,518	2,020,616	2,184,789	2,337,885	2,616,556	2,915,841	3,291,718
Alabama	996,992	1,262,505	1,513,401	1,828,697	2,138,093	2,348,174	2,646,248	2,832,961	3,061,743
Mississippi	827,922	1,131,597	1,289,600	1,551,270	1,797,114	1,790,618	2,009,821	2,183,796	2,178,914
WEST SOUTH CENTRAL	2,029,965	3,334,220	4,740,983	6,532,290	8,784,534	10,242,224	12,176,830	13,064,525	14,537,572
Arkansas	484,471	802,525	1,128,211	1,311,564	1,574,449	1,752,204	1,854,482	1,949,387	1,909,511
Louisiana	726,915	939,946	1,118,588	1,381,625	1,656,388	1,798,509	2,101,593	2,363,880	2,683,516
Oklahoma	. . . .	. . . .	258,657	790,391	1,657,155	2,028,283	2,396,040	2,336,434	2,233,351
Texas	818,579	1,591,749	2,235,527	3,048,710	3,896,542	4,663,228	5,824,715	6,414,824	7,711,194
MOUNTAIN	315,385	653,119	1,213,935	1,674,657	2,633,517	3,336,101	3,701,789	4,150,003	5,074,998
Montana	20,595	39,159	142,924	243,329	376,053	548,889	537,606	559,456	591,024
Idaho	14,999	32,610	88,548	161,772	325,594	431,866	445,032	524,873	588,637
Wyoming	9,118	20,789	62,555	92,531	145,965	194,402	225,565	250,742	290,529
Colorado	39,864	194,327	413,249	539,700	799,024	939,629	1,035,791	1,123,296	1,325,089
New Mexico	91,874	119,565	160,282	195,310	327,301	360,350	423,317	531,818	681,187
Arizona	9,658	40,440	88,243	122,931	204,354	334,162	435,573	499,261	749,587
Utah	86,786	143,963	210,779	276,749	373,351	449,396	507,847	550,310	688,862
Nevada	42,491	62,266	47,355	42,335	81,875	77,407	91,058	110,247	160,083
PACIFIC	675,125	1,114,578	1,888,334	2,416,692	4,192,304	5,566,871	8,194,433	9,733,262	14,486,527
Washington	23,955	75,116	357,232	518,103	1,141,990	1,356,621	1,563,396	1,736,191	2,378,963
Oregon	90,923	174,768	317,704	413,536	672,765	783,389	953,786	1,089,684	1,521,341
California	560,247	864,694	1,213,398	1,485,053	2,377,549	3,426,861	5,677,251	6,907,387	10,586,223

* The population of the United States will be 180,126,000 in July, 1960, according to estimates by the Bureau of the Census.

Immigration, 1820-1955

Area[a]	1820–1830[b]	1831–1840	1841–1850	1851–1860	1861–1870	1871–1880	1881–1890
Europe, total	106,508	495,687	1,597,501	2,452,660	2,065,240	2,272,262	4,737,046
N.W. Europe[c]	95,390	337,285	1,157,436	1,479,669	1,244,174	1,352,191	2,325,663
Central Europe[d]	7,750	152,823	434,731	952,831	797,265	804,121	1,858,495
Eastern Europe[e]	110	283	610	540	2,641	39,632	221,192
Southern Europe[f]	3,258	5,296	4,724	19,620	21,160	76,318	331,696
Asia	15	48	82	41,458	64,630	123,823	68,380
Americas	11,951	33,424	62,469	74,720	166,607	404,039	426,969
Others	33,350	69,165	53,199	29,379	18,281	12,062	14,220
Total	151,824	598,324	1,713,251	2,598,217	2,314,758	2,812,186	5,246,613

Area	1891–1900	1901–1910	1911–1920	1921–1930	1931–1940	1941–1950	1951–1955
Europe, total	3,558,978	8,136,016	4,376,564	2,477,853	348,289	621,704	628,235
N.W. Europe[c]	1,138,340	1,568,537	853,593	871,094	83,906	261,122	193,318
Central Europe[d]	1,194,579	2,486,764	1,050,414	854,742	162,736	272,401	325,799
Eastern Europe[e]	521,826	1,769,570	1,012,478	163,683	9,048	5,082	4,059
Southern Europe[f]	704,233	2,311,145	1,460,179	588,334	92,599	83,099	105,059
Asia	71,236	243,567	192,559	97,400	15,344	31,780	42,385
Americas	38,972[g]	361,888	1,143,671	1,516,716	160,037	354,804	392,353
Others	18,378[g]	21,018	23,017	15,240	4,761	26,751	24,665
Total	3,687,564	8,762,489	5,735,811	4,107,209	528,431	1,035,039	1,087,638

[a] Area of last permanent residence.
[b] Immigration 1783–1820 estimated at 250,000.
[c] Includes British Isles, Scandinavia, France, Switzerland, and Low Countries.
[d] Includes Germany, Poland, and Austria-Hungary (after 1920, states into which Austria-Hungary was divided, i.e., Yugoslavia, Czechoslovakia, Austria, and Hungary).
[e] Includes Russia, Baltic countries, Bulgaria, Rumania, and Turkey in Europe.
[f] Includes Italy, Greece, Spain, Portugal, and miscellaneous smaller countries.
[g] American immigration included in "others" in 1892 and 1893.

PICTURE CREDITS FOR DOUBLE-PAGE SPREADS

Chapter 1

top left, Library of Congress; *center left,* Bettmann Archive; *lower left,* Library of Congress; *center,* Library of Congress; *right,* National Portrait Gallery, London.

Chapter 2

left, Bettmann Archive; *top right,* Brown Bros.; *center right,* Bettmann Archive; *lower right,* Culver Service.

Chapter 3

top left, Charles Phelps Cushing; *center left,* Charles Phelps Cushing; *lower left,* courtesy of Ruth Strickland, University of Indiana; *right background,* Library of Congress; *right foreground,* National Park Service.

Chapter 4

top left, National Gallery of Art (from painting given by Miss Marian B. Maurice); *center left,* Library of Congress; *lower left,* Library of Congress; *left background,* National Archives; *top right,* National Park Service; *lower right,* both from Library of Congress.

Chapter 5

left page, both from National Archives; *top right,* Chase Manhattan Bank Museum of Moneys of the World; *lower right,* Culver Service.

Chapter 6

left side of left page, Brown Bros.; *right side of left page,* Culver Service; *top right,* Library of Congress; *lower right,* Library of Congress.

Chapter 7

top left, Mellon Collection, National Gallery of Art; *center left,* Museum of the City of N.Y.; *lower left,* Culver Service; *top right,* Library of Congress; *center right,* Brown Bros.; *lower right,* Philip Gendreau.

Chapter 8

top left, National Park Service; *lower left,* Mellon Collection, National Gallery of Art; Bureau of Public Roads; *top right,* Culver Service; *lower right,* Culver Service.

Chapter 9

top left, Brown Bros.; *center left,* Culver Service; *lower left,* Charles Phelps Cushing; *right,* Philip Gendreau.

Chapter 10

left side of left page, Library of Congress; *right side of left page, top,* The Corcoran Gallery of Art; *center,* Library of Congress; *bottom,* Library of Congress; *right page,* Bettmann Archive.

Chapter 11

top left, International Harvester Co.; *center left,* Smithsonian Institution; *lower left,* Smithsonian Institution; *top right,* International Harvester Co.; *center right,* Smithsonian Institution; *lower right,* International Harvester Co.

Chapter 12

left, Brown Bros.; *right background,* New-York Historical Society; *top right,* Culver Service; *center right,* Brown Bros.; *lower right,* Culver Service.

Chapter 13

top left, National Archives; *center left,* Bachrach, from Culver Service; *lower left,* Culver Service; *right,* Culver Service.

Chapter 14

top left, Library of Congress; *center left,* Library of Congress; *lower left,* Brown Bros.; *left side of right page,* Culver Service; *right side of right page,* Library of Congress.

Chapter 15

top left, Architect of the Capitol, Washington, D.C.; *center left,* both from Na-

685

tional Archives; *lower left,* Library of Congress; *right,* Library of Congress.

Chapter 16

top left, Library of Congress; *center left,* Culver Service; *lower left,* Culver Service; *top right,* Library of Congress; *center right,* National Archives; *lower right,* Culver Service.

Chapter 17

top left, U.S. Department of Labor; *lower left,* Association of American Railroads; Library of Congress; *top right,* Bureau of Mines, U.S. Department of the Interior; *lower right,* U.S. Department of Labor.

Chapter 18

top left, Library of Congress; *lower left,* Library of Congress; *top right,* Culver Service; *center right,* Brown Bros.; *lower right,* Brown Bros.

Chapter 19

top left, International Harvester Co.; *center left,* International Harvester Co.; *lower left,* Library of Congress; *top right,* Ray Stannard Baker Collection, Library of Congress; *lower right,* Library of Congress.

Chapter 20

top left, National Archives; *center left,* Kansas State Historical Society; *lower left,* Bureau of Reclamation, U.S. Department of the Interior; *top right,* Nebraska State Historical Society; *lower right,* Association of American Railroads.

Chapter 21

top left, National Archives; *lower left,* both from Library of Congress; *top right,* National Archives; *lower right,* National Archives.

Chapter 22

top left, U.S. Department of Labor; *center left,* Detroit Collection, Library of Congress; *lower left,* U.S. Department of Labor; *right,* photo by Lewis Hine, George Eastman House, Rochester, N.Y.

Chapter 23

top left, cartoon by W. A. Rogers, Library of Congress; *lower left,* National Archives; *top right,* Culver Service; *lower right,* National Archives.

Chapter 24

left, Baltimore *Sun; top right,* Culver Service; Brown Bros.; *center right,* both Brown Bros.; *lower right,* Culver Service.

Chapter 25

top left, Wide World; *center left,* Wide World; *lower left,* International News Photo; *center right,* Wide World; *lower right,* Wide World.

Chapter 26

top left, United Press Photo; *center left,* International News Photo; *lower left,* Wide World; *top right,* Tennessee Valley Authority; *center right,* U.S. Department of Agriculture; *lower right,* U.S. Department of Agriculture.

Chapter 27

top left, Wide World; *lower left,* Acme; *top right,* official U.S. Navy photo; *center right,* U.S. Army (Signal Corps) photo; *lower left,* U.S. Army.

Chapter 28

top left, U.S. Coast Guard official photo; *center left,* official U.S. Navy photo; *lower left,* U.S. Army; *top right,* U.S. Army; *lower right,* both U.S. Army.

Chapter 29

top left, Wide World; *center and lower left,* official U.S. Air Force photos, released by Department of Defense; *top right,* Library of Congress; *center right,* Wide World; *lower right,* U.S. Army.

Chapter 30

left side of left page, Carew, from Monkmeyer Press Photo; *right side of left page,* Wide World; *right page, top left,* Monkmeyer Press Photo; *right page, top right,* Jack Rosen, PIX; *center right,* Wide World; *lower right,* United Press Photo.

Index

Abilene, Kansas, cow town, 424; (map), 425
Abolition, program and methods of movement, 254; northern attitude towards, 255–256
Abolitionists, free speech granted to, 244
Acheson, Dean, as Secretary of State, 607
Adams, Charles Francis, American ambassador in England, 331
Adams, John, and Treaty of Paris, 78; elected President, 126, 135, 669; Cabinet, 673; negotiates peace, 138–139
Adams, John Quincy, early career, 172; abilities, 172; Secretary of State, 163; defends Jackson, 161; and Monroe Doctrine, 170; elected President, 151, 172, 669; (photograph), 172; Cabinet, 674; failure of his presidential program, 172–173; and election campaign of 1828; charges against, 174; and sectional controversy, 212; on freedom of speech, 255
Adams, Samuel, and Committee of Correspondence, 67; and Tea Party, 68
Adams, Samuel Hopkins, muckraker author, 457
Adams-Onis treaty (1819) with Spain, 161
Adamson Act for railroad employees, 478
Adkins v. Children's Hospital (decision), minimum wage, 505
Adult education, institutes for, 250
Africa, partition of, 439
Agrarian radicals favor imperialism, 440
Agricultural Adjustment Acts (AAA), for crop curtailment, 537, 549–551; criticism of program, 551
Agricultural Marketing Act, 520, 529, 530
Agriculture, growth of, 1800–1860, 224; in South, 226–227; depressed condition of, 1860–1900, 399, 405; interdependence with industry, 399; benefits to Europe, 399; and balance of payments to Europe, 400; production, factors favoring, 401; prices, 1880–1896 (chart), 402; depressed condition of, 1929, 522; (diagram), 522; under New Deal, 548–551; surplus problem in mid-1950s, 618 (*See also* Farmers)
Alabama, Confederate cruiser, 331
Alabama, development of, 188; secession of, 311; claims arbitrated with Great Britain, 432, 433
Alamo, The, Texas shrine (picture), 271
Alaska, Russian sovereignty over, 170; purchase of, 433; gains statehood (1959), 445
Albany Congress, plan of federations, 43
Alcorn, J. L., cooperation with Negroes, 340
Alcott, Louisa May, on John Brown, 305
Alder Gulch, Mont., gold mining center, 419
Alexander VI, Pope, arbiter of newly discovered lands, 5
Alien Act of 1798, 137, 138
Alien and Sedition Acts, passed, 126; expiration of, 143
Alliance system of Truman and Eisenhower, 607–608; results of, 608

Alliance treaty with France (1777), signed, 56
Altgeld, John P., political reformer, 390; Populist principles of, 413
Alton Observer, antislavery paper, 256
Amalgamated Clothing Workers, industrial union of, 547
Amendments to the United States Constitution, Appendix II, 658–667; first ten, or Bill of Rights, 118, 658–659; eleventh, jurisdiction of federal courts, 660; twelfth, presidential elections, 140, 660–661; thirteenth, abolition of slavery, 338, 344, 661; fourteenth, Negro rights, 338, 346, 661–663; fifteenth, Negro suffrage, 338, 663; sixteenth, income tax, 453, 470, 663; seventeenth, direct election of senators, 453, 470, 664; eighteenth, prohibition, 664; nineteenth, woman suffrage, 665; twentieth, terms of President and Congress, 520, 532, 665; twenty-first, repeal of prohibition, 666; twenty-second, third presidential term forbidden, 666–667
American Anti-Slavery Society, formed, 244; program, 254; growth, 256
American Colonization Society, operations, 254
"American democratic faith," and "manifest destiny," 245, 268
American Expeditionary Force (AEF) in World War I, 489
American Federation of Labor, organized, 358, 374; supports LaFollette in 1924, 503; growth in membership (1932–1941), 547–548; conflict with CIO, 547 (*See also* Labor; Unions)
American Fur Company, power and influence, 191–192
American Insurance Company v. Canter (decision), 167
American Mercury, periodical, 516
American Party or Know-Nothings, 253
American Peace Society founded, 244
American people, characteristics of, 627
American Philosophical Society founded, 42, 52
American Railway Union and Pullman strike, 410
American Revolution, and democracy, 82; radicals in, 81, 82, 92; democratic aspects of, 86; administration in, 87; inflation during, 88; illicit trade in, 88–89; profiteering in, 88; problem of supply in, 89–90; control of economic activities, 89; public service in, 90–91; counterrevolutionary movement during, 91–97; attitude of conservatives toward, 92–93; conservatives gain control, 94; democratic gains of, 98; treatment of loyalists in, 98; achievements of government during, 100 (*See also* War for Independence)
American Sugar Refining Company and political contributions, 392
American System of Henry Clay, 163
American system and the New Deal, 558
American Temperance Society founded, 244
American Tobacco Trust prosecuted by Taft, 470

American virtues, 637–638
Americanism, roots of, in colonial America, 52, 53; as a way of life, 629, 633
Amnesty Act (1872), effects of, 351
Amnesty Proclamation, Lincoln's, 342
Amphibious warfare in Pacific, 590
Anaconda strategy in Civil War, 319–321
Andros, Sir Edmund, and Dominion of New England, 17
Anglican Church, in Virginia, 44, 45; disestablishment, 81
Annapolis convention (1786), and problem of Union, 101; purposes and results of, 109
Anthony, Susan B., temperance reform, 252
Antietam, battle of, checks Confederates, 310
Antifederalists oppose the Constitution, 116
Antimonopoly political party, 391
Anti-Redeemer movement in South, 354–355
Antislavery crusade, nature and scope of, 253; origins of, 253; programs of, 253
Anti-Slavery Society, American, 244; New England, 254
"Appeal of the Independent Democrats," by Salmon P. Chase, 307
Appeasement and Japanese public opinion, 577, 578
Appeasement policy, failure of, to bring peace, 564; abandonment of, towards Soviet Russia, 606 (See also Munich Pact)
Appomattox, surrender of Lee, 310, 323
Arab-Israeli feud involving refugees, 621
Arabic sunk by Germans, 483
Arbitration, use of, by United States and Great Britain, 433–434
Archangel, supply line to, 583
Architecture, early national (illustrations), 85
Argonne Forest, World War I battle, 489
Aristocracy, in Virginia, 43–45; control of, in early state constitutions, 85
Aristocrats, in American Revolution, 81; and Stamp Act Congress, 81
Arizona territory, 419
Arkansas, development of, 188
Armada, Spanish, defeated by British, 1, 9
Arminianism described, 46
Armistice of 1918 with Germany, 480, 492
Army of Northern Virginia, Confederate, 321
Army of the Potomac, Union, 321
Arnold, Benedict, assault on Quebec, 73
Arthur, Chester A., becomes President, 379; Cabinet, 676
Article X in League of Nations Covenant, 495–496
Articles of Confederation, adopted, 81; central government, 86; lack of sanctions in, 86; defects as a system of government, 87; control of taxation under, 87; proposal to amend, 94, 96; democratic progress under, 98–99; financial difficulties under, 107; disposition of government debts, 111; inadequacy demonstrated, 106–107
Aryan supremacy myth, 439
"Ashcan school" of art, 461
Asia, partition of, 439; spread of Communism in, 605, 608, 620, 621
Assemblies, colonial, importance, 39, 40
Assumption applied to state debts, 122
Assumption Act, passed, 101; bargain with Jefferson, 112 (See also Hamilton, Alexander)

Astor, John Jacob, fabulous career of, 191
Atlantic Monthly magazine, limited appeal of, 250, 456
Atomic energy for peaceful uses (photograph), 629
Atomic uranium bomb, 596, 609; first test at Bikini atoll (photograph), 608
Atrocities, in Cuba, 441; in Filipino war, 444; in World War I, propaganda, 482
Automobile industry in 1920s, 523

Babe Ruth, home run king, 514
Back country during American Revolution, 92
Bacon, Nathaniel, 35, 36
Bacon's Rebellion, causes, 35, 36
Bagot, Charles, British Minister to United States, 161
Bailey v. Drexel Furniture Co. (decision), child labor, 505
Balance of power, in Atlantic, threatened by Germans, 570; destroyed by World War II, 604
"Balance of terror" in mid-twentieth century, 623
Ballinger-Pinchot controversy over conservation, 472
Baltimore, Lord, Maryland proprietor, plans, powers, 21–23
Baltimore (view of, in 1752), 53; British repulsed at, 158
Baltimore and Ohio railroad, 235
Bancroft, George, historian, 262n.
Bank of the United States, First, chartered, 101, 123; arguments for and against, 124
Bank of the United States, Second, chartered, 151, 164; expired, 157
Bankers, investment, and railroad capitalization, 365, 366
Banking crisis of 1933, 520, 532, 540, 541
Banks, failure of, in 1929, 525
Baptists, success on frontier, 199
Bates, Edward, presidential aspirant in 1860, 308
Bear Flag Republic in California, 280
Beard, Charles A., historian, criticizes American Constitution, 460
Belgium, invasion of, by Germans, 480, 482
Bell, John C., Constitutional Union party nominee in 1860, 306
Bellamy, Edward, Looking Backward, socialist novel, 376
Belleau Wood, World War I battle, 489
Benson, Ezra Taft, opposes farm subsidies, 617; becomes political issue, 617
Benton, Senator Thomas H., opposes Foot Resolution, 216
Berkeley, Sir William, and Bacon's Rebellion, 35, 36
Berlin and problem of disengagement in Europe (1959–1960), 622
Bernstorff, Count von, German ambassador, 483
Bessemer, Sir Henry, blast furnace for steel, 237; first plant, 358
Bible Society, American, 253
Big business (see Business)
"Big stick" policy of Theodore Roosevelt, 451; renounced in Latin America, 511
Bigelow Papers by Lowell, 255
Bill of Rights, significance in America, 15; in Federal Constitution, enacted and ratified, 101;

controversy over, 116; limitations on Congress, 118
Bill of Rights, Virginia, adopted, 81
Birney, James G., antislavery editor, 254, 256; candidate of Liberty party, 270
Black Codes in southern states (1865), 338, 344–345
Black Hills, Dakota mining center, 419; Deadwood, city in, 419
Black Reconstruction, failure of, 349
Black Republicans, political issue, 301–302
Blackhawk War, 188
Blacklist of workers, 373
Blacklists used by British in World War I, 485
Blaine, James G., defeated by Cleveland, 379, 384; and spoils system, 385; "Half-Breeds" leader, 386; Pan-American policy, 434–435
Blair, Francis P., newspaper editor, 209
Bland-Allison Act, silver coinage, 398, 408; operation of, 408–409
"Bleeding Kansas," 299, 300
"Bleeding Sumner," political issue, 301
Blithedale Romance by Nathaniel Hawthorne, 260
Blockade, "paper," issue with England (1793–1812), 132; British, and Napoleonic Wars, 148; British, in World War I, 485, 486; in Civil War, 317, 319, 321; success of, 334
Bloomer, Amelia, dress reform advocate, 252
Blue Eagle of the NRA, 544
Board of Trade, England, 60
Bohr, Niels, Danish atomic scientist, 596
Bolsheviks, Russian radical communists, 488; seize power, 480
Bonus Army, "Bonus Expeditionary Force," in Washington, 520, 531; demands of, 531; (photographs), 530–531
Book of Mormon, 193
"Boomers," Oklahoma pioneers, 429
"Boondoggling," uneconomic projects, 545
Boone, Daniel, explores Kentucky (1769–1770), 176; role on the frontier, 181
Bootleg liquor traffic, 514
Borah, William E., isolationist, 500
Border states, significance in Civil War, 316; contest for, 316
Bosses, political, feature of the Gilded Age, 380; in cities, 382, 391–393; methods of operation, 392–393; code of conduct, 391–392; target of progressive reformers, 454; persistence into twentieth century, 394 (See also Tweed Ring)
Boston massacre, 56; (illustration), 67
Boston Port Bill, 68
Boston Tea Party, 56, 68
Bounty system in Civil War, "jumpers" and "brokers," 327
Bourbons, southern, identified, 354; program, 354; and Negroes, 354
Boxer uprising in China, consequences of, 447
Boycott against British, 67; by First Continental Congress, 70
Bradford House, Massachusetts (illustration), 36
Bragg, General Braxton, gains initiative in Kentucky, 319, 325
Brain trust, use of, by Franklin Roosevelt, 538, 539, 541
Brandeis, Justice Louis D., concept of law, 460
Brazil, aid from United States to, 436

Breckenridge, John C., radical Democratic nominee in 1860, 306, 670
Brest-Litovsk, Russo-German treaty, 488
Brisbane, Albert, popularizes Fourierism, 260
British East India Company and tea monopoly, 68
British legislation for colonies, 1763–1774 (chart), 64
British strategy in American Revolution, 72
Brook Farm settlement established, 244, 260
Brooks, Congressman Preston, assault on Sumner, 284, 300–301; (picture), 300; reaction to, 301
Brown, John, in Kansas, 300; raid on Harpers Ferry, 284, 300, 304–305
Brown v. Board of Education (1954) (decision), segregation, 618
Brown v. Maryland (decision), 167
Bryan, William J., nominated for President, 398; significance of his 1896 election campaign, 414, 671; and peace with Spain, 444; criticizes policies of T. Roosevelt, 466; defeated in 1908, 469; Secretary of State, opposes Wilson's policies, 484; resignation, 485; and Scopes trial, 500, 514
Bryce, James, The American Commonwealth, on democratic government, 394
Buchanan, James, nominated by Democrats, 301; elected President, 302, 670; and secession, 312; Cabinet, 675
Budget, federal, and New Deal spending, 556
Buena Vista, battle of, 280
Buffalo, plains, and Indians, 422; slaughter of, 422
Bull market, Wall Street in 1920s, 515
Bull Moose rejoin Republicans, 500
Bull Run, battle of, 310, 321–323
Bullwhackers, drivers, 420
Bunau-Varilla, M. Philippe, plans Panama revolution, 449
Bunker Hill, battle of, 72
Burgoyne, General John, battles at Saratoga, 75
Burns, Anthony, fugitive slave, 294
Burnside, Ambrose E., Union commander, defeated, 323
"Burnt-over District," revival area, 259–260
Burr, Aaron, duel with Alexander Hamilton, 126; election of 1800, 140, 668; and plot, 183, 190
Burritt, Elihu, the Learned Blacksmith, 253; reform projects, 253
Business, big, achievements and philosophy of, 370; growth of (chart), 471; and government during World War II, 582; and Supreme Court, 376

Cabet, Étienne, A Voyage to Icaria, 260
Cabinet, President's, development of, 120; members of each, listed, Appendix V, 673–679
Calhoun, Floride, boycotts Peggy Eaton, 213
Calhoun, John C., early career of, 214; introduces Bank recharter bill, 164; in Monroe's cabinet, 163, 673; favors internal improvements, 165; Vice President with J. Q. Adams and Jackson, 674; breach with Jackson, 213; opposes tariff of 1828, 214; writes "South Carolina Exposition and Protest," 214; nullification theory of, 214; Tyler's Secretary of State, 270–271, 674; and Texas issue, 271–272; attitude of, towards Mexican acquisitions, 281; and Compromise of 1850, 288–291; and antislavery thought, 258;

on Northern-Southern economic cooperation, 352; and states' rights issue, 286; warning on freeing slaves, 340

California, trails to, 196; statehood, 196; acquired, 176; gold discovered in, 176; gold rush, 196; conquered in Mexican War, 280; conquest of (map), 282; Japanese school question in, 448

Calvin, John, *Institutes of Christian Religion,* 42

Calvinism, religious beliefs, 24, 25

Cambridge Platform, Congregational, 25

Cameron, Simon, presidential aspirant in 1860, 308

Camp meetings, frontier religious feature, 198–199

Campaigns, political, contributions to, publicity for, 470 (*See also* Elections)

Canada, issue in War of 1812, 155; invasions of, in War of 1812, 157–158

Canadians, attitude toward American Revolution, 73

Canals, era of building, 232–234; (map), 233; in Illinois, 233–234; in Ohio, 233; Pennsylvania system, 233; failure of, 234

Canning, George, and Monroe Doctrine, 170

Cannon, Joseph G., Speaker of House, powers curbed, 472

Cantigny, World War I battle, 489

Capital in colonial period, 30

Capitalist system, advantages of, 360; saved by New Deal, 541; American, achievements of, 628–629

Capitol building at Washington, in 1800 (picture), 142; in 1830 (picture), 173

Capone, Al, Chicago gangster, 514

CARE relief program, 638

Caribbean, policy of Theodore Roosevelt, 448–451; United States in (map), 450

Carnegie, Andrew, steel magnate, career, 368; mass production developed, 368–369; success, 368–369; author of *Triumphant Democracy,* 368

Carolinas, colony, charter granted, 19; provisions, 23

"Carpet-bag" rule in Reconstruction period, 349; and corruption, 349–350

Carson City, Nev., mining town, 418

"Cash-and-carry" principle in Neutrality Act, 566

Cass, Lewis, on "manifest destiny," 268; Secretary of War under Jackson, 624; defeated for President in 1848, 288; vote, 670

Catholics, Roman, missions in Oregon, 193; and public education, 248–249

Cattle, range, beginning of industry, 417, 424; expansion, 424–425; decline, 417, 424–425

Cattle trails on Great Plains (map), 425

Cattlemen's Land Law (1916), 429

Censorship, during Civil War, 330; in World War I, 489, 501

Central America, "dollar diplomacy" in, 451

Central Pacific railroad, chartered, 333; construction of, 420

Century magazine, limited appeal of, 456

Ceresco, utopian community in Wisconsin, 260

Cervera, Admiral, Spanish commander in Cuba, 442

Chamberlain, D. H., "carpet-bag" governor, 350

Chamberlain, Neville, British Prime Minister, signs Munich Pact, 560, 563

Change, persistence of, in America, 634

Channing, William Ellery, author, 261; and abolition, 255

Charles I, King of England, reign, 7; executed, 16

Charles II, King of England, reign, 1, 7, 16

Charles River Bridge case, significance of, 219–220

Charleston captured by British, 77

Charleston & Hamburg, first steam railroad, 235

Chase, Salmon P., and 1860 Republican Convention, 307; Secretary of Treasury under Lincoln, 675; heads radicals in Lincoln's cabinet, 331; Chief Justice, dates, 680; and impeachment of President Johnson, 348

Chase, Samuel, Supreme Court Justice, impeachment of, 126, 145

Chattanooga captured by Union armies, significance, 327

Checks and balances, in Constitution, 112; in American system of government, 631

Cherry Creek, Colorado, gold rush, 418

Chesapeake-Leopard incident, 126, 148

Cheyenne Club, stockmen's headquarters, 427

Chiang Kai-shek, Chinese nationalist leader, fails to unite China, 593; overthrown by Communists, 608, 609; flight to Formosa, 609

Chicago, University of, founded by John D. Rockefeller, 396

Child labor, in factories, 240; proposed amendment to Constitution, 667

Child labor bill voided by Supreme Court, 478

Children's Bureau established, 470

Chile, revolution of 1891, and United States, 435

Chillicothe, Ohio, beginnings of, 186

China, trade, beginnings of, 105; partition of, 437; defeated by Japan (1894–1895), 446; concessions to Great Powers, 446; impending partition, 446; Open Door policy declared by Secretary John Hay, 432, 446–447; war with Japan (1937–1945), 562; Communist movement in, 593; Nationalist, 608–609; Communist, in postwar world, 606, 608–609; opposed by United States, 612; intervenes in Korean war, 612

Chinese, exclusion of, 513

Church of England (*see* Anglican Church)

Churchill, Winston, American novelist, 457

Churchill, Winston, British Prime Minister, greatness of, as leader, 570

Cincinnati, beginnings and development of, 186; (map), 186

Civil liberties, preservation of, in America, 630

Civil Rights Bill passed over Johnson's veto, 345

Civil rights cases (1883), effects of, 618

Civil Service Commission created, 386 (*See also* Merit system; Patronage; Spoils system)

Civil service reform, political issue, 385–386

Civil War, American, causes of, 284–287; Confederate advantages, 317; advantages of North, 317–318; importance of industry in, 318; importance of railroads in, 318; element of leadership in, 318–319; Anaconda plan of strategy, 319–320; eastern theater, terrain, 321; major campaigns (map), 320; principal offensives in eastern theater (map), 322; peninsular campaign, 322–323; western theater, campaigns in, 324–326; offensives in Mississippi Valley (map), 326; principal offensive drives in Central South (map), 335; description of soldiers of, 327–330, end of war in East, 310, 323; Union troops withdrawn from South, 338, 352; significance of, 310, 336 (*See also* Border states; Confederacy)

Civil war, English, in 17th century, 16

Civilization in the United States, critical symposium on, 516

Clark, George Rogers, conquers Northwest, 77, 78

Clark, William, associate of Meriwether Lewis in Lewis and Clark expedition, 189

Class conflict in American colonies, 34–36 (*See also* Sectionalism)

Clay, Henry, Speaker of House, 163; and "American System," 163; and Missouri Compromise, 169; alliance with John Quincy Adams, 172; Compromise Tariff of 1833, 275; presidential candidate, in 1824, 669; in 1832, 669; in 1844, 273, 670; and Compromise of 1850, 290, 291; death of, 284, 297

Clayton Antitrust Act, passed, 453; provisions, 478

Clayton-Bulwer Treaty on inter-American canal, 448–449

Clemenceau, Georges, at Paris Peace Conference, 493

Clemens, Samuel (*see* Twain, Mark)

Cleveland, Grover, elected President, 1884, 379, 670; defeated, 1888, 379, 388, 671; reelected, 1892, 379, 671; Cabinets, 676–677; and tariff issue, 387–388; Cuban policy of, 441; suppresses Pullman strike, 373–374; and panic of 1893, 409–410; deal with bankers, 410; repeal of Sherman Silver Act, 410; repudiated by Democrats in 1896, 413; and Venezuela boundary dispute, 436

Cleveland, Ohio, beginnings of, 185; (map), 186

Clinton, De Witt, and public schools in New York, 248

Clinton, Sir Henry, British commander in American Revolution, 76

Coal used as fuel, 238

Coal strike, anthracite, settled by T. Roosevelt, 467

Coercive Acts (*see* Intolerable Acts)

Cohens v. Virginia (decision), 166

Coinage system in United States established, 123

Coke, Sir Edward, upholds common law, 12; influence on Declaration of Independence, 74

"Cold war" between Soviet Russia and the United States, 607; stalemate in, issue in 1952 election, 613; influence on American thinking, 615

Colleges on American frontier, 199–200 (*See also* Education)

Collier's, muckraker periodical, 456

Colombia rejects Panama canal treaty, 432

Colonies, American, economic activity (map), 29; British legislation for (1763–1774) (chart), 64

Colonies, British, establishment of, in America (chronological chart), 22

Colorado, territory, organization and development of, 418; plateaus of, 418

Columbia River, reached by Lewis and Clark, 189; flood control and power projects, 554

Columbus, Christopher, voyage to New World, 1, 5; significance of, 2

Command of Army Act, control taken from President, 348

Commerce, colonial, British regulations of, 30; and Navigation Acts, 31–32; post-Revolutionary, review of, 105; defined by Supreme Court, 166–167

Commerce and Labor, Department of, established, 467; divided, 470

Committee for Industrial Organization (CIO), formed, 537, 547–548; growth in membership (1932–1941), 548

Committees of Correspondence, colonial, 67

Committees of Safety and Correspondence favor secession, 289

Common law, English, 12–13

Common man, cult of, in America, 627

Commonwealth v. Hunt (decision), right to strike legalized, 223, 242

Commonwealth and Southern, electric power holding company, 553

Communism, fear of, in 1920s, 512; in Asia, 605, 608, 620, 621; charge of, against Truman administration, 614; issue in 1952 campaign, 614

Communists seize control in Russia, 560–561

Compact, government formed in Kentucky and Tennessee, 181 (*See also* Social compact)

Compromise of 1850, issues in, 288; debates on, 288–291; enacted, 284, 292; accepted in South, 295

Compromise of 1877, significance of, 352

Comstock lode discovered, 1859, 418

Concentration camp, Nazi, at Belsen (photograph), 594

Concord, battle of, 56, 70; (map), 72

Confederacy, Constitution framed, 310; advantages of, in Civil War, 317; problem of loyalty in, 315; conscription in, 328; strategy of defense in Civil War, 319; opposition to war in, 330; courts England, 331–332; failure, 332; transportation breakdown in, 336; failure abroad, 310; collapse, 327, 334

Confederation (*see* Articles of Confederation)

Confiscation Act sets slave policy in Civil War, 331

Congregational Church, polity, 46

Congress, United States, first session of, 101; problems of, 120; opposition to Lincoln's Reconstruction policy, 342–343; quarrel with President Johnson, 338, 342–346; refuses to admit southern representatives, 338, 345

Congressional reconstruction (*see* Reconstruction)

Conkling, Roscoe, and spoils system, 385; "Stalwarts" leader, 386; quarrel with Garfield, 386

Connecticut, first settlement of, 19

"Conquered provinces" policy applied to South, 347

Conscription, problem in Confederacy, 328; in American Civil War, 327–328

Conservation, problem arises, 429–430; policy of T. Roosevelt, 468; White House Conference on, 468; policy of President Taft, 470; Carey Act for state irrigation projects, 417, 429; Newlands Act for federal projects, 417, 429–430; projects in Columbia River basin, 554; Civilian Conservation Corps (CCC), work of, 554; Soil Conservation Service (1934), 554; TVA program of, 554

Conservation Commission, National, 468

Conservatism in Old South, 258

Conservatives, view of American Revolution, 92–93; control of American Revolution, 94–95

Constitution, United States, annotated text with amendments, 646–667; signers, 657; amending processes, 115; provision for national authority, 111; framework of government, 113; federal judiciary, 113–114; and balanced government, 112; composition of House and Senate, 113; control of appropriations, 113; treaty power, 115; election of President and Vice President, 113, 660, 661; powers of President, 113; "elastic" clauses, 111; "necessary and proper" clause, 116; limitations on the states, 111; ratification provisions, 115; contests, 117; favored by business classes and speculators, 111; objections to, 116; ratifying conventions, votes in (map), 116; undemocratic features, 112; slavery, 270; democratization of, 118; adaptation to modern times, 118; strength of, 627

Constitution, warship, 160

Constitutional Convention, significance of, 84; meeting of, 101; membership, 109, 110; conservative character of, 110; agreement on fundamentals, 110

Constitutions, state, framing of, 81, 83–84; general provisions, 84; conservative, 85; radical, 84

Construction industry, in 1920s, 523; in Great Depression, 529*n.*

Consumption as factor in the Great Depression, 523

Continental Congress, First, at Philadelphia, 70, 81; Declaration of Grievances, 70; Second, becomes a government, 71, 81; travels of (map), 91

Continental money (currency) worthless, 81

Contraband issue with England (1793–1812), 132

Contract defined by Supreme Court, 165–166

Contract labor, importation of, and status, 371

Contract Labor Law (1864), 341

Contributions, political, by corporations, 392

Cooke, Jay, railroad financier, 365

Coolidge, Calvin, Vice President, becomes President, 500, 502, 671; reputation, 502, 503; nominated for President, 502, 503; Cabinet, 678; attitude toward war debts, 507

Cooper, James Fenimore, deplores lack of literary tradition, 261

Cooper Union, New York, 250

Copernicus, Nikolaus, Polish astronomer, 42, 50

Copperheads oppose Civil War in North, 330

Cornwallis, General Charles, to Yorktown, 77; surrender, 56, 78

Corporate finance, beginnings of, 238

Corporations, form of organization, 362; advantages of, 238–239; effects of, 362; and fourteenth amendment, 358

Corporations, Bureau of, established, 467

Corruption, political, in Gilded Age, 380–382, 384; reasons for, 382–383; pattern of, 391

Cosmopolitan, muckraker periodical, 456

Cotton, John, controversy with Roger Williams, 26

Cotton, southern staple, 227; cultivation, 228; marketing, 228; significance in Civil War, 317, 319

Cotton gin, invented, 223, 228; effects on slavery, 266

Cotton mills (*see* Textiles)

Council of National Defense, World War I, 489

Counterrevolution movement during American Revolution, 91–97

Country Life Commission, National, 468

"Court packing bill," of F. D. Roosevelt, 556

Courts, lower federal, provided, 121

Covenant of Grace, Puritan belief, 24

Cow towns on Great Plains, 424–425

Cowboy, as a historical figure, 424; his environment, 424 (*See also* Cattle; Cattlemen's Land Law)

Cowpens, battle of, 77

Cox, James M., nominated by Democrats, 501; defeated, 671

Coxey, Jacob S., leader of industrial army, 398, 410

Crawford, William H., Secretary of Treasury, 163, 673; defeated for President, 669

Credit, colonial, 29; extension of facilities by New Deal, 541–542

Crédit mobilier, political scandal, 379, 382

Creel, George, World War I propaganda chief, 489

Crèvecoeur, St. Jean de, *Letters from an American Farmer,* 54, 200

Crime, increase of, in America, 633

"Crime against Kansas" speech by Charles Sumner, 300

"Crime of '73," silver demonetized, 398

Critical period defined, 101

"Critical year" elections of 1866, 345, 346

Crittenden Compromise, failure of, 313

Croly, Herbert, author of *The Promise of American Life,* significance of, 474; attacks *laissez faire,* 459

Cromwell, Oliver, Lord Protector of England, 1; and English Civil War, 16

Crop insurance, provision for, in AAA program, 550

Crop-lien system in South, 355

Crops, food, in South, 229

"Cross of Gold" speech by Bryan, 413

Cruisers, Confederate, built in Britain, 331; protested by United States, 331

Crusades, significance of, 3–4

Cuba, American investments in, 434; 1895 revolt against Spain, 440; American reaction to, 440; Ten Years' War, 440; revolutionary junta in New York, 441; American administration of, 445; independence granted, 445; Platt amendment to Cuban constitution, 432, 445

Cultural differences in American colonies, 43

Culture, American, plea for, by Emerson, 244; level of, 633; in Gilded Age, 394–396; debt to Europe, 396

Cumberland settlement in Tennessee (*see* Nashville)

Cumberland Road, opposed by presidents, 164–165; importance of, 232

Currency in American Revolution, 88

Currency Act (1764), 64

Curtis, George W., editor and reformer, 385

Cutler, Manasseh, Ohio Company agent, 184

Czechoslovakia becomes Soviet satellite state, 607

Dairying in East, 226
Dakotas, homesteader rush to, 426; admitted as states, 427
Dark Ages, 1
Darrow, Clarence, and Scopes trial, 500, 514
Dartmouth College v. Woodward (decision), 151, 166
Darwin, Charles, doctrine of evolution, 375
Darwinism, social, and free enterprise, 375
Daugherty, Harry M., and Warren G. Harding, 501; Attorney General, 502
Davis, Jefferson, views on secession, 286; plans transcontinental railroad, 298; career, 313–314; contrast with Lincoln, 313–314; (photograph), 314; as war leader, 318–319; handicaps and difficulties as President of Confederacy, 315
Davis, John W., Democratic nominee in 1924, 502–503, 671
Dawes Act, new Indian policy, 417, 423; objectives, 423; results, 423
Dawes Plan for German reparations, 508
Deadwood, Dakota, mining metropolis, 419
Debs, Eugene, and Pullman strike, 374; becomes Socialist, 376; Socialist candidate in 1912, 476, 671
Debt, national, and Alexander Hamilton, 122; increase of, under New Deal, 555
Declaration of Independence, adopted, 56; contents, 74; signing (illustration), 74; text of, 642–644; signers, 644, 645
Declaratory Act, 64, 65
Deere, John, steel plow invented by, 223, 225
Delaware ratifies Constitution, 101
De Leon, Daniel, revolutionary Socialist, 376
Democracy, and American Revolution, 82; Jeffersonian, characterized, 141–142; and frontier, 176–177; Jacksonian, 202–222; in America, Judge Learned Hand's words on, 626; as persistent factor in American history, 627
Democratic party (*see* Democrats)
Democrats, defeat in 1840, 270; and 1844 campaign, 272; effects of Mexican War, 281–283; and "final settlement" of 1850, 292; platform of 1852, 292; party division in 1860, 284, 306; in Reconstruction period, 341; in Gilded Age, 380, 383; repudiate Cleveland in 1896, 413; nominate Bryan (1896), 413; nominate Wilson, 474; party split in 1924, 502 (*See also* Elections; New Deal)
Dempsey-Tunney prize fight, 511
Denmark conquered by Germany, 560–569
Departments and bureaus, government (*see* under various names)
Depression, post-Revolutionary, 104–105; economic, and War of 1812, 153; of 1873, 358; of 1893, 398, 408–409; Cleveland's attitude toward, 409, 543
    Great, of 1929–1933, 520–521; causes of, 521, 526–527; significance of, 521, 525–526; as cause of wars and revolutions, 528; prolongation of, 532; effects of, 532–533; as destructive force, 533–535
    postwar, anticipated, 603–604 (*See also* Recession)
Desegregation in public schools, 619
Deseret, State of, in Utah, 195
Desert, Great American, settlement of, 426

Desert Land Act, 417, 428
Destruction in South after Civil War, 339
Detroit, effects of Great Depression on, 534
Devaluation of dollar, 543
Dewey, Admiral George, destroys Spanish fleet, 442
Dewey, John, philosopher, *The Old Individualism and the New*, 535, 536
Dewey, Thomas E., Republican presidential candidate (1948), 610, 672
Dial, The, literary periodical, 250
Díaz, Porfirio, Mexican dictator, 434; overthrown, 481
Dickens, Charles, popularity as author, 261
Dickinson, John, on taxation of the colonies, 66; and American Revolution, 82
Dinwiddie, Robert, Virginia governor, and issue of taxation, 14
Disallowance, royal veto power, 60, 65, 66
Discovery, Age of, preparations for, 2–4
Discrimination, racial, and world opinion, 636–637
Dissenters, religious, in England as colonists, 11
Dix, Dorothea, interest in the insane, 250–252
Dodge City, Kansas, cow town, 425
"Dollar diplomacy" repudiated by Wilson, 482
"Dollar-a-year" men in government war service, 581
Dominion of New England, 17
Doniphan, Colonel A. W., leads expeditionary force in Mexican War, 279
"Dooley, Mr.," and Democrats, 383; on Spanish-American War, 442; on reform crusades, 461; on Payne-Aldrich tariff, 471
Dos Passos, John, novelist, 515
Douglas, Stephen A., role in Compromise of 1850, 292; and Kansas-Nebraska Act, 296–297; condemned, 297; and transcontinental railroad, 296–298; Freeport Doctrine, 304; Democratic nominee in 1860, 306, 670; conciliates the South, 312
Douglass, Frederick, Negro antislavery leader, 255–256
Draft dodging in Civil War, 327
Drake, Francis, voyage around world, 1, 9
Dred Scott decision, 284, 303–304
Dreiser, Theodore, novelist, 458, 516
Drew, Daniel, railroad manipulator, 363, 364
Droughts in Great Plains, 427
Duane, James, and American Revolution, 82
Dubinsky, David, president, International Ladies' Garment Workers, 547
Dulles, John Foster, Secretary of State with Eisenhower (photograph), 621
Dumbarton Oaks Conference, preliminary to United Nations, 597
Dutch, in Hudson River region, 5; expelled from East Indies by Japan, 575–576

East Germany, Russian satellite state, 605
East India Company, British, and tea monopoly, 68
Eaton, Senator John H., and Peggy O'Neale, Eaton affair, 212–213
Eaton, Peggy, disrupts Jackson's cabinet, 213
Economic activity, control of, in American Revolution, 89

Economic issues in mid-twentieth century, 615–618

Economic organization, European cooperation, 606

Economic systems, northern and southern (1860) compared, 285–286

Economic theory, reappraisal of, in Depression, 528, 532–533 (*See also* Keynes, John Maynard)

Economic welfare, mass, as goal in United States, 628

Economy, national (1860), interdependence of, 242; weaknesses in (1929), 522–524; (diagram), 526; in mid-1950s, 616

Education, in colonial America, 52; public, expansion of, 247; shortage of facilities for, in schools and colleges, 634–635; reform in universities, 396 (*See also* Colleges; Institutes; Libraries; Lyceum movement; Schools; Universities)

Edwards, Jonathan, philosophical writing, 42; clergyman and preacher, 48; author of *A Narrative of Surprising Conversions*, 48

Egypt attacked by Great Britain and France, 621

Einstein, Albert, theory of relativity, 395; (photograph), 576

Eisenhower, Dwight D., American commander in Europe, 587; as national idol, 614; as political leader, 615; elected President in 1952 and 1956, 614, 672; crusader for peace, 615; and economic issues, 615–618; and Middle East crisis, 621–622; Cabinet, 679

El Alamein, battle of, 585, 587

Elections (congressional), 1866 (versus President Johnson), 347; 1918 (versus President Wilson), 493; 1958 (versus President Eisenhower), 616

Elections (presidential), 1788, 101, 119; 1792, 101, 119; 1796, 126, 135; 1800, 126, 139–140, (map), 139; 1804, 104; 1808, 151; 1812, 153; 1816, 151, 163; 1820, 163; 1824, 172, 202; 1828, 174, 202, (map), 208; 1832, 202, 206, (map), 216; 1836, 202; 1840, 265, 269–270; 1844, 265, 273; 1848, 284, 288; 1852, 284, 298; 1856, 301–302; 1860, 308–309; 1864, 310, 334; 1868, 338, 349, 379; 1872, 338, 351, 379; 1876, 338, 351–352, 379, (map), 384; 1880, 379; 1884, 379; 1888, 379; 1892, 379; 1896, 398, 414–415, (map), 414; 1900, 443–444; 1904, 453, 465–466; 1908, 453, 469; 1912, 453, 475; 1916, 480, 485–486, (map), 485; 1920, 480, 500–501; 1924, 500, 502; 1928, 500, 506; 1932, 520, 531–532, 538; 1936, 537, 554, 555; 1940, 560, 573; 1944, 596; 1948, 601, 609–610; 1952, 601, 613–614; 1956, 601; Appendix IV, 669–672

Electricity for factory power, 358

Elizabeth I, becomes ruler of England, 1; governmental policies, 8–10

Elkins Act, rebate legislation, 467

Ely, Richard T., economist, attacks *laissez faire*, 455

Emancipation of slaves, begins, 81; gradualism or "immediatism," 254–255 (*See also* Abolition; Slavery)

Emancipation Proclamation, preliminary, 310; final, 310, 331

Embargo, Jefferson's, passed, 126; provisions, 148; attacked in New England, 148; success of, 152

Embargo on strategic goods to Japan, beginning of, in 1940, 575–576; effects on Japan, 577

Emergency Fleet Corporation, World War I, 489

Emerson, Ralph Waldo, Phi Beta Kappa Address, 244; and abolition, 255; author, 262–263; (photograph), 262; on Fugitive Slave Law, 294; on John Brown, 305

Emigrant Aid Society aids migration to Kansas, 299

Empress of China, vessel in China trade, 105

England, ancientness of, 1–2; on eve of colonization, 6–11; and settlement of New World, 6–10; and War of 1812, 151; Privy Council, 60; colonial administration, 60–62; Board of Trade, 60; House of Commons and taxation, 61; and international law, 132 (*See also* Great Britain)

English Church, 1 (*See also* Anglican Church)

English heritage, contributions to American liberty, 11–15

Enlightenment, intellectual revolution, 42; nature of, 50–52; and reform, 245

Entail abolished, 81, 98

Equality, social, as American achievement, 628

"Era of Good Feelings," 165; and political confusion, 211

Erie Canal, 188, 232

Erie Railroad, fight for control of, 364

ERP (*see* European Recovery Program)

Erskine fiasco, 151

Europe, contemporary, progress of cooperation in, 623

European age, passing of, 631–632; effects of, on United States, 632

European Recovery Program, announcement by Secretary Marshall, 601; provisions of, 607; Russian criticism of, 607

"Ever-normal granary" crop control program in AAA, 550

Excise tax, proposed by Hamilton, 122; repealed, 143

Executive departments, creation of, 120

Expansion, territorial, before 1860, areas occupied, 267; causes for, 267–268; and "manifest destiny," 267–268, 276–277; attitude of President Polk, 276

Exploration and discovery of New World, preparations for, 2–4

Ezekiel, Mordecai, New Deal economist, 539

Factor, broker for marketing cotton, 228

Factories, conditions in, before 1860, 240

Factors, persistent, in American history, 627–628

Factory system in New England, 361

Fair Labor Standards Act, minimum wage and hours law, 537, 548

Faith as American virtue, 638

Fall, Albert B., Secretary of Interior, and oil scandals, 502

Fall line, 36

Fallen Timbers, battle of, 134

Family life, effects of Great Depression on, 534

Far East, Washington Conference agreements, 509; Manchurian crisis of 1931, 511 (*See also* China; Indo-China; Japan; Korea)

"Far Eastern Munich" rejected by Japan, 577

Farley, James A., politician, 538
Farm bloc in Congress, 504
Farm Board, activities of, under Herbert Hoover, 530
Farm Credit Administration, New Deal measure, 541
Farmers, colonial, 28–29; western, problems of, 225–226; grievances against railroads, 365; grievances of, 400; decline of prices, 401; and railroads, 401; rate grievances, 401–402; taxation, 402–403; lack of credit facilities, 403; and interest rates, 403; currency and money supply, 403–404; silver, 405; tariff, 405; depression in Coolidge era, 503, 504; debt relief under New Deal, 551; increase in income, 550 (See also Agriculture; Homesteaders)
Farmers' alliance movements, 398
Farragut, Admiral David G., Mississippi River campaign, 325
Fascists, seize power in Italy, 561; establish totalitarian government, 561
Faubus, Orval, segregationist Governor of Arkansas, 619–620
Faulkner, William, author, 515; and desegregation, 620
Fear, hysterics of 1920s, 512; as factor in Depression, 527; F. D. Roosevelt on, 540; of war (cartoon), 565
Federal Deposit Insurance Corporation (FDIC), 541
Federal Farm Loan Bank Act (1916), provisions, 477
Federal Highway Act (1916), 477
Federal Reserve Act, listed, 453; purposes and provisions, 477
Federal Reserve Board, and credit regulation, 523; becomes political issue, 1950s, 617
Federal system under Articles of Confederation, 87
Federal Trade Commission (FTC), purposes of, 478
Federalist papers, 101; support Constitution, 113, 116
Federalists, political party, opposition to, 124; split in, 139; conciliated by Jefferson, 143; New England, and War of 1812, 153; demise, 163
Fermi, Enrico, Italian atomic scientist, 596
Feudalism, described, 3; industrial, in South, 356
Fifteenth Amendment submitted to states, 338, 349
"Fifty-four Forty or Fight" as political issue, 276
Filipino insurrection against Americans, 444
Fillmore, Millard, becomes President, 284; nominated by Know-Nothing party, 301, 670; Cabinet, 675
Finance, corporate, beginnings, 238
Finland attacked by Russia, 569
"Fireside chat" of Franklin D. Roosevelt, first, 541
Fisk, James, railraod manipulator, 363, 364
Fitzhugh, George, status after Civil War, 339
5:5:3 naval ratio agreement, 509
Fletcher v. Peck (decision), 165
Flood control program of TVA, 554
Florida, Spanish in, 6; question of, 1783–1819 (map), 162; and disputed election of 1876, 352; real estate boom and bust, 1920s, 515

Florida, West, claimed by Jefferson, 147; American seizure of, 152; acquisition of, 151, 161–162
Foch, Marshall Ferdinand, allied Commander-in-Chief, 492
Foot, Senator Samuel A., resolution on public lands, 216
Force Bill, passed against South Carolina, 115
Ford, Henry, and mass production, 515
Fordney-McCumber tariff act of 1922, 503
Forks of the Ohio, strategic value, 56, 57
Fort Donelson taken by Grant, 325
Fort Duquesne, 57; evacuated by French, 59
Fort Henry taken by Grant, 325
Fort McHenry, British repelled at, 158
Fort Sumter, attacked, 310, 316; significance of, 316
Forts, frontier, under British control, 130; ceded, 133–134
Fourier, Charles, social reformer, 260
Fourteen Points proposed by Wilson, 480, 491, 492
Fourteenth Amendment, proclaimed, 338; provisions of, 346; later application, 346; and Congressional reconstruction, 347; and business corporations, 358, 376
France, areas colonized in New World, 6; expulsion from North America (1763), 60, 61 (See also French and Indian War); alliance with United States (1778), 56, 76; and war threat (1798), 136; undeclared war with (1798–1800), 137; treaty of 1800 with, 126, 138; German attack repulsed in World War I, 489, 490; western front (pictures), 490–491; American troops sent to (1918), 489; defeat of, by Germany in World War II, 569; signs armistice with Germany, 569–570; formation of Vichy regime in, 570; defeated in Indo-China by Japanese, 575; grants naval bases to Japan in Southeast Asia, 576; invasion of Egypt by (1956), 601, 621, 622; repulsed, 622
Franco, Francisco, defeats Spanish Republic, 562
Franklin, Benjamin, experiments, 42; many-sided genius, 51; and French alliance, 76; and Treaty of Paris, 78
Franklin, state of, 182
Free enterprise concept in America, 375 (See also Laissez-faire)
Free School Society organized in New York, 244, 248
"Free ships make free goods," issue with England, (1793–1812), 132
Free Silver movement, 408; in Populist party platform, 411, 412; issue in 1896, 412
Free Soil political party, appears, 265; in 1848 election, 288; gains balance of power, 290
Freedmen in postwar South, 339–340
Freedmen's Bureau, bill passed over Johnson's veto, 345, 347; discontinued, 338, 351
Freedom, basic, in America, 627; political, 630; of discussion, 630; of thought, 630
Freedom of religion, 50; Virginia statute for, 101
Freedom of seas, issue in War of 1812, 153
Freedom of speech, and abolitionists, 244, 256–257; defended by John Quincy Adams, 255
Freedom of thought in old South, 257–258

Freighters, overland, 419–420

Frémont, Captain John C., expedition to California, 280; nominated by Republicans, 284, 301, 670

French and Indian War, beginning, 56; significance, 56; basic issues, 57

French Revolution, beginning of, 126, 129; popularity of, in United States, 129–130; issue in party strife, 130–131

Freneau, Philip, newspaper editor, 137

Frick, H. C., and Homestead strike, 373; (pictures), 374

Frisch, Otto, Jewish atomic scientist, 596

Frontier, influence in America, 19, 622, 627; characteristics, 197; pastimes, 197–198; personalities, 197; religion on, 198–199; posts, dispute with England, 130, 133–134; social experiments, 199; thesis of Frederick J. Turner, 176–177; settlements in New England, 177–178; census reports, end of, 417; end of significance, 430

Frontiers, new, in America, 629–630

Fruit growing in East, 226

Fugitive Slave Law, of 1793, 290; of 1850, 291, 293–294

Fundamentalism in religion, 514

Funding Act, 101 (See also Hamilton, Alexander)

Fur trade issue with British, 130

Fur traders, importance of, 190 (See also American Fur Company; Astor, John Jacob; Hudson's Bay Company)

Gadsden Purchase, treaty, 284; and transcontinental railroad, 298

Gag Resolution denies right of petition, 256

Gage, General Thomas, at Lexington and Concord, 70

Galileo, Italian scientist, 42, 50

Galloway, Joseph, plan of reconciliation, 70

Gangsterism in 1920s, 511, 514

Garfield, James A., elected President, 379, 386, 670; assassinated, 379, 386; Cabinet, 676

Garland, Hamlin, nineteenth-century novelist, 395

Garner, John Nance, Vice President with F. D. Roosevelt, 538

Garrison, William Lloyd, abolitionist and publisher of Liberator, 254; urges disunion, 255

Generosity as American virtue, 637–638

Genêt, Edmond, French envoy, 126; reception of, 131; dismissal of, 131–132

George, David Lloyd (see Lloyd George, David)

George, Henry, publishes Progress and Poverty, 358; single tax idea, 376–377

Georgia, founded, 19; claims jurisdiction over Indians, 173; secession of, 311

Germain, Lord, and War for Independence, 72

Germans, migration to American colonies, 33, 34; settlements on frontier, 177

Germany (See also World War I); Nazi dictatorship established in, 561; rearmament of, 561; occupation of Rhineland zone, 562–563; annexation of Austria, 563; persecution of Jews by Nazis, 568

   in World War II, seizure of Czechoslovakian provinces, 560, 563–564; pact with Soviet, 560, 564, 585; invasion of Poland starts World War II, 560, 564; conquest of Denmark and

Norway, 560, 569; seizure of Belgium and Holland, 569; defeat of France, 560, 569; repulsed by British, 571; invasion of Russia, 574, 585–586; control of Mediterranean at Sicily, 584; defeated in North Africa, 585, 587; defeat and surrender at Stalingrad, 580, 586; plot to assassinate Hitler, 593; concentration camp at Belsen (photograph), 594; allied surrender terms for, 580, 595–596; Battle of the Bulge, 595; final defense of Berlin, 595 (See also World War II)

   after World War II, unification problem, 622 (See also East Germany; Hitler, Adolf; West German Republic)

Gettysburg, battle of, 310; Confederate defeat, 323

Ghent, treaty of, 151, 160

Gibbons v. Ogden (decision), 166

Giddings, Joshua, antislavery Congressman, 288

Gila River Valley purchased from Mexico, 417 (See also Gadsden Purchase)

Gilded Age, named by Mark Twain, 381; cultural aspects, 394–397

Globe, Washington, party newspaper, 209

"Glorious Revolution" in England (1688), 1, 16–17

Godey's Lady's Book, magazine, 250

Godkin, E. L., editor, 385

Gold and money supply, 404

Gold rush, California, 196; Pikes Peak (Colorado), 417, 418; Montana, 417–419; Nevada, 417–419; Idaho, 419; Arizona, 419; Black Hills (Dakota), 419

Gold standard, international, abandonment of, 524, 525

Gold Standard Act, passed 1900, 398

"Golden twenties," 521

Gompers, Samuel, and American Federation of Labor, 374

"Good Neighbor" policy, inaugurated by President Hoover, 511, 528

GOP (see Republican party)

Gould, Jay, railroad manipulator, 363, 364

Governing classes, and American Revolution, 81; and Stamp Act Congress, 81

Government, distrust of, by Americans, 83

Governors, in American colonies, 60, 61; in early state constitutions, 85

Gradualism, emancipation program, 255 (See also Slavery)

Grady, Henry W., and new South, 354

Grand Coulee Dam, Columbia River project (picture), 634

"Grandfather" clauses, suffrage restriction, 356

Grange, founded, 406; objectives, 406; cooperatives, 406; in politics, 406–407; and railroad regulation, 406–407; laws, 406–407; law cases decided (1877), 398, 407

Grant, General Ulysses S., Union commander-in-chief, 323–324; (photograph), 324; career, 324; strategy in Civil War, 324–325; captures Vicksburg, 325; elected President (1868), 338, 349, 379, 670; reelected over Greeley (1872), 338, 351, 379, 384; and political scandals, 382–383; Cabinet, 675–676

"Grantism," 383

Grasshopper invasions on Great Plains, 427

Great American Desert, settlement of, 426
Great Awakening, beginning at Northampton, Mass., 48; influence on frontiers, 49–50
Great Basin, 417
Great Britain, treaty of 1818 with, 161; Oregon treaty with, 265, 276; and Confederate cruisers, 331; signs Munich Pact, 563; seeks alliance with Soviet Russia, 564
    in World War II, German air attacks on, 571; defeats Germans in North Africa, 585
        invasion of Egypt by (1956), 622; repulsed by United Nations, 622; occupation of Jordan (1958), 622 (See also England)
Great Plains, 189; topography and climate, 417
Greece and western civilization, 2
Greeley, Horace, editor New York Tribune, 250; defeated for President by Grant, 351, 384, 670
Green, William, president, American Federation of Labor, 528, 547
Greenback political party, 390–391, 398, 408
Greenville, treaty line of (map), 186
Greenwich Village, "Bohemian" community, 517
Guadalupe Hidalgo, treaty with Mexico, 265, 281
Guam acquired, 432, 443
Guilford Courthouse, battle, 77

"Half-Breeds," political wing, 386
Half-way Covenant adopted, 46
Hamilton, Alexander, plan for a Constitution, 110; rebuffed by House of Representatives, 120; political philosophy, 121; Report on the Public Credit, 122; funding plan and excise tax, 122; and mint, 123; and Bank of the United States, 123; Report on Manufactures, 123; compared with Jefferson, 128–129; and French Revolution, 129
Hamlet, James, fugitive slave, 294
Hancock, Thomas, great wealth, 99
Hand, Judge Learned, on American democracy, 626
Hanna, Marcus A. (Mark), McKinley campaign manager, 415; opinion of T. Roosevelt, 463
Harding, Warren G., nomination of, 500–501; elected President, 500, 671; reputation, 502; scandals, 502; death, 500, 502; Cabinet, 678 (See also Republican party)
Harper's monthly magazine, 250, 385, 456
Harrison, Benjamin, elected President, 379, 388, 671; Cabinet, 676
Harrison, William Henry, and western Indian policy, 154; general in War of 1812, 157; elected President, 265, 269–270, 670; death of, 270; Cabinet, 674
Hartford Convention (1780), resolutions of, 94
Hartford Convention (1814), 151, 157; failure of, of, 211
Harvard College, founded, 42; (illustration), 47
Hawaii, annexation defeated under Cleveland, 432, 438; republic established, 438; Hawaiian revolution of 1891, 437–438; acquisition of, 437; gains statehood in 1959, 445, 667
Hawthorne, Nathaniel, Blithedale Romance, 260; (photograph), 261
Hay-Pauncefote Treaty on inter-American canal, 432, 449
Hayes, Rutherford B., wins disputed election (1876), 338, 379, 670; and civil service reform, 384–385; career, 385–386; (photograph),

385; withdraws troops from the South, 352; suppresses strikes, 373; Cabinet, 676
Haymarket riots in Chicago, 373
Hayne, Senator Robert Y., debate with Webster, 216
Head rights system in Virginia, 24; discarded, 35
"Heartland," industrial area of United States, 358–359
Helena, Mont., mining center, 419
"Hell on wheels," railroad construction towns, 421
Hemingway, Ernest, novelist, 515, 516
Henderson, Richard, settlement in Kentucky, 180–181
Henry VII, King of England, reign of, 6–8
Henry VIIII, King of England, accession, 1; reign of, 6–7
Henry the Navigator, Prince of Portugal, 5
Henry, Patrick, refusal to attend Constitutional Convention, 109
Hepburn Act, railroad rate regulation, 453, 467
Hermitage, home of Andrew Jackson, 204
Herrick, Robert, muckraker novelist, 458
High Commission, Court of, in England, 11
High school, public, beginnings, 247
Hillman, Sidney, president, Amalgamated Clothing Workers, 547
Hiroshima destroyed by atom bomb (1945), 596
Hitler, Adolf, plans for German expansion, 562; seizes Rhineland area, 560, 563; annexes Austria, 563; gains Czechoslovakian provinces at Munich, 563; defeats France in World War II, 569–570; invasion of Russia, 574; bombing of England, 584; attempted assassination of, 593; suicide of, 595 (See also Germany)
Holladay, Ben, transportation mogul, 419
Holmes, Justice Oliver Wendell, and business, 376; concept of law, 460; (photograph), 462
Home Owners' Loan Corporation (HOLC), 541
Homestead, Penna., steel strike, 373; (pictures), 374
Homestead Act, 184–185; in politics, 298–299; passed, 1860, 332; and Republicans, 341; enlarged act for arid states, 429
Homesteaders, on Great Plains, 426; boom period, 426; hardships, 427; depression, 427
Hooker, General Joseph, defeated at Chancellorsville, 323
Hoover, Herbert, Republican nominee in 1928, 506; career and Secretary of Commerce, 506; elected President, 506, 678; and "Good Neighbor" policy, 511; career and reputation, 528; social philosophy of, 528, 529; (photograph), 529; attitude toward unemployment relief, 530; Cabinet, 678
Hopkins, Harry, New Deal leader, 539; administration of WPA, 544
Hopkinson, Joseph, song writer, 136
House, Colonel Edward M., peace mission to England, 486
House of Commons in England, 61
Howe, General William, battle of Long Island, 75; British capture of Philadelphia, 75
Howells, William Dean, nineteenth-century novelist, 395
Hudson's Bay Company in Oregon, 192, 275

Hughes, Charles Evans, Secretary of State, and Washington Disarmament Conference, 509

Hull, Cordell, Senator and Secretary of State, 538

"Hundred Days," New Deal emergency Congress, significance of, 542

Hungary, revolution in, suppressed by Soviet Russia, 601, 622

Hydrogen bomb, destructive threat of, 609

Icarian settlements, utopian movement, 260

Ickes, Harold, New Deal leader, 539; Secretary of Interior and Director of PWA, 545–546

Idaho, territory, 419; statehood, 427

I'll Take My Stand, southern manifesto on modern society, 518

Illinois, slavery legalized, 187; early development, 188; canal system, 233–234

Immigrants, effects on labor, 240; and industrial revolution, 359, 361; and labor, 371; percentage of, in population (1820–1860), 371; and urban growth, 381; and social Darwinism, 381; in Mulberry Street, New York City (picture), 380; influence of, in American history, 627

Immigration, restrictions in 1921 and 1924, 500, 513; quota system adopted, 513–514; 1840–1941 (diagram), 513; settlements on Great Plains, 426–427; Japanese and California, 448; 1820–1955 (chart), 685

Impeachment, in England, 13; used by Jefferson, 126, 144–145; of President Johnson, 338 (photograph), 348

Imperialism, revival of interest in, reasons for, 440; issue in 1900 election, 443 (See also Aryan supremacy; Mahan, Alfred; Manifest destiny; Roosevelt, Theodore; Social Darwinism)

Implements, farm, 224, 225

Import, proposal for levy under Articles of Confederation, 94, 96, 97

Impressment, issue with England, 1793–1812, 132; 1806–1807, 148, 153

Income, distribution of, in 1920s, 523; national and farmers, 399; national, per capita, 1870–1950 (diagram), 557

Incorporation laws passed by states, 217, 220–221

Indentured servants in American colonies, 33

Independence, Declaration of (see Declaration of Independence)

Independent treasury established, 273; political issue, 273

Indians, trade in French and Indian War, 57; as factor in War of 1812, 153–154; removals and land cessions, 154, 173, 176, 188; Seminole, 161; Sioux, 417; Plains, 422; obtain citizenship, 423; Indian Territory opened for settlers, 428–429; merged with Oklahoma, 429; Dawes Act, 417, 423; Indian Reorganization Act of 1924, 423–424; Act of 1934, 417

Indigo, colonial product, 27

Indo-China, civil war in (1954), 601, 620

Industrial growth in nineteenth century, 453–454; accompanying evils, 453–454

Industrial production in Great Depression (diagram), 532

Industrial revolution, effects on labor, 372

Industrial unions (see Committee for Industrial Organization)

Industrial Workers of the World (IWW), 376, 504, 512

Industry, expansion of, 1800–1860, 223; "revolution," 1850–1910, 358–362; "heartland" region, significance of, 358–359; in South, characteristics of, 358; corporate organization, 312; rapid growth, 1860–1900, 398; factors favoring, 398; interdependence with agriculture, 399; in World War I, 489; "the second industrial revolution," 514; Truman's attempt to seize steel industry, 603; diffusion of, in mid-twentieth century, 634; depressed conditions in (1929), 522–523; automobile, in 1920s, 522–523; construction, in 1920s, 523; power of, at end of nineteenth century, 454 (See also Monopoly; Trusts; names of specific corporations)

Inflation, and American Revolution, 88; monetary, issue in mid-1950s, 616–617; efforts to control, 617; problem of, in United States, 602–603

Injunction, use of, in labor disputes, 374; prohibited, 505; in Pullman strike, 410

Installment plan system of buying, 526

Institutes for adult education, 250

Insurgents, revolt in Republican Party, 473

Intellectual ferment in 1830s, 244–245; (map), 256

Interchangeable parts for machinery, 237

Internal improvements, favored by Calhoun, 163; and sectionalism (chart), 212; bill of 1846, vetoed by Polk, 274–275

International Ladies' Garment Workers, industrial union of, 547

Internationalism, United States as pattern of, 638

Interposition, doctrine of, 148

Interstate Commerce Act, passed, 365, 379; weaknesses, 365, 390; implications of, 407–408

Intervention, American policy in Central America, 451

Intolerable Acts, passed, 56; provisions, 64, 68; applied to Massachusetts, 70

Intolerance, Puritan, 25; racial and religious, feature of 1920s, 513

Investment, capital, as factor in modern economy, 523; in Europe in 1920s, 525

"Invisible government," 382; attacked by progressive reformers, 454 (See also Bosses)

Iron, furnace for pig iron, 223, 237; manufactures in South before 1860, 239; ore, Mesabi range deposits, 358–359

Iron Act, colonial, 31

Iroquois in French and Indian War, 57

Irrigation, Carey Act, 417, 429–430; Newlands Act, 429–430; used by Mormons, 430; projects in Columbia River valley, 554

Irving, Washington, author, 261

"Island hopping" in Pacific, 590

Isolation, period of, 1865–1898, 432; reasons for, 433–434; mood of 1920s, reasons for, 507; and Republicans, 500–501

Isolationism, definition of term, 565n.; prevalence of sentiment after World War I, 565, 566; causes of, 565; and Neutrality Acts, 567; "Isolated Isolationist" (cartoon), 573; abandonment of, 636

Israel, feud with Arabs over refugees, 621–622; invasion of Egypt by, 622; withdrawal of, 622

Italian cities and Crusades, 3
Italy, invades Ethiopia, 562; attacks France, 569; in World War II, extent of conquests, 583–584; checked by Greeks in Balkans, 584; defeated by British in North Africa, 584; defeat of navy, 584; final conquest of (1943–1944), 588 (*See also* Mussolini, Benito)
IWW (*see* Industrial Workers of the World)

Jackson, Andrew, ancestry, 203–204; career, 203–204; Florida campaign, 162; defeats southwest Indians, 188; wins battle of New Orleans, 159; election campaign of 1828, 174, 669, Cabinet, 674; ushers in new democracy, 201–202; first modern President, 205; significance of his presidency, 221–222; military reputation, asset, 204–205; reliance on newspapers and editors, 209; "Kitchen Cabinet," 209; reelected 1828, 215; proclamation against nullification in South Carolina, 215; and *laissez faire* doctrine, 218; veto of Maysville Road bill, significance, 217; veto of Bank recharter bill, significance, 218–219
Jackson, General Thomas J. (Stonewall), defeats McClellan before Richmond, 323
Jacksonian democracy, borrowed from Jefferson, 203; bases of, 218; and majority rule, 203; use of political patronage, 208; suffrage broadened, 205–206; increased interest in politics, 206–207; role of party press, 209; "rotation in office," 207–208; "spoils system," 207–209; justification for, 209; and economic freedom, 203, 217; historic significance of, 221–222
James I, King of England, first Stuart King, 1; date, 7; on religion, 11
James II, King of England, 1; date, 7
James, Henry, nineteenth-century philosopher, 395; and pragmatism, 396
Jamestown, Virginia colony, 19, 20
Japan, war with Russia, 447–448; and Washington Conference agreements, 509; clash with China in Manchuria, 511; aggressive policy of, inaugurated in Far East (1931), 560–561; invades Manchuria and creates satellite state, 561; joins Rome-Berlin axis, 564; terminates Washington naval agreements, 561; withdraws from League of Nations, 562; invades North China, 562; establishes "Co-Prosperity Sphere" in Southeast Asia, 575; secret code broken by United States, 576; opposed by United States in China policy, 575–577; attack on Pearl Harbor, 560, 577; conquests after Pearl Harbor, 581–582; final defeat of, in Pacific war, 590–593, 597–598; suicide dive bombers (photograph), 592; World War II surrender of, 602
Japanese immigrants excluded (1924), 514n.
Jay, John, and Treaty of Paris, 78; (map), 134; treaty with England, 126, 133–134
"Jazz age" of 1920s, 511
Jefferson, Thomas, description and appraisal of, 126–127; Secretary of State, 126, 129, 673; and Hamiltonian program, 127–129; arguments against the Bank, 124; opposition to Hamiltonian program, 124; fear of monopoly, 124; Vice President, 135; political theory of, 126–129, 141; elected President, 1800, 126, 669; 1804, 146; Cabinet, 673; presidential policies, 142–143; conciliates Federalists, 143; retirement, 149; opposition to slavery, 266; opinion on Missouri Compromise, 285
Jefferson, state of, 418
Jefferson Day dinner, political crisis, 217
Jeffersonian Republican party, formed, 139; in 1815, 163
Jews, persecution of, by Nazis, 568; number murdered, 594n.
"Jim Crow" laws in South, 356; discriminatory practices against Negroes, 618; breakdown of, in higher education, 618 (*See also* Segregation)
Johns Hopkins University, founded, 379; graduate school, 395, 396
Johnson, Andrew (photograph), 343; early career, 343; social attitudes, 343–344; political views, 344; failure as leader, 346; becomes President, 1865, 338; quarrels with Congress, 338, 342, 343–346; Reconstruction program blocked by Congress, 344–345; impeachment of, 338, 348; Cabinet, 675; impeachment managers (photograph), 348
Johnson, Hiram M., isolationist, 500
Johnson, General Hugh, NRA administration, 544
Johnson, Tom, reform mayor of Cleveland, 461
Johnston, General Joseph E., replaced by Lee, 323
Joint Committee on Reconstruction, 345
Joint Defense Board with Canada in World War II, 571
Joint-stock companies, agencies in colonization, 4, 8, 20
Jones, Samuel ("Golden Rule"), reform mayor of Toledo, 461
Josephson, Matthew, *Portrait of the Artist as American,* 517
Judicial review, and Constitution, 114; controversy, 167
Judiciary Act of 1789, provisions, 121
Judiciary Act of 1801 repealed, 143
Jury, trial by, 13
Justices of peace, county officers, 39
Juvenile delinquency, problem of, 633
Juveniles in 1920s, 514

Kamikaze, Japanese suicide bombing (picture), 592
Kansas, "bleeding," issue, 284, 299–300; statehood, 418; homesteader rush to, 426
Kansas-Nebraska Act, passed, 284; effects of, 297
Kearny, Colonel Stephen, expedition to California, 280
Keating-Owen child labor bill voided, 478
Kelley, Oliver Hudson, founder of Grange, 406
Kellogg-Briand Peace Pact of 1928, 500; signing (picture), 510; significance of, 510
Kelly, William, invents blast furnace, 237
Kentucky, first settlements in, 181; statehood, 182–183; secession defeated, 316
Kentucky and Virginia Resolutions, passed, 126; contents, 138
Keynes, John Maynard, *The General Theory of Employment, Interest, and Money,* 528; advocates deficit spending, 545–546; and recovery under New Deal, 558
"Keynesian revolution" as permanent feature of American system, 633
King's College (Columbia University), 45

King's Mountain, battle, 77
"Kitchen Cabinet" of Andrew Jackson, 209
Knickerbocker school, New York group of authors, 261
Knights of Labor, organized, 358; growth and decline, 373
Knights of White Camelia, organized in postwar South, 351
Know-Nothing political party, 244, 253
Knudson, William, head, Office of Production Management, 581
Korea, partitioned in World War II, 610; outbreak of war in (1950), 601, 610; military actions of United Nations, 611–612; intervention by Communist China, outcome, 612; effects and significance of, 613
Korea, North, pro-Communist puppet state, 605; refugee children (picture), 613
Kossuth, Louis, Hungarian patriot in America, 246
Ku Klux Klan, organized, 338, 351; revival of, in 1920s, 500, 502, 513; (picture), 512

Labor, problem in colonial period, 32, 33; "contract" status of, 321; division of, 238; factory worker before 1860, 240–241; shortage of, in agriculture, 224; ten-hour day in government work granted, 242; discontent in 1920s, 504; under New Deal, 546–547; cooperation with management in World War II, 582; unions (see Unions)
Labor parties, early, influence of, 241; weaknesses, 241–242
LaFollette, Robert M., political reformer, 390; and Interstate Commerce Act, 390; reform governor of Wisconsin, 461; progressive leader, 472–473; isolationist, 500; heads Farmer-Labor ticket in 1924, 503
LaFollette Seamen's Act (1915), 478
Laissez faire, basis of Jackson's economic policy, 218–219; in postwar South, 340; challenged by "Social Gospel," 377; Democratic principle, 380; and Interstate Commerce Act, 408; attacks on, 454–455, 459; decline in progressive era, 464; attitude of Herbert Hoover toward, 529; effects of Great Depression on, 535
Lancastrian system of instruction in public schools, 248
Land, influence in America, 23, 24, 40; colonial systems of, 24; western claims and cessions by states (map), 99; claims, western, ceded by states, 102; public, policies 1785–1862 (chart), 185; prices, and sectionalism (chart), 212; policies of the United States, 1865–1916 (chart), 428
Land Act for cattlemen, 429
Land banks, colonial, 29; controversy in Massachusetts, 38
Land Law of 1820, 176
Land Ordinance of 1785, provisions, 102–103
Landon, Alfred M., Republican candidate in 1936, 555, 672
Lane Seminary, abolitionist center, 255
Latter Day Saints (see Mormons)
Law, American, relation to English law, 12; English concepts of, 12
Lawrence, Kans., sack of, 299–300
League of Nations, idea of, 494–495; organization of, 495; opposition to, in Senate, 495–496; defeated in Senate, 497; issue in 1920 campaign, 501
Learning, valuation of, in America, 629
Lease, Mary Elizabeth, populist leader, 411
Lebanon occupied by United States Marines (1958), 622
Lee, Richard Henry, resolution for independence, 74; leading antifederalist, 116
Lee, General Robert E., and initiative in Civil War, 319; becomes Confederate commander, 323; second northern offensive, 323; defeated at Gettysburg, 323; (photograph), 323; surrender of, 323
Legal protections in American system of government, 631
Legislatures, colonial, 68; in early state constitutions, 85
Lehigh Coal Company, pioneer company, 238
Leisure time, problem of, in America, 633
Lend-lease aid program for Allies, 560, 573–574
Lenin, Nikolai, Russian Communist leader, 488
Lewis, John L., president, United Mine Workers, 547
Lewis, Sinclair, novelist, 515, 516; Babbitt, 517; Nobel prize winner, 518
Lewis and Clark explore far West, 146, 176, 189; (map), 190
Lewiston, Idaho, mining center, 419
Lexington, battle of, 56, 70; (illustration), 71; (map), 72
Lexington, Mass., normal school established, 249
Liberal Republicans, political party, significance of, 351; oppose President Grant, 384
Liberator, abolitionist newspaper, 254
Liberty League, anti-New Deal Republican organization, 555
Liberty Party, appearance of, 265; in campaign of 1840, 270; strength in 1840, 273
Libraries, public and subscription, 250
Lien laws to protect labor, 241
Lilienthal, David, New Deal leader, 539; director of TVA, 553
Liliuokalani, Hawaiian queen, 437; deposed, 438
Lincoln, Abraham, opposes Mexican War, 281; debates with Douglas, 284, 304; reputation in 1860, 307; minority president in 1860, 308; political career, 314; appearance, 314; position in 1861, 314; elected President, 284, 670; Cabinet, 675; concept of Union, 286–287, 315; use of patronage, 315; difficulties with Seward, 315; and Fort Sumter, 316; war preparations, 316; leadership of, in Civil War, 318–319; and "a government of the people," 336; reelected, 310; assassination of, 310, 338; policy toward slaves in Civil War, 350–351; Reconstruction program, 341–343
Lindbergh, Charles A., transatlantic flight (1927), 511, 514
Lippman, Walter, author and journalist, 518
Literary tradition, lack of, in United States, 261
Literature, creative, in 1920s, 515; contemporary American, quality of, 636
Little Rock, Ark., school segregation in, 619–620
Livestock, improvement of, 225
Living standards, improvement of, during World War II, 581; as goal in America, 628

Lloyd, Henry Demarest, attacks trusts, 389; and "good society," 390
Lloyd George, David, at Paris Peace Conference, 492–493
Loans to Allies in World War I, 484
Local government, colonial, in South, 39
Lochner v. New York (decision), 462
Locke, John, *Two Treatises on Civic Government,* influence in America, 17; writings, 42, 51; and revolution, 47; and the Enlightenment, 51; his philosophy, 51; and Declaration of Independence, 74
Locomotive, steam, 235 (illustration), 235
Lodge, Henry Cabot, reservations to League Covenant, 496
"Log cabin" political campaign, 265, 269–270; (illustration), 269
Log rolling on frontier, 198
London, Jack, muckraking novelist, 458
London Economic Conference, significance of, 542
Long, Huey P., Louisiana "Kingfish" and Senator, 535; "share the wealth" program, 548
Long Island, battle of, 75
Longfellow, Henry W., and abolition, 255
Longstreet, General James B., Confederate commander, 324
Louisiana, and disputed election of 1876, 352
Louisiana Purchase, 126, 145, 176; constitutional question, 146; historical background of, 145–146; (map), 145; significance of, 146
Lovejoy, Elijah, antislavery editor, 256
Lowell, James Russell, abolitionist, 255
Lowell, Mass., cotton mills, 223; ideal conditions in, 240–241
Lowell Institute, Boston, 250
Lowndes, William, introduces tariff bill, 163
Loyalists, in North Carolina, 38; treatment of, during American Revolution, 82, 98; property confiscated, 81
Lundy, Benjamin, antislavery editor, 254
Lusitania sunk by Germans, 483
Luther, Martin, and Protestant revolt, 42
Lyceum movement, significance and influence, 250

Macadam, John L., road builder, 232
MacArthur, Douglas, conquers Philippines, 592; commander in Korean War, 611
McCardle case, *habeas corpus* decision, 347
McCarthy, Joseph R., Senator from Wisconsin, 614; struggle with White House, 615; censured by Senate, 615
McClellan, General George B., peninsular campaign, 323; Democratic candidate in 1864, 334
McClure's, muckraker periodical, 456
McCulloch v. Maryland (decision), 151, 166
MacDonough, Captain Thomas, repulses British on Lake Champlain, 158
McGuffey, William, *Eclectic Readers,* 249
Machinery, factory, power-driven, 223
McKinley, William, Republican nominee in 1896, 413; "front porch" campaign, 415; elected President, 415, 671; Cabinet, 677; intervenes in Cuba, 441; declares war on Spain, 441; assassinated, 447, 453, 463
McKinley tariff bill, 389
McLoughlin, Dr. John, Hudson's Bay Company agent, 192

McNary-Haugen farm bill, vetoed by Coolidge, 500, 504
Macon's Bill, No. 2, 151, 152
Macune, C. W., plan for currency reform, 412
Madison, James, "Father of the Constitution," 109; notes on the Constitution, 110; split with Hamilton, 124; elected President, 151, 669; Cabinet, 673
Magazines, early monthlies, 250
Magellan, Ferdinand, voyage, 1, 5
Magna Carta, granted, 1; and American rights, 14–15
"Magna Carta" of labor, 478
Mahan, Captain Alfred T., urges American expansion, 439
Maine, boundary adjusted, 161; and Missouri Compromise, 168; adopts prohibition, 252
Maine, battleship, sunk in Havana, 441; "Remember the Maine" slogan, 441
Malta, British base successfully defended, 584
Manassas, first battle of, 321 (*See also* Bull Run)
Manchuria, Japan-China crisis of 1931, 511; stripped by Soviet Russia, 605
"Manifest destiny," phrase appears, 265; justifications for, 267–268; and law of nature, 268; and James K. Polk, 276; revival of, in 1890s, 439
Manila Bay, battle of, 439, 442
Mann, Horace, school reforms, 244, 247, 249
Mann-Elkins Act, railroad regulation, 470
Manufactures, Report on, by Alexander Hamilton, 101, 123
Manufactures, development (1840–1860), 239; areas of concentration, 239; growth of, in United States, Germany, England, compared (chart), 362
Marbury v. Madison (decision), 126, 144
March, William, novelist, 635
Margin buying in stock market, 523
Marietta, first settlement in Ohio, 184
Markets, for agricultural products, in North, 224; in South, 226–228; and industrial revolution, 360
Marshall, George C., Chief of Staff, testimony on Pearl Harbor attack, 578; in World War II, 587; and ERP program, 606
Marshall, John, Chief Justice, and judicial review, 114; influence, 163; great decisions, 164–167; attacks on, 167
Marx, Karl, and labor movement, 375; and capitalism, 376
Maryland, first settlement, 19; secession defeated, 311, 316
"Mass" as symbol of modern America, 635
Mass production in industry, 515
Massachusetts, colony, and Intolerable Acts, 70; repeal of law allowing religious instruction, 244; effect of law on Catholics, 248
Massachusetts Bay settlement, 19
"Massive resistance," segregation movement in Virginia, 620
Mather, Increase and Cotton, defenders of Puritanism, 46, 47
Maximilian, Emperor of Mexico, 434
Maysville Road bill, veto by Andrew Jackson, 217–218, 232
Meade, General George B., Union commander at Gettysburg, 323

Meat Inspection Act, federal, 468
Mechanical corn picker (illustration), 617
Mechanics' institutes, adult schools, 250
Mediation proposal of Woodrow Wilson, 480, 486
Medieval civilization and medieval synthesis, 1
Meitner, Lise, atomic scientist, 596
Mellon Art Gallery, Washington, D.C., 397
Melville, Herman, author, 262
Mencken, Henry L., author, 511, 516–517
Mercantilism, basic principles, 30, 31; effects on the colonies, 30–32
"Merit system," 385 (See also Civil Service Commission)
Merrimac, battle with Monitor, 318
Mesabi range, iron ore, 358–359
Methodists, mission in Oregon, 193; success on frontier, 199
Mexican War, origins of, 265, 277; military campaigns, 278–280, 282; unpopularity of, 280–281; political effects, 281–283
Mexico, Spanish conquest of, 5; French intervention in, 432–434; American investments in, 434; revolution of 1911, 481
Mexico City captured by General Scott, 265, 280
Michelson and Morley, experiments in light, 395
Michigan, statehood, 188
Middle colonies, agriculture, 28
Middle East, Egyptian crisis of 1956, 601, 621–622; Lebanon-Jordan crisis of 1958, 622
Midway Island, claimed, 443; battle of, 590
Millbury, Mass., first lyceum started in, 250
Miller, Henry, and "massism," 635
Milligan, ex parte, Supreme Court decision, 347
Mining, spread of, 419 (See also Gold rush)
Minnesota, development, 188; statehood, 189
Minorities, rights of, in America, 631
Mint, establishment of, 123
Minutemen in American Revolution, 72
Miranda, Francisco, Latin American leader, 137
Missiles, nuclear warheads, 609
Mississippi, development of, 188; "Black Code," 344–345
Mississippi River, problem of, during Confederation, 107; mouth controlled by Spanish, 130, Union control of, 270
Missouri, development of, 188; secession defeated, 316
Missouri Compromise, 151; background of, 168; merits of, 169; significance, 170; effect on attitudes toward slavery, 266; relation to Civil War, 285; repeal of, 297; declared unconstitutional, 303
Missouri Fur Company, 190
Molasses Act, colonial, 32
Money, in American Revolution, 88; coinage system established, 123; kinds of, 1860–1900, 403–405; farmers' grievances concerning, 404
"Money trust" investigated, 370
Monitor, gunboat, significance of, 318
Monopoly, Standard Oil Company of Ohio, 365–368; United States Steel Company, 368–369; tariff as form of, 387; investigation of, 389; issue in politics, 1888, 389; under Theodore Roosevelt, 466; Sherman Anti-Trust law, 390–391; Clayton Anti-Trust Act, 478; extent of (chart), 367

Monroe, James, elected President, 151, 217, 669; Cabinet, 673; achievements, 163
Monroe Doctrine, 151; background of, 170; principles, 171; opposed by Latin America, 435; extended by Cleveland, 436; Roosevelt corollary to, 432, 449–451
Montana, territory, 419; statehood, 427
Montdidier, World War I battle, 489
Montesquieu, Baron de, influence in America, 58; influence on American Constitution, 113
Montgomery, Bernard, British general, defeats Germans in North Africa, 585, 587
Montgomery, General Richard, killed at Quebec battle, 73
Monticello, home of Jefferson, 142, 149
Morgan, J. P., and railroad consolidation, 365–366; forms United States Steel Company, 369; as a great power, 370
Morgenthau, Henry S., Jr., plan for defeat of Germany, 594
Morgenthau, Henry S., Sr., favors harsh peace with Germany, 491
Mormons, persecutions and migrations, 193–194; migrations (map), 195; migration to Utah, 195–196; organize state, 195; war with United States, 195; social organization, 195–196; church founded, 244; tabernacle (picture), 194
Morocco, crisis of 1905–1906, and Theodore Roosevelt, 480–481
Morrill Land Grant Act for land grant colleges (1862), 332; and Republicans, 341
Morrill Tariff Act of 1861, significance, 332
Morris, Robert, and American Revolution, 82; leader of conservatives, 95; Superintendent of Finance in 1781, 96; creates Bank of North America, 96; plan to strengthen Articles of Confederation, 96–97; great wealth, 99
Morse, Samuel F. B., invents telegraph, 236
Morton, Oliver P., Republican boss, 383
Motley, John Lothrop, historian, 262n.
Mott, Lucretia, reform leader, 252
Mount Holyoke, first women's college, 244, 249
Muckraker periodicals, 456–457; writers, 457, 458
"Mud-sill" theory concerning slavery, 258
Mugwump revolt in GOP (1884), 379, 386
Mulberry Street, New York City, ca. 1900 (picture), 380
Mule skinners, drivers, 420
Munich pact, signed, 563; defense of, 563; signatories (picture), 563; effect of, on United States policy, 568
Munn v. Illinois, Granger case, 407
Munsey's, periodical, 456
Muscle Shoals, power site, 552
Mussolini, Benito, Italian fascist leader, 561; attacks Ethiopia, 562; defies League of Nations, 562; makes alliance with Hitler, 562; failure of Mediterranean offensive, 585; deposition of, 588; captured and executed, 595 (See also Italy)
Mutiny by soldiers in Philadelphia, 81
Myers, Gustavus, muckraker and historian, 460

Nagasaki destroyed by atom bomb (1945), 596
Napoleon Bonaparte, Continental System, 148
Napoleon III of France intervenes in Mexico, 434

Napoleonic Wars, effects of renewal on United States, 148; end of, 151

Nashville, Tenn., beginning of settlement, 181; government formed, 181; and desegregation, 620

Nashville convention and crisis of 1850, 290

Nasser, Abdel, Egyptian nationalist leader, 621; nationalizes Suez Canal, 621

Nathan, Robert, New Deal economist, 539

Nation, The, periodical, 385

National Association for Advancement of Colored People (NAACP), to defend civil rights, 619

National Banking Acts (1863–1864), and Republicans, 341; provisions, 353; operation of, 404

National City Bank and "money trust," 370

National income, redistribution of, under New Deal, 545, 546

National Labor Relations Board (NLRB), to safeguard collective bargaining, 537, 546

National Progressive Republican League formed (1912), 472

National Prohibition Party, 505

National Recovery Administration (NRA), purposes and administration of, 543–544; declared unconstitutional, 544

National Republicans, political party (see Whigs)

National Road, importance, 232

National Socialist party, takes control in Germany, 561; policies of, 561 (See also Germany; Hitler, Adolf)

Nationalism, American, rise of, after 1815, 162–165; New, program launched by Theodore Roosevelt, 474–475

Nationalist China, American policy toward, 608–609; established on Formosa, 609

Nativism, anti-Catholic, 252; and immigrant labor, 371; movement in 1920s, 512

Natural law, English concept of, 12

Natural rights, English concept of, 12

Naturalization Act of 1798, 137; repealed, 143

Naval disarmament, Washington Conference agreements, 509

Navigation, improvements in technical devices, 4

Navigation Acts, purposes and provisions, 31; benefits to colonies, 32

Navy, British, in World War I, 485

Navy, United States (see various wars, e.g., World War II)

Navy Department established, 137

Nazi rule in Germany (see Germany)

Nebraska, "bleeding" in, 299; homesteader rush to, 426

Negroes, intimidated in South, 351; effects of Great Depression on, 534–535 (See also Freedmen; Segregation; Slavery; Slaves; Suffrage)

Nelson, Donald M., head of War Production Board, 581

Neutral rights, issue with England (1793–1812), 132–133

Neutrality, proclamation of (1793), 126, 130; policies in World War I, 483–485

Neutrality Act of 1935, 565–566

Neutrality Act of 1937, provisions of, 566; failure of policy, 566–567; debate over, in Congress, 568; invoked against European belligerents (1939), 568–569

Neutrals, plight of (1805–1807), 148

Nevada, mining rush in, 418; statehood, 419

New Deal, and Herbert Hoover, 529; sources of, 520, 538–539; launching of, 550–551; identification of leaders, 539; emergency program of, 540–542; legislation, principal measures listed, 537 (See also individual agencies, laws, and projects); recovery program of, 543–545; progress under, 557–558; and capitalist system, 541, 558

New England, colonial, fisheries, 28; shipping and commerce, 28; triangular trade, 28; social classes, 36; township system, 36, 37; town meetings, 40;
opposition to embargo, 148–149; opposition to War of 1812, 157; frontier towns, 177–178; factory system in, 361

New England Confederation, 19, 43

New Hampshire ratifies Constitution, 101

New Harmony, utopian settlement in Indiana, 244, 260

"New Lights" defined, 49

New Mexico, acquired, 176; and Compromise of 1850, 289, 291

New Orleans, battle of, 151, 158

New York Central railroad, consolidation of, 365

New York Herald, newspaper, 250

New York Sun, newspaper, 249

New York Tribune, influence of, 250

Newlands Act, federal irrigation projects, 417; and Reclamation Service, 468

Newspapers, first published in Boston, 42; use of party press, 209; spread of daily, 249; in New York, 249–250

Newton, Isaac, laws of motion, 42, 50, 51

Nonintercourse Act, provisions, 151; renewal of, against Great Britain, 152

"Normalcy" and President Harding, 500

Norris, Frank, novelist, 458

Norris, George W., Senator, public power advocate, 558

Norris–La Guardia Act, use of injunctions in labor disputes, 505

North, Lord, British Prime Minister, peace proposals, 76

"North American Phalanx" in New Jersey, 260

North American Review, limited appeal of, 456

North Atlantic Treaty Organization (NATO), launched, 601; and problem of European union, 623

North Carolina, Regulator movement, 38, 179; secession of, 316

Northampton, Mass., revival of religion at, 48

Northern Pacific Railroad, transcontinental line, 421

Northern Securities Company dissolved, 466

Northwest, Old, governmental provisions, 183; system of land survey, 184; prices of land, 184–185; pattern of settlement, 185–186; Virginian influence, 186; later development, 188; divided with states, 188–189; (map), 180

Northwest frontier posts held by British, 107

Northwest Ordinance (1787), 101; provisions, 103–104; significance of, 104, 183

Northwestern Alliance of farmers, 411

Norway conquered by Germany, 560, 569
Nullification, in Virginia and Kentucky Resolutions, 138; theory formulated by Calhoun, 214; purposes of, 215

Oberlin College, first coeducational college, 249
Ogden, Utah, junction point of transcontinental railroads, 421
Ohio, first settlement in, 176; pattern of settlement, 184; (map), 186; significance as a western community, 187; statehood, 187; first constitution, 187; bill of rights, 187; canal system in, 233
Ohio Company of Boston, speculative purchase, 184; (map), 186
Ohio Company of Virginia, grant from British Crown, 57
"Ohio Gang," Harding crowd, 502
Oil, discovery of, 358
O. K., origin of expression, 270
Oklahoma, territory organized, 429; statehood, 429; opened for settlers, 417, 423, 429
"Old Lights" defined, 29
Old Northwest (see Northwest)
Old South, conservatism, 258–259; social structure in, 258–259
Old Spanish Trail, 192
Old West, located and described, 177; settlement of, 177; consequences of, 177
Olney, Richard, and extension of Monroe Doctrine, 436
Omaha Beach, Normandy invasion site, 590
Open Door, notes sent, 432, 447
Open Door policy guaranteed by Washington Conference, 509
Open shop principle and labor, 504
Operation Overlord, cross-channel offensive, 590
Oregon, joint occupation of, 161, 275; agreement, 192–193; Spanish claims acquired, 162; acquired from Britain, 176; boundaries of, 192; claimants of, 192; statehood, 193; migrations to, 193; American and British rivalry, 275; acquisition by United States, 265, 275–276; as political issue, 276
Oregon Trail (map), 191
Organization for European Economic Cooperation (OEEC), 606
Osborn v. Bank of the United States (decision), 166
Osgood, Samuel, opposes plan of Robert Morris, 97
Owen, Robert, New Harmony settlement, 244, 260
Owen, Robert Dale, Scottish philanthropist, 260

Pacific Coast valleys, 418
Pacific Islands acquired by United States (map), 438
Pacific Railway act passed, 417, 420 (See also Transcontinental railroad)
Pacific War (see United States, and World War II)
Packing industry, division of labor in, 238
Paine, Thomas, Common Sense, 73; attitude toward conservatives during American Revolution, 93
Palmer, A. Mitchell, and censorship, 501
Panama, revolution in (1903), 432
Panama Canal controversy with Colombia, 449

Panama Congress and John Quincy Adams, 172–173
Pan-American Conference, first (1889), 432; in Washington, 435
Panic of 1819, 151, 164; effects on West, 164; and sectional animosity, 211; basis for, 211–212
Panic of 1837, effects of, 246; campaign issue, 270
Panic of 1893, 398, 409
Paper money in colonies, 29, 30
Parcel Post established, 470
Paris, treaty of 1763, 56, 59
Paris, treaty of 1783, U.S. wins independence, 56; terms, 78–79; (map), 79
Parish, local unit of government, 39
"Parity prices" in farm program, 550
Parliament, English, growth, 13; in Tudor period, 13; tradition in America, 13–14; control over finance, 14
Parochial schools denied public support, 249
Partnership form of organization, 362
Party system (see Political system)
Patronage, political, under Jackson, 208; Washington's views, 209; policy of Lincoln, 315; and President Garfield, 386
Patrons of Husbandry (see Grange)
Paxton Boys in Pennsylvania, 19, 37, 179
Payne Aldrich Tariff, passed, 453, 471–472; effects of, 472
Peabody Institute, Baltimore, 250
Peace, American Society founded, 244
Peace, universal, as American goal, 638
"Peace without victory," 1916 election slogan, 486
Peaceable coercion policy of Thomas Jefferson, 149; success of, 152
Pearl Harbor, before bombing (photograph), 576; Japanese attack on, 577; debate on, 577, 578
Pendleton Civil Service Act, passed, 379; provisions, 386
Pengree, Hazen, reform mayor of Detroit, 461
Peninsular campaign, Civil War, Union forces defeated, 310
Penn, William, colonizer, 26
Pennsylvania founded, 19, 26
Pennsylvania Dutch, 33, 34
Pennsylvania system, canals, 232–233
"Penny press," newspapers, 249
Peoples' Party, 379 (See also Populists)
Perkins, Frances, Secretary of Labor, 539
Perry, Oliver H., wins battle of Lake Erie, 158
Pershing, General John J., American Commander-in-Chief, 489; favors harsh peace with Germany, 491
Personal liberty laws, 290, 294; significance of, 294
Peru, Spanish conquest of, 5
Petition, right of, 256–257
Petition of Right (1628), significance in America, 15
Phalanx, social system of Fourier, 260
Philadelphia Convention (see Constitutional Convention)
Philanthropist, antislavery newspaper, 258
Philip II, King of Spain, challenges British, 9; defeat of Invincible Armada, 9
Philippines, Spanish conquest of, 5; acquired from Spain, 432, 443; acquisition of, opposed by Americans, 444; American administration in,

445; self-government in, 446; independence, 446; reconquest of, in Pacific war, 592
Phillips, David Graham, muckraker author, 457
Philosophy of successful businessmen, 370
Pickering, Judge John, impeachment of, 126, 144–145
Piedmont, 36
Pierce, Franklin, elected President, 284, 298, 670; Cabinet, 675
Pike, Zebulon, explores Southwest, 176, 190; at Santa Fé, 192
Pikes Peak Gold Rush, 417, 418
Pinckney, Thomas, Federalist candidate, 135; vote, 669
Pinckney treaty with Spain, 126, 135, 183
Pitt, William, British war leader, 59; favors American colonies, 72
Pittsburgh, 56
Pizarro, Francisco, Spanish conquistador in Peru, 5
Plains, Great (see Great Plains)
Plantation, cotton (illustration), 227
Platt, Thomas, on bosses, 391; his power, 392
Platt amendment to Cuban constitution, 432, 445
Plessy v. Ferguson (decision), Jim Crow law, significance of, 618
Plow, steel, 223; development of, 225
"Plumed Knight," James G. Blaine, 386
Plymouth settlement, 19, 25
Poe, Edgar Allan, author, 262
Poetry magazine, 516
Political life in late colonial period, 39–40
Political parties in postbellum South after Civil War, 338
Political reform in progressive era, 461–462
Political system, American, two-party, 535, 630; strength of, 630–631
Politics, party, in Gilded Age, lack of issues in, 379–380; conservative leadership in, 379; professionalization of, 380; degeneration of, 381–382; caliber of politicians in, 382–383 (See also Democrats; Republican party)
Polk, James K., elected President, 265, 273, 670; Cabinet, 674; platform, 273; career, 273; veto of Rivers and Harbors bill, 265; political consequences of veto, 274–275; and "manifest destiny," 276; and expansion, 276; and Oregon issue, 276; and Mexico, 277; declares war on Mexico, 278
Polygamy issue with Mormons, 195
"Pony Express," 417; success of, 420
Poor Richard's Almanack published, 42
Poor whites, antagonism towards Negroes, 340
Pope, General John, Union commander defeated, 323
Popular sovereignty doctrine, 288, 291, 296, 299–300
Population of United States, 1790–1950 (table) Appendix VII, 681–684; shifts of, in 1950s, 634–635
Populists, movement grows, 398, 410–412; political party organized, 391, 411, 427; platform in 1892, 411–412; nomination of Bryan by, 398, 413–414; successes, 412–413; significance of, 415–416; in South, 355; and Democrats, 389, 413–414
Port Hudson, surrender of, to Unionists, significance, 325

Porter, David B., Mississippi River campaign, 325
Portsmouth, Russo-Japanese treaty, 432, 448
Portuguese sail around Africa, 1, 5
"Positive good," proslavery theory, 258
Postal Savings Banks established, 470
Potsdam Conference, formulates peace plans, 596; and occupation plans, 605
Poverty, abolition of, as American achievement, 628
Power vacuum and role of United States, 632
Pragmatism, defined, 459; influence on progressive movement, 459; of philosopher John Dewey and the New Deal, 536
Prairies, farming on, 226
Predestination, religious belief of Puritans, 24, 45
Preemption, land laws, 184, 185; law passed (1841), 176; repealed, 428
Prescott, William H., historian, 262n.
Presidents, of United States, controversy over title, 119–120; list of, Appendix V, 673–679
Prices, agricultural products (1880–1896) (chart), 402; decline of in 1890s, 405; consumer (1940–1951); (diagram), 582; increase in level of, 602–603
Primogeniture abolished, 98
Prince Henry of Portugal, the Navigator, 5
Privateers in War of 1812, 160
Privy Council, English, 60
Processing tax used in AAA program, 549
Proclamation of 1763, 56, 63; (map), 69
Progress and Poverty, book, 358; popularity of, 376
Progressive era, beginning of, 453–456; middle-class leadership, 455–456; attitude toward working class, 456; influence of intellectuals, 460; artistic phase, 460–461; city reform, 461; height of, 461–462
Progressive party, "Bull Moose," 473; of Henry Wallace, 609
Prohibition, adopted in Maine, 252; Constitutional amendment, 500, 664; amendment repealed, 666; political issue in 1920s, 502, 505–506
Prohibition, National Party, 505
Propaganda, use of, in World War I, 483, 489
Proprietary colonies, 21, 22
Proprietors as colonizers, 21
Proslavery thought (see Slavery)
Prosperity during World War II, 581–582
Protestant Association formed, 252
"Protestant Crusade," anti-Catholic movement, 252; demonstrations, 253
Protestantism and reform movement, 246
Public Information Bureau in World War I, 489
Public School Department formed in New York, 244
Public School Society organized, 248
Public Works Administration (PWA), purposes and accomplishments, 545
Public works program under Herbert Hoover, 529
Puerto Rico, acquired, 432, 443; American administration of, 445; self-rule granted, 445
Pujo committee to investigate "money trust," 370
Pullman Company strike, 1892, suppressed, 373–374; strike, 1894, 398, 410
Pump-priming under New Deal, 545
Pure Food and Drug Act, 453, 468

"Purge" attempt by F. D. Roosevelt in 1938 elections, 557

Puritanism, in Rhode Island, 25; in New England, diversifications, 45; influence in America, 47, 48; liberalized, 259

Puritans, theology, 24, 46; heritage in America, 628; revolution and English Civil War, 1, 16

Quadruple Alliance, suppresses revolutions, 170; threat to America, 170

Quakers, persecution in New England, 19, 26; in Pennsylvania, religious beliefs, 26

Quay, Matthew, political boss, 391-392

Quebec, attacked in American Revolution, 73; captured by British, 56, 59

Quebec Act, 64, 68; (map), 69

Quitrents, 22-23n.; abolished, 98

Quota system for immigrants, 513-514

Race riots in South (1866), 346

Racial discrimination and world opinion, 636-637

Radicals, in American Revolution, 81, 82, 92; checked in Constitution, 111; Republican, in Reconstruction period, 338, 342-343, 345

Railroads, early, 223, 235-236; public hostility toward, 236; capital investment in, 236; transcontinental, plans for, 298; in Civil War, 317; subsidization of, 341, 420; federal land grants for (map), 363; transcontinental, completed, 358, 360, 420-421; in American "heartland," 362-363; malpractices of organizers, 363-364; need of consolidation and capital, 363, 365; and farmers, 365, 401; increase in mileage, 1860-1890 (table), 365; increasing efficiency of, 401; rate discriminations, 401-402; attacked by Grangers, 406-407; problem of regulation of, 407; and Interstate Commerce Act, 407; coordination of, in World War I, 489

Rakes, hay, 224

Raleigh, Sir Walter (illustration), 11; colony at Roanoke Island, 19

Ranchers, frontier of, 424, 425 (See also Cattle)

Randolph, John, characterized, 146-147; (picture), 147; attacks President Jefferson, 147-148

Range cattle (see Cattle)

"Rationalization" (rationalizing) of business processes, 366

Realism in nineteenth-century literature, 395

Reapers, use of, 223, 225

Rebates, railroad, and Standard Oil Company, 367

Recession, post-World War II, 603-604, 616

Reclamation, policy of Cleveland, 430; policy of T. Roosevelt, 430

Reconstruction, acts for, passed, 338, 347; Congressional, military occupation, 347; and Supreme Court, 347; "carpet-bag" rule during, 349-350; failure to solve economic problems, 350; democratic gains, 353; in Arkansas, Louisiana, Tennessee, Virginia, 342; post-Civil War program of Republicans, 341

Reconstruction Finance Corporation (RFC), 520, 529, 531

"Red scare," in 1920s, 500, 501, 512; issue in 1952 election, 613

Redeemers, southern, program, 354; and Negroes, 354

Reform movements, 1830-1850, roots of, 245-246; types of, before 1860, 251; in progressive era, basic philosophy of, 455-456, 461-463 (See also Muckraker; New Deal; Progressive era)

Regulators in North Carolina, 19, 38, 179

Religion, importance of, in colonial life, 244; as mainspring of reform, 245; on American frontier, 198-199; instruction of, forbidden in public schools, 244 (See also various denominations, e.g., Baptists; Mormons)

Religious liberty, and Great Awakening, 50; Virginia statute for, 101

Reparations, German, World War I, 493-494; Dawes Plan and Young Plan, 508

Representative government in Virginia, 20, 21

Republican (Jeffersonian) party, consolidated, 139

Republican party, birth of (1854), 284, 297; and transcontinental railroad, 298-299; wins western farmers in 1860, 298-299; platform of 1860 enacted into law, 332-333; domination of, in Reconstruction period, 341-342; in Gilded Age, 380; and campaign of 1896, 413-414; return to conservatism (1920), 500-501; and labor unions, 505; and Taft-Hartley law, 601, 603, 609

Resumption Act, 1875, effects, 408

Revels, Hiram R., Negro senator, 1870-1871 (photograph), 350

Revenue Acts, British (1764, 1765, 1767), 56, 63-65

Revivals, religious, frontier phenomena, 198-199; during Civil War, 330

Revolution (see American Revolution)

Revolutions, English, relationship to American liberties, 15-17

Rhode Island founded, 19

Rice, in Carolinas and Georgia, 27; southern staple, 227-228; cultivation of, 228

Richardson, Henry Hobson, architect, 395

Ridgway, Matthew, United Nations commander in Korea, 612

Rights, natural, English concept, 12; common law, 13

Rivers and Harbors Convention (1846), 275

Roads, plank, built, 223; improvements in, and expansion of, 232

Roanoke Island colony, 19

"Roaring forties," aspects of, 265

"Robber barons," industrial and financial, 392, 460; and philanthropy, 396

Robertson, James, western leader in Watauga, 180

Robinson, Edwin Arlington, poet, 516

Rockefeller, John D., career, 367; business organizer, 367; business practices, 367; "rationalizes" oil business, 367-368; attitude toward lawmakers, 382; founder of University of Chicago, 396

Rocky Mountain Fur Company, 190-191

Roman Empire and western civilization, 2

Romanticism and reform, 245

Rommel, Erwin, German commander in North Africa, 585; offensive against British, 585, 587; defeated at El Alamein, 585; flight of, 588

Roosevelt, Eleanor, wife of F. D. Roosevelt, 537, 539

Roosevelt, Franklin D., early career, 501, 537–538; Secretary of Navy, 538; Governor of New York, 538; elected President, 520, 532, 538; vote, 672; Cabinet, 678–679; (photograph), 538; qualities as leader, 539; use of "brain trust," 538; inaugural address, 540; elected for third term, 573, 672; death of, 601 (*See also* New Deal; World War II)

Roosevelt, Theodore, background, 463; characteristics, 463; early career, 464; author, 464; Vice President, 464, 677; expansionist, 439; in Spanish-American War, 442; becomes President, 447, 453, 463, 671; Cabinet, 677; and Russo-Japanese War, 447–448; wins Nobel Peace Prize, 448; and Japan, 448; and Panama Canal, 448–449; (picture), 448; Caribbean policy, 449–451; as progressive leader, 464, 466; and trusts, 465–466; "Teddy and the Trusts" (cartoon), 465; nominated by "Bull Moose" party, 473; vote, 671; "New Nationalism," 474; and first Morocco crisis, 480; attacks Wilson's peace terms, 491

Roosevelt corollary to Monroe Doctrine, 451
Ross, Edward A., sociologist, 459
Rough Riders at San Juan Hill, 442
Roughing It, Mark Twain classic, 418–419
Routes westward, 1800 (map), 178
Royal Air Force, British, repulses German air attack, (World War II), 571
Royal Exchange, London (illustration), 15
Royce, Josiah, nineteenth-century philosopher, 395, 396
Rubber, synthetic, war product, 581
"Rule of reason" announced by Supreme Court, 470
Rule of 1756, issue with England (1793–1812), 132
Rural Electrification Administration (REA), New Deal Agency, 553
Rush-Bagot agreement, 161
Russell, Charles E., muckraker author, 457
Russell, Lillian, Gilded Age idol, 381
Russell, Majors, and Waddel, overland freighters, 420
Russia, claims on Pacific coast, 170; war with Japan, 447–448; member of Quadruple Alliance, 170; and Monroe Doctrine, 170; Bolshevik revolution (1917), 480, 488; peace with Germany (1918), 488 (*See also* Soviet Russia)
Russo-Finnish War, 569

Sacco-Vanzetti trials and executions, 512; significance, 512
"Safety valve" theory of Frederick J. Turner, 430
St. Lawrence Seaway, 634
St. Mihiel, World War I battle, 489
Salem, Mass., witchcraft delusion, 19
Salt Lake, Mormon settlement at, 194
Samoa, contest for, 437; tripartite agreement with Germany and England, 437; acquisition of, 432, 437
San Francisco, in gold rush, 196; fabulous development of, 196–197; Vigilance Committee, 197
San Francisco Conference organizes United Nations, 597
San Juan Hill, battle of, 442
Santa Fe Railroad, transcontinental line, 421

Santa Fé trade, development and importance of, 192; acquired by Americans, 192
Santa Fé Trail, opened, 176; (map), 191
Santiago Bay, battle of, 442
Santo Domingo, Grant's interest in, 433; intervention in, by Theodore Roosevelt, 451
Sarajevo, prelude to World War I, 480
Saratoga, battle, 1777, 56; significance of, 75; (map), 75
Satellite states, Soviet system of, 605, 607
Savannah captured by British, 77
Schechter case, NRA decision, 544
Schools, parochial, denied public support, 249
Schools, public, land provided for, 102–103; provision for, 184; struggle for, and opposition to, 247–248; spread of, 248; democratic influence of, 249 (*See also* Education; High school; Mann, Horace)
Schurz, Carl, and tariff issue, 387
Scioto Company in Ohio, 185–186; failure of, 186
Scopes, John, trial at Dayton, Tenn., 500, 514, 516
Scotch-Irish, migration to America, 33, 34; on frontier, 177
Scott, Dred, decision, 284
Scott, Sir Walter, popularity as author, 261
Scott, General Winfield, invasion of Mexico, 279–280; defeated for presidency, 284; vote, 670; Anaconda plan of strategy in Civil War, 319–321
Scribner's magazine, limited appeal of, 456
"Sea dogs," English navigators, 9
Sea power urged by Captain Mahan, 439
Secession, Calhoun's substitute for, 215; issue in South Carolina, 284, 289, 310; issue in other states, 311–312, 316; rejection by upper South, causes for, 311–312; course of (map), 312; efforts at compromise, 312–313; as viewed by President Buchanan, 313
Sectional conflict in colonial period, 34–36; in Pennsylvania, 37; in New York, 37; in Massachusetts, 38
Sectionalism, interior versus coast, 178–179; conflict of issues in Northeast, West, South, in 1820s, 212–213
Securities and Exchange Commission (SEC), securities and stock market regulation, 551–552
Seddon, James A., Virginia aristocrat, on John Brown's raid, 305
Sedition Act of 1918, 489
Sedition Law of 1798, 137–138
Segregation, racial, favored by Wilson, 478; issue in public schools, 618–620; legislation to preserve, 619; case of Little Rock, Ark., 619–620
Selectmen in New England, 40
Self-government in English colonies, 20
Separatists, religious group in England, 10; beliefs, 25; at Plymouth, 25
Sevier, John, western leader, in Watauga, 180; in Franklin, 182
Seward, William H., views on slavery, 307; Republican leader, 307–308; (photograph), 307; heads conservatives in Lincoln's cabinet, 331; Secretary of State, 315, 675; negotiations with Confederacy, 315; plan to avert Civil War, 315; and purchase of Alaska, 432; expansionist views, 433
Shantung, Japanese withdrawal from, 509

Sharecroppers in South, 355

Shays' Rebellion (1786), 101, 179; significance of, 108

Sherman, General William T., march through Georgia, 310, 327

Sherman Anti-Trust Act, passed, 358; provisions, 390

Sherman Silver Purchase Act, 398; repealed, 398, 408

Shiloh, battle of, 325

Shipping Board, World War I, 489

Ships, sailing, decline of, 223; steam, on ocean, 223

Silver, Bland Allison Act, 398; Sherman Silver Purchase Act, 398; Free Silver movement, 408; demonetized, the "crime of '73," 398, 405; production (1878-1895) (chart), 408

Sinclair, Upton, publishes The Jungle, 458

Single tax and Henry George, 376, 377

Sioux Indians, war with, 417

Slave trade, African, in colonial period, 28; protected in Constitution, 114; pressure for reopening of, 287; interstate, 230, 291; in District of Columbia, 290, 291

Slaveholders, number of, 226; (chart), 229

Slavery, attitude toward, in Virginia, 44; abolished in Vermont, 81; and United States Constitution, 270; fear of, 287; legalized in Illinois, 187; status of, in 1820 (map), 169; and Missouri Compromise, 168-169; as economic system, 231; effects of, on South, 231; abolished in British Empire, 254; southern defense of, 257-258; issue in "roaring forties," 265-266; change in attitudes toward, 266; expansion into Southwest, 266; and tariff issue (1846), 274; issue in Mexican War, 281; and Compromise of 1850, 266; status of, in western territories, 285; as cause of Civil War, 285-287; status of, in 1860, 287; in District of Columbia, 288, 290, 291; in upper South, 311-312; Lincoln opposes extension of, 313; and Crittenden Compromise, 313; during Civil War, 330; Lincoln's policy toward, 331; division in Lincoln's cabinet, 351; abolished by Thirteenth Amendment, 338; text of Thirteenth Amendment, 661

Slaves, introduction of Negro, in American colonies, 33, 35; need of, in southern labor system, 229-230; numbers of, 230; hiring of, 230; care of, 230-231; discipline system, 230; runaway, number in 1860, 287, 293

Slidell, John, mission to Mexico, failure of, 277

Sloat, Commodore J. G., expedition to California, 280

Slums, prominence of, among immigrants, 381

Smart Set magazine, 516

Smith, Alfred E., and Democratic split in 1924, 502; Democratic candidate in 1928, 506; career, 506; Governor of New York, 506; political views, 506; defeated, 506, 672

Smith, J. Allen, political scientist, criticizes American Constitution, 460

Smith, Jedediah, fur trader and explorer, 190

Smith, Joseph, Mormon prophet, 193; murdered, 194

Smoot-Hawley Tariff Act of 1924, 503, 508; effects of, 508; as cause of Depression, 520, 524

Smuggling during embargo, 149

Social aspects of 1920s, 511-515

Social compact and early state constitutions, 84

Social Darwinism, and immigrants, 381; and "manifest destiny," 439; attacked by progressives, 458

Social gospel, challenges laissez faire, 377; in progressive era, 455

Social organization and industrial revolution, 360-362

Social Security Act (1935), provisions, 537, 548, 555

Social standards, decline of, in 1920s, 514

Social welfare legislation in progressive era, 462

Socialist Labor political party, 376

Socialists imprisoned during World War I, 489

Society, colonial, diversities in, 43; in North and South compared, 258

Soil, exhaustion, colonial, 35; improvement of, 225; in South, 229

Soldier, in Civil War, 327; equipment, 328; combat tactics, 328; concessions to, 329; conduct of, 330

"Solid South," origin of, 353

Sons of Liberty in American Revolution, 81-82

South, manufactures before 1860, 239; postwar, northern economic system introduced, 338; property destruction in, 339; industrial revolution in, 339; shift of political control in, 339; social change in, 339

South Carolina, nullifies tariff of 1832, 215; secession of, 284, 310; and disputed election of 1876, 352

"South Carolina Exposition and Protest," 214

South Pass located, 189, 191

Southern Alliance of farmers, 411

Southern nationalism and slavery, 259

Southern Overland Mail, stagecoach line, 419

Southern Pacific Railroad, part of transcontinental system, 421

Southwest, Old, geography and topography, 179; social pattern in, 179; settlement of, 179; (map), 180; defeat and removal of Indians, 188

Soviet Russia, refuses alliance with British, 564; makes alliance with Germany, 560, 564; attacks Finland, 569; expelled from League of Nations, 569; invited to conquer Manchuria, 593, 596, 597; declares war on Japan, 596; problem of relations with, after World War II, 604-605; satellite states, system of, 605; postwar suspicion of, 606; failure to cooperate with United Nations, 606; "containment" policy toward, 606; crushes Hungarian revolt (1956), 622

Spain, Golden Age of, 5; expulsion of Moslems from, 5; in Age of Discovery, 5; areas colonized in New World, 6; aid from, in American Revolution, 76; cedes Florida, 151, 162; outbreak of Civil War in (1936), 562

Spanish-American War, 432; causes of, 441; popular enthusiasm for, 441; opposed by business leaders, 441; military aspects, 442; American acquisitions by Treaty of Paris, 443

SPARS in armed forces, 582

Speaker in British House of Commons, 13

Speculation in stock market (1929), 523

Speech, freedom of, for abolitionists, 244; defended by John Quincy Adams, 255

Spencer, Herbert, and social Darwinism, 375

Spirit of Laws, by Montesquieu, 52

"Spoils system" under Jackson, 207–208; removals from office, 209; justification for, 209; in practice, 385; and President Hayes, 385

"Square Deal" program of T. Roosevelt, 467, 468

Stagecoach, transcontinental, 419

Stalin, Joseph, death of, 614

Stalingrad, battle of, 580, 586

"Stalwarts," political wing, 386

Stamp Act (1765), 56, 63, 64; repealed, 56

Stamp Act Congress, 63, 64; and ruling classes, 81

Standard of living in United States, 360

Standard Oil Company, growth of monopoly, 365–367; prosecuted by Taft, 470

Standard Oil trust formed, 358

Stanford University, significance of, 397

Stanton, Edwin M., Secretary of War, 347, 675

Stanton, Elizabeth Cady, reform leader, 252

Staple Act, colonial, 31

"Star Spangled Banner" written, 158

State constitutions (see Constitutions)

States, dates of admission to Union, Appendix III, 668; limitations on, in federal Constitution, 111; reserved rights under Constitution, 118; rights, as issue in Civil War, 286–287; rights, in Confederacy, 330

Steam engine, use of, in industry, 238

Steamboat, invented, 223, 234; on western rivers, 234; technical improvements in, 234–235; accidents and hazards, 234–235

Steel, first Bessemer plant, 358

Steel industry, and Andrew Carnegie, 368–370; and J. P. Morgan, 369

Steffens, Lincoln, muckraker author and journalist, 457; on city administration, 461; *Shame of the Cities*, 393

Stephens, Alexander, views on secession, 286

Stevens, Thaddeus, near-dictator, 347; and educational reform, 248

Stevenson, Adlai, Democratic presidential candidate in 1952, 601, 614, 672

Stilwell, Joseph, general in Pacific War, 593; condemns Chiang Kai-shek, 593

Stimson, Henry L., Secretary of State, and Kellogg-Briand Pact, 510

Stock Growers Association, Wyoming, 426

Stock market, 1929 crash, 520, 525; regulation of, under New Deal, 551–552

Stowe, Harriet Beecher, *Uncle Tom's Cabin*, 255, 295; (photograph), 295

Strikes, on railroads (1877), 358; in Chicago (1886), and riots, 358, 373; at Homestead steel works (1892), 373; Pullman (1892), suppressed by Cleveland, 373–374; Pullman (1894), 398, 410; in steel industry (1919–1920), 504; after World War II, 603

Stuart dynasty in England, royal succession (chart), 7

Submarine, in World War I, 483; German pledge on use of, 483; "unrestricted," 480, 486–487 (*See also* World War I)

Subsidies for railroads, 420–421

"Suburbias" and shifting population, 634

Suez Canal, crisis over (1956), 601, 621–622

Suffrage, broadening of, under Jackson, 205–206; increase of voters in 1840, 269; in Reconstruction era, 355; Negro, problem in postwar South, 342; Negro, denied by states, 344; granted by

"carpet-bag" governments, 349; methods of excluding Negroes, 355–356; woman suffrage granted by Nineteenth Amendment, 665

Sugar, southern staple, 227–228

Sugar Act, 1764, British, 56, 64

Sumner, Charles, succeeds Webster in Senate, 298; assaulted by Representative Brooks, 284, 300–301; (picture), 300; reaction to, 301; views on Negro problem, 340; and "merit system," 385

Sumner, William Graham, and social Darwinism, 375

Supreme Court, established, 121; jurisdiction of, 121; attacks on, 167; and Reconstruction, 347; favors big business, 376; and New Deal, 555; challenged by F. D. Roosevelt, 556; and desegregation, 618; chief justices listed, Appendix VI, 680

Surplus, agricultural, problem of, in mid-1950s, 618; as persistent problem, 632

Survey, land, provision for, 102; rectangular system (diagram), 103

Swanscombe man, 1

Symmes purchase in Ohio (map), 186

Taft, Senator Robert A., bid for presidency in 1952, 614

Taft, William H., elected President over Bryan, 453, 469, 671; Cabinet, 677; antitrust prosecutions, 466; qualifications, 469, 470

Taft-Hartley Law passed, 601, 603, 609

Talleyrand, French foreign minister, 136

Tallmadge, James, amendment to Missouri bill, 168

Tammany Hall, social services of, 393

Taney, Roger B., Chief Justice, decides Charles River Bridge case, 219; Dred Scott decision, 303–304

Tappan, Arthur and Lewis, antislavery leaders, 254

Tarbell, Ida, muckraker author, 457

Tariff, proposal for, by Hamilton, 123; first bill, 123; (1816), significance of, 163; (1828), "of Abominations," 164, 214; and sectionalism, 211–212; (chart), 212; compromise bill of 1833, 215; corn laws repealed by British, 223; issue in Polk administration, 274; Walker bill of 1846, 274; steady increases after Civil War, 341; McKinley bill of 1890 passed, 379, 389; and Grover Cleveland, 387; issue in 1888 election, 387; case for and against, 387–388; protective, and farmers, 405; Wilson-Gorman Act and Cuban sugar, 440; Payne-Aldrich bill (1909), 453, 471–472; consequences of, 471–472; Fordney-McCumber Act of 1922, 503; Smoot-Hawley Act of 1924, 503; as persistent problem, 632

Tariff Commission created, 470

Taverns, importance of, in early West, 198

Taxation, and representation, in England, 13; in colonial Virginia, 14; power in American colonies, 61; under Articles of Confederation, 87; grievances of farmers, 402–403

Taylor, General Zachary, elected President, 265, 288, 670; Cabinet, 675; campaigns in northern Mexico, 277–278, 280; great popularity of, 279; and Compromise of 1850, 290; death of, 284, 292

Tea Act, American colonies, 64, 68

Teapot Dome oil scandals, 502; (cartoon), 503
Tecumseh, Indian Chief, and Indian confederation, 154; relations with British, 154
Telegraph reaches Pacific coast, 420
Temperance, American Society, founded, 244, 251; movement, progress of, 251–252; (illustration), 251
Ten Nights in a Bar Room, 252
Tenant farming in South, 355
Tennessee, secession of, 316
Tennessee Valley (map), 552
Tennessee Valley Authority (TVA), reclamation projects, 537, 552; "yardstick" for electricity rates, 553; effects of, 553–554; flood control program, 554
Tenure of Office Act passed, 338, 348
Terror, "balance of," in mid-twentieth century, 623
Texas, title to, relinquished, 162; gains independence, 176; annexed, 176, 265, 271–273; annexation treaty defeated, 271; campaign issue in 1844, 265, 271–272; annexation and slavery issue, 272; boundary dispute with New Mexico, 289, 291; (map), 277
Texas v. White (decision), 347
Textiles, beginning of industry in New England, 237; inventions and technical improvements in manufacture of, 237
Theocracy in American colonies, 24, 25
Thirteenth Amendment frees slaves, 332, 338, 344, 661
"Thirty-six Thirty" line in Missouri Compromise, 168; proposal to restore, 313
Thomas, George H., Union general, 327
Thomas, Senator Jesse, and Missouri Compromise, 168
Thoreau, Henry D., 244, 262; *Walden,* 244; and abolition, 255; on John Brown, 305
Threshers, steam-powered, 223, 225
Thurmond, Strom, Dixiecrat candidate, 610
Tidewater, description and characteristics, 36
Tilden, Samuel J., defeated by Hayes (1876), 379, 384–385
Timber Culture Act (1873), 417, 428
Timber and Stone Act, 428
Tippecanoe, battle of, 151, 154
Titusville, Penna., oil discovered, 358
Tobacco, in Virginia, 20; southern staple, 227
Tobacco colonies, 27
Tocqueville, Alexis de, on religion in America, 245; on democracy in America, 246–247
Tolerance as American virtue, 638
Toleration, growth of, in American colonies, 50
Toleration Act, English, provisions, 16
Town meetings, New England, 40
Townsend, Francis G., old age pension plan, 548
Townshend acts (1767), 56, 64, 66, 67
Township system in New England, 36, 37
Tract Society, American, 253
Trade, foreign, balance of, 1919–1952 (diagram), 524; with Allies in World War I, 484; exports (chart), 484
Trade unions legalized, 223 (*See also* Unions)
Trails, western (*see* California; Mormons; Old Spanish Trail; Oregon Trail, Santa Fé Trail)
Trans-Allegheny West, population in 1783, 100–102; state land claims in, 102
Transcendentalism, philosophy, 262

Transcontinental railroad, bill passed (1862) 333; completed, 417, 420–421 (*See also* Rail roads)
Trans-Mississippi West, described, 189; explora tion of, 189–190; last frontiers in, 417–429
Transportation, expansion before 1860, 232–237 effects of, 237–238 (*See also* Canals; Rail roads; Roads)
Transylvania, colony in Kentucky (map), 180 beginnings, 180; voided, 181
Treasury, independent, 273
Treasury Department, special status of, 120
Treaties (*see* United States, treaties)
Triangular trade, colonial, 28
Triumphant Democracy, by Andrew Carnegie 368
Trotsky, Leon, Russian Communist leader, 488
Truck gardening in East, 226
Truman, Harry S., as United States Senator, 601 elected Vice President, 596, 601; succeeds to Presidency, 601; grave problems confronting, 602; at Potsdam Conference, 596, 602; atomic bomb decision, 602; seizure of steel industry blocked, 603; foreign policy, 607–608; Fair Deal program, 609; opposition to, 609; "whistle stop" campaign of 1948, 610; elected President 601, 610, 672; Cabinet, 679
Truman Doctrine, aid program, 601, 607
Trust, Standard Oil, formed, 358
Trusts, Sherman Anti-Trust Act passed, 358; number of, in 1900, 454; prosecutions by T. Roosevelt, 466; prosecutions by Taft, 466, 470 (*See also* Monopoly)
Tudor dynasty in England, beginnings, 1; significance in age of colonization, 6–9; (dynastic chart), 7; achievements of, 8–9
Tugwell, Rexford G., New Deal leader, 539
Turner, Frederick Jackson, frontier thesis, 176; "safety valve" theory, 430
Turnpikes, corporations, 232
Twain, Mark, 395; names the "Gilded Age," 381; *Roughing It* published, 419
Tweed Ring in New York City, 379, 382, 384; (picture), 392; operations, 393
Twelfth Amendment, provisions, 140, 660
Two-party system (*see* Political system)
Tyler, John, elected Vice President, 674; becomes President, 265, 270; Cabinet, 674; breach with Whig leaders, 270; and annexation of Texas, 270–271

Uncle Tom's Cabin, published, 244, 255; popularity of, 295
"Unconditional Surrender," Grant, origin of, 325
Underground Railroad for fugitive slaves, 294
Underwood Tariff (1913), significance of, 453, 476–477
Unemployment, in 1920s, 522; in Great Depression, 520, 530, 534; during 1958 recession, 616
Union Pacific railroad, chartered, 333; construction of, 421
Union Party, coalition, in 1864, 334; nominates Lincoln and Andrew Johnson, 334
Union of Soviet Socialist Republics (*see* Soviet Russia)
Unions (labor), beginnings of, and handicaps before Civil War, 241; early public attitude to-

ward, 241; boom period in 1830s, 242; right to strike legalized, 242; weakness of, in South, 356; obstacles to formation of, after Civil War, 372; attitude of courts toward, 372; blacklist of workers, 373; industrial, secede from AFL, 537, 547; growth of, under New Deal (diagram), 547; fining of United Mine Workers, 603; and Taft-Hartley Law, 603 (*See also* Industrial Workers of the World; Injunction; Open shop; Strikes; "Yellow dog" labor contracts)

Unitarians, church founded, 244; weakness of, in South, 258

United Mine Workers, industrial union of, 147

United Nations, proposals for, 597; machinery of, 598; difficulties confronting, 598; military action in Korea (map), 611; restores *status quo* in Egypt, 622

United States, achievements of, 627; change and progress in, since colonial days, 626; genius of, 627

World War I, mobilization measures for, 488–489; military actions, 489–490 (*See also* World War I)

World War II, effect of, on United States, 570–571; preparations for, 570–571; conscription law, 571; Joint Defense Board with Canada, 571; aid short of war, 571–572; destroyers for bases, deal with Britain (1940), 560, 571–572; bases acquired by United States (map), 572; lend-lease aid, 573; defense of Iceland, 574; Atlantic convoys, 574; Pearl Harbor bombed by Japanese, 577; enters war, 580; mobilization measures, 581–582; holding action in Pacific, 583; supply lines established, 583; North African campaign, 586–587 (*See also* World War II); plan of strategy for European invasion, 587

World War II, Pacific War, United States strategy (map), 591; Burma campaign, 593; MacArthur's conquest of the Philippines, 592; New Guinea, attack on, by Americans, 583, 586; conquered, 591, 592; Midway Island, battle for, 583, 590; Coral Sea, battle of, 580, 583, 590; Guadalcanal invaded by Marines, 583, 586; taken, 590; "Operation Shoestring," campaign designation, 591; "island hopping" conquests, 591–592; Iwo Jima campaign, 592; Okinawa campaign, 592

in post-war period, demobilization after World War II, 599, 602, 604; restoration of Europe, 623; relations with Soviet Russia, 603–604; policies toward Communist China, 610–612; intervenes in Middle East (1958), 622

population, 1790–1950 (table) Appendix VII, 681–684

treaties, in chronological order, identified by countries, 1778 with France, 56, 76; 1783 with Great Britain, 56, 78–79; 1794 with Great Britain, 126, 133–134; 1795 with Spain, 126; 1795 with Northwest Indians, 134–135; 1800 with France, 126, 138; 1815 with Great Britain, 120; 1818 with Great Britain, 265; 1819 with Spain, 162; 1846 with Great Britain, 276; 1848 with Mexico, 265, 281; 1871 with Great Britain, 433; 1898 with Spain, 432, 442–444; 1921 with Germany, 497

United States Sanitary Commission, 329

United States Steel Company, organized, 369; power of, 454

Universal Brotherhood, League of, 253

Universities, state, land grant in Ohio, 184; growth of, 635

Urban problems in mid-twentieth century, 635

Urbanization, 1870–1910, 380; increase of urban population, 380

U'Ren, William S., Oregon reformer, 461–462

Utah, acquired, 176; admitted as state, 417, 668; in Compromise of 1850, 291 (*See also* Mormons)

Utah Beach, Normandy invasion site, 590

"Utah" war with Mormons, 195

Utilitarianism as American characteristic, 628

Utilities Holding Company Act for regulation of electric power business, 552

Utopianism, and spirit of reform, 259; characteristics of, 260

Valley Forge, Washington at, 76

Van Buren, Martin, elected President, 202, 670; grants ten-hour day to workers, 242; and panic of 1837, 270; and Peggy Eaton affair, 293; Cabinet, 674

Vanderbilt, Cornelius, railroad manipulator, 363–364; residence at Newport, R.I. (picture), 394

Vans Murray, William, minister to Holland, 138; negotiates French treaty, 138

Veblen, Thorstein, pioneer in economics, 396; attacks conventional beliefs, 460

Venezuela boundary dispute, with Britain, 432; with British Guiana, 436

Vera Cruz occupied by Americans, 480, 481

Verdun, battle of, 486

Vermont, slavery abolished in, 81

Versailles, Treaty of, differences among Allies in regard to, 492–493; provisions of, 493; defeated in Senate, 480, 496

Vestry, colonial, 39

Vicksburg, Union's victory, significance of, 325

Villa, Pancho, Mexican guerilla leader, 481

Virgin Islands purchased, 480, 482

Virginia, aristocracy, origins of, 43, 44; House of Burgesses, 19–21; bill of rights, 81; law against entail, 81; statute of religious freedom, 101; attitude of, towards slavery in 1840s, 266; secession of, 316; program of "massive resistance" to segregation, 620

Virginia City, Nev., mining town, 418–419

Virginia Company, joint stock, 20, 21

Virginia and Kentucky Resolutions, passed, 126; contents of, 138

Virtues, American, 637–638

Voting rights (*see* Suffrage)

Wabash Railroad v. Illinois, 407

WACS in armed forces, 582

Wade, Benjamin, and impeachment of Andrew Johnson, 348

Wade-Davis Bill, plan for Reconstruction, 342; vetoed by Lincoln, 342

Wages in 1920s, 523

Wages and hours, regulation of, 548

Wagner Act (1935), unions and collective bargaining legalized, 546; validated by Supreme Court, 547

"Wakarusa War" in Kansas, 299

Wake Island claimed, 443

Wallace, Henry, New Deal leader, 539; Secretary of Agriculture, 549; opposes Truman, 609; forms Progressive party, 609

Waltham, Mass., cotton mills, 223, 240–241

War debts, issue in 1920s, 507; (cartoon), 508

War of 1812, declared, 151, 153; causes of, 153–155; indifference toward, 156–157; opposed by New England, 157; American plan of offensives, 157–158; British invasion of Chesapeake Bay, 158

campaign maps, northern campaigns, 156; Chesapeake campaign, 158; Jackson's campaigns in southwest, 159;

naval operations in, 159–160; failure of British to control lakes, 158; ended by Treaty of Ghent, 160; results for United States, 161

"War Hawks," leaders of, 155; and "manifest destiny" in 1812, 155

War for Independence, British attitude toward, 72; Canadian attitude toward, 73; popular indifference toward, 71, 72; French and Spanish aid, 76; alliance with France, 78; attack on Quebec, 73; southern operations (map), 77; significance of, 78 (See also American Revolution)

War Production Board, work of, in World War II, 581

"War for Southern Independence," 288 (See also Civil War)

Ward, Lester, pioneer sociologist, 396; condemns laissez faire, 459

Wars, eighteenth-century, in Europe and America, 58; (chart), 59; American campaigns (maps), 58

Wars of the Roses in England, 8

Washington, George, Anglican, 44; appointed Commander-in-Chief, 71; leadership, 73; proposal to give dictatorial powers to, 94; inaugurated President (1789), 101, 119; reelected, 1792, 101, 669; Cabinet, 673; executive mansion in New York (picture), 120; neutrality proclamation, 126, 130; reputation attacked, 133–134; retirement, 135; views on patronage, 209

Washington, statehood, 427

Washington, treaty of, with Great Britain, 433

Washington Conference, disarmament, 509

Washington Peace Conference (1861), failure of, 313

WASPS in armed services, 583

Watauga, settlement of, 179–180; government established, 180; annexed to North Carolina, 180; significance of, 180

Waterpower, use of, 238

WAVES in armed services, 582

"Waving the Bloody Shirt," Republican slogan, 341

Wayne, Anthony, defeats Indians, 134

Wealth, dominance of ideal of, 381; and "social set," 381; and "four hundred," 381; distribution of, at end of nineteenth century, 454–455

Weapons in Civil War, 329

Webster, Daniel, denounces embargo, 148; debate with Hayne, 216; and Compromise of 1850,

290, 291; Seventh of March speech, 292; death, 284, 297

Weld, Theodore, antislavery leader, 254–255

Welfare, amounts spent by private and public sources (diagram), 637

Welfare state as permanent feature of American system, 633

Wellington, Duke of, and War of 1812, 156

Wells, Fargo & Company, stage line, 419

West, routes to, in 1800 (map), 178; in American history, 176–177 (See also Frontier; Trans-Allegheny West; Trans-Mississippi West; Turner, Frederick Jackson)

West Florida, factor in War of 1812, 155

West German Republic created, 605 (See also Germany)

West Indies, commerce closed, 105

West Point, prominence of graduates in Civil War, 323–324

Western lands ceded by states, 81

Western Reserve, settlement of, in Ohio, 185; (map), 186

Wharton, Edith, writer, 516

Whigs, English, philosophy of government, 82

Whigs, political party, in "log cabin" campaign, 265, 269; program, 221; and Mexican War, 282; in eclipse, 284

Whisky Rebellion, 124, 126, 128

Whisky Ring scandal, 379, 382, 383

White House, first presidential mansion in New York (illustration), 120

White rule restored in South, 350–351

Whitefield, George, and Great Awakening, 49

Whitman, Dr. Marcus, Presbyterian missionary in Oregon, 193

Whitman, Walt, on Wilmot Proviso, 282; Leaves of Grass published, 244, 262

Whitney, Eli, invents cotton gin, 223, 228; interchangeable-parts system, 223, 237

Whittier, John G., abolitionist, 255; ode to Webster, 292

Wilderness, battle of the, 310

Wilderness Road to Kentucky (map), 178

William and Mary College founded, 42

Williams, Roger, religious beliefs, 26, 46; founds Rhode Island, 19, 25; attacks intolerance, 42

Willkie, Wendell, and public power issue, 553; Republican nominee for President in 1940, defeated, 573, 672

Wilmot Proviso, introduced in Congress, 265, 281; as political issue, 281–283; leagues, 282; and Nashville Convention (1850), 290

Wilson, Woodrow, early career, 473; at Johns Hopkins University, 396; at Princeton, 473; Governor of New Jersey, 474; elected President, 453, 476, 671; Cabinet, 677–678; Wilson with Taft (photograph), 476; "New Freedom," 474; views on trust problem, 475; intervention in Haiti and San Domingo, 482; as party leader, 476; reform program, 477–478; peace proposals of 1916, 480, 486; intervention in Mexico, 481; neutrality policies in World War I, 484–485; severs diplomatic relations with Germany, 487; war message, 487; declares war aims, 488; at Paris Peace Conference, 492–493; battle for League of Nations, 497–498; collapse of, 501

Wilson-Gorman Tariff act, factor in Cuban revolt, 440

Winona, Minn., Taft's tariff speech at, 472

Wisconsin, statehood, 188

Wise, John, clergyman, defends liberty, 42, 47; and Congregational Church polity, 46, 47

Witchcraft at Salem, Mass., 19

Wolfe, James, captures Quebec, 59

Women, colleges for, 249; leaders in reform movement, 252; crusade for rights of, 252; in Civil War service, 329–330; auxiliary forces in World War II, 582; votes for, granted by Nineteenth Amendment, 665

Women's clubs advocate reform, 455

Wool, General John E., commands expeditionary force in Mexican War, 279

Works Progress Administration (WPA), purposes and program, 544–545; accomplishments, 545; employment of artists (picture), 545

World in 1490 and 1580 (map), 4

World Court rejected, 508

World missions of America, belief in concept of, 637

World War I, outbreak of, 480; responsibility for, 482, 507; United States declares war, 480, 487–488; war aims of, 488; mobilization, 489; western front 1914–1916 (map), 487; American sector (photographs), 490–491; armistice terms to Germany, 494; results, 492; and significance, 497–498; American casualties, 489; American economic supremacy, 498; issue of war debts, 507 (*See also* France; League of Nations; Russia; Versailles treaty; Wilson, Woodrow)

World War II, background of, in Europe, 560–561; in Asia, 561–562; German successes on western front, 569–571; operational areas (map), 584; main Allied thrusts in European theater (map), 588; United States participation in, 580–583, 586–596; final Allied strategy in, 588–589; D-Day, invasion of Europe (photograph), 589; defeat of Italy, 588; German surrender, May, 1945, 580, 595; Japanese surrender, August, 1945, 580, 597, 602; division of postwar world into two spheres, 606 (*See also* United States, World War II)

Wright, Frank Lloyd, modern architect, 395

Wyoming, statehood, 427; great cattle center, 425

Wyoming Stock Growers Association, 425–426; services of, 426

XYZ affair with France, 126, 136

Yalta Conference, formulates peace plans, 597; and occupation plans, 605; violated by Russia, 605

"Yardstick" for electricity rates, 553; effects of, 553–554

"Yellow dog" labor contracts, 373

Yellow journalism and Spanish-American War, 441

Young, Brigham, Mormon leader, 194–195; (photograph), 194

Young Plan for German reparations, 508

Zimmerman note, proposal to Mexico, 487

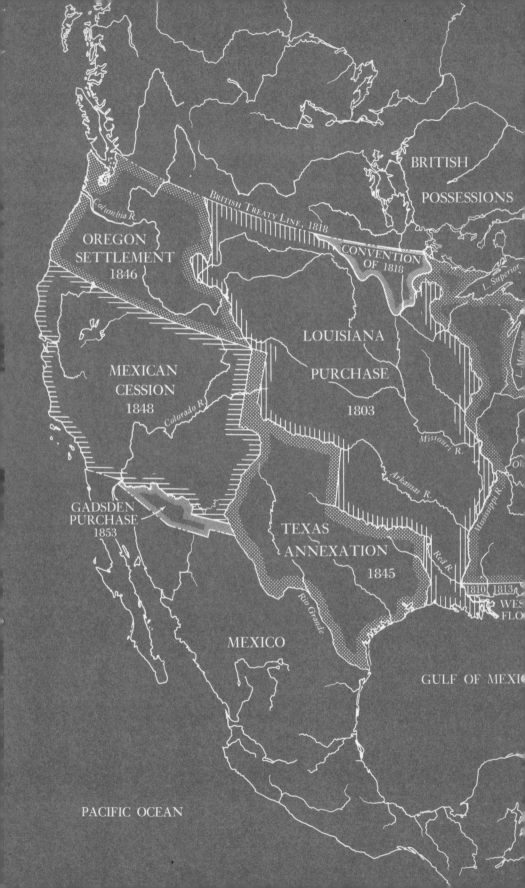